The BOOK of MORMON
STUDY GUIDE

START TO FINISH
REVISED EDITION

THOMAS R. VALLETTA
GENERAL EDITOR

BRUCE L. ANDREASON	JOHN L. FOWLES
RICHARD O. CHRISTENSEN	RYAN C. JENKINS
LEE L. DONALDSON	ROBERT E. LUND
MARK E. EASTMOND	GEORGE R. SIMS
BRUCE G. STEWART	

ASSOCIATE EDITORS

DESERET
BOOK

SALT LAKE CITY, UTAH

Library of Congress Cataloging-in-Publication Data

Names: Valletta, Thomas R., editor.
Title: The Book of Mormon study guide : start to finish / Thomas R. Valletta, general editor ; associate editors: Bruce L. Andreason, Richard O. Christensen, Lee L. Donaldson, Mark E. Eastmond, John L. Fowles, Ryan C. Jenkins, Robert E. Lund, George R. Sims, Bruce G. Stewart.
Description: Salt Lake City, Utah : Deseret Book, [2019] | Includes bibliographical references and index.
Identifiers: LCCN 2019016872 | ISBN 9781629726236 (paperbound)
Subjects: LCSH: Book of Mormon—Study and teaching. | The Church of Jesus Christ of Latter-day Saints—Doctrines. | Mormon Church—Doctrines.
Classification: LCC BX8627 .B645 2019 | DDC 289.3/22076—dc23
LC record available at https://lccn.loc.gov/2019016872

Printed in China
RR Donnelley, Dongguan, China

10 9 8 7 6 5 4 3 2 1

CONTENTS

INTRODUCTION TO
THE BOOK OF MORMON STUDY GUIDE

The Prophet Joseph Smith testified "that the Book of Mormon was the most correct of any book on earth, and the keystone of our religion, and a man would get nearer to God by abiding by its precepts, than by any other book" (*Joseph Smith* [manual], 57). In addition, President Ezra Taft Benson declared that "every Latter-day Saint should make the study of [the Book of Mormon] a lifetime pursuit" ("Book of Mormon Is the Word of God," 5).

The Book of Mormon Study Guide was developed to help Latter-day Saints fulfill this prophetic challenge to make the study of the Book of Mormon a "lifetime pursuit." It is an innovative approach to empower more experienced students of the scriptures to grow in their understanding and application of the "most correct book on earth." *The Book of Mormon Study Guide* provides students and teachers of the scriptures with thought-provoking questions and edifying insights into the Book of Mormon, as well as helpful approaches to studying, pondering, and applying doctrine and principles. Here, all in one place, students and teachers have access to prophetic statements and inspirational commentary from General Authorities, as well as insightful gospel scholarship from hundreds of sources.

What will I find in this book?

As a companion to your study of the Book of Mormon, *The Book of Mormon Study Guide* will provide a treasure trove of inspiring and enlightening words from prophets, apostles, other Church leaders, and numerous respected gospel scholars. In addition to providing inspiring prophetic commentary, this volume includes insights into historical and cultural background and context, discussions of the language of the scriptures, the organization and background of the text, the symbolism, and unique literary qualities of the Book of Mormon. Beyond these aids designed to help you better understand the scriptures, you will also find invitations to personally ponder and apply the truths presented. As President Dallin H. Oaks taught, "In contrast to the institutions of the world, which teach us to *know* something, the gospel of Jesus Christ challenges us to *become* something" ("Challenge to Become," 32). To assist you in more effectively focusing on the holy scriptures, the full text of the Book of Mormon is provided. Pertinent questions are placed alongside the verses that they spring from, followed by helpful commentary which responds to the questions and illuminates the scriptural passage. No other scripture commentary provides such a wide variety of help to understand and apply the scriptures in one place.

The eBook contains additional quotations from authoritative sources that will add to the richness of your study of the Book of Mormon. An icon in both the physical book and the eBook indicates where additional information may be accessed from within the eBook.

How can studying the Book of Mormon benefit me and my family?

President Ezra Taft Benson testified: "The purpose of the Book of Mormon is stated on the title page. It is 'to the convincing of the Jew and Gentile that Jesus is the Christ, the Eternal God.' . . .

"The Book of Mormon brings men to Christ through two basic means. First, it tells in a plain manner of Christ and His gospel. It testifies of His divinity and of the necessity for a Redeemer and the need of our putting trust in Him. . . .

"Second, the Book of Mormon exposes the enemies of Christ. It confounds false doctrines and lays down contention (see 2 Ne. 3:12). It fortifies the humble followers of Christ against the evil designs, strategies, and doctrines of the devil in our day" ("Book of Mormon Is the Word of God," 3).

In another discourse, President Ezra Taft Benson warned that those who do not continually study the Book of Mormon place their soul in jeopardy. They neglect that which could give them spiritual nourishment and protection throughout their life. He also made the following impressive promises: "There are three great reasons why Latter-day Saints should make the study of the Book of Mormon a lifetime pursuit.

"The *first* is that the Book of Mormon is the keystone of our religion. . . . A keystone is the central stone in an arch. It holds all the other stones in place, and if removed, the arch crumbles. . . .

"The *second* great reason why we must make the Book of Mormon a center focus of study is that it was written for our day. The Nephites never had the book; neither did the Lamanites of ancient times. It was meant for us. . . .

"The *third* reason why the Book of Mormon is of such value to Latter-day Saints is given in the same statement by the Prophet Joseph Smith cited previously. He said, 'I told the brethren that the Book of Mormon was the most correct of any book on earth, and the keystone of our religion, and a man would get nearer to God by abiding by its precepts, than by any other book' (*History of the Church*, 4:461). That is the third reason for studying the book. It helps us draw nearer to God. . . .

"It is not just that the Book of Mormon teaches us truth, though it indeed does that. It is not just that the Book of Mormon bears testimony of Christ, though it indeed does that, too. But there is something more. There is a power in the book which will begin to flow into your lives the moment you begin a serious study of the book. You will find greater power to resist temptation.

"You will find the power to avoid deception. You will find the power to stay on the strait and narrow path. The scriptures are called 'the words of life' (D&C 84:85), and nowhere is that more true than it is of the Book of Mormon. When you begin to hunger and thirst after those words, you will find life in greater and greater abundance" ("Book of Mormon—Keystone of Our Religion," 5–7).

It is our sincere hope that *The Book of Mormon Study Guide* will enhance your study of the Book of Mormon and encourage you to make its study a "lifetime pursuit." May we all share in the experiences and blessings of reading the scriptures, of which President Thomas S. Monson said: "I never tire of reading [the scriptures]. I am lifted spiritually whenever I search the scriptures. These holy words of truth and love give guidance to my life and point the way to eternal perfection.

"As we read and ponder the scriptures, we will experience the sweet whisperings of the Spirit to our souls. We can find answers to our questions. We learn of the blessings which come through keeping God's commandments. We gain a sure testimony of our Heavenly Father and our Savior, Jesus Christ, and of Their love for us. When scripture study is combined with our prayers, we can of a certainty know that the gospel of Jesus Christ is true" ("We Never Walk Alone," 122).

THE
BOOK OF MORMON

AN ACCOUNT WRITTEN BY
THE HAND OF MORMON
UPON PLATES
TAKEN FROM THE PLATES OF NEPHI

Wherefore, it is an abridgment of the record of the people of Nephi, and also of the Lamanites—Written to the Lamanites, who are a remnant of the house of Israel; and also to Jew and Gentile—Written by way of commandment, and also by the spirit of prophecy and of revelation—Written and sealed up, and hid up unto the Lord, that they might not be destroyed—To come forth by the gift and power of God unto the interpretation thereof—Sealed by the hand of Moroni, and hid up unto the Lord, to come forth in due time by way of the Gentile—The interpretation thereof by the gift of God.

An abridgment taken from the Book of Ether also, which is a record of the people of Jared, who were scattered at the time the Lord confounded the language of the people, when they were building a tower to get to heaven—Which is to show unto the remnant of the house of Israel what great things the Lord hath done for their fathers; and that they may know the covenants of the Lord, that they are not cast off forever—And also to the convincing of the Jew and Gentile that JESUS is the CHRIST, the ETERNAL GOD, manifesting himself unto all nations—And now, if there are faults they are the mistakes

Did Joseph Smith write the Title Page? The Prophet Joseph Smith said, "I wish to mention here that the title-page of the Book of Mormon is a literal translation, taken from the very last leaf, on the left hand side of the collection or book of plates, which contained the record which has been translated, the language of the whole running the same as all Hebrew writing in general [that is, from right to left]; and that said title page is not by any means a modern composition, either of mine or of any other man who has lived or does live in this generation" (*Joseph Smith* [manual], 60–61).

By what process was the Book of Mormon translated? "Many who read the Book of Mormon understandably desire to know more about its coming forth, including the actual process of translation. This was certainly so with faithful and loyal Hyrum Smith. Upon inquiring, Hyrum was told by the Prophet Joseph that 'it was not intended to tell the world all the particulars of the coming forth of the Book of Mormon' and that 'it was not expedient for him to relate these things' (*History of the Church*, 1:220). Thus what we do know about the actual coming forth of the Book of Mormon is adequate, but it is not comprehensive" (Maxwell, "By the Gift and Power of God," 39). ◉

Was Joseph Smith a Gentile? Elder Bruce R. McConkie explained: "We have heretofore identified the Jews as both the nationals of the kingdom of Judah and as their lineal descendants, all this without reference to tribal affiliation. And we have said, within this usage of terms, that all other people are Gentiles, including the lost and scattered remnants of the kingdom of Israel in whose veins the precious blood of him whose name was Israel does in fact flow. Thus Joseph Smith, of the tribe of Ephraim, the chief and foremost tribe of Israel itself, was the Gentile by whose hand the Book of Mormon came forth, and the members of The Church of Jesus Christ of Latter-day Saints, who have the gospel and who are of Israel by blood descent, are the Gentiles who carry salvation to the Lamanites and to the Jews. The Lamanites, having come out from Jerusalem, are in fact Jews, although they are not the Jews of whom we speak when we divide mankind into the two camps of Jews and Gentiles" (McConkie, *Millennial Messiah*, 233).

Why was the Book of Mormon written? Following the phrase "Which is to show . . ." is a list of several reasons why the Book of Mormon was brought to light in our day. How have you seen those purposes fulfilled? Which of those reasons has had the greatest impact in your life? What might you do to help accomplish those purposes in the lives of others?

To what sort of "mistakes" was Mormon referring? Mormon was referring to the "mistakes of men" and was "not referring to their theology. They made no apology for the doctrines they taught" (Pearson and Bankhead, *Building Faith with the Book of Mormon*, 30). ●

How long did it take Joseph to translate the record? "Recent research has shown more clearly than ever before that the Book of Mormon as we now have it was translated in a stunningly short amount of time. There was no time for outside research, rewriting, or polishing. Many contemporaneous historical documents sustain and validate the accuracy of Joseph Smith's account of the coming forth of the Book of Mormon. . . .

"A span of no more than sixty-five to seventy-five total days was likely involved in translating the Book of Mormon as we now have it, for an overall average of about seven to eight pages per day, conservatively estimated" (Welch and Rathbone, "How Long Did It Take to Translate the Book of Mormon?" 1–4).

of men; wherefore, condemn not the things of God, that ye may be found spotless at the judgment-seat of Christ.

TRANSLATED BY JOSEPH SMITH, Jun.

INTRODUCTION

The Book of Mormon is a volume of holy scripture comparable to the Bible. It is a record of God's dealings with ancient inhabitants of the Americas and contains the fulness of the everlasting gospel.

The book was written by many ancient prophets by the spirit of prophecy and revelation. Their words, written on gold plates, were quoted and abridged by a prophet-historian named Mormon. The record gives an account of two great civilizations. One came from Jerusalem in 600 B.C. and afterward separated into two nations, known as the Nephites and the Lamanites. The other came much earlier when the Lord confounded the tongues at the Tower of Babel. This group is known as the Jaredites. After thousands of years, all were destroyed except the Lamanites, and they are among the ancestors of the American Indians.

The crowning event recorded in the Book of Mormon is the personal ministry of the Lord Jesus Christ among the Nephites soon after His resurrection. It puts forth the doctrines of the gospel, outlines the plan of salvation, and tells men what they must do to gain peace in this life and eternal salvation in the life to come.

After Mormon completed his writings, he delivered the account to his son Moroni, who added a few words of his own and hid up the plates in the Hill Cumorah. On September 21, 1823, the same Moroni, then a glorified,

What adjustments were made to the Introduction in the 2013 edition of the Latter-day Saint scriptures? The following is from churchofjesuschrist.org under "Summary of adjustments introduced in the 2013 edition of the scriptures":

"Intro., par. 1, sent. 2—Changed 'a record of God's dealings with the ancient inhabitants of the Americas' to 'a record of God's dealings with ancient inhabitants of the Americas,' deleting *the* in 'with the ancient inhabitants' to provide clarity and greater accuracy.

"Intro., par. 1, sent. 2—Deleted the phrase 'as does the Bible' to provide clarity and accuracy. . . .

"Intro., par. 2, last sentence—Changed the phrase 'they are the principal ancestors' to 'they are among the ancestors,' providing clarity and greater accuracy."

Reference: "Scripture Adjustments"

What is the "fulness" of the gospel? "The Lord Himself has stated that the Book of Mormon contains the 'fulness of the gospel of Jesus Christ' (D&C 20:9). That does not mean it contains every teaching, every doctrine ever revealed. Rather, it means that in the Book of Mormon we will find the fulness of those doctrines required for our salvation" (Benson, *A Witness and a Warning*, 18).

How might Moroni have felt about his meetings with Joseph Smith, which began on 21 September 1823? We often reflect on how Joseph might have felt when the angel Moroni appeared to him, but how might Moroni have felt? How long had he waited to finally tell someone about the record he had buried more than fourteen hundred years before? This priceless record, which had been preserved by so much sacrifice, was about to come to light and fulfill its destiny. What would you have been thinking and feeling if you had been Moroni on your way to meet young Joseph? How might this influence the way you approach this sacred volume?

What did Joseph mean by "the most correct" book? "'The most correct of any book on earth' was a bold statement to make in Joseph Smith's day, let alone in our day of sophisticated publication. The statement is still applicable, for the Lord has never rescinded it nor cast doubt upon it....

"Its correctness must be attributed to the Lord's hand operative in its translation, an event that was, as Isaiah described it, a 'marvelous work and a wonder' (Isa. 29:13–14)" (Nyman, "Most Correct Book," 21). ●

Why is the Book of Mormon essential to bring us nearer to God? "Our homes are not as strong unless we are using [the Book of Mormon] to bring our children to Christ. Our families may be corrupted by worldly trends and teachings unless we know how to use the book to expose and combat falsehoods in socialism, rationalism, etc.... Social, ethical, cultural, or educational converts will not survive under the heat of the day unless their taproots go down to the fulness of the gospel which the Book of Mormon contains" (Benson, "Book of Mormon Is the Word of God," 5).

Will God give a personal testimony to those who seek for it? "The Lord has made it plain in a number of scriptures how he feels about the Book of Mormon; he and his prophets testify to us that it is true (see, for example, Moro. 10:28–29; 2 Ne. 33:10–11; D&C 17:6; D&C 18:2–3). Yet he still invites every reader to seek personal confirmation from him of these testimonies" (Cook, "Moroni's Promise," 15).

resurrected being, appeared to the Prophet Joseph Smith and instructed him relative to the ancient record and its destined translation into the English language.

In due course the plates were delivered to Joseph Smith, who translated them by the gift and power of God. The record is now published in many languages as a new and additional witness that Jesus Christ is the Son of the living God and that all who will come unto Him and obey the laws and ordinances of His gospel may be saved.

Concerning this record the Prophet Joseph Smith said: "I told the brethren that the Book of Mormon was the most correct of any book on earth, and the keystone of our religion, and a man would get nearer to God by abiding by its precepts, than by any other book."

In addition to Joseph Smith, the Lord provided for eleven others to see the gold plates for themselves and to be special witnesses of the truth and divinity of the Book of Mormon. Their written testimonies are included herewith as "The Testimony of Three Witnesses" and "The Testimony of Eight Witnesses."

We invite all men everywhere to read the Book of Mormon, to ponder in their hearts the message it contains, and then to ask God, the Eternal Father, in the name of Christ if the book is true. Those who pursue this course and ask in faith will gain a testimony of its truth and divinity by the power of the Holy Ghost. (See Moroni 10:3–5.)

Those who gain this divine witness from the Holy Spirit will also come to know by the same power that Jesus Christ is the Savior of the world, that Joseph Smith is His revelator and prophet in these last days, and that The Church of Jesus Christ of Latter-day Saints is the Lord's kingdom once again established on the earth, preparatory to the Second Coming of the Messiah.

THE TESTIMONY OF THREE WITNESSES

Be it known unto all nations, kindreds, tongues, and people, unto whom this work shall come: That we, through the grace of God the Father, and our Lord Jesus Christ, have seen the plates which contain this record, which is a record of the people of Nephi, and also of the Lamanites, their brethren, and also of the people of Jared, who came from the tower of which hath been spoken. And we also know that they have been translated by the gift and power of God, for his voice hath declared it unto us; wherefore we know of a surety that the work is true. And we also testify that we have seen the engravings which are upon the plates; and they have been shown unto us by the power of God, and not of man. And we declare with words of soberness, that an angel of God came down from heaven, and he brought and laid before our eyes, that we beheld and saw the plates, and the engravings thereon; and we know that it is by the grace of God the Father, and our Lord Jesus Christ, that we beheld and bear record that these things are true. And it is marvelous in our eyes. Nevertheless, the voice of the Lord commanded us that we should bear record of it; wherefore, to be obedient unto the commandments of God, we bear testimony of these things. And we know that if we are faithful in Christ, we shall rid our garments of the blood of all men, and be found spotless before the judgment-seat of Christ, and

Who were these witnesses? "When Joseph Smith first obtained the gold plates, he was told to show them to no one. As translation progressed, he and those assisting him learned . . . that three special witnesses would know, by the power of God, 'that these things are true' and that several besides himself would see the plates and testify to their existence (Ether 5:2–4; 2 Ne. 27:12–13; D&C 5:11–13). The testimonies of the witnesses affirm that these things occurred. . . .

"Most of these eleven witnesses were members of the large Smith and Whitmer families—families who had assisted in guarding and in translating the ancient record" (Ludlow, *Encyclopedia of Mormonism*, 1:214).

How important were the Three Witnesses to the Prophet Joseph Smith? Lucy Mack Smith, mother of the Prophet Joseph Smith, recalled that shortly after the Three Witnesses received their manifestation concerning the truthfulness of the plates, Joseph exclaimed, "Father, mother, you do not know how happy I am: the Lord has now caused the plates to be shown to three more besides myself. They have seen an angel, who has testified to them, and they will have to bear witness to the truth of what I have said, for now they know for themselves, that I do not go about to deceive the people, and I feel as if I was relieved of a burden which was almost too heavy for me to bear, and it rejoices my soul, that I am not any longer to be entirely alone in the world" (*History of Joseph Smith by His Mother*, 152; see also "Lucy Mack Smith, History, 1845," from *The Joseph Smith Papers*).

How were the experiences of the witnesses different? "As one compares the testimony of the Three Witnesses with that of the group of Eight Witnesses, it is instructive to contrast the supernatural experience of the former with the more natural and yet still significant experience of the latter. The Three Witnesses were shown the plates by an angel who turned the pages for their examination, and they heard the voice of God bearing testimony of the work. The Eight Witnesses, on the other hand, 'handled' and 'hefted' the plates which were shown them by Joseph Smith himself. Both types of witnesses are important to satisfy a variety of people" (Cowan, *Doctrine and Covenants*, 41).

Did any of the Three Witnesses ever deny his testimony? "Each of the three had ample reason and opportunity to renounce his testimony if it had been false, or to equivocate on details if any had been inaccurate. As is well known, because of disagreements or jealousies involving other leaders of the Church, each one of these three witnesses was excommunicated from The Church of Jesus Christ of Latter-day Saints by about eight years after the publication of their testimony. All three went their separate ways, with no common interest to support a collusive effort. Yet to the end of their lives—periods ranging from 12 to 50 years after their excommunications—not one of these witnesses deviated from his published testimony or said anything that cast any shadow on its truthfulness" (Oaks, "The Witness: Martin Harris," 37).

Why were witnesses required? "To fulfil the law of witnesses, the Lord commanded others . . . to bear record of the divinity of the Book of Mormon. Two groups, known as the Three Witnesses and as the Eight Witnesses, have left their solemn testimonies . . . which are published with each copy of the book itself" (McConkie, *Mormon Doctrine*, 841).

shall dwell with him eternally in the heavens. And the honor be to the Father, and to the Son, and to the Holy Ghost, which is one God. Amen.

OLIVER COWDERY
DAVID WHITMER
MARTIN HARRIS

THE TESTIMONY OF EIGHT WITNESSES

Be it known unto all nations, kindreds, tongues, and people, unto whom this work shall come: That Joseph Smith, Jun., the translator of this work, has shown unto us the plates of which hath been spoken, which have the appearance of gold; and as many of the leaves as the said Smith has translated we did handle with our hands; and we also saw the engravings thereon, all of which has the appearance of ancient work, and of curious workmanship. And this we bear record with words of soberness, that the said Smith has shown unto us, for we have seen and hefted, and know of a surety that the said Smith has got the plates of which we have spoken. And we give our names unto the world, to witness unto the world that which we have seen. And we lie not, God bearing witness of it.

Christian Whitmer
Jacob Whitmer
Peter Whitmer, Jun.
John Whitmer
Hiram Page
Joseph Smith, Sen.
Hyrum Smith
Samuel H. Smith

Why did the Eight Witnesses heft the plates? "Eight farmers and artisans publicly reported that Joseph Smith had shown them ancient plates of the Book of Mormon. A practical group who worked with their hands, they were better able to evaluate the 'appearance of gold' and the 'curious workmanship' than eight picked at random from a modern city" (Anderson, *Investigating the Book of Mormon Witnesses*, 123).

In addition, "the Eight Witnesses were tradesmen and farmers who worked with materials and would recognize a clumsy counterfeit" (Anderson, "Attempts to Redefine the Experience of the Eight Witnesses", 205).

Did any of the Eight Witnesses ever deny his testimony? "In spite of the fact that most of them eventually had serious differences with Joseph Smith or even left the Church, all maintained the veracity of their original witness of the truth of the Book of Mormon and its divine origins" (Reynolds, "Authorship of the Book of Mormon," 3). ✚

THE TESTIMONY OF THE PROPHET JOSEPH SMITH

The testimony of the Prophet Joseph is an abbreviated version of the more complete history found in Joseph Smith–History in the Pearl of Great Price. He recounts the visits of the angel Moroni informing him about the plates of the Book of Mormon, his responsibility to translate them, and the opposition he would face in accomplishing that task.

What is the significance of Moroni's visits? "Second only to the visit of the Father and the Son, the visit of Moroni to young Joseph Smith marks the most wonderful fulfillment of latter-day prophecy. John the Revelator foresaw 'another angel fly in the midst of heaven, having the everlasting gospel to preach unto them that dwell on the earth' (Revelation 14:6). In 1831 the Lord confirmed Moroni's fulfillment of this prophecy when he declared, 'I have sent forth mine angel flying through the midst of heaven, having the everlasting gospel, who hath appeared unto some and hath committed it unto man' (D&C 133:36)" (Williams, "Insights from Moroni's Visits in 1823," 47). ◆

The Prophet Joseph Smith's own words about the coming forth of the Book of Mormon are:

"On the evening of the . . . twenty-first of September [1823] . . . I betook myself to prayer and supplication to Almighty God. . . .

"While I was thus in the act of calling upon God, I discovered a light appearing in my room, which continued to increase until the room was lighter than at noonday, when immediately a personage appeared at my bedside, standing in the air, for his feet did not touch the floor.

"He had on a loose robe of most exquisite whiteness. It was a whiteness beyond anything earthly I had ever seen; nor do I believe that any earthly thing could be made to appear so exceedingly white and brilliant. His hands were naked, and his arms also, a little above the wrist; so, also, were his feet naked, as were his legs, a little above the ankles. His head and neck were also bare. I could discover that he had no other clothing on but this robe, as it was open, so that I could see into his bosom.

"Not only was his robe exceedingly white, but his whole person was glorious beyond description, and his countenance truly like lightning. The room was exceedingly light, but not so very bright as immediately around his person. When I first looked upon him, I was afraid; but the fear soon left me.

"He called me by name, and said unto me

that he was a messenger sent from the presence of God to me, and that his name was Moroni; that God had a work for me to do; and that my name should be had for good and evil among all nations, kindreds, and tongues, or that it should be both good and evil spoken of among all people.

"He said there was a book deposited, written upon gold plates, giving an account of the former inhabitants of this continent, and the source from whence they sprang. He also said that the fulness of the everlasting Gospel was contained in it, as delivered by the Savior to the ancient inhabitants;

"Also, that there were two stones in silver bows—and these stones, fastened to a breastplate, constituted what is called the Urim and Thummim—deposited with the plates; and the possession and use of these stones were what constituted 'seers' in ancient or former times; and that God had prepared them for the purpose of translating the book. . . .

"Again, he told me, that when I got those plates of which he had spoken—for the time that they should be obtained was not yet fulfilled—I should not show them to any person; neither the breastplate with the Urim and Thummim; only to those to whom I should be commanded to show them; if I did I should be destroyed. While he was conversing with me about the plates, the vision was opened to my mind that I could see the place where the plates were deposited, and that so clearly and distinctly that I knew the place again when I visited it.

"After this communication, I saw the light in the room begin to gather immediately around the person of him who had been speaking to me, and it continued to do so until the room was again left dark, except just around him; when, instantly I saw, as it were, a conduit open right up into heaven, and he ascended till he entirely disappeared,

What was the essence of the message delivered by Moroni? "Moroni quoted or paraphrased more than thirty scriptural passages. Perhaps the most concise statement summarizing all that Moroni taught that evening comes to us in the words of Oliver Cowdery. In one of his several letters to W. W. Phelps, he explained that Moroni outlined the 'blessings, promises and covenants to Israel, and the great manifestations of favor to the world, in the ushering in of the fulness of the gospel, to prepare the way for the second advent of the Messiah, when he comes in the glory of the Father with the holy angels' [see also Joseph Smith–History 1:54]" (Williams, "Insights from Moroni's Visits in 1823," 52–53). ⊕

and the room was left as it had been before this heavenly light had made its appearance.

"I lay musing on the singularity of the scene, and marveling greatly at what had been told to me by this extraordinary messenger; when, in the midst of my meditation, I suddenly discovered that my room was again beginning to get lighted, and in an instant, as it were, the same heavenly messenger was again by my bedside.

"He commenced, and again related the very same things which he had done at his first visit, without the least variation; which having done, he informed me of great judgments which were coming upon the earth, with great desolations by famine, sword, and pestilence; and that these grievous judgments would come on the earth in this generation. Having related these things, he again ascended as he had done before.

"By this time, so deep were the impressions made on my mind, that sleep had fled from my eyes, and I lay overwhelmed in astonishment at what I had both seen and heard. But what was my surprise when again I beheld the same messenger at my bedside, and heard him rehearse or repeat over again to me the same things as before; and added a caution to me, telling me that Satan would try to tempt me (in consequence of the indigent circumstances of my father's family), to get the plates for the purpose of getting rich. This he forbade me, saying that I must have no other object in view in getting the plates but to glorify God, and must not be influenced by any other motive than that of building his kingdom; otherwise I could not get them.

"After this third visit, he again ascended into heaven as before, and I was again left to ponder on the strangeness of what I had just experienced; when almost immediately after the heavenly messenger had ascended from me for the third time, the cock crowed, and I found that day was approaching, so that our interviews must have occupied the whole of that night.

"I shortly after arose from my bed, and, as usual, went to the necessary labors of the day; but, in attempting to work as at other times, I found my strength so exhausted as to render me entirely unable. My father, who was laboring along with me, discovered something to be wrong with me, and told me to go home. I started with the intention of going to the house; but, in attempting to cross the fence out of the field where we were, my strength entirely failed me, and I fell helpless on the ground, and for a time was quite unconscious of anything.

"The first thing that I can recollect was a voice speaking unto me, calling me by name. I looked up, and beheld the same messenger standing over my head, surrounded by light as before. He then again related unto me all that he had related to me the previous night, and commanded me to go to my father and tell him of the vision and commandments which I had received.

"I obeyed; I returned to my father in the field, and rehearsed the whole matter to him. He replied to me that it was of God, and told me to go and do as commanded by the messenger. I left the field, and went to the place where the messenger had told me the plates were deposited; and owing to the distinctness of the vision which I had had concerning it, I knew the place the instant that I arrived there.

"Convenient to the village of Manchester, Ontario county, New York, stands a hill of considerable size, and the most elevated of any in the neighborhood. On the west side of this hill, not far from the top, under a stone of considerable size, lay the plates, deposited in a stone box. This stone was thick and rounding in the middle on the upper side, and thinner towards the edges, so that the middle part of it was visible above the ground, but the edge all around was covered with earth.

"Having removed the earth, I obtained a lever, which I got fixed under the edge of the stone, and with a little exertion raised it up. I looked in, and there indeed did I behold the plates, the Urim and Thummim, and the breastplate, as stated by the messenger. The box in which they lay was formed by laying stones together in some kind of cement. In the bottom of the box were laid two stones crossways of the box, and on these stones lay the plates and the other things with them.

"I made an attempt to take them out, but was forbidden by the messenger, and was again informed that the time for bringing them forth had not yet arrived, neither would it, until four years from that time; but he told me that I should come to that place precisely in one year from that time, and that he would there meet with me, and that I should continue to do so until the time should come for obtaining the plates.

"Accordingly, as I had been commanded, I went at the end of each year, and at each time I found the same messenger there, and received instruction and intelligence from him at each of our interviews, respecting what the Lord was going to do, and how and in what manner his kingdom was to be conducted in the last days....

"At length the time arrived for obtaining the plates, the Urim and Thummim, and the breastplate. On the twenty-second day of September, one thousand eight hundred and twenty-seven, having gone as usual at the end of another year to the place where they were deposited, the same heavenly messenger delivered them up to me with this charge: that I should be responsible for them; that if I should let them go carelessly, or through any neglect of mine, I should be cut off; but that if I would use all my endeavors to preserve them, until he, the messenger, should call for them, they should be protected.

"I soon found out the reason why I had received such strict charges to keep them safe, and why it was that the messenger had said that when I had done what was required at my hand, he would call for them. For no sooner was it known that I had them, than the most strenuous exertions were used to get them from me. Every stratagem that could be invented was resorted to for that purpose. The persecution became more bitter and severe than before, and multitudes were on the alert continually to get them from me if possible. But by the wisdom of God, they remained safe in my hands, until I had accomplished by them what was required at my hand. When, according to arrangements, the messenger called for them, I delivered them up to him; and he has them in his charge until this day, being the second day of May, one thousand eight hundred and thirty-eight."

For a more complete account, see Joseph Smith—History in the Pearl of Great Price.

The ancient record thus brought forth from the earth as the voice of a people speaking from the dust, and translated into modern speech by the gift and power of God as attested by Divine affirmation, was first published to the world in the year 1830 as THE BOOK OF MORMON.

A BRIEF EXPLANATION ABOUT THE BOOK OF MORMON

Why are we told about the different metal record plates comprising the Book of Mormon? "The Book of Mormon is a complex text with a complicated history. It is primarily an abridgment of several earlier records by its chief editor and namesake, Mormon. All these records are referred to as 'plates' because they were engraved on thin sheets of metal. Various source documents were used by Mormon in his compilation, leading to abrupt transitions and chronological disjunctions that can confuse readers. However, when one is aware of the history of the text, these are consistent and make good sense" (Ludlow, *Encyclopedia of Mormonism*, 1:195).

What do we know about the small plates? "Soon after the arrival of the original colony from Jerusalem, which was somewhere around 590 B.C., the young prophet Nephi was commanded by the Lord to prepare a record for the history of his people. This record was the large plates of Nephi that we have been discussing. Then, about twenty years later, the Lord commanded him to prepare the small plates of Nephi as an exclusively religious record. . . . [2 Nephi 5:28–33].

"The sacred record that we know of as the small plates of Nephi is indebted to a yet earlier volume that the colony of Lehi brought from Jerusalem in 600 B.C. This previous work, known as the brass plates of Laban, probably set the pattern for the Nephite practice of preserving their most precious writings on metal plates. It also appears to have influenced the language of some of these works (Mosiah 1:4; compare 1 Nephi 1:2 and Mormon 9:32–33). About one-third of the small plates of Nephi is directly or indirectly related to the brass plates of Laban. About one-fourth is quoted from that record verbatim" (Ricks, "The Small Plates of Nephi and the Words of Mormon," 213–14).

What do we know about the large plates? "They were the official continuous chronicle of the Nephites

The Book of Mormon is a sacred record of peoples in ancient America and was engraved upon metal plates. Sources from which this record was compiled include the following:

1. *The Plates of Nephi,* which were of two kinds: the small plates and the large plates. The former were more particularly devoted to spiritual matters and the ministry and teachings of the prophets, while the latter were occupied mostly by a secular history of the peoples concerned (1 Nephi 9:2–4). From the time of Mosiah, however, the large plates also included items of major spiritual importance.

2. *The Plates of Mormon,* which consist of an abridgment by Mormon from the large plates of Nephi, with many commentaries. These plates also contained a continuation of the history by Mormon and additions by his son Moroni.

3. *The Plates of Ether,* which present a history of the Jaredites. This record was abridged by Moroni, who inserted comments of his own and incorporated the record with the general history under the title "Book of Ether."

4. *The Plates of Brass* brought by the people of Lehi from Jerusalem in 600 B.C. These contained "the five books of Moses, . . . and also a record of the Jews from the beginning, . . . down to the commencement of the reign of Zedekiah, king of

Judah; and also the prophecies of the holy prophets" (1 Nephi 5:11–13). Many quotations from these plates, citing Isaiah and other biblical and non-biblical prophets, appear in the Book of Mormon.

The Book of Mormon comprises fifteen main parts or divisions, known, with one exception, as books, usually designated by the name of their principal author. The first portion (the first six books, ending with Omni) is a translation from the small plates of Nephi. Between the books of Omni and Mosiah is an insert called the Words of Mormon. This insert connects the record engraved on the small plates with Mormon's abridgment of the large plates.

The longest portion, from Mosiah through Mormon chapter 7, is a translation of Mormon's abridgment of the large plates of Nephi. The concluding portion, from Mormon chapter 8 to the end of the volume, was engraved by Mormon's son Moroni, who, after finishing the record of his father's life, made an abridgment of the Jaredite record (as the book of Ether) and later added the parts known as the book of Moroni.

In or about the year A.D. 421, Moroni, the last of the Nephite prophet-historians, sealed the sacred record and hid it up unto the Lord, to be brought forth in the latter days, as predicted by the voice of God through His ancient prophets. In A.D. 1823, this same Moroni, then a resurrected personage, visited the Prophet Joseph Smith and subsequently delivered the engraved plates to him.

About this edition: The original title page, immediately preceding the contents page, is taken from the plates and is part of the sacred text. Introductions in a non-italic typeface, such as in 1 Nephi and immediately preceding Mosiah chapter 9, are also part of the sacred text. Introductions in italics, such as in

from the time they left Jerusalem (c. 600 B.C.) until they were destroyed (A.D. 385). Apparently the large plates were divided into books, each named for its primary author. These plates 'contained a "full account of the history of [Nephi's] people" (1 Ne. 9:2, 4; 2 Ne. 4:14; Jacob 1:2–3), the genealogy of Lehi (1 Ne. 19:2) and the "more part" of the teachings of the resurrected Jesus Christ to the Nephite nation (3 Ne. 26:7).' . . . Begun as basically a secular history, they later became a combined record, mingling a thousand years of Nephite history and religious experiences" (Ludlow, *Encyclopedia of Mormonism*, 1:199).

What do we know about the plates of Ether? "These twenty-four gold plates were a record of ancient Jaredites, inhabitants of the Americas before the Nephites. This particular people left the Tower of Babel at the time of the confusion of tongues. Their prophet-leaders were led to the ocean, where they constructed eight peculiar barges. These were driven by the wind across the waters to America, where the Jaredites became a large and powerful nation. After many centuries, wickedness and wars led to a final war of annihilation. During that final war, Ether, a prophet of God, wrote their history and spiritual experiences on twenty-four gold plates, perhaps relying on earlier Jaredite records" (Ludlow, *Encyclopedia of Mormonism*, 1:200).

What do we learn from quotations from the brass plates? "Although the translation of these quotations generally follows the wording of the King James Version of the Bible, there are many significant differences, which may indicate the existence of older textual sources. . . . It is also evident from the scriptural quotations in the Book of Mormon that the plates of brass contained a more extensive record of the writings of Hebrew prophets than does the present Old Testament. For example, the Book of Mormon includes prophecies of Joseph of Egypt that are not found in the Bible, as well as writings of Zenos, Zenock, Neum, and Ezias, prophets who are not specifically named in the Old Testament" (Ludlow, *Encyclopedia of Mormonism*, 1:198).

chapter headings, are not original to the text but are study helps included for convenience in reading.

Some minor errors in the text have been perpetuated in past editions of the Book of Mormon. This edition contains corrections that seem appropriate to bring the material into conformity with prepublication manuscripts and early editions edited by the Prophet Joseph Smith.

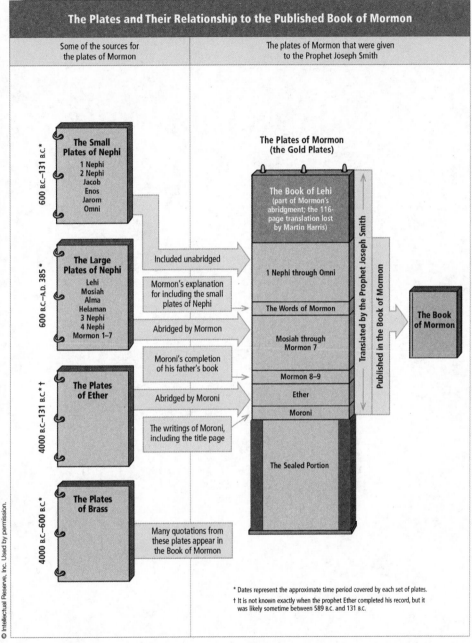

The Plates and Their Relationship to the Published Book of Mormon

Some of the sources for the plates of Mormon	The plates of Mormon that were given to the Prophet Joseph Smith

600 B.C.–131 B.C.*

The Small Plates of Nephi
1 Nephi
2 Nephi
Jacob
Enos
Jarom
Omni

The Plates of Mormon (the Gold Plates)

The Book of Lehi (part of Mormon's abridgment; the 116-page translation lost by Martin Harris)

Included unabridged

600 B.C.–A.D. 385*

The Large Plates of Nephi
Lehi
Mosiah
Alma
Helaman
3 Nephi
4 Nephi
Mormon 1–7

1 Nephi through Omni

Mormon's explanation for including the small plates of Nephi

The Words of Mormon

Abridged by Mormon

Mosiah through Mormon 7

Moroni's completion of his father's book

Mormon 8–9

4000 B.C.–131 B.C.*†

The Plates of Ether

Abridged by Moroni

Ether

Moroni

The writings of Moroni, including the title page

The Sealed Portion

Translated by the Prophet Joseph Smith

Published in the Book of Mormon

The Book of Mormon

4000 B.C.–600 B.C.*

The Plates of Brass

Many quotations from these plates appear in the Book of Mormon

* Dates represent the approximate time period covered by each set of plates.

† It is not known exactly when the prophet Ether completed his record, but it was likely sometime between 589 B.C. and 131 B.C.

THE FIRST BOOK OF NEPHI
HIS REIGN AND MINISTRY

Introduction

Nephi, son of Lehi, wrote 1 Nephi about thirty years after the events described in this book occurred (see 2 Nephi 5:30). Using his father's record and his own experiences (see 1 Nephi 1:17), Nephi related the account of his family leaving their home in the land of Jerusalem about 600 B.C. and traveling through the wilderness and across the ocean to the promised land. His inspired record was intended for at least three groups of people: his own people, the covenant people in the last days, and all of Heavenly Father's children (see 2 Nephi 33:3, 13). Nephi's full intent in writing was to persuade all "to come unto the God of Abraham, and the God of Isaac, and the God of Jacob, and be saved" (1 Nephi 6:4). Using the teachings revealed in both his father's and his own vision of the tree of life, Nephi's writings reveal the way for all mankind to partake of the love of God and receive eternal life. This book also contains many illustrations that the "tender mercies of the Lord are over all" those who exercise faith in him (1 Nephi 1:20).

An account of Lehi and his wife Sariah, and his four sons, being called, (beginning at the eldest) Laman, Lemuel, Sam, and Nephi. The Lord warns Lehi to depart out of the land of Jerusalem, because he prophesieth unto the people concerning their iniquity and they seek to destroy his life. He taketh three days' journey into the wilderness with his family. Nephi taketh his brethren and returneth to the land of Jerusalem after the record of the Jews. The account of their sufferings. They take the daughters of Ishmael to wife. They take their families and depart into the wilderness. Their sufferings and afflictions in the wilderness. The course of their travels. They come to the large waters. Nephi's brethren rebel against him. He confoundeth them, and buildeth a ship. They call the name of the place Bountiful. They cross the large waters into the promised land, and so forth. This is according to the account of Nephi; or in other words, I, Nephi, wrote this record.

The superscription to 1 Nephi, which appears just under the title of the book, was part of the ancient record translated by the Prophet Joseph Smith and dictated by him to his scribe (see also, for example, 2 Nephi, Mosiah 9, and Alma 5).

Distinct from the superscription is the chapter summary, which is presented in italics between the chapter number and the beginning of the scriptural text. Chapter summaries, originally added in the 1920 edition of the Book of Mormon, give the reader an overview of what each chapter contains.

1 Nephi 1:1–3. Nephi Begins His Record

What does *goodly* mean? (1:1) *Goodly* has a few definitions in the 1828 edition of Webster's *American Dictionary of the English Language*. The first two definitions include the following:

"1. Being of a handsome form; beautiful; graceful; as a goodly person; goodly raiment; goodly houses. . . .

"2. Pleasant; agreeable; desirable; as goodly days."

"A proposed etymology of the Book of Mormon name Nephi is that it derives from the ancient Egyptian word nfr, which as an adjective means 'good,' 'fine,' or 'goodly' and as a noun denotes 'kindness' or 'goodness.'" (Bowen, "Internal Textual Evidence for the Egyptian Origin of Nephi's Name, 11). ⊕

What do "goodly parents" teach? (1:1) "Fathers, here is a divine pattern: As the leader of the family, Lehi first taught by example. He led out in righteousness—in conversion to Christ. Then he taught by word, saying, 'Believe as I believe'" (Benson, "Worthy Fathers, Worthy Sons," *Ensign*, Nov. 1985, 35). As partners in teaching their children, the Lord has invited mothers to teach the gospel. President Russell M. Nelson invited mothers to teach from the scriptures and promised "that the heavens will open to you. The Lord will bless you with increased inspiration and revelation. . . . Please teach those whom you love what you are learning from the scriptures" ("Sisters' Participation in the Gathering of Israel," *Ensign*, Nov. 2018, 69). ⊕

What was "the learning of the Jews and the language of the Egyptians"? (1:2) "The most natural interpretation of Nephi's statement is that he was writing Egyptian the way the Jews had learned to write it. . . . That Nephi specifies his writing is according to 'the learning of the Jews' indicates that he has some awareness that there are differences in how the Egyptians themselves write and use their language. He may be referring to the differences in script, in word order, in the incorporation of some Hebrew linguistic elements" (Rappleye, "Learning Nephi's Language: Creating a Context," 158–59). ⊕

CHAPTER 1

Nephi begins the record of his people—Lehi sees in vision a pillar of fire and reads from a book of prophecy—He praises God, foretells the coming of the Messiah, and prophesies the destruction of Jerusalem—He is persecuted by the Jews. About 600 B.C.

1 I, Nephi, having been born of goodly parents, therefore I was taught somewhat in all the learning of my father; and having seen many afflictions in the course of my days, nevertheless, having been highly favored of the Lord in all my days; yea, having had a great knowledge of the goodness and the mysteries of God, therefore I make a record of my proceedings in my days.

2 Yea, I make a record in the language of my father, which consists of the learning of the Jews and the language of the Egyptians.

3 And I know that the record which I make is true; and I make it with mine own hand; and I make it according to my knowledge.

4 For it came to pass in the commencement of the first year of the reign of Zedekiah, king of Judah, (my father, Lehi, having dwelt at Jerusalem in all his days); and in that same year there came many prophets, prophesying unto the people that they must repent, or the great city Jerusalem must be destroyed.

5 Wherefore it came to pass that my father, Lehi, as he went forth prayed unto the Lord, yea, even with all his heart, in behalf of his people.

6 And it came to pass as he prayed unto the Lord, there came a pillar of fire and dwelt upon a rock before him; and he saw and heard much; and because of the things which he saw and heard he did quake and tremble exceedingly.

Why did Nephi say that he wrote his record by his own hand? (1:3) "Several of the books in the Book of Mormon begin or end with a statement by the author certifying that he is the author of his work. Often he tells what is to come in the following pages or explains or marks the end of what has just been said. . . . Dozens of editorial entries like these are found in the Book of Mormon. What purposes do they serve?

"Statements like these are known in ancient documents as colophons. . . . These textual elements functioned in antiquity somewhat like a copyright or seal of approval" (Welch, "Colophons in the Book of Mormon," 13).

1 Nephi 1:4–5. Lehi Prays for His People

Why does the Book of Mormon repeatedly use the phrase "it came to pass"? (1:4) Biblical scholars have long known that the phrase "it came to pass" is a good translation of a common Hebrew element. Hugh Nibley points out that "it happened that" or "it came to pass" are also "standard Egyptian practice." "In Egyptian," according to Hugh Nibley, "these expressions were not merely adornments . . . they are a grammatical necessity and may not be omitted. At any rate they are much commoner in Egyptian than in the Bible, just as they are much commoner in the Book of Mormon. However bad they are in English, they are nothing to be laughed at in Egyptian" (*Since Cumorah*, 150). ⊕

When did the events in Jerusalem involving the prophet Lehi occur? (1:4) "According to the Bible (2 Chronicles 36:11), Zedekiah was twenty-one years old when he was made king over the kingdom of Judah by Nebuchadnezzar, the leader of the Babylonian empire. However, the exact date of Zedekiah's ascension to the throne is not mentioned in the Bible, although nearly all of the scholars agree it must have been within a few years of 600 b.c. The Book of Mormon seems to indicate that the year 600 b.c. is correct for the [ascension of Zedekiah and the] departure of Lehi from Jerusalem (see 1 Nephi 10:4 and 19:8)" (Ludlow, *Companion to Your Study of the Book of Mormon*, 89). ⊕

1 Nephi 1:6–16. Lehi Sees in Vision a Pillar of Fire and Reads from a Book of Prophecy

What did the "pillar of fire" that "dwelt upon a rock" represent? (1:6) "Lehi prayed unto the Lord and, in response, 'there came a pillar of fire and dwelt upon a rock before him' (1 Ne. 1:6). The pillar of fire is a symbol of Deity representing the presence and glory of the Lord that appears not only here in Lehi's vision but in other places in Scripture.

"One of the most famous appearances of the pillar of fire that Bible readers recognize is during the Exodus of the children of Israel from Egypt (e.g. Ex. 13:21-22). The Israelites knew, when they saw the pillar of fire, that the Lord was with them and that He was leading and guiding them" (Book of Mormon Central, "Pillar of Fire").

How is Lehi's vision consistent with the visions of other ancient prophets? (1:8) Lehi's vision of "God seated on his throne among the council of his heavenly hosts" is "fully consistent with the spiritual experiences of other Israelite prophets of his day." Many prophets "expressed their visions in terms of participating in an assembly in heaven and receiving the judgments of that council concerning God's will about the destiny of man and the world (see, for example, 1 Kings 22:19–22; Isaiah 6:1–10; 40:1–8; Job 1:6–12; 2:1–6; Zechariah 1:8–13; 3:1–7; 6:1–8; Jeremiah 23:18)" (Welch, "Lehi's Council Vision," 24). ✚

What book did Lehi read? (1:11) While it is not known what book Lehi read, one commentary suggests: "This heavenly record of doom and destiny which Lehi is given to read may well be the same book as that read by Ezekiel, John the Revelator and others of the prophets. In the book given to Ezekiel he read of 'lamentations, and mourning, and woe' (Ezekiel 2:10), which were to come upon the ungodly. . . . That which Lehi read in the book dealt primarily with the destruction that was to come upon the unrepentant nation of Judah" (McConkie and Millet, *Doctrinal Commentary*, 1:26–27). ✚

7 And it came to pass that he returned to his own house at Jerusalem; and he cast himself upon his bed, being overcome with the Spirit and the things which he had seen.

8 And being thus overcome with the Spirit, he was carried away in a vision, even that he saw the heavens open, and he thought he saw God sitting upon his throne, surrounded with numberless concourses of angels in the attitude of singing and praising their God.

9 And it came to pass that he saw One descending out of the midst of heaven, and he beheld that his luster was above that of the sun at noon-day.

10 And he also saw twelve others following him, and their brightness did exceed that of the stars in the firmament.

11 And they came down and went forth upon the face of the earth; and the first came and stood before my father, and gave unto him a book, and bade him that he should read.

12 And it came to pass that as he read, he was filled with the Spirit of the Lord.

13 And he read, saying: Wo, wo, unto Jerusalem, for I have seen thine abominations! Yea, and many things did my father read concerning Jerusalem—that it should be destroyed, and the inhabitants thereof; many should perish by the sword, and many should be carried away captive into Babylon.

14 And it came to pass that when my father had read and seen many great and marvelous things, he did exclaim many things unto the Lord; such as: Great and marvelous are thy

works, O Lord God Almighty! Thy throne is high in the heavens, and thy power, and goodness, and mercy are over all the inhabitants of the earth; and, because thou art merciful, thou wilt not suffer those who come unto thee that they shall perish!

15 And after this manner was the language of my father in the praising of his God; for his soul did rejoice, and his whole heart was filled, because of the things which he had seen, yea, which the Lord had shown unto him.

16 And now I, Nephi, do not make a full account of the things which my father hath written, for he hath written many things which he saw in visions and in dreams; and he also hath written many things which he prophesied and spake unto his children, of which I shall not make a full account.

What part of 1 Nephi contains the record of Lehi? (1:16) "Lehi, as Jeremiah and other prophets, kept a record of his visions, dreams and prophecies, his public discourses and his talks to his children; Nephi does not intend or propose to copy his record in full. He gives part of it in an abridged form, as an introduction to his own story. 1 Nephi 1:18 to the end of chapter 8 seems to be a synopsis of the record of Lehi. His own record would then begin with chapter 9" (Reynolds and Sjodahl, *Commentary on the Book of Mormon*, 1:10).

Jerusalem in Lehi's Day

Courtesy Church History Museum.

The City of Jerusalem, *by James Fairman*

1 Nephi 1:17–20. Lehi Prophesies of the Destruction of Jerusalem

How does Lehi's call follow the pattern of the calls of other ancient prophets? (1:19) Lehi's prophetic call follows a pattern similar to the commissions of other prophets in the scriptures. As Elder Jeffrey R. Holland outlined it, Lehi "prays, has a vision, sees heavenly messengers (apparently including Jesus), receives a book, [and] is rejected by most people" ("Daddy, Donna, and Nephi," 9). ◎

What wickedness led to the destruction of Jerusalem? (1:19) "Jeremiah tells us that [Jerusalem's] inhabitants had become so sensual and materialistic that they had lost all sense of divine values: 'They are wise to do evil, but to do good they have no knowledge' (Jer. 4:22).

"'They be all adulterers,' Jeremiah said about the mores of that generation (Jer. 9:2)....

"The people's preoccupation with sensuality was matched by their covetousness and dishonesty. Jeremiah lamented, 'From the least of them even unto the greatest of them every one is given to covetousness; and from the prophet even unto the priest every one dealeth falsely' (Jer. 6:13)" (Meservy, "Jerusalem at the Time of Lehi and Jeremiah," 23). ◎

In what ways does the Lord manifest His tender mercy in our lives? (1:20) Elder David A. Bednar described the "tender mercies of the Lord" as "very personal and individualized blessings, strength, protection, assurances, guidance, loving-kindness, consolation, support, and spiritual gifts which we receive from and because of and through the Lord Jesus Christ." Elder Bednar further testified that "the tender

17 But I shall make an account of my proceedings in my days. Behold, I make an abridgment of the record of my father, upon plates which I have made with mine own hands; wherefore, after I have abridged the record of my father then will I make an account of mine own life.

18 Therefore, I would that ye should know, that after the Lord had shown so many marvelous things unto my father, Lehi, yea, concerning the destruction of Jerusalem, behold he went forth among the people, and began to prophesy and to declare unto them concerning the things which he had both seen and heard.

19 And it came to pass that the Jews did mock him because of the things which he testified of them; for he truly testified of their wickedness and their abominations; and he testified that the things which he saw and heard, and also the things which he read in the book, manifested plainly of the coming of a Messiah, and also the redemption of the world.

20 And when the Jews heard these things they were angry with him; yea, even as with the prophets of old, whom they had cast out, and stoned, and slain; and they also sought his life, that they might take it away. But behold, I, Nephi, will show unto you that the tender mercies of the Lord are over all those

whom he hath chosen, because of their faith, to make them mighty even unto the power of deliverance.

CHAPTER 2

Lehi takes his family into the wilderness by the Red Sea—They leave their property—Lehi offers a sacrifice to the Lord and teaches his sons to keep the commandments—Laman and Lemuel murmur against their father—Nephi is obedient and prays in faith; the Lord speaks to him, and he is chosen to rule over his brethren. About 600 B.C.

1 For behold, it came to pass that the Lord spake unto my father, yea, even in a dream, and said unto him: Blessed art thou Lehi, because of the things which thou hast done; and because thou hast been faithful and declared unto this people the things which I commanded thee, behold, they seek to take away thy life.

2 And it came to pass that the Lord commanded my father, even in a dream, that he should take his family and depart into the wilderness.

3 And it came to pass that he was obedient unto the word of the Lord, wherefore he did as the Lord commanded him.

4 And it came to pass that he departed into the wilderness. And he left his house, and the land of his inheritance, and his gold, and his silver, and his precious things, and took nothing with him, save it were his family, and provisions, and tents, and departed into the wilderness.

mercies of the Lord are real and that they do not occur randomly or merely by coincidence. Faithfulness and obedience enable us to receive these important gifts and, frequently, the Lord's timing helps us to recognize them" ("Tender Mercies of the Lord," 99–100). ⊕

In what ways have you discerned the Lord's hand at times in your life? (1:20) When have you received "the tender mercies of the Lord" because of your faith in Jesus Christ? How can you improve in recognizing moments of divine "tender mercy" in your life?

1 Nephi 2:1–8. Lehi Obeys the Lord's Command to Leave Jerusalem

Why do some actions bring divine approval but also intense opposition? (2:1) On the one hand God says Lehi is blessed "because of the things which [he] has done," but on the other, "because [he] has been faithful," residents of Jerusalem "seek to take away [his] life." Can you think of an act (or choice) that led to your being blessed by the Lord but persecuted by others?

Why did Lehi have so many significant dreams? (2:2) "It is certain that divine messages have often been communicated to man by means of dreams" (Reynolds and Sjodahl, *Commentary on the Book of Mormon*, 1:24). Though it is not apparent in this case whether Lehi received two dreams or one, it is obvious that the Lord not only teaches and inspires but also gives commands "even in a dream." ⊕

What does Lehi's choice of provisions reveal about his perspective? (2:4) Of all that Lehi could choose from to take into the wilderness—gold, silver, and other precious things—the prophet took only his family and provisions for them to subsist. President Gordon B. Hinckley declared: "The family is divine. It was instituted by our Heavenly Father. It encompasses the most sacred of all relationships. Only through its organization can the purposes of the Lord be fulfilled" (*Teachings of Gordon B. Hinckley*, 206). Both Lehi's focus on his family and his swift obedience demonstrate his trust in the Lord. ⊕

How long and how far did Lehi's colony travel? (2:5)
"The nearest point of the Red Sea to Jerusalem is over
two hundred miles. It is not stated how many days the
family spent getting to the Red Sea, but it must have
been around two weeks plus the three days. Although
they would be hurrying, they would also have been
careful not to attract attention" (Nyman, *I, Nephi, Wrote
This Record*, 48).

Why does Lehi say "a river of water"? (2:6) The
phrase "river of water," which sounds odd to speakers of English, provides remarkable evidence that the
Prophet Joseph Smith actually translated this ancient
text as he stated. "Although the term 'river of water'
probably seemed foreign to Joseph Smith . . . , the use
of the term in the Book of Mormon is consistent with
both modern and ancient Hebrew and with other
Semitic languages of the Middle East. Different words
are used in these languages to differentiate between
(1) a riverbed that has water flowing in it and (2) a
dry riverbed. This is one of many examples that prove
the Book of Mormon is translation literature" (Ludlow,
Companion to Your Study of the Book of Mormon, 92–93).

**Why did Lehi build an altar and make an offering?
(2:7)** Lehi lived the law of Moses. "According to the
Mosaic law, an altar was to be built either of earth
or stones not 'polluted' by any tools (Ex. 20:24, 25)"
(Reynolds and Sjodahl, *Commentary on the Book of
Mormon*, 1:26).

"The phrase 'altar of stones' derives from Mosaic
Law (see Ex. 20:24–25; Deut. 27:5–7). On the character
of Lehi's altar . . . that in accord with the law of Moses,
it must have been of unhewn field stones" (Brown,
"What Were Those Sacrifices Offered by Lehi?", 8). ◉

1 Nephi 2:9–15. Lehi Counsels Laman and Lemuel to Be Faithful

**Why did Lehi name a river and a valley after his
oldest sons? (2:9–10)** At first glance some might
think Lehi was leaving his mark on the region by
naming a river after Laman and a valley after Lemuel.
However, Lehi was more interested in inspiring his
sons than in leaving family place names. He hoped
these comparisons would lead his sons to more obedience to God's commandments and more interest in
the Lord God, "the foundation of all righteousness."
Unfortunately, "such parallels, like parables, fall too
often upon deaf ears and do not find place in the
hearts of the hardened (cf. Matthew 13:13). So it
was with Laman and Lemuel" (McConkie and Millet,
Doctrinal Commentary, 1:32). ◉

5 And he came down by the borders near the
shore of the Red Sea; and he traveled in the
wilderness in the borders which are nearer
the Red Sea; and he did travel in the wilderness with his family, which consisted of my
mother, Sariah, and my elder brothers, who
were Laman, Lemuel, and Sam.

6 And it came to pass that when he had traveled three days in the wilderness, he pitched
his tent in a valley by the side of a river of
water.

7 And it came to pass that he built an altar of
stones, and made an offering unto the Lord,
and gave thanks unto the Lord our God.

8 And it came to pass that he called the name
of the river, Laman, and it emptied into the
Red Sea; and the valley was in the borders
near the mouth thereof.

9 And when my father saw that the waters
of the river emptied into the fountain of
the Red Sea, he spake unto Laman, saying:
O that thou mightest be like unto this river,
continually running into the fountain of all
righteousness!

10 And he also spake unto Lemuel: O that
thou mightest be like unto this valley, firm
and steadfast, and immovable in keeping the
commandments of the Lord!

11 Now this he spake because of the stiffneckedness of Laman and Lemuel; for behold they did murmur in many things against their father, because he was a visionary man, and had led them out of the land of Jerusalem, to leave the land of their inheritance, and their gold, and their silver, and their precious things, to perish in the wilderness. And this they said he had done because of the foolish imaginations of his heart.

12 And thus Laman and Lemuel, being the eldest, did murmur against their father. And they did murmur because they knew not the dealings of that God who had created them.

What is wrong with murmuring? (2:12) Murmuring reveals that the murmurer has a lack of faith or is shortsighted in his understanding of God's plan for his children. Not only did Laman and Lemuel fail to "[know] the dealings of that God who had created them," they knew not God. Elder Neal A. Maxwell taught: "Those of deep faith do not murmur . . . even while in deep difficulties. . . . Murmuring . . . drowns out the various spiritual signals to us" (*Neal A. Maxwell Quote Book*, 219).

A Possible Route of Lehi's Journey

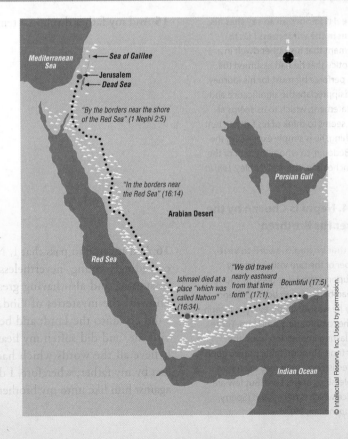

Mediterranean Sea

← Sea of Galilee
← Jerusalem
← Dead Sea

"By the borders near the shore of the Red Sea" (1 Nephi 2:5)

"In the borders near the Red Sea" (16:14)

Persian Gulf

Arabian Desert

Red Sea

Ishmael died at a place "which was called Nahom" (16:34).

"We did travel nearly eastward from that time forth" (17:1).

Bountiful (17:5)

Indian Ocean

Why did Laman and Lemuel believe Jerusalem could not be destroyed? (2:13) David Seely and Fred Woods stated: "The biblical record contains much information that helps us to better understand the attitude of Laman and Lemuel and many of their fellow inhabitants of Jerusalem and to identify the basis for their fervent belief that their city Jerusalem was invincible and impregnable." Their study examines six factors that led to this mistaken idea: (1) the traditions of "That Great City"; (2) misunderstanding of covenant promises; (3) precedent of miraculous preservation during the Assyrian invasion; (4) strong defensive fortifications; (5) the Josiah reformation, which gave them a false sense of security; and (6) false prophets who had misled many ("How Could Jerusalem, 'That Great City,' Be Destroyed?" 595–96). ◐

Who are the "Jews" referred to in verse 13? (2:13) "The term 'Jew' is used in the Book of Mormon with two possible meanings: (1) a descendant of Judah, the son of Jacob (or, perhaps in a more general vein, a member of the house of Israel), and (2) a citizen of the kingdom of Judah of this particular period" (Ludlow, *Companion to Your Study of the Book of Mormon*, 95).

Why would Nephi feel it important to say that his father dwelt in a tent in the wilderness? (2:15) "With the announcement that his 'father dwelt in a tent,' Nephi serves notice that he had assumed the desert way of life, as perforce he must for his journey. Any easterner would appreciate the significance and importance of the statement, which to us seems almost trivial. If Nephi seems to think of his father's tent as the hub of everything, he is simply expressing the view of any normal Bedouin, to whom the tent of the *sheikh* is the sheet anchor of existence" (Nibley, *Lehi in the Desert*, 58). ◐

1 Nephi 2:16–24. Nephi Is Chosen by the Lord to Rule Over His Brethren

What did Nephi do that invited the Lord to visit him? (2:16) "A number of the rare visits made by the Lord to persons upon earth have been to young men—perhaps we had better say to boys. . . . Nephi found the Lord while he was yet a boy, even as Joseph Smith, the boy prophet of this age, found him. These facts should make a lasting impression upon the young people of our time. Through faith, prayer, good works, and patient persistence, men may even now enjoy the personal blessings of the Lord. But few are willing to pay the price which is necessary" (Sperry, *Book of Mormon Compendium*, 99). ◐

13 Neither did they believe that Jerusalem, that great city, could be destroyed according to the words of the prophets. And they were like unto the Jews who were at Jerusalem, who sought to take away the life of my father.

14 And it came to pass that my father did speak unto them in the valley of Lemuel, with power, being filled with the Spirit, until their frames did shake before him. And he did confound them, that they durst not utter against him; wherefore, they did as he commanded them.

15 And my father dwelt in a tent.

16 And it came to pass that I, Nephi, being exceedingly young, nevertheless being large in stature, and also having great desires to know of the mysteries of God, wherefore, I did cry unto the Lord; and behold he did visit me, and did soften my heart that I did believe all the words which had been spoken by my father; wherefore, I did not rebel against him like unto my brothers.

17 And I spake unto Sam, making known unto him the things which the Lord had manifested unto me by his Holy Spirit. And it came to pass that he believed in my words.

18 But, behold, Laman and Lemuel would not hearken unto my words; and being grieved because of the hardness of their hearts I cried unto the Lord for them.

19 And it came to pass that the Lord spake unto me, saying: Blessed art thou, Nephi, because of thy faith, for thou hast sought me diligently, with lowliness of heart.

20 And inasmuch as ye shall keep my commandments, ye shall prosper, and shall be led to a land of promise; yea, even a land which I have prepared for you; yea, a land which is choice above all other lands.

21 And inasmuch as thy brethren shall rebel against thee, they shall be cut off from the presence of the Lord.

22 And inasmuch as thou shalt keep my commandments, thou shalt be made a ruler and a teacher over thy brethren.

23 For behold, in that day that they shall rebel against me, I will curse them even with a sore curse, and they shall have no power over thy seed except they shall rebel against me also.

24 And if it so be that they rebel against me, they shall be a scourge unto thy seed, to stir them up in the ways of remembrance.

What was the difference between Nephi and Laman and Lemuel? (2:17–18) In Nephi's impressive contrast set throughout 1 Nephi 2, we clearly see what led Laman and Lemuel to rebellion and Nephi to obedience. It was a matter of the heart. Verses 16–18 give a key to understanding some of the differences between Nephi and his older brothers: "Nephi sought the Lord early and earnestly and found him; Laman and Lemuel would not so much as begin the spiritual odyssey (see 1 Nephi 15:8–9). Nephi could view things (good and bad, blessings and trials) from an elevated perspective; Laman and Lemuel continued to refuse the vantage of higher ground" (McConkie and Millet, *Doctrinal Commentary*, 1:34).

How can I enjoy blessings similar to Nephi's? (2:19) Nephi was humble and obedient and had faith in the Lord, but because he "sought [the Lord] diligently" he was promised he would prosper and obtain "a land of promise." In what ways can you seek the Lord more diligently?

What additional prophecies did the Lord make concerning the promised land in the New World? (2:20) "Our Father in Heaven planned the coming forth of the Founding Fathers and their form of government as the necessary great prologue leading to the restoration of the gospel. Recall what our Savior Jesus Christ said nearly two thousand years ago when he visited this promised land: "For it is wisdom in the Father that they should be established in this land, and be set up as a free people by the power of the Father, that these things might come forth" (3 Nephi 21:4). America, the land of liberty, was to be the Lord's latter-day base of operations for His restored church" (Ezra Taft Benson, "Our Divine Constitution," 4). ●

Why did the Lord make Nephi a ruler over his older brothers? (2:21–22) Just as Reuben and Esau each lost the birthright to a younger brother (see 1 Chronicles 5:1–2; Hebrews 12:16–17), so Laman lost his right to be "a ruler and [a] teacher over [his] brethren" because of his rebellion against God (see 1 Nephi 3:29). ●

CHAPTER 3

Lehi's sons return to Jerusalem to obtain the plates of brass—Laban refuses to give the plates up—Nephi exhorts and encourages his brethren—Laban steals their property and attempts to slay them—Laman and Lemuel smite Nephi and Sam and are reproved by an angel. About 600–592 B.C.

1 Nephi 3:1–8. Nephi and His Brothers Return to Jerusalem to Obtain the Brass Plates

Why would Lehi use the expression "I have dreamed a dream"? (3:2) "Many words, phrases, and expressions in the religious speeches and writings of Lehi, Nephi, and subsequent Book of Mormon prophets reflect biblical and idiomatic Hebrew rather than nineteenth-century American English . . . usage [,] unnatural in English yet characteristic of the language of Old World prophets as recorded in the Hebrew Bible . . . [and] strongly indicative of the authenticity of the Book of Mormon.

"The cognate accusative is a direct object noun that shares the same root as the preceding verb, as in Joseph 'dreamed a dream' (Genesis 37:5) instead of the more customary English rendering 'Joseph had a dream'" (Parry, "Hebraisms and Other Ancient Peculiarities in the Book of Mormon," 156, 183). ✛

Why are these plates called "plates of brass" rather than brass plates? (3:3) "In many of the Semitic languages (from which we get the thought patterns contained in the Book of Mormon) it is not customary to have the adjective precede the noun. Thus the Book of Mormon mentions the 'plates of brass' of Laban but never refers to the 'brass plates of Laban'" (Ludlow, *Companion to Your Study of the Book of Mormon*, 95). Other examples include "river of water" and "altar of stones" (1 Nephi 2:6–7).

Why do some "murmur" when faced with difficult trials? (3:5) When hard times come, we often forget the Lord's counsel to the Prophet Joseph that "all these things shall give thee experience, and shall be for thy good" (D&C 122:7).

Elder Neal A. Maxwell observed: "Murmuring can block the process of needed tutoring. Yet unappreciated tutoring surely causes murmuring. It is as if we have an unrealistic expectation that life is to flow

1 And it came to pass that I, Nephi, returned from speaking with the Lord, to the tent of my father.

2 And it came to pass that he spake unto me, saying: Behold I have dreamed a dream, in the which the Lord hath commanded me that thou and thy brethren shall return to Jerusalem.

3 For behold, Laban hath the record of the Jews and also a genealogy of my forefathers, and they are engraven upon plates of brass.

4 Wherefore, the Lord hath commanded me that thou and thy brothers should go unto the house of Laban, and seek the records, and bring them down hither into the wilderness.

5 And now, behold thy brothers murmur, saying it is a hard thing which I have required of them; but behold I have not required it of them, but it is a commandment of the Lord.

6 Therefore go, my son, and thou shalt be favored of the Lord, because thou hast not murmured.

7 And it came to pass that I, Nephi, said unto my father: I will go and do the things which the Lord hath commanded, for I know that the Lord giveth no commandments unto the children of men, save he shall prepare a way for them that they may accomplish the thing which he commandeth them.

8 And it came to pass that when my father had heard these words he was exceedingly glad, for he knew that I had been blessed of the Lord.

9 And I, Nephi, and my brethren took our journey in the wilderness, with our tents, to go up to the land of Jerusalem.

10 And it came to pass that when we had gone up to the land of Jerusalem, I and my brethren did consult one with another.

smoothly, featuring an unbroken corridor of green lights leading to vacant parking places just in front of our destinations!" (*Wonderful Flood of Light*, 63–64). ◐

What if you are unsure how to "go and do"? (3:7) President George Albert Smith testified: "The Lord has a way of accomplishing things that we are unable to do, and never asks us to do anything that he does not make the way possible. That is what he told us through Nephi. He will not require anything without preparing the way [1 Nephi 3:7 is quoted].

"If you have something that the Lord asks or expects you to do and you don't know just how to proceed, do your best. Move in the direction that you ought to go; trust the Lord, give him a chance, and he will never fail you" (*Sharing the Gospel*, 15–16). ◐

How can we follow Nephi's example? (3:7) As you analyze your own life's circumstances and the power of your faith, what are some things you could begin to do right now that would help you follow Nephi's example of faith and courage?

1 Nephi 3:9–14. Nephi and His Brothers Fail in Their First Attempt to Obtain the Brass Plates

How long would it have taken the brothers to return to Jerusalem? (3:9) "Young men, as Nephi and his siblings were, traveling on camels with little baggage could reach the city from that distance in four or five days. When the group covered that distance the first time, they took their tents, slowing them (see 1 Nephi 3:9)" (Brown, "Refining the Spotlight on Lehi and Sariah," 48).

Is there a difference between the "land of Jerusalem" and the city of Jerusalem? (3:9) "Lehi 'dwelt at Jerusalem in all his days' (1 Nephi 1:4), yet his sons had to 'go down to the land of our father's inheritance' to pick up their property (1 Nephi 3:16, 22). The apparent anomaly is readily explained by the Amarna Letters, in which we read that 'a city of the land of Jerusalem, Bet-Ninib, has been captured.' It was the rule in Palestine and Syria from ancient times . . . for a large area around a city and all the inhabitants of that area to bear the name of the city. . . . But this was quite unknown at the time the Book of Mormon was written" (Nibley, *Approach to the Book of Mormon*, 101–2). ◐

What does it mean to "cast lots"? (3:11) Anciently, casting lots was an accepted way to determine God's will. It is a little like drawing straws today. "[It] was practiced extensively by the Hebrews of Old Testament times. This authentic and typical use of the custom in the Book of Mormon would indicate again that this part of the story in the Book of Mormon is concerned with a group of people with a Hebrew background and that the Book of Mormon is a translation of an ancient record" (Ludlow, *Companion to Your Study of the Book of Mormon*, 95).

Who was Laban? (3:12–13) The short description of Laban in 1 Nephi 3 is another evidence that the Prophet Joseph translated an ancient record. Hugh Nibley explained: "Laban is described very fully, though casually, by Nephi, and is seen to be the very type and model of a well-known class of public official in the Ancient East. Everything about him is authentic....

"One of the main functions of any governor in the East has always been to hear petitions, and the established practice has ever been to rob the petitioners (or anyone else) wherever possible" (*Approach to the Book of Mormon*, 120–21). ⊕

1 Nephi 3:15–27. The Brothers Fail a Second Time to Obtain the Plates

Why did Nephi swear an oath when seeking to obtain the brass plates? (3:15) "This matter of swearing with an oath in ancient days was far more significant than many of us have realized.

"For instance: Nephi and his brethren were seeking to obtain the brass plates from Laban. Their lives were in peril. Yet Nephi swore this oath: [1 Nephi 3:15 is quoted].

"Thus Nephi made God his partner. If he failed to get the plates, it meant God had failed. And because God does not fail, it was incumbent upon Nephi to get the plates or lay down his life in the attempt" (McConkie, "Doctrine of the Priesthood," 33).

11 And we cast lots—who of us should go in unto the house of Laban. And it came to pass that the lot fell upon Laman; and Laman went in unto the house of Laban, and he talked with him as he sat in his house.

12 And he desired of Laban the records which were engraven upon the plates of brass, which contained the genealogy of my father.

13 And behold, it came to pass that Laban was angry, and thrust him out from his presence; and he would not that he should have the records. Wherefore, he said unto him: Behold thou art a robber, and I will slay thee.

14 But Laman fled out of his presence, and told the things which Laban had done, unto us. And we began to be exceedingly sorrowful, and my brethren were about to return unto my father in the wilderness.

15 But behold I said unto them that: As the Lord liveth, and as we live, we will not go down unto our father in the wilderness until we have accomplished the thing which the Lord hath commanded us.

16 Wherefore, let us be faithful in keeping the commandments of the Lord; therefore let us go down to the land of our father's inheritance, for behold he left gold and silver, and all manner of riches. And all this he hath done because of the commandments of the Lord.

17 For he knew that Jerusalem must be destroyed, because of the wickedness of the people.

18 For behold, they have rejected the words of the prophets. Wherefore, if my father should dwell in the land after he hath been commanded to flee out of the land, behold,

he would also perish. Wherefore, it must needs be that he flee out of the land.

19 And behold, it is wisdom in God that we should obtain these records, that we may preserve unto our children the language of our fathers;

20 And also that we may preserve unto them the words which have been spoken by the mouth of all the holy prophets, which have been delivered unto them by the Spirit and power of God, since the world began, even down unto this present time.

21 And it came to pass that after this manner of language did I persuade my brethren, that they might be faithful in keeping the commandments of God.

22 And it came to pass that we went down to the land of our inheritance, and we did gather together our gold, and our silver, and our precious things.

23 And after we had gathered these things together, we went up again unto the house of Laban.

24 And it came to pass that we went in unto Laban, and desired him that he would give unto us the records which were engraven upon the plates of brass, for which we would give unto him our gold, and our silver, and all our precious things.

25 And it came to pass that when Laban saw our property, and that it was exceedingly great, he did lust after it, insomuch that he thrust us out, and sent his servants to slay us, that he might obtain our property.

26 And it came to pass that we did flee before the servants of Laban, and we were obliged to leave behind our property, and it fell into the hands of Laban.

Why were the records in Laban's possession so important to Lehi's family? (3:19–20) "The Book of Mormon contains a powerful testimony of the importance of scriptural records for the spiritual and intellectual preservation of a nation. The brass plates enabled the Nephites not only to know of and remember the spiritual legacy of ancient Israel but also to have and perpetuate the 'language of [their] fathers.' Later in the Nephite record we learn of the sad tale of the Mulekites, who squandered their possibilities for a time because of their spiritual and intellectual illiteracy, a condition due largely to the lack of a written record (see Omni 1:17; Mosiah 1:3)" (McConkie and Millet, *Doctrinal Commentary*, 1:40).

What can we learn from the failure of the brothers to obtain the plates the first two times? (3:21–28) How did Laman and Lemuel respond to their initial failure? How was that reaction different from Nephi's response? What do these different responses tell you about the character of each of them?

Has the cave been identified where Nephi and his brothers hid? (3:27) Some have claimed that the Khirbet Beit Lei tomb was the brothers' temporary hiding place because of some inscriptions found in the cave. However, according to Dana M. Pike of Brigham Young University, "There is no real basis for such a claim. In addition to the obvious challenges of just reading and dating the inscriptions and the linguistic challenge of relating the name Beit Lei with the name Lehi, this burial chamber seems much too distant from Jerusalem to be a reasonable candidate for the brothers' hiding place" ("Israelite Inscriptions from the Time of Jeremiah and Lehi," 220).

1 Nephi 3:28–31. An Angel Protects Nephi and Sam

What lesson do you learn from how Nephi handled failure? (3:28) Elder Gene R. Cook taught: "Now the brothers had twice failed to obtain their objective. I wonder how strong our faith would be if we were in the same situation. . . .

"After two failures, Nephi still remained strong in the faith. Even when Laman and Lemuel were beating him, he believed. I ask, do *you* still believe when you are being beaten by life? Do you say to the Lord, 'I do not know how I am going to do it, Father, but with thy help I am still going to accomplish thy will.' Or, do you follow the example of Laman and Lemuel who doubted, murmured, feared, and gave up?" (*Living by the Power of Faith*, 46–47). ☉

How does Nephi's deliverance from his brothers' wrath fulfill Nephi's earlier prophecy? (3:29) "Nephi indicated earlier that he would seek to make it clear to the reader that 'the tender mercies of the Lord are over all those whom he hath chosen, because of their faith, to make them mighty even unto the power of deliverance' (1 Nephi 1:20). Here was an occasion when Laman and Lemuel sought to do bodily harm to their younger brothers, and an occasion when the Lord delivered his servants in a miraculous manner, thus verifying the words of the prophet Nephi" (McConkie and Millet, *Doctrinal Commentary*, 1:40).

How could Laman and Lemuel continue to complain after seeing an angel? (3:31) At first it might seem surprising that Laman and Lemuel again resorted to murmuring, even after the appearance of an angel. However, President Joseph Fielding Smith taught: "Personal visitations might become dim as time goes on, but this guidance of the Holy Ghost is renewed and

27 And it came to pass that we fled into the wilderness, and the servants of Laban did not overtake us, and we hid ourselves in the cavity of a rock.

28 And it came to pass that Laman was angry with me, and also with my father; and also was Lemuel, for he hearkened unto the words of Laman. Wherefore Laman and Lemuel did speak many hard words unto us, their younger brothers, and they did smite us even with a rod.

29 And it came to pass as they smote us with a rod, behold, an angel of the Lord came and stood before them, and he spake unto them, saying: Why do ye smite your younger brother with a rod? Know ye not that the Lord hath chosen him to be a ruler over you, and this because of your iniquities? Behold ye shall go up to Jerusalem again, and the Lord will deliver Laban into your hands.

30 And after the angel had spoken unto us, he departed.

31 And after the angel had departed, Laman and Lemuel again began to murmur, saying: How is it possible that the Lord will deliver Laban into our hands? Behold, he is a mighty man, and he can command fifty, yea, even he can slay fifty; then why not us?

continued, day after day, year after year, if we live to be worthy of it" (*Doctrines of Salvation*, 1:44).

Without personal worthiness on the part of Laman and Lemuel, the Spirit could not abide with them, and even the appearance of an angel was not enough to build faith within them.

CHAPTER 4

Nephi slays Laban at the Lord's command and then secures the plates of brass by stratagem— Zoram chooses to join Lehi's family in the wilderness. About 600–592 B.C.

1 And it came to pass that I spake unto my brethren, saying: Let us go up again unto Jerusalem, and let us be faithful in keeping the commandments of the Lord; for behold he is mightier than all the earth, then why not mightier than Laban and his fifty, yea, or even than his tens of thousands?

2 Therefore let us go up; let us be strong like unto Moses; for he truly spake unto the waters of the Red Sea and they divided hither and thither, and our fathers came through, out of captivity, on dry ground, and the armies of Pharaoh did follow and were drowned in the waters of the Red Sea.

3 Now behold ye know that this is true; and ye also know that an angel hath spoken unto you; wherefore can ye doubt? Let us go up; the Lord is able to deliver us, even as our fathers, and to destroy Laban, even as the Egyptians.

4 Now when I had spoken these words, they were yet wroth, and did still continue to murmur; nevertheless they did follow me up until we came without the walls of Jerusalem.

5 And it was by night; and I caused that they should hide themselves without the walls. And after they had hid themselves, I, Nephi, crept into the city and went forth towards the house of Laban.

6 And I was led by the Spirit, not knowing beforehand the things which I should do.

1 Nephi 4:1–3. Nephi Exhorts His Brothers to Have Faith

Why does Nephi refer to Moses and the Exodus? (4:2) The influence of the Exodus is a major theme in the Book of Mormon, much as our pioneer heritage is a common theme to those in the restored Church. "The memory of Israel's exodus from Egypt runs so deeply and clearly in the Book of Mormon that it has naturally drawn the attention of modern students" (Brown, "Exodus Pattern in the Book of Mormon," 75). ●

How could Nephi overcome his brothers' doubt? (4:3) As Nephi recounted Moses's miracle at the Red Sea, he used it as a type, comparable to the situation he and his brothers were in. To inspire his brothers, he "likens" (1 Nephi 19:23) them to the ancient Israelites delivered by the Lord and Laban to the Egyptians.

1 Nephi 4:4–18. Nephi Is Led by the Spirit to Laban

Why didn't the Lord tell Nephi the plan from the beginning? (4:6) President Boyd K. Packer recounted:

"We once had a major decision to make. When our prayers left us uncertain, I went to see Elder Harold B. Lee. . . . He said, 'The problem with you is you want to see the end from the beginning. . . . You must learn to walk a few steps ahead into the darkness, and then the light will turn on and go before you.' That was a life-changing experience from one verse in the Book of Mormon. Haven't you felt at times like Nephi, who said, 'I was led by the Spirit, not knowing beforehand the things which I should do'? (1 Nephi 4:6)" ("Book of Mormon: Another Testament of Jesus Christ," 8).

How might Nephi's example of being "led by the Spirit, not knowing beforehand the things which [he] should do" help you with some of the challenges facing you right now?

Why was Nephi required to kill Laban? (4:10) Elder Jeffrey R. Holland explained: "I believe that story was placed in the very opening verses of a 531-page book and then told in painfully specific detail in order to focus every reader of that record on the absolutely fundamental gospel issue of obedience and submission to the communicated will of the Lord. If Nephi cannot yield to *this terribly painful command*, if he cannot bring himself to obey, then it is entirely probable that he can never succeed or survive in the tasks that lie just ahead" (*On Earth As It Is in Heaven*, 129).

7 Nevertheless I went forth, and as I came near unto the house of Laban I beheld a man, and he had fallen to the earth before me, for he was drunken with wine.

8 And when I came to him I found that it was Laban.

9 And I beheld his sword, and I drew it forth from the sheath thereof; and the hilt thereof was of pure gold, and the workmanship thereof was exceedingly fine, and I saw that the blade thereof was of the most precious steel.

10 And it came to pass that I was constrained by the Spirit that I should kill Laban; but I said in my heart: Never at any time have I shed the blood of man. And I shrunk and would that I might not slay him.

11 And the Spirit said unto me again: Behold the Lord hath delivered him into thy hands. Yea, and I also knew that he had sought to take away mine own life; yea, and he would

God Prepares a Way for His Purposes to Be Fulfilled

The literary repetition in the account of Nephi and his brothers retrieving the brass plates testifies of God's hand in the process of preparing the way to fulfill his purposes. Richard Dilworth Rust wrote: "This quest follows . . . 'the storytelling principle of threefold repetition: a given event happens three times, with a crucial change introduced the third time.'

"In the first of the three visits to Laban, [it was] apparently without a plan. . . . Next, the brothers follow Nephi's plan to offer their gold, silver, and other precious things for the plates of brass. . . . The third time, Nephi goes alone with no plan. . . . Then the Lord's plan goes into effect.

"Each of these efforts is put into motion by a pledge, and the pledges become more and more intense. At the initial request to get the plates, Nephi says to his father, 'I will go and do the things which the Lord hath commanded' (1 Ne. 3:7). After Laman's failure, Nephi increases his initial commitment to go and do what the Lord commanded and applies it to all the brothers: 'As the Lord liveth, and as we live, we will not go down unto our father in the wilderness until we have accomplished the thing which the Lord hath commanded us' (1 Ne. 3:15). When the next plan fails and the older brothers are reproved by an angel for beating their younger brothers, Nephi calls for them all to 'be faithful in keeping the commandments of the Lord' and affirms the power of God by alluding to the great miracle of the Israelites crossing through the Red Sea (1 Ne. 4:1–2). The emphasis has moved from 'I will go and do,' to we will not leave until 'we have accomplished,' to the Lord is 'mightier than Laban and his fifty' and 'the Lord is able to deliver us, even as our fathers, and to destroy Laban, even as the Egyptians' (1 Ne. 4:1, 3).

"Finding Laban drunk in the street, Nephi is three times 'constrained by the Spirit' to kill him (1 Ne. 4:10). The first is a simple injunction: Kill Laban. The second is the impression that the Lord has delivered Laban into Nephi's hands. Nephi thinks of three reasons why he could be justified in taking Laban's life: (1) Laban sought to take away Nephi's own life. (2) Laban would not hearken unto the commands of the Lord. (3) He had taken away property belonging to Nephi's family. The third constraint of the Spirit adds the crucial, convincing element: 'The Lord slayeth the wicked to

not hearken unto the commandments of the Lord; and he also had taken away our property.

12 And it came to pass that the Spirit said unto me again: Slay him, for the Lord hath delivered him into thy hands;

Why was Nephi justified in slaying Laban? (4:12) Joseph Smith declared: "That which is wrong under any circumstance may be and *often is, right under another....* Whatever God requires is right, no matter what it is, although we may not see the reason thereof till long after the events transpire" (*Personal Writings of Joseph Smith*, 508).

13 Behold the Lord slayeth the wicked to bring forth his righteous purposes. It is better that one man should perish than that a nation should dwindle and perish in unbelief.

14 And now, when I, Nephi, had heard these words, I remembered the words of the Lord which he spake unto me in the wilderness, saying that: Inasmuch as thy seed shall keep my commandments, they shall prosper in the land of promise.

Where is there precedent for killing one person to preserve a people? (4:13) Several Old Testament examples that preceded this event with Laban may have given Nephi courage to carry out the command to slay him. "A pivotal example is found in 2 Samuel 20. King David sought the life of Sheba, a rebel guilty of treason. When Sheba took refuge in the city of Abel, Joab, the leader of David's army, demanded that Sheba be released to him. The people of Abel beheaded Sheba instead, and Joab retreated. This episode became an important legal precedent justifying the killing of one person in order to preserve an entire group" (Welch and Parker, "Better That One Man Perish," 17). ✚

bring forth his righteous purposes. It is better that one man should perish than that a nation should dwindle and perish in unbelief' (1 Ne. 4:13).

"Nephi then slays Laban, dresses in his clothes and armor, and with the help of Laban's servant Zoram, gets the brass plates and takes them outside the city wall. There, in calling to his frightened brothers, Nephi reveals his identity to Zoram—whom Nephi holds to keep from fleeing. Nephi then makes three levels of appeal to Zoram. These are introduced by a similar formulaic phrase, moving from sparing Zoram's life, to allowing him freedom, to having a place with Lehi's family:

"'And it came to pass that I spake with him, that if he would hearken unto my words, as the Lord liveth, and as I live, even so that if he would hearken unto our words, we would spare his life. And I spake unto him, even with an oath, that he need not fear; that he should be a free man like unto us if he would go down in the wilderness with us. And I also spake unto him, saying: Surely the Lord hath commanded us to do this thing; and shall we not be diligent in keeping the commandments of the Lord? Therefore, if thou wilt go down into the wilderness to my father thou shalt have place with us' (1 Ne. 4:32–34).

"A three-part pattern is found as well in Sariah's lament to Lehi, with the pattern emphasized by the rhythmical 'Behold ..., and ..., and ...': 'Behold thou hast led us forth from the land of our inheritance [as a so-called visionary man], and my sons are no more, and we perish in the wilderness' (1 Ne. 5:2). This feared decline is counterbalanced by Sariah's three-part praise uttered at the return of her sons. In this utterance she echoes Nephi's initial commitment: 'I also know of a surety that the Lord hath protected my sons, and delivered them out of the hands of Laban, and given them power whereby they could accomplish the thing which the Lord hath commanded them' (1 Ne. 5:8). For his part, Nephi affirms that he and his father obtained the records, searched these scriptures, and carried the records with them so the Lord's commandments could be preserved (1 Ne. 5:21–22)" (*Feasting on the Word*, 27–29).

How did Nephi develop such great faith? (4:18)
Elder Robert D. Hales taught, "Obedience to the laws and ordinances of the gospel is essential to obtain faith in the Lord Jesus Christ" ("Aaronic Priesthood," 39).

1 Nephi 4:19–28. Nephi Obtains the Brass Plates

Who were the elders of the Jews? (4:22) "The Hebrew word translated as 'elder; in the English Bible is *zāqēn* and derives from the Hebrew word for 'beard.' At its most basic definition, then, a biblical 'elder' was an aged ('bearded') and therefore a wise and experienced male who held cultural, political, or religious authority and prestige in Israel. City elders are mentioned especially in the book of Deuteronomy, reflecting the social institutions and civic attitudes that would have been most prominent in Jerusalem in Lehi's day. The 'elders of the Jews' in 1 Nephi 4:22, accordingly, should not necessarily be thought of as elders in the Melchizedek Priesthood. . . . Instead, they were probably senior religious or political bureaucrats

15 Yea, and I also thought that they could not keep the commandments of the Lord according to the law of Moses, save they should have the law.

16 And I also knew that the law was engraven upon the plates of brass.

17 And again, I knew that the Lord had delivered Laban into my hands for this cause—that I might obtain the records according to his commandments.

18 Therefore I did obey the voice of the Spirit, and took Laban by the hair of the head, and I smote off his head with his own sword.

19 And after I had smitten off his head with his own sword, I took the garments of Laban and put them upon mine own body; yea, even every whit; and I did gird on his armor about my loins.

20 And after I had done this, I went forth unto the treasury of Laban. And as I went forth towards the treasury of Laban, behold, I saw the servant of Laban who had the keys of the treasury. And I commanded him in the voice of Laban, that he should go with me into the treasury.

21 And he supposed me to be his master, Laban, for he beheld the garments and also the sword girded about my loins.

22 And he spake unto me concerning the elders of the Jews, he knowing that his master, Laban, had been out by night among them.

23 And I spake unto him as if it had been Laban.

24 And I also spake unto him that I should carry the engravings, which were upon the plates of brass, to my elder brethren, who were without the walls.

25 And I also bade him that he should follow me.

who served as 'community leaders'" (Book of Mormon Central, "Who Were the 'Elders of the Jews' Mentioned by Zoram?").

26 And he, supposing that I spake of the brethren of the church, and that I was truly that Laban whom I had slain, wherefore he did follow me.

Why is using the word *church* not anachronistic? (4:26) Some critics have claimed that the Prophet Joseph made a mistake by using the word *church*. "[The] term 'Church' [would not] sound strange in Jewish ears. The same Greek word [*ecclesia*], as the equivalent of the Hebrew Qahal, 'convocation,' 'the called,' occurs in the Septuagint rendering of the Old Testament, and in 'the Wisdom of the Son of Sirach' (Ecclus, 24.2) and was apparently in familiar use at the time" (Edersheim, *Life and Times of Jesus the Messiah*, 1034).

27 And he spake unto me many times concerning the elders of the Jews, as I went forth unto my brethren, who were without the walls.

28 And it came to pass that when Laman saw me he was exceedingly frightened, and also Lemuel and Sam. And they fled from before my presence; for they supposed it was Laban, and that he had slain me and had sought to take away their lives also.

29 And it came to pass that I called after them, and they did hear me; wherefore they did cease to flee from my presence.

30 And it came to pass that when the servant of Laban beheld my brethren he began to tremble, and was about to flee from before me and return to the city of Jerusalem.

1 Nephi 4:29–38. Zoram Joins Lehi's Family

31 And now I, Nephi, being a man large in stature, and also having received much strength of the Lord, therefore I did seize upon the servant of Laban, and held him, that he should not flee.

What effect does the experience of obtaining the brass plates have on Nephi? (4:31) Nephi, only two chapters earlier, described himself as being "exceedingly young" (1 Nephi 2:16). Now, in 1 Nephi 4:31 he describes himself as a man. It appears that this was a significant turning point for this young prophet.

32 And it came to pass that I spake with him, that if he would hearken unto my words, as the Lord liveth, and as I live, even so that if he would hearken unto our words, we would spare his life.

How binding were oaths in the ancient world? (4:32) "What astonishes the western reader is the miraculous effect of Nephi's oath on Zoram. . . . The reactions of both parties make sense when one realizes that the oath is the one thing that is most sacred and inviolable among the desert people and their descendants. . . .

33 And I spake unto him, even with an oath, that he need not fear; that he should be a free man like unto us if he would go down in the wilderness with us.

"So we see that the only way that Nephi could possibly have pacified the struggling Zoram in an instant was to utter the one oath that no man would dream of breaking, the most solemn of all oaths to the Semite: 'As the Lord liveth, and as I live' (1 Nephi 4:32)" (Nibley, *Approach to the Book of Mormon*, 128–29). ❂

34 And I also spake unto him, saying: Surely the Lord hath commanded us to do this thing; and shall we not be diligent in keeping the commandments of the Lord? Therefore, if thou wilt go down into the wilderness to my father thou shalt have place with us.

35 And it came to pass that Zoram did take courage at the words which I spake. Now Zoram was the name of the servant; and he promised that he would go down into the wilderness unto our father. Yea, and he also made an oath unto us that he would tarry with us from that time forth.

36 Now we were desirous that he should tarry with us for this cause, that the Jews might not know concerning our flight into the wilderness, lest they should pursue us and destroy us.

37 And it came to pass that when Zoram had made an oath unto us, our fears did cease concerning him.

38 And it came to pass that we took the plates of brass and the servant of Laban, and departed into the wilderness, and journeyed unto the tent of our father.

CHAPTER 5

Sariah complains against Lehi—Both rejoice over the return of their sons—They offer sacrifices—The plates of brass contain writings of Moses and the prophets—The plates identify Lehi as a descendant of Joseph—Lehi prophesies concerning his seed and the preservation of the plates. About 600–592 B.C.

1 And it came to pass that after we had come down into the wilderness unto our father, behold, he was filled with joy, and also my mother, Sariah, was exceedingly glad, for she truly had mourned because of us.

2 For she had supposed that we had perished in the wilderness; and she also had complained against my father, telling him that he was a visionary man; saying: Behold thou hast led us forth from the land of our

1 Nephi 5:1–9. Sariah Rejoices When Her Sons Return Safely from Jerusalem

What does the name Sariah mean? (5:1) Jeffrey R. Chadwick pointed out that the name Sariah probably means "Yah (Jehovah) is Prince" ("Names Lehi and Sariah," 34). ●

Why was Sariah so worried? (5:2) Before Sariah "complained" against Lehi, she mourned over her sons (see v. 1), supposing they had "perished in the wilderness." What led to these terrifying thoughts of a loving mother? The known enemies in Jerusalem created by Lehi's divine prophecies might explain much of her

inheritance, and my sons are no more, and we perish in the wilderness.

3 And after this manner of language had my mother complained against my father.

4 And it had come to pass that my father spake unto her, saying: I know that I am a visionary man; for if I had not seen the things of God in a vision I should not have known the goodness of God, but had tarried at Jerusalem, and had perished with my brethren.

5 But behold, I have obtained a land of promise, in the which things I do rejoice; yea, and I know that the Lord will deliver my sons out of the hands of Laban, and bring them down again unto us in the wilderness.

6 And after this manner of language did my father, Lehi, comfort my mother, Sariah, concerning us, while we journeyed in the wilderness up to the land of Jerusalem, to obtain the record of the Jews.

7 And when we had returned to the tent of my father, behold their joy was full, and my mother was comforted.

8 And she spake, saying: Now I know of a surety that the Lord hath commanded my husband to flee into the wilderness; yea, and I also know of a surety that the Lord hath protected my sons, and delivered them out of the hands of Laban, and given them power whereby they could accomplish the thing which the Lord hath commanded them. And after this manner of language did she speak.

9 And it came to pass that they did rejoice exceedingly, and did offer sacrifice and burnt offerings unto the Lord; and they gave thanks unto the God of Israel.

concern. Also, the danger of robbers in the wilderness, the distance to Jerusalem and the time it took to traverse it, and the treacherousness of the terrain contributed to her fears. She had, after all, traveled the route herself and knew its difficulty.

Why would faithful Sariah murmur? (5:3–6) "A hasty and narrow review of these verses could lead a casual reader to conclude that Sariah was a 'murmurer' ... But that approach ignores how women were generally viewed in that culture.... As if the Lord were stretching her to the brink of her faith.... Facing the potential loss of all four of her sons, she 'murmured.'... Children were the focus of life for women in ancient Israel (see Psalms 127:3; 128:3).... Such strong family ties made the tragedy of losing a son especially traumatic—almost insurmountably devastating if a mother like Sariah were to lose all of her sons at one time" (Olson, "Desert Epiphany: Sariah and the Women in 1 Nephi", 7, 9). ✚

Why did Lehi say he had already obtained the land of promise while he was yet in the wilderness? (5:5) Hugh Nibley commented: "'But behold [the tense is important here], I have obtained a land of promise'... already had it, you see. The promise is a promise. All things are present once you have made the transition—once you have accepted it" (*Teachings of the Book of Mormon*, 1:164).

How does the Book of Mormon account depict the growing faith of a righteous mother? (5:8–9) "This verse, where Sariah steps back into unity with her prophet-husband, concludes the Book of Mormon's best-developed description of a woman. In Sariah's role as a mother, we see her hopes, fears, overriding love, and eventually firm faith" (Gardner, *Second Witness*, 1:128).

What is the difference between sacrifice and burnt offerings? (5:9) "The chief question concerning Lehi's sacrifices in the wilderness is how Joseph Smith knew the proper sacrifices that travelers were to offer according to the Mosaic law. The answer is that he did not. But Lehi did. And he offered sacrifices suitable for the occasions noted in Nephi's narrative, including burnt offerings for atonement" (Brown, "New Light from Arabia on Lehi's Trail," 63). The record notes three sacrifices Lehi offered (see 1 Nephi 2:7; 5:9; 7:22) and appropriately express thanksgiving. Lehi is recorded as making burnt offerings twice (see 1 Nephi 5:9; 1 Nephi 7:22). Appropriately, these offerings were made after situations involving sin. ⊕

1 Nephi 5:10–16. The Contents of the Brass Plates

What did the brass plates contain? (5:11–16) "Nephi said that the plates of brass contained 'the five books of Moses' along with a "record of the Jews . . . and also the prophecies of the holy prophets, from the beginning, even down to the commencement of the reign of Zedekiah.' The collection even contained 'many prophecies which have been spoken by the mouth of Jeremiah' (1 Nephi 5:11–13). The 'five books of Moses'" refers to Genesis, Exodus, Leviticus, Numbers, and Deuteronomy. The 'record of the Jews' was likely Joshua, Judges, 1–2 Samuel, and 1–2 Kings. The 'holy prophets' down to the time of Zedekiah may refer to the writings of Isaiah, Hosea, Amos, Micah, Nahum, Habakkuk, and Zephaniah, as well as Jeremiah" (Book of Mormon Central, "What Parts of the Old Testament Were on the Plates of Brass?").

What insights do the brass plates provide to our understanding of the Old Testament? (5:11) The scriptures recorded on the brass plates testified that Old Testament prophets knew the gospel. "What interests us more than the books included on the brass plates is the tone and tenor and general approach to the gospel that they set forth. They are gospel oriented and speak of Christ and the various Christian concepts, which the world falsely assumes to have originated with Jesus and the early apostles" (McConkie, "Doctrinal Restoration," 17).

Why are the contents of the brass plates so vital to us today? (5:13) Nephi prophetically said that many plain and most precious things would be "taken away" from the Bible (1 Nephi 13:26, 28, 29, 40). The importance of the brass plates to the Nephite nation as well as to future readers of the Book of Mormon may be seen, at least partly, in the account of the death of Laban. The life of Laban was taken by the Lord to preserve this version of the Old Testament. Joseph Smith said, "From sundry revelations which had been received, it was apparent that many important points touching the salvation of man, had been taken from

10 And after they had given thanks unto the God of Israel, my father, Lehi, took the records which were engraven upon the plates of brass, and he did search them from the beginning.

11 And he beheld that they did contain the five books of Moses, which gave an account of the creation of the world, and also of Adam and Eve, who were our first parents;

12 And also a record of the Jews from the beginning, even down to the commencement of the reign of Zedekiah, king of Judah;

13 And also the prophecies of the holy prophets, from the beginning, even down to the commencement of the reign of Zedekiah; and also many prophecies which have been spoken by the mouth of Jeremiah.

14 And it came to pass that my father, Lehi, also found upon the plates of brass a genealogy of his fathers; wherefore he knew that he was a descendant of Joseph; yea, even that Joseph who was the son of Jacob, who was sold into Egypt, and who was preserved by the hand of the Lord, that he might preserve his father, Jacob, and all his household from perishing with famine.

15 And they were also led out of captivity and out of the land of Egypt, by that same God who had preserved them.

16 And thus my father, Lehi, did discover the genealogy of his fathers. And Laban also was a descendant of Joseph, wherefore he and his fathers had kept the records.

the Bible, or lost before it was compiled" (*Joseph Smith* [manual], 217).

How was Lehi a descendant of Joseph? (5:14–16) Through the tribe of Manasseh, Lehi was a descendant of Joseph who was sold into Egypt (Alma 10:3). It appears that Ishmael's family was descended from Ephraim. President Franklin D. Richards recounted hearing the Prophet Joseph say that Ishmael's genealogy was recorded in the lost 116 pages of the Book of Mormon manuscript (see "Origin," 425). ⊕

1 Nephi 5:17–22. After Searching the Brass Plates, Lehi Is Filled with the Spirit and Prophesies

How will the brass plates "go forth unto all nations, kindreds, tongues, and people"? (5:18–19) This prophecy by Lehi can be interpreted multiple ways. The doctrines, ideas, and principles from which the prophets of the Book of Mormon taught come directly from the book itself. In this way, the brass plates are going forth to all nations, kindreds, tongues, and peoples (see JS–H 1:33; Alma 37:1–4). Further, Elder Bruce R. McConkie suggested that in a future day "the Lord will raise up a prophet, who will also be a seer and a translator to whom he will give the brass plates that they may be translated for the benefit and blessing of those in all nations" ("Doctrinal Restoration," 16).

What is one of the blessings of searching the scriptures? (5:21) Lehi searched the brass plates from the beginning and found them "desirable," especially regarding preserving a knowledge of the commandments of God. President Spencer W. Kimball wisely counseled the Saints: "I find that when I get casual in my relationships with divinity and when it seems that no divine ear is listening and no divine voice is speaking, that I am far, far away. If I immerse myself in the scriptures the distance narrows and the spirituality returns" (*Teachings of Spencer W. Kimball*, 135).

17 And now when my father saw all these things, he was filled with the Spirit, and began to prophesy concerning his seed—

18 That these plates of brass should go forth unto all nations, kindreds, tongues, and people who were of his seed.

19 Wherefore, he said that these plates of brass should never perish; neither should they be dimmed any more by time. And he prophesied many things concerning his seed.

20 And it came to pass that thus far I and my father had kept the commandments wherewith the Lord had commanded us.

21 And we had obtained the records which the Lord had commanded us, and searched them and found that they were desirable; yea, even of great worth unto us, insomuch that we could preserve the commandments of the Lord unto our children.

22 Wherefore, it was wisdom in the Lord that we should carry them with us, as we journeyed in the wilderness towards the land of promise.

1 Nephi 6:1–6. Nephi Writes Only the Things That Please God

How did Nephi use Lehi's record? (6:1) Nephi mentioned his father's record throughout the small plates. The first ten chapters of 1 Nephi are Nephi's abridgment of his father's record (see also 1 Nephi 1:16–17). ⊕

What was Nephi's major intent throughout his writings? (6:4)

This is Nephi's "first insertion of his current time into his historical narrative. However, it also reminds us that although he is giving us history, it is history with a much more important purpose. Nephi declares: 'For the fulness of mine intent is that I may persuade men to come unto the God of Abraham, and the God of Isaac, and the God of Jacob, and be saved' (1 Ne. 6:4). The recording of Israelite history, and Nephite history, is designed to show the acts of God in the lives of his people" (Gardner, "Musings on the Making of Mormon's Book: 1 Nephi 6").

Why didn't Nephi include things "more pleasing unto the world" in his record? (6:5) "Naturally, some would like to have even more contextual material about the life, times, and culture of the peoples in the Book of Mormon.... No wonder these scriptures fail to please or to impress the world. There are those who prefer details on ancient agriculture to the 'bread of life,' who prefer information on the rising of dynasties to insights on the rising of Jesus from the tomb" (Maxwell, *But for a Small Moment*, 36).

What is Nephi's charge to the future record keepers? (6:6) The small plates contain a record of the spiritual ministry of the Nephites. "Nephi's descendants are remarkably obedient to his instructions. A comparison

CHAPTER 6

Nephi writes of the things of God—Nephi's purpose is to persuade men to come unto the God of Abraham and be saved. About 600–592 B.C.

1 And now I, Nephi, do not give the genealogy of my fathers in this part of my record; neither at any time shall I give it after upon these plates which I am writing; for it is given in the record which has been kept by my father; wherefore, I do not write it in this work.

2 For it sufficeth me to say that we are descendants of Joseph.

3 And it mattereth not to me that I am particular to give a full account of all the things of my father, for they cannot be written upon these plates, for I desire the room that I may write of the things of God.

4 For the fulness of mine intent is that I may persuade men to come unto the God of Abraham, and the God of Isaac, and the God of Jacob, and be saved.

5 Wherefore, the things which are pleasing unto the world I do not write, but the things which are pleasing unto God and unto those who are not of the world.

6 Wherefore, I shall give commandment unto my seed, that they shall not occupy these plates with things which are not of worth unto the children of men.

of the small-plate material (1 Nephi–Omni) with that which remains of the large plates (Mosiah–4 Nephi) shows that the large plates contain a tremendous amount of material on wars and contentions, virtually none of which appears in the small plates. The truly historical information contained in the small plates is limited to 1 Nephi, where it provides the framework for the more important spiritual story, and Omni, where the historical data explains why Nephi's descendants relinquished the records. In between, they record almost exclusively things of the spirit (or, as in Omni, their lack of relevant spiritual experiences to record)" (Gardner, *Second Witness*, 1:139).

CHAPTER 7

Lehi's sons return to Jerusalem and invite Ishmael and his household to join them in their journey—Laman and others rebel—Nephi exhorts his brethren to have faith in the Lord—They bind him with cords and plan his destruction—He is freed by the power of faith—His brethren ask forgiveness—Lehi and his company offer sacrifice and burnt offerings. About 600–592 B.C.

1 And now I would that ye might know, that after my father, Lehi, had made an end of prophesying concerning his seed, it came to pass that the Lord spake unto him again, saying that it was not meet for him, Lehi, that he should take his family into the wilderness alone; but that his sons should take daughters to wife, that they might raise up seed unto the Lord in the land of promise.

2 And it came to pass that the Lord commanded him that I, Nephi, and my brethren, should again return unto the land of Jerusalem, and bring down Ishmael and his family into the wilderness.

3 And it came to pass that I, Nephi, did again, with my brethren, go forth into the wilderness to go up to Jerusalem.

1 Nephi 7:1–5. Lehi's Sons Return to Jerusalem for Ishmael's Family

Why did Lehi send his sons back to Jerusalem for Ishmael and his family? (7:1) "The first divine commandment to men, created in God's image, was: 'Be fruitful, and multiply and replenish the earth, and subdue it' (Gen. 1:28). . . . The commandment to replenish the earth has not been canceled; it will be in force until the entire earth is filled with the children of God.

"God commands the sons of Lehi to go to Jerusalem and bring Ishmael and his family down to the Valley. . . . Both he and Lehi were the descendants of Joseph, Ishmael through Ephraim and Lehi through Manasseh [see 1 Nephi 7:2]. His family consisted of his wife, two sons with their families, and five daughters (v. 6)" (Reynolds and Sjodahl, *Commentary on the Book of Mormon*, 1:55). ☉

Why is it important that Lehi and Ishmael join their families together? (7:2) In 2 Chronicles 15:8–9 we learn that people from the tribes of Ephraim, Manasseh, and Simeon migrated to the kingdom of Judah before the kingdom of Israel was conquered by the Assyrians. Lehi was of the tribe of Manasseh (see Alma 10:3). Elder Erastus Snow noted, "The Prophet Joseph Smith informed us that . . . Ishmael was of the lineage of Ephraim" (in *Journal of Discourses*, 23:184). About 1900 B.C. Jacob blessed Ephraim and Manasseh,

Joseph's sons, saying, "Let my name be named on them . . . and let them grow into a multitude in the midst of the earth" (Genesis 48:16). Jacob foresaw that descendants of Ephraim and Manasseh would be scattered throughout the world (see Genesis 48–49). ⊕

Why was Ishmael's family selected? (7:4) "Lehi, faced with the prospect of a long journey in the wilderness, sent back for Ishmael. . . . The interesting thing is that Nephi takes Ishmael (unlike Zoram) completely for granted, never explaining who he is or how he fits into the picture—the act of sending for him seems to be the most natural thing in the world, as does the marriage of his daughters with Lehi's sons. Since it has ever been the custom among the desert people for a man to marry the daughter of his paternal uncle . . . , it is hard to avoid the impression that Lehi and Ishmael were related" (Nibley, *Lehi in the Desert*, 40).

1 Nephi 7:6–15. Nephi Warns His Brethren Not to Go Back Again to Jerusalem

Why does Nephi recount events for Laman and Lemuel which had just transpired? (7:8–12) Lehi and Nephi experienced frustrations similar to those of earlier prophets who likewise dealt with rebellious souls. Moses once declared to wayward Israel: "Take heed to thyself, and keep thy soul diligently, lest thou forget the things which thine eyes have seen, and lest they depart from thy heart all the days of thy life: but teach them thy sons, and thy sons' sons" (Deuteronomy 4:9). Here Nephi reminded his brothers of all God had done for them to elicit more faith and obedience from his very forgetful brothers.

How could someone forget the experience of seeing an angel? (7:10) "Christ has himself declared that the manifestations we might have of the Spirit of Christ, or from a visitation of an angel, a tangible resurrected being, would not leave the impression and would not convince us and place within us that something which we cannot get away from which we receive through a manifestation of the Holy Ghost.

4 And it came to pass that we went up unto the house of Ishmael, and we did gain favor in the sight of Ishmael, insomuch that we did speak unto him the words of the Lord.

5 And it came to pass that the Lord did soften the heart of Ishmael, and also his household, insomuch that they took their journey with us down into the wilderness to the tent of our father.

6 And it came to pass that as we journeyed in the wilderness, behold Laman and Lemuel, and two of the daughters of Ishmael, and the two sons of Ishmael and their families, did rebel against us; yea, against me, Nephi, and Sam, and their father, Ishmael, and his wife, and his three other daughters.

7 And it came to pass in the which rebellion, they were desirous to return unto the land of Jerusalem.

8 And now I, Nephi, being grieved for the hardness of their hearts, therefore I spake unto them, saying, yea, even unto Laman and unto Lemuel: Behold ye are mine elder brethren, and how is it that ye are so hard in your hearts, and so blind in your minds, that ye have need that I, your younger brother, should speak unto you, yea, and set an example for you?

9 How is it that ye have not hearkened unto the word of the Lord?

10 How is it that ye have forgotten that ye have seen an angel of the Lord?

11 Yea, and how is it that ye have forgotten what great things the Lord hath done for us, in delivering us out of the hands of Laban, and also that we should obtain the record?

12 Yea, and how is it that ye have forgotten that the Lord is able to do all things according to his will, for the children of men, if it so be that they exercise faith in him? Wherefore, let us be faithful to him.

13 And if it so be that we are faithful to him, we shall obtain the land of promise; and ye shall know at some future period that the word of the Lord shall be fulfilled concerning the destruction of Jerusalem; for all things which the Lord hath spoken concerning the destruction of Jerusalem must be fulfilled.

14 For behold, the Spirit of the Lord ceaseth soon to strive with them; for behold, they have rejected the prophets, and Jeremiah have they cast into prison. And they have sought to take away the life of my father, insomuch that they have driven him out of the land.

15 Now behold, I say unto you that if ye will return unto Jerusalem ye shall also perish with them. And now, if ye have choice, go up to the land, and remember the words which I speak unto you, that if ye go ye will also perish; for thus the Spirit of the Lord constraineth me that I should speak.

16 And it came to pass that when I, Nephi, had spoken these words unto my brethren, they were angry with me. And it came to pass that they did lay their hands upon me, for behold, they were exceedingly wroth, and they did bind me with cords, for they sought to take away my life, that they might leave me in the wilderness to be devoured by wild beasts.

17 But it came to pass that I prayed unto the Lord, saying: O Lord, according to my faith which is in thee, wilt thou deliver me from the hands of my brethren; yea, even give me strength that I may burst these bands with which I am bound.

Personal visitations might become dim as time goes on, but this guidance of the Holy Ghost is renewed and continued, day after day, year after year, if we live to be worthy of it" (Smith, *Doctrines of Salvation*, 1:44).

When was Jeremiah first cast into prison? (7:14) "Critics claim that Nephi's mention of Jeremiah being put into prison is anachronistic, since Jeremiah would not have been in prison when Lehi left Jerusalem." However, "Jeremiah was put into prison at least twice during Zedekiah's reign, once soon after Zedekiah ascended the throne [see Jeremiah 37:1, 15]. Jeremiah was released at some point and again able to preach. He was later put into prison again [see Jeremiah 38:1–6, 13, 28]" ("Book of Mormon Anachronisms: Jeremiah Being Put into Prison," fairmormon.org). ⊕

1 Nephi 7:16–22. Nephi Is Protected from His Brothers

What can we learn from Nephi asking for strength? (7:17) Elder David A. Bednar taught: "The implication of this episode for each of us is straightforward. As you and I come to understand and employ the enabling power of the Atonement in our personal lives, we will pray and seek for strength to change our circumstances rather than praying for our circumstances to be changed" ("The Atonement and the Journey of Mortality," 43–44). ⊕

When have you needed the Lord's deliverance?
(7:18) Nephi, according to his faith, was delivered
from his brothers' evil intentions of physical harm to
him. Elder L. Tom Perry stated: "Many of the stories
of the Book of Mormon are stories of deliverance"
("Power of Deliverance," 94).

Reflect upon a time when the Lord delivered you
or a family member from physical harm or a difficult
trial.

Why did Ishmael's daughter and her mother plead-
ing for Nephi soften his brothers' hearts? (7:19)
"The mother and one of the daughters pleaded with
them. This is a thing that no Arab under any circumstance can resist. If a mother or daughter from another
tribe pleads, you are under obligation—even if it is
your worst enemy. It's the chivalric oath. The rules of
chivalry in the Middle Ages were adopted during the
Crusades and taken back [to Europe] in the time of
Edward I. They were taken from the Arabs" (Nibley,
Teachings of the Book of Mormon, 1:169).

What does *frankly* mean? (7:21) Webster's 1828
American Dictionary of the English Language defines
frankly as meaning "freely and without constraint."

18 And it came to pass that when I had said
these words, behold, the bands were loosed
from off my hands and feet, and I stood
before my brethren, and I spake unto them
again.

19 And it came to pass that they were angry with me again, and sought to lay hands
upon me; but behold, one of the daughters
of Ishmael, yea, and also her mother, and
one of the sons of Ishmael, did plead with
my brethren, insomuch that they did soften
their hearts; and they did cease striving to
take away my life.

20 And it came to pass that they were sorrowful, because of their wickedness, insomuch that they did bow down before me,
and did plead with me that I would forgive
them of the thing that they had done against
me.

21 And it came to pass that I did frankly forgive them all that they had done, and I did
exhort them that they would pray unto the
Lord their God for forgiveness. And it came
to pass that they did so. And after they had
done praying unto the Lord we did again
travel on our journey towards the tent of our
father.

22 And it came to pass that we did come
down unto the tent of our father. And after I
and my brethren and all the house of Ishmael
had come down unto the tent of my father,
they did give thanks unto the Lord their
God; and they did offer sacrifice and burnt
offerings unto him.

CHAPTER 8

Lehi sees a vision of the tree of life—He partakes of its fruit and desires his family to do likewise—He sees a rod of iron, a strait and narrow path, and the mists of darkness that enshroud men—Sariah, Nephi, and Sam partake of the fruit, but Laman and Lemuel refuse. About 600–592 B.C.

1 And it came to pass that we had gathered together all manner of seeds of every kind, both of grain of every kind, and also of the seeds of fruit of every kind.

2 And it came to pass that while my father tarried in the wilderness he spake unto us, saying: Behold, I have dreamed a dream; or, in other words, I have seen a vision.

3 And behold, because of the thing which I have seen, I have reason to rejoice in the Lord because of Nephi and also of Sam; for I have reason to suppose that they, and also many of their seed, will be saved.

4 But behold, Laman and Lemuel, I fear exceedingly because of you; for behold, methought I saw in my dream, a dark and dreary wilderness.

5 And it came to pass that I saw a man, and he was dressed in a white robe; and he came and stood before me.

6 And it came to pass that he spake unto me, and bade me follow him.

1 Nephi 8:1–8. Lehi Sees a Vision of His Family and the Tree of Life

Why is seed gathering recorded here? (8:1) "The gathering of 'the seeds of fruit of every kind' prepares our minds for the central symbol of Lehi's dream: the fruit of the tree of life, a fruit 'desirable above all other fruit' (verse 12); the 'seeds' anticipate Lehi's concern for his own 'seed' (verse 3); and the repetition of 'every kind' foreshadows the many kinds of people and paths in the dream. The gathering of the seeds also suggests that they were ready for a long journey that would take years, and that this was therefore the right time for Lehi to receive his historic vision" (Packard and Packard, *Feasting upon the Word*, 14).

Why should we study Lehi's dream? (8:2) President Boyd K. Packer taught why each member of the Church should read and reread Lehi's dream: "You may think that Lehi's dream or vision has no special meaning for you, but it does. You are in it; all of us are in it.... Lehi's dream or vision of the iron rod has in it everything a Latter-day Saint needs to understand the test of life.... Read the dream or vision carefully; then read it again" ("Finding Ourselves in Lehi's Dream," 22).

Who was the man dressed in a white robe? (8:5) Neither Lehi nor Nephi identifies the man in the white robe. Many assume it was an angel or perhaps Jesus Christ. Heavenly beings wearing white robes and standing before prophets is consistent with the experience of Joseph Smith when Moroni, who was wearing an "exceedingly white" robe (JS–H 1:32), appeared to him, and also that of Daniel, who saw in vision "a man clothed in linen" who stood before him (Daniel 10:5 [2–12]). Lehi does not give the interpretation of every symbol in his dream but rather focuses on the outcome of his family members' choices.

How and when was the darkness dispersed for Lehi? (8:7–8) "[Lehi] knew that the fruit of that tree was 'desirable to make one happy,' the sweetest and most important fruit of life and eternity, and he was anxious to reach and partake of it. Before he could realize this blessing, however, he was required to pass through a 'dark and dreary waste,' traveling 'for the space of many hours in darkness.' Earnestly praying to the Lord, holding fast to the iron rod which was the word of God, resisting the 'temptations of the devil' and the mockery of the proud and cynical, Lehi overcame the darkness and found the light. Only then did he taste the inspiration, the soul-filling joy of the love of God" (Hanks, "Conquer the Darkness," 321). ⊕

1 Nephi 8:9–20. Lehi Sees a Tree with White Fruit, a Rod of Iron, and a Strait and Narrow Path

How does Lehi overcome the darkness? (8:9) How is the large and spacious field like the world? How can prayer help us dispel the darkness and see the world more clearly?

What does the tree represent? (8:10–11) Elder Jeffrey R. Holland suggested that "the tree of life . . . [is a symbol] of Christ's redemption. . . . The life, mission, and atonement of Christ are the ultimate manifestations of the Tree of Life" (*Christ and the New Covenant*, 160–61; see Griggs, "Tree of Life in Ancient Cultures," 26–31; see also commentary in this volume on 1 Nephi 11:13–25). ⊕

How did Lehi describe the fruit? (8:11–12) How do you feel when you ponder the Atonement of Jesus Christ and the love that Heavenly Father and His Son, Jesus Christ, have for you? How would you describe the blessings of the Atonement?

What experiences create an anxious desire in parents for their children to partake of the Savior's Atonement? (8:12) "Parents who have, through gospel living, partaken of the fruit of the tree (which is the love of God) and who know the sweet sense of surrender in the kingdom of God will also be stirred, as Lehi was, for they too will be anxious, exceedingly anxious, that their families should partake also. Those who have known the sweetness of service in the kingdom and who have looked at life through the lens of the gospel will ever be restless with a divine discontent until their families do partake of that precious fruit and thereby witness for themselves" (Maxwell, *That My Family Should Partake*, 1).

7 And it came to pass that as I followed him I beheld myself that I was in a dark and dreary waste.

8 And after I had traveled for the space of many hours in darkness, I began to pray unto the Lord that he would have mercy on me, according to the multitude of his tender mercies.

9 And it came to pass after I had prayed unto the Lord I beheld a large and spacious field.

10 And it came to pass that I beheld a tree, whose fruit was desirable to make one happy.

11 And it came to pass that I did go forth and partake of the fruit thereof; and I beheld that it was most sweet, above all that I ever before tasted. Yea, and I beheld that the fruit thereof was white, to exceed all the whiteness that I had ever seen.

12 And as I partook of the fruit thereof it filled my soul with exceedingly great joy; wherefore, I began to be desirous that my family should partake of it also; for I knew that it was desirable above all other fruit.

13 And as I cast my eyes round about, that perhaps I might discover my family also, I beheld a river of water; and it ran along, and it was near the tree of which I was partaking the fruit.

14 And I looked to behold from whence it came; and I saw the head thereof a little way off; and at the head thereof I beheld your mother Sariah, and Sam, and Nephi; and they stood as if they knew not whither they should go.

15 And it came to pass that I beckoned unto them; and I also did say unto them with a loud voice that they should come unto me, and partake of the fruit, which was desirable above all other fruit.

16 And it came to pass that they did come unto me and partake of the fruit also.

17 And it came to pass that I was desirous that Laman and Lemuel should come and partake of the fruit also; wherefore, I cast mine eyes towards the head of the river, that perhaps I might see them.

18 And it came to pass that I saw them, but they would not come unto me and partake of the fruit.

19 And I beheld a rod of iron, and it extended along the bank of the river, and led to the tree by which I stood.

What does the river of water represent? (8:13) "Lehi next discovered a river of water that 'ran along, and . . . was near the tree of which [he] was partaking the fruit.' This river represented filthiness, as well as 'hell' and 'the depths thereof.' So much was [Lehi's] mind swallowed up in other things [Lehi was deeply concerned for his family] that he beheld not the filthiness of the water' (1 Nephi 12:16; 1 Nephi 15:27)" (McConkie and Millet, *Doctrinal Commentary*. 1:56).

In what ways does Lehi's invitation to his family parallel the Lord's invitation to each one of us? (8:14–16) "Throughout the scriptures, the Lord says, 'Come unto me.'. . . These are the very words that Lehi uses when he invites his family to partake of the fruit. . . . Lehi is a loving father who invites his children to come unto him, just as we are constantly being invited to come unto God" (Osguthorpe, "Power of Inspired Invitations," 3). ⊙

What example does Lehi provide for parents whose children are disobedient? (8:17–18) Lehi never gave up on his disobedient sons. Elder David A. Bednar wrote, "Faithful parents may find strength to endure as they follow the examples of other righteous parents with disobedient children. In the Book of Mormon, Father Lehi consistently and constantly encouraged his wayward sons to turn to the Lord . . . [As] Lehi was about to depart this earth, yet he still invited and enticed his wayward sons to "hearken unto [his] words" (2 Nephi 1:12)" ("Faithful Parents and Wayward Children," *Ensign*, Mar. 2014, 32–33).

What does the rod of iron represent? (8:19) "The term rod of iron is found in Psalm 2:9 and in three passages in the book of Revelation [Revelation 2:27; 12:5; 19:15]. . . . All of them imply that the rod is a symbol of ruling power. . . . Anciently, the rod was used both for correction and for gentle guidance. . . . The rod [is] both a source of support (as the word of God) and a weapon of defense. . . . By comparing the word of God with a . . . rod, the prophets have shown us that there is both strength and love in obedience to the Lord" (Tvedtnes, "*Rod* and *Sword* as the Word of God," 48–55). ⊙

Is there a difference between *strait and straight*?
(8:20) *Strait* can mean "a narrow passage, strict or rigorous," whereas *straight* can mean a "straight line" (*Webster's Ninth New Collegiate Dictionary*, 1163–64). In Lehi's vision, the strait path, if faithfully followed, led to the tree and the fruit—which are representations of the redemption of Jesus Christ and ultimately eternal life.

"The strait and narrow path, though clearly marked, is a path, not a freeway nor an escalator. Indeed, there are times when the only way the strait and narrow path can be followed is on one's knees! And we are to help each other along the path" (Maxwell, "A Brother Offended," 38).

1 Nephi 8:21–34. Lehi Sees Numberless Concourses of People

Who are the groups of people represented in Lehi's dream? (8:21) Four groups are identified in Lehi's dream: Group 1 (1 Nephi 8:21–23) is made up of individuals who start on the path to the tree but are lost in the mist; Group 2 (1 Nephi 8:24–25, 28) is those who reach the tree (and taste the fruit) by holding onto the rod but fall away when they are mocked by the people in the great and spacious building; Group 3 (1 Nephi 8:29–30, 33) is those who continually hold fast to the iron rod, fall down, and partake of the fruit of the tree, and stay; and Group 4 (1 Nephi 8:26–27, 31–33) is those who desire the great and spacious building more than they desire the tree and its fruit.

What do you think it means to cling to the word of God compared to continually holding fast to the word of God? (8:24–30) Elder David A. Bednar noted that the group identified in verses 24 to 28 were only "clinging to the rod of iron" and that after partaking of "the fruit of the tree," they became ashamed, fell away, and were lost. He stated that "even with faith, commitment, and the word of God, this group eventually was lost—perhaps because they only periodically read or studied or searched the scriptures. *Clinging* to the rod of iron suggests to me only occasional 'bursts' of study or irregular dipping rather than consistent, ongoing immersion in the word of God" ("Lehi's Dream: Holding Fast to the Rod," 35). ⊙

Why were individuals ashamed even after partaking of the fruit? (8:25) How could people in this group have made it that far and then succumb to fear and shame? Why are some people so fearless in their love for the gospel and their defense of it? How can we live day-to-day unashamed of the gospel of Jesus Christ?

20 And I also beheld a strait and narrow path, which came along by the rod of iron, even to the tree by which I stood; and it also led by the head of the fountain, unto a large and spacious field, as if it had been a world.

21 And I saw numberless concourses of people, many of whom were pressing forward, that they might obtain the path which led unto the tree by which I stood.

22 And it came to pass that they did come forth, and commence in the path which led to the tree.

23 And it came to pass that there arose a mist of darkness; yea, even an exceedingly great mist of darkness, insomuch that they who had commenced in the path did lose their way, that they wandered off and were lost.

24 And it came to pass that I beheld others pressing forward, and they came forth and caught hold of the end of the rod of iron; and they did press forward through the mist of darkness, clinging to the rod of iron, even until they did come forth and partake of the fruit of the tree.

25 And after they had partaken of the fruit of the tree they did cast their eyes about as if they were ashamed.

26 And I also cast my eyes round about, and beheld, on the other side of the river of water, a great and spacious building; and it stood as it were in the air, high above the earth.

27 And it was filled with people, both old and young, both male and female; and their manner of dress was exceedingly fine; and they were in the attitude of mocking and pointing their fingers towards those who had come at and were partaking of the fruit.

28 And after they had tasted of the fruit they were ashamed, because of those that were scoffing at them; and they fell away into forbidden paths and were lost.

29 And now I, Nephi, do not speak all the words of my father.

30 But, to be short in writing, behold, he saw other multitudes pressing forward; and they came and caught hold of the end of the rod of iron; and they did press their way forward, continually holding fast to the rod of iron, until they came forth and fell down and partook of the fruit of the tree.

31 And he also saw other multitudes feeling their way towards that great and spacious building.

32 And it came to pass that many were drowned in the depths of the fountain; and many were lost from his view, wandering in strange roads.

33 And great was the multitude that did enter into that strange building. And after they did enter into that building they did point the finger of scorn at me and those that were

What does the great and spacious building offer? (8:26) Elder Glenn L. Pace taught: "The great and spacious building stands in opposition to the tree of life, which represents the love of God and the blessings of the Atonement of Jesus Christ. . . . Let me make it completely clear that the people in that building have absolutely nothing to offer except instant, short-term gratification inescapably connected to long-term sorrow and suffering. The commandments you observe were not given by a dispassionate God to prevent you from having fun, but by a loving Father in Heaven who wants you to be happy while you are living on this earth as well as in the hereafter" ("They're Not Really Happy," 40).

Why is mocking dangerous? (8:27) The attitude of mocking can be contagious and distracting even to some members of the Church. Elder Neal A. Maxwell said: "A few members of the Church . . . [abandon] an oasis to search for water in the desert. Some of these few will doubtless become critics, and they will be welcomed into the 'great and spacious building.' Henceforth, however, so far as their theological accommodations are concerned, they are in a spacious but third-rate hotel. All dressed up, as the Book of Mormon says, 'exceedingly fine' (1 Ne 8:27), they have no place to go" ("The Book of Mormon: A Great Answer to 'the Great Question,'" 11).

What blessings come from holding fast to the rod of iron? (8:30) President Ezra Taft Benson taught of the blessings that come from holding fast to the iron rod, or the word of God: "[Lehi] saw that if people would hold fast to that rod, they could avoid the rivers of filthiness, stay away from the forbidden paths, stop from wandering in the strange roads that lead to destruction. . . . [It] has the power to fortify the Saints and arm them with the Spirit so they can resist evil, hold fast to the good, and find joy in this life" ("Power of the Word," 80).

Why did this group of people fall down before they partook of the fruit? (8:30) Elder Kim B. Clark noted, "I believe they fell to their knees and humbled themselves before the Lord. They prayed to the Father in the name of Jesus Christ, with expressions of gratitude and repentance. When we humble ourselves before the Lord with a broken heart and contrite spirit, we open our hearts and souls to His redeeming and strengthening power. He blesses us with forgiveness, cleanses us from sin, changes our hearts and strengthens us in our mortal journey on the strait and narrow path" ("Three Invitations").

1 Nephi 8:35–38. Lehi Exhorts His Family with All the Feeling of a Tender Parent

What does it mean to be "cast off from the presence of the Lord"? (8:36) To be *cast off* in this sense is to suffer spiritual death, which is "to die as pertaining to, or to be separated [cast off] from, righteousness—to be alienated from the things of God (Alma 12:16, 32; 40:26)" (Bible Dictionary, "Death," 626).

Why did Lehi "continually exhort" Laman and Lemuel, even when they would not listen? (8:37–38) Elder Robert D. Hales taught: "Lehi did not lose the blessing of feasting at the tree of life because Laman and Lemuel refused to partake of its fruit. Sometimes as parents we feel we have failed when our children make mistakes or stray. Parents are never failures when they do their best to love, teach, pray, and care for their children. Their faith, prayers, and efforts will be consecrated to the good of their children" ("With All the Feeling of a Tender Parent," 88).

1 Nephi 9:1–6. Nephi Makes Two Sets of Records

What are the differences between the two sets of plates? (9:2–4) Nephi describes two different sets of plates he was commanded to make. "Although Nephi had already begun a record of the secular history of his people, the Lord inspired him to make a second record containing the religious history of his people.

partaking of the fruit also; but we heeded them not.

34 These are the words of my father: For as many as heeded them, had fallen away.

35 And Laman and Lemuel partook not of the fruit, said my father.

36 And it came to pass after my father had spoken all the words of his dream or vision, which were many, he said unto us, because of these things which he saw in a vision, he exceedingly feared for Laman and Lemuel; yea, he feared lest they should be cast off from the presence of the Lord.

37 And he did exhort them then with all the feeling of a tender parent, that they would hearken to his words, that perhaps the Lord would be merciful to them, and not cast them off; yea, my father did preach unto them.

38 And after he had preached unto them, and also prophesied unto them of many things, he bade them to keep the commandments of the Lord; and he did cease speaking unto them.

CHAPTER 9

Nephi makes two sets of records—Each is called the plates of Nephi—The larger plates contain a secular history; the smaller ones deal primarily with sacred things. About 600–592 B.C.

1 And all these things did my father see, and hear, and speak, as he dwelt in a tent, in the valley of Lemuel, and also a great many more things, which cannot be written upon these plates.

2 And now, as I have spoken concerning these plates, behold they are not the plates upon which I make a full account of the history of my people; for the plates upon which I make a full account of my people I have given the name of Nephi; wherefore, they are

called the plates of Nephi, after mine own name; and these plates also are called the plates of Nephi.

3 Nevertheless, I have received a commandment of the Lord that I should make these plates, for the special purpose that there should be an account engraven of the ministry of my people.

4 Upon the other plates should be engraven an account of the reign of the kings, and the wars and contentions of my people; wherefore these plates are for the more part of the ministry; and the other plates are for the more part of the reign of the kings and the wars and contentions of my people.

The following list outlines the differences and similarities between the two accounts:

"1. [1 Nephi 9 is] an account taken directly from the small plates.

"2. When Nephi used the term *these* he was referring to the small plates.

"3. When Nephi used the term *those* or *other* he was referring to the large plates.

"4. The large plates were first made about 590 B.C.

"5. The small plates were made 20 years later, about 570 B.C.

"6. Nephi's explanation of why the Lord commanded him to make a second record (the small plates) is in 1 Nephi 9:5.

"7. The large plates cover a period from 570 B.C.–A.D. 385 and cover the account of kings, wars, and history.

"8. The small plates cover a period from 570–130 B.C. and give an account of the Nephite ministry" (*Book of Mormon Student Manual* [2009], 23–24).

Anciently, who else wrote on metal plates? (9:3)
"A prominent late-nineteenth-century critic of the Book of Mormon wrote, 'No such records were ever engraved upon golden plates, or any other plates, in the early ages.' Had he known Hebrew, he would have known that Isaiah 8:1 speaks of writing on a polished metal plate with an engraving tool; the terms are mistranslated 'roll' and 'pen' in the King James Bible. . . .

"Ancient inscribed plates of gold, silver, copper, and lead have been found in such diverse places as China, Java (an Indonesian island), Thailand, India, Pakistan, Portugal, Spain, Italy, Greece, Morocco, Turkey, Iran, Lebanon, Crete, and Korea" (Tvedtnes, *Book of Mormon and Other Hidden Books*, 149). ✪

Why isn't the Book of Mormon a history book? (9:4)
"Often the Book of Mormon is described as a history of some ancient inhabitants of the Americas. If it were called a spiritual history, that description might be appropriate but in the traditional use of the term it is incorrect to call the Book of Mormon a history. Neither the Book of Mormon itself nor the Doctrine and Covenants ever calls it a history book. In fact, the Book of Mormon goes to some length to say that it is not a history; the history of the Nephite people was engraved upon another set of plates, commonly referred to as the large plates of Nephi (Jacob 1:2–8; 1 Ne. 9:2–4)" (Nyman, *Most Correct Book*, 31).

For what reasons did the Lord ask Nephi to make the plates? (9:5–6) "Because the small plates of Nephi . . . were used to fill the gap caused by the loss of the 116 pages . . . I wonder if we have simply supposed that that one episode is all that was meant by the statement about 'wise purposes.' I think it was only one of several wise purposes yet to be experienced" (Matthews, "Power and the Purpose of the Written Record," 115–16). ◑

Why do we not always know "why" before we obey a commandment? (9:5–6) Nephi made another set of plates without knowing why. Adam obediently offered animal sacrifices after he was sent out of the Garden of Eden. After many days, an angel asked him why he obeyed. Adam replied, "I know not, save the Lord commanded me." Only after his obedience was Adam taught why the commandment had been given (see Moses 5:4–7). What commandments are you asked to obey without understanding why? How might your obedience when you "know not" bless you?

How does "the Lord knoweth all things"? (9:6) "God does not live in the dimension of time as do we. We are not only hampered by our finiteness (experiential and intellectual), but also by being in the dimension of time. Moreover, God, since 'all things are present' with him, is not simply predicting based solely on the past. In ways that are not clear to us, he *sees* rather than *foresees* the future, because all things are at once present before him" (Maxwell, *Things As They Really Are*, 29; see also 2 Nephi 2:24; 9:20; Mosiah 4:9; Mormon 8:17).

1 Nephi 10:1–3. Lehi Prophesies about the Destruction of Jerusalem

5 Wherefore, the Lord hath commanded me to make these plates for a wise purpose in him, which purpose I know not.

6 But the Lord knoweth all things from the beginning; wherefore, he prepareth a way to accomplish all his works among the children of men; for behold, he hath all power unto the fulfilling of all his words. And thus it is. Amen.

CHAPTER 10

Lehi predicts that the Jews will be taken captive by the Babylonians—He tells of the coming among the Jews of a Messiah, a Savior, a Redeemer—Lehi tells also of the coming of the one who should baptize the Lamb of God—Lehi tells of the death and resurrection of the Messiah—He compares the scattering and gathering of Israel to an olive tree—Nephi speaks of the Son of God, of the gift of the Holy Ghost, and of the need for righteousness. About 600–592 B.C.

1 And now I, Nephi, proceed to give an account upon these plates of my proceedings, and my reign and ministry; wherefore, to proceed with mine account, I must speak somewhat of the things of my father, and also of my brethren.

2 For behold, it came to pass after my father had made an end of speaking the words of his dream, and also of exhorting them to all diligence, he spake unto them concerning the Jews—

3 That after they should be destroyed, even that great city Jerusalem, and many be carried away captive into Babylon, according to the own due time of the Lord, they should return again, yea, even be brought back out of captivity; and after they should be brought back out of captivity they should possess again the land of their inheritance.

4 Yea, even six hundred years from the time that my father left Jerusalem, a prophet would the Lord God raise up among the Jews—even a Messiah, or, in other words, a Savior of the world.

5 And he also spake concerning the prophets, how great a number had testified of these things, concerning this Messiah, of whom he had spoken, or this Redeemer of the world.

6 Wherefore, all mankind were in a lost and in a fallen state, and ever would be save they should rely on this Redeemer.

Why does Lehi speak "concerning the Jews"? (10:2) "As is typical of epics, many narratives in the Book of Mormon begin in the middle of the action, with the interest being on *why* something happens rather than on *what* happens. We know the ending of the Nephite story from the beginning. Lehi recounts to his children the Babylonian captivity, the coming of the Messiah, the travels of his people to the land of promise, the time when the Gentiles would receive the fulness of the gospel, and the final return of the remnants of the house of Israel to the Messiah (1 Ne. 10)" (Rust, *Feasting on the Word*, 60).

Why did the Babylonians carry the Jews away from Jerusalem? (10:3) "Few understand why Israel and Judah were deported instead of just put under tribute. . . . Each country's gods were considered to be indigenous, with no power outside their own land. . . . Finding themselves in a new land, where their ancient gods had no power, the captive people would lose all hope of being led to freedom from their . . . conquerors. Meanwhile, their homelands would have been resettled by another conquered people, making it even more unlikely that the captives could ever hope to recover their former position" (Tvedtnes, "Why Were Israel and Judah Carried Away Captive?" *Ensign*, Aug. 1982, 25–26).

1 Nephi 10:4–11. Lehi Prophesies about the Coming of John the Baptist and the Messiah

Why did Nephi include many teachings of his father, Lehi? (10:4–11) The 116 pages of manuscript lost by Martin Harris included the record known as the "Book of Lehi" (headnote to D&C 3). Fortunately, many of Lehi's teachings and testimony were preserved in the record of his son Nephi. "Nephi recorded significant portions of his father's teachings in his own record on the small plates, and that glimpse of Lehi's experience adds to the reader's views of the Savior of the world" (Holland, *Christ and the New Covenant*, 36). ☉

Why does the Book of Mormon speak so often of the fall of Adam and our fallen condition? (10:6) President Ezra Taft Benson explained: "The Book of Mormon Saints knew that the plan of redemption must start with the account of the fall of Adam. . . .

Just as a man does not really desire food until he is hungry, so he does not desire the salvation of Christ until he knows why he needs Christ. No one adequately and properly knows why he needs Christ until he understands and accepts the doctrine of the Fall and its effect upon all mankind. And no other book in the world explains this vital doctrine nearly as well as the Book of Mormon" (*A Witness and a Warning*, 33).

What did Lehi know regarding John the Baptist? (10:7–10) Lehi saw in vision the ministry of John the Baptist and foretold what John would testify of. "[His] words indicate that Lehi had an accurate foreknowledge concerning the activities, message, and geographical area of operation of John the Baptist" (Matthews, *Burning Light*, 5–6).

© fik47 / Thinkstock

Jesus was baptized "in Bethabara, beyond Jordan" (1 Nephi 10:9).

What is the significance of Bethabara? (10:9) Bethabara in Hebrew means "house of the ford." It is the "place where John baptized in the Jordan River, the exact site of which is unknown today, although traditionally it is near Jericho. It was at this location that John baptized Jesus, beheld the Holy Ghost descend in the sign of a dove, and was interviewed by a delegation of priests and Levites from Jerusalem (John 1:19–34; 1 Ne. 10:7–10). [See] JST, John 1:34, which indicates that all of the above events were done at Bethabara, whereas the KJV leaves the matter in question" (Bible Dictionary, "Bethabara," 603).

Who are the Gentiles? (10:11) "Israelites are called Gentiles in those scriptures which speak of the gospel going first to the Gentiles and then to the Jews in the last days. Thus the Book of Mormon came forth by way of the Gentile; Joseph Smith was the Gentile who brought it forth; and the United States is a Gentile nation. This is an instance of all men being divided into two categories—Jews and Gentiles, with the Jews

7 And he spake also concerning a prophet who should come before the Messiah, to prepare the way of the Lord—

8 Yea, even he should go forth and cry in the wilderness: Prepare ye the way of the Lord, and make his paths straight; for there standeth one among you whom ye know not; and he is mightier than I, whose shoe's latchet I am not worthy to unloose. And much spake my father concerning this thing.

9 And my father said he should baptize in Bethabara, beyond Jordan; and he also said he should baptize with water; even that he should baptize the Messiah with water.

10 And after he had baptized the Messiah with water, he should behold and bear record that he had baptized the Lamb of God, who should take away the sins of the world.

11 And it came to pass after my father had spoken these words he spake unto my brethren concerning the gospel which should be preached among the Jews, and also concerning the dwindling of the Jews in unbelief. And after they had slain the Messiah, who should come, and after he had been slain he

should rise from the dead, and should make himself manifest, by the Holy Ghost, unto the Gentiles.

12 Yea, even my father spake much concerning the Gentiles, and also concerning the house of Israel, that they should be compared like unto an olive tree, whose branches should be broken off and should be scattered upon all the face of the earth.

13 Wherefore, he said it must needs be that we should be led with one accord into the land of promise, unto the fulfilling of the word of the Lord, that we should be scattered upon all the face of the earth.

14 And after the house of Israel should be scattered they should be gathered together again; or, in fine, after the Gentiles had received the fulness of the Gospel, the natural branches of the olive tree, or the remnants of the house of Israel, should be grafted in, or come to the knowledge of the true Messiah, their Lord and their Redeemer.

15 And after this manner of language did my father prophesy and speak unto my brethren, and also many more things which I do not write in this book; for I have written as many of them as were expedient for me in mine other book.

16 And all these things, of which I have spoken, were done as my father dwelt in a tent, in the valley of Lemuel.

17 And it came to pass after I, Nephi, having heard all the words of my father, concerning the things which he saw in a vision, and also the things which he spake by the power of the Holy Ghost, which power he received by faith on the Son of God—and the Son of God was the Messiah who should come—I, Nephi, was desirous also that I might see,

being those who are descendants of the Kingdom of Judah. This categorizes the Lost Tribes of Israel as Gentiles, though, in fact, they are of the literal blood of Israel" (McConkie, *A New Witness for the Articles of Faith*, 518).

1 Nephi 10:12–16. Lehi Prophesies about the Scattering and Gathering of Israel

Why does Lehi compare the house of Israel to an olive tree? (10:12, 14) "The first mention of the olive in the Book of Mormon is found in Lehi's prediction of the Babylonian captivity . . . [see 1 Nephi 10:12, 14]. In this passage, Lehi probably drew upon Zenos's allegory, found on the plates of brass. In incredible horticultural detail, that allegory compares the house of Israel to an olive tree. Yet that Old World information was apparently lost among Lehi's descendants in the New World. After the fifth chapter of Jacob, the olive is not mentioned again in the Book of Mormon" (Hess, "Recent Notes about Olives in Antiquity," 115). ◉

Why was Israel scattered upon the face of the earth? What will bring about their gathering? (10:12–14) Jesus Christ taught that the tribes of Israel were removed from their homeland and "scattered forth upon the face of the earth because of their unbelief" (3 Nephi 16:4). He explained that they will return when they are "brought to a knowledge of me, their Redeemer" (3 Nephi 16:4; see also 3 Nephi 20:30–33). ◉

1 Nephi 10:17–22. Nephi Desires to Know More about the Son of God

How did Nephi seek to understand Lehi's revelation? (10:17) President Ezra Taft Benson explained that "Nephi had listened to his father, had believed his father, but he wanted to know through the same source his father knew—revelation. . . . It takes revelation to perceive revelation. So Nephi diligently sought the Lord and received a revelation which reaffirmed the revelation his father had given to the family" ("Worthy Fathers, Worthy Sons," 35–36).

What did Nephi's desire to "see, and hear, and know" regarding the things described by his father lead him to do? (10:17) Do you seek after gospel and spiritual truths like Nephi? How does your desire for guidance from the Holy Ghost influence you? Consider the counsel of President Dallin H. Oaks: "Desires dictate our priorities, priorities shape our choices, and choices determine our actions" ("Desires," 45).

When was the "way," or the plan of salvation, prepared for us? (10:18) President Russell M. Nelson taught: "Before the foundation of the earth, the plan of salvation was prepared. It included the glorious possibility of a divine inheritance in the kingdom of God" ("How Firm Our Foundation," 75).

When was the "foundation of the world"? (10:18) "This 'foundation' was the creation, or organizing, of the earth. Known also as 'the beginning of time,' it included the pre-earth councils" (Brewster, *Doctrine and Covenants Encyclopedia*, 193).

What is the meaning of "one eternal round"? (10:19) Elder Bruce R. McConkie explained: "When our revelations say of Christ, 'From eternity to eternity he is the same, and his years never fail' (D&C 76:4), they mean that from one preexistence to the next he does not vary, his course is one eternal round. They mean, for instance, that from our premortal or preexistent state to the day when the exalted among us provide a preexistence for our spirit children, he is the same" (*Promised Messiah*, 166).

What is meant by the expression that "no unclean thing can dwell with God"? (10:21) "In the Book of Mormon, being clean is important. . . . This verse suggests that doing 'wickedly' is symbolically connected to being unclean. . . . One of the main issues with being unclean was that it meant that a person had to be separated from other people. . . . (see Leviticus 11:24–40). . . . This connection between spiritual and physical uncleanness implies that if someone is cut off from the physical presence of the people of God for being physically unclean, then they would be cut off spiritually from God Himself for being spiritually unclean until that condition of impurity was removed. Amulek explained this in Alma 11:37" (Book of Mormon Central, "How Is the Day of Atonement Understood in the Book of Mormon?").

and hear, and know of these things, by the power of the Holy Ghost, which is the gift of God unto all those who diligently seek him, as well in times of old as in the time that he should manifest himself unto the children of men.

18 For he is the same yesterday, today, and forever; and the way is prepared for all men from the foundation of the world, if it so be that they repent and come unto him.

19 For he that diligently seeketh shall find; and the mysteries of God shall be unfolded unto them, by the power of the Holy Ghost, as well in these times as in times of old, and as well in times of old as in times to come; wherefore, the course of the Lord is one eternal round.

20 Therefore remember, O man, for all thy doings thou shalt be brought into judgment.

21 Wherefore, if ye have sought to do wickedly in the days of your probation, then ye are found unclean before the judgment-seat of God; and no unclean thing can dwell with God; wherefore, ye must be cast off forever.

22 And the Holy Ghost giveth authority that I should speak these things, and deny them not.

Introduction to 1 Nephi 11 through 1 Nephi 14

The record of Nephi's vision begins in 1 Nephi 11:1 and concludes in 1 Nephi 14. The vision might be called "Nephi's vision until the end of time," for it covers the history of this world from the birth of Jesus Christ and extends through the Second Coming and the Millennium. The angel allowed Nephi to write only a part of this vision, leaving the remainder to be written by the Apostle John (see commentary in this volume on 1 Nephi 14:18–28). The original manuscript and early printings of the Book of Mormon lack any chapter breaks in this material, further emphasizing the vision's unity. Reading these chapters as a whole may help you better comprehend the full meaning of the vision.

CHAPTER 11

Nephi sees the Spirit of the Lord and is shown in vision the tree of life—He sees the mother of the Son of God and learns of the condescension of God—He sees the baptism, ministry, and crucifixion of the Lamb of God—He sees also the call and ministry of the Twelve Apostles of the Lamb. About 600–592 B.C.

1 For it came to pass after I had desired to know the things that my father had seen, and believing that the Lord was able to make them known unto me, as I sat pondering in mine heart I was caught away in the Spirit of the Lord, yea, into an exceedingly high mountain, which I never had before seen, and upon which I never had before set my foot.

2 And the Spirit said unto me: Behold, what desirest thou?

3 And I said: I desire to behold the things which my father saw.

4 And the Spirit said unto me: Believest thou that thy father saw the tree of which he hath spoken?

5 And I said: Yea, thou knowest that I believe all the words of my father.

6 And when I had spoken these words, the Spirit cried with a loud voice, saying: Hosanna to the Lord, the most high God; for he is God over all the earth, yea, even above all. And blessed art thou, Nephi, because thou

1 Nephi 11:1–12. Nephi Sees a Vision of the Tree of Life

What blessings can come from pondering and meditation? (11:1) "I think we pay too little attention to the value of meditation, a principle of devotion. . . . Meditation is the language of the soul. It is defined as 'a form of private devotion or spiritual exercise, consisting in deep, continued reflection on some religious theme.' Meditation is a form of prayer. . . . Meditation is one of the most secret, most sacred doors through which we pass into the presence of the Lord" (McKay, "Consciousness of God," 80). ●

Why did Nephi go to a mountain? (11:1) "The Lord often uses mountains to reveal his mysteries when there are no temples" (Nyman, *I, Nephi, Wrote This Record*, 137; see also Moses 7:2–3; 1:1–2; Matthew 17:1–9). ●

Who was Nephi conversing with in this vision? (11:1–2) It is unknown whether the "Spirit" referred to in this verse is the Holy Ghost or the premortal personage of Jesus Christ (see McConkie, *Mormon Doctrine*, 752; *Mortal Messiah*, 1:413–14; Talmage, *Articles of Faith*, 159–60; Roberts, *Seventy's Course in Theology*, 5:60n2).

Why did the Spirit cry out "Hosanna"? (11:6) "*HOSHA-NA* in Hebrew [means] 'Save now' or 'Oh, save!'" (Woodbury, "Origin and Uses of the Sacred Hosanna Shout," 18). The first use of the Hosanna Shout recorded in scripture was in the premortal council "when . . . all the sons of God shouted for joy" (Job 38:7). The multitudes in Jerusalem shouted hosanna to honor Jesus Christ as He rode into the city for the last time (Matthew 21:9). Today, when temples are dedicated those attending shout hosanna in unison. This shout of worship honors the saving and redeeming power of Jesus Christ. It is not surprising that the Spirit would shout hosanna to rejoice in the important details of the Savior's life about to be revealed to Nephi. ⊕

What does the tree of life symbolize? (11:7) Elder Jeffrey R. Holland suggested that "the tree of life . . . [is a symbol] of Christ's redemption. . . . The life, mission, and atonement of Christ are the ultimate manifestations of the Tree of Life" (*Christ and the New Covenant*, 160–61; see also Griggs, "Tree of Life in Ancient Cultures," 26–31).

1 Nephi 11:13–25. Nephi Learns of God's Great Love for His Children

Who is the virgin Nephi sees? (11:13) In this vision, Nephi learned what ancient prophets testified: the Savior's mother would be a virgin (see Isaiah 7:14). Later, other Book of Mormon prophets revealed that her name would be Mary (see Mosiah 3:8; Alma 7:10). ⊕

believest in the Son of the most high God; wherefore, thou shalt behold the things which thou hast desired.

7 And behold this thing shall be given unto thee for a sign, that after thou hast beheld the tree which bore the fruit which thy father tasted, thou shalt also behold a man descending out of heaven, and him shall ye witness; and after ye have witnessed him ye shall bear record that it is the Son of God.

8 And it came to pass that the Spirit said unto me: Look! And I looked and beheld a tree; and it was like unto the tree which my father had seen; and the beauty thereof was far beyond, yea, exceeding of all beauty; and the whiteness thereof did exceed the whiteness of the driven snow.

9 And it came to pass after I had seen the tree, I said unto the Spirit: I behold thou hast shown unto me the tree which is precious above all.

10 And he said unto me: What desirest thou?

11 And I said unto him: To know the interpretation thereof—for I spake unto him as a man speaketh; for I beheld that he was in the form of a man; yet nevertheless, I knew that it was the Spirit of the Lord; and he spake unto me as a man speaketh with another.

12 And it came to pass that he said unto me: Look! And I looked as if to look upon him, and I saw him not; for he had gone from before my presence.

13 And it came to pass that I looked and beheld the great city of Jerusalem, and also other cities. And I beheld the city of Nazareth; and in the city of Nazareth I beheld a virgin, and she was exceedingly fair and white.

14 And it came to pass that I saw the heavens open; and an angel came down and stood before me; and he said unto me: Nephi, what beholdest thou?

15 And I said unto him: A virgin, most beautiful and fair above all other virgins.

16 And he said unto me: Knowest thou the condescension of God?

What is the condescension of God? (11:16) Elder Bruce R. McConkie wrote, "'The condescension of God,' of which the scriptures speak, means that the Immortal Father—the glorified, exalted, enthroned ruler of the universe—came down from his station of dominion and power to become the Father of a Son who would be born of Mary, 'after the manner of the flesh'" (*A New Witness for the Articles of Faith*, 111).

17 And I said unto him: I know that he loveth his children; nevertheless, I do not know the meaning of all things.

How does a knowledge of the goodness of God help us face life's difficulties? (11:17) "Nephi had a great knowledge of the goodness of God, hence Nephi's firm declaration: 'I know that [God] loveth his children; nevertheless, I do not know the meaning of all things' (1 Ne. 1:1; 1 Ne. 11:17). If we have a love of God and know His goodness, we will trust Him, even when we are puzzled or perplexed" (Maxwell, "Lessons from Laman and Lemuel," 6).

18 And he said unto me: Behold, the virgin whom thou seest is the mother of the Son of God, after the manner of the flesh.

19 And it came to pass that I beheld that she was carried away in the Spirit; and after she had been carried away in the Spirit for the space of a time the angel spake unto me, saying: Look!

20 And I looked and beheld the virgin again, bearing a child in her arms.

What does "after the manner of the flesh" mean? (11:18) "But there is one person, one person only— and that was his firstborn spirit offspring, the Lord Jehovah—who was destined to come into mortality with God our Father, an immortal person, as the parent of his mortal body, and, of course, with Mary, a mortal individual, as the mother of his mortal body" (McConkie, "Behold the Condescension of God," 36.

21 And the angel said unto me: Behold the Lamb of God, yea, even the Son of the Eternal Father! Knowest thou the meaning of the tree which thy father saw?

How literally do we believe that the Lamb of God is the very Son of the Eternal Father? (11:21) "Without overstepping the bounds of propriety by saying more than is appropriate, let us say this: God the Almighty, the Maker and Preserver and Upholder of all things; . . . God the Almighty, who is infinite and eternal, elects, in his fathomless wisdom, to beget a Son, an Only Son, the Only Begotten in the flesh. God, who is infinite and immortal, condescends to step down from his throne, to join with one who is finite and mortal in bringing forth, 'after the manner of the flesh,' the Mortal Messiah" (McConkie, *Mortal Messiah*, 1:314–15).

How is the love of God manifest in us? (11:22) The Apostle John explained expectations of those who would claim forgiveness and redemption through the atonement of Jesus Christ: "Hereby perceive we the love of God, because he laid down his life for us: and we ought to lay down [our] lives for the brethren. But whoso hath this world's good, and seeth his brother have need, and shutteth up his bowels [of compassion] from him, how dwelleth the love of God in him? My little children, let us not love in word, neither in tongue; but in deed and in truth. And hereby we know that we are of the truth, and shall assure our hearts before him" (1 John 3:13–19).

How do I hold fast to the rod of iron? (11:25) President Boyd K. Packer taught: "If you hold to the rod, you can *feel* your way forward with the gift of the Holy Ghost, conferred upon you at the time you were confirmed a member of the Church. The Holy Ghost will comfort you. You will be able to feel the influence of angels, as Nephi did, and feel your way through life. The Book of Mormon has been my iron rod" ("Finding Ourselves in Lehi's Dream," 22).

1 Nephi 11:26–33. Nephi Learns of the Condescension of Jesus Christ

Why would the Holy Ghost "abide upon him in the form of a dove"? (11:27) "The sign of the dove was instituted before the creation of the world, a witness for the Holy Ghost, and the devil cannot come in the sign of a dove. The Holy Ghost is a personage, and is in the form of a personage. It does not confine itself to the form of the dove, but in sign of the dove. The Holy Ghost cannot be transformed into a dove; but the sign of a dove was given to John to signify the truth of the deed, as the dove is an emblem or token of truth and innocence" (*Joseph Smith* [manual], 81; see also Abraham, Facsimile 2, no. 7).

22 And I answered him, saying: Yea, it is the love of God, which sheddeth itself abroad in the hearts of the children of men; wherefore, it is the most desirable above all things.

23 And he spake unto me, saying: Yea, and the most joyous to the soul.

24 And after he had said these words, he said unto me: Look! And I looked, and I beheld the Son of God going forth among the children of men; and I saw many fall down at his feet and worship him.

25 And it came to pass that I beheld that the rod of iron, which my father had seen, was the word of God, which led to the fountain of living waters, or to the tree of life; which waters are a representation of the love of God; and I also beheld that the tree of life was a representation of the love of God.

26 And the angel said unto me again: Look and behold the condescension of God!

27 And I looked and beheld the Redeemer of the world, of whom my father had spoken; and I also beheld the prophet who should prepare the way before him. And the Lamb of God went forth and was baptized of him; and after he was baptized, I beheld the heavens open, and the Holy Ghost come down out of heaven and abide upon him in the form of a dove.

28 And I beheld that he went forth ministering unto the people, in power and great glory; and the multitudes were gathered together to hear him; and I beheld that they cast him out from among them.

29 And I also beheld twelve others following him. And it came to pass that they were carried away in the Spirit from before my face, and I saw them not.

30 And it came to pass that the angel spake unto me again, saying: Look! And I looked,

and I beheld the heavens open again, and I saw angels descending upon the children of men; and they did minister unto them.

31 And he spake unto me again, saying: Look! And I looked, and I beheld the Lamb of God going forth among the children of men. And I beheld multitudes of people who were sick, and who were afflicted with all manner of diseases, and with devils and unclean spirits; and the angel spake and showed all these things unto me. And they were healed by the power of the Lamb of God; and the devils and the unclean spirits were cast out.

32 And it came to pass that the angel spake unto me again, saying: Look! And I looked and beheld the Lamb of God, that he was taken by the people; yea, the Son of the everlasting God was judged of the world; and I saw and bear record.

33 And I, Nephi, saw that he was lifted up upon the cross and slain for the sins of the world.

34 And after he was slain I saw the multitudes of the earth, that they were gathered together to fight against the apostles of the Lamb; for thus were the twelve called by the angel of the Lord.

35 And the multitude of the earth was gathered together; and I beheld that they were in a large and spacious building, like unto the building which my father saw. And the angel of the Lord spake unto me again, saying: Behold the world and the wisdom thereof; yea, behold the house of Israel hath gathered together to fight against the twelve apostles of the Lamb.

Why is Nephi's use of the title "Lamb of God" significant? (11:31) The title "Lamb of God" is uniquely associated with visions of the end of time. The title is most closely associated with the Apostle John in the New Testament. All but two references to Jesus Christ as the Lamb (Acts 8:32; 1 Peter 1:19) are in the Apostle John's writings—principally the book of Revelation. Nephi saw the same vision and of the 72 references to Jesus Christ as the Lamb in the Book of Mormon, 57 (or approximately 80 percent) are in 1 Nephi 10–14, which in the 1830 edition were all one chapter (1 Nephi 3). This proportion is important in connecting Nephi's vision with that of John (see commentary in this volume on 1 Nephi 14:18–28). ✛

Why did Joseph Smith change verse 32? (11:32) "The first edition of the Book of Mormon states 'the everlasting God was judged.'... instead of 'the Son of the everlasting God.' Joseph Smith apparently added 'the Son of' to avoid confusion, but the doctrine is not changed as the Nephites understood that 'There is a God, and he is Christ, and he cometh in the fulness of his own time' (2 Nephi 11:7)" (Nyman, *I, Nephi, Wrote This Record*, 149n16).

1 Nephi 11:34–36. Wicked People Fight against Jesus's Apostles

What causes the "house of Israel" to fight against the Twelve Apostles? (11:35) "The world is still fighting the apostles of the Lamb because they represent the truth and the world rejects the truth. Even those of the house of Israel at times will gather to fight against the twelve" (Nyman, "The Judgment Seat of Christ," 208-09). Sister Eliza R. Snow added, "Many who had been humble and faithful to the performance of every duty—ready to go and come at every call of the Priesthood—were getting haughty in their spirits, and lifted up in the pride of their hearts. As the Saints drank in the love and spirit of the world, the Spirit of the Lord withdrew from their hearts" (Biography and Family Record of Lorenzo Snow, 20).

What is pride? (11:36) "The central feature of pride is enmity—enmity toward God and enmity toward our fellowmen. Enmity means 'hatred toward, hostility to, or a state of opposition.' It is the power by which Satan wishes to reign over us. Pride is essentially competitive in nature. We pit our will against God's.... [The proud] pit their perceptions of truth against God's great knowledge, their abilities versus God's priesthood power, their accomplishments against His mighty works.... The proud wish God would agree with them. They aren't interested in changing their opinions to agree with God's" (Benson, "Beware of Pride," 4). ☉

What will happen to those who fight against the Twelve Apostles? (11:36) Spiritual destruction awaits those who fight against the Lord's anointed: "Cursed are all those that shall lift up the heel against mine anointed . . . and cry they have sinned when they have not sinned before me, saith the Lord, but have done that which was meet in mine eyes, and which I commanded them. But those who cry transgression do it because they are the servants of sin.... And those who swear falsely against my servants, . . . wo unto them; because they have offended my little ones they shall be severed from the ordinances of mine house. . . . They shall not have right to the priesthood, nor their posterity after them from generation to generation" (D&C 121:16–21).

1 Nephi 12:1–5. Nephi Sees the Future of the Nephites and Lamanites

How do we know America is a chosen land or land of promise? (12:1) "The destiny of America was divinely decreed. The events that established our great nation were foreknown to God and revealed to prophets of old. As in an enacted drama, the players who came on the scene were rehearsed and selected for their parts.... As one looks back upon what we call our history, there is a telling theme that occurs again and again in this drama. It is that God governs in the affairs of this nation.... Secular scholarship, though useful, provides an incomplete and sometimes inaccurate view of our history. The real story of America is one that shows the hand of God in our nation's beginning" (Benson, *This Nation Shall Endure*, 12, 16). ☉

How many times have wars been recorded in the Book of Mormon? (12:2) "John W. Welch has identified at least 15 major wars or conflicts that spanned the history of Book of Mormon peoples.... Wars and the politics of war were an integral part of history in

36 And it came to pass that I saw and bear record, that the great and spacious building was the pride of the world; and it fell, and the fall thereof was exceedingly great. And the angel of the Lord spake unto me again, saying: Thus shall be the destruction of all nations, kindreds, tongues, and people, that shall fight against the twelve apostles of the Lamb.

CHAPTER 12

Nephi sees in vision the land of promise; the righteousness, iniquity, and downfall of its inhabitants; the coming of the Lamb of God among them; how the Twelve Disciples and the Twelve Apostles will judge Israel; and the loathsome and filthy state of those who dwindle in unbelief. About 600–592 B.C.

1 And it came to pass that the angel said unto me: Look, and behold thy seed, and also the seed of thy brethren. And I looked and beheld the land of promise; and I beheld multitudes of people, yea, even as it were in number as many as the sand of the sea.

2 And it came to pass that I beheld multitudes gathered together to battle, one against the other; and I beheld wars, and rumors of wars, and great slaughters with the sword among my people.

3 And it came to pass that I beheld many generations pass away, after the manner of wars and contentions in the land; and I beheld many cities, yea, even that I did not number them.

4 And it came to pass that I saw a mist of darkness on the face of the land of promise; and I saw lightnings, and I heard thunderings, and earthquakes, and all manner of tumultuous noises; and I saw the earth and the rocks, that they rent; and I saw mountains tumbling into pieces; and I saw the plains of the earth, that they were broken up; and I saw many cities that they were sunk; and I saw many that they were burned with fire; and I saw many that did tumble to the earth, because of the quaking thereof.

5 And it came to pass after I saw these things, I saw the vapor of darkness, that it passed from off the face of the earth; and behold, I saw multitudes who had not fallen because of the great and terrible judgments of the Lord.

6 And I saw the heavens open, and the Lamb of God descending out of heaven; and he came down and showed himself unto them.

7 And I also saw and bear record that the Holy Ghost fell upon twelve others; and they were ordained of God, and chosen.

8 And the angel spake unto me, saying: Behold the twelve disciples of the Lamb, who are chosen to minister unto thy seed.

9 And he said unto me: Thou rememberest the twelve apostles of the Lamb? Behold they are they who shall judge the twelve tribes of Israel; wherefore, the twelve ministers of thy seed shall be judged of them; for ye are of the house of Israel.

the Book of Mormon. . . . Most military events in the Book of Mormon have both religious and political importance. The Nephites did not dichotomize their world between church and state as we do. Ancient peoples generally viewed war as a contest between the gods of one people and the gods of another" (Book of Mormon Central, "Why Are There So Many War Chapters in the Book of Mormon?").

How did Nephi's vision foreshadow future events among the Nephites? (12:4–5) "Many are drowned in the depths of the fountain or lost in the mist of darkness, connected for Nephi with the 'mist of darkness on the face of the land of promise' that he prophesied would be part of the great destruction preceding the appearance of the Lamb of God (1 Nephi 12:4). . . . The vision also projects figuratively the destruction of the Nephite people as a result of pride and temptations, but the full sweep of history on the promised land leads to the restoration of other scripture and to Christ's manifesting himself to all nations (1 Nephi 12:17–19; 13:38–42)" (Rust, *Feasting on the Word*, 209).

1 Nephi 12:6–12. Nephi Sees Jesus Christ Appear to the Righteous Nephites

How was the church organized among the Nephites? (12:7) "[The Book of Mormon] tells us that our Savior made His appearance upon this continent after His resurrection; that He planted the Gospel here in all its fulness, and richness, and power, and blessing; that they had Apostles, Prophets, Pastors, Teachers, and Evangelists, the same order, the same priesthood, the same ordinances, gifts, powers, and blessings, as were enjoyed on the eastern continent" (*Joseph Smith* [manual], 64).

What will be the duties of the Twelve Apostles in Jerusalem? (12:9–10) "Instead of the Lord pointing out what should be the duties of these Apostles, while here in this temporal existence, he pointed out the more important duties that would devolve upon them in the next state. The simple duties of this life were nothing compared to those of the world to come.

... The Twelve Nephite Apostles had a knowledge of some other, future duties to be performed in the world to come. 'Know ye, that you shall be judges of this people. What manner of men ought ye to be. Verily, I say unto you, even as I am'" (Orson Pratt, in *Journal of Discourses*, 19:116). ⊕

What do garments made white through the blood of Jesus Christ represent? (12:10) "To have one's garments made white in the blood of the Lamb is to be made free from sin and its effects, this through sincere repentance and submission to the will of the Master. It is to be cleansed and sanctified, to be made pure and holy—fit to dwell in the presence of God and angels. Such a state comes through subscribing to the ordinances of the gospel and thereafter yielding one's heart unto God. . . . These are persons whose garments are free from the blood of the world because of the blood of him who overcame the world" (McConkie and Millet, *Doctrinal Commentary*, 1:87).

What does it mean that four generations "passed away in righteousness"? (12:12) "During the Nephite 'mini-millennium' there were no contentions or divisions among the people. Within about 160 years after the ministry of the Savior, however, one group began to call itself Lamanites. By A.D. 210 pride entered into the Church, 'and from that time forth they did have their goods and their substance no more common among them' (4 Nephi 1:20, 24–25)" (McConkie and Millet, *Doctrinal Commentary*, 1:87).

1 Nephi 12:13–19. Nephi Sees His Descendants Fall into Temptation and Pride

10 And these twelve ministers whom thou beholdest shall judge thy seed. And, behold, they are righteous forever; for because of their faith in the Lamb of God their garments are made white in his blood.

11 And the angel said unto me: Look! And I looked, and beheld three generations pass away in righteousness; and their garments were white even like unto the Lamb of God. And the angel said unto me: These are made white in the blood of the Lamb, because of their faith in him.

12 And I, Nephi, also saw many of the fourth generation who passed away in righteousness.

13 And it came to pass that I saw the multitudes of the earth gathered together.

14 And the angel said unto me: Behold thy seed, and also the seed of thy brethren.

15 And it came to pass that I looked and beheld the people of my seed gathered together in multitudes against the seed of my brethren; and they were gathered together to battle.

16 And the angel spake unto me, saying: Behold the fountain of filthy water which thy father saw; yea, even the river of which he spake; and the depths thereof are the depths of hell.

17 And the mists of darkness are the temptations of the devil, which blindeth the eyes, and hardeneth the hearts of the children of men, and leadeth them away into broad roads, that they perish and are lost.

18 And the large and spacious building, which thy father saw, is vain imaginations and the pride of the children of men. And a great and a terrible gulf divideth them; yea, even the word of the justice of the Eternal God, and the Messiah who is the Lamb of God, of whom the Holy Ghost beareth record, from the beginning of the world until this time, and from this time henceforth and forever.

19 And while the angel spake these words, I beheld and saw that the seed of my brethren did contend against my seed, according to the word of the angel; and because of the pride of my seed, and the temptations of the devil, I beheld that the seed of my brethren did overpower the people of my seed.

20 And it came to pass that I beheld, and saw the people of the seed of my brethren that they had overcome my seed; and they went forth in multitudes upon the face of the land.

21 And I saw them gathered together in multitudes; and I saw wars and rumors of wars among them; and in wars and rumors of wars I saw many generations pass away.

22 And the angel said unto me: Behold these shall dwindle in unbelief.

23 And it came to pass that I beheld, after they had dwindled in unbelief they became a dark, and loathsome, and a filthy people, full of idleness and all manner of abominations.

What are the "vain imaginations" of men? (12:18) "Every day we see allurements of one kind or another that tell us what we have is not enough. Someone or something is forever telling us we need to be more handsome or more wealthy, more applauded or more admired than we see ourselves as being. We are told we haven't collected enough possessions or gone to enough fun places. We are bombarded with the message that on the world's scale of things we have been weighed in the balance and found wanting" (Holland, "The Other Prodigal," 64).

1 Nephi 12:20–23. Nephi Sees the Lamanites Overcome the Nephites

Why did the future Lamanites dwindle in unbelief? (12:22) Lamanites consistently sought to destroy the records and traditions of the Nephites (see Enos 1:13–14). Moroni's burial of the record effectively removed scripture from the Lamanites. Elder Sheldon F. Child reflected: "Without scriptures, not only do nations perish, but families and individuals dwindle in unbelief. Daily scripture study helps us to anchor our faith in Christ. They truly testify of Him" ("Sure Foundation," 8).

Previously, the Lord had commanded the death of Laban and the retrieval of the brass plates so that Lehi's posterity would not "perish in unbelief" (see 1 Nephi 4:13).

What does the darkness that came upon the Lamanites symbolize? (12:23) This was a spiritual condition of filthiness governed by their agency. Hugh Nibley noted: "Notice that they became that way. It wasn't a miraculous change overnight. It is never referred to in that sense. It's a cultural thing" (*Teachings of the Book of Mormon*, 1:5).

CHAPTER 13

Nephi sees in vision the church of the devil set up among the Gentiles, the discovery and colonizing of America, the loss of many plain and precious parts of the Bible, the resultant state of gentile apostasy, the restoration of the gospel, the coming forth of latter-day scripture, and the building up of Zion. About 600–592 B.C.

1 And it came to pass that the angel spake unto me, saying: Look! And I looked and beheld many nations and kingdoms.

2 And the angel said unto me: What beholdest thou? And I said: I behold many nations and kingdoms.

3 And he said unto me: These are the nations and kingdoms of the Gentiles.

4 And it came to pass that I saw among the nations of the Gentiles the formation of a great church.

5 And the angel said unto me: Behold the formation of a church which is most abominable above all other churches, which slayeth the saints of God, yea, and tortureth them and bindeth them down, and yoketh them with a yoke of iron, and bringeth them down into captivity.

6 And it came to pass that I beheld this great and abominable church; and I saw the devil that he was the founder of it.

7 And I also saw gold, and silver, and silks, and scarlets, and fine-twined linen, and all manner of precious clothing; and I saw many harlots.

1 Nephi 13:1–9. An Angel Shows Nephi the Great and Abominable Church Persecuting the Saints

Who are the nations of the Gentiles? (13:3) "The word *Gentiles* means 'the nations' and eventually came to be used to mean all those not of the house of Israel. . . . As used throughout the scriptures it has a dual meaning, sometimes to designate peoples of non-Israelite lineage, and other times to designate nations that are without the gospel, even though there may be some Israelite blood therein. This latter usage is especially characteristic of the word as used in the Book of Mormon" (Bible Dictionary, "Gentile," 650).

What is the "great and abominable church"? (13:5) Elder Bruce R. McConkie explained that "the great and abominable church" or "the church of the devil is the world; it is all the carnality and evil to which fallen man is heir; it is every unholy and wicked practice; it is every false religion, every supposed system of salvation which does not actually save and exalt man in the highest heaven of the celestial world. It is every church except the true church, whether parading under a Christian or a pagan banner" (*Doctrinal New Testament Commentary*, 3:551).

What are the desires of the "great and abominable church"? (13:6–9) From Nephi's vision, we see some of the general characteristics associated with the great and abominable church. The Prophet Joseph Smith stated: "in relation to the kingdom of God, the devil always sets up his kingdom at the very same time in opposition to God" (*Joseph Smith* [manual], 25). ◉

8 And the angel spake unto me, saying: Behold the gold, and the silver, and the silks, and the scarlets, and the fine-twined linen, and the precious clothing, and the harlots, are the desires of this great and abominable church.

9 And also for the praise of the world do they destroy the saints of God, and bring them down into captivity.

10 And it came to pass that I looked and beheld many waters; and they divided the Gentiles from the seed of my brethren.

11 And it came to pass that the angel said unto me: Behold the wrath of God is upon the seed of thy brethren.

12 And I looked and beheld a man among the Gentiles, who was separated from the seed of my brethren by the many waters; and I beheld the Spirit of God, that it came down and wrought upon the man; and he went forth upon the many waters, even unto the seed of my brethren, who were in the promised land.

13 And it came to pass that I beheld the Spirit of God, that it wrought upon other Gentiles; and they went forth out of captivity, upon the many waters.

14 And it came to pass that I beheld many multitudes of the Gentiles upon the land of promise; and I beheld the wrath of God, that it was upon the seed of my brethren; and they were scattered before the Gentiles and were smitten.

15 And I beheld the Spirit of the Lord, that it was upon the Gentiles, and they did prosper and obtain the land for their inheritance; and I beheld that they were white, and exceedingly fair and beautiful, like unto my people before they were slain.

16 And it came to pass that I, Nephi, beheld that the Gentiles who had gone forth out of

1 Nephi 13:10–14. An Angel Shows Nephi That the Spirit Will Lead Columbus and Others to the Promised Land

Why was Columbus inspired of heaven? (13:12) "Observe Christopher Columbus in his silent meditations; mark his untiring and faithful observations . . . ! Inspired of the Almighty God of heaven, he encountered the ridicule and jeer of a faithless and unbelieving world. . . . The time had arrived for the discovery to be made. Millions of spirits in the spirit world, who had not yet taken bodies . . . were waiting with anxious eye for the area of heaven-born intelligences to be extended or opened to the gaze of mortal eye, that there might be room for them to come down and play their part. . . . The Spirit Angel was their guardian and their guide, and was with them on the stormy deep" (Orson Hyde, in *Journal of Discourses*, 7:108). ✛

1 Nephi 13:15–19. Nephi Sees the Lord Deliver Some Gentiles from All Other Nations

What type of men founded America? (13:15) "Those men who laid the foundation of this American government and signed the Declaration of Independence were the best spirits the God of heaven could find on the face of the earth. They were choice spirits, not wicked men. General Washington and all the men that labored for the purpose were inspired of the Lord. . . . Every one of those men that signed the Declaration of Independence, with General Washington, called upon me, as an Apostle of the Lord Jesus Christ . . .

two consecutive nights, and demanded at my hands that I should go forth and attend to the ordinances of the House of God for them" (Woodruff, in Conference Report, Apr. 1898, 89). ⊕

Who were the "mother Gentiles" gathered to battle? (13:17) The American Revolutionists were the target of the mother Gentiles. "We are not talking about righteousness here. We are not talking about just the English . . . either. Remember, there were the French and the Spanish—the French and Indian War and the Spanish wars. All the wars of succession in Europe had their reflections on this continent. Remember, George Washington had to fight both the French and the British" (Nibley, *Teachings of the Book of Mormon*, 1:198).

How was the power of God manifest in American Independence? (13:18) Benjamin Franklin described the crucial role prayer played in the formative days of the American nation: "In the beginning of the Contest with Britain, when we were sensible of danger we had daily prayer in this room for the divine protection. Our prayers, Sir, were heard—and they were graciously answered. All of us who were engaged in the struggle must have observed frequent instances of a superintending providence in our favor. . . . I have lived, Sir, a long time, and the longer I live, the more convincing proofs I see of this truth—that God Governs in the affairs of men" ("Motion for Prayers in the Convention," 1138). ⊕

How were the early colonists delivered from all other nations? (13:19) "Nephi saw in vision also the coming of the Pilgrims, who came to escape religious persecution. He foresaw the coming to America of peoples from many nations, their wars and contentions. . . . Thus the American colonies attained their independence and set up the government of the United States, all under the divine intervention of God in preparing this land for its divine destiny" (Tanner, "If They Will But Serve the God of the Land," 49).

1 Nephi 13:20–23. Nephi Sees That the Colonists Who Journey to the Promised Land Take the Bible with Them

What was the book carried forth by the Gentiles? (13:20) "We note that the early settlers of America, including the Puritans [and] Pilgrims, and also early Catholic settlers, brought with them the Bible. . . . Those on the Mayflower brought a Geneva Bible

captivity did humble themselves before the Lord; and the power of the Lord was with them.

17 And I beheld that their mother Gentiles were gathered together upon the waters, and upon the land also, to battle against them.

18 And I beheld that the power of God was with them, and also that the wrath of God was upon all those that were gathered together against them to battle.

19 And I, Nephi, beheld that the Gentiles that had gone out of captivity were delivered by the power of God out of the hands of all other nations.

20 And it came to pass that I, Nephi, beheld that they did prosper in the land; and I beheld a book, and it was carried forth among them.

21 And the angel said unto me: Knowest thou the meaning of the book?

22 And I said unto him: I know not.

23 And he said: Behold it proceedeth out of the mouth of a Jew. And I, Nephi, beheld it; and he said unto me: The book that thou beholdest is a record of the Jews, which contains the covenants of the Lord, which he hath made unto the house of Israel; and it also containeth many of the prophecies of the holy prophets; and it is a record like unto the engravings which are upon the plates of brass, save there are not so many; nevertheless, they contain the covenants of the Lord, which he hath made unto the house of Israel; wherefore, they are of great worth unto the Gentiles.

24 And the angel of the Lord said unto me: Thou hast beheld that the book proceeded forth from the mouth of a Jew; and when it proceeded forth from the mouth of a Jew it contained the fulness of the gospel of the Lord, of whom the twelve apostles bear record; and they bear record according to the truth which is in the Lamb of God.

25 Wherefore, these things go forth from the Jews in purity unto the Gentiles, according to the truth which is in God.

[1560, 1599]. . . . This was the same translation that . . . came before the King James Version was in wide circulation. Many of the Catholic immigrants to America brought the English version of the Vulgate, known as the Rheims-Douai version and was translated into English in 1582, a few years before the King James Version and at about the same time as the other Protestant Bibles" (Matthews, "Establishing the Truth of the Bible," 203–4).

How extensive were the writings on the brass plates? (13:23) "The plates of brass contained a record beginning with the five books of Moses down to Jeremiah—only a portion of the time period of the Old Testament and none of the New—yet the reduced version of the whole Bible—the Bible with which we are acquainted, containing both the Old and New Testaments—is 'not so many' as the record on the plates of brass" (Matthews, "Establishing the Truth of the Bible," 205). The writings of Zenos (Jacob 5; Alma 33) and Zenock (Alma 33), for example, were preserved on the brass plates but did not survive in the current Bible (see commentary in this volume for 1 Nephi 5:10–16).

1 Nephi 13:24–29. Nephi Sees That Many Plain and Precious Things Are Taken Out of the Bible

In what condition were these sacred records as they went forth from the Jews? (13:25) "The angel's words are plain and to the point: When the biblical records were originally written by the Jewish prophets and apostles, they contained the fulness of the gospel. When these records went to the Gentiles, some valuable plain and precious things were taken out of them. That this reduction was deliberate and not simply caused by carelessness or by the difficulties encountered by transcription and translation is further emphasized by the angel (see verse 28)" (Matthews, "Establishing the Truth of the Bible," 204).

What did Nephi see as the "great and abominable church"? (13:26) "The phrase *great and abominable church* means an immense assembly or association of people bound together by their loyalty to that which God hates. Most likely this will be a religious association involved specifically in sexual immorality and/or idolatry (that is, false worship—abandoning the God of Israel and worshipping anything else). . . . It would appear that . . . Nephi is describing a specific historical institution as the great and abominable church. To this we must add the information given in Doctrine and Covenants 86:1–4, which states that the great and abominable church did its work after the Apostles had fallen asleep, that is, around the end of the first century A.D" (Robinson, "Early Christianity and 1 Nephi 13–14," 178–81). ✪

Was the corruption of the Bible accidental? (13:27) "If the foregoing words say anything, they say that the alteration of the text was *deliberate* and intentional and extensive and for unholy and wicked purposes. It is plain also that the corruption of the text was not simply a matter of interpretation, or an awkward rendering of a few passages. It was not simply 'lost in the translation.' The words of the angel specify that '*many plain and precious things are taken away*' from and 'out of' the 'book of the Lamb of God' (1 Nephi 13:26, 28, 29, 32, 34)" (Matthews, "Establishing the Truth of the Bible," 205). ✪

What effect does the loss of "precious" and "plain" truths have upon us? (13:29) "When precious truths are removed, we are hindered in knowing the verities of scripture in two ways: (1) we do not have access to the materials which are removed; and (2) we are often unable to properly discern the true intents and meanings of that which is left, meanings which frequently are made clear by the missing scripture. In short, the greatest commentary upon scripture is scripture; if we have lost valuable elements of the revealed plan, the 'key of knowledge' is not available to open the otherwise mysterious doors of understanding" (McConkie and Millet, *Doctrinal Commentary*, 1:99).

26 And after they go forth by the hand of the twelve apostles of the Lamb, from the Jews unto the Gentiles, thou seest the formation of that great and abominable church, which is most abominable above all other churches; for behold, they have taken away from the gospel of the Lamb many parts which are plain and most precious; and also many covenants of the Lord have they taken away.

27 And all this have they done that they might pervert the right ways of the Lord, that they might blind the eyes and harden the hearts of the children of men.

28 Wherefore, thou seest that after the book hath gone forth through the hands of the great and abominable church, that there are many plain and precious things taken away from the book, which is the book of the Lamb of God.

29 And after these plain and precious things were taken away it goeth forth unto all the nations of the Gentiles; and after it goeth forth unto all the nations of the Gentiles, yea, even across the many waters which thou hast seen with the Gentiles which have gone forth out of captivity, thou seest—because of the many plain and precious things which have been taken out of the book, which were plain unto the understanding of the children of men, according to the plainness which is in the Lamb of God—because of these things which are taken away out of the gospel of the Lamb, an exceedingly great many do stumble, yea, insomuch that Satan hath great power over them.

30 Nevertheless, thou beholdest that the Gentiles who have gone forth out of captivity, and have been lifted up by the power of God above all other nations, upon the face of the land which is choice above all other lands, which is the land that the Lord God hath covenanted with thy father that his seed should have for the land of their inheritance; wherefore, thou seest that the Lord God will not suffer that the Gentiles will utterly destroy the mixture of thy seed, which are among thy brethren.

31 Neither will he suffer that the Gentiles shall destroy the seed of thy brethren.

32 Neither will the Lord God suffer that the Gentiles shall forever remain in that awful state of blindness, which thou beholdest they are in, because of the plain and most precious parts of the gospel of the Lamb which have been kept back by that abominable church, whose formation thou hast seen.

33 Wherefore saith the Lamb of God: I will be merciful unto the Gentiles, unto the visiting of the remnant of the house of Israel in great judgment.

34 And it came to pass that the angel of the Lord spake unto me, saying: Behold, saith the Lamb of God, after I have visited the remnant of the house of Israel—and this remnant of whom I speak is the seed of thy father—wherefore, after I have visited them in judgment, and smitten them by the hand of the Gentiles, and after the Gentiles do stumble exceedingly, because of the most plain and precious parts of the gospel of the Lamb which have been kept back by that abominable church, which is the mother of harlots, saith the Lamb—I will be merciful unto the Gentiles in that day, insomuch that I will bring forth unto them, in mine own power, much of my gospel, which shall be plain and precious, saith the Lamb.

1 Nephi 13:30–34. In the Latter Days, the True Gospel Will Again Be Revealed to the Gentiles

What is the "awful state of blindness"? (13:32) "This passage involves two changes. The first deals with the word order. The original manuscript reads, 'state of awful wickedness,' which Oliver Cowdery initially copied into [the Printer's Manuscript] as 'awful state of woundedness,' but then immediately corrected the word order to 'state of awful woundedness,' making [the Printer's Manuscript] agree with [the Original Manuscript]. The 1830 edition followed the original reading. But in his editing . . . for the 1837 edition, Joseph Smith restored the initial order found in [the Printer's Manuscript] and then replaced the word *woundedness* with *blindness*—that is, 'awful state of blindness.' . . . Textually there is clear evidence linking spiritual blindness with a state of wickedness" (Skousen, *Analysis of Textual Variants*, 290–91).

How much of the Lord's gospel is contained in the Book of Mormon? (13:34) "The Book of Mormon contains the 'fulness of the gospel of Jesus Christ' (D&C 20:9) . . . and of the principles of that gospel (faith, repentance, baptism, the gift of the Holy Ghost, endurance to the end, resurrection, and judgment (3 Nephi 27:13–21; D&C 76:40–42). . . . The Book of Mormon does not contain—nor does it claim to do so—the fulness of *gospel doctrine*. . . . Rather, its stated purpose is to bring men and women to Christ, to center their attention in the God of Israel" (McConkie and Millet, *Doctrinal Commentary*, 1:102).

1 Nephi 13:35–37. Jesus Christ Will Visit the Descendants of Nephi and Give Them His True Gospel

What does "Zion" mean in the Book of Mormon? (13:37) "In the Book of Mormon we encounter . . . an unusual form and meaning for the word *Zion*. In an Old Testament setting, Zion usually has reference to the holy mount or, by extension, to the city of Jerusalem. Here and in numerous other places (e.g., 2 Nephi 26:29–31; 2 Nephi 28:20–21, 24; 3 Nephi 16:16–18), Zion seems to represent the gathering place of the believers, the society of the pure in heart, the setting for the Saints" (McConkie and Millet, *Doctrinal Commentary*, 1:103; see also Mosiah 15:14–18; Isaiah 52:7).

1 Nephi 13:38–42. The Book of Mormon and Other Modern Scriptures Prove to the World That the Bible Is True

What are the "other books" Nephi saw come forth? (13:39) "The Lord in his foreknowledge provided a way to counteract the work of the devil in taking away the plain and precious things. He brought forth other scriptures, The Book of Mormon, The Doctrine and Covenants, The Pearl of Great Price. . . . There were four purposes of the Lord in bringing forth these other records. . . . First, . . . to establish the truth of the records of the prophets. . . . Second, to make known the plain and precious parts that had been lost. . . . Third, to 'make known . . . that the Lamb of God is the Son of the Eternal Father. . . .' Fourth . . . to make known that 'all men must come unto (Christ) or they cannot be saved'" (Nyman, *I, Nephi, Wrote This Record*, 184).

35 For, behold, saith the Lamb: I will manifest myself unto thy seed, that they shall write many things which I shall minister unto them, which shall be plain and precious; and after thy seed shall be destroyed, and dwindle in unbelief, and also the seed of thy brethren, behold, these things shall be hid up, to come forth unto the Gentiles, by the gift and power of the Lamb.

36 And in them shall be written my gospel, saith the Lamb, and my rock and my salvation.

37 And blessed are they who shall seek to bring forth my Zion at that day, for they shall have the gift and the power of the Holy Ghost; and if they endure unto the end they shall be lifted up at the last day, and shall be saved in the everlasting kingdom of the Lamb; and whoso shall publish peace, yea, tidings of great joy, how beautiful upon the mountains shall they be.

38 And it came to pass that I beheld the remnant of the seed of my brethren, and also the book of the Lamb of God, which had proceeded forth from the mouth of the Jew, that it came forth from the Gentiles unto the remnant of the seed of my brethren.

39 And after it had come forth unto them I beheld other books, which came forth by the power of the Lamb, from the Gentiles unto them, unto the convincing of the Gentiles and the remnant of the seed of my brethren, and also the Jews who were scattered upon all the face of the earth, that the records of the prophets and of the twelve apostles of the Lamb are true.

40 And the angel spake unto me, saying: These last records, which thou hast seen among the Gentiles, shall establish the truth of the first, which are of the twelve apostles of the Lamb, and shall make known the plain and precious things which have been taken away from them; and shall make known to all kindreds, tongues, and people, that the Lamb of God is the Son of the Eternal Father, and the Savior of the world; and that all men must come unto him, or they cannot be saved.

41 And they must come according to the words which shall be established by the mouth of the Lamb; and the words of the Lamb shall be made known in the records of thy seed, as well as in the records of the twelve apostles of the Lamb; wherefore they both shall be established in one; for there is one God and one Shepherd over all the earth.

42 And the time cometh that he shall manifest himself unto all nations, both unto the Jews and also unto the Gentiles; and after he has manifested himself unto the Jews and also unto the Gentiles, then he shall manifest himself unto the Gentiles and also unto the Jews, and the last shall be first, and the first shall be last.

How does the Book of Mormon establish the truth of the Bible? (13:40) "It is not only desirable that the Book of Mormon should substantiate the Bible and supply certain missing parts, it is absolutely *necessary* for eternal justice. It appears that in the economy of God there must be more than one witness for the truths that are taught to mankind. Without a second or third witness, the law cannot be binding on the day of judgment. . . . Not just the truth of the Bible as history and as a cultural record, but to establish . . . and prove that the testimony of Jesus Christ contained in the scriptures is true and correct" (Matthews, "Establishing the Truth of the Bible," 211–12).

Who will be last and who will be first? (13:42) "The Gospel of Jesus Christ is to go forth to the world according to a divinely established timetable. . . . In the last days . . . the gospel was restored . . . [in] a 'gentile' nation; from the Latter-day Saints it shall eventually go preferentially to the Jews and to all the tribes of Israel. Thus, those who were once *first* in receiving the gospel in the meridian of time . . . shall . . . be *last* to receive the message of salvation. . . . Those who were *last* to receive the missionary thrust in the first century—the Gentiles—are honored to be the *first* recipients . . . in the dispensation of the fulness of times" (McConkie and Millet, *Doctrinal Commentary*, 1:104–5).

CHAPTER 14

An angel tells Nephi of the blessings and cursings to fall upon the Gentiles—There are only two churches: the Church of the Lamb of God and the church of the devil—The Saints of God in all nations are persecuted by the great and abominable church—The Apostle John will write concerning the end of the world. About 600–592 B.C.

1 Nephi 14:1–9. An Angel Tells Nephi about Blessings and Punishments That Will Come upon the Gentiles in the Last Days

By what means shall Israel cease to be confounded? (14:2) "With the restoration of things plain and precious, Israel need no more be scattered or confounded. The Book of Mormon in particular is the instrument prepared by God to bring about the gathering of Israel in the last days in two ways: (1) it provides a *description* of Israel's condition—the causes for the scattering as well as the means whereby she is to be gathered; and (2) it provides the specific *prescription* for accomplishing the task of gathering—namely, through the Book of Mormon itself. In short, the Book of Mormon is the scriptural record ordained to accomplish 'the Father's work' (3 Nephi 21)" (McConkie and Millet, *Doctrinal Commentary*, 1:107).

1 And it shall come to pass, that if the Gentiles shall hearken unto the Lamb of God in that day that he shall manifest himself unto them in word, and also in power, in very deed, unto the taking away of their stumbling blocks—

2 And harden not their hearts against the Lamb of God, they shall be numbered among the seed of thy father; yea, they shall be numbered among the house of Israel; and they shall be a blessed people upon the promised land forever; they shall be no more brought down into captivity; and the house of Israel shall no more be confounded.

3 And that great pit, which hath been digged for them by that great and abominable church, which was founded by the devil and his children, that he might lead away the souls of men down to hell—yea, that great pit which hath been digged for the destruction of men shall be filled by those who digged it, unto their utter destruction, saith the Lamb of God; not the destruction of the soul, save it be the casting of it into that hell which hath no end.

4 For behold, this is according to the captivity of the devil, and also according to the justice of God, upon all those who will work wickedness and abomination before him.

5 And it came to pass that the angel spake unto me, Nephi, saying: Thou hast beheld that if the Gentiles repent it shall be well

with them; and thou also knowest concerning the covenants of the Lord unto the house of Israel; and thou also hast heard that whoso repenteth not must perish.

6 Therefore, wo be unto the Gentiles if it so be that they harden their hearts against the Lamb of God.

7 For the time cometh, saith the Lamb of God, that I will work a great and a marvelous work among the children of men; a work which shall be everlasting, either on the one hand or on the other—either to the convincing of them unto peace and life eternal, or unto the deliverance of them to the hardness of their hearts and the blindness of their minds unto their being brought down into captivity, and also into destruction, both temporally and spiritually, according to the captivity of the devil, of which I have spoken.

8 And it came to pass that when the angel had spoken these words, he said unto me: Rememberest thou the covenants of the Father unto the house of Israel? I said unto him, Yea.

9 And it came to pass that he said unto me: Look, and behold that great and abominable church, which is the mother of abominations, whose founder is the devil.

10 And he said unto me: Behold there are save two churches only; the one is the church of the Lamb of God, and the other is the church of the devil; wherefore, whoso belongeth not to the church of the Lamb of God belongeth to that great church, which is the mother of abominations; and she is the whore of all the earth.

11 And it came to pass that I looked and beheld the whore of all the earth, and she sat upon many waters; and she had dominion over all the earth, among all nations, kindreds, tongues, and people.

Why is the "marvelous work" described as being everlasting? (14:7) "The 'marvelous work' of the latter days was to be 'everlasting' in its consequences; the choice between salvation and damnation would be final and irrevocable (1 Nephi 14:7). For, in the final analysis there have been but two paths lying before the family of God. All walk one or the other (2 Nephi 2: 27-29)" (Turner, "The Prophet Nephi," 89).

1 Nephi 14:10–12. Nephi Learns That There Are Only Two Churches

Why will there be only two churches? (14:10) The "Proclamation of the Twelve Apostles" in 1845 declared: "As this work progresses in its onward course, and becomes more and more an object of political and religious interest and excitement, no king, ruler, or subject, no community or individual, will stand *neutral*. All will at length be influenced by one spirit or the other; and all will take sides either for or against the kingdom of God, and the fulfillment of the prophets, in the great restoration and return of his long dispersed covenant people" (in Clark, *Messages of the First Presidency*, 1:257).

What will be the influence of the members of the Church in the last days? (14:12) "This pertains to a day yet future. The saints of the Most High are not yet, as a people and with organized congregations, established upon all the face of the earth. When the day comes that they are, they still will not compare in power with the forces of evil. Even then, as Nephi foresaw, 'their dominions upon the face of the earth were small, because of the wickedness of the great whore whom I saw'" (McConkie, *Millennial Messiah*, 55).

1 Nephi 14:13–17. Nephi Sees That the Church of the Devil Will Persecute the Saints of God

What are the characteristics of the great war of the last days? (14:13) "Where is this war? Where is it fought? It is waged every day in our communities and our nations. It is waged over airwaves and print. It is waged in quiet and subtle ways, but is a war nonetheless. Anything that takes us down the 'other' path cannot lead us to salvation. We live on a battlefield. While the vision of the discovery of the New World was describing a particular war (or set of wars), this one is symbolic, rather than literal" (Gardner, *Second Witness*, 1:249).

What constitutes the work of the Father? (14:17) "The 'work of the Father'—the work of gathering Israel (see 3 Nephi 21:1–8), the missionary thrust of the Latter-day Saints—shall go forward with accelerated force when the Lord has displaced the devil and cleansed the earth of the violence and wickedness on its surface. All Israel, the ten tribes included, shall then be gathered in great numbers (see 2 Nephi 30:7–15;

12 And it came to pass that I beheld the church of the Lamb of God, and its numbers were few, because of the wickedness and abominations of the whore who sat upon many waters; nevertheless, I beheld that the church of the Lamb, who were the saints of God, were also upon all the face of the earth; and their dominions upon the face of the earth were small, because of the wickedness of the great whore whom I saw.

13 And it came to pass that I beheld that the great mother of abominations did gather together multitudes upon the face of all the earth, among all the nations of the Gentiles, to fight against the Lamb of God.

14 And it came to pass that I, Nephi, beheld the power of the Lamb of God, that it descended upon the saints of the church of the Lamb, and upon the covenant people of the Lord, who were scattered upon all the face of the earth; and they were armed with righteousness and with the power of God in great glory.

15 And it came to pass that I beheld that the wrath of God was poured out upon that great and abominable church, insomuch that there were wars and rumors of wars among all the nations and kindreds of the earth.

16 And as there began to be wars and rumors of wars among all the nations which belonged to the mother of abominations, the angel spake unto me, saying: Behold, the wrath of God is upon the mother of harlots; and behold, thou seest all these things—

17 And when the day cometh that the wrath of God is poured out upon the mother of harlots, which is the great and abominable church of all the earth, whose founder is the devil, then, at that day, the work of the Father shall commence, in preparing the way for the fulfilling of his covenants, which he hath made to his people who are of the house of Israel.

18 And it came to pass that the angel spake unto me, saying: Look!

19 And I looked and beheld a man, and he was dressed in a white robe.

20 And the angel said unto me: Behold one of the twelve apostles of the Lamb.

21 Behold, he shall see and write the remainder of these things; yea, and also many things which have been.

22 And he shall also write concerning the end of the world.

23 Wherefore, the things which he shall write are just and true; and behold they are written in the book which thou beheld proceeding out of the mouth of the Jew; and at the time they proceeded out of the mouth of the Jew, or, at the time the book proceeded out of the mouth of the Jew, the things which were written were plain and pure, and most precious and easy to the understanding of all men.

24 And behold, the things which this apostle of the Lamb shall write are many things which thou hast seen; and behold, the remainder shalt thou see.

25 But the things which thou shalt see hereafter thou shalt not write; for the Lord God hath ordained the apostle of the Lamb of God that he should write them.

26 And also others who have been, to them hath he shown all things, and they have written them; and they are sealed up to come forth in their purity, according to the truth which is in the Lamb, in the own due time of the Lord, unto the house of Israel.

27 And I, Nephi, heard and bear record, that the name of the apostle of the Lamb was John, according to the word of the angel.

3 Nephi 21:24–28)" (McConkie and Millet, *Doctrinal Commentary*, 1:113).

1 Nephi 14:18–30. Nephi Sees the Mission of the Apostle John

Who was the apostle of the Lamb seen by Nephi? (14:20) "While Nephi saw the remainder of the world's history, it was left to John the Apostle of Jesus to write [see v. 27]. This undoubtedly referred to the Book of Revelation in the New Testament, and affirms the authorship of this book which is questioned by the Christian world. Originally the things written by John were plain and pure, and easy to be understood (v. 23)" (Nyman, *I, Nephi, Wrote This Record*, 195; see also commentary in this volume on 1 Nephi 11:31).

Who else has seen the events of the last days? (14:26) "This [verse] seems to be a specific reference to the vision had by the Brother of Jared and the record made and sealed up by him (see Ether 3:22-27). When the day comes—no doubt it will be millennial—that the people of the earth rend the veil of unbelief that covers the hearts and minds of even many of the faithful, then shall the panoramic vision given to Nephi, as well as those given to Adam, Enoch, Noah, Mahonri Moriancumer, Abraham, Moses, Joseph Smith, and others, be open to all the obedient (2 Nephi 27:10–11; Ether 4:6–7, 15)" (McConkie and Millett, *Doctrinal Commentary*, 1:115).

28 And behold, I, Nephi, am forbidden that I should write the remainder of the things which I saw and heard; wherefore the things which I have written sufficeth me; and I have written but a small part of the things which I saw.

29 And I bear record that I saw the things which my father saw, and the angel of the Lord did make them known unto me.

30 And now I make an end of speaking concerning the things which I saw while I was carried away in the Spirit; and if all the things which I saw are not written, the things which I have written are true. And thus it is. Amen.

CHAPTER 15

Lehi's seed are to receive the gospel from the Gentiles in the latter days—The gathering of Israel is likened unto an olive tree whose natural branches will be grafted in again—Nephi interprets the vision of the tree of life and speaks of the justice of God in dividing the wicked from the righteous. About 600–592 B.C.

1 And it came to pass that after I, Nephi, had been carried away in the Spirit, and seen all these things, I returned to the tent of my father.

2 And it came to pass that I beheld my brethren, and they were disputing one with another concerning the things which my father had spoken unto them.

3 For he truly spake many great things unto them, which were hard to be understood, save a man should inquire of the Lord; and they being hard in their hearts, therefore they did not look unto the Lord as they ought.

4 And now I, Nephi, was grieved because of the hardness of their hearts, and also, because of the things which I had seen, and knew they must unavoidably come to pass because of the great wickedness of the children of men.

1 Nephi 15:1–11. Nephi's Brothers Cannot Understand Their Father's Dream

Why couldn't Laman and Lemuel understand the things spoken by Lehi? (15:2–7) Elder Neal A. Maxwell explained: "This failure to believe in a revealing God was especially basic. Some moderns who wish to distance themselves from God try placing His pavilion firmly in the past. By believing in such a disabled God, people can do pretty much as they please. It is then not many steps further to saying there is no God, therefore no law and no sin! (see 2 Ne. 2:13; see also Alma 30:28)" ("Lessons from Laman and Lemuel," 6). ☉

5 And it came to pass that I was overcome because of my afflictions, for I considered that mine afflictions were great above all, because of the destruction of my people, for I had beheld their fall.

6 And it came to pass that after I had received strength I spake unto my brethren, desiring to know of them the cause of their disputations.

7 And they said: Behold, we cannot understand the words which our father hath spoken concerning the natural branches of the olive tree, and also concerning the Gentiles.

8 And I said unto them: Have ye inquired of the Lord?

9 And they said unto me: We have not; for the Lord maketh no such thing known unto us.

10 Behold, I said unto them: How is it that ye do not keep the commandments of the Lord? How is it that ye will perish, because of the hardness of your hearts?

11 Do ye not remember the things which the Lord hath said?—If ye will not harden your hearts, and ask me in faith, believing that ye shall receive, with diligence in keeping my commandments, surely these things shall be made known unto you.

12 Behold, I say unto you, that the house of Israel was compared unto an olive tree, by the Spirit of the Lord which was in our father; and behold are we not broken off from

Is it possible to righteously feel our life's circumstances are too severe? (15:5) Elder Neal A. Maxwell explained that we may "feel that our particular assemblage of affliction is perhaps larger than that of anyone else. Nephi recorded this indicator of how he once felt [see 1 Nephi 15:5]. . . . Nephi's capacity to lament genuinely over the wickedness of his colleagues is a reflection of his highly developed love for his associates and fellowmen" (*Even As I Am*, 92).

How do we receive a knowledge of truth? (15:11) "In one of those difficult times that the faithful and dedicated young Nephi had with his rebellious brothers, he reminded them of the following guide to obtaining a testimony. . . .

"First, *don't harden your heart*. Seek to know. In other words, have an intense, consuming desire to know. . . . Second, *ask in faith*. In your study of the scriptures, have you noted how many times the phrase 'believing that ye shall receive' accompanies the commandment of praying and asking? . . . Third, *keep the commandments*. I think that the words of the Book of Mormon point out the blessings that we can obtain if we abound in good works" (Albrea, "Your Own Personal Testimony," 42). ☉

1 Nephi 15:12–20. The Lord Promises to Gather the Scattered People of the House of Israel

How did Nephi distinguish between the Jews and the Gentiles? (15:12–13) "Both Lehi and Nephi divide all men into two camps, Jews and Gentiles. The Jews were either the nationals of the kingdom of Judah or their descendants; all others were considered to be Gentiles. Thus, we [members of the Church] are the Gentiles of whom this scripture speaks; we are the ones who have received the fulness of the gospel; and we shall take it to the Lamanites, who are Jews, because their fathers came from Jerusalem and from the kingdom of Judah" (McConkie, *New Witness*, 556). Elder Bruce R. McConkie also identified one Gentile who would greatly assist in the Restoration: "Joseph Smith . . . was the Gentile by whose hand the Book of Mormon came forth, and the members of The Church of Jesus Christ of Latter-day Saints . . . are the Gentiles who carry salvation to the Lamanites and to the Jews" (*Millennial Messiah*, 233).

the house of Israel, and are we not a branch of the house of Israel?

13 And now, the thing which our father meaneth concerning the grafting in of the natural branches through the fulness of the Gentiles, is, that in the latter days, when our seed shall have dwindled in unbelief, yea, for the space of many years, and many generations after the Messiah shall be manifested in body unto the children of men, then shall the fulness of the gospel of the Messiah come unto the Gentiles, and from the Gentiles unto the remnant of our seed—

14 And at that day shall the remnant of our seed know that they are of the house of Israel, and that they are the covenant people of the Lord; and then shall they know and come to the knowledge of their forefathers, and also to the knowledge of the gospel of their Redeemer, which was ministered unto their fathers by him; wherefore, they shall come to the knowledge of their Redeemer and the very points of his doctrine, that they may know how to come unto him and be saved.

15 And then at that day will they not rejoice and give praise unto their everlasting God, their rock and their salvation? Yea, at that day, will they not receive the strength and nourishment from the true vine? Yea, will they not come unto the true fold of God?

16 Behold, I say unto you, Yea; they shall be remembered again among the house of Israel; they shall be grafted in, being a natural branch of the olive tree, into the true olive tree.

17 And this is what our father meaneth; and he meaneth that it will not come to pass until after they are scattered by the Gentiles; and he meaneth that it shall come by way of the Gentiles, that the Lord may show his power unto the Gentiles, for the very cause that he shall be rejected of the Jews, or of the house of Israel.

18 Wherefore, our father hath not spoken of our seed alone, but also of all the house of Israel, pointing to the covenant which should be fulfilled in the latter days; which covenant the Lord made to our father Abraham, saying: In thy seed shall all the kindreds of the earth be blessed.

19 And it came to pass that I, Nephi, spake much unto them concerning these things; yea, I spake unto them concerning the restoration of the Jews in the latter days.

20 And I did rehearse unto them the words of Isaiah, who spake concerning the restoration of the Jews, or of the house of Israel; and after they were restored they should no more be confounded, neither should they be scattered again. And it came to pass that I did speak many words unto my brethren, that they were pacified and did humble themselves before the Lord.

21 And it came to pass that they did speak unto me again, saying: What meaneth this thing which our father saw in a dream? What meaneth the tree which he saw?

22 And I said unto them: It was a representation of the tree of life.

23 And they said unto me: What meaneth the rod of iron which our father saw, that led to the tree?

24 And I said unto them that it was the word of God; and whoso would hearken unto the word of God, and would hold fast unto it, they would never perish; neither could the temptations and the fiery darts of the adversary overpower them unto blindness, to lead them away to destruction.

25 Wherefore, I, Nephi, did exhort them to give heed unto the word of the Lord; yea, I did exhort them with all the energies of my soul, and with all the faculty which I possessed, that they would give heed to the word

Who is "all the house of Israel" spoken of by Lehi? (15:18) "Lehi and his seed are not the only branch to be grafted into the olive tree. All of the branches of the house of Israel will be grafted in. The allegory of Zenos speaks of three natural branches. Nephi spoke to his brothers of one of the two other natural branches, 'the restoration of the Jews in the latter days' (v. 19). . . . The other branch, the lost tribes, will be identified. . . . The covenant made to Abraham will be fulfilled in the latter days through the grafting in of the natural branches and in offering of the blessings of the gospel to all nations as Abraham was promised (v. 18)" (Nyman, *I, Nephi, Wrote This Record*, 222; see also commentary in this volume on Jacob 5:39).

1 Nephi 15:21–36. Nephi Answers His Brothers' Questions

What does the tree represent? (15:21) "In response to the inquiry of his brothers . . . Nephi told them that it represented the tree of life. The tree of life was first spoken of in the creation account. It was the tree in the midst of the Garden of Eden, the fruit of which contained the power of everlasting life (Genesis 2:9; 3:22–24). . . . The tree was a symbolic representation of Christ, its fruits symbolizing the saving principles of his gospel" (McConkie and Millet, *Doctrinal Commentary*, 1:120).

How does the word of God protect us from the "fiery darts of the adversary"? (15:24) "When Laman and Lemuel asked, 'What meaneth the rod of iron?' Nephi answered, 'It was the word of God; and [note this promise] *whoso would hearken unto the word of God, and would hold fast unto it, they would never perish; neither could the temptations and the fiery darts of the adversary overpower them unto blindness, to lead them away to destruction'* (1 Ne. 15:23–24; italics added). Not only will the word of God lead us to the fruit which is desirable above all others, but in the word of God and through it we can find the power to resist temptation, the power to thwart the work of Satan and his emissaries" (Benson, "Power of the Word," 80).

What is the state of the righteous as opposed to that of the wicked? (15:28) Whether in this life or the next, the righteous and the wicked occupy different spaces. President Joseph F. Smith saw that the Savior "could not" go among the ungodly during his mission to the spirit world (D&C 138:37). These were the "ungodly and the unrepentant who had defiled themselves while in the flesh" (D&C 138:20). Those who had rejected the "testimonies and the warnings of ancient prophets" did not "behold his presence, nor look upon his face. Where they were, darkness reigned" (D&C 138:21–22). The "spirits of the just who had been faithful in the testimony of Jesus while they lived in mortality" (D&C 138:12) beheld the face of the Lord and "rejoiced in their redemption, and bowed the knee and acknowledged the Son of God as their Redeemer" (D&C 138:23).

When and how will every man be judged? (15:32) "'Every man may act in doctrine and principle . . . according to the moral agency which I have given unto him, that every man may be accountable for his own sins in the day of judgment' (D&C 101:78; see also Mosiah 3:24).

"As all will be resurrected, your physical body will then be restored to its proper and perfect frame (see Alma 11:43; Alma 40:23). The day of your resurrection will be a day of judgment that will determine the kind of life you shall have hereafter.

"That judgment will consider not only your actions, but also your innermost intent and heartfelt desires. Your everyday thoughts have not been lost. Scriptures speak of the 'bright recollection' (Alma 11:43) and 'perfect remembrance' (Alma 5:18) that your mind will provide in times of divine judgment" (Nelson, "Choices," 75).

of God and remember to keep his commandments always in all things.

26 And they said unto me: What meaneth the river of water which our father saw?

27 And I said unto them that the water which my father saw was filthiness; and so much was his mind swallowed up in other things that he beheld not the filthiness of the water.

28 And I said unto them that it was an awful gulf, which separated the wicked from the tree of life, and also from the saints of God.

29 And I said unto them that it was a representation of that awful hell, which the angel said unto me was prepared for the wicked.

30 And I said unto them that our father also saw that the justice of God did also divide the wicked from the righteous; and the brightness thereof was like unto the brightness of a flaming fire, which ascendeth up unto God forever and ever, and hath no end.

31 And they said unto me: Doth this thing mean the torment of the body in the days of probation, or doth it mean the final state of the soul after the death of the temporal body, or doth it speak of the things which are temporal?

32 And it came to pass that I said unto them that it was a representation of things both temporal and spiritual; for the day should come that they must be judged of their works, yea, even the works which were done by the temporal body in their days of probation.

33 Wherefore, if they should die in their wickedness they must be cast off also, as to the things which are spiritual, which are pertaining to righteousness; wherefore, they must be brought to stand before God, to be judged of their works; and if their works have been filthiness they must needs be filthy; and if they be filthy it must needs be that they cannot dwell in the kingdom of God; if so, the kingdom of God must be filthy also.

34 But behold, I say unto you, the kingdom of God is not filthy, and there cannot any unclean thing enter into the kingdom of God; wherefore there must needs be a place of filthiness prepared for that which is filthy.

35 And there is a place prepared, yea, even that awful hell of which I have spoken, and the devil is the preparator of it; wherefore the final state of the souls of men is to dwell in the kingdom of God, or to be cast out because of that justice of which I have spoken.

36 Wherefore, the wicked are rejected from the righteous, and also from that tree of life, whose fruit is most precious and most desirable above all other fruits; yea, and it is the greatest of all the gifts of God. And thus I spake unto my brethren. Amen.

CHAPTER 16

The wicked take the truth to be hard—Lehi's sons marry the daughters of Ishmael—The Liahona guides their course in the wilderness—Messages from the Lord are written on the Liahona from time to time—Ishmael dies; his family murmurs because of afflictions. About 600–592 B.C.

1 And now it came to pass that after I, Nephi, had made an end of speaking to my brethren, behold they said unto me: Thou hast declared unto us hard things, more than we are able to bear.

2 And it came to pass that I said unto them that I knew that I had spoken hard things against the wicked, according to the truth; and the righteous have I justified, and testified that they should be lifted up at the last day; wherefore, the guilty taketh the truth to be hard, for it cutteth them to the very center.

Why are the righteous and the wicked separated? (15:34) "Both the justice of God and the laws of nature mandate a division of the wicked from the righteous. The warmth and glory of the noonday sun and midnight's shield of darkness are not compatible companions—light and darkness will never meet, Christ and Satan will never shake hands. The separation of the righteous from the wicked in the world to come is foreshadowed by their separation in mortality. This life, like the one to follow, has its children of light and its children of darkness. The citizens of both kingdoms prepare themselves here for the nature of the society of which they will be a part both in and after death" (McConkie and Millet, *Doctrinal Commentary*, 1:121).

1 Nephi 16:1–6. Wicked People Do Not Like to Hear the Truth

Why do the guilty and the wicked take "the truth to be hard"? (16:1–3) "The scriptures testify that the proud are easily offended and hold grudges (see 1 Ne. 16:1–3). They withhold forgiveness to keep another in their debt and to justify their injured feelings. The proud do not receive counsel or correction easily (see Prov. 15:10; Amos 5:10). Defensiveness is used by them to justify and rationalize their frailties and failures (see Matt. 3:9; John 6:30–59)" (Benson, "Beware of Pride," 6).

Why did Nephi correct and exhort his brothers?
(16:4) "Nephi declared truth to his disobedient brothers in an effort to help them turn their hearts to God. Those who offend the Spirit through wickedness often take offense when given inspired correction or chastisement. Elder Neal A. Maxwell . . . explained why we should accept the Lord's correction even if it is painful: 'God is not only there in the mildest expressions of His presence, but also in those seemingly harsh expressions. For example, when truth "cutteth . . . to the very center" (1 Nephi 16:2), this may signal that spiritual surgery is underway, painfully severing pride from the soul'" (*Book of Mormon Student Manual* [2009], 34). ●

How do you take correction from others? (16:4) In what ways can you improve when others offer to help you improve?

Why does Nephi mention his father's tent and the valley of Lemuel? (16:6) After leaving their home in Jerusalem, Lehi's family lived in the valley of Lemuel (see 1 Nephi 2:10). The reader is now alerted that several years have passed. "After an extended narrative consisting of his father's dream, his own vision, and his exposition to his brothers . . . Nephi must now return to his family's mundane travel narrative. As a transitional device, he repeats the marker he has used earlier: these things were done 'as my father dwelt in a tent in the valley which he called Lemuel'" (Gardner, *Second Witness*, 1:269). ●

1 Nephi 16:7–8. Lehi's Sons Marry the Daughters of Ishmael

Why was it so important to return to Jerusalem for Ishmael's daughters? (16:7) Lehi realized, like all biblical patriarchs, that marriage is central to the plan of God. Nephi records that all eligible sons and daughters were given in marriage. "After reading about the marriages between Lehi's and Ishmael's families, we are told that Lehi had fulfilled all the commandments the Lord had given him (see 1 Nephi 16:8). Marriage is central to the Lord's plans for His children.

3 And now my brethren, if ye were righteous and were willing to hearken to the truth, and give heed unto it, that ye might walk uprightly before God, then ye would not murmur because of the truth, and say: Thou speakest hard things against us.

4 And it came to pass that I, Nephi, did exhort my brethren, with all diligence, to keep the commandments of the Lord.

5 And it came to pass that they did humble themselves before the Lord; insomuch that I had joy and great hopes of them, that they would walk in the paths of righteousness.

6 Now, all these things were said and done as my father dwelt in a tent in the valley which he called Lemuel.

7 And it came to pass that I, Nephi, took one of the daughters of Ishmael to wife; and also, my brethren took of the daughters of Ishmael to wife; and also Zoram took the eldest daughter of Ishmael to wife.

The First Presidency and the Quorum of the Twelve Apostles declared the Lord's view on marriage: 'The family is ordained of God. Marriage between man and woman is essential to His eternal plan' ('The Family: A Proclamation to the World,' 102)" (*Book of Mormon Student Manual* [2009], 34). ⊕

8 And thus my father had fulfilled all the commandments of the Lord which had been given unto him. And also, I, Nephi, had been blessed of the Lord exceedingly.

Why does Nephi say he was exceedingly blessed? (16:8) "This verse leaves the impression that Lehi had been commanded of the Lord to see that his sons were properly married. The antecedent of Nephi's expression that he had been 'blessed of the Lord exceedingly' seems to have been his marriage. If this is the case, it is a touching tribute to his wife, who, according to Hebrew tradition, remains unnamed" (McConkie and Millet, *Doctrinal Commentary*, 1:123–24).

9 And it came to pass that the voice of the Lord spake unto my father by night, and commanded him that on the morrow he should take his journey into the wilderness.

1 Nephi 16:9–17. The Liahona Guides Lehi's Family on Their Journey to the Promised Land

10 And it came to pass that as my father arose in the morning, and went forth to the tent door, to his great astonishment he beheld upon the ground a round ball of curious workmanship; and it was of fine brass. And within the ball were two spindles; and the one pointed the way whither we should go into the wilderness.

What are some of the characteristics to remember about the Liahona? (16:10) "First, the Liahona was a gift from God. . . . Second, it was neither mechanical nor self-operating. It was not a mechanism but worked solely by the power of God and solely according to their faith. It wasn't magic; a magic thing would work by itself. Third, it only worked in response to faith, diligence, and the heed of those who followed it. Fourth, there was something ordinary and familiar about it" (Nibley, *Teachings of the Book of Mormon*, 1:4–5). ⊕

11 And it came to pass that we did gather together whatsoever things we should carry into the wilderness, and all the remainder of our provisions which the Lord had given unto us; and we did take seed of every kind that we might carry into the wilderness.

12 And it came to pass that we did take our tents and depart into the wilderness, across the river Laman.

13 And it came to pass that we traveled for the space of four days, nearly a south-southeast direction, and we did pitch our tents again; and we did call the name of the place Shazer.

What does the word *Shazer* mean? (16:13) Hugh Nibley taught: "'And we did call the name of the place Shazer.' . . . *Shajar* is a clump of trees; it's pronounced *shazer*, of course. It's a group of trees in the desert. Well, naturally, the place they would park next would be where there were some trees, some water, etc. So they camped in a place called Shazer, 'the trees'" (*Teachings of the Book of Mormon*, 1:7–8).

14 And it came to pass that we did take our bows and our arrows, and go forth into the wilderness to slay food for our families; and after we had slain food for our families we did return again to our families in the wilderness, to the place of Shazer. And we did go forth again in the wilderness, following the same direction, keeping in the most fertile parts of the wilderness, which were in the borders near the Red Sea.

15 And it came to pass that we did travel for the space of many days, slaying food by the way, with our bows and our arrows and our stones and our slings.

16 And we did follow the directions of the ball, which led us in the more fertile parts of the wilderness.

17 And after we had traveled for the space of many days, we did pitch our tents for the space of a time, that we might again rest ourselves and obtain food for our families.

What can we learn from how the Liahona operated? (16:16) "As we study and ponder the purposes of the Liahona and the principles by which it operated, I testify that we will receive inspiration suited to our individual and family circumstances and needs. We can and will be blessed with ongoing direction from the Holy Ghost" (Bednar, "That We May Always Have His Spirit," 30).

1 Nephi 16:18–23. Nephi Breaks His Bow, and Lehi's Family Suffers

What was the significance of the bow in the culture of Lehi's family? (16:18) "Bows were symbols of political power. One thinks of Odysseus bending the bow to prove himself. An overlord would break the bow of a disobedient vassal to symbolically put the rebel in his place (see also Jeremiah 49:35; 51:56). That detail is significant in 1 Nephi 16. Nephi's bow broke, and the bows of Laman and Lemuel lost their springs, but when Nephi fashioned a new bow, making him the only one in camp with a bow, his brothers soon accused Nephi of having political ambitions (see 1 Nephi 16:37–38)" (Hamblin, "Nephi's Bows and Arrows," 41).

Was it possible for Nephi to have a steel bow? (16:18) References to steel in the Book of Mormon include "references to metal weapons.... Two are references to Near East weapons: 'the blade [of Laban's sword] was of the most precious steel' (1 Nephi 4:9), and Nephi's bow was made of 'fine steel' (1 Nephi 16:18). The existence of steel (that is, carburized iron) weapons in the Near East in the early sixth century B.C. has been clearly demonstrated. Robert Maddin writes, 'To sum up, by the beginning of the seventh century B.C.... blacksmiths of the eastern Mediterranean had mastered two of the processes that make iron

18 And it came to pass that as I, Nephi, went forth to slay food, behold, I did break my bow, which was made of fine steel; and after I did break my bow, behold, my brethren were angry with me because of the loss of my bow, for we did obtain no food.

19 And it came to pass that we did return without food to our families, and being much fatigued, because of their journeying, they did suffer much for the want of food.

a useful material for tools and weapons: carburizing and quenching' ['How the Iron Age Began,' 131]" (Hamblin and Merrill, "Swords in the Book of Mormon," 345–46). ⊕

20 And it came to pass that Laman and Lemuel and the sons of Ishmael did begin to murmur exceedingly, because of their sufferings and afflictions in the wilderness; and also my father began to murmur against the Lord his God; yea, and they were all exceedingly sorrowful, even that they did murmur against the Lord.

21 Now it came to pass that I, Nephi, having been afflicted with my brethren because of the loss of my bow, and their bows having lost their springs, it began to be exceedingly difficult, yea, insomuch that we could obtain no food.

22 And it came to pass that I, Nephi, did speak much unto my brethren, because they had hardened their hearts again, even unto complaining against the Lord their God.

23 And it came to pass that I, Nephi, did make out of wood a bow, and out of a straight stick, an arrow; wherefore, I did arm myself with a bow and an arrow, with a sling and with stones. And I said unto my father: Whither shall I go to obtain food?

24 And it came to pass that he did inquire of the Lord, for they had humbled themselves because of my words; for I did say many things unto them in the energy of my soul.

25 And it came to pass that the voice of the Lord came unto my father; and he was truly chastened because of his murmuring against

Why did Laman and Lemuel "murmur exceedingly"? (16:20–22) "Easily riled and quick to complain, they could scarcely remember their last rescue long enough to meet their next difficulty. Instead, lacking gospel perspective, the situational cares of the day, like worry over a broken bow, of all things, dominated the things of eternity" (Maxwell, "Lessons from Laman and Lemuel," 8). ⊕

How do you react when others murmur or complain? (16:22) Can you remember times when you heard others, including loved ones, complain about their situation in life? How do you generally respond? Do you seek to help them turn to the Lord, as Nephi did?

Why did Nephi still follow Lehi even though he had murmured? (16:23) Elder Marion D. Hanks emphasized Nephi's great character as a faithful son in how he approached this crisis: "What to do? . . . Nephi went to his father and said, 'Dad, the Lord has blessed you. You are his servant. I need to know where to go to get food. Dad, you ask him, will you?' Oh, he could have gone to his own knees. He could have taken over. I count this one of the really significant lessons of life in the book . . . a son who had strength enough . . . [to] say, 'You ask God, will you?' because somehow he knew this is how you make men strong" ("Steps to Learning," 7). ⊕

1 Nephi 16:24–32. The Liahona Works according to the Faith, Diligence, and Heed the Family Gives unto God

the Lord, insomuch that he was brought down into the depths of sorrow.

26 And it came to pass that the voice of the Lord said unto him: Look upon the ball, and behold the things which are written.

27 And it came to pass that when my father beheld the things which were written upon the ball, he did fear and tremble exceedingly, and also my brethren and the sons of Ishmael and our wives.

28 And it came to pass that I, Nephi, beheld the pointers which were in the ball, that they did work according to the faith and diligence and heed which we did give unto them.

29 And there was also written upon them a new writing, which was plain to be read, which did give us understanding concerning the ways of the Lord; and it was written and changed from time to time, according to the faith and diligence which we gave unto it. And thus we see that by small means the Lord can bring about great things.

30 And it came to pass that I, Nephi, did go forth up into the top of the mountain, according to the directions which were given upon the ball.

31 And it came to pass that I did slay wild beasts, insomuch that I did obtain food for our families.

32 And it came to pass that I did return to our tents, bearing the beasts which I had slain; and now when they beheld that I had obtained food, how great was their joy! And it came to pass that they did humble themselves before the Lord, and did give thanks unto him.

33 And it came to pass that we did again take our journey, traveling nearly the same course as in the beginning; and after we had traveled for the space of many days we did pitch our

How did the Liahona work? (16:28–29) While he was counseling his son Helaman, Alma said: "And it did work for them according to their faith in God; therefore, if they had faith to believe that God could cause that those spindles should point the way they should go, behold, it was done" (Alma 37:40). If, on the other hand, "they were slothful, and forgot to exercise their faith and diligence then those marvelous works ceased, and they did not progress in their journey; therefore, they tarried in the wilderness, or did not travel a direct course, and were afflicted with hunger and thirst, because of their transgressions" (Alma 37:41–42; see also Alma 37:38–47). ✛

1 Nephi 16:33–39. Ishmael Dies, and Part of the Family Rebels against Lehi and Nephi

tents again, that we might tarry for the space of a time.

34 And it came to pass that Ishmael died, and was buried in the place which was called Nahom.

35 And it came to pass that the daughters of Ishmael did mourn exceedingly, because of the loss of their father, and because of their afflictions in the wilderness; and they did murmur against my father, because he had brought them out of the land of Jerusalem, saying: Our father is dead; yea, and we have wandered much in the wilderness, and we have suffered much affliction, hunger, thirst, and fatigue; and after all these sufferings we must perish in the wilderness with hunger.

36 And thus they did murmur against my father, and also against me; and they were desirous to return again to Jerusalem.

37 And Laman said unto Lemuel and also unto the sons of Ishmael: Behold, let us slay our father, and also our brother Nephi, who has taken it upon him to be our ruler and our teacher, who are his elder brethren.

38 Now, he says that the Lord has talked with him, and also that angels have ministered unto him. But behold, we know that he lies unto us; and he tells us these things, and he worketh many things by his cunning arts, that he may deceive our eyes, thinking, perhaps, that he may lead us away into some strange wilderness; and after he has led us away, he has thought to make himself a king and a ruler over us, that he may do with us according to his will and pleasure. And after this manner did my brother Laman stir up their hearts to anger.

39 And it came to pass that the Lord was with us, yea, even the voice of the Lord came and did speak many words unto them, and did chasten them exceedingly; and after they

What does *Nahom* mean? (16:34) "There are two Semitic language roots suggested by the Book of Mormon Nahom: *nhm* . . . in Arabic as *nahama*, 'sigh, groan, moan, especially with another.' In Hebrew, the root *nhm* is often used for 'mourning' someone else's death or 'consoling' the bereaved" (Aston and Aston, "Lehi's Trail and Nahom Revisited," 48).

Where is Nahom? (16:34) There is ample physical evidence documenting the location of both ancient and modern Nahom. The place Nahom was a burial site prior to Lehi's leaving Jerusalem, and it still exists today. "'Nahom' was already the name of the area where his father-in-law, Ishmael, was buried. . . . It was natural and appropriate to mention the tribal place-name in recording and recalling the death and burial that took place there. At just the right location to link directionally to and access the place that they would call 'Bountiful,' the rare name NHM still exists today and is now firmly documented back through the centuries to before Nephi's day" (Aston, "History of NaHoM," 94). ⊕

This altar is located at the place some have identified as the site of ancient Nahom, where Ishmael was buried (see 1 Nephi 16:34).

were chastened by the voice of the Lord they did turn away their anger, and did repent of their sins, insomuch that the Lord did bless us again with food, that we did not perish.

CHAPTER 17

Nephi is commanded to build a ship—His brethren oppose him—He exhorts them by recounting the history of God's dealings with Israel—Nephi is filled with the power of God—His brethren are forbidden to touch him, lest they wither as a dried reed. About 592–591 B.C.

1 And it came to pass that we did again take our journey in the wilderness; and we did travel nearly eastward from that time forth. And we did travel and wade through much affliction in the wilderness; and our women did bear children in the wilderness.

2 And so great were the blessings of the Lord upon us, that while we did live upon raw meat in the wilderness, our women did give plenty of suck for their children, and were strong, yea, even like unto the men; and they began to bear their journeyings without murmurings.

3 And thus we see that the commandments of God must be fulfilled. And if it so be that the children of men keep the commandments of God he doth nourish them, and strengthen them, and provide means whereby they can accomplish the thing which he has commanded them; wherefore, he did provide means for us while we did sojourn in the wilderness.

1 Nephi 17:1–6. The Lord Helps Lehi's Family Travel through the Wilderness to Bountiful

Why did Lehi's family change directions in the wilderness? (17:1) "If we take literally Nephi's statement that they traveled 'nearly eastward' to Bountiful, the trade route is ruled out, for it soon veers in a pronounced southeast direction.... Nephi's repeated emphasis (1 Nephi 17:1, 2, 6) on the hardships and difficulties of the journey are unmistakable hints confirming that a course almost due east from the Jawf [valley] was maintained. This direction took them somewhat north of the trade route, traveling first across the band of wasteland that lies between the shifting sand dunes of the southern edge of the vast 'Empty Quarter' and the smaller Saba'tayn desert, then onto an extended area of plateau. Here they would have been moving in areas far from known routes" (Aston and Aston, *In the Footsteps of Lehi*, 31–32). ⊕

Why did they live on raw meat? (17:2) "The culture patterns of this area in correlation with the hints in the Book of Mormon are impressive. Spicy, raw, partially dried meat is still consumed in the area today. The Arabs call it 'bastern,' which literally means raw meat" (Allen, *Exploring the Lands of the Book of Mormon*, 266).

"It was the custom of experienced travelers in Arabia that they never built a fire, as it could attract the attention of a prowling, raiding party. As a result, they ate much of their food raw, as recorded in the Book of Mormon (1 Nephi 17:2). Attacking and plundering camps still seems to be the chief object of some Arab tribes" (Cheesman, "Lehi's Journeys," 245). ⊕

4 And we did sojourn for the space of many years, yea, even eight years in the wilderness.

5 And we did come to the land which we called Bountiful, because of its much fruit and also wild honey; and all these things were prepared of the Lord that we might not perish. And we beheld the sea, which we called Irreantum, which, being interpreted, is many waters.

6 And it came to pass that we did pitch our tents by the seashore; and notwithstanding we had suffered many afflictions and much difficulty, yea, even so much that we cannot write them all, we were exceedingly rejoiced when we came to the seashore; and we called the place Bountiful, because of its much fruit.

7 And it came to pass that after I, Nephi, had been in the land of Bountiful for the space of many days, the voice of the Lord came unto me, saying: Arise, and get thee into the mountain. And it came to pass that I arose and went up into the mountain, and cried unto the Lord.

8 And it came to pass that the Lord spake unto me, saying: Thou shalt construct a ship, after the manner which I shall show thee, that I may carry thy people across these waters.

9 And I said: Lord, whither shall I go that I may find ore to molten, that I may make tools to construct the ship after the manner which thou hast shown unto me?

10 And it came to pass that the Lord told me whither I should go to find ore, that I might make tools.

11 And it came to pass that I, Nephi, did make a bellows wherewith to blow the fire, of the skins of beasts; and after I had made a bellows, that I might have wherewith to blow the fire, I did smite two stones together that I might make fire.

Where is the land Bountiful? (17:5–6) "Incredible as it seems, the south coast of the Arabian peninsula from Perim to Sur has only one place in its entire length of 1,400 miles that meets that description. It is a tiny sickle of land curved around a little bay, about 28 miles long and only 7 miles wide, backed by the Qara Mountains. . . . We repeat, this is the only place on the whole Arabian peninsula seashore which receives significant rainfall and where large trees grow—and it is known to have been this way for well over two thousand years" (Hilton, "In Search of Lehi's Trail," 50–51). ☉

1 Nephi 17:7–16. The Lord Commands Nephi to Build a Ship

Why did Nephi ask the Lord for "ore"? (17:9) "This is one of the more interesting stories we have in the scriptures because it tells of an instance in which the Lord provided help but then stepped aside to allow one of His sons to exercise his own initiative. I have sometimes wondered what would have happened if Nephi had asked the Lord for tools instead of a place to find the ore to make the tools. I doubt the Lord would have honored Nephi's request. You see, the Lord knew that Nephi could make the tools, and it is seldom the Lord will do something for us that we can do for ourselves" (Perry, "Becoming Self-Reliant," 64).

Why did the Lord tell Lehi's family not to make much fire? (17:12–13) Others who traveled in the same Arab land said "they never dared build a fire on the open plain where it 'would attract the attention of a prowling raiding party over long distances and invite a night attack.' . . . That is, fires are not absolutely out of the question, but rare and risky—not much fire, was Lehi's rule" (Nibley, *Lehi in the Desert*, 72–73).

How is the Lord our light? (17:13–14) "If it were not for the Light of Jesus Christ and His gospel, we would be doomed to the destruction of darkness. . . .

"The Lord is our light and, literally, our salvation. . . . His light will form a protective shield between you and the darkness of the adversary as you live worthy of it. . . . learn to claim the protective light of the gospel as your own.

"You may wonder, 'How can I do that?' There is only one way: you must learn to generate that light each day by believing on Jesus Christ and following His commandments. . . .

"The generation of spiritual light comes from daily spiritual pedaling. It comes from praying, studying the scriptures, fasting, and serving" (Hales, "Out of the Darkness into His Marvelous Light," 70).

1 Nephi 17:17–22. Nephi's Brothers Speak against Him

Why did Laman and Lemuel rejoice in Nephi's sorrows? (17:18–22) Elder Neal A. Maxwell observed Laman and Lemuel's resentment of Nephi: "Hence, encrusted Laman and Lemuel seldom responded to the tenderness of others. They were strangers to empathy, that eternal attribute. When Lehi exhorted them with all the feeling of a tender or trembling parent, the effects were usually more resentment, evoking cruel responses to parents and siblings (see 1 Ne. 8:37). When Nephi displayed sorrow over their behavior, Laman and Lemuel were 'glad' that he was sorry (see

12 For the Lord had not hitherto suffered that we should make much fire, as we journeyed in the wilderness; for he said: I will make thy food become sweet, that ye cook it not;

13 And I will also be your light in the wilderness; and I will prepare the way before you, if it so be that ye shall keep my commandments; wherefore, inasmuch as ye shall keep my commandments ye shall be led towards the promised land; and ye shall know that it is by me that ye are led.

14 Yea, and the Lord said also that: After ye have arrived in the promised land, ye shall know that I, the Lord, am God; and that I, the Lord, did deliver you from destruction; yea, that I did bring you out of the land of Jerusalem.

15 Wherefore, I, Nephi, did strive to keep the commandments of the Lord, and I did exhort my brethren to faithfulness and diligence.

16 And it came to pass that I did make tools of the ore which I did molten out of the rock.

17 And when my brethren saw that I was about to build a ship, they began to murmur against me, saying: Our brother is a fool, for he thinketh that he can build a ship; yea, and he also thinketh that he can cross these great waters.

18 And thus my brethren did complain against me, and were desirous that they might not labor, for they did not believe that I could build a ship; neither would they believe that I was instructed of the Lord.

19 And now it came to pass that I, Nephi, was exceedingly sorrowful because of the hardness of their hearts; and now when they saw that I began to be sorrowful they were glad in their hearts, insomuch that they did rejoice over me, saying: We knew that ye could not construct a ship, for we knew that ye were lacking in judgment; wherefore, thou canst not accomplish so great a work.

20 And thou art like unto our father, led away by the foolish imaginations of his heart; yea, he hath led us out of the land of Jerusalem, and we have wandered in the wilderness for these many years; and our women have toiled, being big with child; and they have borne children in the wilderness and suffered all things, save it were death; and it would have been better that they had died before they came out of Jerusalem than to have suffered these afflictions.

21 Behold, these many years we have suffered in the wilderness, which time we might have enjoyed our possessions and the land of our inheritance; yea, and we might have been happy.

22 And we know that the people who were in the land of Jerusalem were a righteous people; for they kept the statutes and judgments of the Lord, and all his commandments, according to the law of Moses; wherefore, we know that they are a righteous people; and our father hath judged them, and hath led us away because we would hearken unto his words; yea, and our brother is like unto him. And after this manner of language did my brethren murmur and complain against us.

23 And it came to pass that I, Nephi, spake unto them, saying: Do ye believe that our fathers, who were the children of Israel, would have been led away out of the hands of the Egyptians if they had not hearkened unto the words of the Lord?

24 Yea, do ye suppose that they would have been led out of bondage, if the Lord had not

1 Ne. 17:19). Admonitions were bad enough, but to have them come from Nephi!" ("Lessons from Laman and Lemuel," Nov. 1999, 8).

1 Nephi 17:23–43. Nephi Explains How God Helped the Children of Israel

Why does Nephi refer to Moses and the Exodus story of the Israelites? (17:24) "Book of Mormon prophets used imagery of the Exodus to teach and illustrate numerous truths, including trusting in God (see 1 Nephi 17:23–35), the final gathering (see 2 Nephi 6:14–18), spiritual bondage and deliverance (see 2 Nephi 9:8–11), the resurrection (see Alma 36:28–29), and the power of God (see Helaman 8:11–15)" (Valletta, "The Exodus," 181). ●

What does Nephi's recitation of the Exodus imply about the Bible ? (17:25) "The so-called higher critics of the Bible have raised the question as to whether or not the miracles of the exodus of Israel under Moses actually happened as they are recorded in the Old Testament (see Exodus 14:19–20, 26–31; 16:4, 15; 17:5–6; Numbers 21:6–9). However, the Book of Mormon substantiates the actuality of these miraculous events (1 Nephi 17:23, 26, 28, 29, 30, 41). . . . Nephi's knowledge of these miracles came from the authentic account on the brass plates of Laban (1 Nephi 5:11). . . . Once again the Book of Mormon serves as a witness to its companion scripture, the Bible" (Ludlow, *Companion to Your Study of the Book of Mormon*, 115).

What lessons are learned from Nephi's use of scripture examples? (17:27) "Let's learn a great lesson from what transpired with Nephi. He started to recount the things that had happened that they all knew were a part of their heritage. He went back to the coming of the children of Israel out of Egypt. He said: 'You know what happened. There they were right against the Red Sea with the Egyptians coming, and the Lord saved them' (see 1 Ne. 17:26–27). . . . He was trying to . . . develop faith in the Lord. And the way to do it is to recount the examples of faith that have happened in our history and in our heritage and with our people" (Tuttle, "Developing Faith," 66).

commanded Moses that he should lead them out of bondage?

25 Now ye know that the children of Israel were in bondage; and ye know that they were laden with tasks, which were grievous to be borne; wherefore, ye know that it must needs be a good thing for them, that they should be brought out of bondage.

26 Now ye know that Moses was commanded of the Lord to do that great work; and ye know that by his word the waters of the Red Sea were divided hither and thither, and they passed through on dry ground.

27 But ye know that the Egyptians were drowned in the Red Sea, who were the armies of Pharaoh.

28 And ye also know that they were fed with manna in the wilderness.

29 Yea, and ye also know that Moses, by his word according to the power of God which was in him, smote the rock, and there came forth water, that the children of Israel might quench their thirst.

30 And notwithstanding they being led, the Lord their God, their Redeemer, going before them, leading them by day and giving light unto them by night, and doing all things for them which were expedient for man to receive, they hardened their hearts and blinded their minds, and reviled against Moses and against the true and living God.

31 And it came to pass that according to his word he did destroy them; and according to his word he did lead them; and according to his word he did do all things for them; and there was not any thing done save it were by his word.

32 And after they had crossed the river Jordan he did make them mighty unto the driving out of the children of the land, yea, unto the scattering them to destruction.

33 And now, do ye suppose that the children of this land, who were in the land of promise, who were driven out by our fathers, do ye suppose that they were righteous? Behold, I say unto you, Nay.

34 Do ye suppose that our fathers would have been more choice than they if they had been righteous? I say unto you, Nay.

35 Behold, the Lord esteemeth all flesh in one; he that is righteous is favored of God. But behold, this people had rejected every word of God, and they were ripe in iniquity; and the fulness of the wrath of God was upon them; and the Lord did curse the land against them, and bless it unto our fathers; yea, he did curse it against them unto their destruction, and he did bless it unto our fathers unto their obtaining power over it.

36 Behold, the Lord hath created the earth that it should be inhabited; and he hath created his children that they should possess it.

37 And he raiseth up a righteous nation, and destroyeth the nations of the wicked.

38 And he leadeth away the righteous into precious lands, and the wicked he destroyeth, and curseth the land unto them for their sakes.

39 He ruleth high in the heavens, for it is his throne, and this earth is his footstool.

40 And he loveth those who will have him to be their God. Behold, he loved our fathers, and he covenanted with them, yea, even Abraham, Isaac, and Jacob; and he remembered the covenants which he had made;

Does God favor one person over another? (17:35) "'Of a truth,' Peter declared, 'God is no respecter of persons: but in every nation he that feareth him, and worketh righteousness, is accepted with him' (Acts 10:34–35). He loves all of his children. But his love is not unconditional in the sense of treating all of his children alike; men and women are rewarded or punished according to their works (see Romans 2:11; Colossians 3:25). Indeed, even though 'the Lord esteemeth all flesh in one,' as Nephi reminded us, 'he that is righteous is favored of God' (1 Nephi 17:35)" (McConkie and Millet, *Doctrinal Commentary*, 1:309). ☉

Why was the earth created? (17:36) God created the earth to bless his children. "Think of our physical sustenance. It is truly heaven-sent. The necessities of air, food, and water all come to us as gifts from a loving Heavenly Father. The earth was created to support our brief sojourn in mortality [see 1 Nephi 17:36]. We were born with a capacity to grow, love, marry, and form families. Marriage and family are ordained of God. The family is the most important social unit in time and in eternity. Under God's great plan of happiness, families can be sealed in temples and be prepared to return to dwell in His holy presence forever" (Nelson, "Thanks Be to God," 77). ☉

What does a footstool represent? (17:39) "The Lord refers to the earth as his footstool (D&C 38:17; 1 Ne. 17:39; Moses 6:9, 44). A footstool is a low stool upon which to rest one's feet. It is symbolic of subjection, something beneath one and over which power is exercised. For example, God speaks of making a footstool of one's enemies (Matt. 22:44; Acts 2:35). James warns the Saints against treating the poor as one's footstool (James 2:3)" (Brewster, *Doctrine and Covenants Encyclopedia*, 191).

wherefore, he did bring them out of the land of Egypt.

41 And he did straiten them in the wilderness with his rod; for they hardened their hearts, even as ye have; and the Lord straitened them because of their iniquity. He sent fiery flying serpents among them; and after they were bitten he prepared a way that they might be healed; and the labor which they had to perform was to look; and because of the simpleness of the way, or the easiness of it, there were many who perished.

42 And they did harden their hearts from time to time, and they did revile against Moses, and also against God; nevertheless, ye know that they were led forth by his matchless power into the land of promise.

43 And now, after all these things, the time has come that they have become wicked, yea, nearly unto ripeness; and I know not but they are at this day about to be destroyed; for I know that the day must surely come that they must be destroyed, save a few only, who shall be led away into captivity.

1 Nephi 17:44–47. Nephi Tells His Brothers about Their Great Wickedness

Are we accountable for the desires of our hearts? (17:44) "Men will be judged by their works and by the desires of their hearts (see Alma 41:3; D&C 137:9). Nephi's wicked brothers would have killed him and their father had not the Lord intervened, for which desires they will be fully accountable come the day of judgment" (McConkie and Millet, *Doctrinal Commentary*, 1:137).

How does the Holy Ghost communicate to us? (17:45) "Perhaps the single greatest thing I learned from reading the Book of Mormon is that the voice of the Spirit comes as a *feeling* rather than a sound. You will learn, as I have learned, to 'listen' for that voice that is *felt* rather than *heard*. . . . Some critics have said that these verses are in error because you hear words; you do not *feel* them. But if you know anything at all about spiritual communication, you know that the best word to describe what takes place is the word *feeling*" (Packer, "Counsel to Youth," 17). ☉

44 Wherefore, the Lord commanded my father that he should depart into the wilderness; and the Jews also sought to take away his life; yea, and ye also have sought to take away his life; wherefore, ye are murderers in your hearts and ye are like unto them.

45 Ye are swift to do iniquity but slow to remember the Lord your God. Ye have seen an angel, and he spake unto you; yea, ye have heard his voice from time to time; and he hath spoken unto you in a still small voice, but ye were past feeling, that ye could not feel his words; wherefore, he has spoken unto you like unto the voice of thunder, which did cause the earth to shake as if it were to divide asunder.

46 And ye also know that by the power of his almighty word he can cause the earth that it shall pass away; yea, and ye know that by his word he can cause the rough places to be made smooth, and smooth places shall be broken up. O, then, why is it, that ye can be so hard in your hearts?

47 Behold, my soul is rent with anguish because of you, and my heart is pained; I fear lest ye shall be cast off forever. Behold, I am full of the Spirit of God, insomuch that my frame has no strength.

48 And now it came to pass that when I had spoken these words they were angry with me, and were desirous to throw me into the depths of the sea; and as they came forth to lay their hands upon me I spake unto them, saying: In the name of the Almighty God, I command you that ye touch me not, for I am filled with the power of God, even unto the consuming of my flesh; and whoso shall lay his hands upon me shall wither even as a dried reed; and he shall be as naught before the power of God, for God shall smite him.

49 And it came to pass that I, Nephi, said unto them that they should murmur no more against their father; neither should they withhold their labor from me, for God had commanded me that I should build a ship.

50 And I said unto them: If God had commanded me to do all things I could do them. If he should command me that I should say unto this water, be thou earth, it should be earth; and if I should say it, it would be done.

51 And now, if the Lord has such great power, and has wrought so many miracles among the children of men, how is it that he cannot instruct me, that I should build a ship?

52 And it came to pass that I, Nephi, said many things unto my brethren, insomuch that they were confounded and could not

1 Nephi 17:48–55. Nephi, Filled with the Lord's Power, Shocks His Brothers

Can we show the same faith and trust in God as Nephi did? (17:50) "Here is an example of faith and courage which, if we can emulate, will do much to help us through our doubting and discouragement, for we serve the same God that Nephi served, and He will sustain us even as he sustained Nephi if we will serve him even as Nephi served him" (Romney, in Conference Report, Apr. 1949, 40).

contend against me; neither durst they lay their hands upon me nor touch me with their fingers, even for the space of many days. Now they durst not do this lest they should wither before me, so powerful was the Spirit of God; and thus it had wrought upon them.

Why were Laman and Lemuel shocked by the Lord? (17:53) "In 1 Nephi when Nephi was so filled with the Spirit of God as he preached to his brethren with such power that they durst not 'lay their hands upon [him] nor touch [him] with their fingers, even for the space of many days' (1 Nephi 17:48–52). Following these days, the Lord instructed Nephi to stretch forth his hand to his brethren and he would shock them as a witness of the power of God within him. Nephi's compliance with this instruction caused his brothers to shake before him and acknowledge the power of God (1 Nephi 17: 53–55). Such power is irrefutable even to the wicked, and it is available to those who exercise faith" (Nyman, "Lehi and Nephi: Faith unto Salvation," 72–73).

53 And it came to pass that the Lord said unto me: Stretch forth thine hand again unto thy brethren, and they shall not wither before thee, but I will shock them, saith the Lord, and this will I do, that they may know that I am the Lord their God.

54 And it came to pass that I stretched forth my hand unto my brethren, and they did not wither before me; but the Lord did shake them, even according to the word which he had spoken.

55 And now, they said: We know of a surety that the Lord is with thee, for we know that it is the power of the Lord that has shaken us. And they fell down before me, and were about to worship me, but I would not suffer them, saying: I am thy brother, yea, even thy younger brother; wherefore, worship the Lord thy God, and honor thy father and thy mother, that thy days may be long in the land which the Lord thy God shall give thee.

CHAPTER 18

The ship is finished—The births of Jacob and Joseph are mentioned—The company embarks for the promised land—The sons of Ishmael and their wives join in revelry and rebellion—Nephi is bound, and the ship is driven back by a terrible tempest—Nephi is freed, and by his prayer the storm ceases—The people arrive in the promised land. About 591–589 B.C.

1 Nephi 18:1–4. Nephi and His Brothers Build a Ship

What do we learn about revelation in Nephi's experience of building a ship? (18:1–2) "Most frequently, revelation comes in small increments over time and is granted according to our desire, worthiness, and preparation. . . . [Nephi] did not learn how to build a ship of curious workmanship all at one time; rather,

1 And it came to pass that they did worship the Lord, and did go forth with me; and we did work timbers of curious workmanship. And the Lord did show me from time to time

after what manner I should work the timbers of the ship.

2 Now I, Nephi, did not work the timbers after the manner which was learned by men, neither did I build the ship after the manner of men; but I did build it after the manner which the Lord had shown unto me; wherefore, it was not after the manner of men.

3 And I, Nephi, did go into the mount oft, and I did pray oft unto the Lord; wherefore the Lord showed unto me great things.

4 And it came to pass that after I had finished the ship, according to the word of the Lord, my brethren beheld that it was good, and that the workmanship thereof was exceedingly fine; wherefore, they did humble themselves again before the Lord.

5 And it came to pass that the voice of the Lord came unto my father, that we should arise and go down into the ship.

6 And it came to pass that on the morrow, after we had prepared all things, much fruits and meat from the wilderness, and honey in abundance, and provisions according to that which the Lord had commanded us, we did go down into the ship, with all our loading and our seeds, and whatsoever thing we had brought with us, every one according to his age; wherefore, we did all go down into the ship, with our wives and our children.

Nephi was shown by the Lord 'from time to time after what manner [he] should work the timbers of the ship' (1 Nephi 18:1)" (Bednar, "Spirit of Revelation," 88). ☉

Why is it significant to note that Nephi went to the mountain often for instructions? (18:3) Nephi's sacred mountain can be compared to our temple today. "The temple is a house of learning. Much of the instruction imparted in the temple is symbolic and learned by the Spirit. This means we are taught from on high. Temple covenants and ordinances are a powerful symbol of Christ and His atonement. We all receive the same instruction, but our understanding of the meaning of the ordinances and covenants will increase as we return to the temple often with the attitude of learning and contemplating the eternal truths taught" (Allred, "Holy Temples, Sacred Covenants," 113).

1 Nephi 18:5–7. Lehi and His Family Set Sail for the Promised Land

To whom was the Lord communicating and why? (18:5) "It was for Nephi to receive revelation on the building of the ship and for his father to receive the revelation that the time had come for the family to begin their journey. In the economy of heaven revelations are granted according to one's stewardship or right to receive it (see *Teachings [of the Prophet Joseph Smith]*, 21). Revelations that effectually place someone in a position to manipulate or dominate others do not have heaven as their source" (McConkie and Millet, *Doctrinal Commentary*, 1:141).

Why did they enter the ship according to their age? (18:6) "It was a sacred moment and a breathlessly exciting one. After years of overland travel they were now actually going to brave the timeless challenge of the seas. It was their final great test of faith, and they were ready for the test. For reasons not apparent to one reared in a western tradition they seem to have sought expression for the dignity and solemnity of the occasion by forming a ceremonial procession and filing aboard their ship according to the ancient patriarchal order. Nephi's allusion to the detail marks the outcropping of a Hebrew custom at a point in the narrative where we least expected it" (Ricks, *Book of Mormon Commentary*, 217).

In addition to Jacob and Joseph, were there other children born in the wilderness? (18:7) "We are here informed that two sons, Jacob and Joseph, were born to Lehi in the wilderness. . . . They were eight years in the wilderness (see 1 Ne. 17:20). Those that entered the ship were, Lehi and Sariah, his wife; Laman and his wife; Lemuel and his wife; Sam and his wife; Nephi and his wife; . . . two sons of Ishmael and their families (1 Ne. 7:6); Zoram and his wife (1 Ne. 16:7); Jacob and Joseph and others who may have been born in the wilderness. Elder George Reynolds . . . estimates the entire number that landed in the land of promise at from 60 to 80 souls" (Reynolds and Sjodahl, *Commentary on the Book of Mormon*, 185).

1 Nephi 18:8–14. Nephi Is Bound, and a Terrible Storm Nearly Sinks the Ship

Why do Laman and Lemuel constantly say, "We will not that our younger brother shall be a ruler over us"? (18:10) "Several experiences in the Book of Mormon indicate that the law of primogeniture (where the first-born son has special rights and privileges) was part of the belief and tradition of Lehi and his colony. Note particularly the following references in this regard: 1 Nephi 18:10; 2 Nephi 5:3; Mosiah 10:11–15" (Ludlow, *Companion to Your Study of the Book of Mormon*, 116). ☉

7 And now, my father had begat two sons in the wilderness; the elder was called Jacob and the younger Joseph.

8 And it came to pass after we had all gone down into the ship, and had taken with us our provisions and things which had been commanded us, we did put forth into the sea and were driven forth before the wind towards the promised land.

9 And after we had been driven forth before the wind for the space of many days, behold, my brethren and the sons of Ishmael and also their wives began to make themselves merry, insomuch that they began to dance, and to sing, and to speak with much rudeness, yea, even that they did forget by what power they had been brought thither; yea, they were lifted up unto exceeding rudeness.

10 And I, Nephi, began to fear exceedingly lest the Lord should be angry with us, and smite us because of our iniquity, that we should be swallowed up in the depths of the sea; wherefore, I, Nephi, began to speak to them with much soberness; but behold they were angry with me, saying: We will not that our younger brother shall be a ruler over us.

11 And it came to pass that Laman and Lemuel did take me and bind me with cords, and they did treat me with much harshness; nevertheless, the Lord did suffer it that he might show forth his power, unto the fulfilling of his word which he had spoken concerning the wicked.

12 And it came to pass that after they had bound me insomuch that I could not move, the compass, which had been prepared of the Lord, did cease to work.

13 Wherefore, they knew not whither they should steer the ship, insomuch that there arose a great storm, yea, a great and terrible tempest, and we were driven back upon the waters for the space of three days; and they began to be frightened exceedingly lest they should be drowned in the sea; nevertheless they did not loose me.

14 And on the fourth day, which we had been driven back, the tempest began to be exceedingly sore.

15 And it came to pass that we were about to be swallowed up in the depths of the sea. And after we had been driven back upon the waters for the space of four days, my brethren began to see that the judgments of God were upon them, and that they must perish save that they should repent of their iniquities; wherefore, they came unto me, and loosed the bands which were upon my wrists, and behold they had swollen exceedingly; and also mine ankles were much swollen, and great was the soreness thereof.

16 Nevertheless, I did look unto my God, and I did praise him all the day long; and I did not murmur against the Lord because of mine afflictions.

17 Now my father, Lehi, had said many things unto them, and also unto the sons of Ishmael; but, behold, they did breathe out much threatenings against anyone that should speak for me; and my parents being stricken in years, and having suffered much grief because of their children, they were

1 Nephi 18:15–20. The Power of God Causes Nephi's Brothers to Untie Him

What effect does the storm have on the rebellious brethren? (18:15) "The storm amounts to a spiritual sledgehammer, finally getting the brothers' attention. Only when the situation was absolutely desperate did they make a connection between their plight and the binding of Nephi. They may not even have seen that binding Nephi caused the problem, only that he had demonstrated a connection with [Jehovah] in the past and that they now needed divine intervention" (Gardner, *Second Witness*, 1:318).

What purpose is there in Nephi's suffering on the ship? (18:16) "Particularly notable to me is Nephi's endurance. Continually receiving the wrath of his brothers, he was bound for four days on the boat coming to the promised land. . . . Although the purpose of the suffering is not always apparent at the time, the Prophet Joseph had a singularly spiritual experience as he lingered in Liberty Jail. The Lord comforted him: 'My son, peace be unto thy soul; thine adversity and thine afflictions shall be but a small moment; And then, if thou endure it well, God shall exalt thee on high; thou shalt triumph over all thy foes' [D&C 121:7–8]" (Edwards, "That They Might Know Thee," 66).

brought down, yea, even upon their sick-beds.

18 Because of their grief and much sorrow, and the iniquity of my brethren, they were brought near even to be carried out of this time to meet their God; yea, their grey hairs were about to be brought down to lie low in the dust; yea, even they were near to be cast with sorrow into a watery grave.

19 And Jacob and Joseph also, being young, having need of much nourishment, were grieved because of the afflictions of their mother; and also my wife with her tears and prayers, and also my children, did not soften the hearts of my brethren that they would loose me.

20 And there was nothing save it were the power of God, which threatened them with destruction, could soften their hearts; where-fore, when they saw that they were about to be swallowed up in the depths of the sea they repented of the thing which they had done, insomuch that they loosed me.

21 And it came to pass after they had loosed me, behold, I took the compass, and it did work whither I desired it. And it came to pass that I prayed unto the Lord; and after I had prayed the winds did cease, and the storm did cease, and there was a great calm.

22 And it came to pass that I, Nephi, did guide the ship, that we sailed again towards the promised land.

23 And it came to pass that after we had sailed for the space of many days we did ar-rive at the promised land; and we went forth upon the land, and did pitch our tents; and we did call it the promised land.

24 And it came to pass that we did begin to till the earth, and we began to plant seeds; yea, we did put all our seeds into the earth, which we had brought from the land of

Why must some, like Laman and Lemuel, be compelled to be humble? (18:20) Alma taught that those who are compelled to be humble are blessed if it brings them to repentance. What do you think are the blessings for those who repent without being compelled? (see Alma 32:13–16, 25).

1 Nephi 18:21–25. Nephi Sails the Ship Safely to the Promised Land

Where did Lehi first land? (18:23) The "promised land" meant the Americas. "Since the publication of the Book of Mormon in 1830, members and leaders . . . have expressed numerous opinions about the specific locations of the events discussed in the book. Some believe that the history depicted in the Book of Mormon—with the exception of the events in the Near East—occurred in North America, while others believe that it occurred in Central America or South America. Although Church members continue to discuss such theories today, the Church's only position

Jerusalem. And it came to pass that they did grow exceedingly; wherefore, we were blessed in abundance.

25 And it came to pass that we did find upon the land of promise, as we journeyed in the wilderness, that there were beasts in the forests of every kind, both the cow and the ox, and the ass and the horse, and the goat and the wild goat, and all manner of wild animals, which were for the use of men. And we did find all manner of ore, both of gold, and of silver, and of copper.

CHAPTER 19

Nephi makes plates of ore and records the history of his people—The God of Israel will come six hundred years from the time Lehi left Jerusalem—Nephi tells of His sufferings and crucifixion—The Jews will be despised and scattered until the latter days, when they will return unto the Lord. About 588–570 B.C.

1 And it came to pass that the Lord commanded me, wherefore I did make plates of ore that I might engraven upon them the record of my people. And upon the plates which I made I did engraven the record of my father, and also our journeyings in the

is that the events the Book of Mormon describes took place in the ancient Americas. . . .

"The Church does not take a position on the specific geographic locations of Book of Mormon events in the ancient Americas. President M. Russell Ballard . . . reminded members that 'the Book of Mormon is not a textbook on topography. Speculation on the geography of the Book of Mormon may mislead instead of enlighten; such a study can be a distraction from its divine purpose'" ("Book of Mormon Geography," *Gospel Topics*). ⊕

Did Lehi's colony travel after arriving in America? (18:25) "'As we journeyed in the wilderness.' I understand this to mean that as soon as Lehi and his company had taken care of their first harvest they continued their journey 'in the wilderness,' which in this case would mean the bench land, or the mountain regions" (Reynolds and Sjodahl, *Commentary on the Book of Mormon*, 189). Traveling after their first arrival leaves open the likely possibility that they could have lived in various lands and areas in the Americas before settling in the land of their first inheritance.

Were there horses in America before Columbus? (18:25) "There was controversy regarding horses in the Western Hemisphere before Columbus arrived. However, modern archaeological discoveries have shed new light on the subject: 'Fossil remains of true horses, differing but very slightly from the smaller and inferior breeds of those now existing, are found abundantly in deposits of the most recent geological age, in almost every part of America'" (*Book of Mormon Student Manual* [2009], 40). ⊕

1 Nephi 19:1–6. Nephi Makes Metal Plates

wilderness, and the prophecies of my father; and also many of mine own prophecies have I engraven upon them.

2 And I knew not at the time when I made them that I should be commanded of the Lord to make these plates; wherefore, the record of my father, and the genealogy of his fathers, and the more part of all our proceedings in the wilderness are engraven upon those first plates of which I have spoken; wherefore, the things which transpired before I made these plates are, of a truth, more particularly made mention upon the first plates.

3 And after I had made these plates by way of commandment, I, Nephi, received a commandment that the ministry and the prophecies, the more plain and precious parts of them, should be written upon these plates; and that the things which were written should be kept for the instruction of my people, who should possess the land, and also for other wise purposes, which purposes are known unto the Lord.

4 Wherefore, I, Nephi, did make a record upon the other plates, which gives an account, or which gives a greater account of the wars and contentions and destructions of my people. And this have I done, and commanded my people what they should do after I was gone; and that these plates should be handed down from one generation to another, or from one prophet to another, until further commandments of the Lord.

5 And an account of my making these plates shall be given hereafter; and then, behold, I proceed according to that which I have spoken; and this I do that the more sacred things may be kept for the knowledge of my people.

6 Nevertheless, I do not write anything upon plates save it be that I think it be sacred. And now, if I do err, even did they err of old; not that I would excuse myself because of other

What is the distinction in these verses between "these plates" and "other plates"? (19:3–4) Nephi again explains the difference and purpose for creating two sets of plates. "These plates" refers to the small plates, and "other plates" refers to the large plates (see 1 Nephi 9:1–6).

Why is it important to record that which is sacred? (19:5) "Inspiration carefully recorded shows God that His communications are sacred to us. Recording will also enhance our ability to recall revelation. Such recording of direction of the Spirit should be protected from loss or intrusions by others" (Scott, "How to Obtain Revelation and Inspiration," 46).

men, but because of the weakness which is in me, according to the flesh, I would excuse myself.

7 For the things which some men esteem to be of great worth, both to the body and soul, others set at naught and trample under their feet. Yea, even the very God of Israel do men trample under their feet; I say, trample under their feet but I would speak in other words—they set him at naught, and hearken not to the voice of his counsels.

8 And behold he cometh, according to the words of the angel, in six hundred years from the time my father left Jerusalem.

9 And the world, because of their iniquity, shall judge him to be a thing of naught; wherefore they scourge him, and he suffereth it; and they smite him, and he suffereth it. Yea, they spit upon him, and he suffereth it, because of his loving kindness and his long-suffering towards the children of men.

10 And the God of our fathers, who were led out of Egypt, out of bondage, and also were preserved in the wilderness by him, yea, the God of Abraham, and of Isaac, and the God of Jacob, yieldeth himself, according to the words of the angel, as a man, into the hands of wicked men, to be lifted up, according to the words of Zenock, and to be crucified, according to the words of Neum, and to be buried in a sepulchre, according to the words of Zenos, which he spake concerning the three days of darkness, which should be a sign given of his death unto those who should inhabit the isles of the sea, more especially given unto those who are of the house of Israel.

11 For thus spake the prophet: The Lord God surely shall visit all the house of Israel at that day, some with his voice, because of their righteousness, unto their great joy and salvation, and others with the thunderings

1 Nephi 19:7–17. Nephi Prophesies of the Sufferings and Crucifixion of Jesus Christ

How do people trample the God of Israel under their feet? (19:7) "To trample the God of Israel under our feet or setting at naught his words has been a problem in every age of the world. To set at naught his words is to ignore them either by failure to listen or refusal to read them. To not hearken is to be aware of what they teach, but to not do as they say. The Lord condemned the early Church in a similar manner" (Nyman, *I, Nephi, Wrote This Record*, 290).

How can an understanding of Nephi's writing style provide insight into his intended message? (19:10) "The Book of Mormon is replete with parallelisms. The poetic patterns serve, as they do in the Bible, to emphasize messages. . . . Sometimes the two alternating lines will repeat more than once: such a structure is called a repeated alternate parallelism. . . .

"**A** The God of Jacob, yieldeth himself,
　"**B** according to the words of the angel,
"**A** as a man, into the hands of wicked men, to be lifted up,
　"**B** according to the words of Zenock,
"**A** and to be crucified,
　"**B** according to the words of Neum,
"**A** and to be buried in a sepulchre,
　"**B** according to the words of Zenos"
(Parry, "Hebrew Literary Patterns in the Book of Mormon," 60).

Who were Neum, Zenock, and Zenos? (19:10) "Although these prophets are not mentioned in the Bible, their teachings and prophecies were apparently included on the plates of brass (1 Ne. 19:21). The number of years by which these men predated Lehi cannot be determined. Nephi, son of Helaman, listed Zenock,

Zenos, and Ezias as prophets who had testified since the days of Abraham (ca. 1900 B.C.).... Mormon seems to imply that Zenock and Zenos were both descendants of Joseph and ancestors to the Book of Mormon peoples, which would place them later than ca. 1600 B.C. (3 Ne. 10:16–17)" (Ball, "Old Testament Prophets in the Book of Mormon," 260). ○

Why refer to the God of nature? (19:12) One author has described the Savior's suffering thus: "Nature and all her components were joined in horrifying harmony. ... The elements wrenched and writhed in all their fury as undeniable proof of a suffering that was no doubt galactic—that affected every man, every animal, every fish, every plant, and every element in that expanse of space called the universe. The Savior's suffering was like a prodigious boulder thrown into the midst of a glassy pond—the ripples emanating from Gethsemane and Calvary would, as President John Taylor said, 'spread throughout all space' and for the moment 'all eternity [was] pained' (D&C 38:12)" (Callister, *Infinite Atonement*, 126).

What judgment came upon this branch of the house of Israel for rejecting their Messiah? (19:14) "Because of the displeasure of the Father which came upon [the Jews] for rejecting their Redeemer and his Gospel ... they brought upon themselves the hatred of all people.... They have been most surely a hiss and a by-word among the nations.... They are today a standing miracle in their scattered condition, silently testifying to the covenants to Israel and of the divinity of Jesus Christ, yet, themselves, not believing in him" (Smith, *Way to Perfection*, 133). At some point this branch of the house of Israel will return to the Lord, and he will gather them in mercy. ○

1 Nephi 19:18–24. The Scriptures Can Help Us to Remember the Lord

What was Nephi's intention in using the words of ancient prophets? (19:18) "The Nephite tradition centered on the message about Christ. As Nephi often stated, his purpose was to persuade his children to believe in Christ, that they might be saved (see 1 Nephi

and the lightnings of his power, by tempest, by fire, and by smoke, and vapor of darkness, and by the opening of the earth, and by mountains which shall be carried up.

12 And all these things must surely come, saith the prophet Zenos. And the rocks of the earth must rend; and because of the groanings of the earth, many of the kings of the isles of the sea shall be wrought upon by the Spirit of God, to exclaim: The God of nature suffers.

13 And as for those who are at Jerusalem, saith the prophet, they shall be scourged by all people, because they crucify the God of Israel, and turn their hearts aside, rejecting signs and wonders, and the power and glory of the God of Israel.

14 And because they turn their hearts aside, saith the prophet, and have despised the Holy One of Israel, they shall wander in the flesh, and perish, and become a hiss and a byword, and be hated among all nations.

15 Nevertheless, when that day cometh, saith the prophet, that they no more turn aside their hearts against the Holy One of Israel, then will he remember the covenants which he made to their fathers.

16 Yea, then will he remember the isles of the sea; yea, and all the people who are of the house of Israel, will I gather in, saith the Lord, according to the words of the prophet Zenos, from the four quarters of the earth.

17 Yea, and all the earth shall see the salvation of the Lord, saith the prophet; every nation, kindred, tongue and people shall be blessed.

18 And I, Nephi, have written these things unto my people, that perhaps I might persuade them that they would remember the Lord their Redeemer.

19 Wherefore, I speak unto all the house of Israel, if it so be that they should obtain these things.

20 For behold, I have workings in the spirit, which doth weary me even that all my joints are weak, for those who are at Jerusalem; for had not the Lord been merciful, to show unto me concerning them, even as he had prophets of old, I should have perished also.

21 And he surely did show unto the prophets of old all things concerning them; and also he did show unto many concerning us; wherefore, it must needs be that we know concerning them for they are written upon the plates of brass.

22 Now it came to pass that I, Nephi, did teach my brethren these things; and it came to pass that I did read many things to them, which were engraven upon the plates of brass, that they might know concerning the doings of the Lord in other lands, among people of old.

23 And I did read many things unto them which were written in the books of Moses; but that I might more fully persuade them to believe in the Lord their Redeemer I did read unto them that which was written by the prophet Isaiah; for I did liken all scriptures unto us, that it might be for our profit and learning.

24 Wherefore I spake unto them, saying: Hear ye the words of the prophet, ye who are a remnant of the house of Israel, a branch who have been broken off; hear ye the words of the prophet, which were written unto all the house of Israel, and liken them unto yourselves, that ye may have hope as well as your brethren from whom ye have been broken off; for after this manner has the prophet written.

6:4; 19:18; 2 Nephi 25:23)" (Reynolds, "Nephi's Political Testament," 225–26).

What is Isaiah's main message? (19:23–24) As you consider Nephi's statement concerning the importance of Isaiah, what is the main message you should be looking for as you read?

Why is it important to read the scriptures and liken them to ourselves? (19:23) "From events portrayed in the scriptures, new insights will come and principles relevant to your situation will distill upon your heart" (Nelson, "Getting Where You Want to Go," 7). President Brigham Young inquired: "Do you read [the scriptures] as though you stood in the place of the men who wrote them? If you do not feel thus, it is your privilege to do so, that you may be as familiar with the spirit and meaning of the written word of God as you are with your daily walk and conversation" (*Discourses of Brigham Young*, 128).

1 Nephi 20:1–8. The Lord Knows All Things and Uses That Power to Show Us That He Is God

What is the identity of the "House of Jacob [who] come forth out of the waters of Judah"? (20:1) "The phrase 'out of the waters of Judah' refers to those of Judah who are baptized into the Church. The Prophet Joseph Smith added the phrase 'or out of the waters of baptism' to the text in the third edition of the Book of Mormon (1840). This clarifies the meaning of the term 'waters of Judah'" (Nyman, *Great Are the Words of Isaiah*, 170).

What is the concern with these people who call themselves of the holy city? (20:2) "Despite their covenants, these Church members do not lean upon or take hold of the Lord" (Parry et al., *Understanding Isaiah*, 416).

What is meant by the metaphor "thy neck is an iron sinew"? (20:4) Gerald Lund explained: "When Isaiah says, 'thy neck is an iron sinew' (Isa. 48:4) and when Jeremiah notes the people 'made their neck stiff that they may not hear, nor receive instruction' (Jer. 17:23) the image is that of stubborn pride. The reason for this is linked to another function of the neck. It holds the head and turns it. Since the bowing of the head is a sign of humility, to be stiff-necked is the symbol of pride" ("Understanding Scriptural Symbols," 25).

What is one reason the Lord shows future events to his prophets? (20:5) "The Lord shows the future so that false gods will not be worshiped or given credit for the Lord's doings (v. 5). The people of Judah had been shown and told of future events, but they had rejected this knowledge. The Lord knew they would reject it. He told them anyway so they would be accountable for their sins. An understanding of foreknowledge and why it is shared with the prophets is a unique and an important contribution that comes from Isaiah's writing" (Nyman, *I, Nephi, Wrote This Record*, 305). ☉

CHAPTER 20

The Lord reveals His purposes to Israel—Israel has been chosen in the furnace of affliction and is to go forth from Babylon—Compare Isaiah 48. About 588–570 B.C.

1 Hearken and hear this, O house of Jacob, who are called by the name of Israel, and are come forth out of the waters of Judah, or out of the waters of baptism, who swear by the name of the Lord, and make mention of the God of Israel, yet they swear not in truth nor in righteousness.

2 Nevertheless, they call themselves of the holy city, but they do not stay themselves upon the God of Israel, who is the Lord of Hosts; yea, the Lord of Hosts is his name.

3 Behold, I have declared the former things from the beginning; and they went forth out of my mouth, and I showed them. I did show them suddenly.

4 And I did it because I knew that thou art obstinate, and thy neck is an iron sinew, and thy brow brass;

5 And I have even from the beginning declared to thee; before it came to pass I showed them thee; and I showed them for fear lest thou shouldst say—Mine idol hath done them, and my graven image, and my molten image hath commanded them.

6 Thou hast seen and heard all this; and will ye not declare them? And that I have showed thee new things from this time, even hidden things, and thou didst not know them.

7 They are created now, and not from the beginning, even before the day when thou heardest them not they were declared unto thee, lest thou shouldst say—Behold I knew them.

8 Yea, and thou heardest not; yea, thou knewest not; yea, from that time thine ear was not opened; for I knew that thou wouldst deal very treacherously, and wast called a transgressor from the womb.

9 Nevertheless, for my name's sake will I defer mine anger, and for my praise will I refrain from thee, that I cut thee not off.

1 Nephi 20:9–11. Through Our Afflictions the Lord Makes Us His Chosen People

What does the Lord's willingness to spare Israel teach about the power and responsibility of bearing His name? (20:9) "The Lord Jehovah had placed his name and the promise of his power upon the nation of Israel. They were his people; they were to become his peculiar treasure. He had given that name and power to none other, and had no intention of his holy name being forgotten, ignored, or profaned by the surrounding nations. 'I will not suffer my name to be polluted,' he said, 'and I will not give my glory unto another' (1 Ne. 20:4, 8–9, 11)" (Millet, "Nephi on the Destiny of Israel," 78).

Isaiah in the Book of Mormon

"If the Isaiah verses in the Book of Mormon were removed from their present position and collected into one place, [they] would constitute a book with 592 verses, and be larger than what would remain in 12 of the 15 books in the Book of Mormon. The accompanying graph lists the number of verses in each book. . . . Books are listed in order of their size, demonstrating that a book of Isaiah verses would be the fourth largest in the Book of Mormon" (Garner, *Search These Things Diligently*, 68–69).

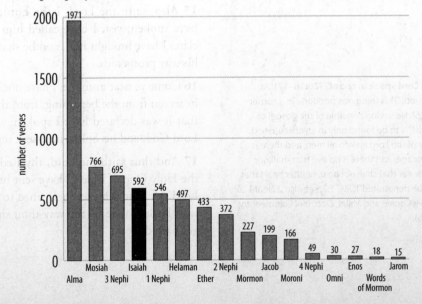

number of verses

Alma	Mosiah	3 Nephi	Isaiah	1 Nephi	Helaman	Ether	2 Nephi	Mormon	Jacob	Moroni	4 Nephi	Omni	Enos	Words of Mormon	Jarom
1971	766	695	592	546	497	433	372	227	199	166	49	30	27	18	15

What is the divine purpose of affliction? (20:10)
"Most of us experience some measure of what the scriptures call 'the furnace of affliction' (Isaiah 48:10; 1 Nephi 20:10). Some are submerged in service to a disadvantaged family member. Others suffer the death of a loved one or the loss or postponement of a righteous goal like marriage or childbearing. Still others struggle with personal impairments or with feelings of rejection, inadequacy, or depression. Through the justice and mercy of a loving Father in Heaven, the refinement and sanctification possible through such experiences can help us achieve what God desires us to become" (Oaks, "Challenge to Become," 33–34).

1 Nephi 20:12–17. The Children of Israel Should Listen to the Lord and His Prophets

What is the significance of the right hand? (20:13)
"There are numerous passages in the scriptures referring to the right hand, indicating that it is a symbol of righteousness and was used in the making of covenants. . . . The right hand or side is called the dexter and the left the sinister. *Dexter* connotes something favorable; *sinister*, something unfavorable or unfortunate" (Smith, *Answers to Gospel Questions*, 1:157–58). ⊕

Does the Lord speak in secret? (20:16–17) "As Paul declared, 'This thing was not done in a corner' (Acts 26:26). No saving principle of the gospel of Jesus Christ, is to be found only in an obscure text. 'The voice of the Lord is unto all men, and there is none to escape; and there is no eye that shall not see neither ear that shall not hear, neither heart that shall not be penetrated' (D&C 1:2; see also 2 Nephi 26: 23–24)" (McConkie and Millet, *Doctrinal Commentary*, 1:155–156).

10 For, behold, I have refined thee, I have chosen thee in the furnace of affliction.

11 For mine own sake, yea, for mine own sake will I do this, for I will not suffer my name to be polluted, and I will not give my glory unto another.

12 Hearken unto me, O Jacob, and Israel my called, for I am he; I am the first, and I am also the last.

13 Mine hand hath also laid the foundation of the earth, and my right hand hath spanned the heavens. I call unto them and they stand up together.

14 All ye, assemble yourselves, and hear; who among them hath declared these things unto them? The Lord hath loved him; yea, and he will fulfil his word which he hath declared by them; and he will do his pleasure on Babylon, and his arm shall come upon the Chaldeans.

15 Also, saith the Lord; I the Lord, yea, I have spoken; yea, I have called him to declare, I have brought him, and he shall make his way prosperous.

16 Come ye near unto me; I have not spoken in secret; from the beginning, from the time that it was declared have I spoken; and the Lord God, and his Spirit, hath sent me.

17 And thus saith the Lord, thy Redeemer, the Holy One of Israel; I have sent him, the Lord thy God who teacheth thee to profit, who leadeth thee by the way thou shouldst go, hath done it.

18 O that thou hadst hearkened to my commandments—then had thy peace been as a river, and thy righteousness as the waves of the sea.

19 Thy seed also had been as the sand; the offspring of thy bowels like the gravel thereof; his name should not have been cut off nor destroyed from before me.

20 Go ye forth of Babylon, flee ye from the Chaldeans, with a voice of singing declare ye, tell this, utter to the end of the earth; say ye: The Lord hath redeemed his servant Jacob.

21 And they thirsted not; he led them through the deserts; he caused the waters to flow out of the rock for them; he clave the rock also and the waters gushed out.

22 And notwithstanding he hath done all this, and greater also, there is no peace, saith the Lord, unto the wicked.

CHAPTER 21

The Messiah will be a light to the Gentiles and will free the prisoners—Israel will be gathered with power in the last days—Kings will be their nursing fathers—Compare Isaiah 49. About 588–570 B.C.

1 And again: Hearken, O ye house of Israel, all ye that are broken off and are driven out because of the wickedness of the pastors of my people; yea, all ye that are broken off, that are scattered abroad, who are of my people, O house of Israel. Listen, O isles, unto me, and hearken ye people from far; the

1 Nephi 20:18–22. Living Righteously Brings Peace

What is the significance of Isaiah's imagery of the river and the waves? (20:18) Lehi used similar imagery as he exhorted his sons Laman and Lemuel (see 1 Nephi 2:8–10). "Those who observe God's commandments experience a peace of conscience that flows continually, even as a river does. Their righteousness will have a rippling and far-flung effect, just as the waves of the sea are set in motion by the forces of nature" (Brewster, *Isaiah Plain and Simple*, 184).

What is the symbolism of *Babylon* and *Chaldeans*? (20:20) "As with other great ancient empires, Babylon's ascendancy to wealth and glory was accompanied by moral decay, wickedness, and iniquity. Babylon's corruption was so extensive that the very name became a symbol for worldliness, spiritual wickedness, and Satan's kingdom" (*Book of Mormon Student Manual* [2009], 46). The Chaldeans were a subgroup of the Babylonian empire. ⊕

Why the warning about leaving Babylon? (20:20) "Why do some of our youth risk engaging in ritual prodigalism, intending to spend a season rebelling and acting out in Babylon and succumbing to that devilishly democratic 'everybody does it'? Crowds cannot make right what God has declared to be wrong. Though planning to return later, many such stragglers find that alcohol, drugs, and pornography will not let go easily. Babylon does not give exit permits gladly. It is an ironic implementation of that ancient boast: 'One soul shall not be lost' (Moses 4:1)" (Maxwell, "Answer Me," 33).

1 Nephi 21:1–7. Jesus Christ and His Prophet Will Gather Israel and Provide Light for the Gentiles

Why does verse 1 differ so dramatically from how the prophecy reads in Isaiah 49? (21:1) "This is a significant textual restoration. It establishes that though the prophet is addressing all the house of Israel, his message is more especially for that part of Israel that had been scattered, not through their own wickedness, but because of the corruption of the Church in the Old World. It was this corruption of the Church and the temple priesthood that caused Lehi and his family to flee" (McConkie and Millet, *Doctrinal Commentary*, 1:158). Jeremiah also prophesied of the wickedness of the pastors and the scattering of the flock (see Jeremiah 23:1–4). ✪

What is the meaning of the servant's mouth being like a sharp sword? (21:2) "A two-edged sword is one which has been sharpened on both sides to make it twice as effective. God's word and the still small voice of the Spirit are even sharper than this, for they are capable of piercing the most pernicious armament and of penetrating to the innermost depths of one's soul (D&C 85:6). When the Lord, or His servants, speak with the sharpness of the sword of their mouths, 'the guilty taketh the truth to be hard, for it cutteth them to the very center' (1 Nephi 16:2)" (Brewster, *Isaiah Plain and Simple*, 190–91).

What does "light to the Gentiles" refer to? (21:6) "The light to the Gentiles is variously defined in the scriptures as Jesus Christ (Isa. 42:6–7; Luke 2:32), the priesthood (D&C 86:11), and Zion (Isa. 60:3). If the servant referred to in this section is not the Messiah himself, he certainly will shine with the light of the Messiah" (Parry et al., *Understanding Isaiah*, 427).

1 Nephi 21:8–12. The House of Israel Will Be Gathered in the Last Days

What are the "desolate heritages" Israel will eventually receive? (21:8) "In considering these words, one would naturally think of the great promises made to Israel that she will inhabit and restore once-fruitful lands that have long lain desolate (Isaiah 61:4). There may, however, be a far more significant meaning attached to this phrase. During their long years of apostasy, have not the children of Israel been deprived of the heritage that might have been theirs had they been worthy? Thus, when they repent and return, will they not then inherit the heritage that has long been desolate?" (Brewster, *Isaiah Plain and Simple*, 194).

Lord hath called me from the womb; from the bowels of my mother hath he made mention of my name.

2 And he hath made my mouth like a sharp sword; in the shadow of his hand hath he hid me, and made me a polished shaft; in his quiver hath he hid me;

3 And said unto me: Thou art my servant, O Israel, in whom I will be glorified.

4 Then I said, I have labored in vain, I have spent my strength for naught and in vain; surely my judgment is with the Lord, and my work with my God.

5 And now, saith the Lord—that formed me from the womb that I should be his servant, to bring Jacob again to him—though Israel be not gathered, yet shall I be glorious in the eyes of the Lord, and my God shall be my strength.

6 And he said: It is a light thing that thou shouldst be my servant to raise up the tribes of Jacob, and to restore the preserved of Israel. I will also give thee for a light to the Gentiles, that thou mayest be my salvation unto the ends of the earth.

7 Thus saith the Lord, the Redeemer of Israel, his Holy One, to him whom man despiseth, to him whom the nations abhorreth, to servant of rulers: Kings shall see and arise, princes also shall worship, because of the Lord that is faithful.

8 Thus saith the Lord: In an acceptable time have I heard thee, O isles of the sea, and in a day of salvation have I helped thee; and I will preserve thee, and give thee my servant for a covenant of the people, to establish the earth, to cause to inherit the desolate heritages;

9 That thou mayest say to the prisoners: Go forth; to them that sit in darkness: Show yourselves. They shall feed in the ways, and their pastures shall be in all high places.

10 They shall not hunger nor thirst, neither shall the heat nor the sun smite them; for he that hath mercy on them shall lead them, even by the springs of water shall he guide them.

11 And I will make all my mountains a way, and my highways shall be exalted.

12 And then, O house of Israel, behold, these shall come from far; and lo, these from the north and from the west; and these from the land of Sinim.

13 Sing, O heavens; and be joyful, O earth; for the feet of those who are in the east shall be established; and break forth into singing, O mountains; for they shall be smitten no more; for the Lord hath comforted his people, and will have mercy upon his afflicted.

Who are those in prison and how will they be set free? (21:9) "The prisoners spoken of are those who are presently confined to a spirit prison or 'state of misery.' These are they who 'chose evil works rather than good' during their earthly sojourn (Alma 40:13–14). Following His death on Calvary, the disembodied Christ went to the spirit world where He organized His righteous followers into a missionary task force to take the gospel to those in the spirit prison (D&C 138:18–21, 28). As these confined spirits accept the gospel, and as saving ordinances are performed in their behalf in holy temples here on earth, the prisoners are set free (D&C 128:22)" (Brewster, *Isaiah Plain and Simple*, 195).

Who will provide for and protect those of the covenant? (21:10) "This passage refers to the Lord's blessings to those who are returning from exile, as well as to those returning from spiritual bondage. Whether in physical or spiritual captivity, they suffer both hunger and thirst, and the heat and sun threaten them; in their deliverance the Lord protects and nourishes them. In all circumstances, it is only through Christ that our spiritual hunger can be satisfied (John 6:35; Alma 31:38; 32:42; 3 Ne. 12:6; 20:8)" (Parry et al., *Understanding Isaiah*, 427).

Has the gathering of scattered Israel from afar begun? (21:12) "This doctrine of the gathering is one of the important teachings of The Church of Jesus Christ of Latter-day Saints. . . . The coming forth of the Book of Mormon is a sign to the entire world that the Lord has commenced to gather Israel and fulfill covenants He made to Abraham, Isaac, and Jacob. We not only teach this doctrine, but we participate in it. We do so as we help to gather the elect of the Lord on both sides of the veil" (Nelson, "Gathering of Scattered Israel," 80). Moses committed the "keys of the gathering of Israel from the four quarters of the earth" to Joseph Smith and Oliver Cowdery (see D&C 110:11).

1 Nephi 21:13–21. The Lord Will Not Forget His Children

Does the Lord forsake and forget those with whom he has covenanted? (21:13–15) Elder Jeffrey R. Holland summarized these verses: "This poetic passage provides yet another reminder of Christ's saving role, that of protective, redeeming parent to Zion's children. He comforts his people and shows mercy when they are afflicted, as any loving father or mother would toward a child. . . . Christ will not forget the children he has redeemed or the covenant he has made with them for salvation in Zion" (*Christ and the New Covenant*, 84).

Why will the Lord never forget His people? (21:15–16) With graphic imagery, Isaiah explained why the Holy One of Israel cares for his children and can never forget them: "The painful reminders of [Christ's] watch care and covenant are the marks of the Roman nails graven upon the palms of his hands, a sign to his disciples in the Old World, his Nephite congregation in the New World, and to us in latter-day Zion that he is the Savior of the world and was wounded in the house of his friends" (Holland, *Christ and the New Covenant*, 84).

Who is the bride in this passage? (21:18) Covenant Israel are the ones the Lord binds to Him. "Israel, therefore, has more than one meaning. There is no divine discrimination except with respect to righteousness, which is the key to being one of the Lord's chosen. While lineal Israel was initially the Lord's betrothed, by the time the marriage takes place, many will have lost their birthright. Others, not Israelite by birth, will have been adopted in with full family status. The symbolic bride, then, will consist of those individuals who have accepted the Lord by individual covenant" (Hart, "The Marriage Metaphor," 24).

Where will the gathering take place? (21:19–21) "The place of gathering has been established, and there is 'none other place appointed,' we are told, 'until the day cometh when there is found no more room for them; and then I have other places which I will appoint unto them, and they shall be called stakes, for the curtains or the strength of Zion' (see D&C 101:20–21; Isaiah 54:2–3; 3 Nephi 22:2–3). The stakes of Zion are the gathering places for latter-day Israel" (McConkie and Millet, *Doctrinal Commentary*, 1:166). The New Jerusalem "will be built upon the American continent" (Articles of Faith 1:10).

1 Nephi 21:22–26. The Gentile Nations Shall Help Gather the House of Israel

What is the Lord's standard and how will it go forth? (21:22) "As the Lord begins the gathering, he will follow a prophesied sequence. First, he will bring the gospel forth to the Gentiles. . . . The Gentiles then have a responsibility to take it to all the nations of

14 But, behold, Zion hath said: The Lord hath forsaken me, and my Lord hath forgotten me—but he will show that he hath not.

15 For can a woman forget her sucking child, that she should not have compassion on the son of her womb? Yea, they may forget, yet will I not forget thee, O house of Israel.

16 Behold, I have graven thee upon the palms of my hands; thy walls are continually before me.

17 Thy children shall make haste against thy destroyers; and they that made thee waste shall go forth of thee.

18 Lift up thine eyes round about and behold; all these gather themselves together, and they shall come to thee. And as I live, saith the Lord, thou shalt surely clothe thee with them all, as with an ornament, and bind them on even as a bride.

19 For thy waste and thy desolate places, and the land of thy destruction, shall even now be too narrow by reason of the inhabitants; and they that swallowed thee up shall be far away.

20 The children whom thou shalt have, after thou hast lost the first, shall again in thine ears say: The place is too strait for me; give place to me that I may dwell.

21 Then shalt thou say in thine heart: Who hath begotten me these, seeing I have lost my children, and am desolate, a captive, and removing to and fro? And who hath brought up these? Behold, I was left alone; these, where have they been?

22 Thus saith the Lord God: Behold, I will lift up mine hand to the Gentiles, and set up my standard to the people; and they shall bring thy sons in their arms, and thy daughters shall be carried upon their shoulders.

23 And kings shall be thy nursing fathers, and their queens thy nursing mothers; they shall bow down to thee with their face towards the earth, and lick up the dust of thy feet; and thou shalt know that I am the Lord; for they shall not be ashamed that wait for me.

24 For shall the prey be taken from the mighty, or the lawful captives delivered?

25 But thus saith the Lord, even the captives of the mighty shall be taken away, and the prey of the terrible shall be delivered; for I will contend with him that contendeth with thee, and I will save thy children.

26 And I will feed them that oppress thee with their own flesh; they shall be drunken with their own blood as with sweet wine; and all flesh shall know that I, the Lord, am thy Savior and thy Redeemer, the Mighty One of Jacob.

CHAPTER 22

Israel will be scattered upon all the face of the earth—The Gentiles will nurse and nourish Israel with the gospel in the last days—Israel will be gathered and saved, and the wicked will burn as stubble—The kingdom of the devil will be destroyed, and Satan will be bound. About 588–570 B.C.

1 And now it came to pass that after I, Nephi, had read these things which were engraven upon the plates of brass, my brethren came unto me and said unto me: What meaneth these things which ye have read? Behold, are they to be understood according to things which are spiritual, which shall

the world. Finally, the testimony of Christ will go to the Jews. As Isaiah saw, through the Gentiles the Lord would 'set up my standard to the people.' . . . It would be through the ministrations of the Gentiles that the generality of the house of Israel would come to the gospel" (Parry and Parry, *Understanding the Signs of the Times,* 62; see D&C 45:9).

What does it mean that the Gentiles will be nursing fathers and mothers? (21:23) "From Nephi we learn that kings and queens are representative of the Gentiles among whom the house of Israel was scattered. We also learn that there is a temporal and a figurative or spiritual fulfillment of Israel's 'nursing' by the Gentiles. [The temporal fulfillment] refers to various attempts, public and private, to assist the Lamanites in the afflictions that followed their scattering. . . . The [spiritual fulfillment refers to the] marvelous work among the Gentiles that would nourish the Lamanites [through] the restored gospel of Jesus Christ" (Nyman, "I Have a Question," 61). ◉

1 Nephi 22:1–7. The Scattering of Israel Is Prophesied

come to pass according to the spirit and not the flesh?

Why do we have prophets? (22:2) "A prophet is a man called by God to be His representative on earth. When a prophet speaks for God, it is as if God were speaking (see D&C 1:38). A prophet is also a special witness for Christ, testifying of His divinity and teaching His gospel. A prophet teaches truth and interprets the word of God. He calls the unrighteous to repentance. He receives revelations and directions from the Lord for our benefit. He may see into the future and foretell coming events so that the world may be warned" (*Gospel Principles*, 47).

What examples can you think of in which the Spirit manifested something to the prophets in our day? (22:2) How has your life been different as a result?

How does the Book of Mormon foreshadow the scattering of the House of Israel? (22:3) "The Bible teaches that some of Abraham's descendants would be scattered 'into all the kingdoms of the earth,' 'among all nations,' and from 'one end of the earth even unto the other' (Deut. 28:25, 37, 64). The Book of Mormon affirms this teaching, declaring that the descendants of Abraham would be 'scattered upon all the face of the earth, and . . . among all nations' (1 Ne. 22:3).

"The Book of Mormon adds to our knowledge of how our Savior's earthly ministry reached out to all of His scattered flock. . . .

"The Book of Mormon is a great witness that the Lord loves all people everywhere. It declares that 'he shall manifest himself unto all nations' (1 Ne. 13:42)" (Oaks, "All Men Everywhere," 79).

What is meant by the statement that the ten tribes of Israel "are already lost"? (22:4) "It ought also to be observed that the lost tribes are not lost in the sense that we do not know where they are. The scriptures plainly tell us they have been scattered among every nation, kindred, tongue, and people. How then are they lost? They are lost temporally in the sense that they are in many instances lost to the lands of their inheritance. Of greater importance, they are lost in a spiritual sense: they are lost to the gospel and its saving ordinances, they are lost to the priesthood and all the blessings that flow from it" (McConkie and Millet, *Doctrinal Commentary*, 1:169–70).

Why was Israel initially scattered? (22:5) "Our Israelite forebears were scattered because they rejected the gospel, defiled the priesthood, forsook

2 And I, Nephi, said unto them: Behold they were manifest unto the prophet by the voice of the Spirit; for by the Spirit are all things made known unto the prophets, which shall come upon the children of men according to the flesh.

3 Wherefore, the things of which I have read are things pertaining to things both temporal and spiritual; for it appears that the house of Israel, sooner or later, will be scattered upon all the face of the earth, and also among all nations.

4 And behold, there are many who are already lost from the knowledge of those who are at Jerusalem. Yea, the more part of all the tribes have been led away; and they are scattered to and fro upon the isles of the sea; and whither they are none of us knoweth, save that we know that they have been led away.

5 And since they have been led away, these things have been prophesied concerning them, and also concerning all those who shall

hereafter be scattered and be confounded, because of the Holy One of Israel; for against him will they harden their hearts; wherefore, they shall be scattered among all nations and shall be hated of all men.

6 Nevertheless, after they shall be nursed by the Gentiles, and the Lord has lifted up his hand upon the Gentiles and set them up for a standard, and their children have been carried in their arms, and their daughters have been carried upon their shoulders, behold these things of which are spoken are temporal; for thus are the covenants of the Lord with our fathers; and it meaneth us in the days to come, and also all our brethren who are of the house of Israel.

7 And it meaneth that the time cometh that after all the house of Israel have been scattered and confounded, that the Lord God will raise up a mighty nation among the Gentiles, yea, even upon the face of this land; and by them shall our seed be scattered.

8 And after our seed is scattered the Lord God will proceed to do a marvelous work among the Gentiles, which shall be of great worth unto our seed; wherefore, it is likened unto their being nourished by the Gentiles and being carried in their arms and upon their shoulders.

the church, and departed from the kingdom. They were scattered because they turned from the Lord, worshipped false gods, and walked in all the ways of the heathen nations. They were scattered because they forsook the Abrahamic covenant, trampled under their feet the holy ordinances, and rejected the Lord Jehovah, who is the Lord Jesus, of whom all their prophets testified. Israel was scattered for apostasy. The Lord in his wrath, because of their wickedness and rebellion, scattered them among the heathen in all the nations of the earth" (McConkie, *New Witness*, 515).

What is the mighty nation among the Gentiles that Nephi foresaw? (22:7) "Our Father in Heaven planned the coming forth of the Founding Fathers and their form of government as the necessary great prologue leading to the restoration of the gospel. . . . America, the land of liberty, was to be the Lord's latter-day base of operations for His restored church" (Benson, "Our Divine Constitution," 4). ◑

How has the United States of America been "a mighty nation"? (22:7) "American Latter-day Saints are not superior in any way to Saints who live in other countries. Many Saints who live in other countries appreciate and respect the United States and her citizens for reaching out with aid and resources" (*Great American Documents for Latter-day Saint Families*, viii). In what ways has the influence of the United States helped fulfill the Lord's purposes in the world? How does the religious liberty of America help the Lord's purposes?

1 Nephi 22:8–12. Israel Shall Be Gathered

How will the Gentiles nourish Lehi's seed? (22:8) "A loving father does not despise his children. These are a chosen people, and this Church has an important part in restoring them to their rightful inheritance. The chasm between what they are and what they will be is opportunity. The gospel furnishes that opportunity; it is ours to give [see also 2 Nephi 10:18]" (Kimball, "Our Paths Have Met Again," 7).

How is the Lord going to make bare his arm in the eyes of all nations? (22:10) "The power of God, here represented as the Lord making bare his arm, will be manifest by the taking of the gospel and its eternal covenants to all the nations and peoples of the earth. That same God who delivered Israel from the might of Egypt will in the latter days show again his power with greater miracles than those witnessed at the hands of Moses.... Missionaries must go to the lands that have not yet received them, until the gospel 'has penetrated every continent, visited every clime, swept every country, and sounded in every ear, till the purposes of God shall be accomplished, and the Great Jehovah shall say the work is done' ([*History of the Church,*] 4:540)" (McConkie and Millet, *Doctrinal Commentary on the Book of Mormon,* 1:172).

How is the Lord bringing about his covenants related to the gathering of Israel? (22:11) "The essence of the gathering is the gathering to the covenants of the gospel of Jesus Christ— ... the same covenants that God made with Israel's great ancestors, Abraham, Isaac, and Jacob.... The idea of a physical return in the scriptures may often be a metaphor for returning to the covenants, accepting the gospel, and joining Christ's church. Geographical relocation plays a lesser role. Today the gathering of Israel is taking place as individuals from all over the earth are gathering to the Church in their own lands" (Jackson, "Comfort My People," 142–43).

1 Nephi 22:13–23. All Who Fight against Zion Will Be Destroyed

How is the prophecy that the unrighteous will "war among themselves" being fulfilled today? (22:13) The prophet Mormon was a firsthand witness in his day of how "it is by the wicked that the wicked are punished" (Mormon 4:5). Also in our day, the Lord has "decreed wars upon the face of the earth, and the wicked shall slay the wicked" (D&C 63:33).

How will those who fight against Zion be destroyed? (22:14) "Israel's triumph over her enemies will occur not because her marching armies defeat

9 And it shall also be of worth unto the Gentiles; and not only unto the Gentiles but unto all the house of Israel, unto the making known of the covenants of the Father of heaven unto Abraham, saying: In thy seed shall all the kindreds of the earth be blessed.

10 And I would, my brethren, that ye should know that all the kindreds of the earth cannot be blessed unless he shall make bare his arm in the eyes of the nations.

11 Wherefore, the Lord God will proceed to make bare his arm in the eyes of all the nations, in bringing about his covenants and his gospel unto those who are of the house of Israel.

12 Wherefore, he will bring them again out of captivity, and they shall be gathered together to the lands of their inheritance; and they shall be brought out of obscurity and out of darkness; and they shall know that the Lord is their Savior and their Redeemer, the Mighty One of Israel.

13 And the blood of that great and abominable church, which is the whore of all the earth, shall turn upon their own heads; for they shall war among themselves, and the sword of their own hands shall fall upon their own heads, and they shall be drunken with their own blood.

14 And every nation which shall war against thee, O house of Israel, shall be turned one against another, and they shall fall into the pit which they digged to ensnare the people of the Lord. And all that fight against Zion shall be destroyed, and that great whore, who hath perverted the right ways of the Lord, yea, that great and abominable church, shall tumble to the dust and great shall be the fall of it.

15 For behold, saith the prophet, the time cometh speedily that Satan shall have no more power over the hearts of the children of men; for the day soon cometh that all the proud and they who do wickedly shall be as stubble; and the day cometh that they must be burned.

16 For the time soon cometh that the fulness of the wrath of God shall be poured out upon all the children of men; for he will not suffer that the wicked shall destroy the righteous.

17 Wherefore, he will preserve the righteous by his power, even if it so be that the fulness of his wrath must come, and the righteous be preserved, even unto the destruction of their enemies by fire. Wherefore, the righteous need not fear; for thus saith the prophet, they shall be saved, even if it so be as by fire.

18 Behold, my brethren, I say unto you, that these things must shortly come; yea, even blood, and fire, and vapor of smoke must come; and it must needs be upon the face of this earth; and it cometh unto men according to the flesh if it so be that they will harden their hearts against the Holy One of Israel.

19 For behold, the righteous shall not perish; for the time surely must come that all they who fight against Zion shall be cut off.

20 And the Lord will surely prepare a way for his people, unto the fulfilling of the words of Moses, which he spake, saying: A prophet shall the Lord your God raise up unto you,

their foes in battle, but because her enemies [the Gentiles, the great and abominable church, the nations that fight against God—call them what you will, the meaning is the same] will be destroyed, simply because every corruptible thing will be consumed at the Second Coming. In that day the Lord will truly fight the battles of his saints, for as he descends from heaven, amid fire and burning, all the proud and they that do wickedly shall be burned as stubble" (McConkie, *New Witness*, 562–63).

Who was the source for Nephi's and Malachi's teachings that the wicked will be burned at the day of judgment? (22:15) "The Book of Mormon also talks about things that are in the book of Malachi, about the earth burning and so on (compare 1 Ne. 22:15 and Mal. 4:1; also 1 Ne. 22:24 with Mal. 4:2), and attributes them to a prophet named Zenos. Now, these portions of the Book of Mormon were written before Malachi was written. This must mean that Nephi (with the brass plates) and Malachi (using Old Testament records) had before them the writings of Zenos and they paraphrased them in the things they were writing" (McConkie, *Doctrines of the Restoration*, 274).

What does it mean that the righteous will be "saved . . . by fire"? (22:17) "Because the wicked will be destroyed by fire at the Second Coming, this verse might seem better worded if it said that the righteous are saved 'from' the fire, rather than 'by' the fire. Another verse of scriptures lends understanding to this idea. At the time of the flood, Noah and his family, in similar language are not saved 'from' the water but 'by' the water (see 1 Peter 3:20). At the time of both events the world was and will be completely cleansed of wickedness—once by water and once by fire. At the first cleansing the earth experienced a baptism of water and at the second cleansing a confirmation of spirit by fire" (Garner, *Search These Things Diligently*, 42).

What is the significance of Moses's prophecy that the Lord would raise up a prophet like unto him? (22:20) "This may well be the most often-quoted messianic prophecy in scripture. It was first uttered by Moses to the children of Israel (Deuteronomy

18:15–19). Nephi quoted it to his people, Peter quoted it in his great discourse on the grounds of Herod's temple (Acts 3:22–23), Christ quoted it to the nation of the Nephites (3 Nephi 21:11), Stephen quoted it while transfigured before the Sanhedrin (Acts 7:37), Moroni quoted it to Joseph Smith (Joseph Smith–History 1:40), and we find it referred to in the revelation given as a preface to the Doctrine and Covenants (D&C 1:14)" (McConkie and Millet, *Doctrinal Commentary*, 1:176).

Why do the righteous not need to fear the future? (22:22) "We need not fear the future. We have every reason to rejoice and little reason to fear. If we follow the promptings of the Spirit, we will be safe, whatever the future holds. We will be shown what to do" (Packer, "Cloven Tongues of Fire," 8).

What are Nephi's last warnings to us? (22:23) "Remember 1 Nephi ends with four things we should never look for. The first thing is gain, the second is power, the third is popularity, and the fourth is the lusts of the flesh. . . . Those are the things, and they all go together. And those are the things everyone is looking for" (Nibley, *Eloquent Witness*, 170).

1 Nephi 22:24–31. The Holy One of Israel (Jesus Christ) Will Lead the Righteous

What is meant by the righteous being compared to "calves of the stall"? (22:24) President Joseph Fielding Smith taught that "Children shall grow up 'as calves of the stall' unto righteousness, that is without sin or the temptations which are so prevalent today" (*The Way to Perfection*, 299).

"Contemplate the difference between a calf that is raised out on the range or in the mountains and one that is raised in a barn. The calf on the range is subject to all the forces of nature: inclement weather, predatory animals, and occasional scarcity of food and water. On the other hand, the calf raised in the barn or in a stall is protected from poor weather and predatory animals. Likewise, food and water are regularly provided. Nephi taught that 'the time cometh speedily that the righteous must be led up as calves

like unto me; him shall ye hear in all things whatsoever he shall say unto you. And it shall come to pass that all those who will not hear that prophet shall be cut off from among the people.

21 And now I, Nephi, declare unto you, that this prophet of whom Moses spake was the Holy One of Israel; wherefore, he shall execute judgment in righteousness.

22 And the righteous need not fear, for they are those who shall not be confounded. But it is the kingdom of the devil, which shall be built up among the children of men, which kingdom is established among them which are in the flesh—

23 For the time speedily shall come that all churches which are built up to get gain, and all those who are built up to get power over the flesh, and those who are built up to become popular in the eyes of the world, and those who seek the lusts of the flesh and the things of the world, and to do all manner of iniquity; yea, in fine, all those who belong to the kingdom of the devil are they who need fear, and tremble, and quake; they are those who must be brought low in the dust; they are those who must be consumed as stubble; and this is according to the words of the prophet.

24 And the time cometh speedily that the righteous must be led up as calves of the stall, and the Holy One of Israel must reign in dominion, and might, and power, and great glory.

25 And he gathereth his children from the four quarters of the earth; and he numbereth his sheep, and they know him; and there shall be one fold and one shepherd; and he shall feed his sheep, and in him they shall find pasture.

26 And because of the righteousness of his people, Satan has no power; wherefore, he cannot be loosed for the space of many years; for he hath no power over the hearts of the people, for they dwell in righteousness, and the Holy One of Israel reigneth.

27 And now behold, I, Nephi, say unto you that all these things must come according to the flesh.

28 But, behold, all nations, kindreds, tongues, and people shall dwell safely in the Holy One of Israel if it so be that they will repent.

29 And now I, Nephi, make an end; for I durst not speak further as yet concerning these things.

30 Wherefore, my brethren, I would that ye should consider that the things which have been written upon the plates of brass are true; and they testify that a man must be obedient to the commandments of God.

31 Wherefore, ye need not suppose that I and my father are the only ones that have testified, and also taught them. Wherefore, if ye shall be obedient to the commandments, and endure to the end, ye shall be saved at the last day. And thus it is. Amen.

of the stall' (1 Nephi 22:24)" (*Book of Mormon Student Manual* (2009), 47).

How will Satan come to have "no power"? (22:26) President George Q. Cannon taught: "Satan will be bound by the power of God; but he will be bound also by the determination of the people of God not to listen to him, not to be governed by him. The Lord will not bind him and take his power from the earth while there are men and women willing to be governed by him. That is contrary to the plan of salvation. To deprive men of their agency is contrary to the purposes of God. . . . If Satan, therefore, has power with man, it is because man yields to his influence" (as cited in Burton, *We Believe*, 56). ⊕

Why does Nephi emphasize repentance so specifically to those who desire to dwell with the Holy One of Israel? (22:28) President Thomas S. Monson assured us: "If any of you has stumbled in your journey, I want you to understand without any question whatsoever that there is a way back. The process is called repentance. Our Savior gave His life to provide you and me that blessed gift. Despite the fact that the repentance path is not easy, the promises are real" ("Dare to Stand Alone," 62).

What was one of Nephi's overall messages in his first book? (22:30–31) It was choosing to obey God and keep His commandments. Joseph F. Smith wrote: "Obedience must be voluntary; it must not be forced; there must be no coercion. Men must not be constrained against their will to obey the will of God; they must obey it because they know it to be right, because they desire to do it, and because it is their pleasure to do it. God delights in the willing heart" (*Gospel Doctrine*, 65).

THE SECOND BOOK OF NEPHI

Introduction

Laman and Lemuel continue their incessant murmuring and again seek to take Nephi's life (2 Nephi 5:4–5). The Lord warns Nephi to separate from his brethren. Nephi leads one group, and the others follow Laman. The groups become known as the Nephites and the Lamanites. Second Nephi contains Lehi's last teachings to his family. It also includes teachings and prophecies of Nephi and his brother Jacob. They were righteous men who taught their people to believe in and follow Christ's teachings. Nephi and Jacob often quoted the words of Isaiah from the brass plates to help their people understand God's purposes and how their arrival in the promised land fulfilled prophecy. The book of 2 Nephi covers the period from about 588 B.C. to about 545 B.C.

"From a literary point of view, we may look upon Second Nephi as the second and last installment of Nephi's 'Memoirs'" (Sperry, *Book of Mormon Compendium*, 144).

What can we expect to learn from 2 Nephi? "Second Nephi is one of the greatest doctrinal books in the canon of scripture. No book within the covers of the Bible . . . can rival it for breadth or purity of doctrine. . . . Standing alone, this book is more than sufficient to justify the testimony that we have been commissioned to bear—among every nation, kindred, tongue, and people—of the restoration of the gospel and the divine mission of the Prophet Joseph Smith" (McConkie and Millet, *Doctrinal Commentary*, 1:181–82).

The superscription to 2 Nephi, which appears just under the title of the book, was part of the ancient record translated by the Prophet Joseph Smith and dictated by him to his scribe (see also, for example, 1 Nephi, Mosiah 9, and Alma 5).

Distinct from the superscription is the chapter summary, which is presented in italics between the chapter number and the beginning of the scriptural text. Chapter summaries, originally added in the 1920 edition of the Book of Mormon, give the reader an overview of what each chapter contains.

2 Nephi 1:1–9. Lehi Prophesies That the Faithful Will Possess the Promised Land

Why did Lehi remind his children "how great things the Lord had done for them"? (1:1) What are some of the great things the Lord had done for Lehi's family? Why do you think it would be important for Lehi's loved ones to remember what the Lord had done for them? What great things has the Lord done for you?

An account of the death of Lehi. Nephi's brethren rebel against him. The Lord warns Nephi to depart into the wilderness. His journeyings in the wilderness, and so forth.

CHAPTER 1

Lehi prophesies of a land of liberty—His seed will be scattered and smitten if they reject the Holy One of Israel—He exhorts his sons to put on the armor of righteousness. About 588–570 B.C.

1 And now it came to pass that after I, Nephi, had made an end of teaching my brethren, our father, Lehi, also spake many things unto them, and rehearsed unto them, how great things the Lord had done for them in bringing them out of the land of Jerusalem.

2 And he spake unto them concerning their rebellions upon the waters, and the mercies of God in sparing their lives, that they were not swallowed up in the sea.

3 And he also spake unto them concerning the land of promise, which they had obtained—how merciful the Lord had been in warning us that we should flee out of the land of Jerusalem.

4 For, behold, said he, I have seen a vision, in which I know that Jerusalem is destroyed; and had we remained in Jerusalem we should also have perished.

5 But, said he, notwithstanding our afflictions, we have obtained a land of promise, a land which is choice above all other lands; a land which the Lord God hath covenanted with me should be a land for the inheritance of my seed. Yea, the Lord hath covenanted this land unto me, and to my children forever, and also all those who should be led out of other countries by the hand of the Lord.

6 Wherefore, I, Lehi, prophesy according to the workings of the Spirit which is in me, that there shall none come into this land save they shall be brought by the hand of the Lord.

7 Wherefore, this land is consecrated unto him whom he shall bring. And if it so be that they shall serve him according to the commandments which he hath given, it shall be a land of liberty unto them; wherefore, they shall never be brought down into captivity; if so, it shall be because of iniquity; for if iniquity shall abound cursed shall be the land for their sakes, but unto the righteous it shall be blessed forever.

8 And behold, it is wisdom that this land should be kept as yet from the knowledge of other nations; for behold, many nations would overrun the land, that there would be no place for an inheritance.

Why does Nephi's account shift from third person to first? (1:3) Nephi's shift from third person to first person is explained by S. Kent Brown: "This account, using Lehi's own words, is clearly a direct quotation from his record. Written from the first person, it is doubtless part of what Nephi referred to when he said that Lehi's record contained 'many things which he prophesied and spake unto his children' (1 Nephi 1:16)" ("Nephi's Use of Lehi's Record," 12).

Nephi's quotation of his father's last words to his family extends to the end of 2 Nephi 3.

What makes the land of America "choice above all other lands"? (1:5) One reason the promised land is considered "choice above all other lands" is that "Zion (the New Jerusalem) will be built upon the American continent" (Articles of Faith 1:10; see also 3 Nephi 21; Ether 13). Another reason is that the Lord would raise up there a mighty nation in the last days. President Gordon B. Hinckley testified: "I marvel at the miracle of America, the land which the God of Heaven long ago declared to be a land choice above all other lands. . . . God bless America, for she is His creation" (*Teachings of Gordon B. Hinckley*, 9–10). ●

What happens to a land that has been consecrated by God? (1:7) There are two very interesting meanings to the word *consecrated*: to be "separated from a common to a sacred use" or "devoted or dedicated to the service and worship of God" (Webster, *American Dictionary*). President Ezra Taft Benson said that America "was to be the Lord's latter-day base of operations for His restored church" ("Our Divine Constitution," 4).

Why wasn't this land of promise overrun by many nations? (1:8) "Columbus's courageous discovery of America at the close of the fifteenth century has compelled the generous and just admiration of the world. The reader of the Book of Mormon is aware that Columbus was directed in his enterprise by the Spirit of God (see 1 Nephi 13:12), as he himself attested. As Columbus was destined in the providence of God to establish the union between the Old and the New worlds, others by that same providence were prohibited from doing so.... The heavens have their timetable and it is not for man to hurry the season of harvest.

"Had the knowledge of the Americas been made known even a century earlier, the religion transplanted to the Western World would have been that of the church of Europe at its lowest stage of decadence. ... with its obsession for gold, silver, silks, scarlets. ... Indeed, it was to escape the chains of bondage and the darkness of religious oppression that people of spiritual nobility emigrated to the new land" (McConkie and Millet, *Doctrinal Commentary*, 1:185).

2 Nephi 1:10–13. Lehi Prophesies of Wickedness and Destruction in the Promised Land

What happens when people living in a land of promise rebel against God? (1:10–12) "The great Book of Mormon societies experienced high levels of civilization and prospered abundantly.... They had many prophets, great revelations, experienced many years of a near-perfect society, and received a lengthy personal visit from the resurrected Lord. But in time they allowed man's wisdom to replace God's revelations and greed to replace love.... Their experience stands as a significant warning of future woes to the nations of the Americas, for the covenant is as much to all of us today as it was to them" (Parrish, "Lehi and the Covenant of the Promised Land," 42). ◉

Why did Lehi urge Laman and Lemuel to remember his words? (1:12) "If we pay close attention to the uses of the word *remember* in the holy scriptures, we will recognize that remembering in the way God intends is a fundamental and saving principle of the gospel. This is so because prophetic admonitions to remember

9 Wherefore, I, Lehi, have obtained a promise, that inasmuch as those whom the Lord God shall bring out of the land of Jerusalem shall keep his commandments, they shall prosper upon the face of this land; and they shall be kept from all other nations, that they may possess this land unto themselves. And if it so be that they shall keep his commandments they shall be blessed upon the face of this land, and there shall be none to molest them, nor to take away the land of their inheritance; and they shall dwell safely forever.

10 But behold, when the time cometh that they shall dwindle in unbelief, after they have received so great blessings from the hand of the Lord—having a knowledge of the creation of the earth, and all men, knowing the great and marvelous works of the Lord from the creation of the world; having power given them to do all things by faith; having all the commandments from the beginning, and having been brought by his infinite goodness into this precious land of promise—behold, I say, if the day shall come that they will reject the Holy One of Israel, the true Messiah, their Redeemer and their God, behold, the judgments of him that is just shall rest upon them.

11 Yea, he will bring other nations unto them, and he will give unto them power, and he will take away from them the lands of their possessions, and he will cause them to be scattered and smitten.

12 Yea, as one generation passeth to another there shall be bloodsheds, and great visitations among them; wherefore, my sons, I would that ye would remember; yea, I would that ye would hearken unto my words.

13 O that ye would awake; awake from a deep sleep, yea, even from the sleep of hell, and shake off the awful chains by which ye are bound, which are the chains which bind the children of men, that they are carried away captive down to the eternal gulf of misery and woe.

14 Awake! and arise from the dust, and hear the words of a trembling parent, whose limbs ye must soon lay down in the cold and silent grave, from whence no traveler can return; a few more days and I go the way of all the earth.

15 But behold, the Lord hath redeemed my soul from hell; I have beheld his glory, and I am encircled about eternally in the arms of his love.

16 And I desire that ye should remember to observe the statutes and the judgments of the Lord; behold, this hath been the anxiety of my soul from the beginning.

17 My heart hath been weighed down with sorrow from time to time, for I have feared, lest for the hardness of your hearts the Lord your God should come out in the fulness of his wrath upon you, that ye be cut off and destroyed forever;

are frequently calls to action: to listen, to see, to do, to obey, to repent [see 2 Nephi 1:12; Mosiah 6:3; Helaman 5:14]. When we remember in God's way, we overcome our human tendency simply to gird for the battle of life and actually engage in the battle itself, doing all in our power to resist temptation and avoid sinning" (Jensen, "Remember and Perish Not," 36).

What is "the sleep of hell"? (1:13) "Physical sleep . . . symbolizes a type of spiritual darkness. Anticipating his eldest sons' problems, Lehi challenges them (and their posterity) to 'awake from a deep sleep, yea, even from the sleep of hell' (2 Nephi 1:13)" (Rust, *Feasting on the Word*, 183).

2 Nephi 1:14–20. Lehi Shares His Testimony with His Children

Does Lehi's language in describing his impending death echo the language of Job? (1:14) "In an attempt to show that Joseph Smith was not the translator of the Book of Mormon, Book of Mormon critics attribute Father Lehi's words in 2 Nephi 1:14 to William Shakespeare. (Lehi lived about 2,100 years before Shakespeare was born.) The critics' reference is to *Hamlet*, Act 3, Scene 1, Lines 79–80: 'But that the dread of something after death, The undiscovered country from whose bourn no traveller returns.' These critics overlook the fact that a similar statement was made by Job. Historian B. H. Roberts suggests that the book of Job could have 'furnished the complete thought and even largely the phraseology to both Lehi and Shakespeare.' The scriptures in Job say, 'Are not my days few? Cease then, and let me alone, that I may take comfort a little, Before I go whence I shall not return, even to the land of darkness and the shadow of death. . . . When a few years are come, then I shall go the way whence I shall not return' (Job 10:20–21; Job 16:22)" (Black, *400 Questions and Answers About the Book of Mormon*, 87–88). ⊕

What are statutes and judgments? (1:16–20) "A statute is a legislative enactment; any authoritatively declared rule, ordinance, decree or law. A judgment may be a sentence pronounced by God as the Supreme Judge" (Reynolds and Sjodahl, *Commentary on the Book of Mormon*, 1:238).

In their simplest form, statutes and judgments refer to God's commandments with the associated punishments or blessings. Later, Nephi tells that his people "did observe to keep the judgments, and the statutes, and the commandments of the Lord" (2 Nephi 5:10).

How would you explain the depth of Lehi's feelings? (1:17–18) "Lehi alludes to times of serious sorrow caused by contemplating his wayward children. While they surely must have understood to some degree the grief they caused Lehi, it is still surprising that Lehi so vulnerably exposes the depths of his fears for them. This is not simply a sermon, but a baring of the soul—a glimpse into the anguished heart of a loving father struggling to raise all of his children in righteousness" (Gardner, *Second Witness*, 2:29). ●

2 Nephi 1:21–29. Lehi Counsels His Sons to Be Righteous Men Who Follow Nephi's Example

What does it mean to "arise from the dust"? (1:21) Elder David A. Bednar taught: "To arise is to come alive, to awaken to things of righteousness through individual conversion and preparation—all of which precedes making a distinctive difference in the lives of others" ("Arise and Shine Forth"). ●

Will a soul (or spirit) really be eternally destroyed? (1:22) "Every soul born into this world shall receive the resurrection and immortality and shall endure forever. Destruction does not mean, then, annihilation. When the Lord says they shall be destroyed, he means that they shall be banished from his presence, that they shall be cut off from the presence of light and truth, and shall not have the privilege of gaining this exaltation; and that is destruction" (Smith, *Doctrines of Salvation*, 2:228).

Why were Laman and Lemuel so resistant to Nephi's words when his only concern was for their good? (1:24–25) Lehi tried to explain that Nephi sought not for power and authority but "[their] own eternal welfare" (verse 25). Still, ancient Israel's long tradition of the birthright and the firstborn was obviously hard for the eldest sons to shake (see Bible Dictionary, "Birthright," 608).

18 Or, that a cursing should come upon you for the space of many generations; and ye are visited by sword, and by famine, and are hated, and are led according to the will and captivity of the devil.

19 O my sons, that these things might not come upon you, but that ye might be a choice and a favored people of the Lord. But behold, his will be done; for his ways are righteousness forever.

20 And he hath said that: Inasmuch as ye shall keep my commandments ye shall prosper in the land; but inasmuch as ye will not keep my commandments ye shall be cut off from my presence.

21 And now that my soul might have joy in you, and that my heart might leave this world with gladness because of you, that I might not be brought down with grief and sorrow to the grave, arise from the dust, my sons, and be men, and be determined in one mind and in one heart, united in all things, that ye may not come down into captivity;

22 That ye may not be cursed with a sore cursing; and also, that ye may not incur the displeasure of a just God upon you, unto the destruction, yea, the eternal destruction of both soul and body.

23 Awake, my sons; put on the armor of righteousness. Shake off the chains with which ye are bound, and come forth out of obscurity, and arise from the dust.

24 Rebel no more against your brother, whose views have been glorious, and who hath kept the commandments from the time that we left Jerusalem; and who hath been an instrument in the hands of God, in bringing us forth into the land of promise; for were it not for him, we must have perished with hunger in the wilderness; nevertheless, ye sought to take away his life; yea, and he hath suffered much sorrow because of you.

25 And I exceedingly fear and tremble because of you, lest he shall suffer again; for behold, ye have accused him that he sought power and authority over you; but I know that he hath not sought for power nor authority over you, but he hath sought the glory of God, and your own eternal welfare.

26 And ye have murmured because he hath been plain unto you. Ye say that he hath used sharpness; ye say that he hath been angry with you; but behold, his sharpness was the sharpness of the power of the word of God, which was in him; and that which ye call anger was the truth, according to that which is in God, which he could not restrain, manifesting boldly concerning your iniquities.

27 And it must needs be that the power of God must be with him, even unto his commanding you that ye must obey. But behold, it was not he, but it was the Spirit of the Lord which was in him, which opened his mouth to utterance that he could not shut it.

28 And now my son, Laman, and also Lemuel and Sam, and also my sons who are the sons of Ishmael, behold, if ye will hearken unto the voice of Nephi ye shall not perish. And if ye will hearken unto him I leave unto you a blessing, yea, even my first blessing.

29 But if ye will not hearken unto him I take away my first blessing, yea, even my blessing, and it shall rest upon him.

30 And now, Zoram, I speak unto you: Behold, thou art the servant of Laban; nevertheless, thou hast been brought out of the land of Jerusalem, and I know that thou art a true friend unto my son, Nephi, forever.

31 Wherefore, because thou hast been faithful thy seed shall be blessed with his seed, that they dwell in prosperity long upon the face of this land; and nothing, save it shall be iniquity among them, shall harm or disturb

What was Lehi's "first blessing"? (1:28–29) Verse 28 marks the beginning of the patriarchal blessings Lehi gave to his sons, which continue through 2 Nephi 4:11. According to the context, Lehi's first blessing was that he and his seed had "obtained a land of promise, a land which is choice above all other lands" and if they "shall keep [God's] commandments, they shall prosper upon the face of this land" (2 Nephi 1:5, 9, 31–32). ⊕

2 Nephi 1:30–32. Lehi Speaks to Zoram

Why does Lehi give Zoram, the servant of Laban, a patriarchal blessing? (1:30–32) "We do not know the ethnic background or bloodline of Zoram, the true friend of Nephi. Being a servant to Laban suggests he was not of the blood of Israel. Regardless, as patriarch of Joseph's branch of Israel, Lehi extends all the blessings of the Lord to this faithful man and to his seed. If he were not of the house of Israel, he was adopted into it. These blessings were to come through the family unit of Nephi (another suggestion that he was not of the blood of Israel), but were conditional upon their keeping the commandments of the Lord" (Nyman, *I, Nephi, Wrote This Record*, 1:379).

their prosperity upon the face of this land forever.

32 Wherefore, if ye shall keep the commandments of the Lord, the Lord hath consecrated this land for the security of thy seed with the seed of my son.

CHAPTER 2

Redemption comes through the Holy Messiah— Freedom of choice (agency) is essential to existence and progression—Adam fell that men might be—Men are free to choose liberty and eternal life. About 588–570 B.C.

1 And now, Jacob, I speak unto you: Thou art my firstborn in the days of my tribulation in the wilderness. And behold, in thy childhood thou hast suffered afflictions and much sorrow, because of the rudeness of thy brethren.

2 Nevertheless, Jacob, my firstborn in the wilderness, thou knowest the greatness of God; and he shall consecrate thine afflictions for thy gain.

3 Wherefore, thy soul shall be blessed, and thou shalt dwell safely with thy brother, Nephi; and thy days shall be spent in the service of thy God. Wherefore, I know that thou art redeemed, because of the righteousness of thy Redeemer; for thou hast beheld that in the fulness of time he cometh to bring salvation unto men.

4 And thou hast beheld in thy youth his glory; wherefore, thou art blessed even as they unto whom he shall minister in the flesh; for the Spirit is the same, yesterday, today, and forever. And the way is prepared from the fall of man, and salvation is free.

2 Nephi 2:1–4. Lehi Speaks to His Son Jacob

What does it mean to "consecrate" our afflictions for our gain? (2:2) "It is in our extremities that we become acquainted with God, which is life's greatest blessing. The soul of the righteous is sanctified through suffering" (McConkie and Millet, *Doctrinal Commentary*, 1:190). ●

When was this time that Christ was to bring salvation? (2:3) "The expression used here has reference to the day of Christ's mortal ministry, usually designated as the meridian of time" (McConkie and Millet, *Doctrinal Commentary*, 1:191). ●

In what way is salvation free? (2:4) "Salvation, which is exaltation, which is eternal life, is free. It is not something for which we can barter, nor is it something that may be purchased with money. Neither is it, in the strictest sense, something that may be *earned*. More correctly, salvation is a gift, a gift most precious, something gloriously transcendent that may only be inherited (D&C 6:13; 14:7). . . .

"When the prophets who lived before the coming of our Lord in the flesh spoke of salvation being free, they were in effect declaring the same doctrine that would come from the apostles and prophets after the ministry of Jesus that we are saved by the grace of Christ. That is to say, free salvation is salvation by grace" (Millet, *Grace Works*, 13).

5 And men are instructed sufficiently that they know good from evil. And the law is given unto men. And by the law no flesh is justified; or, by the law men are cut off. Yea, by the temporal law they were cut off; and also, by the spiritual law they perish from that which is good, and become miserable forever.

6 Wherefore, redemption cometh in and through the Holy Messiah; for he is full of grace and truth.

7 Behold, he offereth himself a sacrifice for sin, to answer the ends of the law, unto all those who have a broken heart and a contrite spirit; and unto none else can the ends of the law be answered.

8 Wherefore, how great the importance to make these things known unto the inhabitants of the earth, that they may know that there is no flesh that can dwell in the presence of God, save it be through the merits, and mercy, and grace of the Holy Messiah, who layeth down his life according to the flesh, and taketh it again by the power of the Spirit, that he may bring to pass the resurrection of the dead, being the first that should rise.

9 Wherefore, he is the firstfruits unto God, inasmuch as he shall make intercession for all the children of men; and they that believe in him shall be saved.

2 Nephi 2:5–10. All People Can Be Saved through the Atonement of Jesus Christ

What is the most important message we can take to the world? (2:5–10) "When all is said and done, when all of history is examined, when the deepest depths of the human mind have been explored, nothing is so wonderful, so majestic, so tremendous as this act of grace when the Son of the Almighty . . . [who] gave His life in ignomy and pain so that all of the sons and daughters of God of all generations of time, every one of whom must die, might walk again and live eternally. He did for us what none of us could do for ourselves" (Hinckley, "The Wonderous and True Story of Christmas," 4).

"The 'Messiah theme' is prevalent in the teachings of Lehi to his children (see 2 Nephi 1–4). . . . In his specific instructions to Jacob (chapter 2), Lehi reviewed for his spiritually alert son the process of redemption that 'cometh in and through the Holy Messiah [who] is full of grace and truth' (v. 6). These instructions about the nature of sin, the Fall, opposition in all things, the Law, righteousness, happiness, and agency comprise one of the greatest discourses on the calling of the Messiah in holy writ. Indeed, Lehi's sermon is surpassed only by Jacob's own discourse in 2 Nephi 9" (Van Orden, "Law of Witnesses," 310–11).

What are the "ends of the law"? (2:7) "At one end of the law is mercy in all its compassionate splendor, at the other is justice in all its stern reality. The Atonement is the one act in recorded history that demonstrated the maximum mercy, yet never robbed justice of one ounce of payment. The Atonement ran the full gamut of the law, end to end, mercy to justice. It was all-inclusive, infinite, so to speak, in its compliance with the law" (Callister, *Infinite Atonement*, 314).

What does the word *intercession* mean? (2:9–10) Intercession is an "interposition between parties at variance, with a view to reconciliation" (Webster, *American Dictionary*). In other words, the Savior intercedes with God on behalf of God's children. ⊕

2 Nephi 2:11–16. There Must Be Opposition in All Things

Why was it necessary to have "opposition in all things"? (2:11–13) "When man and beast were created, an opposition was set up—the forbidden fruit in opposition to the tree of life, the one being sweet and the other bitter. Man was thus left as a free agent to act for himself by choosing one or the other (2:15, 16)" (Sperry, *Book of Mormon Compendium*, 149). ☉

What did Lehi mean by "a compound in one" and how might it affect "an opposition in all things"? (2:11–12) President Dallin H. Oaks explained: "Without opposition in all things, we could not achieve righteousness. All things would be a 'compound in one,' a mixture—no distinction between wickedness and holiness. In that state of innocence, mankind would be 'having no joy, for they knew no misery; doing no good, for they knew no sin' (2 Nephi 2:23)" ("Free Agency and Freedom," 8). Such a condition would have destroyed "the wisdom of God and his eternal purposes" (2 Nephi 2:12).

Why did Lehi explain his doctrine regarding "opposition in all things" in such detail? (2:13) "The law of opposites creates a condition in which there are 'things . . . to act [or] be acted upon.'

"Lehi's essential teaching is not simply that opposites exist but that they function to create situations in which 'things' either act or are acted upon. While we typically concentrate on the opposed conditions, it is really this 'acting' that is the point of Lehi's argument. The opposites merely provide the field in which 'acting upon' occurs" (Gardner, *Second Witness*, 44).

10 And because of the intercession for all, all men come unto God; wherefore, they stand in the presence of him, to be judged of him according to the truth and holiness which is in him. Wherefore, the ends of the law which the Holy One hath given, unto the inflicting of the punishment which is affixed, which punishment that is affixed is in opposition to that of the happiness which is affixed, to answer the ends of the atonement—

11 For it must needs be, that there is an opposition in all things. If not so, my firstborn in the wilderness, righteousness could not be brought to pass, neither wickedness, neither holiness nor misery, neither good nor bad. Wherefore, all things must needs be a compound in one; wherefore, if it should be one body it must needs remain as dead, having no life neither death, nor corruption nor incorruption, happiness nor misery, neither sense nor insensibility.

12 Wherefore, it must needs have been created for a thing of naught; wherefore there would have been no purpose in the end of its creation. Wherefore, this thing must needs destroy the wisdom of God and his eternal purposes, and also the power, and the mercy, and the justice of God.

13 And if ye shall say there is no law, ye shall also say there is no sin. If ye shall say there is no sin, ye shall also say there is no righteousness. And if there be no righteousness there be no happiness. And if there be no righteousness nor happiness there be no punishment nor misery. And if these things are not there is no God. And if there is no God we are not, neither the earth; for there could have been no creation of things, neither to act nor to be acted upon; wherefore, all things must have vanished away.

14 And now, my sons, I speak unto you these things for your profit and learning; for there is a God, and he hath created all things, both the heavens and the earth, and all things that in them are, both things to act and things to be acted upon.

15 And to bring about his eternal purposes in the end of man, after he had created our first parents, and the beasts of the field and the fowls of the air, and in fine, all things which are created, it must needs be that there was an opposition; even the forbidden fruit in opposition to the tree of life; the one being sweet and the other bitter.

16 Wherefore, the Lord God gave unto man that he should act for himself. Wherefore, man could not act for himself save it should be that he was enticed by the one or the other.

17 And I, Lehi, according to the things which I have read, must needs suppose that an angel of God, according to that which is written, had fallen from heaven; wherefore, he became a devil, having sought that which was evil before God.

18 And because he had fallen from heaven, and had become miserable forever, he sought also the misery of all mankind. Wherefore, he said unto Eve, yea, even that old serpent, who is the devil, who is the father of all lies, wherefore he said: Partake of the forbidden fruit, and ye shall not die, but ye shall be as God, knowing good and evil.

19 And after Adam and Eve had partaken of the forbidden fruit they were driven out of the garden of Eden, to till the earth.

20 And they have brought forth children; yea, even the family of all the earth.

Why couldn't man "act for himself" without opposition? (2:15–16) "One of the principal purposes of mortality is for man to have the opportunity to learn the difference between right and wrong and between good and evil. This knowledge is necessary to gain the spiritual maturity to make righteous choices. . . . We came to mortal life to encounter resistance. It is part of the plan for our eternal progress. Without temptation, sickness, pain, and sorrow, there could be no goodness, virtue, appreciation for well-being, or joy. The law of opposition makes freedom of choice possible" (*Teachings of Howard W. Hunter*, 77–78). ❂

2 Nephi 2:17–26. Adam Fell That Men Might Be

What is the meaning of the word *devil*? (2:17) "This word [devil] is from the Greek 'diabolos,' which means 'calumniator,' or 'accuser.' Here it stands for the Hebrew 'satan,' which means an enemy, an adversary. Cast out of heaven, the enemy became an accuser, he became satan, yea, even the devil, the father of lies, to deceive and to blind men (Mosiah 4:4)" (Reynolds and Sjodahl, *Commentary on the Book of Mormon*, 1:247).

What tactic did Satan use when tempting Eve? (2:18) "Deceit is often most effective when blended with truth" (McConkie and Millet, *Doctrinal Commentary*, 1:197). President Brigham Young said: "The devil had truth in his mouth as well as lies when he came to Mother Eve. . . . She did eat, her eyes were opened, and she saw good and evil" (in *Journal of Discourses*, 12:70).

What is a deeper meaning to the Eden story? (2:19) "The events associated with the Garden of Eden make it the archetype of our temples. Here Adam received the priesthood, here Adam and Eve walked and talked with God; here our first parents were eternally married by God himself; here they learned of the tree of good and evil and of the tree of life; here they were taught the law of sacrifice and clothed in garments of skin; and from here they ventured into the lone and dreary world that they and their posterity might prove themselves worthy to return again to that divine presence" (McConkie, *Gospel Symbolism*, 258).

How does one explain the ages attributed to the ancient patriarchs (or prophets)? (2:21) "One can hardly read the ages attributed to the ancient patriarchs without a sense of wonder. Methuselah, we are told, lived nine hundred and sixty-nine years (Moses 8:7), Adam, nine hundred and thirty years (Moses 6:12), Noah lived to be nine hundred and fifty years (Genesis 9:29), and so on. The question is frequently asked whether the ancient year was of the same length as in our modern calendar. Lehi seemed to affirm such to be the case. Their days were 'prolonged' and 'their time was lengthened,' by the command of God, we are told" (McConkie and Millet, *Doctrinal Commentary*, 1:198–99). ●

What is the difference between a transgression and a sin? (2:22) "[The] contrast between a sin and a transgression reminds us of the careful wording in the second article of faith: 'We believe that men will be punished for their own sins, and not for Adam's transgression' (italics added). It also echoes a familiar distinction in the law. Some acts, like murder, are crimes because they are inherently wrong. Other acts, like operating without a license, are crimes only because they are legally prohibited. Under these distinctions, the act that produced the Fall was not a sin—inherently wrong—but a transgression—wrong because it was formally prohibited. These words . . . seems meaningful in the circumstances of the Fall" (Oaks, "'Great Plan of Happiness,'" 73).

What is meant by a "state of innocence"? (2:23) "He [Adam] had knowledge, of course. He could speak. He could converse. There were many things he could be taught and was taught; but under the conditions in which he was living at that time it was impossible for him to visualize or understand the power of good and evil. He did not know what pain was. He did not know

21 And the days of the children of men were prolonged, according to the will of God, that they might repent while in the flesh; wherefore, their state became a state of probation, and their time was lengthened, according to the commandments which the Lord God gave unto the children of men. For he gave commandment that all men must repent; for he showed unto all men that they were lost, because of the transgression of their parents.

22 And now, behold, if Adam had not transgressed he would not have fallen, but he would have remained in the garden of Eden. And all things which were created must have remained in the same state in which they were after they were created; and they must have remained forever, and had no end.

23 And they would have had no children; wherefore they would have remained in a state of innocence, having no joy, for they knew no misery; doing no good, for they knew no sin.

How Would You Describe the State of Adam and Eve in Eden?

"When Adam and Eve were in the Garden of Eden, they lived in a state of innocence—meaning they only had a limited knowledge of good and evil. Lehi described their condition as follows: 'Wherefore they would have remained in a state of innocence, having no joy, for they knew no misery; doing no good, for they knew no sin' (2 Nephi 2:23).

"Suppose for a moment my wife and I invited one of you good Saints from California to drive to our home in Utah. Further suppose I asked you to drive in neutral.

"You might smile and respond, 'That's not possible.'

"What if I further replied, 'Just push the accelerator all the way to the floor—you know, as they say, "Push the pedal to the metal."'

"You might respond, 'That would make no difference. I cannot reach your destination until I put my car in gear.'

"So it was with Adam and Eve. They were in a state of spiritual neutral and could not progress toward their divine destiny until they were cast out of the garden and thus put in spiritual gear" (Callister, "Our Identity and Our Destiny").

24 But behold, all things have been done in the wisdom of him who knoweth all things.

25 Adam fell that men might be; and men are, that they might have joy.

26 And the Messiah cometh in the fulness of time, that he may redeem the children of men from the fall. And because that they are redeemed from the fall they have become free forever, knowing good from evil; to act for themselves and not to be acted upon, save it be by the punishment of the law at the great and last day, according to the commandments which God hath given.

27 Wherefore, men are free according to the flesh; and all things are given them which are expedient unto man. And they are free to choose liberty and eternal life, through the

what sorrow was; and a thousand other things that have come to us in this life that Adam did not know in the Garden of Eden and could not understand and would not have known had he remained there" (Smith, *Doctrines of Salvation*, 1:107–8). ⊕

How can men have joy in a fallen world? (2:23–26)
"Father Lehi taught that if the Fall had not taken place, Adam and Eve 'would have remained in a state of innocence, having no joy, for they knew no misery' (2 Nephi 2:23). Without the experience of opposition in mortality . . . there would be no happiness or misery (verse 11). Therefore, Father Lehi continued, after God had created all things, "to bring about his eternal purposes . . . it must needs be that there was an opposition. . . . His teaching on this part of the plan of salvation concludes with these words:

"'Behold, all things have been done in the wisdom of him who knoweth all things.

"'Adam fell that men might be; and men are, that they might have joy' (verses 24–25).

"Opposition in the form of difficult circumstances we face in mortality is also part of the plan that furthers our growth in mortality" (Oaks, "Opposition in All Things," 115). ⊕

What is the relationship between the fall of man and the Atonement of Jesus Christ? (2:25–26)
President Russell M. Nelson taught us the importance of understanding the fall of Adam in conjunction with the Atonement of Jesus Christ: "The Fall of Adam (and Eve) constituted the mortal creation and brought about the required changes in their bodies . . .

"But mortal life, glorious as it is, was never the ultimate objective of God's plan. Life and death here on planet Earth were merely means to an end—not the end for which we were sent. . . .

"The Atonement of Jesus Christ became the immortal creation. He volunteered to answer the ends of a law previously transgressed. And by the shedding of His blood, His and our physical bodies could become perfected. . . .

"The Fall required the Atonement" ("The Atonement," 33–35).

2 Nephi 2:27–30. Because of the Savior's Atonement, All Mankind Can Choose Eternal Life or Eternal Death

Why does Lehi refer to Jesus Christ as the "great Mediator"? (2:27) Elder Jeffrey R. Holland observed: "For each accountable person, transgression against eternal law has been committed, and the subsequent judgment has been passed. We, like our parents before us, have 'sinned, and come short of the glory of God' (Romans 3:23). But we have a merciful judge and a compassionate, sacrificing Mediator. They have given us time to repent and thereby alter our sentence. Our judge and our advocate are doing everything possible, within the allowable limits of justice, to give us a way out of our plight. If we truly wish to sidestep the spiritual death penalty, we may" (*Christ and the New Covenant*, 210).

How does Lehi clarify the two choices daily before each of us? (2:28–29) We are free to choose between good and evil. We may choose liberty and eternal life by following Jesus Christ or we can choose captivity and death by following Satan. What counsel did Lehi give that helps you choose eternal life rather than eternal death?

2 Nephi 3:1–3. Lehi Blesses His Son Joseph

Why is sorrow part of Heavenly Father's plan? (3:1) "Learning to endure times of disappointment, suffering, and sorrow is part of our on-the-job training. These experiences, while often difficult to bear at the time, are precisely the kinds of experiences that stretch our understanding, build our character, and increase our compassion for others" (Wirthlin, "Come What May, and Love It," 27).

great Mediator of all men, or to choose captivity and death, according to the captivity and power of the devil; for he seeketh that all men might be miserable like unto himself.

28 And now, my sons, I would that ye should look to the great Mediator, and hearken unto his great commandments; and be faithful unto his words, and choose eternal life, according to the will of his Holy Spirit;

29 And not choose eternal death, according to the will of the flesh and the evil which is therein, which giveth the spirit of the devil power to captivate, to bring you down to hell, that he may reign over you in his own kingdom.

30 I have spoken these few words unto you all, my sons, in the last days of my probation; and I have chosen the good part, according to the words of the prophet. And I have none other object save it be the everlasting welfare of your souls. Amen.

CHAPTER 3

Joseph in Egypt saw the Nephites in vision—He prophesied of Joseph Smith, the latter-day seer; of Moses, who would deliver Israel; and of the coming forth of the Book of Mormon. About 588–570 B.C.

1 And now I speak unto you, Joseph, my last-born. Thou wast born in the wilderness of mine afflictions; yea, in the days of my greatest sorrow did thy mother bear thee.

2 And may the Lord consecrate also unto thee this land, which is a most precious land, for thine inheritance and the inheritance of thy seed with thy brethren, for thy security forever, if it so be that ye shall keep the commandments of the Holy One of Israel.

3 And now, Joseph, my last-born, whom I have brought out of the wilderness of mine afflictions, may the Lord bless thee forever, for thy seed shall not utterly be destroyed.

4 For behold, thou art the fruit of my loins; and I am a descendant of Joseph who was carried captive into Egypt. And great were the covenants of the Lord which he made unto Joseph.

5 Wherefore, Joseph truly saw our day. And he obtained a promise of the Lord, that out of the fruit of his loins the Lord God would raise up a righteous branch unto the house of Israel; not the Messiah, but a branch which was to be broken off, nevertheless, to be remembered in the covenants of the Lord that the Messiah should be made manifest unto them in the latter days, in the spirit of power, unto the bringing of them out of darkness unto light—yea, out of hidden darkness and out of captivity unto freedom.

6 For Joseph truly testified, saying: A seer shall the Lord my God raise up, who shall be a choice seer unto the fruit of my loins.

How do we know that Joseph's seed was not "utterly destroyed"? (3:3) "The descendants of Joseph, the son of Lehi, were known as Nephites during much of the period covered by the Book of Mormon. However, when the Book of Mormon records the destruction of the Nephite nation (Mormon 6–8), this does not mean that all of the descendants of Joseph were destroyed. . . . That [Lehi's] promise was literally fulfilled is indicated by the Lord when he said to Joseph Smith in 1828 that the Book of Mormon had to be translated and published so that it might go forth unto the 'Josephites' (see D&C 3:17)" (Ludlow, *Companion to Your Study of the Book of Mormon*, 128–29).

2 Nephi 3:4–15. Joseph of Egypt Prophesies of a Seer Named Joseph in the Latter Days

How was Lehi related to Joseph who was sold into Egypt? (3:4) Joseph who was sold into Egypt had two sons: Ephraim and Manasseh (see Genesis 48:4–5). Lehi learned from the brass plates "a genealogy of his fathers" and "knew that he was a descendant of Joseph" (1 Nephi 5:14). Later, Alma stated that Lehi was a descendant of Manasseh (see Alma 10:3).

What evidence do we have that Joseph, who was sold into Egypt, saw the last days? (3:5) "This great prophecy is also found in the Joseph Smith Translation of Genesis 50:24–38, which contains the words uttered by Joseph on his deathbed" (Tvedtnes, "Ancient Texts," 238).

Who or what is this "righteous branch"? (3:5) "Here, Lehi explains that Joseph did not refer to the Messiah, but to some one who was to be broken off from his genealogical tree and yet to be remembered in the latter days. . . . Joseph in Egypt uses a common term when he speaks of Lehi as a branch that was to be broken off the main tree, but to be restored in the latter days by the Messiah" (Reynolds and Sjodahl, *Commentary on the Book of Mormon*, 1:252–53).

What can we learn from what Joseph of Egypt saw of Joseph Smith's latter-day work? (3:6) "Joseph of Egypt also saw in vision the work and labors of the Prophet Joseph Smith. A knowledge of Joseph Smith and his role as the great prophet of the Restoration was had by many of the ancient prophets, but to none was it known in greater detail than to his progenitor, Jacob's son Joseph. Here the latter-day Joseph was referred to as a 'choice seer' unto the tribes of Ephraim and Manasseh" (McConkie and Millet, *Doctrinal Commentary*, 1:205). ●

Prophecy in 2 Nephi 3	Possible Fulfillments
"A seer shall the Lord my God raise up, who shall be a choice seer unto the fruit of my loins" (verse 6).	The Lord said that Joseph Smith Jr. was to "be called a seer, a translator, a prophet" (D&C 21:1) and that Joseph was appointed to stand at the head of this dispensation (see D&C 110:16; 112:32).
"He shall be esteemed highly among the fruit of thy loins" (verse 7).	Millions of descendants of the Book of Mormon people recognize Joseph Smith as the prophet of the Restoration.
"He shall do a work for the fruit of thy loins . . . , which shall be of great worth unto them" (verse 7).	Many of the children of Lehi have been blessed by the light of the gospel that was restored by the Prophet Joseph Smith.
"He shall do none other work, save the work which I shall command him" (verse 8).	Joseph Smith's life focused upon doing the will of the Lord. For example, in the beginning of his ministry he was commanded to translate the Book of Mormon: "And you have a gift to translate the plates; and this is the first gift that I bestowed upon you; and I have commanded that you should pretend to no other gift until my purpose is fulfilled in this; for I will grant unto you no other gift until it is finished" (D&C 5:4).
"He shall be great like unto Moses" (verse 9).	Moses gathered Israel from Egypt to the promised land. Joseph Smith was given keys by Moses to gather Israel: "Therefore, I will raise up unto my people a man, who shall lead them like as Moses led the children of Israel" (D&C 103:16). This is one of many ways that Joseph Smith was like Moses.
"I give power to bring forth my word unto the seed of thy loins" (verse 11).	Joseph Smith translated and gave the children of Lehi the record of their ancestors (see D&C 3; 5; 10), as well as many other revelations.
"That which shall be written by the fruit of thy loins, and . . . that which shall be written by the fruit of the loins of Judah, shall grow together, unto the confounding of false doctrines" (verse 12).	The Book of Mormon and other modern revelations give plain and authoritative clarification on many principles and doctrines of the gospel recorded in the Bible (see D&C 20:8–15; 42:12).
"Out of weakness he shall be made strong" (verse 13).	A humble farm boy became the prophet of the Restoration.
"They that seek to destroy him shall be confounded" (verse 14).	As promised by the Lord (see 3 Nephi 21:10), the Prophet Joseph Smith was preserved until he had accomplished his mission (see D&C 121:16–22).
"His name shall be called after me; and it shall be after the name of his father" (verse 15).	Joseph Smith Jr., son of Joseph Smith Sr., was named after his father (see Joseph Smith—History 1:4).
"For the thing [the gospel and its ordinances], which the Lord shall bring forth by his hand, by the power of the Lord shall bring my people unto salvation" (verse 15).	It is through the restoration of the Church and the Lord's ordinances that the Prophet Joseph Smith showed us how to obtain eternal life.

(*Book of Mormon Student Manual* [2009], 56.)

7 Yea, Joseph truly said: Thus saith the Lord unto me: A choice seer will I raise up out of the fruit of thy loins; and he shall be esteemed highly among the fruit of thy loins. And unto him will I give commandment that he shall do a work for the fruit of thy loins, his brethren, which shall be of great worth unto them, even to the bringing of them to the knowledge of the covenants which I have made with thy fathers.

8 And I will give unto him a commandment that he shall do none other work, save the work which I shall command him. And I will make him great in mine eyes; for he shall do my work.

9 And he shall be great like unto Moses, whom I have said I would raise up unto you, to deliver my people, O house of Israel.

10 And Moses will I raise up, to deliver thy people out of the land of Egypt.

11 But a seer will I raise up out of the fruit of thy loins; and unto him will I give power to bring forth my word unto the seed of thy loins—and not to the bringing forth my word only, saith the Lord, but to the convincing them of my word, which shall have already gone forth among them.

12 Wherefore, the fruit of thy loins shall write; and the fruit of the loins of Judah shall write; and that which shall be written by the fruit of thy loins, and also that which shall be written by the fruit of the loins of Judah, shall grow together, unto the confounding of false doctrines and laying down of contentions, and establishing peace among the fruit of thy loins, and bringing them to the knowledge of their fathers in the latter days, and also to the knowledge of my covenants, saith the Lord.

13 And out of weakness he shall be made strong, in that day when my work shall commence among all my people, unto the

What evidence is there that Joseph Smith's latter-day work blessed the seed of Joseph of old? (3:7–8) "We praise [Joseph Smith] for his capacity to commune not only with Jehovah but also with other personages of heaven. So many visited, gave keys, and tutored that 'choice seer' raised up in the latter days (see 2 Nephi 3:6–7). When Father Smith blessed young Joseph in 1834, he declared that ancient Joseph in Egypt saw this latter-day seer. Ancient Joseph wept when he realized how the work of the Prophet Joseph would bless the earlier Joseph's numerous posterity" (*Teachings of Howard W. Hunter*, 190). ✛

In what ways was Joseph Smith "like unto Moses"? (3:8–11) "The Prophet Joseph Smith is here compared to Moses. The comparison is striking. (1) Both saw and spoke with Jehovah. (2) Both were liberators who led multitudes in exodus for the sake of liberty from oppression. (3) Both were law-givers by divine inspiration. (4) Both were prophets and seers. (5) Both performed mighty miracles. (6) Both encountered opposition, from 'friends' and enemies. (7) Both depended largely on a brother for success: Moses on Aaron; Joseph on Hyrum" (Reynolds and Sjodahl, *Commentary on the Book of Mormon*, 1:253). ✛

How will the writings of Joseph and Judah "grow together"? (3:12) Joseph's writings are in the Book of Mormon and Judah's are in the Bible. "We invite all men everywhere to read the Book of Mormon. . . . The Bible sits on the pulpit of hundreds of different religious sects. The Book of Mormon . . . verifies and clarifies the Bible. It removes stumbling blocks, it restores many plain and precious things. We testify that when used together, the Bible and the Book of Mormon confound false doctrines, lay down contentions, and establish peace (see 2 Ne. 3:12)" (*Teachings of Ezra Taft Benson*, 63). ✛

How will the enemies of the latter-day seer be "confounded"? (3:13–14) "This promise the Lord has kept, even although the Prophet Joseph suffered martyrdom. 'Confounded' means 'confused,' 'put to shame,' 'defeated.' That has always been the fate of the enemies of the servants of the Lord" (Reynolds and Sjodahl, *Commentary on the Book of Mormon*, 1:255). ⊕

How widely known is Joseph of Egypt's prophecy concerning the latter-day Joseph who the Lord would raise up? (3:15) Brother Tad R. Callister wrote of a fascinating Jewish tradition about the latter-day Joseph who would be named after his father: "The Jews have a tradition, somewhat distorted with time but nonetheless noteworthy, that in the last days (i.e., in the days when Elijah reappears), a Messiah ben Joseph will prepare the way for their Messiah. Some of the traditions hold that he will be a descendant of Joseph who was sold into Egypt, that he will be of the seed of Ephraim, that he will meet a violent death, and that he will be slain by the 'Antichrist' (i.e., those who oppose Christ's work)" (*Inevitable Apostasy and the Promised Restoration*, 460). ⊕

2 Nephi 3:16–25. Lehi Tells His Son Joseph That His Seed Will Be Preserved and Accept the Book of Mormon

Is "by the finger of mine own hand" figurative or literal? (3:17) Here Lehi compared Moses and a latter-day seer. "Lehi speaks of writing done by the finger of God when he tells of the vision the Lord had given to Joseph of Egypt: 'I will write unto him my law, by the finger of mine own hand,' no doubt referring to Moses (2 Nephi 3:17). This same image is of course found in Exodus 31:18 and Deuteronomy 9:10, which refer to 'tables of stone written with the finger of God'" (Seely, "Image of the Hand of God," 143).

Who are these verses speaking about and how far-reaching will his writings be? (3:18–19) This verse speaks of the Prophet Joseph Smith. Lehi understood from the writings of Joseph of Egypt that "eventually, a special seer would bring to pass 'much restoration unto the house of Israel, and unto the seed of thy brethren' (2 Nephi 3:24). Lehi also prophesied that the record his people kept would spread to the survivors of his

restoring thee, O house of Israel, saith the Lord.

14 And thus prophesied Joseph, saying: Behold, that seer will the Lord bless; and they that seek to destroy him shall be confounded; for this promise, which I have obtained of the Lord, of the fruit of my loins, shall be fulfilled. Behold, I am sure of the fulfilling of this promise;

15 And his name shall be called after me; and it shall be after the name of his father. And he shall be like unto me; for the thing, which the Lord shall bring forth by his hand, by the power of the Lord shall bring my people unto salvation.

16 Yea, thus prophesied Joseph: I am sure of this thing, even as I am sure of the promise of Moses; for the Lord hath said unto me, I will preserve thy seed forever.

17 And the Lord hath said: I will raise up a Moses; and I will give power unto him in a rod; and I will give judgment unto him in writing. Yet I will not loose his tongue, that he shall speak much, for I will not make him mighty in speaking. But I will write unto him my law, by the finger of mine own hand; and I will make a spokesman for him.

18 And the Lord said unto me also: I will raise up unto the fruit of thy loins; and I will make for him a spokesman. And I, behold, I will give unto him that he shall write the writing of the fruit of thy loins, unto the fruit of thy loins; and the spokesman of thy loins shall declare it.

19 And the words which he shall write shall be the words which are expedient in my wisdom should go forth unto the fruit of thy loins. And it shall be as if the fruit of thy loins had cried unto them from the dust; for I know their faith.

20 And they shall cry from the dust; yea, even repentance unto their brethren, even after many generations have gone by them. And it shall come to pass that their cry shall go, even according to the simpleness of their words.

21 Because of their faith their words shall proceed forth out of my mouth unto their brethren who are the fruit of thy loins; and the weakness of their words will I make strong in their faith, unto the remembering of my covenant which I made unto thy fathers.

22 And now, behold, my son Joseph, after this manner did my father of old prophesy.

23 Wherefore, because of this covenant thou art blessed; for thy seed shall not be destroyed, for they shall hearken unto the words of the book.

24 And there shall rise up one mighty among them, who shall do much good, both in word and in deed, being an instrument in the hands of God, with exceeding faith, to work mighty wonders, and do that thing which is great in the sight of God, unto the bringing to pass much restoration unto the house of Israel, and unto the seed of thy brethren.

25 And now, blessed art thou, Joseph. Behold, thou art little; wherefore hearken unto the words of thy brother, Nephi, and it shall be done unto thee even according to the words which I have spoken. Remember the words of thy dying father. Amen.

seed and then to all parts of the world (see 2 Nephi 3:18–21)" (Brown, "Nephi's Use of Lehi's Record," 12). ❂

Who shall cry from the dust? (3:20) The phrase "they shall cry from the dust" "refers to the Book of Mormon. It is a divine promise that, by means of this volume, although its words are simple (v. 20) and weak (v. 21) the descendants of Joseph will be converted to the covenants God made with their fathers" (Reynolds and Sjodahl, *Commentary on the Book of Mormon*, 1:256).

Who is the "mighty one" to rise among the descendants of Lehi's son, Joseph? (3:24) "Lehi recapitulates the promises made to the seed of Joseph of Egypt, emphasizing the role of the 'choice seer' [mighty one] whom we know to be the Prophet Joseph Smith—the great prophet of the Restoration" (McConkie and Millet, *Doctrinal Commentary*, 1:212).

What is the origin of the word *amen*? (3:25) "This familiar word is an adjective, meaning, 'true,' or 'faithful.' In Rev. 3:14 Christ is called, 'the Amen, the true and faithful witness'" (Reynolds and Sjodahl, *Commentary on the Book of Mormon*, 1:257). ❂

2 Nephi 4:1–2. Joseph of Egypt Prophesies concerning the Future

What makes Joseph's prophecies so remarkable? (4:1–2) "The stature of Joseph of Egypt as a prophet remains little known even to Latter-day Saints. From the text restored by Joseph Smith to the book of Genesis we learn that Joseph enjoyed the personal presence of the Lord Jehovah . . . (see JST, Genesis 50:24, 34, 36). . . . We learn that he knew of the destiny of Lehi and his family and of the destiny of Joseph Smith. The detail of the knowledge had by the ancient Joseph is remarkable" (McConkie and Millet, *Doctrinal Commentary*, 1:213). ⊕

2 Nephi 4:3–14. Lehi Blesses His Children and Dies

How did Lehi's blessing make it possible for Laman's and Lemuel's children to avoid the punishment of their parents? (4:3–9) "Lehi blessed the posterity of both Laman and Lemuel that if they came to be cursed in the future because they followed the teachings of their parents, the curse would be taken from them and 'answered upon the heads of [their] parents' (4:6). Lehi based this blessing on the doctrine that children who are brought up in the way they should go would 'not depart from it' (v. 5), but because Laman and Lemuel had not taught their children correctly, their sins will be upon their heads" (Nyman, "Come to Understanding and Learn Doctrine," 22). ⊕

CHAPTER 4

Lehi counsels and blesses his posterity—He dies and is buried—Nephi glories in the goodness of God—Nephi puts his trust in the Lord forever. About 588–570 B.C.

1 And now, I, Nephi, speak concerning the prophecies of which my father hath spoken, concerning Joseph, who was carried into Egypt.

2 For behold, he truly prophesied concerning all his seed. And the prophecies which he wrote, there are not many greater. And he prophesied concerning us, and our future generations; and they are written upon the plates of brass.

3 Wherefore, after my father had made an end of speaking concerning the prophecies of Joseph, he called the children of Laman, his sons, and his daughters, and said unto them: Behold, my sons, and my daughters, who are the sons and the daughters of my first-born, I would that ye should give ear unto my words.

4 For the Lord God hath said that: Inasmuch as ye shall keep my commandments ye shall prosper in the land; and inasmuch as ye will not keep my commandments ye shall be cut off from my presence.

5 But behold, my sons and my daughters, I cannot go down to my grave save I should leave a blessing upon you; for behold, I know that if ye are brought up in the way ye should go ye will not depart from it.

6 Wherefore, if ye are cursed, behold, I leave my blessing upon you, that the cursing may be taken from you and be answered upon the heads of your parents.

7 Wherefore, because of my blessing the Lord God will not suffer that ye shall perish;

wherefore, he will be merciful unto you and unto your seed forever.

8 And it came to pass that after my father had made an end of speaking to the sons and daughters of Laman, he caused the sons and daughters of Lemuel to be brought before him.

9 And he spake unto them, saying: Behold, my sons and my daughters, who are the sons and the daughters of my second son; behold I leave unto you the same blessing which I left unto the sons and daughters of Laman; wherefore, thou shalt not utterly be destroyed; but in the end thy seed shall be blessed.

10 And it came to pass that when my father had made an end of speaking unto them, behold, he spake unto the sons of Ishmael, yea, and even all his household.

11 And after he had made an end of speaking unto them, he spake unto Sam, saying: Blessed art thou, and thy seed; for thou shalt inherit the land like unto thy brother Nephi. And thy seed shall be numbered with his seed; and thou shalt be even like unto thy brother, and thy seed like unto his seed; and thou shalt be blessed in all thy days.

12 And it came to pass after my father, Lehi, had spoken unto all his household, according to the feelings of his heart and the Spirit of the Lord which was in him, he waxed old. And it came to pass that he died, and was buried.

13 And it came to pass that not many days after his death, Laman and Lemuel and the sons of Ishmael were angry with me because of the admonitions of the Lord.

Why do Sam's descendants appear to be combined with Nephi's? (4:11) "It appears that when he blessed Joseph with an interest in the land (2 Nephi 3:2), Lehi was creating in Joseph and in his posterity a durable right to possess some specific share of the land. By the same token, [in 2 Nephi 4:11] Lehi was saying that Sam would not have a separate tribal interest in a particular part of the land, but would merge legally and tribally with the seed of Nephi. Consequently, there are Josephites in the Book of Mormon, but never any Samites" (Welch, "Lehi's Last Will and Testament," 72). ⊕

What does it mean to "wax old"? (4:12) "This is perfectly good English, although now archaic. It means, 'he became exhausted,' 'tired out' (see Deut. 29:5; Heb. 8:13).

"Lehi's last act in mortality was to bless his posterity. And, let no one regard this as a mere formality. A father's blessing by the power of the Priesthood is a draft on the unlimited resources of heaven, which our Eternal Father has obligated himself to honor" (Reynolds and Sjodahl, *Commentary on the Book of Mormon*, 1:261–62).

What are the "other plates" Nephi referred to? (4:13–14) "Lehi had scarcely been laid away when Nephi was again the object of the wrath of his elder brothers and the sons of Ishmael (4:13). This was because of the admonitions of the Lord which he had cited to them. Many of his sayings to them, as well as those of his father, were written upon the Large Plates. Nephi says that he wrote the things of his soul upon 'these,' meaning the Small Plates of Nephi (4:15)" (Sperry, *Book of Mormon Compendium*, 152).

2 Nephi 4:15–35. Nephi Writes the Things of His Soul

What do we know about this intense expression of Nephi's heart? (4:15–35) "One of the intimate glimpses we get of Nephi's soul is found in 4:16–35, which passage we may call 'The Psalm of Nephi.' It is the only psalm in the Book of Mormon....

"This is a true psalm in both form and ideas. Its rhythm is comparable to the notable cadence of David's poems. It not only praises God but lays bare to us the very depths of Nephi's soul. A study of this psalm reveals how the scriptures delighted Nephi. The influence upon him of the Books of Isaiah, Jeremiah, Lamentations, and the Psalms is very apparent to the student of scripture" (Sperry, *Book of Mormon Compendium*, 152–53). ◐

Why is it necessary to ponder on the things we have experienced? (4:16) "The scriptures are one of our greatest treasures. They contain God's instructions to His people from the beginning of time. In a world so full of the doctrines of men, how grateful we are to have a sure anchor on which to build our faith!" (Perry, "Back to Gospel Basics," 92).

"Pondering a scripture ... gives great direction to life.... Pondering a passage of scripture can be a key to unlock revelation and the guidance and inspiration of the Holy Ghost. Scriptures can calm an agitated soul, giving peace, hope, and a restoration of confidence in one's ability to overcome the challenges of life" (Scott, "Power of Scripture," 6).

Why did Nephi refer to himself as "wretched"? (4:17) "Rationalization is the intellectual drug that anesthetizes the sting of conscience.... Nephi saw the danger signals in the lives of Laman and Lemuel when he noted, '[God] hath spoken unto you in a still small voice, but ye were past feeling' (1 Nephi 17:45). Contrast that with Nephi's lamentation: 'O wretched man that I am! ... My heart groaneth because of my sins; nevertheless, I know in whom I have trusted' (2 Nephi 4:17, 19). It is hard to imagine those words from a prophet of God. Nephi's life was one of devotion and obedience, yet he was ever more conscious

14 For I, Nephi, was constrained to speak unto them, according to his word; for I had spoken many things unto them, and also my father, before his death; many of which sayings are written upon mine other plates; for a more history part are written upon mine other plates.

15 And upon these I write the things of my soul, and many of the scriptures which are engraven upon the plates of brass. For my soul delighteth in the scriptures, and my heart pondereth them, and writeth them for the learning and the profit of my children.

16 Behold, my soul delighteth in the things of the Lord; and my heart pondereth continually upon the things which I have seen and heard.

17 Nevertheless, notwithstanding the great goodness of the Lord, in showing me his great and marvelous works, my heart exclaimeth: O wretched man that I am! Yea, my heart sorroweth because of my flesh; my soul grieveth because of mine iniquities.

of the distance still to be traveled for perfection. The more spiritual an individual becomes, the more sensitive he becomes to his imperfections. The better he becomes, the worse he realizes he was" (Callister, *Infinite Atonement*, 181).

What does it mean to be "beset" by sins? (4:18) "Nephi uses this word in the same sense the Old Testament writers which he had read used it, viz., 'encompassed about,' or, 'surrounded by.' See Judges 19:22; Ps. 22:12; and Hos. 11:12" (Reynolds and Sjodahl, *Commentary on the Book of Mormon*, 1:265).

18 I am encompassed about, because of the temptations and the sins which do so easily beset me.

19 And when I desire to rejoice, my heart groaneth because of my sins; nevertheless, I know in whom I have trusted.

20 My God hath been my support; he hath led me through mine afflictions in the wilderness; and he hath preserved me upon the waters of the great deep.

Why is there usually a wilderness involved when God delivers His people? (4:20) "When God frees people from bondage, leading them out into and then through the wilderness often seems to be the way he does it. The pattern of escape into a wilderness is found in the Book of Mormon in the stories of Moses, Lehi, Nephi, Mulek, Mosiah, Limhi, Alma, the Anti-Nephi-Lehies, Jared, and King Omer. Responses to the wilderness were dramatically different. It seemed to be a spiritual as much as a physical testing ground. For righteous Nephi, the wilderness was a place for receiving revelation, but Laman and Lemuel feared perishing in it" (Rust, "Book of Mormon Imagery," 137). ✪

21 He hath filled me with his love, even unto the consuming of my flesh.

22 He hath confounded mine enemies, unto the causing of them to quake before me.

23 Behold, he hath heard my cry by day, and he hath given me knowledge by visions in the night-time.

How can recognizing God's influence in our life change our attitude? (4:23) "From the depressing contemplation of weaknesses and shortcomings, Nephi now directs his thoughts toward God. Then the depression vanishes. He counts the many blessings God has bestowed upon him from the day he accompanied his father out of Jerusalem" (Reynolds and Sjodahl, *Commentary on the Book of Mormon*, 1:265).

24 And by day have I waxed bold in mighty prayer before him; yea, my voice have I sent up on high; and angels came down and ministered unto me.

25 And upon the wings of his Spirit hath my body been carried away upon exceedingly high mountains. And mine eyes have beheld great things, yea, even too great for man; therefore I was bidden that I should not write them.

26 O then, if I have seen so great things, if the Lord in his condescension unto the children of men hath visited men in so much mercy, why should my heart weep and my soul linger in the valley of sorrow, and my flesh waste away, and my strength slacken, because of mine afflictions?

What makes being "carried away upon exceedingly high mountains" so significant? (4:25) "All who have been entrusted with a 'high mountain' or temple experience have been given knowledge that they are not at liberty to share. There are many sacred truths revealed to those worthy and ready to receive them that are 'not lawful for man to utter; neither is man capable to make them known, for they are only to be seen and understood by the power of the Holy Spirit, which God bestows on those who love him, and purify themselves before him' (D&C 76:115–16)" (McConkie and Millet, *Doctrinal Commentary*, 1:217–18).

What were the consequences of Nephi's anger?
(4:27–29) "In this paragraph Nephi further opens his heart, and makes it clear that it was anger that had 'beset' him.... That was the 'iniquity,' the 'sin,' that caused his flesh to 'waste away,' and opened his heart to the adversary, to destroy his peace" (Reynolds and Sjodahl, *Commentary on the Book of Mormon*, 1:266). ●

What does it mean to be "strict in the plain road"?
(4:32) "Gospel covenants are to be lived with exactness and honor. It is not for man to dictate the terms of salvation. Too many have been too willing to rewrite the terms of eternal covenants into which they have entered. It has been observed that to almost live the commandments is to almost receive the promised blessings" (McConkie and Millet, *Doctrinal Commentary*, 1:220).

27 And why should I yield to sin, because of my flesh? Yea, why should I give way to temptations, that the evil one have place in my heart to destroy my peace and afflict my soul? Why am I angry because of mine enemy?

28 Awake, my soul! No longer droop in sin. Rejoice, O my heart, and give place no more for the enemy of my soul.

29 Do not anger again because of mine enemies. Do not slacken my strength because of mine afflictions.

30 Rejoice, O my heart, and cry unto the Lord, and say: O Lord, I will praise thee forever; yea, my soul will rejoice in thee, my God, and the rock of my salvation.

31 O Lord, wilt thou redeem my soul? Wilt thou deliver me out of the hands of mine enemies? Wilt thou make me that I may shake at the appearance of sin?

32 May the gates of hell be shut continually before me, because that my heart is broken and my spirit is contrite! O Lord, wilt thou not shut the gates of thy righteousness before me, that I may walk in the path of the low valley, that I may be strict in the plain road!

33 O Lord, wilt thou encircle me around in the robe of thy righteousness! O Lord, wilt thou make a way for mine escape before mine enemies! Wilt thou make my path straight before me! Wilt thou not place a stumbling block in my way—but that thou wouldst clear my way before me, and hedge not up my way, but the ways of mine enemy.

34 O Lord, I have trusted in thee, and I will trust in thee forever. I will not put my trust in the arm of flesh; for I know that cursed is he that putteth his trust in the arm of flesh. Yea, cursed is he that putteth his trust in man or maketh flesh his arm.

35 Yea, I know that God will give liberally to him that asketh. Yea, my God will give me, if I ask not amiss; therefore I will lift up my voice unto thee; yea, I will cry unto thee, my God, the rock of my righteousness. Behold, my voice shall forever ascend up unto thee, my rock and mine everlasting God. Amen.

CHAPTER 5

The Nephites separate themselves from the Lamanites, keep the law of Moses, and build a temple—Because of their unbelief, the Lamanites are cut off from the presence of the Lord, are cursed, and become a scourge unto the Nephites. About 588–559 B.C.

1 Behold, it came to pass that I, Nephi, did cry much unto the Lord my God, because of the anger of my brethren.

2 But behold, their anger did increase against me, insomuch that they did seek to take away my life.

3 Yea, they did murmur against me, saying: Our younger brother thinks to rule over us; and we have had much trial because of him; wherefore, now let us slay him, that we may not be afflicted more because of his words. For behold, we will not have him to be our ruler; for it belongs unto us, who are the elder brethren, to rule over this people.

4 Now I do not write upon these plates all the words which they murmured against me. But it sufficeth me to say, that they did seek to take away my life.

5 And it came to pass that the Lord did warn me, that I, Nephi, should depart from them and flee into the wilderness, and all those who would go with me.

What does it mean to ask amiss? (4:35) *Amiss* "means 'wrong' or 'improper' (2 Chron. 6:37). To ask 'not amiss' is, therefore, to ask for that which is right and proper. 'Ye ask, and receive not, because ye ask amiss, that ye may consume it upon your lusts' (James 4:3)" (Reynolds and Sjodahl, *Commentary on the Book of Mormon*, 1:268).

2 Nephi 5:1–9. Nephi and the Faithful Flee into the Wilderness

Why did Laman and Lemuel reject Nephi's leadership? (5:1–3) Referring to 1 Nephi 2:12, Elder Neal A. Maxwell taught: "Early on, Laman rejected the role he should have played, and, instead, wanted to be 'top dog in the manger,' resenting all the while Nephi's spiritual leadership. Lemuel was not only Laman's dutiful satellite, but he was also his enabler by allowing himself to be 'stirred up' by Laman (see 1 Ne. 16:37–38)."

Elder Maxwell concluded, "Hence Laman and Lemuel became rebels instead of leaders, resentful instead of righteous—all because of their failure to understand either the character or the purposes of God and His dealings with His children" ("Lessons from Laman and Lemuel," 8). ◉

What examples do we see here of the Lord's merciful deliverance? (5:5–6) When Nephi began his record, he promised, "I, Nephi, will show unto you that the tender mercies of the Lord are over all those whom he hath chosen, *because of their faith*, to make them mighty even unto the power of deliverance" (1 Nephi 1:20; emphasis added). Here in 2 Nephi 5 we have another example of those "tender mercies of the Lord" as Nephi and the faithful who followed him are warned to flee. For a modern example of that same promise to the Prophet Joseph Smith, see Doctrine and Covenants 122:9.

What do we know of Nephi's sisters? (5:6) "This is the only specific mention of 'sisters' found in the Book of Mormon. That Nephi mentions 'sisters' in the plural means that at least two went with him. He does not refer to these sisters as the wives of Ishmael's sons. And those married sisters, who had rebelled from the time they first came out of Jerusalem, would probably not have left their husbands to go with Nephi without his mentioning the fact. More likely, the sisters who accompanied Nephi were younger, born in the wilderness" (Hurd, *Our Sisters in the Latter-day Scriptures*, 10). ⊕

What is the significance of the name "the people of Nephi"? (5:9) "These events mark the formation of the Nephite nation. The taking upon themselves the name of Nephi was a symbolic action which affirmed that Nephi's God was their God and that Nephi's faith was their faith" (McConkie and Millet, *Doctrinal Commentary*, 1:222). ⊕

2 Nephi 5:10–18. The Nephites Keep the Commandments and Are Blessed

What are the blessings of prosperity? (5:10–11) "Nephi told of his people's success in raising their flocks, herds, and crops. Often we associate prosperity with tangible blessings, such as wealth or the material things of the world. President Heber J. Grant (1856–1945) taught about what true prosperity is: 'When I say prosperity I am not thinking of it in terms of dollars and cents alone. . . . What I count as real prosperity . . . is the growth in a knowledge of God, and in a testimony, and in the power to live the gospel and to inspire our families to do the same. That is prosperity of the truest kind' (*Ensign*, Nov. 1998, 59)" (*Book of Mormon Student Manual* [2009], 61).

6 Wherefore, it came to pass that I, Nephi, did take my family, and also Zoram and his family, and Sam, mine elder brother and his family, and Jacob and Joseph, my younger brethren, and also my sisters, and all those who would go with me. And all those who would go with me were those who believed in the warnings and the revelations of God; wherefore, they did hearken unto my words.

7 And we did take our tents and whatsoever things were possible for us, and did journey in the wilderness for the space of many days. And after we had journeyed for the space of many days we did pitch our tents.

8 And my people would that we should call the name of the place Nephi; wherefore, we did call it Nephi.

9 And all those who were with me did take upon them to call themselves the people of Nephi.

10 And we did observe to keep the judgments, and the statutes, and the commandments of the Lord in all things, according to the law of Moses.

11 And the Lord was with us; and we did prosper exceedingly; for we did sow seed, and we did reap again in abundance. And we began to raise flocks, and herds, and animals of every kind.

12 And I, Nephi, had also brought the records which were engraven upon the plates of brass; and also the ball, or compass, which was prepared for my father by the hand of the Lord, according to that which is written.

13 And it came to pass that we began to prosper exceedingly, and to multiply in the land.

14 And I, Nephi, did take the sword of Laban, and after the manner of it did make many swords, lest by any means the people who were now called Lamanites should come upon us and destroy us; for I knew their hatred towards me and my children and those who were called my people.

15 And I did teach my people to build buildings, and to work in all manner of wood, and of iron, and of copper, and of brass, and of steel, and of gold, and of silver, and of precious ores, which were in great abundance.

16 And I, Nephi, did build a temple; and I did construct it after the manner of the temple of Solomon save it were not built of so many precious things; for they were not to be found upon the land, wherefore, it could not be built like unto Solomon's temple. But the manner of the construction was like unto the temple of Solomon; and the workmanship thereof was exceedingly fine.

17 And it came to pass that I, Nephi, did cause my people to be industrious, and to labor with their hands.

18 And it came to pass that they would that I should be their king. But I, Nephi, was desirous that they should have no king; nevertheless, I did for them according to that which was in my power.

19 And behold, the words of the Lord had been fulfilled unto my brethren, which he spake concerning them, that I should be their

What is the relationship between faith and self-reliance? (5:14) Nephi testified that "the Lord was with us" (2 Nephi 5:11). Why then does Nephi feel the people need to "make many swords" to defend themselves against the Lamanites? What is the relationship between relying on the Lord and working to care for yourself? (see James 2:14–26; D&C 38:28–30). Why might Heavenly Father prefer that we work and struggle rather than expect him to do everything for us? (see D&C 122:7–8; Hebrews 12:6–11). What are some things you can do now that will help you overcome trials in your life?

What do the frequent "and of" phrases teach us? (5:15) As another proof of the Book of Mormon's authenticity, "Hebrew uses conjunctions much more frequently than English does. One clear example of this can be found in lists of items. In English, the conjunction *and* is normally used only before the last item in a list, such as *wood, iron, copper, and brass.* But Hebrew usually uses a conjunction before each item. The Book of Mormon contains many examples of this Hebrew-like usage, such as this one found in 2 Nephi 5:15: 'in all manner *of* wood, *and of* iron, *and of* copper, *and of* brass, *and of* steel, *and of* gold, *and of* silver, *and of* precious ores'" (Tvedtnes, "Hebrew Background," 82). ✪

How is Nephi's temple building another evidence that the Book of Mormon is an ancient record? (5:16–18) "Several studies have recently demonstrated that kings and temples were closely connected in antiquity....

"Becoming a king, issuing laws or judgments, and performing many other acts of legal consequence in the ancient world were virtually unthinkable without a temple....

"Temples were similarly prominent in the royal and legal landscapes of Nephite civilization. This invites the observation that Nephi's construction of a temple in the city of Nephi directly paved the way for him, two verses later, to become king (see 2 Nephi 5:16–18)" (Lundquist and Welch, "Kingship and Temple," 66). ✪

2 Nephi 5:19–25. The Lamanites Are Cursed Because They Break the Commandments

What was the curse and what caused it? (5:20–24)

"1. What was the curse?

"The curse is clearly defined in verse 20 as being 'cut off from the presence of the Lord.'

"2. What caused the curse?

"According to verse 21, the cause of the curse came 'because of their iniquity' and 'hardened . . . hearts.' Since the days of Adam's Fall, wickedness has resulted in being cut off from the presence of the Lord (see 1 Nephi 2:21; 2 Nephi 4:4; 9:6; Alma 9:13; Ether 10:11)" (*Book of Mormon Student Manual* [2009], 62). ●

2 Nephi 5:26–34. Nephi Makes Another Set of Plates

What priesthood did the Nephites have? (5:26) "The Nephites were descendants of Joseph. Lehi discovered this when reading the brass plates. He was a descendant of Manasseh, and Ishmael, who accompanied him with his family, was of the tribe of Ephraim. . . .

ruler and their teacher. Wherefore, I had been their ruler and their teacher, according to the commandments of the Lord, until the time they sought to take away my life.

20 Wherefore, the word of the Lord was fulfilled which he spake unto me, saying that: Inasmuch as they will not hearken unto thy words they shall be cut off from the presence of the Lord. And behold, they were cut off from his presence.

21 And he had caused the cursing to come upon them, yea, even a sore cursing, because of their iniquity. For behold, they had hardened their hearts against him, that they had become like unto a flint; wherefore, as they were white, and exceedingly fair and delightsome, that they might not be enticing unto my people the Lord God did cause a skin of blackness to come upon them.

22 And thus saith the Lord God: I will cause that they shall be loathsome unto thy people, save they shall repent of their iniquities.

23 And cursed shall be the seed of him that mixeth with their seed; for they shall be cursed even with the same cursing. And the Lord spake it, and it was done.

24 And because of their cursing which was upon them they did become an idle people, full of mischief and subtlety, and did seek in the wilderness for beasts of prey.

25 And the Lord God said unto me: They shall be a scourge unto thy seed, to stir them up in remembrance of me; and inasmuch as they will not remember me, and hearken unto my words, they shall scourge them even unto destruction.

26 And it came to pass that I, Nephi, did consecrate Jacob and Joseph, that they should be priests and teachers over the land of my people.

27 And it came to pass that we lived after the manner of happiness.

28 And thirty years had passed away from the time we left Jerusalem.

29 And I, Nephi, had kept the records upon my plates, which I had made, of my people thus far.

30 And it came to pass that the Lord God said unto me: Make other plates; and thou shalt engraven many things upon them which are good in my sight, for the profit of thy people.

31 Wherefore, I, Nephi, to be obedient to the commandments of the Lord, went and made these plates upon which I have engraven these things.

32 And I engraved that which is pleasing unto God. And if my people are pleased with the things of God they will be pleased with mine engravings which are upon these plates.

33 And if my people desire to know the more particular part of the history of my people they must search mine other plates.

34 And it sufficeth me to say that forty years had passed away, and we had already had wars and contentions with our brethren.

CHAPTER 6

Jacob recounts Jewish history: The Babylonian captivity and return; the ministry and crucifixion of the Holy One of Israel; the help received from the Gentiles; and the Jews' latter-day restoration when they believe in the Messiah. About 559–545 B.C.

1 The words of Jacob, the brother of Nephi, which he spake unto the people of Nephi:

2 Behold, my beloved brethren, I, Jacob, having been called of God, and ordained after the manner of his holy order, and having

"Therefore there were no Levites who accompanied Lehi to the Western Hemisphere. Under these conditions the Nephites officiated by virtue of the Melchizedek Priesthood from the days of Lehi to the days of the appearance of our Savior among them. [The] fact that plural terms *priests and teachers* were used indicates that this was not a reference to the definite office in the priesthood . . . but it was a general assignment to teach, direct, and admonish the people" (Smith, *Answers to Gospel Questions*, 1:124).

What "other plates" did Nephi make? (5:30–32) These "other plates" of which Nephi is speaking are the small plates of Nephi, upon which "Nephi desired the limited room on this smaller set of plates for 'the things of God,' the things of greatest worth unto the children of men. Such matters as genealogy—certainly of importance—are to be found on the large plates. Nephi's hope and intent? 'That I may persuade men to come unto the God of Abraham and the God of Isaac, and the God of Jacob, and be saved.' Some things simply are more valuable and more conducive to bringing men to Jehovah, who is Christ the Lord" (McConkie and Millet, *Doctrinal Commentary*, 1:51). ✪

2 Nephi 6:1–5. Jacob Writes under Nephi's Direction

What does it mean to be ordained after "his holy order"? (6:2) "The phrase 'his holy order' refers to the higher or Melchizedek Priesthood [see JST, Genesis 14:27–29]" (McConkie and Millet, *Doctrinal Commentary*, 1:227).

How is the Book of Mormon a witness for Isaiah?
(6:4) "In the academic world, where scholarship has
displaced the spirit of revelation, it is argued that
Isaiah could speak only of events pertaining to his
own day and that his writings are to be so interpreted.
This is the reason why the world so tenaciously argues
for a second Isaiah—they refuse to acknowledge that
Isaiah could have known of future events described
in his writings. Among the household of faith the
ceaseless tides of revealed truth waste away such
sand-castle theology" (McConkie and Millet, *Doctrinal
Commentary*, 1:227).

Why is Isaiah quoted so often by Jacob and Nephi?
(6:4–5) "It is obvious that Nephi esteemed highly the
messages found in Isaiah's writings and felt them significant enough to duplicate, for he had declared: 'I do
not write anything upon plates save it be that I think
it be sacred' (1 Nephi 19:6). Certainly Nephi would
not use the precious space on his metallic plates to
write something he did not consider to be of great
importance to future readers of his laboriously written
record" (Brewster, *Isaiah Plain & Simple*, 176). ◉

2 Nephi 6:6–13. Jacob Explains the Prophecies of Isaiah

been consecrated by my brother Nephi, unto
whom ye look as a king or a protector, and
on whom ye depend for safety, behold ye
know that I have spoken unto you exceedingly many things.

3 Nevertheless, I speak unto you again; for
I am desirous for the welfare of your souls.
Yea, mine anxiety is great for you; and ye
yourselves know that it ever has been. For I
have exhorted you with all diligence; and I
have taught you the words of my father; and
I have spoken unto you concerning all things
which are written, from the creation of the
world.

4 And now, behold, I would speak unto you
concerning things which are, and which are
to come; wherefore, I will read you the words
of Isaiah. And they are the words which my
brother has desired that I should speak unto
you. And I speak unto you for your sakes,
that ye may learn and glorify the name of
your God.

5 And now, the words which I shall read
are they which Isaiah spake concerning all
the house of Israel; wherefore, they may be
likened unto you, for ye are of the house of
Israel. And there are many things which have
been spoken by Isaiah which may be likened
unto you, because ye are of the house of
Israel.

6 And now, these are the words: Thus saith
the Lord God: Behold, I will lift up mine
hand to the Gentiles, and set up my standard
to the people; and they shall bring thy sons
in their arms, and thy daughters shall be carried upon their shoulders.

7 And kings shall be thy nursing fathers, and
their queens thy nursing mothers; they shall

bow down to thee with their faces towards the earth, and lick up the dust of thy feet; and thou shalt know that I am the Lord; for they shall not be ashamed that wait for me.

8 And now I, Jacob, would speak somewhat concerning these words. For behold, the Lord has shown me that those who were at Jerusalem, from whence we came, have been slain and carried away captive.

9 Nevertheless, the Lord has shown unto me that they should return again. And he also has shown unto me that the Lord God, the Holy One of Israel, should manifest himself unto them in the flesh; and after he should manifest himself they should scourge him and crucify him, according to the words of the angel who spake it unto me.

10 And after they have hardened their hearts and stiffened their necks against the Holy One of Israel, behold, the judgments of the Holy One of Israel shall come upon them. And the day cometh that they shall be smitten and afflicted.

11 Wherefore, after they are driven to and fro, for thus saith the angel, many shall be afflicted in the flesh, and shall not be suffered to perish, because of the prayers of the faithful; they shall be scattered, and smitten, and hated; nevertheless, the Lord will be merciful unto them, that when they shall come to the knowledge of their Redeemer, they shall be gathered together again to the lands of their inheritance.

12 And blessed are the Gentiles, they of whom the prophet has written; for behold, if it so be that they shall repent and fight not against Zion, and do not unite themselves to that great and abominable church, they shall be saved; for the Lord God will fulfil his covenants which he has made unto his children; and for this cause the prophet has written these things.

Why was Jerusalem destroyed and the Jews scattered, and when can they return?(6:8–11) "The rejection of their Messiah caused the southern kingdom or the nation of Judah to be 'scattered,' 'smitten,' and 'hated.' Such was to be their lot until that time came when once again they 'come to the knowledge of their Redeemer.' . . . It would be shortsighted to suppose that this promise was fulfilled in the Jews alone.

"Repetitiously we are told in the Book of Mormon that none have rights or promises to lands of inheritance until they have accepted Jesus as the Christ and accorded their lives with his teachings . . . Book of Mormon prophets . . . were insistent that the Jews must first return to Christ and accept the Holy One of Israel before they would have claim upon the covenants made with their ancient fathers" (McConkie and Millet, *Doctrinal Commentary*, 1:230).

2 Nephi 6:14–18. Israel Will Be Brought Back to Jesus Christ at His Second Coming

When will the Messiah "manifest himself unto them in power and great glory"? (6:14–15) The "second time" referred to in these verses is at the Second Coming. "The Messiah will come just as Judah faces imminent defeat at the hands of her enemies. This time he shall come, as the scriptures record, in power and great glory and save his people from complete annihilation. Zechariah wrote: 'Then shall the Lord go forth and fight against those nations, as when he fought in the day of battle' (Zech. 14:3). Then will the people who survive the refiner's fire believe in the true Messiah, even Jesus Christ" (Galbraith et al., *Jerusalem*, 361).

Who are the "prey" and the "mighty"? (6:16–18) "The context of [Isa. 49:24, which Jacob is quoting] tells us that *prey/captives* refers to God's 'covenant people,' who are in bondage to the gentiles. The *mighty* (called 'the terrible' in [Isaiah] 49:25) could also refer to Satan, who makes us his captives when we sin. The prey shall indeed be 'taken from the mighty,' by God, who is mightier than all.

"The description of being made captive by legal right may suggest that Israel was taken legitimately according to the rules of warfare, or that she is captive to Satan according to the law of justice. But, in his mercy, God's claim to his children supersedes the claims of all others" (Parry et al., *Understanding Isaiah*, 436).

How will Israel be redeemed? (6:16–18) "From this oracle we learn that it will not be guns or planes or military strategy or battlefield courage that redeems Israel; Jesus the Christ will deliver and redeem his people—both temporally and spiritually" (McConkie and Millet, *Doctrinal Commentary on the Book of Mormon*, 1:232).

13 Wherefore, they that fight against Zion and the covenant people of the Lord shall lick up the dust of their feet; and the people of the Lord shall not be ashamed. For the people of the Lord are they who wait for him; for they still wait for the coming of the Messiah.

14 And behold, according to the words of the prophet, the Messiah will set himself again the second time to recover them; wherefore, he will manifest himself unto them in power and great glory, unto the destruction of their enemies, when that day cometh when they shall believe in him; and none will he destroy that believe in him.

15 And they that believe not in him shall be destroyed, both by fire, and by tempest, and by earthquakes, and by bloodsheds, and by pestilence, and by famine. And they shall know that the Lord is God, the Holy One of Israel.

16 For shall the prey be taken from the mighty, or the lawful captive delivered?

17 But thus saith the Lord: Even the captives of the mighty shall be taken away, and the prey of the terrible shall be delivered; for the Mighty God shall deliver his covenant people. For thus saith the Lord: I will contend with them that contendeth with thee—

18 And I will feed them that oppress thee, with their own flesh; and they shall be drunken with their own blood as with sweet wine; and all flesh shall know that I the Lord am thy Savior and thy Redeemer, the Mighty One of Jacob.

CHAPTER 7

Jacob continues reading from Isaiah: Isaiah speaks messianically—The Messiah will have the tongue of the learned—He will give His back to the smiters—He will not be confounded—Compare Isaiah 50. About 559–545 B.C.

1 Yea, for thus saith the Lord: Have I put thee away, or have I cast thee off forever? For thus saith the Lord: Where is the bill of your mother's divorcement? To whom have I put thee away, or to which of my creditors have I sold you? Yea, to whom have I sold you? Behold, for your iniquities have ye sold yourselves, and for your transgressions is your mother put away.

2 Wherefore, when I came, there was no man; when I called, yea, there was none to answer. O house of Israel, is my hand shortened at all that it cannot redeem, or have I no power to deliver? Behold, at my rebuke I dry up the sea, I make their rivers a wilderness and their fish to stink because the waters are dried up, and they die because of thirst.

3 I clothe the heavens with blackness, and I make sackcloth their covering.

4 The Lord God hath given me the tongue of the learned, that I should know how to speak a word in season unto thee, O house of Israel. When ye are weary he waketh morning by morning. He waketh mine ear to hear as the learned.

2 Nephi 7:1–3. The Lord Does Not Give Up on His People

Why was Israel cast off? (7:1) "It was the custom in ancient Israel for some creditors to take the children of their debtors and sell them as slaves . . . (Ex. 21:7–8; Neh. 5:1–5; Matt. 18:25). But the Lord has no creditors—he is in debt to no one—and he has not sold Israel into slavery. Ultimately, God and Israel are separated because of Israel's choices, not God's. . . .

"The children of Israel have sold themselves into the bondage of sin. And the mother has been set aside, or divorced, because of unfaithfulness. Perhaps the children here represent the sons and daughters of the covenant, and perhaps the mother represents the nation of Israel as a whole" (Parry et al., *Understanding Isaiah*, 440).

Can the Savior really deliver me? (7:2–3) Speaking of the power of the Atonement to deliver each one of us, Elder Jeffrey R. Holland said: "However late you think you are, however many chances you think you have missed, however many mistakes you feel you have made or talents you think you don't have, or however far from home and family and God you feel you have traveled, I testify that you have not traveled beyond the reach of divine love. It is not possible for you to sink lower than the infinite light of Christ's Atonement shines" ("Laborers in the Vineyard," 33). ⊕

What does it mean to cover the heavens with sackcloth? (7:3) "*Sackcloth* is the clothing of mourning. Here, the darkness of the heavens may symbolize the mourning of the wicked at the second coming of Christ. Or it may symbolize the mourning of the righteous, and of the heavens and earth" (Parry et al., *Understanding Isaiah*, 441).

2 Nephi 7:4–9. Isaiah Prophesies of the Mortal Ministry of Jesus Christ, the Messiah

To whom is Isaiah referring? (7:4–9) "Isa. 50:4–9 [2 Ne. 7:4–9] is known as a 'servant song' (other servant songs are found in [Isa.] 42:1–9; 49:1–7; 52:13–15; 53:1–12). The servant in this case seems to be Christ in the meridian of time. As the headnote to this chapter in the Latter-day Saint edition of the Bible says, 'Isaiah speaks Messianically—Messiah shall have the tongue of the learned.' These verses also apply to Isaiah or to any true servant of the Lord who obeys despite persecution" (Parry et al., *Understanding Isaiah*, 441). ✚

2 Nephi 7:10–11. Those Who Trust in the Lord Shall Walk in His Light

Who walks in darkness and has no light? (7:10–11) "Those who kindle fires and gird themselves with firebrands—that is, those who conspire evil and plan the destruction of the faithful or who walk by their own lights—shall be trapped by their own snares. They shall come to a sorrowful end" (Sperry, *Book of Mormon Compendium*, 158). ✚

How might this chapter apply to me? (7:1–11) Do you know people who choose to rely on their own light instead of the revelations from God? Have you, at times, chosen to do things that are contrary to what the Lord and His prophets have said? What sorrow has come or will come as a result? What different choices would lead to happiness instead?

2 Nephi 8:1–8. The Lord Calls Israel to Receive Salvation

What is the "rock" and how it is hewn and digged? (8:1–2) "Our origins, ancestry, or heritage. Our rock and quarry are Abraham and Sarah, from whom we descend. Ultimately, of course, the rock we come from is God the Father, and Christ, who is called the Rock

5 The Lord God hath opened mine ear, and I was not rebellious, neither turned away back.

6 I gave my back to the smiter, and my cheeks to them that plucked off the hair. I hid not my face from shame and spitting.

7 For the Lord God will help me, therefore shall I not be confounded. Therefore have I set my face like a flint, and I know that I shall not be ashamed.

8 And the Lord is near, and he justifieth me. Who will contend with me? Let us stand together. Who is mine adversary? Let him come near me, and I will smite him with the strength of my mouth.

9 For the Lord God will help me. And all they who shall condemn me, behold, all they shall wax old as a garment, and the moth shall eat them up.

10 Who is among you that feareth the Lord, that obeyeth the voice of his servant, that walketh in darkness and hath no light?

11 Behold all ye that kindle fire, that compass yourselves about with sparks, walk in the light of your fire and in the sparks which ye have kindled. This shall ye have of mine hand—ye shall lie down in sorrow.

CHAPTER 8

Jacob continues reading from Isaiah: In the last days, the Lord will comfort Zion and gather Israel—The redeemed will come to Zion amid great joy—Compare Isaiah 51 and 52:1–2. About 559–545 B.C.

1 Hearken unto me, ye that follow after righteousness. Look unto the rock from whence ye are hewn, and to the hole of the pit from whence ye are digged.

2 Look unto Abraham, your father, and unto Sarah, she that bare you; for I called him alone, and blessed him.

3 For the Lord shall comfort Zion, he will comfort all her waste places; and he will make her wilderness like Eden, and her desert like the garden of the Lord. Joy and gladness shall be found therein, thanksgiving and the voice of melody.

4 Hearken unto me, my people; and give ear unto me, O my nation; for a law shall proceed from me, and I will make my judgment to rest for a light for the people.

5 My righteousness is near; my salvation is gone forth, and mine arm shall judge the people. The isles shall wait upon me, and on mine arm shall they trust.

6 Lift up your eyes to the heavens, and look upon the earth beneath; for the heavens shall vanish away like smoke, and the earth shall wax old like a garment; and they that dwell therein shall die in like manner. But my salvation shall be forever, and my righteousness shall not be abolished.

7 Hearken unto me, ye that know righteousness, the people in whose heart I have written my law, fear ye not the reproach of men, neither be ye afraid of their revilings.

8 For the moth shall eat them up like a garment, and the worm shall eat them like wool. But my righteousness shall be forever, and my salvation from generation to generation.

9 Awake, awake! Put on strength, O arm of the Lord; awake as in the ancient days. Art thou not he that hath cut Rahab, and wounded the dragon?

at least thirty-four times in the scriptures" (Parry et al., *Understanding Isaiah*, 450).

How will the land of Zion be changed in the Millennium? (8:3–6) "[The Lord] will change the area of Palestine physically . . . and he will give the people a spirit of joy and gladness. . . .

"In the last days, then, Zion will be established and blessed. . . . God's law will go forth from her . . . and his righteousness will dwell there. . . . His judgment will punish the wicked and bless the righteous. . . . When Christ comes, ushering in the Millennium, the heavens and the earth as we know them will be destroyed, as will the wicked, but the Lord's promises to the faithful will never end" (Parry et al., *Understanding Isaiah*, 447–48). ✦

How should we handle social pressure? (8:7–8) "You can't please God without upsetting Satan, so you will get pressure from those he tempts to do wrong. . . . It is natural to want to be accepted by peers, to be part of a group—some even join gangs because of that desire to belong, but they lose their freedom, and some lose their lives. . . . You don't need to compromise your standards to be accepted by good friends. The more obedient you are, the more you stand for true principles, the more the Lord can help you overcome temptation. You can also help others because they will feel your strength. Let them know about your standards by consistently living them" (Scott, "Making the Right Choices," 37).

2 Nephi 8:9–16. If Israel Will Turn to the Lord, He Will Give Them Great Blessings

What are Rahab and the dragon? (8:9–10) "The 'dragon' is easily identified as Satan (Revelation 12:7–9; 20:2). The identity of 'Rahab' is a little more difficult. Some scholars suggest Rahab represents Egypt while others say it is a sea monster representing Satan.

Footnote reference 'c' in [2 Nephi 8:9] cites Isaiah 27:1 as a cross-reference, which speaks of 'leviathan that crooked serpent.' The footnote identifies 'leviathan' as 'a legendary sea-monster representing the forces of chaos that opposed the Creator'" (Brewster, *Isaiah Plain and Simple*, 221).

Who are the "redeemed of the Lord"? (8:11) "The 'redeemed of the Lord' who were to 'return, and come with singing unto Zion' with 'everlasting joy' are identified in the Doctrine and Covenants as the Latter-day Saints (see D&C 45:71; 66:11; 101:18). The return has begun, but it will not be completed until the center place of Zion is built up 'that the prophets might be fulfilled' (D&C 101:19)" (Nyman, *Great Are the Words of Isaiah*, 196).

The Prophet Joseph Smith taught that during the Millennium, "the earth will be renewed and receive its paradisiacal glory" (Articles of Faith 1:10).

"During the Millennium, Satan will be bound. This means he will not have power to tempt those who are living at that time (see D&C 101:28). The 'children shall grow up without sin unto salvation' (D&C 45:58). 'Because of the righteousness of [the Lord's] people, Satan has no power; wherefore, he cannot be loosed for the space of many years; for he hath no power over the hearts of the people, for they dwell in righteousness, and the Holy One of Israel reigneth' (1 Nephi 22:26)" (*Gospel Principles*, 265–66). ✦

2 Nephi 8:17–20. Two Prophets in the Last Days Will Teach and Comfort the Jews

Why has Jerusalem suffered so long? (8:17) "To drink of such a cup is to taste the bitterness eventually experienced by the wicked and unrepentant. Dregs are the last remaining and least desirable sediments that settle to the bottom of a cup of liquid. The great Nephite prophet-king [Benjamin] taught that those who drink of such a cup do so because their works are evil and mercy has lost her claim on them (Mosiah 3:24–27)" (Brewster, *Isaiah Plain and Simple*, 224).

Why are there "none to guide" Jerusalem ? (8:17–19) "The Lord calls on Jerusalem, or the people of Israel, to wake from their spiritual slumber and turn from

10 Art thou not he who hath dried the sea, the waters of the great deep; that hath made the depths of the sea a way for the ransomed to pass over?

11 Therefore, the redeemed of the Lord shall return, and come with singing unto Zion; and everlasting joy and holiness shall be upon their heads; and they shall obtain gladness and joy; sorrow and mourning shall flee away.

12 I am he; yea, I am he that comforteth you. Behold, who art thou, that thou shouldst be afraid of man, who shall die, and of the son of man, who shall be made like unto grass?

13 And forgettest the Lord thy maker, that hath stretched forth the heavens, and laid the foundations of the earth, and hast feared continually every day, because of the fury of the oppressor, as if he were ready to destroy? And where is the fury of the oppressor?

14 The captive exile hasteneth, that he may be loosed, and that he should not die in the pit, nor that his bread should fail.

15 But I am the Lord thy God, whose waves roared; the Lord of Hosts is my name.

16 And I have put my words in thy mouth, and have covered thee in the shadow of mine hand, that I may plant the heavens and lay the foundations of the earth, and say unto Zion: Behold, thou art my people.

17 Awake, awake, stand up, O Jerusalem, which hast drunk at the hand of the Lord the cup of his fury—thou hast drunken the dregs of the cup of trembling wrung out—

18 And none to guide her among all the sons she hath brought forth; neither that taketh her by the hand, of all the sons she hath brought up.

19 These two sons are come unto thee, who shall be sorry for thee—thy desolation and destruction, and the famine and the sword—and by whom shall I comfort thee?

20 Thy sons have fainted, save these two; they lie at the head of all the streets; as a wild bull in a net, they are full of the fury of the Lord, the rebuke of thy God.

21 Therefore hear now this, thou afflicted, and drunken, and not with wine:

22 Thus saith thy Lord, the Lord and thy God pleadeth the cause of his people; behold, I have taken out of thine hand the cup of trembling, the dregs of the cup of my fury; thou shalt no more drink it again.

23 But I will put it into the hand of them that afflict thee; who have said to thy soul: Bow down, that we may go over—and thou hast laid thy body as the ground and as the street to them that went over.

24 Awake, awake, put on thy strength, O Zion; put on thy beautiful garments, O Jerusalem, the holy city; for henceforth there shall no more come into thee the uncircumcised and the unclean.

25 Shake thyself from the dust; arise, sit down, O Jerusalem; loose thyself from the bands of thy neck, O captive daughter of Zion.

the sins that have brought the Lord's fierce anger. . . . The people have become so wicked that there is 'none to guide her among all [her] sons'" (Parry et al., *Understanding Isaiah*, 456).

What guidance is Jerusalem missing? (8:18) The phrase "none to guide her among all the sons she hath brought forth" may describe not only a lack of leadership but also may describe a lack of priesthood leadership.

Who are "these two sons"? (8:19–20) In the Doctrine and Covenants we read that they are "two prophets that are to be raised up to the Jewish nation in the last days, at the time of the restoration, and to prophesy to the Jews after they are gathered and have built the city of Jerusalem in the land of their fathers" (D&C 77:15). ☉

2 Nephi 8:21–25. At the Point of Their Destruction, the Lord Will Personally Save the Jews

What is the Lord's promise to Jerusalem? (8:21–25) After Isaiah describes Judah as drunken with iniquity and afflicted for rebellion, "we are then confronted with the figure of an advocate or lawyer, one who pleads the case of his people and removes 'the cup of trembling' and bitter dregs from Judah's lips. The cup of trembling and bitter dregs represent Judah's scattering and affliction. Judah, however, must act in her own behalf. Mercy and forgiveness are not a one-way street, and she must repent and change her ways in order for God's redeeming power to take effect. Literally, she must awaken, arise, put on strength, and loose the bands around her neck [see D&C 52:1–2]" (Gentry, "God Will Fulfill His Covenants," 171–72). ☉

What message does Isaiah have for you in this chapter? (8:1–25) Isaiah's (and Jacob's) testimony is that God will keep his promises and will do whatever it takes to rescue and save his people as long as they are willing to repent. What does this teach about how the Lord feels about you? What would you say to someone who felt that the Lord did not care about them or that they had strayed too far to ever return?

CHAPTER 9

Jacob explains that the Jews will be gathered in all their lands of promise—The Atonement ransoms man from the Fall—The bodies of the dead will come forth from the grave, and their spirits from hell and from paradise—They will be judged—The Atonement saves from death, hell, the devil, and endless torment—The righteous are to be saved in the kingdom of God—Penalties for sins are set forth—The Holy One of Israel is the keeper of the gate. About 559–545 B.C.

1 And now, my beloved brethren, I have read these things that ye might know concerning the covenants of the Lord that he has covenanted with all the house of Israel—

2 That he has spoken unto the Jews, by the mouth of his holy prophets, even from the beginning down, from generation to generation, until the time comes that they shall be restored to the true church and fold of God; when they shall be gathered home to the lands of their inheritance, and shall be established in all their lands of promise.

3 Behold, my beloved brethren, I speak unto you these things that ye may rejoice, and lift up your heads forever, because of the blessings which the Lord God shall bestow upon your children.

4 For I know that ye have searched much, many of you, to know of things to come; wherefore I know that ye know that our flesh must waste away and die; nevertheless, in our bodies we shall see God.

2 Nephi 9:1–3. The House of Israel Will Be Gathered to Their Promised Lands

How will the house of Israel be gathered? (9:1–3)
President Russell M. Nelson taught that we participate in the gathering of the house of Israel today through both missionary work and temple work: "This doctrine of the gathering is one of the important teachings of The Church of Jesus Christ of Latter-day Saints. . . . The coming forth of the Book of Mormon is a sign to the entire world that the Lord has commenced to gather Israel and fulfill covenants He made to Abraham, Isaac, and Jacob. We not only teach this doctrine, but we participate in it. We do so as we help to gather the elect of the Lord on both sides of the veil" ("The Gathering of Scattered Israel," 80). ●

2 Nephi 9:4–12. The Atonement Delivers Us from the Effects of the Fall of Adam

What Is the Importance of 2 Nephi 9?

President Joseph Fielding Smith emphasized this chapter: "One of the most enlightening discourses ever delivered in regard to the atonement is found in the ninth chapter of 2 Nephi in the Book of Mormon. It is the counsel given by Jacob, brother of Nephi. It should be carefully read by every person seeking salvation" (*Answers to Gospel Questions*, 4:57). Brother Robert J. Matthews added, "This address contains insights relative to the fall of Adam and to the need for the redemption wrought by Jesus that are not stated with such clarity in any other place" ("The Atonement of Jesus Christ," 179).

5 Yea, I know that ye know that in the body he shall show himself unto those at Jerusalem, from whence we came; for it is expedient that it should be among them; for it behooveth the great Creator that he suffereth himself to become subject unto man in the flesh, and die for all men, that all men might become subject unto him.

6 For as death hath passed upon all men, to fulfil the merciful plan of the great Creator, there must needs be a power of resurrection, and the resurrection must needs come unto man by reason of the fall; and the fall came by reason of transgression; and because man became fallen they were cut off from the presence of the Lord.

7 Wherefore, it must needs be an infinite atonement—save it should be an infinite atonement this corruption could not put on incorruption. Wherefore, the first judgment which came upon man must needs have remained to an endless duration. And if so, this flesh must have laid down to rot and to crumble to its mother earth, to rise no more.

8 O the wisdom of God, his mercy and grace! For behold, if the flesh should rise no more our spirits must become subject to that angel who fell from before the presence of the Eternal God, and became the devil, to rise no more.

What does it mean to be "subject unto" Christ? (9:5) President Dallin H. Oaks explained: "Being subject to our Savior means that if our sins are to be forgiven through His Atonement, we must comply with the conditions He has prescribed, including faith, repentance, and baptism. The fulfillment of these conditions depends on our desires, our choices, and our actions. 'He cometh into the world that he may save all men if they will hearken unto his voice' (2 Ne. 9:21).

"The Lord provides a way for all His children, and He desires that each of us come unto Him [see Moroni 10:32]" ("All Men Everywhere," 79).

Why do the scriptures refer to this act as Adam's "transgression"? (9:6) President Dallin H. Oaks taught: "Some Christians condemn Eve for her act, concluding that she and her daughters are somehow flawed by it. Not the Latter-day Saints! Informed by revelation, we celebrate Eve's act and honor her wisdom and courage in the great episode called the Fall [see McConkie, 'Eve and the Fall,' 67–68]. . . . Elder Joseph Fielding Smith said: 'I never speak of the part Eve took in this fall as a sin, nor do I accuse Adam of a sin. . . . This was a transgression of the law, but not a sin . . . for it was something that Adam and Eve had to do!' [*Doctrines of Salvation*, 1:114–15]" ("Great Plan of Happiness," 73). ✪

What is meant by an "infinite atonement"? (9:7) Brother Tad R. Callister explained: "The phrase 'infinite atonement' or 'infinite sacrifice' may refer to an atonement or sacrifice by a God, a being who is infinite in knowledge, power, and glory. Amulek makes that connection when he observes that the 'great and last sacrifice will be the Son of God, yea, infinite and eternal' (Alma 34:14). Accordingly, the Atonement is 'infinite' because its source is 'infinite.' But the Atonement is infinite in other ways as well" (*Infinite Atonement*, 58). ✪

What does the word *atonement* mean? (9:7) President Boyd K. Packer explained: "The English word *atonement* is really three words: *at-one-ment*, which means to set at one; one with God; to reconcile, to conciliate, to expiate.

"But did you know that the word *atonement* appears only once in the English New Testament? [Romans 5:8–11] . . .

"Only once in the New Testament but 39 times in the Book of Mormon. What better witness that the Book of Mormon is indeed another testament of Jesus Christ?" ("Who Is Jesus Christ?" 15). ✪

Why, without a resurrection, would we become devils? (9:9) "What if a man had lived a good life, a commendable and noble life—why would such a one be subject to Satan in the world of spirits? . . . Simply stated, if Christ did not rise from the grave—as he stated he would do—then he was not the promised Messiah. If Christ has not the power to save the body from death, then he surely has not the power to save the spirit from hell. If he did not break the bands of death in the Resurrection, then our hope of deliverance from sin through the Atonement is futile and unfounded" (Millet, *Power of the Word*, 90). ⊕

Why are death and hell described as "this awful monster"? (9:10) "Nephi describes in a graphic way why death and hell are considered to be such awful monsters. Without the atonement of Christ, we would stay permanently in the state of death and hell, 'to an endless duration.' Our bodies would have been 'laid down to rot and to crumble to . . . mother earth, to rise no more.' Under those circumstances, our spirits would 'become subject' to Satan, and 'must have become like unto him, and we become devils, . . . to remain with the father of lies, in misery, like unto himself' (2 Nephi 9:7–9). No wonder he felt to exclaim, 'How great the goodness of our God!'" (Parry and Parry, *Understanding Death and the Resurrection*, 145).

How is the Atonement a "supreme act of goodness"? (9:10–12) Elder Bruce R. McConkie testified: "The most important doctrine I can declare, and the

9 And our spirits must have become like unto him, and we become devils, angels to a devil, to be shut out from the presence of our God, and to remain with the father of lies, in misery, like unto himself; yea, to that being who beguiled our first parents, who transformeth himself nigh unto an angel of light, and stirreth up the children of men unto secret combinations of murder and all manner of secret works of darkness.

10 O how great the goodness of our God, who prepareth a way for our escape from the grasp of this awful monster; yea, that monster, death and hell, which I call the death of the body, and also the death of the spirit.

11 And because of the way of deliverance of our God, the Holy One of Israel, this death, of which I have spoken, which is the temporal, shall deliver up its dead; which death is the grave.

12 And this death of which I have spoken, which is the spiritual death, shall deliver up its dead; which spiritual death is hell; wherefore, death and hell must deliver up their dead, and hell must deliver up its captive spirits, and the grave must deliver up its

The Atonement of Jesus Christ

The Unconditional Results of Adam's Fall
• The earth is in a fallen condition.
• Physical death—We have mortal bodies that will die (2 Ne. 9:6).
• Spiritual death—Because we are born into a fallen world, we are separated spiritually from our Heavenly Father (2 Ne. 9:6).

The Unconditional Blessings of the Atonement of Jesus Christ
• All who have ever lived will be resurrected with an immortal physical body (2 Ne. 9:10–13; Alma 11:42–43).
• All will be brought back into God's presence for judgment (2 Ne. 9:14–15; Helaman 14:15–17).
• The earth will be made celestial (D&C 88:18–20).

(See *Book of Mormon Seminary Student Study Guide*, 37.)

The Conditional Results of Mankind's Personal Fall
• As we become accountable for our choices, our sins make us unworthy to live in our Heavenly Father's presence (2 Ne. 9:16; Mosiah 16:2–5).

The Conditional Blessings of the Atonement of Christ
• If we develop faith in Jesus Christ, repent, and are baptized, we are cleansed from our sins and through the gift of the Holy Ghost can be sanctified and worthy to remain in Heavenly Father's presence and become as He is (2 Ne. 9:17–18; Alma 34:13–17; Moroni 10:32–33).

captive bodies, and the bodies and the spirits of men will be restored one to the other; and it is by the power of the resurrection of the Holy One of Israel.

most powerful testimony I can bear, is of the atoning sacrifice of the Lord Jesus Christ.

"His atonement is the most transcendent event that ever has or ever will occur from Creation's dawn through all the ages of a never-ending eternity.

"It is the supreme act of goodness and grace that only a god could perform. Through it, all of the terms and conditions of the Father's eternal plan of salvation became operative.

"Through it are brought to pass the immortality and eternal life of man" ("Purifying Power of Gethsemane," 9). ☉

2 Nephi 9:13–20. After the Resurrection, All Will Be Judged, and the Righteous Will Inherit the Kingdom of God

13 O how great the plan of our God! For on the other hand, the paradise of God must deliver up the spirits of the righteous, and the grave deliver up the body of the righteous; and the spirit and the body is restored to itself again, and all men become incorruptible, and immortal, and they are living souls, having a perfect knowledge like unto us in the flesh, save it be that our knowledge shall be perfect.

14 Wherefore, we shall have a perfect knowledge of all our guilt, and our uncleanness, and our nakedness; and the righteous shall have a perfect knowledge of their enjoyment, and their righteousness, being clothed with purity, yea, even with the robe of righteousness.

15 And it shall come to pass that when all men shall have passed from this first death unto life, insomuch as they have become immortal, they must appear before the judgment-seat of the Holy One of Israel; and then cometh the judgment, and then must they be judged according to the holy judgment of God.

How can our memory be perfect? (9:13–14)
Speaking of the enduring nature of our memories, President John Taylor said: "Man sleeps the sleep of death, but the spirit lives where the record of his deeds is kept—that does not die—man cannot kill it; there is no decay associated with it, and it still retains in all its vividness the remembrance of that which transpired before the separation by death of the body and the ever-living spirit. Man sleeps for a time in the grave, and by-and-by he rises again from the dead and goes to judgment; and then the secret thoughts of all men are revealed before Him with whom we have to do; we cannot hide them (in *Journal of Discourses*, 2:78–79). ☉

Are we resurrected before or after the Final Judgment? (9:15) "The united spirits and bodies of men become incorruptible and immortal, having a perfect knowledge like unto us in the flesh, except that their knowledge shall be perfect. . . . Men, having become immortal, must now appear before the judgment-seat of the Holy One of Israel to be judged according to the holy judgment of God. Those who are righteous shall be righteous still, but those who are filthy—the devil and his angels—shall go away into the torment prepared for them, which shall be likened unto a 'lake of fire and brimstone' (2 Nephi 9:15,16; cf. Alma 34:35; Alma 40:13,14; D&C 76:36–38)" (Sperry, *Book of Mormon Compendium*, 169).

What is the nature of the torment of the wicked?
(9:16) The Prophet Joseph Smith taught: "The great misery of departed spirits in the world of spirits ... is to know that they come short of the glory that others enjoy and that they might have enjoyed themselves, and they are their own accusers....

"The torment of disappointment in the mind of man is as exquisite as a lake burning with fire and brimstone" (*Joseph Smith* [manual], 224).

What are the "crosses of the world" we must endure? (9:18) The Prophet Joseph Smith's inspired translation of Matthew 16:24 explains: "And now for a man to take up his cross, is to deny himself all ungodliness, and every worldly lust, and keep my commandments" (JST Matthew 16:26).

Why is it essential that God be omniscient? (9:20)
"We read in the Prophet Joseph Smith's *Lectures on Faith* ... 'that without the knowledge of all things, God would not be able to save any portion of his creatures; for it is by reason of the knowledge which he has of all things, from the beginning to the end, that enables him to give that understanding to his creatures by which they are made partakers of eternal life; and if it were not for the idea existing in the minds of men that God had all knowledge it would be impossible for them to exercise faith in him'" (Maxwell, *All These Things Shall Give Thee Experience*, 6–7). ☉

16 And assuredly, as the Lord liveth, for the Lord God hath spoken it, and it is his eternal word, which cannot pass away, that they who are righteous shall be righteous still, and they who are filthy shall be filthy still; wherefore, they who are filthy are the devil and his angels; and they shall go away into everlasting fire, prepared for them; and their torment is as a lake of fire and brimstone, whose flame ascendeth up forever and ever and has no end.

17 O the greatness and the justice of our God! For he executeth all his words, and they have gone forth out of his mouth, and his law must be fulfilled.

18 But, behold, the righteous, the saints of the Holy One of Israel, they who have believed in the Holy One of Israel, they who have endured the crosses of the world, and despised the shame of it, they shall inherit the kingdom of God, which was prepared for them from the foundation of the world, and their joy shall be full forever.

19 O the greatness of the mercy of our God, the Holy One of Israel! For he delivereth his saints from that awful monster the devil, and death, and hell, and that lake of fire and brimstone, which is endless torment.

20 O how great the holiness of our God! For he knoweth all things, and there is not anything save he knows it.

2 Nephi 9:21–40. The Righteous Will Inherit the Kingdom of God, and the Wicked Will Suffer the Penalties for Sin

21 And he cometh into the world that he may save all men if they will hearken unto his voice; for behold, he suffereth the pains of all men, yea, the pains of every living creature, both men, women, and children, who belong to the family of Adam.

22 And he suffereth this that the resurrection might pass upon all men, that all might stand before him at the great and judgment day.

23 And he commandeth all men that they must repent, and be baptized in his name, having perfect faith in the Holy One of Israel, or they cannot be saved in the kingdom of God.

24 And if they will not repent and believe in his name, and be baptized in his name, and endure to the end, they must be damned; for the Lord God, the Holy One of Israel, has spoken it.

25 Wherefore, he has given a law; and where there is no law given there is no punishment; and where there is no punishment there is no condemnation; and where there is no condemnation the mercies of the Holy One of Israel have claim upon them, because of the atonement; for they are delivered by the power of him.

26 For the atonement satisfieth the demands of his justice upon all those who have not the law given to them, that they are delivered from that awful monster, death and hell, and the devil, and the lake of fire and brimstone, which is endless torment; and they are restored to that God who gave them breath, which is the Holy One of Israel.

27 But wo unto him that has the law given, yea, that has all the commandments of God, like unto us, and that transgresseth them,

Why was it necessary for Jesus Christ to suffer for all men in order to save them? (9:21) "Not only did Christ keep the law perfectly, but he suffered the penalty for all violations as though he himself were guilty of them. Thus he satisfied the law of justice in both dimensions" (Lund, "The Fall of Man and His Redemption" 92).

What happens to those who die without the truth? (9:25–27) "Jacob points out that when men have knowledge of the gospel they are required of the Lord to use that knowledge and repent of their sins. Those who do not have knowledge for whatever reason (either because of infancy, lack of mental ability, or perhaps they were never taught) are automatically covered by the Atonement. . . .

"'Those who have not the law given unto them' include little children, and Jacob explains that such are rescued by the Atonement. King Benjamin and Mormon also taught the same doctrine regarding children (Mosiah 3:11–16; Moroni 8:5–20). This is a great contrast to the prominent doctrine of original sin held by many Christian denominations" (Matthews, "Atonement of Jesus Christ," 183). ✪

Why did Jacob choose the evils he did in pronouncing his "woes" against wrongdoing? (9:27–38) "Jacob apparently had the Decalogue [the Ten

Commandments] of Deuteronomy 5 or Exodus 20 in mind when he wrote [2 Nephi 9:27–38]. The prohibitions against worshiping images, committing murder or adultery, and bearing false witness (see Exodus 20:4–6, 13–14, 16) are clearly present in Jacob's sixth through ninth woes. Jacob's summary in these ten 'woes' is much more than a thoughtless copy of the biblical ideals. Whereas the Decalogue gave the law, Jacob goes one step further by stressing the consequences of breaking the law. Furthermore, Jacob's principles have been tailored as revelation to his people and to their needs" (Welch, "Jacob's Ten Commandments," 69–70). ⊕

Why must we learn to control our thoughts?
(9:39–40) "Mental control must be stronger than physical appetites or desires of the flesh. As thoughts

and that wasteth the days of his probation, for awful is his state!

28 O that cunning plan of the evil one! O the vainness, and the frailties, and the foolishness of men! When they are learned they think they are wise, and they hearken not unto the counsel of God, for they set it aside, supposing they know of themselves, wherefore, their wisdom is foolishness and it profiteth them not. And they shall perish.

29 But to be learned is good if they hearken unto the counsels of God.

30 But wo unto the rich, who are rich as to the things of the world. For because they are rich they despise the poor, and they persecute the meek, and their hearts are upon their treasures; wherefore, their treasure is their god. And behold, their treasure shall perish with them also.

31 And wo unto the deaf that will not hear; for they shall perish.

32 Wo unto the blind that will not see; for they shall perish also.

33 Wo unto the uncircumcised of heart, for a knowledge of their iniquities shall smite them at the last day.

34 Wo unto the liar, for he shall be thrust down to hell.

35 Wo unto the murderer who deliberately killeth, for he shall die.

36 Wo unto them who commit whoredoms, for they shall be thrust down to hell.

37 Yea, wo unto those that worship idols, for the devil of all devils delighteth in them.

38 And, in fine, wo unto all those who die in their sins; for they shall return to God, and behold his face, and remain in their sins.

39 O, my beloved brethren, remember the awfulness in transgressing against that

Holy God, and also the awfulness of yielding to the enticings of that cunning one. Remember, to be carnally-minded is death, and to be spiritually-minded is life eternal.

40 O, my beloved brethren, give ear to my words. Remember the greatness of the Holy One of Israel. Do not say that I have spoken hard things against you; for if ye do, ye will revile against the truth; for I have spoken the words of your Maker. I know that the words of truth are hard against all uncleanness; but the righteous fear them not, for they love the truth and are not shaken.

41 O then, my beloved brethren, come unto the Lord, the Holy One. Remember that his paths are righteous. Behold, the way for man is narrow, but it lieth in a straight course before him, and the keeper of the gate is the Holy One of Israel; and he employeth no servant there; and there is none other way save it be by the gate; for he cannot be deceived, for the Lord God is his name.

42 And whoso knocketh, to him will he open; and the wise, and the learned, and they that are rich, who are puffed up because of their learning, and their wisdom, and their riches—yea, they are they whom he despiseth; and save they shall cast these things away, and consider themselves fools before God, and come down in the depths of humility, he will not open unto them.

43 But the things of the wise and the prudent shall be hid from them forever—yea, that happiness which is prepared for the saints.

44 O, my beloved brethren, remember my words. Behold, I take off my garments, and I shake them before you; I pray the God of my salvation that he view me with his all-searching eye; wherefore, ye shall know at the last day, when all men shall be judged of their works, that the God of Israel did witness that

are brought into complete harmony with revealed truth, actions will then become appropriate.

"The timeless proverb is as true now as when it was first spoken: 'For as he thinketh in his heart, so is he' (Prov. 23:7).

"Each of us, with discipline and effort, has the capacity to control his thoughts and his actions. This is part of the process of developing spiritual, physical, and emotional maturity" (Hinckley, "Reverence and Morality," 47).

2 Nephi 9:41–54. Jacob Invites All to Come unto Christ and to Receive His Blessings

Why is Jesus the "keeper of the gate"? (9:41) "I will tell you . . . out of the conviction of my soul . . . what I think the major reason is [why he 'employeth no servant there'], as contained in another Book of Mormon scripture which says he waits for you 'with open arms' (Mormon 6:17). That's why he's there! . . . That imagery is too powerful to brush aside. . . . He does wait for us with open arms, because his love of us is perfect" (Maxwell, "But a Few Days," 7). ✪

Why does God insist on humility? (9:42) Speaking of the importance of humility when facing trials, President Henry B. Eyring taught: "If you'll remember that the key to not being diverted from serving God is humility, then you'll understand that some of those days when you thought things were going badly were a great blessing. You might not have sought them, but if you react to such days by recognizing your dependence on God, you could actually be in a better situation than if everything had gone extremely well. Too much success, in fact, could lead you into a more difficult trial because it could make you arrogant" (*To Draw Closer to God*, 85). ✪

Why do the scriptures use contrasting symbols such as "chains" and "the rock" to teach about the devil and God? (9:45) Symbols can be powerful teaching tools. "The chains of the devil . . . are referred to as 'awful chains' (2 Ne. 1:13), 'everlasting chains' (2 Ne. 28:19), 'chains of hell' (Alma 5:9), and 'chains of death' (D&C 138:18). These diabolical fetters are utilized by Satan to encircle and bind those unrepentant souls who allow him to control their lives" (McConkie and Parry, *A Guide to Scriptural Symbols*, 29). The "rock," on the other hand, is "an often-used metaphor conveying such ideas as permanence, solidity, steadfastness, strength, refuge, reliability and so on. In these and similiar senses both God and Christ are spoken of as the Rock" (*Gospel Symbolism*, 269).

What is a harrow? (9:47) "A harrow is a frame with spikes through it. When pulled across the ground, it rips and tears into the soil. The scriptures frequently speak of souls and minds being 'harrowed up' with guilt" (Packer, "Touch of the Master's Hand," 23).

How does the Lord change our hearts? (9:49–52) Notice how Jacob's love for God changed his heart (2 Nephi 9:49). President Ezra Taft Benson said: "Why did God put the first commandment first? Because He knew that if we truly loved Him we would want to keep all of His other commandments. . . .

"When we put God first, all other things fall into their proper place or drop out of our lives. Our love of the Lord will govern the claims for our affection, the demands on our time, the interests we pursue, and the order of our priorities" ("The Great Commandment— Love the Lord," 4). ●

I shook your iniquities from my soul, and that I stand with brightness before him, and am rid of your blood.

45 O, my beloved brethren, turn away from your sins; shake off the chains of him that would bind you fast; come unto that God who is the rock of your salvation.

46 Prepare your souls for that glorious day when justice shall be administered unto the righteous, even the day of judgment, that ye may not shrink with awful fear; that ye may not remember your awful guilt in perfectness, and be constrained to exclaim: Holy, holy are thy judgments, O Lord God Almighty—but I know my guilt; I transgressed thy law, and my transgressions are mine; and the devil hath obtained me, that I am a prey to his awful misery.

47 But behold, my brethren, is it expedient that I should awake you to an awful reality of these things? Would I harrow up your souls if your minds were pure? Would I be plain unto you according to the plainness of the truth if ye were freed from sin?

48 Behold, if ye were holy I would speak unto you of holiness; but as ye are not holy, and ye look upon me as a teacher, it must needs be expedient that I teach you the consequences of sin.

49 Behold, my soul abhorreth sin, and my heart delighteth in righteousness; and I will praise the holy name of my God.

50 Come, my brethren, every one that thirsteth, come ye to the waters; and he that hath no money, come buy and eat; yea, come buy wine and milk without money and without price.

51 Wherefore, do not spend money for that which is of no worth, nor your labor for that which cannot satisfy. Hearken diligently unto me, and remember the words which I have spoken; and come unto the Holy One of Israel, and feast upon that which perisheth not, neither can be corrupted, and let your soul delight in fatness.

52 Behold, my beloved brethren, remember the words of your God; pray unto him continually by day, and give thanks unto his holy name by night. Let your hearts rejoice.

53 And behold how great the covenants of the Lord, and how great his condescensions unto the children of men; and because of his greatness, and his grace and mercy, he has promised unto us that our seed shall not utterly be destroyed, according to the flesh, but that he would preserve them; and in future generations they shall become a righteous branch unto the house of Israel.

54 And now, my brethren, I would speak unto you more; but on the morrow I will declare unto you the remainder of my words. Amen.

CHAPTER 10

Jacob explains that the Jews will crucify their God—They will be scattered until they begin to believe in Him—America will be a land of liberty where no king will rule—Reconcile yourselves to God and gain salvation through His grace. About 559–545 B.C.

1 And now I, Jacob, speak unto you again, my beloved brethren, concerning this righteous branch of which I have spoken.

2 For behold, the promises which we have obtained are promises unto us according to the flesh; wherefore, as it has been shown

What does it mean to "come buy wine and milk without money and without price"? (9:50) "Salvation is available to all men, not just a select few. . . . 'All mankind may be saved, by obedience to the laws and ordinances of the Gospel' (Third Article of Faith). God is no respecter of persons; 'he inviteth them all to come unto him and partake of his goodness; and he denieth none that come unto him, black and white, bond and free, male and female; and he remembereth the heathen; and all are alike unto God, both Jew and Gentile' (2 Ne. 26:33). The eternal call of the Eternal God is: 'Ho, every one that thirsteth, come ye to the waters, and he that hath no money; come ye, buy, and eat; yea, come, buy wine and milk without money and without price' (Isa. 55:1), for 'salvation is free!' (2 Ne. 2:4)" (McConkie, *Doctrinal New Testament Commentary*, 3:416–17).

What do the Savior's condescensions mean to you? (9:53) Elder Jeffrey R. Holland taught: "The Atonement was the foreordained but voluntary act of the Only Begotten Son of God in which He offered His life and spiritual anguish as a redeeming ransom for the effect of the Fall of Adam upon all mankind and for the personal sins of all who repent" ("Atonement of Jesus Christ," 34).

What does it mean to you that Jesus *volunteered* to redeem you? What can you volunteer to do for Him in return?

2 Nephi 10:1–2. Lamanites Will Return to the Savior in the Last Days

What will bring a "true knowledge of their Redeemer" to Lehi's children? (10:2) "That which would give the latter-day Israelites the knowledge of their Redeemer, more than any single source, is, of course, the Book of Mormon. . . . Jacob's testimony clearly fits Nephi's stated purpose and also constitutes a glorious witness within the application of the divine law of witnesses" (Van Orden, "Law of Witnesses," 314).

2 Nephi 10:3–6. Christ Will Die at the Hands of Wicked Men

What further light does the Prophet Joseph Smith shed on the crucifixion of Jesus Christ at the hands of wicked men? (10:3) "The Prophet Joseph Smith said that if Jesus had come to earth and preached the same 'rough things' and the 'same doctrine' in the Prophet's day as he did to the Jews, that generation too would put him to death. It is noted that while the King James Version is quite clear in depicting Jesus' troubles with the Jewish leaders, the Joseph Smith Translation and the Book of Mormon are even more explicit and pronounced. These later sources give us a more detailed and enhanced concept of the magnitude of the conflict than we could have obtained from the King James Version alone" (Matthews, *Behold the Messiah*, 271).

Why was this earth selected for the performance of the Atonement? (10:4) Brother Tad R. Callister wrote: "Following are three possibilities. The first possibility is that Christ may have come to this earth to counterbalance its great wickedness. . . .

"A second possible reason Christ came to our world may be that no other world was wicked enough to crucify their God. . . .

"There exists at least a third possibility as to why Christ came to this particular earth. Perhaps here he would find a comprehensive cross-section of his children, from the best to the worst—representatives of whom would be witnesses of his Atonement" (*Infinite Atonement*, 90–93).

What happens when God's people disobey? (10:6) "In writing of the Jews, who here symbolize all the house of Israel . . . 'after they have hardened their hearts and stiffened their necks against the Holy One of Israel, behold, the judgments of the Holy One of Israel shall come upon them . . . ; they shall be scattered, and smitten, and hated' (2 Nephi 6:9–11). . . . Of course the same result was prophesied for the Nephites. Nephi the son of Helaman predicted that, unless the Nephites repented of their wickedness, the God of Israel would, instead of gathering his people, scatter them (see Helaman 7:19)" (Millet, "Gathering of Israel," 189). ✪

unto me that many of our children shall perish in the flesh because of unbelief, nevertheless, God will be merciful unto many; and our children shall be restored, that they may come to that which will give them the true knowledge of their Redeemer.

3 Wherefore, as I said unto you, it must needs be expedient that Christ—for in the last night the angel spake unto me that this should be his name—should come among the Jews, among those who are the more wicked part of the world; and they shall crucify him—for thus it behooveth our God, and there is none other nation on earth that would crucify their God.

4 For should the mighty miracles be wrought among other nations they would repent, and know that he be their God.

5 But because of priestcrafts and iniquities, they at Jerusalem will stiffen their necks against him, that he be crucified.

6 Wherefore, because of their iniquities, destructions, famines, pestilences, and bloodshed shall come upon them; and they who shall not be destroyed shall be scattered among all nations.

2 Nephi 10:7–9. Israel Will Be Gathered When They Believe in Christ

7 But behold, thus saith the Lord God: When the day cometh that they shall believe in me, that I am Christ, then have I covenanted with their fathers that they shall be restored in the flesh, upon the earth, unto the lands of their inheritance.

Must the Jews first accept Jesus Christ before they are gathered "unto the lands of their inheritance"? (10:7) In this verse the Lord himself gave an order to the gathering with the words "when . . . they shall believe in me" followed by "then . . . they shall be restored . . . unto the lands of their inheritance." The resurrected Savior taught the same order to those in the promised land (see 3 Nephi 20:30–33). Elder Bruce R. McConkie said: "The present assembling of people of Jewish ancestry into the Palestinian nation of Israel is not the scriptural gathering of Israel or of Judah. . . . A political gathering is not a spiritual gathering. . . . No one is ever gathered with Israel until they accept the Crucified One" (*New Witness*, 519, 564).

How would this gathering take place? (10:8) Although the ultimate fulfillment of the gathering of Israel is spiritual, temporal forces, often political, may play a role in setting the stage for the gathering. "In March 1842 Elder Orson Hyde wrote the offices of the *Millennial Star* and offered these insights regarding the gathering of the Jews: 'It was by political power and influence that the Jewish nation was broken down, and her subjects dispersed abroad; and I will here hazard the opinion, that by political power and influence they will be gathered and built up; and further, that England is destined in the wisdom and economy of heaven to stretch forth the arm of political power, and advance in the front ranks of this glorious enterprise' (Roberts, *Comprehensive History of the Church*, 2:168–69). This inspired comment was fulfilled in the twentieth century" (Brewster, *Behold, I Come Quickly*, 129–30). ◉

8 And it shall come to pass that they shall be gathered in from their long dispersion, from the isles of the sea, and from the four parts of the earth; and the nations of the Gentiles shall be great in the eyes of me, saith God, in carrying them forth to the lands of their inheritance.

9 Yea, the kings of the Gentiles shall be nursing fathers unto them, and their queens shall become nursing mothers; wherefore, the promises of the Lord are great unto the Gentiles, for he hath spoken it, and who can dispute?

2 Nephi 10:10–19. The Americas Will Be Blessed and Protected So the Gospel Can Prosper

10 But behold, this land, said God, shall be a land of thine inheritance, and the Gentiles shall be blessed upon the land.

How do we know the Americas are a land of inheritance for many of scattered Israel? (10:10) "With the translation of the Book of Mormon many of the descendants of Joseph were made known. Who could have made that great discovery without a revelation from the Lord? . . . That remnant now found among the Lamanites shall eventually partake of the blessings of the gospel. They shall unite with the remnant which is being gathered from among the nations and they shall be blessed of the Lord forever" (Smith, *Way to Perfection*, 121). ◉

Why is a land of liberty so important? (10:11) "The Americas were destined in the providences of the Lord to be a place of liberty so that in them the gospel might be restored and from them its saving message go forth to all the world. Such a destiny is facilitated by the absence of monarchic governments, which usually have been synonymous with oppression and the lack of religious freedom. Christ is our king, and if, as Lehi prophesied, we 'serve him according to the commandments which he hath given, it shall be a land of liberty' which shall never know captivity, and in it the righteous 'shall be blessed forever'" (McConkie and Millet, *Doctrinal Commentary*, 1:268).

Is the Lord's promise to protect Zion from her enemies conditional? (10:13) President Spencer W. Kimball explained that if those living in this promised land hope to avoid perishing, they must "'serve the God of this land who is Jesus Christ' (Ether 2:12). There is only one way. That infallible cure is simply righteousness, obedience, Godliness, honor, and integrity. There is no other cure. Mountains of arms and ammunitions will not guarantee safety, for enemies can also build fortifications and missiles and bomb shelters" (in Conference Report, Oct. 1961, 31). ◉

Where do you stand in the conflict between God and the adversary? (10:16) Referring to the spiritual war between good and evil, Elder Bruce R. McConkie stated: "Now there neither are nor can be any neutrals in this war. Every member of the Church is on one side or the other. . . . We are either for the Church or we are against it. We either take its part or we take the consequences. We cannot survive spiritually with one foot in the Church and the other in the world. We must make the choice. It is either the Church or the world. There is no middle ground. And the Lord loves a courageous man who fights openly and boldly in his army" ("Be Valiant in the Fight of Faith," 34).

How was this prophecy fulfilled? (10:18) "One has only to consider the manner in which the early Europeans, following their arrival on this side of the ocean, treated the Lamanites to see how the Gentiles afflicted Jacob's seed. In spite of this, gentile hearts have been softened at times to come to the aid of the Lamanites in North and South America" (Gentry, "God Will Fulfill His Covenants," 174). ◉

11 And this land shall be a land of liberty unto the Gentiles, and there shall be no kings upon the land, who shall raise up unto the Gentiles.

12 And I will fortify this land against all other nations.

13 And he that fighteth against Zion shall perish, saith God.

14 For he that raiseth up a king against me shall perish, for I, the Lord, the king of heaven, will be their king, and I will be a light unto them forever, that hear my words.

15 Wherefore, for this cause, that my covenants may be fulfilled which I have made unto the children of men, that I will do unto them while they are in the flesh, I must needs destroy the secret works of darkness, and of murders, and of abominations.

16 Wherefore, he that fighteth against Zion, both Jew and Gentile, both bond and free, both male and female, shall perish; for they are they who are the whore of all the earth; for they who are not for me are against me, saith our God.

17 For I will fulfil my promises which I have made unto the children of men, that I will do unto them while they are in the flesh—

18 Wherefore, my beloved brethren, thus saith our God: I will afflict thy seed by the hand of the Gentiles; nevertheless, I will soften the hearts of the Gentiles, that they shall be like unto a father to them; wherefore, the Gentiles shall be blessed and numbered among the house of Israel.

19 Wherefore, I will consecrate this land unto thy seed, and them who shall be numbered among thy seed, forever, for the land of their inheritance; for it is a choice land, saith God unto me, above all other lands, wherefore I will have all men that dwell thereon that they shall worship me, saith God.

20 And now, my beloved brethren, seeing that our merciful God has given us so great knowledge concerning these things, let us remember him, and lay aside our sins, and not hang down our heads, for we are not cast off; nevertheless, we have been driven out of the land of our inheritance; but we have been led to a better land, for the Lord has made the sea our path, and we are upon an isle of the sea.

21 But great are the promises of the Lord unto them who are upon the isles of the sea; wherefore as it says isles, there must needs be more than this, and they are inhabited also by our brethren.

22 For behold, the Lord God has led away from time to time from the house of Israel, according to his will and pleasure. And now behold, the Lord remembereth all them who have been broken off, wherefore he remembereth us also.

23 Therefore, cheer up your hearts, and remember that ye are free to act for yourselves—to choose the way of everlasting death or the way of eternal life.

How is America "a choice land"? (10:19) President Joseph Fielding Smith testified: "No nation has been more greatly blessed than has the United States. We live in a land which has been called choice above all other lands by divine pronouncement (1 Ne. 2:20; 2 Ne. 10:19; Ether 2:7). The Lord has watched over it with a jealous care and has commanded its people to serve Him lest His wrath be kindled against them and His blessings be withdrawn" (in Conference Report, Apr. 1943, 11). ⊕

2 Nephi 10:20–25. The Lord Will Guide the Faithful to the Promised Land

Why should we "not hang down our heads"? (10:20) "We are Heavenly Father's children. He wants to be a part of our lives, to bless us, and to help us. He will heal our wounds, dry our tears, and help us along our path to return to His presence. As we look to Him, He will lead us. . . . I bear testimony that sins are forgiven and burdens are lightened as we look to Christ. 'Let us remember him, . . . and not hang down our heads,' for, as President Monson said, 'It is better to look up'" (Cook, "It's Better to Look Up," 35).

Who are the others of the House of Israel which the Lord has led away from time to time? (10:22) Many modern scholars believe that "immigration from Asia across the Pacific Ocean and Islands in the south, and the Bering Strait in the north, furnished America with a mixed population thousands of years ago. . . . The evidence in favor of this opinion is also a testimony to the authenticity of the record in the Book of Mormon of the voyage of Lehi, and the information that 'The Lord did bring Mulek into the land North' (Hel. 6:10), and this further revelation that the Lord has, from time to time, led colonies of Israelites from their main home to distant parts of the world" (Reynolds and Sjodahl, *Commentary on the Book of Mormon*, 1:319).

How do faith and agency work together? (10:23) "It will take unshakable faith in the Lord Jesus Christ to choose the way to eternal life. It is by using that faith we can know the will of God. It is by acting on that faith we build the strength to do the will of God. And it is by exercising that faith in Jesus Christ that we can resist temptation and gain forgiveness through the Atonement" (Eyring, "Spiritual Preparedness," 38).

What can we learn from Jacob's conclusion? (10:25)
Jacob began his two sermons speaking about "an infinite atonement" (2 Nephi 9:7). "Note that Jacob closes his sermon with a final testimony that it is through the Atonement of Christ alone that man can gain an entrance into the eternal kingdom of God, there to praise him for his grace divine. That is the sum and substance of the sermon. And it is stated in sentences which, through their beauty of literary style bear the marks of divine inspiration in every word" (Reynolds and Sjodahl, *Commentary on the Book of Mormon*, 320).

2 Nephi 11:1–3. Isaiah, Nephi, and Jacob See the Redeemer

What does it mean to "liken" the scriptures? (11:2)
"I believe what Nephi meant by 'liken . . .' was that [Isaiah's words] could be directly applied" (Eyring, "Book of Mormon Will Change Your Life," 10). ✪

How are Nephi, Jacob, and Isaiah like the Three Witnesses to the Book of Mormon? (11:3) Elder Jeffrey R. Holland noted: "Those three witnesses were to be Oliver Cowdery, David Whitmer, and Martin Harris . . . and their testimony is forever fixed to the opening pages of the Book of Mormon. . . . In keeping with this same covenantal principle, it is interesting to note that there were three earlier witnesses—special witnesses—not only of the divine origins of the Book of Mormon but also of Divinity himself. These early witnesses were Nephi, Jacob, and Isaiah, and it is not by coincidence that their testimonies appear so conspicuously at the beginning of this ancient record" (*Christ and the New Covenant*, 31–32).

24 Wherefore, my beloved brethren, reconcile yourselves to the will of God, and not to the will of the devil and the flesh; and remember, after ye are reconciled unto God, that it is only in and through the grace of God that ye are saved.

25 Wherefore, may God raise you from death by the power of the resurrection, and also from everlasting death by the power of the atonement, that ye may be received into the eternal kingdom of God, that ye may praise him through grace divine. Amen.

CHAPTER 11

Jacob saw his Redeemer—The law of Moses typifies Christ and proves He will come. About 559–545 B.C.

1 And now, Jacob spake many more things to my people at that time; nevertheless only these things have I caused to be written, for the things which I have written sufficeth me.

2 And now I, Nephi, write more of the words of Isaiah, for my soul delighteth in his words. For I will liken his words unto my people, and I will send them forth unto all my children, for he verily saw my Redeemer, even as I have seen him.

3 And my brother, Jacob, also has seen him as I have seen him; wherefore, I will send their words forth unto my children to prove unto them that my words are true. Wherefore, by the words of three, God hath said, I will establish my word. Nevertheless, God sendeth more witnesses, and he proveth all his words.

2 Nephi 11:4–8. Nephi Delights in Christ and the Plan of Redemption

What is a type? (11:4) A type is a "person, event, or ritual with likeness to another person, event, or ritual of greater importance which is to follow. The term antitype describes the future fulfillment, while typology is the study of types. True types will have noticeable points of resemblance, show evidence of divine appointment, and be prophetic of future events" (McConkie, *Gospel Symbolism*, 274). ⊕

4 Behold, my soul delighteth in proving unto my people the truth of the coming of Christ; for, for this end hath the law of Moses been given; and all things which have been given of God from the beginning of the world, unto man, are the typifying of him.

5 And also my soul delighteth in the covenants of the Lord which he hath made to our fathers; yea, my soul delighteth in his grace, and in his justice, and power, and mercy in the great and eternal plan of deliverance from death.

6 And my soul delighteth in proving unto my people that save Christ should come all men must perish.

What do we learn from these three prophets? (11:6) Elder Jeffrey R. Holland taught: "After reading Nephi, Jacob, and Isaiah, we know two things in bold, powerful strokes—(1) that Jesus is the Christ, the Son of the living God, and (2) that God will keep his covenant promises with the remnants of the house of Israel. These two themes constitute the very purpose of the Book of Mormon, and that is precisely what these three prophets teach so emphatically in the Book of Mormon material we have from them" ("For a Wise Purpose," 14). ⊕

7 For if there be no Christ there be no God; and if there be no God we are not, for there could have been no creation. But there is a God, and he is Christ, and he cometh in the fulness of his own time.

8 And now I write some of the words of Isaiah, that whoso of my people shall see these words may lift up their hearts and rejoice for all men. Now these are the words, and ye may liken them unto you and unto all men.

CHAPTER 12

Isaiah sees the latter-day temple, gathering of Israel, and millennial judgment and peace— The proud and wicked will be brought low at the Second Coming—Compare Isaiah 2. About 559–545 B.C.

1 The word that Isaiah, the son of Amoz, saw concerning Judah and Jerusalem:

2 And it shall come to pass in the last days, when the mountain of the Lord's house shall be established in the top of the mountains, and shall be exalted above the hills, and all nations shall flow unto it.

2 Nephi 12:1–4. Isaiah Prophesies of a Latter-day Temple in the Tops of the Mountains

What do these verses teach us about latter-day temples? (12:2) "This prophecy speaks to us in our day. The gathering of Israel, temples, and temple service are the principal themes in this section; we will 'flow' upwards to the temple mountain, learn of God's ways (in the temple), and walk in God's paths (in the temple). In addition, temple service and worship ([Isaiah] 2:2–3) are directly connected to worldwide peace and prosperity ([Isaiah] 2:4); that is, temple attendance ([Isaiah] 2:2) results in peace ([Isaiah] 2:4), a desire to learn of God ([Isaiah] 2:3), and a willingness to walk in his light ([Isaiah] 2:5). Micah presents the same prophecy in his writings (Micah 4:1–3)" (Parry et al., *Understanding Isaiah*, 24). ✚

What is "the mountain of the Lord's house"? (12:2) "Isaiah spoke of 'the mountain of the Lord's house [being] established in the top of the mountains' in the last days (Isa. 2:2–3; 2 Ne. 12:2–3). Speaking of the Salt Lake Temple during general conference, Elder LeGrand Richards said: 'This temple on this temple block is that house of the God of Jacob' ([Conference Report], Oct. 1975, 77)" (Brewster, *Doctrine and Covenants Encyclopedia*, 372). ✚

What is the law that will go forth? (12:3) President Harold B. Lee taught: "Years ago . . . I heard in [an] inspired prayer of the First Presidency a definition of the meaning of the term 'out of Zion shall go forth the law.' Note what they said: 'We thank thee that thou has revealed to us that those who gave us our constitutional form of government were men wise in thy sight and that thou didst raise them up for the very purpose of putting forth that sacred document [the Constitution of the United States; see D&C 101:80]. . . . We pray that kings and rulers and the peoples of all nations . . . adopt similar governmental systems, thus to fulfil the ancient prophecy of Isaiah'" ("Way to Eternal Life," 15).

When will men leave their weapons of war? (12:4) "This would be an ideal world, filled with righteousness, if all men would keep these two great commandments [to love God and others]; but men have turned away from the true worship of the Living God. They do not love their neighbor as themselves. Because of this condition wickedness prevails in the earth. Nations rise against nations, and war has plagued the earth from the beginning. This condition will continue until the coming of Jesus Christ as Lord of lords and King of kings" (Smith, *Answers to Gospel Questions*, 3:49–50). ✚

3 And many people shall go and say, Come ye, and let us go up to the mountain of the Lord, to the house of the God of Jacob; and he will teach us of his ways, and we will walk in his paths; for out of Zion shall go forth the law, and the word of the Lord from Jerusalem.

4 And he shall judge among the nations, and shall rebuke many people: and they shall beat their swords into plow-shares, and their spears into pruning-hooks—nation shall not lift up sword against nation, neither shall they learn war any more.

2 Nephi 12:5–11. The Wicked and the Proud Will Be Humbled at the Second Coming

5 O house of Jacob, come ye and let us walk in the light of the Lord; yea, come, for ye have all gone astray, every one to his wicked ways.

6 Therefore, O Lord, thou hast forsaken thy people, the house of Jacob, because they be replenished from the east, and hearken unto soothsayers like the Philistines, and they please themselves in the children of strangers.

7 Their land also is full of silver and gold, neither is there any end of their treasures; their land is also full of horses, neither is there any end of their chariots.

8 Their land is also full of idols; they worship the work of their own hands, that which their own fingers have made.

9 And the mean man boweth not down, and the great man humbleth himself not, therefore, forgive him not.

10 O ye wicked ones, enter into the rock, and hide thee in the dust, for the fear of the Lord and the glory of his majesty shall smite thee.

11 And it shall come to pass that the lofty looks of man shall be humbled, and the haughtiness of men shall be bowed down, and the Lord alone shall be exalted in that day.

How does a person walk in the light? (12:5) Elder David A. Bednar promised: "As you appropriately seek for and apply unto the spirit of revelation, I promise you will 'walk in the light of the Lord' (Isaiah 2:5; 2 Nephi 12:5). Sometimes the spirit of revelation will operate immediately and intensely, other times subtly and gradually, and often so delicately you may not even consciously recognize it. But regardless of the pattern whereby this blessing is received, the light it provides will illuminate and enlarge your soul, enlighten your understanding (see Alma 5:7; 32:28), and direct and protect you and your family" ("Spirit of Revelation," 90).

Why does Isaiah express concern over the endless treasures and that the land is "full of horses [and] chariots"? (12:7) "'Their land also is full of . . . treasures; their land is also full of horses [and] chariots.' Isaiah refers here to their reliance on wealth and military power, rather than trusting in and remembering their God" (Brewster, *Isaiah Plain and Simple*, 16).

How does the addition of the word *not* in 2 Nephi 12:9 clarify the corresponding verse in Isaiah 2:9? (12:9) The Book of Mormon clarifies the corresponding verse in Isaiah 2:9 with the addition of the word *not* in two places. This verse shows "that the ordinary man and the great man do not humble themselves before God" (Parry et al., *Understanding Isaiah*, 29n15).

How does the Book of Mormon clarify this verse? (12:10) "2 Ne. 12:10 and JST, Isa. 2:10 clarify the subject of this verse [Isa. 2:10] with the addition of this phrase ["O ye wicked ones"], referring to the wicked of the earth" (Parry et al., *Understanding Isaiah*, 33).

How will we see ourselves when He comes? (12:11) President Henry B. Eyring explained: "This [verse] is describing a day when the Savior will come, a day we all look for. . . . This scripture says that in that day, all of us who thought we were special and wonderful will seem smaller, and the Lord will be exalted. We will see better who He is, how much we love Him, and how humble we should be. . . . We need Him, and the faith we have in Him makes us see Him as great and exalted and ourselves as small and dependent" ("Book of Mormon Will Change Your Life," 10–11).

2 Nephi 12:12–22. Isaiah Describes the Second Coming

How are these verses different from the corresponding verses of Isaiah in the King James Version of the Bible? (12:12–16) "The Book of Mormon adds five phrases in these few verses, four of which stress the universality of the judgment. . . . The fifth addition in verse 16 is also found in the early Greek version of the Old Testament, the Septuagint. . . . Since the prophet Joseph Smith did not know Greek, and since there is no evidence that he had access to a copy of the Septuagint [the Greek translation of the Old Testament] when he completed his Book of Mormon translation in 1829, this addition supports the fact that Joseph Smith translated the Isaiah portion in the Book of Mormon from a more authentic ancient text" (Ludlow, *Isaiah*, 90–91). ✪

What do the cedars and oaks represent? (12:13) "Verses 12–16 emphasize the status symbols of ancient times. The 'cedars of Lebanon'—symbols of strength, splendor, and glory (v. 13)—provided beautiful, fragrant wood for major Israelite buildings such as Solomon's Temple (*Interpreter's Dictionary of the Bible*, 1:545). The 'oaks of Bashan' (v. 13) came from the wooded areas east of the Sea of Galilee and were an important local source of hardwood, often a rare commodity in Palestine. . . . Isaiah prophesies that the Lord will abase all these superficial symbols of wealth and power" (Ludlow, *Isaiah*, 91). ✪

Why does Isaiah mention moles and bats? (12:20) "The imagery of verse 20 is striking: the people will throw their gold and silver idols to moles and bats, animals who are blind from living so long in darkness. The irony of this is that people who understood the material value of the precious metals, and should also have seen the spiritual impotence of the idols, will throw these precious items to animals who will not be able to see them at all" (Ludlow, *Isaiah*, 92).

Why does Isaiah highlight the ragged rocks? (12:21) "The proud and the haughty are found in the clefts and tops of rocks (Isa. 2:19; Jer. 49:16; Obad. 1:3). In times of trouble the wicked choose to flee into the rocks of the earth, rejecting Jehovah, who is the 'Rock of Israel' (2 Sam. 23:3) and the 'Rock of Heaven' (Moses 7:53). Meanwhile, the righteous build on the rock of Christ and will never fall (Matt. 7:24–27). It is possible that the clefts of the rocks mentioned in Isa. 2:21 will be produced by the earthquake mentioned in Isa. 2:19" (Parry et al., *Understanding Isaiah*, 34–35).

12 For the day of the Lord of Hosts soon cometh upon all nations, yea, upon every one; yea, upon the proud and lofty, and upon every one who is lifted up, and he shall be brought low.

13 Yea, and the day of the Lord shall come upon all the cedars of Lebanon, for they are high and lifted up; and upon all the oaks of Bashan;

14 And upon all the high mountains, and upon all the hills, and upon all the nations which are lifted up, and upon every people;

15 And upon every high tower, and upon every fenced wall;

16 And upon all the ships of the sea, and upon all the ships of Tarshish, and upon all pleasant pictures.

17 And the loftiness of man shall be bowed down, and the haughtiness of men shall be made low; and the Lord alone shall be exalted in that day.

18 And the idols he shall utterly abolish.

19 And they shall go into the holes of the rocks, and into the caves of the earth, for the fear of the Lord shall come upon them and the glory of his majesty shall smite them, when he ariseth to shake terribly the earth.

20 In that day a man shall cast his idols of silver, and his idols of gold, which he hath made for himself to worship, to the moles and to the bats;

21 To go into the clefts of the rocks, and into the tops of the ragged rocks, for the fear of the Lord shall come upon them and the majesty of his glory shall smite them, when he ariseth to shake terribly the earth.

22 Cease ye from man, whose breath is in his nostrils; for wherein is he to be accounted of?

CHAPTER 13

Judah and Jerusalem will be punished for their disobedience—The Lord pleads for and judges His people—The daughters of Zion are cursed and tormented for their worldliness—Compare Isaiah 3. About 559–545 B.C.

1 For behold, the Lord, the Lord of Hosts, doth take away from Jerusalem, and from Judah, the stay and the staff, the whole staff of bread, and the whole stay of water—

2 The mighty man, and the man of war, the judge, and the prophet, and the prudent, and the ancient;

3 The captain of fifty, and the honorable man, and the counselor, and the cunning artificer, and the eloquent orator.

4 And I will give children unto them to be their princes, and babes shall rule over them.

5 And the people shall be oppressed, every one by another, and every one by his neighbor; the child shall behave himself proudly against the ancient, and the base against the honorable.

6 When a man shall take hold of his brother of the house of his father, and shall say: Thou

2 Nephi 13:1–12. The Ruin of Judah and Jerusalem Is Foretold

What were the consequences of sins? (13:1) "Isaiah prophesies that anarchy and ruin will come upon the inhabitants of Jerusalem and Judah because of the sinful nature of their inhabitants. . . . Anarchy may also come because of the Lord's removing the supply of bread and water (famine or drought), or by the loss of righteous leadership in the region, for God, we are told, will remove the region's luminaries, and children, babes, and women will become the rulers. These prophecies seem to have a double application, referring to judgments against ancient Judah as well as against the wicked in the last days" (Parry et al., *Understanding Isaiah*, 36).

Why does Isaiah list these influential people? (13:2–3) "Isaiah lists eleven types of people as a way to represent all who have achieved community honor and status, whether religious (prophets), civic (judges), political (men of war), artistic (craftsmen and orators), or in wisdom (older men). The nation will be left without military might (mighty man, man of war, captain of fifty), spiritual guidance (prophets), wise men (ancients), justice (judges), and artisans (skilled craftsmen). All these will be removed from Jerusalem" (Parry et al., *Understanding Isaiah*, 38).

Why are the children mentioned as leaders? (13:4) "Judah's lack of leadership will be evident with the need to place the young and inexperienced—those who lack maturity and understanding—in these vital positions. Another possibility is the placement of outsiders in ruling positions over the Jews—outsiders who lack an understanding (as children do) of the Jewish culture and religious heritage (2 Nephi 13:4)" (Brewster, *Isaiah Plain and Simple*, 24–25).

Why does the society break down? (13:5) "Without proper leadership, the whole society disintegrates into chaos, and the people oppress each other. Instead of love between neighbors, there is fear. This ironic twist of events displays the reversal of moral and social values that will also occur in the latter days. Good becomes evil (2 Nephi 15:20/Isaiah 5:20), children 'behave . . . proudly' to the elderly, and the base defame the honorable (v. 5). Truly, Satan's influence perverts the natural truth and order of earthly life. In his hands, items of darkness are made to seem as light, words of deceit are presented as truth, and ways of wickedness are accepted as behavioral standards" (Ludlow, *Unlocking Isaiah*, 94).

What conditions create this leadership crisis? (13:7) "Isaiah continues to describe the scarcity of leadership that faces the Israelites in ancient and latter days, explaining that men will evade leadership and welfare responsibilities for their own family members. They plead, 'In my house there is neither bread nor clothing; make me not a ruler' (v. 7). This not only portrays cowardice, but it also underscores an inability to accept moral responsibility because of selfishness or wickedness. As Isaiah describes this people, there are just too many cowardly, self-centered men among them, and thus the whole society suffers" (Ludlow, *Unlocking Isaiah*, 94–95).

How does sin affect our countenances? (13:9) Elder Spencer V. Jones described how sin affects our countenance: "At times, consequences of sin may appear to be very subtle to the sinner. We may even convince ourselves . . . that no one will be able to detect our sins and that they are well concealed. But always to our Heavenly Father and often to spiritually sensitive leaders, parents, and friends, our sins are glaringly apparent.

"While attending a youth fireside with Elder Richard G. Scott, I noticed five youths scattered among the congregation whose countenances or body language almost screamed that something was spiritually amiss in their lives. After the meeting, when I mentioned the five youths to Elder Scott, he simply replied, 'There were eight'" ("Overcoming the Stench of Sin," 88).

2 Nephi 13:13–15. The Lord Judges Israel

What are the Savior's roles in judging His people? (13:13) "Jesus Christ has two legal roles in the heavenly courts. The first is as an attorney or advocate: 'Jesus Christ the righteous' is the 'advocate with the Father' (1 Jn. 2:1) who pleads the case of righteous souls. . . . Jesus Christ's second role is as the judge in this divine court (Mosiah 3:10; Moro. 10:34; Moses 6:57), who passes judgment on the wicked. Standing was important in the ancient Israelite courtroom, where the judge stood to pronounce judgment" (Parry et al., *Understanding Isaiah*, 42–43).

hast clothing, be thou our ruler, and let not this ruin come under thy hand—

7 In that day shall he swear, saying: I will not be a healer; for in my house there is neither bread nor clothing; make me not a ruler of the people.

8 For Jerusalem is ruined, and Judah is fallen, because their tongues and their doings have been against the Lord, to provoke the eyes of his glory.

9 The show of their countenance doth witness against them, and doth declare their sin to be even as Sodom, and they cannot hide it. Wo unto their souls, for they have rewarded evil unto themselves!

10 Say unto the righteous that it is well with them; for they shall eat the fruit of their doings.

11 Wo unto the wicked, for they shall perish; for the reward of their hands shall be upon them!

12 And my people, children are their oppressors, and women rule over them. O my people, they who lead thee cause thee to err and destroy the way of thy paths.

13 The Lord standeth up to plead, and standeth to judge the people.

14 The Lord will enter into judgment with the ancients of his people and the princes thereof; for ye have eaten up the vineyard and the spoil of the poor in your houses.

15 What mean ye? Ye beat my people to pieces, and grind the faces of the poor, saith the Lord God of Hosts.

16 Moreover, the Lord saith: Because the daughters of Zion are haughty, and walk with stretched-forth necks and wanton eyes, walking and mincing as they go, and making a tinkling with their feet—

17 Therefore the Lord will smite with a scab the crown of the head of the daughters of Zion, and the Lord will discover their secret parts.

18 In that day the Lord will take away the bravery of their tinkling ornaments, and cauls, and round tires like the moon;

19 The chains and the bracelets, and the mufflers;

20 The bonnets, and the ornaments of the legs, and the headbands, and the tablets, and the ear-rings;

21 The rings, and nose jewels;

22 The changeable suits of apparel, and the mantles, and the wimples, and the crisping-pins;

23 The glasses, and the fine linen, and hoods, and the veils.

24 And it shall come to pass, instead of sweet smell there shall be stink; and instead of a girdle, a rent; and instead of well set hair, baldness; and instead of a stomacher, a girding of sackcloth; burning instead of beauty.

25 Thy men shall fall by the sword and thy mighty in the war.

26 And her gates shall lament and mourn; and she shall be desolate, and shall sit upon the ground.

2 Nephi 13:16–26. The Daughters of Zion Are Punished for Their Wickedness

Who are the daughters of Zion? (13:16) "In these verses one can see a good example of dualism.... Isaiah shows that the wickedness prevailing in Israel and Judah included the women, who were proud, arrogant, and more concerned with their clothing, jewels, and personal appearance than with righteousness. But these verses can also be applied in the latter days, when women will once more lose sight of proper priorities" (*Old Testament Student Manual*, 140).

What is the scab? (13:17) "These terms reflect the Lord's judgment on Israel. Baldness is one of God's judgments on the wicked (Jer. 47:4–5; 48:37; Ezek. 7:18), and it may refer to the 'humiliating punishment known among the Babylonians' in which the hair of the forehead would be shaved off. In addition, since the Hebrew word for atonement means 'covering,' an uncovered head may point to one who has lost some of the privileges of the Atonement" (Parry et al., *Understanding Isaiah*, 43–44).

What judgments will Israel receive for disobedience? (13:18–26) "The prophet intimates the conditions under which the finery will be removed.... In short, these women who delight in their immodest exposure are rewarded with indecent and rude exposure at the hands of the Babylonian conquerors, who molest and rape, thus discovering 'their secret parts' (Isa. 3:17). That the destruction outlined in these verses will come through invading armies is supported by the last verses of the chapter" (Ludlow, *Isaiah*, 108). ●

Do these judgments apply to us? (13:26) "I have been hoping ... that the sayings contained in that chapter would never apply to the daughters of Zion in our day; but I believe they will," declared President Wilford Woodruff. "Some of the daughters of Zion do not seem willing to forsake the fashions of Babylon.... Think not, ye elders of Israel, ye sons and daughters of Zion, that we are going to live after the order of Babylon always. We are not. We shall be chastised and afflicted, and shall feel the chastening rod of the Almighty, unless we serve the Lord our God, and build up his kingdom" (*Discourses of Wilford Woodruff*, 226–27).

2 Nephi 14:1–6. The Lord Blesses the Righteous

Why will seven women take hold of one man?
(14:1) "In a Semitic society, the greatest disgrace for a woman was to be barren. Isaiah describes a time when women will support themselves financially, but seek a husband who will make it possible for them to achieve the honor of motherhood" (Ludlow, *Unlocking the Old Testament*, 149). ⊕

Who are the "escaped of Israel"? (14:2–5) "The previous chapter speaks of judgments against the 'daughters of Zion.' This one deals with those who have survived God's judgments. The survivors are those who are the 'escaped of Israel and Judah' and have been 'left in Zion,' to be 'written among the living in Jerusalem.' The survivors will love and participate in the ordinances of the Lord's temple, for they will be 'called holy' (the term holy is generally connected to the temple), their filth and iniquity will be removed, and the same elements (cloud, smoke, fire, glory) that attended and protected the ancient Israelite temples will exist among them in Zion" (Parry et al., *Understanding Isaiah*, 47). ⊕

What might the blood and filth represent? (14:4) "In scripture a number of standard ideas are associated with blood, including . . . impurity or guilt (see Leviticus 12:5; 15:19, 25). . . . Our Savior, in atoning for the sins of all (thereby ridding the world of sin and death upon conditions of repentance), had the blood literally squeezed out of him. In this context, perhaps, blood is not a multiplicity of different shadows, but one complete symbol for the cycle of mortality, sins, and redemption" (Gaskill, *Lost Language of Symbolism*, 29–31).

What is one way that God comes to the aid of Latter-day Israel? (14:5–6) "Just as a king's throne is covered with a canopy, so will it be becoming for our Lord the King to have a canopy over his Zion. . . .

"Isaiah ends the chapter (14:6) by giving a description of simple comforts and protection the Lord will provide for his people in Zion. There will be provided a pavilion for shade by day from the heat, and for a refuge and a shelter from storm. Some authorities think that 'heat' and 'storm' symbolize enemy attacks, but I think such a view is highly unlikely when applied to a glorified, redeemed Zion" (Sperry, *Book of Mormon Compendium*, 184).

CHAPTER 14

Zion and her daughters will be redeemed and cleansed in the millennial day—Compare Isaiah 4. About 559–545 B.C.

1 And in that day, seven women shall take hold of one man, saying: We will eat our own bread, and wear our own apparel; only let us be called by thy name to take away our reproach.

2 In that day shall the branch of the Lord be beautiful and glorious; the fruit of the earth excellent and comely to them that are escaped of Israel.

3 And it shall come to pass, they that are left in Zion and remain in Jerusalem shall be called holy, every one that is written among the living in Jerusalem—

4 When the Lord shall have washed away the filth of the daughters of Zion, and shall have purged the blood of Jerusalem from the midst thereof by the spirit of judgment and by the spirit of burning.

5 And the Lord will create upon every dwelling-place of mount Zion, and upon her assemblies, a cloud and smoke by day and the shining of a flaming fire by night; for upon all the glory of Zion shall be a defence.

6 And there shall be a tabernacle for a shadow in the daytime from the heat, and for a place of refuge, and a covert from storm and from rain.

CHAPTER 15

The Lord's vineyard (Israel) will become deso-
late, and His people will be scattered—Woes
will come upon them in their apostate and
scattered state—The Lord will lift an ensign
and gather Israel—Compare Isaiah 5. About
559–545 B.C.

1 And then will I sing to my well-beloved a
song of my beloved, touching his vineyard.
My well-beloved hath a vineyard in a very
fruitful hill.

2 And he fenced it, and gathered out the
stones thereof, and planted it with the choicest vine, and built a tower in the midst of it,
and also made a wine-press therein; and he
looked that it should bring forth grapes, and
it brought forth wild grapes.

3 And now, O inhabitants of Jerusalem, and
men of Judah, judge, I pray you, betwixt me
and my vineyard.

4 What could have been done more to
my vineyard that I have not done in it?
Wherefore, when I looked that it should
bring forth grapes it brought forth wild
grapes.

5 And now go to; I will tell you what I will
do to my vineyard—I will take away the
hedge thereof, and it shall be eaten up; and I
will break down the wall thereof, and it shall
be trodden down;

6 And I will lay it waste; it shall not be
pruned nor digged; but there shall come up
briers and thorns; I will also command the
clouds that they rain no rain upon it.

7 For the vineyard of the Lord of Hosts is
the house of Israel, and the men of Judah his
pleasant plant; and he looked for judgment,
and behold, oppression; for righteousness,
but behold, a cry.

2 Nephi 15:1–7. Isaiah's Song of the Lord's Vineyard

What kind of a song did Isaiah sing? (15:1–7) "In
verses 1 to 7 of this chapter, Isaiah gives us his famous
'Song of the Vineyard,' variously described as a parable
or an allegory. By means of it the prophet effectively
portrays to his people the love, energy, and kindness
which God has extended to them, but which they have
repaid with base ingratitude and rebellious conduct.
Because of this, they are threatened with dire retribution" (Sperry, *Book of Mormon Compendium*, 185).

**What is the meaning of the Book of Mormon
change to this verse? (15:1)** "The Book of Mormon
introduces the parable with the words 'and then' in
place of the KJV 'now.' This modification identifies the
time period of [Isaiah] chapter 5 as the same period
spoken of in [Isaiah] chapters 2 and 4, the last days.
However, the parable is a general description of the
house of Israel and the house of Judah, the causes of
their captivity, and why the Lord is angry with them.
What the Lord will do to correct their situation will
happen in the last days" (Nyman, *I, Nephi, Wrote This
Record*, 602).

**What is meant by the phase "what could have been
done more to my vineyard"? (15:3–4)** "The declaration 'what could have been done more to my vineyard'
is the same phrase used by the master of the vineyard
in the allegory of Zenos (see Jacob 5:47). Although
Zenos refers to the whole vineyard, and not just the
'pleasant plant' of Judah as designated by Isaiah, both
conditions show that the Lord gives full opportunity
within the framework of man's agency, wherein man
must choose and do his part" (Nyman, *Great Are the
Words of Isaiah*, 43).

**What happens to Israel's protection when they turn
from the Lord? (15:5)** "The wall, hedge, and watch-
tower (three elements designed to protect a vineyard)
signify God's protection of the house of Israel.
Nevertheless, God has removed them ([Isaiah] 5:2)
[2 Ne. 15:5] so that wild beasts and invading armies
trample the vineyard" (Parry et al., *Understanding
Isaiah*, 53).

2 Nephi 15:8–30. The Six Woes to Come upon Israel Are Foretold, and a Promise to Gather Israel Is Made

What does "wo" mean? (15:8) "The word *wo* denotes distress, affliction, or something of an adverse nature. 'Wo unto [them]' simply means that adversity will befall the individual[s] upon whom or about whom the 'wo' is spoken" (Brewster, *Doctrine and Covenants Encyclopedia*, 644).

What evil practice is the Lord concerned about when condemning Israel for joining "house to house, till there can be no place"? (15:8) "They, the insatiable, would not rest till, after every smaller piece of landed property had been swallowed by them, the whole land had come into their possession, and no one beside themselves was settled in the land [Job 22:8]. Such covetousness was all the more reprehensible, because the law of Israel had provided so very stringently and carefully, that as far as possible there should be an equal distribution of the soil, and that hereditary family property should be inalienable" (Keil and Delitzsch, *Commentary on the Old Testament*, 7:1:166).

What are the consequences for disregarding the Lord's counsel? (15:11–14) "The Lord here condemns not only drinking, but the riotous lifestyle associated with it (v. 12; see also D&C 59:20–21). Verse 13 tells us that this type of behavior leads to captivity and thirst. It could be a pronouncement of a physical captivity and destruction to come upon the people, or of a spiritual captivity that leads to 'hell,' with the idea of 'thirst' representing a lack of the Spirit (see Amos 8:11–12; John 7:37–39). Verse 14 then promises a definite spiritual punishment: the word *hell* in Hebrew is *sheol*, meaning 'grave,' 'underworld,' 'spirit world,' or 'spirit prison'" (Ludlow, *Isaiah*, 118–19).

What are the symptoms of spiritual famine? (15:13) It has been said that a person's choice to sin is a vain attempt to use worldliness to satisfy spiritual hunger. Elder Jeffrey R. Holland put it this way: "In our contemporary success and sophistication we, too, may walk away from the vitally crucial bread of eternal life; we may actually *choose* to be spiritually malnourished, willfully indulging in a kind of spiritual anorexia" (*Trusting Jesus*, 11).

What might cause a personal spiritual famine? Think of the times in your life when you have spiritually feasted. What can you do to feast more often and, thus, sin less? ●

8 Wo unto them that join house to house, till there can be no place, that they may be placed alone in the midst of the earth!

9 In mine ears, said the Lord of Hosts, of a truth many houses shall be desolate, and great and fair cities without inhabitant.

10 Yea, ten acres of vineyard shall yield one bath, and the seed of a homer shall yield an ephah.

11 Wo unto them that rise up early in the morning, that they may follow strong drink, that continue until night, and wine inflame them!

12 And the harp, and the viol, the tabret, and pipe, and wine are in their feasts; but they regard not the work of the Lord, neither consider the operation of his hands.

13 Therefore, my people are gone into captivity, because they have no knowledge; and their honorable men are famished, and their multitude dried up with thirst.

14 Therefore, hell hath enlarged herself, and opened her mouth without measure; and their glory, and their multitude, and their pomp, and he that rejoiceth, shall descend into it.

15 And the mean man shall be brought down, and the mighty man shall be humbled, and the eyes of the lofty shall be humbled.

16 But the Lord of Hosts shall be exalted in judgment, and God that is holy shall be sanctified in righteousness.

17 Then shall the lambs feed after their manner, and the waste places of the fat ones shall strangers eat.

18 Wo unto them that draw iniquity with cords of vanity, and sin as it were with a cart rope;

What does the image of drawing iniquity with a cord symbolize? (15:18) "Isaiah condemned those who think they can give up one sin and yet cling tenaciously to others. 'Woe unto them that draw iniquity with cords of vanity, and sin as it were with a cart rope' (Isa. 5:18). Occasionally we cut the 'cords of vanity' and let go of a favorite sin, but all too often we only periodically cast off from our cart a sin here and there rather than just letting go of the cart rope" (Top, *Peculiar Treasure*, 160).

19 That say: Let him make speed, hasten his work, that we may see it; and let the counsel of the Holy One of Israel draw nigh and come, that we may know it.

Who is asking God to speed up or " hasten his work"? (15:19) In this context, Isaiah notes that "The wicked ask God to quickly reveal his work to them, so that they may know and acknowledge it. Their motive is probably curiosity . . . or perhaps they are being sarcastic and mocking "(Parry et al., *Understanding Isaiah*, 57–58). ●

20 Wo unto them that call evil good, and good evil, that put darkness for light, and light for darkness, that put bitter for sweet, and sweet for bitter!

How does Isaiah's warning help us avoid deception in our day? (15:20) "An increasing number of opinion leaders and followers deny the existence of the God of Abraham, Isaac, and Jacob and revere only the gods of secularism. Many in positions of power and influence deny the right and wrong defined by divine decree. Even among those who profess to believe in right and wrong, there are 'them that call evil good, and good evil' (Isaiah 5:20; 2 Nephi 15:20). Many also deny individual responsibility and practice dependence on others" (Oaks, "Preparation for the Second Coming," 9–10).

What are some additional examples you see in which good and right are being attacked as bad and wrong?

21 Wo unto the wise in their own eyes and prudent in their own sight!

22 Wo unto the mighty to drink wine, and men of strength to mingle strong drink;

What is a curse for being "wise in [your] own eyes"? (15:21) "As the Lord communicates with the meek and submissive, fewer decibels are required, and more nuances are received. Even the most meek, like Moses (see Numbers 12:3), learn overwhelming things they 'never had supposed' (Moses 1:10). But it is only the meek mind which can be so shown and so stretched— not those, as Isaiah wrote, who 'are wise in their own eyes' (Isaiah 5:21; see also 2 Nephi 9:29 and 15:21)" (Maxwell, "Willing to Submit," 71).

23 Who justify the wicked for reward, and take away the righteousness of the righteous from him!

What does it mean to "take away the righteousness of the righteous"? (15:23) "How many fewer devotees of the First Amendment would there be if, for instance, there were not so much profit in pornography? The words of Isaiah may have some special application to our time. . . . We must never make the error of assuming that the wicked believe in tolerant pluralism—in a 'live and let live' philosophy. Misery may crave company, but darkness detests light. Evil people are not polite pluralists—they are predators, as Lot found out in Sodom. Hitler's hatred of the Jews did not remain a private gripe. Private immorality finally makes itself manifest publicly" (Maxwell, *Wherefore Ye Must Press Forward*, 9–10).

What is the "ensign"? (15:26) "The word 'ensign' is rich in meaning. The King James Bible translators used it to mean a signal, sign, identifying symbol, standard, or banner. Hence, we read the biblical prophecy that in the last days the Lord would 'set up an ensign for the nations' (Isa. 11:12), a standard to which Israel and the righteous of all nations might gather in preparation for the Millennium (Isa. 5:26; 18:3; 31:6–9; 49:22; 62:10; Zech. 9:16). In latter-day scriptures, 'ensign' symbolizes such 'standards' as the new and everlasting covenant (D&C 45:9), the gospel of salvation (D&C 49:8–9; 2 Ne. 29:2), the latter-day Zion (D&C 64:41–43), and The Church of Jesus Christ of Latter-day Saints (D&C 115:4–6)" (Ludlow, *Encyclopedia of Mormonism*, 1:461).

What did Isaiah see in connection with the gathering of Israel? (15:27) "[Isaiah] saw that the Lord would gather Israel quickly and with speed, that they would not even have time to loosen the shoe latchets of their shoes, or to slumber or sleep (see Isaiah 5:27). Imagine a statement like that way back in the days of Isaiah, thousands of years ago, with their means of transportation at that time!" (Richards, "Prophets and Prophecy," 52).

What do the bows and arrows represent? (15:28) "The bows and arrows of the righteous who gather in Zion symbolize the protection that God will provide for them as they return. Similar imagery was used when God brought ancient Israel out of Egypt (symbolic of the world) into the land of promise (Num. 24:8)" (Parry et al., *Understanding Isaiah*, 61).

What is the prey? (15:29–30) To Isaiah, the "prey" could "depict missionaries traveling to the ends of the earth to gather converts who are safely enfolded within Zion's tent" (Brewster, *Isaiah Plain and Simple*, 53). In this context, the prey (both missionaries and converts) are carried away safely from darkness and protected in the light.

24 Therefore, as the fire devoureth the stubble, and the flame consumeth the chaff, their root shall be rottenness, and their blossoms shall go up as dust; because they have cast away the law of the Lord of Hosts, and despised the word of the Holy One of Israel.

25 Therefore, is the anger of the Lord kindled against his people, and he hath stretched forth his hand against them, and hath smitten them; and the hills did tremble, and their carcasses were torn in the midst of the streets. For all this his anger is not turned away, but his hand is stretched out still.

26 And he will lift up an ensign to the nations from far, and will hiss unto them from the end of the earth; and behold, they shall come with speed swiftly; none shall be weary nor stumble among them.

27 None shall slumber nor sleep; neither shall the girdle of their loins be loosed, nor the latchet of their shoes be broken;

28 Whose arrows shall be sharp, and all their bows bent, and their horses' hoofs shall be counted like flint, and their wheels like a whirlwind, their roaring like a lion.

29 They shall roar like young lions; yea, they shall roar, and lay hold of the prey, and shall carry away safe, and none shall deliver.

30 And in that day they shall roar against them like the roaring of the sea; and if they look unto the land, behold, darkness and sorrow, and the light is darkened in the heavens thereof.

CHAPTER 16

Isaiah sees the Lord—Isaiah's sins are for-
given—He is called to prophesy—He prophesies
of the rejection by the Jews of Christ's teach-
ings—A remnant will return—Compare Isaiah
6. About 559–545 B.C.

1 In the year that king Uzziah died, I saw
also the Lord sitting upon a throne, high and
lifted up, and his train filled the temple.

2 Above it stood the seraphim; each one had
six wings; with twain he covered his face,
and with twain he covered his feet, and with
twain he did fly.

3 And one cried unto another, and said:
Holy, holy, holy, is the Lord of Hosts; the
whole earth is full of his glory.

4 And the posts of the door moved at the
voice of him that cried, and the house was
filled with smoke.

5 Then said I: Wo is unto me! for I am undone; because I am a man of unclean lips; and
I dwell in the midst of a people of unclean
lips; for mine eyes have seen the King, the
Lord of Hosts.

6 Then flew one of the seraphim unto me,
having a live coal in his hand, which he had
taken with the tongs from off the altar;

7 And he laid it upon my mouth, and said:
Lo, this has touched thy lips; and thine iniquity is taken away, and thy sin purged.

2 Nephi 16:1–7. Isaiah Is Made Worthy to Stand before the Lord

**Why did Isaiah see a vision of "the Lord sitting
upon a throne"? (16:1)** This type of vision is known
as a throne theophany. "Many ancient Near Eastern
accounts show the messenger delivering the identical words he received from the council [he becomes
a courier]. . . . That council, its decrees, its intimate
confidences, and the heavenly principles upon which
this council was based, were known in Hebrew as the
sod (Greek *mysterion*), and knowing the *sod* conferred great power and wisdom" (Welch, "Calling of a
Prophet," 40–41). ✛

What are seraphim? (16:2–3) "Isaiah communicates his vision in symbolic terms. Just as Yahweh's
[Jehovah's] robe symbolically but not literally fills the
temple, so these beings are symbolic. . . . [Seraphim]
is a transliteration of the Hebrew, meaning 'burning
ones.' This connotation has been lost in translation,
but 'burning' would have illustrated their glory and
marked them as celestial beings. Each seraph used
its wings for flight, but its symbolic function—the
more important—is to mark them as celestial beings"
(Gardner, *Second Witness*, 2:241).

Why is "holy" repeated three times? (16:3) "Both
in poetry and prose, repetition is the hallmark of the
Hebraic style. It is such a dominant element in Hebraic
writing that it can even be seen in the grammar of the
language . . . the way Hebrew supplies the force of a
superlative by repetition, as in Exodus 30:10, which literally reads, 'It is a holiness of holinesses unto the Lord'
(translated in English as 'It is most holy unto the Lord'),
and as in the threefold repetition of Isaiah 6:3: 'Holy,
holy, holy is the Lord of hosts' [2 Ne. 16:3]" (Barney,
"Understanding Old Testament Poetry," 51).

**Why did an angel lay a live coal upon Isaiah's lips?
(16:6–7)** "The live coal that touches Isaiah's lips symbolizes the purging of his sins, just as our ordinances
of baptism and the sacrament physically represent
acts of spiritual power" (Ludlow, *Isaiah*, 131).

2 Nephi 16:8–13. Isaiah Is Called to Minister to Israel, but Israel Will Reject His Message

In what ways was Isaiah's call similar to that of Jesus's? (16:8–13) "In many ways, Isaiah and Jesus faced comparable and extremely difficult teaching situations. Isaiah was the last great prophet to address assembled Israel. During his ministry, the Ten Tribes were taken captive; they later fled to the north and became lost.... Given this wide time period and recognizing the wide range of spiritual attitudes that the readers of his work would have, Isaiah was challenged to find the means to teach such a diversified audience. ... Jesus faced a similar challenge during his earthly ministry. He needed to impart special knowledge to his 'elect' apostles and disciples, while at the same time teaching the multitudes" (Ludlow, *Isaiah*, 133–34).

What is symbolically being taught about the spiritual condition of Israel's heart, ears, and eyes? (16:10) President Harold B. Lee explained: "One is converted when he sees with his eyes what he ought to see; when he hears with his ears what he ought to hear; and when he understands with his heart what he ought to understand. And what he ought to see, hear, and understand is truth—eternal truth—and then practice it. That is conversion. But when he fails to see, and fails to hear, and fails to understand truth and apply it in his life for some reason, then that man has lost his faith. He has lost his testimony because of something he has done" (*Stand Ye in Holy Places*, 92).

How did the Lord answer Isaiah's question about how long Judah would be scattered? (16:11–13) "This is clearly a prophecy that, although the cities of Judah will be destroyed and the inhabitants scattered, a remnant of that 'holy seed' will return to inhabit the land.... Isaiah's analogy of a tree's being pruned by animals eating the leaves, and by natural casting off of the dead leaves, indicates that the tenth to return will be a new generation" (Nyman, *Great Are the Words of Isaiah*, 52).

What is a teil tree? (16:13) "A rare English word for lime or linden tree (Isa. 6:13). Elsewhere the Heb. word used is incorrectly translated oak" (Bible Dictionary, "Teil tree," 734).

Why did Isaiah refer to a teil tree in his writings? (16:13) "Isaiah associated the oak and the terebinth (teal-tree [or teil-tree]) not only with apostasy but also

8 Also I heard the voice of the Lord, saying: Whom shall I send, and who will go for us? Then I said: Here am I; send me.

9 And he said: Go and tell this people—Hear ye indeed, but they understood not; and see ye indeed, but they perceived not.

10 Make the heart of this people fat, and make their ears heavy, and shut their eyes— lest they see with their eyes, and hear with their ears, and understand with their heart, and be converted and be healed.

11 Then said I: Lord, how long? And he said: Until the cities be wasted without inhabitant, and the houses without man, and the land be utterly desolate;

12 And the Lord have removed men far away, for there shall be a great forsaking in the midst of the land.

13 But yet there shall be a tenth, and they shall return, and shall be eaten, as a teil tree, and as an oak whose substance is in them when they cast their leaves; so the holy seed shall be the substance thereof.

with restoration. Both kinds of trees are robust and cannot be destroyed merely by chopping them down, for the remaining stumps will regenerate the tree by sending forth new shoots . . . (Isa. 6:12–13).

"Accordingly, Isaiah taught that a part of Israel would return like the oak and the terebinth, which though they are eaten or consumed (*hayetah lebaer*) right to their substance or stumps (*matzebeth*), yet they possess a seed in them that can regenerate" (Ball, "Isaiah's Imagery of Plants and Planting," 29).

CHAPTER 17

Ephraim and Syria wage war against Judah— Christ will be born of a virgin—Compare Isaiah 7. About 559–545 B.C.

1 And it came to pass in the days of Ahaz the son of Jotham, the son of Uzziah, king of Judah, that Rezin, king of Syria, and Pekah the son of Remaliah, king of Israel, went up toward Jerusalem to war against it, but could not prevail against it.

2 And it was told the house of David, saying: Syria is confederate with Ephraim. And his heart was moved, and the heart of his people, as the trees of the wood are moved with the wind.

3 Then said the Lord unto Isaiah: Go forth now to meet Ahaz, thou and Shearjashub thy son, at the end of the conduit of the upper pool in the highway of the fuller's field;

2 Nephi 17:1–9. The Kings of Syria and Israel Join Together to Battle against the Kingdom of Judah

What is the significance in these verses of Isaiah having named his son Shear-jashub? (17:3) "Shear-jashub, who was named prophetically (Hebrew, 'a remnant shall return'; Hosea 1:6–9), was a son of Isaiah and the prophetess, and the elder brother of Maher-shalal-hash-baz. The Lord commanded Isaiah to take Shear-jashub with him to meet King Ahaz at the upper pool because the boy was to become a living symbol to the Jews ([Isaiah] 8:18) and a reminder to the Israelites that a remnant would return to their land and their God" (Parry et al., *Understanding Isaiah*, 71).

Why was Ahaz at the "upper pool" and what is a "fuller's field"? (17:3) "Ahaz may have been checking the city's water supply in case of a siege during war" (*Book of Mormon Student Manual* [2009], 82).

The meaning of the phrase "in the highway of the fuller's field" refers to a 'launderer's field near the stream below the pool of Siloam' ([KJV] Isaiah 7:3, footnote c). Fullers were those who cleansed and whitened garments in large tubs" (Brewster, *Isaiah Plain and Simple*, 65).

What is a smoking firebrand? (17:4) "A firebrand is smoldering wood. The might and majesty of Rezin and Pekah, who were once burning fires with the power to consume, were now nothing more than smoldering embers. The tails may symbolize two animals who are retreating from a battle" (Parry et al., *Understanding Isaiah*, 71).

When did "Ephraim" (representing the ten tribes of Israel) become "broken" or lost? (17:8) This prophecy was "fulfilled when Ephraim fell in 721 B.C. King Sargon II of Assyria deported her citizens, the ten tribes of Israel, to the north countries" (Parry et al., *Understanding Isaiah*, 72). ✛

2 Nephi 17:10–16. The Lord Offers a Sign to King Ahaz

Why did the Lord tell Ahaz to ask Him for a "sign"? (17:11) "The sign was a prophecy that received both immediate and later fulfillment ([Isaiah] 8:3–7). In the Old Testament . . . signs were 'frequently offered by a prophet so that someone may know that God [was] fulfilling the promises he [had] made' ([Isaiah] 37:30; 38:7; 1 Sam. 2:34; 10:7–9). . . . God indeed gave Ahaz the greatest sign in the universe, one that dealt with the Messiah, who would be called Immanuel" (Parry et al., *Understanding Isaiah*, 75). ✛

What did the Lord want Ahaz to understand about the sign He gave? (17:14–15) "In the Hebrew, a definite article precedes the term translated as 'virgin' or 'young woman,' indicating that she is the virgin and not just a virgin or any young woman" (Ludlow, *Isaiah*, 144). ✛

4 And say unto him: Take heed, and be quiet; fear not, neither be faint-hearted for the two tails of these smoking firebrands, for the fierce anger of Rezin with Syria, and of the son of Remaliah.

5 Because Syria, Ephraim, and the son of Remaliah, have taken evil counsel against thee, saying:

6 Let us go up against Judah and vex it, and let us make a breach therein for us, and set a king in the midst of it, yea, the son of Tabeal.

7 Thus saith the Lord God: It shall not stand, neither shall it come to pass.

8 For the head of Syria is Damascus, and the head of Damascus, Rezin; and within three-score and five years shall Ephraim be broken that it be not a people.

9 And the head of Ephraim is Samaria, and the head of Samaria is Remaliah's son. If ye will not believe surely ye shall not be established.

10 Moreover, the Lord spake again unto Ahaz, saying:

11 Ask thee a sign of the Lord thy God; ask it either in the depths, or in the heights above.

12 But Ahaz said: I will not ask, neither will I tempt the Lord.

13 And he said: Hear ye now, O house of David; is it a small thing for you to weary men, but will ye weary my God also?

14 Therefore, the Lord himself shall give you a sign—Behold, a virgin shall conceive, and shall bear a son, and shall call his name Immanuel.

15 Butter and honey shall he eat, that he may know to refuse the evil and to choose the good.

16 For before the child shall know to refuse the evil and choose the good, the land that

thou abhorrest shall be forsaken of both her kings.

17 The Lord shall bring upon thee, and upon thy people, and upon thy father's house, days that have not come from the day that Ephraim departed from Judah, the king of Assyria.

18 And it shall come to pass in that day that the Lord shall hiss for the fly that is in the uttermost part of Egypt, and for the bee that is in the land of Assyria.

19 And they shall come, and shall rest all of them in the desolate valleys, and in the holes of the rocks, and upon all thorns, and upon all bushes.

20 In the same day shall the Lord shave with a razor that is hired, by them beyond the river, by the king of Assyria, the head, and the hair of the feet; and it shall also consume the beard.

21 And it shall come to pass in that day, a man shall nourish a young cow and two sheep;

22 And it shall come to pass, for the abundance of milk they shall give he shall eat butter; for butter and honey shall every one eat that is left in the land.

2 Nephi 17:17–25. Both Syria and Israel Will Be Captured by Egypt and Assyria

What is the symbolism of the fly and the bee? (17:18) "The stinging bees represent the massive armies of Egyptians and Assyrians that would eventually destroy Israel and Syria and then later attack Judah. The pesky flies represent Egyptian armies that would also come into Judah as they counterattacked the Assyrians" (Ludlow, *Unlocking Isaiah in the Book of Mormon*, 130).

Who is the "razor that is hired"? (17:20) "The Assyrian king and his armies represent the Lord's hired razor. The symbol of the razor refers to the fact that the Assyrians forced war prisoners to become slaves, humiliating and dishonoring them by shaving them from head to toe. Hence the fly and bee metaphors in [Isaiah] 7:18 and the razor metaphor foretell that 'no part of the land ([Isaiah] 7:18–19), no part of the person ([Isaiah] 7:20) will be free of enemy occupation'" (Parry et al., *Understanding Isaiah*, 78).

Why would Isaiah use "butter and honey" to describe a land laid waste? (17:22) "Butter and honey may seem like luxury items, but the land was laid waste by the Assyrians (see 2 Nephi 17:23). Consequently, the survivors had to live off the land like nomadic Bedouins with no crops to eat. Butter and honey likely referred to the curdled yogurt that would come from goats or sheep and any wild honey that could be found" (*Book of Mormon Student Manual* [2009], 84).

Signs Given to Israel of the Coming of the Messiah

Themes	Isaiah 7:14–17 [2 Nephi 17:14–17]	Isaiah 8:3–7 [2 Nephi 18:3–7]	Matthew 1:21
Mother	Virgin (14)	Prophetess (3)	She (Mary)
Conception	Shall conceive (14)	Conceived (3)	Bring forth
Child is a son	Bear a son (14)	Bare a son (3)	A son
Naming of son	Call his name Immanuel (14)	Call his name Maher-shalal-hash-baz (3)	Call his name Jesus

(Parry et al., *Understanding Isaiah*, 74)

What did the imagery of "briers and thorns" teach Judah? (17:23–25) "The cultivated fields will return to a wild state and therefore become a location for hunters. Farming, the basis of civilization, will give way to hunting. . . . These waste fields, in Isaiah's culture, signified not only the failure of food, but also the failure of organized society. . . . Verse 25 continues the contrast of social upheaval, symbolized by the lack of agricultural cultivation, with former fields becoming range for livestock (the civilized becoming wild)" (Gardner, *Second Witness*, 2:256).

2 Nephi 18:1–7. Samaria and Damascus Will Be Conquered by Assyria

What does the name of Isaiah's son Maher-shalal-hash-baz mean? (18:1) Isaiah's child's Hebrew name means "to speed to the spoil, he hasteneth the prey" (see footnote 18:1*b*), indicating the swiftness by which the Assyrian army will vanquish both Syria and Israel.

Who did Isaiah select to be witnesses to his words? (18:2) Notice that Uriah and Zechariah become witnesses for Isaiah's teachings.

The Lord provides witnesses for his work. President Henry B. Eyring taught: "The Apostle Paul wrote, 'In the mouth of two or three witnesses shall every word be established' (2 Corinthians 13:1). One of the ways we may know that the warning is from the Lord is that the law of witnesses, authorized witnesses, has been invoked. When the words of prophets seem repetitive, that should rivet our attention and fill our hearts with gratitude to live in such a blessed time" ("Safety in Counsel," 6).

How is Isaiah trying to warn Israel that this prophecy will be fulfilled in a very short time? (18:4) "Isaiah's prophecy concerning the pending invasion of Assyria will be fulfilled within two or three years. The time element is set forth in the prophecy that Assyria will capture Damascus, Syria, Samaria, and Israel before Maher-shalal-hash-baz is able to say My father, and my mother. (Young children are able to say simple

23 And it shall come to pass in that day, every place shall be, where there were a thousand vines at a thousand silverlings, which shall be for briers and thorns.

24 With arrows and with bows shall men come thither, because all the land shall become briers and thorns.

25 And all hills that shall be digged with the mattock, there shall not come thither the fear of briers and thorns; but it shall be for the sending forth of oxen, and the treading of lesser cattle.

CHAPTER 18

Christ will be as a stone of stumbling and a rock of offense—Seek the Lord, not peeping wizards—Turn to the law and to the testimony for guidance—Compare Isaiah 8. About 559–545 B.C.

1 Moreover, the word of the Lord said unto me: Take thee a great roll, and write in it with a man's pen, concerning Maher-shalal-hash-baz.

2 And I took unto me faithful witnesses to record, Uriah the priest, and Zechariah the son of Jeberechiah.

3 And I went unto the prophetess; and she conceived and bare a son. Then said the Lord to me: Call his name, Maher-shalal-hash-baz.

4 For behold, the child shall not have knowledge to cry, My father, and my mother, before the riches of Damascus and the spoil of Samaria shall be taken away before the king of Assyria.

5 The Lord spake also unto me again, saying:

phrases . . . near the age of two.) The prophecy was fulfilled in 734–732 B.C. when Tiglath-pileser, king of Assyria, captured the Galilee region, the Jezreel Valley, and Transjordan, and plundered their riches" (Parry et al., *Understanding Isaiah*, 82).

6 Forasmuch as this people refuseth the waters of Shiloah that go softly, and rejoice in Rezin and Remaliah's son;

7 Now therefore, behold, the Lord bringeth up upon them the waters of the river, strong and many, even the king of Assyria and all his glory; and he shall come up over all his channels, and go over all his banks.

Why did Isaiah refer to "waters" in this prophecy? (18:6–7) "Isaiah describes and then contrasts two forms of waters—the soft, rolling waters of Shiloah, located near the temple mount of Jerusalem, and the waters of the Euphrates, a great river that often floods out of control. The waters of Shiloah are controlled and inviting, whereas the Euphrates is dangerous and destructive. The waters of Shiloah bring life to those who drink them; the Euphrates brings death to those who are swept up in its flood" (Parry et al., *Understanding Isaiah*, 83). ⊕

8 And he shall pass through Judah; he shall overflow and go over, he shall reach even to the neck; and the stretching out of his wings shall fill the breadth of thy land, O Immanuel.

9 Associate yourselves, O ye people, and ye shall be broken in pieces; and give ear all ye of far countries; gird yourselves, and ye shall be broken in pieces; gird yourselves, and ye shall be broken in pieces.

10 Take counsel together, and it shall come to naught; speak the word, and it shall not stand; for God is with us.

11 For the Lord spake thus to me with a strong hand, and instructed me that I should not walk in the way of this people, saying:

12 Say ye not, A confederacy, to all to whom this people shall say, A confederacy; neither fear ye their fear, nor be afraid.

13 Sanctify the Lord of Hosts himself, and let him be your fear, and let him be your dread.

14 And he shall be for a sanctuary; but for a stone of stumbling, and for a rock of offense to both the houses of Israel, for a gin and a snare to the inhabitants of Jerusalem.

2 Nephi 18:8–17. Assyria Will Attack Jerusalem, but God Will Save His People

What is the meaning of a "stone of stumbling" and a "rock of offense"? (18:14–15) "When the stone of Israel comes, he shall be a sanctuary for the righteous; they shall find peace and safety under the shelter of his gospel; but he shall be a Stone of Stumbling and a Rock of Offense (as also a gin and a snare) to the rebellious and disobedient in Jerusalem and in all Israel. They shall stumble and fall because of him; they shall take offense because of his teachings and be condemned and broken and snared and taken for rejecting them" (McConkie, *Doctrinal New Testament Commentary*, 3:292–93). ⊕

How can disciples "bind up the testimony" and "seal the law"? (18:16) "These actions fit into a divine sequence: the Saints must first receive their endowments, then warn the world's inhabitants of God's coming judgments, which will be followed by the binding up of the testimony and the sealing of the law; finally the judgments of God will come (see D&C 88:84; 109:38, 46; 133:72). After the Lord's people have testified to and warned the nations, they will figuratively 'bind,' 'tie up,' or 'shut up' their testimonies and 'affix [a] seal' to the law of God (the prophetic word)" (Parry et al., *Understanding Isaiah*, 88).

What blessings come as we "wait upon the Lord"? (18:17) "If we are going to do our duty, we are going to need the powers of heaven. And if we are going to be given access to the powers of heaven, we are going to have to learn to wait upon the Lord.

"The word *wait* in scriptural language means to hope for or anticipate. Surely the great prophet Isaiah meant that, and I think he meant more, when he made us a glorious promise. . . . 'They that wait upon the Lord shall renew their strength, they shall mount up with wings as eagles; they shall run, and not be weary; and they shall walk, and not faint' (Isaiah 40:31)" (Eyring, *To Draw Closer to God*, 96).

2 Nephi 18:18–22. Trust in the Lord and in the Scriptures for Guidance

Why must we carefully choose our sources of revelation? (18:19) "When people request revelation from sources not of God, such as the various forms of witchcraft enumerated in verse 19 . . . these sources are to be tested according to the law (of Moses) and the testimony (of the prophets). Elder Ezra Taft Benson quoted this scripture as a key for not being deceived and said that this great truth from Isaiah was so important that it was included in the Book of Mormon. . . . President Joseph Fielding Smith quoted verse 19 as an example of the Lord's warning Israel not to seek after 'familiar spirits' or other 'devices prevalent among the heathen nations'" (Nyman, *Great Are the Words of Isaiah*, 65–66). ⊕

15 And many among them shall stumble and fall, and be broken, and be snared, and be taken.

16 Bind up the testimony, seal the law among my disciples.

17 And I will wait upon the Lord, that hideth his face from the house of Jacob, and I will look for him.

18 Behold, I and the children whom the Lord hath given me are for signs and for wonders in Israel from the Lord of Hosts, which dwelleth in Mount Zion.

19 And when they shall say unto you: Seek unto them that have familiar spirits, and unto wizards that peep and mutter—should not a people seek unto their God for the living to hear from the dead?

20 To the law and to the testimony; and if they speak not according to this word, it is because there is no light in them.

21 And they shall pass through it hardly bestead and hungry; and it shall come to pass that when they shall be hungry, they shall fret themselves, and curse their king and their God, and look upward.

22 And they shall look unto the earth and behold trouble, and darkness, dimness of anguish, and shall be driven to darkness.

CHAPTER 19

Isaiah speaks messianically—The people in darkness will see a great light—Unto us a child is born—He will be the Prince of Peace and will reign on David's throne—Compare Isaiah 9. About 559–545 B.C.

1 Nevertheless, the dimness shall not be such as was in her vexation, when at first he lightly afflicted the land of Zebulun, and the land of Naphtali, and afterwards did more grievously afflict by the way of the Red Sea beyond Jordan in Galilee of the nations.

2 The people that walked in darkness have seen a great light; they that dwell in the land of the shadow of death, upon them hath the light shined.

3 Thou hast multiplied the nation, and increased the joy—they joy before thee according to the joy in harvest, and as men rejoice when they divide the spoil.

4 For thou hast broken the yoke of his burden, and the staff of his shoulder, the rod of his oppressor.

5 For every battle of the warrior is with confused noise, and garments rolled in blood; but this shall be with burning and fuel of fire.

6 For unto us a child is born, unto us a son is given; and the government shall be upon his shoulder; and his name shall be called, Wonderful, Counselor, The Mighty God, The Everlasting Father, The Prince of Peace.

2 Nephi 19:1–7. Jesus Christ Will Bring Light into a Darkened World

What was the light these people "that walk in darkness" would see? (19:1–2) "Israel's consolation is ever the hope of their Messiah—he who will sit upon the throne of David and reign in everlasting peace. In the midst of his prophetic description of the night of Israel's sorrows and apostate darkness, Isaiah saw a great light, the latter-day David, even Jesus the Christ, the acceptance of whom would bring to an end the vexations of Judah and Ephraim" (McConkie and Millet, *Doctrinal Commentary*, 1:281).

Why does the Book of Mormon omit the word *not* from Isaiah 9:3? (19:3) "The Book of Mormon changes the meaning of this statement by deleting the word 'not' before 'increased the joy.' The children of Israel, as promised to father Abraham (Abraham 2:9–10), will become numerous. Their joy will be great in the birth of the promised Christ child. Isaiah compares their joy to that received at the harvest festival, a time of national rejoicing, or when soldiers are victorious" (Brewster, *Isaiah Plain and Simple*, 88).

What do Christ's name-titles teach us? (19:6–7) This passage is one of the greatest messianic prophecies ever given of the coming of the Savior of the world. He is the Son of the Everlasting Father, He is the great Counselor, the Prince of Peace.

What do these name-titles tell you about Jesus Christ? How does knowing these characteristics and other scriptural declarations of Jesus Christ help you in your devotion and service to Him?

Who is the individual Isaiah is prophesying about in these verses? (19:6–7) "Some scholars believe that the leader promised by Isaiah in chapter 9 [2 Nephi 19] was Hezekiah. Hezekiah was indeed a righteous king, for he both helped bring Judah to a higher spiritual plane and brought a partial peace to the land. Still, Isaiah was merely using Hezekiah as a type, a figure of the future Messiah. . . . When the Israelites heard of Isaiah's prophecy, they knew it applied to Hezekiah and that they would enjoy a period of peace, but some of them also knew that its full realization would come only in the birth and life of the Messiah, the perfect king" (Ludlow, *Isaiah*, 155).

2 Nephi 19:8–21. The Lord's Anger Is against Israel

What does "we will build with hewn stones" represent? (19:10) "This is indicative of the pride and arrogance of the people. They boast they will replace the destroyed bricks and wood with materials of higher quality" (Brewster, *Isaiah Plain and Simple*, 91).

What does it mean that the Lord's "hand is stretched out still"? (19:12) "Latter-day Saints typically understand the Lord's outstretched hand as a sign of His mercy toward Israel. . . . Within the ancient Israelite and broader ancient Near Eastern context, the meaning of this phrase was quite the opposite. . . . 'The Hebrew is . . . clear on the subject. The idiom is *yado netuya*, which means that the hand is hanging over, threatening, or bent'" (Welch et al., *Knowing Why*, 115). ⊕

What was Isaiah prophesying about as he described the cutting off of Israel's head and tail? (19:14–15) "Because of apostasy, the Lord will cut off the government, elder, or man of rank ('head . . . the ancient and honourable') [Isaiah 9:15] and the false prophets ('tail'). The leaders ('branch') and the followers ('rush' or reed) will be cut off" (Brewster, *Isaiah Plain and Simple*, 92–93).

It should be noted that the word *honourable* has been omitted from the rendering of Isaiah's words in 2 Nephi 19:15, which clarifies that the corrupted leaders were not honorable.

7 Of the increase of government and peace there is no end, upon the throne of David, and upon his kingdom to order it, and to establish it with judgment and with justice from henceforth, even forever. The zeal of the Lord of Hosts will perform this.

8 The Lord sent his word unto Jacob and it hath lighted upon Israel.

9 And all the people shall know, even Ephraim and the inhabitants of Samaria, that say in the pride and stoutness of heart:

10 The bricks are fallen down, but we will build with hewn stones; the sycamores are cut down, but we will change them into cedars.

11 Therefore the Lord shall set up the adversaries of Rezin against him, and join his enemies together;

12 The Syrians before and the Philistines behind; and they shall devour Israel with open mouth. For all this his anger is not turned away, but his hand is stretched out still.

13 For the people turneth not unto him that smiteth them, neither do they seek the Lord of Hosts.

14 Therefore will the Lord cut off from Israel head and tail, branch and rush in one day.

15 The ancient, he is the head; and the prophet that teacheth lies, he is the tail.

16 For the leaders of this people cause them to err; and they that are led of them are destroyed.

17 Therefore the Lord shall have no joy in their young men, neither shall have mercy on their fatherless and widows; for every one of them is a hypocrite and an evildoer, and every mouth speaketh folly. For all this his anger is not turned away, but his hand is stretched out still.

18 For wickedness burneth as the fire; it shall devour the briers and thorns, and shall kindle in the thickets of the forests, and they shall mount up like the lifting up of smoke.

19 Through the wrath of the Lord of Hosts is the land darkened, and the people shall be as the fuel of the fire; no man shall spare his brother.

20 And he shall snatch on the right hand and be hungry; and he shall eat on the left hand and they shall not be satisfied; they shall eat every man the flesh of his own arm—

21 Manasseh, Ephraim; and Ephraim, Manasseh; they together shall be against Judah. For all this his anger is not turned away, but his hand is stretched out still.

CHAPTER 20

The destruction of Assyria is a type of the destruction of the wicked at the Second Coming—Few people will be left after the Lord comes again—The remnant of Jacob will return in that day—Compare Isaiah 10. About 559–545 B.C.

1 Wo unto them that decree unrighteous decrees, and that write grievousness which they have prescribed;

2 To turn away the needy from judgment, and to take away the right from the poor of my people, that widows may be their prey, and that they may rob the fatherless!

What does verse 16 teach us about apostasy? (19:16) "In spite of the dire predictions that await them, and the predicament in which they find themselves, the people stubbornly refuse to repent and return to the Lord of Hosts. They are led by corrupt leaders who lead them astray. The scriptures remind us that 'when the wicked rule the people mourn' (D&C 98:9; see also Proverbs 29:2). Because of their apostasy, they will be destroyed and scattered" (Brewster, *Isaiah Plain and Simple,* 92).

Why are the people referred to as "the fuel of the fire"? (19:18–19) "In 2 Nephi 19:5 the bloody battle gear is fuel for the fire in preparation for the joy and peace of the 'great light' (v. 2). In contrast, the fuel for the fire in verses 18–19 is wickedness, including the people who continue in darkness to the point of not sparing even their own brother" (*Book of Mormon Student Manual* [2009], 87).

2 Nephi 20:1–6. The Children of Israel Become Very Wicked, and the Lord Will Not Protect Them

Why is it important not to "turn away" the poor and the needy? (20:2) President Spencer W. Kimball taught: "We hear reports from time to time of older men and women who, in the sunset of their lives, are neglected by their families and their neighbors.... We hope family members, quorums, Relief Society officers, bishops, and others, using the Lord's own way, will make certain that they are not inadvertently neglecting such needy people. The ways the world has of helping the poor are not often the Lord's way. We must render help in the Lord's way, but let us do it! ... Surely [ward members], quorum leaders, and bishops can be more effective in both ascertaining and responding to the needs of these individuals" (*Teachings of Spencer W. Kimball*, 367–68).

How did the Lord use Assyria to punish Israel? (20:5–6) "In His mercy the Lord sent prophets repeatedly to call His people to repentance. When the prophets were rejected, the Lord allowed Assyria to become a punishing rod to His people. When that purpose had been fulfilled, the Lord then punished Assyria for its wickedness (see 2 Nephi 20:12) by the hand of another nation, Babylon" (*Book of Mormon Student Manual* [2009], 87).

2 Nephi 20:7–19. Assyria's Pride Will Be Destroyed in One Day

What do each of these Israelite cities have in common? (20:9–11) "As the king of Assyria and his armies moved southward, they first destroyed Carchemish, then Calno, then Arpad, and finally conquered Samaria in 721 B.C. The newly conquered cities paid deference, taxes, and tribute to Assyria's king....

"The proud king glorifies himself by proclaiming that he has founded a kingdom of people who produce and worship idols that are even superior to those found in Israel (Samaria) and Judah (Jerusalem)....

"Assyria destroyed the Northern Kingdom of Israel and prepared to destroy Judah, represented here by her capital city, Jerusalem" (Parry et al., *Understanding Isaiah*, 105).

3 And what will ye do in the day of visitation, and in the desolation which shall come from far? to whom will ye flee for help? and where will ye leave your glory?

4 Without me they shall bow down under the prisoners, and they shall fall under the slain. For all this his anger is not turned away, but his hand is stretched out still.

5 O Assyrian, the rod of mine anger, and the staff in their hand is their indignation.

6 I will send him against a hypocritical nation, and against the people of my wrath will I give him a charge to take the spoil, and to take the prey, and to tread them down like the mire of the streets.

7 Howbeit he meaneth not so, neither doth his heart think so; but in his heart it is to destroy and cut off nations not a few.

8 For he saith: Are not my princes altogether kings?

9 Is not Calno as Carchemish? Is not Hamath as Arpad? Is not Samaria as Damascus?

10 As my hand hath founded the kingdoms of the idols, and whose graven images did excel them of Jerusalem and of Samaria;

11 Shall I not, as I have done unto Samaria and her idols, so do to Jerusalem and to her idols?

12 Wherefore it shall come to pass that when the Lord hath performed his whole work upon Mount Zion and upon Jerusalem, I will punish the fruit of the stout heart of the king of Assyria, and the glory of his high looks.

13 For he saith: By the strength of my hand and by my wisdom I have done these things; for I am prudent; and I have moved the borders of the people, and have robbed their treasures, and I have put down the inhabitants like a valiant man;

14 And my hand hath found as a nest the riches of the people; and as one gathereth eggs that are left have I gathered all the earth; and there was none that moved the wing, or opened the mouth, or peeped.

15 Shall the ax boast itself against him that heweth therewith? Shall the saw magnify itself against him that shaketh it? As if the rod should shake itself against them that lift it up, or as if the staff should lift up itself as if it were no wood!

16 Therefore shall the Lord, the Lord of Hosts, send among his fat ones, leanness; and under his glory he shall kindle a burning like the burning of a fire.

17 And the light of Israel shall be for a fire, and his Holy One for a flame, and shall burn and shall devour his thorns and his briers in one day;

18 And shall consume the glory of his forest, and of his fruitful field, both soul and body; and they shall be as when a standard-bearer fainteth.

19 And the rest of the trees of his forest shall be few, that a child may write them.

20 And it shall come to pass in that day, that the remnant of Israel, and such as are escaped of the house of Jacob, shall no more again stay upon him that smote them, but shall stay upon the Lord, the Holy One of Israel, in truth.

21 The remnant shall return, yea, even the remnant of Jacob, unto the mighty God.

22 For though thy people Israel be as the sand of the sea, yet a remnant of them shall return; the consumption decreed shall overflow with righteousness.

23 For the Lord God of Hosts shall make a consumption, even determined in all the land.

Who or what are the "fat ones"? (20:16) "Yahweh [Jehovah] will humble the boastful Assyria of verses 7–14. The Assyrian fortunes will be reversed. Their fat (prosperity) will become lean, and their glory, a burning (fires of destruction)" (Gardner, *Second Witness*, 2:282).

In what way is the Lord's light also a fire? (20:17–19) "God is a light to his people, but a burning flame to his enemies" (Reynolds and Sjodahl, *Commentary on the Book of Mormon*, 1:354). Isaiah illustrates here that the day would come when the Holy One would return as a light to Israel but a flame that "shall burn and shall devour his thorns and briers [Assyria] in one day" (2 Nephi 20:17).

2 Nephi 20:20–27. The Remnant of Israel Will Return to the Lord and Be Saved

What is the remnant and when will they return? (20:20–21) "Isaiah uses the term remnant to describe two distinct groups of Israelites: he talks about a remnant that remains in the land after the Assyrian destruction and promises the return of a future righteous remnant. The two groups are called the historical remnant and the eschatological remnant respectively. The historical remnant is the group present from a past event (such as the Assyrian invasions), while the eschatological remnant is the group that will emerge from a future action of God and have the qualifications of a latter-day, millennial society" (Ludlow, *Isaiah*, 164). ⊕

What is the "consumption" that is "decreed"? (20:22–23) The "consumption decreed" refers to the Second Coming of Jesus Christ, when "all flesh shall see [Him] together" and "all the face of the earth, shall be consumed" (D&C 101:23–24).

24 Therefore, thus saith the Lord God of Hosts: O my people that dwellest in Zion, be not afraid of the Assyrian; he shall smite thee with a rod, and shall lift up his staff against thee, after the manner of Egypt.

25 For yet a very little while, and the indignation shall cease, and mine anger in their destruction.

26 And the Lord of Hosts shall stir up a scourge for him according to the slaughter of Midian at the rock of Oreb; and as his rod was upon the sea so shall he lift it up after the manner of Egypt.

27 And it shall come to pass in that day that his burden shall be taken away from off thy shoulder, and his yoke from off thy neck, and the yoke shall be destroyed because of the anointing.

What is the "anointing" that will destroy the Assyrian yoke? (20:27) "This may refer to the Messiah (Hebrew 'anointed one') who was anointed with olive oil and the Holy Ghost (Acts 10:38). In addition, [this passage] contains symbols that represent Jesus the Messiah, including rock, rod, and the removal of the yoke and burden (Matt. 11:28–29)" (Parry et al., *Understanding Isaiah*, 112).

2 Nephi 20:28–34. The Assyrian Army Invades Israel but Is Destroyed by the Lord to Save Jerusalem

Why does Isaiah list several cities of Judah? (20:28–32) "The mighty Assyrian army marches southward toward Jerusalem, destroying and sacking all towns and villages in its path. Isaiah identifies several cities whose inhabitants cry out with fear as they flee from the Assyrians: Aiath, Migron, Michmash, Geba, Ramah, Gibeah, Laish, Anathoth, Madmenah, Gebim, and Nob. The army lays up supplies at Michmash and stops at Nob to rest. Finally the angry army halts before Jerusalem and makes a threatening gesture toward the sacred mount of Judah, the temple mount" (Parry et al., *Understanding Isaiah*, 112). ☉

Why will the Lord "lop the bough" of Assyria? (20:33–34) "Assyria would be as the axe [2 Ne. 20:15] in the hand of the Lord to hew down a corrupt tree, but, supposing that the power was in themselves, they too would be felled by him whom they mocked. Their destruction was but a type and forewarning to modern idolaters, those who fail to acknowledge the hand of the Lord but rather trust in the arm of flesh. Their ruination at the time of Christ's return is certain, while the righteous remnant of Israel, those who have

28 He is come to Aiath, he is passed to Migron; at Michmash he hath laid up his carriages.

29 They are gone over the passage; they have taken up their lodging at Geba; Ramath is afraid; Gibeah of Saul is fled.

30 Lift up the voice, O daughter of Gallim; cause it to be heard unto Laish, O poor Anathoth.

31 Madmenah is removed; the inhabitants of Gebim gather themselves to flee.

32 As yet shall he remain at Nob that day; he shall shake his hand against the mount of the daughter of Zion, the hill of Jerusalem.

33 Behold, the Lord, the Lord of Hosts shall lop the bough with terror; and the high ones of stature shall be hewn down; and the haughty shall be humbled.

34 And he shall cut down the thickets of the forests with iron, and Lebanon shall fall by a mighty one.

CHAPTER 21

The stem of Jesse (Christ) will judge in righteousness—The knowledge of God will cover the earth in the Millennium—The Lord will raise an ensign and gather Israel—Compare Isaiah 11. About 559–545 B.C.

1 And there shall come forth a rod out of the stem of Jesse, and a branch shall grow out of his roots.

2 And the Spirit of the Lord shall rest upon him, the spirit of wisdom and understanding, the spirit of counsel and might, the spirit of knowledge and of the fear of the Lord;

3 And shall make him of quick understanding in the fear of the Lord; and he shall not judge after the sight of his eyes, neither reprove after the hearing of his ears.

4 But with righteousness shall he judge the poor, and reprove with equity for the meek of the earth; and he shall smite the earth with the rod of his mouth, and with the breath of his lips shall he slay the wicked.

5 And righteousness shall be the girdle of his loins, and faithfulness the girdle of his reins.

6 The wolf also shall dwell with the lamb, and the leopard shall lie down with the kid, and the calf and the young lion and fatling together; and a little child shall lead them.

7 And the cow and the bear shall feed; their young ones shall lie down together; and the lion shall eat straw like the ox.

trusted in the Lord, will greet their returning king with anthems of praise" (McConkie and Millet, *Doctrinal Commentary*, 1:281).

2 Nephi 21:1–5. The Stem, or Branch, of Jesse Will Come Forth to Judge in Righteousness

Who is the "stem of Jesse"? (21:1–5) The Lord clearly revealed that the stem of Jesse is Jesus Christ (D&C 113:1–2). He is also referred to as the "Branch." Elder Bruce R. McConkie taught: "'Behold, the days come, saith the Lord, that I will raise unto David a righteous Branch, and a King shall reign and prosper'... (Jer. 23:3–6). That is to say, the King who shall reign personally upon the earth during the Millennium shall be the Branch who grew out of the house of David.... He is the Lord Jehovah, even him whom we call Christ" (McConkie, *Promised Messiah*, 193). ✪

Who is the rod that will come "out of the stem of Jesse"? (21:1) The Doctrine and Covenants gives us the answer: "It is a servant in the hands of Christ, who is partly a descendant of Jesse as well as of Ephraim, or of the house of Joseph, on whom there is laid much power" (D&C 113:4). Latter-day Saint scholar Sidney B. Sperry observed "that the 'rod' was Joseph Smith, believing that the Prophet, out of modesty, hesitated to name himself directly.... As the 'rod' or 'servant in the hands of Christ,' Joseph Smith fits naturally into Isaiah's prophecy, and it is easy to understand why Moroni quoted and explained Isaiah 11 to him [see Joseph Smith–History 1:40]" ("Problem of the 'Rod' and the 'Root of Jesse,'" 869–914; see also *Doctrine and Covenants Student Manual*, 283). ✪

2 Nephi 21:6–9. The Glorious Conditions of the Millennium Are Prophesied

What is the meaning of the wild and tame animals? (21:6–8) "Six animals are listed.... Three are wild carnivores (wolf, leopard, lion) that feed on the three tame animals (lamb, kid, calf). The wild animals, which are ferocious, aggressive, and vicious, are a threat to mankind; the tame animals are docile, submissive, and useful to man. This passage may be taken literally; or the wolf, leopard, and lion may represent those who foment war and murder; the lamb, kid, and calf may symbolize meek and peaceful people" (Parry et al., *Understanding Isaiah*, 119). ⊕

How will the earth someday be "full of the knowledge of the Lord"? (21:9) Elder Orson Pratt testified: "The knowledge of God will then cover the earth as the waters cover the mighty deep. There will be no place of ignorance, no place of darkness, no place for those that will not serve God. Why? Because Jesus, the Great Creator, and also the Great Redeemer, will be himself on the earth, and his holy angels will be on the earth, and all the resurrected Saints that have died in former dispensations will all come forth, and they will be on the earth" (in *Journal of Discourses*, 21:324–25). ⊕

2 Nephi 21:10–16. Israel and the Gentiles Shall Gather to the Lord's Ensign

Who is the "root of Jesse"? (21:10) "The Doctrine and Covenants identifies this individual as 'a descendant of Jesse, as well as of Joseph, unto whom rightly belongs the priesthood, and the keys of the kingdom, for an ensign, and for the gathering of my people in the last days' (D&C 113:5-6)" (Brewster, *Isaiah Plain and Simple*, 112).

When will the Lord gather Israel "the second time"? (21:11–12) Joseph Smith wrote: "The time has at last arrived when the God of Abraham, of Isaac, and of Jacob, has set his hand again the second time to recover the remnants of his people, . . . and with them to bring in the fulness of the Gentiles, and establish that covenant with them, which was promised when their sins should be taken away" (*History of the Church*, 1:313).

How can the phrase "ensign for the nations" be understood? (21:12) "There is safety and protection in the Church. . . . The principles of the gospel taught in the Church and learned from the scriptures become a guide for each of us individually and for our families.

"We know that the homes we establish, and those of our descendants, will be the refuge spoken of in the revelations—the 'light,' the 'standard,' the 'ensign' for all nations, and the 'refuge' against the gathering storms

8 And the sucking child shall play on the hole of the asp, and the weaned child shall put his hand on the cockatrice's den.

9 They shall not hurt nor destroy in all my holy mountain, for the earth shall be full of the knowledge of the Lord, as the waters cover the sea.

10 And in that day there shall be a root of Jesse, which shall stand for an ensign of the people; to it shall the Gentiles seek; and his rest shall be glorious.

11 And it shall come to pass in that day that the Lord shall set his hand again the second time to recover the remnant of his people which shall be left, from Assyria, and from Egypt, and from Pathros, and from Cush, and from Elam, and from Shinar, and from Hamath, and from the islands of the sea.

12 And he shall set up an ensign for the nations, and shall assemble the outcasts of Israel, and gather together the dispersed of Judah from the four corners of the earth.

To What Time Periods Do Isaiah's Prophecies Speak?

President Dallin H. Oaks taught: "The book of Isaiah contains numerous prophecies that seem to have multiple fulfillments. One seems to involve the people of Isaiah's day or the circumstances of the next generation. Another meaning, often symbolic, seems to refer to events in the meridian of time. . . . Still another meaning or fulfillment of the same prophecy seems to relate to the events attending the Second Coming of the Savior. The fact that many of these prophecies can have multiple meanings underscores the importance of our seeking revelation from the Holy Ghost to help us interpret them" ("Scripture Reading and Revelation," 8).

(see D&C 115:5–6; Isaiah 11:12; 2 Nephi 21:12). The ensign to which all of us are to rally is Jesus Christ, . . . whose Church this is" (Packer, "Defense and Refuge," 88).

13 The envy of Ephraim also shall depart, and the adversaries of Judah shall be cut off; Ephraim shall not envy Judah, and Judah shall not vex Ephraim.

14 But they shall fly upon the shoulders of the Philistines towards the west; they shall spoil them of the east together; they shall lay their hand upon Edom and Moab; and the children of Ammon shall obey them.

15 And the Lord shall utterly destroy the tongue of the Egyptian sea; and with his mighty wind he shall shake his hand over the river, and shall smite it in the seven streams, and make men go over dry shod.

16 And there shall be a highway for the remnant of his people which shall be left, from Assyria, like as it was to Israel in the day that he came up out of the land of Egypt.

How will "the remnant of his people" or the ten lost tribes return? (21:13–16)

"In the coming Millennial day, Israel—which . . . had been divided into two divisive, warring, rebellious kingdoms: the Kingdom of Israel, with its Ten Tribes and the Kingdom of Judah, with the residue; two kingdoms long since destroyed and taken captive, . . . scattered in all the earth—Israel shall again become one nation, upon the mountains of Israel. . . . After the Lord returns, a highway shall be cast up—Isaiah calls it the way of holiness where none of the unclean can pass, meaning that it is the strait and narrow path leading to eternal life—and upon this highway the Ten Tribes shall return" (McConkie, *New Witness*, 641–42). ●

CHAPTER 22

In the millennial day all men will praise the Lord—He will dwell among them—Compare Isaiah 12. About 559–545 B.C.

1 And in that day thou shalt say: O Lord, I will praise thee; though thou wast angry with me thine anger is turned away, and thou comfortedst me.

2 Behold, God is my salvation; I will trust, and not be afraid; for the Lord Jehovah is my strength and my song; he also has become my salvation.

3 Therefore, with joy shall ye draw water out of the wells of salvation.

2 Nephi 22:1–6. In the Millennium All People Will Praise the Lord

To what "day" does Isaiah refer in this brief chapter? (22:1–6) In the millennial day, "The redeemed remnant will be grateful for forgiveness. Because Israel will turn from sin to repentance, the Lord will turn from punishing her to comforting her. The Lord God Jehovah is not only a source of protecting strength to the once-beleaguered Israel, but He is also the source of her salvation in His role as the Redeeming One, or Savior" (Brewster, *Isaiah Plain and Simple*, 120). ●

What does the water from the wells of salvation symbolize? (22:3) Elder Joseph B. Wirthlin identified the source of living water: "The Lord provides the living water that can quench the burning thirst of those whose lives are parched by a drought of truth. . . . When they drink from the cup of gospel knowledge, their thirst is satisfied as they come to understand our Heavenly Father's great plan of happiness" ("Living Water to Quench Spiritual Thirst," 19). ●

When have you felt the desire to praise the Lord? (22:4–5) How have you "declare[d] his doings" to others? Do you sing the hymns with this purpose?

In what ways can the the the command to "sing unto the Lord" have more than millennial application? (22:5) "The admonition to 'sing unto the Lord' is not one that is reserved for the redeemed remnant of the future. Sacred music invites the Spirit of the Lord into our midst and is a wonderful way in which to worship Deity. Modern revelation reminds us that the Lord's 'soul delighteth in the song of the heart; yea, the song of the righteous is a prayer unto [Him]' (D&C 25:12)" (Brewster, *Isaiah Plain and Simple*, 122).

2 Nephi 23:1–8. Isaiah Foresees the Fall of the Wicked

Who was Babylon and what was its "burden"? (23:1) Isaiah's message to a country called Babylon begins with "the introductory phrase 'The burden of,' which is usually interpreted to mean a message of doom. . . . The basic message is against the old Babylon, which existed before Isaiah's time and became a world power under King Nebuchadnezzar after Assyria's downfall and after the ministry of Isaiah. Babylon became the epitome of wickedness in the ancient world, and was used in both the New Testament and the Doctrine and Covenants as the symbol of the wicked world (see Revelation 14:8; D&C 133:14)" (Nyman, *Great are the Words of Isaiah*, 78).

What is the "banner upon the high mountain"? (23:2) "*Banner* also means 'ensign,' which is found earlier in [Isaiah] 5:26 and 11:10. Anciently, Israel's families and clans gathered with their own banner around the temple of Jehovah (Num. 2:2; Mosiah 2:5–6). Similarly, members of God's kingdom of this dispensation will figuratively lift up the gospel banner upon the mountain (Isa. 18:3; 30:17), which symbolizes the temple, and the nations of the earth will seek after it" (Parry et al., *Understanding Isaiah*, 131). ☉

From where does the Lord muster "the hosts of the battle" to fight against wickedness? (23:4–5) President M. Russell Ballard confirmed that this prophecy of Isaiah, similar to the Lord's charge given shortly after His resurrection to take the gospel to all parts

4 And in that day shall ye say: Praise the Lord, call upon his name, declare his doings among the people, make mention that his name is exalted.

5 Sing unto the Lord; for he hath done excellent things; this is known in all the earth.

6 Cry out and shout, thou inhabitant of Zion; for great is the Holy One of Israel in the midst of thee.

CHAPTER 23

The destruction of Babylon is a type of the destruction at the Second Coming—It will be a day of wrath and vengeance—Babylon (the world) will fall forever—Compare Isaiah 13. About 559–545 B.C.

1 The burden of Babylon, which Isaiah the son of Amoz did see.

2 Lift ye up a banner upon the high mountain, exalt the voice unto them, shake the hand, that they may go into the gates of the nobles.

3 I have commanded my sanctified ones, I have also called my mighty ones, for mine anger is not upon them that rejoice in my highness.

4 The noise of the multitude in the mountains like as of a great people, a tumultuous noise of the kingdoms of nations gathered together, the Lord of Hosts mustereth the hosts of the battle.

5 They come from a far country, from the end of heaven, yea, the Lord, and the weapons of his indignation, to destroy the whole land.

6 Howl ye, for the day of the Lord is at hand; it shall come as a destruction from the Almighty.

7 Therefore shall all hands be faint, every man's heart shall melt;

8 And they shall be afraid; pangs and sorrows shall take hold of them; they shall be amazed one at another; their faces shall be as flames.

9 Behold, the day of the Lord cometh, cruel both with wrath and fierce anger, to lay the land desolate; and he shall destroy the sinners thereof out of it.

10 For the stars of heaven and the constellations thereof shall not give their light; the sun shall be darkened in his going forth, and the moon shall not cause her light to shine.

11 And I will punish the world for evil, and the wicked for their iniquity; I will cause the arrogancy of the proud to cease, and will lay down the haughtiness of the terrible.

12 I will make a man more precious than fine gold; even a man than the golden wedge of Ophir.

of the earth (see Matthew 28:19–20) "is in force today and is the mandate for General Authorities, missionaries, and other members of the Church to travel to the four corners of the world teaching the gospel" ("Hand of Fellowship," 28).

When is the "day of the Lord" Isaiah describes that "shall come as a destruction from the Almighty"? (23:6) "The phrase 'the day of the Lord' is used many times to describe the judgments of the Lord that will punish the wicked and preserve the righteous. In preparation for that day the Lord said, 'If ye are prepared ye shall not fear' (D&C 38:30)" (*Book of Mormon Student Manual* [2009], 90).

"As far as we are concerned, he is speaking of the Second Coming, but the facts and the imagery had their beginning in the ancient destructions" (McConkie, *Millennial Messiah*, 432).

2 Nephi 23:9–13. The Lord Explains His Purpose in Punishing the Wicked

What circumstances will exist when these signs in the heavens appear? (23:10) "Both Isaiah and Joel speak of these signs to be shown forth in the sun, moon, and stars, and seem to place the promised events in the midst of war and desolation. . . .

"Although, as Isaiah seems to say, the desolations are in progress when the signs are given, yet the fulness of the day of wrath, meaning the final day of burning and destruction, shall not come until after the signs are shown forth" (McConkie, *Millennial Messiah*, 410–11).

What kind of people was fine gold used to describe? (23:12) "*Fine* gold (2 Chr. 3:8; Lam. 4:2) is a grade of a higher quality than metal simply referred to as *gold*, and the gold of Ophir (1 Kgs. 9:28; 22:48; Job 28:16) was prized in the ancient Near East because it was a grade of gold of the highest quality. The statement here that man will be *more precious than fine gold* calls to mind two things: a great number of people will be slaughtered during the destructions identified in this section, so that those who remain on the earth will be more scarce than a precious metal like gold; and those who remain after the decreed desolations and survive the furnace of affliction will be purified like gold; they will no longer possess dross (sin)" (Parry et al., *Understanding Isaiah*, 136).

What is meant by the heavens shaking and the earth being removed? (23:13) "To have the heavens shaken and the earth removed was a Jewish figure of speech suggesting a time of great calamity and disaster. Such would be the fall of Babylon. The whole political climate and circumstances of the world would be shaken.

"The prophecy also has a literal fulfillment in the latter days. All things are to be restored. The heavens will flee as the earth is brought back to a condition it once enjoyed. The earth will then receive its paradisiacal glory. Its paradisiacal glory is . . . the millennial condition wherein all life will enjoy continual peace" (*Old Testament Student Manual*, 154).

2 Nephi 23:14–22. Isaiah Describes What Will Happen to the Land and Its People during the Great Destruction

How does Isaiah's description of Babylon's destruction parallel the destruction of the wicked at the Second Coming? (23:14–16, 18) "The wicked will be like a hunted deer [roe, v. 14]; they will flee for their lives during this time . . . and they will be like unprotected sheep, meaning those who have not accepted Jesus as their shepherd may not receive his protection. . . .

"The *sword* [v. 15] represents war and its instruments. . . . In the last days, the wicked will destroy themselves. . . . Their children and wives will find no mercy from the destructive armies [vv. 16, 18]. The murder of children and the ravishing of wives is not new to history but represents here both an increase of the hideous crimes against nature and man's savage inclination" (Parry et al., *Understanding Isaiah*, 137).

What is miraculous about Isaiah's prophecy regarding the eventual desolation of ancient Babylon? (23:19–22) Isaiah prophesied of Babylon's glory and eventual destruction more than 100 years before its rise to world power. "To predict the total devastation and desolation of such a city was remarkable, for some ancient cities, such as Jerusalem . . . , have continued through the centuries and still exist today. But after its conquest by Cyrus, Babylon steadily declined. . . . [Its] silent ruins stand as an eloquent witness that Isaiah spoke with divine accuracy.

13 Therefore, I will shake the heavens, and the earth shall remove out of her place, in the wrath of the Lord of Hosts, and in the day of his fierce anger.

14 And it shall be as the chased roe, and as a sheep that no man taketh up; and they shall every man turn to his own people, and flee every one into his own land.

15 Every one that is proud shall be thrust through; yea, and every one that is joined to the wicked shall fall by the sword.

16 Their children also shall be dashed to pieces before their eyes; their houses shall be spoiled and their wives ravished.

17 Behold, I will stir up the Medes against them, which shall not regard silver and gold, nor shall they delight in it.

18 Their bows shall also dash the young men to pieces; and they shall have no pity on the fruit of the womb; their eyes shall not spare children.

19 And Babylon, the glory of kingdoms, the beauty of the Chaldees' excellency, shall be as when God overthrew Sodom and Gomorrah.

20 It shall never be inhabited, neither shall it be dwelt in from generation to generation: neither shall the Arabian pitch tent there; neither shall the shepherds make their fold there.

21 But wild beasts of the desert shall lie there; and their houses shall be full of doleful creatures; and owls shall dwell there, and satyrs shall dance there.

22 And the wild beasts of the islands shall cry in their desolate houses, and dragons in their pleasant palaces; and her time is near to come, and her day shall not be prolonged. For I will destroy her speedily; yea, for I will be merciful unto my people, but the wicked shall perish.

CHAPTER 24

Israel will be gathered and will enjoy millennial rest—Lucifer was cast out of heaven for rebellion—Israel will triumph over Babylon (the world)—Compare Isaiah 14. About 559–545 B.C.

1 For the Lord will have mercy on Jacob, and will yet choose Israel, and set them in their own land; and the strangers shall be joined with them, and they shall cleave to the house of Jacob.

2 And the people shall take them and bring them to their place; yea, from far unto the ends of the earth; and they shall return to their lands of promise. And the house of Israel shall possess them, and the land of the Lord shall be for servants and handmaids; and they shall take them captives unto whom they were captives; and they shall rule over their oppressors.

3 And it shall come to pass in that day that the Lord shall give thee rest, from thy sorrow, and from thy fear, and from the hard bondage wherein thou wast made to serve.

4 And it shall come to pass in that day, that thou shalt take up this proverb against the king of Babylon, and say: How hath the oppressor ceased, the golden city ceased!

"Spiritual Babylon shall likewise become a waste and desolation when God comes upon the world in judgment and ushers in the millennial reign of Christ (see Revelation 18)" (*Old Testament Student Manual*, 154). ◉

2 Nephi 24:1–3. The Lord Will Gather the House of Israel, Who Will Enjoy Peace during the Millennium

Has Isaiah's prophecy of the gathering of the house of Jacob already been fulfilled? (24:1–3) There are at least three fulfillments of this prophecy: first, when Cyrus the Great of Persia issued an order allowing the Jews to return from Babylon in about 538 B.C.; second, "the modern-day return of the Jews to the Holy Land"; and third, at "the second coming of Christ, when the Jews will accept him as their Savior" (Ludlow, *Isaiah*, 186). ◉

2 Nephi 24:4–11. Using the King of Babylon as a Type for Lucifer, Isaiah Prophesies the Fall of Lucifer and His Kingdom

How does the phrase "in that day" clarify Isaiah's message? (24:4) Both 2 Nephi 24:4 and Joseph Smith's translation of Isaiah 14:4 include the phrase "And it shall come to pass in that day." This phrase is not in Isaiah in the King James Version. This significant change suggests that Isaiah's prophecy applies particularly to the last days (see Ludlow, *Companion to Your Study of the Old Testament*, 291).

5 The Lord hath broken the staff of the wicked, the scepters of the rulers.

6 He who smote the people in wrath with a continual stroke, he that ruled the nations in anger, is persecuted, and none hindereth.

7 The whole earth is at rest, and is quiet; they break forth into singing.

8 Yea, the fir trees rejoice at thee, and also the cedars of Lebanon, saying: Since thou art laid down no feller is come up against us.

9 Hell from beneath is moved for thee to meet thee at thy coming; it stirreth up the dead for thee, even all the chief ones of the earth; it hath raised up from their thrones all the kings of the nations.

10 All they shall speak and say unto thee: Art thou also become weak as we? Art thou become like unto us?

11 Thy pomp is brought down to the grave; the noise of thy viols is not heard; the worm is spread under thee, and the worms cover thee.

12 How art thou fallen from heaven, O Lucifer, son of the morning! Art thou cut down to the ground, which did weaken the nations!

13 For thou hast said in thy heart: I will ascend into heaven, I will exalt my throne above the stars of God; I will sit also upon the mount of the congregation, in the sides of the north;

14 I will ascend above the heights of the clouds; I will be like the Most High.

15 Yet thou shalt be brought down to hell, to the sides of the pit.

Why would other wicked rulers be excited to see the king of Babylon in hell? (24:9–11) "The reception of the tyrant among the dead in Sheol [Hell] is described with vivid imagination. There is excitement and commotion, as there would be in any great center of population in the Orient, waiting for the arrival of a great potentate; only, this time they are expecting one whom they hated in life. Kings rise from their thrones and taunt him with questions, sneeringly: 'Art thou become weak as we?' (v. 10). Where is thy music? Look at the worms all over you!" (Reynolds and Sjodahl, *Commentary on the Book of Mormon*, 1:366).

2 Nephi 24:12–23. Isaiah Compares the Fall of the King of Babylon to Lucifer's Fall from Heaven

How was the fall of the king of Babylon a type of the fall of Lucifer? (24:12–15) "The pride and arrogance of Lucifer, when he rebelled in heaven, provided food for thought anciently, as many nations have stories of war among the gods. Lucifer's pride and fall are alluded to in verses 12 through 14. Likening the fall of the king of Babylon to that of Lucifer evokes images of his arrogance, but it also shows how futile his work will be when it all fails. . . . Just as surely as Lucifer fell, so also will all kingdoms . . . based on pride and rebellion against God" (Meservy, "God Is with Us," 106). ☉

What caused Lucifer's fall? (24:12) "In the premortal council, it was pride that felled Lucifer, 'a son of the morning' (2 Nephi 24:12–15; see also D&C 76:25–27; Moses 4:3)" (Benson, "Beware of Pride," 4).

What are the "sides of the pit"? (24:15) "Figuratively, the remotest parts of hell. John the Revelator tells us that at the commencement of the Millennium the devil will be cast into a bottomless pit with a seal set upon him that will not be broken until the end of the

16 They that see thee shall narrowly look upon thee, and shall consider thee, and shall say: Is this the man that made the earth to tremble, that did shake kingdoms?

17 And made the world as a wilderness, and destroyed the cities thereof, and opened not the house of his prisoners?

18 All the kings of the nations, yea, all of them, lie in glory, every one of them in his own house.

19 But thou art cast out of thy grave like an abominable branch, and the remnant of those that are slain, thrust through with a sword, that go down to the stones of the pit; as a carcass trodden under feet.

20 Thou shalt not be joined with them in burial, because thou hast destroyed thy land and slain thy people; the seed of evil-doers shall never be renowned.

21 Prepare slaughter for his children for the iniquities of their fathers, that they do not rise, nor possess the land, nor fill the face of the world with cities.

22 For I will rise up against them, saith the Lord of Hosts, and cut off from Babylon the name, and remnant, and son, and nephew, saith the Lord.

23 I will also make it a possession for the bittern, and pools of water; and I will sweep it with the besom of destruction, saith the Lord of Hosts.

thousand years, when he will be 'loosed a little season' (Revelation 20:2–3)" (Brewster, *Isaiah Plain and Simple*, 141).

What honors and reward will Satan eventually gain? (24:16–21) "Lucifer will not have any honor such as the mortal kings of earth have, though he will have some temporary power on the earth . . . (v. 16; see Moses 1:19–21). He did not want the doors of the (spirit) prison to be opened (v. 17), but he was powerless against Christ's atoning power. . . . Lucifer will have no tomb ('house' [KJV] or body, v. 19), and he will be thrown into a pit (of outer darkness) without any posterity (v. 20). Finally, he and his sons of perdition will be cast off the earth when it receives its celestial glory (v. 21). The ultimate humiliation is that they will . . . fade into oblivion (v. 20)" (Ludlow, *Isaiah*, 188–89).

What are *bittern* and *besom*? (24:23) "Biblical scholars have difficulty identifying the bittern. . . . The bittern [in this case] is a symbol of a desolate and forsaken land, of an area destroyed by the wrath of the Lord" (McConkie and Parry, *Guide to Scriptural Symbols*, 21).

A besom is a broom (see Isaiah 14:23n). "Just as one sweeps his or her house to eliminate dust and dirt, so will God sweep Babylon of her foul matter so that none remains" (Parry et al., *Understanding Isaiah*, 152).

2 Nephi 24:24–32. God Controls the Destiny of Nations

By using Assyria as an example, what is Isaiah teaching about all wicked nations? (24:24–27) "In addition to his use of the Babylonian Empire as a symbol of spiritual Babylon, Isaiah also sketches the demise of the great Assyrian Empire, which in the days of Hezekiah met crushing defeat upon the hills of Jerusalem at the hands of an angel of destruction (see Isaiah 37:33–38). Assyria also served as a type of the world. In like manner will all evil nations feel the hand of God's judgments" (*Old Testament Student Manual*, 155). ✪

When did King Ahaz die? (24:28) In about 728 B.C., "The Philistines revolted and took several cities in Judah. The Prophet warned them not to exult too soon" (Reynolds and Sjodahl, *Commentary on the Book of Mormon*, 1:368).

What is Palestina? (24:29–32) "These verses reveal the judgment of destruction, which Isaiah lived to witness, against Philistia. The Philistines were long-time enemies of Israel, and warfare between the two peoples had gone on for centuries. . . . In Roman times, the Holy Land was known as Judea until the Jewish revolt of A.D. 132–35, after which the Emperor Hadrian changed the name to Syria Palaestina to show the Jews that they had no claim there any longer.

"The King James Version used the Latin form and called it 'Palestina,' but what is meant is the Philistines, not Palestine, as the terms are used today" (*Old Testament Student Manual*, 155). ✪

What can you do to help establish Zion? (24:32) As Elder D. Todd Christofferson taught: "It will be necessary (1) to become unified in one heart and one mind; (2) to become, individually and collectively, a holy people; and (3) to care for the poor and needy with such effectiveness that we eliminate poverty among us. We cannot wait until Zion comes for these things to happen—Zion will come only as they happen" ("Come to Zion," 38).

What can you personally do to improve in each of these three areas?

24 The Lord of Hosts hath sworn, saying: Surely as I have thought, so shall it come to pass; and as I have purposed, so shall it stand—

25 That I will bring the Assyrian in my land, and upon my mountains tread him under foot; then shall his yoke depart from off them, and his burden depart from off their shoulders.

26 This is the purpose that is purposed upon the whole earth; and this is the hand that is stretched out upon all nations.

27 For the Lord of Hosts hath purposed, and who shall disannul? And his hand is stretched out, and who shall turn it back?

28 In the year that king Ahaz died was this burden.

29 Rejoice not thou, whole Palestina, because the rod of him that smote thee is broken; for out of the serpent's root shall come forth a cockatrice, and his fruit shall be a fiery flying serpent.

30 And the firstborn of the poor shall feed, and the needy shall lie down in safety; and I will kill thy root with famine, and he shall slay thy remnant.

31 Howl, O gate; cry, O city; thou, whole Palestina, art dissolved; for there shall come from the north a smoke, and none shall be alone in his appointed times.

32 What shall then answer the messengers of the nations? That the Lord hath founded Zion, and the poor of his people shall trust in it.

CHAPTER 25

Nephi glories in plainness—Isaiah's prophecies will be understood in the last days—The Jews will return from Babylon, crucify the Messiah, and be scattered and scourged—They will be restored when they believe in the Messiah—He will first come six hundred years after Lehi left Jerusalem—The Nephites keep the law of Moses and believe in Christ, who is the Holy One of Israel. About 559–545 B.C.

1 Now I, Nephi, do speak somewhat concerning the words which I have written, which have been spoken by the mouth of Isaiah. For behold, Isaiah spake many things which were hard for many of my people to understand; for they know not concerning the manner of prophesying among the Jews.

2 For I, Nephi, have not taught them many things concerning the manner of the Jews; for their works were works of darkness, and their doings were doings of abominations.

3 Wherefore, I write unto my people, unto all those that shall receive hereafter these things which I write, that they may know the judgments of God, that they come upon all nations, according to the word which he hath spoken.

4 Wherefore, hearken, O my people, which are of the house of Israel, and give ear unto my words; for because the words of Isaiah are not plain unto you, nevertheless they are plain unto all those that are filled with the spirit of prophecy. But I give unto you a prophecy, according to the spirit which is in me; wherefore I shall prophesy according to the plainness which hath been with me from the time that I came out from Jerusalem with my father; for behold, my soul delighteth in plainness unto my people, that they may learn.

5 Yea, and my soul delighteth in the words of Isaiah, for I came out from Jerusalem, and mine eyes hath beheld the things of the

2 Nephi 25:1–8. Nephi Teaches How to Understand Isaiah

What did Nephi teach "concerning the words . . . of Isaiah"? (25:1–2) "Nephi provided a three-pronged formula for comprehending Isaiah's writings: (1) understand 'the manner of prophesying among the Jews'; (2) be 'filled with the spirit of prophecy'; and (3) live in the days when the prophecies of Isaiah are fulfilled (see 2 Ne. 25:1, 4, 7). Applying one or more of these approaches will help us in searching the words of Isaiah, and we can thereby gain understanding—although it will probably come 'line upon line' and 'precept upon precept,' as Isaiah defined the process of receiving revelation (see Isa. 28:10)" (Nyman, *Great Are the Words of Isaiah*, 8). ☉

What is the spirit of prophecy, and how do we receive it? (25:4) "In the final analysis there is no way, absolutely none, to understand any scripture except to have the same spirit of prophecy that rested upon the one who uttered the truth in its original form. Scripture comes from God by the power of the Holy Ghost. . . . To interpret it, we must be enlightened by the power of the Holy Spirit (2 Pet. 1:20–21). It takes a prophet to understand a prophet, and every faithful member of the Church should have 'the testimony of Jesus' which 'is the spirit of prophecy' (Rev. 19:10)" (McConkie, *Doctrines of the Restoration*, 306). ☉

How might we better understand "the things that were spoken unto the Jews"? (25:5) "[Donald W.] Parry explained that understanding the manner of prophesying among the Jews (see 2 Nephi 25:1) includes understanding how the ancient authors of the Old Testament employed such tools as symbolism, metaphor, poetic devices, and prophetic speech patterns.... Understanding Isaiah and other ancient prophets in this way requires serious mental exercise, including a close and perceptive reading of the text and, whenever possible, being aware of the original language as well as the historical and literary contexts of its composition" (Welch et al., *Knowing Why*, 109).

Who are the Jews spoken of by Nephi? (25:6) "In particular, two major historical groups are of concern to Nephi—Jews and Gentiles. To him, Jews are those descended from the inhabitants of the kingdom of Judah at the time Lehi left Jerusalem, regardless of whether individuals might have had ancestors not of the tribe of Judah (see 2 Nephi 33:8). In terms of this very generalized definition, even one who happened to be descended from one of the ten tribes but who lived around Jerusalem in 600 B.C. would be called a Jew (see 2 Nephi 25:6, 14–15 and 33:8). So in this framework, the Lehite colony—whether Nephite or 'Mulekite'—is a subcategory of the Jews" (Millet, "Gathering of Israel," 187).

How does Nephi help us understand Isaiah's words? (25:7–8) "Nephi added some additional information about understanding the words of Isaiah. He wrote that though the Jews in Jerusalem could understand Isaiah's writings (2 Ne. 25:5), Nephi's own people found them very difficult. He explained why: 'For they know not concerning the manner of prophesying among the Jews' (2 Ne. 25:1).... Though Nephi never explained what he meant by that phrase, still he presented his own style as a contrast. While Isaiah's prophecies were 'not plain,' Nephi . . . wrote 'according to my plainness; in which I know that no man can err' (2 Ne. 25:7)" (Jackson, *1 Nephi to Alma 29*, 138). ✛

2 Nephi 25:9–18. The House of Israel Is Scattered Because of Wickedness and Will Be Gathered When They Choose to Believe in the Savior

In what ways does God warn the wicked before they are destroyed? (25:9) Heavenly Father always gives His children an opportunity to change and repent (for example, see 2 Nephi 17:34–35). President Wilford Woodruff declared: "When those ancient kingdoms and peoples became wicked and corrupt, when they turned away from all that was virtuous and

Jews, and I know that the Jews do understand the things of the prophets, and there is none other people that understand the things which were spoken unto the Jews like unto them, save it be that they are taught after the manner of the things of the Jews.

6 But behold, I, Nephi, have not taught my children after the manner of the Jews; but behold, I, of myself, have dwelt at Jerusalem, wherefore I know concerning the regions round about; and I have made mention unto my children concerning the judgments of God, which hath come to pass among the Jews, unto my children, according to all that which Isaiah hath spoken, and I do not write them.

7 But behold, I proceed with mine own prophecy, according to my plainness; in the which I know that no man can err; nevertheless, in the days that the prophecies of Isaiah shall be fulfilled men shall know of a surety, at the times when they shall come to pass.

8 Wherefore, they are of worth unto the children of men, and he that supposeth that they are not, unto them will I speak particularly, and confine the words unto mine own people; for I know that they shall be of great worth unto them in the last days; for in that day shall they understand them; wherefore, for their good have I written them.

9 And as one generation hath been destroyed among the Jews because of iniquity, even so have they been destroyed from generation to generation according to their iniquities; and never hath any of them been destroyed save it were foretold them by the prophets of the Lord.

10 Wherefore, it hath been told them concerning the destruction which should come upon them, immediately after my father left Jerusalem; nevertheless, they hardened their hearts; and according to my prophecy they have been destroyed, save it be those which are carried away captive into Babylon.

11 And now this I speak because of the spirit which is in me. And notwithstanding they have been carried away they shall return again, and possess the land of Jerusalem; wherefore, they shall be restored again to the land of their inheritance.

12 But, behold, they shall have wars, and rumors of wars; and when the day cometh that the Only Begotten of the Father, yea, even the Father of heaven and of earth, shall manifest himself unto them in the flesh, behold, they will reject him, because of their iniquities, and the hardness of their hearts, and the stiffness of their necks.

13 Behold, they will crucify him; and after he is laid in a sepulchre for the space of three days he shall rise from the dead, with healing in his wings; and all those who shall believe on his name shall be saved in the kingdom of God. Wherefore, my soul delighteth to prophesy concerning him, for I have seen his day, and my heart doth magnify his holy name.

holy, the Lord raised up prophets to warn them; and these prophets . . . warned these nations and cities of the judgments that would overtake them" (in *Collected Discourses*, 1:242).

President Spencer W. Kimball observed: "History repeats itself [2 Ne. 25:9 is cited]. And modern prophets are warning frequently and constantly that people are being destroyed by their own acts" (*Miracle of Forgiveness*, 316). ◉

In what way does the Savior have "healing in his wings"? (25:13) "When scripture records that Christ arose from the grave with 'healing in his wings' (Malachi 4:2; 2 Nephi 25:13; 3 Nephi 25:2), it is an image of his power over death and the blessing that awaits all people because of that power" (Gaskill, *Lost Language of Symbolism*, 59). Elder Richard G. Scott testified: "Your challenge may be a serious physical disability, a struggle with lingering illness, or a daily wrestle with a life-threatening disease. It may have roots in the death of a loved one, the anguish caused by another bound by sin, or come from abuse in any of its evil forms. Whatever the cause, I testify that lasting relief is available on conditions established by the Lord" ("To Be Healed," 7).

The Prophet Nephi's Closing Testimony—2 Nephi 25–33

Elder Jeffrey R. Holland observed: "If we were to identify general sections of scripture that are absolutely central to the mission of the Book of Mormon, I'm not sure that there are any more important pages in the book than those that start with 2 Nephi 25 and conclude with Nephi's testimony at the end of chapter 33. That's only about fifteen pages, and yet it is a strong, central statement giving significance to the purpose of the Book of Mormon: to declare that Jesus is the Christ. This is Nephi's closing testimony. It is, for all intents and purposes, the end of his life" ("That Our Children May Know").

Of which destruction of Jerusalem was Nephi speaking? (25:14) "Nephi is speaking of the destruction of Jerusalem in A.D. 70, a destruction that is not recorded in the New Testament. The Jewish historian Josephus gives one of the most detailed accounts of the Roman siege: 'Now, as soon as the army had no more people to slay or to plunder, because there remained none to be the objects of their fury (for they would not have spared any, had there remained any other work to be done), Caesar gave orders that they should now demolish the entire city and temple.' The destruction of the Holy City led to the scattering of the Jewish people throughout the civilized world" (Black, *400 Questions and Answers*, 107).

What change among the Jews will recover them from their scattered state? (25:15–18) "This prophecy clearly sets forth how the Jews would be scattered among all nations where they would be scourged for many generations until they are persuaded to believe in Christ, the Son of God as their Messiah, at which time the Lord shall set His hand the second time to restore them from their lost and fallen state, even by the doing of a marvelous work and a wonder among the children of men, even through the bringing forth of His word for the purpose of convincing them of the true Messiah, who was rejected by them" (Richards, *Israel! Do You Know?*, 57).

In what way is the Atonement of Jesus Christ infinite? (25:16) In addition to the Atonement being of infinite duration in its effects, "Jesus, who performed the 'infinite atonement,' . . . suffered infinitely and is a fully comprehending Savior, having 'descended below all things' and 'comprehended all things' (2 Ne. 9:7; D&C 88:6)" (Maxwell, "How Choice a Seer!" 101).

When will the Lord "set his hand again . . . to restore his people"? (25:17) "Judah will gather to old Jerusalem in due course. . . . But this gathering will consist of accepting Christ, joining the Church. . . . The present assembling of people of Jewish ancestry into the Palestinian nation of Israel is not the scriptural gathering of Israel or of Judah. It may be prelude thereto, and some of the people so assembled may in due course be gathered into the true church and kingdom of God on earth. . . . But a political gathering is not a spiritual gathering, and the Lord's kingdom is not of this world" (McConkie, *New Witness*, 519; see also commentary in this volume on 1 Nephi 10:12–14).

14 And behold it shall come to pass that after the Messiah hath risen from the dead, and hath manifested himself unto his people, unto as many as will believe on his name, behold, Jerusalem shall be destroyed again; for wo unto them that fight against God and the people of his church.

15 Wherefore, the Jews shall be scattered among all nations; yea, and also Babylon shall be destroyed; wherefore, the Jews shall be scattered by other nations.

16 And after they have been scattered, and the Lord God hath scourged them by other nations for the space of many generations, yea, even down from generation to generation until they shall be persuaded to believe in Christ, the Son of God, and the atonement, which is infinite for all mankind— and when that day shall come that they shall believe in Christ, and worship the Father in his name, with pure hearts and clean hands, and look not forward any more for another Messiah, then, at that time, the day will come that it must needs be expedient that they should believe these things.

17 And the Lord will set his hand again the second time to restore his people from their lost and fallen state. Wherefore, he will proceed to do a marvelous work and a wonder among the children of men.

18 Wherefore, he shall bring forth his words unto them, which words shall judge them at the last day, for they shall be given them for the purpose of convincing them of the true Messiah, who was rejected by them; and unto the convincing of them that they need not look forward any more for a Messiah to come, for there should not any come, save it should be a false Messiah which should deceive the people; for there is save one Messiah spoken of by the prophets, and that Messiah is he who should be rejected of the Jews.

19 For according to the words of the prophets, the Messiah cometh in six hundred years from the time that my father left Jerusalem; and according to the words of the prophets, and also the word of the angel of God, his name shall be Jesus Christ, the Son of God.

20 And now, my brethren, I have spoken plainly that ye cannot err. And as the Lord God liveth that brought Israel up out of the land of Egypt, and gave unto Moses power that he should heal the nations after they had been bitten by the poisonous serpents, if they would cast their eyes unto the serpent which he did raise up before them, and also gave him power that he should smite the rock and the water should come forth; yea, behold I say unto you, that as these things are true, and as the Lord God liveth, there is none other name given under heaven save it be this Jesus Christ, of which I have spoken, whereby man can be saved.

21 Wherefore, for this cause hath the Lord God promised unto me that these things which I write shall be kept and preserved, and handed down unto my seed, from generation to generation, that the promise may

What are the "words" that will be brought to the Jews? (25:18) "Nephi wrote that the Jews would be scattered among all nations and remain scattered until they begin to believe in the atonement of the Son of God. He said that in the due time of the Lord the Nephite record will be presented to them to convince them that Jesus is that true Messiah and Son of God" (Matthews, "Power and the Purpose of the Written Record," 100).

2 Nephi 25:19–23. Only Jesus Christ Can Save Mankind

When did ancient prophets first know that the Messiah was also "Jesus Christ, the Son of God"? (25:19) While the title "Christ" first appears in 2 Nephi 10:3, this is the first time the name-title "Jesus Christ" is used in the Book of Mormon. In both instances, these names were given by angels to the Nephite brothers Jacob and Nephi (see Holland, *Christ and the New Covenant*, 69). However, this is not the first time the name was known to prophets. "The name of the Messiah—revealed to us as Jesus Christ, meaning literally 'Jehovah is salvation, the anointed one'—was known from the very beginning of earth's history [see Moses 6:51–52; 7:50; 8:24; Ether 3:14]" (McConkie and Millet, *Doctrinal Commentary*, 1:292).

What power is found in the name of Jesus Christ? (25:20) "Again making an Old and New Testament connection—which would be fundamental to the prophesied understanding and reconciliation of the Jews—Nephi noted that the same power that saved ancient Israel from the poisonous serpents and brought water from the rock at Meribah was the power to save eternal souls" (Holland, *Christ and the New Covenant*, 46). ❂

What does being "reconciled" mean? (25:23)
"Salvation comes to those fallen men who reconcile themselves to God. Through Christ and by faith, men may be ransomed from their state of sin and spiritual darkness and be restored to one of harmony and unity with their Maker" (McConkie, *New Witness*, 123).

What is the relation between our need to repent and the Lord's grace that saves us? (25:23) "It is not repentance per se that saves man. It is the blood of Jesus Christ that saves us. It is not by our sincere and honest change of behavior alone that we are saved.... True repentance, however, is the condition required so that God's forgiveness can come into our lives" (Uchtdorf, "Point of Safe Return," 100). ⊕

2 Nephi 25:24–30. The Law of Moses Prepared Ancient Israel for Christ

How does the law of Moses relate to Christ? (25:24–27) "Nephi and his fellow prophets knew that salvation was not in the law, but they also understood the importance of obeying it in order to realize the full benefit of Christ's earthly mission to fulfill it, wherein salvation did come. The first law of heaven is obedience, and every dispensation of truth has required such. Certainly the fulness of the gospel requires commandment-keeping every bit as much as the lesser law of Moses....

"In fact, the Book of Mormon does more to bridge dispensations and put the law of Moses in its true perspective—that is, to clarify and emphasize its relationship to the gospel of Jesus Christ—than any other book available" (Holland, *Christ and the New Covenant*, 139–40). ⊕

What is the significance of Jesus Christ in the pages of the Book of Mormon? (25:26) "The central purpose of the Book of Mormon is its testament of Jesus Christ. Of more than 6,000 verses in the Book of Mormon, far more than half refer directly to Him" (Packer, "Book of Mormon: Another Testament of Jesus Christ," 8–9).

"The message, ministry, and Atonement of Jesus Christ, our Savior, are our essential family curriculum. No scripture characterizes our faith better than 2 Nephi 25:26" (Cook, "In Tune with the Music of Faith," 42). ⊕

Why did the law of Moses, important for many generations, eventually become "dead"? (25:27) "The law of Moses was, for the rebellious children of Israel, an Elias, a forerunner, a 'schoolmaster' to Christ. And

be fulfilled unto Joseph, that his seed should never perish as long as the earth should stand.

22 Wherefore, these things shall go from generation to generation as long as the earth shall stand; and they shall go according to the will and pleasure of God; and the nations who shall possess them shall be judged of them according to the words which are written.

23 For we labor diligently to write, to persuade our children, and also our brethren, to believe in Christ, and to be reconciled to God; for we know that it is by grace that we are saved, after all we can do.

24 And, notwithstanding we believe in Christ, we keep the law of Moses, and look forward with steadfastness unto Christ, until the law shall be fulfilled.

25 For, for this end was the law given; wherefore the law hath become dead unto us, and we are made alive in Christ because of our faith; yet we keep the law because of the commandments.

26 And we talk of Christ, we rejoice in Christ, we preach of Christ, we prophesy of Christ, and we write according to our prophecies, that our children may know to what source they may look for a remission of their sins.

27 Wherefore, we speak concerning the law that our children may know the deadness of the law; and they, by knowing the deadness of the law, may look forward unto that life

which is in Christ, and know for what end the law was given. And after the law is fulfilled in Christ, that they need not harden their hearts against him when the law ought to be done away.

28 And now behold, my people, ye are a stiffnecked people; wherefore, I have spoken plainly unto you, that ye cannot misunderstand. And the words which I have spoken shall stand as a testimony against you; for they are sufficient to teach any man the right way; for the right way is to believe in Christ and deny him not; for by denying him ye also deny the prophets and the law.

29 And now behold, I say unto you that the right way is to believe in Christ, and deny him not; and Christ is the Holy One of Israel; wherefore ye must bow down before him, and worship him with all your might, mind, and strength, and your whole soul; and if ye do this ye shall in nowise be cast out.

30 And, inasmuch as it shall be expedient, ye must keep the performances and ordinances of God until the law shall be fulfilled which was given unto Moses.

CHAPTER 26

Christ will minister to the Nephites—Nephi foresees the destruction of his people—They will speak from the dust—The Gentiles will build up false churches and secret combinations—The Lord forbids men to practice priestcrafts. About 559–545 B.C.

1 And after Christ shall have risen from the dead he shall show himself unto you, my children, and my beloved brethren; and the words which he shall speak unto you shall be the law which ye shall do.

2 For behold, I say unto you that I have beheld that many generations shall pass away, and there shall be great wars and contentions among my people.

just as John the Baptist (a living Elias and forerunner of Christ) said, 'He [Christ and the gospel] must increase, but I [John and the law of Moses] must decrease,' so also is an increase of gospel understanding and a decrease in the significance of the law of Moses seen in the pages of the Book of Mormon" (Holland, *Christ and the New Covenant*, 136). ⊕

2 Nephi 26:1–8. Nephi Prophesies to His People of Jesus's Visit to America

What important change is Nephi foretelling? (26:1)
"Nephi is not only predicting Christ's appearance to the Nephites but notes that . . . the law that governs their lives will change. The Nephites will keep the law of Moses until that time. Nephi therefore explains clearly not only the person of the Christ, but also the meaning of Christ in fulfilling the law of Moses. He looks forward to the day when the Messiah will provide a new law. It is interesting that it will be 'the law which ye shall do.' Nephi expects that one must

act according to the law. Now his people act under and according to the law of Moses. After the Messiah comes, they will act under and according to Christ's law" (Gardner, *Second Witness*, 2:352).

How does the destruction of the wicked answer the "cry of the blood of the saints"? (26:3–4) "When a people cast out and slay the prophets and the saints, that people shall perish. Figuratively, Nephi speaks of the blood of the ground crying out and ascending to God against them. In the same context and in words similar to a passage in Malachi 4:1, Nephi speaks of the proud and those who do wickedly being burned in a day that would come (2 Nephi 26:4). The doctrine spoken of is the cleansing of the earth by fire at the second coming of the Lord" (Nyman, "Come to Understanding and Learn Doctrine," 29–30). ✪

Why are those who hearken to the prophets preserved? (26:8) "Nephi observed that the righteous who hearkened unto the words of the prophets would not be destroyed. These observations by Nephi deal with an interesting spiritual law regulating this mortal

3 And after the Messiah shall come there shall be signs given unto my people of his birth, and also of his death and resurrection; and great and terrible shall that day be unto the wicked, for they shall perish; and they perish because they cast out the prophets, and the saints, and stone them, and slay them; wherefore the cry of the blood of the saints shall ascend up to God from the ground against them.

4 Wherefore, all those who are proud, and that do wickedly, the day that cometh shall burn them up, saith the Lord of Hosts, for they shall be as stubble.

5 And they that kill the prophets, and the saints, the depths of the earth shall swallow them up, saith the Lord of Hosts; and mountains shall cover them, and whirlwinds shall carry them away, and buildings shall fall upon them and crush them to pieces and grind them to powder.

6 And they shall be visited with thunderings, and lightnings, and earthquakes, and all manner of destructions, for the fire of the anger of the Lord shall be kindled against them, and they shall be as stubble, and the day that cometh shall consume them, saith the Lord of Hosts.

7 O the pain, and the anguish of my soul for the loss of the slain of my people! For I, Nephi, have seen it, and it well nigh consumeth me before the presence of the Lord; but I must cry unto my God: Thy ways are just.

8 But behold, the righteous that hearken unto the words of the prophets, and destroy them not, but look forward unto Christ with steadfastness for the signs which are given,

notwithstanding all persecution—behold, they are they which shall not perish.

9 But the Son of Righteousness shall appear unto them; and he shall heal them, and they shall have peace with him, until three generations shall have passed away, and many of the fourth generation shall have passed away in righteousness.

10 And when these things have passed away a speedy destruction cometh unto my people; for, notwithstanding the pains of my soul, I have seen it; wherefore, I know that it shall come to pass; and they sell themselves for naught; for, for the reward of their pride and their foolishness they shall reap destruction; for because they yield unto the devil and choose works of darkness rather than light, therefore they must go down to hell.

11 For the Spirit of the Lord will not always strive with man. And when the Spirit ceaseth to strive with man then cometh speedy destruction, and this grieveth my soul.

12 And as I spake concerning the convincing of the Jews, that Jesus is the very Christ, it must needs be that the Gentiles be convinced also that Jesus is the Christ, the Eternal God;

13 And that he manifesteth himself unto all those who believe in him, by the power of the Holy Ghost; yea, unto every nation, kindred, tongue, and people, working mighty miracles, signs, and wonders, among the children of men according to their faith.

earth, showing that the behavior of human beings can affect and influence the so-called 'natural' phenomena. The language of the scriptures also suggests that God uses these 'natural' occurrences to punish or at times to reward his children" (Matthews, "Two Ways in the World," 151). ☉

2 Nephi 26:9–13. Nephi Prophesies That the Resurrected Lord Will Visit His Disciples

What do people put at risk if they "sell themselves for naught"? (26:10) "What shall a man or a woman give in exchange for their souls? (see JST, Matthew 16:27–29). Of what value is a divine birthright? Is anything which may be purchased or extorted in this fallen sphere worth eternal life? Are fame, wealth, title, or power worth the bartering of one's values?" (McConkie and Millet, *Doctrinal Commentary*, 1:302).

Why does losing the Lord's Spirit lead to destruction? (26:11) President Harold B. Lee described the terrible consequences of losing the influence of the Spirit: "One of the most tragic experiences that can come to individuals [is] to have the Lord withdraw His Spirit from us. And when He speaks of His Spirit, it isn't just the Holy Ghost, because many of those spoken of by the prophets had not received the gift of the Holy Ghost. This Spirit to which I refer is the Light of Christ. When withdrawn, it becomes difficult for us to pray, to have direction and guidance, to withstand evil" (*Teachings of Harold B. Lee*, 101). ☉

What "convincing" faith in Jesus Christ must Jews and Gentiles possess? (26:12) "Nephi's own words supply the beginnings of an answer. They must be convinced not only of Christ's messiahship, but that he is (1) the Eternal God, (2) that he manifests himself to all (every nation, kindred, tongue, and people) who believe in him by the power of the Holy Ghost, and (3) that he manifests himself by mighty miracles, signs, and wonders" (Wilcox, "Nephi's Message to the 'Gentiles,'" 272–73).

2 Nephi 26:14–19. Unbelief Will Weaken the Nephites and Lamanites

What is a voice "that hath a familiar spirit"? (26:16) The word "familiar can suggest . . . 'known from constant association.' . . . It is certainly true that the Book of Mormon will have a spirit about it that will be familiar to those who know the Bible. . . . Familiar also has another meaning. . . . The Hebrew behind the 'familiar spirit' in Isaiah 29:4 (King James Version) is 'ob. This Hebrew word denotes, approximately, 'the spirit of a deceased person.' Therefore, a familiar spirit can also mean 'a message from those who have passed on before us'" (Hoskisson, "'Familiar Spirit'"). ✚

Who can feel the "familiar spirit" of the Book of Mormon? (26:16) Elder David A. Bednar emphasized: "Youth of all ages, even infants, can and do respond to the distinctive spirit of the Book of Mormon. Children may not understand all of the words and stories, but they certainly can feel the 'familiar spirit'" ("Watching with All Perseverance," 42).

How might you help others, including children, experience the spirit of the Book of Mormon?

How was this prophecy about "those who have dwindled in unbelief" being "smitten by the hand of the Gentiles" fulfilled? (26:19) "The story of the invasion of America by Europeans in the 16th century is a tragic illustration of the truth of this prophecy" (Reynolds and Sjodahl, Commentary on the Book of Mormon, 1:386). ✚

14 But behold, I prophesy unto you concerning the last days; concerning the days when the Lord God shall bring these things forth unto the children of men.

15 After my seed and the seed of my brethren shall have dwindled in unbelief, and shall have been smitten by the Gentiles; yea, after the Lord God shall have camped against them round about, and shall have laid siege against them with a mount, and raised forts against them; and after they shall have been brought down low in the dust, even that they are not, yet the words of the righteous shall be written, and the prayers of the faithful shall be heard, and all those who have dwindled in unbelief shall not be forgotten.

16 For those who shall be destroyed shall speak unto them out of the ground, and their speech shall be low out of the dust, and their voice shall be as one that hath a familiar spirit; for the Lord God will give unto him power, that he may whisper concerning them, even as it were out of the ground; and their speech shall whisper out of the dust.

17 For thus saith the Lord God: They shall write the things which shall be done among them, and they shall be written and sealed up in a book, and those who have dwindled in unbelief shall not have them, for they seek to destroy the things of God.

18 Wherefore, as those who have been destroyed have been destroyed speedily; and the multitude of their terrible ones shall be as chaff that passeth away—yea, thus saith the Lord God: It shall be at an instant, suddenly—

19 And it shall come to pass, that those who have dwindled in unbelief shall be smitten by the hand of the Gentiles.

2 Nephi 26:20–28. False Churches and Secret Combinations Will Come in the Last Days

20 And the Gentiles are lifted up in the pride of their eyes, and have stumbled, because of the greatness of their stumbling block, that they have built up many churches; nevertheless, they put down the power and miracles of God, and preach up unto themselves their own wisdom and their own learning, that they may get gain and grind upon the face of the poor.

21 And there are many churches built up which cause envyings, and strifes, and malice.

22 And there are also secret combinations, even as in times of old, according to the combinations of the devil, for he is the founder of all these things; yea, the founder of murder, and works of darkness; yea, and he leadeth them by the neck with a flaxen cord, until he bindeth them with his strong cords forever.

23 For behold, my beloved brethren, I say unto you that the Lord God worketh not in darkness.

24 He doeth not anything save it be for the benefit of the world; for he loveth the world, even that he layeth down his own life that he may draw all men unto him. Wherefore, he commandeth none that they shall not partake of his salvation.

What might be the "stumbling block" for the Gentiles? (26:20) "What the 'stumbling block' is, Nephi did not say at that point, but he had used the identical language earlier to explain that the Gentiles would stumble because the Bible had been significantly altered and was thus lacking 'many plain and precious parts' that had been 'taken out' of it (see 1 Ne.13:28–35).

"In view of Nephi's earlier . . . explanation about plain and precious parts being taken from the Bible, we can ascertain that the Gentiles' great 'stumbling block' in the last days would be the lack of knowledge and spiritual understanding because of their imperfect Bible, which is the only scriptural record they have ever had" (Matthews, "Two Ways in the World," 151–52). ✛

What is a flaxen cord that Satan uses to bind us? (26:22) In Nephi's day, "a flaxen cord would [have been] made of fine, light-colored fiber manufactured from flax [unspun fibers of the flax plant]—its individual strands soft and thin and easily broken, but as a cord, soft to the touch yet strong and unyielding. If we continually rationalize our involvement with "little sins" we are being subtly, ever so gently, led away by Satan until eventually we will become bound with his "strong cords" (Williams, "Shield against Evil," 31).

What flaxen cords have you experienced in your life? What is the best way to deal with such temptations?

Why would the Lord give up so much to subject Himself to trials and persecution? (26:24) Elder Alexander B. Morrison stated: "Why did Jesus, the Lord God Omnipotent who sits at the right hand of the Father, creator of worlds without number . . . condescend to come to earth to be born in a manger, live out most of His mortal existence in obscurity . . . proclaiming a message which was violently opposed by many, and finally, betrayed by one of His closest associates, die between two malefactors on Golgotha's somber hill? Nephi . . . understood Christ's motivation. . . . It was love for all of God's children that led Jesus . . . to offer Himself as ransom for the sins of others" ("'For This Cause Came I into the World,'" 25–26).

How extensive is the gift of Christ's Atonement?
(26:25–27, 33) Elder Jeffrey R. Holland said: "Perhaps no other passage in the Book of Mormon conveys more plainly the breadth of Christ's gift for all people everywhere than those which Nephi then recorded. The gift was given freely and would be denied to no one who came to partake of that mercy and salvation" (*Christ and the New Covenant*, 48).

2 Nephi 26:29–33. The Lord Condemns Priestcraft and Commands All Men to Have Charity

What is the difference between *priestcraft* and *priesthood*? (26:29–31) Review the definition of priestcraft in 2 Nephi 26:29 and compare it with President Joseph F. Smith's description of priesthood as "the power of God delegated to man by which man can act in the earth for the salvation of the human family" (*Gospel Doctrine*, 139).

What do you see as the most significant distinction between someone who practices priestcraft and one who honors and exercises priesthood? ❂

What warning is the Lord giving in this verse to those who serve Him? (26:31) "We must not only do what is right. We must act for the right reasons. The modern term is good motive. The scriptures often signify this appropriate mental attitude with the words full purpose of heart or real intent.

"The scriptures make clear that God understands our motives and will judge our actions accordingly. If we do not act for the right reasons, our acts will not be counted for righteousness" (Oaks, *Pure in Heart*, 15).

25 Behold, doth he cry unto any, saying: Depart from me? Behold, I say unto you, Nay; but he saith: Come unto me all ye ends of the earth, buy milk and honey, without money and without price.

26 Behold, hath he commanded any that they should depart out of the synagogues, or out of the houses of worship? Behold, I say unto you, Nay.

27 Hath he commanded any that they should not partake of his salvation? Behold I say unto you, Nay; but he hath given it free for all men; and he hath commanded his people that they should persuade all men to repentance.

28 Behold, hath the Lord commanded any that they should not partake of his goodness? Behold I say unto you, Nay; but all men are privileged the one like unto the other, and none are forbidden.

29 He commandeth that there shall be no priestcrafts; for, behold, priestcrafts are that men preach and set themselves up for a light unto the world, that they may get gain and praise of the world; but they seek not the welfare of Zion.

30 Behold, the Lord hath forbidden this thing; wherefore, the Lord God hath given a commandment that all men should have charity, which charity is love. And except they should have charity they were nothing. Wherefore, if they should have charity they would not suffer the laborer in Zion to perish.

31 But the laborer in Zion shall labor for Zion; for if they labor for money they shall perish.

32 And again, the Lord God hath commanded that men should not murder; that they should not lie; that they should not steal; that they should not take the name of

the Lord their God in vain; that they should not envy; that they should not have malice; that they should not contend one with another; that they should not commit whoredoms; and that they should do none of these things; for whoso doeth them shall perish.

33 For none of these iniquities come of the Lord; for he doeth that which is good among the children of men; and he doeth nothing save it be plain unto the children of men; and he inviteth them all to come unto him and partake of his goodness; and he denieth none that come unto him, black and white, bond and free, male and female; and he remembereth the heathen; and all are alike unto God, both Jew and Gentile.

CHAPTER 27

Darkness and apostasy will cover the earth in the last days—The Book of Mormon will come forth—Three witnesses will testify of the book—The learned man will say he cannot read the sealed book—The Lord will do a marvelous work and a wonder—Compare Isaiah 29. About 559–545 B.C.

1 But, behold, in the last days, or in the days of the Gentiles—yea, behold all the nations of the Gentiles and also the Jews, both those who shall come upon this land and those who shall be upon other lands, yea, even upon all the lands of the earth, behold, they will be drunken with iniquity and all manner of abominations—

2 And when that day shall come they shall be visited of the Lord of Hosts, with thunder and with earthquake, and with a great noise, and with storm, and with tempest, and with the flame of devouring fire.

3 And all the nations that fight against Zion, and that distress her, shall be as a dream of a night vision; yea, it shall be unto them, even

Who are the "bond"? (26:33) "*Bond*—the opposite of free—means more than slavery. It means being bound (in bondage) to anything from which it is difficult to escape. *Bond* includes those whose freedom is restricted by physical or emotional afflictions. *Bond* includes those who are addicted to some substance or practice. *Bond* surely refers to those who are imprisoned by sin—'encircled about' by what another teaching of the Book of Mormon calls 'the chains of hell' (Alma 5:7). *Bond* includes those who are held down by traditions or customs contrary to the commandments of God. . . . Finally, *bond* also includes those who are confined within the boundaries of other erroneous ideas" (Oaks, "All Men Everywhere," 77–78).

2 Nephi 27:1–5. The Last Days Will Be a Time of Great Wickedness

Who are the "nations of the Gentiles" in this context? (27:1) "Both Lehi and Nephi divide all men into two camps, Jews and Gentiles. The Jews were either the nationals of the kingdom of Judah or their descendants; all others were considered to be Gentiles. Thus, we are the Gentiles of whom this scripture speaks; we are the ones who have received the fulness of the gospel; and we shall take it to the Lamanites, who are Jews, because their fathers came from Jerusalem and from the kingdom of Judah" (McConkie, *New Witness*, 556).

Why are nations compared to a "dream of a night vision" and hungry and thirsty men? (27:2–3) In the last days God's "judgments will come upon the wicked after they have rejected the testimonies of the Church's prophets and missionaries" and, like "the Babylonians, Romans, . . . after their day of might and dominance, will fade away as a dream vanishes during the night. . . . The nations that fight against Jerusalem and Zion will, in the end, have no more lasting satisfaction than does a hungry person who only dreams of eating" (Parry et al., *Understanding Isaiah*, 262–63).

Why is the name Ariel found in Isaiah 29:7 changed to Zion here? (27:3) "King James 'Ariel,' a poetic term for Jerusalem, is not to be found in the 2 Nephi 27:3 quotation of Isaiah 29:7. However, it is also absent from the Jewish Aramaic Targum—which replaces it with 'the City.' The Book of Mormon reads *Zion* instead. This fits well, however, since 'Mount Zion' appears at the end of the verse (Isaiah 29:8), and 'Zion' and 'Mount Zion' parallel each other here" (Smith, "Textual Criticism of the Book of Mormon," 78).

2 Nephi 27:6–11. The Book of Mormon Will Come Forth

Who are they who have slumbered? (27:6) To slumber or sleep is a "metaphor for death (1 Cor. 15:6)" (McConkie, *Gospel Symbolism*, 272) and refers to "the Jaredites and Nephites [who] *have slumbered in the dust*, or have died and their bodies have returned to the dust" (Parry et al., *Understanding Isaiah*, 266).

What was the sealed book, and why was it sealed? (27:7–8) The sealed book "seems to refer to the portion of the golden plates that was sealed. Sacred records have been sealed up many times in religious history (Dan. 12:1, 4; Rev. 5:1-14; 1 Ne. 14:26; Ether 3:21-22). . . . The sealed portion of the plates will be revealed in the Lord's own time, but not in the day of wickedness" (Parry et al., *Understanding Isaiah*, 266).

Who is the man to whom "the words of the book" will be delivered? (27:9) This prophecy of Nephi "apparently refers (1) to Joseph Smith's giving a copy of some of the characters to Martin Harris and (2) to the subsequent visit of Martin Harris with Professor Charles Anthon [see 2 Nephi 27:15]. Sometime between December 1827 and February 1828, Joseph Smith copied a number of the characters from the plates in his possession and translated some of them by means of the Urim and Thummim. In February 1828, Martin Harris visited the Prophet in Pennsylvania, obtained a transcript of the characters, and took it to Professor Charles Anthon of New York

as unto a hungry man which dreameth, and behold he eateth but he awaketh and his soul is empty; or like unto a thirsty man which dreameth, and behold he drinketh but he awaketh and behold he is faint, and his soul hath appetite; yea, even so shall the multitude of all the nations be that fight against Mount Zion.

4 For behold, all ye that doeth iniquity, stay yourselves and wonder, for ye shall cry out, and cry; yea, ye shall be drunken but not with wine, ye shall stagger but not with strong drink.

5 For behold, the Lord hath poured out upon you the spirit of deep sleep. For behold, ye have closed your eyes, and ye have rejected the prophets; and your rulers, and the seers hath he covered because of your iniquity.

6 And it shall come to pass that the Lord God shall bring forth unto you the words of a book, and they shall be the words of them which have slumbered.

7 And behold the book shall be sealed; and in the book shall be a revelation from God, from the beginning of the world to the ending thereof.

8 Wherefore, because of the things which are sealed up, the things which are sealed shall not be delivered in the day of the wickedness and abominations of the people. Wherefore the book shall be kept from them.

9 But the book shall be delivered unto a man, and he shall deliver the words of the book, which are the words of those who have slumbered in the dust, and he shall deliver these words unto another;

10 But the words which are sealed he shall not deliver, neither shall he deliver the book. For the book shall be sealed by the power of God, and the revelation which was sealed shall be kept in the book until the own due time of the Lord, that they may come forth; for behold, they reveal all things from the foundation of the world unto the end thereof.

11 And the day cometh that the words of the book which were sealed shall be read upon the house tops; and they shall be read by the power of Christ; and all things shall be revealed unto the children of men which ever have been among the children of men, and which ever will be even unto the end of the earth.

12 Wherefore, at that day when the book shall be delivered unto the man of whom I have spoken, the book shall be hid from the eyes of the world, that the eyes of none shall behold it save it be that three witnesses shall behold it, by the power of God, besides him to whom the book shall be delivered; and they shall testify to the truth of the book and the things therein.

13 And there is none other which shall view it, save it be a few according to the will of God, to bear testimony of his word unto the children of men; for the Lord God hath said that the words of the faithful should speak as if it were from the dead.

14 Wherefore, the Lord God will proceed to bring forth the words of the book; and in the mouth of as many witnesses as seemeth him good will he establish his word; and wo be unto him that rejecteth the word of God!

15 But behold, it shall come to pass that the Lord God shall say unto him to whom he shall deliver the book: Take these words which are not sealed and deliver them to another, that he may show them unto the learned, saying: Read this, I pray thee. And the learned shall say: Bring hither the book, and I will read them.

City" (Ludlow, *Companion to Your Study of the Book of Mormon*, 147–48).

How will this book be read from housetops? (27:11) Some suggest that "Joseph Smith's translation of the Book of Mormon fulfills this prophecy. The book was translated by the power of the Lord. So it would be 'read by the power of Christ.' The missionary effort of spreading the gospel fulfills the prediction that it 'shall read upon the house tops'" (Gardner, *Second Witness*, 2:382). ⊕

2 Nephi 27:12–14. The Book of Mormon Plates Will Be Seen by Special Witnesses

Who were the witnesses to the Book of Mormon plates? (27:12–14) "In 2 Nephi 27:12 the three persons who should behold the record 'by the power of God' evidently are the three special witnesses. In their testimony they declared they had seen an angel, had heard the voice of the Lord, and had been shown the plates 'by the power of God, and not of man.'

"In 2 Nephi 27:13, the few other witnesses who should view the record 'according to the will of God, to bear testimony of his word unto the children of men' evidently include the eight special witnesses" (Ludlow, *Companion to Your Study of the Book of Mormon*, 149). ⊕

2 Nephi 27:15–22. The Book of Mormon Will Be Translated by the Power of God, Not the Learning of Man

What does "sealed" mean? (27:15) "A distinctive legal practice in Israel around 600 B.C. was the use of doubled, sealed, and witnessed documents. These documents had two parts: one was left open for ready access while the other was sealed up for later consultation by the parties. . . . Witnesses were necessary, and their numbers could vary. . . . When and by whom could these seals be opened? It appears that only a judge or another authorized official could break the seals and open the document. . . . Similarly, Nephi envisioned the final Nephite record as having two parts, one sealed and the other not sealed (2 Nephi 27:8, 15)" (Welch, "Doubled, Sealed, and Witnessed Documents").

How was this ancient prophecy fulfilled? (27:15–18) "Here is the prophetic word which attests that Martin Harris's trip to New York was based upon more than his own curiosity or desire for academic substantiation for the Book of Mormon translation. Joseph Smith was commanded of the Lord to send another to New York, and Joseph sent Martin Harris.

"Charles Anthon was indeed a learned man by the world's standards: he was a professor of classics—Greek and Latin—at Columbia University in New York" (McConkie and Millet, *Doctrinal Commentary*, 1:322). ✪

Why would the learned man request that the sealed book be delivered to him? (27:16–18) "The Lord gave the world's 'learned' an opportunity to accept or reject the words of the book. He knew their motivation would be not 'the glory of God' but for 'the glory of the world and to get gain'" (Parry et al., *Understanding Isaiah*, 268).

In what way was Joseph considered "not learned"? (27:19–20) Joseph Smith is the one Isaiah referred to as "not learned" whom the Lord would empower "read

16 And now, because of the glory of the world and to get gain will they say this, and not for the glory of God.

17 And the man shall say: I cannot bring the book, for it is sealed.

18 Then shall the learned say: I cannot read it.

19 Wherefore it shall come to pass, that the Lord God will deliver again the book and the words thereof to him that is not learned; and

Witnesses of the Plates

Three Witnesses

© Intellectual Reserve, Inc. Used by permission.

Oliver Cowdery   David Whitmer   Martin Harris

Eight Witnesses

Christian Whitmer	Hiram Page
Jacob Whitmer	Joseph Smith, Sr.
Peter Whitmer, Jr.	Hyrum Smith
John Whitmer	Samuel H. Smith

The Lord revealed anciently that he would provide witnesses of the "sealed book" or gold plates from which the Book of Mormon would be translated—this so that Joseph Smith "may not be destroyed" and "that [He] might bring about [His] righteous purposes" (D&C 17:4, 9).

the man that is not learned shall say: I am not learned.

20 Then shall the Lord God say unto him: The learned shall not read them, for they have rejected them, and I am able to do mine own work; wherefore thou shalt read the words which I shall give unto thee.

21 Touch not the things which are sealed, for I will bring them forth in mine own due time; for I will show unto the children of men that I am able to do mine own work.

22 Wherefore, when thou hast read the words which I have commanded thee, and obtained the witnesses which I have promised unto thee, then shalt thou seal up the book again, and hide it up unto me, that I may preserve the words which thou hast not read, until I shall see fit in mine own wisdom to reveal all things unto the children of men.

23 For behold, I am God; and I am a God of miracles; and I will show unto the world that I am the same yesterday, today, and forever; and I work not among the children of men save it be according to their faith.

24 And again it shall come to pass that the Lord shall say unto him that shall read the words that shall be delivered him:

25 Forasmuch as this people draw near unto me with their mouth, and with their lips do honor me, but have removed their hearts far from me, and their fear towards me is taught by the precepts of men—

26 Therefore, I will proceed to do a marvelous work among this people, yea, a marvelous work and a wonder, for the wisdom of

the words" of the book with a sealed portion. Elder Jeffrey R. Holland wrote: "[T]his magnificent book [the Book of Mormon] was translated when Joseph Smith was barely a boy, a lad still coming of age. To paraphrase Winston Churchill, 'Some boy. Some book'" (*Christ and the New Covenant*, 344).

Why do you think the Lord commanded Joseph to hide up the plates? (27:21–22) The scriptures record that the Prophet Joseph Smith obediently delivered the plates into the hands of the angel Moroni as commanded (see Joseph Smith–History 1:60). Why would the Lord take away the only tangible evidence that the plates existed? What benefits come to us as we accept the Lord's will and engage the Book of Mormon on faith? What could be the consequences if people could see the plates and still choose to be disobedient?

2 Nephi 27:23–35. The Lord Is a God of Miracles

What does this prophecy of Isaiah indicate about the spiritual condition of the people when the Book of Mormon comes forth? (27:25) Isaiah foresaw a time when people would draw near to God with their mouths only: "The essence of this phrase is hypocrisy: to profess one thing but to do another; to pretend to be something one is not, or to declare a belief in something that is not personally practiced. Some of the Lord's strongest rebukes have been directed at hypocrites whom He has labeled as 'whited sepulchres' (whitewashed tombs), serpents, and vipers (see Matthew 23:23–33)" (Brewster, *Isaiah Plain and Simple*, 167).

What is this "marvelous work"? (27:26) "Isaiah says that the Lord, because of the emptiness of the worship, would perform a 'marvelous work and wonder,' by means of which the wisdom of their wise and the understanding of their prudent would perish and be hid; and Nephi applies this language to the coming forth of the Book of Mormon, as the beginning of a marvelous work and wonder, the effects of which would be the humiliation of the wisdom and learning of the world" (Reynolds and Sjodahl, *Commentary on the Book of Mormon*, 1:399). ⊕

What was the "counsel" they sought to hide? (27:27)
"The Hebrew word *sod*, usually translated as *counsel* in the King James Version of the Bible, may also be rendered as *secret* (see also Amos 3:7). That is, those who 'seek to hide their counsel from the Lord' are those who try desperately to hide their secrets, their secret acts from him who sees and knows all things" (McConkie and Millet, *Doctrinal Commentary*, 1:325–26).

What is significant about this prophecy of Lebanon? (27:28) "This verse also has a symbolic meaning—the forest represents the people of God, and the fruitful field represents their works" (Parry et al., *Understanding Isaiah*, 272). ⊕

What is this book and how will it help the deaf, blind, meek, and poor? (27:29–30) The book is the Book of Mormon. The deaf and blind are those who are not able spiritually to hear God's word or see His truth. President Ezra Taft Benson declared how the Book of Mormon can change that: "There is a power in the book which will begin to flow into your lives the moment you begin a serious study of the book. You will find greater power to resist temptation. You will find the power to avoid deception. You will find the power to stay on the strait and narrow path" (*Teachings of Ezra Taft Benson*, 54).

Who are all of these people who will be "cut off" in the last days? (27:31–34) "Both 'the terrible one' and 'the scorner' are epithets applied to Satan. Because Satan is 'brought to naught,' the time period is clearly the last days. With Satan's powerlessness, the wicked ('all that watch for iniquity') also lose their source of inspiration. Binding Satan also checks the iniquity of the wicked" (Gardner, *Second Witness*, 2:396).

their wise and learned shall perish, and the understanding of their prudent shall be hid.

27 And wo unto them that seek deep to hide their counsel from the Lord! And their works are in the dark; and they say: Who seeth us, and who knoweth us? And they also say: Surely, your turning of things upside down shall be esteemed as the potter's clay. But behold, I will show unto them, saith the Lord of Hosts, that I know all their works. For shall the work say of him that made it, he made me not? Or shall the thing framed say of him that framed it, he had no understanding?

28 But behold, saith the Lord of Hosts: I will show unto the children of men that it is yet a very little while and Lebanon shall be turned into a fruitful field; and the fruitful field shall be esteemed as a forest.

29 And in that day shall the deaf hear the words of the book, and the eyes of the blind shall see out of obscurity and out of darkness.

30 And the meek also shall increase, and their joy shall be in the Lord, and the poor among men shall rejoice in the Holy One of Israel.

31 For assuredly as the Lord liveth they shall see that the terrible one is brought to naught, and the scorner is consumed, and all that watch for iniquity are cut off;

32 And they that make a man an offender for a word, and lay a snare for him that reproveth in the gate, and turn aside the just for a thing of naught.

33 Therefore, thus saith the Lord, who redeemed Abraham, concerning the house of Jacob: Jacob shall not now be ashamed, neither shall his face now wax pale.

34 But when he seeth his children, the work of my hands, in the midst of him, they shall sanctify my name, and sanctify the Holy One of Jacob, and shall fear the God of Israel.

35 They also that erred in spirit shall come to understanding, and they that murmured shall learn doctrine.

CHAPTER 28

Many false churches will be built up in the last days—They will teach false, vain, and foolish doctrines—Apostasy will abound because of false teachers—The devil will rage in the hearts of men—He will teach all manner of false doctrines. About 559–545 B.C.

1 And now, behold, my brethren, I have spoken unto you, according as the Spirit hath constrained me; wherefore, I know that they must surely come to pass.

2 And the things which shall be written out of the book shall be of great worth unto the children of men, and especially unto our seed, which is a remnant of the house of Israel.

3 For it shall come to pass in that day that the churches which are built up, and not unto the Lord, when the one shall say unto the other: Behold, I, I am the Lord's; and the others shall say: I, I am the Lord's; and thus shall every one say that hath built up churches, and not unto the Lord—

4 And they shall contend one with another; and their priests shall contend one with another, and they shall teach with their learning,

Who is the work of God's hands? (27:34) "This phrase recalls the mention of clay in [2 Nephi 27:27]. . . . God is the divine sculptor who forms and molds his people into true disciples; we are the work of his hands" (Parry et al., *Understanding Isaiah*, 273).

How shall those who "err" and "murmur" learn doctrine? (27:35) "Such is the purpose of the Book of Mormon. Members of false churches that err in spirit, who think they have the truth, are brought by the Book of Mormon to the fullness of the gospel. Those who have based their beliefs on isolated verses and obscure passages, and who have wondered and murmured at seeming biblical conflicts, come to learn sound doctrine. . . . All things fall into place because of this *new witness for Christ* and His gospel, this witness which bears the name of the prophet Mormon" (McConkie, *Millennial Messiah*, 174–75). ☉

2 Nephi 28:1–6. False Churches Will Be Built Up in the Last Days

What does it mean to be "constrained" by the Spirit? (28:1) "Urged irresistibly or powerfully; compelled" (Webster, *American Dictionary*).

What is an example of a time when churches and priests contended with each other for converts? (28:4) For a literal latter-day fulfillment of this prophecy, see the account of the Prophet Joseph Smith's experience with "priests" and "churches" recorded in Joseph Smith–History 1:5–6. ⊕

What is the fallacy of those who claim "there is no God today"? (28:5) "A beloved Quaker teacher and writer, Rufus Jones, . . . said: 'Vital religion cannot be maintained and preserved on the theory that God dealt with our human race only in the far past ages, and that the Bible is the only evidence we have that our God is a living, revealing, communicating God. If God ever spoke, He is still speaking. He is the great I Am, not the great He Was' (*A Flash of Eternity*).

"This is a significant expression of fundamental truth. Our own understanding of that principle is that God communicates with his children, and that he has revealed, does now reveal, and will yet reveal many great and important things pertaining to his kingdom" (Hanks, "Loving, Communicating God," 63). ⊕

Why do many in the latter days deny miracles? (28:6) "Numerous and varied have been the approaches used by many for centuries to deny the miraculous. In our day it is common for religious-minded individuals to accept the miracles of the past but to deny the same in this 'enlightened' day. Others seek to provide naturalistic explanations for the miraculous, in order to demonstrate that God and his anointed servants simply work within well-planned but required bounds. The effect of both approaches is a weakening of faith and an increase in the distance between man and God" (McConkie and Millet, *Doctrinal Commentary*, 1:331).

2 Nephi 28:7–14. Many Evil People Will Teach False and Foolish Doctrines

Who are those who will say, "Eat, drink, and be merry"? (28:7–9) "This teaching emphasizes both the humanistic and the hedonistic. It argues that individuals are free to gratify their own carnal desires, to set their own standards of morality, to live for the pleasure of the moment and to do all this without guilt. . . . This evil teaching totally denies the justice of God. It embraces the teachings of the noted anti-Christs Nehor and Korihor" (Largey, "Enemies of Christ," 290). Nevertheless, "do not think that this was [only] said of the world. . . . It is said of members of the Church. Moreover, Nephi warns us that in the last days there will be many who will follow Satan" (Smith, *Seek Ye Earnestly*, 143).

and deny the Holy Ghost, which giveth utterance.

5 And they deny the power of God, the Holy One of Israel; and they say unto the people: Hearken unto us, and hear ye our precept; for behold there is no God today, for the Lord and the Redeemer hath done his work, and he hath given his power unto men;

6 Behold, hearken ye unto my precept; if they shall say there is a miracle wrought by the hand of the Lord, believe it not; for this day he is not a God of miracles; he hath done his work.

7 Yea, and there shall be many which shall say: Eat, drink, and be merry, for tomorrow we die; and it shall be well with us.

8 And there shall also be many which shall say: Eat, drink, and be merry; nevertheless, fear God—he will justify in committing a little sin; yea, lie a little, take the advantage of one because of his words, dig a pit for thy neighbor; there is no harm in this; and do all these things, for tomorrow we die; and if it so be that we are guilty, God will beat us with a few stripes, and at last we shall be saved in the kingdom of God.

9 Yea, and there shall be many which shall teach after this manner, false and vain and foolish doctrines, and shall be puffed up in their hearts, and shall seek deep to hide their counsels from the Lord; and their works shall be in the dark.

10 And the blood of the saints shall cry from the ground against them.

11 Yea, they have all gone out of the way; they have become corrupted.

12 Because of pride, and because of false teachers, and false doctrine, their churches have become corrupted, and their churches are lifted up; because of pride they are puffed up.

13 They rob the poor because of their fine sanctuaries; they rob the poor because of their fine clothing; and they persecute the meek and the poor in heart, because in their pride they are puffed up.

14 They wear stiff necks and high heads; yea, and because of pride, and wickedness, and abominations, and whoredoms, they have all gone astray save it be a few, who are the humble followers of Christ; nevertheless, they are led, that in many instances they do err because they are taught by the precepts of men.

How serious is "a little sin"? (28:8) "Few things extinguish the fervor of the Holy Spirit in the heart of any individual more quickly than does sin. It dulls the spiritual senses, diminishes confidence and personal security, and separates the sinner from the Savior. One who carries the burden of unrepented sin is more likely to rationalize additional disobedience. . . . The simple fact is this: anything that does not draw us closer to God takes us away from Him. We have no middle ground, no foggy gray area where we can sin a little without suffering spiritual decline. That is why we must repent and come to Christ daily on submissive knees" (Wirthlin, "Spiritual Bonfires of Testimony," 36). ☉

What effect can false doctrines have upon the faithful? (28:9) Referring to this verse, President Dallin H. Oaks warned: "Surely you have seen and heard these arguments. . . . They will come at you in classrooms and hallways, in what you read, and in what you see in popular entertainment. Many in the world deny the need for a Savior. Others deny that there is any right or wrong, and they scoff at the idea of sin or a devil. Still others rely on the mercy of God and ignore His justice. The prophet said, 'There shall be many which shall teach after this manner, false and vain and foolish doctrines' (2 Ne. 28:9)" ("Be Not Deceived," 44).

What leads to going "out of the way" and becoming "corrupted"? (28:11–14) "Nephi and Moroni saw that the false teachers would have high heads and stiff necks (v. 14) and would love their money and their substance more than their poor (Mormon 8:37). In their quest for praise and personal gain, they would rob the poor and persecute the meek (2 Nephi 28:13; Mormon 8:33–38). This robbery would occur as the poor fall prey to priestcraft, sacrificing to build fine sanctuaries and supplying their false teachers with costly apparel" (Largey, "Enemies of Christ," 293).

Why will so many go astray? (28:14) "Not only are there apostates within our midst, but there are also apostate doctrines that are sometimes taught in our classes and from our pulpits and that appear in our publications. And these apostate precepts of men cause our people to stumble" (*Teachings of Ezra Taft Benson*, 89–90). ☉

2 Nephi 28:15–17. God Will Punish the Wicked Unless They Repent

What is the meaning of the three woes? (28:15)
"The meaning is that deep or inconsolable grief or misery will attend the commission of some proscribed act, the omission of some required duty, or that such penalty will grow out of an ungodly course of conduct" (McConkie, *Mormon Doctrine*, 843).

The context of this verse is obviously a denunciation of the wicked. The three woes indicate the serious nature of the coming punishment of being "thrust down to hell."

Why does Nephi so strongly condemn the learned and rich? (28:15) "It is easy to see how the rich, learned, and powerful could control the disseminations of religious knowledge, facilitating the teaching of their own doctrines rather than Yahweh's [Jehovah's]. What does not make sense to the modern reader is that the learned and rich should also 'commit whoredoms.'. . . [T]he 'whoredom' of the rich is their congress with the learning of men (instead of Yahweh)—not their sexual habits. They were unfaithful to Yahweh, not to their spouses" (Gardner, *Second Witness*, 2:404–5).

2 Nephi 28:18–20. Satan Will Rage in the Hearts of Men in the Last Days

How will those who fight against Zion be destroyed? (28:18–19) Please see commentary in this volume on 1 Nephi 22:14.

What do we learn from the Book of Mormon about the devil's use of rage to stir up anger? (28:20) "The Lord has warned that from the beginning and throughout history, Satan would stir up people's hearts to anger [see 2 Nephi 28:20; D&C 10:24]. In the Book of Mormon, Laman set a pattern of so murmuring as to stir anger, to stoke rage, and to incite murder [see 1 Ne. 16:37–38]. . . . In the days of Captain Moroni, the apostate Amalickiah inspired 'the hearts of the Lamanites against the people of Nephi' [Alma 48:1]. Amulon and

15 O the wise, and the learned, and the rich, that are puffed up in the pride of their hearts, and all those who preach false doctrines, and all those who commit whoredoms, and pervert the right way of the Lord, wo, wo, wo be unto them, saith the Lord God Almighty, for they shall be thrust down to hell!

16 Wo unto them that turn aside the just for a thing of naught and revile against that which is good, and say that it is of no worth! For the day shall come that the Lord God will speedily visit the inhabitants of the earth; and in that day that they are fully ripe in iniquity they shall perish.

17 But behold, if the inhabitants of the earth shall repent of their wickedness and abominations they shall not be destroyed, saith the Lord of Hosts.

18 But behold, that great and abominable church, the whore of all the earth, must tumble to the earth, and great must be the fall thereof.

19 For the kingdom of the devil must shake, and they which belong to it must needs be stirred up unto repentance, or the devil will grasp them with his everlasting chains, and they be stirred up to anger, and perish;

20 For behold, at that day shall he rage in the hearts of the children of men, and stir them up to anger against that which is good.

the wicked priests of Noah; Nehor; Korihor; and Zoram the apostate . . . were agitators who inspired distrust, fueled controversy, and deepened hatreds" (Wood, "Instruments of the Lord's Peace," 93).

2 Nephi 28:21–32. Satan Will Lead People Away from God with False Teachings

21 And others will he pacify, and lull them away into carnal security, that they will say: All is well in Zion; yea, Zion prospereth, all is well—and thus the devil cheateth their souls, and leadeth them away carefully down to hell.

22 And behold, others he flattereth away, and telleth them there is no hell; and he saith unto them: I am no devil, for there is none— and thus he whispereth in their ears, until he grasps them with his awful chains, from whence there is no deliverance.

23 Yea, they are grasped with death, and hell; and death, and hell, and the devil, and all that have been seized therewith must stand

How does the devil carefully lead people to hell? (28:21–22) "First, he *pacifies*, which means he appeases or placates. Second, he *cheats*, swindles, misleads, fools, or practices fraud upon, which means he deceives by trickery. Third, he *flatters*, which means he compliments excessively and insincerely, especially to win favor. . . . Fourth, he *leads* the way by going in advance, by conducting, escorting, or directing, by causing one to follow a certain course of action or line of thought. . . . Satan thus customizes his dishonesty according to the susceptibility of his target. His favorite approach is whatever works" (Largey, "Enemies of Christ," 297). ✚

Why is there confusion about the devil being real? (28:22–23) "Students of comparative Christianity are well aware that many Christian churches today do not

Satan Is the Master of Illusion

© David Frazier Photography. Used by permission.

"Last summer on a lonely stretch of desert highway, we saw ahead what appeared to be the road covered with water. My children would have wagered their entire savings on that fact. But within a few minutes we were at the distant spot and saw not one drop of water. What an illusion!

"How many things there are in this life that appear to be one way and all of a sudden are the reverse. . . . Satan operates that way. He is the master of illusion. He creates illusions in an attempt to detour, dilute, and divert the power and the attention of the Latter-day Saints from the pure truth of God" (Cook, "Spiritual Guides for Teachers of Righteousness," 25).

teach the actual existence of a devil. This condition was prophesied by Nephi wherein he stated that in the last days the devil would say to the people, 'I am no devil, for there is none' (2 Nephi 28:22). The Book of Mormon and other latter-day scriptures clearly and definitely teach the existence of the devil as a personage of spirit" (Ludlow, *Companion to Your Study of the Book of Mormon*, 151). ⊕

What is meant by the phrase "at ease in Zion"? (28:24–29) The essence of being at ease in Zion is to feel secure. "Much of what Nephi saw can be 'well disguised as the philosophies and tendencies' that permeate the thinking of the world, and much of it seems harmless and well intentioned. . . . Perhaps best known among these is the warning against an attitude of complacency. 'All is well in Zion; yea, Zion prospereth, all is well,' is one of the many lies Satan will tell (2 Nephi 28:21, cf. vv. 24–25). Significantly, this is complacency *within* the Church of Zion" (Welch et al., *Knowing Why*, 132).

What was Nephi trying to teach by indicating that the Lord gives unto us "line upon line"? (28:30) "A careful reading of Isaiah 28:9–13 indicates it may have been the text for Nephi's teachings in this passage. Although Nephi does not identify this passage as a quotation from Isaiah, he does indicate clearly that it is a statement of the Lord. . . . The Lord gives us revelation: as we accept and live by that revelation, we are given more revelation, but if we do not accept what is revealed, we lose the knowledge we have already gained" (Nyman, *Great Are the Words of Isaiah*, 102). ⊕

How do we put our trust in men or make flesh our arm? (28:31) "This revelation echoes the Book of Mormon reference to Isaiah's caution (Isa. 8:10). The prophet Nephi taught the importance of trusting in revelation rather than in 'the precepts of men': 'Cursed is he that putteth his trust in man, or maketh flesh his arm, or shall hearken unto the precepts of men, save their precepts shall be given by the power of the Holy Ghost' (2 Ne. 28:31)" (Oaks, *The Lord's Way*, 21). ⊕

before the throne of God, and be judged according to their works, from whence they must go into the place prepared for them, even a lake of fire and brimstone, which is endless torment.

24 Therefore, wo be unto him that is at ease in Zion!

25 Wo be unto him that crieth: All is well!

26 Yea, wo be unto him that hearkeneth unto the precepts of men, and denieth the power of God, and the gift of the Holy Ghost!

27 Yea, wo be unto him that saith: We have received, and we need no more!

28 And in fine, wo unto all those who tremble, and are angry because of the truth of God! For behold, he that is built upon the rock receiveth it with gladness; and he that is built upon a sandy foundation trembleth lest he shall fall.

29 Wo be unto him that shall say: We have received the word of God, and we need no more of the word of God, for we have enough!

30 For behold, thus saith the Lord God: I will give unto the children of men line upon line, precept upon precept, here a little and there a little; and blessed are those who hearken unto my precepts, and lend an ear unto my counsel, for they shall learn wisdom; for unto him that receiveth I will give more; and from them that shall say, We have enough, from them shall be taken away even that which they have.

31 Cursed is he that putteth his trust in man, or maketh flesh his arm, or shall hearken unto the precepts of men, save their precepts shall be given by the power of the Holy Ghost.

32 Wo be unto the Gentiles, saith the Lord God of Hosts! For notwithstanding I shall lengthen out mine arm unto them from day to day, they will deny me; nevertheless, I will be merciful unto them, saith the Lord God, if they will repent and come unto me; for mine arm is lengthened out all the day long, saith the Lord God of Hosts.

CHAPTER 29

Many Gentiles will reject the Book of Mormon—They will say, We need no more Bible—The Lord speaks to many nations—He will judge the world out of the books which will be written. About 559–545 B.C.

1 But behold, there shall be many—at that day when I shall proceed to do a marvelous work among them, that I may remember my covenants which I have made unto the children of men, that I may set my hand again the second time to recover my people, which are of the house of Israel;

2 And also, that I may remember the promises which I have made unto thee, Nephi, and also unto thy father, that I would remember your seed; and that the words of your seed should proceed forth out of my mouth unto your seed; and my words shall hiss forth unto the ends of the earth, for a standard unto my people, which are of the house of Israel;

What is the meaning of the Lord's arm being lengthened all the day long? (28:32) "There is almost no limit to the Lord's mercy, no end to his longsuffering with his children. 'How merciful is our God unto us,' exulted Jacob, 'for he remembereth the house of Israel, both roots and branches; and he stretches forth his hands unto them all the day long.' Jacob further implored the covenant people to 'repent, and come with full purpose of heart, and cleave unto God as he cleaveth unto you. And while his arm of mercy is extended towards you in the light of the day, harden not your hearts' (Jacob 6:4–5)" (McConkie and Millet, *Doctrinal Commentary*, 1:346). ✛

2 Nephi 29:1–2. In the Last Days, the Book of Mormon Shall Go Forth to the Whole Earth

What does this "marvelous work" teach us about the power of covenants? (29:1) In this verse the Lord reiterates how seriously He takes the covenants He has made with mankind (see also the title page of the Book of Mormon; 3 Nephi 20–21). The Book of Mormon, the restoration of the gospel, and the gathering of Israel are all part of the "marvelous work" God is performing so He can keep His covenants with us. What have you experienced in your life that demonstrates that your Heavenly Father is keeping His promise to bless, guide, and perhaps correct you? How can you better keep the covenants you have made with Him?

How is the Book of Mormon a "standard"? (29:2) "The Book of Mormon is the great standard we are to use. It shows that Joseph Smith was a prophet. It contains the words of Christ, and its great mission is to bring men to Christ, and all other things are secondary. The golden question of the Book of Mormon is 'Do you want to learn more of Christ?' The Book of Mormon is the great finder of the golden contact. It does not contain things which are 'pleasing unto the world' (1 Ne. 6:5), and so the worldly are not interested in it. It is a great sieve" (Benson, "Book of Mormon Is the Word of God," 4). ✛

2 Nephi 29:3–6. Many Gentiles Will Say the Only Scripture They Need Is the Bible

What is wrong with saying "we need no more Bible"? (29:3–6) The statement that there cannot be any more Bible "is its own refutation. The philosopher argues that there can be no absolutes, not realizing that such a pronouncement constitutes an absolute. The false religionist argues that the Bible contains all revelation, not realizing that since the Bible makes no such claim for itself, the only way they could know this would be by revelation. Thus men and women find themselves in the awkward position of claiming a revelation to say that there is no revelation. Such is the confusion of which the kingdom of darkness is made" (McConkie and Millet, *Doctrinal Commentary*, 1:347). ⊙

How should we view the Jews today? (29:4–5) "The true gospel is for all men, Jew and Gentile alike. Those who obey the true gospel love all men, Jew and Gentile alike. That love impels true believers to offer the gospel and all of its blessings, without money and without price, to all of our Father's children. Has this been done through the ages by those who profess to glory in the Jewish Bible and who say that it, and it alone suffices to bring salvation? Rather, as we view Jewish history during the Christian era, we see little but ill will and hate and bloodshed heaped by Christians upon Jews" (McConkie, *New Witness*, 463).

Of what value should we hold the Bible? (29:6) "Since few could afford to own a hand-made Bible, Wycliffe and his followers traveled the country-side with Bible manuscripts for the people to read. Sometimes the people would borrow or rent the scriptures for a day, or even for an hour, because they could not afford to buy a copy. It is said that a load of hay was the going price to rent a Bible for an hour" (Matthews, *A Bible! A Bible!* 6).

2 Nephi 29:7–10. The Bible and the Book of Mormon Witness That God Speaks to All People

3 And because my words shall hiss forth—many of the Gentiles shall say: A Bible! A Bible! We have got a Bible, and there cannot be any more Bible.

4 But thus saith the Lord God: O fools, they shall have a Bible; and it shall proceed forth from the Jews, mine ancient covenant people. And what thank they the Jews for the Bible which they receive from them? Yea, what do the Gentiles mean? Do they remember the travails, and the labors, and the pains of the Jews, and their diligence unto me, in bringing forth salvation unto the Gentiles?

5 O ye Gentiles, have ye remembered the Jews, mine ancient covenant people? Nay; but ye have cursed them, and have hated them, and have not sought to recover them. But behold, I will return all these things upon your own heads; for I the Lord have not forgotten my people.

6 Thou fool, that shall say: A Bible, we have got a Bible, and we need no more Bible. Have ye obtained a Bible save it were by the Jews?

7 Know ye not that there are more nations than one? Know ye not that I, the Lord your God, have created all men, and that I remember those who are upon the isles of the sea; and that I rule in the heavens above and in the earth beneath; and I bring forth my word unto the children of men, yea, even upon all the nations of the earth?

8 Wherefore murmur ye, because that ye shall receive more of my word? Know ye not that the testimony of two nations is a witness unto you that I am God, that I remember one nation like unto another? Wherefore, I speak the same words unto one nation like unto another. And when the two nations shall run together the testimony of the two nations shall run together also.

9 And I do this that I may prove unto many that I am the same yesterday, today, and forever; and that I speak forth my words according to mine own pleasure. And because that I have spoken one word ye need not suppose that I cannot speak another; for my work is not yet finished; neither shall it be until the end of man, neither from that time henceforth and forever.

10 Wherefore, because that ye have a Bible ye need not suppose that it contains all my words; neither need ye suppose that I have not caused more to be written.

11 For I command all men, both in the east and in the west, and in the north, and in the south, and in the islands of the sea, that they shall write the words which I speak unto them; for out of the books which shall be written I will judge the world, every man according to their works, according to that which is written.

12 For behold, I shall speak unto the Jews and they shall write it; and I shall also speak unto the Nephites and they shall write it; and

Why is it important to recognize the Book of Mormon and the Bible as "the testimony of two nations"? (29:8) "There is, however, one great difference between the Bible and the Book of Mormon that shows why some people can disbelieve the Bible and let the matter drop, but disbelieving the Book of Mormon, they find themselves compelled to arise in wrath and defame the Nephite record. It is that people who believe the Bible, as they suppose, can also believe any creed of their choice and belong to any church that suits them. But belief in the Book of Mormon presupposes the acceptance of Joseph Smith as a prophet as well as membership in the church organized by him" (McConkie, *New Witness*, 460). ☉

Why is it important that God does not change? (29:9) "One of the attributes of God is indicated here. He is not subject to changes as we are. He works in accordance with eternal laws, or rules. If he has caused inspired writings to be given to men at any time, he will do so again, when necessary for their guidance. We may expect 'bibles' in different ages and localities" (Reynolds and Sjodahl, *Commentary on the Book of Mormon*, 1:412). ☉

Why is God's word not restricted to only the Bible? (29:9–10) The Prophet Joseph Smith said: "We have what we have, and the Bible contains what it does contain: but to say that God never said anything more to man than is there recorded, would be saying at once that we have at last received a revelation . . . because it is nowhere said in that volume by the mouth of God, that He would not, after giving what is there contained, speak again; and if any man has found out for a fact that the Bible contains all that God ever revealed to man he has ascertained it by an immediate revelation, other than has been previously written by the prophets and apostles" (*History of the Church*, 2:18).

2 Nephi 29:11–14. In the Last Days the Word of the Lord Will Be Available for All to Read

What other nations might God speak to besides the Jews and the Nephites? (29:12–13) "The splendid Book of Mormon advises that a third scriptural witness is yet to come from the lost tribes. . . . Its coming is likely to be even more dramatic than the coming forth of the second testament. Those who doubt or disdain the second testament of Christ will not accept the third either. But believers will then possess a triumphant triad of truth (see 2 Nephi 29:12–14). Were it not for the Book of Mormon, we would not even know about the third set of records!" (Maxwell, "Book of Mormon: A Great Answer to 'The Great Question,'" 15). ⊕

2 Nephi 30:1–2. Only Those Who Repent Are Included among the Covenant People of God

Who are the Lord's covenant people? (30:1–2)

"In all dispensations the Lord's people have been a covenant people and have understood that without righteousness their covenants are null and void.... Never are such promises granted to men in wickedness. If the descendants of Abraham reject Christ they also reject the covenants that Christ made with their ancient father and no longer have claim upon them. If, on the other hand, those not of the lineage of Abraham repent and accept Christ, they become his covenant people and thus rightful heirs to all the promises made to Abraham, the father of the faithful (see Abraham 2:9–11)" (McConkie and Millet, *Doctrinal Commentary*, 1:353–54). ⊕

I shall also speak unto the other tribes of the house of Israel, which I have led away, and they shall write it; and I shall also speak unto all nations of the earth and they shall write it.

13 And it shall come to pass that the Jews shall have the words of the Nephites, and the Nephites shall have the words of the Jews; and the Nephites and the Jews shall have the words of the lost tribes of Israel; and the lost tribes of Israel shall have the words of the Nephites and the Jews.

14 And it shall come to pass that my people, which are of the house of Israel, shall be gathered home unto the lands of their possessions; and my word also shall be gathered in one. And I will show unto them that fight against my word and against my people, who are of the house of Israel, that I am God, and that I covenanted with Abraham that I would remember his seed forever.

CHAPTER 30

Converted Gentiles will be numbered with the covenant people—Many Lamanites and Jews will believe the word and become delightsome—Israel will be restored and the wicked destroyed. About 559–545 B.C.

1 And now behold, my beloved brethren, I would speak unto you; for I, Nephi, would not suffer that ye should suppose that ye are more righteous than the Gentiles shall be. For behold, except ye shall keep the commandments of God ye shall all likewise perish; and because of the words which have been spoken ye need not suppose that the Gentiles are utterly destroyed.

2 For behold, I say unto you that as many of the Gentiles as will repent are the covenant people of the Lord; and as many of the Jews as will not repent shall be cast off; for the Lord covenanteth with none save it be with them that repent and believe in his Son, who is the Holy One of Israel.

3 And now, I would prophesy somewhat more concerning the Jews and the Gentiles. For after the book of which I have spoken shall come forth, and be written unto the Gentiles, and sealed up again unto the Lord, there shall be many which shall believe the words which are written; and they shall carry them forth unto the remnant of our seed.

4 And then shall the remnant of our seed know concerning us, how that we came out from Jerusalem, and that they are descendants of the Jews.

5 And the gospel of Jesus Christ shall be declared among them; wherefore, they shall be restored unto the knowledge of their fathers, and also to the knowledge of Jesus Christ, which was had among their fathers.

6 And then shall they rejoice; for they shall know that it is a blessing unto them from the hand of God; and their scales of darkness shall begin to fall from their eyes; and many generations shall not pass away among them, save they shall be a pure and a delightsome people.

7 And it shall come to pass that the Jews which are scattered also shall begin to believe in Christ; and they shall begin to gather in upon the face of the land; and as many as

2 Nephi 30:3–8. The Book of Mormon Gathers People to Christ

What is the book "written to the Gentiles" that will lead people to the gospel of Jesus Christ? (30:3–5)
"The coming forth of the Book of Mormon is a sign to the entire world that the Lord has commenced to gather Israel and fulfill covenants He made to Abraham, Isaac, and Jacob. . . .

"The Book of Mormon is central to this work. It declares the doctrine of the gathering. It causes people to learn about Jesus Christ, to believe His gospel, and to join His Church. In fact, if there were no Book of Mormon, the promised gathering of Israel would not occur" (Nelson, "Gathering of Scattered Israel," 80). ◉

How could the Nephites be called Jews? (30:4)
"The word *Jew* was used early to refer to the citizens of the kingdom of Judah. However, later it came to refer to all those who were descendants of Judah. . . . Still later the term came to mean essentially 'anyone of the House of Israel who remained in the kingdom of Judah . . . after the time of the scattering of the Ten Tribes.' Thus at the time of the Babylonian captivity . . . even descendants of the other tribes, including Ephraim and Manasseh, were considered by some to be Jews if they were of the house of Israel living in Jerusalem. Thus, Nephi refers to himself and his descendants as being 'of the Jews'" (Ludlow, "Message to the Jews," 242).

Why was "white" changed to "pure"? (30:6) "Prior to the 1981 edition of the Book of Mormon, 2 Nephi 30:6 read 'they [the Lamanites] shall be a white and delightsome people.' The change to a 'pure and delightsome people' is traced to the 1840 edition made under the editorial supervision of the Prophet Joseph Smith. However, for some unknown reason, subsequent editions reverted to the first wording. This background was called to the attention of the First Presidency and the Twelve with the recommendation that the word 'pure' be used in the 1981 edition. These modern-day prophets, seers, and revelators unanimously approved the change as a better expression of the correct meaning of the verse" (Nyman, "Come to Understanding and Learn Doctrine," 33). ◉

When will the Jews begin to believe and gather? (30:7–8) "The Jews 'shall begin to believe in Christ' before he comes the second time. Some of them will accept the gospel and forsake the traditions of their fathers; a few will find in Jesus the fulfillment of their ancient Messianic hopes; but their nation as a whole, their people as the distinct body that they now are in all nations, the Jews as a unit shall not, at that time, accept the word of truth. But a beginning will be made; a foundation will be laid; and then Christ will come and usher in the millennial year of his redeemed" (McConkie, *Millennial Messiah*, 228–29). ◉

2 Nephi 30:9–10. The Lord Will Save the Righteous and Destroy the Wicked at His Second Coming

How will the Lord cause "a great division among the people"? (30:9–10) "Eventually all must choose; all must either accept the Christ testified of in the Book of Mormon or reject him. There is no other Christ, and where Christ is concerned there is no middle ground" (McConkie and Millet, *Doctrinal Commentary*, 1:358).

This prophesied separation is spoken of many times in scripture. Read the following verses and ponder what attitudes and actions separate the righteous from the wicked: Alma 10:22–23; 3 Nephi 21:11; Doctrine and Covenants 1:14; 45:56–57, 64–70; 64:23–24; Moses 7:18; 8:28–30. As you are reading, what does the Spirit encourage you to do? ◉

2 Nephi 30:11–15. Nephi Quotes Isaiah's Millennial Prophecies

What does "girdle of his loins" mean? (30:11) "The Lord is clothed in righteousness and faithfulness; these two qualities represent his very existence. . . . The Lord girds his loins with righteousness as he prepares to do his important work. The loins symbolize the creative powers (Gen. 35:11; 1 Kgs. 8:19; Acts 2:30). These items of clothing, the girdle of the loins and the sash around the waist, are also suggestive of temple ordinances" (Parry et al., *Understanding Isaiah*, 118).

What will bring about this change in nature? (30:12–15) "The peace that will exist among all creatures on the earth is exciting. Flesh-eating and plant-eating animals will be at peace with each other, because all living creatures in that day will be herbivorous, as they were in the Garden of Eden. Truly, 'the wolf also shall dwell with the lamb, and the leopard shall lie down with the kid; and the calf and the young lion and the fatling together; and a little child shall lead them' (Isa. 11:6; see also 11:6–9; Abr. 4:29–30; D&C 101:26, 29)" (Meservy, "God Is with Us," 101). ◉

shall believe in Christ shall also become a delightsome people.

8 And it shall come to pass that the Lord God shall commence his work among all nations, kindreds, tongues, and people, to bring about the restoration of his people upon the earth.

9 And with righteousness shall the Lord God judge the poor, and reprove with equity for the meek of the earth. And he shall smite the earth with the rod of his mouth; and with the breath of his lips shall he slay the wicked.

10 For the time speedily cometh that the Lord God shall cause a great division among the people, and the wicked will he destroy; and he will spare his people, yea, even if it so be that he must destroy the wicked by fire.

11 And righteousness shall be the girdle of his loins, and faithfulness the girdle of his reins.

12 And then shall the wolf dwell with the lamb; and the leopard shall lie down with the kid, and the calf, and the young lion, and the fatling, together; and a little child shall lead them.

13 And the cow and the bear shall feed; their young ones shall lie down together; and the lion shall eat straw like the ox.

14 And the sucking child shall play on the hole of the asp, and the weaned child shall put his hand on the cockatrice's den.

15 They shall not hurt nor destroy in all my holy mountain; for the earth shall be full of the knowledge of the Lord as the waters cover the sea.

© Clint Clearly/Shutterstock.

16 Wherefore, the things of all nations shall be made known; yea, all things shall be made known unto the children of men.

17 There is nothing which is secret save it shall be revealed; there is no work of darkness save it shall be made manifest in the light; and there is nothing which is sealed upon the earth save it shall be loosed.

18 Wherefore, all things which have been revealed unto the children of men shall at that day be revealed; and Satan shall have power over the hearts of the children of men no more, for a long time. And now, my beloved brethren, I make an end of my sayings.

CHAPTER 31

Nephi tells why Christ was baptized—Men must follow Christ, be baptized, receive the Holy Ghost, and endure to the end to be saved—Repentance and baptism are the gate to the strait and narrow path—Eternal life comes to those who keep the commandments after baptism. About 559–545 B.C.

1 And now I, Nephi, make an end of my prophesying unto you, my beloved brethren. And I cannot write but a few things, which I

2 Nephi 30:16–18. During the Millennium, the Lord Will Make Known All Things

What more will be revealed in the Millennium? (30:16–18) "The sealed part of the Book of Mormon will come forth; the brass plates will be translated; the writings of Adam and Enoch and Noah and Abraham and prophets without number will be revealed. We shall learn a thousand times more about the earthly ministry of the Lord Jesus than we now know. We shall learn great mysteries of the kingdom that were not even known to those of old who walked and talked with the Eternal One. We shall learn the details of the creation and the origin of man" (McConkie, *Millennial Messiah*, 676). ⊕

2 Nephi 31:1–3. Nephi Teaches in Plainness

How did the Nephites define the gospel? (31:2)
"Three Book of Mormon passages in particular—
2 Nephi 31:2–32:6; 3 Nephi 11:23–39; 3 Nephi 27:13–21
—define the gospel of Jesus Christ, each in a distinctive six-point formula. This formula states that if people
will (1) believe in Christ, (2) repent of their sins, and (3)
submit to baptism in water . . . , he will (4) pour out his
Spirit upon them and cleanse them of their sins. All
who receive this baptism of fire and of the Holy Ghost
and (5) endure to the end . . . will be found guiltless at
the last day and (6) enter God's kingdom" (Reynolds,
"Gospel As Taught by Nephite Prophets," 257). ⊕

**Why does God speak to man "unto their under-
standing"? (31:3)** "It is impossible for the poor, weak
. . . sinful inhabitants of the earth to receive a revelation from the Almighty in all its perfections. He has
to speak to us in a manner to meet the extent of our
capacities. . . .

"If an angel should come into this congregation
. . . and use the language he uses in heaven, what
would we be benefited? Not any, because we could
not understand a word he said. When angels come to
visit mortals; they have to condescend to and assume,
more or less, the condition of mortals, they have to descend to our capacities in order to communicate with
us" (Brigham Young, in *Journal of Discourses*, 2:314).

2 Nephi 31:4–8. Nephi Prophesies of Jesus's Baptism

What does it mean to "fulfil all righteousness"?
(31:5–6) "Nephi, to dramatize the importance of baptism, wrote that the Savior had to be baptized to 'fulfil
all righteousness' (2 Ne. 31:5). . . .

"Nephi identified four ways in which Christ fulfilled
all righteousness through his baptism: (1) he humbled
himself before the Father (2 Ne. 31:7); (2) he entered
a covenant relationship with the Father, promising
obedience in keeping the commandments (2 Ne.
31:7); (3) he opened to himself the gate to the celestial
kingdom (2 Ne. 31:9); (4) he set a perfect example
for all to follow (2 Ne. 31:10)" (McConkie, "Promise of
Eternal Life," 163–64). ⊕

know must surely come to pass; neither can
I write but a few of the words of my brother
Jacob.

2 Wherefore, the things which I have written sufficeth me, save it be a few words
which I must speak concerning the doctrine
of Christ; wherefore, I shall speak unto you
plainly, according to the plainness of my
prophesying.

3 For my soul delighteth in plainness; for
after this manner doth the Lord God work
among the children of men. For the Lord
God giveth light unto the understanding; for
he speaketh unto men according to their language, unto their understanding.

4 Wherefore, I would that ye should remember that I have spoken unto you concerning
that prophet which the Lord showed unto
me, that should baptize the Lamb of God,
which should take away the sins of the world.

5 And now, if the Lamb of God, he being
holy, should have need to be baptized by water, to fulfil all righteousness, O then, how
much more need have we, being unholy, to
be baptized, yea, even by water!

6 And now, I would ask of you, my beloved
brethren, wherein the Lamb of God did fulfil
all righteousness in being baptized by water?

7 Know ye not that he was holy? But notwithstanding he being holy, he showeth unto
the children of men that, according to the
flesh he humbleth himself before the Father,
and witnesseth unto the Father that he would
be obedient unto him in keeping his commandments.

8 Wherefore, after he was baptized with water the Holy Ghost descended upon him in the form of a dove.

9 And again, it showeth unto the children of men the straitness of the path, and the narrowness of the gate, by which they should enter, he having set the example before them.

10 And he said unto the children of men: Follow thou me. Wherefore, my beloved brethren, can we follow Jesus save we shall be willing to keep the commandments of the Father?

11 And the Father said: Repent ye, repent ye, and be baptized in the name of my Beloved Son.

12 And also, the voice of the Son came unto me, saying: He that is baptized in my name, to him will the Father give the Holy Ghost, like unto me; wherefore, follow me, and do the things which ye have seen me do.

13 Wherefore, my beloved brethren, I know that if ye shall follow the Son, with full purpose of heart, acting no hypocrisy and no deception before God, but with real intent, repenting of your sins, witnessing unto the Father that ye are willing to take upon you the name of Christ, by baptism—yea, by following your Lord and your Savior down into the water, according to his word, behold, then shall ye receive the Holy Ghost; yea, then cometh the baptism of fire and of the Holy Ghost; and then can ye speak with the tongue of angels, and shout praises unto the Holy One of Israel.

What does it mean that the Holy Ghost descended "in the form of a dove"? (31:8) "The sign of the dove was instituted before the creation of the world, a witness for the Holy Ghost, and the devil cannot come in the sign of a dove. The Holy Ghost is a personage, and is in the form of a personage. It does not confine itself to the *form* of the dove, but in the *sign* of the dove. The Holy Ghost cannot be transformed into a dove; but the sign of a dove was given to John to signify the truth of the deed, as the dove is an emblem or token of truth and innocence" (*Joseph Smith* [manual], 81). ●

2 Nephi 31:9–16. Follow the Savior's Example

How does someone "speak with the tongue of angels"? (31:13–14) "Our words, like our deeds, should be filled with faith and hope and charity, the three great Christian imperatives so desperately needed in the world today. With such words, spoken under the influence of the Spirit, tears can be dried, hearts can be healed, lives can be elevated, hope can return, confidence can prevail. . . . It will be with the tongue of angels" (Holland, "The Tongue of Angels," 18). ●

2 Nephi 31:17–21. Endure to the End

What is the baptism "by fire and by the Holy Ghost"? (31:17) "President Marion G. Romney taught that the baptism of fire by the Holy Ghost 'cleanses, heals, and purifies the soul. . . . Faith in the Lord Jesus Christ, repentance, and water baptism are all preliminary and prerequisite to it, but [the baptism of fire] is the consummation' [*Learning for the Eternities*, 133].

"Hence, as we are born again and strive to always have His Spirit to be with us, the Holy Ghost sanctifies and refines our souls as if by fire (see 2 Nephi 31:13–14, 17). Ultimately, we are to stand spotless before God" (Bednar, "Clean Hands and a Pure Heart," 81). ⊕

Once we are in the "strait and narrow path," what else should we be doing? (31:18–20) "Many have been baptized and received a testimony, and have 'gotten into this straight and narrow path,' yet have failed to take the further required step—to 'press forward, *feasting upon the word of Christ*, and endure to the end'" (Kimball, "How Rare a Possession—the Scriptures," 2). ⊕

14 But, behold, my beloved brethren, thus came the voice of the Son unto me, saying: After ye have repented of your sins, and witnessed unto the Father that ye are willing to keep my commandments, by the baptism of water, and have received the baptism of fire and of the Holy Ghost, and can speak with a new tongue, yea, even with the tongue of angels, and after this should deny me, it would have been better for you that ye had not known me.

15 And I heard a voice from the Father, saying: Yea, the words of my Beloved are true and faithful. He that endureth to the end, the same shall be saved.

16 And now, my beloved brethren, I know by this that unless a man shall endure to the end, in following the example of the Son of the living God, he cannot be saved.

17 Wherefore, do the things which I have told you I have seen that your Lord and your Redeemer should do; for, for this cause have they been shown unto me, that ye might know the gate by which ye should enter. For the gate by which ye should enter is repentance and baptism by water; and then cometh a remission of your sins by fire and by the Holy Ghost.

18 And then are ye in this strait and narrow path which leads to eternal life; yea, ye have entered in by the gate; ye have done according to the commandments of the Father and the Son; and ye have received the Holy Ghost, which witnesses of the Father and the Son, unto the fulfilling of the promise which he hath made, that if ye entered in by the way ye should receive.

19 And now, my beloved brethren, after ye have gotten into this strait and narrow path, I would ask if all is done? Behold, I say unto you, Nay; for ye have not come thus far save it were by the word of Christ with unshaken faith in him, relying wholly upon the merits of him who is mighty to save.

20 Wherefore, ye must press forward with a steadfastness in Christ, having a perfect brightness of hope, and a love of God and of all men. Wherefore, if ye shall press forward, feasting upon the word of Christ, and endure to the end, behold, thus saith the Father: Ye shall have eternal life.

21 And now, behold, my beloved brethren, this is the way; and there is none other way nor name given under heaven whereby man can be saved in the kingdom of God. And now, behold, this is the doctrine of Christ, and the only and true doctrine of the Father, and of the Son, and of the Holy Ghost, which is one God, without end. Amen.

CHAPTER 32

Angels speak by the power of the Holy Ghost— Men must pray and gain knowledge for themselves from the Holy Ghost. About 559– 545 B.C.

1 And now, behold, my beloved brethren, I suppose that ye ponder somewhat in your hearts concerning that which ye should do after ye have entered in by the way. But, behold, why do ye ponder these things in your hearts?

2 Do ye not remember that I said unto you that after ye had received the Holy Ghost ye could speak with the tongue of angels? And now, how could ye speak with the tongue of angels save it were by the Holy Ghost?

What does it mean to have hope? (31:20) "Hope is a gift of the Spirit. It is a hope that through the Atonement of Jesus Christ and the power of His Resurrection, we shall be raised unto life eternal and this because of our faith in the Savior. This kind of hope is both a principle of promise as well as a commandment, and, as with all commandments, we have the responsibility to make it an active part of our lives and overcome the temptation to lose hope. . . . The hope of salvation is like a protective helmet; it is the foundation of our faith and an anchor to our souls" (Uchtdorf, "Infinite Power of Hope," 21–22). ☉

2 Nephi 32:1–6. The Holy Ghost Teaches All Things

What is the "tongue of angels"? (32:2) Wrote Latter-day Saint scholar Robert L. Millet: "Several years ago I walked out of our stake center with two of my sons after viewing the satellite broadcast of a general priesthood meeting. . . . I overheard an elderly high priest in our stake say to the man with him, 'Wasn't that powerful! President Gordon B. Hinckley just spoke with the tongue of angels.' . . . [Those born of the Spirit] convey not merely their own will and desires but the mind and will of Christ. Stated more simply, President Gordon B. Hinckley spoke with the tongue of angels. . . . He spoke what angels would have spoken. He delivered what Christ wanted delivered. It was as though angels had come and delivered the message" (*Alive in Christ*, 128–33).

How can we "feast upon the words of Christ"?
(32:3) Two latter-day apostles answered this question.
"All members [of the Church] need to generate an
appetite for gospel sustenance. We must 'hunger and
thirst after righteousness' before we can be filled"
(Ballard, "Feasting at the Lord's Table," 80). "If you and
I are to feast upon the words of Christ, we must study
the scriptures and absorb His words through pondering them and making them a part of every thought
and action" (Hales, "Healing Soul and Body," 15).

What will the gift of the Holy Ghost do for us?
(32:5) "The gift of the Holy Ghost, given to us by our
Heavenly Father and administered by one having
authority, includes the merciful promise: 'If ye will
enter in by the way, and receive the Holy Ghost, it will
show unto you all things what ye should do' (2 Nephi
32:5). Through the constant companionship of the
Holy Ghost, every member of the Church can receive
'the words of Christ' directly (2 Nephi 32:3), at any
time or place. This personal divine guidance helps us
to remain valiant in the testimony of Jesus Christ and
endure to the end of our days. Isn't this wonderful!"
(Uchtdorf, "Have We Not Reason to Rejoice?" 20). ✪

**How can Nephi's declaration that there would
be no more doctrine given until after Christ's
Resurrection apply to us today? (32:6)** "We, the
members of the Church, should heed the admonition of Nephi, for there exists among us the same
stiffneckedness and lack of seeking for knowledge,
yet a clamoring by many for more to be revealed.
Let us learn to observe the revelations already given,
then we may in reason ask for more. We are even now
aware that many of the revelations contained on the
plates from which comes the Book of Mormon, have
been withheld from us because we have not proved
ourselves worthy to receive them" (Smith, *Answers to
Gospel Questions*, 2:204).

2 Nephi 32:7–9. Pray Always

3 Angels speak by the power of the Holy
Ghost; wherefore, they speak the words of
Christ. Wherefore, I said unto you, feast
upon the words of Christ; for behold, the
words of Christ will tell you all things what
ye should do.

4 Wherefore, now after I have spoken these
words, if ye cannot understand them it will
be because ye ask not, neither do ye knock;
wherefore, ye are not brought into the light,
but must perish in the dark.

5 For behold, again I say unto you that if ye
will enter in by the way, and receive the Holy
Ghost, it will show unto you all things what
ye should do.

6 Behold, this is the doctrine of Christ, and
there will be no more doctrine given until
after he shall manifest himself unto you in
the flesh. And when he shall manifest himself
unto you in the flesh, the things which he
shall say unto you shall ye observe to do.

7 And now I, Nephi, cannot say more; the
Spirit stoppeth mine utterance, and I am left
to mourn because of the unbelief, and the
wickedness, and the ignorance, and the stiffneckedness of men; for they will not search
knowledge, nor understand great knowledge,
when it is given unto them in plainness, even
as plain as word can be.

8 And now, my beloved brethren, I perceive that ye ponder still in your hearts; and it grieveth me that I must speak concerning this thing. For if ye would hearken unto the Spirit which teacheth a man to pray, ye would know that ye must pray; for the evil spirit teacheth not a man to pray, but teacheth him that he must not pray.

9 But behold, I say unto you that ye must pray always, and not faint; that ye must not perform any thing unto the Lord save in the first place ye shall pray unto the Father in the name of Christ, that he will consecrate thy performance unto thee, that thy performance may be for the welfare of thy soul.

CHAPTER 33

Nephi's words are true—They testify of Christ—Those who believe in Christ will believe Nephi's words, which will stand as a witness before the judgment bar. About 559–545 B.C.

1 And now I, Nephi, cannot write all the things which were taught among my people; neither am I mighty in writing, like unto speaking; for when a man speaketh by the power of the Holy Ghost the power of the Holy Ghost carrieth it unto the hearts of the children of men.

2 But behold, there are many that harden their hearts against the Holy Spirit, that it hath no place in them; wherefore, they cast many things away which are written and esteem them as things of naught.

3 But I, Nephi, have written what I have written, and I esteem it as of great worth, and especially unto my people. For I pray continually for them by day, and mine eyes water my pillow by night, because of them; and I cry unto my God in faith, and I know that he will hear my cry.

How can you seek the influence of the Holy Ghost in your prayers? (32:8–9) How can you improve in remembering to pray always?

2 Nephi 33:1–5. Nephi Testifies That His Words Are True

What is meant by the Holy Ghost carrying messages "unto the heart"? (33:1) "The power of the Spirit carries the message unto but not necessarily into the heart. A teacher can explain, demonstrate, persuade, and testify, and do so with great spiritual power and effectiveness. Ultimately, however, the content of a message and the witness of the Holy Ghost penetrate into the heart only if a receiver allows them to enter. Learning by faith opens the pathway into the heart" (Bednar, "Seek Learning by Faith," 61).

What can we learn from the depth of Nephi's feelings for his people? (33:3) "In his parting testimony, Nephi . . . mourned about those whose hearts were hardened against the Holy Spirit and the messages of the prophets. . . . Perhaps we would all try harder and live better if we knew how the prophets have mourned over our sins and how the Savior himself has tried personally to bring each one of us to him" (Wells, *The Mount and the Master*, 25).

Why are some angry at the words prophets speak and write? (33:5) One example to consider is that "many reject the Book of Mormon because it testifies against their lifestyles. As Nephi told Laman and Lemuel when they complained that he spoke hard things to them, 'the guilty taketh the truth to be hard, for it cutteth them to the very center' (1 Ne. 16:2)" (Nyman, *Most Correct Book*, 131).

2 Nephi 33:6–9. Nephi's Words Testify of Christ

Was Nephi claiming to be a Jew? (33:8) "Nephi was not suggesting that he was a blood descendant of Judah, but that he was from the country of Judah, for it is clearly stated in the Book of Mormon (Alma 10:3) that Lehi's family was of the tribe of Manasseh. Even in Lehi's time a Jew could be defined variously: progeny of Judah (generic), citizen of the Jewish state (political), and believer in the Jewish religion (covenant). Then as now, to many Israel is a people; to others it is a place or state; and to still others it is an idea, concept, or ideal" (Richardson, "What Is a Jew?" 14).

What is the "strait path" as taught by Nephi? (33:9) "In the Book of Mormon, Nephi is the primary user of the word *path*. In its singular form, the word appears in only thirteen verses, and eleven of those were written by Nephi. In one important instance, he refers to the Savior and the path in the same sentence" (Caldwell, "Path That Leads to Christ," 27). ⊕

4 And I know that the Lord God will consecrate my prayers for the gain of my people. And the words which I have written in weakness will be made strong unto them; for it persuadeth them to do good; it maketh known unto them of their fathers; and it speaketh of Jesus, and persuadeth them to believe in him, and to endure to the end, which is life eternal.

5 And it speaketh harshly against sin, according to the plainness of the truth; wherefore, no man will be angry at the words which I have written save he shall be of the spirit of the devil.

6 I glory in plainness; I glory in truth; I glory in my Jesus, for he hath redeemed my soul from hell.

7 I have charity for my people, and great faith in Christ that I shall meet many souls spotless at his judgment-seat.

8 I have charity for the Jew—I say Jew, because I mean them from whence I came.

9 I also have charity for the Gentiles. But behold, for none of these can I hope except they shall be reconciled unto Christ, and enter into the narrow gate, and walk in the strait path which leads to life, and continue in the path until the end of the day of probation.

2 Nephi 33:10–15. Nephi's Words Are True and Shall Stand as a Witness Before God

10 And now, my beloved brethren, and also Jew, and all ye ends of the earth, hearken unto these words and believe in Christ; and if ye believe not in these words believe in Christ. And if ye shall believe in Christ ye will believe in these words, for they are the words of Christ, and he hath given them unto me; and they teach all men that they should do good.

11 And if they are not the words of Christ, judge ye—for Christ will show unto you, with power and great glory, that they are his words, at the last day; and you and I shall stand face to face before his bar; and ye shall know that I have been commanded of him to write these things, notwithstanding my weakness.

12 And I pray the Father in the name of Christ that many of us, if not all, may be saved in his kingdom at that great and last day.

13 And now, my beloved brethren, all those who are of the house of Israel, and all ye ends of the earth, I speak unto you as the voice of

What is a principal purpose of "these words," or the Book of Mormon? (33:10) "What, then, is the Book of Mormon? It is confirming evidence of the birth, life, and crucifixion of Jesus and of his work as the Messiah and the Redeemer" (Faust, "Keystone of Our Religion," 10). ✪

Why did Nephi invite us to judge whether the Book of Mormon contains the words of Christ? (33:11) Elder Robert E. Wells testified: "Like Joseph Smith, the Book of Mormon is a divine instrument to draw the reader closer to Christ. . . . It has withstood every conceivable test by both skeptical and sincere minds. It is not on trial. We are the ones on trial, being tested by our acceptance or rejection of its truths, teachings, commandments, and declarations (see 2 Nephi 33:11–14)" ("Our Message to the World," 66). ✪

What will you say to Nephi at the judgment bar? (33:11) Nephi said he would meet us at the judgment bar. Interestingly, Jacob and Moroni made very similar promises (see Jacob 6:13; Moroni 10:27).

The Prophet Joseph Smith and the Power of Plainness

Joseph Smith,
by Lewis A. Ramsey

As Brigham Young noted, Joseph Smith, like Nephi, also gloried in plainness: "[Joseph Smith] took heaven, figuratively speaking, and brought it down to earth; and he took the earth, brought it up, and opened up, in plainness and simplicity, the things of God. . . .

"The excellency of the glory of the character of Brother Joseph Smith was that he could reduce heavenly things to the understanding of the finite. When he preached to the people—revealed the things of God, the will of God, the plan of salvation, the purposes of Jehovah, the relation in which we stand to Him and all the heavenly beings, he reduced his teachings to the capacity of every man, woman, and child, making them as plain as a well-defined pathway. This should have convinced every person that ever heard of him of his divine authority and power, for no other man was able to teach as he could, and no person can reveal the things of God, but by the revelations of Jesus Christ" (*Brigham Young* [manual], 344–47).

one crying from the dust: Farewell until that great day shall come.

14 And you that will not partake of the goodness of God, and respect the words of the Jews, and also my words, and the words which shall proceed forth out of the mouth of the Lamb of God, behold, I bid you an everlasting farewell, for these words shall condemn you at the last day.

15 For what I seal on earth, shall be brought against you at the judgment bar; for thus hath the Lord commanded me, and I must obey. Amen.

Why is it important to respect the words of the Book of Mormon? (33:14) President Ezra Taft Benson testified: "Do eternal consequences rest upon our response to this book? Yes, either to our blessing or our condemnation. Every Latter-day Saint should make the study of this book a lifetime pursuit. Otherwise he is placing his soul in jeopardy and neglecting that which could give spiritual and intellectual unity to his whole life. There is a difference between a convert who is built on the rock of Christ through the Book of Mormon and stays hold of that iron rod, and one who is not" (*A Witness and a Warning*, 7–8). ✛

What is noteworthy about the way that Nephi concluded his book? (33:15) President Russell M. Nelson taught: "Nephi was a multifaceted genius. Endowed with great physical stature, he was a prophet, teacher, ruler, colonizer, builder, craftsman, scholar, writer, poet, military leader, and father of nations. Nephi had a sincere desire to know the mysteries of God. He became a special witness and trusted prophet of the Lord. . . . Appropriately, his final testimony closed with the words that could be known as his signature: 'I must obey.'

"Few have spoken so profoundly in behalf of one generation to another. Indeed, Nephi's life and mission were destined to bless us and all people of our day" ("Nephi, Son of Lehi," 15).

What impresses you most in Nephi's final testimony? (33:15) In what ways will you improve because of Nephi's words?

THE BOOK OF JACOB
THE BROTHER OF NEPHI

Introduction

Jacob was Nephi's younger brother. He had unshakable faith, was a faithful teacher of the gospel, and received angelic visitors. Like his brother Nephi, Jacob also saw the Redeemer, Jesus Christ (see 2 Nephi 11:3). At the beginning of his book, Jacob tells the reader that he will record preaching, revelation, and prophesying that are important to inspire the reader to come unto Christ (see Jacob 1:4). Chapter 1 is a prologue, chapters 2 and 3 are his preaching, chapter 4 is an exhortation to study the revelations, and chapters 5 and 6 are prophesying concerning the house of Israel. In chapter 7, Jacob uses preaching, revelation, and prophesying to combat Sherem, the anti-Christ, and testifies of the Atonement of Christ. The time is about fifty-five years after the family left Jerusalem. It was a time of exceeding wealth and resulting pride, which led to many sins, including immorality.

The words of his preaching unto his brethren. He confoundeth a man who seeketh to overthrow the doctrine of Christ. A few words concerning the history of the people of Nephi.

CHAPTER 1

Jacob and Joseph seek to persuade men to believe in Christ and keep His commandments— Nephi dies—Wickedness prevails among the Nephites. About 544–421 B.C.

1 For behold, it came to pass that fifty and five years had passed away from the time that Lehi left Jerusalem; wherefore, Nephi gave me, Jacob, a commandment concerning the small plates, upon which these things are engraven.

The superscription to the book of Jacob, which appears just under the title of the book, was part of the ancient record translated by the Prophet Joseph Smith and dictated by him to his scribe (see also, for example, 1 Nephi, Mosiah 9, and Alma 5).

Distinct from the superscription is the chapter summary, which is presented in italics between the chapter number and the beginning of the scriptural text. Chapter summaries, originally added in the 1920 edition of the Book of Mormon, give the reader an overview of what each chapter contains.

Jacob 1:1–4. Jacob Writes upon the Small Plates Only That Which Is Sacred

What do we know concerning Nephi's brother Jacob? (1:1) Because we know Jacob was born during the eight years Lehi's family wandered in the wilderness, he would have been between forty-seven and fifty-five years of age when he wrote his book. "Some think Jacob a lesser character, yet Elder Neal A. Maxwell calls him the 'great poet-prophet,' and Robert J. Matthews considers Jacob 'the outstanding doctrinal teacher of the Book of Mormon.' Jacob's sensitivity to the challenges women face reminds us of Luke; his empathy for suffering reminds us of Job. Yet his voice is unique—right down to his final adieu" (Conkling, "Gentle Power of Jacob," 7).

Why did Jacob and other Book of Mormon authors choose particular events, details, or stories to include in their sacred record? (1:2) "How often we read the record primarily as a history of a fallen people, failing to remember that it was compiled by inspired prophets for the purpose of helping us come unto Christ. The major writers of the Book of Mormon did not intend it to be a history book at all. . . .

"Each time we read the book we should probably ask ourselves: 'Why did these writers choose these particular stories or events to include in the record? What value are they for us today?'" (Perry, "Blessings Resulting from Reading the Book of Mormon," 7–8).

Why is "heads" used in this verse? (1:4) "The term *head* seems out of place. We would expect something like *most important* to be used. But the expression is readily explainable in terms of Hebrew. The Hebrew word for the head of the body is sometimes used to describe things as *chief* (see Deut. 33:15, Ps. 137:6, and Prov. 1:21) or *precious* (see Amos 6:1, Song 4:14, Ezek. 27:22). This is probably the sense in which Jacob used the word" (Tvedtnes, "Hebrew Background," 90).

Jacob 1:5–8. Jacob and Nephi Write to Persuade Men to Believe in Christ

Why did Jacob have great anxiety for his people? (1:5) "This aversion to sin felt by a particularly sensitive soul helps explain the constant anxiety Jacob feels for his people. Because of 'faith and great anxiety'—an unusual turn of phrase, though not a surprising combination of prophetic feelings—Jacob is shown some of this fate we have mentioned regarding his family. That weighs him down 'with much more desire and anxiety' for the welfare of their souls, a burden so great that he pleads not to be 'shaken from my firmness in the spirit, and stumble because of my over anxiety for you' (Jacob 2:3; 4:18). Whether it be against the anti-Christ or the specter of debilitating sin, Jacob remains 'unshaken'" (Holland, "Jacob the Unshakable," 39).

When did the children of Israel provoke the Lord? (1:7) "At Sinai the children of Israel spurned the privileges of the everlasting gospel and the greater priesthood and thereby rejected the higher counsel which might have been had from the lips of Jehovah through Moses the Lawgiver (see JST, Exodus 34:1–2; JST, Deuteronomy 10:1–2; Psalm 95:10–11). They provoked their Lord and robbed themselves of the sublime association with that holy being who was the God of the covenant fathers. Paul warned the meridian Saints

2 And he gave me, Jacob, a commandment that I should write upon these plates a few of the things which I considered to be most precious; that I should not touch, save it were lightly, concerning the history of this people which are called the people of Nephi.

3 For he said that the history of his people should be engraven upon his other plates, and that I should preserve these plates and hand them down unto my seed, from generation to generation.

4 And if there were preaching which was sacred, or revelation which was great, or prophesying, that I should engraven the heads of them upon these plates, and touch upon them as much as it were possible, for Christ's sake, and for the sake of our people.

5 For because of faith and great anxiety, it truly had been made manifest unto us concerning our people, what things should happen unto them.

6 And we also had many revelations, and the spirit of much prophecy; wherefore, we knew of Christ and his kingdom, which should come.

7 Wherefore we labored diligently among our people, that we might persuade them to come unto Christ, and partake of the goodness of God, that they might enter into his rest, lest by any means he should swear in his wrath they should not enter in, as in the provocation in the days of temptation while the children of Israel were in the wilderness.

8 Wherefore, we would to God that we could persuade all men not to rebel against God, to provoke him to anger, but that all men would believe in Christ, and view his death, and suffer his cross and bear the shame of the world; wherefore, I, Jacob, take it upon me to fulfil the commandment of my brother Nephi.

9 Now Nephi began to be old, and he saw that he must soon die; wherefore, he anointed a man to be a king and a ruler over his people now, according to the reigns of the kings.

10 The people having loved Nephi exceedingly, he having been a great protector for them, having wielded the sword of Laban in their defence, and having labored in all his days for their welfare—

11 Wherefore, the people were desirous to retain in remembrance his name. And whoso should reign in his stead were called by the people, second Nephi, third Nephi, and so forth, according to the reigns of the kings; and thus they were called by the people, let them be of whatever name they would.

12 And it came to pass that Nephi died.

of such spiritual folly (Hebrews 3–4), as did the Lord through Joseph Smith to those of our day in a great revelation on priesthood (D&C 84:19–26)" (McConkie and Millet, *Doctrinal Commentary*, 2:4). ☉

What does it mean to "suffer his cross"? (1:8) "To suffer the cross of Christ is to be willing to bear the burdens of Christian discipleship, particularly of crucifying the 'old man of sin' and putting on Christ. 'If any man will come after me,' Jesus taught his meridian Twelve, 'let him deny himself, and take up his cross and follow me. And now for a man to take up his cross, is to deny himself all ungodliness, and every worldly lust, and keep my commandments' (JST, Matthew 16:25–26; cf. Matthew 10:38; 2 Nephi 9:18; 3 Nephi 12:30)" (McConkie and Millet, *Doctrinal Commentary*, 2:5).

Jacob 1:9–14. Jacob Notes Nephi's Death and the Problems between the Nephites and Lamanites

What does "the sword of Laban" represent? (1:10) "The sword of Laban can . . . be traced as part of the royal regalia that gives authority throughout Nephite history, and later as it appears in the Restoration. The sword of Laban as it is associated with Joseph Smith came to be an additional witness of his authority and of the divine sanction for his work" (Holbrook, "Sword of Laban," 39).

Why were the kings given a new name? (1:11) "Nephi had been appointed as king by the voice of the people nearly half a century earlier. Now, as this great spiritual leader approached the end of his mortal ministry, he chose another to reign in his stead. The people, being desirous to retain his name in remembrance, established a Nephite monarchy, such that subsequent kings would be known by the dynastic title of Second Nephi, Third Nephi, and so on, much like the system used by the Egyptians and the Romans with their Pharaohs and Caesars. The Nephite monarchy continued for almost 500 years, after which a system of judges was established (see Mosiah 29)" (McConkie and Millet, *Doctrinal Commentary*, 2:6).

How has Nephi influenced your life? (1:12) President Heber J. Grant paid a great tribute to Nephi: "I read the Book of Mormon as a young man, and fell in love with Nephi more than with any other character in profane or sacred history that I have ever read of, except the Savior of the world. No other individual has made such a strong impression upon me as did Nephi.

He has been one of the guiding stars of my life" (*Gospel Standards*, 357). Has Nephi, son of Lehi, had a similar profound effect on your own life?

Why does Jacob refer to seven tribes of Lehi's posterity? (1:13) "Jacob clarified that the Nephites and Lamanites were actually divided into seven distinct tribes. The same tribal affiliations are also reported in 4 Nephi 1:37–38 and again in Mormon 1:8–9, suggesting that they functioned as a 'social and legal order that lasted . . . for almost one thousand years.'

"This system of tribal organization likely stemmed from Lehi's final patriarchal blessings, where he specifically blessed and counseled the patriarchs or posterities of each of the seven tribes (see 2 Nephi 2–4). In several ways, Lehi's tribe-defining blessings can be meaningfully compared to the patriarchal blessings given by Abraham, Isaac, and Jacob" (Book of Mormon Central, "Why Did Lehi Divide His People Into Seven Tribes?"). ☉

Jacob 1:15–19. The Nephites Grow in Wickedness

What power comes by being on the Lord's errand? (1:17) "If we are on the Lord's errand, we are entitled to the Lord's help. That divine help, however, is predicated upon our worthiness. To sail safely the seas of mortality, to perform a human rescue mission, we need the guidance of that eternal mariner—even the great Jehovah. We reach out, we reach up, to obtain heavenly help" (Monson, "Your Eternal Voyage," 46). ☉

Under which priesthood were Jacob and Joseph consecrated priests and teachers? (1:18) "The Nephites did not officiate under the authority of the Aaronic Priesthood. They were not descendants of Aaron, and there were no Levites among them. There is no evidence in the Book of Mormon that they held the Aaronic Priesthood . . . but the Book of Mormon tells us definitely, in many places, that the priesthood which they held and under which they officiated was the Priesthood after the holy order, the order of the

13 Now the people which were not Lamanites were Nephites; nevertheless, they were called Nephites, Jacobites, Josephites, Zoramites, Lamanites, Lemuelites, and Ishmaelites.

14 But I, Jacob, shall not hereafter distinguish them by these names, but I shall call them Lamanites that seek to destroy the people of Nephi, and those who are friendly to Nephi I shall call Nephites, or the people of Nephi, according to the reigns of the kings.

15 And now it came to pass that the people of Nephi, under the reign of the second king, began to grow hard in their hearts, and indulge themselves somewhat in wicked practices, such as like unto David of old desiring many wives and concubines, and also Solomon, his son.

16 Yea, and they also began to search much gold and silver, and began to be lifted up somewhat in pride.

17 Wherefore I, Jacob, gave unto them these words as I taught them in the temple, having first obtained mine errand from the Lord.

18 For I, Jacob, and my brother Joseph had been consecrated priests and teachers of this people, by the hand of Nephi.

19 And we did magnify our office unto the Lord, taking upon us the responsibility, answering the sins of the people upon our own heads if we did not teach them the word of God with all diligence; wherefore, by laboring with our might their blood might not come upon our garments; otherwise their blood would come upon our garments, and we would not be found spotless at the last day.

CHAPTER 2

Jacob denounces the love of riches, pride, and unchastity—Men may seek riches to help their fellowmen—The Lord commands that no man among the Nephites may have more than one wife—The Lord delights in the chastity of women. About 544–421 B.C.

1 The words which Jacob, the brother of Nephi, spake unto the people of Nephi, after the death of Nephi:

2 Now, my beloved brethren, I, Jacob, according to the responsibility which I am under to God, to magnify mine office with soberness, and that I might rid my garments of your sins, I come up into the temple this day that I might declare unto you the word of God.

3 And ye yourselves know that I have hitherto been diligent in the office of my calling; but I this day am weighed down with much more desire and anxiety for the welfare of your souls than I have hitherto been.

4 For behold, as yet, ye have been obedient unto the word of the Lord, which I have given unto you.

Son of God. This higher priesthood can officiate in every ordinance of the gospel, and Jacob and Joseph, for instance, were consecrated priests and teachers after this order" (Smith, *Doctrines of Salvation*, 3:86).

What does it mean to "magnify our office"? (1:19)
"The Prophet Joseph was often asked, 'Brother Joseph, what do you mean by magnifying a calling?'

"Joseph replied: 'What does it mean to magnify a calling? It means to build it up in dignity and importance, to make it honorable and commendable in the eyes of all men, to enlarge and strengthen it, to let the light of heaven shine through it to the view of other men. And how does one magnify a calling? Simply by performing the service that pertains to it'" (Monson, *Pathways to Perfection*, 146). ✛

Jacob 2:1–11. Jacob Teaches What God Commanded Him to Say

What was the role of the temple in Nephite society? (2:2) "Public veneration at every holy place was freely offered by the faithful, who gathered often at the temple for religious instruction, coronations, sacrifices, and other sacred rites and crucial functions. . . . Nephite kings were crowned, religious teachings were dispensed, and the plan of salvation was taught; there the people were exhorted to proper behavior, sacrifices symbolizing the atonement of Christ were performed, and religious and legal covenants were made and renewed" (Welch, "The Temple in the Book of Mormon," 298). ✛

How did the spirit of discernment help Jacob know what to teach and warn his people? (2:3–5) How is the same discernment evident in the words and actions of the Lord's servants today? When has a leader's message inspired, challenged, or corrected you to avoid or overcome sin?

Notwithstanding his grief, what motivated Jacob to testify of his people's impending wickedness? (2:6–11) "The invitation to repent is an expression of love.... If we do not invite others to change or if we do not demand repentance of ourselves, we fail in a fundamental duty we owe to one another and to ourselves. A permissive parent, an indulgent friend, a fearful Church leader are in reality more concerned about themselves than the welfare and happiness of those they could help. Yes, the call to repentance is at times regarded as intolerant or offensive and may even be resented, but guided by the Spirit, it is in reality an act of genuine caring" (Christofferson, "Divine Gift of Repentance," 39).

What characteristic of God's nature is taught in these verses? (2:10, 15) "Remember," the Prophet Joseph Smith taught, "God sees the secret springs of human action, and knows the hearts of all living" (*Joseph Smith* [manual], 39). How does knowing this characteristic of God's nature influence you?

What does this statement teach us about Jacob? (2:11) "The power of Jacob's message lies in the simple fact that he was a true messenger of the Father—he inquired of the Lord, sought out the divine will, asked of God. The choice of message was not his. He sought

5 But behold, hearken ye unto me, and know that by the help of the all-powerful Creator of heaven and earth I can tell you concerning your thoughts, how that ye are beginning to labor in sin, which sin appeareth very abominable unto me, yea, and abominable unto God.

6 Yea, it grieveth my soul and causeth me to shrink with shame before the presence of my Maker, that I must testify unto you concerning the wickedness of your hearts.

7 And also it grieveth me that I must use so much boldness of speech concerning you, before your wives and your children, many of whose feelings are exceedingly tender and chaste and delicate before God, which thing is pleasing unto God;

8 And it supposeth me that they have come up hither to hear the pleasing word of God, yea, the word which healeth the wounded soul.

9 Wherefore, it burdeneth my soul that I should be constrained, because of the strict commandment which I have received from God, to admonish you according to your crimes, to enlarge the wounds of those who are already wounded, instead of consoling and healing their wounds; and those who have not been wounded, instead of feasting upon the pleasing word of God have daggers placed to pierce their souls and wound their delicate minds.

10 But, notwithstanding the greatness of the task, I must do according to the strict commands of God, and tell you concerning your wickedness and abominations, in the presence of the pure in heart, and the broken heart, and under the glance of the piercing eye of the Almighty God.

11 Wherefore, I must tell you the truth according to the plainness of the word of God.

For behold, as I inquired of the Lord, thus came the word unto me, saying: Jacob, get thou up into the temple on the morrow, and declare the word which I shall give thee unto this people.

12 And now behold, my brethren, this is the word which I declare unto you, that many of you have begun to search for gold, and for silver, and for all manner of precious ores, in the which this land, which is a land of promise unto you and to your seed, doth abound most plentifully.

13 And the hand of providence hath smiled upon you most pleasingly, that you have obtained many riches; and because some of you have obtained more abundantly than that of your brethren ye are lifted up in the pride of your hearts, and wear stiff necks and high heads because of the costliness of your apparel, and persecute your brethren because ye suppose that ye are better than they.

14 And now, my brethren, do ye suppose that God justifieth you in this thing? Behold, I say unto you, Nay. But he condemneth you, and if ye persist in these things his judgments must speedily come unto you.

15 O that he would show you that he can pierce you, and with one glance of his eye he can smite you to the dust!

16 O that he would rid you from this iniquity and abomination. And, O that ye would listen unto the word of his commands, and let not this pride of your hearts destroy your souls!

17 Think of your brethren like unto yourselves, and be familiar with all and free with your substance, that they may be rich like unto you.

18 But before ye seek for riches, seek ye for the kingdom of God.

19 And after ye have obtained a hope in Christ ye shall obtain riches, if ye seek them;

to say and do only what the Lord would have said and done under similar circumstances" (McConkie and Millet, *Doctrinal Commentary*, 2:12–13).

Jacob 2:12–21. Jacob Warns His People against Pride

Where can the love of wealth lead? (2:13) "Wealth is a jealous master who will not be served halfheartedly and will suffer no rival—not even God. . . . Wealth promises security, power, position, and honors, in fact anything in this world. Above all, the Nephites, like the Romans, saw in it a mark of superiority and would do anything to get hold of it, for to them 'money answereth all things' (Ecclesiastes 10:19). . . . The more important wealth is, the less important it is how one gets it" (Nibley, *Since Cumorah*, 393).

What is meant by "stiff necks and high heads"? (2:13) "A stiff neck suggests stubbornness, and a neck stretched to hold a 'high head' suggests a person trying to elevate himself above his fellows" (Parry and Parry, *Understanding the Signs of the Times*, 206). ✚

In what ways did Jacob counsel the Nephites to make their brethren equal? (2:17–19) "Financial and social equality of man was to be accomplished and safeguarded by a high degree of spirituality. Its success depended largely upon the actual existence of a love for God and fellowmen" (Berrett, *Teachings of the Book of Mormon*, 1:143).

"If we study the scriptures and find out what is in the mind of the Lord, behind the instructions that he has given us about caring for the poor, we will double our efforts" (Romney, *Learning for the Eternities*, 209).

How might we wisely use our riches for good? (2:18–19) "There are many worthy individuals and causes to which we might contribute. We should give generously to the fast offering and humanitarian funds of the Church. And, if we desire our families to live lives of depth and meaning, we must have the courage to examine honestly where our treasures lie and avoid the pitfalls that result from greed, selfishness, and overindulgence" (Christensen, "Greed, Selfishness, and Overindulgence," 11). ✚

What are some ways pride is evident today? (2:20) "Most of us think of pride as self-centeredness, conceit, boastfulness, arrogance, or haughtiness. All of these are elements of the sin, but the heart, or core, is still missing. The central feature of pride is . . . enmity toward God and enmity toward our fellowmen. Enmity means 'hatred toward, hostility to, or a state of opposition.' Pride is a sin that can readily be seen in others but is rarely admitted in ourselves. . . . It is manifest in so many ways, such as faultfinding, gossiping, backbiting, murmuring, living beyond our means, envying, coveting, withholding gratitude and praise that might lift another, and being unforgiving and jealous" (Benson, "Beware of Pride," 4).

Jacob 2:22–35. Unfaithfulness in Marriage Is a Serious Sin

What were the grosser crimes during Jacob's day? (2:22–23) "Sexual wickedness which had become prevalent in Israel, and the consequent abuse of the marriage relations, was, evidently, the reason why the Lord commanded that the children of Lehi should have but one wife. . . . [They] ran into excess and wickedness, as their fathers had done before them. . . . The words 'multiply' and 'greatly' [in Deuteronomy 17:17], evidently imply excess and unreasonable indulgence, as in the case of David and Uriah, and in taking strange women, as in the case of Solomon" (Richards and Little, *Compendium of the Doctrines of the Gospel*, 130–32; see also D&C 132:38).

Were all of David and Solomon's marriages abominable to the Lord? (2:24) This verse is clarified by modern revelation contained in the Doctrine and Covenants: "David also received many wives

and ye will seek them for the intent to do good—to clothe the naked, and to feed the hungry, and to liberate the captive, and administer relief to the sick and the afflicted.

20 And now, my brethren, I have spoken unto you concerning pride; and those of you which have afflicted your neighbor, and persecuted him because ye were proud in your hearts, of the things which God hath given you, what say ye of it?

21 Do ye not suppose that such things are abominable unto him who created all flesh? And the one being is as precious in his sight as the other. And all flesh is of the dust; and for the selfsame end hath he created them, that they should keep his commandments and glorify him forever.

22 And now I make an end of speaking unto you concerning this pride. And were it not that I must speak unto you concerning a grosser crime, my heart would rejoice exceedingly because of you.

23 But the word of God burdens me because of your grosser crimes. For behold, thus saith the Lord: This people begin to wax in iniquity; they understand not the scriptures, for they seek to excuse themselves in committing whoredoms, because of the things which were written concerning David, and Solomon his son.

24 Behold, David and Solomon truly had many wives and concubines, which thing was abominable before me, saith the Lord.

25 Wherefore, thus saith the Lord, I have led this people forth out of the land of Jerusalem, by the power of mine arm, that I might raise up unto me a righteous branch from the fruit of the loins of Joseph.

26 Wherefore, I the Lord God will not suffer that this people shall do like unto them of old.

27 Wherefore, my brethren, hear me, and hearken to the word of the Lord: For there shall not any man among you have save it be one wife; and concubines he shall have none;

28 For I, the Lord God, delight in the chastity of women. And whoredoms are an abomination before me; thus saith the Lord of Hosts.

29 Wherefore, this people shall keep my commandments, saith the Lord of Hosts, or cursed be the land for their sakes.

30 For if I will, saith the Lord of Hosts, raise up seed unto me, I will command my people; otherwise they shall hearken unto these things.

31 For behold, I, the Lord, have seen the sorrow, and heard the mourning of the daughters of my people in the land of Jerusalem, yea, and in all the lands of my people, because of the wickedness and abominations of their husbands.

and concubines, and also Solomon and Moses my servants, as also many others of my servants, from the beginning of creation until this time; and in nothing did they sin save in those things which they received not of me" (D&C 132:38).

Why did the Lord hold the people of Jacob to a higher standard? (2:26) "The promised land is a testing ground offering both great opportunity and corresponding risk. . . . In the Old World are civilizations which were ancient at the time Lehi left Jerusalem, and they still survive, but of those in the land of promise we are told that when they are ripe in iniquity, when the cup is full, they shall be swept off from the land. Compared with other continents this one has no history, no surviving cultures, though far and wide civilizations whose identities remain a mystery have left their ruins and their scattered descendants" (Nibley, "Scriptural Perspectives," 13).

What are "concubines" in the Book of Mormon? (2:27) "Anciently [concubines] were considered to be secondary wives, that is, wives who did not have the same standing in the caste system then prevailing as did those wives who were not called concubines. There were no concubines connected with the practice of plural marriage in this dispensation, because the caste system which caused some wives to be so designated did not exist" (McConkie, *Mormon Doctrine,* 154–55). During the time period of the Book of Mormon, the Lord made it clear through His servant Jacob that having concubines was not approved.

Why does the Lord delight in chastity? (2:28) "The law of chastity is a principle of eternal significance. We must not be influenced by the many voices of the world. We must listen to the voice of the Lord and then determine that we will start to keep his commandments. The world is already beginning to reap the consequences of their abandonment of any standards of morality" (Benson, "Law of Chastity," 4).

What are the costs of unchastity? (2:28–29) What examples have you seen of the heartache and sorrow that comes to those who make immoral choices? How do those choices affect those who love them? What choices can you make to protect yourself from similar mistakes?

32 And I will not suffer, saith the Lord of Hosts, that the cries of the fair daughters of this people, which I have led out of the land of Jerusalem, shall come up unto me against the men of my people, saith the Lord of Hosts.

33 For they shall not lead away captive the daughters of my people because of their tenderness, save I shall visit them with a sore curse, even unto destruction; for they shall not commit whoredoms, like unto them of old, saith the Lord of Hosts.

34 And now behold, my brethren, ye know that these commandments were given to our father, Lehi; wherefore, ye have known them before; and ye have come unto great condemnation; for ye have done these things which ye ought not to have done.

35 Behold, ye have done greater iniquities than the Lamanites, our brethren. Ye have broken the hearts of your tender wives, and lost the confidence of your children, because of your bad examples before them; and the sobbings of their hearts ascend up to God against you. And because of the strictness of the word of God, which cometh down against you, many hearts died, pierced with deep wounds.

CHAPTER 3

The pure in heart receive the pleasing word of God—Lamanite righteousness exceeds that of the Nephites—Jacob warns against fornication, lasciviousness, and every sin. About 544–421 B.C.

1 But behold, I, Jacob, would speak unto you that are pure in heart. Look unto God with firmness of mind, and pray unto him with exceeding faith, and he will console you in your afflictions, and he will plead your cause, and send down justice upon those who seek your destruction.

Why was Jacob sensitive to the plight of the Nephite women and children? (2:35) "Whether or not that was a result of having seen his mother in anguish over the wickedness of her eldest sons we cannot know, but it is interesting that in his unflinching declaration against sexual transgression Jacob quotes a communication from heaven [see 2:31–33, 35]. . . . That is a poetic, profound, 'piercing' indictment, and we have the feeling here that Jacob understood then what we unfortunately understand now—that it is usually (but not always) the woman who suffers most in the tragedy of unchastity and that usually (but not always) it is the transgressing man who causes the 'sobbings of the [women's] hearts to ascend up to God'" (Holland, "Jacob the Unshakable," 41).

Jacob 3:1–2. The Pure in Heart Feast on God's Love

How do we "look unto God with firmness of mind"? (3:1–2) "'Firmness of mind' is to be constant and undeterred in one's progress toward that life which is like God's; it is to have undimmed vision of the plans and purposes of the Almighty; to enjoy peace and confidence in the Master as the tempests rage on all sides. To look to God with firmness of mind is to be, as Nephi said, steadfast in Christ (see 2 Nephi 31:19–20) to pursue an undeviating course" (McConkie and Millet, *Doctrinal Commentary*, 2:24).

2 O all ye that are pure in heart, lift up your heads and receive the pleasing word of God, and feast upon his love; for ye may, if your minds are firm, forever.

3 But, wo, wo, unto you that are not pure in heart, that are filthy this day before God; for except ye repent the land is cursed for your sakes; and the Lamanites, which are not filthy like unto you, nevertheless they are cursed with a sore cursing, shall scourge you even unto destruction.

4 And the time speedily cometh, that except ye repent they shall possess the land of your inheritance, and the Lord God will lead away the righteous out from among you.

5 Behold, the Lamanites your brethren, whom ye hate because of their filthiness and the cursing which hath come upon their skins, are more righteous than you; for they have not forgotten the commandment of the Lord, which was given unto our father—that they should have save it were one wife, and concubines they should have none, and there should not be whoredoms committed among them.

6 And now, this commandment they observe to keep; wherefore, because of this observance, in keeping this commandment, the Lord God will not destroy them, but will be merciful unto them; and one day they shall become a blessed people.

7 Behold, their husbands love their wives, and their wives love their husbands; and their husbands and their wives love their children; and their unbelief and their hatred towards you is because of the iniquity of their fathers; wherefore, how much better are you than they, in the sight of your great Creator?

Jacob 3:3–10. The Nephites Are More Wicked Than the Lamanites

When was Jacob's prophecy fulfilled? (3:4) One fulfillment may have been about three hundred to four hundred years later when the Lord led a group of faithful Nephites out of the land of their inheritance. The prophet Mosiah was inspired to lead away the righteous, and "as many as would hearken unto the voice of the Lord . . . were led by the power of his arm, through the wilderness until they came down into . . . the land of Zarahemla" (see Omni 1:7, 12–13). ⊕

What were the "whoredoms" prevalent among the Nephites during Jacob's ministry? (3:5) Book of Mormon prophets frequently referred to immorality, infidelity, adultery, and all other promiscuous sins among the people as whoredoms. President Joseph F. Smith noted the danger of these sins in our lives: "We believe in one standard of morality for men and women. If purity of life is neglected, all other dangers set in upon us like the rivers of waters when the flood gates are opened" (*Gospel Doctrine*, 313).

How did the Lamanites demonstrate the proper relationship between husbands and wives? (3:7) "Marriage between a man and a woman is ordained of God. . . . The first commandment that God gave to Adam and Eve pertained to their potential for parenthood as husband and wife. . . . Husband and wife have a solemn responsibility to love and care for each other and for their children. . . . Marriage between a man and a woman is essential to His eternal plan" ("The Family: A Proclamation to the World).

Why were the Nephites at this time commanded not to condemn the Lamanites? (3:9) "The Book of Mormon promises that all who receive and act upon the Lord's invitation to 'repent and believe in his Son' become 'the covenant people of the Lord' (2 Ne. 30:2). This is a potent reminder that neither riches nor lineage nor any other privileges of birth should cause us to believe that we are 'better one than another' (Alma 5:54; see also Jacob 3:9). Indeed, the Book of Mormon commands, 'Ye shall not esteem one flesh above another, or one man shall not think himself above another' (Mosiah 23:7)" (Oaks, "All Men Everywhere," 79).

Jacob 3:11–14. The Wicked Stand in Danger of the Second Death

What is the "second death"? (3:11) "The second death, therefore, whatever its nature or extent, is a feature of the final judgment, at which each shall stand in his resurrected body of flesh and bones to receive the sentence of honor or of shame.... We are without scriptural warrant for assuming that the second death is another separation of body and spirit, or that the spirit shall undergo dissolution and cease to be. The spirit of man is eternal; and the resurrected body shall be everlasting.... In what then does the second death consist? ... The second death therefore is final consignment to the dominion of Satan, and, of necessity, banishment from the presence of God and Christ" (Talmage, *Vitality of Mormonism*, 302).

Why did Jacob refer to the small plates made by his brother Nephi as the plates of Jacob? (3:13–14) "The writings of Jacob and his descendants form part of the small plates, a section of the Book of Mormon that Mormon included intact.... After passing into Jacob's hands, the small plates became increasingly focused on the history of Jacob's family rather than on the history of the whole Nephite group.... From Jacob on, the plates were no longer kept by the rulers.... After Nephi, never again do the authors of the small plates occupy a central position in the government. Of course, the small plates were always set aside for spiritual things rather than secular matters" (Tanner, "Jacob and His Descendants as Authors," 52–55).

8 O my brethren, I fear that unless ye shall repent of your sins that their skins will be whiter than yours, when ye shall be brought with them before the throne of God.

9 Wherefore, a commandment I give unto you, which is the word of God, that ye revile no more against them because of the darkness of their skins; neither shall ye revile against them because of their filthiness; but ye shall remember your own filthiness, and remember that their filthiness came because of their fathers.

10 Wherefore, ye shall remember your children, how that ye have grieved their hearts because of the example that ye have set before them; and also, remember that ye may, because of your filthiness, bring your children unto destruction, and their sins be heaped upon your heads at the last day.

11 O my brethren, hearken unto my words; arouse the faculties of your souls; shake yourselves that ye may awake from the slumber of death; and loose yourselves from the pains of hell that ye may not become angels to the devil, to be cast into that lake of fire and brimstone which is the second death.

12 And now I, Jacob, spake many more things unto the people of Nephi, warning them against fornication and lasciviousness, and every kind of sin, telling them the awful consequences of them.

13 And a hundredth part of the proceedings of this people, which now began to be numerous, cannot be written upon these plates; but many of their proceedings are written upon the larger plates, and their wars, and their contentions, and the reigns of their kings.

14 These plates are called the plates of Jacob, and they were made by the hand of Nephi. And I make an end of speaking these words.

CHAPTER 4

All the prophets worshiped the Father in the name of Christ—Abraham's offering of Isaac was in similitude of God and His Only Begotten—Men should reconcile themselves to God through the Atonement—The Jews will reject the foundation stone. About 544–421 B.C.

1 Now behold, it came to pass that I, Jacob, having ministered much unto my people in word, (and I cannot write but a little of my words, because of the difficulty of engraving our words upon plates) and we know that the things which we write upon plates must remain;

2 But whatsoever things we write upon anything save it be upon plates must perish and vanish away; but we can write a few words upon plates, which will give our children, and also our beloved brethren, a small degree of knowledge concerning us, or concerning their fathers—

3 Now in this thing we do rejoice; and we labor diligently to engraven these words upon plates, hoping that our beloved brethren and our children will receive them with thankful hearts, and look upon them that they may learn with joy and not with sorrow, neither with contempt, concerning their first parents.

4 For, for this intent have we written these things, that they may know that we knew of Christ, and we had a hope of his glory many hundred years before his coming; and not only we ourselves had a hope of his glory, but also all the holy prophets which were before us.

5 Behold, they believed in Christ and worshiped the Father in his name, and also we worship the Father in his name. And for this intent we keep the law of Moses, it pointing our souls to him; and for this cause it is

Jacob 4:1–7. All the Prophets Worshipped Heavenly Father in the Name of Christ

Did the Nephites write only on metal plates? (4:2)
"This is an oblique acknowledgment that the majority of their writing was on perishable materials. Note that when those who believed the preaching of Alma were being persecuted by the people of the city of Ammonihah, 'they also brought forth their records which contained the holy scriptures, and cast them into the fire also, that they might be burned and destroyed by fire' (Alma 14:8). Paper seems the obvious substance. . . . Lehi and Nephi would surely have been fully familiar with Egyptian paper made from papyrus . . . considering that they carried only a minimum of materials beyond their subsistence necessities" (Sorenson, "Book of Mormon as a Mesoamerican Record," 417–18). ●

How did Jacob and other ancient prophets signify their hope in Christ? (4:4–5) "Whenever the Lord revealed Himself to men in ancient days, and commanded them to offer sacrifice to Him, . . . it was done that they might look forward in faith to the time of His coming, and rely upon the power of that atonement for a remission of their sins. On this matter the Book of Mormon prophets are quite plain and none plainer than Jacob" (McConkie, "Testimony of Christ through the Ages," 162).

What was the purpose of the law of Moses? (4:5)
"The law was the symbol, Jesus the ultimate reality toward which it pointed. The law was the means, Jesus the end. These simple but pertinent verities are all but lost in the Bible, particularly in the Old Testament. Only through the clarifying and illuminating lenses of the

Book of Mormon do we come to know that the law was anything more than a schoolmaster or teaching device" (McConkie and Millet, *Doctrinal Commentary*, 2:34).

How does one obtain the hope of unshaken faith? (4:6) "Closely associated with having faith is what Jacob calls 'obtaining a hope in Christ' [Jacob 2:19]. . . . His phrase of 'obtaining a hope' is more than just having 'hope' and seems to be the assurance or testimony that one has reached a particular state or spiritual condition and a special relationship with the Lord. . . . In all, the word hope appears 50 times in the Book of Mormon and is used by eight different prophets. Jacob, however, is unique in using it in the sense of obtaining 'a hope,' which is an achievement of something beyond simply 'hoping'" (Matthews, "Jacob," 49–50).

Why is it that the Lord "showeth us our weakness"? (4:7) Elder Neal A. Maxwell observed: "One thing is clear: in stressful situations, our deficiencies become more obvious [Jacob 4:7 and Ether 12:27 are quoted]. Difficulties sometimes put our deficiencies on display; it is then that we must be especially humble if we are to be made strong subsequently" (*Wherefore, Ye Must Press Forward*, 66).

Jacob 4:8–10. We Should Listen to the Lord and Do All That He Commands Us

How can we know the mysteries of God? (4:8) "There are two ways to find truth—both useful, provided we follow the laws upon which they are predicated. The first is the scientific method. It can require analysis of data to confirm a theory or, alternatively, establish a valid principle through experimentation. . . .

"The best way of finding truth is simply to go to the origin of all truth and ask or respond to inspiration. For success, two ingredients are essential: first, unwavering faith in the source of all truth; second, a willingness to keep God's commandments to keep open spiritual communication with Him" (Scott, "Truth: The Foundation of Correct Decisions," 90).

sanctified unto us for righteousness, even as it was accounted unto Abraham in the wilderness to be obedient unto the commands of God in offering up his son Isaac, which is a similitude of God and his Only Begotten Son.

6 Wherefore, we search the prophets, and we have many revelations and the spirit of prophecy; and having all these witnesses we obtain a hope, and our faith becometh unshaken, insomuch that we truly can command in the name of Jesus and the very trees obey us, or the mountains, or the waves of the sea.

7 Nevertheless, the Lord God showeth us our weakness that we may know that it is by his grace, and his great condescensions unto the children of men, that we have power to do these things.

8 Behold, great and marvelous are the works of the Lord. How unsearchable are the depths of the mysteries of him; and it is impossible that man should find out all his ways. And no man knoweth of his ways save it be revealed unto him; wherefore, brethren, despise not the revelations of God.

9 For behold, by the power of his word man came upon the face of the earth, which earth was created by the power of his word. Wherefore, if God being able to speak and the world was, and to speak and man was created, O then, why not able to command the earth, or the workmanship of his hands upon the face of it, according to his will and pleasure?

10 Wherefore, brethren, seek not to counsel the Lord, but to take counsel from his hand. For behold, ye yourselves know that he counseleth in wisdom, and in justice, and in great mercy, over all his works.

11 Wherefore, beloved brethren, be reconciled unto him through the atonement of Christ, his Only Begotten Son, and ye may obtain a resurrection, according to the power of the resurrection which is in Christ, and be presented as the first-fruits of Christ unto God, having faith, and obtained a good hope of glory in him before he manifesteth himself in the flesh.

12 And now, beloved, marvel not that I tell you these things; for why not speak of the atonement of Christ, and attain to a perfect knowledge of him, as to attain to the knowledge of a resurrection and the world to come?

13 Behold, my brethren, he that prophesieth, let him prophesy to the understanding of men; for the Spirit speaketh the truth and lieth not. Wherefore, it speaketh of things as they really are, and of things as they really will be; wherefore, these things are manifested unto us plainly, for the salvation of our souls. But behold, we are not witnesses alone in these things; for God also spake them unto prophets of old.

Jacob 4:11–13. Through the Atonement of Jesus Christ, We Can Live Again with God

What is meant by "first-fruits"? (4:11) "The law of Moses dictated that the firstfruits of the harvest be offered unto the Lord (Deut. 26:2; Prov. 3:9; Num. 18:12–13). These, considered 'holy unto the Lord' (Ezek. 48:14), represent the righteous Saints of the first resurrection. These are they who were first plucked from the grave, those who are first gathered to rise from the dead. . . . Christ is 'the firstfruits of them that slept' (1 Cor. 15:20, 23; 2 Ne. 2:9), and those who arise at the first resurrection 'are Christ's, the first fruits' (D&C 88:97–98)" (McConkie and Parry, *Guide to Scriptural Symbols*, 51).

Why was Jacob so eager to speak of the Atonement? (4:12) "Jacob came by his fascination with the Atonement rightly, beginning with his father Lehi's blessing recorded in 2 Nephi 2. . . . Jacob was in his youth introduced to the grand concepts of the creation of Adam and Eve, the role of moral agency, the inevitability of opposition in all things, the design and purpose of the Fall, the consequence of transgression, the immutability of law, the demands of justice, the gift of mercy and grace, the need for mortality and children, the purpose of probation, and, through it all, the joy of redemption" (Holland, *Christ and the New Covenant*, 64).

What is unique about the word *really* in this verse? (4:13) "The adverb *really* is used only twice in all of scripture, and then only for exceptional emphasis. The great poet-prophet Jacob underscored the manner in which the Spirit teaches us the truth 'of things as they really are, and of things as they really will be.' Jacob's declaration about truth is, of course, consistent with the definition of truth given by the Lord to a later prophet, Joseph Smith: 'And truth is knowledge of things as they are, and as they were, and as they are to come' (D&C 93:24). Thus, while in A.D. 33, Pilate asked Jesus, 'What is truth?' and the Savior did not reply, in A.D. 1833 he did reply (John 18:38)" (Maxwell, *Things As They Really Are*, 1). ⊕

Jacob 4:14–18. The Jews Will Suffer for Rejecting Jesus Christ

What does it mean to look "beyond the mark"?
(4:14–15) "Today there is a tendency among some of us to 'look beyond the mark' rather than to maintain a testimony of gospel basics. We do this when we substitute the philosophies of men for gospel truths, engage in gospel extremism, seek heroic gestures at the expense of daily consecration, or elevate rules over doctrine. Avoiding these behaviors will help us avoid the theological blindness and stumbling that Jacob described" (Cook, "Looking beyond the Mark," 41).

14 But behold, the Jews were a stiffnecked people; and they despised the words of plainness, and killed the prophets, and sought for things that they could not understand. Wherefore, because of their blindness, which blindness came by looking beyond the mark, they must needs fall; for God hath taken away his plainness from them, and delivered unto them many things which they cannot understand, because they desired it. And because they desired it God hath done it, that they may stumble.

15 And now I, Jacob, am led on by the Spirit unto prophesying; for I perceive by the workings of the Spirit which is in me, that by the stumbling of the Jews they will reject the stone upon which they might build and have safe foundation.

16 But behold, according to the scriptures, this stone shall become the great, and the last, and the only sure foundation, upon which the Jews can build.

17 And now, my beloved, how is it possible that these, after having rejected the sure foundation, can ever build upon it, that it may become the head of their corner?

18 Behold, my beloved brethren, I will unfold this mystery unto you; if I do not, by any means, get shaken from my firmness in the Spirit, and stumble because of my over anxiety for you.

CHAPTER 5

Jacob quotes Zenos relative to the allegory of the tame and wild olive trees—They are a likeness of Israel and the Gentiles—The scattering and gathering of Israel are prefigured—Allusions are made to the Nephites and Lamanites and all the house of Israel—The Gentiles will be grafted into Israel—Eventually the vineyard will be burned. About 544–421 B.C.

1 Behold, my brethren, do ye not remember to have read the words of the prophet Zenos, which he spake unto the house of Israel, saying:

2 Hearken, O ye house of Israel, and hear the words of me, a prophet of the Lord.

3 For behold, thus saith the Lord, I will liken thee, O house of Israel, like unto a tame olive tree, which a man took and nourished in his vineyard; and it grew, and waxed old, and began to decay.

4 And it came to pass that the master of the vineyard went forth, and he saw that his olive tree began to decay; and he said: I will prune it, and dig about it, and nourish it, that perhaps it may shoot forth young and tender branches, and it perish not.

5 And it came to pass that he pruned it, and digged about it, and nourished it according to his word.

6 And it came to pass that after many days it began to put forth somewhat a little, young and tender branches; but behold, the main top thereof began to perish.

Jacob 5:1–5. The Master Cares for the Tame Olive Tree (the House of Israel) When It Begins to Decay

What is the key to understanding a parable, an allegory, or any scriptural story? (5:1) The Prophet Joseph Smith declared: "I have a key by which I understand the scriptures. I enquire, what was the question which drew out the answer, or caused Jesus to utter the parable? . . . To ascertain its meaning, we must dig up the root and ascertain what it was that drew the saying out of Jesus" (*History of the Church*, 5:261). ⊙

Who was the prophet Zenos? (5:1–2) "Zenos is one of four Israelite prophets of Old Testament times cited in the Book of Mormon whose writings appeared on the plates of brass but who are not mentioned in the Old Testament (see also Zenock; Neum; and Ezias). Zenos is quoted or mentioned by Nephi (1 Ne. 19:10–17), Jacob (Jacob 5:1–77; 6:1), Alma (Alma 33:3–11,13,15), Amulek (Alma 34:7), Nephi (Hel. 8:19–20), and Mormon (3 Ne. 10:14–17)" (Ludlow, *Encyclopedia of Mormonism*, 4:1623). ⊙

How did the Lord try to reclaim the decaying olive tree (house of Israel)? (5:4) "The Lord of the vineyard, on seeing his now venerable tree and the apostasy therein, outlined a course of action to correct the situation, to rejuvenate the tree. . . . Beginning with prophets such as Moses, Samuel, Elijah, and Isaiah, the Lord attempted to reclaim the house of Israel from apostasy. Even with this effort and only after a period of 'many days,' the Lord met with merely minimal success" (Hoskisson, "Allegory of the Olive Tree," 77–78). ⊙

Jacob 5:6–14. The Master (God) and His Servants (the Prophets) Graft Wild Olive Tree Branches (the Gentiles) into the Tame Olive Tree (the House of Israel)

What do the phrases "young and tender branches" and the "main top thereof began to perish" represent? (5:6) "This phrase ['young and tender branches'] seems to refer to the emergence of a righteous element of the house of Israel, this in the midst of gross wickedness....

"[The phrase 'main top thereof began to perish' may indicate that] the older generation of Israel, steeped in sinful traditions, had become comfortable in their iniquity" (McConkie and Millet, *Doctrinal Commentary*, 2:50).

What does the grafting process and preserving of the fruit represent in the allegory? (5:8) "To be grafted is to come to the knowledge of the true Messiah, join the true Church, and gather where the Saints of God are assembled in that day (see 1 Nephi 10:14).... The 'fruit' which the Lord preserves 'unto himself' seems to be those of Israel who accept the message of the gospel, receive the ordinances of salvation, and endure faithfully to the end" (McConkie and Millet, *Doctrinal Commentary*, 2:52).

7 And it came to pass that the master of the vineyard saw it, and he said unto his servant: It grieveth me that I should lose this tree; wherefore, go and pluck the branches from a wild olive tree, and bring them hither unto me; and we will pluck off those main branches which are beginning to wither away, and we will cast them into the fire that they may be burned.

8 And behold, saith the Lord of the vineyard, I take away many of these young and tender branches, and I will graft them whithersoever I will; and it mattereth not that if it so be that the root of this tree will perish, I may preserve the fruit thereof unto myself; wherefore, I will take these young and tender branches, and I will graft them whithersoever I will.

9 Take thou the branches of the wild olive tree, and graft them in, in the stead thereof;

Allegory of the Olive Tree

Allegories and parables should not be forced to perfectly correlate every item with precision. Note the following possible interpretations for the symbols in Zenos's allegory:

Symbol	Meaning
The vineyard	The world
Tame olive tree	The house of Israel, the Lord's covenant people
Wild olive tree	Gentiles or non-Israel (later in the parable, wild branches represent apostate Israel)
Branches	Groups of people
The roots of the tame olive tree	The gospel covenants and promises the Lord makes with His children, a constant source of strength and life to the faithful
Fruit of the tree	The lives or works of men
Digging, pruning, fertilizing	The Lord's work with His children, which seeks to persuade them to be obedient and produce good fruit
Transplanting the branches	Scattering of groups throughout the world or restoring them to their original position
Grafting	The process of spiritual birth through which one is joined to the covenant
Decaying branches	Wickedness and apostasy
Casting the branches into the fire	The judgment of God

and these which I have plucked off I will cast into the fire and burn them, that they may not cumber the ground of my vineyard.

10 And it came to pass that the servant of the Lord of the vineyard did according to the word of the Lord of the vineyard, and grafted in the branches of the wild olive tree.

11 And the Lord of the vineyard caused that it should be digged about, and pruned, and nourished, saying unto his servant: It grieveth me that I should lose this tree; wherefore, that perhaps I might preserve the roots thereof that they perish not, that I might preserve them unto myself, I have done this thing.

12 Wherefore, go thy way; watch the tree, and nourish it, according to my words.

13 And these will I place in the nethermost part of my vineyard, whithersoever I will, it mattereth not unto thee; and I do it that I may preserve unto myself the natural branches of the tree; and also, that I may lay up fruit thereof against the season, unto myself; for it grieveth me that I should lose this tree and the fruit thereof.

14 And it came to pass that the Lord of the vineyard went his way, and hid the natural branches of the tame olive tree in the nethermost parts of the vineyard, some in one and some in another, according to his will and pleasure.

What is meant by grafting wild olive branches into a tame olive tree? (5:10) "Every person who embraces the gospel becomes of the house of Israel. In other words, they become members of the chosen lineage, or Abraham's children through Isaac and Jacob unto whom the promises were made. The great majority of those who become members of the Church are literal descendants of Abraham through Ephraim, son of Joseph. Those who are not literal descendants of Abraham and Israel must become such, and when they are baptized and confirmed they are grafted into the tree and are entitled to all the rights and privileges as heirs" (Smith, *Doctrines of Salvation*, 3:246).

What does it mean that the Lord will "lay up fruit . . . unto myself"? (5:13) "Superficially the allegory is the story of a man and his olive tree and the man's efforts to restore the deteriorating tree to its former pristine condition. At a deeper level, the allegory treats God's response to Israel's spiritual death, represented by its geographically scattered condition. Separation of the people of Israel from each other indicates that Christ's Atonement is not working in their lives; otherwise, they would live in Zion together. . . . Atonement . . . refers not only to the act of redemption Jesus wrought in Gethsemane and on the cross, but also to the Lord's ongoing labors to bring his children back into oneness with him" (Thomas, "Jacob's Allegory," 12).

Where did the Lord hide or scatter Israel? (5:13–14) "The Lord took branches like the Nephites, like the lost tribes, and like others that the Lord led off that we do not know anything about, to other parts of the earth. He planted them all over his vineyard, which is the world. No doubt he sent some of these branches into Japan, into Korea, into China. . . . [He] grafted them into the wild olives, the Gentiles, and is bringing the Gentiles into the gospel of Jesus Christ" (Smith, *Answers to Gospel Questions*, 4:204–6).

Jacob 5:15–28. After a Long Time, the Master and His Servant Discover That the Tame Olive Tree and All but One of the Natural Branches They Had Planted in the Nethermost Parts of the Vineyard Have Grown Good Fruit

What pleasing discovery does the Lord observe during His second visit to the vineyard? (5:15–18) "After a long time has passed, the master returns to examine the fruit of the vineyard. This time, he finds that the tame olive tree has borne tame fruit despite the wild branches that grew from its trunk. The great strength of the roots has overpowered the wildness of the branches. Perhaps this corresponds to the tremendous growth of the Church during and after the Savior's mortal ministry. A great many among the Gentiles, including numerous Samaritans, were converted and lived the gospel as though they had been born of Israel" (Swiss, "The Tame and Wild Olive Trees—An Allegory of Our Savior's Love," 51).

15 And it came to pass that a long time passed away, and the Lord of the vineyard said unto his servant: Come, let us go down into the vineyard, that we may labor in the vineyard.

16 And it came to pass that the Lord of the vineyard, and also the servant, went down into the vineyard to labor. And it came to pass that the servant said unto his master: Behold, look here; behold the tree.

17 And it came to pass that the Lord of the vineyard looked and beheld the tree in the which the wild olive branches had been grafted; and it had sprung forth and begun to bear fruit. And he beheld that it was good; and the fruit thereof was like unto the natural fruit.

18 And he said unto the servant: Behold, the branches of the wild tree have taken hold of the moisture of the root thereof, that the root thereof hath brought forth much strength; and because of the much strength of the root thereof the wild branches have brought forth tame fruit. Now, if we had not grafted in these branches, the tree thereof would have perished. And now, behold, I shall lay up much fruit, which the tree thereof hath brought forth; and the fruit thereof I shall lay up against the season, unto mine own self.

19 And it came to pass that the Lord of the vineyard said unto the servant: Come, let us go to the nethermost part of the vineyard, and behold if the natural branches of the tree have not brought forth much fruit also, that I may lay up of the fruit thereof against the season, unto mine own self.

20 And it came to pass that they went forth whither the master had hid the natural branches of the tree, and he said unto the servant: Behold these; and he beheld the first that it had brought forth much fruit; and he beheld also that it was good. And he said unto the servant: Take of the fruit thereof, and lay it up against the season, that I may preserve it unto mine own self; for behold, said he, this long time have I nourished it, and it hath brought forth much fruit.

21 And it came to pass that the servant said unto his master: How comest thou hither to plant this tree, or this branch of the tree? For behold, it was the poorest spot in all the land of thy vineyard.

22 And the Lord of the vineyard said unto him: Counsel me not; I knew that it was a poor spot of ground; wherefore, I said unto thee, I have nourished it this long time, and thou beholdest that it hath brought forth much fruit.

23 And it came to pass that the Lord of the vineyard said unto his servant: Look hither; behold I have planted another branch of the tree also; and thou knowest that this spot of ground was poorer than the first. But, behold the tree. I have nourished it this long time, and it hath brought forth much fruit; therefore, gather it, and lay it up against the season, that I may preserve it unto mine own self.

24 And it came to pass that the Lord of the vineyard said again unto his servant: Look hither, and behold another branch also, which I have planted; behold that I have nourished it also, and it hath brought forth fruit.

25 And he said unto the servant: Look hither and behold the last. Behold, this have I planted in a good spot of ground; and I have nourished it this long time, and only a part of the tree hath brought forth tame fruit, and the other part of the tree hath brought forth wild fruit; behold, I have nourished this tree like unto the others.

26 And it came to pass that the Lord of the vineyard said unto the servant: Pluck off the branches that have not brought forth good fruit, and cast them into the fire.

Why does the Lord plant "Israel" all over the vineyard? (5:23–25) Zenos's allegory helps us understand that the scattering of Israel all over the world was a blessing to Israel and to the rest of Heavenly Father's children. President Joseph Fielding Smith taught: "In that parable the olive tree is the House of Israel. . . . In its native land it began to die. So the Lord took branches like the Nephites, like the lost tribes, and like others that the Lord led off that we do not know anything about, to other parts of the earth" (*Answers to Gospel Questions*, 4:204). ☉

What is represented by the tame and the wild fruit? (5:25) "Those who were planted in a choice spot of ground—'a land which is choice above all other lands' (Ether 2:10)—are, of course, Lehi and his family. In general, by the meridian of time only the Nephites had brought forth 'tame fruit'—fruit meet for repentance, lives worthy of the covenant family to which they belong. The Lamanites (meaning, broadly, the unbelievers) had brought forth 'wild fruit,' acts of aggression, deeds of hatred, and a belief in false traditions and doctrines" (McConkie and Millet, *Doctrinal Commentary*, 2:56).

Jacob 5:29–48. After a Long Time, the Master and His Servant Discover That All the Olive Trees Are Growing Bad Fruit

What does "cumber" mean? (5:30–32) *Cumber* means "to trouble; to be troublesome to; to cause trouble or obstruction in, as any thing useless. Thus, brambles [prickly shrubs] cumber a garden or field" (Webster, *American Dictionary*).

What does the phrase "it grieveth me" reveal about the nature of God? (5:32) "A key phrase in the allegory is 'it grieveth me that I should lose this tree,' repeated eight times. . . . The frequent repetition of the line describes the quality of that divine love—it is unfailing, persistent, tenacious. This message of the Lord's love matters as much as, if not more than, the historical details of his plan to redeem Israel" (Tanner, "Jacob and His Descendants as Authors," 61).

27 But behold, the servant said unto him: Let us prune it, and dig about it, and nourish it a little longer, that perhaps it may bring forth good fruit unto thee, that thou canst lay it up against the season.

28 And it came to pass that the Lord of the vineyard and the servant of the Lord of the vineyard did nourish all the fruit of the vineyard.

29 And it came to pass that a long time had passed away, and the Lord of the vineyard said unto his servant: Come, let us go down into the vineyard, that we may labor again in the vineyard. For behold, the time draweth near, and the end soon cometh; wherefore, I must lay up fruit against the season, unto mine own self.

30 And it came to pass that the Lord of the vineyard and the servant went down into the vineyard; and they came to the tree whose natural branches had been broken off, and the wild branches had been grafted in; and behold all sorts of fruit did cumber the tree.

31 And it came to pass that the Lord of the vineyard did taste of the fruit, every sort according to its number. And the Lord of the vineyard said: Behold, this long time have we nourished this tree, and I have laid up unto myself against the season much fruit.

32 But behold, this time it hath brought forth much fruit, and there is none of it which is good. And behold, there are all kinds of bad fruit; and it profiteth me nothing, notwithstanding all our labor; and now it grieveth me that I should lose this tree.

33 And the Lord of the vineyard said unto the servant: What shall we do unto the tree, that I may preserve again good fruit thereof unto mine own self?

34 And the servant said unto his master: Behold, because thou didst graft in the branches of the wild olive tree they have nourished the roots, that they are alive and they have not perished; wherefore thou beholdest that they are yet good.

35 And it came to pass that the Lord of the vineyard said unto his servant: The tree profiteth me nothing, and the roots thereof profit me nothing so long as it shall bring forth evil fruit.

36 Nevertheless, I know that the roots are good, and for mine own purpose I have preserved them; and because of their much strength they have hitherto brought forth, from the wild branches, good fruit.

37 But behold, the wild branches have grown and have overrun the roots thereof; and because that the wild branches have overcome the roots thereof it hath brought forth much evil fruit; and because that it hath brought forth so much evil fruit thou beholdest that it beginneth to perish; and it will soon become ripened, that it may be cast into the fire, except we should do something for it to preserve it.

38 And it came to pass that the Lord of the vineyard said unto his servant: Let us go down into the nethermost parts of the vineyard, and behold if the natural branches have also brought forth evil fruit.

39 And it came to pass that they went down into the nethermost parts of the vineyard. And it came to pass that they beheld that the fruit of the natural branches had become corrupt also; yea, the first and the second and also the last; and they had all become corrupt.

40 And the wild fruit of the last had overcome that part of the tree which brought forth good fruit, even that the branch had withered away and died.

41 And it came to pass that the Lord of the vineyard wept, and said unto the servant:

What does it mean that the ripened fruit is to be cast into the fire? (5:37) "The end comes when, and only when, 'the time is ripe,' when 'the harvest is ripe'; when the people are 'ripe in iniquity.'... Fruit is fully ripe at that moment when further ripening would not mean improvement but only deterioration" (*Nibley on the Timely and the Timeless,* 294).

What can we learn from the fact that the Lord of the Vineyard wept? (5:41) Elder Jeffrey R. Holland taught that the allegory of Zenos, like Enoch's vision of God's creations (see Moses 7), "does more to teach the true nature of God than any theological treatise could ever convey. It also helps us understand much more emphatically that vivid moment in the Book of Mormon allegory of the olive tree, when after digging and dunging, watering and weeding, trimming, pruning, transplanting, and grafting, the great Lord of the vineyard throws down his spade and his pruning shears and weeps, crying out to any who would listen, 'What could I have done more for my vineyard?'

"...What anguish in a parent when His children do not choose Him nor 'the gospel of God' He sent!" ("Grandeur of God," 72).

Where is the good spot of ground? (5:43) "Reference here is to America, a land choice above all others (see verse 25; 1 Nephi 2:20; Ether 2:10)" (McConkie and Millet, *Doctrinal Commentary*, 2:62).

Who were the people who had cumbered the ground? (5:44) "The master reminds his servant of the history of the last planting of the branches in the good spot of ground. Again, in the 1881 footnotes, this last branch of Israel is designated as the 'Nephites'..., along with the good spot as 'America.'... The master continues, reminding the servant that he had 'cut down that which cumbered this [good] spot of ground' so he could plant this branch of Israel (v. 44). In the 1881 edition footnotes, 'that which cumbered' is designated as the 'Jaredites'" (Fowles, "Zenos' Prophetic Allegory," 34). ⊕

What could I have done more for my vineyard?

42 Behold, I knew that all the fruit of the vineyard, save it were these, had become corrupted. And now these which have once brought forth good fruit have also become corrupted; and now all the trees of my vineyard are good for nothing save it be to be hewn down and cast into the fire.

43 And behold this last, whose branch hath withered away, I did plant in a good spot of ground; yea, even that which was choice unto me above all other parts of the land of my vineyard.

44 And thou beheldest that I also cut down that which cumbered this spot of ground, that I might plant this tree in the stead thereof.

45 And thou beheldest that a part thereof brought forth good fruit, and a part thereof brought forth wild fruit; and because I plucked not the branches thereof and cast them into the fire, behold, they have overcome the good branch that it hath withered away.

46 And now, behold, notwithstanding all the care which we have taken of my vineyard, the trees thereof have become corrupted, that they bring forth no good fruit; and these I had hoped to preserve, to have laid up fruit thereof against the season, unto mine own self. But, behold, they have become like unto the wild olive tree, and they are of no worth but to be hewn down and cast into the fire; and it grieveth me that I should lose them.

47 But what could I have done more in my vineyard? Have I slackened mine hand, that I have not nourished it? Nay, I have nourished it, and I have digged about it, and I have pruned it, and I have dunged it; and I

have stretched forth mine hand almost all the day long, and the end draweth nigh. And it grieveth me that I should hew down all the trees of my vineyard, and cast them into the fire that they should be burned. Who is it that has corrupted my vineyard?

48 And it came to pass that the servant said unto his master: Is it not the loftiness of thy vineyard—have not the branches thereof overcome the roots which are good? And because the branches have overcome the roots thereof, behold they grew faster than the strength of the roots, taking strength unto themselves. Behold, I say, is not this the cause that the trees of thy vineyard have become corrupted?

49 And it came to pass that the Lord of the vineyard said unto the servant: Let us go to and hew down the trees of the vineyard and cast them into the fire, that they shall not cumber the ground of my vineyard, for I have done all. What could I have done more for my vineyard?

50 But, behold, the servant said unto the Lord of the vineyard: Spare it a little longer.

51 And the Lord said: Yea, I will spare it a little longer, for it grieveth me that I should lose the trees of my vineyard.

52 Wherefore, let us take of the branches of these which I have planted in the nethermost parts of my vineyard, and let us graft them into the tree from whence they came; and let us pluck from the tree those branches whose fruit is most bitter, and graft in the natural branches of the tree in the stead thereof.

What can the problem of branches "taking strength unto themselves" mean for us? (5:48) "There is great meaning in Jacob's parable for the Church in our generation. Meetings and activities can multiply until they take 'strength unto themselves' at the expense of the gospel—of true worship" (Packer, "Teach Them Correct Principles," 90). President Russell M. Nelson in 2018 introduced changes to strengthen the roots of each member of the Church. He said it was time "to strengthen families and individuals through a home-centered and Church-supported plan to learn doctrine, strengthen faith, and foster greater personal worship" (Nelson, "Opening Remarks," 8). ✦

Jacob 5:49–69. The Master and His Servant Decide to Give All the Olive Trees One More Chance to Grow Good Fruit

How are we to understand the Lord's anguish? (5:49) "The Book of Mormon allegory of the olive tree, when after digging and dunging, watering and weeding, trimming, pruning, transplanting, and grafting, the great Lord of the vineyard throws down his spade and his pruning shears and weeps, crying out to any who would listen, 'What could I have done more for my vineyard?'

"What an indelible image of God's engagement in our lives! What anguish in a parent when His children do not choose Him nor 'the gospel of God' He sent! How easy to love someone who so singularly loves us!" (Holland, "The Grandeur of God," 72).

What will the Lord do with the branches scattered throughout the vineyard? (5:52) "Formerly isolated groups of scattered Israel became one with the main body of Saints in a worldwide Church. This includes such groups as Lehi's posterity and the descendants of the scattered tribes of Israel. There is a union of Israel and Gentiles in the Lord's church" (Jackson, "Nourished by the Good Word of God," 193). ✦

53 And this will I do that the tree may not perish, that, perhaps, I may preserve unto myself the roots thereof for mine own purpose.

54 And, behold, the roots of the natural branches of the tree which I planted whithersoever I would are yet alive; wherefore, that I may preserve them also for mine own purpose, I will take of the branches of this tree, and I will graft them in unto them. Yea, I will graft in unto them the branches of their mother tree, that I may preserve the roots also unto mine own self, that when they shall be sufficiently strong perhaps they may bring forth good fruit unto me, and I may yet have glory in the fruit of my vineyard.

55 And it came to pass that they took from the natural tree which had become wild, and grafted in unto the natural trees, which also had become wild.

56 And they also took of the natural trees which had become wild, and grafted into their mother tree.

57 And the Lord of the vineyard said unto the servant: Pluck not the wild branches from the trees, save it be those which are most bitter; and in them ye shall graft according to that which I have said.

58 And we will nourish again the trees of the vineyard, and we will trim up the branches thereof; and we will pluck from the trees those branches which are ripened, that must perish, and cast them into the fire.

59 And this I do that, perhaps, the roots thereof may take strength because of their goodness; and because of the change of the branches, that the good may overcome the evil.

60 And because that I have preserved the natural branches and the roots thereof, and that I have grafted in the natural branches again into their mother tree, and have preserved the

---

How extensive will the gathering of the Lord's fruit be in the last days? (5:57–68) "We see that as the restored Church began to be established on the earth, the living prophets sought and followed the will of God about how the gospel should go forth among the nations.

"I have lived to see the time foreseen by the prophet Zenos . . . , when the righteous from all nations of the earth would become partakers of the covenant of God with Israel.

"I have seen the good fruit of the gospel blossom in my home continent of Africa. After just 30 years, there are 300,000 Saints" (Sitati, "Blessings of the Gospel Available to All," 104).

What are the "natural branches" and the "mother tree"? (5:60) "The announcement that Israel is to be grafted into 'their mother tree' affirms that the promises embrace literal blood lines. The promise given to Abraham was that it would be the 'literal seed, or the

roots of their mother tree, that, perhaps, the trees of my vineyard may bring forth again good fruit; and that I may have joy again in the fruit of my vineyard, and, perhaps, that I may rejoice exceedingly that I have preserved the roots and the branches of the first fruit—

61 Wherefore, go to, and call servants, that we may labor diligently with our might in the vineyard, that we may prepare the way, that I may bring forth again the natural fruit, which natural fruit is good and the most precious above all other fruit.

62 Wherefore, let us go to and labor with our might this last time, for behold the end draweth nigh, and this is for the last time that I shall prune my vineyard.

63 Graft in the branches; begin at the last that they may be first, and that the first may be last, and dig about the trees, both old and young, the first and the last; and the last and the first, that all may be nourished once again for the last time.

64 Wherefore, dig about them, and prune them, and dung them once more, for the last time, for the end draweth nigh. And if it be so that these last grafts shall grow, and bring forth the natural fruit, then shall ye prepare the way for them, that they may grow.

65 And as they begin to grow ye shall clear away the branches which bring forth bitter fruit, according to the strength of the good

seed of [his] body,' who, in the last days, would hold the priesthood and bear the responsibility to take the message of salvation to all nations (Abraham 2:9, 11). Such are 'lawful heirs, according to the flesh' (D&C 86:9; D&C 103:17–18; D&C 132:30–32)" (McConkie and Millet, *Doctrinal Commentary*, 2:70).

Who are the laborers in the vineyard at the last day? (5:62) "The Savior's call is to you of the rising generation. He is asking for worthy, prepared, faithful young men and young women who will heed the prophet's voice, who will step up and say, as the Savior Himself said, 'Here am I, send me' (Abraham 3:27). The need has never been greater. The field has never been whiter. You are called to go 'this last time' (Jacob 5:62). There is no greater work; there is no greater call than teaching 'all nations, baptizing them in the name of the Father, and of the Son, and of the Holy Ghost' (Matthew 28:19)" (Nielson, "Call to the Rising Generation," 97). ●

Who is the "last" and who is the "first"? (5:63) "The Lord has a divine timetable wherein the gospel is presented to the people on earth. In the meridian of time the gospel went first to the Jews and then to the Gentiles. In our day the message of the Restoration is taken first to the Gentiles (Israelites scattered among and identified with the Gentiles) and then to the house of Israel, meaning specifically the Lamanites and the Jews. Thus the first (the Jews) shall, in the last days, be last; and the last (the Gentiles) shall, in the final dispensation, be first" (McConkie and Millet, *Doctrinal Commentary*, 2:71). ●

What are the different ways the Lord tries to save the tree which is a representation of the house of Israel? (5:64) "*Digging* about suggests the divine structuring of one's environment for individual tutorials. Dunging suggests spiritual nourishing. As to *pruning*, we might understand those painful experiences in which we feel stymied as the divine will operates against our own" (Thomas, "Jacob's Allegory," 17).

What is the purpose of all the work done for the olive tree? (5:64–68) "Clearly this at-one-ment is hard, demanding, and, at times, deeply painful work, as the work of redemption always is. There is digging and dunging. There is watering and nourishing and pruning. And there is always the endless approaches to grafting—all to one saving end, that the trees of the vineyard would 'thrive exceedingly' and become 'one body; . . . the fruits [being] equal' [Jacob 6:73]. . . . It has always been the work of Christ (and his disciples) in every dispensation to gather them, heal them, and unite them with their Master" (Holland, *Christ and the New Covenant*, 165–66).

Jacob 5:70–74. The Master's Servant and Other Servants Work in the Vineyard to Save the Olive Trees and to Gather Much Good Fruit

When is the "last time" in which the vineyard will be nourished? (5:71) Elder Dean L. Larsen, speaking in the priesthood session of general conference in April 1983, quoted from the allegory of the olive tree and then declared: "You have come to the earth when the foundation has been laid for this great work. The gospel has been restored for the last time. The Church has been established in almost every part of the world. The stage is set for the final dramatic scenes to be enacted. You will be the principal players. You are among the last laborers in the vineyard. This is the yoke that is set upon your necks. This is the service for which you are chosen" ("Royal Generation," 33).

and the size thereof; and ye shall not clear away the bad thereof all at once, lest the roots thereof should be too strong for the graft, and the graft thereof shall perish, and I lose the trees of my vineyard.

66 For it grieveth me that I should lose the trees of my vineyard; wherefore ye shall clear away the bad according as the good shall grow, that the root and the top may be equal in strength, until the good shall overcome the bad, and the bad be hewn down and cast into the fire, that they cumber not the ground of my vineyard; and thus will I sweep away the bad out of my vineyard.

67 And the branches of the natural tree will I graft in again into the natural tree;

68 And the branches of the natural tree will I graft into the natural branches of the tree; and thus will I bring them together again, that they shall bring forth the natural fruit, and they shall be one.

69 And the bad shall be cast away, yea, even out of all the land of my vineyard; for behold, only this once will I prune my vineyard.

70 And it came to pass that the Lord of the vineyard sent his servant; and the servant went and did as the Lord had commanded him, and brought other servants; and they were few.

71 And the Lord of the vineyard said unto them: Go to, and labor in the vineyard, with your might. For behold, this is the last time that I shall nourish my vineyard; for the end is nigh at hand, and the season speedily cometh; and if ye labor with your might with me ye shall have joy in the fruit which I shall lay up unto myself against the time which will soon come.

72 And it came to pass that the servants did go and labor with their mights; and the Lord of the vineyard labored also with them; and they did obey the commandments of the Lord of the vineyard in all things.

73 And there began to be the natural fruit again in the vineyard; and the natural branches began to grow and thrive exceedingly; and the wild branches began to be plucked off and to be cast away; and they did keep the root and the top thereof equal, according to the strength thereof.

74 And thus they labored, with all diligence, according to the commandments of the Lord of the vineyard, even until the bad had been cast away out of the vineyard, and the Lord had preserved unto himself that the trees had become again the natural fruit; and they became like unto one body; and the fruits were equal; and the Lord of the vineyard had preserved unto himself the natural fruit, which was most precious unto him from the beginning.

75 And it came to pass that when the Lord of the vineyard saw that his fruit was good, and that his vineyard was no more corrupt, he called up his servants, and said unto them: Behold, for this last time have we nourished my vineyard; and thou beholdest that I have done according to my will; and I have preserved the natural fruit, that it is good, even like as it was in the beginning. And blessed art thou; for because ye have been diligent in laboring with me in my vineyard, and have kept my commandments, and have brought unto me again the natural fruit, that my vineyard is no more corrupted, and the bad is cast away, behold ye shall have joy with me because of the fruit of my vineyard.

76 For behold, for a long time will I lay up of the fruit of my vineyard unto mine own self against the season, which speedily cometh;

How might the Lord be laboring with us in His work? (5:72) "I suspect that many Church members are much more familiar with the nature of the redeeming and cleansing power of the Atonement than they are with the strengthening and enabling power. It is one thing to know that Jesus Christ came to earth to die for us—that is fundamental and foundational to the doctrine of Christ. But we also need to appreciate that the Lord desires, through His Atonement and by the power of the Holy Ghost, to live in us—not only to direct us but also to empower us" (Bednar, "The Atonement and the Journey of Mortality," 42).

Jacob 5:75–77. The Master Will Gather the Good Fruit and Burn the Bad

What does the phrase "a long time" represent at the end of the allegory? (5:75–76) These verses describe "the millennium, wherein the Lord will lay up fruit for a long time....

"The millennium is when Christ will 'dwell in righteousness with men on earth a thousand years' (D&C 29:11; see also Revelation 20:4)" (Nyman, *These Records Are True*, 94–95).

How do the details of Zenos's allegory suggest that Joseph Smith was translating an ancient work? (5:76) "Zenos's mention of planting, . . . pruning, . . . grafting, . . . digging, . . . nourishing, . . . and dunging . . .

as well as the fact that dunging occurs less frequently in the parable than the nourishing, all mark it as an authentic ancient work. . . . Joseph Smith could have known nothing about olives from personal experience. . . . Can it . . . be supposed that Joseph simply guessed right on so many details? And even if he somehow managed to get the details from classical authors, how did he know to put it into the proper Hebrew narrative form?" (Gee and Peterson, "Graft and Corruption," 223–24).

What period of time in the earth's history is represented by the burning of the vineyard? (5:77) This phrase refers to "the end of the millennium, when evil fruit will again appear and the Lord will again gather both the good and the bad together, preserving the good and casting away the bad [see D&C 29:22].

"Following this, the vineyard will be burned (Jacob 5:77). The temporal existence of the earth will then be completed and the program of the house of Israel finished. The earth will then be celestialized [see D&C 88:25–26]" (Nyman, *These Records Are True*, 95).

Jacob 6:1–4. In the Last Days, the Lord Will Save His People

When will God begin again to gather His people? (6:1–2) The coming forth of the Book of Mormon is a sign that God has commenced His work to gather His chosen people a second time (see 3 Nephi 21:1–7). President Russell M. Nelson testified: "This promise of the gathering, woven all through the fabric of the scriptures, will be fulfilled just as surely as were the prophecies of the scattering of Israel" ("Gathering of Scattered Israel," 79).

What are "a gainsaying people"? (6:4) "To say that Israel is 'a gainsaying people' is to say that they are quick to object, to oppose, resist, contradict, or speak against that which comes from God. They are slow

and for the last time have I nourished my vineyard, and pruned it, and dug about it, and dunged it; wherefore I will lay up unto mine own self of the fruit, for a long time, according to that which I have spoken.

77 And when the time cometh that evil fruit shall again come into my vineyard, then will I cause the good and the bad to be gathered; and the good will I preserve unto myself, and the bad will I cast away into its own place. And then cometh the season and the end; and my vineyard will I cause to be burned with fire.

CHAPTER 6

The Lord will recover Israel in the last days— The world will be burned with fire—Men must follow Christ to avoid the lake of fire and brimstone. About 544–421 B.C.

1 And now, behold, my brethren, as I said unto you that I would prophesy, behold, this is my prophecy—that the things which this prophet Zenos spake, concerning the house of Israel, in the which he likened them unto a tame olive tree, must surely come to pass.

2 And the day that he shall set his hand again the second time to recover his people, is the day, yea, even the last time, that the servants of the Lord shall go forth in his power, to nourish and prune his vineyard; and after that the end soon cometh.

3 And how blessed are they who have labored diligently in his vineyard; and how cursed are they who shall be cast out into their own place! And the world shall be burned with fire.

4 And how merciful is our God unto us, for he remembereth the house of Israel, both roots and branches; and he stretches forth his

hands unto them all the day long; and they are a stiffnecked and a gainsaying people; but as many as will not harden their hearts shall be saved in the kingdom of God.

5 Wherefore, my beloved brethren, I beseech of you in words of soberness that ye would repent, and come with full purpose of heart, and cleave unto God as he cleaveth unto you. And while his arm of mercy is extended towards you in the light of the day, harden not your hearts.

6 Yea, today, if ye will hear his voice, harden not your hearts; for why will ye die?

7 For behold, after ye have been nourished by the good word of God all the day long, will ye bring forth evil fruit, that ye must be hewn down and cast into the fire?

8 Behold, will ye reject these words? Will ye reject the words of the prophets; and will ye reject all the words which have been spoken concerning Christ, after so many have spoken concerning him; and deny the good word of Christ, and the power of God, and the gift of the Holy Ghost, and quench the Holy Spirit, and make a mock of the great plan of redemption, which hath been laid for you?

9 Know ye not that if ye will do these things, that the power of the redemption and the resurrection, which is in Christ, will bring you to stand with shame and awful guilt before the bar of God?

to believe, quick to disbelieve" (McConkie and Millet, *Doctrinal Commentary*, 2:78).

Jacob 6:5–7. At the Second Coming, the Earth Will Be Cleansed by Fire

What does it mean to "cleave unto God"? (6:5) Webster's 1828 *American Dictionary of the English Language* defines *cleave* as "to stick; to adhere; to hold to."

"In the Bible we read, 'O Israel, return unto the Lord, thy God, for thou hast stumbled in thine iniquity.' Likewise, Jacob implores his brethren to forsake their evil ways and hold fast to God's commandments, 'as he cleaveth unto you.' This was a call to repentance, and if they would repent with full purpose of heart, that includes going before the Lord in humility, he would be merciful unto them, and would hold them close to his bosom" (Reynolds and Sjodahl, *Commentary on the Book of Mormon*, 1:484–85). ⊕

What does Jacob mean when he asks, "why will ye die?" (6:6) President Franklin D. Richards of the Quorum of the Twelve Apostles testified: "The Lord our God is a God that forgives sin. When Israel went far astray He pleaded with them to turn unto Him. 'Why will ye die?' What the Lord wants is repentance; that is, to turn away from unrighteousness. Not to say you are sorry because you got caught at it. The thing is for you to catch yourself at it. It is more important to you than to anybody else that you should do this, and repent, and work out your salvation. . . . He does not wish that any should perish, but that all should turn unto Him and live" (in *Collected Discourses*, 5:5).

Jacob 6:8–13. Jacob Preaches Repentance and Asks Us to Follow Jesus Christ

What is the "lake of fire and brimstone"? (6:10) "The phrase 'lake of fire and brimstone' . . . is generally used to describe either the place that awaits the unrepentant individual after the Judgment or the mental anguish associated with sin. . . . In reference to mental anguish, the Prophet Joseph Smith said: 'A man is his own tormentor and his own condemner. Hence the saying, They shall go into the lake that burns with fire and brimstone. The torment of disappointment in the mind of man is as exquisite as a lake burning with fire and brimstone'" (*Book of Mormon Student Manual* [2009], 127).

How can we be wise today? (6:12) "I carry in my daily date book a few brief memo sheets. . . . One sheet almost worn out now has nothing more on it than Jacob 6, verse 12: 'O be wise; what can I say more?' Be wise enough to accept appropriate discipline and guidelines. Be wise enough to say the right words at the right time to the right person" (Ashton, *Teaching, Mentoring, and Things of the Spirit*, 5). ☉

What is the "pleasing bar of God"? (6:13) "Every person who has lived or will yet live upon the earth 'shall be brought to stand before the bar of God, to be judged of him according to [his or her] works whether they be good or whether they be evil' (Mosiah 16:10). If our desires have been for righteousness and our works good, then the judgment bar will be pleasing (see Jacob 6:13; Enos 1:27; Moroni 10:34). And at the last day we will 'be rewarded unto righteousness' (Alma 41:6). Conversely, if our desires have been for evil and our works wicked, then the judgment bar will be a cause of dread" (Bednar, "Therefore They Hushed Their Fears," 49).

Jacob 7:1–4. Sherem Preaches That "There Should Be No Christ"

Who was Sherem? (7:1) "[The] antichrist Sherem (Jacob 7) may have been an outsider. Jacob wrote of him, 'there came a man among the people of Nephi' (Jacob 7:1). Does this mean that he was not a Nephite? Jacob further notes 'that he had a perfect knowledge of the language of the people' (Jacob 7:4). Don't all native speakers? This would have been remarkable only if the man were not a Nephite" (Tvedtnes, "Review of 'New Approaches,'" 28). ☉

10 And according to the power of justice, for justice cannot be denied, ye must go away into that lake of fire and brimstone, whose flames are unquenchable, and whose smoke ascendeth up forever and ever, which lake of fire and brimstone is endless torment.

11 O then, my beloved brethren, repent ye, and enter in at the strait gate, and continue in the way which is narrow, until ye shall obtain eternal life.

12 O be wise; what can I say more?

13 Finally, I bid you farewell, until I shall meet you before the pleasing bar of God, which bar striketh the wicked with awful dread and fear. Amen.

CHAPTER 7

Sherem denies Christ, contends with Jacob, demands a sign, and is smitten of God—All of the prophets have spoken of Christ and His Atonement—The Nephites lived out their days as wanderers, born in tribulation, and hated by the Lamanites. About 544–421 B.C.

1 And now it came to pass after some years had passed away, there came a man among the people of Nephi, whose name was Sherem.

2 And it came to pass that he began to preach among the people, and to declare unto them that there should be no Christ. And he preached many things which were flattering unto the people; and this he did that he might overthrow the doctrine of Christ.

3 And he labored diligently that he might lead away the hearts of the people, insomuch that he did lead away many hearts; and he knowing that I, Jacob, had faith in Christ who should come, he sought much opportunity that he might come unto me.

4 And he was learned, that he had a perfect knowledge of the language of the people; wherefore, he could use much flattery, and much power of speech, according to the power of the devil.

5 And he had hope to shake me from the faith, notwithstanding the many revelations and the many things which I had seen concerning these things; for I truly had seen angels, and they had ministered unto me. And also, I had heard the voice of the Lord speaking unto me in very word, from time to time; wherefore, I could not be shaken.

6 And it came to pass that he came unto me, and on this wise did he speak unto me, saying: Brother Jacob, I have sought much opportunity that I might speak unto you; for I have heard and also know that thou goest about much, preaching that which ye call the gospel, or the doctrine of Christ.

What are the characteristics of an anti-Christ? (7:2) "There are certain characteristics of an anti-Christ, certain patterns of belief and practice which we might expect to find among those, like Sherem, who are bent upon overthrowing the doctrine of Christ. Some of these are as follows:

"1) They Deny the Need for Jesus Christ. . . .

"2) They Use Flattery to Win Disciples. . . .

"3) They Accuse the Brethren of Teaching False Doctrine. . . .

"4) They Have a Limited View of Reality. . . .

"5) They Have a Disposition to Misread and Thereby Misrepresent the Scriptures. . . .

"6) They are Sign Seekers" (Millet, "Sherem the Anti-Christ," 176–81). ❸

Why was Sherem's deception so successful? (7:3–4) "Early in Nephite history an ambitious intellectual by the name of Sherem, who was a master of smooth talk and rhetorical tricks and made a great show of being a good and devout church-member, set himself to the task of outshining all others as a Great Mind. . . . The interesting thing about Sherem is his convincing performance as a devout and active churchman who is not attacking the gospel but defending it: no wonder he got a large following!" (Nibley, *Approach to the Book of Mormon*, 302). ❸

Jacob 7:5–12. Sherem Uses the Deceptions of the Devil to Argue with Jacob

What can we learn from the phrase "notwithstanding the many revelations and the many things which I had seen"? (7:5) "Jacob here provides a marvelous pattern for steadfastness in the face of spiritual persecution and intellectual challenge. Only when we have drunk deeply of the waters of life—when we have been grounded in revealed theology, rooted in genuine spiritual experience, and established in the things of God—can we hope to withstand the burning rays of doubt and the scorching thirst of skepticism" (Millet, "Sherem the Anti-Christ," 183–84).

What was Sherem's intent when he confronted Jacob? (7:6) "Sherem . . . said, 'Brother Jacob [speaking to him very benevolently], I have sought much opportunity that I might speak unto you; . . . thou goest about much, preaching . . . the doctrine of Christ [oh, no]. And ye have led away much of this people that they pervert the right way of God, and keep not the law of Moses which is the right way.' See, he is teaching the orthodox way; he's doing what's right. He's Sherem, the defender of the faith of orthodoxy" (Nibley, *Teachings of the Book of Mormon*, 1:5–8).

Why did Sherem attack future prophecies? (7:6–7) "Sherem's words . . . advanced a claim of false prophecy. [He] objected that Jacob had spoken of things too far distant in the future. When Sherem asserted categorically that 'no man knoweth of such things' (Jacob 7:7), he seems to be arguing that prophecies of that nature should not be easily tolerated under the law. . . . Deuteronomy 18:20 requires that a man shall be put to death if he speaks 'in the name of other gods.' Sherem's allegations were not merely vague rhetorical criticisms; they were well-formulated accusations, logically derived from specific provisions of the ancient law. If allowed to stand, these accusations would have justified Jacob's execution" (Welch, "Sherem's Accusations against Jacob," 85–86).

Why didn't Sherem give a direct answer? (7:9) Why does Sherem engage in debate and rhetoric rather than answer the question? How can you recognize Sherem's arguments and tactics today and reject them as Jacob did?

What does Jacob say are the foundations of our faith? (7:9–12) In his confrontation with Sherem, Jacob asks two important questions. First, "Deniest thou the Christ?" Second, "Believest thou the scriptures?" As Sherem begins to dissemble, Jacob "points out three sources of truth—the scriptures, the prophets, and the Holy Ghost—that testify of Christ. They will help us build 'upon the rock of our Redeemer, who is Christ, the Son of God'" (Childs, "A Sure Foundation," 8). These three sources provide both the foundation of our faith and also a defense against the false teachers and teachings that seek to deceive us.

Jacob 7:13–15. Sherem Demands a Sign

What is the solemn warning to those, like Sherem, who demand a sign? (7:13–14) "The Lord has given significant warnings to those who seek signs without faith. To these 'he showeth no signs, only in wrath unto their condemnation' (D&C 63:11). The Book of Mormon contains two illustrations of this principle, and a memorable explanation of how men are condemned by seeking after a sign. Contending with Jacob, the learned Sherem said, 'Show me a sign by this power

7 And ye have led away much of this people that they pervert the right way of God, and keep not the law of Moses which is the right way; and convert the law of Moses into the worship of a being which ye say shall come many hundred years hence. And now behold, I, Sherem, declare unto you that this is blasphemy; for no man knoweth of such things; for he cannot tell of things to come. And after this manner did Sherem contend against me.

8 But behold, the Lord God poured in his Spirit into my soul, insomuch that I did confound him in all his words.

9 And I said unto him: Deniest thou the Christ who shall come? And he said: If there should be a Christ, I would not deny him; but I know that there is no Christ, neither has been, nor ever will be.

10 And I said unto him: Believest thou the scriptures? And he said, Yea.

11 And I said unto him: Then ye do not understand them; for they truly testify of Christ. Behold, I say unto you that none of the prophets have written, nor prophesied, save they have spoken concerning this Christ.

12 And this is not all—it has been made manifest unto me, for I have heard and seen; and it also has been made manifest unto me by the power of the Holy Ghost; wherefore, I know if there should be no atonement made all mankind must be lost.

13 And it came to pass that he said unto me: Show me a sign by this power of the Holy Ghost, in the which ye know so much.

14 And I said unto him: What am I that I should tempt God to show unto thee a sign in the thing which thou knowest to be true? Yet thou wilt deny it, because thou art of the

devil. Nevertheless, not my will be done; but if God shall smite thee, let that be a sign unto thee that he has power, both in heaven and in earth; and also, that Christ shall come. And thy will, O Lord, be done, and not mine.

15 And it came to pass that when I, Jacob, had spoken these words, the power of the Lord came upon him, insomuch that he fell to the earth. And it came to pass that he was nourished for the space of many days.

16 And it came to pass that he said unto the people: Gather together on the morrow, for I shall die; wherefore, I desire to speak unto the people before I shall die.

17 And it came to pass that on the morrow the multitude were gathered together; and he spake plainly unto them and denied the things which he had taught them, and confessed the Christ, and the power of the Holy Ghost, and the ministering of angels.

18 And he spake plainly unto them, that he had been deceived by the power of the devil. And he spake of hell, and of eternity, and of eternal punishment.

19 And he said: I fear lest I have committed the unpardonable sin, for I have lied unto God; for I denied the Christ, and said that I believed the scriptures; and they truly testify of him. And because I have thus lied unto God I greatly fear lest my case shall be awful; but I confess unto God.

of the Holy Ghost, in the which ye know so much.' In this instance a sign was given. He was struck down, confessed his error, and died (Jacob 7:13–20)" (Oaks, *The Lord's Way*, 84).

Jacob 7:16–23. Sherem Confesses the Truth and Gives His Final Speech

What changes in Sherem's rhetoric at the end of his encounter with Jacob? (7:17) "When Sherem is struck down, he abandons his sophisticated subtlety and assumes, at his death, the position Jacob had taken: He 'spake plainly' unto the multitude (the humble preacher, not using much flattery and power of language), he confessed the Christ (prophecy), and he acknowledged the means of acquiring spiritual knowledge, the power of the Holy Ghost (revelation). Both as summarized and then as quoted, Sherem's speech now is plain, not clever, made up of simple sentences and direct declarations. His death seals his confession" (Rust, *Feasting on the Word*, 35–36).

How can we avoid being deceived by the devil? (7:18) How can you recognize and reject Sherem's arguments as Jacob did? Consider the following passages of scripture: "Whoso treasureth up my word, shall not be deceived" (Joseph Smith–Matthew 1:37). "Whoso would hearken unto the word of God, and would hold fast unto it, they would never perish; neither could the temptations and the fiery darts of the adversary overpower them unto blindness, to lead them away to destruction" (1 Nephi 15:24). What are you doing to daily treasure up and hold fast to the holy scriptures?

What is the "unpardonable sin"? (7:19) The Prophet Joseph Smith taught: "All sins shall be forgiven, except the sin against the Holy Ghost; for Jesus will save all except the sons of perdition. What must a man do to commit the unpardonable sin? He must receive the Holy Ghost, have the heavens opened unto him, and know God, and then sin against him. After a man has sinned against the Holy Ghost, there is no repentance for him. He has got to say that the sun does not shine while he sees it; he has got to deny Jesus Christ when the heavens have been opened unto him, and to deny the plan of salvation with his eyes open to the truth of it; and from that time he begins to be an enemy" (*History of the Church*, 6:314). ⊕

How were the people tempted by Sherem's arguments? (7:23) "One reason Sherem, the anti-Christ, was able to deceive the Nephites was that they lacked scriptural knowledge.... Today individuals ... deceive others by their smooth words and scholarly language. These modern Sherems call for such things as modifications in Church doctrine and liberalized moral standards. Some are led into inactivity and even apostasy because they do not search and understand the scriptures as they are illuminated by the light of the Spirit" (Williams, "Book of Mormon and Overcoming Satan," 245–46).

Jacob 7:24–27. The Nephites Live Out Their Days Persecuted by the Lamanites, and Enos Promises to Obey God's Commandments

What was the relationship between the people of Jacob and the Lamanites? (7:24) "Jacob is a child of a house divided. He saw a family feud evolve into a more or less permanent state of internecine civil war. Think of what it meant that Jacob was Laman's and Lemuel's brother. The Lamanites were not distant, faceless, nameless enemies; they were his brothers, nephews, and cousins whose names and families he knew. Remembering this helps me read with more sympathy Jacob's sad parting observation: 'Many means were devised to reclaim and restore the Lamanites to the knowledge of the truth; but it all was vain, for they delighted in wars and bloodshed, and they had an eternal hatred against us, their brethren' (Jacob 7:24)" (Tanner, "Literary Reflections on Jacob and His Descendants," 264).

20 And it came to pass that when he had said these words he could say no more, and he gave up the ghost.

21 And when the multitude had witnessed that he spake these things as he was about to give up the ghost, they were astonished exceedingly; insomuch that the power of God came down upon them, and they were overcome that they fell to the earth.

22 Now, this thing was pleasing unto me, Jacob, for I had requested it of my Father who was in heaven; for he had heard my cry and answered my prayer.

23 And it came to pass that peace and the love of God was restored again among the people; and they searched the scriptures, and hearkened no more to the words of this wicked man.

24 And it came to pass that many means were devised to reclaim and restore the Lamanites to the knowledge of the truth; but it all was vain, for they delighted in wars and bloodshed, and they had an eternal hatred against us, their brethren. And they sought by the power of their arms to destroy us continually.

25 Wherefore, the people of Nephi did fortify against them with their arms, and with all their might, trusting in the God and rock of their salvation; wherefore, they became as yet, conquerors of their enemies.

26 And it came to pass that I, Jacob, began to be old; and the record of this people being kept on the other plates of Nephi, wherefore, I conclude this record, declaring that I have written according to the best of my knowledge, by saying that the time passed away with us, and also our lives passed away like as it were unto us a dream, we being a lonesome and a solemn people, wanderers, cast out from Jerusalem, born in tribulation, in a wilderness, and hated of our brethren, which caused wars and contentions; wherefore, we did mourn out our days.

27 And I, Jacob, saw that I must soon go down to my grave; wherefore, I said unto my son Enos: Take these plates. And I told him the things which my brother Nephi had commanded me, and he promised obedience unto the commands. And I make an end of my writing upon these plates, which writing has been small; and to the reader I bid farewell, hoping that many of my brethren may read my words. Brethren, adieu.

What is the cause of Jacob's deep melancholy? (7:26) Jacob lamented the deep hatred of the Lamanites against his people, even though he tried to reclaim them. "I think there is nothing in the Book of Mormon more moving than this. The prose sounds like a solemn dirge here in verse 26: '. . . hated of our brethren, which caused wars and contentions; wherefore, we did mourn out our days.' . . . This is one of those perennial feuds that you have in the Book of Mormon . . . blood, hatred, despair, and mourning out our days that you find in the Book of Mormon" (Nibley, *Teachings of the Book of Mormon*, 1:10–11).

Why was the word "adieu" used? (7:27) "Some have questioned the use of the French word *adieu* in Jacob 7:27. One author explained:

"'The choice of words came through the manner of the language of Joseph Smith, so that we might have understanding. This is why words not known in Book of Mormon times are found in the translated text.

"'The word *adieu* is defined in a dictionary of Joseph Smith's day as "a farewell; an expression of kind wishes at the parting of friends" [meaning that one commends the other to God] (Noah Webster, *An American Dictionary of the English Language*, 1828). While the word is of French origin, it had found common usage in early nineteenth-century New England' (Edward J. Brandt, 'I Have a Question,' *Ensign*, Oct. 1985, 17)" (*Book of Mormon Student Manual* [2009], 128–29). ●

THE BOOK OF ENOS

The prophet Enos, son of Jacob and grandson of Lehi and Sariah, learned that remission of sins comes through faith in Jesus Christ. The book of Enos shows how a person with faith can pray and receive blessings from his Father in Heaven for himself and for others. About 544–421 B.C.

Enos 1:1–8. Enos Prays and Is Forgiven of His Sins

What were the factors that motivated Enos to seek the Lord? (1:1–2) "What did the righteous fathers of the Book of Mormon teach their sons? They taught them many things, but the overarching message was 'the great plan of the Eternal God'—the Fall, rebirth, Atonement, Resurrection, Judgment, eternal life (see Alma 34:9). Enos said he knew his father was a just man, 'for he taught me . . . —and blessed be the name of my God for it' (Enos 1:1). . . . All truths are not of the same value. The saving truths of salvation are of greatest worth. These truths the fathers taught plainly, frequently, and fervently. Are we fathers doing likewise?" (Benson, "Worthy Fathers, Worthy Sons," 66).

Why did Enos describe his prayer as a "wrestle" before God? (1:2) "Here is no casual prayer; here no trite, worn phrases; here no momentary appeal. All the day long, with seconds turning into minutes, and minutes into hours, and hours into an 'all day long.' But when the sun had set relief had still not come, for repentance is not a single act nor forgiveness an unearned gift. So precious to him was communication with, and approval of, his Redeemer that his determined soul pressed on without ceasing" (Kimball, "Prayer," 9).

CHAPTER 1

Enos prays mightily and gains a remission of his sins—The voice of the Lord comes into his mind, promising salvation for the Lamanites in a future day—The Nephites sought to reclaim the Lamanites—Enos rejoices in his Redeemer. About 420 B.C.

1 Behold, it came to pass that I, Enos, knowing my father that he was a just man—for he taught me in his language, and also in the nurture and admonition of the Lord—and blessed be the name of my God for it—

2 And I will tell you of the wrestle which I had before God, before I received a remission of my sins.

3 Behold, I went to hunt beasts in the forests; and the words which I had often heard my father speak concerning eternal life, and the joy of the saints, sunk deep into my heart.

4 And my soul hungered; and I kneeled down before my Maker, and I cried unto him in mighty prayer and supplication for mine own soul; and all the day long did I cry unto him; yea, and when the night came I did still raise my voice high that it reached the heavens.

5 And there came a voice unto me, saying: Enos, thy sins are forgiven thee, and thou shalt be blessed.

6 And I, Enos, knew that God could not lie; wherefore, my guilt was swept away.

7 And I said: Lord, how is it done?

8 And he said unto me: Because of thy faith in Christ, whom thou hast never before heard nor seen. And many years pass away before he shall manifest himself in the flesh; wherefore, go to, thy faith hath made thee whole.

Why is Enos often used as a model of faith? (1:3) "We cannot find Enos-like faith without our own wrestle before God in prayer. I testify that the reward is worth the effort. Remember the pattern: (1) hear the word of God, spoken and written by His servants; (2) let that word sink deep into your heart; (3) hunger in your soul for righteousness; (4) obediently follow gospel laws . . . and (5) raise your voice in mighty prayer . . . asking in faith to know that Jesus Christ is our Savior. I promise that if you do these things sincerely and unceasingly, the words Christ spoke to His disciples will be fulfilled in your life: . . . 'knock, and it shall be opened unto you' [Matt. 7:7]" (Hales, "Finding Faith in the Lord Jesus Christ," 72).

How can you feel and recognize the voice of the Lord? (1:5) Elder Richard G. Scott taught that when we seek direction through prayer, "the answer comes as a feeling with an accompanying conviction. The Savior defines two separate ways: 'I will tell you in your *mind* and in your *heart*, by the Holy Ghost' [D&C 8:2; emphasis added]. Answers to the mind and heart are messages from the Holy Ghost to our spirits. For me, response to the mind is very specific, like dictated words, while response to the heart is generalized, like a feeling to pray more [see Enos 1:3–5, 9–10]" ("Using the Supernal Gift of Prayer," 9–10). ◉

What do we learn from Enos's experience about the power of the Atonement of Jesus Christ? (1:5–8) "The Redeemer can settle your individual account with justice and grant forgiveness through the merciful path of repentance [see Alma 42:15]. Full repentance is absolutely essential for the Atonement to work its complete miracle in your life. By understanding the Atonement, you will see that God is not a jealous being who delights in persecuting those who misstep. He is an absolutely perfect, compassionate, understanding, patient, and forgiving Father" (Scott, "Finding Forgiveness," 75).

How are our hearts most often changed and purified? (1:7) "For every Paul, for every Enos, and for every King Lamoni, there are hundreds and thousands of people who find the process of repentance much more subtle, much more imperceptible. Day by day they move closer to the Lord, little realizing they are building a godlike life. They live quiet lives of goodness, service, and commitment. They are like the Lamanites, who the Lord said 'were baptized with fire and with the Holy Ghost, and they knew it not' (3 Ne. 9:20)" (Benson, "Mighty Change of Heart," 5).

Enos 1:9–18. Enos Prays for the Nephites and Lamanites

What was the purpose of Enos's prayer before the Lord? (1:9) "After feeling the blessings of the Atonement for himself, Enos prayed for the welfare of his own people, the Nephites, and then for the spiritual welfare of his enemies, the Lamanites. Elder Robert D. Hales spoke about the concern those who have been converted feel for others: 'The scriptures confirm that the truly converted do more than just forsake the enticements of the world. They love God and their fellowmen. Their minds and hearts are centered on the Savior's atoning sacrifice. From the moment of their respective conversions, Enos . . . and others turned wholeheartedly to the task of bringing themselves and their fellowmen to God. Worldly power and possessions lost their former significance' (in Conference Report, Oct. 2000, 6; or *Ensign*, Nov. 2000, 8)" (*Book of Mormon Student Manual* [2009], 131).

Why did Enos pray that God would preserve the records of the Nephites? (1:13–16) Enos knew of the Lamanites' deep hatred for the Nephites and worried they would destroy them and their holy records if possible. Even though the Lamanites rejected the gospel in his day, they might accept it in the latter days. In addition to Enos, the "'holy prophets, yea, and also my disciples [the twelve] desired in their prayers' for the records to come forth (D&C 10:46). The records have come forth and the time has come for the Lamanites to individually accept or reject them according to their agency. They must also be diligent in keeping the Lord's commandments to receive the promised blessings" (Nyman, *These Records Are True*, 128–29).

9 Now, it came to pass that when I had heard these words I began to feel a desire for the welfare of my brethren, the Nephites; wherefore, I did pour out my whole soul unto God for them.

10 And while I was thus struggling in the spirit, behold, the voice of the Lord came into my mind again, saying: I will visit thy brethren according to their diligence in keeping my commandments. I have given unto them this land, and it is a holy land; and I curse it not save it be for the cause of iniquity; wherefore, I will visit thy brethren according as I have said; and their transgressions will I bring down with sorrow upon their own heads.

11 And after I, Enos, had heard these words, my faith began to be unshaken in the Lord; and I prayed unto him with many long strugglings for my brethren, the Lamanites.

12 And it came to pass that after I had prayed and labored with all diligence, the Lord said unto me: I will grant unto thee according to thy desires, because of thy faith.

13 And now behold, this was the desire which I desired of him—that if it should so be, that my people, the Nephites, should fall into transgression, and by any means be destroyed, and the Lamanites should not be destroyed, that the Lord God would preserve a record of my people, the Nephites; even if it so be by the power of his holy arm, that it might be brought forth at some future day unto the Lamanites, that, perhaps, they might be brought unto salvation—

14 For at the present our strugglings were vain in restoring them to the true faith. And they swore in their wrath that, if it were possible, they would destroy our records and us, and also all the traditions of our fathers.

15 Wherefore, I knowing that the Lord God was able to preserve our records, I cried unto him continually, for he had said unto me: Whatsoever thing ye shall ask in faith, believing that ye shall receive in the name of Christ, ye shall receive it.

16 And I had faith, and I did cry unto God that he would preserve the records; and he covenanted with me that he would bring them forth unto the Lamanites in his own due time.

17 And I, Enos, knew it would be according to the covenant which he had made; wherefore my soul did rest.

18 And the Lord said unto me: Thy fathers have also required of me this thing; and it shall be done unto them according to their faith; for their faith was like unto thine.

19 And now it came to pass that I, Enos, went about among the people of Nephi, prophesying of things to come, and testifying of the things which I had heard and seen.

20 And I bear record that the people of Nephi did seek diligently to restore the Lamanites unto the true faith in God. But our labors were vain; their hatred was fixed, and they were led by their evil nature that they became wild, and ferocious, and a blood-thirsty people, full of idolatry and filthiness; feeding upon beasts of prey; dwelling in tents, and wandering about in the wilderness with a short skin girdle about their loins and their heads shaven; and their skill was in the bow, and in the cimeter, and the ax. And many of them did eat nothing save it was raw meat; and they were continually seeking to destroy us.

21 And it came to pass that the people of Nephi did till the land, and raise all manner of grain, and of fruit, and flocks of herds, and flocks of all manner of cattle of every kind, and goats, and wild goats, and also many horses.

Enos 1:19–24. Enos Sees Great Wars between the Nephites and the Lamanites

What are the differences between the Nephites and Lamanites at this time? (1:20–21) "The Nephites sought diligently to make peace with the Lamanites … '[and] the people of Nephi did till the land.' In this one paragraph we learn what the peaceful pursuits of the Nephites were. We would call them, farmers and stockmen. The picture Enos draws of the degradation into which the Lamanites had fallen at this early age is a pitiable one. On the other hand the Nephites were a rural, pastoral people, rich in grain and fruits, flocks and herds. They were industrious in their habits and committed but few offenses" (Reynolds and Sjodahl, *Commentary on the Book of Mormon*, 493–94).

22 And there were exceedingly many prophets among us. And the people were a stiffnecked people, hard to understand.

23 And there was nothing save it was exceeding harshness, preaching and prophesying of wars, and contentions, and destructions, and continually reminding them of death, and the duration of eternity, and the judgments and the power of God, and all these things—stirring them up continually to keep them in the fear of the Lord. I say there was nothing short of these things, and exceedingly great plainness of speech, would keep them from going down speedily to destruction. And after this manner do I write concerning them.

24 And I saw wars between the Nephites and Lamanites in the course of my days.

25 And it came to pass that I began to be old, and an hundred and seventy and nine years had passed away from the time that our father Lehi left Jerusalem.

26 And I saw that I must soon go down to my grave, having been wrought upon by the power of God that I must preach and prophesy unto this people, and declare the word according to the truth which is in Christ. And I have declared it in all my days, and have rejoiced in it above that of the world.

27 And I soon go to the place of my rest, which is with my Redeemer; for I know that in him I shall rest. And I rejoice in the day when my mortal shall put on immortality, and shall stand before him; then shall I see his face with pleasure, and he will say unto me: Come unto me, ye blessed, there is a place prepared for you in the mansions of my Father. Amen.

Why did Enos use harsh words as he preached to the Nephites? (1:23) "It is possible, particularly in a generation only once removed from the fathers who had come from Jerusalem, that Enos saw multiple prophets preaching of coming war as a parallel to the conditions in Jerusalem which led to the Lehite exodus. . . . Enos emphasizes in his preaching the Nephites' persistent tendency to move away from Yahweh's [Jehovah's] path. The call to return was harsh because only the harshness of the penalties kept 'them from going down speedily to destruction'. . . . That path was 'speedy' because it was so tempting. It tempted them away from their religious/cultural heritage, snaring them in a new culture containing new religious ideas which could supplant those they had received from Nephi [and] Jacob" (Gardner, *Second Witness* , 3:23).

Enos 1:25–27. Enos Testifies concerning the Blessings He Will Receive

What does Enos mean by the phrase "in him I shall rest"? (1:25–27) "With increasing temptations, distractions, and distortions, the world attempts to beguile the faithful into dismissing the rich spiritual experiences of one's past, redefining them as foolish deceptions.

"Overcoming the world is remembering, even when we are discouraged, the times we have felt the love and light of the Savior. . . .

"Overcoming the world does not mean we live a cloistered life, protected from the unfairness and difficulties of mortality. Rather, it opens the more expansive view of faith, drawing us to the Savior and His promises.

"While perfection is not complete in this life, overcoming the world keeps our hope aflame that one day we 'shall stand before [our Redeemer]; [and] see his face with pleasure,' and hear His voice: 'Come, ye blessed of my Father, inherit the kingdom prepared for you'" (Andersen, "Overcoming the World," 60–61).

How can we, like Enos, obtain a promise from the Lord to enter a mansion of glory? (1:27) "I should think that all faithful Latter-day Saints 'would want that more sure word of prophecy, that they were sealed in the heavens and had the promise of eternal life in the kingdom of God.' . . . Lehi's grandson Enos so 'hungered after righteousness' that he received this promise" (Romney, "Light of Christ," 66). ☉

THE BOOK OF JAROM

Introduction

Jarom, the son of Enos, continued to keep the record on the small plates of Nephi. The prophets and kings taught the people to keep God's commandments and thus they were protected from their enemies. They emphasized that the purpose of the law of Moses was to look forward to the Messiah. About 399–361 B.C.

CHAPTER 1

The Nephites keep the law of Moses, look forward to the coming of Christ, and prosper in the land—Many prophets labor to keep the people in the way of truth. About 399–361 B.C.

1 Now behold, I, Jarom, write a few words according to the commandment of my father, Enos, that our genealogy may be kept.

2 And as these plates are small, and as these things are written for the intent of the benefit of our brethren the Lamanites, wherefore, it must needs be that I write a little; but I shall not write the things of my prophesying, nor of my revelations. For what could I write more than my fathers have written? For have not they revealed the plan of salvation? I say unto you, Yea; and this sufficeth me.

Jarom 1:1–4. Both Wicked and Righteous Are Found among the Nephites

What does the name Jarom mean? (1:1) *"Jarom* means 'to prosper or to get a good share of something.' It means 'to support one's family properly.' It also means 'to have good luck in business' or 'finding something of value.' It can also mean 'to grasp or snatch something' or 'to be a crook.' That's the way these words do; one meaning leads to the next. They are very rich, but the basic meaning of Jarom is 'to be prosperous, to be happy'" (Nibley, *Teachings of the Book of Mormon*, 1:422).

What do we know of Jarom's use of the phrase "the plan of salvation"? (1:2) Jarom is the first book in the Book of Mormon to use the expression "plan of salvation." President Russell M. Nelson taught: "The entire Creation was planned by God. A council in heaven was once convened in which we participated. There our Heavenly Father announced His divine plan. It is also called the plan of happiness, the plan of salvation, the plan of redemption, the plan of restoration, the plan of mercy, the plan of deliverance, and the everlasting gospel. The purpose of the plan is to provide opportunity for the spirit children of God to progress toward an eternal exaltation" ("The Creation," 84).

What is the symbolic meaning of Jarom's description of his people? (1:3) "*Blind* and *blindness* in the scriptures refers to the spiritual blindness of men—the inability to see the truth. . . .

"The wicked possess an ear that is 'not opened' (Isa. 48:8). They are not responsive unto the things of God. . . .

"The word *heart* pertains to the evil disposition of a man. . . .

"The neck typifies the spirit and attitude of nations and men, usually denoting callousness and hardness. . . . [Stiff necks] are those who are unable to glance sidewards at the concerns of their neighbor or to look upward toward their Creator" (McConkie and Parry, *Guide to Scriptural Symbols*, 21, 43–44, 64, 86).

What allows us to have "communion with the Holy Spirit"? (1:4) "Our feelings of separation from God will diminish as we become more childlike before Him. That is not easy in a world where the opinions of other human beings can have such an effect on our motives. But it will help us recognize this truth: God is close to us and aware of us and never hides from His faithful children.

" . . . Sometimes our insistence on acting according to our own timetable can obscure [God's] will for us." When we're humble, "we [listen to God] when we feel and pray, 'Thy will be done' and 'in Thine own time'" (Erying, "Where Is the Pavilion?" 72–73). ✛

Jarom 1:5–10. The Lord Protects and Blesses the Nephites

What does it mean to profane or blaspheme? (1:5) "Here we learn again that the Nephites were very diligent in keeping the law of Moses. They did not profane or blaspheme; that is, they did not speak or act in any way that would desecrate or make profane (worldly) anything that was holy, especially the name of God, the law, the temple, or its sacred space" (Welch, "Temple in the Book of Mormon," 303).

Why did the Nephites succeed in their battles with the Lamanites? (1:7) "It was not mighty warriors, men mighty in strength, but men mighty in the faith of the Lord that consistently led the Nephites to victory over

3 Behold, it is expedient that much should be done among this people, because of the hardness of their hearts, and the deafness of their ears, and the blindness of their minds, and the stiffness of their necks; nevertheless, God is exceedingly merciful unto them, and has not as yet swept them off from the face of the land.

4 And there are many among us who have many revelations, for they are not all stiffnecked. And as many as are not stiffnecked and have faith, have communion with the Holy Spirit, which maketh manifest unto the children of men, according to their faith.

5 And now, behold, two hundred years had passed away, and the people of Nephi had waxed strong in the land. They observed to keep the law of Moses and the sabbath day holy unto the Lord. And they profaned not; neither did they blaspheme. And the laws of the land were exceedingly strict.

6 And they were scattered upon much of the face of the land, and the Lamanites also. And they were exceedingly more numerous than were they of the Nephites; and they loved murder and would drink the blood of beasts.

7 And it came to pass that they came many times against us, the Nephites, to battle. But our kings and our leaders were mighty men in the faith of the Lord; and they taught the people the ways of the Lord; wherefore, we withstood the Lamanites and swept them away out of our lands, and began to fortify our cities, or whatsoever place of our inheritance.

8 And we multiplied exceedingly, and spread upon the face of the land, and became exceedingly rich in gold, and in silver, and in precious things, and in fine workmanship of wood, in buildings, and in machinery, and also in iron and copper, and brass and steel, making all manner of tools of every kind to till the ground, and weapons of war—yea, the sharp pointed arrow, and the quiver, and the dart, and the javelin, and all preparations for war.

9 And thus being prepared to meet the Lamanites, they did not prosper against us. But the word of the Lord was verified, which he spake unto our fathers, saying that: Inasmuch as ye will keep my commandments ye shall prosper in the land.

10 And it came to pass that the prophets of the Lord did threaten the people of Nephi, according to the word of God, that if they did not keep the commandments, but should fall into transgression, they should be destroyed from off the face of the land.

11 Wherefore, the prophets, and the priests, and the teachers, did labor diligently, exhorting with all long-suffering the people to diligence; teaching the law of Moses, and the intent for which it was given; persuading them to look forward unto the Messiah, and believe in him to come as though he already was. And after this manner did they teach them.

12 And it came to pass that by so doing they kept them from being destroyed upon the face of the land; for they did prick their hearts with the word, continually stirring them up unto repentance.

their blood-drinking enemies, the Lamanites. Faith in God is a weapon more to be feared that the sharpness of a sword or the muscle and sinew that wields it (see also 3 Nephi 3:19)" (McConkie and Millet, *Doctrinal Commentary*, 2:108). ⊕

What can we learn from the preparation of the Nephites for war with the Lamanites? (1:9) Search Jarom 1:4, 5, 7, and 8 to discover what the Nephites did to prepare themselves against their enemies. Then ponder the nature of the enemies, or challenges, you face. What did the Nephites do that might help you face your challenges?

Jarom 1:11–15. Church Leaders Persuade the Nephites to Look to the Lord

What was the purpose of the law of Moses? (1:11) The Book of Mormon beautifully and concisely explains the purpose and intent of the law of Moses. The Bible is less clear on this point. The law of Moses was not an end in itself. The whole purpose and meaning of the law was "persuading them to look forward unto the Messiah" (Jarom 1:11; see also 2 Nephi 25:24, 30; Jacob 4:5; Mosiah 3:15; 12–13; Alma 34:13; 3 Nephi 15:8). ⊕

Why do prophets often "prick [our] hearts" with the word? (1:12) "Jarom speaks with no timidity on the manner in which the Nephite prophets delivered the message of the Lord. They 'threaten the people' in such a manner, he said, as to 'prick their hearts.' To the obedient the book of Jarom promised the blessings of protection; to the disobedient it prophesied destruction. . . .

"'The word of God is quick and powerful, sharper than a two-edged sword, to the dividing asunder of both joints and marrow' (D&C 6:2)" (McConkie and Millet, *Doctrinal Commentary*, 2:105–10).

13 And it came to pass that two hundred and thirty and eight years had passed away—after the manner of wars, and contentions, and dissensions, for the space of much of the time.

14 And I, Jarom, do not write more, for the plates are small. But behold, my brethren, ye can go to the other plates of Nephi; for behold, upon them the records of our wars are engraven, according to the writings of the kings, or those which they caused to be written.

15 And I deliver these plates into the hands of my son Omni, that they may be kept according to the commandments of my fathers.

THE BOOK OF OMNI

Introduction

The book of Omni is the last book on the small plates of Nephi. It covers 230 years and includes the writing of five Nephite scribes. The book is named after the first of those scribes, a grandson of Enos. One of those scribes, Amaleki, wrote the largest portion of Omni, which describes the relationship of the Jaredites, the people of Zarahemla, and King Mosiah's righteous followers (see Omni 1:12–22). Amaleki also emphasized the importance of a written record in preserving both the language of the people and the Lord's teachings through prophets. After inviting all to come unto Christ, Amaleki delivered the plates to King Benjamin.

CHAPTER 1

Omni, Amaron, Chemish, Abinadom, and Amaleki, each in turn, keep the records—Mosiah discovers the people of Zarahemla, who came from Jerusalem in the days of Zedekiah—Mosiah is made king over them—The descendants of Mulek at Zarahemla had discovered Coriantumr, the last of the Jaredites—King Benjamin succeeds Mosiah—Men should offer their souls as an offering to Christ. About 323–130 B.C.

1 Behold, it came to pass that I, Omni, being commanded by my father, Jarom, that I should write somewhat upon these plates, to preserve our genealogy—

2 Wherefore, in my days, I would that ye should know that I fought much with the sword to preserve my people, the Nephites, from falling into the hands of their enemies, the Lamanites. But behold, I of myself am a wicked man, and I have not kept the statutes and the commandments of the Lord as I ought to have done.

3 And it came to pass that two hundred and seventy and six years had passed away, and

Omni 1:1–11. The Records Pass from Omni to Amaron to Chemish to Abinadom

What does the name Omni mean? (1:1) "It means *belonging to Amon*. Remember, *Amon* is the name in the Book of Mormon. There are more Ammon names and Amon compounds than anything else because actually in the time of Lehi *Amon* was the god of the empire. It was the one time when God filled the earth. Amon filled the earth with the Egyptian Empire. They claimed everything, but always in the name of *Amon*. We have songs in which we refer to Adam-ondi-Ahman and *Amon* as an epithet for God. Actually, it means 'the one who is not known, the secret one whom we can't name, whose name is not known to us'" (Nibley, *Teachings of the Book of Mormon*, 1:425).

Why was so little written by the first four writers of the book of Omni? (1:1–11) "Omni kept the record for 44 years. . . . Amaron kept the record for at least 38

years.... Chemish ... did not state how long he kept the record, but ... it was probably less time than the others. Abinadom ... [stated] that there had been wars with the Lamanites and an absence of revelation and prophecy. Perhaps this is the reason these four recorded so little" (Nyman, "To Learn with Joy," 204).

What does it mean to "prosper in the land"? (1:6)
"Certainly prosperity had to do with the physical and spiritual circumstances of the obedient, but beyond that it is used in the framework of deliverance [see Alma 36:1–2]. Notice how closely related the ideas of prosperity and deliverance are. The parallel usage of these two words is not uncommon in the Nephite text (see Omni 1:6–7; Mosiah 2:31; 7:29, 33; Alma 9:9, 13; 36:29–30).... However, prosperity is not without adversity and the text has several examples of individuals who obeyed the commandments and yet sealed their testimonies with their blood (see Mosiah 17:20; Alma 14:18)" (Bassett, "Nephi's Freedom Thesis and the Sons of Helaman," 291–92).

we had many seasons of peace; and we had many seasons of serious war and bloodshed. Yea, and in fine, two hundred and eighty and two years had passed away, and I had kept these plates according to the commandments of my fathers; and I conferred them upon my son Amaron. And I make an end.

4 And now I, Amaron, write the things whatsoever I write, which are few, in the book of my father.

5 Behold, it came to pass that three hundred and twenty years had passed away, and the more wicked part of the Nephites were destroyed.

6 For the Lord would not suffer, after he had led them out of the land of Jerusalem and kept and preserved them from falling into the hands of their enemies, yea, he would not suffer that the words should not be verified, which he spake unto our fathers, saying that: Inasmuch as ye will not keep my commandments ye shall not prosper in the land.

7 Wherefore, the Lord did visit them in great judgment; nevertheless, he did spare the righteous that they should not perish, but did deliver them out of the hands of their enemies.

Who Are the Peoples of Mosiah, Zarahemla, and Coriantumr?

	The People of Mosiah	The People of Zarahemla	The People of Coriantumr
Common name	Nephites	Mulekites (though not a name used in the Book of Mormon)	Jaredites
Where they came from	Left Jerusalem in about 600 B.C.	Left Jerusalem in about 589 B.C.	Left the tower of Babel about 2290 B.C.
Where they lived	South of Zarahemla in the land called Nephi (Helaman 6:10)	Americas, north of the Nephites in the land called Zarahemla (Helaman 6:10)	Americas, far north of Zarahemla in the land called Desolation (Alma 22:30)
Where to read about their history	History recorded throughout the Book of Mormon	Did not keep their own history but merged with the Nephites about 130 B.C.	Account recorded in the book of Ether, in the Book of Mormon

(Adapted from Garner, *Search These Things Diligently*, 127–28)

8 And it came to pass that I did deliver the plates unto my brother Chemish.

9 Now I, Chemish, write what few things I write, in the same book with my brother; for behold, I saw the last which he wrote, that he wrote it with his own hand; and he wrote it in the day that he delivered them unto me. And after this manner we keep the records, for it is according to the commandments of our fathers. And I make an end.

10 Behold, I, Abinadom, am the son of Chemish. Behold, it came to pass that I saw much war and contention between my people, the Nephites, and the Lamanites; and I, with my own sword, have taken the lives of many of the Lamanites in the defence of my brethren.

11 And behold, the record of this people is engraven upon plates which is had by the kings, according to the generations; and I know of no revelation save that which has been written, neither prophecy; wherefore, that which is sufficient is written. And I make an end.

12 Behold, I am Amaleki, the son of Abinadom. Behold, I will speak unto you somewhat concerning Mosiah, who was made king over the land of Zarahemla; for behold, he being warned of the Lord that he should flee out of the land of Nephi, and as many as would hearken unto the voice of the Lord should also depart out of the land with him, into the wilderness—

13 And it came to pass that he did according as the Lord had commanded him. And they departed out of the land into the wilderness, as many as would hearken unto the voice of the Lord; and they were led by many preachings and prophesyings. And they were admonished continually by the word of God; and they were led by the power of his arm, through the wilderness until they came

Omni 1:12–22. Amaleki Starts His Record, and King Mosiah Discovers the People of Zarahemla and Learns of the Jaredites

What is the significance of the name Mosiah? (1:12)
In 1965 biblical scholar John Sawyer, who was not a Latter-day Saint, wrote "that the term *mosiah* was an ancient Hebrew term . . . a 'word invariably implying a champion of justice in a situation of controversy, battle or oppression.'

"Apparently the form of the word Mosiah is a 'hiphil participle' in Hebrew. It occurs in the Hebrew in [several Old Testament texts] that in all probability were on the Plates of Brass. This word, however, was not transliterated into the English by the King James translators, and thus the Hebrew would not have been known to Joseph Smith. . . .

"Sawyer concludes that the term applied to a particular kind of person or role and was sometimes a title designating 'a definite office or position'" (Welch, "What Was a 'Mosiah'?" 105–6). ☉

Why was Mosiah warned to leave the land of Nephi? (1:12–18) Mosiah led his people out of the land because he was "warned of the Lord that he should flee out of the land of Nephi" (Omni 1:12). This divinely directed departure fulfilled Jacob's prophecy that unless the Nephites repented, "the Lord God will lead away the righteous" (Jacob 3:4). One commentary added, "The necessity of the Lord's people fleeing ... and taking refuge in the wilderness seems so often repeated ... that perhaps it ought to be viewed as a prophetic type. Even the Savior fled association with all others for a wilderness respite prior to the commencement of his ministry. ... In a symbolic sense, all who would desire to number themselves among the children of God find it necessary to leave the refinements of the world and find refuge in the simplicity of [what] God created—be it a mountain top or a sacred grove" (McConkie and Millet, *Doctrinal Commentary on the Book of Mormon*, 2:115).

Where was Zarahemla? (1:13) "Don't be concerned over Book of Mormon geography. Some say the Hill Cumorah was in southern Mexico (and someone pushed it down still farther) and not in western New York. Well, if the Lord wanted us to know where it was or where Zarahemla was, He'd have given us latitude and longitude, don't you think? ... The witness of the Book of Mormon is not found in the ruins of Central and South America. They may be outward evidences of a people long since disappeared. The real witness is that which is found in the Book of Mormon itself" (*Teachings of Harold B. Lee*, 155–56).

What is a possible meaning of the name Zarahemla? (1:15) "The name Zarahemla probably derives from the Hebrew *zera'-hemla h*, which has been variously translated as 'seed of compassion' or 'child of grace, pity, or compassion.' It may be that the Mulekite leader was given that name because his ancestor had been rescued when the other sons of King Zedekiah were slain during the Babylonian conquest of Jerusalem. To subsequent Nephite generations, it may even have suggested the deliverance of their own ancestors from Jerusalem prior to its destruction or the anticipation of Christ's coming" (Ricks and Tvedtnes, "Hebrew Origin of Some Book of Mormon Place Names," 259).

Why is living without scriptures spiritually devastating? (1:17) "The untaught can, so quickly, become unbelieving. They form a rising generation who do not understand the words of prophets and who do not believe in the Resurrection of Christ [see Judges 2:10 and Mosiah 26:1–4]. ...

"Holy scriptures testify powerfully, but they also familiarize us with the history of what God has done for His people. This spiritual memory is so essential. ...

"Holy scriptures, when searched and believed, help us to 'remember,' as it were, from the sacred records" (Maxwell, "Richness of the Restoration," 10).

down into the land which is called the land of Zarahemla.

14 And they discovered a people, who were called the people of Zarahemla. Now, there was great rejoicing among the people of Zarahemla; and also Zarahemla did rejoice exceedingly, because the Lord had sent the people of Mosiah with the plates of brass which contained the record of the Jews.

15 Behold, it came to pass that Mosiah discovered that the people of Zarahemla came out from Jerusalem at the time that Zedekiah, king of Judah, was carried away captive into Babylon.

16 And they journeyed in the wilderness, and were brought by the hand of the Lord across the great waters, into the land where Mosiah discovered them; and they had dwelt there from that time forth.

17 And at the time that Mosiah discovered them, they had become exceedingly numerous. Nevertheless, they had had many wars and serious contentions, and had fallen by the sword from time to time; and their language had become corrupted; and they had brought no records with them; and they denied the being of their Creator; and Mosiah, nor the people of Mosiah, could understand them.

18 But it came to pass that Mosiah caused that they should be taught in his language. And it came to pass that after they were taught in the language of Mosiah, Zarahemla gave a genealogy of his fathers, according to his memory; and they are written, but not in these plates.

19 And it came to pass that the people of Zarahemla, and of Mosiah, did unite together; and Mosiah was appointed to be their king.

20 And it came to pass in the days of Mosiah, there was a large stone brought unto him with engravings on it; and he did interpret the engravings by the gift and power of God.

21 And they gave an account of one Coriantumr, and the slain of his people. And Coriantumr was discovered by the people of Zarahemla; and he dwelt with them for the space of nine moons.

22 It also spake a few words concerning his fathers. And his first parents came out from the tower, at the time the Lord confounded the language of the people; and the severity of the Lord fell upon them according to his judgments, which are just; and their bones lay scattered in the land northward.

23 Behold, I, Amaleki, was born in the days of Mosiah; and I have lived to see his death; and Benjamin, his son, reigneth in his stead.

24 And behold, I have seen, in the days of king Benjamin, a serious war and much bloodshed between the Nephites and the Lamanites. But behold, the Nephites did obtain much advantage over them; yea, insomuch that king Benjamin did drive them out of the land of Zarahemla.

25 And it came to pass that I began to be old; and, having no seed, and knowing king Benjamin to be a just man before the Lord, wherefore, I shall deliver up these plates unto him, exhorting all men to come unto

Why did the people of Zarahemla require a new language? (1:17–18) "'The lack of records had been a stumbling block for the Mulekites, in that without them to stabilize their language it had become corrupt . . .' [It] does not seem reasonable that possession of texts would have stopped or even necessarily slowed the pace of linguistic change. More probably, it is simply that, without records, there was no reason to preserve a language whose speakers could communicate only with a group of others that shrank with every generation. There was no reason not to adopt the language of the people among whom the Mulekites found themselves" (Gardner, *Second Witness*, 3:60).

Was writing on stones in ancient America a typical form of record keeping? (1:20) "The Book of Mormon reports the fact that inhabitants of ancient America other than Nephites left stone inscriptions. Particularly, when the Nephites joined the Mulekites in the city of Zarahemla about 200 B.C., a large engraved stone was brought to King Mosiah that merited special mention in the Nephite records (see Omni 1:20). Presumably this was part of a tradition of stone-monument erection, not a lone case" (Sorenson, "Latest Discoveries," 111). ✪

Omni 1:23–26. Amaleki Gives the Plates to King Benjamin

Why did King Benjamin take part in wars? (1:23–26) "Effective military leadership by the king . . . was vital to the society's well-being. . . . Ancient kings fulfilled their duty as guardian of the nation by personally commanding military forces in time of war. . . .

"One of the most important roles of the Hebrew king 'was that of being a leader in war. . . . Primarily it was his duty to defend his people from aggressive action on the part of their neighbors.' . . .

"King Benjamin's military generalship, as well as his personal combat skills on the battlefield, gave the Nephites serious advantage over the Lamanites [see also Words of Mormon 1:13]" (Kerr, "Ancient Aspects of Nephite Kingship," 87–90).

Why was King Benjamin given the small plates? (1:25) "The fact that King Benjamin ruled over the Nephites seems to suggest that the kingship line had moved away from Nephi's descendants. However, this

is not the case. Mormon assures his readers that during the kingship reign of Nephite history 'the kingdom
had been conferred upon none but those who were
descendants of Nephi' (Mosiah 25:13). What is apparent in the names of King Mosiah and King Benjamin is
that the honorific title of Nephi had been discarded.
However, the lineage of Nephite kings remained.
When Amaleki, who did not have children, gave the
small plates to King Benjamin, Benjamin already had
in his possession the large plates of Nephi that contained the secular history of the Nephites" (Black, *400
Questions and Answers*, 129).

What does it mean to "offer your whole souls"?
(1:26) "After we come out of the waters of baptism,
our souls need to be continuously immersed in and
saturated with the truth and the light of the Savior's
gospel. Sporadic and shallow dipping in the doctrine
of Christ and partial participation in His restored
Church cannot produce the spiritual transformation
that enables us to walk in a newness of life. Rather,
fidelity to covenants, constancy of commitment, and
offering our whole soul unto God are required if we
are to receive the blessings of eternity....

   "Total immersion in and saturation with the Savior's
gospel are essential steps in the process of being born
again" (Bednar, "Ye Must Be Born Again," 21).

Omni 1:27–30. A Colony of Nephites Returns to the Land of Nephi

**Why did the land of Nephi continue to be impor-
tant to the people of Mosiah?** (1:27) "After Nephi
fled into the wilderness with his younger brothers and
sisters, they settled in an area that came to be known
as the land of Lehi-Nephi. Several generations later ...
a man named Mosiah took as many righteous people
as would follow him and fled this land. Mosiah and
his people wandered northward until they discovered
the land of Zarahemla, which was inhabited by the
Mulekites.... These two groups united and chose
Mosiah as their king. Nevertheless, Lehi-Nephi continued to be considered the homeland of the Nephites"
(Hurd, *Our Sisters in the Latter-day Scriptures*, 13).

God, the Holy One of Israel, and believe
in prophesying, and in revelations, and in
the ministering of angels, and in the gift of
speaking with tongues, and in the gift of interpreting languages, and in all things which
are good; for there is nothing which is good
save it comes from the Lord: and that which
is evil cometh from the devil.

26 And now, my beloved brethren, I would
that ye should come unto Christ, who is the
Holy One of Israel, and partake of his salvation, and the power of his redemption. Yea,
come unto him, and offer your whole souls
as an offering unto him, and continue in fasting and praying, and endure to the end; and
as the Lord liveth ye will be saved.

27 And now I would speak somewhat concerning a certain number who went up into
the wilderness to return to the land of Nephi;
for there was a large number who were desirous to possess the land of their inheritance.

28 Wherefore, they went up into the wilderness. And their leader being a strong and
mighty man, and a stiffnecked man, wherefore he caused a contention among them;
and they were all slain, save fifty, in the wilderness, and they returned again to the land
of Zarahemla.

29 And it came to pass that they also took
others to a considerable number, and took
their journey again into the wilderness.

30 And I, Amaleki, had a brother, who also
went with them; and I have not since known
concerning them. And I am about to lie
down in my grave; and these plates are full.
And I make an end of my speaking.

THE WORDS OF MORMON

Introduction

Mormon, who lived five hundred years after Amaleki, wrote a brief message as a bridge between the small plates of Nephi (which contained 1 Nephi through Omni) and his abridgment of the large plates of Nephi (Mosiah through 4 Nephi). This message was written just before Mormon passed the records to his son Moroni (Words of Mormon 1:1). Mormon explained that he had completed an abridgment starting with Lehi and ending with King Benjamin. Then he discovered the small plates of Nephi, and though they overlapped the period covered in his abridgment, he felt impressed to include them. He explained that they were "pleasing" to him "because of the prophecies of the coming of Christ" (Words of Mormon 1:3–4). In verse 11, Mormon testified that the sacred record he helped compile will have a role in the judgment of all mankind. Finally, he described King Benjamin and the circumstances leading up to the events recorded in the book of Mosiah (Words of Mormon 1:12–18).

CHAPTER 1

Mormon abridges the large plates of Nephi—
He puts the small plates with the other plates—
King Benjamin establishes peace in the land.
About A.D. 385.

1 And now I, Mormon, being about to deliver up the record which I have been making into the hands of my son Moroni, behold I have witnessed almost all the destruction of my people, the Nephites.

2 And it is many hundred years after the coming of Christ that I deliver these records into the hands of my son; and it supposeth me that he will witness the entire destruction

Words of Mormon 1:1–8. Mormon Includes the Small Plates of Nephi in the Book of Mormon for a Wise Purpose

Why might Mormon have inserted this brief explanation between Omni and Mosiah? (1:1) "The Words of Mormon jumps ahead to about A.D. 385. He writes to bridge the gap between the ending of the smaller plates of Nephi and the book of Mosiah that he has abridged from the larger plates of Nephi.... The abridgment of the plates of Nephi down to the reign of King Benjamin would be the book of Lehi that was translated by Joseph Smith with Martin Harris as his scribe or the one hundred and sixteen pages.... The plates that were found by Mormon were, of course, the smaller plates of Nephi and were translated into what is now the first one hundred and forty-three pages of today's edition of the Book of Mormon" (Nyman, *These Records Are True*, 169–170).

Did Moroni fulfill his father's hopes that he would write "somewhat concerning Christ"? (1:2) "Following this dismaying decline of Nephite civilization documented by his father, Moroni picked up the recorder's task, but he did not write to any living audience. Rather, he directed his final testimony—in fact, three final testimonies—to those who would receive the record in the last days. A book that began with three witnesses of Christ ends the same way but with a difference—with three final declarations of the Savior from the writings of one man [see Mormon 8 and 9; Ether 12; Moroni 1–10]" (Holland, *Christ and the New Covenant*, 323).

Are scriptures that teach of Christ pleasing to you? (1:4) What portions of 1 Nephi through Omni have you found to be of most interest? Why do you think Mormon was particularly impressed with the prophecies of Christ on the small plates of Nephi? As you read the Book of Mormon, marking those verses that teach and testify of the Savior may help you more clearly see how the book truly is another testament of Jesus Christ.

If Mormon could not write "a hundredth part," what did he choose to emphasize? (1:5) "When Mormon abridged these records, he noted that he could not write a 'hundredth part' of their proceedings. Thus, *historical* aspects of the book assume *secondary* significance" (Nelson, "Testimony of the Book of Mormon," 69).

What was the "wise purpose" for including the small plates of Nephi? (1:6–7) "At least six times in the Book of Mormon, the phrase *for a wise purpose* is used in reference to the making, writing, and preserving of the small plates. One such wise purpose—the most obvious one—was to compensate for the future loss of 116 pages of manuscript translated by the Prophet Joseph Smith. . . .

"But there is another 'wise purpose' for the inclusion of these smaller plates in the highly edited material that would constitute the Book of Mormon. In Doctrine and Covenants 10:45 the Lord declared to Joseph Smith, 'Behold, there are many things engraven upon the [small] plates of Nephi which do throw *greater views* upon my gospel'" (Holland, *Christ and the New Covenant*, 34). ◉

of my people. But may God grant that he may survive them, that he may write somewhat concerning them, and somewhat concerning Christ, that perhaps some day it may profit them.

3 And now, I speak somewhat concerning that which I have written; for after I had made an abridgment from the plates of Nephi, down to the reign of this king Benjamin, of whom Amaleki spake, I searched among the records which had been delivered into my hands, and I found these plates, which contained this small account of the prophets, from Jacob down to the reign of this king Benjamin, and also many of the words of Nephi.

4 And the things which are upon these plates pleasing me, because of the prophecies of the coming of Christ; and my fathers knowing that many of them have been fulfilled; yea, and I also know that as many things as have been prophesied concerning us down to this day have been fulfilled, and as many as go beyond this day must surely come to pass—

5 Wherefore, I chose these things, to finish my record upon them, which remainder of my record I shall take from the plates of Nephi; and I cannot write the hundredth part of the things of my people.

6 But behold, I shall take these plates, which contain these prophesyings and revelations, and put them with the remainder of my record, for they are choice unto me; and I know they will be choice unto my brethren.

7 And I do this for a wise purpose; for thus it whispereth me, according to the workings of the Spirit of the Lord which is in me. And now, I do not know all things; but the Lord knoweth all things which are to come; wherefore, he worketh in me to do according to his will.

Book of Mormon Plates and Records

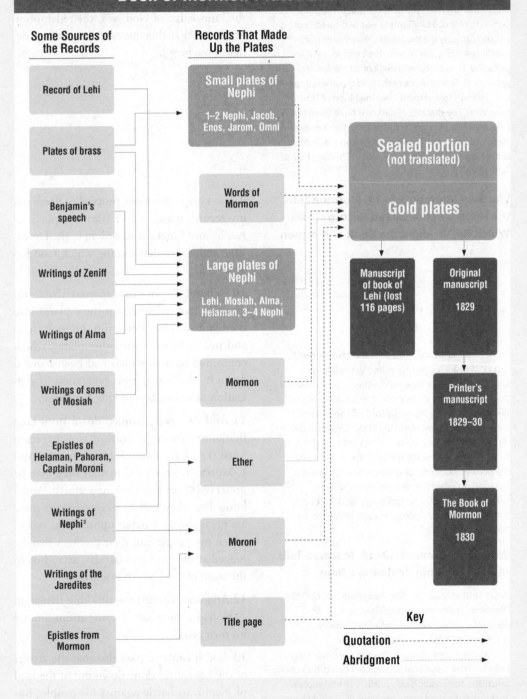

Some Sources of the Records

- Record of Lehi
- Plates of brass
- Benjamin's speech
- Writings of Zeniff
- Writings of Alma
- Writings of sons of Mosiah
- Epistles of Helaman, Pahoran, Captain Moroni
- Writings of Nephi³
- Writings of the Jaredites
- Epistles from Mormon

Records That Made Up the Plates

Small plates of Nephi
1–2 Nephi, Jacob, Enos, Jarom, Omni

Words of Mormon

Large plates of Nephi
Lehi, Mosiah, Alma, Helaman, 3–4 Nephi

Mormon

Ether

Moroni

Title page

Sealed portion (not translated)

Gold plates

Manuscript of book of Lehi (lost 116 pages)

Original manuscript 1829

Printer's manuscript 1829–30

The Book of Mormon 1830

Key

Quotation ·····················►

Abridgment ──────────►

How has Mormon's prayer been answered? (1:8)
One modern-day example of an answer to Mormon's prayer was given by President Gordon B. Hinckley: "When the Mexico City Temple was dedicated, [our people] came by the thousands. They were clean, their faces bright and smiling, their clothes neat and attractive. They bore every mark of education and refinement. There was something of greatness apparent in them. Most of them have the blood of Lehi in their veins. The shackles of darkness have fallen from their eyes, as promised by the prophets of the Book of Mormon. They have become 'a pure and a delightsome people' (2 Ne. 30:6)" ("Rejoice in This Great Era of Temple Building," 54).

Words of Mormon 1:9–11. Mormon Tells the History of the Sacred Records from Which He Abridged the Book of Mormon

From what scriptural records will we be judged? (1:11) "Men are judged according to the light and knowledge they have received—the scriptural records in their possession and also the commandments and divine directives delivered by the legal administrators in their own day. Members of the Church in the dispensation of the fulness of times will be judged by the doctrines and standards set forth in the Bible, the Book of Mormon, the Doctrine and Covenants, the Pearl of Great Price, and words of the living oracles (see D&C 20:13–15; cf. 2 Nephi 33:11; Ether 5:4, 6; Moroni 10:27)" (McConkie and Millet, *Doctrinal Commentary*, 1:290).

Words of Mormon 1:12–18. Mormon Tells More about King Benjamin's Time

What kind of man was King Benjamin? (1:12–18) "Benjamin is almost always referred to as ... King Benjamin.... [He] was remembered primarily as the greatest of all Nephite Kings....

"As the records disclose, Benjamin was righteous, holy, inspired, just, frugal, loving, concerned, humble articulate, and courageous.... [His] son and successor Mosiah declared to the Nephites, 'if ye could have men for your kings who would do even as my father Benjamin did for this people—I say unto you, if this

8 And my prayer to God is concerning my brethren, that they may once again come to the knowledge of God, yea, the redemption of Christ; that they may once again be a delightsome people.

9 And now I, Mormon, proceed to finish out my record, which I take from the plates of Nephi; and I make it according to the knowledge and the understanding which God has given me.

10 Wherefore, it came to pass that after Amaleki had delivered up these plates into the hands of king Benjamin, he took them and put them with the other plates, which contained records which had been handed down by the kings, from generation to generation until the days of king Benjamin.

11 And they were handed down from king Benjamin, from generation to generation until they have fallen into my hands. And I, Mormon, pray to God that they may be preserved from this time henceforth. And I know that they will be preserved; for there are great things written upon them, out of which my people and their brethren shall be judged at the great and last day, according to the word of God which is written.

12 And now, concerning this king Benjamin —he had somewhat of contentions among his own people.

13 And it came to pass also that the armies of the Lamanites came down out of the land of Nephi, to battle against his people. But behold, king Benjamin gathered together his armies, and he did stand against them; and he did fight with the strength of his own arm, with the sword of Laban.

14 And in the strength of the Lord they did contend against their enemies, until they had slain many thousands of the Lamanites. And it came to pass that they did contend against the Lamanites until they had driven them out of all the lands of their inheritance.

15 And it came to pass that after there had been false Christs, and their mouths had been shut, and they punished according to their crimes;

16 And after there had been false prophets, and false preachers and teachers among the people, and all these having been punished according to their crimes; and after there having been much contention and many dissensions away unto the Lamanites, behold, it came to pass that king Benjamin, with the assistance of the holy prophets who were among his people—

17 For behold, king Benjamin was a holy man, and he did reign over his people in righteousness; and there were many holy men in the land, and they did speak the word of God with power and with authority; and they did use much sharpness because of the stiffneckedness of the people—

18 Wherefore, with the help of these, king Benjamin, by laboring with all the might of his body and the faculty of his whole soul, and also the prophets, did once more establish peace in the land.

could always be the case then it would be expedient that ye should always have kings to rule over you' (Mosiah 29:13)" (Welch, "Benjamin, the Man: His Place in Nephite History," 24).

Who are among the "false Christs" in the last days? (1:15) "There may be those deranged persons who suppose they are God, or Christ. . . . None but the lunatic fringe among men, however, will give them a second serious thought. The promise of false Christs who will deceive . . . is a far more subtle and insidious evil.

"A false Christ is not a person. It is a false system of worship, a false church. . . . It is any concept or philosophy that says that redemption, salvation, sanctification, justification, and all of the promised rewards can be gained in any way except that set forth by the apostles and prophets" (McConkie, *Millennial Messiah*, 48).

What are "false prophets"? (1:16) False prophets "teach false doctrine; they neither know nor teach the doctrines of salvation. Rather, they have followed cunningly devised fables that they suppose make up the gospel of Christ, and they preach them as such" (McConkie, *Millennial Messiah*, 71).

Why does Satan use false prophets? (1:16) "Following the Brethren can be more difficult when in some settings wolves are sent among the flock. False prophets will arise, enticing some to follow them, and by their evil works they deceive careless observers into discounting any and all who claim to be prophets. Satan's order of battle is such that if it is necessary to encourage a hundred false prophets in order to obscure the validity of one true prophet, he will gladly do so" (Maxwell, *All These Things Shall Give Thee Experience*, 115).

What does it mean that King Benjamin was a "holy man"? (1:17) *Holy* means "sacred, having a godly character, or spiritually and morally pure. The opposite of holy is common or profane" (Guide to the Scriptures).

"A holy man is a man who prizes the things of the Spirit above all else. He is one who has garnered control over passions and appetites, one who has achieved the victory over self. He is, in addition, one who enjoys communion with the powers of heaven. He is one who is sanctified, who is clean. . . . He is one who finds joy in simple living and rejoices in goodness and truth" (McConkie and Millet, *Doctrinal Commentary*, 2:124–25).

THE BOOK OF MOSIAH

The book of Mosiah represents a change in location for the narrative of the Book of Mormon. The book of Omni tells of Mosiah I and a group of righteous Nephites fleeing persecution in the land of Nephi and settling in a place they called Zarahemla (Omni 1:12–13). Zarahemla had been previously settled by a group called the people of Zarahemla, who had fled Jerusalem under the leadership of Mulek, son of Zedekiah, the last king of Judah (Omni 1:14–15; Mosiah 25:2). The Mulekites and Nephites combined under the leadership of Mosiah. The book of Mosiah recounts various attempts of Nephite people to reconnect. Zeniff and Ammon from Zarahemla, an exploratory party from the land of Nephi, and later Alma, driven into the wilderness by King Noah's army, set out to find other scattered Nephites. Each group of Nephites keeps records. When, at the end of the book of Mosiah, all the records are brought together in Zarahemla, the records from the land of Nephi are inserted into Mosiah's record (Zeniff's record is found in Mosiah 9–22, and Alma's record is found in Mosiah 23–24).

The records that were merged to form the present book of Mosiah have a repeated theme of deliverance and redemption of the Nephite people, who experienced captivity and bondage under Lamanite oppressors. God raised a number of deliverers and inspired them to save His people after they humbled themselves and hearkened unto His word.

The book of Mosiah contains some of the most beloved stories in the Book of Mormon: King Benjamin and his final oration to the people in Zarahemla, Ammon and King Limhi, King Noah and Abinadi, Alma's conversion and the baptisms at the Waters of Mormon, and others. Important teachings include instructions and covenants to become children of Christ, the definition of the office of seer, Jesus Christ as the fulfillment of the law of Moses, the doctrine of the Father and the Son, and the baptismal covenant.

Mosiah 1:1–8. The Scriptures Help the Nephites Understand God and His Commandments

Why was the book of Mosiah written in third person? (1:1) "With the beginning of the book of Mosiah we start our study of Mormon's abridgment of various books that had been written on the large plates of Nephi (2 Nephi 5:8–12). The book of Mosiah and the five books that follow—Alma, Helaman, 3 Nephi, 4 Nephi, and Mormon—were all abridged or condensed by Mormon from the large plates of Nephi, and these abridged versions were written by

CHAPTER 1

King Benjamin teaches his sons the language and prophecies of their fathers—Their religion and civilization have been preserved because of the records kept on the various plates—Mosiah is chosen as king and is given custody of the records and other things. About 130–124 B.C.

1 And now there was no more contention in all the land of Zarahemla, among all the people who belonged to king Benjamin, so that king Benjamin had continual peace all the remainder of his days.

2 And it came to pass that he had three sons; and he called their names Mosiah, and

Helorum, and Helaman. And he caused that they should be taught in all the language of his fathers, that thereby they might become men of understanding; and that they might know concerning the prophecies which had been spoken by the mouths of their fathers, which were delivered them by the hand of the Lord.

3 And he also taught them concerning the records which were engraven on the plates of brass, saying: My sons, I would that ye should remember that were it not for these plates, which contain these records and these commandments, we must have suffered in ignorance, even at this present time, not knowing the mysteries of God.

4 For it were not possible that our father, Lehi, could have remembered all these things, to have taught them to his children, except it were for the help of these plates; for he having been taught in the language of the Egyptians therefore he could read these engravings, and teach them to his children, that thereby they could teach them to their children, and so fulfilling the commandments of God, even down to this present time.

5 I say unto you, my sons, were it not for these things, which have been kept and preserved by the hand of God, that we might read and understand of his mysteries, and have his commandments always before our eyes, that even our fathers would have dwindled in unbelief, and we should have been like unto our brethren, the Lamanites, who know nothing concerning these things, or even do not believe them when they are taught them, because of the traditions of their fathers, which are not correct.

6 O my sons, I would that ye should remember that these sayings are true, and also that these records are true. And behold, also the plates of Nephi, which contain the records

Mormon on the plates that bear his name, the plates of Mormon. These are the same plates that were given to Joseph Smith by the angel Moroni" (Ludlow, *Companion to Your Study of the Book of Mormon*, 173).

How important were the brass plates? (1:3-4) "King Benjamin's recognition of the importance of the plates of brass was based upon the degenerate condition of the Mulekites when his father discovered them . . . (Omni 1:17). The positive influence of the plates of brass was taught by Nephi. . . . Although 'the mysteries of God shall be unfolded unto [you], by the power of the Holy Ghost' (1 Nephi 10:19), if one will 'feast upon the words of Christ [the scriptures] will tell you all things what ye should do'" (Nyman, *These Records Are True*, 191). ◉

Why did King Benjamin consider the Egyptian language so critical? (1:4-5) "Benjamin, Nephi (see 1 Nephi 1:2), and Moroni (see Mormon 9:32) all referred to the Egyptian language. In Mosiah 1:4–6, King Benjamin makes it clear there was a reason his sons needed to learn 'the language of the Egyptians.' It was necessary in order to study the commandments contained on the brass plates and the plates of Nephi (see Mosiah 1:6). From the time of Nephi down to Moroni, the Nephites had a form of the Egyptian language" (*Book of Mormon Student Manual* [2009], 136). ◉

What are the mysteries of God? (1:5) "A mystery is a truth that cannot be known except through divine revelation—a sacred secret. In the days of Paul the important truth that Gentiles were to be admitted to the Kingdom of God without observing the Law of Moses was a 'mystery' (Eph. 1:9–11; Col. 1:25–27). In our day such great truths as those pertaining to the restoration of the Priesthood, the work for the dead, and the re-establishment of the Church are 'mysteries,' because they could not have been discovered except by revelation" (Smith and Sjodahl, *Doctrine and Covenants Commentary*, 141).

and the sayings of our fathers from the time they left Jerusalem until now, and they are true; and we can know of their surety because we have them before our eyes.

7 And now, my sons, I would that ye should remember to search them diligently, that ye may profit thereby; and I would that ye should keep the commandments of God, that ye may prosper in the land according to the promises which the Lord made unto our fathers.

8 And many more things did king Benjamin teach his sons, which are not written in this book.

9 And it came to pass that after king Benjamin had made an end of teaching his sons, that he waxed old, and he saw that he must very soon go the way of all the earth; therefore, he thought it expedient that he should confer the kingdom upon one of his sons.

10 Therefore, he had Mosiah brought before him; and these are the words which he spake unto him, saying: My son, I would that ye should make a proclamation throughout all this land among all this people, or the people of Zarahemla, and the people of Mosiah who dwell in the land, that thereby they may be gathered together; for on the morrow I shall proclaim unto this my people out of mine own mouth that thou art a king and a ruler over this people, whom the Lord our God hath given us.

Mosiah 1:9–14. Benjamin Wants His People to Gather and Make Covenants with the Lord

Why did King Benjamin send out a proclamation?
(1:10) "Every ancient people held [a] yearly assembly, they held it in the new year, and the king presided. When they had the new king, it was the New Age, and they brought their first-fruits. . . . This was not only in Israel, but in at least every other major ancient civilization. Notice he brings them together. . . . He has to send out the proclamation; that's the *heror*. When you get the proclamation, you must come or be banished from the kingdom for three [years]" (Nibley, *Teachings of the Book of Mormon*, 1:448).

Why are the "people of Mosiah" and the "people of Zarahemla" still mentioned as two separate groups? (1:10) "Their cultural distinction, readily apparent by name usage alone, had existed since Mosiah I and his followers first discovered the people of Zarahemla. These 'people of Zarahemla' were the inhabitants of Zarahemla who traced their heritage to Mulek, the son of Zedekiah, while the 'people of Mosiah' (Mosiah 1:10) were the descendants of those who followed Mosiah I, Benjamin's father, when he escaped from a wicked Nephite culture and found Zarahemla. Benjamin desired to unite these two distinct peoples with one name and one purpose" (Black, "King Benjamin: In the Service of God," 38–39). ✪

11 And moreover, I shall give this people a name, that thereby they may be distinguished above all the people which the Lord God hath brought out of the land of Jerusalem; and this I do because they have been a diligent people in keeping the commandments of the Lord.

12 And I give unto them a name that never shall be blotted out, except it be through transgression.

13 Yea, and moreover I say unto you, that if this highly favored people of the Lord should fall into transgression, and become a wicked and an adulterous people, that the Lord will deliver them up, that thereby they become weak like unto their brethren; and he will no more preserve them by his matchless and marvelous power, as he has hitherto preserved our fathers.

14 For I say unto you, that if he had not extended his arm in the preservation of our fathers they must have fallen into the hands of the Lamanites, and become victims to their hatred.

15 And it came to pass that after king Benjamin had made an end of these sayings to his son, that he gave him charge concerning all the affairs of the kingdom.

16 And moreover, he also gave him charge concerning the records which were engraven on the plates of brass; and also the plates of Nephi; and also, the sword of Laban, and the ball or director, which led our fathers through the wilderness, which was prepared by the hand of the Lord that thereby they might be led, every one according to the heed and diligence which they gave unto him.

Why did King Benjamin desire to give his people a new name? (1:11) "Not only was the new name, found in Mosiah 3:8, uniquely and distinctively given for these particular people and for this specific occasion, but, even more importantly, this designation was given to the people, not just to the new king. In traditional Israelite coronations only the king entered into the covenant with God and thereby became his son (see Psalm 2:7). In Benjamin's kingdom, however, every person was allowed to enter into a covenant in connection with Mosiah's coronation (see Mosiah 5:1–5), and thereby they all became God's 'sons, and his daughters' (Mosiah 5:7)" (Welch, "King Benjamin's Speech," 57). ⊕

Why does transgression negate promised blessings? (1:12) "Virtually all God's promises and blessings granted to men or nations in our mortal estate are conditional. Even when conditions are not specifically stated, the very system of salvation implies that there are no unearned blessings (see D&C 132:5–7). . . . In the true sense of the word, there are no covenant people unless a covenant has been made and the conditions of the covenant are honored. There are no covenants with the Lord that do not require obedience and righteousness. . . . No power in heaven or earth, save wickedness only, can sever these familial ties, bringing the forfeiture of the promised inheritance" (McConkie and Millet, *Doctrinal Commentary*, 2:133).

Mosiah 1:15–18. Benjamin Gives Responsibility for the Nephite Kingdom to Mosiah II

What was the significance of the transfer of the records, sword, and Liahona to Mosiah? (1:15–17) "When Benjamin gives Mosiah 'charge concerning the affairs of the kingdom,' we are seeing him transfer political power to Mosiah. Part of that ceremonial transferral of title and authority includes some specific items. . . . Each of these items originated in or near Jerusalem. They are physical proofs that [Jehovah] has preserved this people. They have great interest as historical relics, but their true value is that they are highly charged with religious meaning. . . . These relics serve as physical reminders of the covenant between the people and [Jehovah]" (Gardner, *Second Witness*, 3:109). ⊕

Why did the people gather to the temple? (1:18) "As in the Old World, so in the New World the temple was the focal point of worship among the Lord's people. It was the natural and accepted place to which they gathered to be instructed by their spiritual leaders. It was at the temple site in Bountiful that Christ manifested himself and taught the Nephites following his resurrection in Jerusalem (3 Nephi 11:1, 10). The pattern of the Nephite temples, at least until after the time of Christ's visit, was that of Solomon's temple, the outer court being a place of instruction (see 2 Nephi 5:16; Jacob 1:17)" (McConkie and Millet, *Doctrinal Commentary*, 2:134). ●

Mosiah 2:1–8. The People Gather around the Temple to Hear King Benjamin Speak

How long did it take King Benjamin's people to gather at the temple? (2:1–2) "In Mosiah 1:10, Benjamin asked his son to send out a proclamation for the people to gather 'on the morrow.' The observation has been made that Zarahemla must have been a small country, if all the people in it could have been notified one day to come to conference at the capital the next day," but "the morrow" also "stands for *soon* or *shortly.* . . . In 3 Ne. 1:13 we read that the Lord promised the Prophet Nephi, 'On the morrow come I into the world.' The people understood that. 'They began to know that the Son of God must shortly appear' (verse 17)" (Reynolds and Sjodahl, *Commentary on the Book of Mormon*, 2:34).

Why did the people of King Benjamin offer sacrifice according to the law of Moses? (2:3–4) "While 'sacrifice and burnt offerings according to the law of Moses' were made (Mosiah 2:3), they were made on a daily basis (Mosiah 13:30). They were 'a type and a shadow of things [of Christ] which are to come' (Mosiah 13:10), and also of thanksgiving for their blessings (Mosiah 2:4, compare Leviticus 7:12). It should also

17 Therefore, as they were unfaithful they did not prosper nor progress in their journey, but were driven back, and incurred the displeasure of God upon them; and therefore they were smitten with famine and sore afflictions, to stir them up in remembrance of their duty.

18 And now, it came to pass that Mosiah went and did as his father had commanded him, and proclaimed unto all the people who were in the land of Zarahemla that thereby they might gather themselves together, to go up to the temple to hear the words which his father should speak unto them.

CHAPTER 2

King Benjamin addresses his people—He recounts the equity, fairness, and spirituality of his reign—He counsels them to serve their Heavenly King—Those who rebel against God will suffer anguish like unquenchable fire. About 124 B.C.

1 And it came to pass that after Mosiah had done as his father had commanded him, and had made a proclamation throughout all the land, that the people gathered themselves together throughout all the land, that they might go up to the temple to hear the words which king Benjamin should speak unto them.

2 And there were a great number, even so many that they did not number them; for they had multiplied exceedingly and waxed great in the land.

3 And they also took of the firstlings of their flocks, that they might offer sacrifice and burnt offerings according to the law of Moses;

4 And also that they might give thanks to the Lord their God, who had brought them out of the land of Jerusalem, and who had delivered them out of the hands of their

enemies, and had appointed just men to be their teachers, and also a just man to be their king, who had established peace in the land of Zarahemla, and who had taught them to keep the commandments of God, that they might rejoice and be filled with love towards God and all men.

5 And it came to pass that when they came up to the temple, they pitched their tents round about, every man according to his family, consisting of his wife, and his sons, and his daughters, and their sons, and their daughters, from the eldest down to the youngest, every family being separate one from another.

6 And they pitched their tents round about the temple, every man having his tent with the door thereof towards the temple, that thereby they might remain in their tents and hear the words which king Benjamin should speak unto them;

7 For the multitude being so great that king Benjamin could not teach them all within the walls of the temple, therefore he caused a tower to be erected, that thereby his people might hear the words which he should speak unto them.

8 And it came to pass that he began to speak to his people from the tower; and they could not all hear his words because of the greatness of the multitude; therefore he caused that the words which he spake should be written and sent forth among those that were not under the sound of his voice, that they might also receive his words.

be mentioned that the Nephites operated under the Melchizedek priesthood for 'the law hath become dead' unto them. Nevertheless, they kept it until Christ had fulfilled the law (2 Nephi 25:24–25)" (Nyman, *These Records Are True*, 197).

What would be on your list of blessings for which you are grateful? (2:4) In Mosiah 2:4 we find a list of the blessings the Nephites gave thanks for at the temple. Take a moment and rewrite that verse for yourself. What would you include on your thank-you list?

What did Benjamin and his people do that demonstrates the temple's importance? (2:5–6) "The temple is placed in the center of Israel both literally and symbolically. For ancient Israel, the entire camp was laid out in relationship to the tabernacle, or temple. . . . The temple is a sacred place where God makes himself and his plan known to his people. . . . Like ancient Israel, Benjamin's people 'pitched their tents round about the temple, every man having his tent with the door thereof towards the temple' (Mosiah 2:6). As the word *tent* can also mean household, or people (*Interpreter's Dictionary of the Bible*, 4:572), in a very real sense the families of Benjamin's colony turned toward the temple" (Donaldson, "Benjamin and Noah," 50–51).

In what ways do latter-day prophets figuratively speak from towers to the people? (2:7) President Spencer W. Kimball spoke of modern-day towers: "King Benjamin, that humble but mighty servant of the Lord, called together all the people in the land of Zarahemla, and the multitude was so great that King Benjamin ' . . . caused a tower to be erected, that thereby his people might hear the words which he should speak unto them' (Mosiah 2:7). Our Father in heaven has now provided us mighty towers—radio and television towers with possibilities beyond comprehension—to help fulfill the words of the Lord that 'the sound must go forth from this place unto all the world'" ("When the World Will Be Converted," 10).

What is the significance and impact of King Benjamin's final speech? (2:8) "Benjamin's monumental speech . . . became a type of constitutional document in Nephite culture. . . . The fact that each family was given a copy of this speech . . . facilitated its far-reaching impact. . . . Shortly after Benjamin's death . . . Mosiah sent Ammon and fifteen other emissaries to the Land of Nephi. When they found Limhi and his people, Ammon 'rehearsed unto them the last words which King Benjamin had taught' (Mosiah 8:3), and the people of Limhi followed Benjamin's pattern and 'entered into a covenant with God . . .' (Mosiah 21:31). Almost a century later, Helaman spoke to his sons . . . admonishing them 'to remember . . . the words which King Benjamin spake unto his people'" (Welch, "King Benjamin's Speech," 61). ◉

Mosiah 2:9–17. King Benjamin Explains How and Why He Has Served the People

How does one prepare to learn the mysteries of God? (2:9) "The scriptures repeatedly invite the reader to inquire about and receive an understanding of the mysteries of God (Alma 26:22; D&C 6:11; 42:61). Mysteries are spiritual realities that can be known and understood only by revelation" (Thomas, "Benjamin and the Mysteries of God," 202). King Benjamin invited his people to prepare themselves to seek revelation so they might learn the mysteries of God. He used counsel similar to the Savior, who taught, "Who hath ears to hear, let him hear" (Matt. 13:9; 13:43). Likewise, King Solomon taught, "Incline thine ear unto wisdom, and apply thine heart to understanding" (Proverbs 2:2). King Benjamin knew that "the Spirit pours down upon the souls of those who are prepared to hear" (Thomas, "The Weak Things of the World," 309). ◉

Considering King Benjamin's example, why is service important? (2:10–16) "Every unselfish act of kindness and service increases your spirituality. God would use you to bless others. Your continued spiritual growth and eternal progress are very much wrapped up in your relationships—in how you treat others. Do you indeed love others and become a blessing in their lives? Isn't the measure of the level of your conversion how you treat others? The person who does only those things in the Church that concern himself alone will never reach the goal of perfection. Service to others is what the gospel and exalted life are all about" (Whetten, "Strengthen Thy Brethren," 91).

9 And these are the words which he spake and caused to be written, saying: My brethren, all ye that have assembled yourselves together, you that can hear my words which I shall speak unto you this day; for I have not commanded you to come up hither to trifle with the words which I shall speak, but that you should hearken unto me, and open your ears that ye may hear, and your hearts that ye may understand, and your minds that the mysteries of God may be unfolded to your view.

10 I have not commanded you to come up hither that ye should fear me, or that ye should think that I of myself am more than a mortal man.

11 But I am like as yourselves, subject to all manner of infirmities in body and mind; yet I have been chosen by this people, and consecrated by my father, and was suffered by the hand of the Lord that I should be a ruler and a king over this people; and have been kept and preserved by his matchless power, to serve you with all the might, mind and strength which the Lord hath granted unto me.

12 I say unto you that as I have been suffered to spend my days in your service, even up to this time, and have not sought gold nor silver nor any manner of riches of you;

13 Neither have I suffered that ye should be confined in dungeons, nor that ye should make slaves one of another, nor that ye should murder, or plunder, or steal, or commit adultery; nor even have I suffered that ye should commit any manner of wickedness, and have taught you that ye should keep the commandments of the Lord, in all things which he hath commanded you—

14 And even I, myself, have labored with mine own hands that I might serve you, and that ye should not be laden with taxes, and that there should nothing come upon you which was grievous to be borne—and of all these things which I have spoken, ye yourselves are witnesses this day.

15 Yet, my brethren, I have not done these things that I might boast, neither do I tell these things that thereby I might accuse you; but I tell you these things that ye may know that I can answer a clear conscience before God this day.

16 Behold, I say unto you that because I said unto you that I had spent my days in your service, I do not desire to boast, for I have only been in the service of God.

17 And behold, I tell you these things that ye may learn wisdom; that ye may learn that when ye are in the service of your fellow beings ye are only in the service of your God.

18 Behold, ye have called me your king; and if I, whom ye call your king, do labor to serve you, then ought not ye to labor to serve one another?

What is the relationship between serving others and serving God? (2:17) "'Charity is the pure love of Christ' (Moro. 7:47). The Book of Mormon teaches us that this virtue is 'the greatest of all' (Moro. 7:46). . . . We know from these inspired words that even the most extreme acts of service—such as giving all of our goods to feed the poor—profit us nothing unless our service is motivated by the pure love of Christ. If our service is to be most efficacious, it must be accomplished for the love of God and the love of his children" (Oaks, "Why Do We Serve?" 14).

Mosiah 2:18–26. King Benjamin Explains Why People Should Serve Their Heavenly King

If I am to follow King Benjamin's counsel, whom should I serve? (2:18) Prayerfully ponder Benjamin's call to serve others as the way to serve God. Is there a person who comes to mind? Ask the Lord today to help you find meaningful ways to serve that person. Then notice how that service increases your love for that person and for God.

How do we appropriately thank our Heavenly King? (2:19) Elder Robert D. Hales stated: "Prayer is an essential part of conveying appreciation to our Heavenly Father. He awaits our expressions of gratefulness each morning and night in sincere, simple prayer from our hearts for our many blessings, gifts, and talents" ("Gratitude for the Goodness of God," 64).

Elder Neal A. Maxwell taught: "God is surely pleased when we keep His commandments, and He delights to honor those who serve Him in righteousness (see D&C 76:5)" ("King Benjamin," 61).

What does it mean to be "created of the dust of the earth"? (2:25) In November 1909, the First Presidency (Joseph F. Smith, John R. Winder, and Anthon H. Lund) issued an official statement on the origin of man, which included the following: "Adam, the first

19 And behold also, if I, whom ye call your king, who has spent his days in your service, and yet has been in the service of God, do merit any thanks from you, O how you ought to thank your heavenly King!

20 I say unto you, my brethren, that if you should render all the thanks and praise which your whole soul has power to possess, to that God who has created you, and has kept and preserved you, and has caused that ye should rejoice, and has granted that ye should live in peace one with another—

21 I say unto you that if ye should serve him who has created you from the beginning, and is preserving you from day to day, by lending you breath, that ye may live and move and do according to your own will, and even supporting you from one moment to another—I say, if ye should serve him with all your whole souls yet ye would be unprofitable servants.

22 And behold, all that he requires of you is to keep his commandments; and he has promised you that if ye would keep his commandments ye should prosper in the land; and he never doth vary from that which he hath said; therefore, if ye do keep his commandments he doth bless you and prosper you.

23 And now, in the first place, he hath created you, and granted unto you your lives, for which ye are indebted unto him.

24 And secondly, he doth require that ye should do as he hath commanded you; for which if ye do, he doth immediately bless you; and therefore he hath paid you. And ye are still indebted unto him, and are, and will be, forever and ever; therefore, of what have ye to boast?

25 And now I ask, can ye say aught of yourselves? I answer you, Nay. Ye cannot say that ye are even as much as the dust of the earth; yet ye were created of the dust of the earth; but behold, it belongeth to him who created you.

26 And I, even I, whom ye call your king, am no better than ye yourselves are; for I am also of the dust. And ye behold that I am old, and am about to yield up this mortal frame to its mother earth.

27 Therefore, as I said unto you that I had served you, walking with a clear conscience before God, even so I at this time have caused that ye should assemble yourselves together, that I might be found blameless, and that your blood should not come upon me, when I shall stand to be judged of God of the things whereof he hath commanded me concerning you.

28 I say unto you that I have caused that ye should assemble yourselves together that I might rid my garments of your blood, at this period of time when I am about to go down to my grave, that I might go down in peace, and my immortal spirit may join the choirs above in singing the praises of a just God.

29 And moreover, I say unto you that I have caused that ye should assemble yourselves together, that I might declare unto you that I can no longer be your teacher, nor your king;

30 For even at this time, my whole frame doth tremble exceedingly while attempting to speak unto you; but the Lord God doth support me, and hath suffered me that I should speak unto you, and hath commanded me that I should declare unto you this day, that my son Mosiah is a king and a ruler over you.

31 And now, my brethren, I would that ye should do as ye have hitherto done. As ye have kept my commandments, and also the commandments of my father, and have

of all men, was formed from the 'dust of the ground' (Genesis 2:7).... All mankind ... are born into mortality 'by water, and blood, and the spirit,' and so become 'of dust' living souls (see Moses 6:59). That is ... 'all who have inhabited the earth since Adam have taken bodies and become souls *in like manner*'" (in Clark, *Messages of the First Presidency*, 4:205; italics added).

"We were born of the dust of the earth in the same manner that our first earthly father was born of dust. Our bodies ... were formed from the elements of this earth" (McConkie and Millet, *Doctrinal Commentary*, 2:140).

Mosiah 2:27–41. King Benjamin Explains What Happens to People Who Rebel against God

What are the heavenly choirs? (2:28) "We are told that those who are found guiltless will have the privilege of dwelling in the presence of God, and singing 'ceaseless praises with the choirs above....' The ability to sing and to compose and play music is a divine gift. The very purpose of it is to enable man to praise the Lord and to glorify His name.... There are choirs on the other side, and bands, and John describes their performances as 'the voice of many waters, and as the voice of a great thunder ... and the voice of harpers harping with their harps' (Rev. 14:2)" (Reynolds and Sjodahl, *Commentary on the Book of Mormon*, 2:47).

prospered, and have been kept from falling into the hands of your enemies, even so if ye shall keep the commandments of my son, or the commandments of God which shall be delivered unto you by him, ye shall prosper in the land, and your enemies shall have no power over you.

32 But, O my people, beware lest there shall arise contentions among you, and ye list to obey the evil spirit, which was spoken of by my father Mosiah.

33 For behold, there is a wo pronounced upon him who listeth to obey that spirit; for if he listeth to obey him, and remaineth and dieth in his sins, the same drinketh damnation to his own soul; for he receiveth for his wages an everlasting punishment, having transgressed the law of God contrary to his own knowledge.

34 I say unto you, that there are not any among you, except it be your little children that have not been taught concerning these things, but what knoweth that ye are eternally indebted to your heavenly Father, to render to him all that you have and are; and also have been taught concerning the records which contain the prophecies which have been spoken by the holy prophets, even down to the time our father, Lehi, left Jerusalem;

35 And also, all that has been spoken by our fathers until now. And behold, also, they spake that which was commanded them of the Lord; therefore, they are just and true.

36 And now, I say unto you, my brethren, that after ye have known and have been taught all these things, if ye should transgress and go contrary to that which has been spoken, that ye do withdraw yourselves from the Spirit of the Lord, that it may have no place in you to guide you in wisdom's paths that ye may be blessed, prospered, and preserved—

37 I say unto you, that the man that doeth this, the same cometh out in open rebellion against God; therefore he listeth to obey the evil spirit, and becometh an enemy to all righteousness; therefore, the Lord has no place in him, for he dwelleth not in unholy temples.

38 Therefore if that man repenteth not, and remaineth and dieth an enemy to God, the demands of divine justice do awaken his immortal soul to a lively sense of his own guilt, which doth cause him to shrink from the presence of the Lord, and doth fill his breast with guilt, and pain, and anguish, which is like an unquenchable fire, whose flame ascendeth up forever and ever.

39 And now I say unto you, that mercy hath no claim on that man; therefore his final doom is to endure a never-ending torment.

40 O, all ye old men, and also ye young men, and you little children who can understand my words, for I have spoken plainly unto you that ye might understand, I pray that ye should awake to a remembrance of the awful situation of those that have fallen into transgression.

41 And moreover, I would desire that ye should consider on the blessed and happy state of those that keep the commandments of God. For behold, they are blessed in all things, both temporal and spiritual; and if they hold out faithful to the end they are received into heaven, that thereby they may dwell with God in a state of never-ending happiness. O remember, remember that these things are true; for the Lord God hath spoken it.

How does someone become an "enemy to God"?
(2:37–38) "When someone has committed himself to the kingdom of God and then falls prey to an evil spirit, it is no longer possible for him to remain neutral. He becomes an enemy to the Church and wars against its doctrines. He may leave the Church but he cannot leave it alone. Such is the spirit of the adversary, once a bright and shining star, who rebelled against God and his Only Begotten Son. Satan came out in open warfare against God and all those the Father had chosen to be his rulers (D&C 76:25–29); he brought accusations against 'them before our God day and night' (Revelation 12:10)" (McConkie and Millet, *Doctrinal Commentary*, 2:143).

What is the "unquenchable fire" for the wicked?
(2:38–39) The Prophet Joseph Smith stated: "A man is his own tormentor and his own condemner. Hence the saying, They shall go into the lake that burns with fire and brimstone [see Revelation 21:8]. The torment of disappointment in the mind of man is as exquisite as a lake burning with fire and brimstone. I say, so is the torment of man" (*Joseph Smith* [manual], 224).

How can Heavenly Father's children come to dwell in His presence? (2:41) "The laws and conditions prescribed for the welfare of mankind cannot be changed nor circumvented, because they are divine and were established before the foundation of the world was laid. They are, in fact, the only means by which we can have peace of mind here and gain eternal life hereafter. This is expressed in a great revelation given to the Prophet Joseph, as follows: 'For all who will have a blessing at my hands shall abide the law which was appointed for that blessing, and the conditions thereof, as were instituted from before the foundation of the world' (D&C 132:5)" (Christiansen, "Laws of God Are Blessings," 23–24). ☉

Mosiah 3:1–15. An Angel Teaches King Benjamin about the Life and Atonement of Jesus Christ

What is the importance of this angel's message declared to King Benjamin in this chapter? (3:1–4) Elder Bruce R. McConkie declared that this "angel from heaven recited to King Benjamin what well may be the greatest sermon ever delivered on the atonement of Christ the Lord" (*Promised Messiah*, 232).

What does "all eternity to all eternity" mean? (3:5) President Joseph Fielding Smith explained: "From eternity to eternity means from the spirit existence through the probation which we are in, and then back again to the eternal existence which will follow. . . . We are from eternity; and we will be to eternity everlasting, if we receive the exaltation. . . . Those who become like God will also be from eternity to eternity" (*Doctrines of Salvation*, 1:12). ☉

CHAPTER 3

King Benjamin continues his address—The Lord Omnipotent will minister among men in a tabernacle of clay—Blood will come from every pore as He atones for the sins of the world—His is the only name whereby salvation comes—Men can put off the natural man and become Saints through the Atonement—The torment of the wicked will be as a lake of fire and brimstone. About 124 B.C.

1 And again my brethren, I would call your attention, for I have somewhat more to speak unto you; for behold, I have things to tell you concerning that which is to come.

2 And the things which I shall tell you are made known unto me by an angel from God. And he said unto me: Awake; and I awoke, and behold he stood before me.

3 And he said unto me: Awake, and hear the words which I shall tell thee; for behold, I am come to declare unto you the glad tidings of great joy.

4 For the Lord hath heard thy prayers, and hath judged of thy righteousness, and hath sent me to declare unto thee that thou mayest rejoice; and that thou mayest declare unto thy people, that they may also be filled with joy.

5 For behold, the time cometh, and is not far distant, that with power, the Lord Omnipotent who reigneth, who was, and is from all eternity to all eternity, shall come down from heaven among the children of men, and shall dwell in a tabernacle of clay, and shall go forth amongst men, working mighty miracles, such as healing the sick, raising the dead, causing the lame to walk, the blind to receive their sight, and the deaf to hear, and curing all manner of diseases.

6 And he shall cast out devils, or the evil spirits which dwell in the hearts of the children of men.

7 And lo, he shall suffer temptations, and pain of body, hunger, thirst, and fatigue, even more than man can suffer, except it be unto death; for behold, blood cometh from every pore, so great shall be his anguish for the wickedness and the abominations of his people.

8 And he shall be called Jesus Christ, the Son of God, the Father of heaven and earth, the Creator of all things from the beginning; and his mother shall be called Mary.

9 And lo, he cometh unto his own, that salvation might come unto the children of men even through faith on his name; and even after all this they shall consider him a man, and say that he hath a devil, and shall scourge him, and shall crucify him.

10 And he shall rise the third day from the dead; and behold, he standeth to judge the world; and behold, all these things are done that a righteous judgment might come upon the children of men.

11 For behold, and also his blood atoneth for the sins of those who have fallen by the transgression of Adam, who have died not

What was the extent of the Savior's suffering? (3:7) Jesus Christ is called "the Son because of the flesh, and descended in suffering below that which man can suffer; or, in other words, suffered greater sufferings, and was exposed to more powerful contradictions than any man can be. But, notwithstanding all this, he kept the law of God, and remained without sin" (*Lectures on Faith*, 59). ☼

What other scriptures describe Jesus Christ bleeding from His pores? (3:7) "Luke, the only Gospel-writer who mentions sweat and blood in connection with our Lord's agony in Gethsemane, states that 'his sweat was as it were great drops of blood falling down to the ground' (22:44). Many critical expositors deny that there was an actual extrusion of blood, on the grounds that the evangelist does not positively affirm it. . . . Modern scripture removes all doubt. See D&C 19:16–19 . . . , also 18:11" (Talmage, *Jesus the Christ*, 620).

What is the meaning of the titles "Jesus Christ, the Son of God, the Father of heaven and earth, the Creator of all things from the beginning"? (3:8) "Each of these titles has as its purpose to teach some singular truth about them. Jesus [Hebrew, *Joshua*] is a given name; it means 'Jehovah saves.' Christ is a title meaning 'anointed,' or 'anointed one.' Son of God denominates the reality of Jesus' divine nature. He is in reality God's Son. Father of heaven and earth denotes Christ's role in the creation. The title Creator of all things expands his creative role to embrace all that lives, dies, and is resurrected in and through his atoning sacrifice (see also Mosiah 4:2; 3 Nephi 9:15)" (McConkie and Millet, *Doctrinal Commentary*, 2:147). ☼

Who are Jesus Christ's "own"? (3:9) "Christ coming to 'his own' (v. 9) refers to his being of the tribe of Judah. In 'the words of [Moses'] song' (see Deuteronomy 31:30) we read: 'When the most High divided to the nations their inheritance, when he separated the sons of Adam, he set the bounds of the people according to the number of the children of Israel. For the Lord's portion is his people; Jacob is the lot of his inheritance' (Deuteronomy 32:8–9). Apparently the numbers of each tribe were determined through pre-mortal organization, and Jesus was born into his afore assigned tribe of Judah" (Nyman, *These Records Are True*, 222).

What does it mean to have "ignorantly sinned"? (3:11) "Although the modern mind tends to see sin essentially as a bad choice or an evil intent, the ancient mind included many other dimensions in its concept of sin, such as defilement, accident, error, or misjudgment. . . . In Old Testament times, the concept of sin embraced many nuances of erring, disobeying, missing the mark, bending, rebelling, straying, wandering, or otherwise being at fault, whether consciously or unconsciously" (Welch, "Unintentional Sin," 2). ⊕

How is sin remitted and salvation achieved? (3:12) "It is not repentance per se that saves man. It is the blood of Jesus Christ that saves us. It is not by our sincere and honest change of behavior alone that we are saved, but 'by grace that we are saved, after all we can do' (2 Nephi 25:23). True repentance, however, is the condition required so that God's forgiveness can come into our lives. True repentance makes 'a brilliant day [out] of the darkest night' (Spencer W. Kimball, *The Miracle of Forgiveness* [1969], 362)" (Uchtdorf, "Point of Safe Return," 100).

How did the Savior's sacrifice redeem mankind even before He came to earth and performed His Atonement? (3:13) "The Atonement was clearly efficacious for mortal men who lived after the Savior's ordeal in the Garden and on the cross. But what of mortals who lived before the Savior or even further back in time to spirits of the premortal realm? Does the Atonement reach that far? Is it infinite in time both retroactively and prospectively . . . ? The laws of justice could recognize the benefits of the Atonement before the purchase price was ever paid, because his promise, his pledge, his credit was 'good for it,' and everyone who honored their first estate knew it" (Callister, *Infinite Atonement*, 72–74). ⊕

How was the law of Moses a type and shadow? (3:14–15) "As used in the scriptures, types, which include persons, objects, or events, symbolize future events of even greater magnitude. The prophetic nature of the type is the shadow that it casts. Virtually everything in the law of Moses was, according to divine design, given to teach and testify of Christ and his atoning sacrifice (Alma 34:14). . . . The law of Moses was a grand lesson given by Jehovah himself in which he foretold the events of his mortal ministry with symbols, similitudes, and substitutes" (McConkie and Millet, *Doctrinal Commentary*, 2:151).

knowing the will of God concerning them, or who have ignorantly sinned.

12 But wo, wo unto him who knoweth that he rebelleth against God! For salvation cometh to none such except it be through repentance and faith on the Lord Jesus Christ.

13 And the Lord God hath sent his holy prophets among all the children of men, to declare these things to every kindred, nation, and tongue, that thereby whosoever should believe that Christ should come, the same might receive remission of their sins, and rejoice with exceedingly great joy, even as though he had already come among them.

14 Yet the Lord God saw that his people were a stiffnecked people, and he appointed unto them a law, even the law of Moses.
15 And many signs, and wonders, and types, and shadows showed he unto them, concerning his coming; and also holy prophets spake unto them concerning his coming; and yet they hardened their hearts, and understood not that the law of Moses availeth nothing except it were through the atonement of his blood.

16 And even if it were possible that little children could sin they could not be saved; but I say unto you they are blessed; for behold, as in Adam, or by nature, they fall, even so the blood of Christ atoneth for their sins.

17 And moreover, I say unto you, that there shall be no other name given nor any other way nor means whereby salvation can come unto the children of men, only in and through the name of Christ, the Lord Omnipotent.

18 For behold he judgeth, and his judgment is just; and the infant perisheth not that dieth in his infancy; but men drink damnation to their own souls except they humble themselves and become as little children, and believe that salvation was, and is, and is to come, in and through the atoning blood of Christ, the Lord Omnipotent.

19 For the natural man is an enemy to God, and has been from the fall of Adam, and will be, forever and ever, unless he yields to the enticings of the Holy Spirit, and putteth off the natural man and becometh a saint through the atonement of Christ the Lord, and becometh as a child, submissive, meek, humble, patient, full of love, willing to submit to all things which the Lord seeth fit to inflict upon him, even as a child doth submit to his father.

20 And moreover, I say unto you, that the time shall come when the knowledge of a Savior shall spread throughout every nation, kindred, tongue, and people.

Mosiah 3:16–19. The Natural Man Is an Enemy to God

How does the Savior's Atonement affect little children? (3:16–18) The Prophet Joseph Smith taught: "Children have no sins. Jesus blessed them and said, 'Do what you have seen me do.' Children are all made alive in Christ, and those of riper years through faith and repentance.

"The doctrine of baptizing children, or sprinkling them, or they must welter in hell, is a doctrine not true, not supported in Holy Writ, and is not consistent with the character of God. All children are redeemed by the blood of Jesus Christ, and the moment that children leave this world, they are taken to the bosom of Abraham" (*Joseph Smith* [manual], 94–95). ☻

What does it mean to submit to the Lord? (3:19) "To some degree, the natural man described by King Benjamin is alive and well in each of us (see Mosiah 3:19). The natural man or woman is unrepentant, is carnal and sensual (see Mosiah 16:5; Alma 42:10; Moses 5:13), is indulgent and excessive, and is prideful and selfish. . . .

"In contrast, the 'man [or woman] of Christ' (Helaman 3:29) is spiritual and bridles all passions (see Alma 38:12), is temperate and restrained, and is benevolent and selfless. Men and women of Christ lay hold upon the word of God, deny themselves and take up His cross (see Matthew 16:24; Mark 8:34; Luke 9:23; D&C 56:2), and press forward along a strait and narrow course of faithfulness, obedience, and devotion to the Savior and His gospel" (Bednar, "We Believe in Being Chaste," 42).

Mosiah 3:20–27. God's Mercy Cannot Save Those Who Rebel against God

When will the knowledge of the Savior reach every nation and people? (3:20) "It is the destiny of the Book of Mormon to be the instrument by which this prophecy . . . is to be fulfilled. . . . In the full and complete sense, the fulfillment of this promise is millennial, a time when 'the earth shall be full of the knowledge of the Lord, as the waters cover the sea' (Isaiah 11:9; 2 Nephi 21:9). 'And they shall teach no more every man his neighbour, and every man his brother, saying, Know the Lord: for they shall all know me, from the least of them unto the greatest of them, saith the Lord' (Jeremiah 31:34)" (McConkie and Millet, *Doctrinal Commentary*, 2:154).

Why is torment described as a lake of fire and brimstone? (3:25–27) "The angel's warning of 'their torment as a lake of fire and brimstone' (Mosiah 3:27) is symbolic of the mental anguish they would suffer. The Doctrine and Covenants calls this punishment being 'delivered over to the buffetings of Satan until the day of redemption' (D&C 78:12; 82:21; 104:9–10; 132:26). . . . Wherefore, those with knowledge who commit sin still have hope for salvation after having been through endless punishment and having paid the demands of justice" (Nyman, *These Records Are True*, 232).

21 And behold, when that time cometh, none shall be found blameless before God, except it be little children, only through repentance and faith on the name of the Lord God Omnipotent.

22 And even at this time, when thou shalt have taught thy people the things which the Lord thy God hath commanded thee, even then are they found no more blameless in the sight of God, only according to the words which I have spoken unto thee.

23 And now I have spoken the words which the Lord God hath commanded me.

24 And thus saith the Lord: They shall stand as a bright testimony against this people, at the judgment day; whereof they shall be judged, every man according to his works, whether they be good, or whether they be evil.

25 And if they be evil they are consigned to an awful view of their own guilt and abominations, which doth cause them to shrink from the presence of the Lord into a state of misery and endless torment, from whence they can no more return; therefore they have drunk damnation to their own souls.

26 Therefore, they have drunk out of the cup of the wrath of God, which justice could no more deny unto them than it could deny that Adam should fall because of his partaking of the forbidden fruit; therefore, mercy could have claim on them no more forever.

27 And their torment is as a lake of fire and brimstone, whose flames are unquenchable, and whose smoke ascendeth up forever and ever. Thus hath the Lord commanded me. Amen.

CHAPTER 4

King Benjamin continues his address—Salvation comes because of the Atonement—Believe in God to be saved—Retain a remission of your sins through faithfulness—Impart of your substance to the poor—Do all things in wisdom and order. About 124 B.C.

1 And now, it came to pass that when king Benjamin had made an end of speaking the words which had been delivered unto him by the angel of the Lord, that he cast his eyes round about on the multitude, and behold they had fallen to the earth, for the fear of the Lord had come upon them.

2 And they had viewed themselves in their own carnal state, even less than the dust of the earth. And they all cried aloud with one voice, saying: O have mercy, and apply the atoning blood of Christ that we may receive forgiveness of our sins, and our hearts may be purified; for we believe in Jesus Christ, the Son of God, who created heaven and earth, and all things; who shall come down among the children of men.

3 And it came to pass that after they had spoken these words the Spirit of the Lord came upon them, and they were filled with joy, having received a remission of their sins, and having peace of conscience, because of the exceeding faith which they had in Jesus Christ who should come, according to the words which king Benjamin had spoken unto them.

4 And king Benjamin again opened his mouth and began to speak unto them, saying: My friends and my brethren, my kindred and my people, I would again call your attention, that ye may hear and understand the remainder of my words which I shall speak unto you.

Mosiah 4:1–8. Salvation Comes to Each of Us through the Atonement

What does it mean to be created from the "dust of the earth"? (4:2) "'Dust of the earth' is a scriptural phrase implying far more than mere dirt particles. We are told that man was created from the dust of the earth (see Gen. 2:7). Perhaps another word that would come close to what is implied by dust would be 'the elements of the earth.' In Latter-day Saint theology, we certainly do not believe that God pulled together a pile of mud, formed it into the shape of a man, and breathed life into it. A more accurate statement would be to say that God created the human body from the elements of the earth. Benjamin said then, to paraphrase, that we are not even as much as those elements" (Lund, *Jesus Christ*, 122). ☉

How did King Benjamin's people receive the Spirit and a remission of their sins? (4:3) "Upon hearing King Benjamin's words (see Mosiah 3), which up to this point were apparently given to Benjamin by the Lord through an angel (Mosiah 3:23; Mosiah 4:1), the multitude began to exercise faith in a Savior who was yet to come, as compared with mortals today, who exercise faith in a Savior who has come. The listening and responsive multitude actually received, because of their faith, a remission of their sins (see Mosiah 4:3). They believed, had joy, received a remission of their sins, obtained thereby a peace of conscience, and had strong faith" (Maxwell, "King Benjamin's Manual of Discipleship," 11–12). ☉

Why did King Benjamin stress the goodness of God in his sermon? (4:5) "King Benjamin extolled, again and again, the goodness of God, his matchless power, his wisdom, and his long-suffering. These citings are all the more directional and significant, precisely because we are to strive to become like God and his Son—attribute by attribute—in our discipleship" (Maxwell, "King Benjamin's Manual of Discipleship," 12).

What does it mean that the "atonement . . . was prepared from the foundation of the world"? (4:7) "This is the atonement prepared from the foundation of the earth, going back to the premortal existence when they discussed the creation. . . . This is a biblical expression, too—'the atonement prepared from the foundation of the world'—although Christians ignore that. What was going on then if they prepared a plan at that early time . . . ? The plan was prepared from the foundation of the world. You come here, you have faith, you put your trust in him, and then you do something—keeping his commandments. It is faith that keeps you on the track" (Nibley, *Teachings of the Book of Mormon*, 1:471).

Mosiah 4:9–15. We Must Believe in God to Be Saved

What constitutes a belief in God? (4:9–10) "Benjamin taught his people eight steps, an early sort of the Articles of Faith . . . which appear at the center . . . of the speech (see Mosiah 4:9–10). His eight incremental and sequential steps are (1) believe that he is, (2) believe that he created all things, (3) believe that he has all wisdom and power, (4) honestly admit that man does not comprehend all, (5) believe that you must repent and forsake your sins, (6) humble yourself before God, (7) ask in sincerity of heart for forgiveness, and (8) if you believe these things, see that you do them" (Welch, "King Benjamin's Speech," 75–76).

How can we retain a remembrance of God? (4:11) "How can you and I remember, always, the goodness of God, that we can retain a remission of our sins? The Apostle John recorded what the Savior taught us of a

5 For behold, if the knowledge of the goodness of God at this time has awakened you to a sense of your nothingness, and your worthless and fallen state—

6 I say unto you, if ye have come to a knowledge of the goodness of God, and his matchless power, and his wisdom, and his patience, and his long-suffering towards the children of men; and also, the atonement which has been prepared from the foundation of the world, that thereby salvation might come to him that should put his trust in the Lord, and should be diligent in keeping his commandments, and continue in the faith even unto the end of his life, I mean the life of the mortal body—

7 I say, that this is the man who receiveth salvation, through the atonement which was prepared from the foundation of the world for all mankind, which ever were since the fall of Adam, or who are, or who ever shall be, even unto the end of the world.

8 And this is the means whereby salvation cometh. And there is none other salvation save this which hath been spoken of; neither are there any conditions whereby man can be saved except the conditions which I have told you.

9 Believe in God; believe that he is, and that he created all things, both in heaven and in earth; believe that he has all wisdom, and all power, both in heaven and in earth; believe that man doth not comprehend all the things which the Lord can comprehend.

10 And again, believe that ye must repent of your sins and forsake them, and humble yourselves before God; and ask in sincerity of heart that he would forgive you; and now, if you believe all these things see that ye do them.

11 And again I say unto you as I have said before, that as ye have come to the knowledge of the glory of God, or if ye have known of

his goodness and have tasted of his love, and have received a remission of your sins, which causeth such exceedingly great joy in your souls, even so I would that ye should remember, and always retain in remembrance, the greatness of God, and your own nothingness, and his goodness and long-suffering towards you, unworthy creatures, and humble yourselves even in the depths of humility, calling on the name of the Lord daily, and standing steadfastly in the faith of that which is to come, which was spoken by the mouth of the angel.

12 And behold, I say unto you that if ye do this ye shall always rejoice, and be filled with the love of God, and always retain a remission of your sins; and ye shall grow in the knowledge of the glory of him that created you, or in the knowledge of that which is just and true.

13 And ye will not have a mind to injure one another, but to live peaceably, and to render to every man according to that which is his due.

14 And ye will not suffer your children that they go hungry, or naked; neither will ye suffer that they transgress the laws of God, and fight and quarrel one with another, and serve the devil, who is the master of sin, or who is the evil spirit which hath been spoken of by our fathers, he being an enemy to all righteousness.

15 But ye will teach them to walk in the ways of truth and soberness; ye will teach them to love one another, and to serve one another.

gift of remembrance which comes through the gift of the Holy Ghost: 'But the Comforter, which is the Holy Ghost, whom the Father will send in my name, he shall teach you all things, and bring all things to your remembrance, whatsoever I have said unto you' (John 14:26).

"The Holy Ghost brings back memories of what God has taught us. And one of the ways God teaches us is with his blessings; and so, if we choose to exercise faith, the Holy Ghost will bring God's kindnesses to our remembrance" (Eyring, *To Draw Closer to God*, 77–78).

How do we retain a remission of sins? (4:12) "We retain that remission of sins by faithful observance of covenants we have made with God and through Christlike service to those in need" (McConkie and Millet, *Doctrinal Commentary*, 2:162).

What kind of life does God require of his people? (4:13) "In The Church of Jesus Christ of Latter-day Saints, we follow the formula prescribed by the prophet-king Benjamin. He taught that those who receive a remission of their sins through the atonement of Christ are filled with the love of God and the knowledge of that which is just and true. That kind of person 'will not have a mind to injure one another, but to live peaceably' with all people (Mosiah 4:13).

"That is our method, and salvation and peace for all mankind is our goal.

"Jesus Christ is our Savior. He has taught us the way to live. If we follow him and have goodwill toward all men, we can have peace on earth" (Oaks, "World Peace," 73).

What are our responsibilities to our children? (4:14–15) "Parents have a sacred duty to rear their children in love and righteousness, to provide for their physical and spiritual needs, and to teach them to love and serve one another, [and] to observe the commandments of God" ("The Family: A Proclamation to the World," 102). ⊕

Mosiah 4:16–26. Caring for the Poor Helps Us Maintain Forgiveness of Our Sins

What is the meaning of "succor"? (4:16) "The word *succor* means to aid, assist, and to provide relief to someone in need. It apparently comes from the words *sub-* and *cur*, literally meaning 'to go beneath' or 'to run to help or assist'" (Welch and Ricks, "Complete Text of Benjamin's Speech," 586).

Why is it wrong to "judge" and "condemn" the poor? (4:21–26) "It is for God to be just; it is for his children to be merciful. To judge others as unworthy of our help, and then to withhold it, is to assume a prerogative the Lord has not given us. Everything we have belongs to the Lord. He has *commanded* us to share *his* substance with others. Indeed, it is quite impossible for anyone blessed with the Holy Spirit to do otherwise...

16 And also, ye yourselves will succor those that stand in need of your succor; ye will administer of your substance unto him that standeth in need; and ye will not suffer that the beggar putteth up his petition to you in vain, and turn him out to perish.

17 Perhaps thou shalt say: The man has brought upon himself his misery; therefore I will stay my hand, and will not give unto him of my food, nor impart unto him of my substance that he may not suffer, for his punishments are just—

18 But I say unto you, O man, whosoever doeth this the same hath great cause to repent; and except he repenteth of that which he hath done he perisheth forever, and hath no interest in the kingdom of God.

19 For behold, are we not all beggars? Do we not all depend upon the same Being, even God, for all the substance which we have, for both food and raiment, and for gold, and for silver, and for all the riches which we have of every kind?

20 And behold, even at this time, ye have been calling on his name, and begging for a remission of your sins. And has he suffered that ye have begged in vain? Nay; he has poured out his Spirit upon you, and has caused that your hearts should be filled with joy, and has caused that your mouths should be stopped that ye could not find utterance, so exceedingly great was your joy.

21 And now, if God, who has created you, on whom you are dependent for your lives and for all that ye have and are, doth grant unto you whatsoever ye ask that is right, in faith, believing that ye shall receive, O then, how ye ought to impart of the substance that ye have one to another.

22 And if ye judge the man who putteth up his petition to you for your substance that he perish not, and condemn him, how much more just will be your condemnation for withholding your substance, which doth not belong to you but to God, to whom also your life belongeth; and yet ye put up no petition, nor repent of the thing which thou hast done.

23 I say unto you, wo be unto that man, for his substance shall perish with him; and now, I say these things unto those who are rich as pertaining to the things of this world.

24 And again, I say unto the poor, ye who have not and yet have sufficient, that ye remain from day to day; I mean all you who deny the beggar, because ye have not; I would that ye say in your hearts that: I give not because I have not, but if I had I would give.

25 And now, if ye say this in your hearts ye remain guiltless, otherwise ye are condemned; and your condemnation is just for ye covet that which ye have not received.

26 And now, for the sake of these things which I have spoken unto you—that is, for the sake of retaining a remission of your sins from day to day, that ye may walk guiltless before God—I would that ye should impart of your substance to the poor, every man according to that which he hath, such as feeding the hungry, clothing the naked, visiting the sick and administering to their relief, both spiritually and temporally, according to their wants.

27 And see that all these things are done in wisdom and order; for it is not requisite that a man should run faster than he has strength. And again, it is expedient that he should be diligent, that thereby he might win the prize; therefore, all things must be done in order.

"Worldly wealth is an illusion. No one *possesses* his or her stewardship; all things, including our very lives, belong to the Lord (Mosiah 4:22). To withhold one's substance from the needy or from God's work is to 'covet that which *ye have not received*' (Mosiah 4:25; italics added)" (Turner, "The Great Conversion," 221). ●

Mosiah 4:27–30. We Should Do All Things in Wisdom and Order

How can we apply King Benjamin's counsel to use wisdom and order in serving the Lord? (4:27) Elder Robert D. Hales taught, "As temperate disciples, we live the gospel in a balanced and steady way. We do not 'run faster than [we have] strength' (Mosiah 4:27). Day by day we move forward, undeterred by the refining challenges of mortality....

"We develop patience and trust in the Lord. We are able to rely on His design for our lives, even though we cannot see it with our own natural eyes. Therefore, we can 'be still and know that [He is] God' (Doctrine and Covenants 101:16). When faced with the storms of tribulation, we ask, 'What wouldst Thou have me learn from this experience?' With His plan and purposes in our hearts, we move forward not only enduring all things but also enduring them patiently and well" ("Becoming a Disciple of Our Lord Jesus Christ," 47–48).

Why was borrowing a concern for Benjamin's people? (4:28) "Under Israelite law, failure to return that which a person has borrowed was the equivalent of theft.... It was also important for a person under ancient law to return exactly what he had borrowed; otherwise a dispute could ensue over whether the value of the returned object was equal to the value of the borrowed object" (Welch and Ricks, "Complete Text of Benjamin's Speech," 593).

Why is it unnecessary to list all the ways we may commit sin? (4:29) "Sometimes people quibble about the meaning of scripture and rationalize and justify themselves in doing things they well know they shouldn't do. They sometimes say, for example, that 'Thou shalt not commit adultery' doesn't include all the other kinds and degrees of immoral sins and perversions, or that the Word of Wisdom ... doesn't catalogue all the substances and brand names and all the products and dope and harmful things that have been discovered or concocted that are not good for men....

"The Lord expects us to use wisdom and common sense and not quibble about what obviously isn't good for the body or mind or spirit or morals of man" (Evans, "Should the Commandments Be Rewritten?" 57).

Why does King Benjamin put such emphasis on remembering? (4:30) "The Book of Mormon constantly reminds its readers to remember.... It is evident that 'remembering' is a saving principle of the gospel. Just as faith looks forward in Christ to actualize the present power of his redemption, so remembrance looks back on covenants and gifts from God and keeps the past alive.... Not only man, but also God 'remembers.' He remembers covenants he has made" (Midgley, "O Man, Remember," 127–28). ☉

28 And I would that ye should remember, that whosoever among you borroweth of his neighbor should return the thing that he borroweth, according as he doth agree, or else thou shalt commit sin; and perhaps thou shalt cause thy neighbor to commit sin also.

29 And finally, I cannot tell you all the things whereby ye may commit sin; for there are divers ways and means, even so many that I cannot number them.

30 But this much I can tell you, that if ye do not watch yourselves, and your thoughts, and your words, and your deeds, and observe the commandments of God, and continue in the faith of what ye have heard concerning the coming of our Lord, even unto the end of your lives, ye must perish. And now, O man, remember, and perish not.

CHAPTER 5

The Saints become the sons and daughters of Christ through faith—They are then called by the name of Christ—King Benjamin exhorts them to be steadfast and immovable in good works. About 124 B.C.

1 And now, it came to pass that when king Benjamin had thus spoken to his people, he sent among them, desiring to know of his people if they believed the words which he had spoken unto them.

2 And they all cried with one voice, saying: Yea, we believe all the words which thou hast spoken unto us; and also, we know of their surety and truth, because of the Spirit of the Lord Omnipotent, which has wrought a mighty change in us, or in our hearts, that we have no more disposition to do evil, but to do good continually.

3 And we, ourselves, also, through the infinite goodness of God, and the manifestations of his Spirit, have great views of that which is to come; and were it expedient, we could prophesy of all things.

4 And it is the faith which we have had on the things which our king has spoken unto us that has brought us to this great knowledge, whereby we do rejoice with such exceedingly great joy.

5 And we are willing to enter into a covenant with our God to do his will, and to be obedient to his commandments in all things that he shall command us, all the remainder of our days, that we may not bring upon ourselves a never-ending torment, as has been spoken by the angel, that we may not drink out of the cup of the wrath of God.

Mosiah 5:1–5. The People Feel the Spirit, Believe King Benjamin's Words, and Desire to Follow the Lord

What is the "mighty change" wrought in Benjamin's people? (5:2–3) "As Christians today, we have the opportunity to act straightway, immediately, and decisively, just as Peter and Andrew did: 'they forsook their nets, and followed him.' We too are called upon to leave our nets, to reject worldly habits, customs, and traditions. We are also called to forsake our sins. . . . Denying ourselves of ungodly behavior is the beginning of repentance, which brings a mighty change of heart until 'we have no more disposition to do evil.'

"This change, called conversion, is possible only through the Savior. . . . As we are made new in Christ, our very natures change and we no longer want to go back to our old ways" (Hales, "Being a More Christian Christian," 90).

What constitutes a covenant with God? (5:5) "According to the *Dictionary of New Testament Theology*, the six elements involved in covenant making are (1) the preamble mentioning the names of the partners; (2) a preliminary history of the relationship of those entering the covenant; (3) a basic declaration about the future relationship of the partners; (4) details of the new relationship; (5) an invocation of the respective gods worshipped by both sides to act as witnesses; (6) a pronouncement of curse and blessing ("Covenant"). . . . These steps have their counterparts in Benjamin's speech. See . . . Mosiah 2:20–24, 32–33; 4:1–4; 7–11; 23–25; 5:11–12, 15; 6:3" (Welch and Ricks, "Complete Text of Benjamin's Speech," 598).

Mosiah 5:6–9. We Become Sons and Daughters of Christ by Faith and Obedience

What does it mean to become the children of Christ? (5:7) "Those who come unto Christ also enter into a spiritual child-parent relationship with him. They take upon themselves his name. . . . In this way, the concept of being born again suggests not only a change of heart but also the profound beginning of a new life—a parent-child relationship in which the child develops and grows toward the maturity of being like the parent. . . . The unlimited parental commitment the Savior feels for those who are in this sense his children is anchored deeply in the sacrifice of his Atonement" (Hafen and Hafen, *Belonging Heart*, 143–44). ●

What does it mean to take upon ourselves the name of Christ? (5:8) "Scriptures help us understand that the process of taking upon ourselves the name of Jesus Christ that is commenced in the waters of baptism is continued and enlarged in the house of the Lord. As we stand in the waters of baptism, we look to the temple. As we partake of the sacrament, we look to the temple. We pledge to always remember the Savior and to keep His commandments as preparation to participate in the sacred ordinances of the temple. . . . Thus, in the ordinances of the holy temple we more completely and fully take upon us the name of Jesus Christ" (Bednar, "Honorably Hold a Name and Standing," 98). ●

Mosiah 5:10–15. King Benjamin Encourages the People to Remain Faithful

How important is it to retain the name of Jesus Christ? (5:10–12) President M. Russell Ballard taught how important it is to take upon ourselves the name of Christ: "We take the name of Christ upon us in the waters of baptism. We renew the effect of that baptism each week as we partake of the sacrament, signifying our willingness to take His name upon us and promising always to remember Him (see D&C 20:77, 79).

"Do we realize how blessed we are to take upon us the name of God's Beloved and Only Begotten Son? Do we understand how significant that is? The Savior's name is the only name under heaven by which man can be saved (see 2 Nephi 31:21)" ("The Importance of a Name," 79).

6 And now, these are the words which king Benjamin desired of them; and therefore he said unto them: Ye have spoken the words that I desired; and the covenant which ye have made is a righteous covenant.

7 And now, because of the covenant which ye have made ye shall be called the children of Christ, his sons, and his daughters; for behold, this day he hath spiritually begotten you; for ye say that your hearts are changed through faith on his name; therefore, ye are born of him and have become his sons and his daughters.

8 And under this head ye are made free, and there is no other head whereby ye can be made free. There is no other name given whereby salvation cometh; therefore, I would that ye should take upon you the name of Christ, all you that have entered into the covenant with God that ye should be obedient unto the end of your lives.

9 And it shall come to pass that whosoever doeth this shall be found at the right hand of God, for he shall know the name by which he is called; for he shall be called by the name of Christ.

10 And now it shall come to pass, that whosoever shall not take upon him the name of Christ must be called by some other name; therefore, he findeth himself on the left hand of God.

11 And I would that ye should remember also, that this is the name that I said I should give unto you that never should be blotted out, except it be through transgression; therefore, take heed that ye do not transgress, that the name be not blotted out of your hearts.

12 I say unto you, I would that ye should remember to retain the name written always in

your hearts, that ye are not found on the left hand of God, but that ye hear and know the voice by which ye shall be called, and also, the name by which he shall call you.

13 For how knoweth a man the master whom he has not served, and who is a stranger unto him, and is far from the thoughts and intents of his heart?

14 And again, doth a man take an ass which belongeth to his neighbor, and keep him? I say unto you, Nay; he will not even suffer that he shall feed among his flocks, but will drive him away, and cast him out. I say unto you, that even so shall it be among you if ye know not the name by which ye are called.

15 Therefore, I would that ye should be steadfast and immovable, always abounding in good works, that Christ, the Lord God Omnipotent, may seal you his, that you may be brought to heaven, that ye may have everlasting salvation and eternal life, through the wisdom, and power, and justice, and mercy of him who created all things, in heaven and in earth, who is God above all. Amen.

CHAPTER 6

King Benjamin records the names of the people and appoints priests to teach them—Mosiah reigns as a righteous king. About 124–121 B.C.

1 And now, king Benjamin thought it was expedient, after having finished speaking to the people, that he should take the names of all those who had entered into a covenant with God to keep his commandments.

2 And it came to pass that there was not one soul, except it were little children, but who had entered into the covenant and had taken upon them the name of Christ.

3 And again, it came to pass that when king Benjamin had made an end of all these things, and had consecrated his son Mosiah

In what way did King Benjamin use covenant language in his response to the people? (5:12) "King Benjamin's covenant language in Mosiah 5 figures seminally as an early text to which Jesus was apparently alluding when he articulated in 3 Nephi 18 words that provided the basis for the final form of the Nephite sacrament prayers in Moroni 4–5. A historical, textual relationship exists between the words . . . of King Benjamin, the words of Jesus in 3 Nephi 18, and the phrases used in the Nephite sacrament prayers; the precision and persistence of basic terms throughout all three of these texts . . . speak highly of the faithful and logical orderliness, the linguistic sensitivity, and the progressing revelation and inspiration present in this history" (Welch, "Benjamin's Covenant," 293). ◐

By what means are we sealed unto everlasting salvation? (5:15) "Because it is the power of God that saves men, it includes both what the Lord does for us and what we must do for ourselves to be saved. On his part it is the atonement; on our part it is obedience to all that is given us of God. Thus the gospel includes every truth, every principle, every law—all that men must believe and know. Thus it includes every ordinance, every rite, every performance—all that men must do to please their Maker. Thus it includes every priesthood, every key, every power—all that men must receive to have their acts bound on earth and sealed eternally in the heavens" (McConkie, *Millennial Messiah*, 98). ◐

Mosiah 6:1–7. King Benjamin Serves as a Righteous Example to His People

Why did King Benjamin record the names of his people who entered into the covenant? (6:1–2) "Even as it is an obligation in these latter-days to record the names of those who have covenanted to serve the Lord, so also was it with the Nephites under the rule of King Benjamin. The custom to keep in touch with every Church member through the recording of every name was practiced by all generations of the Nephites. Keeping a record of the membership is an important part of the Gospel Plan [see Moroni 6:4]" (Reynolds and Sjodahl, *Commentary on the Book of Mormon*, 2:87). ◐

What constituted the consecration of Mosiah to be king? (6:3) "Anointing the king with oil is a significant element in the coronation ceremonies in ancient Israel and in the ancient Near East generally. . . . Following Benjamin's address and the renewal of the covenant by the people, Benjamin 'consecrated his son Mosiah to be a ruler and a king over his people' (Mosiah 6:3). The text does not indicate whether this 'consecration' included anointing. However, some ritual act was clearly involved. Other instances in Nephite history indicate that the coronation included anointing (see Jacob 1:9)" (Ricks, "Coronation of Kings," 125).

Why did Mosiah continue doing "all things" that his father had done? (6:6–7) "The covenant they made at the conference held in Zarahemla raised the followers of Nephi to a glory and a prosperity that had not been surpassed in any of their bygone ages: What to them was once a duty, now became a pleasure, and serving the Lord was their delight. We need not wonder at this when we remember that the Nephites, themselves, were a deeply religious and a goodly people. A goodly people are a happy people, and, let us remember, also, 'Happy is the people whose God is the Lord' (Hebrew saying)" (Reynolds and Sjodahl, *Commentary on the Book of Mormon*, 2:86).

Mosiah 7:1–6. Ammon Leads a Search Party to the Land of Lehi-Nephi

Who were the people who went up to dwell in the land of Lehi-Nephi? (7:1) Amaleki, a record keeper during the reigns of King Mosiah and his son, King

to be a ruler and a king over his people, and had given him all the charges concerning the kingdom, and also had appointed priests to teach the people, that thereby they might hear and know the commandments of God, and to stir them up in remembrance of the oath which they had made, he dismissed the multitude, and they returned, every one, according to their families, to their own houses.

4 And Mosiah began to reign in his father's stead. And he began to reign in the thirtieth year of his age, making in the whole, about four hundred and seventy-six years from the time that Lehi left Jerusalem.

5 And king Benjamin lived three years and he died.

6 And it came to pass that king Mosiah did walk in the ways of the Lord, and did observe his judgments and his statutes, and did keep his commandments in all things whatsoever he commanded him.

7 And king Mosiah did cause his people that they should till the earth. And he also, himself, did till the earth, that thereby he might not become burdensome to his people, that he might do according to that which his father had done in all things. And there was no contention among all his people for the space of three years.

CHAPTER 7

Ammon finds the land of Lehi-Nephi, where Limhi is king—Limhi's people are in bondage to the Lamanites—Limhi recounts their history—A prophet (Abinadi) had testified that Christ is the God and Father of all things—Those who sow filthiness reap the whirlwind, and those who put their trust in the Lord will be delivered. About 121 B.C.

1 And now, it came to pass that after king Mosiah had had continual peace for the space of three years, he was desirous to know

concerning the people who went up to dwell in the land of Lehi-Nephi, or in the city of Lehi-Nephi; for his people had heard nothing from them from the time they left the land of Zarahemla; therefore, they wearied him with their teasings.

2 And it came to pass that king Mosiah granted that sixteen of their strong men might go up to the land of Lehi-Nephi, to inquire concerning their brethren.

3 And it came to pass that on the morrow they started to go up, having with them one Ammon, he being a strong and mighty man, and a descendant of Zarahemla; and he was also their leader.

4 And now, they knew not the course they should travel in the wilderness to go up to the land of Lehi-Nephi; therefore they wandered many days in the wilderness, even forty days did they wander.

5 And when they had wandered forty days they came to a hill, which is north of the land of Shilom, and there they pitched their tents.

6 And Ammon took three of his brethren, and their names were Amaleki, Helem, and Hem, and they went down into the land of Nephi.

7 And behold, they met the king of the people who were in the land of Nephi, and in the land of Shilom; and they were surrounded by the king's guard, and were taken, and were bound, and were committed to prison.

8 And it came to pass when they had been in prison two days they were again brought

Benjamin, wrote of a group "who went up into the wilderness to return to the land of Nephi; for there was a large number who were desirous to possess the land of their inheritance." Contention caused them to war among themselves and all but fifty were slain. Later, "a considerable number" of others "took their journey again into the wilderness. And I, Amaleki, had a brother, who also went with them; and I have not since known concerning them" (Omni 1:27–30). Now, after some years, King Mosiah authorized an expedition to find out what happened to them.

What is the significance of the name Ammon appearing in the Book of Mormon? (7:3) Nephi wrote that he made a record "which consists of the learning of the Jews and the language of the Egyptians" (1 Nephi 1:2). King Benjamin and Moroni also described an Egyptian influence in the Book of Mormon writings (see Mosiah 1:4; Mormon 9:32). Hugh Nibley explained that Ammon (or Amon) "is the commonest proper name in the Book of Mormon, and also the commonest and most revered name in the Egyptian Empire" (*Lehi in the Desert*, 23). ✛

What significance might there be in Ammon's people wandering for forty days? (7:4) The number forty has a number of different symbolic meanings in scripture. "In scripture, the number represents a period of trial, testing, probation, or mourning" (Gaskill, *Lost Language of Symbolism*, 137). Ammon's group traveled for forty days to assist Limhi's people, who were in a period of trial, testing, and mourning in their bondage.

The Bible illustrates a related symbol for forty. "In Noah's time, forty days of rain . . . made a new beginning for humanity. . . . Christ fasted forty days before beginning his ministry. . . . These and other biblical parallels create a typology of deliverance following forty days of tribulation. . . . When Ammon arrives, Limhi and his people are sunk in despair. . . . Having suffered greatly and having repented of their sins, they are now rescued" (Larsen, "In His Footsteps," 94–96). ✛

Mosiah 7:7–16. Ammon Is Taken Prisoner and Questioned

1. **Some Nephites seek to reclaim the land of Nephi.** They fight amongst themselves, and the survivors return to Zarahemla. Zeniff is a part of this group. (See Omni 1:27–28; Mosiah 9:1–2.)

2. **Nephite group led by Zeniff** settles among the Lamanites in the land of Nephi (see Omni 1:29–30; Mosiah 9:3–5).

   After Zeniff died, his son Noah reigned in wickedness. Abinadi warned the people to repent. Alma obeyed Abinadi's message and taught it to others near the Waters of Mormon. (See Mosiah 11–18.)

3. **Alma and his people depart** from King Noah and travel to the land of Helam (see Mosiah 18:4–5, 32–35; 23:1–5, 19–20).

   The Lamanites attacked Noah's people in the land of Nephi. Noah's son Limhi reigned while the people lived in bondage to the Lamanites. (See Mosiah 19–20.)

4. **Attempt to find Zarahemla:** Limhi sends a group to find Zarahemla and get help. The group discovers the ruins of a destroyed nation and 24 gold plates. (See Mosiah 8:7–9; 21:25–27.)

5. **Search party led by Ammon** journeys from Zarahemla to find the descendants of those who had gone to the land of Nephi (see Mosiah 7:1–6; 21:22–24).

6. **Limhi's people escape** from bondage and are led by Ammon back to Zarahemla (see Mosiah 22:10–13).

   The Lamanites sent an army after Limhi and his people. After becoming lost in the wilderness, the army discovered Alma and his people in the land of Helam. The Lamanites brought them into bondage. (See Mosiah 22–24.)

7. **Alma's people escape** from bondage and journey to Zarahemla (see Mosiah 24:20–25).

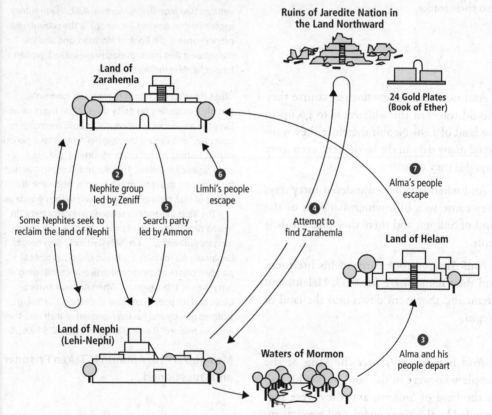

Ruins of Jaredite Nation in the Land Northward

24 Gold Plates (Book of Ether)

Land of Zarahemla

2 Nephite group led by Zeniff

6 Limhi's people escape

Alma's people escape

1 Some Nephites seek to reclaim the land of Nephi

5 Search party led by Ammon

4 Attempt to find Zarahemla

Land of Helam

Land of Nephi (Lehi-Nephi)

Waters of Mormon

3 Alma and his people depart

before the king, and their bands were loosed; and they stood before the king, and were permitted, or rather commanded, that they should answer the questions which he should ask them.

9 And he said unto them: Behold, I am Limhi, the son of Noah, who was the son of Zeniff, who came up out of the land of Zarahemla to inherit this land, which was the land of their fathers, who was made a king by the voice of the people.

10 And now, I desire to know the cause whereby ye were so bold as to come near the walls of the city, when I, myself, was with my guards without the gate?

11 And now, for this cause have I suffered that ye should be preserved, that I might inquire of you, or else I should have caused that my guards should have put you to death. Ye are permitted to speak.

12 And now, when Ammon saw that he was permitted to speak, he went forth and bowed himself before the king; and rising again he said: O king, I am very thankful before God this day that I am yet alive, and am permitted to speak; and I will endeavor to speak with boldness;

13 For I am assured that if ye had known me ye would not have suffered that I should have worn these bands. For I am Ammon, and am a descendant of Zarahemla, and have come up out of the land of Zarahemla to inquire concerning our brethren, whom Zeniff brought up out of that land.

14 And now, it came to pass that after Limhi had heard the words of Ammon, he was exceedingly glad, and said: Now, I know of a surety that my brethren who were in the land of Zarahemla are yet alive. And now, I will rejoice; and on the morrow I will cause that my people shall rejoice also.

Who was Limhi? (7:9) Limhi, the son of wicked King Noah and the grandson of righteous Zeniff, was himself "a righteous man, and he knew that his father [Noah] was wicked. . . . Limhi's life more closely followed his grandfather's. Perhaps he read Zeniff's own record, and learned from him that the people must depend on the Lord, and that it is the king's place to serve his people, not to profit from them. . . . [After King Noah's departure] the people . . . chose [Limhi] to be their king" (Card, "Three Kings and a Captain," 80). ⊕

What does Ammon's introduction suggest about the relationship between the Nephites and the descendants of Zarahemla? (7:13) "Limhi . . . declared his lineage . . . and identified its ultimate authority in Zarahemla. Ammon is no king, but his lineage likewise links him to Zarahemla, both the king (his ancestor) and the land (the current political regime). Ammon, a lineal Zarahemlaite, was entrusted with the mission of finding a dynasty founded by a lineal/cultural Nephite from the original city of Nephi. Such an assignment suggests that the Zarahemlaites were thoroughly accepted as participants in Benjamin's new covenant. Had there been any continuing animosity between the descendants of Nephi and the descendants of Zarahemla, then almost certainly, the mission would have been given to a descendant of Nephi" (Gardner, *Second Witness*, 3:204).

How are taxes and bondage related? (7:15) Mosiah 7:15 "equates slavery and taxation. This isn't surprising considering the Israelite context had a fine distinction between the two. Tax levies could be paid off through forced labor—*corvée*. In fact, this verse should be juxtaposed to Benjamin's speech, proclaiming his prohibition of slavery and not burdening his people with taxes (Mosiah 2:13–14). Benjamin says he prevented slavery and worked with his hands so as not to impose taxes which would be 'grievous to be borne' (Mosiah 2:14). The account later connects taxation and the people's labor (Mosiah 11:6)" (Goff, "Historical Narrative," 92).

Mosiah 7:17–33. Limhi Speaks to His People

What led the people of Zeniff into bondage? (7:18–32) Limhi "identified three reasons why his people were in bondage to the Lamanites. The first was that Zeniff... was overzealous to inherit the land of his fathers... (Mosiah 7:21). To be overzealous means to go beyond what is necessary....

"The second cause... was transgression.... As Joseph Smith taught: 'The moment we revolt at anything which comes from God, the devil takes power.'...

"Limhi's third cause of bondage was the Nephites' slaying of the prophet Abinadi....

"While other things may lead into bondage, these three causes outlined by King Limhi are typical reasons for any time period" (Nyman, "Bondage and Deliverance," 263–64).

When have you put your trust in the God of Abraham, Isaac, and Jacob? (7:19) "The God of Abraham, and Isaac, and Jacob" is clearly Jesus, known as Jehovah in the Old Testament period (see 1 Nephi 10:19). Notice how Limhi urges his people to "put [their] trust in God" to deliver them by reminding them of God's powerful deliverance of ancient Israel. What scripture stories or passages do you find most inspirational and faith building when times are hard and you need encouragement? Which scriptures would you use to encourage a friend or loved one who is struggling?

15 For behold, we are in bondage to the Lamanites, and are taxed with a tax which is grievous to be borne. And now, behold, our brethren will deliver us out of our bondage, or out of the hands of the Lamanites, and we will be their slaves; for it is better that we be slaves to the Nephites than to pay tribute to the king of the Lamanites.

16 And now, king Limhi commanded his guards that they should no more bind Ammon nor his brethren, but caused that they should go to the hill which was north of Shilom, and bring their brethren into the city, that thereby they might eat, and drink, and rest themselves from the labors of their journey; for they had suffered many things; they had suffered hunger, thirst, and fatigue.

17 And now, it came to pass on the morrow that king Limhi sent a proclamation among all his people, that thereby they might gather themselves together to the temple, to hear the words which he should speak unto them.

18 And it came to pass that when they had gathered themselves together that he spake unto them in this wise, saying: O ye, my people, lift up your heads and be comforted; for behold, the time is at hand, or is not far distant, when we shall no longer be in subjection to our enemies, notwithstanding our many strugglings, which have been in vain; yet I trust there remaineth an effectual struggle to be made.

19 Therefore, lift up your heads, and rejoice, and put your trust in God, in that God who was the God of Abraham, and Isaac, and Jacob; and also, that God who brought the children of Israel out of the land of Egypt, and caused that they should walk through the Red Sea on dry ground, and fed them with manna that they might not perish in the wilderness; and many more things did he do for them.

20 And again, that same God has brought our fathers out of the land of Jerusalem, and has kept and preserved his people even until now; and behold, it is because of our iniquities and abominations that he has brought us into bondage.

21 And ye all are witnesses this day, that Zeniff, who was made king over this people, he being over-zealous to inherit the land of his fathers, therefore being deceived by the cunning and craftiness of king Laman, who having entered into a treaty with king Zeniff, and having yielded up into his hands the possessions of a part of the land, or even the city of Lehi-Nephi, and the city of Shilom; and the land round about—

22 And all this he did, for the sole purpose of bringing this people into subjection or into bondage. And behold, we at this time do pay tribute to the king of the Lamanites, to the amount of one half of our corn, and our barley, and even all our grain of every kind, and one half of the increase of our flocks and our herds; and even one half of all we have or possess the king of the Lamanites doth exact of us, or our lives.

23 And now, is not this grievous to be borne? And is not this, our affliction, great? Now behold, how great reason we have to mourn.

24 Yea, I say unto you, great are the reasons which we have to mourn; for behold how many of our brethren have been slain, and their blood has been spilt in vain, and all because of iniquity.

25 For if this people had not fallen into transgression the Lord would not have suffered that this great evil should come upon them. But behold, they would not hearken unto his words; but there arose contentions among them, even so much that they did shed blood among themselves.

What might be a reason Mormon included the story of Limhi and the bondage of his people? (7:20) "One of the main reasons for including Limhi's story in the Book of Mormon is for the lessons it teaches about bondage—the steps leading to it, its different types, what we must do to be delivered from it, and the different degrees of help the Lord gives us in dealing with it" (Williams, "Deliverance from Bondage," 261–62).

What are the dangers in being overzealous? (7:21) "Zeniff's over-zealousness led him to make an unwise agreement with one whose ultimate purpose was to bring these Nephites into bondage.

"While we question the wisdom of Zeniff, we could ask if the same kind of zeal causes people today to make agreements or sign contracts that will ultimately place them in political or financial bondage. Individuals can be over-zealous for material possessions, or they can become so involved in a cause or in their work that they begin to neglect the weightier matters that are most important, such as family, church, and service to others" (Williams, "Deliverance from Bondage," 263). ◉

Was barley common in the ancient Americas? (7:22) "The December 1983 issue of the popular magazine *Science* reported the discovery in Phoenix, Arizona, by professional archaeologists of what they supposed to be pre-Columbian domesticated barley.... This Arizona find is the first direct New World evidence for cultivated pre-Columbian barley in support of the Book of Mormon. Mosiah 9:9 lists barley among several crops that were cultivated by the Nephites in the land of Nephi, and Alma 11:7 singles out barley as the primary grain into which silver and gold were converted in the Nephite system of weights and measures" (Sorenson, "Barley in Ancient America," 130). ◉

What relation is there between sin and bondage? (7:25) "Sin of any kind leads one into bondage—some sins more rapidly than others. Until the murder of the prophet Abinadi, the most serious of Noah's sins was adultery. Immorality has a tremendous tendency to lead one into bondage" (Williams, "Deliverance from Bondage," 264).

Why was the prophet Abinadi killed? (7:26–28)
The prophet described in verses 26–28 is Abinadi. He testified that "God himself should come down among the children of men, and take upon him the form of man" (Mosiah 13:34). "It was for that testimony and for that doctrine that the wicked King Noah ordered Abinadi killed. . . . Abinadi plainly taught . . . that Christ was the God of the Old Testament." Another reason for his death "is the power associated with truth and the terror it strikes in the kingdom of darkness. The very foundations of hell tremble when a fourteen-year-old boy goes into a grove to pray or a humble prophet like Abinadi bears his simple testimony in the streets of the city of Nephi" (McConkie and Millet, *Doctrinal Commentary*, 2:186).

What is the meaning of the word *chaff*? (7:30)
Chaff is the unwanted husk that surrounds the grain. "Anciently, threshers of grain understood well the art of separating the seed from the husks, or chaff. This simple matter was accomplished by tossing the grain into the air. By so doing, the valuable seed immediately returned to the threshing floor, and the slightest breeze would carry the worthless chaff away" (McConkie and Parry, *Guide to Scriptural Symbols*, 28).

What did the "east wind" represent? (7:31) "The east wind is a destructive wind which originates in the east, the symbolic direction of Deity's presence. Also called 'the wind of the Lord' (Hosea 13:15), it is 'prepared' by God (Jonah 4:8) for the purpose of destroying the ungodly and unrighteous" (McConkie and Parry, *Guide to Scriptural Symbols*, 45). The phrase is used only twice in the Book of Mormon, but both references seem consistent with this symbolic biblical usage (see Mosiah 7:31; 12:6). ✪

What must we do to be delivered from physical and spiritual bondage? (7:33) "A person who is guilty of a serious transgression cannot progress, and he is not happy while the guilt is upon him. Until he has confessed and repented he is in bondage" (Tanner, "Our Responsibility to the Transgressor," 78).

26 And a prophet of the Lord have they slain; yea, a chosen man of God, who told them of their wickedness and abominations, and prophesied of many things which are to come, yea, even the coming of Christ.

27 And because he said unto them that Christ was the God, the Father of all things, and said that he should take upon him the image of man, and it should be the image after which man was created in the beginning; or in other words, he said that man was created after the image of God, and that God should come down among the children of men, and take upon him flesh and blood, and go forth upon the face of the earth—

28 And now, because he said this, they did put him to death; and many more things did they do which brought down the wrath of God upon them. Therefore, who wondereth that they are in bondage, and that they are smitten with sore afflictions?

29 For behold, the Lord hath said: I will not succor my people in the day of their transgression; but I will hedge up their ways that they prosper not; and their doings shall be as a stumbling block before them.

30 And again, he saith: If my people shall sow filthiness they shall reap the chaff thereof in the whirlwind; and the effect thereof is poison.

31 And again he saith: If my people shall sow filthiness they shall reap the east wind, which bringeth immediate destruction.

32 And now, behold, the promise of the Lord is fulfilled, and ye are smitten and afflicted.

33 But if ye will turn to the Lord with full purpose of heart, and put your trust in him, and serve him with all diligence of mind, if ye do this, he will, according to his own will and pleasure, deliver you out of bondage.

CHAPTER 8

Ammon teaches the people of Limhi—He learns of the twenty-four Jaredite plates—Ancient records can be translated by seers—No gift is greater than seership. About 121 B.C.

1 And it came to pass that after king Limhi had made an end of speaking to his people, for he spake many things unto them and only a few of them have I written in this book, he told his people all the things concerning their brethren who were in the land of Zarahemla.

2 And he caused that Ammon should stand up before the multitude, and rehearse unto them all that had happened unto their brethren from the time that Zeniff went up out of the land even until the time that he himself came up out of the land.

3 And he also rehearsed unto them the last words which king Benjamin had taught them, and explained them to the people of king Limhi, so that they might understand all the words which he spake.

4 And it came to pass that after he had done all this, that king Limhi dismissed the multitude, and caused that they should return every one unto his own house.

5 And it came to pass that he caused that the plates which contained the record of his people from the time that they left the land of Zarahemla, should be brought before Ammon, that he might read them.

6 Now, as soon as Ammon had read the record, the king inquired of him to know if he could interpret languages, and Ammon told him that he could not.

7 And the king said unto him: Being grieved for the afflictions of my people, I caused that forty and three of my people should take a journey into the wilderness, that thereby they might find the land of Zarahemla, that we

Mosiah 8:1–4. Ammon Teaches the Words of King Benjamin

How did Ammon's teachings prepare Limhi's people to escape from bondage? (8:1–3) The bondage of Limhi's people resulted from their fathers' rejecting the words of Abinadi and putting him to death. "How appropriate that Ammon, who would act as their liberator, first taught and testified to them of the same truths that were rejected when taught by Abinadi. Having seen the fulfillment of Abinadi's prophecy and come into bondage, Limhi's people were now sufficiently humble to accept those truths—truths which would free them from the spiritual bondage that is always associated with rejecting the Lord's servants, and enable them to free themselves from the temporal bondage the Lamanites had imposed upon them" (McConkie and Millet, *Doctrinal Commentary*, 2:188). ☉

Mosiah 8:5–12. Limhi Tells of Finding the Jaredite Record

How were the efforts of Limhi's people to find Zarahemla considered a blessing? (8:8) It is quite probable that those forty-three men returned to King Limhi thinking they had failed because they had not accomplished their intended mission, which was finding Zarahemla. It is also quite possible, however, that the Lord had a very different mission in mind, finding the Jaredite record, and in that they were very successful. Have there been times in your life when, despite your best efforts, everything seemed to go wrong? Is it possible that the Lord had a different direction in mind for you, or other lessons He wanted you to learn, that would bless your life or the lives of others more than what you had in mind would do?

To what great civilization did these ruins and bones belong? (8:8) The ruins discovered by Limhi's people were those left by remnants of the Jaredites. See the map entitled "Overview of the Journeys in Mosiah 7 through 24" in the commentary in this volume on Mosiah 7.

Mosiah 8:13–21. A Seer Is a Revelator and a Prophet

What is the relation between the "interpreters" and the Urim and Thummim? (8:13) The term *interpreters* was used in the Book of Mormon to describe the Urim and Thummim. Prior to the 1835 edition of the Doctrine and Covenants, "the word *interpreters* was used [in Doctrine and Covenants 10:1]. It appears that

might appeal unto our brethren to deliver us out of bondage.

8 And they were lost in the wilderness for the space of many days, yet they were diligent, and found not the land of Zarahemla but returned to this land, having traveled in a land among many waters, having discovered a land which was covered with bones of men, and of beasts, and was also covered with ruins of buildings of every kind, having discovered a land which had been peopled with a people who were as numerous as the hosts of Israel.

9 And for a testimony that the things that they had said are true they have brought twenty-four plates which are filled with engravings, and they are of pure gold.

10 And behold, also, they have brought breastplates, which are large, and they are of brass and of copper, and are perfectly sound.

11 And again, they have brought swords, the hilts thereof have perished, and the blades thereof were cankered with rust; and there is no one in the land that is able to interpret the language or the engravings that are on the plates. Therefore I said unto thee: Canst thou translate?

12 And I say unto thee again: Knowest thou of any one that can translate? For I am desirous that these records should be translated into our language; for, perhaps, they will give us a knowledge of a remnant of the people who have been destroyed, from whence these records came; or, perhaps, they will give us a knowledge of this very people who have been destroyed; and I am desirous to know the cause of their destruction.

13 Now Ammon said unto him: I can assuredly tell thee, O king, of a man that can translate the records; for he has wherewith that he can look, and translate all records that are of ancient date; and it is a gift from

God. And the things are called interpreters, and no man can look in them except he be commanded, lest he should look for that he ought not and he should perish. And whosoever is commanded to look in them, the same is called seer.

14 And behold, the king of the people who are in the land of Zarahemla is the man that is commanded to do these things, and who has this high gift from God.

15 And the king said that a seer is greater than a prophet.

16 And Ammon said that a seer is a revelator and a prophet also; and a gift which is greater can no man have, except he should possess the power of God, which no man can; yet a man may have great power given him from God.

17 But a seer can know of things which are past, and also of things which are to come, and by them shall all things be revealed, or, rather, shall secret things be made manifest, and hidden things shall come to light, and things which are not known shall be made known by them, and also things shall be made known by them which otherwise could not be known.

18 Thus God has provided a means that man, through faith, might work mighty miracles; therefore he becometh a great benefit to his fellow beings.

19 And now, when Ammon had made an end of speaking these words the king rejoiced exceedingly, and gave thanks to God, saying:

while Joseph Smith was laboring on the translation of the Old Testament, he became acquainted with the revelatory device known to the ancients as the Urim and Thummim. Recognizing this term to be the same as the instrument that he had been given to translate the Book of Mormon and use in the receipt of revelation, he adopted the Bible term and added clarification by inserting 'Urim and Thummim' in the approprate texts" (McConkie and Ostler, *Revelations of the Restoration*, 101-102). ⊕

What is a seer? (8:15) Elder John A. Widtsoe described a seer as "one who sees with spiritual eyes. He perceives the meaning of that which seems obscure to others; therefore he is an interpreter and clarifier of eternal truth. He foresees the future from the past and the present. This he does by the power of the Lord operating through him directly, or indirectly with the aid of divine instruments such as the Urim and Thummim. In short, he is one who sees, who walks in the Lord's light with open eyes" (*Evidences and Reconciliations*, 258).

What is a revelator and a prophet? (8:16) Elder John A. Widtsoe taught: "A prophet is a teacher of known truth; a seer is a perceiver of hidden truth; a revelator is a bearer of new truth. In the widest sense, the one most commonly used, the title prophet includes the other titles and makes of the prophet, a teacher, perceiver, and bearer of truth" (*Evidences and Reconciliations*, 258).

In what ways does a seer reveal truths about the past as well as the present and the future? (8:17–18) Think about Joseph Smith's role in bringing forth sacred records from the past. "Through what has been revealed by means of the Book of Mormon, the revelations in the Doctrine and Covenants, the Prophet's translation of the King James Bible, the Book of Abraham, and other inspired prophetic commentary, we sit as it were with a great Urim and Thummim before us, gazing upon the scenes of days gone by. It just may be that the Lord revealed to Joseph Smith as much or more pertaining to the past than he did in regard to the future" (Millet, *Power of the Word*, 266–67).

What do the scriptures mean when speaking of blindness? (8:20) "The figurative usage of the terms *blind* and *blindness* in the scriptures refers to the spiritual blindness of men—the inability to see the truth.... Amulek spoke of those with blind eyes who 'will not understand the words which are spoken' by the prophets (Alma 10:25). Nephi asked of his brothers Laman and Lemuel, 'How is it that ye are so hard in your hearts, and so blind in your minds?' (1 Ne. 7:8).

"According to the scriptures, the devil blinds the spiritual eyes of man (1 Ne. 12:17; 3 Ne. 2:1–2), as do the practices of wicked men (D&C 76:75; 123:12)" (McConkie and Parry, *Guide to Scriptural Symbols*, 21).

Superscription to Mosiah 9

The superscription to Mosiah 9 (which begins "The Record of Zeniff") was part of the ancient record translated by the Prophet Joseph Smith and dictated by him to his scribe (see also, for example, 1 Nephi, 2 Nephi, and Alma 5).

The phrase in italics, "Comprising chapters 9 through 22," is not from the ancient record but was added to the printed Book of Mormon to clarify that the record of Zeniff begins at Mosiah 9 and ends with Mosiah 22.

Mosiah 9:1–3. Zeniff Leads a Group Back to the Land of Nephi

What languages did the Nephites use? (9:1) Much of what we know about the Nephite language comes from descriptions related to their written language. For example, Nephi wrote, "I make a record in the language of my father, which consists of the learning of the Jews and the language of the Egyptians" (1 Nephi 1:2; see also Mormon 9:32–33). "It is evident that Nephite record keepers knew Hebrew and something of Egyptian. It is unknown whether Nephi, Mormon, or Moroni wrote Hebrew in modified Egyptian characters or inscribed their plates in both the Egyptian language and Egyptian characters or whether Nephi wrote in one language and Mormon and Moroni, who lived some nine hundred years later, in another" (Ludlow, *Encyclopedia of Mormonism*, 1:179). ⊕

Doubtless a great mystery is contained within these plates, and these interpreters were doubtless prepared for the purpose of unfolding all such mysteries to the children of men.

20 O how marvelous are the works of the Lord, and how long doth he suffer with his people; yea, and how blind and impenetrable are the understandings of the children of men; for they will not seek wisdom, neither do they desire that she should rule over them!

21 Yea, they are as a wild flock which fleeth from the shepherd, and scattereth, and are driven, and are devoured by the beasts of the forest.

THE RECORD OF ZENIFF—An account of his people, from the time they left the land of Zarahemla until the time that they were delivered out of the hands of the Lamanites.

Comprising chapters 9 through 22.

CHAPTER 9

Zeniff leads a group from Zarahemla to possess the land of Lehi-Nephi—The Lamanite king permits them to inherit the land—There is war between the Lamanites and Zeniff's people. About 200–187 B.C.

1 I, Zeniff, having been taught in all the language of the Nephites, and having had a knowledge of the land of Nephi, or of the land of our fathers' first inheritance, and having been sent as a spy among the Lamanites that I might spy out their forces, that our army might come upon them and destroy them—but when I saw that which was good among them I was desirous that they should not be destroyed.

2 Therefore, I contended with my brethren in the wilderness, for I would that our ruler should make a treaty with them; but he being an austere and a blood-thirsty man commanded that I should be slain; but I

was rescued by the shedding of much blood; for father fought against father, and brother against brother, until the greater number of our army was destroyed in the wilderness; and we returned, those of us that were spared, to the land of Zarahemla, to relate that tale to their wives and their children.

3 And yet, I being over-zealous to inherit the land of our fathers, collected as many as were desirous to go up to possess the land, and started again on our journey into the wilderness to go up to the land; but we were smitten with famine and sore afflictions; for we were slow to remember the Lord our God.

4 Nevertheless, after many days' wandering in the wilderness we pitched our tents in the place where our brethren were slain, which was near to the land of our fathers.

5 And it came to pass that I went again with four of my men into the city, in unto the king, that I might know of the disposition of the king, and that I might know if I might go in with my people and possess the land in peace.

Why would there be a concern with being "over-zealous"? (9:3) Zeniff's misplaced zeal "allowed himself to be deceived by wicked King Laman, which led to the captivity, suffering, and disadvantage of the group of people he led. . . .

"Now let me be clear. We are in favor of correctly focused zeal. We admire courageous leaders and those who are willing to sacrifice or stand for what they know is right. The scriptures are replete with references to zeal, and the word is often attached to Deity. . . .

"Be clear in your priorities, in your understanding, in your faith, and in all your endeavors. Don't be like Zeniff, overzealous and stiff-necked. Be like King Benjamin, who received his message from an angel, and Joseph Smith, who was taught directly by the Lord.

"Do what you do with wisdom and order. Do not run faster or labor more than you have strength and means, but be diligent always" (Samuelson, "Appropriate Zeal," 2–5).

What can we do to ensure we are not "slow to remember the Lord our God"? (9:3) President Henry B. Eyring told of what he did to daily remember the Lord: "I wrote down a few lines every day for years. I never missed a day. . . . Before I would write, I would ponder this question: 'Have I seen the hand of God reaching out to touch us or our children or our family today?' As I kept at it, something began to happen. . . . I would see evidence of what God had done for one of us that I had not recognized in the busy moments of the day. As that happened, and it happened often, I realized that trying to remember had allowed God to show me what He had done" ("O Remember, Remember," 67).

Mosiah 9:4–10. Zeniff Is Deceived by the Lamanite King

What is "sheum"? (9:9) *Sheum* has a possible connection to the ancient Near East. "It is the Old Assyrian name for wheat, which is *she'um* or *e'um*. . . . Even though for Nephites the name evidently did not refer to wheat, as it did at one time in ancient Mesopotamia, its attestation among the names of other cereal grains points to an origin for the term in the ancient Near East. What is not clear, of course, is whether this term came originally from the Jaredites, the Mulekites, or the Nephites" (Welch, "Weighing and Measuring," 43). ✪

What might be the significance of the name King Laman? (9:10) "Evidently the Lamanites have used the same procedure as the Nephites did in their early history of naming their kings after their earliest leader. Jacob 1:11 mentions that the kings who succeeded Nephi were known as 'second Nephi, third Nephi, and so forth, according to the reigns of the kings.' Thus, it should not be too surprising to discover that the king of the Lamanites in approximately 178 B.C. was still known as 'King Laman' (Mosiah 10:6), although the original leader after whom the king was named had lived some four hundred years before. Also, later . . . we discover that the son who succeeded this king is also known as Laman (Mosiah 24:3)" (Ludlow, *Companion to Your Study of the Book of Mormon*, 181).

Mosiah 9:11–19. The Lamanites Attack the People of Zeniff

6 And I went in unto the king, and he covenanted with me that I might possess the land of Lehi-Nephi, and the land of Shilom.

7 And he also commanded that his people should depart out of the land, and I and my people went into the land that we might possess it.

8 And we began to build buildings, and to repair the walls of the city, yea, even the walls of the city of Lehi-Nephi, and the city of Shilom.

9 And we began to till the ground, yea, even with all manner of seeds, with seeds of corn, and of wheat, and of barley, and with neas, and with sheum, and with seeds of all manner of fruits; and we did begin to multiply and prosper in the land.

10 Now it was the cunning and the craftiness of king Laman, to bring my people into bondage, that he yielded up the land that we might possess it.

11 Therefore it came to pass, that after we had dwelt in the land for the space of twelve years that king Laman began to grow uneasy, lest by any means my people should wax strong in the land, and that they could not overpower them and bring them into bondage.

12 Now they were a lazy and an idolatrous people; therefore they were desirous to bring us into bondage, that they might glut

themselves with the labors of our hands; yea, that they might feast themselves upon the flocks of our fields.

13 Therefore it came to pass that king Laman began to stir up his people that they should contend with my people; therefore there began to be wars and contentions in the land.

14 For, in the thirteenth year of my reign in the land of Nephi, away on the south of the land of Shilom, when my people were watering and feeding their flocks, and tilling their lands, a numerous host of Lamanites came upon them and began to slay them, and to take off their flocks, and the corn of their fields.

15 Yea, and it came to pass that they fled, all that were not overtaken, even into the city of Nephi, and did call upon me for protection.

16 And it came to pass that I did arm them with bows, and with arrows, with swords, and with cimeters, and with clubs, and with slings, and with all manner of weapons which we could invent, and I and my people did go forth against the Lamanites to battle.

17 Yea, in the strength of the Lord did we go forth to battle against the Lamanites; for I and my people did cry mightily to the Lord that he would deliver us out of the hands of our enemies, for we were awakened to a remembrance of the deliverance of our fathers.

18 And God did hear our cries and did answer our prayers; and we did go forth in his might; yea, we did go forth against the Lamanites, and in one day and a night we did slay three thousand and forty-three; we did slay them even until we had driven them out of our land.

19 And I, myself, with mine own hands, did help to bury their dead. And behold, to our great sorrow and lamentation, two hundred and seventy-nine of our brethren were slain.

How are the weapons and battles described in the Book of Mormon similar to ancient Mesoamerica? (9:16) "All premodern soldiers fought with roughly similar weapons. Face-to-face, personal combat was standard. Hence swords and other hand-held weapons were key, and armor was common. Missiles like arrows, javelins, and spears were all propelled by muscle power in some way....

"The weapons, tactics, and military operations in the Book of Mormon fit this ancient pattern.... Weapons and armor in the Book of Mormon [are] consistent with patterns in the ancient Near East and Mesoamerica. Nothing in the Nephite record suggests that Joseph Smith could have invented such war stories, based on how fighting was done in his time.

"Warfare in the Book of Mormon consistently sounds like that in Mesoamerica before the European conquerors arrived.... The Book of Mormon leaves out those features of armament frequently mentioned in biblical and classical sources but absent from ancient Mesoamerica" (Hamblin, "Warfare in the Book of Mormon," 243–44).

Why is it vital to remember to call upon the Lord for strength when facing challenges? (9:17–18) Elder David A. Bednar taught how the Lord strengthens our limited abilities: "In the Bible Dictionary we learn that the word *grace* frequently is used in the scriptures to connote a strengthening or enabling power....

"Thus, the enabling and strengthening aspect of the Atonement helps us to see and to do and to become good in ways that we could never recognize or accomplish with our limited mortal capacity....

" ... In the strength of the Lord we can do and endure and overcome all things" (Bednar, "In the Strength of the Lord," 76–77).

CHAPTER 10

King Laman dies—His people are wild and ferocious and believe in false traditions—Zeniff and his people prevail against them. About 187–160 B.C.

1 And it came to pass that we again began to establish the kingdom and we again began to possess the land in peace. And I caused that there should be weapons of war made of every kind, that thereby I might have weapons for my people against the time the Lamanites should come up again to war against my people.

2 And I set guards round about the land, that the Lamanites might not come upon us again unawares and destroy us; and thus I did guard my people and my flocks, and keep them from falling into the hands of our enemies.

3 And it came to pass that we did inherit the land of our fathers for many years, yea, for the space of twenty and two years.

4 And I did cause that the men should till the ground, and raise all manner of grain and all manner of fruit of every kind.

5 And I did cause that the women should spin, and toil, and work, and work all manner of fine linen, yea, and cloth of every kind, that we might clothe our nakedness; and thus we did prosper in the land—thus we did have continual peace in the land for the space of twenty and two years.

6 And it came to pass that king Laman died, and his son began to reign in his stead. And he began to stir his people up in rebellion against my people; therefore they began to prepare for war, and to come up to battle against my people.

7 But I had sent my spies out round about the land of Shemlon, that I might discover their preparations, that I might guard against

Mosiah 10:1–9. Zeniff Prepares His People to Defend Themselves against the Lamanites

What did Zeniff do to help his people live in peace? (10:2–5) "For twenty-two years after the first attack by the Lamanites (see Mosiah 9:14–18), Zeniff and his people had peace in their land. During this time, Zeniff organized guards to keep watch over the land to prevent a surprise attack by the Lamanites. . . . Zeniff understood how to lead his people so that they could live in peace (see 2 Nephi 1:7). . . .

" . . . Zeniff and his people prospered in their righteousness because they remembered the Lord" (Jackson and Tanner, "Zeniff and Noah," 231).

How does the Lord bless our industrious efforts? (10:4–5) Elder Robert D. Hales taught that "joyfully living within our means and preparing for the ups and downs of life" helps us to "be ready for the rainy-day emergencies when they come into our lives." He added: "Happy is the man who lives within his means and is able to save a little for future needs. As we live providently and increase our gifts and talents, we become more self-reliant. Self-reliance is taking responsibility for our own spiritual and temporal welfare and for those whom Heavenly Father has entrusted to our care" ("Gospel Vision of Welfare," 1–2).

them, that they might not come upon my people and destroy them.

8 And it came to pass that they came up upon the north of the land of Shilom, with their numerous hosts, men armed with bows, and with arrows, and with swords, and with cimeters, and with stones, and with slings; and they had their heads shaved that they were naked; and they were girded with a leathern girdle about their loins.

9 And it came to pass that I caused that the women and children of my people should be hid in the wilderness; and I also caused that all my old men that could bear arms, and also all my young men that were able to bear arms, should gather themselves together to go to battle against the Lamanites; and I did place them in their ranks, every man according to his age.

10 And it came to pass that we did go up to battle against the Lamanites; and I, even I, in my old age, did go up to battle against the Lamanites. And it came to pass that we did go up in the strength of the Lord to battle.

11 Now, the Lamanites knew nothing concerning the Lord, nor the strength of the Lord, therefore they depended upon their own strength. Yet they were a strong people, as to the strength of men.

12 They were a wild, and ferocious, and a blood-thirsty people, believing in the tradition of their fathers, which is this—Believing that they were driven out of the land of Jerusalem because of the iniquities of their fathers, and that they were wronged in the wilderness by their brethren, and they were also wronged while crossing the sea;

Why did the Lamanites come to battle wearing only leather about their loins? (10:8) "You notice the standard equipment here—the leather clothing. . . . They had the equipment and their heads shaved, and they were naked except for the leather garments they had on. They were trying to inspire terror, of course, and this is a very important thing.

" . . . The purpose of the military, of course, is to break the enemy's will, not to destroy them. The Lamanites don't want to destroy the Nephites; they want the Nephites to work for them. . . . They want to enslave them" (Nibley, *Teachings of the Book of Mormon*, 2:1).

How did Zeniff's efforts in battle against the Lamanites demonstrate his military leadership? (10:9) "Impressive were King Zeniff's heroics while defending his kingdom against Lamanite invasion [including guards placed 'round about the land' and spies; see Mosiah 10:2, 7]. . . . When the Lamanites finally attacked, Zeniff led virtually the *entire* male population into battle. . . . Thus, although Zeniff's people went 'up in the strength of the Lord to battle' (Mosiah 10:10), victory was due in no small part to King Zeniff's tactical prowess and battlefield valor" (Kerr, "Ancient Aspects of Nephite Kingship," 90).

Mosiah 10:10–18. The Lamanites Teach Their Children to Hate the Nephites

In what way can false traditions keep us from the truth? (10:12) The Lord cautioned, "And that wicked one cometh and taketh away light and truth, through disobedience . . . and because of the tradition of their fathers" (D&C 93:39). President Howard W. Hunter counseled: "Measure whatever anyone else asks you to do, whether it be from your family, loved ones, your cultural heritage, or traditions you have inherited—measure everything against the teachings of the Savior. Where you find a variance from those teachings, set that matter aside and do not pursue it. It will not bring you happiness" (as quoted in Scott, "Removing Barriers to Happiness," 85).

Do you ever place a higher priority on the opinions of friends or family or traditions than on the teachings of Christ? What consequences can come from such action? ❂

Why does the Lord favor any of His children? (10:13) "While the Lord is impartial, yet heaven has its 'favorites' (*Lectures on Faith*, 6:4). They are spoken of as the 'noble and great' (Abr 3:22–23), the 'chosen' (D&C 121:40), the 'sanctified' (D&C 20:34), and so forth. They constitute what Elder Matthew Cowley called 'the aristocracy of righteousness.'... But they are not born aristocrats, they are exalted by merit, not by chance. 'Behold, the Lord esteemeth all flesh in one; he that is righteous is favored of God' (1 Nephi 17:35).... James wrote: 'The effectual fervent prayer of a righteous man availeth much' (James 5:16)" (Turner, "Imperative and Unchanging Nature of God," 216).

How might we be negatively influenced by our lack of understanding God's character and His "dealings"? (10:14) "Failing to understand the 'dealings' of the Lord with His children—meaning His relations with and treatment of His children—is very fundamental.... In fact... this failure affects everything else!

"To misread something so crucial constitutes a failure to know God, who then ends up being wrongly seen as unreachable, uninvolved, uncaring, and unable—a disabled and diminished Deity, really— about whose seeming limitations, ironically, some then quickly complain....

"By believing in such a disabled God, people can do pretty much as they please. It is then not many steps further to saying there is no God, therefore no law and no sin!" (Maxwell, "Lessons from Laman and Lemuel," 6–7).

Why did the Lamanites feel Nephi robbed them when he took the brass plates? (10:15–16) "Nephite kingship was... connected with and was even symbolized or legitimized by possession of certain material objects.... Nephi took the brass plates with him when he abandoned the land of Nephi.... The Lamanites... claimed that by taking them Nephi had 'robbed them'... (Mosiah 10:15–16; compare 2 Nephi 5:3; Alma 20:10, 13). When Benjamin transferred the kingdom to his son Mosiah, he gave Mosiah the brass plates, as well as the plates of Nephi, the sword of Laban, and the Liahona" (Peterson, "Priesthood in Mosiah," 191). ❂

13 And again, that they were wronged while in the land of their first inheritance, after they had crossed the sea, and all this because that Nephi was more faithful in keeping the commandments of the Lord—therefore he was favored of the Lord, for the Lord heard his prayers and answered them, and he took the lead of their journey in the wilderness.

14 And his brethren were wroth with him because they understood not the dealings of the Lord; they were also wroth with him upon the waters because they hardened their hearts against the Lord.

15 And again, they were wroth with him when they had arrived in the promised land, because they said that he had taken the ruling of the people out of their hands; and they sought to kill him.

16 And again, they were wroth with him because he departed into the wilderness as the Lord had commanded him, and took the records which were engraven on the plates of brass, for they said that he robbed them.

17 And thus they have taught their children that they should hate them, and that they should murder them, and that they should rob and plunder them, and do all they could to destroy them; therefore they have an eternal hatred towards the children of Nephi.

18 For this very cause has king Laman, by his cunning, and lying craftiness, and his fair promises, deceived me, that I have brought this my people up into this land, that they may destroy them; yea, and we have suffered these many years in the land.

19 And now I, Zeniff, after having told all these things unto my people concerning the Lamanites, I did stimulate them to go to battle with their might, putting their trust in the Lord; therefore, we did contend with them, face to face.

20 And it came to pass that we did drive them again out of our land; and we slew them with a great slaughter, even so many that we did not number them.

21 And it came to pass that we returned again to our own land, and my people again began to tend their flocks, and to till their ground.

22 And now I, being old, did confer the kingdom upon one of my sons; therefore, I say no more. And may the Lord bless my people. Amen.

CHAPTER 11

King Noah rules in wickedness—He revels in riotous living with his wives and concubines—Abinadi prophesies that the people will be taken into bondage—His life is sought by King Noah. About 160–150 B.C.

1 And now it came to pass that Zeniff conferred the kingdom upon Noah, one of his sons; therefore Noah began to reign in his stead; and he did not walk in the ways of his father.

Mosiah 10:19–22. Zeniff's People Battle the Lamanites

How can we, like Zeniff and his people, be successful in defending ourselves against our enemies? (10:19) "President Spencer W. Kimball issued the following warning: 'When threatened, we become anti-enemy instead of pro-kingdom of God. . . . We forget that if we are righteous the Lord will either not suffer our enemies to come upon us—and this is the special promise to the inhabitants of the land of the Americas (see 2 Ne. 1:7)—or he will fight our battles for us' ('False Gods We Worship,' 6). President Kimball did not say that we should never revert to a military solution, but he connected the military with a spiritual perspective" (Bassett, "Four Faces of Pride in the Book of Mormon," 23). ●

Mosiah 11:1–15. King Noah Rules in Wickedness

What is a concubine? (11:2) "Concubines in the Old Testament 'were considered to be secondary wives, that is, wives who did not have the same standing in the caste system then prevailing as did those wives who were not called concubines' (Bruce R. McConkie, *Mormon Doctrine*, 154). . . . In the time of King Noah, however, the word 'concubines' (Mosiah 11:2) referred to the wicked practice of a man living with more than one woman, in or out of marriage, without God's approval. The word 'whoredoms' (Mosiah 11:2) refers to any perversion of the laws of chastity and virtue" (*Book of Mormon Student Manual* [1989], 62). King Noah abused his power and spent his time in riotous living. ⊕

Why is the account of Noah's excessive taxation included in Zeniff's record? (11:3) One "change in the affairs of Noah's kingdom was a heavy taxation upon the people, one fifth of all they possessed (v. 3). The amount of taxes seems a warning to us as a nation, and to any nation who possesses this land of promise (see Ether 2:12)" (Nyman, *These Records Are True*, 310). In addition, Mormon's inclusion of excessive taxation alerts the reader to the Old Testament code commanding kings not to "multiply to [themselves]" additional wives or gold (see Deuteronomy 17:14–17).

If King Noah's priests held priesthood authority, from whom did they obtain it? (11:5) "The priests of Noah were corrupt and their priesthood one of defilement and debauchery. Of interest but unclear in the Book of Mormon is what authority if any the priests had who were consecrated by Zeniff. Assuming Zeniff to have been properly ordained, it may well be that Alma traced his authority to this source (see Mosiah 18:18)" (McConkie and Millet, *Doctrinal Commentary*, 2:200). ⊕

In what manner was iron used as a "precious" decorative metal? (11:8) "When iron was scarce, it was used as a precious decorative metal. . . . [Often] beds or jeweled boxes were not of solid iron, but they were plated, veneered, or studded with the metal. . . . With such a point in mind, we can reread the account of King Noah, who built many elegant buildings and '*ornamented* them with fine work of wood, and of all manner of precious things, of gold, and of silver, and of *iron*' (Mosiah 11:8; emphasis added). Although a person today would not normally think of using iron as a precious decoration, we can now see that this was actually done in antiquity" (Welch, "Decorative Iron in Early Israel," 133).

2 For behold, he did not keep the commandments of God, but he did walk after the desires of his own heart. And he had many wives and concubines. And he did cause his people to commit sin, and do that which was abominable in the sight of the Lord. Yea, and they did commit whoredoms and all manner of wickedness.

3 And he laid a tax of one fifth part of all they possessed, a fifth part of their gold and of their silver, and a fifth part of their ziff, and of their copper, and of their brass and their iron; and a fifth part of their fatlings; and also a fifth part of all their grain.

4 And all this did he take to support himself, and his wives and his concubines; and also his priests, and their wives and their concubines; thus he had changed the affairs of the kingdom.

5 For he put down all the priests that had been consecrated by his father, and consecrated new ones in their stead, such as were lifted up in the pride of their hearts.

6 Yea, and thus they were supported in their laziness, and in their idolatry, and in their whoredoms, by the taxes which king Noah had put upon his people; thus did the people labor exceedingly to support iniquity.

7 Yea, and they also became idolatrous, because they were deceived by the vain and flattering words of the king and priests; for they did speak flattering things unto them.

8 And it came to pass that king Noah built many elegant and spacious buildings; and he ornamented them with fine work of wood, and of all manner of precious things, of gold, and of silver, and of iron, and of brass, and of ziff, and of copper;

9 And he also built him a spacious palace, and a throne in the midst thereof, all of which was of fine wood and was ornamented with gold and silver and with precious things.

10 And he also caused that his workmen should work all manner of fine work within the walls of the temple, of fine wood, and of copper, and of brass.

11 And the seats which were set apart for the high priests, which were above all the other seats, he did ornament with pure gold; and he caused a breastwork to be built before them, that they might rest their bodies and their arms upon while they should speak lying and vain words to his people.

12 And it came to pass that he built a tower near the temple; yea, a very high tower, even so high that he could stand upon the top thereof and overlook the land of Shilom, and also the land of Shemlon, which was possessed by the Lamanites; and he could even look over all the land round about.

13 And it came to pass that he caused many buildings to be built in the land Shilom; and he caused a great tower to be built on the hill north of the land Shilom, which had been a resort for the children of Nephi at the time they fled out of the land; and thus he did do with the riches which he obtained by the taxation of his people.

14 And it came to pass that he placed his heart upon his riches, and he spent his time in riotous living with his wives and his concubines; and so did also his priests spend their time with harlots.

15 And it came to pass that he planted vineyards round about in the land; and he built wine-presses, and made wine in abundance; and therefore he became a wine-bibber, and also his people.

Why did King Noah build a spacious palace and many buildings? (11:9–13) "An earmark of false religion is its attempt to hide its emptiness in such things as pomp and ceremony, grandeur and elegance. The purpose of great and spacious buildings, ornate in decor, is to create a sense of reverence and awe that otherwise would be lacking. Gold and silver, silks and scarlets, magnificent treasures of art and craftsmanship, buildings of enormous size and expense—such are the trappings of the kingdoms of this world and the cloak of the god of that which is worldly" (McConkie and Millet, *Doctrinal Commentary*, 2:202).

Mosiah 11:16–19. King Noah's Armies Delight in Bloodshed

What can we learn about the spiritual condition of Noah's people from their delighting in bloodshed? (11:18–19) "Mormon is painting a picture of a people in apostasy, from which they will be called to repentance by Abinadi. . . . The set up necessitates our understanding of the fallen nature of Noah and his people. Their sins include the 'pride of their hearts.' They achieved a victory, but ascribe it to their own strength and forget their God. Even worse, they 'did delight in blood, and the shedding of the blood of their brethren'" (Gardner, *Second Witness*, 3:259).

Mosiah 11:20–29. Abinadi Warns the People to Repent or Face Bondage

Who was Abinadi? (11:20) "The prophet Abinadi holds a singular place in the Book of Mormon. He was the first to die as a martyr, and his doctrinal teachings clarify the purpose of the law of Moses, identify the Redeemer, and declare facts about the doctrine of resurrection not previously mentioned in the book. He was capable of exquisite language sparked with fiery metaphor, yet was plainspoken to the point of bluntness.

" . . . So far as we know, he converted but one man, yet that one man (Alma) became the progenitor of a posterity that kept the sacred records and served as the ecclesiastical leaders (and sometimes the political leaders) for the remainder of the Nephites' history, a period of well over four hundred years" (Matthews, "Abinadi," *Ensign*, Apr. 1992, 25–26). ⊕

How can we avoid the spiritual suffering and temporal bondage prophesied by Abinadi? (11:21) "The word of the Lord through Abinadi is as valid for us today as it was for Noah's society. People of all nations must repent or suffer spiritual and temporal bondage" (Jackson and Tanner, "Zeniff and Noah," 235). How

16 And it came to pass that the Lamanites began to come in upon his people, upon small numbers, and to slay them in their fields, and while they were tending their flocks.

17 And king Noah sent guards round about the land to keep them off; but he did not send a sufficient number, and the Lamanites came upon them and killed them, and drove many of their flocks out of the land; thus the Lamanites began to destroy them, and to exercise their hatred upon them.

18 And it came to pass that king Noah sent his armies against them, and they were driven back, or they drove them back for a time; therefore, they returned rejoicing in their spoil.

19 And now, because of this great victory they were lifted up in the pride of their hearts; they did boast in their own strength, saying that their fifty could stand against thousands of the Lamanites; and thus they did boast, and did delight in blood, and the shedding of the blood of their brethren, and this because of the wickedness of their king and priests.

20 And it came to pass that there was a man among them whose name was Abinadi; and he went forth among them, and began to prophesy, saying: Behold, thus saith the Lord, and thus hath he commanded me, saying, Go forth, and say unto this people, thus saith the Lord—Wo be unto this people, for I have seen their abominations, and their wickedness, and their whoredoms; and except they repent I will visit them in mine anger.

21 And except they repent and turn to the Lord their God, behold, I will deliver them into the hands of their enemies; yea, and they shall be brought into bondage; and they shall be afflicted by the hand of their enemies.

22 And it shall come to pass that they shall know that I am the Lord their God, and am a jealous God, visiting the iniquities of my people.

23 And it shall come to pass that except this people repent and turn unto the Lord their God, they shall be brought into bondage; and none shall deliver them, except it be the Lord the Almighty God.

24 Yea, and it shall come to pass that when they shall cry unto me I will be slow to hear their cries; yea, and I will suffer them that they be smitten by their enemies.

25 And except they repent in sackcloth and ashes, and cry mightily to the Lord their God, I will not hear their prayers, neither will I deliver them out of their afflictions; and thus saith the Lord, and thus hath he commanded me.

26 Now it came to pass that when Abinadi had spoken these words unto them they were wroth with him, and sought to take away his life; but the Lord delivered him out of their hands.

have you seen the prophecy in verse 21 come to pass in your own life?

What can we learn about overcoming the bondage of sin from Abinadi's warning to Noah's people? (11:23) Elder Bruce R. McConkie wrote: "Before sinners can repent and gain the inestimable blessings that flow therefrom, they must come to a knowledge of the plan of salvation. Before they can free themselves from the bondage of sin and rejoice in the liberty of the Lord, they must know the part repentance plays in the gospel plan. . . .

"To enable men to escape the bondage of sin, God provided a plan of redemption, a plan of mercy, a plan of repentance. . . .

"Repentance is made available to men through the atoning sacrifice of the Lord Jesus Christ" (McConkie, *New Witness*, 212–14).

Why might it appear that the Lord is sometimes slow to hear our prayers? (11:24) Mosiah 11:24 is comparable in many ways to the Lord's warning to the early Saints in our own dispensation who were chastened and afflicted because of their own transgressions. The Lord revealed to the Prophet Joseph Smith that the suffering Saints in Missouri "were slow to hearken unto the voice of the Lord their God; therefore, the Lord their God is slow to hearken unto their prayers, to answer them in the day of their trouble. In the day of their peace they esteemed lightly my counsel; but, in the day of their trouble, of necessity they feel after me" (D&C 101:7–8).

How does this principle apply to individuals as well as whole groups of people?

What does it mean to repent in sackcloth and ashes? (11:25) "Sackcloth was a coarse, dark cloth made of goat or camel hair. It was typically worn by mourners as a symbol of their grief, humiliation, repentance, or dismay" (Gaskill, *Lost Language of Symbolism*, 74). Wearing sackcloth was often accompanied with "sitting among ashes, or scattering them upon one's person, as a symbol of grief and mourning" (Unger, *New Unger's Bible Dictionary*, 113).

President Spencer W. Kimball described an association between sackcloth, ashes, and the mourning of sin required for full repentance: "To every forgiveness there is a condition. The plaster must be as wide as the sore. The fasting, the prayers, the humility must be equal to or greater than the sin. There must be a broken heart and a contrite spirit. There must be 'sackcloth and ashes.' There must be tears and genuine change of heart" (*Miracle of Forgiveness*, 316).

Mosiah 12:1–8. Abinadi Prophesies the Destruction of King Noah and His People

Why did Abinadi disguise himself? (12:1) "Why did Abinadi go to all the trouble of disguising himself and then promptly identify himself in his opening statement? The answer is he needed the disguise to get inside the city. The people were seeking his life, but he had been commanded of the Lord (v. 1) and put his trust in him. Later he indicates he may have had an inkling of his being put to death (vv. 13:2–9)" (Nyman, *These Records Are True*, 326–27).

27 Now when king Noah had heard of the words which Abinadi had spoken unto the people, he was also wroth; and he said: Who is Abinadi, that I and my people should be judged of him, or who is the Lord, that shall bring upon my people such great affliction?

28 I command you to bring Abinadi hither, that I may slay him, for he has said these things that he might stir up my people to anger one with another, and to raise contentions among my people; therefore I will slay him.

29 Now the eyes of the people were blinded; therefore they hardened their hearts against the words of Abinadi, and they sought from that time forward to take him. And king Noah hardened his heart against the word of the Lord, and he did not repent of his evil doings.

CHAPTER 12

Abinadi is imprisoned for prophesying the destruction of the people and the death of King Noah—The false priests quote the scriptures and pretend to keep the law of Moses—Abinadi begins to teach them the Ten Commandments. About 148 B.C.

1 And it came to pass that after the space of two years that Abinadi came among them in disguise, that they knew him not, and began to prophesy among them, saying: Thus has the Lord commanded me, saying—Abinadi, go and prophesy unto this my people, for they have hardened their hearts against my words; they have repented not of their evil doings; therefore, I will visit them in my anger, yea, in my fierce anger will I visit them in their iniquities and abominations.

2 Yea, wo be unto this generation! And the Lord said unto me: Stretch forth thy hand and prophesy, saying: Thus saith the Lord, it shall come to pass that this generation, because of their iniquities, shall be brought into bondage, and shall be smitten on the cheek;

yea, and shall be driven by men, and shall be slain; and the vultures of the air, and the dogs, yea, and the wild beasts, shall devour their flesh.

3 And it shall come to pass that the life of king Noah shall be valued even as a garment in a hot furnace; for he shall know that I am the Lord.

4 And it shall come to pass that I will smite this my people with sore afflictions, yea, with famine and with pestilence; and I will cause that they shall howl all the day long.

5 Yea, and I will cause that they shall have burdens lashed upon their backs; and they shall be driven before like a dumb ass.

6 And it shall come to pass that I will send forth hail among them, and it shall smite them; and they shall also be smitten with the east wind; and insects shall pester their land also, and devour their grain.

7 And they shall be smitten with a great pestilence—and all this will I do because of their iniquities and abominations.

8 And it shall come to pass that except they repent I will utterly destroy them from off the face of the earth; yet they shall leave a record behind them, and I will preserve them for other nations which shall possess the land; yea, even this will I do that I may discover the abominations of this people to other nations. And many things did Abinadi prophesy against this people.

9 And it came to pass that they were angry with him; and they took him and carried him bound before the king, and said unto the king: Behold, we have brought a man before thee who has prophesied evil concerning thy people, and saith that God will destroy them.

10 And he also prophesieth evil concerning thy life, and saith that thy life shall be as a garment in a furnace of fire.

What meaning is conveyed by comparing King Noah's life to "a garment in a hot furnace"? (12:3) "Abinadi's words fit the pattern of a simile curse, of which he gives examples. Hugh Nibley suggested that Abinadi borrowed from the simile curse in Isaiah 50:9, 11.... Abinadi's curse of King Noah, with the specific mention of fire, was intended to indicate the very serious nature of Noah's sins. Like the diseased garment in Leviticus 13:52, 57, and the useless garment in Isaiah 14:19–20 (another simile curse), he is not to be honored with burial. Instead, he will suffer death by fire, which is the ultimate punishment of the wicked" (Tvedtnes, "As a Garment in a Hot Furnace," 76, 79). ⊕

What is the symbolism of the east wind? (12:6) The "east wind, which bringeth immediate destruction ... is an Old World cultural symbol. The people of the Bible recognized the existence of four prevailing winds as issuing, broadly speaking, from the four cardinal points: north, south, east, and west.... The north wind is cold; the west wind coming from the Mediterranean Sea is moist; the south, warm; and the east, which crosses the sandy wastes of the Arabian Desert before reaching Palestine, can be violent and destructive. It was called 'the wind of the wilderness' (Job 1:19; Jeremiah 13:24; cf. Genesis 41:6, 23, 27; Ezekiel 27:26; Psalm 78:26)" (McConkie and Millet, *Doctrinal Commentary*, 2:187; see also the commentary in this volume on Mosiah 7:31).

Mosiah 12:9–17. Abinadi Is Cast into Prison

Why was Abinadi arrested? (12:9–11) "The trial of Abinadi arose out of the words he spoke to the townspeople within the city of Nephi (Mosiah 12:1–17)..... Two charges were to be leveled against Abinadi by the people: (1) that he had lied concerning the king and (2) that he had falsely prophesied evil about the people" (Welch, *Legal Cases in the Book of Mormon*, 151–58).

Why did the people accuse Abinadi of pretending to prophesy? (12:12) As set forth in Deuteronomy 18:18–20, the law of Moses prescribes the "death penalty for someone who presumes to prophesy and is a false prophet. They are saying that Abinadi has pretended to say this stuff about King Noah and calls it prophecy. This deed is worthy of death, so they should kill him" (Parker, "Abinadi").

Why did Noah hold a council with his priests to decide Abinadi's fate? (12:17) "That Noah shared jurisdiction with his priests is not surprising given the limited judicial role kings played in ancient Israel. Israel's king seldom participated in everyday judicial matters.... Similarly, King Noah participated in Abinadi's trial probably because the case arose in the capital city and involved charges of lying against the king (and his household). Because the claims against Abinadi also involved priestly matters (i.e., the charge of false prophecy against the people), King Noah could not adjudicate the case without respecting the jurisdiction of his priests" (Kerr, "Ancient Aspects of Nephite Kingship," 98). ✪

11 And again, he saith that thou shalt be as a stalk, even as a dry stalk of the field, which is run over by the beasts and trodden under foot.

12 And again, he saith thou shalt be as the blossoms of a thistle, which, when it is fully ripe, if the wind bloweth, it is driven forth upon the face of the land. And he pretendeth the Lord hath spoken it. And he saith all this shall come upon thee except thou repent, and this because of thine iniquities.

13 And now, O king, what great evil hast thou done, or what great sins have thy people committed, that we should be condemned of God or judged of this man?

14 And now, O king, behold, we are guiltless, and thou, O king, hast not sinned; therefore, this man has lied concerning you, and he has prophesied in vain.

15 And behold, we are strong, we shall not come into bondage, or be taken captive by our enemies; yea, and thou hast prospered in the land, and thou shalt also prosper.

16 Behold, here is the man, we deliver him into thy hands; thou mayest do with him as seemeth thee good.

17 And it came to pass that king Noah caused that Abinadi should be cast into prison; and he commanded that the priests should gather themselves together that he might hold a council with them what he should do with him.

Mosiah 12:18–32. Abinadi Defends Himself before the Wicked Priests of King Noah

18 And it came to pass that they said unto the king: Bring him hither that we may question him; and the king commanded that he should be brought before them.

19 And they began to question him, that they might cross him, that thereby they might have wherewith to accuse him; but he answered them boldly, and withstood all their questions, yea, to their astonishment; for he did withstand them in all their questions, and did confound them in all their words.

20 And it came to pass that one of them said unto him: What meaneth the words which are written, and which have been taught by our fathers, saying:

21 How beautiful upon the mountains are the feet of him that bringeth good tidings; that publisheth peace; that bringeth good tidings of good; that publisheth salvation; that saith unto Zion, Thy God reigneth;

22 Thy watchmen shall lift up the voice; with the voice together shall they sing; for they shall see eye to eye when the Lord shall bring again Zion;

23 Break forth into joy; sing together ye waste places of Jerusalem; for the Lord hath comforted his people, he hath redeemed Jerusalem;

24 The Lord hath made bare his holy arm in the eyes of all the nations, and all the ends of the earth shall see the salvation of our God?

Why did the priests want to cross-examine in order to accuse Abinadi? (12:18–19) "What was the thrust of their challenge? It appears that the priests intended, by their direct examination of Abinadi, to catch him in conflict with that scripture (Isaiah 52:7–10) and thereby convict him of false prophecy—a capital offence under the law of Moses (see Deuteronomy 18:20). In essence, they were apparently asking Abinadi why he bore tidings of doom and destruction when Isaiah had declared that the beautiful and true prophet brings good tidings and publishes peace" (Welch, "Isaiah 53, Mosiah 14, and the Book of Mormon," 294).

How did Abinadi withstand all their questions during his trial? (12:19–20) "The trial first focused on the charge of false prophecy. The priests challenged Abinadi to interpret Isaiah 52:7–10. They presumably thought this text showed that God had spoken 'comfort' to their own people. . . . They contended that whereas Isaiah extolled those who brought 'good tidings,' Abinadi spoke ill. Under such interpretation, Abinadi's curses conflicted with Isaiah and were held by the priests to be false and unlawful.

"Abinadi rebutted the priests in several ways. He accused them of misunderstanding and disobeying the law. He extracted from them an admission that salvation requires obedience to the law and then rehearsed to them the Ten Commandments" (Ludlow, *Encyclopedia of Mormonism*, 1:6). ⊕

What does it mean to publish peace and who shall publish it? (12:21) "Peace and good tidings; good tidings and peace . . . are among the ultimate blessings that the gospel of Jesus Christ brings a troubled world and the troubled people who live in it, solutions to personal struggles and human sinfulness, a source of strength for days of weariness and hours of genuine despair. . . . Ultimately it is Christ who is beautiful upon the mountain" (Holland, "Peaceable Things of the Kingdom," 82).

How have you experienced this peace in your life? What can you do to publish peace?

What prophetic statement was the priest of King Noah asking Abinadi to address? (12:21–24) "Having failed to cross up Abinadi, one of the priests asks the meaning of Isaiah 52:7–10 (Mosiah 12:21–24). This question, on the good tidings that bring peace, opened the door for Abinadi to leave the priests without excuse for their teachings to their people. At the same time Abinadi was magnifying his priesthood (see Jacob 1:19). Abinadi does not answer the question of the meaning of the Isaiah passage at this time, but he does so later" (Nyman, *These Records Are True*, 329–30).

What did it mean that the priests "pretend[ed] to teach" and had not "applied" their hearts to understanding? (12:25–27) "Undoubtedly the priests of Noah were men of learning and intellect, yet they had no wisdom, no understanding of the heart. In this they were typical of many who reject the gospel while professing to accept it. In our day it was of professors of religion that the Lord said, 'They draw near to me with their lips, but their hearts are far from me, they teach for doctrines the commandments of men, having a form of godliness, but they deny the power thereof' (Joseph Smith–History 1:19)" (McConkie and Millet, *Doctrinal Commentary*, 2:209). ◉

How does salvation come? (12:31–32) The priests "answer that salvation does come by the law of Moses.

"Abinadi refutes their answer by explaining that salvation comes only through Christ and that the law alone cannot save. He quotes the first two of the ten commandments given to Moses—'Thou shalt have no other God before me' and 'Thou shalt not make unto thee any graven image'—then asks the priests:

"'Have ye done all this? I say unto you, Nay, ye have not' (Mosiah 12:32–37)" (Matthews, "Abinadi," 27). ◉

25 And now Abinadi said unto them: Are you priests, and pretend to teach this people, and to understand the spirit of prophesying, and yet desire to know of me what these things mean?

26 I say unto you, wo be unto you for perverting the ways of the Lord! For if ye understand these things ye have not taught them; therefore, ye have perverted the ways of the Lord.

27 Ye have not applied your hearts to understanding; therefore, ye have not been wise. Therefore, what teach ye this people?

28 And they said: We teach the law of Moses.

29 And again he said unto them: If ye teach the law of Moses why do ye not keep it? Why do ye set your hearts upon riches? Why do ye commit whoredoms and spend your strength with harlots, yea, and cause this people to commit sin, that the Lord has cause to send me to prophesy against this people, yea, even a great evil against this people?

30 Know ye not that I speak the truth? Yea, ye know that I speak the truth; and you ought to tremble before God.

31 And it shall come to pass that ye shall be smitten for your iniquities, for ye have said that ye teach the law of Moses. And what know ye concerning the law of Moses? Doth salvation come by the law of Moses? What say ye?

32 And they answered and said that salvation did come by the law of Moses.

33 But now Abinadi said unto them: I know if ye keep the commandments of God ye shall be saved; yea, if ye keep the commandments which the Lord delivered unto Moses in the mount of Sinai, saying:

34 I am the Lord thy God, who hath brought thee out of the land of Egypt, out of the house of bondage.

35 Thou shalt have no other God before me.

36 Thou shalt not make unto thee any graven image, or any likeness of any thing in heaven above, or things which are in the earth beneath.

37 Now Abinadi said unto them, Have ye done all this? I say unto you, Nay, ye have not. And have ye taught this people that they should do all these things? I say unto you, Nay, ye have not.

CHAPTER 13

Abinadi is protected by divine power—He teaches the Ten Commandments—Salvation does not come by the law of Moses alone—God Himself will make an atonement and redeem His people. About 148 B.C.

1 And now when the king had heard these words, he said unto his priests: Away with this fellow, and slay him; for what have we to do with him, for he is mad.

2 And they stood forth and attempted to lay their hands on him; but he withstood them, and said unto them:

Mosiah 12:33–37. Abinadi Begins to Teach the Ten Commandments

Why did Abinadi emphasize the Ten Commandments? (12:33) "God has not left us alone to flounder over right and wrong in the area of personal ethics and morality. His laws are circumscribed in the Decalogue—the Ten Commandments. These laws embody our relationships with God, family and fellowmen. . . . To disregard them will lead to inevitable personal character loss and ruin" (*Teachings of Ezra Taft Benson*, 353). ●

In modern times, what gods are often placed ahead of Heavenly Father? (12:35) "What other priorities are being 'served' ahead of God by persons—even religious persons—in our day? Consider these possibilities, all common in our world:

"• Cultural and family traditions

"• Political correctness

"• Career aspirations

"• Material possessions

"• Recreational pursuits

"• Power, prominence, and prestige

" . . . The question posed by the second commandment is 'What is our ultimate priority?' Are we serving priorities or gods ahead of the God we profess to worship? Have we forgotten to follow the Savior who taught that if we love Him, we will keep His commandments? (see John 14:15). If so, our priorities have been turned upside down by the spiritual apathy and undisciplined appetites so common in our day" (Oaks, "No Other Gods," 72–75).

Mosiah 13:1–10. Abinadi Is Protected by the Lord

Why would Noah accuse Abinadi of being mad? (13:1) The lives of the Lord's prophets often reflect Jesus Christ's own life. This is the same accusation made against Jesus (see John 10:20). "No insanity defense existed under biblical law. Even a 'mad' person could be punished if he had broken the law. . . . Being 'mad' (*shāg*) was a derogatory label often used to describe the ravings of false prophets in the Old Testament" (Welch, *Legal Cases in the Book of Mormon*, 179).

What spiritual state came over Abinadi? (13:5) "Abinadi, like Stephen in the New Testament, is so filled with the Holy Ghost that he has been transfigured. Of Stephen's defense before a like council in the Old World we read: 'All that sat in the council, looking steadfastly on him, saw his face as it had been the face of an angel' (Acts 6:15). Those rejecting the testimony of Abinadi or Stephen are condemned by that which they have seen, that which they have heard, and that which they have felt within their souls" (McConkie and Millet, *Doctrinal Commentary*, 2:213). ●

What was Abinadi's message? (13:7) Abinadi declared "a prophecy and explanation of the coming of Christ to redeem humankind, and also his answer to the question the priests had asked him about a passage from Isaiah (Mosiah 14–16). His teachings at this juncture constitute five and one-half pages of material in our present Book of Mormon. He cites Moses and Isaiah particularly, and all of the prophets generally, as having taught that God himself would come down from heaven and dwell in the form of a man on the earth and redeem humankind from the Fall" (Matthews, "Abinadi," *Mosiah*, 111).

What is significant about Abinadi's claim that he would be a type and a shadow? (13:10) "The Book of Mormon prophet who probably thought about scriptural symbolism and taught it more effectively than any other is Abinadi. Very early he warned King Noah that whatever he would do to Abinadi would be 'a type and a shadow of things to come'—and indeed it was. ...And ...[Abinadi], like Christ, died lamenting that those who claimed a belief in the law of Moses could not recognize the Messianic teachings ... toward which that law in its purity had always been directed" (Holland, *Christ and the New Covenant*, 171–73).

3 Touch me not, for God shall smite you if ye lay your hands upon me, for I have not delivered the message which the Lord sent me to deliver; neither have I told you that which ye requested that I should tell; therefore, God will not suffer that I shall be destroyed at this time.

4 But I must fulfil the commandments wherewith God has commanded me; and because I have told you the truth ye are angry with me. And again, because I have spoken the word of God ye have judged me that I am mad.

5 Now it came to pass after Abinadi had spoken these words that the people of king Noah durst not lay their hands on him, for the Spirit of the Lord was upon him; and his face shone with exceeding luster, even as Moses' did while in the mount of Sinai, while speaking with the Lord.

6 And he spake with power and authority from God; and he continued his words, saying:

7 Ye see that ye have not power to slay me, therefore I finish my message. Yea, and I perceive that it cuts you to your hearts because I tell you the truth concerning your iniquities.

8 Yea, and my words fill you with wonder and amazement, and with anger.

9 But I finish my message; and then it matters not whither I go, if it so be that I am saved.

10 But this much I tell you, what you do with me, after this, shall be as a type and a shadow of things which are to come.

Mosiah 13:11–24. Abinadi Continues to Teach the Ten Commandments

11 And now I read unto you the remainder of the commandments of God, for I perceive that they are not written in your hearts; I perceive that ye have studied and taught iniquity the most part of your lives.

What does it mean to have the commandments written in our hearts? (13:11) "To have the commandments written in your hearts is a prevalent Old Testament concept. Isaiah invites 'the people in whose heart is written my law' to hearken (Isaiah 51:7). Jeremiah, whose record was only partly upon the plates of brass (see 1 Nephi 5:13), quotes the Lord: 'I will put my law in their inward parts, and write it upon their hearts' (Jeremiah 31:33). Paul quotes the prophecy of Jeremiah (Hebrews 8:8–10) and paraphrases it to the Corinthians (2 Corinthians 3:3). A Proverb advises to 'write [the commandments] upon the table of thine heart' (3:3). The priests of Noah had chosen iniquity rather than following this symbolic internalizing of the commandments" (Nyman, *These Records Are True*, 335–36).

12 And now, ye remember that I said unto you: Thou shalt not make unto thee any graven image, or any likeness of things which are in heaven above, or which are in the earth beneath, or which are in the water under the earth.

Where did Abinadi obtain the Ten Commandments? (13:12–24) "It should be remembered that the brass plates Nephi obtained contained the five books of Moses (see 1 Nephi 5:10–11). This record, which would have contained the Ten Commandments, had been passed down by Nephite prophets and record keepers. Evidently the contents of the brass plates were known to Noah and his priests because they quoted from Isaiah and referred to the law of Moses (see Mosiah 12:20–24, 28)" (*Book of Mormon Student Manual* [1989], 63).

13 And again: Thou shalt not bow down thyself unto them, nor serve them; for I the Lord thy God am a jealous God, visiting the iniquities of the fathers upon the children, unto the third and fourth generations of them that hate me;

14 And showing mercy unto thousands of them that love me and keep my commandments.

15 Thou shalt not take the name of the Lord thy God in vain; for the Lord will not hold him guiltless that taketh his name in vain.

16 Remember the sabbath day, to keep it holy.

17 Six days shalt thou labor, and do all thy work;

Mosiah 13:25–35. The Law of Moses Points to Christ

What does Abinadi teach about the law of Moses and salvation through Jesus Christ? (13:28) "After all our obedience and good works, we cannot be saved from death or the effects of our individual sins without the grace extended by the atonement of Jesus Christ.

18 But the seventh day, the sabbath of the Lord thy God, thou shalt not do any work, thou, nor thy son, nor thy daughter, thy man-servant, nor thy maid-servant, nor thy cattle, nor thy stranger that is within thy gates;

19 For in six days the Lord made heaven and earth, and the sea, and all that in them is; wherefore the Lord blessed the sabbath day, and hallowed it.

20 Honor thy father and thy mother, that thy days may be long upon the land which the Lord thy God giveth thee.

21 Thou shalt not kill.

22 Thou shalt not commit adultery. Thou shalt not steal.

23 Thou shalt not bear false witness against thy neighbor.

24 Thou shalt not covet thy neighbor's house, thou shalt not covet thy neighbor's wife, nor his man-servant, nor his maid-servant, nor his ox, nor his ass, nor anything that is thy neighbor's.

25 And it came to pass that after Abinadi had made an end of these sayings that he said unto them: Have ye taught this people that they should observe to do all these things for to keep these commandments?

26 I say unto you, Nay; for if ye had, the Lord would not have caused me to come forth and to prophesy evil concerning this people.

27 And now ye have said that salvation cometh by the law of Moses. I say unto you that it is expedient that ye should keep the law of Moses as yet; but I say unto you, that the time shall come when it shall no more be expedient to keep the law of Moses.

28 And moreover, I say unto you, that salvation doth not come by the law alone; and were it not for the atonement, which God himself shall make for the sins and iniquities

of his people, that they must unavoidably perish, notwithstanding the law of Moses.

29 And now I say unto you that it was expedient that there should be a law given to the children of Israel, yea, even a very strict law; for they were a stiffnecked people, quick to do iniquity, and slow to remember the Lord their God;

30 Therefore there was a law given them, yea, a law of performances and of ordinances, a law which they were to observe strictly from day to day, to keep them in remembrance of God and their duty towards him.

31 But behold, I say unto you, that all these things were types of things to come.

32 And now, did they understand the law? I say unto you, Nay, they did not all understand the law; and this because of the hardness of their hearts; for they understood not that there could not any man be saved except it were through the redemption of God.

33 For behold, did not Moses prophesy unto them concerning the coming of the Messiah, and that God should redeem his people? Yea, and even all the prophets who have prophesied ever since the world began—have they not spoken more or less concerning these things?

34 Have they not said that God himself should come down among the children of men, and take upon him the form of man, and go forth in mighty power upon the face of the earth?

35 Yea, and have they not said also that he should bring to pass the resurrection of the dead, and that he, himself, should be oppressed and afflicted?

The Book of Mormon makes this clear. It teaches that 'salvation doth not come by the law alone' (Mosiah 13:28). In other words, salvation does not come simply by keeping the commandments. 'By the law no flesh is justified' (2 Ne. 2:5). Even those who try to obey and serve God with all their heart, might, mind, and strength are 'unprofitable servants' (Mosiah 2:21). Man cannot earn his own salvation. He cannot be cleansed by personal suffering for his own sins" (Oaks, "Another Testament of Jesus Christ," 67). ☉

What was the purpose of the law of Moses? (13:30) "Verse 30 states that this law, which included the law of carnal commandments, consisted of a law of ordinances and performances. The ordinances and performances were teaching instruments of the law of carnal commandments. A synonym for the word *carnal* is *flesh*. The law of carnal commandments was, therefore, commandments intended to help the children of Israel to control the flesh—to develop self-control and self-discipline in their lives. It was to help them to get a handle on their lives so they could begin to focus on the basic fundamentals that would lead them to Christ. That was its primary purpose and the spirit and the intent of the law of carnal commandments" (Brandt, "The Law of Moses and the Law of Christ," 136).

Who is the God that shall "come down among the children of men"? (13:33–35) "The term *God* generally refers to our Heavenly Father, and it is Him whom we ultimately worship. It is also true that Jesus Christ is God. . . . 'We claim scriptural authority for the assertion that Jesus Christ was and is God the Creator, the God who revealed Himself to Adam, Enoch, . . . the God of Abraham, Isaac and Jacob . . . from Moses to Malachi; the God of the Old Testament record; and the God of the Nephites. We affirm that Jesus Christ was and is Jehovah, the Eternal One' (*Jesus the Christ*, 3rd ed. [1916], 32)" (*Book of Mormon Student Manual* [1989], 152).

Mosiah 14:1–3. Jesus, the Son of God, Experiences Mortal Life

Why did Abinadi teach Isaiah 53? (14:1) Abinadi poignantly taught "that 'God should redeem his people,' that 'God himself' would come down from heaven, take upon himself by birth the form of a man, and 'go forth in mighty power upon the face of the earth.' To reinforce that declaration Abinadi quoted the 53rd chapter of Isaiah—surely the most powerful and extended passage regarding Christ in all the Old Testament—developing the symbolism of the Savior not so much as a shepherd but as a sheep" (Holland, *Christ and the New Covenant*, 152). ⊕

How did Jesus Christ appear to others? (14:2) "There is no mystique, no dynamic appearance, no halo around his head, thunders do not roll and lightnings do not flash at his appearance. He is the Son of the Highest, but he walks and appears as the offspring of the lowest. He is a man among men, appearing, speaking, dressing, seeming in all outward respects as they are" (McConkie, *Promised Messiah*, 447–78).

In what ways was Jesus Christ despised and rejected? (14:3) "Jesus had come unto his own, and his own received him not! The leaders of the people rejected his words when he preached in the temple at Passover time. The common people of Nazareth hardened their hearts against his words when he spoke to them in their synagogue. And so it would be throughout his whole ministry; save for a few believing souls, he was 'despised and rejected of men' (Isa. 53:3); and eventually his own would lead him before Roman overlords, as they raised their voices in chants of 'Crucify him, Crucify him'" (McConkie, *Mortal Messiah*, 2:27).

Mosiah 14:4–12. Through Suffering the Pains, Sins, and Sorrows of the World, Jesus Christ Works Out the Atonement

How does Jesus Christ know our sorrows? (14:4) Jesus Christ "knows by actual, personal experience, because not only did He suffer pains, afflictions, and temptations of every kind during His second estate, but He took upon Himself our sins as well as our pains,

CHAPTER 14

Isaiah speaks messianically—The Messiah's humiliation and sufferings are set forth—He makes His soul an offering for sin and makes intercession for transgressors—Compare Isaiah 53. About 148 B.C.

1 Yea, even doth not Isaiah say: Who hath believed our report, and to whom is the arm of the Lord revealed?

2 For he shall grow up before him as a tender plant, and as a root out of dry ground; he hath no form nor comeliness; and when we shall see him there is no beauty that we should desire him.

3 He is despised and rejected of men; a man of sorrows, and acquainted with grief; and we hid as it were our faces from him; he was despised, and we esteemed him not.

4 Surely he has borne our griefs, and carried our sorrows; yet we did esteem him stricken, smitten of God, and afflicted.

5 But he was wounded for our transgressions, he was bruised for our iniquities; the chastisement of our peace was upon him; and with his stripes we are healed.

6 All we, like sheep, have gone astray; we have turned every one to his own way; and the Lord hath laid on him the iniquities of us all.

7 He was oppressed, and he was afflicted, yet he opened not his mouth; he is brought as a lamb to the slaughter, and as a sheep before her shearers is dumb so he opened not his mouth.

8 He was taken from prison and from judgment; and who shall declare his generation? For he was cut off out of the land of the living; for the transgressions of my people was he stricken.

9 And he made his grave with the wicked, and with the rich in his death; because he had done no evil, neither was any deceit in his mouth.

sicknesses, and infirmities (see Alma 7:11–12). Thus He knew, not in abstraction but in actuality, 'according to the flesh,' the whole of human suffering. He bore our infirmities before we bore them. He knows perfectly well how to succor us. We can tell Him nothing of pain, temptation, or affliction; He learned 'according to the flesh,' and His triumph was complete!" (Maxwell, *We Will Prove Them Herewith*, 46).

What does the Savior's agony and suffering mean to you personally? (14:4–6) "No member of this Church must ever forget the terrible price paid by our Redeemer who gave His life that all men might live— the agony of Gethsemane, the bitter mockery of His trial, the vicious crown of thorns tearing at His flesh, . . . the cross, the instrument of His torture, the terrible device designed to destroy the Man of Peace. . . .

"We cannot forget that. We must never forget it, for here our Savior, our Redeemer, the Son of God, gave Himself a vicarious sacrifice for each of us" (Hinckley, "Symbol of Our Faith," 4). ⊕

When was Isaiah's prophecy that the Savior "opened not his mouth" fulfilled during His ministry? (14:7) "This prophecy was fulfilled when Jesus appeared before Herod, who 'questioned with him in many words; but he answered him nothing' (Luke 23:9). When Jesus stood before Pilate, Mark records, 'the chief priests accused him of many things: but he answered nothing. And Pilate asked him again, saying, Answerest thou nothing? behold how many things they witness against thee. But Jesus yet answered nothing' (Mark 15:3–5)" (Parry et al., *Understanding Isaiah*, 475–76).

What does the statement "he was taken from prison and from judgment" mean? (14:8) This phrase means that Jesus Christ "was taken by force (Hebrew *'utser*) and without justice (Hebrew *mishpat*)" (Parry et al., *Understanding Isaiah*, 476).

How was Isaiah's prophecy that "he made his grave with the wicked, and with the rich in his death" fulfilled? (14:9) "His grave's being with the wicked is a prophecy of Christ's being crucified between two thieves (see Luke 23:32–33; Matthew 27:38; Mark 15:27; John 19:18). His grave's being with the rich is a prophecy of his being buried in the tomb of the rich man Joseph of Arimathea (see Matthew 27:57–60; Mark 15:42–46; Luke 23:50–53; John 19:38–42)" (Nyman, *Great Are the Words of Isaiah*, 209).

What was pleasing to Heavenly Father about Jesus Christ being bruised? (14:10) "Our Father in Heaven was not pleased with the treatment His Son received at the hands of wicked men, but He was pleased with His Son's willingness to obediently fulfill the great atoning sacrifice" (Brewster, *Isaiah Plain and Simple*, 257).

How did the Messiah "[pour] out his soul unto death"? (14:12) "In Gethsemane, the Savior 'descended below all things' (D&C 88:6) as He bore the burden of sin for every human being. At Golgotha, He 'poured out his soul unto death' (Isaiah 53:12 [and Mosiah 14:12]), and His great heart literally broke with an all-encompassing love for the children of God. When we remember the Savior and His suffering, our hearts too will break in gratitude for the Anointed One" (Porter, "Broken Heart and a Contrite Spirit," 32).

Mosiah 15:1–5. Abinadi Explains How Jesus Christ Can Be Called Both Father and Son

Which member of the Godhead was Abinadi referencing? (15:1) Jesus Christ was the God of the Old Testament and was known as Jehovah. When Abinadi taught that "God himself shall come down among the children of men," he was referring to Jehovah and His mortal ministry (see 1 Nephi 11:16–33; 19:10).

What does it mean that the Savior subjected the flesh to the will of the Father? (15:2) This phrase means that "the will of the Son was swallowed up in the will of the Father. That is, the flesh became subject to the Spirit, the mortal subject to the immortal. 'I seek not mine own will,' Jesus explained, 'but the will of the Father which hath sent me' (John 5:30). Further, 'I came down from heaven, not to do mine own will, but the will of him that sent me' (John 6:38). . . . Jesus did what Elohim would have him to do: he carried out to the full extent the terms and conditions of the plan of the Father" (McConkie and Millet, *Doctrinal Commentary*, 2:229–30).

10 Yet it pleased the Lord to bruise him; he hath put him to grief; when thou shalt make his soul an offering for sin he shall see his seed, he shall prolong his days, and the pleasure of the Lord shall prosper in his hand.

11 He shall see the travail of his soul, and shall be satisfied; by his knowledge shall my righteous servant justify many; for he shall bear their iniquities.

12 Therefore will I divide him a portion with the great, and he shall divide the spoil with the strong; because he hath poured out his soul unto death; and he was numbered with the transgressors; and he bore the sins of many, and made intercession for the transgressors.

CHAPTER 15

How Christ is both the Father and the Son—He will make intercession and bear the transgressions of His people—They and all the holy prophets are His seed—He brings to pass the Resurrection—Little children have eternal life. About 148 B.C.

1 And now Abinadi said unto them: I would that ye should understand that God himself shall come down among the children of men, and shall redeem his people.

2 And because he dwelleth in flesh he shall be called the Son of God, and having subjected the flesh to the will of the Father, being the Father and the Son—

3 The Father, because he was conceived by the power of God; and the Son, because of the flesh; thus becoming the Father and Son—

"Jesus Christ is known as Father by virtue of his role as the Creator. . . . Christ is [also] the Father through spiritual rebirth. . . . Our Lord acted and spoke on behalf of the Almighty Elohim and is therefore known as Father by divine investiture of authority, meaning that [the Father] . . . 'has authorized him to speak in the first person as though he were the original primal Father' (McConkie, *Promised Messiah*, 63). . . . Jesus Christ is Father because Elohim has literally invested his Son with his own attributes and powers" (Millet, "Abinadi's Messianic Sermon," 101). ⊕

How are the Father and the Son one God? (15:4–5) "Abinadi's purpose in this sermon . . . is to declare more than the unity of the Godhead; his is 'the pronouncement of pronouncements, the doctrine of doctrines, the message of messages, which is that Christ is God. And if it were not so, he could not save us' (*Promised Messiah*, 98). . . . Abinadi is declaring the true doctrine of the Incarnation: he is teaching and testifying that God (Jehovah) will become a man (Jesus), that he who was the 'Great Spirit' . . . shall dwell in a tabernacle of clay. . . . Father and Son, Spirit and flesh, are brought together in one to form the 'one God' who is the very Eternal Father of heaven and earth—Jesus Christ" (McConkie and Millet, *Doctrinal Commentary*, 2:230–31). ⊕

4 And they are one God, yea, the very Eternal Father of heaven and of earth.

5 And thus the flesh becoming subject to the Spirit, or the Son to the Father, being one God, suffereth temptation, and yieldeth not to the temptation, but suffereth himself to be mocked, and scourged, and cast out, and disowned by his people.

Mosiah 15:6–9. Abinadi Prophesies of Jesus Christ's Mortal Ministry

6 And after all this, after working many mighty miracles among the children of men, he shall be led, yea, even as Isaiah said, as a sheep before the shearer is dumb, so he opened not his mouth.

7 Yea, even so he shall be led, crucified, and slain, the flesh becoming subject even unto death, the will of the Son being swallowed up in the will of the Father.

What does the phrase "swallowed up in the will of the Father" mean in this verse? (15:7) Aligning our will with God's will requires faith. "The Savior is the perfect example of how to use our agency best. . . . Abinadi aptly described the Savior's submission as 'the will of the Son being swallowed up in the will of the Father' (Mosiah 15:7).

"Submitting one's will to God's is not always easy. . . . The implication is that submitting our will to God's will requires sacrifice and likely some suffering" (Clyde J. Williams, "According to Our Will," 38).

8 And thus God breaketh the bands of death, having gained the victory over death; giving the Son power to make intercession for the children of men—

9 Having ascended into heaven, having the bowels of mercy; being filled with compassion towards the children of men; standing betwixt them and justice; having broken the bands of death, taken upon himself their iniquity and their transgressions, having redeemed them, and satisfied the demands of justice.

Mosiah 15:10–13. The Atonement of Jesus Christ Will Save All Those Who Obey the Words of the Prophets

What does the phrase "who shall declare his generation" mean? (15:10) "One text is the great messianic utterance of Isaiah, which he couched in these simple words: 'Who shall declare his generation?' (Isaiah 53:8). This means, 'Who will give his genesis? Who will reveal his genealogy? Who will give the source from whence he sprang? Who will announce the divinity of the mortal Messiah?' We might also take another text, and this is one that Jesus himself spoke. He said, 'Whose son is he?'... He is the firstborn spirit child of God, our Heavenly Father.... The Lord Jesus, the great Jehovah, the creator of all things under the Father, is the firstborn of all that spirit host" (McConkie, "Who Shall Declare His Generation?" 554–55). ◉

Who are the seed of Jesus Christ? (15:10–13) "Seed is the progeny of the species. Among us men it is our children. The children of the Lord Jesus Christ are those who believe in him and obey his gospel, those who exercise the power given them to become his sons and his daughters, and who as a consequence are adopted into his family.... Included in this group of whom Abinadi speaks are all those who have been faithful from the day of father Adam to that moment; all are members of their Messiah's family.... In

10 And now I say unto you, who shall declare his generation? Behold, I say unto you, that when his soul has been made an offering for sin he shall see his seed. And now what say ye? And who shall be his seed?

11 Behold I say unto you, that whosoever has heard the words of the prophets, yea, all the holy prophets who have prophesied concerning the coming of the Lord—I say unto you, that all those who have hearkened unto their words, and believed that the Lord would redeem his people, and have looked forward to that day for a remission of their sins, I say unto you, that these are his seed, or they are the heirs of the kingdom of God.

12 For these are they whose sins he has borne; these are they for whom he has died, to redeem them from their transgressions. And now, are they not his seed?

Abinadi's Testimony of Christ as the Father and the Son

"One of the grandest messianic sermons ever delivered was Abinadi's defense before King Noah and his wicked priests, particularly that portion constituting chapter fifteen of Mosiah. The first five verses of this chapter are especially poignant and may be understood in light of ... the ministry of Christ as the Father and the Son.... Key doctrinal matters are given in verses one through five:

"1. God himself—Jehovah, the God of ancient Israel—will come to earth, take a physical body, and bring to pass redemption for all men.

"2. Because Jehovah/Jesus Christ will have a physical body and dwell in the *flesh*—like every other mortal son and daughter of God—he will be known as the *Son* of God. On the other hand, because he will be conceived by the power of God and will thus have within him the powers of the *Spirit*, he will be known as the *Father*. This same doctrine is given in a modern revelation through the Prophet Joseph Smith (see D&C 93:4, 12–14).

"3. The will of the Son is to be swallowed up in the will of the Father. That is, the *flesh* will become subject to the *Spirit*, the mortal subject to the immortal. 'I seek not mine own will,' Jesus explained, 'but the will of the Father which hath sent me' (John 5:30; compare 6:38). In short, Jesus will do what the Father would have him do.

"4. Thus Christ will be both the Father and the Son. He will be called the Father because he was conceived by the power of God and inherited all of the divine endowments, particularly immortality, from his exalted Sire. He will be called the Son because of the flesh—his mortal inheritance from his mother, Mary. Therefore Christ will be both *flesh* and *spirit*, both *man* and *God*, both *Son* and *Father*. And they—the Son and the Father, the man and the God, the flesh and the spirit—are to be blended wondrously in one being, Jesus Christ, 'the very Eternal Father of heaven and of earth'" (Millet, *Power of the Word*, 122–23).

13 Yea, and are not the prophets, every one that has opened his mouth to prophesy, that has not fallen into transgression, I mean all the holy prophets ever since the world began? I say unto you that they are his seed.

14 And these are they who have published peace, who have brought good tidings of good, who have published salvation; and said unto Zion: Thy God reigneth!

15 And O how beautiful upon the mountains were their feet!

16 And again, how beautiful upon the mountains are the feet of those that are still publishing peace!

17 And again, how beautiful upon the mountains are the feet of those who shall hereafter publish peace, yea, from this time henceforth and forever!

18 And behold, I say unto you, this is not all. For O how beautiful upon the mountains are the feet of him that bringeth good tidings, that is the founder of peace, yea, even the Lord, who has redeemed his people; yea, him who has granted salvation unto his people;

19 For were it not for the redemption which he hath made for his people, which was prepared from the foundation of the world, I say unto you, were it not for this, all mankind must have perished.

20 But behold, the bands of death shall be broken, and the Son reigneth, and hath power over the dead; therefore, he bringeth to pass the resurrection of the dead.

21 And there cometh a resurrection, even a first resurrection; yea, even a resurrection of those that have been, and who are, and who shall be, even until the resurrection of Christ—for so shall he be called.

22 And now, the resurrection of all the prophets, and all those that have believed in

principle the same thing will apply to all the faithful yet to come, all who shall be spiritually born of him" (McConkie, *Promised Messiah*, 359–60). ⊕

Mosiah 15:14–20. Abinadi Exclaims, "How Beautiful upon the Mountains Are the Feet" of Those Who Speak the Truth about Salvation

What is the meaning of the expression "how beautiful upon the mountains are the feet of him that bringeth good tidings"? (15:15–18) "This expression is found six times in the scriptures. . . . The singular pronoun *him* may refer specifically to Christ, the ultimate source of the gospel's good news. In addition, all those who preach the gospel are beautiful because of the wonderful message they take to others. By the Lord's definition, *mountains* describes the place where the gospel is preached, regardless of the actual physical location in the world. As we read in latter-day revelation: 'Thou shalt declare glad tidings, yea, publish it upon the mountains, and upon every high place, and among every people that thou shalt be permitted to see' (D&C 19:29)" (Parry et al., *Understanding Isaiah*, 464). ⊕

Mosiah 15:21–25. Abinadi Tells Who Will Be Resurrected at the Time of Christ's Resurrection

their words, or all those that have kept the commandments of God, shall come forth in the first resurrection; therefore, they are the first resurrection.

23 They are raised to dwell with God who has redeemed them; thus they have eternal life through Christ, who has broken the bands of death.

24 And these are those who have part in the first resurrection; and these are they that have died before Christ came, in their ignorance, not having salvation declared unto them. And thus the Lord bringeth about the restoration of these; and they have a part in the first resurrection, or have eternal life, being redeemed by the Lord.

25 And little children also have eternal life.

Why does Abinadi include little children in the first resurrection? (15:25) "Little children shall be saved. They are alive in Christ and shall have eternal life. For them the family unit will continue, and the fulness of exaltation is theirs. No blessing shall be withheld. They shall rise in immortal glory, grow to full maturity, and live forever in the highest heaven of the celestial kingdom—all through the merits and mercy and grace of the Holy Messiah, all because of the atoning sacrifice of Him who died that we might live.... Truly it is one of the sweetest and most soul-satisfying doctrines of the gospel!" (McConkie, "Salvation of Little Children," 3–7).

Mosiah 15:26–27. Wicked People Will Not Be Redeemed

How does Abinadi help us to better understand who will be redeemed? (15:26–27) "Redemption, in its highest sense, consists in being delivered from death and sin and inheriting exaltation in the celestial kingdom. While salvation is made available to the penitent and the obedient, 'the wicked remain as though there had been no redemption made, except it be the loosing of the bands of death' (Alma 11:41); that is, the wicked are redeemed only in the sense that they are delivered from hell, eventually escape the perils of the second death, and come forth to a kingdom of glory in the resurrection" (McConkie and Millet, *Doctrinal Commentary*, 2:240).

26 But behold, and fear, and tremble before God, for ye ought to tremble; for the Lord redeemeth none such that rebel against him and die in their sins; yea, even all those that have perished in their sins ever since the world began, that have wilfully rebelled against God, that have known the commandments of God, and would not keep them; these are they that have no part in the first resurrection.

27 Therefore ought ye not to tremble? For salvation cometh to none such; for the Lord hath redeemed none such; yea, neither can the Lord redeem such; for he cannot deny himself; for he cannot deny justice when it has its claim.

28 And now I say unto you that the time shall come that the salvation of the Lord shall be declared to every nation, kindred, tongue, and people.

29 Yea, Lord, thy watchmen shall lift up their voice; with the voice together shall they sing; for they shall see eye to eye, when the Lord shall bring again Zion.

30 Break forth into joy, sing together, ye waste places of Jerusalem; for the Lord hath comforted his people, he hath redeemed Jerusalem.

Mosiah 15:28–31. In the Last Days, Salvation Will Be Declared to All People

Why will watchmen "lift up their voice"? (15:29) "Watchmen are charged with the responsibility of safeguarding the people of the Lord and of keeping the doctrines of His gospel pure. Speaking for himself and others called to serve in the governing councils of The Church of Jesus Christ of Latter-day Saints, President Spencer W. Kimball declared, 'We continue to warn the people and plead with them, for we are watchmen upon the towers, and in our hands we have a trumpet which we must blow loudly and sound the alarm'" (Brewster, *Isaiah Plain and Simple*, 239).

When will the Lord bring again Zion? (15:29) "The building up of Zion is a cause that has interested the people of God in every age; it is a theme upon which prophets, priests and kings have dwelt with peculiar delight; they have looked forward with joyful anticipation to the day in which we live; and fired with heavenly and joyful anticipations they have sung and written and prophesied of this our day; but they died without the sight; we are the favored people that

What Is the Order in the Resurrection?

"In Christ shall all be made alive. . . . But every man in his own order: Christ the firstfruits; afterward they that are Christ's at his coming" (1 Corinthians 15:22–23).

"Who has part in the 'first resurrection'? 'All those that have kept the commandments of God': Those who die 'in their ignorance, not having salvation declared unto them' but who 'would have received it if they had' heard it. 'And little children' [Mosiah 15:22–25; D&C 137:7]" (Garner, *Search These Things Diligently*, 151).

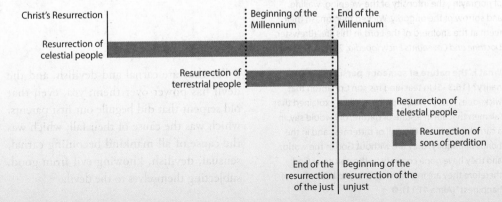

God has made choice of to bring about the Latter-day glory; it is left for us to see, participate in and help to roll forward the Latter-day glory" (*Joseph Smith* [manual], 513). ⊕

What is the meaning of the Lord making bare His arm? (15:31) "In ancient times, men prepared for battle by throwing their cloak away from the shoulder of their fighting arm (Ps. 74:11). At the second coming of Christ, God will make bare his arm when he shows forth his power for all to see (D&C 133:2–3)" (Parry et al., *Understanding Isaiah*, 466).

Mosiah 16:1–6. God Will Save Those Who Repent of Their Sins

What does the phrase "shall see eye to eye" mean? (16:1) "The expression eye to eye is figurative, and here it means that all people, as one, will understand and discern that the judgments of the Lord are just. Their minds will apprehend His justice and unitedly they will sing His praises" (Reynolds and Sjodahl, *Commentary on the Book of Mormon*, 2:177).

What is meant by the phrase "gnash their teeth"? (16:2) "The description of the wicked as 'weeping, wailing and gnashing of teeth' upon their receiving the divine decrees pronounced upon them is common in scripture (D&C 19:5; 85:9; 101:91; 124:8, 52; 133:73; Alma 40:13; Moses 1:22; Matt. 8:12). . . . In the literal sense, the gnashing of teeth consists in grinding and striking the teeth together in anger. This expressive act, indicative of hate and violent animosity was adopted by the prophets as the proverbial way of portraying the intensity of the weeping, wailing, and sorrow of the ungodly. Wicked men gnash their teeth at the anointed of the Lord in this life" (Brewster, *Doctrine and Covenants Encyclopedia*, 213).

What is the nature of someone persisting in carnality? (16:3–5) In teaching his son Corianton that wickedness never was happiness, Alma explained that "all men that are in a state of nature, or I would say, in a carnal state, are in the gall of bitterness and in the bonds of iniquity; they are without God in the world, and they have gone contrary to the nature of God; therefore they are in a state contrary to the nature of happiness" (Alma 41:11). ⊕

31 The Lord hath made bare his holy arm in the eyes of all the nations; and all the ends of the earth shall see the salvation of our God.

CHAPTER 16

God redeems men from their lost and fallen state—Those who are carnal remain as though there were no redemption—Christ brings to pass a resurrection to endless life or to endless damnation. About 148 B.C.

1 And now, it came to pass that after Abinadi had spoken these words he stretched forth his hand and said: The time shall come when all shall see the salvation of the Lord; when every nation, kindred, tongue, and people shall see eye to eye and shall confess before God that his judgments are just.

2 And then shall the wicked be cast out, and they shall have cause to howl, and weep, and wail, and gnash their teeth; and this because they would not hearken unto the voice of the Lord; therefore the Lord redeemeth them not.

3 For they are carnal and devilish, and the devil has power over them; yea, even that old serpent that did beguile our first parents, which was the cause of their fall; which was the cause of all mankind becoming carnal, sensual, devilish, knowing evil from good, subjecting themselves to the devil.

4 Thus all mankind were lost; and behold, they would have been endlessly lost were it not that God redeemed his people from their lost and fallen state.

5 But remember that he that persists in his own carnal nature, and goes on in the ways of sin and rebellion against God, remaineth in his fallen state and the devil hath all power over him. Therefore he is as though there was no redemption made, being an enemy to God; and also is the devil an enemy to God.

6 And now if Christ had not come into the world, speaking of things to come as though they had already come, there could have been no redemption.

7 And if Christ had not risen from the dead, or have broken the bands of death that the grave should have no victory, and that death should have no sting, there could have been no resurrection.

8 But there is a resurrection, therefore the grave hath no victory, and the sting of death is swallowed up in Christ.

9 He is the light and the life of the world; yea, a light that is endless, that can never be darkened; yea, and also a life which is endless, that there can be no more death.

10 Even this mortal shall put on immortality, and this corruption shall put on incorruption, and shall be brought to stand before the bar of God, to be judged of him according to their works whether they be good or whether they be evil—

Why is redemption only in Jesus Christ? (16:6) "One might look for another redeemer; one might speculate as to other possibilities, but it will be in vain. The Savior was not just the best candidate, he was much more—he was the only candidate. The reason is straightforward: he was the only one of the Father's children who came to earth with infinitely divine qualities and thus possessed the infinite power necessary to perform the atoning act. Anyone else simply did not have the power and means to overcome physical and spiritual death" (Callister, *Infinite Atonement*, 331).

Mosiah 16:7–12. We Will All Be Resurrected Either to Endless Life or to Endless Damnation

How can a personal testimony of the reality of the resurrection affect all aspects of our lives? (16:7–8) "The assurance of resurrection and immortality affects how we look on the physical challenges of mortality, how we live our mortal lives, and how we relate to those around us. . . . The assurance of resurrection also gives us a powerful incentive to keep the commandments of God . . . [and] encouragement for us to fulfill our family responsibilities in mortality. . . . Our sure knowledge of a resurrection to immortality also gives us the courage to face our own death. The assurance of immortality also helps us bear the mortal separations involved in the death of our loved ones" (Oaks, "Resurrection," 15). ☉

What is meant by endless damnation? (16:11)
"Abinadi uses the term endless damnation . . . to refer to the resurrected state of all the rebellious, those who come forth in the resurrection of the unjust, those who refused to repent when the gospel was offered to them but who chose to go their own carnal ways, receiving eventually an inheritance in the telestial kingdom. Though they attain a kingdom of glory, yet to all eternity they are damned, cannot go where God and Christ are (D&C 76:112). . . . Their eternal condemnation is to have limitations imposed upon them so that they cannot progress to the state of godhood and gain a fullness of all things" (McConkie, *Mormon Doctrine*, 234–35).

To what do the "arms of mercy" refer? (16:12) "The image of the arm of mercy . . . occurs in Mosiah 16:12; Alma 5:33; 19:36; 29:10; and 3 Nephi 9:14. Each time, the Lord is offering . . . the chance to take full advantage of the Atonement" (Seely, "Image of the Hand of God," 148).

Mosiah 16:13–15. Abinadi Warns King Noah and His Priests to Repent

What is the only certain way back to the presence of our Father in Heaven? (16:13) "An all-wise Father announces the provisions whereby mortals may return to his presence. Jesus Christ is the way. His gospel contains the laws which must be obeyed. In the beginning it was so; during all dispensations thereafter it was the same; it so remains to this hour; and it shall be so everlastingly. There is only one gospel, one plan of salvation, one Christ, one course back to our Father. God does not vary" (McConkie, *Promised Messiah*, 289–90).

How was the law of Moses a shadow of things to come? (16:14) "The modern reader should not see the Mosaic code—anciently or in modern times—as simply a tedious set of religious rituals. . . . [The] historic covenant, given by the hand of God himself . . . [is] an avenue to righteousness, [and] should be seen rather as the unparalleled collection of types, shadows, symbols, and prefigurations of Christ that it is. For that reason it was once . . . a guide to spirituality, a gateway to Christ, a path of strict commandment-keeping that would, through laws of duty and decency, lead to higher laws of holiness on the way to immortality and eternal life" (Holland, *Christ and the New Covenant*, 136–37).

11 If they be good, to the resurrection of endless life and happiness; and if they be evil, to the resurrection of endless damnation, being delivered up to the devil, who hath subjected them, which is damnation—

12 Having gone according to their own carnal wills and desires; having never called upon the Lord while the arms of mercy were extended towards them; for the arms of mercy were extended towards them, and they would not; they being warned of their iniquities and yet they would not depart from them; and they were commanded to repent and yet they would not repent.

13 And now, ought ye not to tremble and repent of your sins, and remember that only in and through Christ ye can be saved?

14 Therefore, if ye teach the law of Moses, also teach that it is a shadow of those things which are to come—

15 Teach them that redemption cometh through Christ the Lord, who is the very Eternal Father. Amen.

CHAPTER 17

Alma believes and writes the words of Abinadi—Abinadi suffers death by fire—He prophesies disease and death by fire upon his murderers. About 148 B.C.

1 And now it came to pass that when Abinadi had finished these sayings, that the king commanded that the priests should take him and cause that he should be put to death.

2 But there was one among them whose name was Alma, he also being a descendant of Nephi. And he was a young man, and he believed the words which Abinadi had spoken, for he knew concerning the iniquity which Abinadi had testified against them; therefore he began to plead with the king that he would not be angry with Abinadi, but suffer that he might depart in peace.

3 But the king was more wroth, and caused that Alma should be cast out from among them, and sent his servants after him that they might slay him.

4 But he fled from before them and hid himself that they found him not. And he being concealed for many days did write all the words which Abinadi had spoken.

5 And it came to pass that the king caused that his guards should surround Abinadi and take him; and they bound him and cast him into prison.

6 And after three days, having counseled with his priests, he caused that he should again be brought before him.

7 And he said unto him: Abinadi, we have found an accusation against thee, and thou art worthy of death.

8 For thou hast said that God himself should come down among the children of men; and now, for this cause thou shalt be put to death unless thou wilt recall all the words which

Mosiah 17:1–4. Alma Believes Abinadi's Words and Is Cast Out from Noah's People

What was the significance of Alma's conversion? (17:1–4) "For about three hundred years, the religious writings of the Nephites centered on Alma and his descendants—his son Alma, his grandson Helaman, his great-grandson Helaman, his second-great-grandson Nephi, and his third-great-grandson Nephi, a disciple of the resurrected Lord. Because Alma hearkened to the words of Abinadi, Alma was able to impact for good the religious course of the Nephites for more than three hundred years" (Black, *400 Questions and Answers*, 141). ⊕

What do we learn from Alma's conversion? (17:2) "Alma knew that he was guilty of the evils Abinadi had laid bare.... Alma felt profoundly and personally the transforming power of the gospel of Jesus Christ. He repented, and he turned with full purpose of heart to do the work of the Lord.... He listened carefully to the preaching of Abinadi.... With a humble heart, with integrity and courage, he 'repented of his sins and iniquities'... through faith in the Lord Jesus Christ.... Alma's change of heart is a powerful example of how repentance through faith in the atonement of the Savior can transform our lives" (Wirthlin, "Alma the Elder," 82). ⊕

Mosiah 17:5–10. Abinadi Is Imprisoned and Then Brought before King Noah

Why was Abinadi sentenced to death for teaching that Jesus Christ would come in the flesh? (17:7–8) "The exact crime for which Abinadi was accused was, 'Thou hast said that God himself should come down among the children of men.' This accusation was only an excuse, a pretext for them to slay righteous Abinadi. King Noah and his priests smarted most because they knew Abinadi spoke truthfully of their wicked ways. Therefore, they wished to be rid of the reproach by doing away with their accuser" (Reynolds and Sjodahl, *Commentary on the Book of Mormon*, 2:361).

What did Abinadi and the Prophet Joseph Smith have in common? (17:10) The following words of the Prophet Joseph Smith about himself also characterize Abinadi: "I understand my mission and business. God Almighty is my shield; and what can man do if God is my friend? I shall not be sacrificed until my time comes; then I shall be offered freely" (*Joseph Smith* [manual], 522–23).

Mosiah 17:11–20. Abinadi Is Put to Death by Fire

Why were the priests so invested in finding Abinadi guilty? (17:11–12) "Noah is shaken by Abinadi's words and the power of the Spirit. The condemnation frightens him to the point that he is on the verge of withdrawing his own decree. But the priests do not allow it. As the focus of Abinadi's accusations was that they had taught false doctrine, they had the greatest hatred for Abinadi. They push Noah by reminding him that Abinadi has spoken against the king. The belief in the king's divinity, common throughout most of the ancient world, made Abinadi's words tantamount to blasphemy. By appealing to Noah's pride (and perhaps subtly reminding him that his own status was challenged), they assured Abinadi's execution" (Gardner, *Second Witness*, 3:317).

What did it mean in Abinadi's day to scourge someone with faggots? (17:13) "We generally say that Abinadi was burned at the stake—and that may be true, although technically it might not be the whole story. . . . Three words in [verse 13] should be noted. The first is that they bound him. . . . The second is that they scourged him. To scourge means to whip, flail, or beat. The third term is faggots. . . . A faggot is a bundle of sticks or twigs. This passage seems to say that Abinadi's tormentors took burning torches and poked him with these, burning his skin until he died" (Matthews, "Abinadi," 103). ☉

thou hast spoken evil concerning me and my people.

9 Now Abinadi said unto him: I say unto you, I will not recall the words which I have spoken unto you concerning this people, for they are true; and that ye may know of their surety I have suffered myself that I have fallen into your hands.

10 Yea, and I will suffer even until death, and I will not recall my words, and they shall stand as a testimony against you. And if ye slay me ye will shed innocent blood, and this shall also stand as a testimony against you at the last day.

11 And now king Noah was about to release him, for he feared his word; for he feared that the judgments of God would come upon him.

12 But the priests lifted up their voices against him, and began to accuse him, saying: He has reviled the king. Therefore the king was stirred up in anger against him, and he delivered him up that he might be slain.

13 And it came to pass that they took him and bound him, and scourged his skin with faggots, yea, even unto death.

14 And now when the flames began to scorch him, he cried unto them, saying:

15 Behold, even as ye have done unto me, so shall it come to pass that thy seed shall cause that many shall suffer the pains that I do suffer, even the pains of death by fire; and this because they believe in the salvation of the Lord their God.

16 And it will come to pass that ye shall be afflicted with all manner of diseases because of your iniquities.

17 Yea, and ye shall be smitten on every hand, and shall be driven and scattered to and fro, even as a wild flock is driven by wild and ferocious beasts.

18 And in that day ye shall be hunted, and ye shall be taken by the hand of your enemies, and then ye shall suffer, as I suffer, the pains of death by fire.

19 Thus God executeth vengeance upon those that destroy his people. O God, receive my soul.

20 And now, when Abinadi had said these words, he fell, having suffered death by fire; yea, having been put to death because he would not deny the commandments of God, having sealed the truth of his words by his death.

CHAPTER 18

Alma preaches in private—He sets forth the covenant of baptism and baptizes at the waters of Mormon—He organizes the Church of Christ and ordains priests—They support themselves and teach the people—Alma and his people flee from King Noah into the wilderness. About 147–145 B.C.

1 And now, it came to pass that Alma, who had fled from the servants of king Noah, repented of his sins and iniquities, and went about privately among the people, and began to teach the words of Abinadi—

2 Yea, concerning that which was to come, and also concerning the resurrection of the dead, and the redemption of the people, which was to be brought to pass through the power, and sufferings, and death of Christ, and his resurrection and ascension into heaven.

How did Mormon become aware of Abinadi's prophecies and their fulfillment? (17:16–18) Abinadi's "predictions of retribution upon his slayers were literally fulfilled, as Mormon was always careful to point out [see Alma 25:9]. The critical reader may wonder how Abinadi's words came to be recorded. It is possible that Alma came on the scene in disguise, or it may be that one of his future converts was present and at a later time reported what happened" (Sperry, *Book of Mormon Compendium*, 311).

What must we understand about the Lord's vengeance? (17:19) Vengeance comes as consequences of disobeying the Lord. In a modern revelation we learn: "For behold, and lo, vengeance cometh speedily upon the ungodly as the whirlwind; and who shall escape it? . . . For the indignation of the Lord is kindled against their abominations and all their wicked works" (D&C 97:22, 24).

Mosiah 18:1–6. Alma Teaches the Words of Abinadi

How involved was Alma in King Noah's way of life? (18:1) "Just how involved Alma was in King Noah's way of life before his conversion we have no way of knowing. We do know, whatever the depth of his transgressions, that his repentance was genuine and the renovation of his soul complete. He lived thereafter a life of unquestioned integrity and kept the laws of God with fidelity and devotion" (McConkie and Millet, *Doctrinal Commentary*, 2:253).

What was Alma's message to the people? (18:1–3) Alma taught the words of Abinadi, which testified of the resurrection and redemption of the people through the power of Jesus Christ. The Prophet Joseph Smith similarly testified: . . ."The fundamental principles of our religion are the testimony of the Apostles and Prophets concerning Jesus Christ, that He died, was buried, and rose again the third day, and ascended into heaven; and all other things which pertain to our religion are only appendages to it" (*Joseph Smith* [manual], 49).

What was the significance of this place called Mormon? (18:4–5) Many people came to a knowledge of their Redeemer at the place called Mormon (see v. 30). Mormon was a beautiful and secluded place where Alma went to privately teach the gospel of Jesus Christ (see v. 30). While there, many entered the waters of baptism and "were filled with the grace of God" (v. 16). With the authority of God, Alma ordained priests and established the church of Christ (see 17–18). Long after Alma and his people left, the waters of Mormon held great significance among many of the Nephite nation (see 3 Nephi 5:12).

Mosiah 18:7–16. Alma Teaches the Covenant of Baptism

Why are these verses important for those seeking to understand the covenant of baptism? (18:8–10) "This declaration by Alma at the Waters of Mormon still stands as the most complete scriptural statement on record as to what the newly baptized commit to do and be" (Holland, *Christ and the New Covenant*, 106). What are the essential aspects of the baptismal covenant, as explained by Alma? How would you evaluate your covenant-keeping with regard to these aspects of the covenant?

Why is it important to be baptized "in the name of the Lord"? (18:10) "Some people are 'baptized . . . for the remission of sins' (D&C 84:64). However, since children who are baptized when they turn eight have no sins, the purpose of baptism that Alma stated—to give testimony of their covenant with the Lord—is the primary purpose of baptism (see also 2 Nephi 31:5–9; Mosiah 21:35; 3 Nephi 7:25). The Prophet Joseph Smith taught, 'Baptism is a sign to God, to angels, and to

3 And as many as would hear his word he did teach. And he taught them privately, that it might not come to the knowledge of the king. And many did believe his words.

4 And it came to pass that as many as did believe him did go forth to a place which was called Mormon, having received its name from the king, being in the borders of the land having been infested, by times or at seasons, by wild beasts.

5 Now, there was in Mormon a fountain of pure water, and Alma resorted thither, there being near the water a thicket of small trees, where he did hide himself in the daytime from the searches of the king.

6 And it came to pass that as many as believed him went thither to hear his words.

7 And it came to pass after many days there were a goodly number gathered together at the place of Mormon, to hear the words of Alma. Yea, all were gathered together that believed on his word, to hear him. And he did teach them, and did preach unto them repentance, and redemption, and faith on the Lord.

8 And it came to pass that he said unto them: Behold, here are the waters of Mormon (for thus were they called) and now, as ye are desirous to come into the fold of God, and to be called his people, and are willing to bear one another's burdens, that they may be light;

9 Yea, and are willing to mourn with those that mourn; yea, and comfort those that stand in need of comfort, and to stand as witnesses of God at all times and in all things, and in all places that ye may be in, even until death, that ye may be redeemed of God, and be numbered with those of the first resurrection, that ye may have eternal life—

10 Now I say unto you, if this be the desire of your hearts, what have you against being baptized in the name of the Lord, as a witness

before him that ye have entered into a covenant with him, that ye will serve him and keep his commandments, that he may pour out his Spirit more abundantly upon you?

11 And now when the people had heard these words, they clapped their hands for joy, and exclaimed: This is the desire of our hearts.

12 And now it came to pass that Alma took Helam, he being one of the first, and went and stood forth in the water, and cried, saying: O Lord, pour out thy Spirit upon thy servant, that he may do this work with holiness of heart.

13 And when he had said these words, the Spirit of the Lord was upon him, and he said: Helam, I baptize thee, having authority from the Almighty God, as a testimony that ye have entered into a covenant to serve him until you are dead as to the mortal body; and may the Spirit of the Lord be poured out upon you; and may he grant unto you eternal life, through the redemption of Christ, whom he has prepared from the foundation of the world.

14 And after Alma had said these words, both Alma and Helam were buried in the water; and they arose and came forth out of the water rejoicing, being filled with the Spirit.

15 And again, Alma took another, and went forth a second time into the water, and baptized him according to the first, only he did not bury himself again in the water.

16 And after this manner he did baptize every one that went forth to the place of Mormon; and they were in number about two hundred and four souls; yea, and they were baptized in the waters of Mormon, and were filled with the grace of God.

heaven that we do the will of God'" (Garner, *Search These Things Diligently*, 154).

What does entering into the baptismal covenant mean? (18:10) "All Latter-day Saints enter the new and everlasting covenant when they enter this Church. They covenant to cease sustaining, upholding and cherishing the kingdom of the Devil and the kingdoms of this world. They enter the new and everlasting covenant to sustain the Kingdom of God and no other kingdom. They take a vow of the most solemn kind, before the heavens and earth, . . . that they will sustain truth and righteousness instead of wickedness and falsehood, and build up the Kingdom of God, instead of the kingdoms of this world" (*Brigham Young*, [manual], 62–63). ◉

How did Alma have authority from God to ordain and baptize? (18:13–15, 18) "We may conclude that Alma held the priesthood before he, with others, became disturbed with King Noah. . . . If he had authority to baptize that is evidence that he had been baptized. Therefore, when Alma baptized himself with Helam that was not a case of Alma baptizing himself, but merely as a token to the Lord of his humility and full repentance. . . . Alma did not organize the Church with the idea that they had no church before that time. They had a church from the days of Lehi, and Alma only set things in order" (Smith, *Answers to Gospel Questions*, 3:203–4). ◉

Mosiah 18:17–23. Alma Organizes the Church of Christ

Who were these priests Alma ordained? (18:18)
President Joseph Fielding Smith explained, "Before the coming of Christ, the Nephites did not have the Aaronic Priesthood" (*Doctrines of Salvation*, 3:87). Therefore, it would be inaccurate to assume that priests in the Book of Mormon were the same as priests in the church today. Prior to the coming of Jesus Christ, priests functioned as part of the high priesthood of the holy order of God.

What does the Lord authorize His servants to teach in our time? (18:19–20) "Teach the principles of my gospel, which are in the Bible and the Book of Mormon, in the which is the fulness of the gospel. [All] shall observe the covenants and church articles to do them, and these shall be their teachings, as they shall be directed by the Spirit. And the Spirit shall be given unto you by the prayer of faith; and if ye receive not the Spirit ye shall not teach. And all this ye shall observe to do as I have commanded concerning your teaching, until the fulness of my scriptures is given" (D&C 42:12–15).

How can we achieve the same unity and love found among Alma and his people? (18:21–22) "The miracle of unity is being granted to us as we pray and work for it in the Lord's way. Our hearts will be knit together in unity. God has promised that blessing to His faithful Saints whatever their differences in background and whatever conflict rages around them. . . . The joy of unity . . . is not solitary. We must seek it and qualify for it with others. . . . He wants us to gather into families. He has established classes, wards, and branches and commanded us to meet together often" (Eyring, "Our Hearts Knit As One," 69).

Mosiah 18:24–30. Church Members Support Each Other in All Things

Why was it important for the priests to labor with their own hands? (18:24) "This is the pattern which had been exemplified by King Benjamin (see Mosiah 2:14) and no doubt by previous spiritual leaders among the Nephites. . . . It has ever been the practice for the great generality of those called to labor in the Lord's vineyard to be required also to earn their daily bread by temporal labor. This necessary feature of mortality ought not be viewed as a spiritual disadvantage. In fact, many of life's greatest spiritual lessons derive from life's challenges and vicissitudes. Spiritual labor is its own reward, a labor not motivated by the

17 And they were called the church of God, or the church of Christ, from that time forward. And it came to pass that whosoever was baptized by the power and authority of God was added to his church.

18 And it came to pass that Alma, having authority from God, ordained priests; even one priest to every fifty of their number did he ordain to preach unto them, and to teach them concerning the things pertaining to the kingdom of God.

19 And he commanded them that they should teach nothing save it were the things which he had taught, and which had been spoken by the mouth of the holy prophets.

20 Yea, even he commanded them that they should preach nothing save it were repentance and faith on the Lord, who had redeemed his people.

21 And he commanded them that there should be no contention one with another, but that they should look forward with one eye, having one faith and one baptism, having their hearts knit together in unity and in love one towards another.

22 And thus he commanded them to preach. And thus they became the children of God.

23 And he commanded them that they should observe the sabbath day, and keep it holy, and also every day they should give thanks to the Lord their God.

24 And he also commanded them that the priests whom he had ordained should labor with their own hands for their support.

25 And there was one day in every week that was set apart that they should gather themselves together to teach the people, and to worship the Lord their God, and also, as often as it was in their power, to assemble themselves together.

idea of temporal remuneration" (McConkie and Millet, *Doctrinal Commentary*, 2:263).

26 And the priests were not to depend upon the people for their support; but for their labor they were to receive the grace of God, that they might wax strong in the Spirit, having the knowledge of God, that they might teach with power and authority from God.

27 And again Alma commanded that the people of the church should impart of their substance, every one according to that which he had; if he have more abundantly he should impart more abundantly; and of him that had but little, but little should be required; and to him that had not should be given.

28 And thus they should impart of their substance of their own free will and good desires towards God, and to those priests that stood in need, yea, and to every needy, naked soul.

29 And this he said unto them, having been commanded of God; and they did walk uprightly before God, imparting to one another both temporally and spiritually according to their needs and their wants.

30 And now it came to pass that all this was done in Mormon, yea, by the waters of Mormon, in the forest that was near the waters of Mormon; yea, the place of Mormon, the waters of Mormon, the forest of Mormon, how beautiful are they to the eyes of them who there came to the knowledge of their Redeemer; yea, and how blessed are they, for they shall sing to his praise forever.

31 And these things were done in the borders of the land, that they might not come to the knowledge of the king.

32 But behold, it came to pass that the king, having discovered a movement among the people, sent his servants to watch them. Therefore on the day that they were assembling

What does it mean to "wax strong"? (18:26) "This phrase appears 12 times in the Book of Mormon and is used positively and negatively in its expression. For example, 'the people began to wax strong in wickedness and abominations' (3 Nephi 2:3).

"To wax means to come to be or to increase in size, strength, or intensity. Thus, to 'wax strong' is to increase in strength or capacity" (Brewster, *Doctrine and Covenants Encyclopedia*, 627).

Why is the temporal welfare of God's children an important part of His kingdom? (18:27–29) "The welfare plan, in any age, is that part of the gospel which is designed, under the then existing circumstances, to care for the temporal needs of the saints on the basis of gospel principles. Such a system is one of the evidences of the divinity of the Lord's Church. Unless and until members of the Church give freely of their means for the support of their less fortunate brethren, they do not develop those attributes of goodness and godliness which prepare them for a celestial inheritance" (McConkie, *Doctrinal New Testament Commentary*, 2:432).

Mosiah 18:31–35. Alma's People Flee from King Noah into the Wilderness

themselves together to hear the word of the Lord they were discovered unto the king.

33 And now the king said that Alma was stirring up the people to rebellion against him; therefore he sent his army to destroy them.

34 And it came to pass that Alma and the people of the Lord were apprised of the coming of the king's army; therefore they took their tents and their families and departed into the wilderness.

35 And they were in number about four hundred and fifty souls.

CHAPTER 19

Gideon seeks to slay King Noah—The Lamanites invade the land—King Noah suffers death by fire—Limhi rules as a tributary monarch. About 145–121 B.C.

1 And it came to pass that the army of the king returned, having searched in vain for the people of the Lord.

2 And now behold, the forces of the king were small, having been reduced, and there began to be a division among the remainder of the people.

3 And the lesser part began to breathe out threatenings against the king, and there began to be a great contention among them.

4 And now there was a man among them whose name was Gideon, and he being a strong man and an enemy to the king, therefore he drew his sword, and swore in his wrath that he would slay the king.

Who informed Alma and his people that King Noah was sending his army to destroy them? (18:34) Alma received a warning from the Lord (see Mosiah 23:1). Many years earlier the Lord warned Nephi that he should depart from Laman and Lemuel and their families and flee into the wilderness (2 Nephi 5:5). Likewise, Mosiah was "warned of the Lord" to flee out of the land of Nephi (Omni 1:12). Like Nephi and his people, Mosiah and his people, Alma and his people were spared destruction by the Lord extending mercy to His covenant people.

Mosiah 19:1–8. Gideon Confronts King Noah

What are the possible reasons for this contention and threatenings to the king? (19:2–3) "Mormon has most certainly omitted an important historical episode somewhere between the story of Abinadi and this point. . . .

"Yet this passage describes a king losing his authority. How has the unity of Noah's people disintegrated into internal factionalism and a reduction of the army? Have unspecified battle losses caused the military reduction? It seems unlikely, since verse 6 specifies a Lamanite attack with no indication of any previous attack. Rather, the army seems to have dwindled through defections. In that case, it would be directly related to the internal dissension. Those who agreed with the dissenters are leaving Noah's service" (Gardner, *Second Witness*, 3:346).

Who was Gideon? (19:4) "Gideon appears abruptly in the narrative, without any background. From his actions, we can easily surmise his military experience. Verse 22 mentions 'men of Gideon,' clearly positioning him as a leader. Mosiah 20:21 shows that Gideon knows Abinadi's prophecy about Noah and his people. These bits of information let us deduce that Gideon

5 And it came to pass that he fought with the king; and when the king saw that he was about to overpower him, he fled and ran and got upon the tower which was near the temple.

6 And Gideon pursued after him and was about to get upon the tower to slay the king, and the king cast his eyes round about towards the land of Shemlon, and behold, the army of the Lamanites were within the borders of the land.

7 And now the king cried out in the anguish of his soul, saying: Gideon, spare me, for the Lamanites are upon us, and they will destroy us; yea, they will destroy my people.

8 And now the king was not so much concerned about his people as he was about his own life; nevertheless, Gideon did spare his life.

9 And the king commanded the people that they should flee before the Lamanites, and he himself did go before them, and they did flee into the wilderness, with their women and their children.

10 And it came to pass that the Lamanites did pursue them, and did overtake them, and began to slay them.

11 Now it came to pass that the king commanded them that all the men should leave their wives and their children, and flee before the Lamanites.

12 Now there were many that would not leave them, but had rather stay and perish with them. And the rest left their wives and their children and fled.

13 And it came to pass that those who tarried with their wives and their children caused that their fair daughters should stand

was a man of physical action, skilled in handling weapons, not a man given to political intrigue" (Gardner, *Second Witness*, 3:347).

Why did Gideon spare King Noah's life? (19:8)
Gideon was a powerful man who knew that the king cared nothing for his people. Nevertheless, he decided to spare the king's life. What does that action say about Gideon? How might the plight of his people have played into his decision? ●

Mosiah 19:9–17. Lamanites Capture Limhi, the Son of King Noah, and His People

What does this event teach us about the moral character of Noah's leadership? (19:11–12) "When we compare the people as the text invites us to do, we contrast the care the men of Limhi showed for their wives and children with the abandonment by the priests of Noah. All of these events define the lack of moral character of the priests. . . . The people of Limhi, on the other hand, 'fought for their lives, and for their wives, and for their children' (Mosiah 20:11). These differences reveal not only the character of the priests of Noah, who abandoned their families rather than fall into Lamanite hands, but also of the Nephites, who decided to face death with their families rather than abandon them" (Goff, "Stealing of the Daughters of the Lamanites," 73).

forth and plead with the Lamanites that they would not slay them.

14 And it came to pass that the Lamanites had compassion on them, for they were charmed with the beauty of their women.

15 Therefore the Lamanites did spare their lives, and took them captives and carried them back to the land of Nephi, and granted unto them that they might possess the land, under the conditions that they would deliver up king Noah into the hands of the Lamanites, and deliver up their property, even one half of all they possessed, one half of their gold, and their silver, and all their precious things, and thus they should pay tribute to the king of the Lamanites from year to year.

16 And now there was one of the sons of the king among those that were taken captive, whose name was Limhi.

17 And now Limhi was desirous that his father should not be destroyed; nevertheless, Limhi was not ignorant of the iniquities of his father, he himself being a just man.

18 And it came to pass that Gideon sent men into the wilderness secretly, to search for the king and those that were with him. And it came to pass that they met the people in the wilderness, all save the king and his priests.

19 Now they had sworn in their hearts that they would return to the land of Nephi, and if their wives and their children were slain, and also those that had tarried with them, that they would seek revenge, and also perish with them.

20 And the king commanded them that they should not return; and they were angry with the king, and caused that he should suffer, even unto death by fire.

21 And they were about to take the priests also and put them to death, and they fled before them.

Why does Mormon use the unusual expression that Limhi was "desirous that his father should not be destroyed"? (19:17) *Antenantiosis* is a figure of speech used here and other places in the Book of Mormon (see Mosiah 2:9; Alma 12:14; 30:21; 34:39; 46:30; 50:27, etc.). "It is the practice of stating a proposition in terms of its opposite ['Limhi *was desirous* that his father should *not* be destroyed']. The result is to express the positive in a very high degree, or as the biblical scholar E. W. Bullinger puts it, 'We thus emphasize that which we seem to lessen.' . . .

"It is an interesting figure of speech, . . . that helps illuminate the forceful effectiveness of many of the prophetic messages of the Book of Mormon" (Call, "Antenantiosis in the Book of Mormon," 96–97).

Mosiah 19:18–29. King Noah's People Put Him to Death

22 And it came to pass that they were about to return to the land of Nephi, and they met the men of Gideon. And the men of Gideon told them of all that had happened to their wives and their children; and that the Lamanites had granted unto them that they might possess the land by paying a tribute to the Lamanites of one half of all they possessed.

23 And the people told the men of Gideon that they had slain the king, and his priests had fled from them farther into the wilderness.

24 And it came to pass that after they had ended the ceremony, that they returned to the land of Nephi, rejoicing, because their wives and their children were not slain; and they told Gideon what they had done to the king.

25 And it came to pass that the king of the Lamanites made an oath unto them, that his people should not slay them.

26 And also Limhi, being the son of the king, having the kingdom conferred upon him by the people, made oath unto the king of the Lamanites that his people should pay tribute unto him, even one half of all they possessed.

27 And it came to pass that Limhi began to establish the kingdom and to establish peace among his people.

28 And the king of the Lamanites set guards round about the land, that he might keep the people of Limhi in the land, that they might not depart into the wilderness; and he did support his guards out of the tribute which he did receive from the Nephites.

29 And now king Limhi did have continual peace in his kingdom for the space of two years, that the Lamanites did not molest them nor seek to destroy them.

What is the meaning of the ceremony spoken of in this verse? (19:24) "Now what ceremony is mentioned in verse 24? Well, it's very clear. Remember these people had left the town, and Gideon had come to catch up with them and punish their leader. Gideon couldn't leave Noah alone—he was on his heels all the time.

"So they were hostile parties who were opposed to each other. One was the refugees, and the other was the avenging party following them, so they were hostile. They couldn't go back home together until they had settled, smoked the peace pipe, and had the ceremony. You have to have a ceremony before you can reach peace with a hostile group. You either fight them or have the ceremony, so that's what they did. They had a peace ceremony" (Nibley, *Teachings of the Book of Mormon*, 2:125).

How does this oath fulfill Abinadi's prophecy? (19:25–26) "The oath made with the Lamanite king by the newly appointed King Limhi (vv. 25–26) fulfilled another of Abinadi's prophecies. The Lord had said through him: 'This generation, because of their iniquities, shall be brought into bondage' (Mosiah 12:2)" (Nyman, *These Records Are True*, 436).

What do we learn from Limhi's succession to the throne? (19:26–29) "Noah . . . did not provide for succession to his throne. Instead, his son Limhi was appointed king by the people after his father's kingdom had collapsed (Mosiah 19:26). There is no record of Noah's ever having taught Limhi about royal responsibilities. Ironically, Limhi's first official act of government was to indenture his people to the Lamanites. Noah's reign brought about his people's bondage and landed his son in a political quagmire" (Donaldson, "Benjamin and Noah," 53–54).

CHAPTER 20

Some Lamanite daughters are abducted by the priests of Noah—The Lamanites wage war upon Limhi and his people—The Lamanite hosts are repulsed and pacified. About 145–123 B.C.

1 Now there was a place in Shemlon where the daughters of the Lamanites did gather themselves together to sing, and to dance, and to make themselves merry.

2 And it came to pass that there was one day a small number of them gathered together to sing and to dance.

3 And now the priests of king Noah, being ashamed to return to the city of Nephi, yea, and also fearing that the people would slay them, therefore they durst not return to their wives and their children.

4 And having tarried in the wilderness, and having discovered the daughters of the Lamanites, they laid and watched them;

5 And when there were but few of them gathered together to dance, they came forth out of their secret places and took them and carried them into the wilderness; yea, twenty and four of the daughters of the Lamanites they carried into the wilderness.

Mosiah 20:1–5. The Wicked Priests of King Noah Carry Away Twenty-Four Daughters of the Lamanites

What is the significance of the practice of the women gathering to dance? (20:1) In ancient Israel, it was a tradition for the maidens of Israel to gather to dance. "This was . . . a 'matrimonial holiday for youth.' . . .

"Following the conclusion of their summer chores in the fields, youths would turn their attention to 'bride-hunting,' and the dance of the maidens. . . .

"Lehi and his people, of course, would have known the earlier traditions of 'dancing and bride-hunting,' and perhaps this sheds light on the time when the priests of Noah carried off twenty-four Lamanite daughters to be their wives" (Welch et al., "Dancing Maidens," 139–40). ✚

What insight into Noah's court can we gain from the twenty-four daughters who were kidnapped? (20:5) "Consider the significance of the number twenty-four in ancient Israel and in the Book of Mormon. Certain numbers were clearly meaningful in antiquity: seven was the number of spiritual perfection (as in the seven seals in the book of Revelation); twelve was a governmental number (as with the twelve tribes, twelve apostles). The number twenty-four, being a multiple of twelve, was associated with heavenly government, *especially priestly judgment* and temple service. . . .

"Apparently there were twenty-four judges on King Noah's court, since Noah and his priests kidnapped twenty-four Lamanite daughters" (Welch, "Number 24," 272–73; emphasis added).

Mosiah 20:6–11. The Lamanites Attack the People of Limhi and Are Defeated

6 And it came to pass that when the Lamanites found that their daughters had been missing, they were angry with the people of Limhi, for they thought it was the people of Limhi.

7 Therefore they sent their armies forth; yea, even the king himself went before his people; and they went up to the land of Nephi to destroy the people of Limhi.

8 And now Limhi had discovered them from the tower, even all their preparations for war did he discover; therefore he gathered his people together, and laid wait for them in the fields and in the forests.

9 And it came to pass that when the Lamanites had come up, that the people of Limhi began to fall upon them from their waiting places, and began to slay them.

10 And it came to pass that the battle became exceedingly sore, for they fought like lions for their prey.

11 And it came to pass that the people of Limhi began to drive the Lamanites before them; yet they were not half so numerous as the Lamanites. But they fought for their lives, and for their wives, and for their children; therefore they exerted themselves and like dragons did they fight.

12 And it came to pass that they found the king of the Lamanites among the number of their dead; yet he was not dead, having been wounded and left upon the ground, so speedy was the flight of his people.

13 And they took him and bound up his wounds, and brought him before Limhi, and said: Behold, here is the king of the Lamanites; he having received a wound has fallen among their dead, and they have left him; and behold, we have brought him before you; and now let us slay him.

14 But Limhi said unto them: Ye shall not slay him, but bring him hither that I may see him. And they brought him. And Limhi said unto him: What cause have ye to come up to war against my people? Behold, my people have not broken the oath that I made unto you; therefore, why should ye break the oath which ye made unto my people?

15 And now the king said: I have broken the oath because thy people did carry away the

Like Limhi on the tower, who are the watchmen on the towers today? (20:8) "Today, we have again apostles, seers, and revelators who are watchmen on the tower, messengers of supernal, healing truth. God speaks to us through them. They are profoundly aware of the different circumstances we members are living in. They are in this world but not of this world. They point the way, and they offer help for our difficulties, not through the wisdom of this world but from an eternal Source" (Uchtdorf, "Heeding the Voice of the Prophets," 6).

What warnings have our apostles and prophets provided recently? In what ways are you responding?

When is war justified? (20:11) "Modern revelation states that we are to 'renounce war and proclaim peace' (D&C 98:16). . . .

"However, we all must also be mindful of another overriding responsibility. . . .

"There are times and circumstances when nations are justified, in fact have an obligation, to fight for family, for liberty, and against tyranny, threat, and oppression" (Hinckley, "War and Peace," 80).

Mosiah 20:12–26. The King of the Lamanites Pleads on Behalf of the People of Limhi

What do we learn about oaths in these verses? (20:12–14) "The probable cause for Limhi's not slaying the injured king was a desire to know why the oath was broken (v. 14). Oaths were sacred in both cultures (see 1 Nephi 4:30–35). The sacredness of oaths is shown in Limhi's determination to find who was responsible for the act (Mosiah 20:16)" (Nyman, *These Records Are True*, 438).

What should we do to help people overcome the serious results of misunderstanding? (20:13–20) The error of the Lamanites nearly led to the annihilation of Limhi's people. The destruction caused by misunderstanding can happen in many areas of life. "There are . . . times when one of the greatest acts of service we can perform is to stop something. The emotional chain of reaction and overreaction can come at us like electric voltage; it is very tempting to simply pass along. But we must say, 'Let it stop with me.' . . . At times we . . . should be stern, sweet sentries willing to expose ourselves to misunderstanding and pain in order to keep undesirable things from spreading any farther" (*Neal A. Maxwell Quote Book*, 315).

daughters of my people; therefore, in my anger I did cause my people to come up to war against thy people.

16 And now Limhi had heard nothing concerning this matter; therefore he said: I will search among my people and whosoever has done this thing shall perish. Therefore he caused a search to be made among his people.

17 Now when Gideon had heard these things, he being the king's captain, he went forth and said unto the king: I pray thee forbear, and do not search this people, and lay not this thing to their charge.

18 For do ye not remember the priests of thy father, whom this people sought to destroy? And are they not in the wilderness? And are not they the ones who have stolen the daughters of the Lamanites?

19 And now, behold, and tell the king of these things, that he may tell his people that they may be pacified towards us; for behold they are already preparing to come against us; and behold also there are but few of us.

20 And behold, they come with their numerous hosts; and except the king doth pacify them towards us we must perish.

21 For are not the words of Abinadi fulfilled, which he prophesied against us—and all this because we would not hearken unto the words of the Lord, and turn from our iniquities?

22 And now let us pacify the king, and we fulfil the oath which we have made unto him; for it is better that we should be in bondage than that we should lose our lives; therefore, let us put a stop to the shedding of so much blood.

23 And now Limhi told the king all the things concerning his father, and the priests that had fled into the wilderness, and attributed the carrying away of their daughters to them.

What was a significant reason why Limhi's people were in bondage to the Lamanites? (20:22)
"Although physical bondage is the most recognizable form of bondage—the Lord often uses it to persuade people to repent—the eternal effects of spiritual bondage are of greater consequence. It was the bondage of sin that ultimately led king Noah's people into physical bondage" (Williams, "Deliverance from Bondage," 266).

24 And it came to pass that the king was pacified towards his people; and he said unto them: Let us go forth to meet my people, without arms; and I swear unto you with an oath that my people shall not slay thy people.

25 And it came to pass that they followed the king, and went forth without arms to meet the Lamanites. And it came to pass that they did meet the Lamanites; and the king of the Lamanites did bow himself down before them, and did plead in behalf of the people of Limhi.

26 And when the Lamanites saw the people of Limhi, that they were without arms, they had compassion on them and were pacified towards them, and returned with their king in peace to their own land.

CHAPTER 21

Limhi's people are smitten and defeated by the Lamanites—Limhi's people meet Ammon and are converted—They tell Ammon of the twenty-four Jaredite plates. About 122–121 B.C.

1 And it came to pass that Limhi and his people returned to the city of Nephi, and began to dwell in the land again in peace.

2 And it came to pass that after many days the Lamanites began again to be stirred up in anger against the Nephites, and they began to come into the borders of the land round about.

3 Now they durst not slay them, because of the oath which their king had made unto Limhi; but they would smite them on their cheeks, and exercise authority over them; and began to put heavy burdens upon their backs, and drive them as they would a dumb ass—

4 Yea, all this was done that the word of the Lord might be fulfilled.

Mosiah 21:1–12. Limhi and His People Lose Three Wars in Their Attempts to Escape from the Lamanites

What prophecy was fulfilled? (21:3–4) "In these verses [Mosiah 21:1–12] we find a more specific detailing of the fulfillment of Abinadi's prophecy relative to the bondage of the people of the city of Nephi (see Mosiah 12:2–8). Though their plight was now most pitiful, we would err to suppose that God had forgotten them. 'As many as I love, I rebuke and chasten,' the Lord said, charging such to 'be zealous therefore, and repent' (Revelation 3:19). To be chastened is to be subjected to pain, suffering, deprivation, or misfortune in order to correct, strengthen, and perfect behavior" (McConkie and Millet, *Doctrinal Commentary*, 2:271–72).

What parallels can we make between our own spiritual challenges or limitations and the bondage of Limhi and his people? (21:5–12) Peace between Limhi and his people and the Lamanites did not last. Eventually the Lamanites oppressed them and "under their exactions and cruelty the condition of King Limhi's subjects grew continually worse, until, at last, they were little better off than were their ancestors in Egypt before Moses arose and delivered them" (Reynolds and Sjodahl, *Commentary on the Book of Mormon*, 2:230).

Have you ever felt ill-treated or persecuted? Where do you turn for help in such situations? Why is the Savior the only one who can deliver you from certain circumstances? ✛

Mosiah 21:13–22. Limhi's People Humble Themselves before the Lord

What is always one of the first steps to relieve physical or spiritual bondage? (21:13) "The first step outlined in the Book of Mormon for removing the chains of bondage is to be humble before the Lord.

5 And now the afflictions of the Nephites were great, and there was no way that they could deliver themselves out of their hands, for the Lamanites had surrounded them on every side.

6 And it came to pass that the people began to murmur with the king because of their afflictions; and they began to be desirous to go against them to battle. And they did afflict the king sorely with their complaints; therefore he granted unto them that they should do according to their desires.

7 And they gathered themselves together again, and put on their armor, and went forth against the Lamanites to drive them out of their land.

8 And it came to pass that the Lamanites did beat them, and drove them back, and slew many of them.

9 And now there was a great mourning and lamentation among the people of Limhi, the widow mourning for her husband, the son and the daughter mourning for their father, and the brothers for their brethren.

10 Now there were a great many widows in the land, and they did cry mightily from day to day, for a great fear of the Lamanites had come upon them.

11 And it came to pass that their continual cries did stir up the remainder of the people of Limhi to anger against the Lamanites; and they went again to battle, but they were driven back again, suffering much loss.

12 Yea, they went again even the third time, and suffered in the like manner; and those that were not slain returned again to the city of Nephi.

13 And they did humble themselves even to the dust, subjecting themselves to the yoke of bondage, submitting themselves to be smitten,

and to be driven to and fro, and burdened, according to the desires of their enemies.

14 And they did humble themselves even in the depths of humility; and they did cry mightily to God; yea, even all the day long did they cry unto their God that he would deliver them out of their afflictions.

15 And now the Lord was slow to hear their cry because of their iniquities; nevertheless the Lord did hear their cries, and began to soften the hearts of the Lamanites that they began to ease their burdens; yet the Lord did not see fit to deliver them out of bondage.

16 And it came to pass that they began to prosper by degrees in the land, and began to raise grain more abundantly, and flocks, and herds, that they did not suffer with hunger.

17 Now there was a great number of women, more than there was of men; therefore king Limhi commanded that every man should impart to the support of the widows and their children, that they might not perish with hunger; and this they did because of the greatness of their number that had been slain.

18 Now the people of Limhi kept together in a body as much as it was possible, and secured their grain and their flocks;

19 And the king himself did not trust his person without the walls of the city, unless he took his guards with him, fearing that he might by some means fall into the hands of the Lamanites.

Because of heartache and the heavy yoke of bondage, Limhi and his people humbled themselves before the Lord (Mosiah 21:13), 'turn[ing] to the Lord with full purpose of heart' as Limhi had instructed (Mosiah 7:33). . . . Limhi's people acknowledged their guilt and turned to the Lord for his help" (Williams, "Deliverance from Bondage," 269).

What does the word humility mean and how can humility lead to our obtaining God's help? (21:14) "Humus is the earth, and humility means 'down to the earth.' *Dhn t3* the Egyptians call it—grinding your forehead in the dirt. You are lowering yourself as low as you can get in the dust" (Nibley, *Teachings of the Book of Mormon*, 2:441).

How is the Lord's timing related to deliverance from sin? (21:15) "The Lord who is patient and long-suffering even with evil may be equally slow to redeem the transgressor. The seeds of iniquity are not easily uprooted; time and suffering are a part of the healing process. The blessings of heaven are not cheaply obtained. One hardly merits the company of Abraham, Isaac, and Jacob and the exalted of all ages by the mere profession of faith or the lamentation for sin. A merely verbal repentance is hardly good training for the discipline necessary in keeping the commandments" (McConkie and Millet, *Doctrinal Commentary*, 2:273). ✪

Why did Limhi's people begin "to prosper by degrees"? (21:16) According to the previous verses in this account, the Lord was slow to answer the prayers of Limhi and his people because of their iniquities. Consider the challenging situation if these developing converts were immediately blessed with all that they desired, including freedom and abundance. Would their faith have continued to grow as steadily as it did? How might we apply Mosiah 21:16 in our own lives today?

20 And he caused that his people should watch the land round about, that by some means they might take those priests that fled into the wilderness, who had stolen the daughters of the Lamanites, and that had caused such a great destruction to come upon them.

21 For they were desirous to take them that they might punish them; for they had come into the land of Nephi by night, and carried off their grain and many of their precious things; therefore they laid wait for them.

22 And it came to pass that there was no more disturbance between the Lamanites and the people of Limhi, even until the time that Ammon and his brethren came into the land.

Mosiah 21:23–36. Limhi and His People Tell Their Story to Ammon and His Men

23 And the king having been without the gates of the city with his guard, discovered Ammon and his brethren; and supposing them to be priests of Noah therefore he caused that they should be taken, and bound, and cast into prison. And had they been the priests of Noah he would have caused that they should be put to death.

24 But when he found that they were not, but that they were his brethren, and had come from the land of Zarahemla, he was filled with exceedingly great joy.

25 Now king Limhi had sent, previous to the coming of Ammon, a small number of men to search for the land of Zarahemla; but they could not find it, and they were lost in the wilderness.

26 Nevertheless, they did find a land which had been peopled; yea, a land which was covered with dry bones; yea, a land which had been peopled and which had been destroyed; and they, having supposed it to be the land of Zarahemla, returned to the land of Nephi, having arrived in the borders of the land not many days before the coming of Ammon.

27 And they brought a record with them, even a record of the people whose bones they had found; and it was engraven on plates of ore.

28 And now Limhi was again filled with joy on learning from the mouth of Ammon that king Mosiah had a gift from God, whereby he could interpret such engravings; yea, and Ammon also did rejoice.

29 Yet Ammon and his brethren were filled with sorrow because so many of their brethren had been slain;

30 And also that king Noah and his priests had caused the people to commit so many sins and iniquities against God; and they also did mourn for the death of Abinadi; and also for the departure of Alma and the people that went with him, who had formed a church of God through the strength and power of God, and faith on the words which had been spoken by Abinadi.

31 Yea, they did mourn for their departure, for they knew not whither they had fled. Now they would have gladly joined with them, for they themselves had entered into a covenant with God to serve him and keep his commandments.

32 And now since the coming of Ammon, king Limhi had also entered into a covenant with God, and also many of his people, to serve him and keep his commandments.

33 And it came to pass that king Limhi and many of his people were desirous to be baptized; but there was none in the land that had authority from God. And Ammon declined doing this thing, considering himself an unworthy servant.

34 Therefore they did not at that time form themselves into a church, waiting upon the Spirit of the Lord. Now they were desirous to become even as Alma and his brethren, who had fled into the wilderness.

Why was Limhi joyful upon hearing that King Mosiah had a special gift from God? (21:28) Limhi expressed joy in the realization that King Mosiah could translate by the gift and power of God. Many in our day find great joy in realizing that the heavens are open and that God speaks to living prophets, seers, and revelators. Consider the friends and family you know and love who need to discover this joy. What is the best way for you to tell them the good news?

Why did Limhi's people desire to be with Alma and his followers? (21:30–31) "It ought not be lost upon the reader that those who joined Alma at the waters of Mormon and entered into the covenant of repentance and baptism escaped the bondage and suffering imposed upon those of the city of Nephi that would cause them to flee into the wilderness. Our story bespeaks the verity that gospel covenants faithfully kept bring both spiritual and temporal freedom, while iniquity brings both spiritual and temporal bondage" (McConkie and Millet, *Doctrinal Commentary*, 2:274).

What modern-day Church history event parallels this event? (21:34) "The history of Latter-day Saints of indigenous African heritage has largely been one of 'waiting on the Lord,' trusting that if they remain faithful, they will 'mount up with wings as eagles' and will 'run and not be weary and walk and not faint.' Since the priesthood revelation of 1978, which was voted as the top story of the century in a *Church News* poll, those of black African ancestry in nations throughout the world have willingly taken their places as an integral part of the Church" (Lloyd, "Revelation Rewarded Those Who Waited").

Mosiah 22:1–8. Gideon Presents His Plan to Deliver the People of Limhi

How do we have access to the same power that made deliverance possible for Limhi's people? (22:2) After Limhi's people arrived in Zarahemla, Alma counseled them "that they should remember that it was the Lord that did deliver them" (Mosiah 25:16). Likewise, we are taught: "The Lord will give relief with divine power when you seek deliverance in humility and *faith in Jesus Christ*. . . . That faith is demonstrated by a willingness to trust His promises given through His prophets and in His scriptures, . . . trust that He will help you use your agency to open the doors. . . . Faith in Christ means we trust Him; we trust His teachings" (Scott, "To Be Healed," 8). ☉

How does Gideon's plan follow the Lord's teachings regarding revelation? (22:3–8) "Limhi's people were now turning to the Lord with full purpose of heart and putting their trust in him. Their trust is exemplified in their devoted study to obtain deliverance from bondage (Mosiah 21:36). The Lord has instructed us to study things out in our minds as part of the revelatory process (D&C 9:8). . . . Gideon, the stalwart defender of righteousness, entered the picture. His study resulted

35 They were desirous to be baptized as a witness and a testimony that they were willing to serve God with all their hearts; nevertheless they did prolong the time; and an account of their baptism shall be given hereafter.

36 And now all the study of Ammon and his people, and king Limhi and his people, was to deliver themselves out of the hands of the Lamanites and from bondage.

CHAPTER 22

Plans are made for the people to escape from Lamanite bondage—The Lamanites are made drunk—The people escape, return to Zarahemla, and become subject to King Mosiah. About 121–120 B.C.

1 And now it came to pass that Ammon and king Limhi began to consult with the people how they should deliver themselves out of bondage; and even they did cause that all the people should gather themselves together; and this they did that they might have the voice of the people concerning the matter.

2 And it came to pass that they could find no way to deliver themselves out of bondage, except it were to take their women and children, and their flocks, and their herds, and their tents, and depart into the wilderness; for the Lamanites being so numerous, it was impossible for the people of Limhi to contend with them, thinking to deliver themselves out of bondage by the sword.

3 Now it came to pass that Gideon went forth and stood before the king, and said unto him: Now O king, thou hast hitherto hearkened unto my words many times when we have been contending with our brethren, the Lamanites.

4 And now O king, if thou hast not found me to be an unprofitable servant, or if thou hast hitherto listened to my words in any degree, and they have been of service to thee, even so I desire that thou wouldst listen to my words at this time, and I will be thy servant and deliver this people out of bondage.

5 And the king granted unto him that he might speak. And Gideon said unto him:

6 Behold the back pass, through the back wall, on the back side of the city. The Lamanites, or the guards of the Lamanites, by night are drunken; therefore let us send a proclamation among all this people that they gather together their flocks and herds, that they may drive them into the wilderness by night.

7 And I will go according to thy command and pay the last tribute of wine to the Lamanites, and they will be drunken; and we will pass through the secret pass on the left of their camp when they are drunken and asleep.

8 Thus we will depart with our women and our children, our flocks, and our herds into the wilderness; and we will travel around the land of Shilom.

9 And it came to pass that the king hearkened unto the words of Gideon.

10 And king Limhi caused that his people should gather their flocks together; and he sent the tribute of wine to the Lamanites; and he also sent more wine, as a present unto them; and they did drink freely of the wine which king Limhi did send unto them.

11 And it came to pass that the people of king Limhi did depart by night into the wilderness with their flocks and their herds, and they went round about the land of Shilom in the wilderness, and bent their course towards the land of Zarahemla, being led by Ammon and his brethren.

in a plan to pay a tribute of wine to the Lamanites and to escape through a secret pass while they were drunken. The plan worked, and the people of Limhi were delivered from bondage by the hand of the Lord" (Nyman, "Bondage and Deliverance," 266).

What do these details tell us about Gideon's knowledge in planning the Nephites' escape? (22:6–7)
"Gideon's knowledge of Lamanite drunkenness tells us that Gideon has some system of espionage. The fact that the Lamanites seem to have frequently, or even habitually, gotten drunk is interesting and may have been interpreted, even among the Lamanites, as a moral failing" (Gardner, *Second Witness*, 3:380). ❂

Mosiah 22:9–16. Limhi's People Are Delivered from the Lamanites

What can we learn from this and other significant journeys in the Book of Mormon? (22:12–13) "All major journeys in the Book of Mormon are allegorical as well as actual, and reflect not only the different kinds of the Lord's deliverances but also the principles on which the deliverances depend. All these journeys typify every person's sojourn on earth and the tasks that each is given to accomplish. Only God has the overview of the journey, and only God knows what will be needed along the way. He offers everything each one needs to succeed in the quest. As the Book of Mormon amply illustrates, however, people must often be persuaded to receive Christ's divine deliverance for their earthly journeys" (Thomas, "Types and Shadows of Deliverance," 186–87).

What significant plates were added to the Nephites' collection? (22:14) "The early history contained in the Book of Mormon is obtained from three sets of plates: the brass plates of Laban, the small plates of Nephi, and the large plates of Nephi. However, when Limhi's people join with the people of King Mosiah in the land of Zarahemla they bring with them two additional sets of plates: (1) their own records, which are known as the record of Zeniff, and (2) the 'records which had been found by the people of Limhi,' which are later identified as the records of Ether (see Ether 1:1–2)" (Ludlow, *Companion to Your Study of the Book of Mormon*, 188).

Superscription to Mosiah 23

The superscription to Mosiah 23 was part of the ancient record translated by the Prophet Joseph Smith and dictated by him to his scribe.

The phrase "Comprising chapters 23 and 24" is not from the ancient record but was added later to clarify which chapters in the book of Mosiah constitute the account of Alma in the land of Helam.

Mosiah 23:1–5. Alma's People Escape into the Wilderness

How should righteous people respond to warnings? (23:1) President Boyd K. Packer shared this insight: "When the Teton dam [built not far from Rexburg, Idaho,] collapsed and unleashed seventeen miles of backed-up water and accumulated debris upon the towns and farms beneath it, only eleven of nearly thirty-five thousand people in the path of

12 And they had taken all their gold, and silver, and their precious things, which they could carry, and also their provisions with them, into the wilderness; and they pursued their journey.

13 And after being many days in the wilderness they arrived in the land of Zarahemla, and joined Mosiah's people, and became his subjects.

14 And it came to pass that Mosiah received them with joy; and he also received their records, and also the records which had been found by the people of Limhi.

15 And now it came to pass when the Lamanites had found that the people of Limhi had departed out of the land by night, that they sent an army into the wilderness to pursue them;

16 And after they had pursued them two days, they could no longer follow their tracks; therefore they were lost in the wilderness.

An account of Alma and the people of the Lord, who were driven into the wilderness by the people of King Noah.

Comprising chapters 23 and 24.

CHAPTER 23

Alma refuses to be king—He serves as high priest—The Lord chastens His people, and the Lamanites conquer the land of Helam—Amulon, leader of King Noah's wicked priests, rules subject to the Lamanite monarch. About 145–121 B.C.

1 Now Alma, having been warned of the Lord that the armies of king Noah would come upon them, and having made it known to his people, therefore they gathered together their flocks, and took of their grain, and departed into the wilderness before the armies of king Noah.

2 And the Lord did strengthen them, that the people of king Noah could not overtake them to destroy them.

3 And they fled eight days' journey into the wilderness.

4 And they came to a land, yea, even a very beautiful and pleasant land, a land of pure water.

5 And they pitched their tents, and began to till the ground, and began to build buildings; yea, they were industrious, and did labor exceedingly.

6 And the people were desirous that Alma should be their king, for he was beloved by his people.

7 But he said unto them: Behold, it is not expedient that we should have a king; for thus saith the Lord: Ye shall not esteem one flesh above another, or one man shall not think himself above another; therefore I say unto you it is not expedient that ye should have a king.

8 Nevertheless, if it were possible that ye could always have just men to be your kings it would be well for you to have a king.

9 But remember the iniquity of king Noah and his priests; and I myself was caught in a snare, and did many things which were abominable in the sight of the Lord, which caused me sore repentance;

the flood died. Why? Because they were warned; and more importantly, because they heeded the warning instantly. . . .

"We, too, have been warned. It seems almost against our natures to accept warning or guidance from others. There are, however, times when, regardless of how much we know, our very existence depends upon paying attention to those who guide us" (*That All May Be Edified*, 203).

What does the escape of Alma's people illustrate about what the Lord will do for His people? (23:1–2) Nephi promised to show us that "the tender mercies of the Lord are over all those whom he has chosen, because of their faith, to make them mighty even unto the power of deliverance" (1 Nephi 1:20).

How does this verse in Mosiah 23:2 illustrate the truth of that promise?

What principle did Mormon emphasize as he related the history of Alma and his people settling in a new land? (23:5) Being industrious or hardworking has always been expected of the Lord's people (see Genesis 3:19). "The aim of the Church is to help the people to help themselves. Work is to be re-enthroned as the ruling principle of the lives of our Church membership" (Grant, in Conference Report, Oct. 1936, 3).

Mosiah 23:6–13. Alma Refuses to Be King

What is the inherent danger in having a leader with great power? (23:6–13) "Alma wisely denied his people's offer of kingship and taught them to treasure their liberty and freedom, especially their freedom 'from the bonds of iniquity' into which King Noah and his wicked priests had led them. 'Even so,' he said, 'I desire that ye should stand fast in this liberty wherewith ye have been made free' (Mosiah 23:4, 6, 13). Alma's caution to his people applies to all of us today. We must be ever vigilant to ensure that our government leaders serve us well in protecting our liberty and freedom, including our freedom 'from the bonds of iniquity'" (Wirthlin, "Alma the Elder," 90).

Why must we not esteem ourselves above others? (23:7) "The Book of Mormon promises that all who receive and act upon the Lord's invitation to 'repent and believe in his Son' become 'the covenant people of the Lord' (2 Ne. 30:2). This is a potent reminder that neither riches nor lineage nor any other privileges of birth should cause us to believe that we are 'better one than another' (Alma 5:54; see also Jacob 3:9)" (Oaks, "All Men Everywhere," 79).

How does tribulation bless us? (23:10) Elder D. Todd Christofferson noted: "The very experience of enduring chastening can refine us and prepare us for greater spiritual privileges" ("'As Many As I Love,'" 98).

President John Taylor observed: "I used to think, if I were the Lord, I would not suffer people to be tried as they are. But I have changed my mind on that subject. Now I think I would, if I were the Lord, because it purges out the meanness and corruption that stick around the Saints, like flies around molasses" (in *Journal of Discourses*, 5:115). ⊕

How do we achieve and maintain the blessings of liberty and freedom? (23:13) "In all ages when the people of God listened to the voice and counsel of apostles and prophets, they enjoyed the blessings growing out of human freedom, and the tyranny and oppression of kings and rulers was impossible. There never was a kingly power placed over ancient Israel except against the remonstrance of the prophets" (Erastus Snow, in *Journal of Discourses*, 23:233).

Mosiah 23:14–18. Alma Organizes the Church of Jesus Christ

Why should we trust only teachers and leaders who are men of God? (23:14) "The care we take in the choice of a physician ought to be nothing in comparison with the caution we take in the choice of those with whom we trust our eternal well-being. A wise father observed that he would rather trust his sheep to the care of a wolf than his children to a teacher who did not willingly keep the commandments of God" (McConkie and Millet, *Doctrinal Commentary*, 2:280).

Was there a church among the Nephites before Alma? (23:16) "In the part of the Book of Mormon where we first read that Alma was the 'founder of their church,' the pronoun *their* refers only to the people who were with Alma in the wilderness; it does not refer to the entire Nephite nation" (Ludlow, *Companion to Your Study of the Book of Mormon*, 189).

How do we watch over each other? (23:18) Just as church leaders in Alma's day "did watch over their people," modern prophets have asked us to do the same through ministering. "The ways in which we can love and minister to one another are limitless. Every child of God is unique; therefore, effective ministering must be highly individualized and led by the Spirit. . . . As we commit to being flexible and then prayerfully consider how to best love and serve others, we will be blessed with the inspiration and knowledge we need to minister as the Savior did" ("What Is Ministering?" ChurchofJesusChrist.org).

10 Nevertheless, after much tribulation, the Lord did hear my cries, and did answer my prayers, and has made me an instrument in his hands in bringing so many of you to a knowledge of his truth.

11 Nevertheless, in this I do not glory, for I am unworthy to glory of myself.

12 And now I say unto you, ye have been oppressed by king Noah, and have been in bondage to him and his priests, and have been brought into iniquity by them; therefore ye were bound with the bands of iniquity.

13 And now as ye have been delivered by the power of God out of these bonds; yea, even out of the hands of king Noah and his people, and also from the bonds of iniquity, even so I desire that ye should stand fast in this liberty wherewith ye have been made free, and that ye trust no man to be a king over you.

14 And also trust no one to be your teacher nor your minister, except he be a man of God, walking in his ways and keeping his commandments.

15 Thus did Alma teach his people, that every man should love his neighbor as himself, that there should be no contention among them.

16 And now, Alma was their high priest, he being the founder of their church.

17 And it came to pass that none received authority to preach or to teach except it were by him from God. Therefore he consecrated all their priests and all their teachers; and none were consecrated except they were just men.

18 Therefore they did watch over their people, and did nourish them with things pertaining to righteousness.

19 And it came to pass that they began to prosper exceedingly in the land; and they called the land Helam.

20 And it came to pass that they did multiply and prosper exceedingly in the land of Helam; and they built a city, which they called the city of Helam.

21 Nevertheless the Lord seeth fit to chasten his people; yea, he trieth their patience and their faith.

22 Nevertheless—whosoever putteth his trust in him the same shall be lifted up at the last day. Yea, and thus it was with this people.

23 For behold, I will show unto you that they were brought into bondage, and none could deliver them but the Lord their God, yea, even the God of Abraham and Isaac and of Jacob.

24 And it came to pass that he did deliver them, and he did show forth his mighty power unto them, and great were their rejoicings.

25 For behold, it came to pass that while they were in the land of Helam, yea, in the city of Helam, while tilling the land round about, behold an army of the Lamanites was in the borders of the land.

26 Now it came to pass that the brethren of Alma fled from their fields, and gathered themselves together in the city of Helam; and they were much frightened because of the appearance of the Lamanites.

27 But Alma went forth and stood among them, and exhorted them that they should not be frightened, but that they should

Mosiah 23:19–39. Alma's People Are Put in Bondage to the Lamanites

Why was the land and the city where Alma's people dwelt called *Helam*? (23:19–20) It was not uncommon in ancient times for places to be named after relatives or someone held in high regard (see 2 Nephi 5:8). It is likely the land of Helam was named after one of the first converts among the people of King Noah who was baptized by Alma at the waters of Mormon (see Mosiah 18:12).

What blessing comes from chastening? (23:21) "Faith likewise includes faith in God's developmental purposes, for 'the Lord seeth fit to chasten his people; yea, he trieth their patience and their faith' (Mosiah 23:21). Still, some of us have trouble when God's tutoring is applied to us! We plead for exemption more than we do for sanctification, don't we, brothers and sisters?" (Maxwell, "'Lest Ye Be Wearied and Faint in Your Minds,'" 90). ✛

What blessings have you seen in your life from putting your trust in God? (23:22) How does this verse give you hope for your life as you face the future?

What can we learn from Alma's advice to His people in response to their fear? (23:27) "When you're experiencing a severe trial, ask yourself this question: 'Am I trying to do what the Lord would have me do?' If you're not, then adjust your course. But if you are, remember the boy outside the walls of Jerusalem who turned to his brothers and said, 'I will go and do the things which the Lord hath commanded, for I know that the Lord giveth no commandments unto the children of men, save he shall prepare a way for them that they may accomplish the thing which he commandeth them' (1 Nephi 3:7)" (Eyring, *To Draw Closer to God*, 86). ✪

remember the Lord their God and he would deliver them.

28 Therefore they hushed their fears, and began to cry unto the Lord that he would soften the hearts of the Lamanites, that they would spare them, and their wives, and their children.

29 And it came to pass that the Lord did soften the hearts of the Lamanites. And Alma and his brethren went forth and delivered themselves up into their hands; and the Lamanites took possession of the land of Helam.

30 Now the armies of the Lamanites, which had followed after the people of king Limhi, had been lost in the wilderness for many days.

31 And behold, they had found those priests of king Noah, in a place which they called Amulon; and they had begun to possess the land of Amulon and had begun to till the ground.

32 Now the name of the leader of those priests was Amulon.

33 And it came to pass that Amulon did plead with the Lamanites; and he also sent forth their wives, who were the daughters of the Lamanites, to plead with their brethren, that they should not destroy their husbands.

34 And the Lamanites had compassion on Amulon and his brethren, and did not destroy them, because of their wives.

35 And Amulon and his brethren did join the Lamanites, and they were traveling in the wilderness in search of the land of Nephi when they discovered the land of Helam, which was possessed by Alma and his brethren.

36 And it came to pass that the Lamanites promised unto Alma and his brethren, that if they would show them the way which led to the land of Nephi that they would grant unto them their lives and their liberty.

37 But after Alma had shown them the way that led to the land of Nephi the Lamanites would not keep their promise; but they set guards round about the land of Helam, over Alma and his brethren.

38 And the remainder of them went to the land of Nephi; and a part of them returned to the land of Helam, and also brought with them the wives and the children of the guards who had been left in the land.

39 And the king of the Lamanites had granted unto Amulon that he should be a king and a ruler over his people, who were in the land of Helam; nevertheless he should have no power to do anything contrary to the will of the king of the Lamanites.

CHAPTER 24

Amulon persecutes Alma and his people—They are to be put to death if they pray—The Lord makes their burdens seem light—He delivers them from bondage, and they return to Zarahemla. About 145–120 B.C.

1 And it came to pass that Amulon did gain favor in the eyes of the king of the Lamanites; therefore, the king of the Lamanites granted unto him and his brethren that they should be appointed teachers over his people, yea, even over the people who were in the land of Shemlon, and in the land of Shilom, and in the land of Amulon.

2 For the Lamanites had taken possession of all these lands; therefore, the king of the Lamanites had appointed kings over all these lands.

3 And now the name of the king of the Lamanites was Laman, being called after the name of his father; and therefore he was called king Laman. And he was king over a numerous people.

Mosiah 24:1–7. Amulon and His People Teach the Nephite Language to the Lamanites

How was it a blessing that the Lamanites learned the Nephite language? (24:4) "The priests of Amulon were commissioned to teach the Nephite language to the Lamanites (Mosiah 24:1–7). One cannot help but wonder if the Lord's hand was not involved in this assignment. While they did not teach the law of Moses or the words of Abinadi (they were not qualified anyway), did they not prepare the way for the future Nephite missionaries, the sons of Mosiah, to proclaim the gospel among the Lamanites?" (Nyman, "Bondage and Deliverance," 264). ◐

What can we learn from the Lamanites as they acquired the wisdom of the world but not the knowledge of God? (24:5–7) "I want to emphasize several principles of wisdom. First, in our age of information and knowledge, we must seek after wisdom. Wisdom is multidimensional and comes in different sizes and colors. Wisdom gained early brings enormous blessings. Wisdom in one area may not be transferable to another. And finally, the wisdom of the world, while in many cases very valuable, is most valuable when it humbly bows to the wisdom of God" (Andersen, "Reverence for God Is the Beginning of Wisdom," 34). ◐

Mosiah 24:8–12. Amulon Persecutes Alma and His Followers

Why would nonbelievers prohibit prayer? (24:11) "How bitter is the irony that so many dissipate their energies in fighting a God whose existence they refuse to admit! Had Amulon not feared the God of Alma and his people, he would not have feared their prayers. The death ban on prayer is assuredly an admission on his part of the efficacy of prayer and the reality of Israel's God" (McConkie and Millet, *Doctrinal Commentary*, 2:287).

4 And he appointed teachers of the brethren of Amulon in every land which was possessed by his people; and thus the language of Nephi began to be taught among all the people of the Lamanites.

5 And they were a people friendly one with another; nevertheless they knew not God; neither did the brethren of Amulon teach them anything concerning the Lord their God, neither the law of Moses; nor did they teach them the words of Abinadi;

6 But they taught them that they should keep their record, and that they might write one to another.

7 And thus the Lamanites began to increase in riches, and began to trade one with another and wax great, and began to be a cunning and a wise people, as to the wisdom of the world, yea, a very cunning people, delighting in all manner of wickedness and plunder, except it were among their own brethren.

8 And now it came to pass that Amulon began to exercise authority over Alma and his brethren, and began to persecute him, and cause that his children should persecute their children.

9 For Amulon knew Alma, that he had been one of the king's priests, and that it was he that believed the words of Abinadi and was driven out before the king, and therefore he was wroth with him; for he was subject to king Laman, yet he exercised authority over them, and put tasks upon them, and put task-masters over them.

10 And it came to pass that so great were their afflictions that they began to cry mightily to God.

11 And Amulon commanded them that they should stop their cries; and he put guards over them to watch them, that whosoever should be found calling upon God should be put to death.

12 And Alma and his people did not raise their voices to the Lord their God, but did pour out their hearts to him; and he did know the thoughts of their hearts.

13 And it came to pass that the voice of the Lord came to them in their afflictions, saying: Lift up your heads and be of good comfort, for I know of the covenant which ye have made unto me; and I will covenant with my people and deliver them out of bondage.

14 And I will also ease the burdens which are put upon your shoulders, that even you cannot feel them upon your backs, even while you are in bondage; and this will I do that ye may stand as witnesses for me hereafter, and that ye may know of a surety that I, the Lord God, do visit my people in their afflictions.

15 And now it came to pass that the burdens which were laid upon Alma and his brethren were made light; yea, the Lord did strengthen them that they could bear up their burdens with ease, and they did submit cheerfully and with patience to all the will of the Lord.

16 And it came to pass that so great was their faith and their patience that the voice of the Lord came unto them again, saying: Be of good comfort, for on the morrow I will deliver you out of bondage.

17 And he said unto Alma: Thou shalt go before this people, and I will go with thee and deliver this people out of bondage.

18 Now it came to pass that Alma and his people in the night-time gathered their flocks together, and also of their grain; yea, even all the night-time were they gathering their flocks together.

19 And in the morning the Lord caused a deep sleep to come upon the Lamanites, yea, and all their task-masters were in a profound sleep.

20 And Alma and his people departed into

Why does the idea that God knows our thoughts trouble some people? (24:12) Why does that idea trouble some people? (consider D&C 1:1–3). In what ways could it be a blessing that God knows what is in our minds and hearts?

Mosiah 24:13–25. The Lord Hears the Cries of Alma and His People and Delivers Them from Bondage

How does the Lord ease our burdens? (24:14) "The people who followed Alma were in bondage to wicked oppressors. When they prayed for relief, the Lord told them He would deliver them eventually, but in the meantime He would ease their burdens 'that even you cannot feel them upon your backs, even while you are in bondage; and this will I do that ye may stand as witnesses . . . that I, the Lord God, do visit my people in their afflictions' (Mosiah 24:14). In that case the people did not have their burdens removed, but the Lord strengthened them so that 'they could bear up their burdens with ease' (v. 15)" (Oaks, "He Heals the Heavy Laden," 8).

the wilderness; and when they had traveled all day they pitched their tents in a valley, and they called the valley Alma, because he led their way in the wilderness.

21 Yea, and in the valley of Alma they poured out their thanks to God because he had been merciful unto them, and eased their burdens, and had delivered them out of bondage; for they were in bondage, and none could deliver them except it were the Lord their God.

22 And they gave thanks to God, yea, all their men and all their women and all their children that could speak lifted their voices in the praises of their God.

23 And now the Lord said unto Alma: Haste thee and get thou and this people out of this land, for the Lamanites have awakened and do pursue thee; therefore get thee out of this land, and I will stop the Lamanites in this valley that they come no further in pursuit of this people.

24 And it came to pass that they departed out of the valley, and took their journey into the wilderness.

25 And after they had been in the wilderness twelve days they arrived in the land of Zarahemla; and king Mosiah did also receive them with joy.

CHAPTER 25

The descendants of Mulek at Zarahemla become Nephites—They learn of the people of Alma and of Zeniff—Alma baptizes Limhi and all his people—Mosiah authorizes Alma to organize the Church of God. About 120 B.C.

1 And now king Mosiah caused that all the people should be gathered together.

2 Now there were not so many of the children of Nephi, or so many of those who were descendants of Nephi, as there were of the people of Zarahemla, who was a descendant

How does Alma's journey in the wilderness compare to Moses's exodus? (24:24) "The Exodus served as more than an affirmation of God's power for these two groups [Alma's group and King Limhi's group (see Mosiah 22)] in bondage. It served as a pattern for their escape as well" (Brown, "The Exodus," 56). ✱

Mosiah 25:1–4. King Mosiah Gathers His People

Who was Mulek? (25:1–2) "Mulek, the son of Zedekiah, is mentioned several times in the Book of Mormon (see Mosiah 25:2; Helaman 6:10; 8:21) but not in the Bible—at least not in a way that people have recognized, until just recently. Biblical scholarship now bears out this Book of Mormon claim: King Zedekiah had a son named *Mulek*" (Smith, "New Information about Mulek," 142). ✱

Limhi's Bondage and Deliverance	Alma's Bondage and Deliverance
Limhi's group was placed under bondage with much bloodshed (21:5–12).	Alma's group was placed under bondage with no bloodshed (23:35–38; 24:9).
The Lord was slow to hear their cries because they had been slow to hear Him (21:15).	The Lord was not slow to hear their cries (24:10–13).
The Lord softened the Lamanites' hearts so they eased the burdens of Limhi's group (21:15).	The Lord physically eased the burdens of Alma's group (24:14–15).
They prospered by degrees as their faith increased (21:16).	The Lord visited them in their afflictions (24:14).
Gideon devised a plan of escape (22:9).	The Lord said, "I will deliver you" (24:16).
They got the guards drunk (22:7, 10).	The Lord put the guards to sleep (24:19).
They needed to have Ammon lead them to Zarahemla (22:11).	The Lord led them to Zarahemla (24:23–25).

"As this chart shows, because Alma and his people had been humbled by the word of God rather than being compelled to be humble by their bondage as Limhi's group had been, the Lord made the bondage of Alma and his people much easier to endure. The message for us is that it is better to repent sooner than later. The slower we are to hearken to the Lord, the slower he must be in responding to our needs. How reassuring it must have been to Alma's people to experience the miracle of not feeling the burdens which were placed upon their backs. They could have no question in their minds about whose power it was that delivered them and led them back to the land of Zarahemla.

"The question may be asked why Alma's group was put into bondage since they had repented, had made covenants, and had served the Lord for some time. The answer seems to go back to Abinadi's prophecy. When he first came to the Nephites in the land of Nephi, he warned that they would be brought into bondage, if they did not repent (see Mosiah 11:21). This warning went unheeded until Abinadi returned two years later. His warning then proclaimed that they would be brought into bondage, and if they still refused to repent they would be destroyed (see Mosiah 12:2, 8). It was at this time that Alma was converted and began to teach the words of Abinadi secretly to those Nephites who would listen. Thus, even though Alma and his people had repented, it was still necessary that Abinadi's first prophecy be fulfilled" (Williams, "Deliverance from Bondage," 271). http://gospelink.com/library/document/28290).v

Who were the people of Zarahemla? (25:2) "When [Mosiah₁] I led the more righteous portion of the Nephites northward from the land of Lehi-Nephi (about 200 B.C.) he found [the people of Zarahemla]. . . . It was discovered that the people of Zarahemla were the descendants of a colony which had been led by the Lord out of Jerusalem in the year when that city was destroyed by the king of Babylon (587 B.C.). After wandering in the wilderness they were brought across the ocean and landed in the Americas. In the years that followed, they migrated southward to the place where they were found by Mosiah" (McConkie and Millet, *Doctrinal Commentary*, 2:287–88).

What influence did Mulek's descendants have on Nephite history? (25:2) "If the Book of Mormon story is truly analogous to the biblical, we should expect that some of the Mulekites objected to Nephite rule and occasionally rebelled against those in power. There is, in fact, evidence that the rebellious king-men and Nehors may have been Mulekites" (Tvedtnes, "Book of Mormon Tribal Affiliation and Military Castes," 298). ✇

Mosiah 25:5–13. King Mosiah Reads the Records to His People

How could the record cover the time that Alma left Zarahemla if Alma was born in the land of Nephi? (25:6) "A first possibility is that the phrase 'Alma and his brethren' includes the group's ancestors as well as all who were ever part of the colonization effort. . . . A second possibility is that Alma and other members of his group did originally come from the land of Zarahemla. If the events that Amaleki recorded in the book of Omni are chronological, then Zeniff's group left during the early years of Benjamin's reign. Because Limhi's group returned soon after Benjamin's death, the time between the two events may have been no longer than the length of Benjamin's reign" (Cazier, "I Have a Question," 60–61). ✇

of Mulek, and those who came with him into the wilderness.

3 And there were not so many of the people of Nephi and of the people of Zarahemla as there were of the Lamanites; yea, they were not half so numerous.

4 And now all the people of Nephi were assembled together, and also all the people of Zarahemla, and they were gathered together in two bodies.

5 And it came to pass that Mosiah did read, and caused to be read, the records of Zeniff to his people; yea, he read the records of the people of Zeniff, from the time they left the land of Zarahemla until they returned again.

6 And he also read the account of Alma and his brethren, and all their afflictions, from the time they left the land of Zarahemla until the time they returned again.

7 And now, when Mosiah had made an end of reading the records, his people who tarried in the land were struck with wonder and amazement.

8 For they knew not what to think; for when they beheld those that had been delivered out of bondage they were filled with exceedingly great joy.

9 And again, when they thought of their brethren who had been slain by the Lamanites they were filled with sorrow, and even shed many tears of sorrow.

10 And again, when they thought of the immediate goodness of God, and his power in

delivering Alma and his brethren out of the hands of the Lamanites and of bondage, they did raise their voices and give thanks to God.

11 And again, when they thought upon the Lamanites, who were their brethren, of their sinful and polluted state, they were filled with pain and anguish for the welfare of their souls.

12 And it came to pass that those who were the children of Amulon and his brethren, who had taken to wife the daughters of the Lamanites, were displeased with the conduct of their fathers, and they would no longer be called by the names of their fathers, therefore they took upon themselves the name of Nephi, that they might be called the children of Nephi and be numbered among those who were called Nephites.

13 And now all the people of Zarahemla were numbered with the Nephites, and this because the kingdom had been conferred upon none but those who were descendants of Nephi.

14 And now it came to pass that when Mosiah had made an end of speaking and reading to the people, he desired that Alma should also speak to the people.

15 And Alma did speak unto them, when they were assembled together in large bodies, and he went from one body to another, preaching unto the people repentance and faith on the Lord.

16 And he did exhort the people of Limhi and his brethren, all those that had been delivered out of bondage, that they should remember that it was the Lord that did deliver them.

17 And it came to pass that after Alma had taught the people many things, and had made an end of speaking to them, that king Limhi was desirous that he might be baptized; and all his people were desirous that they might be baptized also.

Does this disowning of parents foreshadow the hereafter? (25:12) "No one wants to bear a name that has been dishonored. Their action typifies that which is to happen in the world to come. Those whose fathers have no place in the kingdom of God will, like links of a chain, be removed, while their righteous seed will unite themselves with those of their progenitors worthy of that honor" (McConkie and Millet, *Doctrinal Commentary*, 2:289).

Mosiah 25:14–24. Alma Preaches the Gospel, Baptizes Converts, and Organizes the Church in Zarahemla

What is significant about Alma's introduction to the people of Zarahemla in this verse? (25:14) "Much information that Mormon does not tell us can be surmised from this verse, in which Mosiah publicly introduces Alma to the people. Modern readers of the Book of Mormon are so familiar with Alma that his immediate public role does not seem surprising, but it should be. In contrast to Alma, Limhi apparently moves into a secondary position in his own community (the city and land of Gideon) even though he had been a king" (Gardner, *Second Witness*, 3:421). ☉

Why is it so important to remember the divine source of our deliverance? (25:16) "When you look in the dictionary for the most important word, do you know what it is? It could be *remember*. Because all of you have made covenants—you know what to do and you know how to do it—our greatest need is to remember. That is why everyone goes to sacrament meeting every Sabbath day—to take the sacrament and listen to the priests pray that 'they may always remember him and keep his commandments which he has given them.' Remember is the word. Remember is the program" (Kimball, "Circles of Exaltation").

Is this a step toward separating church from state?
(25:19) "King Mosiah granted Alma the right to 'establish churches throughout all the land of Zarahemla' and authorized him 'to ordain priests and teachers over every church' (Mosiah 25:19)—a prerogative heretofore pertaining only to kingship. The overall organization was called the 'church,' but it was made up of subordinate local units also called 'churches.' There were seven of these local units in Zarahemla alone (Mosiah 25:22–23). Indeed, Mosiah gave Alma authority over the Church (Mosiah 26:8), thus effectively delegating to another man a major portion of the sacral authority which had traditionally been attached to the Nephite throne" (Peterson, "Priesthood in Mosiah," 202–3). ●

How united were these different churches?
(25:21–22) "'The Church is the same wherever you go!' I grew up hearing this from returning vacationers and from missionaries reporting their missions. And I understood what they meant. They didn't mean that the same hymns were sung elsewhere—though they were—or that everyone used the same lesson manuals, or that everyone thought the same. They meant the gospel felt the same wherever they went. This resulted from the presence of the Holy Spirit, which is the universal way we recognize the things of God" (Hlavaty, "Religion of Moses and the Book of Mormon," 105).

18 Therefore, Alma did go forth into the water and did baptize them; yea, he did baptize them after the manner he did his brethren in the waters of Mormon; yea, and as many as he did baptize did belong to the church of God; and this because of their belief on the words of Alma.

19 And it came to pass that king Mosiah granted unto Alma that he might establish churches throughout all the land of Zarahemla; and gave him power to ordain priests and teachers over every church.

20 Now this was done because there were so many people that they could not all be governed by one teacher; neither could they all hear the word of God in one assembly;

21 Therefore they did assemble themselves together in different bodies, being called churches; every church having their priests and their teachers, and every priest preaching the word according as it was delivered to him by the mouth of Alma.

22 And thus, notwithstanding there being many churches they were all one church, yea, even the church of God; for there was nothing preached in all the churches except it were repentance and faith in God.

23 And now there were seven churches in the land of Zarahemla. And it came to pass that whosoever were desirous to take upon them the name of Christ, or of God, they did join the churches of God;

24 And they were called the people of God. And the Lord did pour out his Spirit upon them, and they were blessed, and prospered in the land.

CHAPTER 26

Many members of the Church are led into sin by unbelievers—Alma is promised eternal life—Those who repent and are baptized gain forgiveness—Church members in sin who repent and confess to Alma and to the Lord will be forgiven; otherwise, they will not be numbered among the people of the Church. About 120–100 B.C.

1 Now it came to pass that there were many of the rising generation that could not understand the words of king Benjamin, being little children at the time he spake unto his people; and they did not believe the tradition of their fathers.

2 They did not believe what had been said concerning the resurrection of the dead, neither did they believe concerning the coming of Christ.

3 And now because of their unbelief they could not understand the word of God; and their hearts were hardened.

4 And they would not be baptized; neither would they join the church. And they were a separate people as to their faith, and remained so ever after, even in their carnal and sinful state; for they would not call upon the Lord their God.

5 And now in the reign of Mosiah they were not half so numerous as the people of God; but because of the dissensions among the brethren they became more numerous.

6 For it came to pass that they did deceive many with their flattering words, who were in the church, and did cause them to commit many sins; therefore it became expedient that those who committed sin, that were in the church, should be admonished by the church.

Mosiah 26:1–6. Members of the Church Are Led into Sin by Unbelievers

How can faith be preserved in the rising generation? (26:1–4) "No charge in the kingdom is more important than to build faith in youth. Each child in each generation chooses faith or disbelief. Faith is not an inheritance; it is a choice. Those who believed King Benjamin learned that. Many of their children chose later not to believe. The scriptures give as a reason, 'for they would not call upon the Lord their God' (Mosiah 26:4). . . . Teach doctrine and recount stories of faith and courage. I hope your students will remember the doctrine and the stirring stories. But most of all . . . your students will be more inclined to 'inquire of the Lord,' because of their experiences with you" (Eyring, "Helping Students Inquire of the Lord"). ●

What are some reasons why some individuals must be "admonished by the church"? (26:6) "Bishops and branch presidents and stake, mission, and district presidents have a responsibility to help members overcome transgression through repentance. . . . The purposes of disciplinary councils are to save the souls of transgressors, protect the innocent, and safeguard the purity, integrity, and good name of the Church ("Church Disciplinary Councils," *True to the Faith* (2004), 37–38). ●

Mosiah 26:7–13. The Leaders Try to Decide How to Work with Members Who Sin

Who were the priests and teachers? (26:7)
"Reference to 'priests and teachers' in the Book of Mormon should not be confused with the office of priest or the office of teacher as known to us in the Aaronic Priesthood today" (McConkie and Millet, *Doctrinal Commentary*, 1:225).

"In all dispensations it is the duty of those called to bear the priesthood to 'watch over the church always, and be with and strengthen them; and see *that there is no iniquity in the church*, neither hardness with each other, neither lying, backbiting, nor evil speaking; and see that the church meet together often, and also see that all the members do their duty' (D&C 20:53–55; italics added)" (McConkie and Millet, *Doctrinal Commentary*, 2:295).

Why did Mosiah refuse to judge? (26:12) "Old habits die hard. Alma, who claimed anti-monarchical views, turned to the monarch for assistance in solving a grievous ecclesiastical problem. But he had miscalculated king Mosiah II, for he was probably Alma's greatest convert to the anti-monarchical position. And, at least in this instance, Mosiah was a more consistent partisan of that stance than was the high priest. He refused to become involved in the kind of religious-ecclesiastical issue that he had put onto Alma's shoulders" (Peterson, "Church Discipline in the Book of Mosiah," 205). ⊙

How does Alma's troubled spirit and fear of doing wrong indicate how meek he was? (26:13) "Meekness is a defining attribute of the Redeemer and is distinguished by righteous responsiveness, willing submissiveness, and strong self-restraint" (Bednar, "Meek and Lowly of Heart," 32). How was Alma's response righteous, submissive, and illustrative of self-restraint?

7 And it came to pass that they were brought before the priests, and delivered up unto the priests by the teachers; and the priests brought them before Alma, who was the high priest.

8 Now king Mosiah had given Alma the authority over the church.

9 And it came to pass that Alma did not know concerning them; but there were many witnesses against them; yea, the people stood and testified of their iniquity in abundance.

10 Now there had not any such thing happened before in the church; therefore Alma was troubled in his spirit, and he caused that they should be brought before the king.

11 And he said unto the king: Behold, here are many whom we have brought before thee, who are accused of their brethren; yea, and they have been taken in divers iniquities. And they do not repent of their iniquities; therefore we have brought them before thee, that thou mayest judge them according to their crimes.

12 But king Mosiah said unto Alma: Behold, I judge them not; therefore I deliver them into thy hands to be judged.

13 And now the spirit of Alma was again troubled; and he went and inquired of the Lord what he should do concerning this matter, for he feared that he should do wrong in the sight of God.

Mosiah 26:14–32. The Lord Blesses Alma and Instructs Him How to Work with Members Who Sin

14 And it came to pass that after he had poured out his whole soul to God, the voice of the Lord came to him, saying:

15 Blessed art thou, Alma, and blessed are they who were baptized in the waters of Mormon. Thou art blessed because of thy exceeding faith in the words alone of my servant Abinadi.

16 And blessed are they because of their exceeding faith in the words alone which thou hast spoken unto them.

17 And blessed art thou because thou hast established a church among this people; and they shall be established, and they shall be my people.

18 Yea, blessed is this people who are willing to bear my name; for in my name shall they be called; and they are mine.

19 And because thou hast inquired of me concerning the transgressor, thou art blessed.

20 Thou art my servant; and I covenant with thee that thou shalt have eternal life; and thou shalt serve me and go forth in my name, and shalt gather together my sheep.

21 And he that will hear my voice shall be my sheep; and him shall ye receive into the church, and him will I also receive.

What does it mean to pour out our souls to God? (26:14) "There are moments that matter, occasions when a supplicant is poignantly aware of the need for divine direction. Though we are continually dependent on the light of heaven to illuminate our paths, there are occasions that require a sure answer, occasions in which we 'pour out our whole souls' in prayer—we implore with an intensity and petition with a passion. Even our Master, at the time of his greatest test, 'prayed more earnestly' (Luke 22:44)" (McConkie and Millet, *Doctrinal Commentary*, 2:295).

What blessings come from working with transgressors? (26:19) "Fearing to do wrong in the sight of God, Alma poured out his whole soul to God and pled with Him for answers as to how to handle the transgressors. Because of Alma's great love for his fellowman and his fervent desire to do God's will, the Lord blessed him mightily, even with a promise of eternal life. Then the Lord explained to him why his pleading for understanding in judgment was so important, saying: 'This is my Church. It is my name through which they will be saved. It is through my sacrifice. It is I who will judge'" (Mickelsen, "Atonement, Repentance, and Dirty Linen," 10).

What covenant or promise did the Lord give Alma? (26:20) The Prophet Joseph Smith explained the great promise Alma received from the Lord: "After a person has faith in Christ, repents of his sins, and is baptized for the remission of his sins and receives the Holy Ghost, . . . then let him continue to . . . [seek] after righteousness, and living by every word of God, and the Lord will soon say unto him, Son, thou shalt be exalted. When the Lord has thoroughly proved him, and finds that the man is determined to serve Him at all hazards, then the man will find his calling and his election made sure, then it will be his privilege to receive the other Comforter" (*History of the Church,* 3:380).

How does one hear the Savior's voice? (26:25–28)
Doctrine and Covenants 1:38 reminds us that the Lord's servants speak His voice. Likewise, Doctrine and Covenants 18:33–36 helps us understand that Jesus Christ also speaks to us through His latter-day scriptures when we read them with His Spirit.

How do we know if our repentance is sincere?
(26:29) "We begin with a dictionary's definition that to repent is 'to turn from sin . . . to feel sorrow [and] regret.' To repent from sin is not easy. But the prize is worth the price. Repentance needs to be done one step at a time. Humble prayer will facilitate each essential step. As prerequisites to forgiveness, there must first be recognition, remorse, then confession. 'By this ye may know if a man repenteth of his sins—behold, he will confess them and forsake them'" (Nelson, "Repentance and Conversion," 102). ✦

How does the Church bless the transgressor?
(26:29–30) President Dallin H. Oaks explained: "The objective of church discipline is to facilitate repentance, . . . to qualify a transgressor for the mercy of God and the salvation made possible through the

22 For behold, this is my church; whosoever is baptized shall be baptized unto repentance. And whomsoever ye receive shall believe in my name; and him will I freely forgive.

23 For it is I that taketh upon me the sins of the world; for it is I that hath created them; and it is I that granteth unto him that believeth unto the end a place at my right hand.

24 For behold, in my name are they called; and if they know me they shall come forth, and shall have a place eternally at my right hand.

25 And it shall come to pass that when the second trump shall sound then shall they that never knew me come forth and shall stand before me.

26 And then shall they know that I am the Lord their God, that I am their Redeemer; but they would not be redeemed.

27 And then I will confess unto them that I never knew them; and they shall depart into everlasting fire prepared for the devil and his angels.

28 Therefore I say unto you, that he that will not hear my voice, the same shall ye not receive into my church, for him I will not receive at the last day.

29 Therefore I say unto you, Go; and whosoever transgresseth against me, him shall ye judge according to the sins which he has committed; and if he confess his sins before thee and me, and repenteth in the sincerity of his heart, him shall ye forgive, and I will forgive him also.

30 Yea, and as often as my people repent will I forgive them their trespasses against me.

atonement of Jesus Christ. Consequently, church discipline is not an instrument of punishment but a catalyst for change. The purpose of the suffering that must occur as part of the process of repentance is not to *punish* the transgressor, but to *change* him. The broken heart and contrite spirit required to 'answer the ends of the law' introduce the repentant transgressor to the change necessary to conform his life to the pattern prescribed by his Redeemer" (*The Lord's Way*, 224).

Must the offender repent before we forgive? (26:31) Modern revelation clarifies that we are "required to forgive all men" (D&C 64:10).

President Spencer W. Kimball said: "Remember that we must forgive even if our offender did not repent and ask forgiveness.... Do we follow that commandment or do we sulk in our bitterness, waiting for our offender to learn of it and to kneel to us in remorse? ... No bitterness of past frictions can be held in memory if we forgive with all our hearts" (in Conference Report, Oct. 1949, 132–33).

Mosiah 26:33–39. Alma Judges the People

Does being appointed by God to be a spiritual judge over His people include the responsibility of forgiving sins? (26:33) "The bishop, and others in comparable positions, can forgive in the sense of waiving the penalties. In our loose connotation we sometimes call this forgiveness, but it is not forgiveness in the sense of 'wiping out' or absolution. The waiver means, however, that the individual will not need to be tried again for the same error, and that he may become active and have fellowship with the people of the Church. In receiving the confession and waiving the penalties the bishop is representing the Lord....

"It is the Lord, however, who forgives sin" (Kimball, *Miracle of Forgiveness*, 332).

What does it mean to have one's name blotted out? (26:35–36) "That is, they were cut off from the Church; their names were removed from the records of the Church; it would be as though no baptism had taken place, no remission of sins had been granted, no promises given" (McConkie and Millet, *Doctrinal Commentary*, 2:301).

31 And ye shall also forgive one another your trespasses; for verily I say unto you, he that forgiveth not his neighbor's trespasses when he says that he repents, the same hath brought himself under condemnation.

32 Now I say unto you, Go; and whosoever will not repent of his sins the same shall not be numbered among my people; and this shall be observed from this time forward.

33 And it came to pass when Alma had heard these words he wrote them down that he might have them, and that he might judge the people of that church according to the commandments of God.

34 And it came to pass that Alma went and judged those that had been taken in iniquity, according to the word of the Lord.

35 And whosoever repented of their sins and did confess them, them he did number among the people of the church;

36 And those that would not confess their sins and repent of their iniquity, the same were not numbered among the people of the church, and their names were blotted out.

37 And it came to pass that Alma did regulate all the affairs of the church; and they began again to have peace and to prosper exceedingly in the affairs of the church, walking

What does it mean to "pray without ceasing"?
(26:39) "It means simply that you continue in the practice of prayer. [Saying] 'he constantly brushed his teeth' doesn't mean he did it twenty-four hours a day. The interesting thing is that in a Semitic language like Arabic, the only way you can say *continually*, or *go on doing a thing* is *lāzalla* or *lam yazil/mā zalla, he did not cease. Mā zalla yaktubu*, "he did not cease writing," means he wrote from time to time, or he wrote regularly. . . . When it says, 'they continued in prayer without ceasing,' that doesn't mean they had a monastic fanaticism here, or anything like that" (Nibley, *Teachings of the Book of Mormon*, 2:183).

Mosiah 27:1–7. King Mosiah Forbids Persecution and Inequality

How can we preserve religious freedom today?
(27:2–3) In answering this question, Elder Quentin L. Cook replied: "First, be a righteous example. You must not be in camouflage as to who you are and what you believe. . . .

"Religious freedom all over the world is also under attack. It is important for us to become well educated on this issue and assume responsibility for ensuring that the religious freedom we have inherited is passed on to future generations. We must work together to both protect religious freedom and restore morality. . . .

circumspectly before God, receiving many, and baptizing many.

38 And now all these things did Alma and his fellow laborers do who were over the church, walking in all diligence, teaching the word of God in all things, suffering all manner of afflictions, being persecuted by all those who did not belong to the church of God.

39 And they did admonish their brethren; and they were also admonished, every one by the word of God, according to his sins, or to the sins which he had committed, being commanded of God to pray without ceasing, and to give thanks in all things.

CHAPTER 27

Mosiah forbids persecution and enjoins equality—Alma the younger and the four sons of Mosiah seek to destroy the Church—An angel appears and commands them to cease their evil course—Alma is struck dumb—All mankind must be born again to gain salvation—Alma and the sons of Mosiah declare glad tidings. About 100–92 B.C.

1 And now it came to pass that the persecutions which were inflicted on the church by the unbelievers became so great that the church began to murmur, and complain to their leaders concerning the matter; and they did complain to Alma. And Alma laid the case before their king, Mosiah. And Mosiah consulted with his priests.

2 And it came to pass that king Mosiah sent a proclamation throughout the land round about that there should not any unbeliever persecute any of those who belonged to the church of God.

3 And there was a strict command throughout all the churches that there should be no persecutions among them, that there should be an equality among all men;

4 That they should let no pride nor haughtiness disturb their peace; that every man should esteem his neighbor as himself, laboring with their own hands for their support.

5 Yea, and all their priests and teachers should labor with their own hands for their support, in all cases save it were in sickness, or in much want; and doing these things, they did abound in the grace of God.

6 And there began to be much peace again in the land; and the people began to be very numerous, and began to scatter abroad upon the face of the earth, yea, on the north and on the south, on the east and on the west, building large cities and villages in all quarters of the land.

7 And the Lord did visit them and prosper them, and they became a large and wealthy people.

8 Now the sons of Mosiah were numbered among the unbelievers; and also one of the sons of Alma was numbered among them, he being called Alma, after his father; nevertheless, he became a very wicked and an idolatrous man. And he was a man of many words, and did speak much flattery to the people; therefore he led many of the people to do after the manner of his iniquities.

9 And he became a great hinderment to the prosperity of the church of God; stealing away the hearts of the people; causing much dissension among the people; giving a chance for the enemy of God to exercise his power over them.

10 And now it came to pass that while he was going about to destroy the church of God, for he did go about secretly with the sons of Mosiah seeking to destroy the church, and to lead astray the people of the Lord, contrary to the commandments of God, or even the king—

"Our challenge is to help people without religious faith understand that the protection of moral principles grounded in religion is a great benefit to society and that religious devotion is critical to public virtue" ("Restoring Morality and Religious Freedom," 35–37). ●

Is there a difference between a "wealthy people" and rich individuals? (27:6–7) "There is the paradox again, that these people who don't set their hearts on wealth and don't strive for it at all become a large and wealthy people. Brigham Young said, 'I could easily make this the richest people in the world, but I'm afraid it would destroy them.' It says they were a large and wealthy people; it doesn't say they had great fortunes among them" (Nibley, *Teachings of the Book of Mormon*, 2:185).

Mosiah 27:8–17. An Angel Calls upon Alma the Younger to Repent

What do the enemies of truth want to accomplish? (27:8) "Consistently the doctrines or philosophies of those trying to lead members of the Church astray seek to justify a downward course. Invariably their appeal is in abandoning covenants and standards" (McConkie and Millet, *Doctrinal Commentary*, 2:305). ●

What does dissension look like today? (27:8–10) "Scriptures repeatedly warn that the father of contention opposes the plan of our Heavenly Father. Satan's method relies on the infectious canker of contention. Satan's motive: to gain personal acclaim even over God Himself.

"The work of the adversary may be likened to loading guns in opposition to the work of God. Salvos containing germs of contention are aimed and fired at strategic targets essential to that holy work. These vital targets include—in addition to the individual—the family, leaders of the Church, and divine doctrine" (Nelson, "Canker of Contention," 69). ●

Why was an angel sent to Alma and his companions? (27:11–14) "Mosiah 27:14 provides an example [of how the] prayers of the members of the church for a person have power and meaning and are heard by our Father. More important, the prayers of a faithful parent for a wayward child will be heard and honored by the Lord. He will not violate the agency of the child to choose between good and evil, but He will provide opportunity for repentance and welcome the former sinner back into the fold" (Edwards, "The Kingdom of God and the Kingdoms of Men," 276). ◐

How are the righteous prayers of the Saints heard and answered? (27:14–16) "The Lord has promised that if we ask in faith for that which is right, we shall receive (3 Ne. 18:20). However, he has not promised the manner or the time in which the prayer will be answered. When the angel appeared to Alma the younger and the four sons of Mosiah, the angel made it clear that he had not appeared to them because of their own worthiness. . . . It was primarily because of the faithful prayers of Alma the elder and the other members of the church that the angel appeared to Alma the younger and the four sons of Mosiah" (Ludlow, *Companion to Your Study of the Book of Mormon*, 192).

Why did the angel emphasize that Alma should remember the captivity of his fathers and the great things the Lord had done for them? (27:16) Did Alma do as he was counseled? A few years later while teaching the people of Zarahemla, Alma asked: "Have you sufficiently retained in remembrance the captivity of our fathers? Yea, and have ye sufficiently retained in remembrance his mercy and long-suffering towards them? And moreover, have ye sufficiently retained in remembrance that he has delivered their souls from hell?" (Alma 5:6). There is strong evidence Alma took the angel's directive to heart and likewise extended the challenge to those he taught.

11 And as I said unto you, as they were going about rebelling against God, behold, the angel of the Lord appeared unto them; and he descended as it were in a cloud; and he spake as it were with a voice of thunder, which caused the earth to shake upon which they stood;

12 And so great was their astonishment, that they fell to the earth, and understood not the words which he spake unto them.

13 Nevertheless he cried again, saying: Alma, arise and stand forth, for why persecutest thou the church of God? For the Lord hath said: This is my church, and I will establish it; and nothing shall overthrow it, save it is the transgression of my people.

14 And again, the angel said: Behold, the Lord hath heard the prayers of his people, and also the prayers of his servant, Alma, who is thy father; for he has prayed with much faith concerning thee that thou mightest be brought to the knowledge of the truth; therefore, for this purpose have I come to convince thee of the power and authority of God, that the prayers of his servants might be answered according to their faith.

15 And now behold, can ye dispute the power of God? For behold, doth not my voice shake the earth? And can ye not also behold me before you? And I am sent from God.

16 Now I say unto thee: Go, and remember the captivity of thy fathers in the land of Helam, and in the land of Nephi; and remember how great things he has done for them; for they were in bondage, and he has delivered them. And now I say unto thee, Alma, go thy way, and seek to destroy the church no more, that their prayers may be answered, and this even if thou wilt of thyself be cast off.

17 And now it came to pass that these were the last words which the angel spake unto Alma, and he departed.

18 And now Alma and those that were with him fell again to the earth, for great was their astonishment; for with their own eyes they had beheld an angel of the Lord; and his voice was as thunder, which shook the earth; and they knew that there was nothing save the power of God that could shake the earth and cause it to tremble as though it would part asunder.

19 And now the astonishment of Alma was so great that he became dumb, that he could not open his mouth; yea, and he became weak, even that he could not move his hands; therefore he was taken by those that were with him, and carried helpless, even until he was laid before his father.

20 And they rehearsed unto his father all that had happened unto them; and his father rejoiced, for he knew that it was the power of God.

21 And he caused that a multitude should be gathered together that they might witness what the Lord had done for his son, and also for those that were with him.

22 And he caused that the priests should assemble themselves together; and they began to fast, and to pray to the Lord their God that he would open the mouth of Alma, that he might speak, and also that his limbs might receive their strength—that the eyes of the people might be opened to see and know of the goodness and glory of God.

23 And it came to pass after they had fasted and prayed for the space of two days and two nights, the limbs of Alma received their strength, and he stood up and began to speak unto them, bidding them to be of good comfort:

Mosiah 27:18–31. Alma Repents and Is Forgiven

How is Alma's experience similar to that of Saul/Paul? (27:19–20) " Alma's similarity to Saul/Paul is clear in the physical incapacity that resulted from the visitation (Acts 9:8). Contrary to Saul, however, Alma is completely debilitated. His companions are functional, able to carry him to assistance. Saul was only blind, but Alma was dumb and so weak that he was 'carried helpless.' That he was 'laid' before his father indicates that he was too weak even to sit. This physical weakness apparently resulted from a spiritual struggle, which he recounts later. Perhaps he was so preoccupied with the internal that his body was unable to cope with the external. Whatever the cause, his condition clearly stemmed from his experience with the angel" (Gardner, *Second Witness*, 3:454).

What effect did the righteous prayers of Alma and the people have upon Alma the younger? (27:19–23) "Through the prayers of his father, Alma . . . was now ready to be baptized by fire and the Holy Ghost. He had certainly been baptized by water as a youth, being the son of the head of the church, but had not been baptized by the Spirit. Two days and two nights of purging (v. 23) is not the usual way of being baptized by fire, but Alma . . . was not the usual person. He needed a cleansing of intense fire to purge out the old creature. The assembling of the priests to fast and pray (v. 22) had involved the church in his cleansing, both as participants and as observers of God's power" (Nyman, *These Records Are True*, 491). ⊕

How do fasting and prayer work together? (27:23–24) President Russell M. Nelson taught: "The sweet power of prayer can be intensified by fasting, on occasion, when appropriate to a particular need" ("Sweet Power of Prayer," 7).

What is spiritual birth? (27:24–27) "The spiritual birth comes after the natural birth. It is to die as pertaining to worldliness and carnality and to become a new creature by the power of the Spirit. It is to begin a new life, a life in which we bridle our passions and control our appetites, a life of righteousness, a spiritual life. Whereas we were in a deep abyss of darkness, now we are alive in Christ and bask in the shining rays of his everlasting light. Such is the new birth, the second birth, the birth into the household of Christ" (McConkie, *New Witness*, 282). ⊕

How can we be born again? (27:25) "Sins are remitted not in the waters of baptism, as we say in speaking figuratively, but when we receive the Holy Ghost. It is the Holy Spirit of God that erases carnality and brings us into a state of righteousness. We become clean when we actually receive the fellowship and companionship of the Holy Ghost. It is then that sin and dross and evil are burned out of our souls as though by fire. The baptism of the Holy Ghost is the baptism of fire.... And the Spirit will not dwell in an unclean tabernacle" (McConkie, *New Witness*, 290). ⊕

Must we experience what Alma experienced? (27:29) "We must be cautious as we discuss these remarkable examples. Though they are real and powerful, they are the exception more than the rule. For every Paul, for every Enos, and for every King Lamoni [or Alma the Younger], there are hundreds and thousands of people who find the process of repentance much more subtle, much more imperceptible. Day by day they move closer to the Lord, little realizing they are building a godlike life. They live quiet lives of goodness, service, and commitment. They are like the Lamanites, who the Lord said 'were baptized with fire and with the Holy Ghost, *and they knew it not*' (3 Ne. 9:20; italics added)" (Benson, "Mighty Change of Heart," 5). ⊕

How can "eternal torment" last only three days? (27:28–29) "As to the duration of punishment, we may take assurance that it will be graded according to the sin; and that the conception of every sentence for misdeeds being interminable [unending] is false. ... Any punishment ordained of God is eternal, for He is eternal (D&C 19:12–14). His is a system of endless punishment, for it will always exist as a place or condition prepared for disobedient spirits; yet the infliction of the penalty will have an end in every case of acceptable repentance and reparation" (Talmage, *Articles of Faith*, 60–61).

24 For, said he, I have repented of my sins, and have been redeemed of the Lord; behold I am born of the Spirit.

25 And the Lord said unto me: Marvel not that all mankind, yea, men and women, all nations, kindreds, tongues and people, must be born again; yea, born of God, changed from their carnal and fallen state, to a state of righteousness, being redeemed of God, becoming his sons and daughters;

26 And thus they become new creatures; and unless they do this, they can in nowise inherit the kingdom of God.

27 I say unto you, unless this be the case, they must be cast off; and this I know, because I was like to be cast off.

28 Nevertheless, after wading through much tribulation, repenting nigh unto death, the Lord in mercy hath seen fit to snatch me out of an everlasting burning, and I am born of God.

29 My soul hath been redeemed from the gall of bitterness and bonds of iniquity. I was in the darkest abyss; but now I behold the marvelous light of God. My soul was racked with eternal torment; but I am snatched, and my soul is pained no more.

30 I rejected my Redeemer, and denied that which had been spoken of by our fathers; but now that they may foresee that he will come, and that he remembereth every creature of his creating, he will make himself manifest unto all.

31 Yea, every knee shall bow, and every tongue confess before him. Yea, even at the last day, when all men shall stand to be judged of him, then shall they confess that he is God; then shall they confess, who live without God in the world, that the judgment of an everlasting punishment is just upon them;

and they shall quake, and tremble, and shrink beneath the glance of his all-searching eye.

32 And now it came to pass that Alma began from this time forward to teach the people, and those who were with Alma at the time the angel appeared unto them, traveling round about through all the land, publishing to all the people the things which they had heard and seen, and preaching the word of God in much tribulation, being greatly persecuted by those who were unbelievers, being smitten by many of them.

33 But notwithstanding all this, they did impart much consolation to the church, confirming their faith, and exhorting them with long-suffering and much travail to keep the commandments of God.

34 And four of them were the sons of Mosiah; and their names were Ammon, and Aaron, and Omner, and Himni; these were the names of the sons of Mosiah.

35 And they traveled throughout all the land of Zarahemla, and among all the people who were under the reign of king Mosiah, zealously striving to repair all the injuries which they had done to the church, confessing all their sins, and publishing all the things which they had seen, and explaining the prophecies and the scriptures to all who desired to hear them.

36 And thus they were instruments in the hands of God in bringing many to the knowledge of the truth, yea, to the knowledge of their Redeemer.

37 And how blessed are they! For they did publish peace; they did publish good tidings of good; and they did declare unto the people that the Lord reigneth.

Mosiah 27:32–37. Alma and the Sons of Mosiah Teach the Gospel

What is required of the converted? (27:32–33) "After conversion comes the responsibility and obligation to share the knowledge received with our Father in Heaven's other children. Alma's life was changed, and he became one of the greatest missionaries who ever lived. He taught with power and firsthand knowledge of the plan of redemption. He had learned at the feet of an angel; then he went forth and served" (Perry, "Learning to Serve," 16). ✦

What restitution is required for repentance? (27:35) "Repentance requires a full restitution in the spirit of Zacchaeus, who said, 'If I have taken any thing from any man . . . , I restore him fourfold' (Luke 19:8; see also Leviticus 6:4). . . .

"Restitution comes in many forms. It may involve a return of funds, an apology, prayers offered on behalf of the injured party, making up for years of lost service by redoubling our efforts, or making up for negativism with positive deeds and words. The spirit of repentance demands a restoration of all that is possible, within our power" (Callister, *Infinite Atonement*, 187–88). ✦

Mosiah 28:1–9. Mosiah's Sons Desire to Serve Missions

What are "all these things"? (28:1) "'All these things' that the sons of Mosiah have been doing were attempts to rectify the effects of their preaching against the church in the land of Zarahemla. Because of their privileged position as the sons of the king, they had probably been instrumental in attracting many away from the church in Zarahemla. Therefore, they took their first mission to those whom they had most directly hurt" (Gardner, *Second Witness*, 3:461).

What motivated the sons of Mosiah to serve? (28:3–4) Those who have learned to share the gospel with others "are the grateful disciples of the resurrected Jesus Christ. They know for themselves that the Atonement is real and necessary for all. They have felt cleansed through baptism by those in authority and the receipt of the Holy Ghost for themselves. And because of the peace they have experienced, they are like the sons of Mosiah, 'desirous that salvation should be declared to every creature, for they could not bear that any human soul should perish'" (Eyring, "A Child and a Disciple," 30–31).

CHAPTER 28

The sons of Mosiah go to preach to the Lamanites—Using the two seer stones, Mosiah translates the Jaredite plates. About 92 B.C.

1 Now it came to pass that after the sons of Mosiah had done all these things, they took a small number with them and returned to their father, the king, and desired of him that he would grant unto them that they might, with these whom they had selected, go up to the land of Nephi that they might preach the things which they had heard, and that they might impart the word of God to their brethren, the Lamanites—

2 That perhaps they might bring them to the knowledge of the Lord their God, and convince them of the iniquity of their fathers; and that perhaps they might cure them of their hatred towards the Nephites, that they might also be brought to rejoice in the Lord their God, that they might become friendly to one another, and that there should be no more contentions in all the land which the Lord their God had given them.

3 Now they were desirous that salvation should be declared to every creature, for they could not bear that any human soul should perish; yea, even the very thoughts that any soul should endure endless torment did cause them to quake and tremble.

4 And thus did the Spirit of the Lord work upon them, for they were the very vilest of sinners. And the Lord saw fit in his infinite mercy to spare them; nevertheless they suffered much anguish of soul because of their iniquities, suffering much and fearing that they should be cast off forever.

5 And it came to pass that they did plead with their father many days that they might go up to the land of Nephi.

6 And king Mosiah went and inquired of the Lord if he should let his sons go up among the Lamanites to preach the word.

7 And the Lord said unto Mosiah: Let them go up, for many shall believe on their words, and they shall have eternal life; and I will deliver thy sons out of the hands of the Lamanites.

8 And it came to pass that Mosiah granted that they might go and do according to their request.

9 And they took their journey into the wilderness to go up to preach the word among the Lamanites; and I shall give an account of their proceedings hereafter.

10 Now king Mosiah had no one to confer the kingdom upon, for there was not any of his sons who would accept of the kingdom.

11 Therefore he took the records which were engraven on the plates of brass, and also the plates of Nephi, and all the things which he had kept and preserved according to the commandments of God, after having translated and caused to be written the records which were on the plates of gold which had been found by the people of Limhi, which were delivered to him by the hand of Limhi;

12 And this he did because of the great anxiety of his people; for they were desirous beyond measure to know concerning those people who had been destroyed.

13 And now he translated them by the means of those two stones which were fastened into the two rims of a bow.

14 Now these things were prepared from the beginning, and were handed down from generation to generation, for the purpose of interpreting languages;

15 And they have been kept and preserved by the hand of the Lord, that he should

What were the sons of Mosiah promised? (28:7) "It is not entirely clear in the present text whether those being promised eternal life are the Lamanites who embrace the faith or Mosiah's sons who serve in faith.... Of special interest in the context of our present story, however, are the many passages that promise eternal life to the faithful missionary. One of the first revelations given in our dispensation ... promised those so laboring that through such service they may lay 'up in store' that they perish not, but bring salvation to their own souls (D&C 4:2–4). That is simply to say that we serve to work out our own salvation" (McConkie and Millet, *Doctrinal Commentary*, 2:312).

Mosiah 28:10–20. King Mosiah Translates the Jaredite Plates

Where is the translation of these plates? (28:11–19) "Mosiah's translation of the gold plates discovered by the people of Limhi was evidently made available to the people of Mosiah (Mosiah 28:11, 18), and Mormon promises that an account of this record 'shall be written hereafter; for behold, it is expedient that all people should know the things which are written in this account' (Mosiah 28:19). Mormon's son Moroni later abridges the account contained in these records, and his abridgment appears in our present Book of Mormon as the book of Ether" (Ludlow, *Companion to Your Study of the Book of Mormon*, 192).

What do we know about Mosiah's "two stones"? (28:13–16) See the note and extended link associated with Mosiah 8:13.

discover to every creature who should possess the land the iniquities and abominations of his people;

16 And whosoever has these things is called seer, after the manner of old times.

17 Now after Mosiah had finished translating these records, behold, it gave an account of the people who were destroyed, from the time that they were destroyed back to the building of the great tower, at the time the Lord confounded the language of the people and they were scattered abroad upon the face of all the earth, yea, and even from that time back until the creation of Adam.

18 Now this account did cause the people of Mosiah to mourn exceedingly, yea, they were filled with sorrow; nevertheless it gave them much knowledge, in the which they did rejoice.

19 And this account shall be written hereafter; for behold, it is expedient that all people should know the things which are written in this account.

20 And now, as I said unto you, that after king Mosiah had done these things, he took the plates of brass, and all the things which he had kept, and conferred them upon Alma, who was the son of Alma; yea, all the records, and also the interpreters, and conferred them upon him, and commanded him that he should keep and preserve them, and also keep a record of the people, handing them down from one generation to another, even as they had been handed down from the time that Lehi left Jerusalem.

CHAPTER 29

Mosiah proposes that judges be chosen in place of a king—Unrighteous kings lead their people into sin—Alma the younger is chosen chief judge by the voice of the people—He is also the high priest over the Church—Alma the elder and Mosiah die. About 92–91 B.C.

1 Now when Mosiah had done this he sent out throughout all the land, among all the people, desiring to know their will concerning who should be their king.

2 And it came to pass that the voice of the people came, saying: We are desirous that Aaron thy son should be our king and our ruler.

3 Now Aaron had gone up to the land of Nephi, therefore the king could not confer the kingdom upon him; neither would Aaron take upon him the kingdom; neither were any of the sons of Mosiah willing to take upon them the kingdom.

4 Therefore king Mosiah sent again among the people; yea, even a written word sent he among the people. And these were the words that were written, saying:

5 Behold, O ye my people, or my brethren, for I esteem you as such, I desire that ye should consider the cause which ye are called to consider—for ye are desirous to have a king.

6 Now I declare unto you that he to whom the kingdom doth rightly belong has declined, and will not take upon him the kingdom.

Mosiah 29:1–9. Mosiah's Sons Refuse to Be King

Why did the people request Aaron to be king? (29:2) "The order of the birth of the four sons of Mosiah is never made clear in the Book of Mormon. The listing in Mosiah 27:34 would indicate that Ammon was the first born followed by Aaron, then Omner, and Himni. Also, the fact that Ammon was the leader on their missionary journey to the Lamanites would seem to indicate that Ammon was the eldest (see Alma, chapters 17–26). However, when King Mosiah asked his people to select his successor, they first desired that Aaron should be their king and their ruler (Mosiah 29:1–2). In this single instance it appears as though Aaron may have been the eldest son" (Ludlow, *Companion to Your Study of the Book of Mormon*, 192).

What can we learn from Mosiah's sons' choosing discipleship over kingship? (29:3) Speaking of the relative value of our choices, President Dallin H. Oaks taught: "We should begin by recognizing the reality that just because something is *good* is not a sufficient reason for doing it. The number of good things we can do far exceeds the time available to accomplish them. Some things are better than good, and these are the things that should command priority attention in our lives....

"We have to forego some good things in order to choose others that are better or best because they develop faith in the Lord Jesus Christ and strengthen our families" ("Good, Better, Best," 104–7).

Mosiah 29:10–24. Mosiah Warns of the Dangers of Being Led by a King

What is noteworthy about the new governmental form established by King Mosiah? (29:11) "Important changes occurred in Nephite law and society with the establishment and promulgation of the law of Mosiah in 92 B.C. . . . Details about this significant legal reform . . . embedded in the narrative of the Book of Mormon shows that 'the law of Mosiah' (Alma 11:1) was solidly rooted in ancient Near Eastern ideas and legal tradition. . . .

"Research into the laws and jurisprudence of the ancient Near East sheds light on the legal provisions and procedures reflected in the Book of Mormon. . . . Whoever wrote the Book of Mormon was intimately familiar with the workings of ancient Israelite law and with the Nephite legal system that derived from it" (Welch, "Law of Mosiah," 158–61). ●

What does the comparison of King Benjamin and King Noah teach us? (29:12–18) "The book of Mosiah's penetrating look into the characters of king Benjamin and king Noah illustrates a lesson on

7 And now if there should be another appointed in his stead, behold I fear there would rise contentions among you. And who knoweth but what my son, to whom the kingdom doth belong, should turn to be angry and draw away a part of this people after him, which would cause wars and contentions among you, which would be the cause of shedding much blood and perverting the way of the Lord, yea, and destroy the souls of many people.

8 Now I say unto you let us be wise and consider these things, for we have no right to destroy my son, neither should we have any right to destroy another if he should be appointed in his stead.

9 And if my son should turn again to his pride and vain things he would recall the things which he had said, and claim his right to the kingdom, which would cause him and also this people to commit much sin.

10 And now let us be wise and look forward to these things, and do that which will make for the peace of this people.

11 Therefore I will be your king the remainder of my days; nevertheless, let us appoint judges, to judge this people according to our law; and we will newly arrange the affairs of this people, for we will appoint wise men to be judges, that will judge this people according to the commandments of God.

12 Now it is better that a man should be judged of God than of man, for the judgments of God are always just, but the judgments of man are not always just.

13 Therefore, if it were possible that you could have just men to be your kings, who would establish the laws of God, and judge this people according to his commandments, yea, if ye could have men for your kings who would do even as my father Benjamin did for this people—I say unto you, if this could always be the case then it would be expedient that ye should always have kings to rule over you.

14 And even I myself have labored with all the power and faculties which I have possessed, to teach you the commandments of God, and to establish peace throughout the land, that there should be no wars nor contentions, no stealing, nor plundering, nor murdering, nor any manner of iniquity;

15 And whosoever has committed iniquity, him have I punished according to the crime which he has committed, according to the law which has been given to us by our fathers.

16 Now I say unto you, that because all men are not just it is not expedient that ye should have a king or kings to rule over you.

17 For behold, how much iniquity doth one wicked king cause to be committed, yea, and what great destruction!

18 Yea, remember king Noah, his wickedness and his abominations, and also the wickedness and abominations of his people. Behold what great destruction did come upon them; and also because of their iniquities they were brought into bondage.

19 And were it not for the interposition of their all-wise Creator, and this because of their sincere repentance, they must unavoidably remain in bondage until now.

20 But behold, he did deliver them because they did humble themselves before him; and because they cried mightily unto him he did deliver them out of bondage; and thus doth

righteous and unrighteous uses of power and authority. . . .

"A close look at the book of Mosiah makes it obvious why Mosiah II would have selected these two kings to make his point: Benjamin is the type of a righteous king, Noah the model of a wicked one. King Benjamin's purpose was to bring his people to Christ, while Noah led his people away from Christ. The 'great joy' of Benjamin's people came from the teachings of their righteous king (Mosiah 5:4), whereas the 'sore afflictions' of Noah's reign were the fruits of his evil leadership (Mosiah 12:4)" (Donaldson, "Benjamin and Noah," 49–50).

What is the relationship between humility, faith, and deliverance? (29:20) The prophet Nephi wrote: "The tender mercies of the Lord are over all those whom he hath chosen, because of their faith, to make them mighty even unto the power of deliverance"

(1 Nephi 1:20). Elder David A. Bednar taught: "The Lord's tender mercies do not occur randomly or merely by coincidence. Faithfulness, obedience, and humility invite tender mercies into our lives, and it is often the Lord's timing that enables us to recognize and treasure these important blessings" ("Tender Mercies of the Lord," 100). ⊕

What does history teach us about how difficult it is to replace a corrupt government? (29:21–24) How much blood has been shed in the world in attempts to overthrow corrupt and oppressive rulers? Have those who have thus gained power been better than those they replaced? What are examples of laws being instituted "after the manner of [their] own wickedness"? Why do some choose to be "friends in iniquity" and support a wicked ruler? What can we do to combat such wickedness?

Mosiah 29:25–36. Mosiah Counsels the People to Choose Judges to Rule over Them

What does Mosiah teach us about the "voice of the people"? (29:25–26) "There are various systems of government. The best is theocracy, which is government by divine guidance....

"At this point in Nephite history it was thought wise to shift to the rule of judges, a form of democracy.... Mosiah counseled, 'it is not common that that the voice of the people desireth anything contrary to that which is right.'

"'Governments are only good when the people are good. As founding father John Adams observed, "Our constitution was made for a moral people. It is wholly inadequate to the government of any other" (Federer, *America's God and Country*, 10–11)'" (Bytheway, *Righteous Warriors*, 33–34). ⊕

What are most people in the world choosing today? (29:27) What do the choices and votes of the people of your nation indicate about the

the Lord work with his power in all cases among the children of men, extending the arm of mercy towards them that put their trust in him.

21 And behold, now I say unto you, ye cannot dethrone an iniquitous king save it be through much contention, and the shedding of much blood.

22 For behold, he has his friends in iniquity, and he keepeth his guards about him; and he teareth up the laws of those who have reigned in righteousness before him; and he trampleth under his feet the commandments of God;

23 And he enacteth laws, and sendeth them forth among his people, yea, laws after the manner of his own wickedness; and whosoever doth not obey his laws he causeth to be destroyed; and whosoever doth rebel against him he will send his armies against them to war, and if he can he will destroy them; and thus an unrighteous king doth pervert the ways of all righteousness.

24 And now behold I say unto you, it is not expedient that such abominations should come upon you.

25 Therefore, choose you by the voice of this people, judges, that ye may be judged according to the laws which have been given you by our fathers, which are correct, and which were given them by the hand of the Lord.

26 Now it is not common that the voice of the people desireth anything contrary to that which is right; but it is common for the lesser part of the people to desire that which is not right; therefore this shall ye observe and make it your law—to do your business by the voice of the people.

27 And if the time comes that the voice of the people doth choose iniquity, then is the time that the judgments of God will come

upon you; yea, then is the time he will visit you with great destruction even as he has hitherto visited this land.

28 And now if ye have judges, and they do not judge you according to the law which has been given, ye can cause that they may be judged of a higher judge.

29 If your higher judges do not judge righteous judgments, ye shall cause that a small number of your lower judges should be gathered together, and they shall judge your higher judges, according to the voice of the people.

30 And I command you to do these things in the fear of the Lord; and I command you to do these things, and that ye have no king; that if these people commit sins and iniquities they shall be answered upon their own heads.

31 For behold I say unto you, the sins of many people have been caused by the iniquities of their kings; therefore their iniquities are answered upon the heads of their kings.

32 And now I desire that this inequality should be no more in this land, especially among this my people; but I desire that this land be a land of liberty, and every man may enjoy his rights and privileges alike, so long as the Lord sees fit that we may live and inherit the land, yea, even as long as any of our posterity remains upon the face of the land.

33 And many more things did king Mosiah write unto them, unfolding unto them all the trials and troubles of a righteous king, yea, all the travails of soul for their people, and also all the murmurings of the people to their king; and he explained it all unto them.

34 And he told them that these things ought not to be; but that the burden should come upon all the people, that every man might bear his part.

righteousness of their values? (compare Helaman 5:1–2). What can you do in your nation, in your community, and in your home to be an influence for correct principles and righteous choices? How can you use social media to lift your voice to share goodness and proclaim the gospel of Jesus Christ? (see Bednar, "That We May Always Have His Spirit to Be with Us").

Why should we want to be accountable for our actions? (29:30–32) "Once we have accepted responsibility for our own actions, the grace of God is extended to us. For freedom implies not only accountability but also the ability to repent (see D&C 20:71), and repentance, grounded upon faith in the Lord Jesus Christ, brings sanctification and holiness—the ability to transcend the consequences of our actions and to be restored as children of our Father in Heaven" (Wood, "On the Responsible Self," 29). ●

What is an essential part we bear as citizens in relation to good government? (29:34–38) "We believe that governments were instituted of God for the benefit of man; and that he holds men accountable for their acts in relation to them, both in making laws and administering them, for the good and safety of society' (D&C 134:1). Further, the responsibility for identifying and selecting good men and women to represent them and serve them in government rests with the people.... 'Nevertheless, when the wicked rule the people mourn. Wherefore, honest men and wise men should be sought for diligently, and good men and wise men ye should observe to uphold; otherwise whatsoever is less than these cometh of evil' (D&C 98:8–10)" (McConkie and Millet, *Doctrinal Commentary*, 2:320).

Mosiah 29:37–47. Alma Is Appointed as the First Chief Judge

What adjustment was required for people moving from a monarchy to a system of judges chosen by the voice of the people? (29:38) "People often express a desire for someone to protect and care for them, as if they were unable to care for themselves. Satan cleverly persuades them to relinquish responsibility for their lives—their innate right to exercise their agency within a free environment—to someone else, in exchange for anticipated security. Those who are thus accustomed to submissive security are often hesitant to leap into the arena of civic freedom, where they determine their future by their own choices. If they alone are responsible for their future, whom can they blame for life's frustrations?" (Merrill, "Government by the Voice of the People," 120). ✪

How should we view different types of governments? (29:39) "Mosiah 29 is not a treatise about the superiority of democracy over kingship, but a discussion of fundamental principles of government that should be protected in any form of government. ... Elder Bruce R. McConkie pointed out that religion must be free from any earthly power and subject only to the powers of heaven if it is to have saving power. Thus, governments that inhibit freedom of religion, freedom of worship, and the freedom to choose one's own course curtail and even prevent the choice-making that leads us to salvation" (Edwards, "Kingdom of God and the Kingdoms of Men," 278–79). ✪

Why was Mosiah so esteemed? (29:40) "As a king, he was a father to them, but as a prophet, seer, and revelator, he was the source from whence divine

35 And he also unfolded unto them all the disadvantages they labored under, by having an unrighteous king to rule over them;

36 Yea, all his iniquities and abominations, and all the wars, and contentions, and bloodshed, and the stealing, and the plundering, and the committing of whoredoms, and all manner of iniquities which cannot be enumerated—telling them that these things ought not to be, that they were expressly repugnant to the commandments of God.

37 And now it came to pass, after king Mosiah had sent these things forth among the people they were convinced of the truth of his words.

38 Therefore they relinquished their desires for a king, and became exceedingly anxious that every man should have an equal chance throughout all the land; yea, and every man expressed a willingness to answer for his own sins.

39 Therefore, it came to pass that they assembled themselves together in bodies throughout the land, to cast in their voices concerning who should be their judges, to judge them according to the law which had been given them; and they were exceedingly rejoiced because of the liberty which had been granted unto them.

40 And they did wax strong in love towards Mosiah; yea, they did esteem him more than any other man; for they did not look upon him as a tyrant who was seeking for gain, yea, for that lucre which doth corrupt the soul; for he had not exacted riches of them, neither

had he delighted in the shedding of blood; but he had established peace in the land, and he had granted unto his people that they should be delivered from all manner of bondage; therefore they did esteem him, yea, exceedingly, beyond measure.

41 And it came to pass that they did appoint judges to rule over them, or to judge them according to the law; and this they did throughout all the land.

42 And it came to pass that Alma was appointed to be the first chief judge, he being also the high priest, his father having conferred the office upon him, and having given him the charge concerning all the affairs of the church.

43 And now it came to pass that Alma did walk in the ways of the Lord, and he did keep his commandments, and he did judge righteous judgments; and there was continual peace through the land.

44 And thus commenced the reign of the judges throughout all the land of Zarahemla, among all the people who were called the Nephites; and Alma was the first and chief judge.

45 And now it came to pass that his father died, being eighty and two years old, having lived to fulfil the commandments of God.

46 And it came to pass that Mosiah died also, in the thirty and third year of his reign, being sixty and three years old; making in the whole, five hundred and nine years from the time Lehi left Jerusalem.

47 And thus ended the reign of the kings over the people of Nephi; and thus ended the days of Alma, who was the founder of their church.

wisdom flowed unto them. We must go back to the days of the antediluvian patriarchs to find the peers of these three kings (the two Mosiahs and Benjamin), when monarchs ruled by right divine, and men were prophets, priests, and kings by virtue of heaven's gifts and God's will" (Reynolds and Sjodahl, *Commentary on the Book of Mormon*, 2:291). ●

How democratic was the system of judges? (29:41–42) "Once elected, [Alma] never again submitted himself to the people. After being proclaimed chief judge by the voice of the people, Alma enjoyed life tenure. When he chose to resign because of internal difficulties he selected his own successor (see Alma 4:16). That seems to have been the beginning of a dynasty. In the next succession, the judgeship passed to the chief judge's son and thence 'by right' to the successive sons of the Judges (see Alma 50:39; Hel. 1:13). Although democratic elements were there—the Judges were confirmed by the voice of the people— the 'reign of the Judges,' as the Book of Mormon calls the period, was a far cry from the republican government Joseph Smith knew" (Bushman, "Book of Mormon and the American Revolution," 14–16). ●

How was time reckoned by the Nephites? (29:44) "After Lehi left Jerusalem, time was reckoned according to the date of his departure—e.g., 'fifty years after Lehi left Jerusalem.' . . . With the establishment of the system of the judges we encounter a new reckoning of time among the Nephites—the 'first year of the reign of the judges,' the 'fifteenth year of the reign of the judges,' and so on. This system would be in effect until the sign of the birth of Christ would be given, when they would begin reckoning their time from that point (see 3 Nephi 2:8)" (McConkie and Millet, *Doctrinal Commentary*, 2:320).

THE BOOK OF ALMA
THE SON OF ALMA

Introduction

Alma, often called Alma the Younger by modern readers to distinguish him from his father, became a powerful missionary and teacher after his conversion (see Mosiah 27). His book covers less than forty years of history, from about 91 B.C. to 53 B.C., but its pages compose nearly a third of the Book of Mormon. "The book of Alma . . . breaks down into three logical divisions according to its authorship. The text abridged by Mormon was therefore the product of a father [chapters 1–44] and two of his sons, Helaman [45–62] and Shiblon [63], being sons of the younger Alma" (Sperry, *Book of Mormon Compendium*, 324).

An important teaching in the book of Alma is that the word of God is more powerful than the sword in bringing people to the Lord (see Alma 31:5). Equally important is the teaching that rejecting God's word leads to war and bloodshed.

The superscription to the book of Alma, which appears just under the title, was part of the ancient record translated by the Prophet Joseph Smith and dictated by him to his scribe (see also, for example, 2 Nephi, Mosiah 9, and Alma 5). In contrast to other books within the Book of Mormon, the book of Alma contains "an unusually large number of superscriptions," which appear above "chapters 1, 5, 7, 9, 17, 21, 36, 38, 39, and 45. These superscriptions are of more than passing interest. The fact that they are found over the chapters enumerated and over no others [in the book of Alma] would seem to indicate that Mormon took them from Alma's original text" (Sperry, *Book of Mormon Compendium*, 324). ☉

Alma 1:1–10. Nehor Teaches False Doctrines and Slays Gideon

What impact did the life of King Mosiah have on the people of Nephi? (1:1) "As the book of Mosiah concludes, the people of Nephi have been established under a government of elected judges. Alma, the son of Alma, has been named as the 'first and chief judge.' He is also the presiding officer of the Church.

"It is a good time. The great love felt by the people for King Mosiah has laid a strong foundation for the new government. The Church is well established, and

The account of Alma, who was the son of Alma, the first and chief judge over the people of Nephi, and also the high priest over the Church. An account of the reign of the judges, and the wars and contentions among the people. And also an account of a war between the Nephites and the Lamanites, according to the record of Alma, the first and chief judge.

CHAPTER 1

Nehor teaches false doctrines, establishes a church, introduces priestcraft, and slays Gideon—Nehor is executed for his crimes—Priestcrafts and persecutions spread among the people—The priests support themselves, the people care for the poor, and the Church prospers. About 91–88 B.C.

1 Now it came to pass that in the first year of the reign of the judges over the people of Nephi, from this time forward, king Mosiah having gone the way of all the earth, having

warred a good warfare, walking uprightly before God, leaving none to reign in his stead; nevertheless he had established laws, and they were acknowledged by the people; therefore they were obliged to abide by the laws which he had made.

2 And it came to pass that in the first year of the reign of Alma in the judgment-seat, there was a man brought before him to be judged, a man who was large, and was noted for his much strength.

3 And he had gone about among the people, preaching to them that which he termed to be the word of God, bearing down against the church; declaring unto the people that every priest and teacher ought to become popular; and they ought not to labor with their hands, but that they ought to be supported by the people.

4 And he also testified unto the people that all mankind should be saved at the last day, and that they need not fear nor tremble, but that they might lift up their heads and rejoice; for the Lord had created all men, and had also redeemed all men; and, in the end, all men should have eternal life.

5 And it came to pass that he did teach these things so much that many did believe on his words, even so many that they began to support him and give him money.

6 And he began to be lifted up in the pride of his heart, and to wear very costly apparel, yea, and even began to establish a church after the manner of his preaching.

7 And it came to pass as he was going, to preach to those who believed on his word, he met a man who belonged to the church

the people rejoice 'because of the liberty which had been granted unto them' (Mosiah 29:39)" (Larsen, "Likening the Scriptures unto Us," 2).

Who was this man brought before Alma? (1:2–3)
Nehor was a "successful religious charlatan . . . to whom the unstable listened and the weak-minded flocked. . . . [His] teachings had . . . the interest of novelty to the Nephites. . . . He would save all men in their sins and with their sins. . . . Every man could be a member of his church and yet continue to gratify every vice his nature inclined to" (Reynolds, *Dictionary of the Book of Mormon*, 229). ✚

What approach was Nehor using in his interpretation of the scriptures that we must be cautious about? (1:3) "Indeed, what [Nehor] spoke was not the word of God, but it was what he would have wished the word of God to be. The perverse and the malicious frequently devise their own form of divinity, conjure up their own words of truth, and create their own set of values. They then blaspheme against divine order by stating that their views are heaven-sent and have God's approbation" (McConkie and Millet, *Doctrinal Commentary*, 3:3).

How can we discern Nehor's false doctrines in our day? (1:4–5) "Nehor's words appealed to many of the people; they were easy words because they required neither obedience nor sacrifice. As we face many decisions in life, the easy and popular messages of the world will seem appealing. But when these worldly messages contradict gospel teachings and the still, small voice of the Spirit, we can be 100 percent confident they are wrong. Still, it will take great courage to choose the right" (Perry, *Living with Enthusiasm*, 108–9). ✚

What does costly apparel, repeatedly warned against in the Book of Mormon, represent? (1:6) "Virtually all Book of Mormon incidents of unrighteous wealth or pride manifest themselves in the wearing of costly apparel. Nephi's brother, Jacob, first denounced this practice. . . . When the Nephites began drifting away from Christianity two hundred years after the Lord's appearance in the Americas, the first sign of that drift was costly apparel (4 Ne. 1:24)" (Gardner, *Second Witness*, 4:23).

Why did Nehor react to Gideon so violently? (1:7–9) "The fray began when Gideon 'admonish[ed Nehor] with the words of God' (Alma 1:7). Gideon's words may or may not have had any legal significance at the time they were spoken. On the one hand, the sharp words between Nehor and Gideon may have simply been a heated theological debate. On the other hand, these words may have served a legal function. The law of Jehoshaphat, for example, required 'judges in all the land' to warn 'your brethren that dwell in their cities . . . that they trespass not against the Lord' (2 Chronicles 19:5, 10). This principle, that potential offenders should be warned, . . . certainly could have found its way into Nephite law as well" (Welch, *Legal Cases in the Book of Mormon*, 221). ✚

Alma 1:11–15. Nehor Is Tried and Put to Death

How does priestcraft differ from priesthood? (1:12) "Priesthood and priestcraft are two opposites; one is of God, the other of the devil [see 2 Nephi 26:29]. When ministers claim but do not possess the priesthood; when they set themselves up as lights to their congregations, but do not preach the pure and full gospel; when their interest is in gaining personal popularity and financial gain, rather than in caring for the poor and ministering to the wants and needs of their fellow men—they are engaged, in a greater or lesser degree, in the practice of priestcrafts" (McConkie, *Mormon Doctrine*, 593). ✚

Was Alma alone in speaking of the dangers of priestcraft? (1:12) "The word *priestcraft* (including its plural, *priestcrafts*) is found eight times in scripture. All but one of those are in the Book of Mormon. Jacob prophesied that Jesus would be crucified because of priestcraft (see 2 Nephi 10:5). Alma accused Nehor of introducing priestcraft into the Nephite church and trying to enforce it with the sword (see Alma 1:12, 16). During His visit to the Americas, Jesus spoke of priestcrafts three different times (see 3 Nephi 16:10; 21:19; 30:2)" (Lund, *In Tune*, 134). Alma saw that priestcraft led to spiritual and physical destruction. He felt to use all of his influence to curtail its practice among the people.

of God, yea, even one of their teachers; and he began to contend with him sharply, that he might lead away the people of the church; but the man withstood him, admonishing him with the words of God.

8 Now the name of the man was Gideon; and it was he who was an instrument in the hands of God in delivering the people of Limhi out of bondage.

9 Now, because Gideon withstood him with the words of God he was wroth with Gideon, and drew his sword and began to smite him. Now Gideon being stricken with many years, therefore he was not able to withstand his blows, therefore he was slain by the sword.

10 And the man who slew him was taken by the people of the church, and was brought before Alma, to be judged according to the crimes which he had committed.

11 And it came to pass that he stood before Alma and pled for himself with much boldness.

12 But Alma said unto him: Behold, this is the first time that priestcraft has been introduced among this people. And behold, thou art not only guilty of priestcraft, but hast endeavored to enforce it by the sword; and were priestcraft to be enforced among this people it would prove their entire destruction.

13 And thou hast shed the blood of a righteous man, yea, a man who has done much good among this people; and were we to spare thee his blood would come upon us for vengeance.

14 Therefore thou art condemned to die, according to the law which has been given us by Mosiah, our last king; and it has been acknowledged by this people; therefore this people must abide by the law.

15 And it came to pass that they took him; and his name was Nehor; and they carried him upon the top of the hill Manti, and there he was caused, or rather did acknowledge, between the heavens and the earth, that what he had taught to the people was contrary to the word of God; and there he suffered an ignominious death.

16 Nevertheless, this did not put an end to the spreading of priestcraft through the land; for there were many who loved the vain things of the world, and they went forth preaching false doctrines; and this they did for the sake of riches and honor.

17 Nevertheless, they durst not lie, if it were known, for fear of the law, for liars were punished; therefore they pretended to preach according to their belief; and now the law could have no power on any man for his belief.

18 And they durst not steal, for fear of the law, for such were punished; neither durst they rob, nor murder, for he that murdered was punished unto death.

19 But it came to pass that whosoever did not belong to the church of God began to persecute those that did belong to the church of God, and had taken upon them the name of Christ.

20 Yea, they did persecute them, and afflict them with all manner of words, and this because of their humility; because they were not proud in their own eyes, and because they did impart the word of God, one with another, without money and without price.

21 Now there was a strict law among the people of the church, that there should not any man, belonging to the church, arise and persecute those that did not belong to the church, and that there should be no persecution among themselves.

What is an "ignominious death"? (1:15) *Ignominious* means "very shameful; reproachful; dishonorable; infamous. To be hanged for a crime is ignominious" (Webster, *American Dictionary*). Nehor's "execution took place on the hill Manti, and, from the way which his death is spoken of, we imagine that he was hanged" (Reynolds, *Dictionary of the Book of Mormon*, 230). ⊕

Alma 1:16–22. Priestcraft, False Doctrine, and Persecution Spread among the Nephites

How did Nephite law allow for the growth of Nehor's false teachings? (1:17–18) "Under Nephite religious law, all people were free to believe whatever they desired (see Alma 1:17). The law protected the right of personal belief and even allowed individuals to teach those beliefs as long as others were not forced or injured. An important teaching of the Church was and always will be to eliminate religious intolerance and bigotry. The true saints of God respected Nehor's right to believe and teach as he pleased, but they armed themselves with the word of God so they would not be deceived" (Reeve, "Dealing with Opposition to the Church," 16). ⊕

Why is the Church of God persecuted? (1:19–20) "Although the religions of men are often tolerant of each other, they cannot abide the presence of living prophets and the truths of salvation. Their bitterness and opposition toward Mormonism are an essential witness of its truthfulness. Validity draws the fire. . . .

"If Mormonism were not true, it could be ignored. The fact that Satan and his cohorts cannot leave it alone is an evidence of its truthfulness. There is no neutrality where the truths of salvation are concerned" (McConkie, *Answers*, 54).

How should we react to those who choose to leave the Church? (1:21–22) What are some Christlike ways to respond to those who are antagonistic toward the Church? What can we learn from the experience of the Church in Alma's day as we endure persecution? ⊕

Alma 1:23–33. Church Members Who Are Patient in Trials and Suffering Are Blessed

How can we be strong even when others harden their hearts and withdraw from the Church? (1:23–25) Unlike some Nephites who "withdrew themselves" from the Church, others did "stand fast." "How do you remain 'steadfast and immovable' during a trial of faith? You immerse yourself in the very things that helped build your core of faith: you exercise faith in Christ, you pray, you ponder the scriptures, you repent, you keep the commandments, and you serve others.

"When faced with a trial of faith—whatever you do, you don't step away from the Church! Distancing yourself from the kingdom of God during a trial of faith is like leaving the safety of a secure storm cellar just as the tornado comes into view" (Andersen, "Trial of Your Faith," 40). ○

In what way is today's Church similar to the church among the Nephites? (1:26) "In the Lord's Church the members are a congregation of equals; there are no degrees, no academic titles, no worldly attainments that separate members of the group. . . . The bishop perhaps is a plumber, while his clerk is the vice president of a large corporation. The stake president is a farmer, while his high council is composed of lawyers and physicians and professors" (McConkie and Millet, *Doctrinal Commentary*, 3:9–10).

Why are we taught to impart of our substance to those in need? (1:27) "Providing in the Lord's way humbles the rich, it exalts the poor, and sanctifies both (see D&C 104:15–18). The giver helps those in need by sharing what he has received. The receiver accepts the offering with gratitude. As the receiver rises to his full potential, he then is able to reach out to help others" (Burton, "Go, and Do Thou Likewise," 76).

How have you been influenced when someone has helped you in a time of need? Does it increase in you a desire to help others?

22 Nevertheless, there were many among them who began to be proud, and began to contend warmly with their adversaries, even unto blows; yea, they would smite one another with their fists.

23 Now this was in the second year of the reign of Alma, and it was a cause of much affliction to the church; yea, it was the cause of much trial with the church.

24 For the hearts of many were hardened, and their names were blotted out, that they were remembered no more among the people of God. And also many withdrew themselves from among them.

25 Now this was a great trial to those that did stand fast in the faith; nevertheless, they were steadfast and immovable in keeping the commandments of God, and they bore with patience the persecution which was heaped upon them.

26 And when the priests left their labor to impart the word of God unto the people, the people also left their labors to hear the word of God. And when the priest had imparted unto them the word of God they all returned again diligently unto their labors; and the priest, not esteeming himself above his hearers, for the preacher was no better than the hearer, neither was the teacher any better than the learner; and thus they were all equal, and they did all labor, every man according to his strength.

27 And they did impart of their substance, every man according to that which he had, to the poor, and the needy, and the sick, and the afflicted; and they did not wear costly apparel, yet they were neat and comely.

28 And thus they did establish the affairs of the church; and thus they began to have continual peace again, notwithstanding all their persecutions.

29 And now, because of the steadiness of the church they began to be exceedingly rich, having abundance of all things whatsoever they stood in need—an abundance of flocks and herds, and fatlings of every kind, and also abundance of grain, and of gold, and of silver, and of precious things, and abundance of silk and fine-twined linen, and all manner of good homely cloth.

30 And thus, in their prosperous circumstances, they did not send away any who were naked, or that were hungry, or that were athirst, or that were sick, or that had not been nourished; and they did not set their hearts upon riches; therefore they were liberal to all, both old and young, both bond and free, both male and female, whether out of the church or in the church, having no respect to persons as to those who stood in need.

31 And thus they did prosper and become far more wealthy than those who did not belong to their church.

32 For those who did not belong to their church did indulge themselves in sorceries, and in idolatry or idleness, and in babblings, and in envyings and strife; wearing costly apparel; being lifted up in the pride of their own eyes; persecuting, lying, thieving, robbing, committing whoredoms, and murdering, and all manner of wickedness; nevertheless, the law was put in force upon all those who did transgress it, inasmuch as it was possible.

33 And it came to pass that by thus exercising the law upon them, every man suffering according to that which he had done, they became more still, and durst not commit any wickedness if it were known; therefore, there was much peace among the people of Nephi until the fifth year of the reign of the judges.

What can we learn from faithful Nephites living in this era? (1:31) "It is related in this verse that because of the 'steadiness of the Church' its members became 'far more wealthy than those who did not belong to their' organization" (Reynolds and Sjodahl, *Commentary on the Book of Mormon*, 3:47).

What can you do to show your "steadiness"? In what kinds of ways can the righteous become more "wealthy" than others?

CHAPTER 2

Amlici seeks to be king and is rejected by the voice of the people—His followers make him king—The Amlicites make war on the Nephites and are defeated—The Lamanites and Amlicites join forces and are defeated—Alma slays Amlici. About 87 B.C.

1 And it came to pass in the commencement of the fifth year of their reign there began to be a contention among the people; for a certain man, being called Amlici, he being a very cunning man, yea, a wise man as to the wisdom of the world, he being after the order of the man that slew Gideon by the sword, who was executed according to the law—

2 Now this Amlici had, by his cunning, drawn away much people after him; even so much that they began to be very powerful; and they began to endeavor to establish Amlici to be a king over the people.

3 Now this was alarming to the people of the church, and also to all those who had not been drawn away after the persuasions of Amlici; for they knew that according to their law that such things must be established by the voice of the people.

4 Therefore, if it were possible that Amlici should gain the voice of the people, he, being a wicked man, would deprive them of their rights and privileges of the church; for it was his intent to destroy the church of God.

5 And it came to pass that the people assembled themselves together throughout all the land, every man according to his mind, whether it were for or against Amlici, in separate bodies, having much dispute and wonderful contentions one with another.

Alma 2:1–7. Amlici Is Rejected as King

What do we know about Amlici? (2:1–2) "Soon after the establishment of a system of elected judges among the Nephites, several revolts take place against this type of government. The first of these revolts is headed by Amlici, who, in addition to being an avowed kingman, is also a follower of the order of Nehor and thus advocates priestcraft (Alma 2:1). Although Amlici is not successful in his desire to obtain the kingship, he precipitates a civil war that results in the deaths of over 19,000 people (Alma 2:19)" (Ludlow, *Companion to Your Study of the Book of Mormon*, 194). ✪

Why is Amlici's approach to government considered so dangerous? (2:4) The Prophet Joseph Smith explained: "We deem it a just principle, and it is one the force of which we believe ought to be duly considered by every individual, that all men are created equal, and that all have the privilege of thinking for themselves upon all matters relative to conscience. Consequently, then, we are not disposed, had we the power, to deprive any one of exercising that free independence of mind which heaven has so graciously bestowed upon the human family as one of its choicest gifts" (*Joseph Smith* [manual], 344–45).

What is a "wonderful contention"? (2:5) According to Webster's 1828 *American Dictionary*, another word for "wonderful" is "astonishing."

6 And thus they did assemble themselves together to cast in their voices concerning the matter; and they were laid before the judges.

7 And it came to pass that the voice of the people came against Amlici, that he was not made king over the people.

What danger was inherent in this national vote? (2:7) Review Mosiah 29:26–27. What might have happened to the Nephite nation if the majority of the people had chosen "the persuasions of Amlici"? (verse 3). What implications does this example have for our own day?

Alma 2:8–23. Amlici Causes a War between Nephite Groups

8 Now this did cause much joy in the hearts of those who were against him; but Amlici did stir up those who were in his favor to anger against those who were not in his favor.

9 And it came to pass that they gathered themselves together, and did consecrate Amlici to be their king.

10 Now when Amlici was made king over them he commanded them that they should take up arms against their brethren; and this he did that he might subject them to him.

11 Now the people of Amlici were distinguished by the name of Amlici, being called Amlicites; and the remainder were called Nephites, or the people of God.

12 Therefore the people of the Nephites were aware of the intent of the Amlicites, and therefore they did prepare to meet them; yea, they did arm themselves with swords, and with cimeters, and with bows, and with arrows, and with stones, and with slings, and with all manner of weapons of war, of every kind.

13 And thus they were prepared to meet the Amlicites at the time of their coming. And there were appointed captains, and higher captains, and chief captains, according to their numbers.

14 And it came to pass that Amlici did arm his men with all manner of weapons of war of every kind; and he also appointed rulers

What are the dangers when political factions refuse to be bound by the established laws of the land? (2:8–14) "[The vote] should have ended the matter, but it did not; the turbulent minority, incited by Amlici, would not accept this constitutional decision. They assembled and crowned their favorite as king of the Nephites, and he at once began to prepare for war that he might force the rest of the people to accept him to be their ruler. . . . The two camps were known as Nephites and as Amlicites, and their armies, the members of which had but a short time before dwelt together as brethren, marched against each other" (Reynolds and Sjodahl, *Commentary on the Book of Mormon*, 3:54–55).

and leaders over his people, to lead them to war against their brethren.

15 And it came to pass that the Amlicites came upon the hill Amnihu, which was east of the river Sidon, which ran by the land of Zarahemla, and there they began to make war with the Nephites.

16 Now Alma, being the chief judge and the governor of the people of Nephi, therefore he went up with his people, yea, with his captains, and chief captains, yea, at the head of his armies, against the Amlicites to battle.

17 And they began to slay the Amlicites upon the hill east of Sidon. And the Amlicites did contend with the Nephites with great strength, insomuch that many of the Nephites did fall before the Amlicites.

18 Nevertheless the Lord did strengthen the hand of the Nephites, that they slew the Amlicites with great slaughter, that they began to flee before them.

19 And it came to pass that the Nephites did pursue the Amlicites all that day, and did slay them with much slaughter, insomuch that there were slain of the Amlicites twelve thousand five hundred thirty and two souls; and there were slain of the Nephites six thousand five hundred sixty and two souls.

20 And it came to pass that when Alma could pursue the Amlicites no longer he caused that his people should pitch their tents in the valley of Gideon, the valley being called after that Gideon who was slain by the hand of Nehor with the sword; and in this valley the Nephites did pitch their tents for the night.

21 And Alma sent spies to follow the remnant of the Amlicites, that he might know of their plans and their plots, whereby he might guard himself against them, that he might preserve his people from being destroyed.

What powers did the role of chief judge and governor give Alma? (2:16) "The first chief judge was Alma the Younger. . . . As chief judge, Alma conducted the military affairs of his people and fought in hand-to-hand combat against Amlici, the leader of the insurgents (see Alma 2:29).

"Six years later, however, the previously unmentioned Zoram led the Nephites in battle as their 'chief captain'—a position to which he had been 'appointed' (Alma 16:5). This office was legally constituted as a result of the division of governmental powers that resulted when Alma relinquished the judgment seat. Alma retained control of religious affairs as high priest but conferred power over judicial matters upon Nephihah as chief judge (see Alma 4:16–18). Evidently, military power was given to the chief captain" (Welch, "Law and War in the Book of Mormon," 53–54). ⊕

How much damage can a single person cause among a people? (2:19) "Individuals or groups seeking power over others often engage in war . . . to accomplish their evil desires. For example, Amlici lost a contentious but legitimate election. . . . Consequently, he convinced his constituents to consecrate him king anyway. His first order of business was to command his new subjects to engage in war against their fellow Nephites. The result was a scene of carnage in which tens of thousands were killed. The river Sidon became a watery grave for many lifeless bodies, while the living were driven into the wilderness only to be devoured by wild and ravenous beasts (see Alma 2). Thousands suffered unnecessary violence because one man wanted power over others" (Marsh, "Peace through Christ," 248).

22 Now those whom he had sent out to watch the camp of the Amlicites were called Zeram, and Amnor, and Manti, and Limher; these were they who went out with their men to watch the camp of the Amlicites.

23 And it came to pass that on the morrow they returned into the camp of the Nephites in great haste, being greatly astonished, and struck with much fear, saying:

24 Behold, we followed the camp of the Amlicites, and to our great astonishment, in the land of Minon, above the land of Zarahemla, in the course of the land of Nephi, we saw a numerous host of the Lamanites; and behold, the Amlicites have joined them;

25 And they are upon our brethren in that land; and they are fleeing before them with their flocks, and their wives, and their children, towards our city; and except we make haste they obtain possession of our city, and our fathers, and our wives, and our children be slain.

26 And it came to pass that the people of Nephi took their tents, and departed out of the valley of Gideon towards their city, which was the city of Zarahemla.

27 And behold, as they were crossing the river Sidon, the Lamanites and the Amlicites, being as numerous almost, as it were, as the sands of the sea, came upon them to destroy them.

28 Nevertheless, the Nephites being strengthened by the hand of the Lord, having prayed mightily to him that he would deliver them out of the hands of their enemies, therefore the Lord did hear their cries, and did strengthen them, and the Lamanites and the Amlicites did fall before them.

Alma 2:24–28. The Amlicites Join the Lamanites but Are Defeated by the Nephites

How were these rebellious Nephites able to join forces with the Lamanites so quickly? (2:24–28) "[This] encounter . . . certainly must have required rapid negotiations. That requirement, in turn, implies that there was some system for communicating non-hostile intentions and, furthermore, some recognized mechanism for joining forces. The priests of Noah were able to achieve the same goal quite easily. Therefore, the Amlicites' ethnic identity (as Nephites) was apparently no inherent impediment. Apparently they shared some type of lingua franca that facilitated rapid and clear communication, otherwise the possibility of interpreting the situation as hostile would be strong" (Gardner, *Second Witness*, 4:63). ☉

What can we learn from how the Nephites faced their enemy? (2:24–28) The Nephites faced "a numerous host" but were enabled by God to overcome it. We may not face an army, but we do face numerous tests, trials, and temptations. The Nephites learned that "prayer unlocks the powers of heaven in our behalf" (*Teachings of Gordon B. Hinckley*, 470).

How would you describe "mighty" prayer that unlocks heaven's power?

Alma 2:29–38. Alma and His People Drive the Amlicites and Lamanites from the Land

How unique is the imagery of being "an instrument" in God's hands? (2:30) "This phrase occurs twelve times in the Book of Mormon but not at all in the Old Testament. It refers to servants of the Lord who help bring souls to Christ, often through missionary work. . . . The phrase appears several times for the younger Alma and the sons of Mosiah (see Mosiah 27:36; Alma 2:30; 17:9, 11; 26:3, 15; 29:9; 35:14). The sense of this expression is perfectly logical in relation to other biblical hand-of-God expressions" (Seely, "Image of the Hand of God," 145). ◐

What do we learn about Nephite/Lamanite norms for battle from this incident? (2:31–35) "Unquestionably, the individual battles between Alma and Amlici and the king of the Lamanites are most significant. . . . [The] Lamanite force does not employ its numerical superiority. Rather than a general melee, Alma engages in two personal combats, one with Amlici and one with the Lamanite king.

"Thus, each leader represents his army in a battle of kings, not a battle between the armies themselves. Alma crossed the river with a small number of men under his immediate command and began combat with Amlici. It could not have happened by chance that, in an army as numerous as grains of sand, Alma coincidentally fell on one of two opponents of his own social ranking" (Gardner, *Second Witness*, 4:65–66). ◐

29 And it came to pass that Alma fought with Amlici with the sword, face to face; and they did contend mightily, one with another.

30 And it came to pass that Alma, being a man of God, being exercised with much faith, cried, saying: O Lord, have mercy and spare my life, that I may be an instrument in thy hands to save and preserve this people.

31 Now when Alma had said these words he contended again with Amlici; and he was strengthened, insomuch that he slew Amlici with the sword.

32 And he also contended with the king of the Lamanites; but the king of the Lamanites fled back from before Alma and sent his guards to contend with Alma.

33 But Alma, with his guards, contended with the guards of the king of the Lamanites until he slew and drove them back.

34 And thus he cleared the ground, or rather the bank, which was on the west of the river Sidon, throwing the bodies of the Lamanites who had been slain into the waters of Sidon, that thereby his people might have room to cross and contend with the Lamanites and the Amlicites on the west side of the river Sidon.

35 And it came to pass that when they had all crossed the river Sidon that the Lamanites and the Amlicites began to flee before them, notwithstanding they were so numerous that they could not be numbered.

36 And they fled before the Nephites towards the wilderness which was west and north, away beyond the borders of the land; and the Nephites did pursue them with their might, and did slay them.

37 Yea, they were met on every hand, and slain and driven, until they were scattered on the west, and on the north, until they had reached the wilderness, which was called Hermounts; and it was that part of the wilderness which was infested by wild and ravenous beasts.

38 And it came to pass that many died in the wilderness of their wounds, and were devoured by those beasts and also the vultures of the air; and their bones have been found, and have been heaped up on the earth.

CHAPTER 3

The Amlicites had marked themselves according to the prophetic word—The Lamanites had been cursed for their rebellion—Men bring their own curses upon themselves—The Nephites defeat another Lamanite army. About 87–86 B.C.

1 And it came to pass that the Nephites who were not slain by the weapons of war, after having buried those who had been slain—now the number of the slain were not numbered, because of the greatness of their number—after they had finished burying their dead they all returned to their lands, and to their houses, and their wives, and their children.

2 Now many women and children had been slain with the sword, and also many of their flocks and their herds; and also many of their fields of grain were destroyed, for they were trodden down by the hosts of men.

3 And now as many of the Lamanites and the Amlicites who had been slain upon the bank of the river Sidon were cast into the waters of Sidon; and behold their bones are in the depths of the sea, and they are many.

Alma 3:1–3. The Many Nephites Who Died in Battle Are Buried

Is there an explanation for repeated phrases in some verses? (3:1) "Epanalepsis is the name of a significant literary device known in antiquity. It occurs where an author repeats certain words in the course of a lengthy sentence, to pick up a previous train of thought after a parenthetical aside, to remind the reader of the original idea of the sentence. This technique was noted in antiquity by Demetrius, and it is sometimes called 'resumptive repetition'" (Welch, "Epanalepsis in the Book of Mormon," 165). ☉

What significance does the river Sidon hold in Nephite geography and history? (3:3) The river was a major landmark identifier. It flowed near the city of Zarahemla. In Alma's day many slain bodies were cast into the river after a serious battle. Alma "went from standing face-to-face and sword-to-sword with Amlici near the river of Sidon during a battle to standing face-to-face and hand-in-hand in the river Sidon with those who had repented (see Alma 2:29, 34–35; 3:3; 4:4). The river Sidon was a scene of bloodshed, later to become a place of baptism" (Jenkins, "Peaceable Followers of Christ in Days of War and Contention," 94).

Alma 3:4–19. The Amlicites Mark Themselves and Are Cursed like the Lamanites

What can we learn today from the Amlicites marking themselves? (3:4) "A classic illustration of marking oneself is found in the example of the Amlicites. They did not want to appear as Nephites and 'marked themselves with red in their foreheads after the manner of the Lamanites' (Alma 3:4). . . . Just as these Amlicites began to take on the appearance of the Lamanites, they also began to take on their attitudes. The spiritual principle is, 'You can't act like, think like, and dress like the world. It will cost you spiritually'" (Williams, "Using the Book of Mormon to Meet Today's Challenges," 36). ☉

What is the difference between the "curse" and the "mark" put on the Lamanites? (3:6–9) "The mark placed upon the Lamanites was a dark skin (see Alma 3:6). The curse was not the dark skin but being 'cut off from the presence of the Lord' (2 Nephi 5:20). Notice that in both Alma 3:7 and Alma 3:14 the conjunction *and* is used between the curse and the mark. This implies that they are not the same thing. The people brought the curse upon themselves: 'And even so doth every man that is cursed bring upon himself his own condemnation' (Alma 3:19). Through righteousness the curse may be removed, but the mark may remain as it has with the Lamanites" (*Book of Mormon Student Manual* [2009], 174). ☉

What happened to the meaning of the terms *Nephite* and *Lamanite*? (3:10–12) "After a period of time in Book of Mormon history, lineal descent becomes virtually irrelevant. Basically, Nephites are those who give heed to the prophets, and Lamanites are those who refuse to do so" (McConkie and Millet, *Doctrinal Commentary*, 3:17). ☉

4 And the Amlicites were distinguished from the Nephites, for they had marked themselves with red in their foreheads after the manner of the Lamanites; nevertheless they had not shorn their heads like unto the Lamanites.

5 Now the heads of the Lamanites were shorn; and they were naked, save it were skin which was girded about their loins, and also their armor, which was girded about them, and their bows, and their arrows, and their stones, and their slings, and so forth.

6 And the skins of the Lamanites were dark, according to the mark which was set upon their fathers, which was a curse upon them because of their transgression and their rebellion against their brethren, who consisted of Nephi, Jacob, and Joseph, and Sam, who were just and holy men.

7 And their brethren sought to destroy them, therefore they were cursed; and the Lord God set a mark upon them, yea, upon Laman and Lemuel, and also the sons of Ishmael, and Ishmaelitish women.

8 And this was done that their seed might be distinguished from the seed of their brethren, that thereby the Lord God might preserve his people, that they might not mix and believe in incorrect traditions which would prove their destruction.

9 And it came to pass that whosoever did mingle his seed with that of the Lamanites did bring the same curse upon his seed.

10 Therefore, whosoever suffered himself to be led away by the Lamanites was called under that head, and there was a mark set upon him.

11 And it came to pass that whosoever would not believe in the tradition of the Lamanites, but believed those records which were brought

out of the land of Jerusalem, and also in the tradition of their fathers, which were correct, who believed in the commandments of God and kept them, were called the Nephites, or the people of Nephi, from that time forth—

12 And it is they who have kept the records which are true of their people, and also of the people of the Lamanites.

13 Now we will return again to the Amlicites, for they also had a mark set upon them; yea, they set the mark upon themselves, yea, even a mark of red upon their foreheads.

14 Thus the word of God is fulfilled, for these are the words which he said to Nephi: Behold, the Lamanites have I cursed, and I will set a mark on them that they and their seed may be separated from thee and thy seed, from this time henceforth and forever, except they repent of their wickedness and turn to me that I may have mercy upon them.

15 And again: I will set a mark upon him that mingleth his seed with thy brethren, that they may be cursed also.

16 And again: I will set a mark upon him that fighteth against thee and thy seed.

17 And again, I say he that departeth from thee shall no more be called thy seed; and I will bless thee, and whomsoever shall be called thy seed, henceforth and forever; and these were the promises of the Lord unto Nephi and to his seed.

18 Now the Amlicites knew not that they were fulfilling the words of God when they began to mark themselves in their foreheads; nevertheless they had come out in open rebellion against God; therefore it was expedient that the curse should fall upon them.

19 Now I would that ye should see that they brought upon themselves the curse; and even so doth every man that is cursed bring upon himself his own condemnation.

What is the source of the quotation "I will set a mark upon him"? (3:13–18) "We have searched every reference that is made to God's warning that is recorded upon the Smaller Plates of Nephi, wherein the followers of the older brothers were cursed, and do not find them. Yet, we presume Mormon's quote was word-for-word. Our conclusion is that they were first written upon the larger plates, and that Mormon copied them direct from the original source" (Reynolds and Sjodahl, *Commentary on the Book of Mormon*, 3:62).

How do people bring curses upon themselves? (3:19) "Just as obedience and righteousness bring blessings, so wickedness and rebellion result in cursings.... Cursings are the opposite of blessings, and the greater the opportunity given a people to earn blessings, the more severe will be the cursings heaped upon them, if they do not measure up and gain the proffered rewards" (McConkie, *Mormon Doctrine*, 175). ◐

Alma 3:20–27. The Nephites Drive Away Another Lamanite Army

What possible good can come from so much destruction? (3:26) "The wars and contentions caused by Amlici and his followers had greatly afflicted the Nephites. The loss of their brethren as casualties in battle, not to mention the destruction of flocks, herds, and crops of grain, caused great mourning among the people. But the destruction had at least one good result: it caused much soul-searching among them, because they all felt that the judgments of God had come upon them because of their wickedness and abominations. For a time the Church grew in size because of numerous baptisms performed under the hands of Alma, who was the high priest and chief ecclesiastical authority among the people" (Sperry, *Book of Mormon Compendium*, 329).

What is the lesson regarding man's agency and ultimate judgment? (3:27) "If we list to obey Jesus Christ, as our Master, we walk in the light: we receive peace, happiness, prosperity and the other good blessings of this life, and in the world to come, eternal life in our Father's kingdom. If we choose to follow Lucifer as our master, we shall receive the wages which are his to bestow upon us. On certain occasions those who obey Satan receive as their wages misery, unhappiness, sorrow, and disappointment in this life; and, one might say, on all occasions, they experience the loss of their eternal rewards in the world to come" (Hunter, in Conference Report, Apr. 1952, 123).

20 Now it came to pass that not many days after the battle which was fought in the land of Zarahemla, by the Lamanites and the Amlicites, that there was another army of the Lamanites came in upon the people of Nephi, in the same place where the first army met the Amlicites.

21 And it came to pass that there was an army sent to drive them out of their land.

22 Now Alma himself being afflicted with a wound did not go up to battle at this time against the Lamanites;

23 But he sent up a numerous army against them; and they went up and slew many of the Lamanites, and drove the remainder of them out of the borders of their land.

24 And then they returned again and began to establish peace in the land, being troubled no more for a time with their enemies.

25 Now all these things were done, yea, all these wars and contentions were commenced and ended in the fifth year of the reign of the judges.

26 And in one year were thousands and tens of thousands of souls sent to the eternal world, that they might reap their rewards according to their works, whether they were good or whether they were bad, to reap eternal happiness or eternal misery, according to the spirit which they listed to obey, whether it be a good spirit or a bad one.

27 For every man receiveth wages of him whom he listeth to obey, and this according to the words of the spirit of prophecy; therefore let it be according to the truth. And thus endeth the fifth year of the reign of the judges.

CHAPTER 4

Alma baptizes thousands of converts—Iniquity enters the Church, and the Church's progress is hindered—Nephihah is appointed chief judge—Alma, as high priest, devotes himself to the ministry. About 86–83 B.C.

1 Now it came to pass in the sixth year of the reign of the judges over the people of Nephi, there were no contentions nor wars in the land of Zarahemla;

2 But the people were afflicted, yea, greatly afflicted for the loss of their brethren, and also for the loss of their flocks and herds, and also for the loss of their fields of grain, which were trodden under foot and destroyed by the Lamanites.

3 And so great were their afflictions that every soul had cause to mourn; and they believed that it was the judgments of God sent upon them because of their wickedness and their abominations; therefore they were awakened to a remembrance of their duty.

4 And they began to establish the church more fully; yea, and many were baptized in the waters of Sidon and were joined to the church of God; yea, they were baptized by the hand of Alma, who had been consecrated the high priest over the people of the church, by the hand of his father Alma.

5 And it came to pass in the seventh year of the reign of the judges there were about three thousand five hundred souls that united themselves to the church of God and were baptized. And thus ended the seventh year of the reign of the judges over the people of Nephi; and there was continual peace in all that time.

Alma 4:1–5. Many Nephites Are Humbled Because of the War and Are Baptized into the Church

What is the Book of Mormon chronology with reference to the reign of judges? (4:1) "The sixth year of the reign of the judges would be approximately 87 B.C., since the first year of the reign of the judges occurred 509 years after the departure from Jerusalem. Apparently, both counts overlap in that year rather than having one end and the other begin. In no other way will the time frame fit with the birth of Christ" (Gardner, *Second Witness*, 4:83).

How can affliction and suffering work in our favor? (4:2–3) "It is normal and natural when things go wrong to begin to search for causes, to begin to look carefully at one's attitudes and behaviors to ascertain whether one has offended God. If a person is sincere in his searchings, if he asks God to reveal his weakness, . . . the Lord can awaken him to a remembrance of his duty. . . . That is, the Spirit of Jesus Christ can bring to remembrance commitments, covenants, and divine counsel, thereby placing in vivid relief the ideal and the real in our lives" (McConkie and Millet, *Doctrinal Commentary*, 3:18–19).

How did the effects of war bring the Nephites to Christ? (4:4) "The great losses sustained by the Nephites in war, not of warriors alone, but of women and children, together with the vast amount of their property which was destroyed, had the effect of humbling them and softening their wayward hearts, so that many thousands during the next few years were added to the Church. . . .

"The Church, under the divinely inspired leadership of Alma, who was its Presiding High Priest, or the President of the Church, was more fully established in every Branch throughout the nation. Teachers, priests, and elders were consecrated to administer the sacred ordinances of the Church to all who believed and who took upon themselves the name of Christ" (Reynolds and Sjodahl, *Commentary on the Book of Mormon*, 3:66). ❂

Alma 4:6–14. Many Church Members Become Rich, Proud, and Wicked

What did Church members at the time of Alma set their hearts upon? How is that a warning to us today? (4:6) "Pride again raised its ugly head, as they began to set their hearts upon riches. The wearing of costly apparel (v. 6), scorn and persecution and great contentions (vv. 8–9) are a part and parcel of the problem of pride. It is a reappearing problem throughout the Book of Mormon. Thus, we know why the Lord warned this generation to 'beware of pride, lest ye become as the Nephites of old' (D&C 38:39). Sadly it was worse among the church members than those who were not members (Alma 4:9)" (Nyman, *Record of Alma*, 35–36). ✪

What priesthood did these Nephite priests and teachers hold? (4:7) See commentary in this volume on Jacob 1:18.

Why is pride a stumbling-block for the Church? (4:8–9) See commentary in this volume on 1 Nephi 11:36.

How do members become stumbling-blocks to Church growth? (4:10) "How vain and trifling have been our spirits, our conferences, our councils, our meetings, our private as well as public conversations—too low, too mean, too vulgar, too condescending for the dignified characters of the called and chosen of God, according to the purposes of His will, from before the foundation of the world!" (Smith, *History of the Church*, 3:295–96).

6 And it came to pass in the eighth year of the reign of the judges, that the people of the church began to wax proud, because of their exceeding riches, and their fine silks, and their fine-twined linen, and because of their many flocks and herds, and their gold and their silver, and all manner of precious things, which they had obtained by their industry; and in all these things were they lifted up in the pride of their eyes, for they began to wear very costly apparel.

7 Now this was the cause of much affliction to Alma, yea, and to many of the people whom Alma had consecrated to be teachers, and priests, and elders over the church; yea, many of them were sorely grieved for the wickedness which they saw had begun to be among their people.

8 For they saw and beheld with great sorrow that the people of the church began to be lifted up in the pride of their eyes, and to set their hearts upon riches and upon the vain things of the world, that they began to be scornful, one towards another, and they began to persecute those that did not believe according to their own will and pleasure.

9 And thus, in this eighth year of the reign of the judges, there began to be great contentions among the people of the church; yea, there were envyings, and strife, and malice, and persecutions, and pride, even to exceed the pride of those who did not belong to the church of God.

10 And thus ended the eighth year of the reign of the judges; and the wickedness of the church was a great stumbling-block to those who did not belong to the church; and thus the church began to fail in its progress.

11 And it came to pass in the commencement of the ninth year, Alma saw the

wickedness of the church, and he saw also that the example of the church began to lead those who were unbelievers on from one piece of iniquity to another, thus bringing on the destruction of the people.

12 Yea, he saw great inequality among the people, some lifting themselves up with their pride, despising others, turning their backs upon the needy and the naked and those who were hungry, and those who were athirst, and those who were sick and afflicted.

13 Now this was a great cause for lamentations among the people, while others were abasing themselves, succoring those who stood in need of their succor, such as imparting their substance to the poor and the needy, feeding the hungry, and suffering all manner of afflictions, for Christ's sake, who should come according to the spirit of prophecy;

14 Looking forward to that day, thus retaining a remission of their sins; being filled with great joy because of the resurrection of the dead, according to the will and power and deliverance of Jesus Christ from the bands of death.

15 And now it came to pass that Alma, having seen the afflictions of the humble followers of God, and the persecutions which were heaped upon them by the remainder of his people, and seeing all their inequality, began to be very sorrowful; nevertheless the Spirit of the Lord did not fail him.

16 And he selected a wise man who was among the elders of the church, and gave him power according to the voice of the people, that he might have power to enact laws according to the laws which had been given, and to put them in force according to the wickedness and the crimes of the people.

17 Now this man's name was Nephihah, and he was appointed chief judge; and he sat in

"I beg leave to say unto you, brethren, that ignorance, superstition and bigotry placing itself where it ought not, is oftentimes in the way of the prosperity of this Church" (*Joseph Smith* [manual], 363). ◆

Alma 4:15–18. A New Chief Judge Is Chosen to Replace Alma

How can the Spirit strengthen us in times of trouble? (4:15) "We live in troubled times—very troubled times. We hope, we pray, for better days. But that is not to be. The prophecies tell us that. We will not as a people, as families, or as individuals be exempt from the trials to come. No one will be spared the trials common to home and family, work, disappointment, grief, health, aging, ultimately death.... We need not live in fear of the future. We have every reason to rejoice and little reason to fear. If we follow the promptings of the Spirit, we will be safe, whatever the future holds. We will be shown what to do" (Packer, "Cloven Tongues of Fire," 8).

"Names like Nephihah that end in *-ihah* are interesting. At the time of Lehi, there was a new revival movement begun in Israel led by Josiah. These names that ended in *-ihah* in Israel at that time are Jehovah names. That was the revival of the cult going back to Jehovah. *Ihah* is another form of the name. You find that name later. You find it in Aramaic, too. The name Nephihah would probably be a mixture. They mixed Semitic and Aramaic elements. It might mean 'the Lord is Jehovah'" (Nibley, *Teachings of the Book of Mormon*, 2:263).

Alma 4:19–20. Alma Spends His Time Preaching the Word of God and Bearing Testimony to the People

Why did Alma choose to spend his life serving in God's kingdom? (4:19) "We have experienced the joy of service in our Heavenly Father's kingdom and know the soul-satisfying fulfillment it brings to our lives. I often think of the challenge which Alma faced when he could see the urgent need of the people to be taught the importance of having an understanding of the gospel of our Lord and Savior. At that time he served in two positions, that of chief judge and high priest over all the Church. He had to make a choice between the two in order to maximize his effectiveness in serving the people. . . . He selected for himself the position which would allow him to do the most good for his people" (Perry, "Peaceable Followers of Christ," 72).

What impelled Alma to bear "pure testimony" against his people? (4:19–20) Alma recognized the "wickedness of the Church" (v. 11). He not only felt impelled to do something, but he was under obligation to do something. "Decadence is very demanding and dogmatic, and it is no friend of liberty. Decadence which grew in the soil of tolerance and permissiveness soon seeks to drive out all of these. Then, finally, it reaches a point when, as one prophet declared, 'There was no remedy.' In such moments the prophets of God speak out even more forcibly, doing as Alma did when he began bearing down in pure testimony against the evils of his time (see Alma 4:19). Nothing less will do under those conditions" (Kimball, "Listen to the Prophets," 78).

What is "the holy order of God"? (4:20) See commentary in this volume on Alma 13:1. See also D&C 107:2–4.

the judgment-seat to judge and to govern the people.

18 Now Alma did not grant unto him the office of being high priest over the church, but he retained the office of high priest unto himself; but he delivered the judgment-seat unto Nephihah.

19 And this he did that he himself might go forth among his people, or among the people of Nephi, that he might preach the word of God unto them, to stir them up in remembrance of their duty, and that he might pull down, by the word of God, all the pride and craftiness and all the contentions which were among his people, seeing no way that he might reclaim them save it were in bearing down in pure testimony against them.

20 And thus in the commencement of the ninth year of the reign of the judges over the people of Nephi, Alma delivered up the judgment-seat to Nephihah, and confined himself wholly to the high priesthood of the holy order of God, to the testimony of the word, according to the spirit of revelation and prophecy.

The words which Alma, the High Priest according to the holy order of God, delivered to the people in their cities and villages throughout the land.

Beginning with chapter 5.

CHAPTER 5

To gain salvation, men must repent and keep the commandments, be born again, cleanse their garments through the blood of Christ, be humble and strip themselves of pride and envy, and do the works of righteousness—The Good Shepherd calls His people—Those who do evil works are children of the devil—Alma testifies of the truth of his doctrine and commands men to repent—The names of the righteous will be written in the book of life. About 83 B.C.

1 Now it came to pass that Alma began to deliver the word of God unto the people, first in the land of Zarahemla, and from thence throughout all the land.

2 And these are the words which he spake to the people in the church which was established in the city of Zarahemla, according to his own record, saying:

3 I, Alma, having been consecrated by my father, Alma, to be a high priest over the church of God, he having power and authority from God to do these things, behold, I say unto you that he began to establish a church in the land which was in the borders of Nephi; yea, the land which was called the land of Mormon; yea, and he did baptize his brethren in the waters of Mormon.

4 And behold, I say unto you, they were delivered out of the hands of the people of king Noah, by the mercy and power of God.

5 And behold, after that, they were brought into bondage by the hands of the Lamanites in the wilderness; yea, I say unto you, they were in captivity, and again the Lord did

Superscription to Alma 5

The superscription to Alma 5 was part of the ancient record translated by the Prophet Joseph Smith and dictated by him to his scribe (see also, for example, 2 Nephi, Mosiah 9, and Alma 21).

"This [superscription] appeared in the 1830 [edition of the Book of Mormon]. . . . It is apparently from Mormon's hand and is intended to introduce a quoted record. The original manuscript is not extant at this point (nor for similar introductions at the beginning of our chapters 7 and 9 of Alma).

"The printer's manuscript indicates that these summaries were set off from the rest of the text only by a dash, with the first verse of the text beginning on the same line" (Gardner, *Second Witness*, 4:90).

The phrase "Comprising chapter 5" was added in later editions for clarity.

Alma 5:1–6. Alma Uses the Power of the Word to Teach the People

What is the setting of Alma's discourse in Zarahemla? (5:1) "[Alma 5 is] a long and carefully articulated address delivered presumably over a period of time and on various occasions . . . 'in the city of Zarahemla,' possibly consisting of seven or more congregations (Mosiah 25:23)" (Brown, "Alma's Conversion," 143).

From whom did Alma the Elder receive the priesthood? (5:3) President Joseph Fielding Smith reminded us that "in the Book of Mosiah it is stated definitely that [Alma the Elder] had authority [see Mosiah 18:13]." However, the Book of Mormon does not indicate from whom Alma received his priesthood. President Smith explained, "Remember that the Book of Mormon is an abridgment of former records, and like the Bible, does not furnish many details. If I remember correctly, there is no reference to the baptism of Alma the elder or Helaman nor of Nephi and his brother Jacob, but we know they were baptized as were all the faithful members in the Church" (Smith, *Answers to Gospel Questions*, 3:203–4).

Why does Alma narrate the history of the deliverance of the Nephites? (5:4–5) "Alma intends to draw parallels between this people and his father's church by the Waters of Mormon. First, those Nephites were in bondage to the Lamanites. . . . Second, Yahweh's power delivered Alma's father's people from Lamanite bondage. Alma wanted to emphasize the power of faith and [God's] power to deliver, logically suggesting that [God's] power will also resolve their current situation. Third, Alma's father's converts came to Zarahemla and established 'the church of God,' of which his listeners are members. This statement forcefully brings history into the present. Symbolically, the current church will have the same option as that earlier church, and it, too, may be delivered by [God's] word" (Gardner, *Second Witness*, 4:91).

What did Alma want his people to remember? (5:6) "Many of the things he recited to his brethren were familiar to them. Some . . . of his listeners had undergone . . . the tribulations of which he spoke. . . . Out of all their trials and afflictions, which were many, they all knew whereof Alma spoke. . . .

"All these things out of which the Lord had rescued them and of which Alma reminded them, led to the questions which were uppermost in his mind. . . . Has the remembrance of these things stirred you up to a renewed determination to serve God, even that you keep all His commandments?" (Reynolds and Sjodahl, *Commentary on the Book of Mormon*, 3:75). ⊕

Alma 5:7–13. Alma Explains the Need of Being Born Again in Order to Gain Eternal Life

How are we to awaken others unto God? (5:7) "We need to use the everlasting word to awaken those in deep sleep so they will awake 'unto God.'

"I am deeply concerned about what we are doing to teach the Saints at all levels the gospel of Jesus Christ as completely and authoritatively as do the Book of Mormon and the Doctrine and Covenants. By this I mean teaching the 'great plan of the Eternal God,' to use the words of Amulek (Alma 34:9).

"Are we using the messages and the method of teaching found in the Book of Mormon and other scriptures of the Restoration to teach this great plan of the Eternal God?" (Benson, "The Book of Mormon and the Doctrine and Covenants," 84).

What are the "chains of hell"? (5:7–10) Alma later defines the "chains of hell" as being brought "into subjection unto [the devil], . . . that he might chain you down to everlasting destruction" (Alma 12:6) and as "knowing nothing concerning [God's] mysteries," they are, as a consequence, being "taken captive by the devil, and led by his will down to destruction" (Alma 12:11).

deliver them out of bondage by the power of his word; and we were brought into this land, and here we began to establish the church of God throughout this land also.

6 And now behold, I say unto you, my brethren, you that belong to this church, have you sufficiently retained in remembrance the captivity of your fathers? Yea, and have you sufficiently retained in remembrance his mercy and long-suffering towards them? And moreover, have ye sufficiently retained in remembrance that he has delivered their souls from hell?

7 Behold, he changed their hearts; yea, he awakened them out of a deep sleep, and they awoke unto God. Behold, they were in the midst of darkness; nevertheless, their souls were illuminated by the light of the everlasting word; yea, they were encircled about by the bands of death, and the chains of hell, and an everlasting destruction did await them.

8 And now I ask of you, my brethren, were they destroyed? Behold, I say unto you, Nay, they were not.

9 And again I ask, were the bands of death broken, and the chains of hell which encircled them about, were they loosed? I say unto you, Yea, they were loosed, and their souls did expand, and they did sing redeeming love. And I say unto you that they are saved.

10 And now I ask of you on what conditions are they saved? Yea, what grounds had they to hope for salvation? What is the cause of their being loosed from the bands of death, yea, and also the chains of hell?

11 Behold, I can tell you—did not my father Alma believe in the words which were delivered by the mouth of Abinadi? And was he not a holy prophet? Did he not speak the words of God, and my father Alma believe them?

12 And according to his faith there was a mighty change wrought in his heart. Behold I say unto you that this is all true.

13 And behold, he preached the word unto your fathers, and a mighty change was also wrought in their hearts, and they humbled themselves and put their trust in the true and living God. And behold, they were faithful until the end; therefore they were saved.

14 And now behold, I ask of you, my brethren of the church, have ye spiritually been born of God? Have ye received his image in your countenances? Have ye experienced this mighty change in your hearts?

15 Do ye exercise faith in the redemption of him who created you? Do you look forward with an eye of faith, and view this mortal body raised in immortality, and this corruption raised in incorruption, to stand before God to be judged according to the deeds which have been done in the mortal body?

What is a "mighty change" of heart? (5:10–13)
"Webster says . . . that *conversion* is 'a spiritual and moral *change* attending a *change* of belief with conviction' [italics added]. As used in the scriptures, *converted* generally implies not merely mental acceptance of Jesus and his teachings, but also a motivating faith in him and in his gospel, a faith which works a transformation, an actual *change* in one's understanding of life's meaning and in one's allegiance to God—in interest, in thought, and in conduct. While *conversion* may be accomplished in stages, one is not really converted in the full sense of the term unless and until he is at heart a new person" (Romney, "According to the Covenants," 71). ⊕

Alma 5:14–32. Alma Asks Searching Questions regarding What It Means to Be Born Again

What does it mean to have God's image in our countenance and to have a change of heart? (5:14, 19) "To receive Christ's image in one's countenance means to acquire the Savior's likeness in behavior, to be a copy or reflection of the Master's life. This is not possible without a mighty change in one's pattern of living. It requires, too, a change in feelings, attitudes, desires, and spiritual commitment" (Skinner, "Alma's 'Pure Testimony,'" 301).

"The heart is used by Alma to symbolize the center of affections. By using a question/answer approach, Alma invites his listeners to personally evaluate their conversion to the gospel of Jesus Christ" (Black, *400 Questions and Answers*, 149). ⊕

How do we "exercise faith in the redemption" of Christ? (5:15) "To exercise faith in the redemption of Christ is to have perfect confidence that in Christ is found the power to remit sins, heal souls, raise the dead, and triumph in all that is right and good. It is to trust the simplicity of gospel answers; it is to seek the sanction of heaven on all that one does" (McConkie and Millet, *Doctrinal Commentary*, 3:30).

What does it mean to be judged of mortal deeds? (5:15) "God is sincere in trying to promote their [those outside of the Church] happiness and welfare as well as he is ours, both in regard to this world and the world to come. And hence he will do the best he possibly can with all peoples. But . . . being governed by law, he can only treat them 'according to the deeds done in the body, whether those deeds be good or evil' [JST, 2 Corinthians 5:10]. And when that judgment takes place all men will have to abide its award; there is no appeal from it. No court to which they can have access whereby they can change the decree of the Almighty" (John Taylor, in *Journal of Discourses*, 20:111).

What are the implications of Alma's questions in these verses? (5:16–19) "Alma implies here that the 'exercise of faith in the redemption' [verse 15] of Christ sufficient to bring about the mighty change in one's heart is prerequisite to obtaining a pure heart and clean hands. He also implies that if on the great judgment day one can look up to God with a pure heart and clean hands, he will hear the voice of the Lord saying unto him, 'Come unto me ye blessed'; if he cannot do so, his soul will be filled with guilt and remorse" (Romney, *Learning for the Eternities*, 127). ✛

Will we remember all of our deeds and thoughts after this mortal life? (5:18) "As all will be resurrected, your physical body will then be restored to its proper and perfect frame (see Alma 11:43; Alma 40:23). The day of your resurrection will be a day of judgment that will determine the kind of life you shall have hereafter.

"That judgment will consider not only your actions, but also your innermost intent and heartfelt desires. Your everyday thoughts have not been lost. Scriptures speak of the 'bright recollection' (Alma 11:43) and 'perfect remembrance' (Alma 5:18) that your mind will provide in times of divine judgment" (Nelson, "Choices," 75).

What does it mean to have our garments "washed white"? (5:21–22) "No principle was better understood among the ancient Saints than that no unclean thing could enter the presence of the Lord. Thus the imagery common to the scriptures is to depict the Saints of God, those living righteous lives, as wearing 'robes of righteousness' (2 Nephi 9:14; Revelation 19:8), or 'garments of salvation' (Isaiah 61:10). This imagery is closely associated with the temple, which is the

16 I say unto you, can you imagine to yourselves that ye hear the voice of the Lord, saying unto you, in that day: Come unto me ye blessed, for behold, your works have been the works of righteousness upon the face of the earth?

17 Or do ye imagine to yourselves that ye can lie unto the Lord in that day, and say—Lord, our works have been righteous works upon the face of the earth—and that he will save you?

18 Or otherwise, can ye imagine yourselves brought before the tribunal of God with your souls filled with guilt and remorse, having a remembrance of all your guilt, yea, a perfect remembrance of all your wickedness, yea, a remembrance that ye have set at defiance the commandments of God?

19 I say unto you, can ye look up to God at that day with a pure heart and clean hands? I say unto you, can you look up, having the image of God engraven upon your countenances?

20 I say unto you, can ye think of being saved when you have yielded yourselves to become subjects to the devil?

21 I say unto you, ye will know at that day that ye cannot be saved; for there can no man be saved except his garments are washed white; yea, his garments must be purified until they are cleansed from all stain, through the blood of him of whom it has been spoken by our fathers, who should come to redeem his people from their sins.

22 And now I ask of you, my brethren, how will any of you feel, if ye shall stand before the bar of God, having your garments stained with blood and all manner of filthiness? Behold, what will these things testify against you?

23 Behold will they not testify that ye are murderers, yea, and also that ye are guilty of all manner of wickedness?

24 Behold, my brethren, do ye suppose that such an one can have a place to sit down in the kingdom of God, with Abraham, with Isaac, and with Jacob, and also all the holy prophets, whose garments are cleansed and are spotless, pure and white?

25 I say unto you, Nay; except ye make our Creator a liar from the beginning, or suppose that he is a liar from the beginning, ye cannot suppose that such can have place in the kingdom of heaven; but they shall be cast out for they are the children of the kingdom of the devil.

26 And now behold, I say unto you, my brethren, if ye have experienced a change of heart, and if ye have felt to sing the song of redeeming love, I would ask, can ye feel so now?

27 Have ye walked, keeping yourselves blameless before God? Could ye say, if ye were called to die at this time, within yourselves, that ye have been sufficiently humble? That your garments have been cleansed and made white through the blood of Christ, who will come to redeem his people from their sins?

28 Behold, are ye stripped of pride? I say unto you, if ye are not ye are not prepared to meet God. Behold ye must prepare quickly; for the kingdom of heaven is soon at hand, and such an one hath not eternal life.

earthly representation of the divine presence, or our sought-after heavenly abode. In the temple we are taught, primarily with symbolic representation, how we return to the presence of God (see D&C 109:80)" (McConkie and Millet, *Doctrinal Commentary*, 3:31; see also commentary in this volume on Alma 7:25).

What is the "song of redeeming love"? (5:26) "To sing the song of redeeming love is to joy in the matchless majesty of God's goodness, to know the wonder of his love. It is to sense and know that the Lord is intimately involved with his children and that he cares, really cares, about their well-being. . . .

" . . . All those who have had the burdens of sin, the weight of guilt, and the agonies of bitterness, hostility, or pain removed by the Great Physician shout praises to the Holy One of Israel" (Millet, *Power of the Word*, 232–33).

How will we know if we are prepared for the kingdom of heaven? (5:26–31) "You will have put yourself so often in the Master's service, bringing the cleansing companionship of the Holy Ghost, that you will be on the front row, early, whenever and wherever the Master calls" (Eyring, *To Draw Closer to God*, 58). ☉

What does the phrase "the kingdom of heaven is soon at hand" mean? (5:28) "In one sense this [phrase] meant to the Nephites that Christ, the King of all the earth, would come into mortality (see v. 50; Alma 7:9; 10:20). In another sense it means that each of us, as we face the time of death, must reckon with ourselves in regard to the commandments of God. That is, we know not the day nor the hour in which our experience in mortality will end. Be it a few years or many (as mortals count them), the time spent on earth will seem all too short" (McConkie and Millet, *Doctrinal Commentary*, 3:33).

What is envy and where might it lead? (5:29) "It has been said that envy is the one sin to which no one readily confesses, but just how widespread that tendency can be is suggested in the old Danish proverb, 'If envy were a fever, all the world would be ill.' The parson in Chaucer's *Canterbury Tales* laments it because it is so far-reaching—it can resent anything, including any virtue and talent, and it can be offended by everything, including every goodness and joy. As others seem to grow larger in our sight, we think we must therefore be smaller. So, unfortunately, we occasionally act that way" (Holland, "The Other Prodigal," 63).

It is important to note that in the aftermath of Christ's visit among the Nephites, there were no "envyings" among the people (4 Nephi 1:16). Throughout

29 Behold, I say, is there one among you who is not stripped of envy? I say unto you that such an one is not prepared; and I would that he should prepare quickly, for the hour is close at hand, and he knoweth not when the time shall come; for such an one is not found guiltless.

30 And again I say unto you, is there one among you that doth make a mock of his brother, or that heapeth upon him persecutions?

Stripping Ourselves of Envy

Elder Jeffrey R. Holland
of the Quorum of the
Twelve Apostles

© Intellectual Reserve, Inc. Used by permission.

Elder Jeffrey R. Holland noted how the world conditions us to embrace the sin of envy: "How does this happen, especially when we wish so much that it would not? I think one of the reasons is that every day we see allurements of one kind or another that tell us what we have is not enough. Someone or something is forever telling us we need to be more handsome or more wealthy, more applauded or more admired than we see ourselves as being. We are told we haven't collected enough possessions or gone to enough fun places. We are bombarded with the message that on the *world's* scale of things we have been weighed in the balance and found wanting. Some days it is as if we have been locked in a cubicle of a great and spacious building where the only thing on the TV is a never-ending soap opera entitled *Vain Imaginations*. . . .

"How can we overcome such a tendency so common in almost everyone? For one thing, we can . . . start making our way back to the Father. We should do so with as much haste and humility as we can summon. Along the way we can count our many blessings and we can applaud the accomplishments of others. Best of all, we can serve others, the finest exercise for the heart ever prescribed. But finally these will not be enough. When we are lost, we can 'come to ourselves,' but we may not always be able to 'find ourselves,' and, worlds without end, we cannot 'save ourselves.' Only the Father and His Only Begotten Son can do that. Salvation is in Them only. So we pray that They will help us, that They will 'come out' to meet and embrace us and bring us into the feast They have prepared.

"They will do this! The scriptures are replete with the promise that God's grace is sufficient. This is one arena where no one has to claw or compete. Nephi declares that the Lord 'loveth the [whole] world' and has given salvation freely. . . .

"I testify that no one of us is less treasured or cherished of God than another. I testify that He loves each of us—insecurities, anxieties, self-image, and all. He doesn't measure our talents or our looks; He doesn't measure our professions or our possessions. He cheers on every runner, calling out that the race is against sin, not against each other. I know that if we will be faithful, there is a perfectly tailored robe of righteousness ready and waiting for *everyone*, 'robes . . . made . . . white in the blood of the Lamb' (Revelation 7:14)" ("The Other Prodigal," 63–64).

31 Wo unto such an one, for he is not prepared, and the time is at hand that he must repent or he cannot be saved!

32 Yea, even wo unto all ye workers of iniquity; repent, repent, for the Lord God hath spoken it!

33 Behold, he sendeth an invitation unto all men, for the arms of mercy are extended towards them, and he saith: Repent, and I will receive you.

34 Yea, he saith: Come unto me and ye shall partake of the fruit of the tree of life; yea, ye shall eat and drink of the bread and the waters of life freely;

35 Yea, come unto me and bring forth works of righteousness, and ye shall not be hewn down and cast into the fire—

36 For behold, the time is at hand that whosoever bringeth forth not good fruit, or whosoever doeth not the works of righteousness, the same have cause to wail and mourn.

37 O ye workers of iniquity; ye that are puffed up in the vain things of the world, ye that have professed to have known the ways of righteousness nevertheless have gone astray, as sheep having no shepherd, notwithstanding a shepherd hath called after you and is still calling after you, but ye will not hearken unto his voice!

38 Behold, I say unto you, that the good shepherd doth call you; yea, and in his own name he doth call you, which is the name of Christ; and if ye will not hearken unto the voice of the good shepherd, to the name by which ye are called, behold, ye are not the sheep of the good shepherd.

39 And now if ye are not the sheep of the good shepherd, of what fold are ye? Behold, I say unto you, that the devil is your shepherd, and ye are of his fold; and now, who can deny this? Behold, I say unto you, whosoever denieth this is a liar and a child of the devil.

the rest of the Book of Mormon, however, envy was a persistent problem (see Alma 1:32; 16:18; Helaman 13:22). One of the most important warnings from Book of Mormon prophets is that in the last days, envy will become a great stumbling-block to righteousness and the progress of the Church (see Mormon 8:28; see also 2 Nephi 21:13; 26:21, 32).

Alma 5:33–42. Eternal Life Is Offered to All through the Name of Jesus Christ

Who is invited to come unto the Lord? (5:33–34) Elder Quentin L. Cook said: "We are all equal before God. His doctrine is clear. In the Book of Mormon, we read, 'All are alike unto God,' including 'black and white, bond and free, male and female' (2 Nephi 26:33). Accordingly, all are invited to come to the Lord" (Cook, "The Eternal Everyday," 51). President Russell M. Nelson also stated: "Our message to the world is simple and sincere: We invite all of God's children on both sides of the veil to come unto their Savior, receive the blessings of the holy temple, have enduring joy, and qualify for eternal life" (Nelson, "Let Us All Press On, 118–119).

Who are those not included in the fold of "the good shepherd"? (5:38–39) Joseph Fielding Smith stated that those not of the fold are "all who refuse to receive the fulness of the truth, or abide by the principles and ordinances of the everlasting gospel. They may have received a testimony; they may be able to testify that they *know* that Jesus is the Christ; but in their lives they have refused to accept ordinances which are essential to entrance into the celestial kingdom. They have refused to live the gospel, when they knew it to be true; or have been blinded by tradition; or for other cause have not been willing to walk in the light" (Smith, *Doctrines of Salvation*, 2:28–29). ❂

How are verses 40–41 consistent with other teachings of the Savior's servants? (5:40–41) "All that is good comes from God, and all that is evil comes from the devil (Alma 5:40) is also a New Testament doctrine. The Apostle James taught: 'Every good gift and every perfect gift is from above, and comes down from the Father of lights, with whom there is no variableness, neither shadow of turning' (James 1:17). The concepts that good works come from following the good shepherd and evil works come from following the devil (Alma 5:41), and that we receive wages from whom we follow, were taught in the previous chapter of Alma (see Alma 4:26–27)" (Nyman, *Record of Alma*, 66).

Where does serving Satan lead? (5:42) "Those who do not live the gospel are servants of sin; when they accept the gospel and yield themselves to the cause of righteousness, their sins are forgiven through baptism, and they become the servants of righteousness.

"The fruit of sin is spiritual death.

"The fruit of righteousness is everlasting life.

"'Every man receiveth wages of him whom he listeth to obey' (Alma 3:27). Satan pays his servants with death, spiritual death, death as pertaining to the things of righteousness; Christ rewards those who serve him with life, spiritual life, eternal life, life in the presence of God, enjoying and possessing all that Deity himself has" (McConkie, *Doctrinal New Testament Commentary*, 2:251).

Alma 5:43–49. There Is Value in Having More Than One Witness to the Truth

How do we teach according to God's holy order? (5:44) See commentary in this volume on 2 Nephi 6:2. High priests are to teach the commandments unto the children of men and preach repentance (Alma 13:6, 18). Elders, priests, and teachers are exhorted to teach the principles of the gospel from the Bible and Book of Mormon (see D&C 42:12). Alma counseled his son Shiblon to teach in "boldness, but not overbearance" (Alma 38:12). Those teaching after the holy order of God should live in such a way that the Lord can put words into their hearts and minds (Helaman 13:4–5). When directed by the Lord they are to warn against "every kind of sin, telling them the awful consequences of them" (Jacob 3:12). Those ordained are to teach with all diligence (Jacob 1:19).

Why did Alma testify, in the way he did, that his words were true? (5:45–46) "The crowning, convincing, converting power of gospel teaching is manifest when an inspired teacher says, 'I know by the power of

40 For I say unto you that whatsoever is good cometh from God, and whatsoever is evil cometh from the devil.

41 Therefore, if a man bringeth forth good works he hearkeneth unto the voice of the good shepherd, and he doth follow him; but whosoever bringeth forth evil works, the same becometh a child of the devil, for he hearkeneth unto his voice, and doth follow him.

42 And whosoever doeth this must receive his wages of him; therefore, for his wages he receiveth death, as to things pertaining unto righteousness, being dead unto all good works.

43 And now, my brethren, I would that ye should hear me, for I speak in the energy of my soul; for behold, I have spoken unto you plainly that ye cannot err, or have spoken according to the commandments of God.

44 For I am called to speak after this manner, according to the holy order of God, which is in Christ Jesus; yea, I am commanded to stand and testify unto this people the things which have been spoken by our fathers concerning the things which are to come.

45 And this is not all. Do ye not suppose that I know of these things myself? Behold, I testify unto you that I do know that these things whereof I have spoken are true. And how do ye suppose that I know of their surety?

46 Behold, I say unto you they are made known unto me by the Holy Spirit of God. Behold, I have fasted and prayed many days that I might know these things of myself. And now I do know of myself that they are true; for the Lord God hath made them manifest unto me by his Holy Spirit; and this is the spirit of revelation which is in me.

47 And moreover, I say unto you that it has thus been revealed unto me, that the words which have been spoken by our fathers are true, even so according to the spirit of prophecy which is in me, which is also by the manifestation of the Spirit of God.

48 I say unto you, that I know of myself that whatsoever I shall say unto you, concerning that which is to come, is true; and I say unto you, that I know that Jesus Christ shall come, yea, the Son, the Only Begotten of the Father, full of grace, and mercy, and truth. And behold, it is he that cometh to take away the sins of the world, yea, the sins of every man who steadfastly believeth on his name.

49 And now I say unto you that this is the order after which I am called, yea, to preach unto my beloved brethren, yea, and every one that dwelleth in the land; yea, to preach unto all, both old and young, both bond and free; yea, I say unto you the aged, and also the middle aged, and the rising generation; yea, to cry unto them that they must repent and be born again.

50 Yea, thus saith the Spirit: Repent, all ye ends of the earth, for the kingdom of heaven is soon at hand; yea, the Son of God cometh in his glory, in his might, majesty, power, and dominion. Yea, my beloved brethren, I say unto you, that the Spirit saith: Behold the glory of the King of all the earth; and also the

the Holy Ghost, by the revelations of the Holy Spirit to my soul, that the doctrines I have taught are true.' This divine seal of approval makes the spoken word binding upon the hearers" (McConkie, *Promised Messiah*, 516–17). ⊕

Why did those in ancient times fast? (5:46)
"Anciently, obtaining a testimony was one reason for fasting. The Old Testament and the Book of Mormon tell of people fasting for a variety of reasons: comfort at the death of a loved one (see 2 Sam. 1:12; Alma 30:2); help for the sick (see Matt. 17:18–21); overcoming sin (see Isa. 58:6); and help in missionary work (see Alma 17:9)" (Black, *400 Questions and Answers*, 150–51).

What is the "spirit of revelation"? (5:46–47) "Christ has himself declared that the manifestations we might have of the Spirit of Christ, or from a visitation of an angel, a tangible resurrected being, would not leave the impression and would not convince us and place within us that something which we cannot get away from which we receive through a manifestation of the Holy Ghost. Personal visitations might become dim as time goes on, but this guidance of the Holy Ghost is renewed and continued, day after day, year after year, if we live to be worthy of it" (Smith, *Doctrines of Salvation*, 1:44).

Alma 5:50–62. By Repenting and Living Righteously, We Show the Lord We Follow Him

How close at hand is the "kingdom of heaven"? (5:50) "The ultimate fulfillment of these prophetic words is the establishment of the millennial kingdom, that time when Christ will come in glory, might, majesty, power, and dominion to rule and reign as Lord of lords and King of kings. In a limited sense, however, the kingdom of God would come when Jesus would come to earth in fourscore years' time. In another sense the coming of the heavenly kingdom is equally close for men of all ages. This is so because those who live well, those who choose to repent and honor their God and his Christ—irrespective of when they lived or how long they lived—will obtain citizenship in the heavenly kingdom hereafter" (McConkie and Millet, *Doctrinal Commentary*, 43).

Why is a tree often used as a metaphor in scripture? (5:52) "The axe of a husbandman is used in a symbolic sense by several inspired writers to denote the manner in which barren trees (men) will be destroyed (Luke 3:9; D&C 97:7; Isa. 10:33–34). . . . As a tree often represents a man, so a branch signifies one aspect of a man (Mal. 4:1; Job 29:19; Prov. 11:28; see also John 15:1–6). Therefore, figuratively, a man has roots, leaves, and branches. Concerning the final status of the wicked, it is said that 'his roots shall be dried up beneath, and above shall his branch be cut off' (Job 18:16)" (McConkie and Parry, *A Guide to Scriptural Symbols*, 18, 25).

What is the meaning of things being "vain"? (5:53–54) *Vain* is defined as "empty; worthless; having no substance, value or importance. . . . Elated with a high opinion of one's own accomplishments" (Webster, *American Dictionary*).

King of heaven shall very soon shine forth among all the children of men.

51 And also the Spirit saith unto me, yea, crieth unto me with a mighty voice, saying: Go forth and say unto this people—Repent, for except ye repent ye can in nowise inherit the kingdom of heaven.

52 And again I say unto you, the Spirit saith: Behold, the ax is laid at the root of the tree; therefore every tree that bringeth not forth good fruit shall be hewn down and cast into the fire, yea, a fire which cannot be consumed, even an unquenchable fire. Behold, and remember, the Holy One hath spoken it.

53 And now my beloved brethren, I say unto you, can ye withstand these sayings; yea, can ye lay aside these things, and trample the Holy One under your feet; yea, can ye be puffed up in the pride of your hearts; yea, will ye still persist in the wearing of costly apparel and setting your hearts upon the vain things of the world, upon your riches?

54 Yea, will ye persist in supposing that ye are better one than another; yea, will ye persist in the persecution of your brethren, who humble themselves and do walk after the holy order of God, wherewith they have been brought into this church, having been sanctified by the Holy Spirit, and they do bring forth works which are meet for repentance—

55 Yea, and will you persist in turning your backs upon the poor, and the needy, and in withholding your substance from them?

56 And finally, all ye that will persist in your wickedness, I say unto you that these are they who shall be hewn down and cast into the fire except they speedily repent.

57 And now I say unto you, all you that are desirous to follow the voice of the good shepherd, come ye out from the wicked, and be ye separate, and touch not their unclean things; and behold, their names shall be blotted out, that the names of the wicked shall not be numbered among the names of the righteous, that the word of God may be fulfilled, which saith: The names of the wicked shall not be mingled with the names of my people;

58 For the names of the righteous shall be written in the book of life, and unto them will I grant an inheritance at my right hand. And now, my brethren, what have ye to say against this? I say unto you, if ye speak against it, it matters not, for the word of God must be fulfilled.

59 For what shepherd is there among you having many sheep doth not watch over them, that the wolves enter not and devour his flock? And behold, if a wolf enter his flock doth he not drive him out? Yea, and at the last, if he can, he will destroy him.

60 And now I say unto you that the good shepherd doth call after you; and if you will hearken unto his voice he will bring you into his fold, and ye are his sheep; and he commandeth you that ye suffer no ravenous wolf to enter among you, that ye may not be destroyed.

61 And now I, Alma, do command you in the language of him who hath commanded me, that ye observe to do the words which I have spoken unto you.

62 I speak by way of command unto you that belong to the church; and unto those who do not belong to the church I speak by way of invitation, saying: Come and be baptized unto repentance, that ye also may be partakers of the fruit of the tree of life.

How can the world's uncleanness lead Church members away from their covenants? (5:57, 59–60)
"Drifting away from the course of life marked out by the Lord has occurred as individuals begin to make compromises with the Lord's standard. This is particularly true when the transgression is willful and no repentance occurs. . . . It [begins] as individual members of the Church knowingly [begin] to make compromises with the Lord's standard. They [seek] justification for their diversions in the knowledge that others [are] compromising as well. Those who willfully sin soon seek to establish a standard of their own with which they can feel more comfortable and which justifies their misconduct. They also seek the association of those who are willing to drift with them along this path of self-delusion" (Larsen, "Likening the Scriptures unto Us," 8). ☉

What is the purpose of Church discipline? (5:57)
"When members need to have certain blessings withheld, the Lord's object is to teach as well as to discipline. So probation, disfellowshipment, and excommunication, when they become necessary, are ideally accompanied by eventual reinstatement and restoration of blessings. . . . The purpose is threefold: to save the soul of the transgressor, to protect the innocent, and to safeguard the Church's purity, integrity, and good name" (Ballard, "Chance to Start Over," 12). ☉

Alma 6:1–6. Alma Strengthens the Church in Zarahemla

What priesthood did Alma hold? (6:1) See commentary in this volume on Jacob 1:18.

What was required to reestablish the church in Zarahemla? (6:2–4) "In Zarahemla, Alma admonished the people to change their hearts and then called them to repentance with straightforward questions. When he finished his questioning, he did not invite the members to come to Christ, as he did the nonmembers, but commanded them to repent (Alma 5:62). He even found it necessary to excommunicate those who would not repent because of the pride of their hearts (Alma 6:3). Alma's preaching, the excommunications, and the ordination of new priesthood leaders were apparently all necessary to reestablish the order of the Church again in Zarahemla (Alma 6:2–4)" (Hansen, "Book of Alma as a Prototype," 265–66).

How can Alma's counsel to the church in Zarahemla bless our homes? (6:5–6) "Having a gospel-sharing home will not only be a blessing for those we bring into our homes but for those who live within it. By living in a gospel-sharing home, our testimonies become stronger and our understanding of the gospel improves....

"In gospel-sharing homes we pray for guidance for ourselves, and we pray for the physical and spiritual well-being of others. We pray for the people the missionaries are teaching, for our acquaintances, and for those not of our faith. In the gospel-sharing homes of Alma's time, the people would 'join in fasting and mighty prayer in behalf of the welfare of the souls of those who knew not God' (Alma 6:6)" (Ballard, "Creating a Gospel-Sharing Home," 85).

What are some righteous purposes for a fast? (6:6) The prophet Isaiah admonished those in his day to fast with unselfish purposes. He declared, "Is not this the fast that I have chosen? to loose the bands of

CHAPTER 6

The Church in Zarahemla is cleansed and set in order—Alma goes to Gideon to preach. About 83 B.C.

1 And now it came to pass that after Alma had made an end of speaking unto the people of the church, which was established in the city of Zarahemla, he ordained priests and elders, by laying on his hands according to the order of God, to preside and watch over the church.

2 And it came to pass that whosoever did not belong to the church who repented of their sins were baptized unto repentance, and were received into the church.

3 And it also came to pass that whosoever did belong to the church that did not repent of their wickedness and humble themselves before God—I mean those who were lifted up in the pride of their hearts—the same were rejected, and their names were blotted out, that their names were not numbered among those of the righteous.

4 And thus they began to establish the order of the church in the city of Zarahemla.

5 Now I would that ye should understand that the word of God was liberal unto all, that none were deprived of the privilege of assembling themselves together to hear the word of God.

6 Nevertheless the children of God were commanded that they should gather themselves together oft, and join in fasting and mighty prayer in behalf of the welfare of the souls of those who knew not God.

wickedness, to undo the heavy burdens, and to let the oppressed go free, and that ye break every yoke?" (Isaiah 58:6).

7 And now it came to pass that when Alma had made these regulations he departed from them, yea, from the church which was in the city of Zarahemla, and went over upon the east of the river Sidon, into the valley of Gideon, there having been a city built, which was called the city of Gideon, which was in the valley that was called Gideon, being called after the man who was slain by the hand of Nehor with the sword.

8 And Alma went and began to declare the word of God unto the church which was established in the valley of Gideon, according to the revelation of the truth of the word which had been spoken by his fathers, and according to the spirit of prophecy which was in him, according to the testimony of Jesus Christ, the Son of God, who should come to redeem his people from their sins, and the holy order by which he was called. And thus it is written. Amen.

_____

The words of Alma which he delivered to the people in Gideon, according to his own record.

Comprising chapter 7.

CHAPTER 7

Christ will be born of Mary—He will loose the bands of death and bear the sins of His people—Those who repent, are baptized, and keep the commandments will have eternal life—Filthiness cannot inherit the kingdom of God—Humility, faith, hope, and charity are required. About 83 B.C.

1 Behold my beloved brethren, seeing that I have been permitted to come unto you, therefore I attempt to address you in my language; yea, by my own mouth, seeing that it

Alma 6:7–8. Alma Declares the Gospel in Gideon

What is teaching with the "spirit of prophecy"? (6:8) Declaring the word of God "according to the spirit of prophecy" is to teach the gospel by the power of the Holy Ghost by witnessing one's knowledge of Jesus Christ. John declared that the "testimony of Jesus is the spirit of prophecy" (Revelation 19:10). Joseph Smith explained, "God in his superior wisdom has always given his Saints, wherever he had any on the earth, the same spirit, and that spirit, as John says, is the true spirit of prophecy, which is the testimony of Jesus" (*History of the Church*, 5:400).

Superscription to Alma 7

The superscription to Alma 7 was part of the ancient record translated by the Prophet Joseph Smith and dictated by him to his scribe (see also, for example, 2 Nephi, Mosiah 9, and Alma 21).

The phrase "Comprising chapter 7" was not part of the ancient record but was added later to printed editions of the Book of Mormon.

Alma 7:1–6. Alma Desires That the People of Gideon Be Humble, Obedient, and Believing

How can we have joy even in affliction? (7:3–5)
"Focusing on joy brings God's power into our lives. As in all things, Jesus Christ is our ultimate exemplar, 'who for the joy that was set before him endured the cross' (Hebrews 12:2). Think of that! In order for Him to endure the most excruciating experience ever endured on earth, our Savior focused on joy! . . . Surely it included the joy of cleansing, healing, and strengthening us; the joy of paying for the sins of all who would repent; the joy of making it possible for you and me to return home—clean and worthy—to live with our Heavenly Parents and families. If we focus on the joy that will come to us, or to those we love, what can we endure that presently seems overwhelming, painful, scary, unfair, or simply impossible?" (Nelson, "Joy and Spiritual Survival," 82–83).

is the first time that I have spoken unto you by the words of my mouth, I having been wholly confined to the judgment-seat, having had much business that I could not come unto you.

2 And even I could not have come now at this time were it not that the judgment-seat hath been given to another, to reign in my stead; and the Lord in much mercy hath granted that I should come unto you.

3 And behold, I have come having great hopes and much desire that I should find that ye had humbled yourselves before God, and that ye had continued in the supplicating of his grace, that I should find that ye were blameless before him, that I should find that ye were not in the awful dilemma that our brethren were in at Zarahemla.

4 But blessed be the name of God, that he hath given me to know, yea, hath given unto me the exceedingly great joy of knowing that they are established again in the way of his righteousness.

5 And I trust, according to the Spirit of God which is in me, that I shall also have joy over you; nevertheless I do not desire that my joy over you should come by the cause of so much afflictions and sorrow which I have had for the brethren at Zarahemla, for behold, my joy cometh over them after wading through much affliction and sorrow.

6 But behold, I trust that ye are not in a state of so much unbelief as were your brethren; I trust that ye are not lifted up in the pride of your hearts; yea, I trust that ye have not set your hearts upon riches and the vain things of the world; yea, I trust that you do not worship idols, but that ye do worship the true and the living God, and that ye look forward for the remission of your sins, with an everlasting faith, which is to come.

7 For behold, I say unto you there be many things to come; and behold, there is one thing which is of more importance than they all—for behold, the time is not far distant that the Redeemer liveth and cometh among his people.

8 Behold, I do not say that he will come among us at the time of his dwelling in his mortal tabernacle; for behold, the Spirit hath not said unto me that this should be the case. Now as to this thing I do not know; but this much I do know, that the Lord God hath power to do all things which are according to his word.

9 But behold, the Spirit hath said this much unto me, saying: Cry unto this people, saying—Repent ye, and prepare the way of the Lord, and walk in his paths, which are straight; for behold, the kingdom of heaven is at hand, and the Son of God cometh upon the face of the earth.

10 And behold, he shall be born of Mary, at Jerusalem which is the land of our forefathers, she being a virgin, a precious and chosen vessel, who shall be overshadowed and conceive by the power of the Holy Ghost, and bring forth a son, yea, even the Son of God.

Alma 7:7–13. Alma Prophesies of the Birth and Mission of Jesus Christ

What has always been the principal prophetic message? (7:9) "The doctrine of repentance is as old as the gospel itself. Biblical teachings from the books of Genesis to Revelation teach repentance.... References to repentance are even more frequent in the Book of Mormon.... With the Restoration of the gospel, our Savior has again stressed this doctrine. The word *repent* in any of its forms appears in 47 of the 138 sections of the Doctrine and Covenants!" (Nelson, "Repentance and Conversion," 102). ☉

Why is it significant that Book of Mormon prophets knew the name of the Savior's mortal mother long before His birth? (7:10) "[Mary] was foreordained. There is only one Mary, even as there is only one Christ. We may suppose that she was more highly endowed spiritually than any of her mortal sisters, but with it all, she was a mortal, not a God. Her mission was to bring the Son of God into the world, not to redeem mankind, not to intercede for them. She was destined to be a mother, not a mediator; hers was the blessed privilege, being mortal, to bring into the world Him by whom immortality should come. And blessed is she forever!" (McConkie, *Promised Messiah*, 466).

Why is there no contradiction between the Book of Mormon and Bible concerning the location of the Savior's birth? (7:10) "There is no conflict or contradiction in the Book of Mormon with any truth recorded in the Bible. A careful reading of what Alma said will show that he had no intention of declaring that Jesus would be born *in* Jerusalem. Alma knew better. So did Joseph Smith and those who were associated with him in the bringing forth of the Book of

Mormon. Had Alma said, 'born *in* Jerusalem, the *city* of our fathers,' it would have made all the difference in the world. Then we would have said he made an error. Alma made no mistake, and what he said is true" (Smith, *Answers to Gospel Questions*, 1:174). ✦

How does the Savior know our afflictions and individual transgressions? (7:11–12) "He knows by actual, personal experience, because not only did He suffer pains, afflictions, and temptations of every kind during His second estate, but He took upon Himself our sins as well as our pains, sicknesses, and infirmities. . . . Thus He knew, not in abstraction but in actuality, 'according to the flesh,' the whole of human suffering. He bore our infirmities before we bore them. He knows perfectly well how to succor us. We can tell Him nothing of pain, temptation, or affliction; He learned 'according to the flesh,' and His triumph was complete!" (Maxwell, *We Will Prove Them Herewith*, 46). ✦

What does *succor* mean? (7:12) "[*Succor*] is used often in the scriptures to describe Christ's care for and attention to us. It means literally 'to run to.' What a magnificent way to describe the Savior's urgent effort in our behalf. Even as he calls us to come to him and follow him, he is unfailingly running to help us" (Holland, "Come unto Me," 22).

Alma 7:14–21. To Enter the Kingdom of God, We Must Repent and Keep the Commandments

What does it mean to have our sins washed away? (7:14) "The scriptures seldom speak of having our sins 'washed away' in the waters of baptism (see Acts 22:16; D&C 39:10), though the Saints frequently use this expression to teach the purpose of baptism. Perhaps the more useful analogy is that which attests to the Holy Ghost as the agent, the medium by which sins and dross are burned out of the human soul as though by fire, thus giving rise to the phrase 'baptism by fire.' Sins are remitted not in the waters of baptism, as we say casually, but rather as we receive the cleansing and sanctifying influence of the Spirit in our lives" (McConkie and Millet, *Doctrinal Commentary*, 3:53).

11 And he shall go forth, suffering pains and afflictions and temptations of every kind; and this that the word might be fulfilled which saith he will take upon him the pains and the sicknesses of his people.

12 And he will take upon him death, that he may loose the bands of death which bind his people; and he will take upon him their infirmities, that his bowels may be filled with mercy, according to the flesh, that he may know according to the flesh how to succor his people according to their infirmities.

13 Now the Spirit knoweth all things; nevertheless the Son of God suffereth according to the flesh that he might take upon him the sins of his people, that he might blot out their transgressions according to the power of his deliverance; and now behold, this is the testimony which is in me.

14 Now I say unto you that ye must repent, and be born again; for the Spirit saith if ye are not born again ye cannot inherit the kingdom of heaven; therefore come and be baptized unto repentance, that ye may be washed from your sins, that ye may have faith on the Lamb of God, who taketh away the sins of the world, who is mighty to save and to cleanse from all unrighteousness.

15 Yea, I say unto you come and fear not, and lay aside every sin, which easily doth beset you, which doth bind you down to destruction, yea, come and go forth, and show unto your God that ye are willing to repent of your sins and enter into a covenant with him to keep his commandments, and witness it unto him this day by going into the waters of baptism.

16 And whosoever doeth this, and keepeth the commandments of God from thenceforth, the same will remember that I say unto him, yea, he will remember that I have said unto him, he shall have eternal life, according to the testimony of the Holy Spirit, which testifieth in me.

17 And now my beloved brethren, do you believe these things? Behold, I say unto you, yea, I know that ye believe them; and the way that I know that ye believe them is by the manifestation of the Spirit which is in me. And now because your faith is strong concerning that, yea, concerning the things which I have spoken, great is my joy.

18 For as I said unto you from the beginning, that I had much desire that ye were not in the state of dilemma like your brethren, even so I have found that my desires have been gratified.

19 For I perceive that ye are in the paths of righteousness; I perceive that ye are in the path which leads to the kingdom of God; yea, I perceive that ye are making his paths straight.

20 I perceive that it has been made known unto you, by the testimony of his word, that he cannot walk in crooked paths; neither doth he vary from that which he hath said; neither hath he a shadow of turning from the right to the left, or from that which is right to that which is wrong; therefore, his course is one eternal round.

21 And he doth not dwell in unholy temples; neither can filthiness or anything which is unclean be received into the kingdom of

What is baptism symbolic of? (7:16) "Baptism is an ordinance of profound symbolism. In the purest sense, we are baptized to witness our willingness to accept Christ, to take upon us his name, and to commit ourselves to receive his atonement. We go down into the watery grave as a token and a remembrance of our Master's descent into the tomb of death. We come forth, as did he, unto a newness of life: his a resurrected immortality, ours a sanctified mortality. Having been 'planted . . . in the likeness of his death,' we are thereby 'in the likeness of his resurrection' (Romans 6:3–5)" (McConkie and Millet, *Doctrinal Commentary*, 3:54).

What does it mean to make his paths straight? (7:19) President Gordon B. Hinckley described one way to look at this verse and ones similar to it. He said: "That is what this church is all about—to help us to prepare to follow the way of the Lord, to walk in obedience to His commandments, to get into our lives the spirit of His work, to come to know Him and to love Him, and to seek to do His will. Prepare ye to follow the way of the Lord" (*Teachings of Gordon B. Hinckley*, 470).

Why can we trust Heavenly Father and His Son completely? (7:20) "The Lord does not, nor can He, walk in crooked paths. For Him to do so would mean a changeable god, an inconstant and variable person, on whose word we could not rely. He commands and it is so; He forgives us our trespasses, and we are forgiven. He marks the Way, and He, himself, walks therein, saying as He does so, 'Follow thou Me!' or 'Come after Me' (Matthew 4:19). . . . His paths are not crooked; He does not say one thing and mean another. Neither does He command, and accept something else in its place" (Reynolds and Sjodahl, *Commentary on the Book of Mormon*, 3:137).

Why must our bodies be holy temples, worthy of the Spirit of God? (7:21) "The light of Christ is given to every person born into the world (see John 1:9;

Moroni 7:16; see also D&C 84:46).'And every man whose spirit receiveth not the light is under condemnation' (D&C 93:31). Likewise, the Holy Ghost 'may descend upon [a person] and not tarry with him' (D&C 130:23). . . . Those who drive out the Holy Ghost and the light of Christ will, in the last day, be filthy and 'he who is filthy shall remain in his filthiness' (Alma 7:21) and cannot dwell in the kingdom of God (see 1 Nephi 15:33)" (Nyman, *Record of Alma*, 94).

Alma 7:22–27. Alma Asks the People of Gideon to Follow the Lord

How do we gain these Christlike qualities ?
(7:23–24) *Preach My Gospel* teaches: "The scriptures describe Christlike attributes that are essential for you to eventually develop . . . throughout your life. . . .

"Christlike attributes are gifts from God. They come as you use your agency righteously. Ask your Heavenly Father to bless you with these attributes; you cannot develop them without His help. With a desire to please God, recognize your weaknesses and be willing and anxious to improve" (*Preach My Gospel*, 115).

What does it mean to have spotless garments?
(7:25) "*Garments* are various articles of clothing used to dress the body. They may be worn for utilitarian or religious purposes or both. The Lord made 'coats of skins' for Adam and Eve to cover their nakedness (Gen. 3:21). . . .

"Much that is sacred and symbolical is taught by reference to garments. . . .

"Symbolism is used in latter-day revelation: 'Cleanse your hearts and your garments, lest the blood of this generation be required at your hands,' the Lord says (D&C 112:33; 88:85; 135:5).

"Clean garments are a sign of cleanliness, perfection, and salvation. To gain salvation men must [symbolically] wash their garments in the blood of the Lamb" (McConkie, *Mormon Doctrine*, 303–4; see also commentary in this volume on Alma 5:21–22).

God; therefore I say unto you the time shall come, yea, and it shall be at the last day, that he who is filthy shall remain in his filthiness.

22 And now my beloved brethren, I have said these things unto you that I might awaken you to a sense of your duty to God, that ye may walk blameless before him, that ye may walk after the holy order of God, after which ye have been received.

23 And now I would that ye should be humble, and be submissive and gentle; easy to be entreated; full of patience and long-suffering; being temperate in all things; being diligent in keeping the commandments of God at all times; asking for whatsoever things ye stand in need, both spiritual and temporal; always returning thanks unto God for whatsoever things ye do receive.

24 And see that ye have faith, hope, and charity, and then ye will always abound in good works.

25 And may the Lord bless you, and keep your garments spotless, that ye may at last be brought to sit down with Abraham, Isaac, and Jacob, and the holy prophets who have been ever since the world began, having your garments spotless even as their garments are spotless, in the kingdom of heaven to go no more out.

26 And now my beloved brethren, I have spoken these words unto you according to the Spirit which testifieth in me; and my soul doth exceedingly rejoice, because of the exceeding diligence and heed which ye have given unto my word.

27 And now, may the peace of God rest upon you, and upon your houses and lands, and upon your flocks and herds, and all that you possess, your women and your children, according to your faith and good works, from this time forth and forever. And thus I have spoken. Amen.

CHAPTER 8

Alma preaches and baptizes in Melek—He is rejected in Ammonihah and leaves—An angel commands him to return and cry repentance unto the people—He is received by Amulek, and the two of them preach in Ammonihah. About 82 B.C.

1 And now it came to pass that Alma returned from the land of Gideon, after having taught the people of Gideon many things which cannot be written, having established the order of the church, according as he had before done in the land of Zarahemla, yea, he returned to his own house at Zarahemla to rest himself from the labors which he had performed.

2 And thus ended the ninth year of the reign of the judges over the people of Nephi.

3 And it came to pass in the commencement of the tenth year of the reign of the judges over the people of Nephi, that Alma departed from thence and took his journey over into the land of Melek, on the west of the river Sidon, on the west by the borders of the wilderness.

4 And he began to teach the people in the land of Melek according to the holy order of God, by which he had been called; and he began to teach the people throughout all the land of Melek.

5 And it came to pass that the people came to him throughout all the borders of the land which was by the wilderness side. And they were baptized throughout all the land;

Alma 8:1–5. Alma Returns to Melek, Preaches, and Baptizes

Why is it important that we not labor more than we have strength? (8:1) King Benjamin taught the principle in his address: "And see that all these things are done in wisdom and order; for it is not requisite that a man should run faster than he has strength. And again, it is expedient that he should be diligent, that thereby he might win the prize; therefore, all things must be done in order" (Mosiah 4:27). ❂

Where was the land of Melek? (8:1–3) "The boundaries of this land are very indistinctly stated. . . . However, two things are positively stated . . . namely, that it was west of the River Sidon, and that it extended westward as far as the narrow strip of wilderness which ran north and south between the mountains and the [ocean]. . . . That it embraced a large district of country is proved by the fact that . . . Alma . . . traveled three days' journey on the north of the Land of Melek before he came to the City of Ammonihah. . . . It was *the king's land*. The ancient Phoenician word for king is spelled letter for letter the same as in the Book of Mormon (Melek), and the Hebrew word is almost identical" (Reynolds and Sjodahl, *Commentary on the Book of Mormon*, 3:145). ❂

Alma 8:6–13. Alma's Message Is Rejected at Ammonihah

6 So that when he had finished his work at Melek he departed thence, and traveled three days' journey on the north of the land of Melek; and he came to a city which was called Ammonihah.

7 Now it was the custom of the people of Nephi to call their lands, and their cities, and their villages, yea, even all their small villages, after the name of him who first possessed them; and thus it was with the land of Ammonihah.

8 And it came to pass that when Alma had come to the city of Ammonihah he began to preach the word of God unto them.

9 Now Satan had gotten great hold upon the hearts of the people of the city of Ammonihah; therefore they would not hearken unto the words of Alma.

10 Nevertheless Alma labored much in the spirit, wrestling with God in mighty prayer, that he would pour out his Spirit upon the people who were in the city; that he would also grant that he might baptize them unto repentance.

What can make prayers powerful and effective? (8:10) "There are many reasons our prayers lack power. Sometimes they become routine. Our prayers become hollow when we say similar words in similar ways over and over so often that the words become more of a recitation than a communication. . . . Prayers that do not demand much of your thought will hardly merit much attention from our Heavenly Father. When you find yourself getting into a routine . . . , step back and think. Meditate for a while on the things for which you really are grateful" (Wirthlin, "Improving Our Prayers," 160).

What makes people unwilling to accept gospel truth? (8:11–13) "[Alma] proclaimed those same eternal truths that had been the burden of his message beforehand. He called upon them to repent and believe on the Messiah, Jesus Christ, who would soon come to redeem all those who would accept Him as their Savior. But they would not hearken unto his words. They expressed no desire to be saved in God's Kingdom as Alma exhorted them. Satan, that cunning one, had planted pride and worldly ambition in their hearts, and they wanted neither promise of future reward nor spiritual restraints to interfere with their search for the riches of the earth, or the plaudits of men" (Reynolds and Sjodahl, *Commentary on the Book of Mormon*, 3:147).

11 Nevertheless, they hardened their hearts, saying unto him: Behold, we know that thou art Alma; and we know that thou art high priest over the church which thou hast established in many parts of the land, according to your tradition; and we are not of thy church, and we do not believe in such foolish traditions.

12 And now we know that because we are not of thy church we know that thou hast no power over us; and thou hast delivered up the judgment-seat unto Nephihah; therefore thou art not the chief judge over us.

13 Now when the people had said this, and withstood all his words, and reviled him, and spit upon him, and caused that he should be cast out of their city, he departed thence and took his journey towards the city which was called Aaron.

14 And it came to pass that while he was journeying thither, being weighed down with sorrow, wading through much tribulation and anguish of soul, because of the wickedness of the people who were in the city of Ammonihah, it came to pass while Alma was thus weighed down with sorrow, behold an angel of the Lord appeared unto him, saying:

15 Blessed art thou, Alma; therefore, lift up thy head and rejoice, for thou hast great cause to rejoice; for thou hast been faithful in keeping the commandments of God from the time which thou receivedst thy first message from him. Behold, I am he that delivered it unto you.

16 And behold, I am sent to command thee that thou return to the city of Ammonihah, and preach again unto the people of the city; yea, preach unto them. Yea, say unto them, except they repent the Lord God will destroy them.

17 For behold, they do study at this time that they may destroy the liberty of thy people, (for thus saith the Lord) which is contrary to the statutes, and judgments, and commandments which he has given unto his people.

18 Now it came to pass that after Alma had received his message from the angel of the Lord he returned speedily to the land of Ammonihah. And he entered the city by another way, yea, by the way which is on the south of the city of Ammonihah.

Alma 8:14–18. Alma Is Commanded to Return to Ammonihah

How did the Lord minister to Alma in his weakness and despair? (8:14) "From the beginning down through the dispensations, God has used angels as His emissaries in conveying love and concern for His children. Time in this setting does not allow even a cursory examination of the scriptures or our own latter-day history, which are so filled with accounts of angels ministering to those on earth, but it is rich doctrine and rich history indeed" (Holland, "Ministry of Angels," 29). ✪

Who is the great enemy of freedom? (8:17) "The Lord never destroys a nation 'save it were foretold them by the prophets of the Lord' (2 Nephi 25:9). Again, the influence of Satan was evident. Satan is trying, through his followers, to destroy the freedom of man that God desired his people to have (Alma 8:17; see also Moses 4:1–4)" (Nyman, *Record of Alma*, 100).

Why is prompt obedience important? (8:18) "However much faith to obey God we now have, we will need to strengthen it continually and keep it refreshed constantly. We can do that by deciding now to be more quick to obey and more determined to endure....

"We must decide to obey and then do it. We build the faith to pass the tests of obedience over time and through our daily choices. We can decide now to do quickly whatever God asks of us. And we can decide to be steady in the small tests of obedience which build the faith to carry us through the great tests, which will surely come" (Eyring, "Spiritual Preparedness," 38, 40).

Alma 8:19–27. Alma Meets Amulek

Who was Amulek? (8:21–22) "[Amulek,] son of Giddonah, who was the son of Ishmael, who was a descendant of Aminadi, a descendant of Nephi. He was a man of wealth and importance and was blessed with many relatives. One day, in the latter half of the year as he was journeying to see a very near relation, an angel of the Lord appeared unto him and told him to return to his home for he had to feed a holy prophet of God who was exceeding hungry, he having fasted many days on account of the sins of the people of Ammonihah [Alma 10:7]" (Reynolds and Sjodahl, *Commentary on the Book of Mormon*, 3:152).

What blessings did Alma receive through fasting? (8:26) "At times fasting is appropriate as a strong evidence of our sincerity. As Alma testified to the people of Zarahemla: 'I have fasted and prayed many days that I might know these things of myself. And now I do know of myself that they are true; for the Lord God hath made them manifest unto me by his Holy Spirit' (Alma 5:46). When we fast we humble our souls, which brings us more in tune with God and His holy purposes" (Faust, "Lifeline of Prayer," 60). ⊕

19 And as he entered the city he was an hungered, and he said to a man: Will ye give to an humble servant of God something to eat?

20 And the man said unto him: I am a Nephite, and I know that thou art a holy prophet of God, for thou art the man whom an angel said in a vision: Thou shalt receive. Therefore, go with me into my house and I will impart unto thee of my food; and I know that thou wilt be a blessing unto me and my house.

21 And it came to pass that the man received him into his house; and the man was called Amulek; and he brought forth bread and meat and set before Alma.

22 And it came to pass that Alma ate bread and was filled; and he blessed Amulek and his house, and he gave thanks unto God.

23 And after he had eaten and was filled he said unto Amulek: I am Alma, and am the high priest over the church of God throughout the land.

24 And behold, I have been called to preach the word of God among all this people, according to the spirit of revelation and prophecy; and I was in this land and they would not receive me, but they cast me out and I was about to set my back towards this land forever.

25 But behold, I have been commanded that I should turn again and prophesy unto this people, yea, and to testify against them concerning their iniquities.

26 And now, Amulek, because thou hast fed me and taken me in, thou art blessed; for I was an hungered, for I had fasted many days.

27 And Alma tarried many days with Amulek before he began to preach unto the people.

28 And it came to pass that the people did wax more gross in their iniquities.

29 And the word came to Alma, saying: Go; and also say unto my servant Amulek, go forth and prophesy unto this people, saying—Repent ye, for thus saith the Lord, except ye repent I will visit this people in mine anger; yea, and I will not turn my fierce anger away.

30 And Alma went forth, and also Amulek, among the people, to declare the words of God unto them; and they were filled with the Holy Ghost.

31 And they had power given unto them, insomuch that they could not be confined in dungeons; neither was it possible that any man could slay them; nevertheless they did not exercise their power until they were bound in bands and cast into prison. Now, this was done that the Lord might show forth his power in them.

32 And it came to pass that they went forth and began to preach and to prophesy unto the people, according to the spirit and power which the Lord had given them.

The words of Alma, and also the words of Amulek, which were declared unto the people who were in the land of Ammonihah. And also they are cast into prison, and delivered by the miraculous power of God which was in them, according to the record of Alma.

Comprising chapters 9 through 14.

CHAPTER 9

Alma commands the people of Ammonihah to repent—The Lord will be merciful to the Lamanites in the last days—If the Nephites forsake the light, they will be destroyed by the Lamanites—The Son of God will come soon—He will redeem those who repent, are baptized, and have faith in His name. About 82 B.C.

Alma 8:28–32. Amulek Is Called to Preach the Gospel

How did the Lord show forth His power with these missionaries? (8:30–32) "Filled with the Holy Ghost, these servants of God went forth and valiantly delivered their terrible message. They were strengthened and preserved by power from on High. So greatly were they guarded by heavenly care, that by the grace of God 'they could not be confined in dungeons; neither was it possible that any man could slay them.' In spite of the extreme sufferings they endured, and the gentleness of their ways—they having sensibilities most keen and feelings most poignant—they shunned using their powers until, as a demonstration of God's fearsome strength, [they] burst the bands that when in prison held them tight [Alma 14:10–11, 17–29]" (Reynolds and Sjodahl, *Commentary on the Book of Mormon*, 3:152).

Superscription to Alma 9

The superscription to Alma 9 was part of the ancient record translated by the Prophet Joseph Smith and dictated by him to his scribe (see also, for example, 2 Nephi, Mosiah 9, and Alma 21).

"The [superscription to Alma 9] is included in the printer's manuscript and the 1830 edition. The original manuscript is not extant for this chapter. There is no line break between this introduction and what we have as the first verse.... The separation of the introduction from the text was done as part of the typesetting for the 1830 edition" (Gardner, *Second Witness*, 4:151).

The italicized words "Comprising chapters 9 through 14" were not part of the ancient record but were added later to printed editions of the Book of Mormon.

Alma 9:1–13. Alma Commands the People of Ammonihah to Repent

Why was this account written in the first person? (9:1) "Mormon seems to be quoting here from Alma's own account of his encounter with the people of Ammonihah, an account which presumably was written some time after the preaching" (McConkie and Millet, *Doctrinal Commentary*, 3:64).

What do we learn about the people of Ammonihah as they question "the testimony of one man"? (9:2, 6) Apparently some in Ammonihah knew the law well enough to use it against Alma. As Moses had taught: "One witness shall not rise up against a man for any iniquity, or for any sin, in any sin that he sinneth: at the mouth of two witnesses, or at the mouth of three witnesses, shall the matter be established" (Deuteronomy 19:15). ✪

What traditions of the fathers were forgotten by the people of Ammonihah? (9:7–11) "[The people of Ammonihah] gave little heed to the fact that a *Divine Guidance* had piloted their great ancestor, Lehi, across the ocean to the Land of Zion. They also forgot how many times their repentant brethren had been saved from destruction at the hands of the Lamanites through God's long-suffering and His mercy.

"If it had not been that God had protected and preserved the Ammonihahites, in spite of their many abuses of His grace, Alma cautioned them, that they, too, might have suffered even unto death as had many others" (Reynolds and Sjodahl, *Commentary on the Book of Mormon*, 3:156).

1 And again, I, Alma, having been commanded of God that I should take Amulek and go forth and preach again unto this people, or the people who were in the city of Ammonihah, it came to pass as I began to preach unto them, they began to contend with me, saying:

2 Who art thou? Suppose ye that we shall believe the testimony of one man, although he should preach unto us that the earth should pass away?

3 Now they understood not the words which they spake; for they knew not that the earth should pass away.

4 And they said also: We will not believe thy words if thou shouldst prophesy that this great city should be destroyed in one day.

5 Now they knew not that God could do such marvelous works, for they were a hard-hearted and a stiffnecked people.

6 And they said: Who is God, that sendeth no more authority than one man among this people, to declare unto them the truth of such great and marvelous things?

7 And they stood forth to lay their hands on me; but behold, they did not. And I stood with boldness to declare unto them, yea, I did boldly testify unto them, saying:

8 Behold, O ye wicked and perverse generation, how have ye forgotten the tradition of your fathers; yea, how soon ye have forgotten the commandments of God.

9 Do ye not remember that our father, Lehi, was brought out of Jerusalem by the hand of God? Do ye not remember that they were all led by him through the wilderness?

10 And have ye forgotten so soon how many times he delivered our fathers out of the hands

of their enemies, and preserved them from being destroyed, even by the hands of their own brethren?

11 Yea, and if it had not been for his matchless power, and his mercy, and his longsuffering towards us, we should unavoidably have been cut off from the face of the earth long before this period of time, and perhaps been consigned to a state of endless misery and woe.

12 Behold, now I say unto you that he commandeth you to repent; and except ye repent, ye can in nowise inherit the kingdom of God. But behold, this is not all—he has commanded you to repent, or he will utterly destroy you from off the face of the earth; yea, he will visit you in his anger, and in his fierce anger he will not turn away.

13 Behold, do ye not remember the words which he spake unto Lehi, saying that: Inasmuch as ye shall keep my commandments, ye shall prosper in the land? And again it is said that: Inasmuch as ye will not keep my commandments ye shall be cut off from the presence of the Lord.

14 Now I would that ye should remember, that inasmuch as the Lamanites have not kept the commandments of God, they have been cut off from the presence of the Lord. Now we see that the word of the Lord has been verified in this thing, and the Lamanites have been cut off from his presence, from the beginning of their transgressions in the land.

15 Nevertheless I say unto you, that it shall be more tolerable for them in the day of judgment than for you, if ye remain in your sins, yea, and even more tolerable for them in this life than for you, except ye repent.

16 For there are many promises which are extended to the Lamanites; for it is because of the traditions of their fathers that caused

Why did Alma contrast opposite consequences in this verse? (9:13) "Alma frequently used a highly significant literary technique, a figure of speech called antithetical parallelism, which presents the teaching in plainest terms possible by contrasting it with an opposite" (Parry, "Teaching in Black and White," 282). ✚

Alma 9:14–17. The Lord Promises That Lamanites in the Last Days Will Believe

Why would the Lord be merciful to the Lamanites? (9:14–16) "The promises of the Lord to the Lamanites are sure and certain. Because their sins were so often a result of incorrect traditions (as opposed to the Nephites, who sinned against great light), God will be merciful to them" (McConkie and Millet, *Doctrinal Commentary*, 3:65). ✚

How can a people overcome their own ignorance? (9:16) Each of us must overcome ignorance regardless of it being inherited by the traditions of our fathers or self-inflicted by disobedience or indifference. The

Lord has stated: "Let him that is ignorant learn wisdom by humbling himself and calling upon the Lord his God, that his eyes may be opened that he may see, and his ears opened that he may hear; for my Spirit is sent forth into the world to enlighten the humble and contrite, and to the condemnation of the ungodly" (D&C 136:32–33).

Alma 9:18–25. Alma Warns the People to Repent or Be Destroyed by the Lamanites

What do these verses teach about a person's responsibility to receive light and knowledge? (9:19–22) As you search these verses, notice the phrases that begin with the word *having*. What do these phrases tell you about the people of Ammonihah? What warning does this suggest to anyone who chooses not to live according to revealed light and knowledge?

them to remain in their state of ignorance; therefore the Lord will be merciful unto them and prolong their existence in the land.

17 And at some period of time they will be brought to believe in his word, and to know of the incorrectness of the traditions of their fathers; and many of them will be saved, for the Lord will be merciful unto all who call on his name.

18 But behold, I say unto you that if ye persist in your wickedness that your days shall not be prolonged in the land, for the Lamanites shall be sent upon you; and if ye repent not they shall come in a time when you know not, and ye shall be visited with utter destruction; and it shall be according to the fierce anger of the Lord.

19 For he will not suffer you that ye shall live in your iniquities, to destroy his people. I say unto you, Nay; he would rather suffer that the Lamanites might destroy all his people who are called the people of Nephi, if it were possible that they could fall into sins and transgressions, after having had so much light and so much knowledge given unto them of the Lord their God;

20 Yea, after having been such a highly favored people of the Lord; yea, after having been favored above every other nation, kindred, tongue, or people; after having had all things made known unto them, according to their desires, and their faith, and prayers, of that which has been, and which is, and which is to come;

21 Having been visited by the Spirit of God; having conversed with angels, and having been spoken unto by the voice of the Lord; and having the spirit of prophecy, and the spirit of revelation, and also many gifts, the gift of speaking with tongues, and the gift of preaching, and the gift of the Holy Ghost, and the gift of translation;

22 Yea, and after having been delivered of God out of the land of Jerusalem, by the hand of the Lord; having been saved from famine, and from sickness, and all manner of diseases of every kind; and they having waxed strong in battle, that they might not be destroyed; having been brought out of bondage time after time, and having been kept and preserved until now; and they have been prospered until they are rich in all manner of things—

23 And now behold I say unto you, that if this people, who have received so many blessings from the hand of the Lord, should transgress contrary to the light and knowledge which they do have, I say unto you that if this be the case, that if they should fall into transgression, it would be far more tolerable for the Lamanites than for them.

24 For behold, the promises of the Lord are extended to the Lamanites, but they are not unto you if ye transgress; for has not the Lord expressly promised and firmly decreed, that if ye will rebel against him that ye shall utterly be destroyed from off the face of the earth?

25 And now for this cause, that ye may not be destroyed, the Lord has sent his angel to visit many of his people, declaring unto them that they must go forth and cry mightily unto this people, saying: Repent ye, for the kingdom of heaven is nigh at hand;

26 And not many days hence the Son of God shall come in his glory; and his glory shall be the glory of the Only Begotten of the Father, full of grace, equity, and truth, full of patience, mercy, and long-suffering, quick to hear the cries of his people and to answer their prayers.

27 And behold, he cometh to redeem those who will be baptized unto repentance, through faith on his name.

28 Therefore, prepare ye the way of the Lord, for the time is at hand that all men shall reap

Why would it be more tolerable for the Lamanites to transgress? (9:23) "Alma . . . pointed out that there is a relationship between understanding gospel principles and being accountable for our actions. He warned the wicked Nephites in Ammonihah: ' . . . it would be far more tolerable for the Lamanites than for them' because the Lamanites had sinned in ignorance (Alma 9:23). Elder George Albert Smith similarly declared: 'We will not be judged as our brothers and sisters of the world are judged, but according to the greater opportunities placed in our keeping'" (Cowan, "New Meaning of 'Restoration,'" 205–6).

Alma 9:26–34. Alma Prophesies That Jesus Will Come and Redeem Those Who Believe in Him

How would Jesus "come in his glory" during His mortal sojourn? (9:26) "Jesus Christ enjoyed the glory and power of the Eternal Father while in mortality because he was the Only Begotten Son of the Father in the flesh, because he inherited the powers of the Father from that exalted Sire" (McConkie and Millet, *Doctrinal Commentary*, 3:65–66).

What kind of judgment might we expect from the Lord? (9:27–29) "All of us have made wrong turns along the way. I believe the kind and merciful God, whose children we are, will judge us as lightly as He can for the wrongs that we have done and give us the maximum blessing for the good that we do" (Faust, "Woman, Why Weepest Thou?" 53). ☺

a reward of their works, according to that which they have been—if they have been righteous they shall reap the salvation of their souls, according to the power and deliverance of Jesus Christ; and if they have been evil they shall reap the damnation of their souls, according to the power and captivation of the devil.

29 Now behold, this is the voice of the angel, crying unto the people.

30 And now, my beloved brethren, for ye are my brethren, and ye ought to be beloved, and ye ought to bring forth works which are meet for repentance, seeing that your hearts have been grossly hardened against the word of God, and seeing that ye are a lost and a fallen people.

31 Now it came to pass that when I, Alma, had spoken these words, behold, the people were wroth with me because I said unto them that they were a hard-hearted and a stiff-necked people.

32 And also because I said unto them that they were a lost and a fallen people they were angry with me, and sought to lay their hands upon me, that they might cast me into prison.

33 But it came to pass that the Lord did not suffer them that they should take me at that time and cast me into prison.

34 And it came to pass that Amulek went and stood forth, and began to preach unto them also. And now the words of Amulek are not all written, nevertheless a part of his words are written in this book.

How might Alma's experience help us prepare for missionary service today? (9:30–33) "Unfortunately, Alma's words did not produce a repentant spirit in the people; they were wroth with him and attempted to cast him into prison. But the power of the Lord attended the prophet, and the people were not able to do what they desired (9:31–33)" (Sperry, *Book of Mormon Compendium*, 335). When has the Lord "attended" you as you have shared the gospel with others?

What book was referred to in verse 34? (9:34) "Here, Mormon, the abridger of the account of Alma and Amulek, again notes that only a part of Amulek's words are written in this abridgment" (Reynolds and Sjodahl, *Commentary on the Book of Mormon*, 3:165).

CHAPTER 10

Lehi descended from Manasseh—Amulek recounts the angelic command that he care for Alma—The prayers of the righteous cause the people to be spared—Unrighteous lawyers and judges lay the foundation of the destruction of the people. About 82 B.C.

1 Now these are the words which Amulek preached unto the people who were in the land of Ammonihah, saying:

2 I am Amulek; I am the son of Giddonah, who was the son of Ishmael, who was a descendant of Aminadi; and it was that same Aminadi who interpreted the writing which was upon the wall of the temple, which was written by the finger of God.

3 And Aminadi was a descendant of Nephi, who was the son of Lehi, who came out of the land of Jerusalem, who was a descendant of Manasseh, who was the son of Joseph who was sold into Egypt by the hands of his brethren.

4 And behold, I am also a man of no small reputation among all those who know me; yea, and behold, I have many kindreds and friends, and I have also acquired much riches by the hand of my industry.

5 Nevertheless, after all this, I never have known much of the ways of the Lord, and his mysteries and marvelous power. I said I never had known much of these things; but behold, I mistake, for I have seen much of his mysteries and his marvelous power; yea, even in the preservation of the lives of this people.

6 Nevertheless, I did harden my heart, for I was called many times and I would not hear; therefore I knew concerning these things, yet I would not know; therefore I went on rebelling against God, in the wickedness of my heart, even until the fourth day of this seventh month, which is in the tenth year of the reign of the judges.

Alma 10:1–11. Amulek Tells Who He Is and How He Was Called

Who was Aminadi? (10:2) "This is the only time Aminadi is mentioned, and our present Book of Mormon gives no further details concerning the writing written by the finger of God upon the wall of the temple. Evidently an account of this incident was recorded on the large plates of Nephi, but Mormon did not include it in his abridgment" (Ludlow, *Companion to Your Study of the Book of Mormon*, 198). ⊕

How do we know that Lehi descended from Manasseh? (10:3) Compare this verse with 1 Nephi 5:14. Elder Erastus Snow of the Quorum of the Twelve Apostles said, "The Prophet Joseph informed us that the record of Lehi was contained on the 116 pages that were first translated and subsequently stolen, and of which an abridgment is given us in the first Book of Nephi, which is the record of Nephi individually, he himself being of the lineage of Manasseh; but that Ishmael was of the lineage of Ephraim" (in *Journal of Discourses*, 23:185–86). ⊕

Why are mortals, like Amulek, often reluctant to hear the Lord? (10:5–6) "Amulek . . . is a classic case of an essentially good man being out of touch with the great spiritual realities; he resisted the things of the Spirit because, though he was basically good, he was preoccupied with the cares of the world. When meekness was needed, it was sufficiently there in Amulek. As a result, he became yoked, and he then experienced the costs of discipleship [see Alma 15:16–18]" (Maxwell, *Meek and Lowly*, 12).

7 As I was journeying to see a very near kindred, behold an angel of the Lord appeared unto me and said: Amulek, return to thine own house, for thou shalt feed a prophet of the Lord; yea, a holy man, who is a chosen man of God; for he has fasted many days because of the sins of this people, and he is an hungered, and thou shalt receive him into thy house and feed him, and he shall bless thee and thy house; and the blessing of the Lord shall rest upon thee and thy house.

8 And it came to pass that I obeyed the voice of the angel, and returned towards my house. And as I was going thither I found the man whom the angel said unto me: Thou shalt receive into thy house—and behold it was this same man who has been speaking unto you concerning the things of God.

9 And the angel said unto me he is a holy man; wherefore I know he is a holy man because it was said by an angel of God.

10 And again, I know that the things whereof he hath testified are true; for behold I say unto you, that as the Lord liveth, even so has he sent his angel to make these things manifest unto me; and this he has done while this Alma hath dwelt at my house.

11 For behold, he hath blessed mine house, he hath blessed me, and my women, and my children, and my father and my kinsfolk; yea, even all my kindred hath he blessed, and the blessing of the Lord hath rested upon us according to the words which he spake.

12 And now, when Amulek had spoken these words the people began to be astonished, seeing there was more than one witness who testified of the things whereof they were accused, and also of the things which were to come, according to the spirit of prophecy which was in them.

Alma 10:12–16. Lawyers Try to Deceive Amulek with Their Questions

Why did the hardened people of Ammonihah suddenly become astonished? (10:12) Amulek was a community figurehead. He was aware of their practices and their wickedness. They knew he knew of their true intentions (see Alma 8:17).

These wicked Nephites were determined to destroy the faith of these missionaries, but the fact that "there was more than one witness" was a shock to them.

13 Nevertheless, there were some among them who thought to question them, that by their cunning devices they might catch them in their words, that they might find witness against them, that they might deliver them to their judges that they might be judged according to the law, and that they might be slain or cast into prison, according to the crime which they could make appear or witness against them.

14 Now it was those men who sought to destroy them, who were lawyers, who were hired or appointed by the people to administer the law at their times of trials, or at the trials of the crimes of the people before the judges.

15 Now these lawyers were learned in all the arts and cunning of the people; and this was to enable them that they might be skilful in their profession.

16 And it came to pass that they began to question Amulek, that thereby they might make him cross his words, or contradict the words which he should speak.

17 Now they knew not that Amulek could know of their designs. But it came to pass as they began to question him, he perceived their thoughts, and he said unto them: O ye wicked and perverse generation, ye lawyers and hypocrites, for ye are laying the foundations of the devil; for ye are laying traps and snares to catch the holy ones of God.

18 Ye are laying plans to pervert the ways of the righteous, and to bring down the wrath of God upon your heads, even to the utter destruction of this people.

19 Yea, well did Mosiah say, who was our last king, when he was about to deliver up the kingdom, having no one to confer it upon, causing that this people should be governed by their own voices—yea, well did he say that if the time should come that the voice of

What do we know about lawyers in the Book of Mormon? (10:14–15) In this scriptural account we learn that lawyers were compensated for each day of service before a judge, thus creating an incentive for them to stir up controversy among the people (see Alma 11:20). Their motives were economic, social, and political gain. One would assume there were virtuous lawyers in the Nephite nation; the record is just void of an account.

Alma 10:17–32. Amulek Tells of the Wickedness of the People in Ammonihah

Who were the "holy ones" referred to by Amulek? (10:17) In verse 9 Amulek explained that an angel who appeared to him (see Alma 8:20) referred to Alma as "a holy man." Now, caught up in the power of the Spirit and perceiving the thoughts of the people, he accuses them of "laying traps and snares to catch the *holy ones* of God." Because of his own sincere spiritual awakening, and given his dedicated service to the gospel, Amulek apparently included himself in a select group of individuals, both sanctified and chosen of God: holy men.

Why is it so vital to listen to living prophets? (10:19) When a people choose iniquity and fall into transgression, they face destruction. Nephi, son of Lehi, taught that "as one generation hath been destroyed among the Jews because of iniquity, even so have they been destroyed from generation to generation according to their iniquities; and never hath any of them been destroyed save it were foretold them by the prophets of the Lord" (2 Nephi 25:9). Alma and Amulek were prophets. They were sent to warn the people of Ammonihah of their imminent destruction if they did not repent.

How influential can the prayers of the righteous be? (10:22–23) "Many voices of seducing spirits advocate carnal pleasures and unrestrained physical satisfactions. Our world is now much the same as it was in the days of the Nephite prophet who said: 'if it were not for the prayers of the righteous . . . ye would even now be visited with utter destruction' (Alma 10:22). Of course, there are many upright and faithful who live all the commandments and whose lives and prayers keep the world from destruction" (Kimball, "Voices of the Past," 16).

this people should choose iniquity, that is, if the time should come that this people should fall into transgression, they would be ripe for destruction.

20 And now I say unto you that well doth the Lord judge of your iniquities; well doth he cry unto this people, by the voice of his angels: Repent ye, repent, for the kingdom of heaven is at hand.

21 Yea, well doth he cry, by the voice of his angels that: I will come down among my people, with equity and justice in my hands.

22 Yea, and I say unto you that if it were not for the prayers of the righteous, who are now in the land, that ye would even now be visited with utter destruction; yet it would not be by flood, as were the people in the days of Noah, but it would be by famine, and by pestilence, and the sword.

23 But it is by the prayers of the righteous that ye are spared; now therefore, if ye will cast out the righteous from among you then will not the Lord stay his hand; but in his fierce anger he will come out against you; then ye shall be smitten by famine, and by pestilence, and by the sword; and the time is soon at hand except ye repent.

24 And now it came to pass that the people were more angry with Amulek, and they cried out, saying: This man doth revile against our laws which are just, and our wise lawyers whom we have selected.

25 But Amulek stretched forth his hand, and cried the mightier unto them, saying: O ye wicked and perverse generation, why hath Satan got such great hold upon your hearts? Why will ye yield yourselves unto him that he may have power over you, to blind your eyes, that ye will not understand the words which are spoken, according to their truth?

26 For behold, have I testified against your law? Ye do not understand; ye say that I have spoken against your law; but I have not, but I have spoken in favor of your law, to your condemnation.

27 And now behold, I say unto you, that the foundation of the destruction of this people is beginning to be laid by the unrighteousness of your lawyers and your judges.

28 And now it came to pass that when Amulek had spoken these words the people cried out against him, saying: Now we know that this man is a child of the devil, for he hath lied unto us; for he hath spoken against our law. And now he says that he has not spoken against it.

29 And again, he has reviled against our lawyers, and our judges.

30 And it came to pass that the lawyers put it into their hearts that they should remember these things against him.

31 And there was one among them whose name was Zeezrom. Now he was the foremost to accuse Amulek and Alma, he being one of the most expert among them, having much business to do among the people.

32 Now the object of these lawyers was to get gain; and they got gain according to their employ.

CHAPTER 11

The Nephite monetary system is set forth—Amulek contends with Zeezrom—Christ will not save people in their sins—Only those who inherit the kingdom of heaven are saved—All men will rise in immortality—There is no death after the Resurrection. About 82 B.C.

1 Now it was in the law of Mosiah that every man who was a judge of the law, or those who were appointed to be judges, should receive wages according to the time which they

What can we learn today from this ancient warning regarding unrighteous lawyers and judges? (10:27–30) "One of the signs of moral decay, of apostasy and corruption within a society, is an emphasis on technicalities of law. This comes about when, in order to advance their cause, people seek to play the letter against the spirit of the law and in effect to legalize chicanery. Among the pure in heart God's laws are etched on the soul; they are found written in the countenances and inscribes on the inward parts. Among the perverse, however, law is a means of accomplishing the manipulation of others" (McConkie and Millet, *Doctrinal Commentary*, 3:71). ⊕

What should we consider in Mormon identifying Zeezrom as the main accuser? (10:31) Accusations have always been brought against the Lord's servants and true followers. Satan is referred by John the Beloved as the "accuser of our brethren" (see Revelation 12:10). It would also be worthy to note these words from the revelations given to Joseph Smith: "Cursed are all those that shall lift up the heel against mine anointed, saith the Lord, and cry they have sinned when they have not sinned before me, saith the Lord, but have done that which was meet in mine eyes, and which I commanded them. But those who cry transgression do it because they are the servants of sin, and are the children of disobedience themselves" (D&C 121:16–17).

Alma 11:1–20. The Nephite Judges Were Paid According to Their Labor

What significant changes did the law of Mosiah bring to Nephite society? (11:1–4) "The law of Mosiah departed most significantly from traditional law by providing that judges would be paid for their services (see Alma 11:1). This is not paralleled in other Near Eastern systems, although the fixing of wages for various other laborers was one of the main subjects of several ancient Near Eastern law codes.

"In order to set statutory wages of any kind, it was often necessary for ancient laws to recognize a system of legal exchange equivalents. Thus, the law of Mosiah gave exchange ratios for gold, silver, barley, and all kinds of grain (see Alma 11:7)" (Welch, "Law of Mosiah," 159–60). ●

To what does "pieces of their gold" refer? (11:4–19) The 2013 chapter summary for Alma 11 states: "The Nephite monetary system is set forth." Previous editions of the Book of Mormon used the term "coinage," but in "the text proper, the gold and silver units are referred to as pieces, not coins. . . . The word *coin*, of course, claims more than what the text actually says" (Skousen, *Analysis of Textual Variants*, 1812). ●

What evidence exists for the use of barley in ancient times? (11:7) "The Nephite monetary system was based on a barley standard, with a senine of gold or a senum of silver equal to a measure of barley" (Ludlow, *Companion to Your Study of the Book of Mormon*, 200). The December 1983 issue of *Science* magazine reported the discovery of pre-Columbian domesticated barley in Phoenix, Arizona. This is the

labored to judge those who were brought before them to be judged.

2 Now if a man owed another, and he would not pay that which he did owe, he was complained of to the judge; and the judge executed authority, and sent forth officers that the man should be brought before him; and he judged the man according to the law and the evidences which were brought against him, and thus the man was compelled to pay that which he owed, or be stripped, or be cast out from among the people as a thief and a robber.

3 And the judge received for his wages according to his time—a senine of gold for a day, or a senum of silver, which is equal to a senine of gold; and this is according to the law which was given.

4 Now these are the names of the different pieces of their gold, and of their silver, according to their value. And the names are given by the Nephites, for they did not reckon after the manner of the Jews who were at Jerusalem; neither did they measure after the manner of the Jews; but they altered their reckoning and their measure, according to the minds and the circumstances of the people, in every generation, until the reign of the judges, they having been established by king Mosiah.

5 Now the reckoning is thus—a senine of gold, a seon of gold, a shum of gold, and a limnah of gold.

6 A senum of silver, an amnor of silver, an ezrom of silver, and an onti of silver.

7 A senum of silver was equal to a senine of gold, and either for a measure of barley, and also for a measure of every kind of grain.

8 Now the amount of a seon of gold was twice the value of a senine.

9 And a shum of gold was twice the value of a seon.

10 And a limnah of gold was the value of them all.

11 And an amnor of silver was as great as two senums.

12 And an ezrom of silver was as great as four senums.

13 And an onti was as great as them all.

14 Now this is the value of the lesser numbers of their reckoning—

15 A shiblon is half of a senum; therefore, a shiblon for half a measure of barley.

16 And a shiblum is a half of a shiblon.

17 And a leah is the half of a shiblum.

18 Now this is their number, according to their reckoning.

19 Now an antion of gold is equal to three shiblons.

20 Now, it was for the sole purpose to get gain, because they received their wages according to their employ, therefore, they did stir up the people to riotings, and all manner

first direct New World evidence for cultivated pre-Columbian barley in support of the Book of Mormon. See also commentary in this volume on Mosiah 7:22.

Why was the elaborate Nephite system of weights and measures inserted here? (11:20) Mormon seems to be establishing the significance of the bribe Zeezrom had offered to the Lord's servants—six onties of silver—if they would "deny the existence of a Supreme Being" (see v. 22).

Nephite Weights and Measures

Measures	Ratio	Barley/Grain	Silver	Gold
42		84 shiblon	6 onti (bribe)	6 limnah
7	1:56	14 shiblon	onti	limnah
4	1:32	8 shiblon	ezrom	shum (Alma 11:9) / shun (Alma 11:5)
2	1:16	4 shiblon	amnor	seon
1½	1:12	3 shiblon	3 shiblon	antion
1	1:8	2 shiblon (measure)	senum	senine
½	1:4	shiblon (= ½ measure)	shiblon	
¼	1:2	shiblum	shiblum	
⅛	1:1	leah	leah	

FARMS Staff

Alma 11:21–25. Amulek Calls Zeezrom a Wicked Man

What do these verses reveal about Zeezrom? (11:21–22) "[Zeezrom] sought to intimidate, threaten, weaken, and confuse the prophets by plying the tools of his trade. His first challenge to Alma and Amulek was the temptation of money. As we have already seen, the Nehors put great stock in money, which conferred on them greater status. The essence of priestcraft is to teach false (or even true) doctrine in the pursuit of wealth and power. And so Zeezrom tempted Amulek" (Kramer, "Prophetic Principles for Building Zion," 281).

What can we learn from Amulek's example? (11:23–24) "Amulek's life was heroic, not tragic. . . . We do know that he was blessed with the sure blessings of obedience: the transforming of his life by the power of the atonement of Jesus Christ, the gift to give others the chance to choose that blessing, and the trust which God extends to those He knows will hear, will obey, and then will endure as doers of the word to the point of sacrifice, and beyond. Amulek was blessed with all of that, as we will be if we choose to obey" (Eyring, "Amulek," 112).

How serious was Zeezrom's exorbitant bribe? (11:25) "Before Zeezrom began, he offered Amulek, a man of considerable wealth, a substantial bribe of six onties (Alma 11:22). This was a very large bribe—worth forty-two days of professional labor—large enough that it might not have been taken seriously. Amulek generously discounted Zeezrom's ploy as a disingenuous offer and did not accuse Zeezrom of having made a serious attempt at bribery, but rather accused him of lying (v. 25)" (Welch, *Legal Cases in the Book of Mormon*, 257).

of disturbances and wickedness, that they might have more employ, that they might get money according to the suits which were brought before them; therefore they did stir up the people against Alma and Amulek.

21 And this Zeezrom began to question Amulek, saying: Will ye answer me a few questions which I shall ask you? Now Zeezrom was a man who was expert in the devices of the devil, that he might destroy that which was good; therefore, he said unto Amulek: Will ye answer the questions which I shall put unto you?

22 And Amulek said unto him: Yea, if it be according to the Spirit of the Lord, which is in me; for I shall say nothing which is contrary to the Spirit of the Lord. And Zeezrom said unto him: Behold, here are six onties of silver, and all these will I give thee if thou wilt deny the existence of a Supreme Being.

23 Now Amulek said: O thou child of hell, why tempt ye me? Knowest thou that the righteous yieldeth to no such temptations?

24 Believest thou that there is no God? I say unto you, Nay, thou knowest that there is a God, but thou lovest that lucre more than him.

25 And now thou hast lied before God unto me. Thou saidst unto me—Behold these six onties, which are of great worth, I will give unto thee—when thou hadst it in thy heart to retain them from me; and it was only thy desire that I should deny the true and living God, that thou mightest have cause to destroy me. And now behold, for this great evil thou shalt have thy reward.

Alma 11:26–41. Amulek Explains That We Cannot Be Saved in Our Sins

26 And Zeezrom said unto him: Thou sayest there is a true and living God?

27 And Amulek said: Yea, there is a true and living God.

28 Now Zeezrom said: Is there more than one God?

29 And he answered, No.

30 Now Zeezrom said unto him again: How knowest thou these things?

31 And he said: An angel hath made them known unto me.

32 And Zeezrom said again: Who is he that shall come? Is it the Son of God?

33 And he said unto him, Yea.

34 And Zeezrom said again: Shall he save his people in their sins? And Amulek answered and said unto him: I say unto you he shall not, for it is impossible for him to deny his word.

35 Now Zeezrom said unto the people: See that ye remember these things; for he said there is but one God; yet he saith that the Son of God shall come, but he shall not save his people—as though he had authority to command God.

36 Now Amulek saith again unto him: Behold thou hast lied, for thou sayest that I spake as though I had authority to command God because I said he shall not save his people in their sins.

37 And I say unto you again that he cannot save them in their sins; for I cannot deny his word, and he hath said that no unclean thing can inherit the kingdom of heaven; therefore, how can ye be saved, except ye inherit the kingdom of heaven? Therefore, ye cannot be saved in your sins.

Why did Amulek say there is only one God? (11:26–33) "This is a discussion—a question-and-answer session—that could be difficult to follow. Zeezrom, in his eagerness to trap Amulek in his own words, asks whether there is more than one God. Amulek answers that there is not. Amulek is, of course, speaking entirely of the Savior, of the Lord Jehovah; he is not making reference to our Father in Heaven or to the Godhead" (McConkie and Millet, *Doctrinal Commentary*, 3:75). ☉

Can people be saved *in* their sins? (11:34–37) "Even the Omnipotent One, the Lord Jehovah, cannot save his people *in* their sins. He came on a search-and-rescue mission to save people *from* their sins. But no one, not the least and lowliest of mankind or the mightiest Apostle and prophet, can be saved in sin. Such is the divine decree. Speaking of the Amulek-Zeezrom encounter, Nephi later said: 'For he said unto him that the Lord surely should come to redeem his people. . . . And he hath power given unto him from the Father to redeem them from their sins because of repentance' (Helaman 5:10–11)" (McConkie and Millet, *Doctrinal Commentary*, 3:76). ☉

What does the doctrine of Christ teach us about the Father and the Son? (11:38–39) "The doctrine of Christ with roles as a Father as well as a Son was the source of some confusion and contention in Book of Mormon times. One of the most skillful and cunning of adversaries in the Book of Mormon . . . was Zeezrom. He used the complexity of this doctrine to try to trap new missionary Amulek. . . .

"There are ways in which Christ is so united with his Father that in some assignments he rightfully plays a fatherly role and rightfully bears the title of Father in doing so.

"The fundamental . . . doctrine of the Son-as-Father is illuminated more definitively in the Book of Mormon than in any other revelation" (Holland, *Christ and the New Covenant*, 182–83).

Did the Savior suffer only for believers? (11:40) "Some people have thought that Amulek was teaching that Christ suffered only for those who believe and repent. This is not correct. The scriptures tell us that the Savior 'suffereth the pains of all men, yea, the pains of every living creature, both men, women, and children' (2 Nephi 9:21; see also Mosiah 4:7). If mankind will not repent, however, the Savior indicates that 'my blood shall not cleanse them' (D&C 29:17). Clearly, what Amulek was intending to convey is the fact that the Atonement in part may go unused when the wicked choose not to repent—not that the Savior only suffered for those who would repent" (*Book of Mormon Student Manual* [2009], 187).

In what way are the unrepentant wicked redeemed? (11:41) "In essence, Amulek is saying that the wicked are all resurrected, but they are not redeemed into the presence of God unless they repent of their sins and become spotless before him" (Ludlow, *Companion to Your Study of the Book of Mormon*, 200). ☉

Alma 11:42–46. Amulek Tells Zeezrom That All People Will Be Resurrected and Judged by Their Works

How is the doctrine of restoration related to the Resurrection? (11:43–44) "The spiritual impact of [the] doctrine of restoration is sobering for those who may have believed that Christ's atonement and their resurrection would somehow bring something more than was deserved. Alma made it very clear that if our works are good in this life, and the desires of our hearts are good, then in the Resurrection we will be restored to that which is good. But, by the same token, if our works are evil, then our reward will be the

---

38 Now Zeezrom saith again unto him: Is the Son of God the very Eternal Father?

39 And Amulek said unto him: Yea, he is the very Eternal Father of heaven and of earth, and all things which in them are; he is the beginning and the end, the first and the last;

40 And he shall come into the world to redeem his people; and he shall take upon him the transgressions of those who believe on his name; and these are they that shall have eternal life, and salvation cometh to none else.

41 Therefore the wicked remain as though there had been no redemption made, except it be the loosing of the bands of death; for behold, the day cometh that all shall rise from the dead and stand before God, and be judged according to their works.

42 Now, there is a death which is called a temporal death; and the death of Christ shall loose the bands of this temporal death, that all shall be raised from this temporal death.

43 The spirit and the body shall be reunited again in its perfect form; both limb and joint shall be restored to its proper frame, even as we now are at this time; and we shall be brought to stand before God, knowing even as we know now, and have a bright recollection of all our guilt.

44 Now, this restoration shall come to all, both old and young, both bond and free, both male and female, both the wicked and the righteous; and even there shall not so much as a hair of their heads be lost; but every thing shall be restored to its perfect frame, as it is now, or in the body, and shall be brought and be arraigned before the bar of Christ the Son, and God the Father, and the Holy Spirit, which is one Eternal God, to be judged according to their works, whether they be good or whether they be evil.

45 Now, behold, I have spoken unto you concerning the death of the mortal body, and also concerning the resurrection of the mortal body. I say unto you that this mortal body is raised to an immortal body, that is from death, even from the first death unto life, that they can die no more; their spirits uniting with their bodies, never to be divided; thus the whole becoming spiritual and immortal, that they can no more see corruption.

46 Now, when Amulek had finished these words the people began again to be astonished, and also Zeezrom began to tremble. And thus ended the words of Amulek, or this is all that I have written.

CHAPTER 12

Alma speaks to Zeezrom—The mysteries of God can be given only to the faithful—Men are judged by their thoughts, beliefs, words, and works—The wicked will suffer a spiritual death—This mortal life is a probationary state—The plan of redemption brings to pass the Resurrection and, through faith, a remission of sins—The repentant have a claim on mercy through the Only Begotten Son. About 82 B.C.

1 Now Alma, seeing that the words of Amulek had silenced Zeezrom, for he beheld that Amulek had caught him in his lying and deceiving to destroy him, and seeing that he

restoration of evil in the Resurrection" (Holland, *Christ and the New Covenant*, 242). ◐

What might it be like to be "restored to" a "perfect frame"? (11:44–45) "The exact type of body that resurrected beings will have after the resurrection has not been made clear in the scriptures except that it will be an immortal, glorified body animated by spirit" (Ludlow, *Companion to Your Study of the Book of Mormon*, 201).

What do you personally anticipate in a resurrected body? Can you imagine the level of joy you will experience in such a state of immortality? ◐

How is a resurrected body both physical and spiritual? (11:45) "The word *spiritual* is used here to describe a condition. A resurrected body is a physical body in a *spiritual* condition, as contrasted to a mortal body which is also physical but is not in a spiritual condition: mortal bodies are subject to death and contain blood, but resurrected bodies will never die again and are, as President Joseph Fielding Smith explained, 'quickened by the spirit and not the blood' (*Doctrines of Salvation*, 2:284)" (Matthews, *A Bible! A Bible!* 200; emphasis added).

Alma 12:1–8. Alma Exposes Zeezrom's Evil Plan

Where did Zeezrom's silence, then guilt, followed by inquiry, lead him? (12:1–3) Zeezrom was silenced by the truth. His deception, and subsequently his guilt, were exposed. The psalmist wrote: "Let the lying lips be put to silence; which speak grievous things proudly and contemptuously against the righteous" (Psalm 31:18). Peter wrote to the Saints in his day, "For so is the will of God, that with well doing ye may put to silence the ignorance of foolish men" (1 Peter 2:15). The silence of Zeezrom also reveals a positive nature about his character. He was open to admit his guilt. His heart was not closed to truth. He went from accusing to inquiring; from inquiring to an exceptional servant of the Lord. ●

What can we learn about Satan's use of *subtlety*? (12:4–6) "I think we will witness increasing evidence of Satan's power as the kingdom of God grows stronger. I believe Satan's ever-expanding efforts are some proof of the truthfulness of this work. In the future the opposition will be both more subtle and more open. It will be masked in greater sophistication and cunning, but it will also be more blatant. . . . Some of Satan's most appealing lines are 'Everyone does it'; 'If it doesn't hurt anybody else, it's all right'; 'If you feel all right about it, it's OK'; or 'It's the "in" thing to do.' These subtle entreaties make Satan the great imitator, the master deceiver, the arch counterfeiter, and the great forger" (Faust, "The Great Imitator," 33).

What convinced Zeezrom that Alma and Amulek knew his thoughts? (12:7) Once Alma revealed Zeezrom's "very subtle plan" (v. 4) and declared that he had been "taken in [his] lying and craftiness" (v. 3), "[Zeezrom] was convinced more and more of the power of God [v. 7]."

"This gift of discernment is one of the gifts of the Holy Spirit, and it is through the proper use of this gift that the evils and designs of wicked men are made known to the prophets of God" (Ludlow, *Companion to Your Study of the Book of Mormon*, 202). ●

began to tremble under a consciousness of his guilt, he opened his mouth and began to speak unto him, and to establish the words of Amulek, and to explain things beyond, or to unfold the scriptures beyond that which Amulek had done.

2 Now the words that Alma spake unto Zeezrom were heard by the people round about; for the multitude was great, and he spake on this wise:

3 Now Zeezrom, seeing that thou hast been taken in thy lying and craftiness, for thou hast not lied unto men only but thou hast lied unto God; for behold, he knows all thy thoughts, and thou seest that thy thoughts are made known unto us by his Spirit;

4 And thou seest that we know that thy plan was a very subtle plan, as to the subtlety of the devil, for to lie and to deceive this people that thou mightest set them against us, to revile us and to cast us out—

5 Now this was a plan of thine adversary, and he hath exercised his power in thee. Now I would that ye should remember that what I say unto thee I say unto all.

6 And behold I say unto you all that this was a snare of the adversary, which he has laid to catch this people, that he might bring you into subjection unto him, that he might encircle you about with his chains, that he might chain you down to everlasting destruction, according to the power of his captivity.

7 Now when Alma had spoken these words, Zeezrom began to tremble more exceedingly, for he was convinced more and more of the power of God; and he was also convinced that Alma and Amulek had a knowledge of him, for he was convinced that they knew the thoughts and intents of his heart; for power was given unto them that they might know of these things according to the spirit of prophecy.

8 And Zeezrom began to inquire of them diligently, that he might know more concerning the kingdom of God. And he said unto Alma: What does this mean which Amulek hath spoken concerning the resurrection of the dead, that all shall rise from the dead, both the just and the unjust, and are brought to stand before God to be judged according to their works?

9 And now Alma began to expound these things unto him, saying: It is given unto many to know the mysteries of God; nevertheless they are laid under a strict command that they shall not impart only according to the portion of his word which he doth grant unto the children of men, according to the heed and diligence which they give unto him.

10 And therefore, he that will harden his heart, the same receiveth the lesser portion of the word; and he that will not harden his heart, to him is given the greater portion of the word, until it is given unto him to know the mysteries of God until he know them in full.

11 And they that will harden their hearts, to them is given the lesser portion of the word until they know nothing concerning his mysteries; and then they are taken captive by the devil, and led by his will down to destruction. Now this is what is meant by the chains of hell.

12 And Amulek hath spoken plainly concerning death, and being raised from this mortality to a state of immortality, and being brought before the bar of God, to be judged according to our works.

How does the "preaching of the word" (Alma 31:5) have a tendency to lead people to Christ? (12:8) "We see in this verse an example of the marvelous transformation that can begin to take place because of the power of the word. Zeezrom, only a short time before, had asked baiting, trapping questions. Now that he is confronted by the power of God and having his sins laid open to view, his queries begin to change, to reflect a type of sincere inquiry after the truth" (McConkie and Millet, *Doctrinal Commentary*, 3:82).

Can you think of a time when a passage of scripture had such a profound effect upon you? ◐

Alma 12:9–11. The Mysteries of God Are Unfolded to the Faithful and Obedient

How can we receive of the "mysteries of God"? (12:9–11) "Alma explained the basis on which the gospel is taught to the human family, showing that the mysteries of God are made clear only to the faithful.... Alma's words explain a principle that determines the extent to which the gospel is taught at any one time to any individual or group. It is a matter of readiness based upon the personal desires and preferences of the receivers" (Matthews, "Probationary Nature of Mortality," 48).

What is meant by "mysteries"? (12:11) A mystery is "a spiritual truth that was once hidden but now is revealed and that without special revelation would have remained unknown. It is generally used along with words denoting revelation or publication (Rom. 16:25–26; Eph. 1:9; 3:3–10; Col. 1:26; 4:3; 1 Tim. 3:16)" (Bible Dictionary, "Mystery," 691).

Alma 12:12–18. People Will Be Judged by Their Words, Works, and Thoughts

What attitudes are exhibited by people who harden their hearts against God's word? (12:12–13) "Those who cry out, 'I have enough'; those who refuse to learn more; those who are content to exist at their present level of light and truth, who say essentially, 'Thus far and no further'—these shall live and die in ignorance of the mysteries of God and shall thereby subject themselves to the chains of hell. God is gracious: He provides for us that which we are willing—and thus able—to receive" (McConkie and Millet, *Doctrinal Commentary*, 3:84–85).

How are our words, works, and thoughts recorded and known by God? (12:14) "In a real though figurative sense, the *book of life* is the record of the acts of men as such is written in their own bodies. It is the record engraven on the very bones, sinews, and flesh of the mortal body. That is, every thought, word, and deed has an effect on the human body; all these leave their marks, marks which can be read by Him who is Eternal as easily as the words in a book can be read" (McConkie, *Mormon Doctrine*, 97). ❍

Why does Alma teach by pointing out alternatives? (12:15–16) "It might be said that Alma is beyond eloquence in that he strives for directness and simplicity. . . . A judge himself, in teaching about judgment Alma repeatedly sets forth alternatives: Give heed and diligence to the word and eventually know the mysteries of God; or harden your heart and be taken captive by the devil (Alma 12:9–11). Believe, repent, and be saved; or die in your sins and then die a spiritual death (Alma 12:15–17). Do not provoke the Lord to 'pull down his wrath'; but rather, 'enter into the rest of God' (Alma 12:37)" (Rust, *Feasting on the Word*, 120, 131).

What happens to those who suffer "spiritual death"? (12:17) "The suffering to which the wicked are subjected takes place in the postmortal spirit world. This is hell, both a place and a state of mind. Concerning hell as a state of mind, Joseph Smith explained: 'A man is his own tormenter and his own condemner. Hence the saying, They shall go into the lake that burns with fire and brimstone. The torment of disappointment in the mind of man is as exquisite as a lake burning with fire and brimstone' (*Teachings*, 357)" (McConkie and Millet, *Doctrinal Commentary*, 3:86).

13 Then if our hearts have been hardened, yea, if we have hardened our hearts against the word, insomuch that it has not been found in us, then will our state be awful, for then we shall be condemned.

14 For our words will condemn us, yea, all our works will condemn us; we shall not be found spotless; and our thoughts will also condemn us; and in this awful state we shall not dare to look up to our God; and we would fain be glad if we could command the rocks and the mountains to fall upon us to hide us from his presence.

15 But this cannot be; we must come forth and stand before him in his glory, and in his power, and in his might, majesty, and dominion, and acknowledge to our everlasting shame that all his judgments are just; that he is just in all his works, and that he is merciful unto the children of men, and that he has all power to save every man that believeth on his name and bringeth forth fruit meet for repentance.

16 And now behold, I say unto you then cometh a death, even a second death, which is a spiritual death; then is a time that whosoever dieth in his sins, as to a temporal death, shall also die a spiritual death; yea, he shall die as to things pertaining unto righteousness.

17 Then is the time when their torments shall be as a lake of fire and brimstone, whose flame ascendeth up forever and ever; and then is the time that they shall be chained down to an everlasting destruction, according to the power and captivity of Satan, he having subjected them according to his will.

18 Then, I say unto you, they shall be as though there had been no redemption made; for they cannot be redeemed according to God's justice; and they cannot die, seeing there is no more corruption.

19 Now it came to pass that when Alma had made an end of speaking these words, the people began to be more astonished;

20 But there was one Antionah, who was a chief ruler among them, came forth and said unto him: What is this that thou hast said, that man should rise from the dead and be changed from this mortal to an immortal state, that the soul can never die?

21 What does the scripture mean, which saith that God placed cherubim and a flaming sword on the east of the garden of Eden, lest our first parents should enter and partake of the fruit of the tree of life, and live forever? And thus we see that there was no possible chance that they should live forever.

22 Now Alma said unto him: This is the thing which I was about to explain. Now we see that Adam did fall by the partaking of the forbidden fruit, according to the word of God; and thus we see, that by his fall, all mankind became a lost and fallen people.

23 And now behold, I say unto you that if it had been possible for Adam to have partaken of the fruit of the tree of life at that time, there would have been no death, and the word would have been void, making God a liar, for he said: If thou eat thou shalt surely die.

24 And we see that death comes upon mankind, yea, the death which has been spoken of by Amulek, which is the temporal death; nevertheless there was a space granted unto man in which he might repent; therefore this life became a probationary state; a time to prepare to meet God; a time to prepare for that endless state which has been spoken of by us, which is after the resurrection of the dead.

Alma 12:19–24. Mortal Life Is a Time of Testing for God's Children

What was the doctrinal challenge for Alma in Antionah's argument? (12:20–21) Antionah "thought he would make an irrefutable argument by asking Alma concerning the cherubim with a flaming sword. . . . What Antionah made to appear as conflicting evidence . . . was Alma's forthright declaration that through the Atonement of Christ all men, both righteous and wicked, would gain immortality and therefore *live forever*. Antionah quoted scripture to show that the reason God sent guardians to watch the *Tree of Life* was that our first parents should not enter Eden and partake of its fruit and *live forever*. . . .

"But what Antionah failed to add to his harangue was . . . that the Almighty . . . would not have it that man should live forever in his sins" (Reynolds and Sjodahl, *Commentary on the Book of Mormon*, 3:193).

What are we to understand about mankind being "a lost and fallen people"? (12:22) "Ancient and modern prophets have taught that Adam and Eve's partaking of the forbidden fruit had, and continues to have, significant consequences. . . .

"We know that the Prophet Joseph Smith . . . clearly acknowledged and taught of mankind's fallen nature. . . . During a trip to New York City in October 1832, he wrote a letter to his wife, Emma, in which, in addition to describing the splendor of the city and the accomplishments of the people, he stated: 'The iniquity of the people is printed in every countenance and nothing but the dress of the people makes them look fair and beautiful. All is deformity. There is something in every countenance that is disagreeable, with few exceptions'" (Judd, *Fortunate Fall*, 90–92). ✪

How does a "probationary state" help us? (12:24) "The word *probation* is found only ten times in the Standard Works, and nine of those references are in the Book of Mormon. What an essential doctrine in understanding the Fall and the Atonement, a doctrine of prolonged opportunity for mortal men and women in which the gospel can be taught to and accepted by them . . . !

"In this term of mortal probation (whatever period that may be after eight years of age until the day of death), we have the teachings of the gospel and the commandments of God to guide our time of testing" (Holland, *Christ and the New Covenant*, 209–10).

Alma 12:25–37. All of God's Children Will Be Resurrected Because of the Plan of Redemption

What is meant by the "plan of redemption"? (12:26–27) "Among the most significant of Jesus Christ's descriptive titles is Redeemer. . . . The word *redeem* means to pay off an obligation or a debt. *Redeem* can also mean to rescue or set free as by paying a ransom. If someone commits a mistake and then corrects it or makes amends, we say he has redeemed himself. Each of these meanings suggests different facets of the great Redemption accomplished by Jesus Christ through His Atonement, which includes, in the words of the dictionary, 'to deliver from sin and its penalties, as by a sacrifice made for the sinner'" (Christofferson, "Redemption," 109).

What was Alma suggesting about communication between angels, God, and men? (12:28–30) "I think there are at least two ways to read that . . . phrase from Alma—that 'God conversed with men.' One way is to note that angels came first and then, with men thus spiritually prepared, God conversed directly with them. But another way is to see those phrases as synonymous, that when God sent angels to converse with mortals he was speaking to them, just as if he were personally there doing so" (Holland, "Standard unto My People," 11).

How important is agency in Heavenly Father's plan? (12:31–32) "The plan presupposes mistakes. Under the plan, penalties connected with bad choices, our sins, may be cancelled on condition that we keep the commandments which activate the influence of the Atonement.

"We are commanded to do some things, and we are commanded not to do others in order to merit the redeeming power of that sacrifice, the atonement of Christ. The choice is ours. Alma said, 'God gave unto

25 Now, if it had not been for the plan of redemption, which was laid from the foundation of the world, there could have been no resurrection of the dead; but there was a plan of redemption laid, which shall bring to pass the resurrection of the dead, of which has been spoken.

26 And now behold, if it were possible that our first parents could have gone forth and partaken of the tree of life they would have been forever miserable, having no preparatory state; and thus the plan of redemption would have been frustrated, and the word of God would have been void, taking none effect.

27 But behold, it was not so; but it was appointed unto men that they must die; and after death, they must come to judgment, even that same judgment of which we have spoken, which is the end.

28 And after God had appointed that these things should come unto man, behold, then he saw that it was expedient that man should know concerning the things whereof he had appointed unto them;

29 Therefore he sent angels to converse with them, who caused men to behold of his glory.

30 And they began from that time forth to call on his name; therefore God conversed with men, and made known unto them the plan of redemption, which had been prepared from the foundation of the world; and this he made known unto them according to their faith and repentance and their holy works.

31 Wherefore, he gave commandments unto men, they having first transgressed the first commandments as to things which were temporal, and becoming as gods, knowing good from evil, placing themselves in a state to act, or being placed in a state to act according to their wills and pleasures, whether to do evil or to do good—

32 Therefore God gave unto them commandments, after having made known unto them the plan of redemption, that they should not do evil, the penalty thereof being a second death, which was an everlasting death as to things pertaining unto righteousness; for on such the plan of redemption could have no power, for the works of justice could not be destroyed, according to the supreme goodness of God.

33 But God did call on men, in the name of his Son, (this being the plan of redemption which was laid) saying: If ye will repent, and harden not your hearts, then will I have mercy upon you, through mine Only Begotten Son;

34 Therefore, whosoever repenteth, and hardeneth not his heart, he shall have claim on mercy through mine Only Begotten Son, unto a remission of his sins; and these shall enter into my rest.

35 And whosoever will harden his heart and will do iniquity, behold, I swear in my wrath that he shall not enter into my rest.

36 And now, my brethren, behold I say unto you, that if ye will harden your hearts ye shall not enter into the rest of the Lord; therefore your iniquity provoketh him that he sendeth down his wrath upon you as in the first provocation, yea, according to his word in the last provocation as well as the first, to the everlasting destruction of your souls; therefore, according to his word, unto the last death, as well as the first.

37 And now, my brethren, seeing we know these things, and they are true, let us repent, and harden not our hearts, that we provoke not the Lord our God to pull down his wrath upon us in these his second commandments which he has given unto us; but let us enter into the rest of God, which is prepared according to his word.

them commandments, after having made known unto them the plan of redemption' (Alma 12:32)" (Packer, *Things of the Soul*, 50).

What can we learn from God's manner of teaching His children? (12:32) "Understanding [the] plan of happiness provides us with an eternal perspective and helps us to truly value the commandments, the ordinances, the covenants, and the trials and tribulations. . . . It is interesting to note the sequence in the teaching process. Our Heavenly Father first taught Adam and Eve the plan of redemption, and then He gave them commandments. This is a great truth. Understanding the plan will help people keep the commandments, make better decisions, and have the right motivation" (Pino, "The Eternal Perspective of the Gospel," 119). ⊕

What can we learn from the Book of Mormon's use of the title "the Only Begotten Son"? (12:33–34) *Begotten* means "to be born. To beget is to give birth, to procreate, or to call into being. In the scriptures, these words are often used to mean being born of God. Although Jesus Christ is the only child begotten of the Father in mortality, all people may be spiritually begotten of Christ by accepting Him, obeying His commandments, and becoming new persons through the power of the Holy Ghost" (*Guide to the Scriptures*, "Begotten").

What does it mean to "enter into [God's] rest"? (12:35–37) See commentary in this volume on Alma 13:6.

Alma 13:1–5. Righteous Priesthood Holders Were Called to Hold the Priesthood before They Were Born

How was Alma citing minds "forward"? (13:1) "His use of the word *forward* is unusual, especially in light of the fact that he will speak of people in the past; we would normally say backwards. But actually forward can also mean toward the beginning, toward the front, '[n]ear or at the forepart' (*Webster's*)" (Millet, "Holy Order of God," 64). ✪

What is "his holy order, which was after the order of his Son"? (13:1) "We enter into the holy order of God through receiving the Melchizedek Priesthood, inasmuch as the full name of this sacred authority is '*the Holy Priesthood, after the Order of the Son of God*' (D&C 107:3). At another level, we encounter the holy order of God through receiving the ordinances of the temple, through receiving the endowment and the blessings of eternal marriage" (Millet, "Holy Order of God," 75). "The word *order* appears fourteen times in Alma's teachings about the priesthood in Alma 13; forms of *ordain* appear seven times; and *ordinance* or *ordinances* appears three times. The English words *order*, *ordain*, and *ordinances* all stem from the same root: Latin *ordo*, which means literally a straight row or regular series. To ordain originally meant 'to put in order' and still has the force of that meaning" (Rust, *Feasting on the Word*, 129).

How are priests a pattern for Christ? (13:2) "[All] prophets are types and shadows of the Savior. He was called and prepared from before the foundations of this world. So were they. He speaks the truth. So do they. He offers the words of life. So do they. He preaches as one having authority. So do they. . . . Thus the ancient prophets were living Messianic prophecies" (Millet, "Holy Order of God," 65).

How similar to mortality was the priesthood organization in our premortal life? (13:3) "In regard to the holding of the priesthood in pre-existence, I will say that there was an organization there just as well as

CHAPTER 13

Men are called as high priests because of their exceeding faith and good works—They are to teach the commandments—Through righteousness they are sanctified and enter into the rest of the Lord—Melchizedek was one of these—Angels are declaring glad tidings throughout the land—They will declare the actual coming of Christ. About 82 B.C.

1 And again, my brethren, I would cite your minds forward to the time when the Lord God gave these commandments unto his children; and I would that ye should remember that the Lord God ordained priests, after his holy order, which was after the order of his Son, to teach these things unto the people.

2 And those priests were ordained after the order of his Son, in a manner that thereby the people might know in what manner to look forward to his Son for redemption.

3 And this is the manner after which they were ordained—being called and prepared from the foundation of the world according to the foreknowledge of God, on account

of their exceeding faith and good works; in the first place being left to choose good or evil; therefore they having chosen good, and exercising exceedingly great faith, are called with a holy calling, yea, with that holy calling which was prepared with, and according to, a preparatory redemption for such.

4 And thus they have been called to this holy calling on account of their faith, while others would reject the Spirit of God on account of the hardness of their hearts and blindness of their minds, while, if it had not been for this they might have had as great privilege as their brethren.

5 Or in fine, in the first place they were on the same standing with their brethren; thus this holy calling being prepared from the foundation of the world for such as would not harden their hearts, being in and through the atonement of the Only Begotten Son, who was prepared—

6 And thus being called by this holy calling, and ordained unto the high priesthood of the holy order of God, to teach his commandments unto the children of men, that they also might enter into his rest—

7 This high priesthood being after the order of his Son, which order was from the foundation of the world; or in other words, being

an organization here, and men there held authority. Men chosen to positions of trust in the spirit world held priesthood" (Smith, *Doctrines of Salvation*, 3:81).

What does this passage teach about our choice in the premortal existence to accept or reject the Spirit of God? (13:4) President Joseph Fielding Smith explained the eternal principle of agency: "God gave his children . . . agency even in the [premortal] spirit world, by which the individual spirits had the privilege, just as men have here, of choosing the good and rejecting the evil. . . . The spirits of men were not equal. They may have had an equal start, and we know they were all innocent in the beginning; but the right of . . . agency which was given to them enabled some to outstrip others, and thus, through the eons of immortal existence, to become more intelligent, more faithful, for they were free to act for themselves, to think for themselves, to receive the truth or rebel against it" (*Doctrines of Salvation*, 1:58–59).

What does this phrase "in the first place they were on the same standing" add to our understanding of our status in the premortal world? (13:5) "In the beginning all spirits were created equal. There were none more privileged than were others. All were nurtured at the side of our Heavenly Father. All were blessed with the capability of learning. . . .

"As the spirits grew in the knowledge of that which is just and true, they also grew in the knowledge of the glory of Him that created them" (Reynolds and Sjodahl, *Commentary on the Book of Mormon*, 3:201).

Alma 13:6–13. The Eternal Priesthood Helps Us Gain Salvation

What does it mean to "enter into his rest"? (13:6) "Modern revelation sometimes equates the 'rest' of the Lord with entering into the presence of God, or receiving the 'fulness of his glory' (D&C 84:24). . . .

"This interpretation of 'the rest of God' is consistent with Alma's use of the phrase in his teachings in Ammonihah" (Valletta, "Conflicting Orders," 219).

When did the priesthood begin? (13:7) The Prophet Joseph Smith taught: "The priesthood is an everlasting principle, and existed with God from eternity, and will to eternity, without beginning of days or end of years." It is the "channel through which all knowledge, doctrine, the plan of salvation and every important matter is revealed from heaven" (*Joseph Smith* [manual], 104, 108).

What is the "holy ordinance" by which priesthood holders are ordained? (13:8–9) "*The Laying on of Hands* by which the Priesthood of God is conferred and office in that Priesthood is given is a *Holy Ordinance* which is upheld by the Church of Jesus Christ of Latter-day Saints. How different from any self-appointed calling practiced in many of the churches of the world today is the endowment of the Priesthood by this Holy Ordinance" (Reynolds and Sjodahl, *Commentary on the Book of Mormon*, 3:203). President Benson and others have also emphasized that this holy ordinance is "entering into the fullness of the Melchizedek Priesthood, which is only received in the house of the Lord" (*Ezra Taft Benson* [manual], 170).

How can we be sanctified and have our garments "washed white"? (13:10–11) "As men exercise the priesthood, it has a purifying effect upon them. They become sanctified [holy] and the Atonement of Christ takes away their sins (v. 11). In addition to the priesthood, they are given the Holy Ghost, which is also a sanctifying gift if they receive it. Because of their pure and spotless [divine] nature, they cannot look upon sin without abhorring that sin (v. 12). Nonetheless, as the Prophet Joseph Smith said: 'I love you all; but I hate some of your deeds' (*Teachings of the Prophet Joseph Smith*, 361). Sanctification is not limited to a few, but to all who will magnify the priesthood and be guided by the Holy Ghost" (Nyman, *Record of Alma*, 176). ✪

How might the truth in verse 12 give us hope today? (13:12) Apparently, many in the ancient Church were made pure and fulfilled God's purposes. How can we remain pure and fulfill our purposes amid the challenges of life?

Elder Richard G. Scott testified: "God has a specific plan for your life. He will reveal parts of that plan to you as you look for it with faith and consistent obedience. . . . God's eternal purpose is for you to be successful in this mortal life" ("How to Live Well amid Increasing Evil," 102). What can we do to help fulfill God's purpose for us? ✪

without beginning of days or end of years, being prepared from eternity to all eternity, according to his foreknowledge of all things—

8 Now they were ordained after this manner—being called with a holy calling, and ordained with a holy ordinance, and taking upon them the high priesthood of the holy order, which calling, and ordinance, and high priesthood, is without beginning or end—

9 Thus they become high priests forever, after the order of the Son, the Only Begotten of the Father, who is without beginning of days or end of years, who is full of grace, equity, and truth. And thus it is. Amen.

10 Now, as I said concerning the holy order, or this high priesthood, there were many who were ordained and became high priests of God; and it was on account of their exceeding faith and repentance, and their righteousness before God, they choosing to repent and work righteousness rather than to perish;

11 Therefore they were called after this holy order, and were sanctified, and their garments were washed white through the blood of the Lamb.

12 Now they, after being sanctified by the Holy Ghost, having their garments made white, being pure and spotless before God, could not look upon sin save it were with abhorrence; and there were many, exceedingly great many, who were made pure and entered into the rest of the Lord their God.

13 And now, my brethren, I would that ye should humble yourselves before God, and bring forth fruit meet for repentance, that ye may also enter into that rest.

Alma 13:14–20. Melchizedek Leads His People by Faith and the Power of the Priesthood

14 Yea, humble yourselves even as the people in the days of Melchizedek, who was also a high priest after this same order which I have spoken, who also took upon him the high priesthood forever.

15 And it was this same Melchizedek to whom Abraham paid tithes; yea, even our father Abraham paid tithes of one-tenth part of all he possessed.

16 Now these ordinances were given after this manner, that thereby the people might look forward on the Son of God, it being a type of his order, or it being his order, and this that they might look forward to him for a remission of their sins, that they might enter into the rest of the Lord.

17 Now this Melchizedek was a king over the land of Salem; and his people had waxed strong in iniquity and abomination; yea, they had all gone astray; they were full of all manner of wickedness;

18 But Melchizedek having exercised mighty faith, and received the office of the high priesthood according to the holy order of God, did preach repentance unto his people. And behold, they did repent; and Melchizedek did establish peace in the land in his days; therefore he was called the prince of peace, for he was the king of Salem; and he did reign under his father.

19 Now, there were many before him, and also there were many afterwards, but none were greater; therefore, of him they have more particularly made mention.

Who was Melchizedek? (13:14–16) The meaning of the Hebrew name *Melchizedek* is *"King of Righteousness."* Melchizedek was a "notable prophet and leader who lived about 2000 B.C. He is called the king of Salem (Jerusalem), king of peace, and 'priest of the most High God.' Unfortunately, information concerning him in the Bible is relatively scarce . . . However, latter-day revelation gives us much more about him and his priesthood (see JST Gen. 14:17 [Gen. 14:18, footnote *d*]; JST Gen. 14:25–40; JST Heb. 7:3 [Appendix]; Alma 13:14–19; D&C 84:14; 107:1–4). From these sources we realize something of the greatness of this prophet and the grandeur of his ministry" (Bible Dictionary, "Melchizedek," 730). ✪

What do we learn from Alma about Melchizedek? (13:17–18) Elder Jeffrey R. Holland wrote: "Latter-day Saints know more than most about Melchizedek because of references to him in the thirteenth chapter of Alma in the Book of Mormon. Indeed, in that other 'testament of Jesus Christ,' Melchizedek is clearly a very specific Old Testament type of Jesus Christ that was to come in New Testament times. It is noted that Melchizedek was 'king over the land of [Jeru]Salem,' 'did reign under his father,' 'received the office of the high priesthood' in 'the holy order of God,' 'did preach repentance unto his people,' 'did establish peace,' and 'was called the prince of peace'—all recognized by even the most casual of readers as characteristics of Jesus when He came in mortality" (*For Times of Trouble*, 185). ✪

If "none were greater" than Melchizedek, why does the Bible say so little about him? (13:19) "There were none greater or more wise than Melchizedek, although there were many both before and after him who occupied his exalted office. Yet little is said in the Bible of his greatness, his goodness, or his wisdom. . . .

"The brief passages in the Bible concerning Melchizedek when compared with the greater statement made in the Book of Mormon confirms our belief that a more detailed account of him was purposely, or at least carelessly, left out of the Scriptures by the teachers and leaders of the Jews who many years later came into positions of prominence and power" (Reynolds and Sjodahl, *Commentary on the Book of Mormon*, 3:206). ⊕

What does it mean to *wrest* the scriptures? (13:20) "Webster states that to wrest is to 'turn or twist; to ascribe a wrong meaning or intent to; to deliberately misinterpret or distort.' The Lord warned against wresting the scriptures (D&C 10:63).

"President Joseph Fielding Smith gave the following counsel regarding wresting or misinterpreting the scriptures: 'It is wrong to take one passage of scripture and isolate it from all other teachings dealing with the same subject. We should bring together all that has been said by authority on the question' [*Doctrines of Salvation*, 2:95]" (Brewster, *Doctrine and Covenants Encyclopedia*, 651). Perhaps "one reason the city of Ammonihah had gone into such a spiritual decline was that the people and their leaders had begun to 'wrest,' or distort, the scriptures for their own unrighteous purposes" (Williams, "Using the Book of Mormon," 35).

Alma 13:21–31. Alma Pleads with His People to Repent

What is the "day of salvation"? (13:21) "In one sense, reference [to the day of salvation] is to the day of the Savior's birth. In another sense, to say that 'the day of salvation draweth nigh' is to lay stress upon the importance of preparing in this life for death, that 'night of darkness wherein there can be no labor performed' (Alma 34:33; compare JST, Luke 12:41–44)" (McConkie and Millet, *Doctrinal Commentary*, 3:104–5).

20 Now I need not rehearse the matter; what I have said may suffice. Behold, the scriptures are before you; if ye will wrest them it shall be to your own destruction.

21 And now it came to pass that when Alma had said these words unto them, he stretched forth his hand unto them and cried with a mighty voice, saying: Now is the time to repent, for the day of salvation draweth nigh;

22 Yea, and the voice of the Lord, by the mouth of angels, doth declare it unto all nations; yea, doth declare it, that they may have glad tidings of great joy; yea, and he doth sound these glad tidings among all his people, yea, even to them that are scattered abroad upon the face of the earth; wherefore they have come unto us.

23 And they are made known unto us in plain terms, that we may understand, that we cannot err; and this because of our being wanderers in a strange land; therefore, we are thus highly favored, for we have these glad tidings declared unto us in all parts of our vineyard.

24 For behold, angels are declaring it unto many at this time in our land; and this is for the purpose of preparing the hearts of the children of men to receive his word at the time of his coming in his glory.

25 And now we only wait to hear the joyful news declared unto us by the mouth of angels, of his coming; for the time cometh, we know not how soon. Would to God that it might be in my day; but let it be sooner or later, in it I will rejoice.

26 And it shall be made known unto just and holy men, by the mouth of angels, at the time of his coming, that the words of our fathers may be fulfilled, according to that which they have spoken concerning him, which was according to the spirit of prophecy which was in them.

27 And now, my brethren, I wish from the inmost part of my heart, yea, with great anxiety even unto pain, that ye would hearken unto my words, and cast off your sins, and not procrastinate the day of your repentance;

28 But that ye would humble yourselves before the Lord, and call on his holy name, and watch and pray continually, that ye may not be tempted above that which ye can bear, and thus be led by the Holy Spirit, becoming humble, meek, submissive, patient, full of love and all long-suffering;

29 Having faith on the Lord; having a hope that ye shall receive eternal life; having the love of God always in your hearts, that ye may be lifted up at the last day and enter into his rest.

30 And may the Lord grant unto you repentance, that ye may not bring down his wrath

Why did angelic messengers frequently appear to Book of Mormon people prior to Christ's coming? (13:24–25) "Alma, some three-quarters of a century before Christ was born, posed to his son Corianton this very issue. . . .

"'Is it not as necessary that the plan of redemption should be made known unto this people as well as unto their children?

"'*Is it not as easy at this time for the Lord to send his angel to declare these glad tidings unto us as unto our children, or as after the time of his coming*' (Alma 39:17–19; emphasis added).

"In that little passage of encouragement to a wayward son, Alma gives insight as to the very special encouragement God would provide for those who were born before Christ's mortal ministry" (Holland, "Standard unto My People," 9).

In what ways might this promise that we "may not be tempted above that which [we] can bear" be misinterpreted? (13:28) "[Some] have falsely supposed that they could hurl themselves into the path of sin, enter into forbidden territory, or wander briefly from that road which is strait and narrow—and then be divinely delivered from spiritual destruction. Such people are deceived. They have bought into another of Satan's lies" (McConkie and Millet, *Doctrinal Commentary*, 3:106).

Why is this a dangerous approach to life? How will we avoid this worldly philosophy? In 1 Corinthians 10:13, what does Paul testify about this promise?

What does it mean to "enter into his rest"? (13:29) See commentary in this volume on Alma 13:6.

To what book does this verse refer? (13:31) "'This book' evidently refers to Mormon's own abridgement. The editorial summary for the tenth year, at 15:19, seems to end the entry begun by the preface to chapter nine" (Tvedtnes, "Colophons," 34–35).

Alma 14:1–8. Alma and Amulek Are Brought before the Chief Judge for Teaching the Truth

What do we learn about the people of Ammonihah from this verse? (14:1) "An important item in the religious legacy inherited by the Nephite people was the Holy Scriptures. By way of illustration, the words 'Scriptures' and 'Holy Scriptures' appear forty-one times in the Book of Mormon. . . .

"This treasury of truth apparently had not been seriously consulted by [the people of Ammonihah], however, or its precepts would not have been so outrageously violated" (Reynolds and Sjodahl, *Commentary on the Book of Mormon*, 3:214).

Why did they seek to put Alma and Amulek away in secret? (14:2–3) "The word *privily* here signifies 'privately,' 'in secret,' or 'clandestinely.' The passage suggests either that they were ashamed of what they were about to do, or else, for strategic reasons, that they thought it best to accomplish their murderous designs with as little publicity as possible" (Reynolds and Sjodahl, *Commentary on the Book of Mormon*, 3:216).

upon you, that ye may not be bound down by the chains of hell, that ye may not suffer the second death.

31 And Alma spake many more words unto the people, which are not written in this book.

CHAPTER 14

Alma and Amulek are imprisoned and smitten—The believers and their holy scriptures are burned by fire—These martyrs are received by the Lord in glory—The prison walls are rent and fall—Alma and Amulek are delivered, and their persecutors are slain. About 82–81 B.C.

1 And it came to pass after he had made an end of speaking unto the people many of them did believe on his words, and began to repent, and to search the scriptures.

2 But the more part of them were desirous that they might destroy Alma and Amulek; for they were angry with Alma, because of the plainness of his words unto Zeezrom; and they also said that Amulek had lied unto them, and had reviled against their law and also against their lawyers and judges.

3 And they were also angry with Alma and Amulek; and because they had testified so plainly against their wickedness, they sought to put them away privily.

4 But it came to pass that they did not; but they took them and bound them with strong cords, and took them before the chief judge of the land.

5 And the people went forth and witnessed against them—testifying that they had reviled against the law, and their lawyers and judges of the land, and also of all the people

that were in the land; and also testified that there was but one God, and that he should send his Son among the people, but he should not save them; and many such things did the people testify against Alma and Amulek. Now this was done before the chief judge of the land.

6 And it came to pass that Zeezrom was astonished at the words which had been spoken; and he also knew concerning the blindness of the minds, which he had caused among the people by his lying words; and his soul began to be harrowed up under a consciousness of his own guilt; yea, he began to be encircled about by the pains of hell.

7 And it came to pass that he began to cry unto the people, saying: Behold, I am guilty, and these men are spotless before God. And he began to plead for them from that time forth; but they reviled him, saying: Art thou also possessed with the devil? And they spit upon him, and cast him out from among them, and also all those who believed in the words which had been spoken by Alma and Amulek; and they cast them out, and sent men to cast stones at them.

8 And they brought their wives and children together, and whosoever believed or had been taught to believe in the word of God they caused that they should be cast into the fire; and they also brought forth their records which contained the holy scriptures, and cast them into the fire also, that they might be burned and destroyed by fire.

9 And it came to pass that they took Alma and Amulek, and carried them forth to the place of martyrdom, that they might witness the destruction of those who were consumed by fire.

What does it mean to be "harrowed up"? (14:6) "A harrow is an instrument for tilling the soil although, unlike the plow which makes a single deep furrow, a harrow has numerous teeth and covers a broader area but more shallowly. It breaks up clods and drags out vines and other vegetable encumbrances, so metaphorically, it is a powerful image of becoming submissive and humble" (Gardner, *Second Witness*, 4:232). See also commentary in this volume on 2 Nephi 9:47. ⊕

Why did the people turn on Zeezrom? (14:7) "Knowing that he has employed 'lying words,' Zeezrom's conscience is stung by the doctrines taught and the testimony borne. His effort to right the matter by defending Alma and Amulek, however, is rewarded in the same spirit in which previously he sought to abuse and confound them. Might we say that Satan is no respecter of persons—that he will turn with equal wrath upon one and all who oppose him" (McConkie and Millet, *Doctrinal Commentary*, 3:108). ⊕

What are some possible reasons why the innocent must suffer? (14:8) "Verse 8 probably qualifies for the designation as the most 'painful' passage in the Book of Mormon" (Reynolds and Sjodahl, *Commentary on the Book of Mormon*, 3:218). In what ways would you agree? How would you answer the question, "Why must the innocent suffer?" ⊕

Alma 14:9–13. Alma and Amulek Are Forced to Watch Righteous People Burn to Death

How might this account be an indictment against the city of Ammonihah? (14:9–11) "After being rejected, Alma was instructed to return to preach in the city, to give them the necessary warning that they would be destroyed if they did not repent (see Alma 8:16). Then, acting as the two required eyewitnesses (see Deuteronomy 17:6), Alma and Amulek stood and witnessed the abominable scene of the burning of the faithful, innocent wives and children of their followers (see Alma 14:9). This was a revolting experience, but it completed the case against the city and sealed its fate (see Alma 14:11)" (Welch, "Destruction of Ammonihah," 177–78). ●

Why are the righteous not exempt from suffering and judgment? (14:11) "[It] is a false idea that the Saints will escape all the judgments, whilst the wicked suffer; for all flesh is subject to suffer, and 'the righteous shall hardly escape' [see D&C 63:34]" (*Joseph Smith* [manual], 253). President Spencer W. Kimball provided this insight: "Being human, we would expel from our lives physical pain and mental anguish and assure ourselves of continual ease and comfort, but if we were to close the doors upon sorrow and distress, we might be excluding our greatest friends and benefactors. Suffering can make saints of people as they learn patience, long-suffering, and self-mastery" (*Spencer W. Kimball* [manual], 15).

Alma 14:14–22. Alma and Amulek Are Mocked, Beaten, and Abused

What is the significance of Alma and Amulek being smitten "upon their cheeks"? (14:14–22) "How similar these devils incarnate were to those who mocked the Christ! He too was smitten upon the cheek, gnashed at, and spat upon. He too was artfully questioned by unscrupulous and double-tongued lawyers and priests. He too chose to remain silent rather than dignify their cunning inquisition with answers. And he too was taunted for not having the power to save himself from the agonies of the cross" (McConkie and Millet, *Doctrinal Commentary*, 3:111). ●

10 And when Amulek saw the pains of the women and children who were consuming in the fire, he also was pained; and he said unto Alma: How can we witness this awful scene? Therefore let us stretch forth our hands, and exercise the power of God which is in us, and save them from the flames.

11 But Alma said unto him: The Spirit constraineth me that I must not stretch forth mine hand; for behold the Lord receiveth them up unto himself, in glory; and he doth suffer that they may do this thing, or that the people may do this thing unto them, according to the hardness of their hearts, that the judgments which he shall exercise upon them in his wrath may be just; and the blood of the innocent shall stand as a witness against them, yea, and cry mightily against them at the last day.

12 Now Amulek said unto Alma: Behold, perhaps they will burn us also.

13 And Alma said: Be it according to the will of the Lord. But, behold, our work is not finished; therefore they burn us not.

14 Now it came to pass that when the bodies of those who had been cast into the fire were consumed, and also the records which were cast in with them, the chief judge of the land came and stood before Alma and Amulek, as they were bound; and he smote them with his hand upon their cheeks, and said unto them: After what ye have seen, will ye preach again unto this people, that they shall be cast into a lake of fire and brimstone?

15 Behold, ye see that ye had not power to save those who had been cast into the fire; neither has God saved them because they were of thy faith. And the judge smote them again upon their cheeks, and asked: What say ye for yourselves?

16 Now this judge was after the order and faith of Nehor, who slew Gideon.

17 And it came to pass that Alma and Amulek answered him nothing; and he smote them again, and delivered them to the officers to be cast into prison.

18 And when they had been cast into prison three days, there came many lawyers, and judges, and priests, and teachers, who were of the profession of Nehor; and they came in unto the prison to see them, and they questioned them about many words; but they answered them nothing.

19 And it came to pass that the judge stood before them, and said: Why do ye not answer the words of this people? Know ye not that I have power to deliver you up unto the flames? And he commanded them to speak; but they answered nothing.

20 And it came to pass that they departed and went their ways, but came again on the morrow; and the judge also smote them again on their cheeks. And many came forth also, and smote them, saying: Will ye stand again and judge this people, and condemn

How does Nehor's profession provide yet another example of secret combinations? (14:18) "Here we see the professional hierarchy, performing in unholy combination. The Law and the Church had joined together their infamous hands to weave a steel net from which no dissenter could escape" (Reynolds and Sjodahl, *Commentary on the Book of Mormon*, 3:222).

Trials Beget Growth

President Spencer W. Kimball

By Eldon Keith Linschoten © Intellectual Reserve, Inc. Used by permission.

President Spencer W. Kimball wrote eloquently about trials and suffering:

"If we looked at mortality as the whole of existence, then pain, sorrow, failure, and short life would be calamity. But if we look upon life as an eternal thing stretching far into the premortal past and on into the eternal post-death future, then all happenings may be put in proper perspective.

"Is there not wisdom in his giving us trials that we might rise above them, responsibilities that we might achieve, work to harden our muscles, sorrows to try our souls? Are we not exposed to temptations to test our strength, sickness that we might learn patience, death that we might be immortalized and glorified?

"If all the sick for whom we pray were healed, if all the righteous were protected and the wicked destroyed, the whole program of the Father would be annulled and the basic principle of the gospel, free agency, would be ended. No man would have to live by faith.

"If joy and peace and rewards were instantaneously given the doer of good, there could be no evil—all would do good but not because of the rightness of doing good. There would be no test of strength, no development of character, no growth of powers, no free agency, only satanic controls.

"Should all prayers be immediately answered according to our selfish desires and our limited understanding, then there would be little or no suffering, sorrow, disappointment, or even death, and if these were not, there would also be no joy, success, resurrection, nor eternal life and godhood" (*Spencer W. Kimball* [manual], 15).

our law? If ye have such great power why do ye not deliver yourselves?

21 And many such things did they say unto them, gnashing their teeth upon them, and spitting upon them, and saying: How shall we look when we are damned?

22 And many such things, yea, all manner of such things did they say unto them; and thus they did mock them for many days. And they did withhold food from them that they might hunger, and water that they might thirst; and they also did take from them their clothes that they were naked; and thus they were bound with strong cords, and confined in prison.

23 And it came to pass after they had thus suffered for many days, (and it was on the twelfth day, in the tenth month, in the tenth year of the reign of the judges over the people of Nephi) that the chief judge over the land of Ammonihah and many of their teachers and their lawyers went in unto the prison where Alma and Amulek were bound with cords.

Alma 14:23–29. Alma and Amulek Are Set Free by the Power of God

Where was the land of Ammonihah? (14:23)
The land of Ammonihah was the "country immediately surrounding the city of the same name. It lay between the River Sidon and the Pacific Ocean, but exactly where cannot be determined" (Reynolds and Sjodahl, *Commentary on the Book of Mormon,* 3:146). "The land was to the north of Melek. No intervening lands are mentioned. There is wilderness to the west of Ammonihah. The general assumption . . . is that Ammonihah was to the west as well. The text is ambigious as to exactly where in the north Ammonihah was. It has been assumed that Ammonihah was to the west because Melek was on the west of Zarahemlah. However . . . Alma could [have] gone north from Melek but ended up east of Zarahemla.

"There were 3 other lands adjacent to Ammonihah, Noah, Sidom and Aaron" (Book of Mormon Central, "Ammonihah").

How do the attitudes of these wicked men remind us of those who persecuted and mocked Jesus Christ? (14:24) "Of one thing we have perfect assurance—the last thing wanted by those who demand signs is signs; the last thing wanted by those who demand evidence is evidence. A world of signs and evidences would not soften their hearts. The leaders of the Jews sought signs and Christ gave them signs sufficient to convince any people, yet they rejected him (see 2 Nephi 10:4)" (McConkie and Millet, *Doctrinal Commentary,* 3:113).

24 And the chief judge stood before them, and smote them again, and said unto them: If ye have the power of God deliver yourselves from these bands, and then we will believe that the Lord will destroy this people according to your words.

25 And it came to pass that they all went forth and smote them, saying the same words, even until the last; and when the last had spoken unto them the power of God was upon Alma and Amulek, and they rose and stood upon their feet.

26 And Alma cried, saying: How long shall we suffer these great afflictions, O Lord? O Lord, give us strength according to our faith which is in Christ, even unto deliverance. And they broke the cords with which they were bound; and when the people saw this, they began to flee, for the fear of destruction had come upon them.

27 And it came to pass that so great was their fear that they fell to the earth, and did not obtain the outer door of the prison; and the earth shook mightily, and the walls of the prison were rent in twain, so that they fell to the earth; and the chief judge, and the lawyers, and priests, and teachers, who smote upon Alma and Amulek, were slain by the fall thereof.

28 And Alma and Amulek came forth out of the prison, and they were not hurt; for the Lord had granted unto them power, according to their faith which was in Christ. And they straightway came forth out of the prison; and they were loosed from their bands; and the prison had fallen to the earth, and every soul within the walls thereof, save it were Alma and Amulek, was slain; and they straightway came forth into the city.

29 Now the people having heard a great noise came running together by multitudes to know the cause of it; and when they saw Alma and Amulek coming forth out of the prison, and the walls thereof had fallen to the earth, they were struck with great fear, and fled from the presence of Alma and Amulek even as a goat fleeth with her young from two lions; and thus they did flee from the presence of Alma and Amulek.

What can we learn from Alma and Amulek's ministry in Ammonihah? (14:26–28) Referring to the inspired speeches delivered by Alma and Amulek to the people of Ammonihah, Elder Jeffrey R. Holland wrote: "This is a significant amount of information about the Savior's ministry, especially when we realize it was given in very hostile circumstances and to a very threatening audience." Yet, "in that cruel and violent circumstance, it was faith in Christ that gave Alma and Amulek their strength" (*Christ and the New Covenant*, 116). In other words, the faith that stirred up the wicked enemies of Alma and Amulek also delivered them from trial.

What do the events in Ammonihah illustrate about agency? (14:28–29) The influence of Ammonihah's wicked judges, teachers, and lawyers caused the deaths of many believers. However, their wicked choices eventually brought them disastrous consequences. All choices—both good and evil—have consequences. Agency is a gift from God. "Your use of this gift determines your happiness or misery in this life and in the life to come. You are free to choose and act, but you are not free to choose the consequences of your actions. The consequences may not be immediate, but they will always follow. Choices of good and righteousness lead to happiness, peace, and eternal life, while choices of sin and evil eventually lead to heartache and misery" (*True to the Faith*, 12).

Alma 15:1–5. Alma and Amulek Find Zeezrom Sick Because of His Wickedness

What is the relationship between spiritual and physical sickness? (15:3–4) "There is another part of us, not so tangible, but quite as real as our physical body. This tangible part of us is described as mind, emotion, intellect, temperament, and many other things. Very seldom is it described as spiritual.

"But there is a *spirit* in man; to ignore it is to ignore reality. There are spiritual disorders, too, and spiritual diseases that can cause intense suffering.

"The body and spirit of man are bound together. Often, very often, when there are disorders, it is very difficult to tell which is which" (Packer, "Balm of Gilead," 59). ◉

CHAPTER 15

Alma and Amulek go to Sidom and establish a church—Alma heals Zeezrom, who joins the Church—Many are baptized, and the Church prospers—Alma and Amulek go to Zarahemla. About 81 B.C.

1 And it came to pass that Alma and Amulek were commanded to depart out of that city; and they departed, and came out even into the land of Sidom; and behold, there they found all the people who had departed out of the land of Ammonihah, who had been cast out and stoned, because they believed in the words of Alma.

2 And they related unto them all that had happened unto their wives and children, and also concerning themselves, and of their power of deliverance.

3 And also Zeezrom lay sick at Sidom, with a burning fever, which was caused by the great tribulations of his mind on account of his wickedness, for he supposed that Alma and Amulek were no more; and he supposed that they had been slain because of his iniquity. And this great sin, and his many other sins, did harrow up his mind until it did become exceedingly sore, having no deliverance; therefore he began to be scorched with a burning heat.

4 Now, when he heard that Alma and Amulek were in the land of Sidom, his heart began to take courage; and he sent a message immediately unto them, desiring them to come unto him.

5 And it came to pass that they went immediately, obeying the message which he had sent unto them; and they went in unto the house unto Zeezrom; and they found him upon his bed, sick, being very low with a burning fever; and his mind also was exceedingly sore because of his iniquities; and when

he saw them he stretched forth his hand, and besought them that they would heal him.

6 And it came to pass that Alma said unto him, taking him by the hand: Believest thou in the power of Christ unto salvation?

7 And he answered and said: Yea, I believe all the words that thou hast taught.

8 And Alma said: If thou believest in the redemption of Christ thou canst be healed.

9 And he said: Yea, I believe according to thy words.

10 And then Alma cried unto the Lord, saying: O Lord our God, have mercy on this man, and heal him according to his faith which is in Christ.

11 And when Alma had said these words, Zeezrom leaped upon his feet, and began to walk; and this was done to the great astonishment of all the people; and the knowledge of this went forth throughout all the land of Sidom.

12 And Alma baptized Zeezrom unto the Lord; and he began from that time forth to preach unto the people.

Alma 15:6–12. Alma Blesses and Baptizes Zeezrom

What can we infer from Alma's treatment of Zeezrom? (15:6) "One can sense the implied reconciliation and goodwill of Alma's gesture when he takes hold of Zeezrom's outstretched hand. This sequence of outstretched hand followed by contact seems to indicate that the gesture expresses not only a partial bridging of social distance but also a desire for acceptance through contact. One can posit that the desire for contact as a symbol of acceptance is a consistent aspect of this gesture in the Book of Mormon" (Calabro, "'Stretch Forth Thy Hand and Prophesy,'" 49) ⊕

What can heal the sin-sick soul? (15:6–12) "The atoning sacrifice of Christ, and our full acceptance of it, is the spiritual antidote that heals the wounded soul. It is such an antidote that replaces despair with hope, darkness with light, and turmoil with peace. It was this antidote that worked for Zeezrom. He lay sick with a burning fever. He recounted his many sins, believing there was 'no deliverance' for what he had done. Then Alma posed the tide-turning question, 'Believest thou in the power of Christ unto salvation?' . . . The response was positive. The healing that followed was not only physical but spiritual as well. The prerequisite was a belief in the Atonement of Jesus Christ" (Callister, *Infinite Atonement*, 203). ⊕

What happened to Zeezrom after he was healed? (15:10–11) "Zeezrom was healed of his afflictions due to his belief in Christ. He became a faithful servant of God, spending his time preaching among the people. His name and teachings are referred to by a later Book of Mormon recorder (see Hel. 5:41). There was a city named for him (see Alma 56:13–14)" (Black, *400 Questions and Answers*, 153).

What does Zeezrom's transformation teach us about individuals who seem, at present, hopelessly antagonistic to the truth? (15:12) How might we use this account to help someone who thinks they could never be forgiven for their sins? While we all realize that in Heavenly Father's plan not everyone who is blessed is healed from sickness, what other kinds of healing can come even when physical healing does not? For example, in what ways was Zeezrom healed beyond his physical illness?

Alma 15:13–15. Alma Establishes the Church in Sidom

Did teachers have authority to baptize among the Nephites? (15:13) "There were apparently no Levites among the Nephites. The Nephites were of Joseph and apparently didn't have any Aaronites or Levites, who would have been natural heirs to the Aaronic Priesthood. However, they obeyed the law of Moses. Therefore, we conclude that because the Nephites had the Melchizedek Priesthood, they could do everything the Aaronic Priesthood could do. Since the Aaronic Priesthood was limited to the sons of Aaron, the Nephites could not have functioned in the law of Moses unless they had had the Melchizedek Priesthood" (*Selected Writings of Robert J. Matthews*, 189).

What is the consequence of hard-heartedness? (15:15) "Nephi teaches us, 'When a man speaketh by the power of the Holy Ghost the power of the Holy Ghost carrieth [the message] unto the hearts of the children of men' (2 Nephi 33:1). Please notice how the power of the Spirit carries the message *unto* but not necessarily *into* the heart. A teacher can explain, demonstrate, persuade, and testify, and do so with great spiritual power and effectiveness. Ultimately, however, the content of a message and the witness of the Holy Ghost penetrate into the heart only if a receiver allows them to enter" (Bednar, "Seek Learning by Faith," 1). ⊕

Alma 15:16–19. Alma Provides for Amulek's Needs

Why did Amulek give up so much? (15:16) "Let us here observe, that a religion that does not require the sacrifice of all things never has power sufficient to produce the faith necessary unto life and salvation. . . .

"It is in vain for persons to fancy to themselves that they are heirs with those . . . who have offered their all in sacrifice, and by this means obtain faith in God and favor with him so as to obtain eternal life, unless they, in like manner, offer unto him the same sacrifice" (*Lectures on Faith*, 69). ⊕

13 And Alma established a church in the land of Sidom, and consecrated priests and teachers in the land, to baptize unto the Lord whosoever were desirous to be baptized.

14 And it came to pass that they were many; for they did flock in from all the region round about Sidom, and were baptized.

15 But as to the people that were in the land of Ammonihah, they yet remained a hard-hearted and a stiffnecked people; and they repented not of their sins, ascribing all the power of Alma and Amulek to the devil; for they were of the profession of Nehor, and did not believe in the repentance of their sins.

16 And it came to pass that Alma and Amulek, Amulek having forsaken all his gold, and silver, and his precious things, which were in the land of Ammonihah, for the word of God, he being rejected by those who were once his friends and also by his father and his kindred;

17 Therefore, after Alma having established the church at Sidom, seeing a great check, yea, seeing that the people were checked as to the pride of their hearts, and began to humble themselves before God, and began to assemble themselves together at their sanctuaries to worship God before the altar, watching and praying continually, that they might be delivered from Satan, and from death, and from destruction—

18 Now as I said, Alma having seen all these things, therefore he took Amulek and came over to the land of Zarahemla, and took him to his own house, and did administer unto him in his tribulations, and strengthened him in the Lord.

19 And thus ended the tenth year of the reign of the judges over the people of Nephi.

CHAPTER 16

The Lamanites destroy the people of Ammonihah—Zoram leads the Nephites to victory over the Lamanites—Alma and Amulek and many others preach the word—They teach that after His Resurrection Christ will appear to the Nephites. About 81–77 B.C.

1 And it came to pass in the eleventh year of the reign of the judges over the people of Nephi, on the fifth day of the second month, there having been much peace in the land of Zarahemla, there having been no wars nor contentions for a certain number of years, even until the fifth day of the second month in the eleventh year, there was a cry of war heard throughout the land.

2 For behold, the armies of the Lamanites had come in upon the wilderness side, into the borders of the land, even into the city of Ammonihah, and began to slay the people and destroy the city.

3 And now it came to pass, before the Nephites could raise a sufficient army to drive them out of the land, they had destroyed the people who were in the city of Ammonihah, and also some around the borders of Noah, and taken others captive into the wilderness.

Why did Alma take Amulek home with him to Zarahemla? (15:18) "The turbulent story of a great missionary episode here comes to a gentle close. The anguish through which Alma and Amulek had passed had knit them inseparably together. Their joint missionary activities had been plentifully rewarded. Their harvest had been rich; their influence for good, almost limitless. Alma and Amulek, through the tears of affliction, could look into their hearts and find great joy" (Reynolds and Sjodahl, *Commentary on the Book of Mormon*, 3:231–32).

Alma 16:1–3. The Lamanites Destroy Ammonihah and Take Many Nephite Prisoners

What is significant about the eleventh year, second month, and fifth day in relation to war in the Book of Mormon? (16:1) "When we look carefully at what the Book of Mormon says about war, we find that the many military activities reported did not take place just anytime during the calendar year. Rather, they occurred according to a definite pattern. Certain months were war months while others were not. The complete consistency of this pattern reminds us of how many details the writers of this scripture kept straight....

"For example, Alma 16:1 says that a Lamanite army attacked around the city of Ammonihah on 'the fifth day of the second month in the eleventh year' of the reign of the judges over the Nephites" (Sorenson, "Seasons of War, Seasons of Peace," 249).

Why did the Lamanites attack the unsuspecting Nephites in Ammonihah? (16:2) The Lamanites had been angry with the Nephites for having taken in the people of Ammon, "therefore they swore vengeance upon [them]" (Alma 25:1). Unfortunately for the city of Ammonihah, "being . . . located on the contry's outer fringe, would of necessity have been the first city attacked by the invading horde" (Reynolds and Sjodahl, *Commentary on the Book of Mormon*, 3:233).

Alma 16:4–11. Zoram Leads the Nephites to Victory over the Lamanites

What is the "spirit of prophecy"? (16:5–6) The "spirit of prophecy" is described by Elder Bruce R. McConkie: "Those having prophetic status are people who know by personal revelation that Jesus Christ is the Son of the living God who was crucified for the sins of the world. Having thus gained revelation from the Holy Spirit, they are in a position to gain added revelations that foretell the future or set forth the mind and will and purposes of the Lord in whatever respect is pleasing to Him whose servants they are" (*New Witness*, 349). Think about the challenges you face in life. Perhaps you have challenging trials and hardships. How could following the counsel of modern prophets help you with the struggles you face?

Why was the apostate city of Ammonihah destroyed? (16:9–11) "Alma 16:9–11 records the utter destruction of the wicked city of Ammonihah by Lamanite soldiers. Recent research has uncovered several striking affinities between that account and the ancient Israelite law regarding the annihilation of apostate cities (see Deuteronomy 13:12–16)....

4 Now it came to pass that the Nephites were desirous to obtain those who had been carried away captive into the wilderness.

5 Therefore, he that had been appointed chief captain over the armies of the Nephites, (and his name was Zoram, and he had two sons, Lehi and Aha)—now Zoram and his two sons, knowing that Alma was high priest over the church, and having heard that he had the spirit of prophecy, therefore they went unto him and desired of him to know whither the Lord would that they should go into the wilderness in search of their brethren, who had been taken captive by the Lamanites.

6 And it came to pass that Alma inquired of the Lord concerning the matter. And Alma returned and said unto them: Behold, the Lamanites will cross the river Sidon in the south wilderness, away up beyond the borders of the land of Manti. And behold there shall ye meet them, on the east of the river Sidon, and there the Lord will deliver unto thee thy brethren who have been taken captive by the Lamanites.

7 And it came to pass that Zoram and his sons crossed over the river Sidon, with their armies, and marched away beyond the borders of Manti into the south wilderness, which was on the east side of the river Sidon.

8 And they came upon the armies of the Lamanites, and the Lamanites were scattered and driven into the wilderness; and they took their brethren who had been taken captive by the Lamanites, and there was not one soul of them had been lost that were taken captive. And they were brought by their brethren to possess their own lands.

9 And thus ended the eleventh year of the judges, the Lamanites having been driven out of the land, and the people of Ammonihah were destroyed; yea, every living soul of the Ammonihahites was destroyed, and also their

great city, which they said God could not destroy, because of its greatness.

10 But behold, in one day it was left desolate; and the carcasses were mangled by dogs and wild beasts of the wilderness.

11 Nevertheless, after many days their dead bodies were heaped up upon the face of the earth, and they were covered with a shallow covering. And now so great was the scent thereof that the people did not go in to possess the land of Ammonihah for many years. And it was called Desolation of Nehors; for they were of the profession of Nehor, who were slain; and their lands remained desolate.

12 And the Lamanites did not come again to war against the Nephites until the fourteenth year of the reign of the judges over the people of Nephi. And thus for three years did the people of Nephi have continual peace in all the land.

13 And Alma and Amulek went forth preaching repentance to the people in their temples, and in their sanctuaries, and also in their synagogues, which were built after the manner of the Jews.

14 And as many as would hear their words, unto them they did impart the word of God, without any respect of persons, continually.

15 And thus did Alma and Amulek go forth, and also many more who had been chosen for the work, to preach the word throughout all the land. And the establishment of the church became general throughout the land, in all the region round about, among all the people of the Nephites.

"While Alma clearly lacked both the desire and the power to have the city of Ammonihah destroyed by a Nephite military force, . . . Alma carefully recorded and documented the fact that the inhabitants of Ammonihah had satisfied every element of the crime of being an apostate city. When the justice of God destroyed that city, Alma effectively showed in the record that this fate befell them in accordance with divine law" (Welch, "Destruction of Ammonihah," 176–77). ✛

What is the "Desolation of Nehors"? (16:11)
"Ammonihah and Nehor are symbols—history as prophecy. Ammonihah and Nehor were to the nation of the Nephites what the Book of Mormon is to us—a warning voice! They were types casting shadows upon the cities of Zarahemla, Moroni, Moronihah, Gilgal, Onihah, Mocum, Jerusalem, Gadiandi, Gadiomnah, Jacob, Gimgimno, Jacobugath, Laman, Josh, Gad, and Kishkumen, all of which, like Nehor, had the blood of the prophets and the Saints upon their hands, and all of which were destroyed before the coming of Christ to the Nephites in the meridian dispensation (see 3 Nephi 8, 9)" (McConkie and Millet, *Doctrinal Commentary*, 3:119). ✛

Alma 16:12–17. Alma, Amulek, and Others Preach the Gospel to All Who Will Listen

What does this passage tell us about worship in the new world and the old? (16:13) "The reference to temples in the plural is of special interest because virtually all non-Mormon sources insist that for Israel there was to be but one temple, and that in Jerusalem. We have no interest in reviewing scholarly arguments, but simply observe that such an idea was not shared by the family of Lehi, who were in the Americas only a relatively short time before they began building a temple (see 2 Nephi 5:16)" (McConkie and Millet, *Doctrinal Commentary*, 3:120–21). ✛

Why does the Lord require equality and unity among his people? (16:16) Along with Alma 16:16, consider the following passages: John 17:11, 20–22; 4 Nephi 1:2–3, 15–16; Doctrine and Covenants 38:27; 78:6–7. How does equality and unity invite the Spirit? Why does inequality and contention drive away the Spirit? What does the Spirit suggest we could do to create more unity and equality in our homes, our wards, and our communities?

What is the "true vine"? (16:17) "Of all the analogies and parallelisms which make their appearance in the Scriptures, perhaps none is more frequent than that of the tree or vine, which represents Christ, or the Church, or the source of all truth and authority [see John 15:1–4]....

"Probably the most elaborate and extended analogy developed anywhere in the Scriptures is that of the olive tree, as expounded in Chapters 5 and 6 of the Book of Jacob" (Reynolds and Sjodahl, *Commentary on the Book of Mormon*, 3:240).

Alma 16:18–21. Alma and Other Priests Preach against Evil and Testify of Christ

How might the destruction of Ammonihah, in fulfillment of prophecy, apply to us? (16:21) "Perhaps the central lesson [in Alma 9–16] is that there is a God in heaven to whom people on earth are accountable. He loves us. He has implemented a 'plan of redemption' whereby we can 'be lifted up at the last day and enter into his rest' (Alma 12:33; 13:29). Through his Spirit he reaches out to all: the righteous exemplified in these chapters by Alma and the Ammonihahite believers; the temporarily distracted but decent people like Amulek; and even enemies to the cause of truth, whether they will repent as did Zeezrom, or reject the invitation as did most of the people of Ammonihah. And everyone is accountable for how they respond to that Spirit" (Dahl, "Plan of Redemption—Taught and Rejected," 316). ☉

16 And there was no inequality among them; the Lord did pour out his Spirit on all the face of the land to prepare the minds of the children of men, or to prepare their hearts to receive the word which should be taught among them at the time of his coming—

17 That they might not be hardened against the word, that they might not be unbelieving, and go on to destruction, but that they might receive the word with joy, and as a branch be grafted into the true vine, that they might enter into the rest of the Lord their God.

18 Now those priests who did go forth among the people did preach against all lyings, and deceivings, and envyings, and strifes, and malice, and revilings, and stealing, robbing, plundering, murdering, committing adultery, and all manner of lasciviousness, crying that these things ought not so to be—

19 Holding forth things which must shortly come; yea, holding forth the coming of the Son of God, his sufferings and death, and also the resurrection of the dead.

20 And many of the people did inquire concerning the place where the Son of God should come; and they were taught that he would appear unto them after his resurrection; and this the people did hear with great joy and gladness.

21 And now after the church had been established throughout all the land—having got the victory over the devil, and the word of God being preached in its purity in all the land, and the Lord pouring out his blessings upon the people—thus ended the fourteenth year of the reign of the judges over the people of Nephi.

An account of the sons of Mosiah, who rejected their rights to the kingdom for the word of God, and went up to the land of Nephi to preach to the Lamanites; their sufferings and deliverance—according to the record of Alma.

Comprising chapters 17 through 27.

CHAPTER 17

The sons of Mosiah have the spirit of prophecy and of revelation—They go their several ways to declare the word to the Lamanites—Ammon goes to the land of Ishmael and becomes the servant of King Lamoni—Ammon saves the king's flocks and slays his enemies at the water of Sebus. Verses 1–3, about 77 B.C.; verse 4, about 91–77 B.C.; and verses 5–39, about 91 B.C.

1 And now it came to pass that as Alma was journeying from the land of Gideon southward, away to the land of Manti, behold, to his astonishment, he met with the sons of Mosiah journeying towards the land of Zarahemla.

2 Now these sons of Mosiah were with Alma at the time the angel first appeared unto him; therefore Alma did rejoice exceedingly to see his brethren; and what added more to his joy, they were still his brethren in the Lord; yea, and they had waxed strong in the knowledge of the truth; for they were men of a sound understanding and they had searched the scriptures diligently, that they might know the word of God.

3 But this is not all; they had given themselves to much prayer, and fasting; therefore

Superscription to Alma 17

The superscription to Alma 17 was part of the ancient record translated by the Prophet Joseph Smith and dictated by him to his scribe (see also, for example, 2 Nephi, Mosiah 9, and Alma 36).

"This [superscription, or preface,] is part of the 1830 edition.... Mormon specifies that, while it discusses the sons of Mosiah, it comes from Alma's record. A similar preface appears before our chapter 21; although its source is not cited, it must also be from Alma's record. These prefaces inform us that Alma's record contains either insertions or copies of other source records. The two separate headings give accounts from two separate sub-records contained in the larger record of Alma. It is also possible that the 'record' was oral rather than written" (Gardner, *Second Witness*, 4:259).

The italicized words "Comprising chapters 17 through 27" were not part of the ancient record but were added later to printed editions of the Book of Mormon.

Alma 17:1–5. The Sons of Mosiah Prepare Spiritually to Serve a Mission among the Lamanites

Why is scripture study vital in our day? (17:2–3)
"In order to come unto Christ and be perfected in him, each person needs to receive a testimony of the Lord's words. Some individuals falter because they fail to open the books, others because they read casually. As one would expect, there is a difference between diligent searching or 'pondering over the scriptures' and casual reading....

"There are certain blessings obtained when one searches the scriptures. As a person studies the words of the Lord and obeys them, he or she draws closer to the Savior and obtains a greater desire to live a righteous life. The power to resist temptation increases, and spiritual weaknesses are overcome. Spiritual wounds are healed" (Bateman, "Coming unto Christ," 27). ☉

What is the "altar of God"? (17:4) The altar of God is "a place of worship, most frequently associated with making sacrifices and entering into or renewing covenants. Always found in temples, altars are a place of the divine presence. Anciently, they were built on raised ground so that there was a ritual ascent as one approached the place of worship. Among the Book of Mormon peoples they were a place where one called upon God and confessed sins (Alma 17:4). In the Bible they are clearly seen as the place from which prayers were to ascend to heaven" (McConkie, *Gospel Symbolism*, 251).

Why did these faithful missionaries suffer such trials? (17:5) "So often in life a deserved blessing is quickly followed by a needed stretching. Spiritual exhilaration may be quickly followed by a vexation or temptation. Were it otherwise, extended spiritual reveries or immunities from adversity might induce in us a regrettable forgetfulness of others in deep need. The sharp, side-by-side contrast of the sweet and the bitter is essential until the very end of this brief, mortal experience. Meanwhile, even routine, daily life provides sufficient sandpaper to smooth our crustiness and polish our rough edges, if we are meek" (Maxwell, "Enduring Well," 7). ✦

Alma 17:6–17. The Sons of Mosiah Set Out on Their Mission to the Lamanites

they had the spirit of prophecy, and the spirit of revelation, and when they taught, they taught with power and authority of God.

4 And they had been teaching the word of God for the space of fourteen years among the Lamanites, having had much success in bringing many to the knowledge of the truth; yea, by the power of their words many were brought before the altar of God, to call on his name and confess their sins before him.

5 Now these are the circumstances which attended them in their journeyings, for they had many afflictions; they did suffer much, both in body and in mind, such as hunger, thirst and fatigue, and also much labor in the spirit.

6 Now these were their journeyings: Having taken leave of their father, Mosiah, in the first year of the judges; having refused the kingdom which their father was desirous to confer upon them, and also this was the minds of the people;

7 Nevertheless they departed out of the land of Zarahemla, and took their swords, and their spears, and their bows, and their arrows, and their slings; and this they did that they might provide food for themselves while in the wilderness.

8 And thus they departed into the wilderness with their numbers which they had selected, to go up to the land of Nephi, to preach the word of God unto the Lamanites.

9 And it came to pass that they journeyed many days in the wilderness, and they fasted much and prayed much that the Lord would grant unto them a portion of his Spirit to go with them, and abide with them, that they might be an instrument in the hands of God to bring, if it were possible, their brethren, the Lamanites, to the knowledge of the truth, to the knowledge of the baseness of the traditions of their fathers, which were not correct.

10 And it came to pass that the Lord did visit them with his Spirit, and said unto them: Be comforted. And they were comforted.

11 And the Lord said unto them also: Go forth among the Lamanites, thy brethren, and establish my word; yet ye shall be patient in long-suffering and afflictions, that ye may show forth good examples unto them in me, and I will make an instrument of thee in my hands unto the salvation of many souls.

12 And it came to pass that the hearts of the sons of Mosiah, and also those who were with them, took courage to go forth unto the Lamanites to declare unto them the word of God.

13 And it came to pass when they had arrived in the borders of the land of the Lamanites, that they separated themselves and departed one from another, trusting in the Lord that they should meet again at the close of their harvest; for they supposed that great was the work which they had undertaken.

14 And assuredly it was great, for they had undertaken to preach the word of God to a wild and a hardened and a ferocious people; a people who delighted in murdering the Nephites, and robbing and plundering them; and their hearts were set upon riches, or upon gold and silver, and precious stones; yet

How can we become instruments in God's hands? (17:9) "I have learned that a person does not need to have a Church calling, an invitation to help someone, or even good health to become an instrument in God's hands.... The prophets and the scriptures teach us how.

"First of all, we must have love for God's children. When the lawyer asked the Savior, 'Master, which is the great commandment?' the Savior replied:

"'Thou shalt love the Lord thy God with all thy heart, and with all thy soul, and with all thy mind.

"'This is the first and great commandment.

"'And the second is like unto it, Thou shalt love thy neighbour as thyself' (Matthew 22:36–39)" (Clarke, "Becoming Instruments in the Hands of God," 97–98). ◑

How do we trust in the Lord? (17:13) "This life is an experience in profound trust—trust in Jesus Christ, trust in His teachings, trust in our capacity as led by the Holy Spirit to obey those teachings for happiness now and for a purposeful, supremely happy eternal existence. To trust means to obey willingly without knowing the end from the beginning (see Prov. 3:5–7). To produce fruit, your trust in the Lord must be more powerful and enduring than your confidence in your own personal feelings and experience" (Scott, "Trust in the Lord," 17). ◑

Where did the philosophy of murder for the purpose of getting gain originate? (17:14) From the very beginning Satan taught Cain the "great secret, that I may murder and get gain" (Moses 5:31). Then with that philosophy he killed his brother Abel and said, "Surely the flocks of my brother falleth into my hands" (Moses 5:33). Where in our day do you see people, groups, organizations, whether private or public, that are willing to cause or allow harm to others as long as there is profit in it? What can you do to avoid being a part of that Satan-inspired philosophy?

How important is it for us to understand God's plan and Christ's role in that plan? (17:16) "The center of the plan is the Lord Jesus Christ. Reject or ignore Him, and the great plan of happiness cannot function in your behalf. His life was dedicated in His premortal existence, through mortality, and even on into the eternal worlds to establishing the Father's plan to our blessing and benefit. The cost to the Master was monumental. Think of the pain of Gethsemane and of His suffering on Calvary. This should give us some concept of the enormous importance of the plan of redemption" (Porter, "Our Destiny," 65). ☉

Alma 17:18–25. Ammon Travels to the Land of Ishmael and Becomes a Servant to King Lamoni

How are missionaries set apart and blessed today? (17:18) "Today, all missionaries are set apart and given individual, distinctive blessings. Most missionaries have also had patriarchal blessings giving individual guidance and promises. These personal guidelines will bring success to each missionary. [We] see the effectiveness of [these] requirements in the lives of the sons of Mosiah and those who went with them" (Nyman, *Record of Alma*, 237).

they sought to obtain these things by murdering and plundering, that they might not labor for them with their own hands.

15 Thus they were a very indolent people, many of whom did worship idols, and the curse of God had fallen upon them because of the traditions of their fathers; notwithstanding the promises of the Lord were extended unto them on the conditions of repentance.

16 Therefore, this was the cause for which the sons of Mosiah had undertaken the work, that perhaps they might bring them unto repentance; that perhaps they might bring them to know of the plan of redemption.

17 Therefore they separated themselves one from another, and went forth among them, every man alone, according to the word and power of God which was given unto him.

18 Now Ammon being the chief among them, or rather he did administer unto them, and he departed from them, after having blessed them according to their several stations, having imparted the word of God unto them, or administered unto them before his departure; and thus they took their several journeys throughout the land.

19 And Ammon went to the land of Ishmael, the land being called after the sons of Ishmael, who also became Lamanites.

20 And as Ammon entered the land of Ishmael, the Lamanites took him and bound him, as was their custom to bind all the Nephites who fell into their hands, and carry them before the king; and thus it was left to the pleasure of the king to slay them, or to retain them in captivity, or to cast them into prison, or to cast them out of his land, according to his will and pleasure.

21 And thus Ammon was carried before the king who was over the land of Ishmael; and his name was Lamoni; and he was a descendant of Ishmael.

22 And the king inquired of Ammon if it were his desire to dwell in the land among the Lamanites, or among his people.

23 And Ammon said unto him: Yea, I desire to dwell among this people for a time; yea, and perhaps until the day I die.

24 And it came to pass that king Lamoni was much pleased with Ammon, and caused that his bands should be loosed; and he would that Ammon should take one of his daughters to wife.

25 But Ammon said unto him: Nay, but I will be thy servant. Therefore Ammon became a servant to king Lamoni. And it came to pass that he was set among other servants to watch the flocks of Lamoni, according to the custom of the Lamanites.

26 And after he had been in the service of the king three days, as he was with the Lamanitish servants going forth with their flocks to the place of water, which was called the water of Sebus, and all the Lamanites drive their flocks hither, that they may have water—

27 Therefore, as Ammon and the servants of the king were driving forth their flocks to this place of water, behold, a certain number of the Lamanites, who had been with their flocks to water, stood and scattered the flocks of Ammon and the servants of the king, and they scattered them insomuch that they fled many ways.

Why would Lamoni offer one of his daughters to a hated Nephite? (17:24) "It would have been a political coup, of course, for Lamoni to marry his daughter to a Nephite prince. But the issue is more complex than we might appreciate at first. Both men seemed to understand that Ammon's new status in the Lamanite realm could be linked to Ammon's former status back home, that of a prince. But Ammon refused to allow his royal standing to enter into the discussion" (Brown, *Voices from the Dust*, 95).

How was Ammon a type or symbol of Jesus Christ? (17:25) "In retrospect, one recognizes that the temptations placed before Ammon were the same as those that would later be offered to Christ in a more enticing manner. . . . Like the Savior, Ammon did not give in to these worldly pleasures. Both the Savior and Ammon had greater missions to accomplish" (Fronk, "Show Forth Good Examples in Me," 328). ⊕

Alma 17:26–39. Ammon Shows Forth the Power of God by Saving the King's Flocks

What did Ammon do to create a teaching moment in order to share the gospel? (17:28–29) "The servants of the Lord pray and petition the heavens for teaching moments, for those special occasions when the power and goodness of God and his word can be manifest. The spirit of readiness and receptivity must be had by those outside the faith before the message of truth can be delivered and accepted" (McConkie and Millet, *Doctrinal Commentary*, 3:131).

How does this story confirm that the Book of Mormon is an ancient book and not simply Joseph Smith's creation? (17:33) "How could [the Lamanites] get away with that? Didn't [the king] have enough men to protect them if this happened regularly? Well, for one thing the Lamanites played the game for sport; it was more than meat that they were after, for 'they delighted in the destruction of their brethren; and for this cause they stood to scatter the flocks of the king' (Alma 17:35). They thought it was great sport. The Arabs have a saying, 'If we cease *ghaza*, we will cease to live. A *ghaza* is a *raid;* our word *raid* is from the Arabic *ghaza*. They must raid or life isn't worth living. 'Life is raiding'" (Nibley, *Teachings of the Book of Mormon*, 2:368). ⊕

28 Now the servants of the king began to murmur, saying: Now the king will slay us, as he has our brethren because their flocks were scattered by the wickedness of these men. And they began to weep exceedingly, saying: Behold, our flocks are scattered already.

29 Now they wept because of the fear of being slain. Now when Ammon saw this his heart was swollen within him with joy; for, said he, I will show forth my power unto these my fellow-servants, or the power which is in me, in restoring these flocks unto the king, that I may win the hearts of these my fellow-servants, that I may lead them to believe in my words.

30 And now, these were the thoughts of Ammon, when he saw the afflictions of those whom he termed to be his brethren.

31 And it came to pass that he flattered them by his words, saying: My brethren, be of good cheer and let us go in search of the flocks, and we will gather them together and bring them back unto the place of water; and thus we will preserve the flocks unto the king and he will not slay us.

32 And it came to pass that they went in search of the flocks, and they did follow Ammon, and they rushed forth with much swiftness and did head the flocks of the king, and did gather them together again to the place of water.

33 And those men again stood to scatter their flocks; but Ammon said unto his brethren: Encircle the flocks round about that they flee not; and I go and contend with these men who do scatter our flocks.

34 Therefore, they did as Ammon commanded them, and he went forth and stood to contend with those who stood by the waters of Sebus; and they were in number not a few.

35 Therefore they did not fear Ammon, for they supposed that one of their men could slay him according to their pleasure, for they knew not that the Lord had promised Mosiah that he would deliver his sons out of their hands; neither did they know anything concerning the Lord; therefore they delighted in the destruction of their brethren; and for this cause they stood to scatter the flocks of the king.

36 But Ammon stood forth and began to cast stones at them with his sling; yea, with mighty power he did sling stones amongst them; and thus he slew a certain number of them insomuch that they began to be astonished at his power; nevertheless they were angry because of the slain of their brethren, and they were determined that he should fall; therefore, seeing that they could not hit him with their stones, they came forth with clubs to slay him.

37 But behold, every man that lifted his club to smite Ammon, he smote off their arms with his sword; for he did withstand their blows by smiting their arms with the edge of his sword, insomuch that they began to be astonished, and began to flee before him; yea, and they were not few in number; and he caused them to flee by the strength of his arm.

38 Now six of them had fallen by the sling, but he slew none save it were their leader with his sword; and he smote off as many of their arms as were lifted against him, and they were not a few.

39 And when he had driven them afar off, he returned and they watered their flocks and returned them to the pasture of the king, and then went in unto the king, bearing the arms which had been smitten off by the sword of Ammon, of those who sought to slay him; and they were carried in unto the king for a testimony of the things which they had done.

How was the Lord's protection of Ammon similar to another well-known Book of Mormon account? (17:33–39) Ammon's miraculous protection paralleled the protection offered to the sons of Helaman. Both accounts illustrate the Lord's fulfillment of His promise of divine deliverance. Speaking of the stripling warriors, one writer observed, "Their faith in their mothers' words echoed the same courage that Ammon . . . displayed at the waters of Sebus against impossible odds (Alma 17:29–37). Just like the stripling warriors, Ammon faced the Lamanites armed with little more than the promise [to] a righteous parent (Alma 17:35; Mosiah 28:7–8)" (Bassett, "Nephi's Freedom Thesis and the Sons of Helaman," 298).

Why does it seem that Ammon's arm was so much stronger? (17:37) "In antiquity the arm invoked ideas of power or strength, both human (see 2 Nephi 4:34; 19:20; D&C 1:19) and divine (see Enos 1:13; D&C 3:8; 15:2). . . .

"Occasionally the scriptures mention righteous men as God's emissaries on earth and in so doing state metaphorically that their arms symbolize God's arm (see D&C 35:13–14; 1 Nephi 22:10–11)" (Gaskill, *Lost Language of Symbolism*, 28).

Why did the servants take the severed arms to the king? (17:39) "The practice of cutting off the arms or other body parts of enemies, specifically as a testimony of the conquest of victims, is attested in the ancient Near East. . . . On the decorated Gates of Shalmaneser III (858–824 b.c.), Assyrian troops are shown cutting off the heads, feet, and hands of vanquished enemies. . . . This practice seems related to that of the astounded servants of King Lamoni, who took the arms that had been cut off by Ammon into the king as 'a testimony' of what Ammon had done" (Lundquist and Welch, "Ammon and Cutting Off the Arms of Enemies," 180). ◉

Alma 18:1–11. King Lamoni Thinks That Ammon Is the Great Spirit

CHAPTER 18

King Lamoni supposes that Ammon is the Great Spirit—Ammon teaches the king about the Creation, God's dealings with men, and the redemption that comes through Christ—Lamoni believes and falls to the earth as if dead. About 90 B.C.

1 And it came to pass that king Lamoni caused that his servants should stand forth and testify to all the things which they had seen concerning the matter.

2 And when they had all testified to the things which they had seen, and he had learned of the faithfulness of Ammon in preserving his flocks, and also of his great power in contending against those who sought to slay him, he was astonished exceedingly, and said: Surely, this is more than a man. Behold, is not this the Great Spirit who doth send such great punishments upon this people, because of their murders?

3 And they answered the king, and said: Whether he be the Great Spirit or a man, we know not; but this much we do know, that he cannot be slain by the enemies of the king; neither can they scatter the king's flocks when he is with us, because of his expertness and great strength; therefore, we know that he is a friend to the king. And now, O king, we do not believe that a man has such great power, for we know he cannot be slain.

4 And now, when the king heard these words, he said unto them: Now I know that it is the Great Spirit; and he has come down at this time to preserve your lives, that I might not slay you as I did your brethren. Now this is the Great Spirit of whom our fathers have spoken.

5 Now this was the tradition of Lamoni, which he had received from his father, that there was a Great Spirit. Notwithstanding they believed in a Great Spirit, they supposed that

Why did Lamoni suddenly question his own actions? (18:4–5) "Prophets, both ancient and modern, have taught that the Spirit of Christ [or light of Christ] is *preparatory* in purpose. It prepares God's children to receive the temporary witness of the Holy Ghost, followed by the more constant Gift of the Holy Ghost, which is bestowed upon those who are baptized (see D&C 130:23). An example of this progression can be identified in the Book of Mormon account of the conversion of king Lamoni. Even though Lamoni had the autocratic authority of a king and had been taught that 'whatsoever [he] did was right,' the text suggests that he still knew it was wrong to slay those servants

whatsoever they did was right; nevertheless, Lamoni began to fear exceedingly, with fear lest he had done wrong in slaying his servants;

6 For he had slain many of them because their brethren had scattered their flocks at the place of water; and thus, because they had had their flocks scattered they were slain.

7 Now it was the practice of these Lamanites to stand by the waters of Sebus to scatter the flocks of the people, that thereby they might drive away many that were scattered unto their own land, it being a practice of plunder among them.

8 And it came to pass that king Lamoni inquired of his servants, saying: Where is this man that has such great power?

9 And they said unto him: Behold, he is feeding thy horses. Now the king had commanded his servants, previous to the time of the watering of their flocks, that they should prepare his horses and chariots, and conduct him forth to the land of Nephi; for there had been a great feast appointed at the land of Nephi, by the father of Lamoni, who was king over all the land.

10 Now when king Lamoni heard that Ammon was preparing his horses and his chariots he was more astonished, because of the faithfulness of Ammon, saying: Surely there has not been any servant among all my servants that has been so faithful as this man; for even he doth remember all my commandments to execute them.

11 Now I surely know that this is the Great Spirit, and I would desire him that he come in unto me, but I durst not.

he judged had not served him well [Alma 18:5]" (Judd, "Spirit of Christ," 136). ⊕

What does this story teach us about the authenticity of the Book of Mormon? (18:6–7) Hugh Nibley wrote of the similarities between the customs of the Lamanites and the Bedouins of Arabia, with whom Lehi and Ishmael would have been familiar or perhaps were even related to. Referring to the scattering at the waters of Sebus, Dr. Nibley wrote: "If ever there was an authentic piece of Bedouin mischief that is it. And of course it led to fights and reprisals in the best desert manner (Alma 18:6). Among others these rascals scattered the flocks of their own king and yet continued active in the social and political life of the community—how weak and poorly organized a government, and how typical of the East! (Alma 17:26–27; 19:21)" (*Approach to the Book of Mormon*, 73–74). ⊕

Why was Ammon not present? (18:8–11) "He was keeping the commandment of the king. . . . The king's son understood the value of total service. He knew that the glory of his previous actions was the Lord's, but he also knew that he could be a faithful and worthy servant himself by filling all the commandments of the king. So when the servants told the king that Ammon was preparing his horses and his chariots, he was more astonished because of the faithfulness of Ammon, and he said, 'Surely there has not been any servant among all my servants that has been so faithful as this man; for even he doth remember all my commandments to execute them' (Alma 18:10)" (Featherstone, "King's Son," 37–38). ⊕

Alma 18:12–23. Ammon Answers King Lamoni's Questions

How may "Rabbanah" compare to Biblical words?
(18:13) "The Lamanite word 'Rabbanah,' meaning
'powerful or great king,' is strikingly similar to other
Semitic words having essentially the same meaning. For
example, the New Testament word *rabboni* clearly refers
to one who is a leader (John 20:16). Also the word *rabbi*,
which is used frequently by Jewish people, designates
'one who teaches or leads.' That the spoken language
of both the Nephites and the Lamanites is derived from
the Hebrew is made quite clear in several places in
the Book of Mormon. In fact, even as late as the fourth
century A.D. one Book of Mormon prophet said, '. . . if
our plates had been sufficiently large we should have
written in Hebrew' (Mormon 9:33)" (Ludlow, *Companion
to Your Study of the Book of Mormon*, 207).

What role can silence play in teaching the gospel?
(18:14) Ammon allowed for silence before he instructed the king. Modern missionaries are instructed
to allow silence to permit the Spirit to teach: "Do not
be afraid of silence. People often need time to think
about and reply to questions or to express what they
are feeling. You might pause after you have asked a
question, after sharing a spiritual experience, or when
people are having difficulty expressing themselves. Be
sure to give people time to complete their thoughts
before you respond, and do not interrupt while they
are talking" (*Preach My Gospel*, 185).

Why did the Spirit reveal Lamoni's thoughts?
(18:16) "After caring for the king's horses, Ammon
came before king Lamoni. Awe-struck by Ammon's
power and ability, the king was fearful of speaking to
him (see Alma 18:11–15). It was in this circumstance
that Ammon relied on the Spirit to enable him to
perceive king Lamoni's thoughts (see Alma 18:16).
Ammon could then determine how to respond
to Lamoni and his unspoken concerns" (Williams,
"Instruments in the Hands of God," 98). ○

12 And it came to pass that when Ammon
had made ready the horses and the chariots
for the king and his servants, he went in unto
the king, and he saw that the countenance of
the king was changed; therefore he was about
to return out of his presence.

13 And one of the king's servants said unto
him, Rabbanah, which is, being interpreted,
powerful or great king, considering their
kings to be powerful; and thus he said unto
him: Rabbanah, the king desireth thee to
stay.

14 Therefore Ammon turned himself unto
the king, and said unto him: What wilt thou
that I should do for thee, O king? And the
king answered him not for the space of an
hour, according to their time, for he knew
not what he should say unto him.

15 And it came to pass that Ammon said
unto him again: What desirest thou of me?
But the king answered him not.

16 And it came to pass that Ammon, being
filled with the Spirit of God, therefore he
perceived the thoughts of the king. And he
said unto him: Is it because thou hast heard
that I defended thy servants and thy flocks,
and slew seven of their brethren with the
sling and with the sword, and smote off the
arms of others, in order to defend thy flocks
and thy servants; behold, is it this that causeth thy marvelings?

17 I say unto you, what is it, that thy marvelings are so great? Behold, I am a man, and
am thy servant; therefore, whatsoever thou
desirest which is right, that will I do.

18 Now when the king had heard these words, he marveled again, for he beheld that Ammon could discern his thoughts; but notwithstanding this, king Lamoni did open his mouth, and said unto him: Who art thou? Art thou that Great Spirit, who knows all things?

19 Ammon answered and said unto him: I am not.

20 And the king said: How knowest thou the thoughts of my heart? Thou mayest speak boldly, and tell me concerning these things; and also tell me by what power ye slew and smote off the arms of my brethren that scattered my flocks—

21 And now, if thou wilt tell me concerning these things, whatsoever thou desirest I will give unto thee; and if it were needed, I would guard thee with my armies; but I know that thou art more powerful than all they; nevertheless, whatsoever thou desirest of me I will grant it unto thee.

22 Now Ammon being wise, yet harmless, he said unto Lamoni: Wilt thou hearken unto my words, if I tell thee by what power I do these things? And this is the thing that I desire of thee.

23 And the king answered him, and said: Yea, I will believe all thy words. And thus he was caught with guile.

Who did the king think Ammon was? (18:18–19)
President Ezra Taft Benson related a story about a man who, heading home late on a busy Christmas eve, stopped to assist a crippled boy in need. After helping, as the man started to leave the boy asked, "'Are you Jesus Christ?'

"By the look on his face, it was obvious the commuter was embarrassed by the question. But he smiled and said, 'No, son, I am not Jesus Christ. But I am trying hard to do what He would do if He were here'" (*Come unto Christ*, 42).

How did Ammon gain such influence? (18:22–23)
"Ponder these points as you feel the influence of Ammon's teachings, his ministry and great example:
   "1. The desire of his heart was to bring people to God [Alma 17:29].
   "2. He was always a servant, a minister. He was out among the people [Alma 17:25].
   "3. He prepared himself by fasting, studying the scriptures, and prayer [Alma 17:2–3].
   "4. He went forth believing he could make a difference with the help of God [Alma 17:13].
   "5. He anxiously looked for every possible opportunity to serve [Alma 17:29].
   "6. He kept all of the commandments [Alma 18:10].
   "7. As a result of doing all of these things, he taught with power and authority and established the Church of God [Alma 18:24–19:35]" (Paramore, "They Taught and Did Minister One to Another," 70).

What is the meaning of the word *guile* in verse 23?
(18:23) "Although the word *guile* is frequently used to mean 'deceitful cunning' or 'treachery,' it can also denote the use of strategy. It is evidently used in the latter sense in Alma 18:23; in other words, Ammon *planned* or *used strategy* in arranging the questions he asked King Lamoni" (Ludlow, *Companion to Your Study of the Book of Mormon*, 207). ✛

Alma 18:24–39. Ammon Teaches Lamoni the Plan of Salvation

How do we teach someone who doesn't even know about God? (18:24–35) "It took a series of explanations to convince Lamoni that Ammon was not the Lord. First, Ammon flatly declared, 'I am not' (Alma 18:19). Next, Ammon taught Lamoni who God was and about his attributes (Alma 18:24–32). He explained his own calling from God and the gifts of the Spirit that helped him accomplish the Lord's work (Alma 18:33–35). Finally, Ammon taught Lamoni the gospel from the scriptures, specifically explaining the creation, the fall, and the atonement (Alma 18:38–39)" (Fronk, "Show Forth Good Examples in Me," 325).

24 And Ammon began to speak unto him with boldness, and said unto him: Believest thou that there is a God?

25 And he answered, and said unto him: I do not know what that meaneth.

26 And then Ammon said: Believest thou that there is a Great Spirit?

27 And he said, Yea.

28 And Ammon said: This is God. And Ammon said unto him again: Believest thou that this Great Spirit, who is God, created all things which are in heaven and in the earth?

29 And he said: Yea, I believe that he created all things which are in the earth; but I do not know the heavens.

30 And Ammon said unto him: The heavens is a place where God dwells and all his holy angels.

31 And king Lamoni said: Is it above the earth?

32 And Ammon said: Yea, and he looketh down upon all the children of men; and he knows all the thoughts and intents of the heart; for by his hand were they all created from the beginning.

33 And king Lamoni said: I believe all these things which thou hast spoken. Art thou sent from God?

34 Ammon said unto him: I am a man; and man in the beginning was created after the image of God, and I am called by his Holy Spirit to teach these things unto this people, that they may be brought to a knowledge of that which is just and true;

35 And a portion of that Spirit dwelleth in me, which giveth me knowledge, and also power according to my faith and desires which are in God.

36 Now when Ammon had said these words, he began at the creation of the world, and also the creation of Adam, and told him all the things concerning the fall of man, and rehearsed and laid before him the records and the holy scriptures of the people, which had been spoken by the prophets, even down to the time that their father, Lehi, left Jerusalem.

37 And he also rehearsed unto them (for it was unto the king and to his servants) all the journeyings of their fathers in the wilderness, and all their sufferings with hunger and thirst, and their travail, and so forth.

38 And he also rehearsed unto them concerning the rebellions of Laman and Lemuel, and the sons of Ishmael, yea, all their rebellions did he relate unto them; and he expounded unto them all the records and scriptures from the time that Lehi left Jerusalem down to the present time.

39 But this is not all; for he expounded unto them the plan of redemption, which was prepared from the foundation of the world; and he also made known unto them concerning the coming of Christ, and all the works of the Lord did he make known unto them.

40 And it came to pass that after he had said all these things, and expounded them to the king, that the king believed all his words.

41 And he began to cry unto the Lord, saying: O Lord, have mercy; according to thy abundant mercy which thou hast had upon the people of Nephi, have upon me, and my people.

Why start teaching with the doctrines of Creation, Fall, and Atonement? (18:36) "Elder Bruce R. McConkie called these [the Creation, the Fall, and the Atonement] 'the three pillars of eternity' and the 'greatest events that have ever occurred in all eternity.' He explained: 'If we can gain an understanding of them, then the whole eternal scheme of things will fall into place, and we will be in a position to work out our own salvation. . . . These three are the foundations upon which all things rest. Without any one of them all things would lose their purpose and meaning and the plans and designs of Deity would come to naught' ('Three Pillars of Eternity')" (Fronk, "Show Forth Good Examples in Me," 325). ✚

What does Ammon's approach to teaching the scriptures suggest to latter-day teachers of youth? (18:36) "He used the scriptures from both the Old and New Worlds as his basic source (Alma 18:36–39). Ammon's straightforward doctrinal approach calls to mind President J. Reuben Clark Jr.'s comment about how not to teach our spiritually alert youth, 'There is no need for gradual approaches, for "bed-time" stories, for coddling, for patronizing, or for any of the other childish devices.' If Ammon could teach doctrine from the scriptures to a wicked Lamanite who barely knew God existed, surely students in modern Zion deserve to be taught in the same way. Conversion comes, as Mormon explains in Alma 32, when we hear the word of God taught by the power of the Holy Ghost" (Hansen, "Book of Alma as a Prototype," 269).

Alma 18:40–43. King Lamoni Believes Ammon and Desires to Be Forgiven

How is mercy made possible? (18:41) "By eternal law, mercy cannot be extended save there be one who is both willing and able to assume our debt and pay the price and arrange the terms for our redemption.

"Unless there is a mediator, . . . the full weight of justice untempered, unsympathetic, must, positively must fall on us. The full recompense for every transgression, however minor or however deep, will be exacted from us to the uttermost farthing.

"But know this: Truth, glorious truth, proclaims there is such a Mediator.

"'For there is one God, and one mediator between God and men, the man Christ Jesus' (1 Tim. 2:5).

"Through Him mercy can be fully extended to each of us without offending the eternal law of justice" (Packer, "The Mediator," 55–56). ⊕

What is the meaning of the king's almost deathlike state? (18:42–43) "From what we can deduce from scriptural writ, it appears that a trance is a state in which the body and its functions become quiescent in order that the full powers of the Spirit may be centered on the revelations of heaven. Freed from the fetters of a mortal body, man's spirit can be ushered into the divine presence; it can hear what otherwise could not be heard and see what otherwise could not be seen—even the visions of eternity and even the Almighty himself" (McConkie and Millet, *Doctrinal Commentary*, 3:140).

Alma 19:1–11. For Three Days, King Lamoni Is Overcome by the Spirit

What was happening to Lamoni? (19:1) "While Lamoni's body took on the appearance of death for three days, his spirit was very much alive and actively learning. Parallel ordeals of the same length of time are found throughout scripture. . . . Alma the Younger was unable to speak or move during the three days of his spiritual awakening (Mosiah 27:18–25). Paul received his sight after being blind three days . . . (Acts 9:8–9). Christ used Jonah's three-days' experience in the belly of a great fish to teach His death and resurrection to the Pharisees (Matt. 12:40). Each of these incidents points to the death and resurrection of the Messiah, whose body was in the tomb for three days while his spirit was in the spirit world" (Fronk, "Show Forth Good Examples in Me," 325). ⊕

How does the queen show love for her husband? (19:5) "In the story of Ammon's missionary work among the Lamanites there is one statement the unusual language of which sometimes evokes mirth in a student when he first hears it, but which to me is one of the most sacred and provocative verses in all the record. . . .

"The love of this faithful wife for her beloved husband seems typical to me of the love which will obtain in the heavenly kingdom and which should here characterize our relationships with those dear to us" (Hanks, in Conference Report, Apr. 1957, 125–29).

42 And now, when he had said this, he fell unto the earth, as if he were dead.

43 And it came to pass that his servants took him and carried him in unto his wife, and laid him upon a bed; and he lay as if he were dead for the space of two days and two nights; and his wife, and his sons, and his daughters mourned over him, after the manner of the Lamanites, greatly lamenting his loss.

CHAPTER 19

Lamoni receives the light of everlasting life and sees the Redeemer—His household falls into a trance, and many see angels—Ammon is preserved miraculously—He baptizes many and establishes a church among them. About 90 B.C.

1 And it came to pass that after two days and two nights they were about to take his body and lay it in a sepulchre, which they had made for the purpose of burying their dead.

2 Now the queen having heard of the fame of Ammon, therefore she sent and desired that he should come in unto her.

3 And it came to pass that Ammon did as he was commanded, and went in unto the queen, and desired to know what she would that he should do.

4 And she said unto him: The servants of my husband have made it known unto me that thou art a prophet of a holy God, and that thou hast power to do many mighty works in his name;

5 Therefore, if this is the case, I would that ye should go in and see my husband, for he has been laid upon his bed for the space of two days and two nights; and some say that he is not dead, but others say that he is dead and that he stinketh, and that he ought to be placed in the sepulchre; but as for myself, to me he doth not stink.

6 Now, this was what Ammon desired, for he knew that king Lamoni was under the power of God; he knew that the dark veil of unbelief was being cast away from his mind, and the light which did light up his mind, which was the light of the glory of God, which was a marvelous light of his goodness—yea, this light had infused such joy into his soul, the cloud of darkness having been dispelled, and that the light of everlasting life was lit up in his soul, yea, he knew that this had overcome his natural frame, and he was carried away in God—

7 Therefore, what the queen desired of him was his only desire. Therefore, he went in to see the king according as the queen had desired him; and he saw the king, and he knew that he was not dead.

8 And he said unto the queen: He is not dead, but he sleepeth in God, and on the morrow he shall rise again; therefore bury him not.

9 And Ammon said unto her: Believest thou this? And she said unto him: I have had no witness save thy word, and the word of our servants; nevertheless I believe that it shall be according as thou hast said.

10 And Ammon said unto her: Blessed art thou because of thy exceeding faith; I say unto thee, woman, there has not been such great faith among all the people of the Nephites.

11 And it came to pass that she watched over the bed of her husband, from that time even until that time on the morrow which Ammon had appointed that he should rise.

12 And it came to pass that he arose, according to the words of Ammon; and as he arose, he stretched forth his hand unto the woman, and said: Blessed be the name of God, and blessed art thou.

13 For as sure as thou livest, behold, I have seen my Redeemer; and he shall come forth,

What is the "light of the glory of God"? (19:6) "We have no better illustration of the full operation of the light of Christ upon an investigator of the gospel than what happened to King Lamoni [see Alma 19:6]. Thereafter, Lamoni was baptized and received the gift of the Holy Ghost.

"There is really no excuse for men to reject the gospel message. When they do so, it is because of spiritual blindness or because their deeds are evil and they love darkness rather than light. If they would but hearken to the voice of conscience, to the voice of the light within them, to the voice of the Spirit, they would come unto Christ and receive the Holy Ghost" (McConkie, *New Witness*, 261). ⊕

How did Lamoni's wife manifest faith? (19:9–11) "The Apostle Paul wrote to the Romans, 'Faith cometh by hearing, and hearing by the word of God.' . . . The first step to finding faith in the Lord Jesus Christ is to let His word—spoken by the mouth of His servants, the prophets—touch your heart. But it is not enough merely to let those words wash over you, as if they alone could transform you. We must do our part" (Hales, "Finding Faith in the Lord Jesus Christ," 72).

How did the queen show she believed Ammon's words? Think about a challenge you face that requires faith. What do you think God expects you to do to show you believe?

Alma 19:12–17. The King's Household and Ammon Are Overcome by the Spirit

How does the Lord use a trance to teach? (19:12–16) "The story of Ammon and Lamoni affirms religious trances as a legitimate revelatory device. Lamoni, as already noted, came forth from his trance testifying that he had seen the Redeemer and then prophesied relative to the Savior's birth and the necessity of all mankind believing on his name. The testimony of his servants was that while they were in this state of physical insensibility, angels instructed them in the principles of salvation and their obligation to live righteously. Indeed, they experienced a change of heart and no longer had a desire to do evil. Such is the state in which the power of God overcomes the 'natural frame' and one is 'carried away in God'" (McConkie and Millet, *Doctrinal Commentary*, 3:141). ✛

Who was Abish and how was she converted? (19:16) "If for no other reason, Abish, the Lamanitish woman, is distinguished because her actual name appears in the Book of Mormon....

"The brief account of the conversion of Abish is not clear. The statement that Abish had been converted 'unto the Lord for many years, on account of a remarkable vision of her father' (Alma 19:16) may have two possible interpretations. One interpretation is that Abish herself had this vision and in her vision she saw her father. Another possible interpretation is that the vision was actually had by the father of Abish. Regardless of which interpretation is correct, this conversion of Abish plays an important role in converting large numbers of Lamanites" (Ludlow, *Companion to Your Study of the Book of Mormon*, 207). ✛

How does Abish's vision demonstrate God's foreknowledge? (19:17) "Visions are not idly given by the Lord but reserved for specific purposes. One of the Lord's purposes for visions is 'preparing men for salvation.' The case of Abish cannot be seen as an exception, for she was prepared to help her people come

and be born of a woman, and he shall redeem all mankind who believe on his name. Now, when he had said these words, his heart was swollen within him, and he sunk again with joy; and the queen also sunk down, being overpowered by the Spirit.

14 Now Ammon seeing the Spirit of the Lord poured out according to his prayers upon the Lamanites, his brethren, who had been the cause of so much mourning among the Nephites, or among all the people of God because of their iniquities and their traditions, he fell upon his knees, and began to pour out his soul in prayer and thanksgiving to God for what he had done for his brethren; and he was also overpowered with joy; and thus they all three had sunk to the earth.

15 Now, when the servants of the king had seen that they had fallen, they also began to cry unto God, for the fear of the Lord had come upon them also, for it was they who had stood before the king and testified unto him concerning the great power of Ammon.

16 And it came to pass that they did call on the name of the Lord, in their might, even until they had all fallen to the earth, save it were one of the Lamanitish women, whose name was Abish, she having been converted unto the Lord for many years, on account of a remarkable vision of her father—

17 Thus, having been converted to the Lord, and never having made it known, therefore, when she saw that all the servants of Lamoni had fallen to the earth, and also her mistress, the queen, and the king, and Ammon lay prostrate upon the earth, she knew that it was the power of God; and supposing that this opportunity, by making known unto the people what had happened among them, that by beholding this scene it would cause them to believe in the power of God, therefore she ran forth from house to house, making it known unto the people.

18 And they began to assemble themselves together unto the house of the king. And there came a multitude, and to their astonishment, they beheld the king, and the queen, and their servants prostrate upon the earth, and they all lay there as though they were dead; and they also saw Ammon, and behold, he was a Nephite.

19 And now the people began to murmur among themselves; some saying that it was a great evil that had come upon them, or upon the king and his house, because he had suffered that the Nephite should remain in the land.

20 But others rebuked them, saying: The king hath brought this evil upon his house, because he slew his servants who had had their flocks scattered at the waters of Sebus.

21 And they were also rebuked by those men who had stood at the waters of Sebus and scattered the flocks which belonged to the king, for they were angry with Ammon because of the number which he had slain of their brethren at the waters of Sebus, while defending the flocks of the king.

22 Now, one of them, whose brother had been slain with the sword of Ammon, being exceedingly angry with Ammon, drew his sword and went forth that he might let it fall upon Ammon, to slay him; and as he lifted the sword to smite him, behold, he fell dead.

23 Now we see that Ammon could not be slain, for the Lord had said unto Mosiah, his father: I will spare him, and it shall be

to a knowledge of salvation. When she witnessed the condition of the king's court, she recognized the power of God and knew what she must do. Her testimony as a Lamanite strengthened the testimony of Ammon, a Nephite foreigner, and satisfied the law of witnesses (D&C 6:28)" (Fronk, "Show Forth Good Examples in Me," 326–27).

Alma 19:18–24. Ammon's Life Is Saved by the Lord

Why did the Lord spare Ammon? (19:22–23) "The Lord has promised his servants in this dispensation that He would go before them and 'be on [their] right hand and on [their] left' and preserve them as they seek to spread the gospel throughout the nations of the earth (see D&C 84:88; 35:13–15). Undoubtedly this promise holds true unless one is 'appointed unto death' or, as in some cases, 'the Lord suffereth the righteous to be slain that his justice and judgment may come upon the wicked' (see D&C 42:48; Alma 60:13)" (Williams, "Instruments in the Hands of God," 98–99). ⊕

unto him according to thy faith—therefore, Mosiah trusted him unto the Lord.

24 And it came to pass that when the multitude beheld that the man had fallen dead, who lifted the sword to slay Ammon, fear came upon them all, and they durst not put forth their hands to touch him or any of those who had fallen; and they began to marvel again among themselves what could be the cause of this great power, or what all these things could mean.

25 And it came to pass that there were many among them who said that Ammon was the Great Spirit, and others said he was sent by the Great Spirit;

Alma 19:25–36. All Who Are Carried Away by the Spirit Awake and Begin to Teach the Gospel

26 But others rebuked them all, saying that he was a monster, who had been sent from the Nephites to torment them.

27 And there were some who said that Ammon was sent by the Great Spirit to afflict them because of their iniquities; and that it was the Great Spirit that had always attended the Nephites, who had ever delivered them out of their hands; and they said that it was this Great Spirit who had destroyed so many of their brethren, the Lamanites.

28 And thus the contention began to be exceedingly sharp among them. And while they were thus contending, the woman servant who had caused the multitude to be gathered together came, and when she saw the contention which was among the multitude she was exceedingly sorrowful, even unto tears.

29 And it came to pass that she went and took the queen by the hand, that perhaps she might raise her from the ground; and as soon as she touched her hand she arose and stood upon her feet, and cried with a loud voice, saying: O blessed Jesus, who has saved me from an awful hell! O blessed God, have mercy on this people!

30 And when she had said this, she clasped her hands, being filled with joy, speaking many words which were not understood; and when she had done this, she took the king, Lamoni, by the hand, and behold he arose and stood upon his feet.

31 And he, immediately, seeing the contention among his people, went forth and began to rebuke them, and to teach them the words which he had heard from the mouth of Ammon; and as many as heard his words believed, and were converted unto the Lord.

32 But there were many among them who would not hear his words; therefore they went their way.

33 And it came to pass that when Ammon arose he also administered unto them, and also did all the servants of Lamoni; and they did all declare unto the people the selfsame thing—that their hearts had been changed; that they had no more desire to do evil.

34 And behold, many did declare unto the people that they had seen angels and had conversed with them; and thus they had told them things of God, and of his righteousness.

35 And it came to pass that there were many that did believe in their words; and as many as did believe were baptized; and they became a righteous people, and they did establish a church among them.

What is the ultimate source of conversion for those who will hear the message? (19:31) "Those who experience the mighty change in their hearts are converted by hearing the word of God when it is accompanied by a witness of the Holy Ghost. Some . . . may conclude that it was the miraculous show of power that gave Lamoni's people . . . their testimonies. We misunderstand the faith of these people and the power of the word of God if that is what we conclude. Alma the Younger and Lamoni had similar miraculous spiritual awakenings. Alma bore witness that it was the Holy Spirit who gave him his testimony, not the angel (Alma 5:45–46). Those born of God do not require miracles for conversion but respond to the teachings of the Spirit (Alma 19:35–36)" (Fronk, "Show Forth Good Examples in Me," 333).

How do we lose the desire to sin? (19:33) "That mighty change is reported time after time in the Book of Mormon. The way it is wrought and what the person becomes are always the same. The words of God in pure doctrine go down deep into the heart by the power of the Holy Ghost. The person pleads with God in faith. The repentant heart is broken and the spirit contrite. Sacred covenants have been made. Then God keeps His covenant to grant a new heart and a new life, in His time. . . . Whether the miracle comes in a moment or over years, as is far more common, it is the doctrine of Jesus Christ that drives the change" (Eyring, "We Must Raise Our Sights," 16–17). ●

Why did all those converted bear a similar testimony? (19:34–35) "Once they understand the gospel plan, converts know to whom they must turn for mercy and forgiveness. Notice the initial exclamations made by those who repented and were born again. When Lamoni regained consciousness, he stood and bore witness of the Savior (Alma 19:13), as did his queen (Alma 19:29). Many people have an intense desire to bear witness of Christ once they have experienced the blessings of his atonement. This witness may be given in words, but as has been illustrated in these chapters of the Book of Mormon, people witness Christ's reality frequently and powerfully by their lives.

They take the Lord's request to heart: 'Show forth good examples unto them in me' (Alma 17:11)" (Fronk, "Show Forth Good Examples in Me," 333).

What is meant by the often-used scriptural imagery of the Lord's arm being extended? (19:36) "The outstretched arm is always a symbol of God's power being exercised, whether in creation (see Jeremiah 32:17), judgment (see Jeremiah 21:5; 1 Nephi 20:14; 2 Nephi 8:5; Mosiah 12:24; D&C 1:14), or deliverance of his people (see Deuteronomy 4:34; 26:8; Mosiah 29:20; D&C 133:67)" (Gaskill, *Lost Language of Symbolism*, 28). In this case, God is reaching out to repentant Lamanites who had committed many serious sins. How might this account benefit those who think they have sinned so seriously that God has rejected them? What is required of all who would be clean again?

Alma 20:1–7. The Lord Sends Ammon to Deliver His Brethren from Prison

Who, like Ammon, can hear the "voice of the Lord"? (20:2) "The spirit of revelation is available to every person who receives by proper priesthood authority the saving ordinances of baptism by immersion for the remission of sins and the laying on of hands for the gift of the Holy Ghost—and who is acting in faith to fulfill the priesthood injunction to 'receive the Holy Ghost.' This blessing is not restricted to the presiding authorities of the Church; rather, it belongs to and should be operative in the life of every man, woman, and child who reaches the age of accountability and enters into sacred covenants. Sincere desire and worthiness invite the spirit of revelation into our lives" (Bednar, "Spirit of Revelation," 87). ◉

Is the Lord's strength always available to us? (20:4) "The restored gospel of Jesus Christ gives us help in knowing how to qualify for the strength of the Lord as we deal with adversity. . . .

"We need strength beyond ourselves to keep the commandments in whatever circumstance life brings

36 And thus the work of the Lord did commence among the Lamanites; thus the Lord did begin to pour out his Spirit upon them; and we see that his arm is extended to all people who will repent and believe on his name.

CHAPTER 20

The Lord sends Ammon to Middoni to deliver his imprisoned brethren—Ammon and Lamoni meet Lamoni's father, who is king over all the land—Ammon compels the old king to approve the release of his brethren. About 90 B.C.

1 And it came to pass that when they had established a church in that land, that king Lamoni desired that Ammon should go with him to the land of Nephi, that he might show him unto his father.

2 And the voice of the Lord came to Ammon, saying: Thou shalt not go up to the land of Nephi, for behold, the king will seek thy life; but thou shalt go to the land of Middoni; for behold, thy brother Aaron, and also Muloki and Ammah are in prison.

3 Now it came to pass that when Ammon had heard this, he said unto Lamoni: Behold, my brother and brethren are in prison at Middoni, and I go that I may deliver them.

4 Now Lamoni said unto Ammon: I know, in the strength of the Lord thou canst do all things. But behold, I will go with thee to the land of Middoni; for the king of the land of Middoni, whose name is Antiomno, is a

friend unto me; therefore I go to the land of Middoni, that I may flatter the king of the land, and he will cast thy brethren out of prison. Now Lamoni said unto him: Who told thee that thy brethren were in prison?

5 And Ammon said unto him: No one hath told me, save it be God; and he said unto me—Go and deliver thy brethren, for they are in prison in the land of Middoni.

6 Now when Lamoni had heard this he caused that his servants should make ready his horses and his chariots.

7 And he said unto Ammon: Come, I will go with thee down to the land of Middoni, and there I will plead with the king that he will cast thy brethren out of prison.

8 And it came to pass that as Ammon and Lamoni were journeying thither, they met the father of Lamoni, who was king over all the land.

9 And behold, the father of Lamoni said unto him: Why did ye not come to the feast on that great day when I made a feast unto my sons, and unto my people?

10 And he also said: Whither art thou going with this Nephite, who is one of the children of a liar?

11 And it came to pass that Lamoni rehearsed unto him whither he was going, for he feared to offend him.

12 And he also told him all the cause of his tarrying in his own kingdom, that he did not go unto his father to the feast which he had prepared.

13 And now when Lamoni had rehearsed unto him all these things, behold, to his astonishment, his father was angry with him, and said: Lamoni, thou art going to deliver these Nephites, who are sons of a liar. Behold, he robbed our fathers; and now his children

to us. For some it may be poverty, but for others it may be prosperity. It may be the ravages of age or the exuberance of youth. The combination of trials and their duration are as varied as are the children of our Heavenly Father. No two are alike. But what is being tested is the same, at all times in our lives and for every person: will we do whatsoever the Lord our God will command us?" (Eyring, "In the Strength of the Lord," 16–17). ✚

Alma 20:8–22. Ammon and Lamoni Meet Lamoni's Father

How do false traditions lead people astray? (20:10–13) "Faulty memory bequeathed to the Lamanite children the wicked and abominable traditions of their fathers, which when repeated time and time again made it easy for wicked and ambitious rulers to lead them astray. We may imagine that with each telling, these unwritten memorials assumed greater and more evil proportions, and in this way, every passing generation of Lamanites inherited more and more which was but the invention of diseased and depraved hearts. Thus, again, their imperfect traditions delivered a treacherous blow to the Lamanites for they therein became the victims of their own degraded beliefs" (Reynolds and Sjodahl, *Commentary on the Book of Mormon*, 3:159).

How do we know that Lamoni was converted and had a change of heart? (20:15–16) "His determination not to kill his best friend reveals to our senses the real change that had come into Lamoni's heart. He was willing to incur his father's wrath to protect the innocent. Before Ammon's visit, Lamoni exhibited all those qualities which mark the savage breast, or which fixed *a life without God.* He was proud and haughty, cruel and overbearing, superstitious and irrational; his word was law. But now he was gentle and considerate, firm in keeping the commandments of God" (Reynolds and Sjodahl, *Commentary on the Book of Mormon*, 3:284–85).

Why might the king lose his soul? (20:17–18) "Ammon's statement implies that the king would have been guilty of murder. Joseph Smith taught that one guilty of murder, 'one that sheds innocent blood, cannot have forgiveness' (*Teachings*, 339). Such a one would be guilty of the unforgivable sin, one for which the atonement of Christ cannot bring remission of sins" (McConkie and Millet, *Doctrinal Commentary*, 3:148). ◉

are also come amongst us that they may, by their cunning and their lyings, deceive us, that they again may rob us of our property.

14 Now the father of Lamoni commanded him that he should slay Ammon with the sword. And he also commanded him that he should not go to the land of Middoni, but that he should return with him to the land of Ishmael.

15 But Lamoni said unto him: I will not slay Ammon, neither will I return to the land of Ishmael, but I go to the land of Middoni that I may release the brethren of Ammon, for I know that they are just men and holy prophets of the true God.

16 Now when his father had heard these words, he was angry with him, and he drew his sword that he might smite him to the earth.

17 But Ammon stood forth and said unto him: Behold, thou shalt not slay thy son; nevertheless, it were better that he should fall than thee, for behold, he has repented of his sins; but if thou shouldst fall at this time, in thine anger, thy soul could not be saved.

18 And again, it is expedient that thou shouldst forbear; for if thou shouldst slay thy son, he being an innocent man, his blood would cry from the ground to the Lord his God, for vengeance to come upon thee; and perhaps thou wouldst lose thy soul.

19 Now when Ammon had said these words unto him, he answered him, saying: I know that if I should slay my son, that I should shed innocent blood; for it is thou that hast sought to destroy him.

20 And he stretched forth his hand to slay Ammon. But Ammon withstood his blows, and also smote his arm that he could not use it.

21 Now when the king saw that Ammon could slay him, he began to plead with Ammon that he would spare his life.

22 But Ammon raised his sword, and said unto him: Behold, I will smite thee except thou wilt grant unto me that my brethren may be cast out of prison.

23 Now the king, fearing he should lose his life, said: If thou wilt spare me I will grant unto thee whatsoever thou wilt ask, even to half of the kingdom.

24 Now when Ammon saw that he had wrought upon the old king according to his desire, he said unto him: If thou wilt grant that my brethren may be cast out of prison, and also that Lamoni may retain his kingdom, and that ye be not displeased with him, but grant that he may do according to his own desires in whatsoever thing he thinketh, then will I spare thee; otherwise I will smite thee to the earth.

25 Now when Ammon had said these words, the king began to rejoice because of his life.

26 And when he saw that Ammon had no desire to destroy him, and when he also saw the great love he had for his son Lamoni, he was astonished exceedingly, and said: Because this is all that thou hast desired, that I would release thy brethren, and suffer that my son Lamoni should retain his kingdom, behold, I will grant unto you that my son may retain his kingdom from this time and forever; and I will govern him no more—

27 And I will also grant unto thee that thy brethren may be cast out of prison, and thou and thy brethren may come unto me, in my kingdom; for I shall greatly desire to see thee. For the king was greatly astonished at the words which he had spoken, and also at the words which had been spoken by his son Lamoni, therefore he was desirous to learn them.

Alma 20:23–30. Ammon's Brethren Are Released from Prison

What was Ammon's most effective weapon? (20:26)
"It is significant that it was not Ammon's strength or his ability to speak which had the greatest effect upon Lamoni's father. Rather, it was the great love Ammon showed for Lamoni, even being willing to defend him from physical harm, which so deeply affected Lamoni's father. . . . Love has the effect of opening the hearts of individuals. In the Lord's instructions through the prophet Joseph Smith, we are taught that love is among those characteristics which qualify one for the work of teaching the gospel (see D&C 4:5). The more we allow love to permeate our service to the Lord the more successful our efforts will be" (Williams, "Instruments in the Hands of God," 101).

What is it about a testimony of the gospel that gives one the patience to endure trials and suffering? (20:28–29) In today's world, the almost universal cry is for justice, and if that is denied, then the demand is for retribution and vengeance. What have you learned from the example set by "the brethren of Ammon"? What other examples have you seen of faith in God and love for His children enabling a person to endure injustice and suffering? What are the fruits of such forbearance both for the sufferer and those whose actions caused the suffering? What seems to be Heavenly Father's most common method of helping us develop patience? Is there someone in your life who could be blessed by your patient service?

Who were these "more hardened" people? (20:30) The more hardened people "had fallen into the hands of the Amalekites and the Amulonites (see Alma 21:1–4). We know that Amulon was one of the wicked priests of Noah (Mosiah 23:32). The present text is silent as to the identity of Amaleki" (McConkie and Millet, *Doctrinal Commentary*, 3:149–50). ⊕

Superscription to Alma 21

The superscription to Alma 21 was part of the ancient record translated by the Prophet Joseph Smith and dictated by him to his scribe (see also, for example, 2 Nephi, Mosiah 9, and Alma 36).

The italicized words "Comprising chapters 21 through 25" were not part of the ancient record but were added later to printed editions of the Book of Mormon.

Alma 21:1–10. Aaron Teaches the Wicked Nephites Who Live among the Lamanites

28 And it came to pass that Ammon and Lamoni proceeded on their journey towards the land of Middoni. And Lamoni found favor in the eyes of the king of the land; therefore the brethren of Ammon were brought forth out of prison.

29 And when Ammon did meet them he was exceedingly sorrowful, for behold they were naked, and their skins were worn exceedingly because of being bound with strong cords. And they also had suffered hunger, thirst, and all kinds of afflictions; nevertheless they were patient in all their sufferings.

30 And, as it happened, it was their lot to have fallen into the hands of a more hardened and a more stiffnecked people; therefore they would not hearken unto their words, and they had cast them out, and had smitten them, and had driven them from house to house, and from place to place, even until they had arrived in the land of Middoni; and there they were taken and cast into prison, and bound with strong cords, and kept in prison for many days, and were delivered by Lamoni and Ammon.

An account of the preaching of Aaron, and Muloki, and their brethren, to the Lamanites. *Comprising chapters 21 through 25.*

CHAPTER 21

Aaron teaches the Amalekites about Christ and His Atonement—Aaron and his brethren are imprisoned in Middoni—After their deliverance, they teach in the synagogues and make many converts—Lamoni grants religious freedom to the people in the land of Ishmael. About 90–77 B.C.

1 Now when Ammon and his brethren separated themselves in the borders of the land of the Lamanites, behold Aaron took his journey towards the land which was called by the Lamanites, Jerusalem, calling it after the land of their fathers' nativity; and it was away joining the borders of Mormon.

2 Now the Lamanites and the Amalekites and the people of Amulon had built a great city, which was called Jerusalem.

3 Now the Lamanites of themselves were sufficiently hardened, but the Amalekites and the Amulonites were still harder; therefore they did cause the Lamanites that they should harden their hearts, that they should wax strong in wickedness and their abominations.

4 And it came to pass that Aaron came to the city of Jerusalem, and first began to preach to the Amalekites. And he began to preach to them in their synagogues, for they had built synagogues after the order of the Nehors; for many of the Amalekites and the Amulonites were after the order of the Nehors.

5 Therefore, as Aaron entered into one of their synagogues to preach unto the people, and as he was speaking unto them, behold there arose an Amalekite and began to

Who were the "Amalekites and the people of Amulon"? (21:2) "The Amalekites are mentioned for the first time in Alma 21:2; the exact source of their name is never made clear in the Book of Mormon. The Amulonites mentioned here are the descendants and the followers of Amulon, the wicked priest of King Noah (Mosiah 23:31–35; Mosiah 24:3–4). Both of these groups of people believed in the 'order of the Nehors' (Alma 21:4; read also Alma 1:2–6, 15–16), and they were so hardened in wickedness that only one Amalekite and no Amulonites were converted by the four sons of Mosiah and their companions (Alma 23:14)" (Ludlow, *Companion to Your Study of the Book of Mormon*, 208).

Why do the wicked react so strongly against divine messengers? (21:3) The Prophet Joseph Smith provided insights from his own experience: "But behold the words of the Savior: 'If the light which is in you become darkness, behold how great is that darkness.' Look at the dissenters. Again, 'If you were of the world the world would love its own.' . . . But they speak all manner of evil of us falsely, for no other reason than that we have been endeavoring to teach the fullness of the Gospel of Jesus Christ" (*Teachings of the Prophet Joseph Smith*, 124).

Were synagogues known before or after Lehi left Jerusalem? (21:4) "They are mentioned among both Nephites and the Lamanites under dissident Nephite influence (Alma 21:4–5; 32:1–12; Helaman 3:9, 14; Moroni 7:1). Many historians have maintained that synagogues were not known among the Jews until well after Lehi had left Palestine. Another group of experts, however, now argue that the synagogue predated Lehi's departure. They propose that when King Josiah carried out his sweeping reforms of Jewish worship in order to clean out pagan intrusions, he closed the old sanctuaries (2 Kings 23). The centralization of worship in Jerusalem from 621 B.C. onward, with many Jews thereby denied a share in temple worship, must inevitably have led to the establishment of non-sacrificial places of assembly" (Sorenson, *Ancient American Setting*, 235). ⊕

Generally, why do angels not appear to the wicked? (21:5) "In harmony with the order of heaven, angels appear unto 'just and holy men' (see Alma 13:26; D&C 67:10–13). The Savior's teaching as recorded in Luke

16:29–31 is relevant here. Clearly, those who will not hear the word of God as preached by one such as Aaron will not hear it if preached by one who has come back from the dead. The issue is the message, not the messenger" (McConkie and Millet, *Doctrinal Commentary*, 3:151).

What did the order of the Nehors believe? (21:6–8) "The order of the Nehors [see Alma 21:4] believed that meeting together constituted a worship of God (see Alma 21:6). They held that God would save all men (see Alma 21:6) and denied the coming of Jesus Christ, for they did not believe that future events could be known (see Alma 21:7–8). Their beliefs were abhorrent to the righteous and to God" (Black, *400 Questions and Answers*, 156).

Why did Aaron begin by asking about the coming of Jesus Christ? (21:7) "Aaron has gone to the heart of erroneous Nehorite theology, which denies the doctrine of the Atoning Messiah" (Gardner, *Second Witness*, 4:324).

What was the doctrinal difference between the beliefs of the Nephites and those of the Nehors? (21:8) "The Amalekite reveals the doctrinal difference between the Nephites and the Nehors, first by denying an important doctrine, then by denying that there is any evidence for it, and finally by impugning the tradition that would encourage belief in that doctrine. By stating that these are 'thy fathers and also . . . our fathers,' the Amalekite is not only dismissing belief in the Atoning Messiah but also in revelation ('concerning . . . that which is to come')" (Gardner, *Second Witness*, 4:324).

Why has a correct understanding of Christ's Atonement been so central since the beginning of man? (21:9) President Wilford Woodruff noted: "The very first principle was faith in the Messiah; this was the first principle ever taught to man. When Adam, after being driven from the garden of Eden, went to Adam-ondi-Ahman to offer sacrifice, the angel of the Lord asked him why he did so. Adam replied that he did not know. . . . He was then told that the blood . . . should be spilt upon the altar as a type of the great and last sacrifice. . . . The first principle, then, ever taught to Father Adam was faith in the Messiah, who was to come in the meridian of time to lay down his life for the redemption of man" (*Discourses of Wilford Woodruff*, 18).

contend with him, saying: What is that thou hast testified? Hast thou seen an angel? Why do not angels appear unto us? Behold are not this people as good as thy people?

6 Thou also sayest, except we repent we shall perish. How knowest thou the thought and intent of our hearts? How knowest thou that we have cause to repent? How knowest thou that we are not a righteous people? Behold, we have built sanctuaries, and we do assemble ourselves together to worship God. We do believe that God will save all men.

7 Now Aaron said unto him: Believest thou that the Son of God shall come to redeem mankind from their sins?

8 And the man said unto him: We do not believe that thou knowest any such thing. We do not believe in these foolish traditions. We do not believe that thou knowest of things to come, neither do we believe that thy fathers and also that our fathers did know concerning the things which they spake, of that which is to come.

9 Now Aaron began to open the scriptures unto them concerning the coming of Christ, and also concerning the resurrection of the dead, and that there could be no redemption for mankind save it were through the death and sufferings of Christ, and the atonement of his blood.

10 And it came to pass as he began to expound these things unto them they were angry with him, and began to mock him; and they would not hear the words which he spake.

Alma 21:11–17. The Sons of Mosiah and Their Friends Are Persecuted as They Preach the Gospel to the Lamanites

11 Therefore, when he saw that they would not hear his words, he departed out of their synagogue, and came over to a village which was called Ani-Anti, and there he found Muloki preaching the word unto them; and also Ammah and his brethren. And they contended with many about the word.

12 And it came to pass that they saw that the people would harden their hearts, therefore they departed and came over into the land of Middoni. And they did preach the word unto many, and few believed on the words which they taught.

13 Nevertheless, Aaron and a certain number of his brethren were taken and cast into prison, and the remainder of them fled out of the land of Middoni unto the regions round about.

14 And those who were cast into prison suffered many things, and they were delivered by the hand of Lamoni and Ammon, and they were fed and clothed.

15 And they went forth again to declare the word, and thus they were delivered for the first time out of prison; and thus they had suffered.

16 And they went forth whithersoever they were led by the Spirit of the Lord, preaching the word of God in every synagogue of the Amalekites, or in every assembly of the Lamanites where they could be admitted.

17 And it came to pass that the Lord began to bless them, insomuch that they brought many to the knowledge of the truth; yea, they did convince many of their sins, and of the traditions of their fathers, which were not correct.

What should missionaries do when people refuse to listen to their message? (21:11–12) The Prophet Joseph Smith wrote: "Let the Elders be exceedingly careful about unnecessarily disturbing and harrowing up the feelings of the people. Remember that your business is to preach the Gospel in all humility and meekness, and warn sinners to repent and come to Christ.

"Avoid contentions and vain disputes with men of corrupt minds, who do not desire to know the truth. . . . If they receive not your testimony in one place, flee to another, . . . cast no reflections, nor throw out any bitter sayings. If you do your duty, it will be just as well with you, as though all men embraced the Gospel" (*History of the Church*, 1:468).

Why are there so many examples of bondage in the Book of Mormon? (21:13–15) "Again and again, individuals or peoples in the Book of Mormon are delivered from captivity. Sometimes they are physically enslaved; other times the captivity is of the mind and spirit; or the two may be connected. . . . Bondage often seems to be necessary to prepare a person for conversion or salvation. After Aaron is freed (Alma 21:14–17), he and his brothers are tremendously successful" (Rust, *Feasting on the Word*, 177).

How does the Spirit direct missionary work in these latter days? (21:16) Missionaries are counseled to "have faith that you will receive personal revelation to guide you from day to day. The Holy Ghost will help you in every aspect of your work" (*Preach My Gospel*, 90). Can you think of times when the Spirit led you to share the gospel with another? How else has the Spirit assisted you in being a member missionary? ●

How is Alma 21:17 a fulfillment of the Lord's promises in Alma 17:10–11? (21:17) Compare Doctrine and Covenants 58:4. When have you seen the Lord's blessings come to you after you have faithfully endured trials? How can these verses help you have courage to face the trials you are currently experiencing or adversities yet to come?

Alma 21:18–23. Ammon and Lamoni Return to the Land of Ishmael to Strengthen the Church

What does Lamoni's refusal to let Ammon become his servant indicate about the king? (21:19)
"Lamoni as king could have been jealous of Ammon and his ability to garner such obedience and respect among the Lamanite people. But there is no sign of such a feeling, only love and compassion for Ammon. . . . Lamoni forbade Ammon to serve him and asked him to preach to his people instead (Alma 21:19, 23). It is rare to see one of such authority and position as Lamoni be as accepting and teachable before one so traditionally inferior" (Fronk, "Show Forth Good Examples in Me," 328).

18 And it came to pass that Ammon and Lamoni returned from the land of Middoni to the land of Ishmael, which was the land of their inheritance.

19 And king Lamoni would not suffer that Ammon should serve him, or be his servant.

20 But he caused that there should be synagogues built in the land of Ishmael; and he caused that his people, or the people who were under his reign, should assemble themselves together.

21 And he did rejoice over them, and he did teach them many things. And he did also declare unto them that they were a people who were under him, and that they were a free people, that they were free from the oppressions of the king, his father; for that his father had granted unto him that he might reign over the people who were in the land of Ishmael, and in all the land round about.

22 And he also declared unto them that they might have the liberty of worshiping the Lord their God according to their desires, in whatsoever place they were in, if it were in the land which was under the reign of king Lamoni.

23 And Ammon did preach unto the people of king Lamoni; and it came to pass that he did teach them all things concerning things pertaining to righteousness. And he did exhort them daily, with all diligence; and they gave heed unto his word, and they were zealous for keeping the commandments of God.

CHAPTER 22

Aaron teaches Lamoni's father about the Creation, the Fall of Adam, and the plan of redemption through Christ—The king and all his household are converted—The division of the land between the Nephites and the Lamanites is explained. About 90–77 B.C.

1 Now, as Ammon was thus teaching the people of Lamoni continually, we will return to the account of Aaron and his brethren; for after he departed from the land of Middoni he was led by the Spirit to the land of Nephi, even to the house of the king which was over all the land save it were the land of Ishmael; and he was the father of Lamoni.

2 And it came to pass that he went in unto him into the king's palace, with his brethren, and bowed himself before the king, and said unto him: Behold, O king, we are the brethren of Ammon, whom thou hast delivered out of prison.

3 And now, O king, if thou wilt spare our lives, we will be thy servants. And the king said unto them: Arise, for I will grant unto you your lives, and I will not suffer that ye shall be my servants; but I will insist that ye shall administer unto me; for I have been somewhat troubled in mind because of the generosity and the greatness of the words of thy brother Ammon; and I desire to know the cause why he has not come up out of Middoni with thee.

4 And Aaron said unto the king: Behold, the Spirit of the Lord has called him another way; he has gone to the land of Ishmael, to teach the people of Lamoni.

5 Now the king said unto them: What is this that ye have said concerning the Spirit of the Lord? Behold, this is the thing which doth trouble me.

Alma 22:1–16. Aaron Is Led by the Spirit to King Lamoni's Father

Is there a pattern between the statements "repent and be saved" and "repent not and be cast off"? (22:6) This pattern is known as an antithetic parallelism which "is characterized by an opposition or contrast of thoughts, or an antithesis between two lines. . . . The opposites in this simple summation of the gospel plan are evident: *repent ye* contrasts with *ye will not repent*, and *saved* stands opposite to *cast off*" (Parry, "Hebraisms and Other Peculiarities in the Book of Mormon," 161–62).

What is the purpose of reminding inhabitants that God brought earlier peoples to new homelands? (22:9) "Israel followed the custom of retelling the Exodus experience to remind them of their dependence on God. The transplanted Israelites in the New World continued the same kind of memory, but with a twist. They not only remembered the acts of God among the Israelites fleeing Egypt, they also retold the story of the journey of Lehi and his family through the desert and to the new promised land. Eight times in the Book of Mormon, the Exodus was recalled. Lehi's journey from Jerusalem is referred to at least ten times. Even the Lamanites may have followed this custom to an extent (see Alma 22:9)" (Szink, "Nephi and the Exodus," 49).

What scriptures did Aaron use? (22:12–13) "The scriptures Aaron was using are still from an 'Old Testament' era, yet the sacred writings speak clearly of Christ's coming, his atonement and resurrection— further evidence of the loss of plain and precious truths from our present Bible. To king Lamoni's father 'Aaron did expound . . . the scriptures from the creation of Adam, laying the fall of man before him, and their carnal state and also the plan of redemption, which was prepared from the foundation of the world, through Christ, for all whosoever would believe on his name'" (Holland, *Christ and the New Covenant*, 119).

How does understanding man's carnal state help us learn the need for the Atonement? (22:13) "Just as soil needs preparation for a seed, so does a human heart for the word of God to take root. . . . Aaron, one

6 And also, what is this that Ammon said— If ye will repent ye shall be saved, and if ye will not repent, ye shall be cast off at the last day?

7 And Aaron answered him and said unto him: Believest thou that there is a God? And the king said: I know that the Amalekites say that there is a God, and I have granted unto them that they should build sanctuaries, that they may assemble themselves together to worship him. And if now thou sayest there is a God, behold I will believe.

8 And now when Aaron heard this, his heart began to rejoice, and he said: Behold, assuredly as thou livest, O king, there is a God.

9 And the king said: Is God that Great Spirit that brought our fathers out of the land of Jerusalem?

10 And Aaron said unto him: Yea, he is that Great Spirit, and he created all things both in heaven and in earth. Believest thou this?

11 And he said: Yea, I believe that the Great Spirit created all things, and I desire that ye should tell me concerning all these things, and I will believe thy words.

12 And it came to pass that when Aaron saw that the king would believe his words, he began from the creation of Adam, reading the scriptures unto the king—how God created man after his own image, and that God gave him commandments, and that because of transgression, man had fallen.

13 And Aaron did expound unto him the scriptures from the creation of Adam, laying the fall of man before him, and their

carnal state and also the plan of redemption, which was prepared from the foundation of the world, through Christ, for all whosoever would believe on his name.

14 And since man had fallen he could not merit anything of himself; but the sufferings and death of Christ atone for their sins, through faith and repentance, and so forth; and that he breaketh the bands of death, that the grave shall have no victory, and that the sting of death should be swallowed up in the hopes of glory; and Aaron did expound all these things unto the king.

15 And it came to pass that after Aaron had expounded these things unto him, the king said: What shall I do that I may have this eternal life of which thou hast spoken? Yea, what shall I do that I may be born of God, having this wicked spirit rooted out of my breast, and receive his Spirit, that I may be filled with joy, that I may not be cast off at

of the great missionaries in the Book of Mormon, knew how to teach that way. You remember how he taught King Lamoni's father, the old king. The king's heart had already been prepared by seeing love and humility in the way Aaron's brother had treated Lamoni, his son. But even with that preparation of the old king's heart, Aaron taught the word of God in a way to emphasize God's love and our need for him" (Eyring, *To Draw Closer to God*, 186–87). ◉

What does it mean that man "[can] not merit anything of himself"? (22:14) "Man cannot earn his own salvation. He cannot be cleansed by personal suffering for his own sins" (Oaks, "Another Testament of Christ"). ◉

What does this verse teach us about the spiritual growth in Lamoni's father? (22:15) "Lamoni's father was so impressed with the message of the gospel that he said to Aaron, 'I will give up *all* that I possess, yea, I will forsake my kingdom, that I may receive this great joy' (Alma 22:15; emphasis added). In contrast, when Lamoni's father was earlier faced with the fear of death, he promised Ammon up to '*half* of the kingdom' if he would spare him (Alma 20:23; emphasis added). It is interesting to note that the king's value of physical life was only half that of the value he placed on principles that would affect him eternally" (Williams, "Instruments in the Hands of God," 102).

Three Pillars of Eternity

Elder Bruce R. McConkie stated: "The three pillars of eternity, the three events, preeminent and transcendent above all others, are the creation, the fall, and the atonement. These three are the foundations upon which all things rest. Without any one of them all things would lose their purpose and meaning, and the plans and designs of Deity would come to naught" ("Three Pillars of Eternity"). The chart below shows how all three pillars are included in Aaron's masterful discourse in Alma 22.

Creation	Fall	Atonement of Jesus Christ
Verses 10–11. God created the heavens and the earth. Verse 12. God created man in His own image.	Verses 12–13. Because of transgression, man is fallen and is in a carnal state. Verse 14. Fallen man cannot "merit anything of himself."	Verse 13. The plan of redemption was prepared during the premortal existence for all who would believe on His name. Verse 14. "The sufferings and death of Christ atone for [our] sins, through faith and repentance." Verse 14. Christ's Atonement breaks the bands of death (all will be resurrected).

the last day? Behold, said he, I will give up all that I possess, yea, I will forsake my kingdom, that I may receive this great joy.

16 But Aaron said unto him: If thou desirest this thing, if thou wilt bow down before God, yea, if thou wilt repent of all thy sins, and will bow down before God, and call on his name in faith, believing that ye shall receive, then shalt thou receive the hope which thou desirest.

Alma 22:17–18. The King Offers a Sincere Prayer

How does the preaching of the word touch the heart? (22:17) "Many of us live or work in an environment where humility is often misunderstood and considered a weakness. Not many corporations or institutions include humility as a value statement or a desired characteristic of their management. Yet as we learn about the workings of God, the power of a humble and submissive spirit becomes apparent. In the kingdom of God, greatness begins with humility and submissiveness. These companion virtues are the first critical steps to opening the doors to the blessings of God and the power of the priesthood. It matters not who we are or how lofty our credentials appear. Humility and submissiveness to the Lord, coupled with a grateful heart, are our strength and our hope" (Edgley, "Empowerment of Humility," 98).

Why is it necessary to give away all our sins? (22:18) "So it is that real, personal sacrifice never was placing an animal on the altar. Instead, it is a willingness to put the animal in us upon the altar and letting it be consumed! Such is the 'sacrifice unto the Lord . . . of a broken heart and a contrite spirit,' (D&C 59:8), a prerequisite to taking up the cross, while giving 'away all [our] sins' in order to 'know God' (Alma 22:18) for the denial of self precedes the full acceptance of Him" (Maxwell, "Deny Yourselves of All Ungodliness," 68).

Alma 22:19–26. The Lamanite King Is Converted

17 And it came to pass that when Aaron had said these words, the king did bow down before the Lord, upon his knees; yea, even he did prostrate himself upon the earth, and cried mightily, saying:

18 O God, Aaron hath told me that there is a God; and if there is a God, and if thou art God, wilt thou make thyself known unto me, and I will give away all my sins to know thee, and that I may be raised from the dead, and be saved at the last day. And now when the king had said these words, he was struck as if he were dead.

19 And it came to pass that his servants ran and told the queen all that had happened unto the king. And she came in unto the king; and when she saw him lay as if he were dead, and also Aaron and his brethren standing as though they had been the cause of his fall, she was angry with them, and commanded that her servants, or the servants of the king, should take them and slay them.

20 Now the servants had seen the cause of the king's fall, therefore they durst not lay their hands on Aaron and his brethren; and they pled with the queen saying: Why commandest thou that we should slay these men, when behold one of them is mightier than us all? Therefore we shall fall before them.

21 Now when the queen saw the fear of the servants she also began to fear exceedingly, lest there should some evil come upon her. And she commanded her servants that they should go and call the people, that they might slay Aaron and his brethren.

22 Now when Aaron saw the determination of the queen, he, also knowing the hardness of the hearts of the people, feared lest that a multitude should assemble themselves together, and there should be a great contention and a disturbance among them; therefore he put forth his hand and raised the king from the earth, and said unto him: Stand. And he stood upon his feet, receiving his strength.

23 Now this was done in the presence of the queen and many of the servants. And when they saw it they greatly marveled, and began to fear. And the king stood forth, and began to minister unto them. And he did minister unto them, insomuch that his whole household were converted unto the Lord.

24 Now there was a multitude gathered together because of the commandment of the queen, and there began to be great murmurings among them because of Aaron and his brethren.

25 But the king stood forth among them and administered unto them. And they were pacified towards Aaron and those who were with him.

26 And it came to pass that when the king saw that the people were pacified, he caused that Aaron and his brethren should stand

Why did Aaron take the king by the hand? (22:22)
"Twice in the Book of Mormon, when individuals fell as if dead under the influence of the Spirit of the Lord, someone raised them by grasping their hand. This happened to Lamoni and his wife (Alma 19:29–30) and later to Lamoni's father (Alma 22:18–22), each of whom came to know the Lord during the experience. While there are no exact parallels in the Bible, in Revelation 1:17 the apostle John falls down as dead before the risen Christ, who then lays his right hand upon him and tells him not to fear. Closer parallels to the Book of Mormon stories are found in various pseudepigraphic texts unavailable to Joseph Smith" (Tvedtnes, *Most Correct Book*, 198). ✛

Alma 22:27–35. The Lands of the Nephites and the Lamanites

How was the land divided? (22:27–31) "During the days of Alma and General Moroni, Book of Mormon lands consisted of three sectors that could be considered Nephite, Lamanite, and former Jaredite. The depopulated Jaredite lands comprised the land northward; Nephite and Lamanite lands lay in the land southward. Nephite lands, known as the land of Zarahemla, were sandwiched between the ancient Jaredite lands to the north and the Lamanite land of Nephi to the south" (Clark, "Evaluating Nephite Geographies," 1). ✚

Why was this place considered the land of their "first inheritance"? (22:28) Hugh Nibley explained the significance of "first inheritance": "Not only does Lehi leave 'the land of his inheritance' (1 Nephi 2:4) but whenever his people wish to establish a new society they first of all make sure to allot and define the lands of their inheritance, which first allotment is regarded as inalienable. No matter where a group or family move to in later times, the first land allotted to them is always regarded as 'the land of their inheritance'" (Nibley, *An Approach to the Book of Mormon*, 100). ✚

forth in the midst of the multitude, and that they should preach the word unto them.

27 And it came to pass that the king sent a proclamation throughout all the land, amongst all his people who were in all his land, who were in all the regions round about, which was bordering even to the sea, on the east and on the west, and which was divided from the land of Zarahemla by a narrow strip of wilderness, which ran from the sea east even to the sea west, and round about on the borders of the seashore, and the borders of the wilderness which was on the north by the land of Zarahemla, through the borders of Manti, by the head of the river Sidon, running from the east towards the west—and thus were the Lamanites and the Nephites divided.

28 Now, the more idle part of the Lamanites lived in the wilderness, and dwelt in tents; and they were spread through the wilderness on the west, in the land of Nephi; yea, and also on the west of the land of Zarahemla, in the borders by the seashore, and on the west in the land of Nephi, in the place of their fathers' first inheritance, and thus bordering along by the seashore.

29 And also there were many Lamanites on the east by the seashore, whither the Nephites had driven them. And thus the Nephites were nearly surrounded by the Lamanites; nevertheless the Nephites had taken possession of all the northern parts of the land bordering on the wilderness, at the head of the river Sidon, from the east to the west, round about on the wilderness side; on the north, even until they came to the land which they called Bountiful.

30 And it bordered upon the land which they called Desolation, it being so far northward that it came into the land which had been peopled and been destroyed, of whose bones we have spoken, which was discovered by the people of Zarahemla, it being the place of their first landing.

31 And they came from there up into the south wilderness. Thus the land on the northward was called Desolation, and the land on the southward was called Bountiful, it being the wilderness which is filled with all manner of wild animals of every kind, a part of which had come from the land northward for food.

32 And now, it was only the distance of a day and a half's journey for a Nephite, on the line Bountiful and the land Desolation, from the east to the west sea; and thus the land of Nephi and the land of Zarahemla were nearly surrounded by water, there being a small neck of land between the land northward and the land southward.

33 And it came to pass that the Nephites had inhabited the land Bountiful, even from the east unto the west sea, and thus the Nephites in their wisdom, with their guards and their armies, had hemmed in the Lamanites on the south, that thereby they should have no more possession on the north, that they might not overrun the land northward.

34 Therefore the Lamanites could have no more possessions only in the land of Nephi, and the wilderness round about. Now this was wisdom in the Nephites—as the Lamanites were an enemy to them, they would not suffer their afflictions on every hand, and also that they might have a country whither they might flee, according to their desires.

35 And now I, after having said this, return again to the account of Ammon and Aaron, Omner and Himni, and their brethren.

CHAPTER 23

Religious freedom is proclaimed—The Lamanites in seven lands and cities are converted—They call themselves Anti-Nephi-Lehies and are freed from the curse—The Amalekites and the Amulonites reject the truth. About 90–77 B.C.

Alma 23:1–3. The King of the Lamanites Declares Freedom of Religion

What should our role be in preserving freedom so the gospel can be taught? (23:1) "Be an advocate for religious freedom and morality. This is a time when those who feel accountable to God for their conduct feel under siege by a secular world. You understand the moral principles that are under attack and the need to defend morality. Religious freedom all over the world is also under attack. It is important for your generation to become well educated on this issue and assume responsibility for ensuring that the religious freedom you have inherited is passed on to future generations. We must work together to both protect religious freedom and restore morality. Please understand this is not an effort to coerce religious belief. As John Locke asserted, religious worship does not have value unless it is voluntary" (Cook, "Restoration of Morality and Religious Freedom").

What was the extent of Nephite influence upon this Lamanite king? (23:1–3) "Early in Book of Mormon history, King Benjamin set forth a five-part legal series prohibiting (1) murder, (2) plunder, (3) theft, (4) adultery, and (5) any manner of wickedness. This five-part list, which first appears in Mosiah 2:13, uniformly reappears seven other times in the Book of Mormon (see Mosiah 29:36; Alma 23:3; 30:10; Helaman 3:14; 6:23; 7:21; and Ether 8:16). Apparently the Nephites viewed Benjamin's set of laws as setting a formulaic precedent" (Welch, "Textual Consistency," 23).

What role would these converts play in Nephite history? (23:3) "The sons of these people of Ammon were the army of Helaman, who helped fight the nonconverted Lamanites (see Alma 56:3–6). So the strength of the army of Helaman really began with their parents, who were the people of Ammon" (Matsumori, "A Lesson from the Book of Mormon," 76).

Alma 23:4–15. Thousands of Lamanites Are Converted to the Lord

1 Behold, now it came to pass that the king of the Lamanites sent a proclamation among all his people, that they should not lay their hands on Ammon, or Aaron, or Omner, or Himni, nor either of their brethren who should go forth preaching the word of God, in whatsoever place they should be, in any part of their land.

2 Yea, he sent a decree among them, that they should not lay their hands on them to bind them, or to cast them into prison; neither should they spit upon them, nor smite them, nor cast them out of their synagogues, nor scourge them; neither should they cast stones at them, but that they should have free access to their houses, and also their temples, and their sanctuaries.

3 And thus they might go forth and preach the word according to their desires, for the king had been converted unto the Lord, and all his household; therefore he sent his proclamation throughout the land unto his people, that the word of God might have no obstruction, but that it might go forth throughout all the land, that his people might be convinced concerning the wicked traditions of their fathers, and that they might be convinced that they were all brethren, and that they ought not to murder, nor to plunder, nor to steal, nor to commit adultery, nor to commit any manner of wickedness.

4 And now it came to pass that when the king had sent forth this proclamation, that Aaron and his brethren went forth from city to city, and from one house of worship to another, establishing churches, and consecrating priests and teachers throughout the land among the Lamanites, to preach and to teach the word of God among them; and thus they began to have great success.

5 And thousands were brought to the knowledge of the Lord, yea, thousands were brought to believe in the traditions of the Nephites; and they were taught the records and prophecies which were handed down even to the present time.

6 And as sure as the Lord liveth, so sure as many as believed, or as many as were brought to the knowledge of the truth, through the preaching of Ammon and his brethren, according to the spirit of revelation and of prophecy, and the power of God working miracles in them—yea, I say unto you, as the Lord liveth, as many of the Lamanites as believed in their preaching, and were converted unto the Lord, never did fall away.

7 For they became a righteous people; they did lay down the weapons of their rebellion, that they did not fight against God any more, neither against any of their brethren.

8 Now, these are they who were converted unto the Lord:

9 The people of the Lamanites who were in the land of Ishmael;

10 And also of the people of the Lamanites who were in the land of Middoni;

11 And also of the people of the Lamanites who were in the city of Nephi;

12 And also of the people of the Lamanites who were in the land of Shilom, and who were in the land of Shemlon, and in the city of Lemuel, and in the city of Shimnilom.

13 And these are the names of the cities of

How is this a standard for modern missionary efforts? (23:6) President Gordon B. Hinckley taught that "missionaries have a responsibility to those they baptize to help them be 'faithful and true, dyed-in-the-wool Latter-day Saints, with a conviction in their hearts concerning the truth of this great work. . . .

"'Do all you can to see that those whom you baptize are not baptisms only but solid true converts to this Church who will remain so. . . .

"'The Book of Mormon speaks of missionaries who taught so faithfully and so well that those they baptized never did fall away. . . . Now that ought to be our standard and our motto. . . .

"'I don't believe there is any reason why a convert to this Church should leave again in a short time'" ("Bring in Solid Converts; Help Them Remain"). ◉

What are our weapons of rebellion? (23:7) "To set aside cherished 'weapons of rebellion' such as selfishness, pride, and disobedience requires more than merely believing and knowing. Conviction, humility, repentance, and submissiveness precede the abandonment of our weapons of rebellion. Do you and I still possess weapons of rebellion that keep us from becoming converted unto the Lord? If so, then we need to repent now" (Bednar, "Converted unto the Lord," 108–9).

the Lamanites which were converted unto the Lord; and these are they that laid down the weapons of their rebellion, yea, all their weapons of war; and they were all Lamanites.

14 And the Amalekites were not converted, save only one; neither were any of the Amulonites; but they did harden their hearts, and also the hearts of the Lamanites in that part of the land wheresoever they dwelt, yea, and all their villages and all their cities.

15 Therefore, we have named all the cities of the Lamanites in which they did repent and come to the knowledge of the truth, and were converted.

16 And now it came to pass that the king and those who were converted were desirous that they might have a name, that thereby they might be distinguished from their brethren; therefore the king consulted with Aaron and many of their priests, concerning the name that they should take upon them, that they might be distinguished.

17 And it came to pass that they called their names Anti-Nephi-Lehies; and they were called by this name and were no more called Lamanites.

18 And they began to be a very industrious people; yea, and they were friendly with the Nephites; therefore, they did open a correspondence with them, and the curse of God did no more follow them.

Alma 23:16–18. The Converted Lamanites Desire a New Name

What does the term "Anti-Nephi-Lehies" mean? (23:17) "Book of Mormon scholars suggested a variety of definitions for *Anti-Nephi-Lehies*. George Reynolds and Janne Sjodahl suggest that the word *anti* means a 'mountain' or 'hill' and conclude that the name 'Anti-Nephi-Lehies may mean that they were located in a hilly or mountainous country'—the land of Nephi and Lehi. Hugh Nibley suggests 'a Semitic and common Indo-European root corresponding to *anti* that means "in the face of" or "facing," as of one facing a mirror, and by extension either "one who opposes" or "one who imitates." Stephen Ricks suggests, 'The name "Anti" of Anti-Nephi-Lehies may be a reflex of the Egyptian *nty* "he of, the one of." Thus, rather than having the sense "against," it has the meaning "the one of Nephi and Lehi"'" (Black, *400 Questions and Answers,* 159).

What effect did these Lamanites' conversion have on their personal work ethic? (23:18) "The Lord works from the inside out. The world works from the outside in. The world would take people out of the slums. Christ takes the slums out of people, and then they take themselves out of the slums. The world would mold men by changing their environment. Christ changes men, who then change their environment. The world would shape human behavior, but Christ can change human nature" (Benson, "Born of God," 5). ☉

CHAPTER 24

The Lamanites come against the people of God—The Anti-Nephi-Lehies rejoice in Christ and are visited by angels—They choose to suffer death rather than to defend themselves—More Lamanites are converted. About 90–77 B.C.

1 And it came to pass that the Amalekites and the Amulonites and the Lamanites who were in the land of Amulon, and also in the land of Helam, and who were in the land of Jerusalem, and in fine, in all the land round about, who had not been converted and had not taken upon them the name of Anti-Nephi-Lehi, were stirred up by the Amalekites and by the Amulonites to anger against their brethren.

2 And their hatred became exceedingly sore against them, even insomuch that they began to rebel against their king, insomuch that they would not that he should be their king; therefore, they took up arms against the people of Anti-Nephi-Lehi.

3 Now the king conferred the kingdom upon his son, and he called his name Anti-Nephi-Lehi.

4 And the king died in that selfsame year that the Lamanites began to make preparations for war against the people of God.

5 Now when Ammon and his brethren and all those who had come up with him saw the preparations of the Lamanites to destroy their brethren, they came forth to the land of Midian, and there Ammon met all his brethren; and from thence they came to the land of Ishmael that they might hold a council with Lamoni and also with his brother Anti-Nephi-Lehi, what they should do to defend themselves against the Lamanites.

6 Now there was not one soul among all the people who had been converted unto the Lord that would take up arms against their

Alma 24:1–5. The Lamanites Attack the People of Anti-Nephi-Lehi

What compelled the Lamanites to war against the people of Anti-Nephi-Lehi? (24:1–2) "Those who chose to war against the Anti-Nephi-Lehies had lost no freedoms by the conversion of their brethren; they had forfeited no rights. Wickedness hates righteousness and must, by its nature, war against it" (McConkie and Millet, *Doctrinal Commentary*, 3:166).

Why did the king give his son a new name? (24:3–5) "When Ammon successfully converted Lamoni and his people, it was necessary for them, and the Lamanites converted by the other sons of Mosiah, to make significant changes in their lives. The first step for the converted Lamanites was to call themselves Anti-Nephi-Lehies, a name chosen after Lamoni's father, the king over all the land, consulted with 'Aaron and many of their priests' regarding a name whereby 'they might be distinguished from their brethren' (see Alma 23:16–17). To strengthen this separation further, on his deathbed Lamoni's father conferred the kingdom upon his other son and changed that son's name to Anti-Nephi-Lehi (see Alma 24:2–3, 5)" (Coutts, "From a Convert's Viewpoint," 427–28).

Alma 24:6–10. The Anti-Nephi-Lehies Rejoice in Christ

How do we explain this people's reluctance to defend themselves? (24:6) "The absolute duty to go to war applied only in fighting against an *enemy*. Deuteronomy 20:1–2, instructing the Israelite leader to speak to his troops in a holy tongue when they go up to battle against an *enemy*, was interpreted in the Talmud as not applying in a conflict against other Israelites.... A similar feeling may be reflected in the Ammonite reluctance to 'take up arms against their brethren' (Alma 24:6, 18; 27:23; italics added)" (Welch, "Exemption from Military Duty," 190).

What must we do to receive God's forgiveness? (24:10) "To forgive yourself and others, you must trust the Atonement of Jesus Christ. The prophet Zenock prayed, 'Thou art angry, O Lord, with this people, because they will not understand thy mercies which thou hast bestowed upon them because of thy Son' (Alma 33:16). Our Father in Heaven is saddened when we limit the power of His Son's atoning sacrifice. As you exercise faith in Jesus Christ, you can have your guilt 'swept away'" (Perkins, "Great and Wonderful Love," 77).

Alma 24:11–19. The People of Anti-Nephi-Lehi Refuse to Fight the Lamanites

Why were the converted Lamanites forgiven of serious sin? (24:11) "This chapter is a remarkable tribute to the Lamanite converts. The world today desperately needs such peacemakers. A rather remarkable fact that we should also notice in this chapter is that God not only permitted many Lamanites to repent of their murders, but also seems to have forgiven them (vss. 10, 11). This may be justified on the grounds that the Lamanites before their conversion had little spiritual light and were ignorant of the consequences of their misdeeds" (Sperry, *Book of Mormon Compendium*, 343).

brethren; nay, they would not even make any preparations for war; yea, and also their king commanded them that they should not.

7 Now, these are the words which he said unto the people concerning the matter: I thank my God, my beloved people, that our great God has in goodness sent these our brethren, the Nephites, unto us to preach unto us, and to convince us of the traditions of our wicked fathers.

8 And behold, I thank my great God that he has given us a portion of his Spirit to soften our hearts, that we have opened a correspondence with these brethren, the Nephites.

9 And behold, I also thank my God, that by opening this correspondence we have been convinced of our sins, and of the many murders which we have committed.

10 And I also thank my God, yea, my great God, that he hath granted unto us that we might repent of these things, and also that he hath forgiven us of those our many sins and murders which we have committed, and taken away the guilt from our hearts, through the merits of his Son.

11 And now behold, my brethren, since it has been all that we could do (as we were the most lost of all mankind) to repent of all our sins and the many murders which we have committed, and to get God to take them away from our hearts, for it was all we could do to repent sufficiently before God that he would take away our stain—

12 Now, my best beloved brethren, since God hath taken away our stains, and our swords have become bright, then let us stain our swords no more with the blood of our brethren.

13 Behold, I say unto you, Nay, let us retain our swords that they be not stained with the blood of our brethren; for perhaps, if we should stain our swords again they can no more be washed bright through the blood of the Son of our great God, which shall be shed for the atonement of our sins.

14 And the great God has had mercy on us, and made these things known unto us that we might not perish; yea, and he has made these things known unto us beforehand, because he loveth our souls as well as he loveth our children; therefore, in his mercy he doth visit us by his angels, that the plan of salvation might be made known unto us as well as unto future generations.

15 Oh, how merciful is our God! And now behold, since it has been as much as we could do to get our stains taken away from us, and our swords are made bright, let us hide them away that they may be kept bright, as a testimony to our God at the last day, or at the day that we shall be brought to stand before him to be judged, that we have not stained our swords in the blood of our brethren since he imparted his word unto us and has made us clean thereby.

16 And now, my brethren, if our brethren seek to destroy us, behold, we will hide away our swords, yea, even we will bury them deep in the earth, that they may be kept bright, as a testimony that we have never used them, at the last day; and if our brethren destroy us, behold, we shall go to our God and shall be saved.

How can a sword be stained? (24:12–13) "Although today we speak of 'stainless steel,' in Joseph Smith's day, metals were not generally thought of as becoming stained. Staining was a term that generally applied to wood, cloth, or other substances subject to discoloration. . . . If the Nephite swords were the Mesoamerican *macuahuitl* with a wooden shaft, blood would naturally stain and discolor the wood when an enemy was wounded. . . . Thus the metaphor of the great mercy of God in removing bloodstains from the swords becomes much more powerful and understandable if it refers to wood stained with blood, which only a miracle would remove, rather than if it refers to metal stained with blood, which a piece of cloth would clean" (Hamblin and Merrill, "Swords in the Book of Mormon," 342).

What does the burying of weapons represent?
(24:17–18) "The simile curse is a type of curse that
appears in ancient Near Eastern, Old Testament, and
Book of Mormon texts. It consists of two parts: (1) an
event (e.g., 'Just as this wax is burned by fire') and
(2) an application of that event to the subject of the
curse (e.g., 'so shall Arpad be burned'). In ancient Near
Eastern texts, simile curses appear in written treaties
and were often part of a ritual acted out during a
treaty ceremony.... [An] example of a group ritual
occurs in the Book of Mormon when the Anti-Nephi-
Lehies bury their weapons of war as a token of their
decision never again to take up arms against their
brethren" (Morrise, "Simile Curses," 124–35).

**In what other instances did Book of Mormon writ-
ers correct themselves?** (24:19) "Concerning the
converted Lamanites, Mormon had written that 'they
buried their weapons of peace.' Then, evidently realizing that he had not intended exactly what he had
written, he added 'or they buried the weapons of war,
for peace.' Other examples of similar changes in the
Book of Mormon are found in Mosiah 7:8, Alma 50:32,
Helaman 3:33, and 3 Nephi 16:4" (Ludlow, *Companion
to Your Study of the Book of Mormon*, 210).

Alma 24:20–30. Many Lamanites Are Converted by the Example of the People of Anti-Nephi-Lehi

**What makes the action of the Anti-Nephi-Lehies
so astonishing and inspiring?** (24:21–22) Elder
Jeffrey R. Holland explained, "These Anti-Nephi-Lehies,
once a hardened and bloodthirsty people, accepted
the gospel totally and became 'distinguished for their
zeal towards God, and also towards men; for they were
perfectly honest and upright in all things; and they
were firm in the faith of Christ, even unto the end.

"'... And they never did look upon death with any
degree of terror, for their hope and views of Christ and
the resurrection; therefore, death was swallowed up to
them by the victory of Christ over it' (Alma 27:27–28)"
(Holland, *Christ and the New Covenant*, 120).

17 And now it came to pass that when the
king had made an end of these sayings, and
all the people were assembled together, they
took their swords, and all the weapons which
were used for the shedding of man's blood,
and they did bury them up deep in the earth.

18 And this they did, it being in their view
a testimony to God, and also to men, that
they never would use weapons again for the
shedding of man's blood; and this they did,
vouching and covenanting with God, that
rather than shed the blood of their brethren they would give up their own lives; and
rather than take away from a brother they
would give unto him; and rather than spend
their days in idleness they would labor abundantly with their hands.

19 And thus we see that, when these Lamanites were brought to believe and to know the
truth, they were firm, and would suffer even
unto death rather than commit sin; and thus
we see that they buried their weapons of peace,
or they buried the weapons of war, for peace.

20 And it came to pass that their brethren, the
Lamanites, made preparations for war, and
came up to the land of Nephi for the purpose
of destroying the king, and to place another in
his stead, and also of destroying the people of
Anti-Nephi-Lehi out of the land.

21 Now when the people saw that they were
coming against them they went out to meet
them, and prostrated themselves before them
to the earth, and began to call on the name of
the Lord; and thus they were in this attitude
when the Lamanites began to fall upon them,
and began to slay them with the sword.

22 And thus without meeting any resistance,
they did slay a thousand and five of them;
and we know that they are blessed, for they
have gone to dwell with their God.

23 Now when the Lamanites saw that their brethren would not flee from the sword, neither would they turn aside to the right hand or to the left, but that they would lie down and perish, and praised God even in the very act of perishing under the sword—

24 Now when the Lamanites saw this they did forbear from slaying them; and there were many whose hearts had swollen in them for those of their brethren who had fallen under the sword, for they repented of the things which they had done.

25 And it came to pass that they threw down their weapons of war, and they would not take them again, for they were stung for the murders which they had committed; and they came down even as their brethren, relying upon the mercies of those whose arms were lifted to slay them.

26 And it came to pass that the people of God were joined that day by more than the number who had been slain; and those who had been slain were righteous people, therefore we have no reason to doubt but what they were saved.

27 And there was not a wicked man slain among them; but there were more than a thousand brought to the knowledge of the truth; thus we see that the Lord worketh in many ways to the salvation of his people.

28 Now the greatest number of those of the Lamanites who slew so many of their brethren were Amalekites and Amulonites, the greatest number of whom were after the order of the Nehors.

29 Now, among those who joined the people of the Lord, there were none who were Amalekites or Amulonites, or who were of the order of Nehor, but they were actual descendants of Laman and Lemuel.

What does this account teach us about turning the other cheek? (24:22–27) "While the message of the story is not to insist on universal pacifism, we do learn that by not returning aggressions from others we can have a profound effect on them. Literally, we can change their hearts when we follow Christ's example and turn the other cheek. Our examples as peaceable followers of Christ inspire others to follow him" (Perry, *Living with Enthusiasm*, 127–28).

How can good come from conflict? (24:27) The worst circumstances can be turned for our good through faith in God. "Notwithstanding the evil and the tragedy, I see a silver thread shining through the dark and bloody tapestry of conflict. I see the finger of the Lord plucking some good from the evil designs of the adversary" (Hinckley, in Conference Report, Apr. 1968, 21).

Why do apostates persecute the Saints? (24:30)
"When once that light which was in them is taken from them, they become as much darkened as they were previously enlightened, and then, no marvel, if all their power should be enlisted against the truth, and they, Judas-like, seek the destruction of those who were their greatest benefactors" (*Joseph Smith* [manual], 321). ⊕

Alma 25:1–3. The Lamanites Attack the Nephites

What are the positive effects of not seeking vengeance? (25:1–2) "Let us, as disciples of Jesus Christ, return good for evil. Let us not seek revenge or allow our wrath to overcome us. . . . Remember: in the end, it is the merciful who obtain mercy" (Uchtdorf, "Merciful Obtain Mercy," 74).

What can we do to embrace these principles?

Alma 25:4–12. The Children of King Noah's Wicked Priests Perish by Fire

What happened to the children of Noah's former priests? (25:4–9) "In a somber aftermath, we learn of the terrible fate of the former priests and their sons. . . . When the Nephite force ambushed the Lamanite army, it both killed 'almost all the seed of Amulon and his brethren, who were the priests of Noah,' and drove the remainder deeper into the wilderness where a rift occurred among the Lamanite soldiers. . . . After an ensuing mutiny, termed a 'contention in the wilderness,' 'the Lamanites' began 'to hunt' and kill 'the seed of Amulon and his brethren' (Alma 25:8). In a mournful ending to this episode, the record sadly observes that 'they are hunted at this day by the Lamanites' (Alma 25:9)" (Brown, "Marriage and Treaty in the Book of Mormon," 110). ⊕

30 And thus we can plainly discern, that after a people have been once enlightened by the Spirit of God, and have had great knowledge of things pertaining to righteousness, and then have fallen away into sin and transgression, they become more hardened, and thus their state becomes worse than though they had never known these things.

CHAPTER 25

Lamanite aggressions spread—The seed of the priests of Noah perish as Abinadi prophesied—Many Lamanites are converted and join the people of Anti-Nephi-Lehi—They believe in Christ and keep the law of Moses. About 90–77 B.C.

1 And behold, now it came to pass that those Lamanites were more angry because they had slain their brethren; therefore they swore vengeance upon the Nephites; and they did no more attempt to slay the people of Anti-Nephi-Lehi at that time.

2 But they took their armies and went over into the borders of the land of Zarahemla, and fell upon the people who were in the land of Ammonihah and destroyed them.

3 And after that, they had many battles with the Nephites, in the which they were driven and slain.

4 And among the Lamanites who were slain were almost all the seed of Amulon and his brethren, who were the priests of Noah, and they were slain by the hands of the Nephites;

5 And the remainder, having fled into the east wilderness, and having usurped the power and authority over the Lamanites, caused that many of the Lamanites should perish by fire because of their belief—

6 For many of them, after having suffered much loss and so many afflictions, began to be stirred up in remembrance of the words

which Aaron and his brethren had preached to them in their land; therefore they began to disbelieve the traditions of their fathers, and to believe in the Lord, and that he gave great power unto the Nephites; and thus there were many of them converted in the wilderness.

7 And it came to pass that those rulers who were the remnant of the children of Amulon caused that they should be put to death, yea, all those that believed in these things.

8 Now this martyrdom caused that many of their brethren should be stirred up to anger; and there began to be contention in the wilderness; and the Lamanites began to hunt the seed of Amulon and his brethren and began to slay them; and they fled into the east wilderness.

9 And behold they are hunted at this day by the Lamanites. Thus the words of Abinadi were brought to pass, which he said concerning the seed of the priests who caused that he should suffer death by fire.

10 For he said unto them: What ye shall do unto me shall be a type of things to come.

11 And now Abinadi was the first that suffered death by fire because of his belief in God; now this is what he meant, that many should suffer death by fire, according as he had suffered.

12 And he said unto the priests of Noah that their seed should cause many to be put to death, in the like manner as he was, and that they should be scattered abroad and slain, even as a sheep having no shepherd is driven and slain by wild beasts; and now behold, these words were verified, for they were driven by the Lamanites, and they were hunted, and they were smitten.

13 And it came to pass that when the Lamanites saw that they could not overpower the Nephites they returned again to their own

Alma 25:13–17. Many Lamanites Repent and Join the Anti-Nephi-Lehies

Who were the "people of God"? (25:13) "The name and description of the community (or church) in the Book of Mormon was People of God, or Covenant People of the Lord. Those names, as well as a complex of related language, are linked with the making and renewal of the covenant binding the faithful to God. The covenant was at times renewed through rituals involving the entire community. Those rituals admonished and constituted, as they did with ancient Israel, what the Book of Mormon calls 'ways of remembrance' (1 Nephi 2:24)" (Midgley, "Prophetic Messages or Dogmatic Theology?" 98).

How do types point us to Christ? (25:15) "The Anti-Nephi-Lehies obeyed the law of Moses, believing that it was a type of Christ's coming (Alma 25:15). Obeying the law strengthened their faith in Christ: [Alma 25:15–16 is quoted].

"This is one of the finest statements in the scriptures about the role of the law of Moses as a 'type,' a symbol or pattern, of the mission of Christ. The faithful Book of Mormon people observed the law of Moses while looking forward to the coming of Christ and while living gospel principles and ordinances. They knew that salvation did not come by the law of Moses but through Christ; yet the law strengthened their faith in Christ and taught them of him through the spirit of prophecy" (Jackson and Matthews, "Lamanite Converts Firm in the Faith of Christ," 335). ●

How did the Nephites' obedience to the law differ from that of the Jews? (25:16) "Nephites, though separated from their forebears and kindred by oceans of water, yet kept the law of Moses (2 Ne. 5:10; Jarom 1:5; Hel. 15:5). But they did so with a proper understanding, knowing that salvation was in Christ who should come and that 'the law of Moses was a type of his coming' (Alma 25:15–16)....To them the law was not an end in itself, but a means to an end. The blindness of their Jewish relatives in the Old World came 'by looking beyond the mark' (Jacob 4:14), meaning they did not have a proper perspective of the law and know how it was designed to lead them to Christ and his gospel" (McConkie, *Promised Messiah*, 420).

What does Mormon teach us about being a servant of God? (25:17) "God's servants are only instruments in his hands. Mormon's statement that God 'verified his word unto [the sons of Mosiah] in every particular' (Alma 25:17) coupled with the reminder of Abinadi's death (Alma 25:11) should cause us to note that God allowed Abinadi to die as a martyr yet protected the sons of Mosiah from death just as he had promised them (Mosiah 28:7). Abinadi and the sons of Mosiah had different assignments; both fulfilled those assignments" (Hansen, "Book of Alma as a Prototype," 270–71).

land; and many of them came over to dwell in the land of Ishmael and the land of Nephi, and did join themselves to the people of God, who were the people of Anti-Nephi-Lehi.

14 And they did also bury their weapons of war, according as their brethren had, and they began to be a righteous people; and they did walk in the ways of the Lord, and did observe to keep his commandments and his statutes.

15 Yea, and they did keep the law of Moses; for it was expedient that they should keep the law of Moses as yet, for it was not all fulfilled. But notwithstanding the law of Moses, they did look forward to the coming of Christ, considering that the law of Moses was a type of his coming, and believing that they must keep those outward performances until the time that he should be revealed unto them.

16 Now they did not suppose that salvation came by the law of Moses; but the law of Moses did serve to strengthen their faith in Christ; and thus they did retain a hope through faith, unto eternal salvation, relying upon the spirit of prophecy, which spake of those things to come.

17 And now behold, Ammon, and Aaron, and Omner, and Himni, and their brethren did rejoice exceedingly, for the success which they had had among the Lamanites, seeing that the Lord had granted unto them according to their prayers, and that he had also verified his word unto them in every particular.

CHAPTER 26

Ammon glories in the Lord—The faithful are strengthened by the Lord and are given knowledge—By faith men may bring thousands of souls unto repentance—God has all power and comprehends all things. About 90–77 B.C.

1 And now, these are the words of Ammon to his brethren, which say thus: My brothers and my brethren, behold I say unto you, how great reason have we to rejoice; for could we have supposed when we started from the land of Zarahemla that God would have granted unto us such great blessings?

2 And now, I ask, what great blessings has he bestowed upon us? Can ye tell?

3 Behold, I answer for you; for our brethren, the Lamanites, were in darkness, yea, even in the darkest abyss, but behold, how many of them are brought to behold the marvelous light of God! And this is the blessing which hath been bestowed upon us, that we have been made instruments in the hands of God to bring about this great work.

4 Behold, thousands of them do rejoice, and have been brought into the fold of God.

5 Behold, the field was ripe, and blessed are ye, for ye did thrust in the sickle, and did reap with your might, yea, all the day long did ye labor; and behold the number of your sheaves! And they shall be gathered into the garners, that they are not wasted.

6 Yea, they shall not be beaten down by the storm at the last day; yea, neither shall they be harrowed up by the whirlwinds; but when the storm cometh they shall be gathered together in their place, that the storm cannot penetrate to them; yea, neither shall they be

Alma 26:1–9. Ammon Speaks of the Blessings He Received as a Missionary

What great blessings has God bestowed upon us? (26:1–2) Why is it important to take time as we do the Lord's work to ponder His hand in our efforts?

How can we rejoice as these people did? (26:4) In the modern revelation the Lord has promised that, like the sons of Mosiah, we will have great joy with those we bring into the kingdom, even if it is only one soul (see D&C 18:15–16). Who is there in your circle of acquaintances that you would like to rejoice with in the kingdom of God? What is one step you can take to begin to introduce them to the gospel?

How are converts like sheaves? (26:5) Sheaves are "stalks of wheat, rye, oats or barley bound together" (Webster, *American Dictionary*). "Agricultural imagery—sowing, reaping, harvesting—is often related by the prophets to missionary work" (McConkie and Parry, *Guide to Scriptural Symbols,* 99). Elder David A. Bednar taught, "The sheaves in this analogy represent newly baptized members of the Church. The garners are the holy temples" ("Honorably Hold a Name and Standing," *Ensign,* May 2009, 97). ☉

What do the garners that protect the sheaves represent? (26:5–7) "The great garner into which the sheaves should be gathered is the holy temple" (Maxwell, "Make Calling Focus of Your Mission," 4).

driven with fierce winds whithersoever the enemy listeth to carry them.

7 But behold, they are in the hands of the Lord of the harvest, and they are his; and he will raise them up at the last day.

8 Blessed be the name of our God; let us sing to his praise, yea, let us give thanks to his holy name, for he doth work righteousness forever.

9 For if we had not come up out of the land of Zarahemla, these our dearly beloved brethren, who have so dearly beloved us, would still have been racked with hatred against us, yea, and they would also have been strangers to God.

10 And it came to pass that when Ammon had said these words, his brother Aaron rebuked him, saying: Ammon, I fear that thy joy doth carry thee away unto boasting.

11 But Ammon said unto him: I do not boast in my own strength, nor in my own wisdom; but behold, my joy is full, yea, my heart is brim with joy, and I will rejoice in my God.

Alma 26:10–13. Ammon Tells Aaron That Their Missionary Success Came Because of God's Power

What is the difference between rejoicing and boasting? (26:10–11) "Ammon's expression of his joy caused Aaron to voice concern that perhaps Ammon was beginning to boast of his success (see Alma 26:10). However, through Ammon's reply we can discern the principles upon which true joy is founded. . . . Divine joy is available to all who are willing to serve the Lord with the same degree of commitment as Ammon and his companions" (Williams, "Instruments in the Hands of God," 103). ❂

When do our hearts become "brim with joy"? (26:11) "When we reach a point of consecration, our afflictions will be swallowed up in the joy of Christ. It does not mean we won't have afflictions, but they will be put in a perspective that permits us to deal with them. With our steady pursuit of joy and with each increasing measure of righteousness, we will experience one more drop of delight—one drop after another—until, in the words of a prophet, our hearts are 'brim with joy' (Alma 26:11). At last, the soul's cup finally runs over!" (Maxwell, "Brim with Joy," 13).

Why is it important to remember that we are nothing without the Lord? (26:12) "Everything is given by God. All talent, creativity, ability, insight, and strength comes from him. In our own strength we can do nothing, as Ammon admitted to his brother (see Alma 26:10–12). When we seek the praise of man more than the praise of God, it will become easy to fall" (Ashton, "Neither Boast of Faith Nor Mighty Works," 67). ❂

12 Yea, I know that I am nothing; as to my strength I am weak; therefore I will not boast of myself, but I will boast of my God, for in his strength I can do all things; yea, behold, many mighty miracles we have wrought in this land, for which we will praise his name forever.

13 Behold, how many thousands of our brethren has he loosed from the pains of hell; and

they are brought to sing redeeming love, and this because of the power of his word which is in us, therefore have we not great reason to rejoice?

14 Yea, we have reason to praise him forever, for he is the Most High God, and has loosed our brethren from the chains of hell.

15 Yea, they were encircled about with everlasting darkness and destruction; but behold, he has brought them into his everlasting light, yea, into everlasting salvation; and they are encircled about with the matchless bounty of his love; yea, and we have been instruments in his hands of doing this great and marvelous work.

16 Therefore, let us glory, yea, we will glory in the Lord; yea, we will rejoice, for our joy is full; yea, we will praise our God forever. Behold, who can glory too much in the Lord? Yea, who can say too much of his great power, and of his mercy, and of his long-suffering towards the children of men? Behold, I say unto you, I cannot say the smallest part which I feel.

17 Who could have supposed that our God would have been so merciful as to have snatched us from our awful, sinful, and polluted state?

18 Behold, we went forth even in wrath, with mighty threatenings to destroy his church.

19 Oh then, why did he not consign us to an awful destruction, yea, why did he not let the sword of his justice fall upon us, and doom us to eternal despair?

20 Oh, my soul, almost as it were, fleeth at the thought. Behold, he did not exercise his justice upon us, but in his great mercy hath brought us over that everlasting gulf of death and misery, even to the salvation of our souls.

Alma 26:14–22. Ammon Praises God for Delivering Him from Sin

How does God encircle His children with love? (26:15) "God has spoken to Joseph Smith for the purpose of blessing all of God's children with His mercy and love, even in times of uncertainties and insecurities, of wars and rumors of wars, of natural and personal disasters. The Savior said, 'Behold, mine arm of mercy is extended towards you, and whosoever will come, him will I receive' (3 Nephi 9:14). And all who accept this invitation will be 'encircled about with the matchless bounty of his love' (Alma 26:15)" (Uchtdorf, "Fruits of the First Vision," 38). ✦

How do we communicate what we feel? (26:16) "The Holy Ghost will help us by transmitting our feelings, teachings, and testimonies to others—even when, inadequate of ourselves, we cannot speak 'the smallest part which [we] feel' (Alma 26:16). In so many of life's situations, do we not genuinely yearn to be able to connect, especially with those we love the most? Or with others who have played special roles in our lives?" (Maxwell, *Promise of Discipleship*, 95).

What effect does the Atonement have on those who have repented? (26:17) "When memory of prior mistakes encroached upon Ammon's mind, he turned his thoughts to Jesus Christ and the miracle of forgiveness. Then his suffering was replaced with joy, gratitude, and thanksgiving for the Savior's love and forgiveness. Please, go and do likewise. Do it now so that you can enjoy peace of conscience and peace of mind with all their attendant blessings" (Scott, "Peace of Conscience and Peace of Mind," 18).

Why does the natural man fail to see the things of God? (26:21) "Paul explained that 'the natural man receiveth not the things of the Spirit of God: for they are foolishness unto him: neither *can* he know them, because they are spiritually discerned' (1 Corinthians 2:14; italics added). In exulting over the Lord's infinite mercy—in His willingness to snatch His children from evil and forgive their sins—Ammon said: 'What natural man is there that knoweth these things? I say unto you, there is none that knoweth these things, save it be the penitent' (Alma 26:21).... 'How difficult it is to teach the natural man,' Brigham Young declared, 'who comprehends nothing more than that which he sees with the natural eye!'" (Millet, *Power of the Word*, 75).

What are the "mysteries of God"? (26:22) "There are in the gospel such things as mysteries. A mystery is, of course, some truth which is not understood. All the principles of the gospel and all truth pertaining to the salvation of men are simple when understood. Until it is understood, however, a simple truth may be a great mystery....

"To understand spiritual things, a man must have spiritual discernment, that is, guidance by the Holy Ghost. For this reason we are confirmed and receive the gift of the Holy Ghost" (Smith, *Doctrines of Salvation*, 1:296–97).

Alma 26:23–34. Ammon Reminds His Brothers about Some of Their Missionary Experiences

21 And now behold, my brethren, what natural man is there that knoweth these things? I say unto you, there is none that knoweth these things, save it be the penitent.

22 Yea, he that repenteth and exerciseth faith, and bringeth forth good works, and prayeth continually without ceasing—unto such it is given to know the mysteries of God; yea, unto such it shall be given to reveal things which never have been revealed; yea, and it shall be given unto such to bring thousands of souls to repentance, even as it has been given unto us to bring these our brethren to repentance.

23 Now do ye remember, my brethren, that we said unto our brethren in the land of Zarahemla, we go up to the land of Nephi, to preach unto our brethren, the Lamanites, and they laughed us to scorn?

24 For they said unto us: Do ye suppose that ye can bring the Lamanites to the knowledge of the truth? Do ye suppose that ye can convince the Lamanites of the incorrectness of the traditions of their fathers, as stiffnecked a people as they are; whose hearts delight in the shedding of blood; whose days have been spent in the grossest iniquity; whose ways have been the ways of a transgressor from the beginning? Now my brethren, ye remember that this was their language.

25 And moreover they did say: Let us take up arms against them, that we destroy them and their iniquity out of the land, lest they overrun us and destroy us.

26 But behold, my beloved brethren, we came into the wilderness not with the intent to destroy our brethren, but with the intent that perhaps we might save some few of their souls.

27 Now when our hearts were depressed, and we were about to turn back, behold, the Lord comforted us, and said: Go amongst thy brethren, the Lamanites, and bear with patience thine afflictions, and I will give unto you success.

28 And now behold, we have come, and been forth amongst them; and we have been patient in our sufferings, and we have suffered every privation; yea, we have traveled from house to house, relying upon the mercies of the world—not upon the mercies of the world alone but upon the mercies of God.

29 And we have entered into their houses and taught them, and we have taught them in their streets; yea, and we have taught them upon their hills; and we have also entered into their temples and their synagogues and taught them; and we have been cast out, and mocked, and spit upon, and smote upon our cheeks; and we have been stoned, and taken and bound with strong cords, and cast into prison; and through the power and wisdom of God we have been delivered again.

30 And we have suffered all manner of afflictions, and all this, that perhaps we might be the means of saving some soul; and we supposed that our joy would be full if perhaps we could be the means of saving some.

31 Now behold, we can look forth and see the fruits of our labors; and are they few? I say unto you, Nay, they are many; yea, and we can witness of their sincerity, because of their love towards their brethren and also towards us.

32 For behold, they had rather sacrifice their lives than even to take the life of their enemy; and they have buried their weapons of war

What can (or should) we do when our hearts are depressed? (26:27) "There are times when you simply have to righteously hang on and outlast the devil until his depressive spirit leaves you. As the Lord told the Prophet Joseph Smith: 'Thine adversity and thine afflictions shall be but a small moment; and then, if thou endure it well, God shall exalt thee on high' (D&C 121:7–8). To press on in noble endeavors, even while surrounded by a cloud of depression, will eventually bring you out on top into the sunshine" (Benson, "Do Not Despair," 68). ☉

How can Ammon's experiences strengthen modern missionaries? (26:29) "I was reading again the twenty-sixth chapter of Alma and the story of Ammon's mission. I read out loud, as I sometimes do, trying to put myself in the position of the characters in the book. . . . The Spirit spoke to my soul, saying, Did you notice? Everything that happened to Ammon happened to you. . . . And then on that day as I read, the Spirit testified to me again. . . . No one but a missionary could have written this story. Joseph Smith could never have known what it was like to be a missionary to the Lamanites, for no one he knew had ever done such a thing before" (Howard, "Ammon," 124–25). ☉

Alma 26:35–37. We Can Rejoice Because of the Goodness of God

Why is it vital that God "has all power"? (26:35) "Unless God had power over all things, and was able by his power to control all things, and thereby deliver his creatures who put their trust in him from the power of all beings that might seek their destruction, whether in heaven, on earth, or in hell, men could not be saved" (*Lectures on Faith*, 52).

"Mercy is granted . . . as it is with all blessings, to those who comply with the law upon which its receipt is predicated (see D&C 130:20–21)" (McConkie and Millet, *Doctrinal Commentary*, 3:184).

What does this reference to "wanderers" teach us? (26:36) Regarding wanderers, Nibley said: "The Nephites never ceased to think of themselves in those melancholy terms. Five hundred years after Jacob, Alma could write that his people were both blessed and sorrowful in their wandering state. . . . 'God,' he says, 'has been mindful of this people, who are a branch of the tree of Israel, and has been lost from its body in a strange land; yea, I say, blessed be the name of my God, who has been mindful of us, wanderers in a strange land' (Alma 26:36)" (Nibley, *Approach to the Book of Mormon*, 142). ☉

In what way is God "mindful of every people"? (26:37) "It is convenient to imagine all the righteous in one camp and the wicked in another, and this has been the usual and comfortable interpretation of the Book of Mormon—it is the good guys versus the bad guys. But this is exactly what the Book of Mormon tells us to avoid. God plays no favorites. Nephi rebukes his brothers for believing that because they are Jews they are righteous; God does not judge by party, he tells them; a good man is good and a bad one is bad, according to his own behavior: 'Behold, the Lord esteemeth all flesh in one; he that is righteous is favored of God' (1 Nephi 17:35)" (Nibley, *Prophetic Book of Mormon*, 506).

deep in the earth, because of their love towards their brethren.

33 And now behold I say unto you, has there been so great love in all the land? Behold, I say unto you, Nay, there has not, even among the Nephites.

34 For behold, they would take up arms against their brethren; they would not suffer themselves to be slain. But behold how many of these have laid down their lives; and we know that they have gone to their God, because of their love and of their hatred to sin.

35 Now have we not reason to rejoice? Yea, I say unto you, there never were men that had so great reason to rejoice as we, since the world began; yea, and my joy is carried away, even unto boasting in my God; for he has all power, all wisdom, and all understanding; he comprehendeth all things, and he is a merciful Being, even unto salvation, to those who will repent and believe on his name.

36 Now if this is boasting, even so will I boast; for this is my life and my light, my joy and my salvation, and my redemption from everlasting wo. Yea, blessed is the name of my God, who has been mindful of this people, who are a branch of the tree of Israel, and has been lost from its body in a strange land; yea, I say, blessed be the name of my God, who has been mindful of us, wanderers in a strange land.

37 Now my brethren, we see that God is mindful of every people, whatsoever land they may be in; yea, he numbereth his people, and his bowels of mercy are over all the earth. Now this is my joy, and my great thanksgiving; yea, and I will give thanks unto my God forever. Amen.

CHAPTER 27

The Lord commands Ammon to lead the people of Anti-Nephi-Lehi to safety—Upon meeting Alma, Ammon's joy exhausts his strength—The Nephites give the Anti-Nephi-Lehies the land of Jershon—They are called the people of Ammon. About 90–77 B.C.

1 Now it came to pass that when those Lamanites who had gone to war against the Nephites had found, after their many struggles to destroy them, that it was in vain to seek their destruction, they returned again to the land of Nephi.

2 And it came to pass that the Amalekites, because of their loss, were exceedingly angry. And when they saw that they could not seek revenge from the Nephites, they began to stir up the people in anger against their brethren, the people of Anti-Nephi-Lehi; therefore they began again to destroy them.

3 Now this people again refused to take their arms, and they suffered themselves to be slain according to the desires of their enemies.

4 Now when Ammon and his brethren saw this work of destruction among those whom they so dearly beloved, and among those who had so dearly beloved them—for they were treated as though they were angels sent from God to save them from everlasting destruction—therefore, when Ammon and his brethren saw this great work of destruction, they were moved with compassion, and they said unto the king:

5 Let us gather together this people of the Lord, and let us go down to the land of Zarahemla to our brethren the Nephites, and flee out of the hands of our enemies, that we be not destroyed.

6 But the king said unto them: Behold, the Nephites will destroy us, because of the many murders and sins we have committed against them.

Alma 27:1–12. Ammon Asks the Lord How to Save the Anti-Nephi-Lehies

Why would the converted Lamanites call themselves "Anti-Nephi-Lehies"? (27:2) If Joseph Smith were simply writing a fictional story, why would he choose this name? "Dr. Hugh Nibley has found 'a Semitic and common Indo-European root corresponding to *anti* that means 'in the face of' or 'facing' as of one facing a mirror, and by extension either 'one who opposes' or 'one who imitates.' . . . Thus the term 'Anti-Nephi-Lehies' might refer to those who imitate the teachings of the descendants of Nephi and Lehi" (Ludlow, *Companion to Your Study of the Book of Mormon*, 209–10; see also Alma 23:17). ⊕

How are missionaries like angels? (27:4) The Lord has stated that missionaries, like Alma and his brethren, are like unto angels or messengers from heaven. Missionaries and angels preach the gospel of repentance. Modern-day missionaries are to "go forth in the power of my Spirit, preaching my gospel, two by two, in my name, lifting up your voices as with the sound of a trump, declaring my word like unto angels of God" (D&C 42:6). ⊕

What do we know about Mosiah's law regarding slavery? (27:9) "The law of Mosiah . . . prohibited slavery in the land of Zarahemla, for Ammon assured his converts that 'it is against the law of our brethren, which was established by my father, that there should be any slaves among them' (Alma 27:9). Previously it had been only by royal benevolence that slavery was not allowed in Zarahemla (see Mosiah 2:13)" (Welch, "Law of Mosiah," 160).

Alma 27:13–19. Ammon and His Brothers Meet Alma on Their Way Home

Why would Ammon's request "try the hearts" of the Nephites? (27:15) "The conversion of the warmongering Lamanites who became the Anti-Nephi-Lehies was remarkable. But just as remarkable was the instant forgiveness of the Nephites, who apparently had friends and relatives who had been killed by the Anti-Nephi-Lehies prior to their conversion (see Alma

7 And Ammon said: I will go and inquire of the Lord, and if he say unto us, go down unto our brethren, will ye go?

8 And the king said unto him: Yea, if the Lord saith unto us go, we will go down unto our brethren, and we will be their slaves until we repair unto them the many murders and sins which we have committed against them.

9 But Ammon said unto him: It is against the law of our brethren, which was established by my father, that there should be any slaves among them; therefore let us go down and rely upon the mercies of our brethren.

10 But the king said unto him: Inquire of the Lord, and if he saith unto us go, we will go; otherwise we will perish in the land.

11 And it came to pass that Ammon went and inquired of the Lord, and the Lord said unto him:

12 Get this people out of this land, that they perish not; for Satan has great hold on the hearts of the Amalekites, who do stir up the Lamanites to anger against their brethren to slay them; therefore get thee out of this land; and blessed are this people in this generation, for I will preserve them.

13 And now it came to pass that Ammon went and told the king all the words which the Lord had said unto him.

14 And they gathered together all their people, yea, all the people of the Lord, and did gather together all their flocks and herds, and departed out of the land, and came into the wilderness which divided the land of Nephi from the land of Zarahemla, and came over near the borders of the land.

15 And it came to pass that Ammon said unto them: Behold, I and my brethren will go forth into the land of Zarahemla, and ye shall remain here until we return; and we will try the hearts of our brethren, whether they will that ye shall come into their land.

16 And it came to pass that as Ammon was going forth into the land, that he and his brethren met Alma, over in the place of which has been spoken; and behold, this was a joyful meeting.

17 Now the joy of Ammon was so great even that he was full; yea, he was swallowed up in the joy of his God, even to the exhausting of his strength; and he fell again to the earth.

18 Now was not this exceeding joy? Behold, this is joy which none receiveth save it be the truly penitent and humble seeker of happiness.

19 Now the joy of Alma in meeting his brethren was truly great, and also the joy of Aaron, of Omner, and Himni; but behold their joy was not that to exceed their strength.

20 And now it came to pass that Alma conducted his brethren back to the land of Zarahemla; even to his own house. And they went and told the chief judge all the things that had happened unto them in the land of Nephi, among their brethren, the Lamanites.

21 And it came to pass that the chief judge sent a proclamation throughout all the land, desiring the voice of the people concerning the admitting their brethren, who were the people of Anti-Nephi-Lehi.

22 And it came to pass that the voice of the people came, saying: Behold, we will give up the land of Jershon, which is on the east by the sea, which joins the land Bountiful, which is on the south of the land Bountiful; and this land Jershon is the land which we will give unto our brethren for an inheritance.

23 And behold, we will set our armies between the land Jershon and the land Nephi, that we may protect our brethren in the land Jershon; and this we do for our brethren, on account of their fear to take up arms against

27:6). Conversion involves a mighty change of heart, a process experienced by both Anti-Nephi-Lehies and Nephites alike" (Condie, *Your Agency: Handle with Care*, 106).

What does *penitent* mean? (27:18) The word *penitent* means "suffering pain or sorrow of heart on account of sins, crimes or offenses; contrite; sincerely affected by a sense of guilt and resolving on amendment of life" (Webster, *American Dictionary*). ⊕

Alma 27:20–24. The Nephites Provide a Safe Home for the Lamanite Converts

What does the name Jershon mean? (27:22) "The name, though not found in the Bible, has an authentic Hebrew origin, the root . . . meaning 'to inherit.' . . .

"It is in this light that we should understand the words in Alma 27:22 ('and this land Jershon is the land which we will give unto our brethren for an inheritance'), Alma 27:24 ('that they may inherit the land Jershon')" (Ricks and Tvedtnes, "Hebrew Origins of Some Book of Mormon Place Names," 257–58).

In what way is repentance "sore"? (27:23) "What does it mean to repent? We begin with a dictionary's definition that to repent is 'to turn from sin . . . to feel sorrow [and] regret.' To repent from sin is not easy. But the prize is worth the price" (Nelson, "Repentance and Conversion," 102). ⊕

their brethren lest they should commit sin; and this their great fear came because of their sore repentance which they had, on account of their many murders and their awful wickedness.

24 And now behold, this will we do unto our brethren, that they may inherit the land Jershon; and we will guard them from their enemies with our armies, on condition that they will give us a portion of their substance to assist us that we may maintain our armies.

Alma 27:25–30. The Anti-Nephi-Lehies Become Known as the People of Ammon

25 Now, it came to pass that when Ammon had heard this, he returned to the people of Anti-Nephi-Lehi, and also Alma with him, into the wilderness, where they had pitched their tents, and made known unto them all these things. And Alma also related unto them his conversion, with Ammon and Aaron, and his brethren.

26 And it came to pass that it did cause great joy among them. And they went down into the land of Jershon, and took possession of the land of Jershon; and they were called by the Nephites the people of Ammon; therefore they were distinguished by that name ever after.

27 And they were among the people of Nephi, and also numbered among the people who were of the church of God. And they were also distinguished for their zeal towards God, and also towards men; for they were perfectly honest and upright in all things; and they were firm in the faith of Christ, even unto the end.

28 And they did look upon shedding the blood of their brethren with the greatest abhorrence; and they never could be prevailed upon to take up arms against their brethren; and they never did look upon death with any degree of terror, for their hope and views of Christ and the resurrection; therefore, death

Why is being "perfectly honest" a fundamental value in the gospel? (27:27) "Honesty is the basis of a true Christian life. For Latter-day Saints, honesty is an important requirement for entering the Lord's holy temple. Honesty is embedded in the covenants that we make in the temple. Each Sunday as we partake of the holy emblems of the Savior's flesh and blood, we again renew our basic and sacred covenants—which encompass honesty. As Latter-day Saints we have a sacred obligation to not only teach the principles of honesty, but also to live them.... Honesty should be among the most fundamental values that govern our everyday living" (Edgley, "Three Towels and a 25-Cent Newspaper," 74). ☉

was swallowed up to them by the victory of Christ over it.

29 Therefore, they would suffer death in the most aggravating and distressing manner which could be inflicted by their brethren, before they would take the sword or cimeter to smite them.

30 And thus they were a zealous and beloved people, a highly favored people of the Lord.

CHAPTER 28

The Lamanites are defeated in a tremendous battle—Tens of thousands are slain—The wicked are consigned to a state of endless woe; the righteous attain a never-ending happiness. About 77–76 B.C.

1 And now it came to pass that after the people of Ammon were established in the land of Jershon, and a church also established in the land of Jershon, and the armies of the Nephites were set round about the land of Jershon, yea, in all the borders round about the land of Zarahemla; behold the armies of the Lamanites had followed their brethren into the wilderness.

2 And thus there was a tremendous battle; yea, even such an one as never had been known among all the people in the land from the time Lehi left Jerusalem; yea, and tens of thousands of the Lamanites were slain and scattered abroad.

3 Yea, and also there was a tremendous slaughter among the people of Nephi; nevertheless, the Lamanites were driven and scattered, and the people of Nephi returned again to their land.

4 And now this was a time that there was a great mourning and lamentation heard throughout all the land, among all the people of Nephi—

How do we become favored of the Lord? (27:30)
Nephi taught that "the Lord esteemeth all flesh in one" (1 Nephi 17:35) and "denieth none that come unto him" (2 Nephi 26:33), yet "he that is righteous is favored of God" (1 Nephi 17:35). Why? The Lord explained to the Prophet Joseph Smith an eternal principle: "I, the Lord, am bound when ye do what I say; but when you do not what I say, ye have no promise" (D&C 82:10). Through our obedience to Him, we become *bound* to Him and become His servants. Like the people of Ammon, we become beloved, "a highly favored people of the Lord" (Alma 27:30).

Alma 28:1–7. The Lamanites Are Defeated in a Great Battle

How can those in "great mourning and lamentation" over the loss of their loved ones find comfort and hope? (28:4–5) The Prophet Joseph Smith explained: "More painful to me are the thoughts of annihilation than death. If I have no expectation of seeing my father, mother, brothers, sisters and friends again, my heart would burst in a moment, and I should go down to my grave.

"The expectation of seeing my friends in the morning of the resurrection cheers my soul and makes me bear up against the evils of life. It is like their taking a long journey, and on their return we meet them with increased joy" (*Joseph Smith* [manual], 176). The Lord further clarified that we should mourn only for those who do not have a hope of a glorious resurrection (see D&C 42:45–47).

To what might "a time of solemnity" refer? (28:6)
In the language of the Prophet Joseph Smith's day, "a time of solemnity" could have had reference to "a religious ceremony; [or] a ritual performance attended with religious reverence; [such] as the solemnity of a funeral" (Webster, *American Dictionary*).

Alma 28:8–14. The Wicked Who Die Are Miserable, but the Righteous Receive Great Joy

How can we experience joy while having afflictions? (28:8) Elder Hafen relates this to what he calls "Lehi's paradox: 'He shall consecrate thine afflictions for thy gain.'" Elder Hafen further explains: "There is a link between sorrow, toil, affliction, and 'incomprehensible joy.' Otherwise, there may only be innocence—'having no joy, for they knew no misery' (2 Nephi 2:23)" (Hafen, *Broken Heart*, 70).

5 Yea, the cry of widows mourning for their husbands, and also of fathers mourning for their sons, and the daughter for the brother, yea, the brother for the father; and thus the cry of mourning was heard among all of them, mourning for their kindred who had been slain.

6 And now surely this was a sorrowful day; yea, a time of solemnity, and a time of much fasting and prayer.

7 And thus endeth the fifteenth year of the reign of the judges over the people of Nephi;

8 And this is the account of Ammon and his brethren, their journeyings in the land of Nephi, their sufferings in the land, their sorrows, and their afflictions, and their incomprehensible joy, and the reception and safety of the brethren in the land of Jershon. And now may the Lord, the Redeemer of all men, bless their souls forever.

9 And this is the account of the wars and contentions among the Nephites, and also the wars between the Nephites and the Lamanites; and the fifteenth year of the reign of the judges is ended.

10 And from the first year to the fifteenth has brought to pass the destruction of many thousand lives; yea, it has brought to pass an awful scene of bloodshed.

11 And the bodies of many thousands are laid low in the earth, while the bodies of many thousands are moldering in heaps upon the face of the earth; yea, and many thousands are mourning for the loss of their kindred, because they have reason to fear,

according to the promises of the Lord, that they are consigned to a state of endless wo.

12 While many thousands of others truly mourn for the loss of their kindred, yet they rejoice and exult in the hope, and even know, according to the promises of the Lord, that they are raised to dwell at the right hand of God, in a state of never-ending happiness.

13 And thus we see how great the inequality of man is because of sin and transgression, and the power of the devil, which comes by the cunning plans which he hath devised to ensnare the hearts of men.

14 And thus we see the great call of diligence of men to labor in the vineyards of the Lord; and thus we see the great reason of sorrow, and also of rejoicing—sorrow because of death and destruction among men, and joy because of the light of Christ unto life.

CHAPTER 29

Alma desires to cry repentance with angelic zeal—The Lord grants teachers for all nations—Alma glories in the Lord's work and in the success of Ammon and his brethren. About 76 B.C.

1 O that I were an angel, and could have the wish of mine heart, that I might go forth and speak with the trump of God, with a voice to shake the earth, and cry repentance unto every people!

2 Yea, I would declare unto every soul, as with the voice of thunder, repentance and the plan of redemption, that they should repent and come unto our God, that there might not be more sorrow upon all the face of the earth.

3 But behold, I am a man, and do sin in my wish; for I ought to be content with the things which the Lord hath allotted unto me.

What can we learn from Mormon's use of the phrase: "thus we see"? (28:13) The phrase "thus we see" is used by Mormon "over twenty times to insert moral conclusions in the sections he wrote or abridged (i.e., Alma 12:21; 24:19; 28:13; 30:60; 46:8; 50:19; Helaman 3:28; 6:34–36; 12:3). Moroni used the phrase only once (see Ether 14:25)" (Keller, "Mormon and Moroni as Authors and Abridgers," 270–71). ☉

What should we do to be more diligent in the Lord's service? (28:14) "The challenge is to be more profitable servants in the Lord's vineyard. This applies to all of us, whatever our age, and not alone to those who are preparing to serve as full-time missionaries, for to each of us comes the mandate to share the gospel of Christ.

"May I suggest a formula that will ensure our success: first, search the scriptures with diligence; second, plan your life with purpose (and, I might add, plan your life regardless of your age); third, teach the truth with testimony; and fourth, serve the Lord with love" (Monson, "Come All Ye Sons of God," 66). ☉

Alma 29:1–3. Alma Desires to Preach the Gospel

How does repentance rescue us from sorrow? (29:1–2) "Only repentance leads to the sunlit uplands of a better life. And, of course, only through repentance do we gain access to the atoning grace of Jesus Christ and salvation. Repentance is a divine gift, and there should be a smile on our faces when we speak of it. It points us to freedom, confidence, and peace. Rather than interrupting the celebration, the gift of repentance is the cause for true celebration" (Christofferson, "Divine Gift of Repentance," 38). ☉

What does it mean to be content with what the Lord has allotted to us? (29:3) "Alma said, 'But behold . . . I ought to be content with the things which the Lord hath allotted unto me.' However, note the often ignored, but tutoring, verse that follows: 'Now, seeing that I know these things, why should I desire more than to perform the work to which I have been called?' (Alma 29:3, 6). To develop that kind of justifiable contentment to better use our existing opportunities—is obviously one of our challenges, particularly so when we seem to be in a 'flat' period of life. We may feel underused, underwhelmed, and underappreciated even though we are ignoring unused opportunities for service all about us" (Maxwell, *Notwithstanding My Weakness*, 115–16).

Alma 29:4–8. Men Receive Good or Evil according to Their Desires

How do our desires relate to our accountability? (29:4) "*Desire* denotes a real longing or craving. Hence righteous desires are much more than passive preferences or fleeting feelings. Of course our genes, circumstances, and environments matter very much, and they shape us significantly. Yet there remains an inner zone in which we are sovereign, unless we abdicate. In this zone lies the essence of our individuality and our personal accountability. . . .

"Like it or not, therefore, reality requires that we acknowledge our responsibility for our desires. . . .

"Some of our present desires, therefore, need to be diminished and then finally dissolved" (Maxwell, "'According to the Desire of [Our] Hearts,'" 21–22). ◑

How does God "teach His word" to all nations? (29:8) Elder Orson F. Whitney taught: "'The Lord will open their eyes in His own due time. God is using more than one people for the accomplishment of His great and marvelous work. The Latter-day Saints cannot do it all. It is too vast, too arduous for any one people. . . . We have no quarrel with the Gentiles. They are our partners in a certain sense' (Conference Report, April 1928, 59)" (Benson, "Civic Standards for the Faithful Saints," 59).

4 I ought not to harrow up in my desires the firm decree of a just God, for I know that he granteth unto men according to their desire, whether it be unto death or unto life; yea, I know that he allotteth unto men, yea, decreeth unto them decrees which are unalterable, according to their wills, whether they be unto salvation or unto destruction.

5 Yea, and I know that good and evil have come before all men; he that knoweth not good from evil is blameless; but he that knoweth good and evil, to him it is given according to his desires, whether he desireth good or evil, life or death, joy or remorse of conscience.

6 Now, seeing that I know these things, why should I desire more than to perform the work to which I have been called?

7 Why should I desire that I were an angel, that I could speak unto all the ends of the earth?

8 For behold, the Lord doth grant unto all nations, of their own nation and tongue, to teach his word, yea, in wisdom, all that he seeth fit that they should have; therefore we see that the Lord doth counsel in wisdom, according to that which is just and true.

9 I know that which the Lord hath commanded me, and I glory in it. I do not glory of myself, but I glory in that which the Lord hath commanded me; yea, and this is my glory, that perhaps I may be an instrument in the hands of God to bring some soul to repentance; and this is my joy.

10 And behold, when I see many of my brethren truly penitent, and coming to the Lord their God, then is my soul filled with joy; then do I remember what the Lord has done for me, yea, even that he hath heard my prayer; yea, then do I remember his merciful arm which he extended towards me.

11 Yea, and I also remember the captivity of my fathers; for I surely do know that the Lord did deliver them out of bondage, and by this did establish his church; yea, the Lord God, the God of Abraham, the God of Isaac, and the God of Jacob, did deliver them out of bondage.

12 Yea, I have always remembered the captivity of my fathers; and that same God who delivered them out of the hands of the Egyptians did deliver them out of bondage.

13 Yea, and that same God did establish his church among them; yea, and that same God hath called me by a holy calling, to preach the word unto this people, and hath given me much success, in the which my joy is full.

14 But I do not joy in my own success alone, but my joy is more full because of the success of my brethren, who have been up to the land of Nephi.

15 Behold, they have labored exceedingly, and have brought forth much fruit; and how great shall be their reward!

16 Now, when I think of the success of these my brethren my soul is carried away, even to the separation of it from the body, as it were, so great is my joy.

Alma 29:9–17. Alma Rejoices in Missionary Work

How can being "an instrument in the hands of God" bring us great joy? (29:9) "Joy cometh in the morning to those who have earned the night's rest of a laborer. One of life's sweetest returns is the privilege of rendering significant service of worth to others. To be able to do for fellow human beings something they could not do for themselves brings matchless satisfaction. Years of preparation are worth it.

"And joy is derived in Church service. Alma so expressed this thought: 'That perhaps I may be an instrument in the hands of God to bring some soul to repentance . . . is my joy' (Alma 29:9)" (Nelson, "Joy Cometh in the Morning," 68).

Who is the Lord God? (29:11) "He was known as Jehovah by the Old Testament prophets (see Abraham 1:16; Exodus 6:3). The prophets were shown of His coming: 'Behold the Lamb of God, yea, even the Son of the Eternal Father!' (1 Nephi 11:21; see also John 1:14). His mother was told, 'Call his name Jesus. . . . He shall be . . . called the Son of the Highest' (Luke 1:31–32)" (Packer, "Who Is Jesus Christ?" 13).

Why is the word *remember* used so many times in the scriptures? (29:12) "Memory is a powerful motivator to righteousness. The repentant sinner need only remember the agony and suffering through which he once passed on the road to spiritual recovery. . . . And a free people need only reflect seriously upon a time when the living God miraculously delivered them or their ancestors from bondage" (McConkie and Millet, *Doctrinal Commentary*, 3:198–99).

17 And now may God grant unto these, my brethren, that they may sit down in the kingdom of God; yea, and also all those who are the fruit of their labors that they may go no more out, but that they may praise him forever. And may God grant that it may be done according to my words, even as I have spoken. Amen.

CHAPTER 30

Korihor, the anti-Christ, ridicules Christ, the Atonement, and the spirit of prophecy—He teaches that there is no God, no fall of man, no penalty for sin, and no Christ—Alma testifies that Christ will come and that all things denote there is a God—Korihor demands a sign and is struck dumb—The devil had appeared to Korihor as an angel and taught him what to say—Korihor is trodden down and dies. About 76–74 B.C.

Alma 30:1–5. The Nephites Live Righteously after the War

1 Behold, now it came to pass that after the people of Ammon were established in the land of Jershon, yea, and also after the Lamanites were driven out of the land, and their dead were buried by the people of the land—

2 Now their dead were not numbered because of the greatness of their numbers; neither were the dead of the Nephites numbered—but it came to pass after they had buried their dead, and also after the days of fasting, and mourning, and prayer, (and it was in the sixteenth year of the reign of the judges over the people of Nephi) there began to be continual peace throughout all the land.

3 Yea, and the people did observe to keep the commandments of the Lord; and they were strict in observing the ordinances of God, according to the law of Moses; for they were taught to keep the law of Moses until it should be fulfilled.

What kind of peace does obedience always bring? (30:3–5) "Whenever a people live the gospel, whenever they live in harmony with the statutes and ordinances God has given them, whenever they follow the light of their consciences and subscribe to the rules and standards established for those of the household of faith, they come to know the peace of

4 And thus the people did have no disturbance in all the sixteenth year of the reign of the judges over the people of Nephi.

5 And it came to pass that in the commencement of the seventeenth year of the reign of the judges, there was continual peace.

6 But it came to pass in the latter end of the seventeenth year, there came a man into the land of Zarahemla, and he was Anti-Christ, for he began to preach unto the people against the prophecies which had been spoken by the prophets, concerning the coming of Christ.

7 Now there was no law against a man's belief; for it was strictly contrary to the commands of God that there should be a law which should bring men on to unequal grounds.

8 For thus saith the scripture: Choose ye this day, whom ye will serve.

9 Now if a man desired to serve God, it was his privilege; or rather, if he believed in God it was his privilege to serve him; but if he did not believe in him there was no law to punish him.

10 But if he murdered he was punished unto death; and if he robbed he was also punished; and if he stole he was also punished; and if he committed adultery he was also punished; yea, for all this wickedness they were punished.

11 For there was a law that men should be judged according to their crimes. Nevertheless, there was no law against a man's belief; therefore, a man was punished only for the crimes which he had done; therefore all men were on equal grounds.

the Spirit. Keeping the commandments brings the quiet assurance that one's course in life is pleasing in the sight of God, a consciousness of victory over self which we know as spirituality. 'Learn of me, and listen to my words; walk in the meekness of my Spirit, and you shall have peace in me' (D&C 19:23)" (McConkie and Millet, *Doctrinal Commentary*, 3:200).

Alma 30:6–11. The Law Allows Korihor to Revile against the Church and Its Leaders

What are some of the characteristics and motives of an anti-Christ? (30:6) "An antichrist is an opponent of Christ; he is one who is in opposition to the true gospel, the true Church, and the true plan of salvation (1 John 2:19; 4:4–6). He is one who offers salvation to men on some other terms than those laid down by Christ. Sherem (Jac. 7:1–23), Nehor (Alma 1:2–16), and Korihor (Alma 30:6–60) were antichrists who spread their delusions among the Nephites" (McConkie, *Doctrinal New Testament Commentary*, 3:381). ☉

How do anti-Christs manipulate man's laws for their own benefit? (30:7–9) "Korihor was perfectly free to teach the people anything he chose, for 'there was no law against a man's belief; for it was strictly contrary to the commands of God that there should be a law which should bring men on to unequal grounds' (Alma 30:7). 'Now if a man desired to serve God, it was his privilege, . . . but if he did not believe in him there was no law to punish him' (Alma 30:9) or to put him at a disadvantage, for the idea was that 'all men were on equal grounds' (Alma 30:11)" (Nibley, *Prophetic Book of Mormon*, 342–43). ☉

Alma 30:12–18. Korihor Tries to Convince the People Not to Believe in Christ or His Teachings

Why is Mormon's insertion of the story of Korihor so valuable to us today? (30:12) "If Mormon had included nothing but those [Korihor's] teachings, they would have been of great value to us. But he did more than that. He also included Alma's answer to Korihor....

"The first thing to note is that Alma does not get into a philosophical debate with Korihor. He does not talk about metaphysics or axiology or epistemology. He does not allow himself to get pulled onto the ground that Korihor tries to define as the area of debate. There is a great lesson in that. Alma teaches that we should combat false philosophies with revelation and doctrine, not with academic debate" (Lund, "Anti-Christ in the Book of Mormon," 121–22).

What do Korihor's teachings have in common with false teachings of our day? (30:12–17) Chauncey Riddle once explored how three of Korihor's arguments seduce people today: "The first is that 'it is possible to know all truth through the senses—by experience and observation.' The second is a humanist position that 'the solutions to our problems lie in sharp thinking and realistic approaches to life,' and success is defined 'in terms of wealth, social status, political power, and the glutting of the senses.' A third argument is relativist: since so-called commandments and laws 'are but social conveniences to give power to priests, the only important thing in life is to do what you want to do—if you can get away with it'" (Rust, *Feasting on the Word*, 36–37). ❂

What could the phrase "management of the creature" mean? (30:17) "When we talk about 'the management of the creature,' that's a perfect expression. It's the manipulation of people as if they were items or products. You can manipulate everything with the psychology of salesmanship. It is the manipulation, the management of the creature" (Nibley, *Teachings of the Book of Mormon*, 2:424). ❂

12 And this Anti-Christ, whose name was Korihor, (and the law could have no hold upon him) began to preach unto the people that there should be no Christ. And after this manner did he preach, saying:

13 O ye that are bound down under a foolish and a vain hope, why do ye yoke yourselves with such foolish things? Why do ye look for a Christ? For no man can know of anything which is to come.

14 Behold, these things which ye call prophecies, which ye say are handed down by holy prophets, behold, they are foolish traditions of your fathers.

15 How do ye know of their surety? Behold, ye cannot know of things which ye do not see; therefore ye cannot know that there shall be a Christ.

16 Ye look forward and say that ye see a remission of your sins. But behold, it is the effect of a frenzied mind; and this derangement of your minds comes because of the traditions of your fathers, which lead you away into a belief of things which are not so.

17 And many more such things did he say unto them, telling them that there could be no atonement made for the sins of men, but every man fared in this life according to the management of the creature; therefore every man prospered according to his genius, and that every man conquered according to his strength; and whatsoever a man did was no crime.

18 And thus he did preach unto them, leading away the hearts of many, causing them to lift up their heads in their wickedness, yea, leading away many women, and also men, to commit whoredoms—telling them that when a man was dead, that was the end thereof.

19 Now this man went over to the land of Jershon also, to preach these things among the people of Ammon, who were once the people of the Lamanites.

20 But behold they were more wise than many of the Nephites; for they took him, and bound him, and carried him before Ammon, who was a high priest over that people.

21 And it came to pass that he caused that he should be carried out of the land. And he came over into the land of Gideon, and began to preach unto them also; and here he did not have much success, for he was taken and bound and carried before the high priest, and also the chief judge over the land.

22 And it came to pass that the high priest said unto him: Why do ye go about perverting the ways of the Lord? Why do ye teach this people that there shall be no Christ, to interrupt their rejoicings? Why do ye speak against all the prophecies of the holy prophets?

23 Now the high priest's name was Giddonah. And Korihor said unto him: Because I do not teach the foolish traditions of your fathers, and because I do not teach this people to bind themselves down under the foolish ordinances and performances which are laid down by ancient priests, to usurp power and authority over them, to keep them in ignorance, that they may not lift up their heads, but be brought down according to thy words.

Alma 30:19–29. The People of Jershon Refuse to Believe Korihor's Lies

What type of "freedom" was Korihor offering? (30:22–24) "Korihor claims the protection of law in a free nation to teach the doctrines of disbelief, disrespect, and disobedience. He attempts to convince people that they are in bondage, for if he can successfully do so they will naturally turn to him as a liberator or redeemer. His then is a liberation movement. He is going to free them from the burden of commandments and gospel commitments. Whereas the gospel declares that the knowledge of revealed truths brings freedom, Korihor contends that freedom really means being without the constraints of righteousness" (McConkie and Millet, *Sustaining and Defending the Faith*, 88–89). ⊕

The False Teachings of Korihor

1. No Christ (verse 12)
2. No man can know of anything which is to come (verse 13)
3. Prophecies are foolish tradition of your fathers (verse 14)
4. You cannot know of things which you do not see (verse 15)
5. Remission of sins is simply a product of a frenzied or deranged mind (verse 16)
6. There is no Atonement (verse 17)
7. Everyone fares in this life according to his management (verse 17)
8. Man prospers by his genius (verse 17)
9. Every man conquers according to his strength (verse 17)
10. Whatsoever a man does is no crime (verse 17)

What is wrong with the argument that righteous traditions result in the loss of "rights and privileges"? (30:27) "Korihor was arguing, as men and women have falsely argued from the beginning of time, that to take counsel from the servants of God is to surrender God-given rights of independence. But the argument is false because it misrepresents reality. When we reject the counsel which comes from God, we do not choose to be independent of outside influence. We choose another influence" (Eyring, "Finding Safety in Counsel," 25). ✛

Why is it important to understand the impact that critics can have on members of the Church? (30:29) "Later Alma encountered Korihor . . . I think, not unlike some things that are happening in the Church today. Not too many days ago, in a moment of great concern over a rapid series of events that demonstrated the challenge of those within the Church who have that feeling of criticism and challenge and apostasy, I had an impression, as revelations are. It was strong and it was clear, because lingering in my mind was: 'Why? Why—when we need so much to be united?' And there came the answer: 'It is permitted to be so now that the sifting might take place, and it will have negligible effect upon the Church'" (Packer, "Great Plan of Happiness"). ✛

24 Ye say that this people is a free people. Behold, I say they are in bondage. Ye say that those ancient prophecies are true. Behold, I say that ye do not know that they are true.

25 Ye say that this people is a guilty and a fallen people, because of the transgression of a parent. Behold, I say that a child is not guilty because of its parents.

26 And ye also say that Christ shall come. But behold, I say that ye do not know that there shall be a Christ. And ye say also that he shall be slain for the sins of the world—

27 And thus ye lead away this people after the foolish traditions of your fathers, and according to your own desires; and ye keep them down, even as it were in bondage, that ye may glut yourselves with the labors of their hands, that they durst not look up with boldness, and that they durst not enjoy their rights and privileges.

28 Yea, they durst not make use of that which is their own lest they should offend their priests, who do yoke them according to their desires, and have brought them to believe, by their traditions and their dreams and their whims and their visions and their pretended mysteries, that they should, if they did not do according to their words, offend some unknown being, who they say is God—a being who never has been seen or known, who never was nor ever will be.

29 Now when the high priest and the chief judge saw the hardness of his heart, yea, when they saw that he would revile even against God, they would not make any reply to his words; but they caused that he should be bound; and they delivered him up into the hands of the officers, and sent him to the land of Zarahemla, that he might be brought before Alma, and the chief judge who was governor over all the land.

30 And it came to pass that when he was brought before Alma and the chief judge, he did go on in the same manner as he did in the land of Gideon; yea, he went on to blaspheme.

31 And he did rise up in great swelling words before Alma, and did revile against the priests and teachers, accusing them of leading away the people after the silly traditions of their fathers, for the sake of glutting on the labors of the people.

32 Now Alma said unto him: Thou knowest that we do not glut ourselves upon the labors of this people; for behold I have labored even from the commencement of the reign of the judges until now, with mine own hands for my support, notwithstanding my many travels round about the land to declare the word of God unto my people.

33 And notwithstanding the many labors which I have performed in the church, I have never received so much as even one senine for my labor; neither has any of my brethren, save it were in the judgment-seat; and then we have received only according to law for our time.

34 And now, if we do not receive anything for our labors in the church, what doth it profit us to labor in the church save it were to declare the truth, that we may have rejoicings in the joy of our brethren?

35 Then why sayest thou that we preach unto this people to get gain, when thou, of thyself, knowest that we receive no gain? And now, believest thou that we deceive this people, that causes such joy in their hearts?

36 And Korihor answered him, Yea.

37 And then Alma said unto him: Believest thou that there is a God?

Alma 30:30–42. Alma Testifies to Korihor of the Truth

What does it mean to blaspheme? (30:30)

Blasphemy "generally denotes contemptuous speech concerning God or concerning something that stands in a sacred relation toward God, such as His temple, His law, or His prophet.... The punishment for willful and intentional blasphemy was death by stoning (Lev. 24:11–16; John 10:31–33; Acts 7:58)" (Bible Dictionary, "Blasphemy," 608).

What would it take to prove there is no God? (30:40)
"Alma takes Korihor's own philosophy and catches him in a trap of his own making. Korihor teaches that we can know only what we can see (see Alma 30:15). But when questioned, Korihor categorically denies that he believes there is a God. . . . Korihor is not consistent in his own thinking. If we truly can know only those things for which we have empirical evidence, then we cannot teach there is no God unless we have evidence for that belief. And Korihor has no evidence" (Lund, "Countering Korihor's Philosophy," 21). ✚

Alma 30:43–50. Korihor Asks for a Sign and Is Cursed

Why is seeking for a sign so wrong? (30:43) "The sign-seekers, the God-tempters, presume to put the Almighty on trial by challenging him to prove his own existence. Korihor typified them: 'Except ye show me a sign, I will not believe' (Alma 30:48). In their pride, the Korihors of this world set up the preconditions under which they may condescend to believe. But it is all a sham; their insistence on signs is not meant to foster faith but to justify doubt. And the seed of faith will never grow in the soil of doubt. Where there is a will to doubt, a heavenly sign or evidence will be ignored, rejected, or rationalized away" (Turner, "Faith unto Salvation," 21–22). ✚

How do the miracle of the earth's existence and the order of the heavens bear testimony that there is a God? (30:44) "Can any man who has walked beneath the stars at night, can anyone who has seen the touch of spring upon the land doubt the hand of divinity in creation? So observing the beauties of the earth, one is wont to speak as did the Psalmist: 'The heavens declare the glory of God; and the firmament sheweth his handywork. Day unto day uttereth speech, and night unto night sheweth knowledge' (Ps. 19:1–2).

38 And he answered, Nay.

39 Now Alma said unto him: Will ye deny again that there is a God, and also deny the Christ? For behold, I say unto you, I know there is a God, and also that Christ shall come.

40 And now what evidence have ye that there is no God, or that Christ cometh not? I say unto you that ye have none, save it be your word only.

41 But, behold, I have all things as a testimony that these things are true; and ye also have all things as a testimony unto you that they are true; and will ye deny them? Believest thou that these things are true?

42 Behold, I know that thou believest, but thou art possessed with a lying spirit, and ye have put off the Spirit of God that it may have no place in you; but the devil has power over you, and he doth carry you about, working devices that he may destroy the children of God.

43 And now Korihor said unto Alma: If thou wilt show me a sign, that I may be convinced that there is a God, yea, show unto me that he hath power, and then will I be convinced of the truth of thy words.

44 But Alma said unto him: Thou hast had signs enough; will ye tempt your God? Will ye say, Show unto me a sign, when ye have the testimony of all these thy brethren, and also all the holy prophets? The scriptures are laid before thee, yea, and all things denote there is a God; yea, even the earth, and all things that are upon the face of it, yea, and its motion, yea, and also all the planets which move in their regular form do witness that there is a Supreme Creator.

45 And yet do ye go about, leading away the hearts of this people, testifying unto them there is no God? And yet will ye deny against all these witnesses? And he said: Yea, I will deny, except ye shall show me a sign.

46 And now it came to pass that Alma said unto him: Behold, I am grieved because of the hardness of your heart, yea, that ye will still resist the spirit of the truth, that thy soul may be destroyed.

47 But behold, it is better that thy soul should be lost than that thou shouldst be the means of bringing many souls down to destruction, by thy lying and by thy flattering words; therefore if thou shalt deny again, behold God shall smite thee, that thou shalt become dumb, that thou shalt never open thy mouth any more, that thou shalt not deceive this people any more.

48 Now Korihor said unto him: I do not deny the existence of a God, but I do not believe that there is a God; and I say also, that ye do not know that there is a God; and except ye show me a sign, I will not believe.

49 Now Alma said unto him: This will I give unto thee for a sign, that thou shalt be struck dumb, according to my words; and I say, that in the name of God, ye shall be struck dumb, that ye shall no more have utterance.

50 Now when Alma had said these words, Korihor was struck dumb, that he could not have utterance, according to the words of Alma.

51 And now when the chief judge saw this, he put forth his hand and wrote unto Korihor, saying: Art thou convinced of the power of God? In whom did ye desire that Alma should show forth his sign? Would ye

"All of beauty in the earth bears the fingerprint of the Master Creator" (Hinckley, "Be Not Faithless," 59).

What is the purpose of Church discipline? (30:47) Similar to Alma disciplining Korihor, there are times when members of the Church who teach and promote false doctrine are disciplined. "Members sometimes ask why Church disciplinary councils are held. The purpose is threefold: to save the soul of the transgressor, to protect the innocent, and to safeguard the Church's purity, integrity, and good name" (Ballard, "Chance to Start Over," 15).

What do we learn about Korihor when he asked for a sign to produce belief? (30:48) The Prophet Joseph Smith warned: "Whenever you see a man seeking after a sign, you may set it down that he is an adulterous man" (*History of the Church*, 3:385).

He later recalled: "When I was preaching in Philadelphia, a Quaker called out for a sign. I told him to be still. After the sermon, he again asked for a sign. I told the congregation the man was an adulterer; that a wicked and adulterous generation seeketh after a sign; and that the Lord had said to me in a revelation, that any man who wanted a sign was an adulterous person. 'It is true,' cried one, 'for I caught him in the very act,' which the man afterwards confessed, when he was baptized" (*History of the Church*, 5:268).

Alma 30:51–55. The Devil Told Korihor What to Teach

that he should afflict others, to show unto thee a sign? Behold, he has showed unto you a sign; and now will ye dispute more?

52 And Korihor put forth his hand and wrote, saying: I know that I am dumb, for I cannot speak; and I know that nothing save it were the power of God could bring this upon me; yea, and I always knew that there was a God.

53 But behold, the devil hath deceived me; for he appeared unto me in the form of an angel, and said unto me: Go and reclaim this people, for they have all gone astray after an unknown God. And he said unto me: There is no God; yea, and he taught me that which I should say. And I have taught his words; and I taught them because they were pleasing unto the carnal mind; and I taught them, even until I had much success, insomuch that I verily believed that they were true; and for this cause I withstood the truth, even until I have brought this great curse upon me.

54 Now when he had said this, he besought that Alma should pray unto God, that the curse might be taken from him.

55 But Alma said unto him: If this curse should be taken from thee thou wouldst again lead away the hearts of this people; therefore, it shall be unto thee even as the Lord will.

56 And it came to pass that the curse was not taken off of Korihor; but he was cast out, and went about from house to house begging for his food.

57 Now the knowledge of what had happened unto Korihor was immediately published throughout all the land; yea, the proclamation was sent forth by the chief judge to all the people in the land, declaring unto those who had believed in the words of Korihor that they must speedily repent, lest the same judgments would come unto them.

How does the devil recruit anti-Christs to lead us astray? (30:53) "Since the spring of 1820, Lucifer has led a relentless attack against the Latter-day Saints and their leaders. A parade of anti-Christs, anti-Mormons, and apostate groups have appeared on the scene. Many are still among us and have released new floods of lies and false accusations. These faith-killers and testimony-thieves use personal contacts, the printed word, electronic media, and other means of communication to sow doubts and to disturb the peace of true believers" (Asay, "Opposition to the Work," 67).

Alma 30:56–60. Korihor Suffers a Horrible Death

58 And it came to pass that they were all convinced of the wickedness of Korihor; therefore they were all converted again unto the Lord; and this put an end to the iniquity after the manner of Korihor. And Korihor did go about from house to house, begging food for his support.

59 And it came to pass that as he went forth among the people, yea, among a people who had separated themselves from the Nephites and called themselves Zoramites, being led by a man whose name was Zoram—and as he went forth amongst them, behold, he was run upon and trodden down, even until he was dead.

60 And thus we see the end of him who perverteth the ways of the Lord; and thus we see that the devil will not support his children at the last day, but doth speedily drag them down to hell.

CHAPTER 31

Alma heads a mission to reclaim the apostate Zoramites—The Zoramites deny Christ, believe in a false concept of election, and worship with set prayers—The missionaries are filled with the Holy Spirit—Their afflictions are swallowed up in the joy of Christ. About 74 B.C.

1 Now it came to pass that after the end of Korihor, Alma having received tidings that the Zoramites were perverting the ways of the Lord, and that Zoram, who was their leader, was leading the hearts of the people to bow down to dumb idols, his heart again began to sicken because of the iniquity of the people.

2 For it was the cause of great sorrow to Alma to know of iniquity among his people; therefore his heart was exceedingly sorrowful because of the separation of the Zoramites from the Nephites.

Why were the story, teachings, and fate of Korihor recorded in the Book of Mormon? (30:60) The Book of Mormon was written for our day. Later in his own book, Mormon says, "I speak unto you [latter-day readers] as if ye were present" (Mormon 8:35). "We did not borrow the Book of Mormon from the ancients; they wrote it to us. We are the audience Mormon and Moroni addressed as they chose what was to be included in this scriptural record. They told us the story of Korihor because they knew that we would have our Korihors. The Korihor of the Book of Mormon story is but the prototype of our modern anti-Christs" (McConkie and Millet, *Sustaining and Defending the Faith*, 96). ✪

Alma 31:1–7. Alma Decides to Preach the Gospel to the Zoramites

What is a dumb idol? (31:1) A dumb idol is something that does not speak in response to worshippers' devotion. There is no revelation from a dumb idol. What are some material things man seeks that could be called dumb idols?

Why does the "preaching of the word" lead people to do good? (31:5) "True doctrine, understood, changes attitudes and behavior. The study of the doctrines of the gospel will improve behavior quicker than a study of behavior will improve behavior" (Packer, "Do Not Fear," 79).

Alma 31:8–23. The Zoramites Fall Away from the True Beliefs and Practices of the Church

3 Now the Zoramites had gathered themselves together in a land which they called Antionum, which was east of the land of Zarahemla, which lay nearly bordering upon the seashore, which was south of the land of Jershon, which also bordered upon the wilderness south, which wilderness was full of the Lamanites.

4 Now the Nephites greatly feared that the Zoramites would enter into a correspondence with the Lamanites, and that it would be the means of great loss on the part of the Nephites.

5 And now, as the preaching of the word had a great tendency to lead the people to do that which was just—yea, it had had more powerful effect upon the minds of the people than the sword, or anything else, which had happened unto them—therefore Alma thought it was expedient that they should try the virtue of the word of God.

6 Therefore he took Ammon, and Aaron, and Omner; and Himni he did leave in the church in Zarahemla; but the former three he took with him, and also Amulek and Zeezrom, who were at Melek; and he also took two of his sons.

7 Now the eldest of his sons he took not with him, and his name was Helaman; but the names of those whom he took with him were Shiblon and Corianton; and these are the names of those who went with him among the Zoramites, to preach unto them the word.

8 Now the Zoramites were dissenters from the Nephites; therefore they had had the word of God preached unto them.

9 But they had fallen into great errors, for they would not observe to keep the commandments of God, and his statutes, according to the law of Moses.

10 Neither would they observe the performances of the church, to continue in prayer and supplication to God daily, that they might not enter into temptation.

11 Yea, in fine, they did pervert the ways of the Lord in very many instances; therefore, for this cause, Alma and his brethren went into the land to preach the word unto them.

12 Now, when they had come into the land, behold, to their astonishment they found that the Zoramites had built synagogues, and that they did gather themselves together on one day of the week, which day they did call the day of the Lord; and they did worship after a manner which Alma and his brethren had never beheld;

13 For they had a place built up in the center of their synagogue, a place for standing, which was high above the head; and the top thereof would only admit one person.

14 Therefore, whosoever desired to worship must go forth and stand upon the top thereof, and stretch forth his hands towards heaven, and cry with a loud voice, saying:

15 Holy, holy God; we believe that thou art God, and we believe that thou art holy, and that thou wast a spirit, and that thou art a spirit, and that thou wilt be a spirit forever.

16 Holy God, we believe that thou hast separated us from our brethren; and we do not believe in the tradition of our brethren, which was handed down to them by the childishness of their fathers; but we believe that thou hast elected us to be thy holy children; and also thou hast made it known unto us that there shall be no Christ.

17 But thou art the same yesterday, today, and forever; and thou hast elected us that we shall be saved, whilst all around us are elected to be cast by thy wrath down to hell; for the which holiness, O God, we thank thee; and we also

Why is it important for us to know that synagogues existed in the Book of Mormon? (31:12) "The Book of Mormon . . . lends credence to the idea that synagogues, at least as places of worship, were known to Israel before the departure of Lehi from Jerusalem. . . . Jacob Weingreen writes: 'It would be natural to suppose that, following upon the enforcement of Josiah's edict, religious services continued to be held outside Jerusalem, but now without sacrifices. . . . These must . . . have constituted the basis of the synagogue service of later times.' . . .

" . . . We do not know what Hebrew or other word the Nephites or Zoramites used in naming their places of worship" (Welch, "Synagogues in the Book of Mormon," 194–95). See also commentary on Alma 21:4.

thank thee that thou hast elected us, that we may not be led away after the foolish traditions of our brethren, which doth bind them down to a belief of Christ, which doth lead their hearts to wander far from thee, our God.

18 And again we thank thee, O God, that we are a chosen and a holy people. Amen.

19 Now it came to pass that after Alma and his brethren and his sons had heard these prayers, they were astonished beyond all measure.

20 For behold, every man did go forth and offer up these same prayers.

21 Now the place was called by them Rameumptom, which, being interpreted, is the holy stand.

22 Now, from this stand they did offer up, every man, the selfsame prayer unto God, thanking their God that they were chosen of him, and that he did not lead them away after the tradition of their brethren, and that their hearts were not stolen away to believe in things to come, which they knew nothing about.

23 Now, after the people had all offered up thanks after this manner, they returned to their homes, never speaking of their God again until they had assembled themselves together again to the holy stand, to offer up thanks after their manner.

What does "Rameumptom" mean? (31:21)
"*Rameumptom* has at least one Semitic root: *ram*, which refers to a 'high place' like the Hill Ramah (see Ether 15:11). 'In modern Israel are the town of Ramallah, located in the tops of the Judean hills just north of Jerusalem, and Rameem, which literally means "the heights" and is located on the top of the hills near the Lebanese border' (Ludlow, *Companion to Your Study of the Book of Mormon*, 213).

"Once a week, the apostate Zoramites stood on the Rameumptom to offer prayers extolling their greatness. Their prayers were memorized and self-serving. In the prayers, Zoramites told of their belief that God was a spirit and had elected them to be saved. Among their other apostate beliefs was that religious practices were to be observed only one day a week" (Black, *400 Questions and Answers*, 160).

What did the prayer on the Rameumpton illustrate about the Zoramites? (31:22–23) "Pride is the great sin of self-elevation. It is for so many a personal Rameumptom, a holy stand that justifies envy, greed, and vanity (see Alma 31:21). In a sense, pride is the original sin, for before the foundations of this earth, pride felled Lucifer, a son of the morning 'who was in authority in the presence of God' (D&C 76:25). If pride can corrupt one as capable and promising as this, should we not examine our own souls as well?" (Uchtdorf, "Pride and the Priesthood," 56).

24 Now when Alma saw this his heart was grieved; for he saw that they were a wicked and a perverse people; yea, he saw that their hearts were set upon gold, and upon silver, and upon all manner of fine goods.

25 Yea, and he also saw that their hearts were lifted up unto great boasting, in their pride.

26 And he lifted up his voice to heaven, and cried, saying: O, how long, O Lord, wilt thou suffer that thy servants shall dwell here below in the flesh, to behold such gross wickedness among the children of men?

27 Behold, O God, they cry unto thee, and yet their hearts are swallowed up in their pride. Behold, O God, they cry unto thee with their mouths, while they are puffed up, even to greatness, with the vain things of the world.

28 Behold, O my God, their costly apparel, and their ringlets, and their bracelets, and their ornaments of gold, and all their precious things which they are ornamented with; and behold, their hearts are set upon them, and yet they cry unto thee and say— We thank thee, O God, for we are a chosen people unto thee, while others shall perish.

29 Yea, and they say that thou hast made it known unto them that there shall be no Christ.

30 O Lord God, how long wilt thou suffer that such wickedness and infidelity shall be among this people? O Lord, wilt thou give me strength, that I may bear with mine infirmities. For I am infirm, and such wickedness among this people doth pain my soul.

31 O Lord, my heart is exceedingly sorrowful; wilt thou comfort my soul in Christ. O Lord, wilt thou grant unto me that I may have strength, that I may suffer with patience these afflictions which shall come upon me, because of the iniquity of this people.

Alma 31:24–38. Alma Prays for Help in Teaching the Zoramites

What do we learn from Alma's prayer for the people and his "fellow laborers"? (31:30–35) "The enabling power of the Atonement strengthens us to do and be good and to serve beyond our own individual desire and natural capacity....

"In Alma 31, Alma is directing a mission to reclaim the apostate Zoramites....

"Notice the plea for strength in Alma's personal prayer: 'O Lord, wilt thou grant unto me *that I may have strength*, that I may suffer with patience these afflictions which shall come upon me, because of the iniquity of this people' (Alma 31:31; emphasis added)....

"Alma did not pray to have his afflictions removed. He knew he was an agent of the Lord, and he prayed for the power to act and affect his situation" (Bednar, "Atonement and the Journey of Mortality," 42–45). ⊕

Why does the Lord sometimes allow us to suffer undeserved afflictions? (31:33) "Much of our suffering is not necessarily our fault. Unexpected events, contradicting or disappointing circumstances, interrupting illness, and even death surround us and penetrate our mortal experience. Additionally, we may suffer afflictions because of the actions of others (see Alma 31:31, 33). . . . Opposition is part of Heavenly Father's plan of happiness. We all encounter enough to bring us to an awareness of our Father's love and of our need for the Savior's help" (Richards, "Atonement Covers All Pain," 15).

32 O Lord, wilt thou comfort my soul, and give unto me success, and also my fellow laborers who are with me—yea, Ammon, and Aaron, and Omner, and also Amulek and Zeezrom, and also my two sons—yea, even all these wilt thou comfort, O Lord. Yea, wilt thou comfort their souls in Christ.

33 Wilt thou grant unto them that they may have strength, that they may bear their afflictions which shall come upon them because of the iniquities of this people.

34 O Lord, wilt thou grant unto us that we may have success in bringing them again unto thee in Christ.

35 Behold, O Lord, their souls are precious, and many of them are our brethren; therefore, give unto us, O Lord, power and wisdom that we may bring these, our brethren, again unto thee.

36 Now it came to pass that when Alma had said these words, that he clapped his hands upon all them who were with him. And behold, as he clapped his hands upon them, they were filled with the Holy Spirit.

37 And after that they did separate themselves one from another, taking no thought for themselves what they should eat, or what they should drink, or what they should put on.

38 And the Lord provided for them that they should hunger not, neither should they thirst; yea, and he also gave them strength, that they should suffer no manner of afflictions, save it were swallowed up in the joy of Christ. Now this was according to the prayer of Alma; and this because he prayed in faith.

CHAPTER 32

Alma teaches the poor whose afflictions had humbled them—Faith is a hope in that which is not seen which is true—Alma testifies that angels minister to men, women, and children—Alma compares the word unto a seed—It must be planted and nourished—Then it grows into a tree from which the fruit of eternal life is picked. About 74 B.C.

1 And it came to pass that they did go forth, and began to preach the word of God unto the people, entering into their synagogues, and into their houses; yea, and even they did preach the word in their streets.

2 And it came to pass that after much labor among them, they began to have success among the poor class of people; for behold, they were cast out of the synagogues because of the coarseness of their apparel—

3 Therefore they were not permitted to enter into their synagogues to worship God, being esteemed as filthiness; therefore they were poor; yea, they were esteemed by their brethren as dross; therefore they were poor as to things of the world; and also they were poor in heart.

4 Now, as Alma was teaching and speaking unto the people upon the hill Onidah, there came a great multitude unto him, who were those of whom we have been speaking, of whom were poor in heart, because of their poverty as to the things of the world.

5 And they came unto Alma; and the one who was the foremost among them said unto him: Behold, what shall these my brethren

Alma 32:1–6. Alma Preaches the Gospel among the Poor

Why were the poor cast out? (32:2) "Bad religion breeds bad societies. The Zoramites created a class system that ostracized their less fortunate brothers and sisters from the very synagogues they had built. But—as has been the case from time immemorial—it was these downtrodden souls who proved most responsive to the message of Alma and his companions. Impoverished 'as to things of the world,' they are described as 'poor in heart' or 'lowly in heart' (Alma 32:3–4, 8). That is, they were dispirited and quite hopeless. Alma 'beheld that their afflictions had truly humbled them, and that they were in a preparation to hear the word' (Alma 32:6)" (Turner, "Faith unto Salvation," 19).

What does *dross* mean? (32:3) According to the dictionary, *dross* means "waste matter; refuse; any worthless matter separated from the better part; impure matter" (Webster, *American Dictionary*).

do, for they are despised of all men because of their poverty, yea, and more especially by our priests; for they have cast us out of our synagogues which we have labored abundantly to build with our own hands; and they have cast us out because of our exceeding poverty; and we have no place to worship our God; and behold, what shall we do?

6 And now when Alma heard this, he turned him about, his face immediately towards him, and he beheld with great joy; for he beheld that their afflictions had truly humbled them, and that they were in a preparation to hear the word.

What are some preparatory experiences that prepare a people to "hear the word"? (32:6) "Building faith is often preceded by shaping circumstances, benefiting those who are 'in a preparation to hear the word' (Alma 32:6). These beginnings require at least a 'desire to believe,' and then comes the exercising of a 'particle of faith' (Alma 32:27).

"As we 'give place' and plant the seed of faith, it grows discernibly. We are invigorated as it enlightens and swells (see Alma 32:28–30). We become our own internal auditors, confirming this increase in our faith. It is better to so nourish our faith in what seems to be an ordinary process than to experience extraordinary things only to stumble later over life's ordinary challenges" (Maxwell, "'Lest Ye Be Wearied and Faint in Your Minds,'" 89).

Alma 32:7–16. Alma Teaches about Humility

7 Therefore he did say no more to the other multitude; but he stretched forth his hand, and cried unto those whom he beheld, who were truly penitent, and said unto them:

8 I behold that ye are lowly in heart; and if so, blessed are ye.

9 Behold thy brother hath said, What shall we do?—for we are cast out of our synagogues, that we cannot worship our God.

10 Behold I say unto you, do ye suppose that ye cannot worship God save it be in your synagogues only?

11 And moreover, I would ask, do ye suppose that ye must not worship God only once in a week?

Can we worship only in a church or other dedicated building? (32:10) "The needy Zoramites told Alma they could not worship God because they had been cast out of their synagogues. Alma's reply was, 'Do ye suppose that ye cannot worship God save it be in your synagogues only?' [Alma 31:10]. . .

"What he was saying to the Zoramites, . . . is that if we do have testimonies we should bear them with us seven days a week. . . . We show our testimonies by our actions" (Higbee, "Five Ways to Bear Testimony," 89).

12 I say unto you, it is well that ye are cast out of your synagogues, that ye may be humble, and that ye may learn wisdom; for it is necessary that ye should learn wisdom; for it is because that ye are cast out, that ye are despised of your brethren because of your exceeding poverty, that ye are brought to a lowliness of heart; for ye are necessarily brought to be humble.

13 And now, because ye are compelled to be humble blessed are ye; for a man sometimes, if he is compelled to be humble, seeketh repentance; and now surely, whosoever repenteth shall find mercy; and he that findeth mercy and endureth to the end the same shall be saved.

14 And now, as I said unto you, that because ye were compelled to be humble ye were blessed, do ye not suppose that they are more blessed who truly humble themselves because of the word?

15 Yea, he that truly humbleth himself, and repenteth of his sins, and endureth to the end, the same shall be blessed—yea, much more blessed than they who are compelled to be humble because of their exceeding poverty.

16 Therefore, blessed are they who humble themselves without being compelled to be humble; or rather, in other words, blessed is he that believeth in the word of God, and is baptized without stubbornness of heart, yea, without being brought to know the word, or even compelled to know, before they will believe.

17 Yea, there are many who do say: If thou wilt show unto us a sign from heaven, then we shall know of a surety; then we shall believe.

Why is it important to be humble? (32:12) "Humility is teachableness—an ability to realize that all virtues and abilities are not concentrated in one's self. . . .

"Humility is never accusing nor contentious. . . .

"Humility is repentant and seeks not to justify its follies. It is forgiving others in the realization that there may be errors of the same kind or worse chalked up against itself. . . .

"Humility makes no bid for popularity and notoriety; demands no honors. . . .

"It is not self-abasement—the hiding in the corner, the devaluation of everything one does or thinks or says; but it is the doing of one's best in every case and leaving of one's acts, expressions, and accomplishments to largely speak for themselves" (Kimball, "Humility"). ⊕

Why must humility precede repentance? (32:13–16) "Spiritual humility—the recognition of one's dependence upon God for all things temporal and spiritual, coupled with a willingness to accept his law—is a precondition for true repentance. Some achieve this humility only after they have been 'compelled to be humble' by those 'slings and arrows of outrageous fortune' of which Hamlet soliloquized. Some do so only after they have been brought face-to-face with the stark truth about themselves and the God they defied, or never knew.

"Some will never learn humility and, therefore, never repent even when they stand before God with a 'perfect knowledge' of their guilt and uncleanness" (Turner, *Faith unto Salvation*, 19–20). ⊕

Alma 32:17–43. Alma Teaches about Faith

18 Now I ask, is this faith? Behold, I say unto you, Nay; for if a man knoweth a thing he hath no cause to believe, for he knoweth it.

19 And now, how much more cursed is he that knoweth the will of God and doeth it not, than he that only believeth, or only hath cause to believe, and falleth into transgression?

20 Now of this thing ye must judge. Behold, I say unto you, that it is on the one hand even as it is on the other; and it shall be unto every man according to his work.

21 And now as I said concerning faith—faith is not to have a perfect knowledge of things; therefore if ye have faith ye hope for things which are not seen, which are true.

22 And now, behold, I say unto you, and I would that ye should remember, that God is merciful unto all who believe on his name; therefore he desireth, in the first place, that ye should believe, yea, even on his word.

23 And now, he imparteth his word by angels unto men, yea, not only men but women also. Now this is not all; little children do have words given unto them many times, which confound the wise and the learned.

24 And now, my beloved brethren, as ye have desired to know of me what ye shall do because ye are afflicted and cast out—now I do not desire that ye should suppose that I mean to judge you only according to that which is true—

25 For I do not mean that ye all of you have been compelled to humble yourselves; for I verily believe that there are some among you who would humble themselves, let them be in whatsoever circumstances they might.

26 Now, as I said concerning faith—that it was not a perfect knowledge—even so it is with my words. Ye cannot know of their surety at first, unto perfection, any more than faith is a perfect knowledge.

Why is faith an essential prerequisite for gaining spiritual knowledge? (32:21) "In keeping faith I hope you are able to know that there are some things that must be taken on faith; and that, in our insatiable quest for knowledge, always preparatory to and preliminary to gaining spiritual knowledge there is the exercise of faith. As the prophet Moroni said, 'Dispute not because ye see not, for ye receive no witness until after the trial of your faith' (Ether 12:6)" (Packer, *Let Not Your Heart Be Troubled*, 147–48). ●

Why does God send angels? (32:23) "In times of special need, He sent angels, divine messengers, to bless His children, reassure them that heaven was always very close and that His help was always very near" (Holland, "Ministry of Angels," 29). ●

27 But behold, if ye will awake and arouse your faculties, even to an experiment upon my words, and exercise a particle of faith, yea, even if ye can no more than desire to believe, let this desire work in you, even until ye believe in a manner that ye can give place for a portion of my words.

28 Now, we will compare the word unto a seed. Now, if ye give place, that a seed may be planted in your heart, behold, if it be a true seed, or a good seed, if ye do not cast it out by your unbelief, that ye will resist the Spirit of the Lord, behold, it will begin to swell within your breasts; and when you feel these swelling motions, ye will begin to say within yourselves—It must needs be that this is a good seed, or that the word is good, for it beginneth to enlarge my soul; yea, it beginneth to enlighten my understanding, yea, it beginneth to be delicious to me.

29 Now behold, would not this increase your faith? I say unto you, Yea; nevertheless it hath not grown up to a perfect knowledge.

30 But behold, as the seed swelleth, and sprouteth, and beginneth to grow, then you must needs say that the seed is good; for behold it swelleth, and sprouteth, and beginneth to grow. And now, behold, will not this strengthen your faith? Yea, it will strengthen your faith: for ye will say I know that this is a good seed; for behold it sprouteth and beginneth to grow.

31 And now, behold, are ye sure that this is a good seed? I say unto you, Yea; for every seed bringeth forth unto its own likeness.

32 Therefore, if a seed groweth it is good, but if it groweth not, behold it is not good, therefore it is cast away.

33 And now, behold, because ye have tried the experiment, and planted the seed, and it swelleth and sprouteth, and beginneth to

How is desire an essential characteristic that leads to belief? (32:27) "Some may say, 'I cannot believe; I am not a religious person.' Just consider, God promises us divine help even if we have only a desire to believe, but it has to be a true and not a pretended desire" (Uchtdorf, "Power of a Personal Testimony," 38). ✚

How is truth delicious once it is received? (32:28) Joseph Smith stated: "I can taste the principles of eternal life, and so can you. They are given to me by the revelations of Jesus Christ; and I know that when I tell you these words of eternal life as they are given to me, you taste them, and I know that you believe them. You say honey is sweet, and so do I. I can also taste the spirit of eternal life. I know that it is good; and when I tell you of these things which were given me by inspiration of the Holy Spirit, you are bound to receive them as sweet, and rejoice more and more" (*Joseph Smith* [manual], 525).

How is the development of faith like unto the growth of a seed? (32:33) "My experience has been that a testimony does not burst upon us suddenly. Rather, it grows. . . .

"Do not be disappointed if you have read and reread and yet have not received a powerful witness. You may be somewhat like the disciples spoken of in the Book of Mormon who were filled with the power of God in great glory 'and they knew it not' (3 Nephi 9:20)" (Packer, "Book of Mormon: Another Testament of Jesus Christ—Plain and Precious Things," 8).

How does the seed of faith and testimony grow? (32:37–40) "When Alma compared the word of God to a seed, he explained that the seed grows into a fruit-bearing tree gradually, as a result of our 'faith, and [our] diligence, and patience, and long-suffering' (Alma 32:43). It's true that some blessings come right away: soon after we plant the seed in our hearts, it begins to swell and sprout and grow, and by this we know that the seed is good. From the very moment we set foot upon the pathway of discipleship, seen and unseen blessings from God begin to attend us" (Uchtdorf, "Way of the Disciple," 76). ✦

Where does Alma's tree of life grow? (32:40–41) "Alma states that continued nourishment will cause

grow, ye must needs know that the seed is good.

34 And now, behold, is your knowledge perfect? Yea, your knowledge is perfect in that thing, and your faith is dormant; and this because you know, for ye know that the word hath swelled your souls, and ye also know that it hath sprouted up, that your understanding doth begin to be enlightened, and your mind doth begin to expand.

35 O then, is not this real? I say unto you, Yea, because it is light; and whatsoever is light, is good, because it is discernible, therefore ye must know that it is good; and now behold, after ye have tasted this light is your knowledge perfect?

36 Behold I say unto you, Nay; neither must ye lay aside your faith, for ye have only exercised your faith to plant the seed that ye might try the experiment to know if the seed was good.

37 And behold, as the tree beginneth to grow, ye will say: Let us nourish it with great care, that it may get root, that it may grow up, and bring forth fruit unto us. And now behold, if ye nourish it with much care it will get root, and grow up, and bring forth fruit.

38 But if ye neglect the tree, and take no thought for its nourishment, behold it will not get any root; and when the heat of the sun cometh and scorcheth it, because it hath no root it withers away, and ye pluck it up and cast it out.

39 Now, this is not because the seed was not good, neither is it because the fruit thereof would not be desirable; but it is because your ground is barren, and ye will not nourish the tree, therefore ye cannot have the fruit thereof.

40 And thus, if ye will not nourish the word, looking forward with an eye of faith to the fruit thereof, ye can never pluck of the fruit of the tree of life.

41 But if ye will nourish the word, yea, nourish the tree as it beginneth to grow, by your faith with great diligence, and with patience, looking forward to the fruit thereof, it shall take root; and behold it shall be a tree springing up unto everlasting life.

42 And because of your diligence and your faith and your patience with the word in nourishing it, that it may take root in you, behold, by and by ye shall pluck the fruit thereof, which is most precious, which is sweet above all that is sweet, and which is white above all that is white, yea, and pure above all that is pure; and ye shall feast upon this fruit even until ye are filled, that ye hunger not, neither shall ye thirst.

43 Then, my brethren, ye shall reap the rewards of your faith, and your diligence, and patience, and long-suffering, waiting for the tree to bring forth fruit unto you.

CHAPTER 33

Zenos taught that men should pray and worship in all places, and that judgments are turned away because of the Son—Zenock taught that mercy is bestowed because of the Son—Moses had lifted up in the wilderness a type of the Son of God. About 74 B.C.

1 Now after Alma had spoken these words, they sent forth unto him desiring to know whether they should believe in one God, that they might obtain this fruit of which he had spoken, or how they should plant the seed, or the word of which he had spoken, which he said must be planted in their hearts; or in what manner they should begin to exercise their faith.

2 And Alma said unto them: Behold, ye have said that ye could not worship your God

the seed to grow into the tree of life with fruit that is exceedingly white, sweet, and pure—'a tree springing up unto everlasting life' (Alma 32:41; see also 32:26–42). In Alma's example, the tree of life grows within each person to change his or her heart and soul. Holding fast to the iron rod in Lehi's dream is the equivalent" (Bateman, "Coming unto Christ," 28).

Why does Alma repeat the pronoun "your" when teaching about faith? (32:42) "In lists the Hebrew language repeats the possessive pronoun (e.g., their, our, your, thy, his, her) before each of the nouns to which it refers, a convention that is uncommon in English usage....

"[Examples] of the repeated possessive pronoun in the Book of Mormon include *your* four times in Mosiah 4:30, *their* eight times in Mosiah 11:3, *your* three times in Alma 32:42, *our* nine times in Alma 44:5, *thy* four times in Alma 38:3, and *their* twelve times in Helaman 3:14" (Parry, "Hebraisms and Other Ancient Peculiarities in the Book of Mormon," 179–80).

Alma 33:1–11. Alma Quotes the Prophet Zenos on How to Worship

How should we worship and how will we be blessed for doing so? (33:2) "To worship God is to give Him our love, reverence, service, and devotion. . . . Worship not only shows our love for God and commitment to Him, it gives us strength to keep His commandments. Through worship we grow in knowledge and faithfulness. If we place any person or thing above the love of God, we worship that thing or person. This is called idolatry (see Exodus 20:3–6)" (*True to the Faith*, 188). ☉

Why does Alma appeal to the example of "Zenos, the prophet of old"? (33:3–7) "From these verses written by Zenos in the form of a prayer, literally a psalm of thanksgiving, we obtain a sketch of his prophetic activities. Because of his witness of the Redeemer, Zenos was put to death by his enemies (see Helaman 8:19). Alma quotes the psalm because it illustrates the propriety of praying in whatever circumstance one finds oneself, be it wilderness, fields, home, or closet. In so doing, he places special emphasis on the mercy extended to men through the atonement of the Son of God" (McConkie and Millet, *Doctrinal Commentary*, 3:240).

What is one of Alma's purposes in quoting Zenos? (33:5) "Alma's purpose in quoting Zenos was to show that they did not have to go to their synagogue to pray or worship. The Lord had heard Zenos's prayer in every possible place, the wilderness, his field, his house, in the closet in his house, and even in the midst of the Lord's congregations. It was not where he prayed, but how sincerely he prayed to the Lord that was mercifully answered under trying circumstances" (Nyman, *Record of Alma*, 424).

What is the value of secret prayer? (33:8) Said President John Taylor: "At [an] early period of my life I learned to approach God. Many a time I have gone into the fields and concealing myself behind some bush, would bow before the Lord and call upon him to guide and direct me. And he heard my prayer. . . . It would not hurt you . . . to call upon the Lord in your secret places, as I did. That was the spirit which I had when a little boy. And God has led me from one thing to another" (in *Journal of Discourses*, 22:315).

How might have Zenos's afflictions led to his sincerity in calling forth the mercy of the Lord? (33:11) "Often afflictions lead some to sincerity! When

because ye are cast out of your synagogues. But behold, I say unto you, if ye suppose that ye cannot worship God, ye do greatly err, and ye ought to search the scriptures; if ye suppose that they have taught you this, ye do not understand them.

3 Do ye remember to have read what Zenos, the prophet of old, has said concerning prayer or worship?

4 For he said: Thou art merciful, O God, for thou hast heard my prayer, even when I was in the wilderness; yea, thou wast merciful when I prayed concerning those who were mine enemies, and thou didst turn them to me.

5 Yea, O God, and thou wast merciful unto me when I did cry unto thee in my field; when I did cry unto thee in my prayer, and thou didst hear me.

6 And again, O God, when I did turn to my house thou didst hear me in my prayer.

7 And when I did turn unto my closet, O Lord, and prayed unto thee, thou didst hear me.

8 Yea, thou art merciful unto thy children when they cry unto thee, to be heard of thee and not of men, and thou wilt hear them.

9 Yea, O God, thou hast been merciful unto me, and heard my cries in the midst of thy congregations.

10 Yea, and thou hast also heard me when I have been cast out and have been despised by mine enemies; yea, thou didst hear my cries, and wast angry with mine enemies, and thou didst visit them in thine anger with speedy destruction.

11 And thou didst hear me because of mine afflictions and my sincerity; and it is because of thy Son that thou hast been thus merciful

unto me, therefore I will cry unto thee in all mine afflictions, for in thee is my joy; for thou hast turned thy judgments away from me, because of thy Son.

12 And now Alma said unto them: Do ye believe those scriptures which have been written by them of old?

13 Behold, if ye do, ye must believe what Zenos said; for, behold he said: Thou hast turned away thy judgments because of thy Son.

14 Now behold, my brethren, I would ask if ye have read the scriptures? If ye have, how can ye disbelieve on the Son of God?

15 For it is not written that Zenos alone spake of these things, but Zenock also spake of these things—

16 For behold, he said: Thou art angry, O Lord, with this people, because they will not understand thy mercies which thou hast bestowed upon them because of thy Son.

17 And now, my brethren, ye see that a second prophet of old has testified of the Son of God, and because the people would not understand his words they stoned him to death.

18 But behold, this is not all; these are not the only ones who have spoken concerning the Son of God.

19 Behold, he was spoken of by Moses; yea, and behold a type was raised up in the wilderness, that whosoever would look upon it might live. And many did look and live.

our souls have been stretched; when our bodies or our hearts have been racked with pain and frustration; when our present hopes have been dashed; when there is no place to go but to God for comfort—at such a time our words more truly reflect and mirror the soul's sincere desire" (McConkie and Millet, *Doctrinal Commentary*, 3:240). ⊕

Alma 33:12–23. Alma Quotes the Words of Prophets That Testify of Jesus Christ

How do the scriptures strengthen our testimonies of Jesus Christ? (33:12–14) Think about the ways you feel your belief in the scriptures has blessed your life. Who do you know that would most likely appreciate those same blessings? How might you share your testimony with them? Consider writing about or discussing with someone how the scriptures have helped you understand and rely on the Atonement of Jesus Christ.

What did Zenos and Zenock clearly teach about Jesus Christ? (33:13–18) "The Book of Mormon tells us more about the usage of the name the Son of God by Old Testament prophets than does that volume of Holy Writ itself. . . . Fragmentary as our records are, it is nonetheless clear that all of the prophets of Old Testament times knew and taught that the promised Messiah would be the Son of God" (McConkie, *Promised Messiah*, 143–45).

What mercies does God bestow on us because of His Son? (33:16) "I have learned there are many who believe Jesus is the Son of God and that he is the Savior of the World, but they do not believe that he can save them. They believe in his identity, but not in his power to cleanse and to purify and to save. . . . As our understanding of the Atonement increases, our ability to forgive ourselves and others increases as well. When we more fully understand the depths to which the Savior descended, the breadth to which he reached, and the heights to which he ascended, we can more readily accept that our own sins are within the vast sphere of his conquered domain" (Callister, *Infinite Atonement*, 197).

What is a type? (33:19) President Dallin H. Oaks explained that a type is "a likeness or reminder of something else" ("Bible Stories," 37). Joseph Fielding McConkie described a type as "a person, event, or ritual with likeness to another person, event, or ritual of greater importance which is to follow. The term *antitype* describes future fulfillment, while *typology* is the study of types. True types will have noticeable points of resemblance, show evidence of divine appointment, and be prophetic of future events" (*Gospel Symbolism*, 274).

What is "this word" we are to plant in our hearts? (33:22–23) "The seed or word is the life and mission of Jesus Christ, the central feature being His terrible suffering for the sins of the world and His humiliating death by crucifixion" (Judd, "Parables of Matthew 13," 76).

In what ways have you planted the Lord's Atonement in your heart?

What does God promise us if we trust Him with our burdens? (33:23) "Life presses all kinds of burdens on each of us, some light but others relentless and heavy. People struggle every day under burdens that tax their souls.... They can be emotionally or physically ponderous. They can be worrisome, oppressive, and exhausting. And they can continue for years.... Through it all, the Savior offers us sustaining strength and support, and in His own time and way, He offers deliverance.... Mercifully, the Son of God offers us deliverance from the bondage of our sins, which are among the heaviest of all the burdens we bear" (Clayton, "That Your Burdens May Be Light," 12–13).

20 But few understood the meaning of those things, and this because of the hardness of their hearts. But there were many who were so hardened that they would not look, therefore they perished. Now the reason they would not look is because they did not believe that it would heal them.

21 O my brethren, if ye could be healed by merely casting about your eyes that ye might be healed, would ye not behold quickly, or would ye rather harden your hearts in unbelief, and be slothful, that ye would not cast about your eyes, that ye might perish?

22 If so, wo shall come upon you; but if not so, then cast about your eyes and begin to believe in the Son of God, that he will come to redeem his people, and that he shall suffer and die to atone for their sins; and that he shall rise again from the dead, which shall bring to pass the resurrection, that all men shall stand before him, to be judged at the last and judgment day, according to their works.

23 And now, my brethren, I desire that ye shall plant this word in your hearts, and as it beginneth to swell even so nourish it by your faith. And behold, it will become a tree, springing up in you unto everlasting life. And then may God grant unto you that your burdens may be light, through the joy of his Son. And even all this can ye do if ye will. Amen.

CHAPTER 34

Amulek testifies that the word is in Christ unto salvation—Unless an atonement is made, all mankind must perish—The whole law of Moses points toward the sacrifice of the Son of God—The eternal plan of redemption is based on faith and repentance—Pray for temporal and spiritual blessings—This life is the time for men to prepare to meet God—Work out your salvation with fear before God. About 74 B.C.

1 And now it came to pass that after Alma had spoken these words unto them he sat down upon the ground, and Amulek arose and began to teach them, saying:

2 My brethren, I think that it is impossible that ye should be ignorant of the things which have been spoken concerning the coming of Christ, who is taught by us to be the Son of God; yea, I know that these things were taught unto you bountifully before your dissension from among us.

3 And as ye have desired of my beloved brother that he should make known unto you what ye should do, because of your afflictions; and he hath spoken somewhat unto you to prepare your minds; yea, and he hath exhorted you unto faith and to patience—

4 Yea, even that ye would have so much faith as even to plant the word in your hearts, that ye may try the experiment of its goodness.

5 And we have beheld that the great question which is in your minds is whether the word be in the Son of God, or whether there shall be no Christ.

Alma 34:1–7. Amulek Adds His Witness to Alma's

How were the Nephites taught "bountifully" concerning the coming of Jesus Christ and His Atonement? (34:2) "The testimonies of Nephi, Jacob, and Isaiah have been given as the three great early witnesses . . . declaring their testimony of Christ. . . . Obviously, prophets coming later had their affirmations strengthened by these three, and so the reinforcing, prophetic declarations of Christ unfold throughout the Book of Mormon.

"In fact, the theme 'Jesus is the Christ,' which runs throughout the Book of Mormon, suggests that one way of reading and remembering this sacred record is to move, in effect, from one teaching about the Savior to the next" (Holland, *Christ and the New Covenant*, 95).

What did Amulek identify as the "great question"? (34:5) "The Book of Mormon provides resounding and great answers to what Amulek designated as 'the great question'; namely, is there really a redeeming Christ? (Alma 34:5–6). The Book of Mormon with clarity and with evidence says, 'Yes! Yes! Yes!' Moreover, in its recurring theme, the book even declares that 'all things which have been given of God from the beginning of the world, unto man, are the typifying of [Christ]' (2 Ne 11:4). . . . He, before whom all things—past, present, and future—are continually, has chosen to tell us about the 'gospel'—the transcending 'good news,' the resplendent answers to 'the great question'" (Maxwell, "Book of Mormon: A Great Answer to 'the Great Question,'" 1).

Why is Jesus Christ the only way of salvation?
(34:6) "Surely there is no salvation to be found in the worship of false gods. Certainly no benefit can accrue from spurious or delusive doctrine. Even that which is innocently ignorant is without the power to bless. Sincerity, however pure it may be, cannot remit sins, raise the dead, or create a celestial kingdom. . . . Christ addressed the issue in his intercessory prayer: 'And this is life eternal,' he said, 'that they might know thee the only true God, and Jesus Christ, whom thou hast sent' (John 17:3). The bloodline must be pure—eternal life can only be the offspring of eternal truth" (McConkie, "Chosen Vessels and the Order of the Priesthood," 179).

Alma 34:8–12. Amulek Testifies of the Atonement of Jesus Christ

What can we learn from Amulek's example of testifying? (34:8) "Some of us are naturally reserved and timid about bearing our testimony with words. Perhaps we should not be so timid. . . . When we do bear testimony, we should testify with a spirit of humility. Perhaps we do not always remember that it is the power of the Spirit that carries our testimony into the hearts of others. Our testimony is our own. It cannot be challenged by someone else. It is personal and real to us. But it is the Holy Spirit that gives a similar witness to another" (Faust, "Importance of Bearing Testimony," 4). ⊕

What did Amulek want the people to understand about the Savior's sacrifice? (34:10) "It was . . . infinite in that all humankind would be saved from never-ending death. It was infinite in terms of His immense suffering. It was infinite in time, putting an end to the preceding prototype of animal sacrifice. It was infinite in scope—it was to be done once for all. . . . And the mercy of the Atonement extends not only to an infinite number of people, but also to an infinite number of worlds created by Him. . . . It was infinite beyond any human scale of measurement or mortal comprehension. Jesus was the only one who could offer such an infinite atonement, since He was born of a mortal mother and an immortal Father. Because of that unique birthright, Jesus was an infinite Being" (Nelson, "The Atonement," 35). ⊕

6 And ye also beheld that my brother has proved unto you, in many instances, that the word is in Christ unto salvation.

7 My brother has called upon the words of Zenos, that redemption cometh through the Son of God, and also upon the words of Zenock; and also he has appealed unto Moses, to prove that these things are true.

8 And now, behold, I will testify unto you of myself that these things are true. Behold, I say unto you, that I do know that Christ shall come among the children of men, to take upon him the transgressions of his people, and that he shall atone for the sins of the world; for the Lord God hath spoken it.

9 For it is expedient that an atonement should be made; for according to the great plan of the Eternal God there must be an atonement made, or else all mankind must unavoidably perish; yea, all are hardened; yea, all are fallen and are lost, and must perish except it be through the atonement which it is expedient should be made.

10 For it is expedient that there should be a great and last sacrifice; yea, not a sacrifice of man, neither of beast, neither of any manner of fowl; for it shall not be a human sacrifice; but it must be an infinite and eternal sacrifice.

11 Now there is not any man that can sacrifice his own blood which will atone for the sins of another. Now, if a man murdereth, behold will our law, which is just, take the life of his brother? I say unto you, Nay.

12 But the law requireth the life of him who hath murdered; therefore there can be nothing which is short of an infinite atonement which will suffice for the sins of the world.

13 Therefore, it is expedient that there should be a great and last sacrifice, and then shall there be, or it is expedient there should be, a stop to the shedding of blood; then shall the law of Moses be fulfilled; yea, it shall be all fulfilled, every jot and tittle, and none shall have passed away.

14 And behold, this is the whole meaning of the law, every whit pointing to that great and last sacrifice; and that great and last sacrifice will be the Son of God, yea, infinite and eternal.

15 And thus he shall bring salvation to all those who shall believe on his name; this being the intent of this last sacrifice, to bring about the bowels of mercy, which overpowereth justice, and bringeth about means unto men that they may have faith unto repentance.

16 And thus mercy can satisfy the demands of justice, and encircles them in the arms of safety, while he that exercises no faith unto repentance is exposed to the whole law of the demands of justice; therefore only unto him that has faith unto repentance is brought about the great and eternal plan of redemption.

17 Therefore may God grant unto you, my brethren, that ye may begin to exercise your faith unto repentance, that ye begin to call upon his holy name, that he would have mercy upon you;

Alma 34:13–16. The Atonement of Jesus Christ Shall Fulfill the Law of Moses

Why was Christ's sacrifice considered "that great and last sacrifice"? (34:14) "The Zoramites, in spite of their apostasy from the Nephite Church of God, . . . took with them a belief in the Law of Moses which they had garbled, and which they evidently did not understand. The Law of Moses required the rendering of sacrifice wherein animals . . . were offered in token of the 'great and last Sacrifice' which 'will be the Son of God, yea, infinite and eternal,' Amulek said. That great and last Sacrifice of the Son of God wherein His blood will be spilled to atone for the sins of all men will put a 'stop to the shedding of blood.' To this end, that is the 'great and last Sacrifice of the Son of God' every ordinance, performance, and sacrifice, of that Law was pointed" (Reynolds and Sjodahl, *Commentary on the Book of Mormon*, 4:107).

How does Jesus Christ's sacrifice satisfy both mercy and the demands of justice? (34:15–16) "Only an omniscient, all-loving God could have both roles of advocate (pleading for the petitioner) and judge (deciding the ultimate fate of the petitioner). This is because He possesses a perfect balance of the qualities of justice and mercy and all other divine attributes that make Him perfect, or complete, in all the Godly virtues" (Maxwell, *One More Strain of Praise*, 33–34).

Alma 34:17–29. Amulek Teaches the People to Pray for Mercy and Serve Others

Why did Amulek express hope that God would grant unto them to exercise "faith unto repentance"? (34:17) "The combination of faith in Christ plus faith unto repentance is vitally important. . . . Apparently faith great enough to move mountains is not required; faith enough to speak in tongues or to heal the sick is not needed; all that we need is enough faith to recognize that we have sinned and need to repent of our sins, to feel remorse for them, and to desire to sin no more but to please Christ the Lord. Then the greatest miracle of all, the Atonement, whereby Christ rescues us from our deserved punishment, is in effect in our behalf" (Wells, "Liahona Triad," 6–7).

How might Amulek's repetitive use of the word *cry* **influence your prayers?** (34:18–26) "Amulek's instructions on prayer are made memorable by the anaphora (initial repetition) of 'cry,' by frequent amplification . . . and by the progressive development of prayer from 'call' to 'cry' to 'pour out your souls'" (Rust, *Feasting on the Word*, 96–97).

What power might we experience in family prayer? (34:21) "Think of the power for good as you gather your family together and thank God for all of his blessings. Think of the eternal significance of daily thanking him for each member of your family and asking him to guide and bless and protect each one. Think of the strength that will come to your family as, daily, one member or another pours out his or her soul in love to God for other family members" (Groberg, "Power of Family Prayer," 50). ✪

Why does Amulek highlight "closets," "secret places," and the "wilderness" as specific locations for prayer? (34:26) "The mention of 'closets and secret places' is a clear reference to the . . . custom of the ancient Hebrew of having special shrines or prayer-rooms in their houses. . . . But what we wish especially to notice here is that 'your wilderness' is a normal and natural part of the Nephite scene, with people going into the wilderness on regular business, where they are admonished to pray as in other places" (Nibley, *Approach to the Book of Mormon*, 404).

How should we live after pleading for the Lord's mercy in our own behalf? (34:28–29) "To be converted, you must not only open your heart to a knowledge of the gospel and the love of God, you must practice the gospel law. You cannot fully understand or appreciate it unless you personally apply it in your life. Jesus said that He came to serve, not to be served. So it must be with you. You must look outward and care about others. You can be compassionate; you can be friendly; you can share; you can help others in a hundred small ways. As you do, the gospel of Jesus Christ will become a part of you" (Christofferson, "When Thou Art Converted," 12).

18 Yea, cry unto him for mercy; for he is mighty to save.

19 Yea, humble yourselves, and continue in prayer unto him.

20 Cry unto him when ye are in your fields, yea, over all your flocks.

21 Cry unto him in your houses, yea, over all your household, both morning, mid-day, and evening.

22 Yea, cry unto him against the power of your enemies.

23 Yea, cry unto him against the devil, who is an enemy to all righteousness.

24 Cry unto him over the crops of your fields, that ye may prosper in them.

25 Cry over the flocks of your fields, that they may increase.

26 But this is not all; ye must pour out your souls in your closets, and your secret places, and in your wilderness.

27 Yea, and when you do not cry unto the Lord, let your hearts be full, drawn out in prayer unto him continually for your welfare, and also for the welfare of those who are around you.

28 And now behold, my beloved brethren, I say unto you, do not suppose that this is all; for after ye have done all these things, if ye turn away the needy, and the naked, and visit not the sick and afflicted, and impart of your substance, if ye have, to those who stand in need—I say unto you, if ye do not any of these things, behold, your prayer is vain, and availeth you nothing, and ye are as hypocrites who do deny the faith.

29 Therefore, if ye do not remember to be charitable, ye are as dross, which the refiners do cast out, (it being of no worth) and is trodden under foot of men.

30 And now, my brethren, I would that, after ye have received so many witnesses, seeing that the holy scriptures testify of these things, ye come forth and bring fruit unto repentance.

31 Yea, I would that ye would come forth and harden not your hearts any longer; for behold, now is the time and the day of your salvation; and therefore, if ye will repent and harden not your hearts, immediately shall the great plan of redemption be brought about unto you.

32 For behold, this life is the time for men to prepare to meet God; yea, behold the day of this life is the day for men to perform their labors.

33 And now, as I said unto you before, as ye have had so many witnesses, therefore, I beseech of you that ye do not procrastinate the day of your repentance until the end; for after this day of life, which is given us to prepare for eternity, behold, if we do not improve our time while in this life, then cometh the night of darkness wherein there can be no labor performed.

34 Ye cannot say, when ye are brought to that awful crisis, that I will repent, that I will return to my God. Nay, ye cannot say this; for that same spirit which doth possess your bodies at the time that ye go out of this life,

Alma 34:30–36. We Must Spend Our Lives Preparing to Meet the Lord

How can we prepare to meet God? (34:32) "Thank God for one more day! For what? For the opportunity to take care of some unfinished business; to repent; to right some wrongs; to influence for good some wayward child; to reach out to someone who cried for help—in short, thank God for one more day to prepare to meet God. Don't try to live too many days ahead. Seek for strength to attend to the problems of today. Do all that you can do and leave the rest to God, the Father of us all. It is not enough to say I will do my best, but rather, I will do everything that is within my power; I will do all that is necessary" (Lee, *Stand Ye in Holy Places*, 239). ☉

What does procrastinating living gospel principles cost us? (34:33) President Joseph Fielding Smith warned: "Procrastination, as it may be applied to gospel principles, is the thief of eternal life, which is life in the presence of the Father and the Son. There are many among us, even members of the Church, who feel that there is no need for haste in the observance of gospel principles and the keeping of the commandments" (in Conference Report, Apr. 1969, 121).

Why is it wise to not delay our repentance? (34:33) "According to Oliver B. Huntington the Prophet Joseph Smith said that 'a man can do as much in this life in one year as he can do in ten years in the spirit world without the body.' If . . . a person has enjoyed the privileges of gospel understanding but chooses in this life to deny or defy that light, to reject the truth and avoid the works of righteousness when he knows better, it becomes extremely difficult for him to turn around, to change directions at the time of death" (McConkie and Millet, *Doctrinal Commentary*, 3:256). ⊕

What does the term "seal you his" mean? (34:35)
"To those who die in their wicked state, not having repented, the scriptures say the devil shall seal them as his own (see Alma 34:35), which means that until they have paid the uttermost farthing for what they have done, they shall not be redeemed from his grasp. When they shall have been subjected to the buffetings of Satan sufficient to have satisfied justice, then they shall be brought forth out of the grasp of Satan and shall be assigned to that place in our Father's celestial, terrestrial, or telestial world merited by their life here upon this earth" (*Teachings of Harold B. Lee*, 59).

Who will claim your everlasting soul? (34:35)
Contrast Alma 34:35 with Mosiah 5:15. What can you do in order for the Savior to seal you His?

Alma 34:37–41. Amulek Encourages the People to Obey the Lord and Follow Him

Why is it important to live a life centered in Jesus Christ? (34:38) "Can you imagine how your life would improve if you lived in thanksgiving daily? Can you imagine how your life would improve if others did the same? Do you think the world would be a happier place? less stressful? less angry? more spiritual?" (Wirthlin, "Live in Thanksgiving Daily," 8–9).

What are the heaven-sent blessings that you are most grateful for? What happens to your mood and your motivation when you keep those blessings foremost in your mind? ⊕

that same spirit will have power to possess your body in that eternal world.

35 For behold, if ye have procrastinated the day of your repentance even until death, behold, ye have become subjected to the spirit of the devil, and he doth seal you his; therefore, the Spirit of the Lord hath withdrawn from you, and hath no place in you, and the devil hath all power over you; and this is the final state of the wicked.

36 And this I know, because the Lord hath said he dwelleth not in unholy temples, but in the hearts of the righteous doth he dwell; yea, and he has also said that the righteous shall sit down in his kingdom, to go no more out; but their garments should be made white through the blood of the Lamb.

37 And now, my beloved brethren, I desire that ye should remember these things, and that ye should work out your salvation with fear before God, and that ye should no more deny the coming of Christ;

38 That ye contend no more against the Holy Ghost, but that ye receive it, and take upon you the name of Christ; that ye humble yourselves even to the dust, and worship God, in whatsoever place ye may be in, in spirit and in truth; and that ye live in thanksgiving daily, for the many mercies and blessings which he doth bestow upon you.

39 Yea, and I also exhort you, my brethren, that ye be watchful unto prayer continually, that ye may not be led away by the temptations of the devil, that he may not overpower you, that ye may not become his subjects at the last day; for behold, he rewardeth you no good thing.

40 And now my beloved brethren, I would exhort you to have patience, and that ye bear with all manner of afflictions; that ye do not revile against those who do cast you out because of your exceeding poverty, lest ye become sinners like unto them;

41 But that ye have patience, and bear with those afflictions, with a firm hope that ye shall one day rest from all your afflictions.

CHAPTER 35

The preaching of the word destroys the craft of the Zoramites—They expel the converts, who then join the people of Ammon in Jershon—Alma sorrows because of the wickedness of the people. About 74 B.C.

1 Now it came to pass that after Amulek had made an end of these words, they withdrew themselves from the multitude and came over into the land of Jershon.

2 Yea, and the rest of the brethren, after they had preached the word unto the Zoramites, also came over into the land of Jershon.

3 And it came to pass that after the more popular part of the Zoramites had consulted together concerning the words which had been preached unto them, they were angry because of the word, for it did destroy their craft; therefore they would not hearken unto the words.

4 And they sent and gathered together throughout all the land all the people, and consulted with them concerning the words which had been spoken.

5 Now their rulers and their priests and their teachers did not let the people know concerning their desires; therefore they found out privily the minds of all the people.

6 And it came to pass that after they had found out the minds of all the people, those who were in favor of the words which had been spoken by Alma and his brethren were

Alma 35:1–7. The Converted Zoramites Are Cast Out

Why was the land of Jershon a place of refuge for Alma and Amulek? (35:1–2) "Jershon is a logical location, since it is closer than Zarahemla. They would have depended on the generosity of those whom they visited to feed and house them. Apparently their message had appealed to the poorest Zoramites, who were therefore the least able to offer hospitality, especially for a sustained period. Most Zoramites were completely unsympathetic. . . . The welcoming support of Jershon would have been sustaining to them" (Gardner, *Second Witness*, 4:488).

What was the Zoramite craft that was destroyed? (35:3) The craft refers to priestcraft (see 2 Nephi 26:28–29). "When preaching the Gospel is made a craft, when ministering its precepts becomes a business, or when its blessings are known only to the rich, its mercies and its comforts flee and what is left is merely a sham, a make-believe in which there is no soul, no holy promptings" (Reynolds and Sjodahl, *Commentary on the Book of Mormon*, 4:82).

Alma 35:8–13. The Zoramites and the Lamanites Begin a War against the Nephites

Why did the wicked Zoramites threaten the people of Ammon? (35:8–10) The Savior explained to his apostles and disciples why some people get angry and violent when the truth is preached: "If the world hate you, ye know that it hated me before it hated you. If ye were of the world, the world would love his own: but because ye are not of the world, but I have chosen you out of the world, therefore the world hateth you. . . . If they have persecuted me, they will also persecute you. . . . He that hateth me hateth my Father also" (John 15:18–23).

Would we be as brave in a similar situation? Why did the people of Ammon not fear the Zoramites? (see Alma 24:16–19). What is the relationship between the level of our obedience and our susceptibility to fear? What do we know about the power of God that makes the threats of the wicked less troubling? What can we do to face with more faith and less fear the difficult times prophesied for our future? ●

cast out of the land; and they were many; and they came over also into the land of Jershon.

7 And it came to pass that Alma and his brethren did minister unto them.

8 Now the people of the Zoramites were angry with the people of Ammon who were in Jershon, and the chief ruler of the Zoramites, being a very wicked man, sent over unto the people of Ammon desiring them that they should cast out of their land all those who came over from them into their land.

9 And he breathed out many threatenings against them. And now the people of Ammon did not fear their words; therefore they did not cast them out, but they did receive all the poor of the Zoramites that came over unto them; and they did nourish them, and did clothe them, and did give unto them lands for their inheritance; and they did administer unto them according to their wants.

10 Now this did stir up the Zoramites to anger against the people of Ammon, and they began to mix with the Lamanites and to stir them up also to anger against them.

11 And thus the Zoramites and the Lamanites began to make preparations for war against the people of Ammon, and also against the Nephites.

12 And thus ended the seventeenth year of the reign of the judges over the people of Nephi.

13 And the people of Ammon departed out of the land of Jershon, and came over into the land of Melek, and gave place in the land of Jershon for the armies of the Nephites, that they might contend with the armies of the Lamanites and the armies of the Zoramites; and thus commenced a war betwixt the Lamanites and the Nephites, in the eighteenth year of the reign of the judges; and an account shall be given of their wars hereafter.

14 And Alma, and Ammon, and their brethren, and also the two sons of Alma returned to the land of Zarahemla, after having been instruments in the hands of God of bringing many of the Zoramites to repentance; and as many as were brought to repentance were driven out of their land; but they have lands for their inheritance in the land of Jershon, and they have taken up arms to defend themselves, and their wives, and children, and their lands.

15 Now Alma, being grieved for the iniquity of his people, yea for the wars, and the bloodsheds, and the contentions which were among them; and having been to declare the word, or sent to declare the word, among all the people in every city; and seeing that the hearts of the people began to wax hard, and that they began to be offended because of the strictness of the word, his heart was exceedingly sorrowful.

16 Therefore, he caused that his sons should be gathered together, that he might give unto them every one his charge, separately, concerning the things pertaining unto righteousness. And we have an account of his commandments, which he gave unto them according to his own record.

Alma 35:14–16. Alma Prepares to Counsel His Three Sons

How can we overcome our fear of inviting others to repent even though we know some will be offended because of "the strictness of the word"? (35:15) "The invitation to repent is an expression of love. . . . If we do not invite others to change or if we do not demand repentance of ourselves, we fail in a fundamental duty we owe to one another and to ourselves. A permissive parent, an indulgent friend, a fearful Church leader are in reality more concerned about themselves than the welfare and happiness of those they could help. Yes, the call to repentance is at times regarded as intolerant or offensive and may even be resented, but guided by the Spirit, it is in reality an act of genuine caring" (Christofferson, "Divine Gift of Repentance," 39).

Why did Mormon include Alma's commandments and counsel to his sons? (35:16) "Where does a prophet begin to change things? What could he do to turn things around in the land? Notice that he did not begin with a general conference, though he was the prophet, nor did he call a press conference to gather public support. He chose instead to start at home. In fact, perhaps Mormon, in making his abridgment, felt this point was so critical for us as a latter-day people to understand that he put aside his account of wars and difficulties that Alma faced in governing his people and instead detailed in his transcript how a prophet may have helped change the entire social order. He began at home!" (Anderson and Anderson, "One by One," 55).

Superscription to Alma 36

The superscription to Alma 36 was part of the ancient record translated by the Prophet Joseph Smith and dictated by him to his scribe (see also, for example, 2 Nephi, Mosiah 9, and Alma 38).

The italicized words "Comprising chapters 36 and 37" were not part of the ancient record but were added later to printed editions of the Book of Mormon.

Alma 36:1–5. Alma Bears Testimony to His Son Helaman

What does it mean, in the Book of Mormon, to prosper if we keep the commandments? (36:1–2) "To understand this promise we need to define the word *prosper* in a Book of Mormon context. Certainly prosperity had to do with the physical and spiritual circumstances of the obedient, but beyond that it is used in the framework of deliverance. . . . Notice how closely related the ideas of prosperity and deliverance are. The parallel usage of these two words is not uncommon in the Nephite text (see Omni 1:6–7; Mosiah 2:31; 7:29, 33; Alma 9:9, 13; 36:29–30)" (Bassett, "Nephi's Freedom Thesis and the Sons of Helaman," 291–92). ⊕

What is meant by "carnal"? (36:4) "The word *carnal* is used in the Book of Mormon to distinguish between that of the flesh and that of the spirit. It does not necessarily infer sin, but when it is contrasted with spirit it sometimes is so intended. It comes from the Latin *carnis*, which means flesh" (Reynolds and Sjodahl, *Commentary on the Book of Mormon*, 4:138).

Alma 36:6–30. Alma Tells Helaman His Own Conversion Story

Why does God send angels? (36:6) "In the very beginning, God established a pattern of his teaching

The commandments of Alma to his son Helaman.

Comprising chapters 36 and 37.

CHAPTER 36

Alma testifies to Helaman of his conversion after seeing an angel—He suffered the pains of a damned soul; he called upon the name of Jesus, and was then born of God—Sweet joy filled his soul—He saw concourses of angels praising God—Many converts have tasted and seen as he has tasted and seen. About 74 B.C.

1 My son, give ear to my words; for I swear unto you, that inasmuch as ye shall keep the commandments of God ye shall prosper in the land.

2 I would that ye should do as I have done, in remembering the captivity of our fathers; for they were in bondage, and none could deliver them except it was the God of Abraham, and the God of Isaac, and the God of Jacob; and he surely did deliver them in their afflictions.

3 And now, O my son Helaman, behold, thou art in thy youth, and therefore, I beseech of thee that thou wilt hear my words and learn of me; for I do know that whosoever shall put their trust in God shall be supported in their trials, and their troubles, and their afflictions, and shall be lifted up at the last day.

4 And I would not that ye think that I know of myself—not of the temporal but of the spiritual, not of the carnal mind but of God.

5 Now, behold, I say unto you, if I had not been born of God I should not have known these things; but God has, by the mouth of his holy angel, made these things known unto me, not of any worthiness of myself;

6 For I went about with the sons of Mosiah, seeking to destroy the church of God; but behold, God sent his holy angel to stop us by the way.

7 And behold, he spake unto us, as it were the voice of thunder, and the whole earth did tremble beneath our feet; and we all fell to the earth, for the fear of the Lord came upon us.

8 But behold, the voice said unto me: Arise. And I arose and stood up, and beheld the angel.

9 And he said unto me: If thou wilt of thyself be destroyed, seek no more to destroy the church of God.

10 And it came to pass that I fell to the earth; and it was for the space of three days and three nights that I could not open my mouth, neither had I the use of my limbs.

11 And the angel spake more things unto me, which were heard by my brethren, but I did not hear them; for when I heard the words—If thou wilt be destroyed of thyself, seek no more to destroy the church of God—I was struck with such great fear and amazement lest perhaps I should be destroyed, that I fell to the earth and I did hear no more.

12 But I was racked with eternal torment, for my soul was harrowed up to the greatest degree and racked with all my sins.

13 Yea, I did remember all my sins and iniquities, for which I was tormented with the

men by way of angels. It started with the first man, Adam [Moses 5:6–8 is quoted]. . . . The basic relationship between the Son of God and man was announced and taught by an angel. This system of teaching has been repeated over and over again. The Book of Mormon furnishes the best examples of the use of angels as teachers [Mosiah 3:2–3 and Alma 19:34 are quoted]" (McConkie, *Angels*, 34–35).

What does *racked* mean? (36:12, 16) The dictionary defines *racked* as "strained to the utmost" (Webster, *American Dictionary*).

Differences between Alma's Accounts of His Conversion

"Some readers of the Book of Mormon have claimed there is a discrepancy in the accounts of the conversion of Alma as recorded in Mosiah 27:23 and Alma 36:10. It is true that one account mentions 'two days and two nights' and the other says 'three days and three nights,' but there is no apparent discrepancy because they are not referring to exactly the same thing. In the account in the book of Mosiah the time element clearly refers to the period of fasting by the priests; no exact length of time is indicated for Alma's unconscious state. Note the major details of the account: After Alma was confronted by an angel and realized the enormity of his sins, he fell to the earth almost as if dead. Then he was carried to his father in this helpless condition. The father of Alma then called in the priests of the church and 'after they had fasted and prayed for the space of two days and two nights, the limbs of Alma received their strength, and he stood up' (Mosiah 27:22–23). In the account in the book of Alma, however, the term 'three days and three nights' clearly refers to the total time Alma could not open his mouth nor use his limbs (Alma 36:10)" (Ludlow, *Companion to Your Study of the Book of Mormon*, 217–18).

In what way was Alma's example a form of murder? (36:14) "As Alma mentions later to his son Corianton, the murder of a human physical body is a grave sin. However, an even more serious sin is to murder the spiritual life of a person or, in other words, to purposely lead one away from the saving principles of the gospel. Concerning such people Alma says: ' . . . whosoever murdereth against the light and knowledge of God, it is not easy for him to obtain forgiveness' (Alma 39:6)" (Ludlow, *Companion to Your Study of the Book of Mormon*, 218).

What is the purpose of painful consequences associated with sin? (36:16) "It is not uncommon to find men and women in the world who feel remorse for the things they do wrong. . . . Godly sorrow is a gift of the Spirit. It is a deep realization that our actions have offended our Father and our God. It is the sharp and keen awareness that our behavior caused the Savior, He who knew no sin, even the greatest of all, to endure agony and suffering. . . . This very real mental and spiritual anguish is what the scriptures refer to as having 'a broken heart and a contrite spirit.' Such a spirit is the absolute prerequisite for true repentance" (Benson, "Mighty Change of Heart," 4).

How was Alma finally converted? (36:17–18) "I am . . . impressed with the repetition of the name 'Jesus Christ, Son of God' at the very center of the chapter. This unquestionably had deep significance for Alma. It is one of the best examples of any ancient author succeeding in placing the most important concept at the central or turning point of his passage. . . . For the central turning point of his conversion came precisely when he called

pains of hell; yea, I saw that I had rebelled against my God, and that I had not kept his holy commandments.

14 Yea, and I had murdered many of his children, or rather led them away unto destruction; yea, and in fine so great had been my iniquities, that the very thought of coming into the presence of my God did rack my soul with inexpressible horror.

15 Oh, thought I, that I could be banished and become extinct both soul and body, that I might not be brought to stand in the presence of my God, to be judged of my deeds.

16 And now, for three days and for three nights was I racked, even with the pains of a damned soul.

17 And it came to pass that as I was thus racked with torment, while I was harrowed up by the memory of my many sins, behold, I remembered also to have heard my father prophesy unto the people concerning the coming of one Jesus Christ, a Son of God, to atone for the sins of the world.

Chiasmus

"*Chiasmus*, sometimes called an inverted parallelism, is a Hebrew literary form where words or ideas are arranged in a certain order and then repeated in reverse order. This repetition emphasizes important ideas and words. In addition, the writer's main idea is often located at the center of the chiasmus.

"Alma used chiasmus to tell the story of his conversion to his son Helaman. The presence of Semitic literary forms such as chiasmus in the Book of Mormon is an external witness that the book is what the Prophet Joseph Smith taught that it is: a translation of an ancient text written in a Middle Eastern language.

"The following chart will help you recognize the chiasmus in Alma 36. For convenience, positions are designated in the chart from left to right, starting with the letter A and ending with the letter P. Thus, the thought expressed in the beginning verse of the chiasmus, Alma 36:1 (labeled position *A*), is repeated in the last verse of the chiasmus, Alma 36:30 (also in position *A*). The thought in Alma 36:2 (labeled position *D*) is repeated in verse 29 (also in position *D*), and so forth.

A. Give ear to my words (v. 1)

  B. Keep the commandments of God, and ye shall prosper in the land (v. 1)

    C. Do as I have done (v. 2)

      D. Remember the captivity of our fathers, for they were in bondage (v. 2)

        E. He surely did deliver them (v. 2)

          F. Trust in God (v. 3)

            G. Supported in their trials, and their troubles, and their afflictions (v. 3)

              H. Lifted up at the last day (v. 3)

                I. I would not that ye think that I know of myself— but of God (v. 4)

                  J. Born of God (v. 5)

                    K. I went about seeking to destroy the church of God (v. 6)

                      L. Neither had I the use of my limbs (v. 10)

                        M. I thought that I might not be brought to the presence of my God (v. 15)

                          N. The pains of a damned soul (v. 16)

                            O. Harrowed up by the memory of my many sins (v. 17)

                              P. I remembered one Jesus Christ, a Son of God (v. 17)

                              P. I cried within my heart: O Jesus, thou Son of God (v. 18)

                            O. Harrowed up by the memory of my sins no more (v. 19)

                          N. Joy as exceeding as was my pain (v. 20)

                        M. My soul did long to be there (in the presence of God) (v. 22)

                      L. My limbs received strength again (v. 23)

                    K. I labored to bring souls to repentance (v. 24)

                  J. Born of God (v. 26)

              I. My knowledge is of God (v. 26)

            H. Supported under trials, troubles, and afflictions (v. 27)

          G. Trust in him (v. 27)

        F. He will deliver me and raise me up (vv. 27–28)

      E. He has delivered them out of bondage and captivity (v. 28)

      D. Retain a remembrance of their captivity (v. 29)

    C. Know as I do know (v. 30)

  B. Keep the commandments of God, and ye shall prosper (v. 30)

A. This according to his word (v. 30)

"Notice that the central message of the chiasmus focuses on the time in Alma's life when he experienced great pain and sorrow and turned to Jesus Christ for relief (see Alma 36:17–18)" (*Book of Mormon Student Manual* [2009], 232).

John W. Welch, the scholar who first wrote about chiasmus in the Book of Mormon, observed: "Rarely in Book of Mormon studies has a concept captured the imagination and fascination of scholars and readers more than has the presence of chiasmus in that book. The basic concept of chiasmus is readily grasped, and in certain texts its presence can be easily and obviously demonstrated. Novice readers may spot the clear and simple examples of chiasmus without difficulty, although puzzling over the task of unraveling, digesting, and displaying the more complex and sometimes nebulous examples of chiasmus challenges even the most sophisticated literary analysts. Many people, in studying both the Bible and the Book of Mormon, have found the search for chiasms to be almost irresistible. Some people are intrinsically fascinated by the form and are propelled by the prospects of discovering some new aspect of their text, of uncovering some new insight into its meaning, or of adding some new level of appreciation for the possible organizing structures that lie embedded behind the words of its passages" ("What Does Chiasmus in the Book of Mormon Prove?" 200–202). http://maxwellinstitute.byu.edu/publications/books/?bookid=41&chapid=188

upon the name of Jesus Christ and asked for mercy. Nothing was more important than this in Alma's conversion. . . . He makes it the center of this magnificent composition" (Welch, "Masterpiece," 118).

What does the expression "gall of bitterness" symbolize? (36:18) "Gall, a poisonous plant, denotes an extremely bitter thing. The 'gall of bitterness' speaks of hell, or the 'darkest abyss'" (McConkie and Parry, *Guide to Scriptural Symbols*, 57).

What great blessings come to those who truly repent of sin? (36:19) "Satan will try to make us believe that our sins are not forgiven because we can remember them. Satan is a liar; he tries to blur our vision and lead us away from the path of repentance and forgiveness. God did not promise that we would not remember our sins. Remembering will help us avoid making the same mistakes again. But if we stay true and faithful, the memory of our sins will be softened over time. This will be part of the needed healing and sanctification process" (Uchtdorf, "Point of Safe Return," 101).

What does *exquisite* imply? (36:21) The dictionary states that one meaning of *exquisite* is "being in the highest degree; complete" (Webster, *American Dictionary*).

What changes take place for those who have been born of God? (36:23–24) "When we have undergone this mighty change, which is brought about only through faith in Jesus Christ and through the operation of the Spirit upon us, it is as though we have become a new person. Thus, the change is likened to a new birth. . . . You have forsaken lives of sin, sometimes deep and offensive sin, and through applying the blood of Christ in your lives, have become clean. You have no more disposition to return to your old ways" (Benson, "Mighty Change of Heart," 4).

How do we develop the ability to "taste" in a spiritual sense? (36:24, 26) "'Taste,' in the spiritual sense, involves the capacity to savor joy, sweetness,

18 Now, as my mind caught hold upon this thought, I cried within my heart: O Jesus, thou Son of God, have mercy on me, who am in the gall of bitterness, and am encircled about by the everlasting chains of death.

19 And now, behold, when I thought this, I could remember my pains no more; yea, I was harrowed up by the memory of my sins no more.

20 And oh, what joy, and what marvelous light I did behold; yea, my soul was filled with joy as exceeding as was my pain!

21 Yea, I say unto you, my son, that there could be nothing so exquisite and so bitter as were my pains. Yea, and again I say unto you, my son, that on the other hand, there can be nothing so exquisite and sweet as was my joy.

22 Yea, methought I saw, even as our father Lehi saw, God sitting upon his throne, surrounded with numberless concourses of angels, in the attitude of singing and praising their God; yea, and my soul did long to be there.

23 But behold, my limbs did receive their strength again, and I stood upon my feet, and did manifest unto the people that I had been born of God.

24 Yea, and from that time even until now, I have labored without ceasing, that I might bring souls unto repentance; that I might bring them to taste of the exceeding joy of which I did taste; that they might also be born of God, and be filled with the Holy Ghost.

25 Yea, and now behold, O my son, the Lord doth give me exceedingly great joy in the fruit of my labors;

26 For because of the word which he has imparted unto me, behold, many have been born of God, and have tasted as I have tasted, and have seen eye to eye as I have seen; therefore they do know of these things of which I have spoken, as I do know; and the knowledge which I have is of God.

27 And I have been supported under trials and troubles of every kind, yea, and in all manner of afflictions; yea, God has delivered me from prison, and from bonds, and from death; yea, and I do put my trust in him, and he will still deliver me.

28 And I know that he will raise me up at the last day, to dwell with him in glory; yea, and I will praise him forever, for he has brought our fathers out of Egypt, and he has swallowed up the Egyptians in the Red Sea; and he led them by his power into the promised land; yea, and he has delivered them out of bondage and captivity from time to time.

29 Yea, and he has also brought our fathers out of the land of Jerusalem; and he has also, by his everlasting power, delivered them out of bondage and captivity, from time to time even down to the present day; and I have always retained in remembrance their captivity; yea, and ye also ought to retain in remembrance, as I have done, their captivity.

30 But behold, my son, this is not all; for ye ought to know as I do know, that inasmuch as ye shall keep the commandments of God ye shall prosper in the land; and ye ought to know also, that inasmuch as ye will not keep the commandments of God ye shall be cut off from his presence. Now this is according to his word.

goodness, and light, for they are 'discernible.' Even so, we are not only to possess the capacity to discern and distinguish thusly; we are also to use our agency so that we come to prefer, and even strongly desire, the taste of gospel goodness, sweetness, and joy.... Only those who have significantly developed the tastebuds of the soul will be even partially prepared for the incredible beauties of the world ahead" (Maxwell, *One More Strain of Praise*, 84–85).

What does Alma know? How did he gain that knowledge? (see also verses 3, 26). To what extent do you know what Alma knows? How did you gain your testimony?

CHAPTER 37

The plates of brass and other scriptures are preserved to bring souls to salvation—The Jaredites were destroyed because of their wickedness—Their secret oaths and covenants must be kept from the people—Counsel with the Lord in all your doings—As the Liahona guided the Nephites, so the word of Christ leads men to eternal life. About 74 B.C.

Alma 37:1–12. Alma Teaches Helaman the Importance of the Sacred Records

1 And now, my son Helaman, I command you that ye take the records which have been entrusted with me;

2 And I also command you that ye keep a record of this people, according as I have done, upon the plates of Nephi, and keep all these things sacred which I have kept, even as I have kept them; for it is for a wise purpose that they are kept.

3 And these plates of brass, which contain these engravings, which have the records of the holy scriptures upon them, which have the genealogy of our forefathers, even from the beginning—

How were the brass plates to be "handed down from one generation to another"? (37:3–4) "The brass plates . . . were the scriptures of the Nephites, and we suppose that multiple copies were made by the Nephites in order that all the people might have access to the written word of the Lord. At least a portion of this sacred record shall go to all the world through the dissemination of the Book of Mormon. . . . Eventually, however, this prophecy shall be fulfilled in a day yet future . . . when God raises up, through his appointed channels, a prophet, seer, and revelator, who will also be a translator" (McConkie and Millet, *Doctrinal Commentary*, 3:272–73).

4 Behold, it has been prophesied by our fathers, that they should be kept and handed down from one generation to another, and be kept and preserved by the hand of the Lord until they should go forth unto every nation, kindred, tongue, and people, that they shall know of the mysteries contained thereon.

5 And now behold, if they are kept they must retain their brightness; yea, and they will retain their brightness; yea, and also shall all the plates which do contain that which is holy writ.

6 Now ye may suppose that this is foolishness in me; but behold I say unto you, that by small and simple things are great things brought to pass; and small means in many instances doth confound the wise.

What are the "small means" through which the Lord accomplishes His purposes? (37:6–7) "We observe vast, sweeping world events; however, we must remember that the purposes of the Lord in our personal lives generally are fulfilled through the small and simple things and not the momentous and spectacular. . . . We need to have family and personal prayers;

7 And the Lord God doth work by means to bring about his great and eternal purposes; and by very small means the Lord doth confound the wise and bringeth about the salvation of many souls.

8 And now, it has hitherto been wisdom in God that these things should be preserved; for behold, they have enlarged the memory of this people, yea, and convinced many of the error of their ways, and brought them to the knowledge of their God unto the salvation of their souls.

9 Yea, I say unto you, were it not for these things that these records do contain, which are on these plates, Ammon and his brethren could not have convinced so many thousands of the Lamanites of the incorrect tradition of their fathers; yea, these records and their words brought them unto repentance; that is, they brought them to the knowledge of the Lord their God, and to rejoice in Jesus Christ their Redeemer.

10 And who knoweth but what they will be the means of bringing many thousands of them, yea, and also many thousands of our stiffnecked brethren, the Nephites, who are now hardening their hearts in sin and iniquities, to the knowledge of their Redeemer?

11 Now these mysteries are not yet fully made known unto me; therefore I shall forbear.

12 And it may suffice if I only say they are preserved for a wise purpose, which purpose is known unto God; for he doth counsel in wisdom over all his works, and his paths are straight, and his course is one eternal round.

13 O remember, remember, my son Helaman, how strict are the commandments of God. And he said: If ye will keep my commandments ye shall prosper in the land—but if ye keep not his commandments ye shall be cut off from his presence.

study the scriptures, particularly the Book of Mormon; hold family home evenings; follow the admonition of the Savior to love one another; and be thoughtful, kind, and gentle within the family. Through these and other similar small and simple things, we have the promise that our lives will be filled with peace and joy" (Ballard, "Small and Simple Things," 6–8). ✪

How do the scriptures enlarge our memory? (37:8) "The scriptures enlarge our memory by helping us always to remember the Lord and our relationship to Him and the Father. . . . The scriptures also enlarge our memory by helping us not forget what we and earlier generations have learned. . . . Those who either don't have or ignore the recorded word of God eventually cease to believe in Him and forget the purpose of their existence. You will remember how important it was for Lehi's people to take the brass plates with them when they left Jerusalem. These scriptures were key to their knowledge of God and the coming Redemption of Christ" (Christofferson, "Blessing of Scripture," 33). ✪

Alma 37:13–20. Helaman Learns What Will Happen to Him if He Breaks the Commandments of God

What does "strict" imply? (37:13) "The word *strict* here does not seem to imply difficulty so much as straightness or narrowness. To walk in the strict ways of the Lord is to stay on course, to navigate the straight and narrow path with care and caution" (McConkie and Millet, *Doctrinal Commentary*, 3:275).

How do we avoid Satan's attempt to "sift [us] as chaff"? (37:15–16) "Praying always opens the door for divine help to 'conquer Satan.' Each time Jesus alerts priesthood holders to 'beware, for Satan desireth to sift [you],' He prescribes prayer as the temptation-countering action (see D&C 52:12–15; see also Luke 22:31–32; Alma 37:15–17; 3 Nephi 18:18–19)" (Perkins, "Beware concerning Yourselves," 54–55).

Where, and in what form, will the power of "these things" lead? (37:18–19) "[The Book of Mormon] will proclaim the everlasting gospel; it will gather Israel; it will build the New Jerusalem; it will prepare a people for the Second Coming; it will usher in the Millennium—at least it will play such an important part in all of these that its value and power can scarcely be overstated" (McConkie, *Millennial Messiah*, 171).

14 And now remember, my son, that God has entrusted you with these things, which are sacred, which he has kept sacred, and also which he will keep and preserve for a wise purpose in him, that he may show forth his power unto future generations.

15 And now behold, I tell you by the spirit of prophecy, that if ye transgress the commandments of God, behold, these things which are sacred shall be taken away from you by the power of God, and ye shall be delivered up unto Satan, that he may sift you as chaff before the wind.

16 But if ye keep the commandments of God, and do with these things which are sacred according to that which the Lord doth command you, (for you must appeal unto the Lord for all things whatsoever ye must do with them) behold, no power of earth or hell can take them from you, for God is powerful to the fulfilling of all his words.

17 For he will fulfil all his promises which he shall make unto you, for he has fulfilled his promises which he has made unto our fathers.

18 For he promised unto them that he would preserve these things for a wise purpose in him, that he might show forth his power unto future generations.

19 And now behold, one purpose hath he fulfilled, even to the restoration of many thousands of the Lamanites to the knowledge of the truth; and he hath shown forth his power in them, and he will also still show forth his power in them unto future generations; therefore they shall be preserved.

20 Therefore I command you, my son Helaman, that ye be diligent in fulfilling all my words, and that ye be diligent in keeping the commandments of God as they are written.

21 And now, I will speak unto you concerning those twenty-four plates, that ye keep them, that the mysteries and the works of darkness, and their secret works, or the secret works of those people who have been destroyed, may be made manifest unto this people; yea, all their murders, and robbings, and their plunderings, and all their wickedness and abominations, may be made manifest unto this people; yea, and that ye preserve these interpreters.

22 For behold, the Lord saw that his people began to work in darkness, yea, work secret murders and abominations; therefore the Lord said, if they did not repent they should be destroyed from off the face of the earth.

23 And the Lord said: I will prepare unto my servant Gazelem, a stone, which shall shine forth in darkness unto light, that I may discover unto my people who serve me, that I may discover unto them the works of their brethren, yea, their secret works, their works of darkness, and their wickedness and abominations.

24 And now, my son, these interpreters were prepared that the word of God might be fulfilled, which he spake, saying:

25 I will bring forth out of darkness unto light all their secret works and their abominations; and except they repent I will destroy them from off the face of the earth; and I will bring to light all their secrets and abominations, unto every nation that shall hereafter possess the land.

26 And now, my son, we see that they did not repent; therefore they have been destroyed, and thus far the word of God has

Alma 37:21–31. Alma Tells Helaman about the Jaredite People Who Made the Twenty-Four Gold Plates

Who and what is Gazelem? (37:23) "The servant Gazelem . . . is unidentified, but Gazelam was one of the names used in early printings of the Doctrine and Covenants as a code name for Joseph Smith. Of it, Elder [Bruce R.] McConkie wrote, 'with reference to the name Gazelam, it is interesting to note that Alma in directing Helaman to preserve both the Urim and Thummim and the plates containing the Book of Ether, says that such record will be brought to light by the Lord's servant Gazelem, who will use "a stone" in his translation work. . . . It may be that Gazelem is a variant spelling of Gazelam and that Alma's reference is to the Prophet Joseph Smith who did . . . bring forth part . . . of the Ether record' (*Mormon Doctrine*, 307–8)" (Esplin, "Millions Shall Know Brother Joseph Again," 176). ❂

What is significant about "these interpreters"? (37:24) "'Joseph Smith received the same Urim and Thummim had by the Brother of Jared,' wrote Elder Bruce R. McConkie, 'for it was the one expressly provided for the translation of the Jaredite and Nephite records (D&C 10:1; D&C 17:1; Ether 3:22–28)' (*Mormon Doctrine*, 818)." Hence, in September 1823 the angel Moroni, in terms consistent with the descriptions above, informed the Prophet that 'there were two stones in silver bows—and these stones, fastened to a breastplate, constituted what is called the Urim and Thummim—deposited with the plates; and the possession and use of these stones were what constituted seers in ancient or former times; and that God had prepared them for the purpose of translating the book' (Joseph Smith–History 1:35)" (Nyman, *Most Correct Book*, 16–17).

What was Alma's concern regarding the secret plans and oaths practiced by those in secret combinations? (37:28–31) "Alma feared that his people upon learning such oaths and signs as were administered to each other among the Jaredites, would like them fall into all kinds of iniquity and therein encourage wickedness among them. He knew that a curse had been placed by the Lord upon all the Land of America 'that destruction shall come upon all those workers of darkness, according to the power of God, when they are fully ripe; therefore I desire that this people might not be destroyed' (Alma 37:28)" (Reynolds and Sjodahl, *Commentary on the Book of Mormon*, 4:162–63). ⊕

been fulfilled; yea, their secret abominations have been brought out of darkness and made known unto us.

27 And now, my son, I command you that ye retain all their oaths, and their covenants, and their agreements in their secret abominations; yea, and all their signs and their wonders ye shall keep from this people, that they know them not, lest peradventure they should fall into darkness also and be destroyed.

28 For behold, there is a curse upon all this land, that destruction shall come upon all those workers of darkness, according to the power of God, when they are fully ripe; therefore I desire that this people might not be destroyed.

29 Therefore ye shall keep these secret plans of their oaths and their covenants from this people, and only their wickedness and their murders and their abominations shall ye make known unto them; and ye shall teach them to abhor such wickedness and abominations and murders; and ye shall also teach them that these people were destroyed on account of their wickedness and abominations and their murders.

30 For behold, they murdered all the prophets of the Lord who came among them to declare unto them concerning their iniquities; and the blood of those whom they murdered did cry unto the Lord their God for vengeance upon those who were their murderers; and thus the judgments of God did come upon these workers of darkness and secret combinations.

31 Yea, and cursed be the land forever and ever unto those workers of darkness and secret combinations, even unto destruction, except they repent before they are fully ripe.

32 And now, my son, remember the words which I have spoken unto you; trust not those secret plans unto this people, but teach them an everlasting hatred against sin and iniquity.

33 Preach unto them repentance, and faith on the Lord Jesus Christ; teach them to humble themselves and to be meek and lowly in heart; teach them to withstand every temptation of the devil, with their faith on the Lord Jesus Christ.

34 Teach them to never be weary of good works, but to be meek and lowly in heart; for such shall find rest to their souls.

35 O, remember, my son, and learn wisdom in thy youth; yea, learn in thy youth to keep the commandments of God.

36 Yea, and cry unto God for all thy support; yea, let all thy doings be unto the Lord, and whithersoever thou goest let it be in the Lord; yea, let all thy thoughts be directed unto the Lord; yea, let the affections of thy heart be placed upon the Lord forever.

37 Counsel with the Lord in all thy doings, and he will direct thee for good; yea, when thou liest down at night lie down unto the Lord, that he may watch over you in your sleep; and when thou risest in the morning let thy heart be full of thanks unto God; and if ye do these things, ye shall be lifted up at the last day.

38 And now, my son, I have somewhat to say concerning the thing which our fathers call a ball, or director—or our fathers called it Liahona, which is, being interpreted, a compass; and the Lord prepared it.

39 And behold, there cannot any man work after the manner of so curious a workmanship.

Alma 37:32–37. Alma Tells Helaman What He Should Teach the People

What does it mean to learn wisdom? (37:35) "The word *wisdom* in the Book of Mormon is used to denote the wise or effective use of knowledge; it not only concerns the acquisition of knowledge, but also the right use of knowledge. . . . Wise indeed is the person who will learn the commandments of God and then obey them so he can receive the promised blessings" (Ludlow, *Companion to Your Study of the Book of Mormon*, 219).

How can each of us further apply Alma's counsel on praying? (37:36–37) "Seek to know God in your closets, call upon him in the fields. Follow the directions of the Book of Mormon, and pray over, and for your families, your cattle, your flocks, your herds, your corn, and all things that you possess; ask the blessing of God upon all your labors, and everything that you engage in" (*Joseph Smith* [manual], 130).

"Be virtuous and pure; be men of integrity and truth; keep the commandments of God; and then you will be able more perfectly to understand the difference between right and wrong—between the things of God and the things of men" (*Joseph Smith* [manual], 162).

Alma 37:38–47. The Liahona Led Lehi's Family to the Promised Land

How was the Liahona a "shadow" and a "type"? (37:38–47) "The Liahona was a tangible instrument that was prepared by the Lord to assist Lehi's family in their travels. . . . By interpretation, the Liahona means 'compass' (Alma 37:38). . . . Working according to the collective faith, heed, and diligence that Lehi's family gave to the Lord, the Liahona included various communications from God. . . .

" . . . Alma taught his son Helaman that the tangible Liahona was a shadow, type, or symbol, of spiritual guidance. . . . Alma likened the compass to the 'word of Christ, which will point to you a straight course to eternal bliss'" (Millet, et al., *LDS Beliefs*, 390–91).

What is one way the working of the Liahona may be applied today? (37:40) "The same Lord who provided a Liahona for Lehi provides for you and for me today a rare and valuable gift to give direction to our lives, to mark the hazards to our safety, and to chart the way. . . . The gift to which I refer is known as your patriarchal blessing" (Monson, "Your Patriarchal Blessing," 65).

In what ways do you see your patriarchal blessing as a valuable gift that gives direction to your life? How does it work according to your faith?

Why should we remember that the Liahona worked by "small means"? (37:41) "Great and marvelous events seem to motivate us, but small things often do not hold our attention. . . . Is our journey sometimes impeded when we forget the importance of small things? Do we realize that small events and choices determine the direction of our lives just as small helms determine the direction of great ships?" (Ballard, "Small and Simple Things," 8).

What does it mean to look to God and live? (37:43–47) "The call of the Book of Mormon is always 'Look that ye might live.' Whether that is to look up to a staff held aloft by a prophet of God or down upon a personal, sphere-like Liahona, it is the same. They mark the way of eternal life. Indeed, they are similitudes of the Way of Eternal Life. All things are the typifying of Christ" (Holland, *Christ and the New Covenant*, 177). ☉

And behold, it was prepared to show unto our fathers the course which they should travel in the wilderness.

40 And it did work for them according to their faith in God; therefore, if they had faith to believe that God could cause that those spindles should point the way they should go, behold, it was done; therefore they had this miracle, and also many other miracles wrought by the power of God, day by day.

41 Nevertheless, because those miracles were worked by small means it did show unto them marvelous works. They were slothful, and forgot to exercise their faith and diligence and then those marvelous works ceased, and they did not progress in their journey;

42 Therefore, they tarried in the wilderness, or did not travel a direct course, and were afflicted with hunger and thirst, because of their transgressions.

43 And now, my son, I would that ye should understand that these things are not without a shadow; for as our fathers were slothful to give heed to this compass (now these things were temporal) they did not prosper; even so it is with things which are spiritual.

44 For behold, it is as easy to give heed to the word of Christ, which will point to you a straight course to eternal bliss, as it was for our fathers to give heed to this compass, which would point unto them a straight course to the promised land.

45 And now I say, is there not a type in this thing? For just as surely as this director did bring our fathers, by following its course, to the promised land, shall the words of Christ, if we follow their course, carry us beyond this vale of sorrow into a far better land of promise.

46 O my son, do not let us be slothful because of the easiness of the way; for so was it with our fathers; for so was it prepared for them, that if they would look they might live; even so it is with us. The way is prepared, and if we will look we may live forever.

47 And now, my son, see that ye take care of these sacred things, yea, see that ye look to God and live. Go unto this people and declare the word, and be sober. My son, farewell.

The commandments of Alma to his son Shiblon.

Comprising chapter 38.

CHAPTER 38

Shiblon was persecuted for righteousness' sake—Salvation is in Christ, who is the life and the light of the world—Bridle all your passions. About 74 B.C.

1 My son, give ear to my words, for I say unto you, even as I said unto Helaman, that inasmuch as ye shall keep the commandments of God ye shall prosper in the land; and inasmuch as ye will not keep the commandments of God ye shall be cut off from his presence.

2 And now, my son, I trust that I shall have great joy in you, because of your steadiness and your faithfulness unto God; for as you have commenced in your youth to look to the Lord your God, even so I hope that you will continue in keeping his commandments; for blessed is he that endureth to the end.

3 I say unto you, my son, that I have had great joy in thee already, because of thy faithfulness and thy diligence, and thy patience and thy long-suffering among the people of the Zoramites.

4 For I know that thou wast in bonds; yea, and I also know that thou wast stoned for the word's sake; and thou didst bear all these

Why does Alma admonish his son to "declare the word" to the people and be sober? (37:47) "The gospel message is a voice of gladness, a declaration of good news, a proclamation of peace. It has been delivered to make of us a happy people. But we are also under obligation to take seriously the manner in which the message is presented. Souls are at stake" (McConkie and Millet, *Doctrinal Commentary*, 3:283).

Superscription to Alma 38

The superscription to Alma 38 was part of the ancient record translated by the Prophet Joseph Smith and dictated by him to his scribe (see also, for example, 2 Nephi, Mosiah 9, and Helaman).

The italicized words "Comprising chapter 38" were not part of the ancient record but were added later to printed editions of the Book of Mormon.

Alma 38:1–5. Alma Praises Shiblon for His Faithfulness

What does *give ear* mean? (38:1) "To 'give ear' is to devote the sense of hearing to the search for truth, or in other words, to 'listen' or 'to give attention, lest any word escape'" (Smith and Sjodahl, *Doctrine and Covenants Commentary*, 373).

What do *steadiness* and *faithfulness* denote? (38:2) "Steadiness bespeaks spiritual balance and constancy of course. It aptly describes those who are well rooted in the principles of the gospel and who are dependable in fulfilling assignments. It is a manifestation of spiritual maturity and is independent of office or calling" (McConkie and Millet, *Doctrinal Commentary*, 3:285).

What helped Shiblon get through persecution as a servant of Jesus Christ? (38:4) In like circumstances, the Prophet Joseph Smith declared: "Know assuredly, dear brethren, that it is for the testimony of Jesus that we are in bonds and in prison.... Therefore God hath made broad our shoulders for the burden. We glory in our tribulation, because we know that God is with us, that He is our friend, and that He will save our souls" (*Joseph Smith* [manual], 375).

How can trusting in God deliver us from trials? (38:5) "It isn't as bad as you sometimes think it is. It all works out. Don't worry. I say that to myself every morning. It will all work out. If you do your best, it will all work out. Put your trust in God, and move forward with faith and confidence in the future. The Lord will not forsake us.... If we will put our trust in Him, if we will pray to Him, if we will live worthy of His blessings, He will hear our prayers" (Hinckley, "Latter-day Counsel," 73).

Alma 38:6–9. Alma Remembers His Own Trials

What brings forgiveness of sin? (38:8) "From this scripture you can see that suffering does not bring forgiveness. That comes through faith in Jesus Christ and obedience to His teachings so that His gift of redemption can work its miracle" (Scott, "Peace of Conscience and Peace of Mind," 17).

Why is there only one way to salvation? (38:9) "Regardless of how mortals view Him ... there is no other saving and atoning name under heaven (Mosiah 3:17; Moses 6:52). 'O remember, remember ... that there is no other way nor means whereby man can be saved, only through the atoning blood of Jesus Christ, who shall come; yea, remember that he cometh to redeem the world' (Helaman 5:9). All other 'gods' but Him will finally fail and fall, including all the 'ism' gods of this world and the many secular Caesars who, as we see currently, continue to come and go in 'an hour of pomp, an hour of show'" (Maxwell, *Men and Women of Christ*, 35).

things with patience because the Lord was with thee; and now thou knowest that the Lord did deliver thee.

5 And now my son, Shiblon, I would that ye should remember, that as much as ye shall put your trust in God even so much ye shall be delivered out of your trials, and your troubles, and your afflictions, and ye shall be lifted up at the last day.

6 Now, my son, I would not that ye should think that I know these things of myself, but it is the Spirit of God which is in me which maketh these things known unto me; for if I had not been born of God I should not have known these things.

7 But behold, the Lord in his great mercy sent his angel to declare unto me that I must stop the work of destruction among his people; yea, and I have seen an angel face to face, and he spake with me, and his voice was as thunder, and it shook the whole earth.

8 And it came to pass that I was three days and three nights in the most bitter pain and anguish of soul; and never, until I did cry out unto the Lord Jesus Christ for mercy, did I receive a remission of my sins. But behold, I did cry unto him and I did find peace to my soul.

9 And now, my son, I have told you this that ye may learn wisdom, that ye may learn of me that there is no other way or means whereby man can be saved, only in and through Christ. Behold, he is the life and the light of the world. Behold, he is the word of truth and righteousness.

10 And now, as ye have begun to teach the word even so I would that ye should continue to teach; and I would that ye would be diligent and temperate in all things.

11 See that ye are not lifted up unto pride; yea, see that ye do not boast in your own wisdom, nor of your much strength.

12 Use boldness, but not overbearance; and also see that ye bridle all your passions, that ye may be filled with love; see that ye refrain from idleness.

13 Do not pray as the Zoramites do, for ye have seen that they pray to be heard of men, and to be praised for their wisdom.

14 Do not say: O God, I thank thee that we are better than our brethren; but rather say: O Lord, forgive my unworthiness, and remember my brethren in mercy—yea, acknowledge your unworthiness before God at all times.

15 And may the Lord bless your soul, and receive you at the last day into his kingdom, to sit down in peace. Now go, my son, and teach the word unto this people. Be sober. My son, farewell.

Alma 38:10–15. Alma Gives Advice to Missionaries

What does this verse reveal about Shiblon's initial teaching as a missionary? (38:10) "Shiblon's decorum in the mission field among the Zoramites was ample proof to his father that Shiblon was prepared to continue the work of the ministry in teaching and admonishing unto righteousness. 'Be diligent and temperate in all things'; by that Alma meant be zealous in your work, but temper your fervor in the things you proclaim with wisdom, 'and be guided by regard for other men's faith'" (Reynolds and Sjodahl, *Commentary on the Book of Mormon*, 4:186).

How can we use boldness appropriately? (38:12) Elder Carlos E. Asay observed: "I believe that Alma was advocating a type of confidence relating to a commission received of God and a confidence relating to a righteous life. If a missionary or member really believes that he or she is an agent of the Lord and engaged in the Lord's business, that person's confidence and boldness will wax strong, providing he or she is doing things according to the will of the Lord (see D&C 64:29; Prov. 28:1)" (*Seven M's of Missionary Service*, 72).

What does it mean to bridle all our passions? (38:12) "Is self-denial wise because there is something wrong with our passions, or because there is something right with our passions? Alma taught his son: 'See that ye bridle all your passions, *that ye may be filled with love*' (Alma 38:12; emphasis added). He did not say we should suppress or eliminate our passions but rather *bridle* them—harness, channel, and focus them. Why? Because disciplining our passions makes possible a *richer, deeper love*.

"Yet in today's world, where people clamor for rights and freedom, the reasons behind self-denial are often lost. Many unmarried members of the Church yearn for fulfillment of righteous feelings and desires, and the world tells them that waiting to explore those desires is unnecessary" (Hafen, "Bridle All Your Passions," 14). ●

Superscription to Alma 39

The superscription to Alma 39 was part of the ancient record translated by the Prophet Joseph Smith and dictated by him to his scribe (see also, for example, 2 Nephi, Mosiah 9, and Helaman).

The italicized words "Comprising chapters 39 through 42" were not part of the ancient record but were added later to printed editions of the Book of Mormon.

Alma 39:1–6. Alma Speaks of Serious Sins

What are the dangers of boasting of our own strength and wisdom? (39:2) "It is not that Corianton went throughout the streets of Antionum (among the Zoramites) bragging about himself and extolling his virtues. Instead, what he appears to have done is to assume that he possessed strength and wisdom of his own, independent of that strength and wisdom which come from God. In the parlance of our day, Corianton said, 'I can handle it!' Unwilling to trust in the power and ways of the Omnipotent One, Corianton was left to his own resources. He thought he knew better. He felt confident he had the willpower to deal with any eventuality. He fell" (McConkie and Millet, *Doctrinal Commentary*, 3:288).

Who was Isabel? (39:3) "Alma does not mention doctrinal errors that Corianton started to believe but rather his 'go[ing] after' the harlot Isabel. . . . She was apparently a Lamanite. To reach her, Corianton had to physically move toward the Lamanites, but he also moved culturally in that direction. He abandoned his mission, not to return to Zarahemla, his home, but to head in the opposite direction both physically and spiritually. Considering the fact that only six women in the Book of Mormon are named (and three of them, Eve, Sarah, and Mary, are biblical women), it is remarkable that Isabel's name is recorded. This fact alone suggests her importance but doesn't give us enough of a hint to know why she was sufficiently important to name" (Gardner, *Second Witness*, 4:563).

The commandments of Alma to his son Corianton.

Comprising chapters 39 through 42.

CHAPTER 39

Sexual sin is an abomination—Corianton's sins kept the Zoramites from receiving the word—Christ's redemption is retroactive in saving the faithful who preceded it. About 74 B.C.

1 And now, my son, I have somewhat more to say unto thee than what I said unto thy brother; for behold, have ye not observed the steadiness of thy brother, his faithfulness, and his diligence in keeping the commandments of God? Behold, has he not set a good example for thee?

2 For thou didst not give so much heed unto my words as did thy brother, among the people of the Zoramites. Now this is what I have against thee; thou didst go on unto boasting in thy strength and thy wisdom.

3 And this is not all, my son. Thou didst do that which was grievous unto me; for thou didst forsake the ministry, and did go over into the land of Siron among the borders of the Lamanites, after the harlot Isabel.

4 Yea, she did steal away the hearts of many; but this was no excuse for thee, my son. Thou shouldst have tended to the ministry wherewith thou wast entrusted.

5 Know ye not, my son, that these things are an abomination in the sight of the Lord; yea, most abominable above all sins save it be the shedding of innocent blood or denying the Holy Ghost?

6 For behold, if ye deny the Holy Ghost when it once has had place in you, and ye know that ye deny it, behold, this is a sin which is unpardonable; yea, and whosoever murdereth against the light and knowledge of God, it is not easy for him to obtain forgiveness; yea, I say unto you, my son, that it is not easy for him to obtain a forgiveness.

7 And now, my son, I would to God that ye had not been guilty of so great a crime. I would not dwell upon your crimes, to harrow up your soul, if it were not for your good.

8 But behold, ye cannot hide your crimes from God; and except ye repent they will stand as a testimony against you at the last day.

9 Now my son, I would that ye should repent and forsake your sins, and go no more after the lusts of your eyes, but cross yourself in all these things; for except ye do this ye can in nowise inherit the kingdom of God.

What are sexual sins and why are they so serious? (39:5) "The Lord's standard regarding sexual purity is clear and unchanging. Do not have any sexual relations before marriage, and be completely faithful to your spouse after marriage. . . . In God's sight, sexual sins are extremely serious. They defile the sacred power God has given us to create life. The prophet Alma taught that sexual sins are more serious than any other sins except murder or denying the Holy Ghost (see Alma 39:5). . . . Before marriage, do not participate in passionate kissing, lie on top of another person, or touch the private, sacred parts of another person's body, with or without clothing. Do not do anything else that arouses sexual feelings" (*For the Strength of Youth* [booklet, 2011], 35–36). ☉

What is the unpardonable sin? (39:6) The Prophet Joseph Smith taught, "All sins shall be forgiven, except the sin against the Holy Ghost; for Jesus will save all except the sons of perdition. What must a man do to commit the unpardonable sin? He must receive the Holy Ghost, have the heavens opened unto him, and know God, and then sin against him. After a man has sinned against the Holy Ghost, there is no repentance for him. He has got to say that the sun does not shine while he sees it; he has got to deny Jesus Christ when the heavens have been opened unto him" (*History of the Church*, 6:314).

Alma 39:7–14. Corianton Is Counseled to Repent

Why do some people try to hide their sins? (39:8) "Do not take comfort in the fact that your transgressions are not known by others. That is like an ostrich with his head buried in the sand. He sees only darkness and feels comfortably hidden. In reality he is ridiculously conspicuous. Likewise our every act is seen by our Father in Heaven and His Beloved Son. They know everything about us. . . . I invite each one of you to thoughtfully review your life. . . . Is there a dark corner that needs to be cleaned out? . . . When it is quiet and you can think clearly, does your conscience tell you to repent?" (Scott, "Finding Forgiveness," 77).

What might "lust of your eyes" mean today? (39:9) "'The lusts of your eyes.' In our day, what does that expression mean?

"Movies, television programs, and video recordings that are both suggestive and lewd.

"Magazines and books that are obscene and pornographic.

"We counsel you . . . not to pollute your minds with such degrading matter, for the mind through which this filth passes is never the same afterwards. Don't see R-rated movies or vulgar videos or participate in any entertainment that is immoral, suggestive, or pornographic" (Benson, "To the 'Youth of the Noble Birthright,'" 45). ⊕

What does "cross yourself" mean? (39:9) "The phrase 'cross yourself,' as used in Alma 39:9, is not familiar to us today. However, in Webster's 1828 dictionary, we find the following helpful definitions that relate to Alma's counsel to his son: 'To erase, to cancel, to counteract, to stop, to preclude' (Noah Webster's first edition of *An American Dictionary of the English Language*, 1828). All of these actions apply well to what one must do to avoid moral transgression, the topic Alma was teaching his son Corianton. Refer also to the footnote for Alma 39:9b, which refers to self-mastery" (*Book of Mormon Student Manual* [2009], 62).

How does our example affect missionary work? (39:11) Think of the associations you have had with others in your lifetime. "As in the time of Alma, the bad conduct of a few members slows the work" (Maxwell, "Net Gathers of Every Kind," 66). On the other hand, the power of good examples often leads people to investigate the Church. "Whenever you step over the line in an immoral act or in doing any other evil thing, the Church is that much weaker. . . . When you stand true and faithful, it is that much stronger. Each one of you counts" (Hinckley, "Stand True and Faithful," 94). What more might we do to help others come unto Christ?

How can a parent admonish and show love as Alma did? (39:12) "After this severe rebuke, Alma the loving father became Alma the teacher. He knew that 'the preaching of the word had a great tendency to lead the people to do that which was just—yea, it had had more powerful effect upon the minds of the people than the sword, or anything else' (Alma 31:5). So Alma taught Corianton. He spoke first of Christ" (Packer, "I Will Remember Your Sins No More," 25).

What does it mean to fully "turn to the Lord"? (39:13) "Serious transgression such as immorality requires the help of one who holds keys of authority, such as a bishop . . . to quietly work out the repentance process. . . . Do not make the mistake to believe that because you have confessed a serious

Oh, remember, and take it upon you, and cross yourself in these things.

10 And I command you to take it upon you to counsel with your elder brothers in your undertakings; for behold, thou art in thy youth, and ye stand in need to be nourished by your brothers. And give heed to their counsel.

11 Suffer not yourself to be led away by any vain or foolish thing; suffer not the devil to lead away your heart again after those wicked harlots. Behold, O my son, how great iniquity ye brought upon the Zoramites; for when they saw your conduct they would not believe in my words.

12 And now the Spirit of the Lord doth say unto me: Command thy children to do good, lest they lead away the hearts of many people to destruction; therefore I command you, my son, in the fear of God, that ye refrain from your iniquities;

13 That ye turn to the Lord with all your mind, might, and strength; that ye lead away the hearts of no more to do wickedly; but rather return unto them, and acknowledge your faults and that wrong which ye have done.

14 Seek not after riches nor the vain things of this world; for behold, you cannot carry them with you.

15 And now, my son, I would say somewhat unto you concerning the coming of Christ. Behold, I say unto you, that it is he that surely shall come to take away the sins of the world; yea, he cometh to declare glad tidings of salvation unto his people.

16 And now, my son, this was the ministry unto which ye were called, to declare these glad tidings unto this people, to prepare their minds; or rather that salvation might come unto them, that they may prepare the minds of their children to hear the word at the time of his coming.

17 And now I will ease your mind somewhat on this subject. Behold, you marvel why these things should be known so long beforehand. Behold, I say unto you, is not a soul at this time as precious unto God as a soul will be at the time of his coming?

18 Is it not as necessary that the plan of redemption should be made known unto this people as well as unto their children?

19 Is it not as easy at this time for the Lord to send his angel to declare these glad tidings unto us as unto our children, or as after the time of his coming?

transgression, you have repented of it. That is an essential step, but it is not all that is required. Nor assume that because someone did not ask you all the important details of a transgression, you need not mention them. You personally must make sure that the bishop or stake president understands those details so that he can help you properly through the process of repentance for full forgiveness" (Scott, "The Power of Righteousness," 69–70). ✚

Alma 39:15–19. The Atonement of Jesus Christ Is for All Those Who Repent

How does Jesus Christ's foreknowledge affect our redemption? (39:15–19) "The great Jehovah contemplated the whole of the events connected with the earth, pertaining to the plan of salvation, before it rolled into existence . . . ; the past, the present, and the future were and are, with Him, one eternal 'now'; He knew of the fall of Adam, . . . of the depth of iniquity that would be connected with the human family . . . ; He comprehended the fall of man, and his redemption; He knew the plan of salvation and pointed it out; He was acquainted with the situation of all nations and with their destiny; . . . He knows the situation of both the living and the dead, and has made ample provision for their redemption" (*Joseph Smith* [manual], 406–7). ✚

CHAPTER 40

Christ brings to pass the resurrection of all men—The righteous dead go to paradise and the wicked to outer darkness to await the day of their resurrection—All things will be restored to their proper and perfect frame in the Resurrection. About 74 B.C.

1 Now my son, here is somewhat more I would say unto thee; for I perceive that thy mind is worried concerning the resurrection of the dead.

2 Behold, I say unto you, that there is no resurrection—or, I would say, in other words, that this mortal does not put on immortality, this corruption does not put on incorruption—until after the coming of Christ.

3 Behold, he bringeth to pass the resurrection of the dead. But behold, my son, the resurrection is not yet. Now, I unfold unto you a mystery; nevertheless, there are many mysteries which are kept, that no one knoweth them save God himself. But I show unto you one thing which I have inquired diligently of God that I might know—that is concerning the resurrection.

4 Behold, there is a time appointed that all shall come forth from the dead. Now when this time cometh no one knows; but God knoweth the time which is appointed.

Alma 40:1–5. All Will Be Resurrected Because of the Atonement of Jesus Christ

Why was Corianton concerned about the resurrection? (40:1) "Alma made it very clear that if our works are good in this life, and the desires of our hearts are good, then in the Resurrection we will be restored to that which is good. But, by the same token, if our works are evil, then our reward will be the restoration of evil in the Resurrection. To Corianton, who apparently was taking casually some of these 'points of doctrine,' Alma expressed strongly that no one should fallaciously assume that the restorative powers of the Resurrection could restore one 'from sin to happiness.' That can never be, for 'wickedness never was happiness'" (Holland, *Christ and the New Covenant*, 242–43).

What insight did Alma teach Corianton about the resurrection? (40:1–2) One of the unique teachings of Alma to his son Corianton was the truth of mulitiple resurrections and individual times for the resurrections for the dead. President Boyd K. Packer noted: "Corianton was 'worried concerning the resurrection of the dead' (Alma 40:1).

"Alma had inquired of God concerning the Resurrection and told Corianton of the First Resurrection and of other resurrections. 'There is a time appointed that all shall come forth from the dead' (Alma 40:4)" (Packer, "I Will Remember Your Sins No More," 25). ◉

Alma Teaches Corianton about the Resurrection (Alma 40–42)

1. Alma 40:1–2 There will be no Resurrection until after the coming of Jesus Christ.
2. Alma 40:3 Jesus Christ brings the Resurrection.
3. Alma 40:4 There is a time appointed for all people to be resurrected.
4. Alma 40:6–9 There is a period of time between death and the Resurrection.
5. Alma 40:11–12 Righteous spirits await the Resurrection in a state of happiness called paradise.
6. Alma 40:13–14 The wicked await the Resurrection in darkness and fear of judgment.
7. Alma 40:16–19 Those who lived before Jesus Christ are resurrected before those who live after Him. The righteous are resurrected before the wicked; see John 5:29; D&C 88:95–102.
8. Alma 40:23; 41:2 When the spirit and body are reunited, every limb, joint, hair, and part of the physical body will be restored to its proper place.
9. Alma 42:23 The Atonement makes the Resurrection possible, and the Resurrection brings everyone back into the presence of God to be judged.

5 Now, whether there shall be one time, or a second time, or a third time, that men shall come forth from the dead, it mattereth not; for God knoweth all these things; and it sufficeth me to know that this is the case—that there is a time appointed that all shall rise from the dead.

6 Now there must needs be a space betwixt the time of death and the time of the resurrection.

7 And now I would inquire what becometh of the souls of men from this time of death to the time appointed for the resurrection?

8 Now whether there is more than one time appointed for men to rise it mattereth not; for all do not die at once, and this mattereth not; all is as one day with God, and time only is measured unto men.

9 Therefore, there is a time appointed unto men that they shall rise from the dead; and there is a space between the time of death and the resurrection. And now, concerning this space of time, what becometh of the souls of men is the thing which I have inquired diligently of the Lord to know; and this is the thing of which I do know.

10 And when the time cometh when all shall rise, then shall they know that God knoweth all the times which are appointed unto man.

11 Now, concerning the state of the soul between death and the resurrection—Behold, it has been made known unto me by an angel, that the spirits of all men, as soon as they are departed from this mortal body, yea, the spirits of all men, whether they be good or evil, are taken home to that God who gave them life.

12 And then shall it come to pass, that the spirits of those who are righteous are received into a state of happiness, which is called

Alma 40:6–14. The Spirit World Has a Place for Both Wicked and Righteous People

Why were the specific times appointed for resurrection not a great concern for Alma? (40:7–8) "After testifying to Corianton of the reality of the Resurrection, such concerns did not matter to Alma, for he said 'all is as one day with God' (Alma 40:8). The Prophet Joseph Smith . . . revealed that for God all things 'are manifest, past, present, and future, and are continually before the Lord' (D&C 130:7). . . . The past, the present, and the future were and are, with Him, one eternal 'now' (*History of the Church*, 4:597)" (*Book of Mormon Student Manual* [2009], 242). ⊕

In what sense are we "taken home" to God? (40:9–11) "If at death we enter the spirit world, not God's actual presence, how are we to understand Alma's words? President Joseph Fielding Smith . . . explained that Alma did not necessarily mean that we are brought back into God's presence: 'These words of Alma (40:11) as I understand them, do not intend to convey the thought that all spirits go back into the presence of God for an assignment to a place of peace or a place of punishment and before him receive their individual sentence. 'Taken home to God' (compare Ecclesiastes 12:7) simply means that their mortal existence has come to an end, and they have returned to the world of spirits'" (*Book of Mormon Student Manual*, [2009], 242). ⊕

What is the state of the righteous and the wicked between death and resurrection? (40:11–14) "When the physical body dies, the spirit continues to live. In the spirit world, the spirits of the righteous 'are received into a state of happiness, which is called paradise, a state of rest, a state of peace, where they shall rest from all their troubles and from all care, and sorrow' (Alma 40:12). A place called spirit prison is reserved for 'those who [have] died in their sins, without a knowledge of the truth, or in transgression, having rejected the prophets' (D&C 138:32). The spirits in prison are [taught the gospel]. . . . If they accept . . . they will be welcomed into paradise" (*True to the Faith*, 46–47).

paradise, a state of rest, a state of peace, where they shall rest from all their troubles and from all care, and sorrow.

13 And then shall it come to pass, that the spirits of the wicked, yea, who are evil—for behold, they have no part nor portion of the Spirit of the Lord; for behold, they chose evil works rather than good; therefore the spirit of the devil did enter into them, and take possession of their house—and these shall be cast out into outer darkness; there shall be weeping, and wailing, and gnashing of teeth, and this because of their own iniquity, being led captive by the will of the devil.

14 Now this is the state of the souls of the wicked, yea, in darkness, and a state of awful, fearful looking for the fiery indignation of the wrath of God upon them; thus they remain in this state, as well as the righteous in paradise, until the time of their resurrection.

15 Now, there are some that have understood that this state of happiness and this state of misery of the soul, before the resurrection, was a first resurrection. Yea, I admit it may be termed a resurrection, the raising of the spirit

Alma 40:15–20. The Righteous Saints Who Die before the Time of Jesus Christ Will Be Resurrected with Him

When is the first resurrection? (40:15–20) The first resurrection, which is also referred to as the Resurrection of the Just, began with the resurrection of Jesus Christ and continues through the Second Coming. "Those coming forth in the morning of this resurrection do so with celestial bodies and shall inherit

Where Is the Spirit World? (40:11–14)

"President Brigham Young taught that when individuals die they 'all pass through the veil from this state and go into the world of spirits; and there they dwell waiting for their final destiny' (*Discourses of Brigham Young*, 376). This world of spirits, as taught by President Young, is very close:

"'It is not beyond the sun, but is *on this earth* that was organized for the people that have lived and that do and will live upon it. . . .

"'Where is the spirit world? It is right here. Do the good and evil spirits go together? Yes, they do. Do they both inhabit one kingdom? Yes, they do. Do they go to the sun? No. Do they go beyond the boundaries of the organized earth? No, they do not' (*Discourses of Brigham Young*, 376; italics added). . . .

"The wicked and the righteous live together in the spirit world much the same as they do in mortality, not that the righteous do the things of wickedness, nor that the wicked enjoy the blessings bestowed on the righteous, but that the righteous may preach the gospel to the wicked. If they accept it, they too may lay claim upon the blessings of the Lord through the Atonement. Elder Bruce R. McConkie wrote:

"'Although there are two spheres within the one spirit world, there is now some intermingling of the righteous and the wicked who inhabit those spheres; and when the wicked spirits repent, they leave their prison-hell and join the righteous in paradise. Hence, we find Joseph Smith saying: "Hades, sheol, paradise, spirits in prison, are all one: it is a world of spirits. The righteous and the wicked all go to the same world of spirits until the resurrection" (*Teachings*, 310)' (*Mormon Doctrine*, 762)" (*Doctrine and Covenants Student Manual*, 2001, 445).

or the soul and their consignation to happiness or misery, according to the words which have been spoken.

16 And behold, again it hath been spoken, that there is a first resurrection, a resurrection of all those who have been, or who are, or who shall be, down to the resurrection of Christ from the dead.

17 Now, we do not suppose that this first resurrection, which is spoken of in this manner, can be the resurrection of the souls and their consignation to happiness or misery. Ye cannot suppose that this is what it meaneth.

18 Behold, I say unto you, Nay; but it meaneth the reuniting of the soul with the body, of those from the days of Adam down to the resurrection of Christ.

19 Now, whether the souls and the bodies of those of whom has been spoken shall all be reunited at once, the wicked as well as the righteous, I do not say; let it suffice, that I say that they all come forth; or in other words, their resurrection cometh to pass before the resurrection of those who die after the resurrection of Christ.

20 Now, my son, I do not say that their resurrection cometh at the resurrection of Christ; but behold, I give it as my opinion, that the souls and the bodies are reunited, of the righteous, at the resurrection of Christ, and his ascension into heaven.

21 But whether it be at his resurrection or after, I do not say; but this much I say, that there is a space between death and the resurrection of the body, and a state of the soul in happiness or in misery until the time which is appointed of God that the dead shall come forth, and be reunited, both soul and body, and be brought to stand before God, and be judged according to their works.

a celestial glory; these are they who are Christ's, the first fruits. Those coming forth in the afternoon of this resurrection do so with terrestrial bodies and consequently shall inherit that kingdom; they are described as being Christ's at this coming. All who have been resurrected so far have received celestial bodies; the coming forth of terrestrial beings does not commence until after the Second Coming (D&C 76:50–80; 88:95–99)" (McConkie, *Doctrinal New Testament Commentary*, 1:196).

Alma 40:21–26. Bodies Are Resurrected to Their Perfect State

How do we come forth in the resurrection? (40:23)
"Resurrection is the reuniting of the spirit with the body in a perfect, immortal state, no longer subject to disease or death (see Alma 11:42–45)" (*True to the Faith*, 139).

"From the day of the resurrection, the body will develop until it reaches the full measure of the stature of its spirit, whether it be male or female" (Smith, *Gospel Doctrine*, 24). President Smith also records that "the body will come forth as it is laid to rest, for there is no growth nor development in the grave. As it is laid down, so will it arise" (Smith, *Gospel Doctrine*, 449). ☉

What is the awful death that comes upon the wicked? (40:26) The "awful death" refers to the second death, which is a permanent death that prevents one from entering into glory: "The scriptures sometimes speak of salvation from the second death. The second death is the final spiritual death—being cut off from righteousness and denied a place in any kingdom of glory (see Alma 12:32; D&C 88:24). This second death will not come until the Final Judgment, and it will come to very few (see D&C 76:31–37). Almost every person who has ever lived on the earth is assured salvation from the second death (see D&C 76:40–45)" (*True to the Faith*, 153).

What does it mean that they drink the dregs of a bitter cup? (40:26) "That is, they face the full effects of the justice of the Almighty God (Mosiah 3:26). A justice which could have been mitigated by their own repentance through the divine grace of the Holy One of Israel" (McConkie and Millet, *Doctrinal Commentary*, 3:303).

Alma 41:1–7. We Are Judged according to Our Works and the Desires of Our Hearts

What does it mean to wrest the scriptures? (41:1) *Wrested* means "pulled with twisting; distorted; perverted" (Webster, *American Dictionary*). "To wrest the scriptures is to twist or interpret them to mean differently than they were intended. Peter, in the New Testament, warns of the 'unlearned and unstable' wresting the Apostle Paul's epistles 'as they do also the other scriptures, unto their destruction' (2 Peter

22 Yea, this bringeth about the restoration of those things of which has been spoken by the mouths of the prophets.

23 The soul shall be restored to the body, and the body to the soul; yea, and every limb and joint shall be restored to its body; yea, even a hair of the head shall not be lost; but all things shall be restored to their proper and perfect frame.

24 And now, my son, this is the restoration of which has been spoken by the mouths of the prophets—

25 And then shall the righteous shine forth in the kingdom of God.

26 But behold, an awful death cometh upon the wicked; for they die as to things pertaining to things of righteousness; for they are unclean, and no unclean thing can inherit the kingdom of God; but they are cast out, and consigned to partake of the fruits of their labors or their works, which have been evil; and they drink the dregs of a bitter cup.

CHAPTER 41

In the Resurrection men come forth to a state of endless happiness or endless misery—Wickedness never was happiness—Carnal men are without God in the world—Every person receives again in the Restoration the characteristics and attributes acquired in mortality. About 74 B.C.

1 And now, my son, I have somewhat to say concerning the restoration of which has been spoken; for behold, some have wrested the scriptures, and have gone far astray because of this thing. And I perceive that thy mind has been worried also concerning this thing. But behold, I will explain it unto thee.

2 I say unto thee, my son, that the plan of restoration is requisite with the justice of God; for it is requisite that all things should be restored to their proper order. Behold, it is requisite and just, according to the power and resurrection of Christ, that the soul of man should be restored to its body, and that every part of the body should be restored to itself.

3 And it is requisite with the justice of God that men should be judged according to their works; and if their works were good in this life, and the desires of their hearts were good, that they should also, at the last day, be restored unto that which is good.

4 And if their works are evil they shall be restored unto them for evil. Therefore, all things shall be restored to their proper order, every thing to its natural frame—mortality raised to immortality, corruption to incorruption—raised to endless happiness to inherit the kingdom of God, or to endless misery to inherit the kingdom of the devil, the one on one hand, the other on the other—

5 The one raised to happiness according to his desires of happiness, or good according to his desires of good; and the other to evil according to his desires of evil; for as he has desired to do evil all the day long even so shall he have his reward of evil when the night cometh.

6 And so it is on the other hand. If he hath repented of his sins, and desired righteousness until the end of his days, even so he shall be rewarded unto righteousness.

7 These are they that are redeemed of the Lord; yea, these are they that are taken out, that are delivered from that endless night of darkness; and thus they stand or fall; for behold, they are their own judges, whether to do good or do evil.

3:16). Wisely, Alma does not give us the false premises that had led many away. To quote these premises may plant seeds of doubt, and such has never been a substitute for truth" (Nyman, *Record of Alma*, 538).

What did Alma teach about the desires of the heart? (41:2–7) "The attributes by which we shall be judged one day are all spiritual. (The spirit, not the body, is the active, responsible component of the soul. Without the spirit, the body is dead [see James 2:26]. It is the spirit, therefore, that chooses good or evil and will be held accountable for both the positive and negative attributes it possesses at the Final Judgment [see Alma 41:3–7].) . . . Your spirit, coupled with and housed in your body, is able to develop and manifest these attributes in ways that are vital to your eternal progression" (Nelson, "Thanks Be to God," 79). ✪

Alma 41:8–11. Wickedness Never Was Happiness

Why can wickedness never bring happiness? (41:10–11) President Ezra Taft Benson warned, "You cannot do wrong and feel right" ("To the Rising Generation," 5).

"Truly the statement of Alma, an inspired prophet and compassionate father, is borne out in their lives: 'wickedness never was happiness.'

"If you are ever tempted to experiment with the alluring offerings of Lucifer, first calmly analyze the inevitable consequences of such choices, and your life will not be shattered. You cannot ever sample those things that are forbidden of God as destructive of happiness and corrosive to spiritual guidance without tragic results" (Scott, "How to Live Well amid Increasing Evil," 102). ⊕

Alma 41:12–15. Our Choices Will Bring Happiness or Misery in the Next Life

8 Now, the decrees of God are unalterable; therefore, the way is prepared that whosoever will may walk therein and be saved.

9 And now behold, my son, do not risk one more offense against your God upon those points of doctrine, which ye have hitherto risked to commit sin.

10 Do not suppose, because it has been spoken concerning restoration, that ye shall be restored from sin to happiness. Behold, I say unto you, wickedness never was happiness.

11 And now, my son, all men that are in a state of nature, or I would say, in a carnal state, are in the gall of bitterness and in the bonds of iniquity; they are without God in the world, and they have gone contrary to the nature of God; therefore, they are in a state contrary to the nature of happiness.

12 And now behold, is the meaning of the word restoration to take a thing of a natural state and place it in an unnatural state, or to place it in a state opposite to its nature?

13 O, my son, this is not the case; but the meaning of the word restoration is to bring back again evil for evil, or carnal for carnal, or devilish for devilish—good for that which

Hebrew Parallel Structures

Donald W. Parry, a Latter-day Saint scholar, identified a Hebrew parallelistic structure in Alma 41:13–15 that focuses on "mercy":

"a Therefore, my son, see that you are *merciful* unto your brethren;
  b deal *justly*,
    c judge *righteously*,
      d and do *good* continually;
        e and if *ye do* all these things
          f then *shall ye receive* your reward;
a yea, ye shall have *mercy* restored unto you again;
  b ye shall have *justice* restored unto you again;
    c ye shall have a *righteous* judgment restored unto you again;
      d and ye shall have *good* rewarded unto you again.
        e For that which *ye do* send out
          f *shall return unto you* again, and be restored; (extended alternate)"
(*The Book of Mormon Text Reformatted according to Parallelistic Patterns*, 291–92).

is good; righteous for that which is righteous; just for that which is just; merciful for that which is merciful.

14 Therefore, my son, see that you are merciful unto your brethren; deal justly, judge righteously, and do good continually; and if ye do all these things then shall ye receive your reward; yea, ye shall have mercy restored unto you again; ye shall have justice restored unto you again; ye shall have a righteous judgment restored unto you again; and ye shall have good rewarded unto you again.

15 For that which ye do send out shall return unto you again, and be restored; therefore, the word restoration more fully condemneth the sinner, and justifieth him not at all.

CHAPTER 42

Mortality is a probationary time to enable man to repent and serve God—The Fall brought temporal and spiritual death upon all mankind—Redemption comes through repentance—God Himself atones for the sins of the world—Mercy is for those who repent—All others are subject to God's justice—Mercy comes because of the Atonement—Only the truly penitent are saved. About 74 B.C.

1 And now, my son, I perceive there is somewhat more which doth worry your mind, which ye cannot understand—which is concerning the justice of God in the punishment of the sinner; for ye do try to suppose that it is injustice that the sinner should be consigned to a state of misery.

2 Now behold, my son, I will explain this thing unto thee. For behold, after the Lord God sent our first parents forth from the garden of Eden, to till the ground, from whence

How does Alma understand the word "restoration"? (41:15) "Bad habits are easily formed, but not so easily broken. Are we yielding to our evil habits, thinking they are only trifles after all, and we will get rid of them in the grave? Do we expect that our bodies will be cleansed in the grave, and we shall come forth with perfect and sanctified bodies in the resurrection? There are some among us who teach such things and excuse themselves for their practices, saying that they will be cleansed in the grave. Alma taught a very different doctrine. He said to Corianton: 'Do not suppose . . . that ye shall be restored from sin to happiness . . . the word restoration more fully condemneth the sinner' (Alma 41:10, 15)" (Smith, in Conference Report, Apr. 1969, 121). ●

Alma 42:1–15. The Fall of Adam Was Vital to Heavenly Father's Plan

Why did Alma teach Corianton the doctrine of the justice of God? (42:1) "Alma 42 contains some of the most magnificent doctrine on the Atonement [of Jesus Christ] in all scripture. Alma helped Corianton understand that it is not an 'injustice that the sinner should be consigned to a state of misery. . . .'

"Alma's teachings are most instructive. . . . Seen in their true light, the glorious blessings of repentance and adherence to the Savior's teachings are monumentally important. It is not unfair to be clear, as Alma was with Corianton, about the consequences of sinful choices and lack of repentance" (Cook, "Valiant in the Testimony of Jesus," 40).

Why was the Fall an essential part of the plan? (42:2–5) "Some people believe Adam and Eve committed a serious sin when they ate of the tree of knowledge of good and evil. However, latter-day scriptures help us understand that their Fall was a necessary step in the plan of life and a great blessing to all of us. Because of the Fall, we are blessed with physical bodies, the right to choose between good and evil, and the opportunity to gain eternal life. None of these privileges would have been ours had Adam and Eve remained in the garden" (*Gospel Principles*, 29).

How did partaking of the forbidden fruit help Adam and Eve to progress? (42:3–5) "Having partaken of the tree of the knowledge of good and evil—that is, having obtained the capacity to distinguish between opposites, and being able now to understand the difference between good and evil—Adam had, on this matter, become as God. Thereafter, through the righteous exercise of agency, Adam could pursue a course that would eventually endow him with a fulness of the Father. 'As to the fall,' Elder Bruce R. McConkie wrote, 'Eve partook without full understanding; Adam partook knowing that unless he did so, he and Eve could not have children and fulfill the commandment they had received to multiply and replenish the earth' (*New Witness*, 86)" (McConkie and Millet, *Doctrinal Commentary*, 3:311).

What would have been the consequences of partaking of the tree of life for Adam and Eve in the garden? (42:5) "In comparing the laws of justice and mercy, had Adam and Eve partaken of the tree of life, they would have become immortal beings at that time. Just as the forbidden fruit changed them into mortal beings . . . , the fruit of the tree of life would have changed them into immortal beings (Alma 42:5). This was the eternal law, or the attribute of justice according to eternal law. On the other hand, the law of mercy protected Adam and Eve from the tree of life so they could have an opportunity to repent and serve God (v. 4). The plan of salvation was for man to fall 'that men might be' (2 Nephi 2:25). Had there been no fall 'they would have had no children' (2 Nephi 2:23), and the earth would not have been populated. The Lord 'created the earth that it should be inhabited; and he hath created his [spirit] children that they should possess it' (1 Nephi 17:36). Therefore, the great plan of salvation would have been frustrated had there been no probationary time (Alma 42:4–5)" (Nyman, *Record of Alma*, 550).

What is the purpose of the probationary state? (42:6–12) "You are now experiencing mortal life. Your spirit is united with your body, giving you opportunities to grow and develop in ways that were

they were taken—yea, he drew out the man, and he placed at the east end of the garden of Eden, cherubim, and a flaming sword which turned every way, to keep the tree of life—

3 Now, we see that the man had become as God, knowing good and evil; and lest he should put forth his hand, and take also of the tree of life, and eat and live forever, the Lord God placed cherubim and the flaming sword, that he should not partake of the fruit—

4 And thus we see, that there was a time granted unto man to repent, yea, a probationary time, a time to repent and serve God.

5 For behold, if Adam had put forth his hand immediately, and partaken of the tree of life, he would have lived forever, according to the word of God, having no space for repentance; yea, and also the word of God would have been void, and the great plan of salvation would have been frustrated.

6 But behold, it was appointed unto man to die—therefore, as they were cut off from the tree of life they should be cut off from the

face of the earth—and man became lost forever, yea, they became fallen man.

7 And now, ye see by this that our first parents were cut off both temporally and spiritually from the presence of the Lord; and thus we see they became subjects to follow after their own will.

8 Now behold, it was not expedient that man should be reclaimed from this temporal death, for that would destroy the great plan of happiness.

9 Therefore, as the soul could never die, and the fall had brought upon all mankind a spiritual death as well as a temporal, that is, they were cut off from the presence of the Lord, it was expedient that mankind should be reclaimed from this spiritual death.

10 Therefore, as they had become carnal, sensual, and devilish, by nature, this probationary state became a state for them to prepare; it became a preparatory state.

11 And now remember, my son, if it were not for the plan of redemption, (laying it aside) as soon as they were dead their souls were miserable, being cut off from the presence of the Lord.

12 And now, there was no means to reclaim men from this fallen state, which man had brought upon himself because of his own disobedience;

13 Therefore, according to justice, the plan of redemption could not be brought about, only on conditions of repentance of men in this probationary state, yea, this preparatory state; for except it were for these conditions, mercy could not take effect except it should destroy the work of justice. Now the work of justice could not be destroyed; if so, God would cease to be God.

14 And thus we see that all mankind were fallen, and they were in the grasp of justice;

not possible in your premortal life. This part of your existence is a time of learning in which you can prove yourself, choose to come unto Christ, and prepare to be worthy of eternal life. It is also a time when you can help others find the truth and gain a testimony of the plan of salvation" (*True to the Faith*, 116). ◉

What became the nature of man after the Fall? (42:10) "After the fall of Adam, man became carnal, sensual, and devilish by nature; he became fallen man (Moses 5:13; 6:49; Mosiah 16:1–4; Alma 42:10; D&C 20:20). All accountable persons on earth inherit this fallen state, this probationary state, this state in which worldly things seem desirable to the carnal nature. Being in this state, 'the natural man is an enemy to God,' until he conforms to the great plan of redemption and is born again to righteousness (Mosiah 3:19). Thus all mankind would remain lost and fallen forever were it not for the atonement of our Lord (Alma 42:4–14)" (McConkie, *Mormon Doctrine*, 267).

What is the justice of God? (42:13–15) "Justice has many meanings. One is balance. A popular symbol of justice is scales in balance. Thus, when the laws of man have been violated, justice usually requires that a punishment be imposed, a penalty that will restore the balance [to the scales]. . . . [The] laws of God are likewise concerned with justice. The idea of justice as what one deserves is the fundamental premise of all scriptures that speak of men's being judged according to their works" (Oaks, "Sins, Crimes, and Atonement," 1).

Alma 42:16–26. Sorrow for Sin Is Part of Repentance

What does justice demand? (42:17) Justice demands "the unfailing consequence of blessings for righteous thoughts and acts, and punishment for unrepented sin. Justice is an eternal law that requires a penalty each time a law of God is broken (Alma 42:13–24). The sinner must pay the penalty if he does not repent (Mosiah 2:38–39; D&C 19:17). If he does repent, the Savior pays the penalty through the Atonement, invoking mercy (Alma 34:16)" ("Justice," *Guide to the Scriptures*, ChurchofJesusChrist.org).

Why is there pain and remorse when we sin? (42:18) "All of us sometime, and some of us much of the time, suffer remorse of conscience from things we did wrong or things left undone. That feeling of guilt is to the spirit what pain is to the physical body. . . . We all make mistakes. Sometimes we harm ourselves and seriously injure others in ways that we alone cannot repair. We break things that we alone cannot fix. It is then in our nature to feel guilt and humiliation and suffering, which we alone cannot cure. That is when the healing power of the Atonement will help" (Packer, "Touch of the Master's Hand," 22–23).

Could God actually cease to be God? (42:22, 25) Alma knew eternal laws could not be violated and he was teaching this doctrine to Corianton. In an effort to teach his son, Alma used rhetorical questions to make his point. Alma highlights the doctrines of mercy and justice by asking Corianton the impossible: "What, do ye suppose that mercy can rob justice?" He adds emphasis to the impossible by stating: "If so, God would

yea, the justice of God, which consigned them forever to be cut off from his presence.

15 And now, the plan of mercy could not be brought about except an atonement should be made; therefore God himself atoneth for the sins of the world, to bring about the plan of mercy, to appease the demands of justice, that God might be a perfect, just God, and a merciful God also.

16 Now, repentance could not come unto men except there were a punishment, which also was eternal as the life of the soul should be, affixed opposite to the plan of happiness, which was as eternal also as the life of the soul.

17 Now, how could a man repent except he should sin? How could he sin if there was no law? How could there be a law save there was a punishment?

18 Now, there was a punishment affixed, and a just law given, which brought remorse of conscience unto man.

19 Now, if there was no law given—if a man murdered he should die—would he be afraid he would die if he should murder?

20 And also, if there was no law given against sin men would not be afraid to sin.

21 And if there was no law given, if men sinned what could justice do, or mercy either, for they would have no claim upon the creature?

22 But there is a law given, and a punishment affixed, and a repentance granted; which repentance, mercy claimeth; otherwise, justice claimeth the creature and executeth the law, and the law inflicteth the punishment; if not so, the works of justice would be destroyed, and God would cease to be God.

23 But God ceaseth not to be God, and mercy claimeth the penitent, and mercy cometh because of the atonement; and the atonement bringeth to pass the resurrection of the dead; and the resurrection of the dead bringeth back men into the presence of God; and thus they are restored into his presence, to be judged according to their works, according to the law and justice.

24 For behold, justice exerciseth all his demands, and also mercy claimeth all which is her own; and thus, none but the truly penitent are saved.

25 What, do ye suppose that mercy can rob justice? I say unto you, Nay; not one whit. If so, God would cease to be God.

26 And thus God bringeth about his great and eternal purposes, which were prepared from the foundation of the world. And thus cometh about the salvation and the redemption of men, and also their destruction and misery.

27 Therefore, O my son, whosoever will come may come and partake of the waters of life freely; and whosoever will not come the same is not compelled to come; but in the last day it shall be restored unto him according to his deeds.

28 If he has desired to do evil, and has not repented in his days, behold, evil shall be done unto him, according to the restoration of God.

29 And now, my son, I desire that ye should let these things trouble you no more, and only let your sins trouble you, with that trouble which shall bring you down unto repentance.

cease to be God." Alma is not wondering or actually suggesting that God would cease to be God. Rather, Alma knew as did Moroni, that "God . . . [is] an unchangeable Being . . . [and] he changeth not" (Mormon 9:19). How does knowing God will never change or cease to be, increase our faith in Him?

How can justice be satisfied? (42:24–26) "By eternal law, mercy cannot be extended save there be one who is both willing and able to assume our debt and pay the price and arrange the terms for our redemption. Unless there is a mediator . . . the full weight of justice untempered, unsympathetic, must . . . fall on us. The full recompense for every transgression, however minor or however deep, will be exacted from us. . . . But know this: Truth, glorious truth, proclaims there is such a Mediator. 'For there is one God, and one mediator between God and men, the man Christ Jesus' (1 Tim. 2:5). Through Him mercy can be fully extended to each of us without offending the eternal law of justice" (Packer, "The Mediator," 54–56).

Alma 42:27–31. The Justice of God Requires That Those Who Do Not Repent Suffer the Consequences of Their Choices

Why did Alma counsel Corianton to let his sins trouble him? (42:29) "There is an appropriate guilt, a proper remorse of conscience, that men and women must enjoy if they are to remain on that strait and narrow path that leads ultimately to eternal life. There is a fine line between the devil's dissonance (which is evil and demoralizing) and divine discontent (which is of God and is a source for gradual and constant improvement). . . . No one wants to feel any more guilt than is appropriate. But no one seeking salvation would want to feel any less than is necessary. . . . 'For godly sorrow worketh repentance to salvation,' while 'the sorrow of the world worketh death' (2 Corinthians 7:10–11; compare Mormon 2:13)" (McConkie and Millet, *Doctrinal Commentary*, 3:319).

What would happen if Corianton continued to excuse himself in his transgressions? (42:30) "To change is difficult.... Repentance is turning away from some things, such as dishonesty, pride, anger, and impure thoughts, and turning toward other things, such as kindness, unselfishness, patience, and spirituality. It is 're-turning' toward God.... We then are allowed to choose: will we repent, or will we pull the shades down over our open window into heaven? Alma warned, 'Do not endeavor to excuse yourself in the least point' (Alma 42:30). When we 'pull the shades down,' we stop believing that spiritual voice inviting us to change. We pray but we listen less. Our prayers lack that faith that leads to repentance (see Alma 34:17–18)" (Andersen, "Repent . . . That I May Heal You," 41). ☉

What will one seek as they accept the justice of God? (42:30) "Real happiness lies not in denying the justice of God or trying to circumvent the consequences of sin but in repentance and forgiveness through the atoning grace of the Son of God (see Alma 42)" (Christofferson, "Blessing of Scripture," 34).

Alma 43:1–8. The Lamanites Attack the Nephites to Put Them in Bondage

Did Corianton also go forth and preach the gospel? (43:1) "Tellingly, Corianton was obviously included with the other two 'sons of Alma' who began preaching. We must conclude, therefore, that Corianton truly repented, followed his father's admonitions, embraced this new call to the ministry. Confirmation of this conclusion is that he joined Helaman and Shiblon in preaching God's word (Alma 49:30)" (Gardner, *Second Witness*, 4:563).

Why is the preaching of the word so vital? (43:2) "The essence of the Book of Alma is captured when

30 O my son, I desire that ye should deny the justice of God no more. Do not endeavor to excuse yourself in the least point because of your sins, by denying the justice of God; but do you let the justice of God, and his mercy, and his long-suffering have full sway in your heart; and let it bring you down to the dust in humility.

31 And now, O my son, ye are called of God to preach the word unto this people. And now, my son, go thy way, declare the word with truth and soberness, that thou mayest bring souls unto repentance, that the great plan of mercy may have claim upon them. And may God grant unto you even according to my words. Amen.

CHAPTER 43

Alma and his sons preach the word—The Zoramites and other Nephite dissenters become Lamanites—The Lamanites come against the Nephites in war—Moroni arms the Nephites with defensive armor—The Lord reveals to Alma the strategy of the Lamanites—The Nephites defend their homes, liberties, families, and religion—The armies of Moroni and Lehi surround the Lamanites. About 74 B.C.

1 And now it came to pass that the sons of Alma did go forth among the people, to declare the word unto them. And Alma, also, himself, could not rest, and he also went forth.

2 Now we shall say no more concerning their preaching, except that they preached the word, and the truth, according to the spirit of prophecy and revelation; and they preached after the holy order of God by which they were called.

3 And now I return to an account of the wars between the Nephites and the Lamanites, in the eighteenth year of the reign of the judges.

4 For behold, it came to pass that the Zoramites became Lamanites; therefore, in the commencement of the eighteenth year the people of the Nephites saw that the Lamanites were

Mormon writes, 'And now, as the preaching of the word had a great tendency to lead the people to do that which is just—yea, it had had more powerful effect upon the minds of the people than the sword, or anything else' (Alma 31:5). The first two-thirds of the book of Alma illustrates the power of the word. The last third of the book portrays the great wars and the effect of the sword upon the Nephites. The two ways are masterfully contrasted. The word is taught and then comes the sword. . . . The word of the gospel must be preached in all the world before the final sword of destruction" (Donaldson, "'After the Manner of Their Language'").

Why did Mormon include a large amount of detail regarding war? (43:3) President Ezra Taft Benson explained, "From the Book of Mormon we learn how disciples of Christ live in times of war" ("Book of Mormon—Keystone of Our Religion," 7). ◉

Lessons Learned from the "War Chapters"

"Given the constraints of space on Mormon's abridgment of the large plates, why would he devote so much time to a discussion of war? . . . Though the list below is by no means exhaustive, we might consider the following important lessons.

"1. *The Christian's attitude toward war.* 'War is basically selfish,' President David O. Mckay stated. 'Its roots feed in the soil of envy, hatred, desire for domination. Its fruit, therefore, is always bitter. . . . War impels you to hate your enemies. The Prince of Peace says, love your enemies. War says, curse them that curse you. The Prince of Peace says, pray for them that curse you. War says, injure and kill them that hate you. The risen Lord says, do good to them that hate you.' . . .

"2. *The importance of righteous military leaders.* The Nephite military leaders were not bloodthirsty. They hated war and hated the thought of shedding the blood of their brethren . . . [and appointed] '(save it were in their times of wickedness) some one that had the spirit of revelation and also prophecy' (3 Nephi 3:19). . . .

"3. *Our attitude toward constituted government.* . . . The Lord has instructed us that Latter-day Saints in the United States are to be subject to the powers [of government]. Though some of Moroni's actions might be offensive to the more pacifistic of this modern age, he acted in harmony with what he felt was his and others' duty to God, even to the point of compelling dissenters to take up arms in support of the government during war (see Alma 51:15–16). . . .

"4. *The power and influence of a righteous home.* Because righteousness was central to the maintenance of the government, proper training in the home, in the family setting, was absolutely necessary. This is illustrated beautifully in the lives of Helaman's two thousand stripling warriors. . . .

"5. *A person's external circumstances need not determine his attitude or his faithfulness.* One of the vital messages of the Book of Mormon is that one can remain untainted from the sins of the world, no matter what the extent of the degradation of the day. . . .

"6. *Why God allows the righteous to be slain.* War is ugly. Its effects are poignant and painful. Its reach is devastating. It rushes into premature death a great many of the sons and daughters of God. . . .

"7. *A prophetic pattern of what is to come.* Though it is not pleasant to entertain such a thought, it may be that the chapters on warfare have been preserved to prepare us for things to come" (McConkie and Millet, *Doctrinal Commentary*, 3:321–27).

Who were the Amalekites? (43:6) The Amalekites were Nephites who separated themselves from the Nephites and were described as more hardened than Lamanites (see Alma 21:3) and during Nephite-Lamanite wars the Amalekites were "appointed captains because of murderous dispositions," (Index to the Triple Combination, s.v. "Amalekites"; see also Alma 43:6). They helped build the city Jerusalem (see Alma 21:2). The Amalekites were after the order of Nehors (see Alma 21:4) and thus rejected Christ and the faithful tradition of the Nephite fathers.

What tactics of Satan can you find illustrated in Zerahemnah's actions? (43:7–8) A quick reading of these verses might give the impression that the "them" Zerahemnah wanted to bring into subjection and usurp power over referred to the Nephites. Actually, he wanted power over the Lamanites so he could use them to conquer the Nephites. What methods or tools did Zerahemnah use to subject the Lamanites to his will? What examples have you seen in our day, perhaps even in your own life, of people doing wicked or foolish things because they allowed themselves to get angry?

Alma 43:9–14. The Nephites Fight for Their Families, Their Freedoms, and the Right to Worship the Lord

What are just reasons to go to war? (43:9) "President David O. McKay taught: 'There are . . . two conditions which may justify a truly Christian man to enter— mind you, I say enter, not begin—a war: (1) An attempt to dominate and to deprive another of his free agency, and (2) Loyalty to his country. Possibly there is a third, viz., Defense of a weak nation that is being unjustly crushed by a strong, ruthless one. . . . Paramount among these reasons, of course, is the defense of man's freedom. An attempt to rob man of his free agency caused dissension even in heaven. . . . To deprive an intelligent human being of his free

coming upon them; therefore they made preparations for war; yea, they gathered together their armies in the land of Jershon.

5 And it came to pass that the Lamanites came with their thousands; and they came into the land of Antionum, which is the land of the Zoramites; and a man by the name of Zerahemnah was their leader.

6 And now, as the Amalekites were of a more wicked and murderous disposition than the Lamanites were, in and of themselves, therefore, Zerahemnah appointed chief captains over the Lamanites, and they were all Amalekites and Zoramites.

7 Now this he did that he might preserve their hatred towards the Nephites, that he might bring them into subjection to the accomplishment of his designs.

8 For behold, his designs were to stir up the Lamanites to anger against the Nephites; this he did that he might usurp great power over them, and also that he might gain power over the Nephites by bringing them into bondage.

9 And now the design of the Nephites was to support their lands, and their houses, and their wives, and their children, that they might preserve them from the hands of their enemies; and also that they might preserve their rights and their privileges, yea, and also their liberty, that they might worship God according to their desires.

10 For they knew that if they should fall into the hands of the Lamanites, that whosoever should worship God in spirit and in truth, the true and the living God, the Lamanites would destroy.

11 Yea, and they also knew the extreme hatred of the Lamanites towards their brethren, who were the people of Anti-Nephi-Lehi, who were called the people of Ammon—and they would not take up arms, yea, they had entered into a covenant and they would not break it—therefore, if they should fall into the hands of the Lamanites they would be destroyed.

12 And the Nephites would not suffer that they should be destroyed; therefore they gave them lands for their inheritance.

13 And the people of Ammon did give unto the Nephites a large portion of their substance to support their armies; and thus the Nephites were compelled, alone, to withstand against the Lamanites, who were a compound of Laman and Lemuel, and the sons of Ishmael, and all those who had dissented from the Nephites, who were Amalekites and Zoramites, and the descendants of the priests of Noah.

14 Now those descendants were as numerous, nearly, as were the Nephites; and thus the Nephites were obliged to contend with their brethren, even unto bloodshed.

15 And it came to pass as the armies of the Lamanites had gathered together in the land of Antionum, behold, the armies of the Nephites were prepared to meet them in the land of Jershon.

16 Now, the leader of the Nephites, or the man who had been appointed to be the chief captain over the Nephites—now the chief captain took the command of all the armies of the Nephites—and his name was Moroni;

17 And Moroni took all the command, and the government of their wars. And he was

agency is to commit the crime of the ages'" (*Doctrine and Covenants Student Manual*, 230–34).

What was the situation of the Nephites when the Lamanites came to war against them? (43:13–14)
"The number of Nephite dissenters who became Lamanites was almost as large as the number of Nephites who remained true (see Alma 43:14). This large number, combined with the Lamanite armies, placed the Nephites at a serious numerical disadvantage (see Alma 43:51; see also Mosiah 25:3; Alma 2:27, 35). Relying on their faith, however, the Nephites trusted that God would strengthen them during their battles against overwhelming odds, just as He had done for Gideon's army (see Judges 7–9), Elisha (see 2 Kings 6:15–23), King Benjamin (see Words of Mormon 1:14), and Alma (see Alma 2:27–35)" (*Book of Mormon Student Manual* [2009], 249).

Alma 43:15–28. Captain Moroni Prepares for the Lamanites' Attack

Who was Moroni? (43:16) Moroni lived during the period 74 B.C. to 57 B.C. and was one of the most faithful and righteous men in Nephite history (see Alma 48:17). "Moroni, only twenty-five years old, was appointed leader over the Nephites (Alma 43:16–17) and immediately proved his ability by equipping his men with armor, an unexpected innovation" and for years outmanuevered his enemies with his superior tactics (England, "Moroni and His Captains," 32). Moroni insisted that his men fight with honor in order to qualify for the Lord's blessing of strength during battle. Mormon's placement of Moroni gives the reader a striking contrast to the differences between wicked Amalickiah and the righteous Captain Moroni. ⊕

How did Captain Moroni's innovations affect the war? (43:18–21) "Preparation is the mark of a good leader. To be prepared requires anticipation of the future, and Captain Moroni was always prepared for war against the Lamanites (Alma 43:18–21). As the account continues, the Lamanites copy the Nephites' innovative methods, but . . . Captain Moroni was a step ahead and always prepared with some new methods of defense that the Lamanites had not anticipated. On the other hand, the Lamanites still used their basic age-old customs of warfare (see Enos 1:20; Mosiah 10:8; Alma 3:5). They relied on the arm of human strength while Captain Moroni relied on the Lord" (Nyman, *Record of Helaman*, 20).

What can we learn from this brief episode of Moroni seeking and receiving revelatory direction from the prophet Alma? (43:22–24) "Alma not only learned gospel principles and doctrines by faith; he also received information on current events. For example, in the year 74 b.c., the Lamanite armies were invading the land of the Nephites. But, says the record, 'they durst not come against the Nephites in the borders of Jershon. . . . And it came to pass that the word of the Lord came unto Alma . . . that the armies of the Lamanites were marching round about in the wilderness. . . . And those messengers went and delivered the message unto Moroni' (Alma 43:22–24). Moroni, acting upon the information, sent his armies into the land of Manti, where they met the Lamanites and defeated them" (Romney, *Learning for the Eternities*, 77).

only twenty and five years old when he was appointed chief captain over the armies of the Nephites.

18 And it came to pass that he met the Lamanites in the borders of Jershon, and his people were armed with swords, and with cimeters, and all manner of weapons of war.

19 And when the armies of the Lamanites saw that the people of Nephi, or that Moroni, had prepared his people with breastplates and with arm-shields, yea, and also shields to defend their heads, and also they were dressed with thick clothing—

20 Now the army of Zerahemnah was not prepared with any such thing; they had only their swords and their cimeters, their bows and their arrows, their stones and their slings; and they were naked, save it were a skin which was girded about their loins; yea, all were naked, save it were the Zoramites and the Amalekites;

21 But they were not armed with breastplates, nor shields—therefore, they were exceedingly afraid of the armies of the Nephites because of their armor, notwithstanding their number being so much greater than the Nephites.

22 Behold, now it came to pass that they durst not come against the Nephites in the borders of Jershon; therefore they departed out of the land of Antionum into the wilderness, and took their journey round about in the wilderness, away by the head of the river Sidon, that they might come into the land of Manti and take possession of the land; for they did not suppose that the armies of Moroni would know whither they had gone.

23 But it came to pass, as soon as they had departed into the wilderness Moroni sent spies into the wilderness to watch their camp;

and Moroni, also, knowing of the prophecies of Alma, sent certain men unto him, desiring him that he should inquire of the Lord whither the armies of the Nephites should go to defend themselves against the Lamanites.

24 And it came to pass that the word of the Lord came unto Alma, and Alma informed the messengers of Moroni, that the armies of the Lamanites were marching round about in the wilderness, that they might come over into the land of Manti, that they might commence an attack upon the weaker part of the people. And those messengers went and delivered the message unto Moroni.

25 Now Moroni, leaving a part of his army in the land of Jershon, lest by any means a part of the Lamanites should come into that land and take possession of the city, took the remaining part of his army and marched over into the land of Manti.

26 And he caused that all the people in that quarter of the land should gather themselves together to battle against the Lamanites, to defend their lands and their country, their rights and their liberties; therefore they were prepared against the time of the coming of the Lamanites.

27 And it came to pass that Moroni caused that his army should be secreted in the valley which was near the bank of the river Sidon, which was on the west of the river Sidon in the wilderness.

28 And Moroni placed spies round about, that he might know when the camp of the Lamanites should come.

29 And now, as Moroni knew the intention of the Lamanites, that it was their intention to destroy their brethren, or to subject them and bring them into bondage that they might establish a kingdom unto themselves over all the land;

Alma 43:29–44. The Lamanites Are Caught between Two Nephite Armies

What were the tactics used by Moroni in defending his people? (43:29–30) "The Nephite military leaders were not bloodthirsty. They hated war and hated the thought of shedding the blood of their brethren. They utilized clever strategy regularly, not only to win the war more rapidly but also to save lives on both sides (see Alma 43:29–30). Later in the story Mormon points out that 'it was the custom among all the

Nephites to appoint for their chief captains, (save it were in their times of wickedness) some one that had the spirit of revelation and also prophecy' (3 Nephi 3:19)" (McConkie and Millet, *Doctrinal Commentary*, 3:322–23).

Why were the Nephites' liberty, land, and religion important enough to risk dying to defend? (43:30) What would you be willing to defend even at the risk of losing your life?

30 And he also knowing that it was the only desire of the Nephites to preserve their lands, and their liberty, and their church, therefore he thought it no sin that he should defend them by stratagem; therefore, he found by his spies which course the Lamanites were to take.

31 Therefore, he divided his army and brought a part over into the valley, and concealed them on the east, and on the south of the hill Riplah;

32 And the remainder he concealed in the west valley, on the west of the river Sidon, and so down into the borders of the land Manti.

33 And thus having placed his army according to his desire, he was prepared to meet them.

34 And it came to pass that the Lamanites came up on the north of the hill, where a part of the army of Moroni was concealed.

35 And as the Lamanites had passed the hill Riplah, and came into the valley, and began to cross the river Sidon, the army which was concealed on the south of the hill, which was led by a man whose name was Lehi, and he led his army forth and encircled the Lamanites about on the east in their rear.

36 And it came to pass that the Lamanites,

Leaders of the Lamanites (Alma 43–Helaman 1)

Reference	Lamanite Leader	Was He a Lamanite?
Alma 43:5–8	Zerahemnah (chief captain)	Probably Zoramite
Alma 46:3–7	Amalickiah (king)	Zoramite, Nephite dissenter
Alma 52:3	Ammoron (king)	Zoramite, Nephite dissenter
Helaman 1:15	Coriantumr (chief captain)	Nephite dissenter
Helaman 1:16	Tubaloth (king)	Zoramite, son of Nephite dissenter

when they saw the Nephites coming upon them in their rear, turned them about and began to contend with the army of Lehi.

37 And the work of death commenced on both sides, but it was more dreadful on the part of the Lamanites, for their nakedness was exposed to the heavy blows of the Nephites with their swords and their cimeters, which brought death almost at every stroke.

38 While on the other hand, there was now and then a man fell among the Nephites, by their swords and the loss of blood, they being shielded from the more vital parts of the body, or the more vital parts of the body being shielded from the strokes of the Lamanites, by their breastplates, and their armshields, and their head-plates; and thus the Nephites did carry on the work of death among the Lamanites.

39 And it came to pass that the Lamanites became frightened, because of the great destruction among them, even until they began to flee towards the river Sidon.

40 And they were pursued by Lehi and his men; and they were driven by Lehi into the waters of Sidon, and they crossed the waters of Sidon. And Lehi retained his armies upon the bank of the river Sidon that they should not cross.

41 And it came to pass that Moroni and his army met the Lamanites in the valley, on the other side of the river Sidon, and began to fall upon them and to slay them.

42 And the Lamanites did flee again before them, towards the land of Manti; and they were met again by the armies of Moroni.

43 Now in this case the Lamanites did fight exceedingly; yea, never had the Lamanites been known to fight with such exceedingly great strength and courage, no, not even from the beginning.

Why would Mormon note the "strength and courage" with which the Lamanites fought? (43:43)
President Russell M. Nelson observed that a "theme in the scriptures requisite for significant accomplishment is difficult to summarize in one word, so I shall link two to describe it—strength and courage. Repeatedly,

scriptures yoke these attributes of character together, especially when difficult challenges are to be conquered (see Deuteronomy 31:6, 7, 23; Joshua 1:6, 7, 9, 18; 10:25; 1 Chronicles 22:13, 28:20; 2 Chronicles 32:7; Psalms 27:14, 31:24; Alma 43:43, 53:20)" ("With God Nothing Shall Be Impossible," 35).

Alma 43:45–54. The Nephites Fight for a Better Cause and Rely upon the Lord for Help

How were the Nephites justified in going to war against the Lamanites? (43:45–48) "I mention another plain and precious insight that did not come with the first reading in the Book of Mormon. When I was 18 years old, I was inducted into the military. While I had no reason to wonder about it before, I became very concerned if it was right for me to go to war. In time, I found my answer in the Book of Mormon: . . . 'Ye shall defend your families even unto bloodshed. Therefore for this cause were the Nephites contending with the Lamanites, to defend themselves, and their families, and their lands, their country, and their rights, and their religion' (Alma 43:45–47). Knowing this, I could serve willingly and with honor" (Packer, "Book of Mormon: Another Testament of Jesus Christ—Plain and Precious Things," 7–8). ⊕

What did Captain Moroni understand about the law of war as revealed by the Lord? (43:46–47) "The source of what the Lord had said (vv. 46–47) was undoubtedly the plates of brass. . . . The ancients had been taught the law of war. . . . There are two parts of the law quoted by Mormon. . . . The lifting of the standard of peace is a condition presented to the aggressor. In Captain Moroni's situation, the lifting of the standard is recorded in the forty-fourth chapter of Alma. . . . The second part of the law of war [is] the defending of your families even unto bloodshed. . . . The significant point of this part of the law is that you do not have to wait for three offenses to defend yourself, your family, or your personal rights (v. 47)" (Nyman, *Record of Helaman*, 25–26).

44 And they were inspired by the Zoramites and the Amalekites, who were their chief captains and leaders, and by Zerahemnah, who was their chief captain, or their chief leader and commander; yea, they did fight like dragons, and many of the Nephites were slain by their hands, yea, for they did smite in two many of their head-plates, and they did pierce many of their breastplates, and they did smite off many of their arms; and thus the Lamanites did smite in their fierce anger.

45 Nevertheless, the Nephites were inspired by a better cause, for they were not fighting for monarchy nor power but they were fighting for their homes and their liberties, their wives and their children, and their all, yea, for their rites of worship and their church.

46 And they were doing that which they felt was the duty which they owed to their God; for the Lord had said unto them, and also unto their fathers, that: Inasmuch as ye are not guilty of the first offense, neither the second, ye shall not suffer yourselves to be slain by the hands of your enemies.

47 And again, the Lord has said that: Ye shall defend your families even unto bloodshed. Therefore for this cause were the Nephites contending with the Lamanites, to defend themselves, and their families, and their lands, their country, and their rights, and their religion.

48 And it came to pass that when the men of Moroni saw the fierceness and the anger of the Lamanites, they were about to shrink and flee from them. And Moroni, perceiving their intent, sent forth and inspired their hearts with these thoughts—yea, the thoughts of their lands, their liberty, yea, their freedom from bondage.

49 And it came to pass that they turned upon the Lamanites, and they cried with one voice unto the Lord their God, for their liberty and their freedom from bondage.

50 And they began to stand against the Lamanites with power; and in that selfsame hour that they cried unto the Lord for their freedom, the Lamanites began to flee before them; and they fled even to the waters of Sidon.

51 Now, the Lamanites were more numerous, yea, by more than double the number of the Nephites; nevertheless, they were driven insomuch that they were gathered together in one body in the valley, upon the bank by the river Sidon.

52 Therefore the armies of Moroni encircled them about, yea, even on both sides of the river, for behold, on the east were the men of Lehi.

53 Therefore when Zerahemnah saw the men of Lehi on the east of the river Sidon, and the armies of Moroni on the west of the river Sidon, that they were encircled about by the Nephites, they were struck with terror.

54 Now Moroni, when he saw their terror, commanded his men that they should stop shedding their blood.

CHAPTER 44

Moroni commands the Lamanites to make a covenant of peace or be destroyed—Zerahemnah rejects the offer, and the battle resumes—Moroni's armies defeat the Lamanites. About 74–73 B.C.

1 And it came to pass that they did stop and withdrew a pace from them. And Moroni said unto Zerahemnah: Behold, Zerahemnah, that we do not desire to be men of blood. Ye know that ye are in our hands, yet we do not desire to slay you.

2 Behold, we have not come out to battle against you that we might shed your blood

Alma 44:1–7. Moroni Offers Peace

What does "maintenance of the sacred word of God" mean? (44:1–5) "It is noteworthy that sometimes the term 'word' was used synonymously with 'covenant' (e.g., Num 30:2; Deut 33:9; 1 Chron 16:15; Ps 105:8). This may be a result of the binding nature of the revealed word of God (compare Ex 13:16; Deut 11:18). In our own dispensation, the Lord has revealed: 'For of him unto whom much is given much is required; and he who sins against the greater light shall receive the greater condemnation' (D&C 82:3). Phrases such as 'keeping the commandments' (Alma 48:15), and 'maintenance of the sacred word of God' (Alma 44:5), are the scriptural equivalent of living the covenants of the Lord (Alma 46:21)" (Valletta, "Captain and the Covenant," 227).

What did Captain Moroni understand about obtaining the Lord's sanction during times of war? (44:1–7) "Captain Moroni was not guilty of the first offense according to the law of war (Alma 43:46; D&C 98:34). His speech to his captive audience included several important declarations relative to the law of war. First, the Nephites did not desire to shed blood, the Lamanites had initiated the war (D&C 98:34). Second, they did not want to bring the Lamanites into bondage, which was the Lamanite design of the war (Alma 44:2). The third point was about God and his people, certainly the most important declaration of all (vv. 2–4)" (Nyman, *Record of Helaman*, 28–29). ⊕

Why did Moroni want to disarm the enemy? (44:6) Citing the Prussian military authority Karl von Clausewitz, Hugh Nibley wrote: "'The disarming of the enemy—this object of war in the abstract, [is the] final means of attaining the political object.' In the Book of Mormon, Moroni often requires the enemy to lay down their arms and lets them go home. There are no reprisals or anything similar (see Alma 44:6, 15, 20; 52:37). The test comes when they lay down their arms—then they know your will has dominated over theirs. So Clausewitz says, the 'disarming of the enemy—this [is the] object of war' [*War, Politics, and Power*, 91]. Moroni was satisfied when the enemy laid down their arms" (Nibley, "Warfare and the Book of Mormon," 129).

for power; neither do we desire to bring any one to the yoke of bondage. But this is the very cause for which ye have come against us; yea, and ye are angry with us because of our religion.

3 But now, ye behold that the Lord is with us; and ye behold that he has delivered you into our hands. And now I would that ye should understand that this is done unto us because of our religion and our faith in Christ. And now ye see that ye cannot destroy this our faith.

4 Now ye see that this is the true faith of God; yea, ye see that God will support, and keep, and preserve us, so long as we are faithful unto him, and unto our faith, and our religion; and never will the Lord suffer that we shall be destroyed except we should fall into transgression and deny our faith.

5 And now, Zerahemnah, I command you, in the name of that all-powerful God, who has strengthened our arms that we have gained power over you, by our faith, by our religion, and by our rites of worship, and by our church, and by the sacred support which we owe to our wives and our children, by that liberty which binds us to our lands and our country; yea, and also by the maintenance of the sacred word of God, to which we owe all our happiness; and by all that is most dear unto us—

6 Yea, and this is not all; I command you by all the desires which ye have for life, that ye deliver up your weapons of war unto us, and we will seek not your blood, but we will spare your lives, if ye will go your way and come not again to war against us.

7 And now, if ye do not this, behold, ye are in our hands, and I will command my men that they shall fall upon you, and inflict the wounds of death in your bodies, that ye may become extinct; and then we will see who

shall have power over this people; yea, we will see who shall be brought into bondage.

8 And now it came to pass that when Zerahemnah had heard these sayings he came forth and delivered up his sword and his cimeter, and his bow into the hands of Moroni, and said unto him: Behold, here are our weapons of war; we will deliver them up unto you, but we will not suffer ourselves to take an oath unto you, which we know that we shall break, and also our children; but take our weapons of war, and suffer that we may depart into the wilderness; otherwise we will retain our swords, and we will perish or conquer.

9 Behold, we are not of your faith; we do not believe that it is God that has delivered us into your hands; but we believe that it is your cunning that has preserved you from our swords. Behold, it is your breastplates and your shields that have preserved you.

10 And now when Zerahemnah had made an end of speaking these words, Moroni returned the sword and the weapons of war, which he had received, unto Zerahemnah, saying: Behold, we will end the conflict.

11 Now I cannot recall the words which I have spoken, therefore as the Lord liveth, ye shall not depart except ye depart with an oath that ye will not return again against us to war. Now as ye are in our hands we will spill your blood upon the ground, or ye shall submit to the conditions which I have proposed.

12 And now when Moroni had said these words, Zerahemnah retained his sword, and he was angry with Moroni, and he rushed forward that he might slay Moroni; but as he raised his sword, behold, one of Moroni's soldiers smote it even to the earth, and it broke by the hilt; and he also smote Zerahemnah that he took off his scalp and it fell to the earth. And Zerahemnah withdrew from before them into the midst of his soldiers.

Alma 44:8–16. Zerahemnah Refuses Peace

Why did Zerahemnah refuse to swear an oath to Moroni? (44:8–9) "It is important to note that Moroni invoked the name of God in the brief covenant-making ceremony he enacted with Zerahemnah (Alma 44:4). Invoking the name of a deity to witness and ratify a covenant or oath was standard procedure in ancient Near Eastern oath-making ceremonies. The understanding anciently was that if a party failed to keep the covenant, then that party would face divine retribution. This might explain why Zerahemnah initially refused to make an oath he knew he couldn't (or wouldn't) keep. He may have feared God at least enough to anticipate divine wrath should he fail to keep the covenant, even if he disbelieved it was God who granted the Nephites victory (Alma 44:9)" (Book of Mormon Central, "Why Would Zerahemnah Not Swear an Oath to Moroni?").

13 And it came to pass that the soldier who stood by, who smote off the scalp of Zerahemnah, took up the scalp from off the ground by the hair, and laid it upon the point of his sword, and stretched it forth unto them, saying unto them with a loud voice:

14 Even as this scalp has fallen to the earth, which is the scalp of your chief, so shall ye fall to the earth except ye will deliver up your weapons of war and depart with a covenant of peace.

15 Now there were many, when they heard these words and saw the scalp which was upon the sword, that were struck with fear; and many came forth and threw down their weapons of war at the feet of Moroni, and entered into a covenant of peace. And as many as entered into a covenant they suffered to depart into the wilderness.

16 Now it came to pass that Zerahemnah was exceedingly wroth, and he did stir up the remainder of his soldiers to anger, to contend more powerfully against the Nephites.

Alma 44:17–24. Moroni's Army Defeats Zerahemnah's Army

17 And now Moroni was angry, because of the stubbornness of the Lamanites; therefore he commanded his people that they should fall upon them and slay them. And it came to pass that they began to slay them; yea, and the Lamanites did contend with their swords and their might.

18 But behold, their naked skins and their bare heads were exposed to the sharp swords of the Nephites; yea, behold they were pierced and smitten, yea, and did fall exceedingly fast before the swords of the Nephites; and they began to be swept down, even as the soldier of Moroni had prophesied.

19 Now Zerahemnah, when he saw that they were all about to be destroyed, cried mightily unto Moroni, promising that he would covenant and also his people with them, if they would spare the remainder of their lives, that they never would come to war again against them.

20 And it came to pass that Moroni caused that the work of death should cease again among the people. And he took the weapons of war from the Lamanites; and after they had entered into a covenant with him of peace they were suffered to depart into the wilderness.

21 Now the number of their dead was not numbered because of the greatness of the number; yea, the number of their dead was exceedingly great, both on the Nephites and on the Lamanites.

22 And it came to pass that they did cast their dead into the waters of Sidon, and they have gone forth and are buried in the depths of the sea.

23 And the armies of the Nephites, or of Moroni, returned and came to their houses and their lands.

24 And thus ended the eighteenth year of the reign of the judges over the people of Nephi. And thus ended the record of Alma, which was written upon the plates of Nephi.

Why did Captain Moroni stop the fighting? (44:20) "Captain Moroni 'did not delight in bloodshed' (Alma 48:11) even though he was justified in taking another person's life while defending his country. He reluctantly fought the Lamanites for many years (see Alma 48:22). When he did fight, he maintained charity for all, including those on the opposing side. The record states that Captain Moroni stopped the battle on more than one occasion in order to spare as many lives as possible (see Alma 43:54–44:1–2; 55:19). Lives were taken reluctantly and with sorrow that 'their brethren [were sent] out of this world … unprepared to meet their God' (Alma 48:23)" (*Book of Mormon Student Manual* [2009], 251).

How is the book of Alma organized? (44:24) "The book of Alma begins with a preface and ends with a summary statement in the last verse. In between there are a number of subdivisions set off by editorial statements. Mormon divided his abridgment of the book of Alma into (1) the record of Alma, which ends at 44:24 with 'And thus ended the record of Alma'; (2) the record of Helaman, which is introduced by a preface between chapters 44 and 45 and which ends with an editorial statement in the last verse of chapter 62; and (3) the record of Shiblon, which is marked by statements at its beginning in 63:1 and its end at 63:11" (Tvedtnes, "Colophons," 34).

Superscription to Alma 45

In Mormon's superscription preceding the war chapters in Alma, just prior to Alma 45, Mormon tells us that we are about to read several chapters that deal with wars and dissensions. President Ezra Taft Benson gave insight on these chapters: "From the Book of Mormon we learn how disciples of Christ live in times of war" (*Teachings of Ezra Taft Benson*, 59).

The superscription to Alma 45 was part of the ancient record translated by the Prophet Joseph Smith and dictated by him to his scribe (see also, for example, 2 Nephi, Mosiah 9, and Helaman).

The italicized words "Comprising chapters 45 through 62" were not part of the ancient record but were added later to printed editions of the Book of Mormon.

Alma 45:1–8. Helaman Believes in Jesus Christ and Is Willing to Keep His Commandments

Why did the Nephites fast and pray in giving thanks to the Lord? (45:1) President Gordon B. Hinckley illustrated that gratitude can be expressed with fasting. He read a letter written by a woman who said, "Most of my fasts are 'thankful' fasts" ("Save the Children," 54).

President Russell M. Nelson spoke similarly of prayer: "I did not fully appreciate the significance of prayerful greetings until I became a father.... Now I sense how our Heavenly Father may appreciate our prayers, morning and night. But I can imagine the pangs of his sorrow because of silence from any of his children. To me, such ingratitude seems comparable to sullen goldfish oblivious to kind providers who sprinkle food in their bowl" ("Joy Cometh in the Morning," 69).

What can a parent learn from Alma's interview with his son? (45:2–3) "Alma's interview with Helaman is a classic.... It is a short, three-question, forty-five-second exchange between father and son....

"This short, informative, and inspiring interview must have pleased Alma greatly. Not only had he communicated heart-to-heart and soul-to-soul with his son, but the son had openly declared his faith and pledged his devotion....

"I wonder if our interviews with our children are as inspirational and building as the one between Alma and Helaman" (Asay, "Parent-Child Interviews," 14).

The account of the people of Nephi, and their wars and dissensions, in the days of Helaman, according to the record of Helaman, which he kept in his days.

Comprising chapters 45 through 62.

CHAPTER 45

Helaman believes the words of Alma—Alma prophesies the destruction of the Nephites—He blesses and curses the land—Alma may have been taken up by the Spirit, even as Moses—Dissension grows in the Church. About 73 B.C.

1 Behold, now it came to pass that the people of Nephi were exceedingly rejoiced, because the Lord had again delivered them out of the hands of their enemies; therefore they gave thanks unto the Lord their God; yea, and they did fast much and pray much, and they did worship God with exceedingly great joy.

2 And it came to pass in the nineteenth year of the reign of the judges over the people of Nephi, that Alma came unto his son Helaman and said unto him: Believest thou the words which I spake unto thee concerning those records which have been kept?

3 And Helaman said unto him: Yea, I believe.

4 And Alma said again: Believest thou in Jesus Christ, who shall come?

5 And he said: Yea, I believe all the words which thou hast spoken.

6 And Alma said unto him again: Will ye keep my commandments?

7 And he said: Yea, I will keep thy commandments with all my heart.

8 Then Alma said unto him: Blessed art thou; and the Lord shall prosper thee in this land.

9 But behold, I have somewhat to prophesy unto thee; but what I prophesy unto thee ye shall not make known; yea, what I prophesy unto thee shall not be made known, even until the prophecy is fulfilled; therefore write the words which I shall say.

10 And these are the words: Behold, I perceive that this very people, the Nephites, according to the spirit of revelation which is in me, in four hundred years from the time that Jesus Christ shall manifest himself unto them, shall dwindle in unbelief.

11 Yea, and then shall they see wars and pestilences, yea, famines and bloodshed, even until the people of Nephi shall become extinct—

12 Yea, and this because they shall dwindle in unbelief and fall into the works of darkness, and lasciviousness, and all manner of iniquities; yea, I say unto you, that because they shall sin against so great light and knowledge, yea, I say unto you, that from that day, even the fourth generation shall not all pass away before this great iniquity shall come.

Alma 45:9–14. Alma Prophesies of the Destruction of the Nephites

What is the spirit of revelation of which Alma spoke? (45:10) "The spirit of revelation that imbued Alma's whole being was the power within him to make known the future and also to interpret the past. The spirit of revelation is the forerunner of prophecy; in fact, they are counterparts. Prophecy fulfilling by way of promise what the spirit of revelation makes known" (Reynolds and Sjodahl, *Commentary on the Book of Mormon*, 5:27). ●

How widespread was this falling away from the truth? (45:11–12) "It was foreseen that the powers of evil would be permitted to prevail in the west as in the east. . . .

"An earlier prophecy relating to the degradation of the surviving remnant of Lehi's descendants, was uttered by Nephi, as a result of a revelation communicated to him through angelic visitation [1 Nephi 12:19–23 is quoted]. . . .

"The scriptures . . . show that widespread apostasy from the Church was foreseen; that the corruption of the Church itself was likewise foreknown; and that on both hemispheres a general apostasy was foretold" (Talmage, *Great Apostasy*, 32–33).

Why is lasciviousness so damning? (45:12) *Lasciviousness* is "irregular indulgence of animal desires or the tendency to excite lust, and promote irregular indulgence" (Webster, *American Dictionary*).

"President Harold B. Lee has called our attention to the phrase 'past feeling' which is used several places in the scriptures. In Ephesians, Paul links it to lasciviousness that apparently so sated its victims that they sought 'uncleanness with greediness'" (Maxwell, *For the Power Is in Them*, 22).

What leads a person into these works of darkness and iniquities? (45:12) Alma identifies five steps by which people fall into apostasy: (1) they dwindle in unbelief; (2) they fall into works of darkness; (3) lust and indulgence become a way of life; (4) they are attracted to all manner of iniquity; and (5), they sin against the light and knowledge they have received. What are we doing to avoid these pitfalls of apostasy? What are we doing to strengthen our faith?

Alma 45:15–19. Alma Gives a Final Blessing to His Sons

How does Alma's prophecy of God's blessing apply to these latter-days? (45:15–16) "If we will keep the commandments of God—live as he has directed and does now direct, through his prophets—we will continue to have His protecting hand over us. But we must be true to the eternal verities, the great Christian virtues that God has revealed. Then, and only then, will we be safe as a nation and as individuals. God grant that the faithfulness of the Latter-day Saints will provide the balance of power to save this nation in time of crisis" (Benson, *This Nation Shall Endure*, 145).

What happened to Moses and Alma the Younger? (45:18–19) "The scriptural inference is that Moses also was translated as was Alma. [Alma 45:18–19 is quoted.] . . .

"It is a very reasonable thought to believe that both Moses and Alma, like Elijah and John, were translated to accomplish some work which the Lord had in store for them at some future day" (Smith, *Answers to Gospel Questions*, 5:38). ❂

13 And when that great day cometh, behold, the time very soon cometh that those who are now, or the seed of those who are now numbered among the people of Nephi, shall no more be numbered among the people of Nephi.

14 But whosoever remaineth, and is not destroyed in that great and dreadful day, shall be numbered among the Lamanites, and shall become like unto them, all, save it be a few who shall be called the disciples of the Lord; and them shall the Lamanites pursue even until they shall become extinct. And now, because of iniquity, this prophecy shall be fulfilled.

15 And now it came to pass that after Alma had said these things to Helaman, he blessed him, and also his other sons; and he also blessed the earth for the righteous' sake.

16 And he said: Thus saith the Lord God—Cursed shall be the land, yea, this land, unto every nation, kindred, tongue, and people, unto destruction, which do wickedly, when they are fully ripe; and as I have said so shall it be; for this is the cursing and the blessing of God upon the land, for the Lord cannot look upon sin with the least degree of allowance.

17 And now, when Alma had said these words he blessed the church, yea, all those who should stand fast in the faith from that time henceforth.

18 And when Alma had done this he departed out of the land of Zarahemla, as if to go into the land of Melek. And it came to pass that he was never heard of more; as to his death or burial we know not of.

19 Behold, this we know, that he was a righteous man; and the saying went abroad in the church that he was taken up by the Spirit, or buried by the hand of the Lord, even as Moses. But behold, the scriptures saith the Lord took

Moses unto himself; and we suppose that he has also received Alma in the spirit, unto himself; therefore, for this cause we know nothing concerning his death and burial.

20 And now it came to pass in the commencement of the nineteenth year of the reign of the judges over the people of Nephi, that Helaman went forth among the people to declare the word unto them.

21 For behold, because of their wars with the Lamanites and the many little dissensions and disturbances which had been among the people, it became expedient that the word of God should be declared among them, yea, and that a regulation should be made throughout the church.

22 Therefore, Helaman and his brethren went forth to establish the church again in all the land, yea, in every city throughout all the land which was possessed by the people of Nephi. And it came to pass that they did appoint priests and teachers throughout all the land, over all the churches.

23 And now it came to pass that after Helaman and his brethren had appointed priests and teachers over the churches that there arose a dissension among them, and they would not give heed to the words of Helaman and his brethren;

24 But they grew proud, being lifted up in their hearts, because of their exceedingly great riches; therefore they grew rich in their own eyes, and would not give heed to their words, to walk uprightly before God.

Alma 45:20–24. Helaman Begins to Teach the People and Call Them to Repentance

What role did prophets have in times of war? (45:22) "In Moroni's day it was not merely the secular authorities (generals and chief judges) who established the peace. The high priest of the church, Helaman, worked closely with Moroni to quell dissent. Before the lengthy Nephite-Lamanite wars began, he tried to set the church in order because the dissensions that soon were to plague the nation were evident in the church (Alma 45:20–22). Just as Moroni, the great general, prayed and preached powerfully (Alma 46:16–27), Helaman, the great prophet, took up the sword and led an army (the 2000 stripling warriors) (Alma 56–58). The establishment of peace did not merely mean that the Lamanites were defeated, but also that the gospel was widely preached" (Wardle, "Dissent," 67).

Alma 46:1–10. Amalickiah Seeks to Be King

Who were the people who refused to follow Helaman's teachings and sought to kill him? (46:1–2) These dissenters consisted of "those who refused all instruction, 'because of their exceedingly great riches' (Alma 45:24), [and] 'gathered together' as a hate-group—'exceeding wroth'—to plan the extremist measures against those who stood in their way.... Then there were passionate monarchists, who not only were 'in favor of kings' but, being of 'high birth, ... sought to be kings' (Alma 51:8)—everyone in line for the throne. After them were those who may not have claimed royal blood but nevertheless 'professed the blood of nobility'—whether they could prove it or not (Alma 51:21)" (Nibley, *Prophetic Book of Mormon*, 333).

Who was Amalickiah and what were his desires and strategies? (46:3) "Amalickiah is one of a line of brilliant trouble-makers who keep things stirred up.... Beginning with Laman and Lemuel we meet in order Sherem, Amulon, Nehor, Amlici, Zeezrom, Korihor, Zerahemnah, and now, neither last nor least, Amalickiah. All of these men had certain traits in common: all were personally ambitious and unscrupulous, aspiring to be either king or the religious head of the people; all were powerful speakers and clever propagandists, skilled in the use of 'flattering words'; all sought to undermine, if they could not seize, the highest authority of the church and state, being particularly opposed to popular government and drawing their support from those who sought to overthrow it" (Nibley, *Since Cumorah*, 302). ⊕

CHAPTER 46

Amalickiah conspires to be king—Moroni raises the title of liberty—He rallies the people to defend their religion—True believers are called Christians—A remnant of Joseph will be preserved—Amalickiah and the dissenters flee to the land of Nephi—Those who will not support the cause of freedom are put to death. About 73–72 B.C.

1 And it came to pass that as many as would not hearken to the words of Helaman and his brethren were gathered together against their brethren.

2 And now behold, they were exceedingly wroth, insomuch that they were determined to slay them.

3 Now the leader of those who were wroth against their brethren was a large and a strong man; and his name was Amalickiah.

4 And Amalickiah was desirous to be a king; and those people who were wroth were also desirous that he should be their king; and they were the greater part of them the lower judges of the land, and they were seeking for power.

5 And they had been led by the flatteries of Amalickiah, that if they would support him and establish him to be their king that he would make them rulers over the people.

6 Thus they were led away by Amalickiah to dissensions, notwithstanding the preaching of Helaman and his brethren, yea, notwithstanding their exceedingly great care over the church, for they were high priests over the church.

7 And there were many in the church who believed in the flattering words of Amalickiah, therefore they dissented even from the church; and thus were the affairs of the people of Nephi exceedingly precarious and dangerous, notwithstanding their great victory which they had had over the Lamanites, and their great rejoicings which they had had because of their deliverance by the hand of the Lord.

8 Thus we see how quick the children of men do forget the Lord their God, yea, how quick to do iniquity, and to be led away by the evil one.

9 Yea, and we also see the great wickedness one very wicked man can cause to take place among the children of men.

10 Yea, we see that Amalickiah, because he was a man of cunning device and a man of many flattering words, that he led away the hearts of many people to do wickedly; yea, and to seek to destroy the church of God, and to destroy the foundation of liberty which God had granted unto them, or which blessing God had sent upon the face of the land for the righteous' sake.

11 And now it came to pass that when Moroni, who was the chief commander of the armies of the Nephites, had heard of these dissensions, he was angry with Amalickiah.

12 And it came to pass that he rent his coat; and he took a piece thereof, and wrote upon it—In memory of our God, our religion, and freedom, and our peace, our wives, and our children—and he fastened it upon the end of a pole.

13 And he fastened on his head-plate, and his breastplate, and his shields, and girded on his armor about his loins; and he took the pole, which had on the end thereof his rent coat, (and he called it the title of liberty) and

Why did the Nephites keep finding themselves at war? (46:7–10) "The irony of the wars in the book of Alma is that the Nephites were righteous enough to win the wars, but not righteous enough to prevent them from taking place. According to President Spencer W. Kimball, God had given a special promise to the Nephites which is valid to all the peoples of America: if they would stay sufficiently righteous, they would not have to fight ("False Gods We Worship," 6). . . . Both the war with Zerahemnah and the one with Amalickiah began at a time when many Nephites, including members of the Church, had hardened their hearts (Alma 35:15–16; 45:20–24)" (Hansen, "Book of Alma as a Prototype," 278). ◐

Alma 46:11–18. Captain Moroni Raises the Title of Liberty

What does Captain Moroni's example teach us about standing up to evil? (46:11–13) "It does not take long for a people who are full of pride to 'forget the Lord their God' and 'be led away by the evil one' (Alma 46:8). One wicked individual can cause great wickedness to take place among such a people (see Alma 46:9).

"On the other hand, one righteous person can make a difference in such a setting. Captain Moroni reacted to this situation by making a banner. . . . He prayed fervently to the Lord. . . . This became such an important time for Moroni that he challenged all his supporters to 'enter into a covenant' (Alma 46:20)" (Garrett, "Inspired by a Better Cause," 75). What opportunities do we have to make a difference for righteousness with those around us?

How is freedom related to regard for "our God, [and] our religion"? (46:12) "The only way we can keep our freedom is through our personal righteousness—by handling that freedom responsibly" (*Teachings of Howard W. Hunter*, 169).

"Freedom and liberty are part of the gospel plan. Any program or philosophy that would destroy a person's free agency is not of God. . . .

"Freedom is an inherited, God-given principle. It has always been planned that God should have in His plan that men should be free. . . .

"Righteousness, as the Book of Mormon states, is the indispensable ingredient to liberty" (*Teachings of Ezra Taft Benson*, 83, 573, 588). ⊕

Why is the word *Christian* in the Book of Mormon? (46:13) "It should be remembered that the Book of Mormon is a translation of an ancient Nephite text. The English word 'Christian' is not the word that was originally on the Nephite record, but is the English word that Joseph Smith used when translating the original Nephite word. The word 'Christian' simply means 'Christ-believer' in common use and in the Book of Mormon. We don't know what the original Nephite word was for 'Christian', but it signified something like 'Christ-believer'. The word 'Christ' is a Greek word that means the same thing as the Hebrew word 'Messiah.' . . . [thus] anyone who believed [the] prophecies would have been a 'Messiah-believer'. Therefore, all pre-Christian era Israelites who believed in the coming Messiah/Christ were Christians in this sense" (Fairmormon.org, "Is it an anachronism that the Book of Mormon teaches that Christians existed before Christ?").

What was the ancient importance of taking upon oneself a new name? (46:13–15) "As in the Old Testament, renaming is also understood to be part of a covenant in Nephite culture. When Moroni rallies the people of Nephi with the title of liberty, 'all those who were true believers in Christ *took upon them*, gladly, *the name of Christ*, or Christians as they were called . . . ' (Alma 46:15; emphasis added). . . . In the Book of Mormon the making of covenants is usually connected with taking the name of Christ upon one's self. This practice connects the idea of renaming as a change of nature with the idea of renaming as adoption, because a new name was also an indication of adoption in the ancient Near East" (Lane, "The Lord Will Redeem His People," 47–48).

he bowed himself to the earth, and he prayed mightily unto his God for the blessings of liberty to rest upon his brethren, so long as there should a band of Christians remain to possess the land—

14 For thus were all the true believers of Christ, who belonged to the church of God, called by those who did not belong to the church.

15 And those who did belong to the church were faithful; yea, all those who were true believers in Christ took upon them, gladly, the name of Christ, or Christians as they were called, because of their belief in Christ who should come.

16 And therefore, at this time, Moroni prayed that the cause of the Christians, and the freedom of the land might be favored.

17 And it came to pass that when he had poured out his soul to God, he named all the land which was south of the land Desolation, yea, and in fine, all the land, both on the north and on the south—A chosen land, and the land of liberty.

18 And he said: Surely God shall not suffer that we, who are despised because we take upon us the name of Christ, shall be trodden down and destroyed, until we bring it upon us by our own transgressions.

Alma 46:19–22. The Righteous Covenant to Uphold Their Freedom and the Church of God

19 And when Moroni had said these words, he went forth among the people, waving the rent part of his garment in the air, that all might see the writing which he had written upon the rent part, and crying with a loud voice, saying:

20 Behold, whosoever will maintain this title upon the land, let them come forth in the strength of the Lord, and enter into a covenant that they will maintain their rights, and their religion, that the Lord God may bless them.

21 And it came to pass that when Moroni had proclaimed these words, behold, the people came running together with their armor girded about their loins, rending their garments in token, or as a covenant, that they would not forsake the Lord their God; or, in other words, if they should transgress the commandments of God, or fall into transgression, and be ashamed to take upon them the name of Christ, the Lord should rend them even as they had rent their garments.

22 Now this was the covenant which they made, and they cast their garments at the feet of Moroni, saying: We covenant with our God, that we shall be destroyed, even as our brethren in the land northward, if we shall fall into transgression; yea, he may cast us at the feet of our enemies, even as we have cast our garments at thy feet to be trodden under foot, if we shall fall into transgression.

How is the original 1830 Book of Mormon edition wording of this verse evidence of its authenticity? (46:19–22) Critics of the Book of Mormon point out that the original wording in this verse—"waving the rent"—does not include the word *part*. Since a *rent* is the hole, not the piece torn from the cloth, and one cannot write on a hole, they claim that the book is in error. They charge that "part" was later added for deception. However, Hebrew scholar John A. Tvedtnes explained that "Hebrew does not have to add the word *part* to a verbal substantive like *rent* as English requires. . . . In the verse . . . *rent* would mean *rent thing* or *rent part*" ("Hebrew Background," 78). ●

Why did Moroni and his followers rend their clothing as part of their covenant? (46:20–22) "Rending or tearing clothes is customary in ancient oaths. Terrence Szink has found comparable rites in the ancient world (*Warfare in the Book of Mormon*, 35–45). He suggests that the oath of the Nephite army described in Alma 46:21–22 is similar to a number of Near Eastern oaths that have two characteristics. First, they are self-execrative in nature: the party making the covenant or treaty takes upon himself a conditional curse, swearing that, if he fails to fulfill his part of the agreement, he is willing to endure a specified punishment. Second, they are accompanied by various rites that in some way symbolized the punishment to be inflicted" (Valletta, "Captain and the Covenant," 234–35). ●

Why would someone cast his clothing at another's feet? (46:21–22) "While twentieth-century readers correctly view this moment as a time of great patriotism, it is important to note that any such feelings of the Nephites were founded in their covenants. . . . Hugh Nibley has said 'treading on one's garments while making a covenant' follows a 'forgotten but peculiar old Jewish rite' ("Freemen" 335–36)" (Valletta, "Captain and the Covenant," (234–35). ●

Alma 46:23–33. Moroni Inspires His People to Fight for Their Freedom, and Amalickiah Flees

What was Moroni teaching by referring to Joseph's coat? (46:23–24) Moroni spoke of "an incident in the life of Joseph of Egypt which has been lost to the Bible record. He told them that as Joseph's coat had been rent into many pieces by his brothers in their bitterness, so his people would be rent by their dissenting brothers if they were not true to their covenant. Moroni then said that Jacob had prophesied before his death using the remnants of Joseph's coat as a type. Jacob noted that part of what had been brought him had decayed, while part of it had been preserved, and he prophesied that part of the seed or remnant of Joseph would likewise be destroyed, while part would be preserved" (McConkie, *Gospel Symbolism*, 172).

Was Moroni justified in physically restraining the dissenters? (46:28–33) "There are times when firmness, even physical compulsion, is necessary to stop dissenters....

"In times of war, when internal rebellions threaten the lives and liberties of the people, when ample opportunity to repent has been afforded, the use of military force under righteous leadership to put down treacherous dissent has been justified....

23 Moroni said unto them: Behold, we are a remnant of the seed of Jacob; yea, we are a remnant of the seed of Joseph, whose coat was rent by his brethren into many pieces; yea, and now behold, let us remember to keep the commandments of God, or our garments shall be rent by our brethren, and we be cast into prison, or be sold, or be slain.

24 Yea, let us preserve our liberty as a remnant of Joseph; yea, let us remember the words of Jacob, before his death, for behold, he saw that a part of the remnant of the coat of Joseph was preserved and had not decayed. And he said—Even as this remnant of garment of my son hath been preserved, so shall a remnant of the seed of my son be preserved by the hand of God, and be taken unto himself, while the remainder of the seed of Joseph shall perish, even as the remnant of his garment.

25 Now behold, this giveth my soul sorrow; nevertheless, my soul hath joy in my son, because of that part of his seed which shall be taken unto God.

26 Now behold, this was the language of Jacob.

27 And now who knoweth but what the remnant of the seed of Joseph, which shall perish as his garment, are those who have dissented from us? Yea, and even it shall be ourselves if we do not stand fast in the faith of Christ.

28 And now it came to pass that when Moroni had said these words he went forth, and also sent forth in all the parts of the land where there were dissensions, and gathered together all the people who were desirous to maintain their liberty, to stand against Amalickiah and those who had dissented, who were called Amalickiahites.

29 And it came to pass that when Amalickiah saw that the people of Moroni were more numerous than the Amalickiahites—and he also saw that his people were doubtful concerning the justice of the cause in which they had undertaken—therefore, fearing that he should not gain the point, he took those of his people who would and departed into the land of Nephi.

30 Now Moroni thought it was not expedient that the Lamanites should have any more strength; therefore he thought to cut off the people of Amalickiah, or to take them and bring them back, and put Amalickiah to death; yea, for he knew that he would stir up the Lamanites to anger against them, and cause them to come to battle against them; and this he knew that Amalickiah would do that he might obtain his purposes.

31 Therefore Moroni thought it was expedient that he should take his armies, who had gathered themselves together, and armed themselves, and entered into a covenant to keep the peace—and it came to pass that he took his army and marched out with his tents into the wilderness, to cut off the course of Amalickiah in the wilderness.

32 And it came to pass that he did according to his desires, and marched forth into the wilderness, and headed the armies of Amalickiah.

33 And it came to pass that Amalickiah fled with a small number of his men, and the remainder were delivered up into the hands of Moroni and were taken back into the land of Zarahemla.

34 Now, Moroni being a man who was appointed by the chief judges and the voice of the people, therefore he had power according to his will with the armies of the Nephites, to establish and to exercise authority over them.

"The righteous only resort to slaying dissenters when the dissenters had undertaken to do something that immediately and seriously threatened the lives and liberties of the righteous innocent who would not agree with the dissenters" (Wardle, "Dissent," 60–63).

Alma 46:34–41. Moroni Establishes Peace Again in the Land

Why were the Amalickiahites who did not enter into the covenant put to death? (46:35) "The fiction has been diligently cultivated that Moroni on this occasion put all the pacifists to death. Those put to death were not those who had refused to take up arms to defend their country, but those who had taken up arms to attack it and who were on their way to join the enemy across the border, glad in their hearts when they heard that the Lamanites were coming down to battle against their country; they were dissenters to the enemy. Pacifists? They were all members of Amalickiah's army, armed to their teeth on their way to join the enemy when Moroni caught them. . . . Armed violence, not pacifism, had been their program from the beginning" (Nibley, *Approaching Zion*, 98–99). ✪

How can our generation plant the "standard of liberty" in our own land and time? (46:36) President Ezra Taft Benson explained: "This is our need today—to plant the standard of liberty among our people throughout the Americas.

"While this incident occurred some seventy years B.C., the struggle went on through one thousand years covered by this sacred Book of Mormon record. In fact, the struggle for liberty is a continuing one—it is with us in a very real sense today right here on this choice land of the Americas" (in Conference Report, Oct. 1962, 14–15).

If our lives were to end today, would we go "out of the world rejoicing"? (46:39) Elder Jeffrey R. Holland explained that these people died rejoicing because they knew "firmly that their souls had been redeemed by the Lord Jesus Christ, whose name they had taken upon themselves and whose gospel they had tried to defend" (*Christ and the New Covenant*, 128).

Do Elder Holland's words describe you? How does knowing you have taken Christ's name upon you influence you each day? What opportunities have you had to defend His gospel?

What helped cure the illness of the Book of Mormon people? (46:40) "The plants and roots which God had prepared could conquer the fevers. . . . Quinine wasn't discovered until 1840. Nobody knew that the quinine bark would cure these fevers until then. They didn't know what could cure them. They didn't know about mosquitoes or anything else. . . .

35 And it came to pass that whomsoever of the Amalickiahites that would not enter into a covenant to support the cause of freedom, that they might maintain a free government, he caused to be put to death; and there were but few who denied the covenant of freedom.

36 And it came to pass also, that he caused the title of liberty to be hoisted upon every tower which was in all the land, which was possessed by the Nephites; and thus Moroni planted the standard of liberty among the Nephites.

37 And they began to have peace again in the land; and thus they did maintain peace in the land until nearly the end of the nineteenth year of the reign of the judges.

38 And Helaman and the high priests did also maintain order in the church; yea, even for the space of four years did they have much peace and rejoicing in the church.

39 And it came to pass that there were many who died, firmly believing that their souls were redeemed by the Lord Jesus Christ; thus they went out of the world rejoicing.

40 And there were some who died with fevers, which at some seasons of the year were very frequent in the land—but not so much so with fevers, because of the excellent qualities of the many plants and roots which God had prepared to remove the cause of diseases,

to which men were subject by the nature of the climate—

41 But there were many who died with old age; and those who died in the faith of Christ are happy in him, as we must needs suppose.

CHAPTER 47

Amalickiah uses treachery, murder, and intrigue to become king of the Lamanites—The Nephite dissenters are more wicked and ferocious than the Lamanites. About 72 B.C.

1 Now we will return in our record to Amalickiah and those who had fled with him into the wilderness; for, behold, he had taken those who went with him, and went up in the land of Nephi among the Lamanites, and did stir up the Lamanites to anger against the people of Nephi, insomuch that the king of the Lamanites sent a proclamation throughout all his land, among all his people, that they should gather themselves together again to go to battle against the Nephites.

2 And it came to pass that when the proclamation had gone forth among them they were exceedingly afraid; yea, they feared to displease the king, and they also feared to go to battle against the Nephites lest they should lose their lives. And it came to pass that they would not, or the more part of them would not, obey the commandments of the king.

3 And now it came to pass that the king was wroth because of their disobedience; therefore he gave Amalickiah the command of that part of his army which was obedient unto his commands, and commanded him that he should go forth and compel them to arms.

4 Now behold, this was the desire of Amalickiah; for he being a very subtle man to do evil therefore he laid the plan in his heart to dethrone the king of the Lamanites.

There are these occasional flashes of background in the Book of Mormon, which for the most part concentrate intently on the issues of salvation. But here it just happens to note in passing . . . that it was fever country and there were diseases to which men were subject by the nature of the climate, which was tropical and humid. The fevers were held under control by the most excellent quality of the plants" (Nibley, *Teachings of the Book of Mormon*, 3:65).

Alma 47:1–16. Amalickiah Is Given Authority over the Lamanite Army and Plans to Dethrone the Lamanite King

How much did the Lamanites understand about Amalickiah's cunning? (47:1–13) "[Amalickiah] 'did stir up the Lamanites to anger against the people of Nephi,' to such a degree that the Lamanite king ordered a general mobilization for war (Alma 47:1). Such an order to a people who had just had their fill of war was coolly received, and most of the people refused to obey it (Alma 47:2) and organized a huge protest-meeting at the marshalling area at Onidah, electing a king for themselves on a no-war platform (Alma 47:5–6). . . . The fact that . . . [Lehonti] had to be urged four times before he would risk a secret meeting with Amalickiah shows that the latter already had something of a reputation as a smooth operator" (Nibley, *Since Cumorah*, 305).

5 And now he had got the command of those parts of the Lamanites who were in favor of the king; and he sought to gain favor of those who were not obedient; therefore he went forward to the place which was called Onidah, for thither had all the Lamanites fled; for they discovered the army coming, and, supposing that they were coming to destroy them, therefore they fled to Onidah, to the place of arms.

6 And they had appointed a man to be a king and a leader over them, being fixed in their minds with a determined resolution that they would not be subjected to go against the Nephites.

7 And it came to pass that they had gathered themselves together upon the top of the mount which was called Antipas, in preparation to battle.

8 Now it was not Amalickiah's intention to give them battle according to the commandments of the king; but behold, it was his intention to gain favor with the armies of the Lamanites, that he might place himself at their head and dethrone the king and take possession of the kingdom.

9 And behold, it came to pass that he caused his army to pitch their tents in the valley which was near the mount Antipas.

10 And it came to pass that when it was night he sent a secret embassy into the mount Antipas, desiring that the leader of those who were upon the mount, whose name was Lehonti, that he should come down to the foot of the mount, for he desired to speak with him.

11 And it came to pass that when Lehonti received the message he durst not go down to the foot of the mount. And it came to pass that Amalickiah sent again the second time, desiring him to come down. And it came to

How do some people try to seduce us to leave the high ground of light and truth? (47:7–16) "By arguments and accusations, some people bait us to leave the high ground. The high ground is where the light is. It's where we see the first light of morning and the last light in the evening. It is the safe ground. It is true and where knowledge is. Sometimes others want us to come down off the high ground and join them in a theological scrum in the mud. These few contentious individuals are set on picking religious fights, online or in person. We are always better staying on the higher ground of mutual respect and love" (Hales, "Christian Courage," 74). ⊕

pass that Lehonti would not; and he sent again the third time.

12 And it came to pass that when Amalickiah found that he could not get Lehonti to come down off from the mount, he went up into the mount, nearly to Lehonti's camp; and he sent again the fourth time his message unto Lehonti, desiring that he would come down, and that he would bring his guards with him.

13 And it came to pass that when Lehonti had come down with his guards to Amalickiah, that Amalickiah desired him to come down with his army in the night-time, and surround those men in their camps over whom the king had given him command, and that he would deliver them up into Lehonti's hands, if he would make him (Amalickiah) a second leader over the whole army.

14 And it came to pass that Lehonti came down with his men and surrounded the men of Amalickiah, so that before they awoke at the dawn of day they were surrounded by the armies of Lehonti.

15 And it came to pass that when they saw that they were surrounded, they pled with Amalickiah that he would suffer them to fall in with their brethren, that they might not be destroyed. Now this was the very thing which Amalickiah desired.

16 And it came to pass that he delivered his men, contrary to the commands of the king. Now this was the thing that Amalickiah desired, that he might accomplish his designs in dethroning the king.

17 Now it was the custom among the Lamanites, if their chief leader was killed, to appoint the second leader to be their chief leader.

18 And it came to pass that Amalickiah caused that one of his servants should administer poison by degrees to Lehonti, that he died.

Alma 47:17–30. Amalickiah Gains Control of the Lamanite Army by Lying

Why do you think Mormon described Lehonti's death this way instead of simply saying he was poisoned? (47:18) Lehonti was poisoned by degrees. Have you ever noticed Satan attempting to spiritually "poison" you by degrees? "Satan . . . seeks to deceive us about right and wrong and persuade us that there is no such thing as sin. This detour typically starts off with what seems to be only a small departure: 'Just try it once. One beer or one cigarette or one porno movie won't hurt.' What all of these departures have in common is that each of them is addictive. Addiction is a condition in which we surrender part of our power of choice" (Oaks, "Be Not Deceived," 44).

What is a "token of peace"? (47:23) A *token* is "a sign; something intended to represent or indicate another thing or an event. Thus the rainbow is a *token* of God's covenant established with Noah" (Webster, *American Dictionary*).

It is ironic that the "token of peace" preceded the king's death. Amalickiah "sent his servants to greet the king, seemingly to pay him reverence. . . . As was also a custom among the Lamanites, they bowed down to the ground to show their homage to him. Everything went as protocol among them provided. The king put forth his hand to raise them from their position of nothingness, and when he raised the first, the servant immediately stabbed him in the heart" (Reynolds and Sjodahl, *Commentary on the Book of Mormon*, 5:45–46).

19 Now, when Lehonti was dead, the Lamanites appointed Amalickiah to be their leader and their chief commander.

20 And it came to pass that Amalickiah marched with his armies (for he had gained his desires) to the land of Nephi, to the city of Nephi, which was the chief city.

21 And the king came out to meet him with his guards, for he supposed that Amalickiah had fulfilled his commands, and that Amalickiah had gathered together so great an army to go against the Nephites to battle.

22 But behold, as the king came out to meet him Amalickiah caused that his servants should go forth to meet the king. And they went and bowed themselves before the king, as if to reverence him because of his greatness.

23 And it came to pass that the king put forth his hand to raise them, as was the custom with the Lamanites, as a token of peace, which custom they had taken from the Nephites.

24 And it came to pass that when he had raised the first from the ground, behold he stabbed the king to the heart; and he fell to the earth.

25 Now the servants of the king fled; and the servants of Amalickiah raised a cry, saying:

26 Behold, the servants of the king have stabbed him to the heart, and he has fallen and they have fled; behold, come and see.

27 And it came to pass that Amalickiah commanded that his armies should march forth and see what had happened to the king; and when they had come to the spot, and found the king lying in his gore, Amalickiah pretended to be wroth, and said: Whosoever loved the king, let him go forth, and pursue his servants that they may be slain.

28 And it came to pass that all they who loved the king, when they heard these words, came forth and pursued after the servants of the king.

29 Now when the servants of the king saw an army pursuing after them, they were frightened again, and fled into the wilderness, and came over into the land of Zarahemla and joined the people of Ammon.

30 And the army which pursued after them returned, having pursued after them in vain; and thus Amalickiah, by his fraud, gained the hearts of the people.

31 And it came to pass on the morrow he entered the city Nephi with his armies, and took possession of the city.

32 And now it came to pass that the queen, when she had heard that the king was slain— for Amalickiah had sent an embassy to the queen informing her that the king had been slain by his servants, that he had pursued them with his army, but it was in vain, and they had made their escape—

33 Therefore, when the queen had received this message she sent unto Amalickiah, desiring him that he would spare the people of the city; and she also desired him that he should come in unto her; and she also desired him that he should bring witnesses with him to testify concerning the death of the king.

34 And it came to pass that Amalickiah took the same servant that slew the king, and all them who were with him, and went in unto the queen, unto the place where she sat; and they all testified unto her that the king was slain by his own servants; and they said also: They have fled; does not this testify against them? And thus they satisfied the queen concerning the death of the king.

35 And it came to pass that Amalickiah sought the favor of the queen, and took her

Alma 47:31–36. Amalickiah, through Deception, Gains Control of the Entire Lamanite Kingdom

What can the dissenters among the Nephites teach us? (47:36) "There are the dissenters who leave the Church, either formally or informally, but who cannot leave it alone. Usually anxious to please worldly galleries, they are critical or at least condescending towards the Brethren. They not only seek to steady the ark but also on occasion give it a hard shove! Often having been taught the same true doctrines as the faithful, they have nevertheless moved in the direction of dissent (see Alma 47:36). They have minds hardened by pride (see Daniel 5:20)" (Maxwell, *Men and Women of Christ*, 4). ◆

Alma 48:1–6. Amalickiah's Desire for Power Causes War between the Nephites and the Lamanites

What tactics did Amalickiah use to inspire the hesitant Lamanites to attack the Nephites? (48:1–3) Amalickiah's "big problem . . . was to get the Lamanites to fight for him, and no professional public-relations office could have done a more skillful job than he did. 'He did appoint men to speak unto the Lamanites from their towers, against the Nephites' (Alma 48:1)— trained orators delivering set speeches from the official information centers; accusing, always accusing" (Nibley, *Since Cumorah*, 305).

unto him to wife; and thus by his fraud, and by the assistance of his cunning servants, he obtained the kingdom; yea, he was acknowledged king throughout all the land, among all the people of the Lamanites, who were composed of the Lamanites and the Lemuelites and the Ishmaelites, and all the dissenters of the Nephites, from the reign of Nephi down to the present time.

36 Now these dissenters, having the same instruction and the same information of the Nephites, yea, having been instructed in the same knowledge of the Lord, nevertheless, it is strange to relate, not long after their dissensions they became more hardened and impenitent, and more wild, wicked and ferocious than the Lamanites—drinking in with the traditions of the Lamanites; giving way to indolence, and all manner of lasciviousness; yea, entirely forgetting the Lord their God.

CHAPTER 48

Amalickiah incites the Lamanites against the Nephites—Moroni prepares his people to defend the cause of the Christians—He rejoices in liberty and freedom and is a mighty man of God. About 72 B.C.

1 And now it came to pass that, as soon as Amalickiah had obtained the kingdom he began to inspire the hearts of the Lamanites against the people of Nephi; yea, he did appoint men to speak unto the Lamanites from their towers, against the Nephites.

2 And thus he did inspire their hearts against the Nephites, insomuch that in the latter end of the nineteenth year of the reign of the judges, he having accomplished his designs thus far, yea, having been made king over the Lamanites, he sought also to reign over all the land, yea, and all the people who were in the land, the Nephites as well as the Lamanites.

3 Therefore he had accomplished his design, for he had hardened the hearts of the Lamanites and blinded their minds, and stirred them up to anger, insomuch that he had gathered together a numerous host to go to battle against the Nephites.

4 For he was determined, because of the greatness of the number of his people, to overpower the Nephites and to bring them into bondage.

5 And thus he did appoint chief captains of the Zoramites, they being the most acquainted with the strength of the Nephites, and their places of resort, and the weakest parts of their cities; therefore he appointed them to be chief captains over his armies.

6 And it came to pass that they took their camp, and moved forth toward the land of Zarahemla in the wilderness.

7 Now it came to pass that while Amalickiah had thus been obtaining power by fraud and deceit, Moroni, on the other hand, had been preparing the minds of the people to be faithful unto the Lord their God.

8 Yea, he had been strengthening the armies of the Nephites, and erecting small forts, or places of resort; throwing up banks of earth round about to enclose his armies, and also building walls of stone to encircle them about, round about their cities and the borders of their lands; yea, all round about the land.

9 And in their weakest fortifications he did place the greater number of men; and thus he did fortify and strengthen the land which was possessed by the Nephites.

10 And thus he was preparing to support their liberty, their lands, their wives, and their

Why were Zoramites chosen as leaders in the war against the Nephites? (48:5) "The Zoramites had likely been military leaders among the Nephites prior to their defection to the Lamanites. . . . In the same account, we learn that it was the Zoramite chief captains who had introduced shields, breastplates, and armor (thick clothing) to the Lamanites [see Alma 49:6]. These implements had aided the Nephites during previous battles against the Lamanites (e.g., Alma 43:19–21)" (Tvedtnes, "Book of Mormon Tribal Affiliation and Military Castes," 320).

Alma 48:7–10. Moroni Prepares the Nephites for War with the Lamanites

What can we learn from Moroni's preparation of his people to be faithful to the Lord? (48:7) How do we prepare our minds to be faithful to God? Why is having a spiritually and mentally sound mind needful today? What are we doing to keep ourselves worthy of the Spirit to guide us toward uplifting thoughts when others are trying to lead us to impure ideas?

In addition to spiritual preparation, when is physical preparation for war justified? (48:8–10) Two days before his martyrdom, the Prophet Joseph Smith declared: "There is one principle which is eternal; it is the duty of all men to protect their lives and the lives of the household, whenever necessity requires, and no power has a right to forbid it" (*History of the Church*, 6:605).

President Gordon B. Hinckley taught: "We are people of peace. We are followers of the Christ who was and is the Prince of Peace. But there are times when we must stand up for right and decency, for freedom and civilization, just as Moroni rallied his people in his day to the defense of their wives, their children, and the cause of liberty" ("Times in Which We Live," 72).

Alma 48:11–20. Moroni Rejoices in Liberty and Freedom

What do we learn from this description of Moroni? (48:11–13, 17) "Mormon masterfully abridged the scriptural record about Moroni, ... demonstrating to his anticipated readers that this was a man most needed not only for his day, but also for our own. ... Captain Moroni endures as a model of courage and righteousness to many Latter-day Saints. ...

"In Mormon's view, Captain Moroni exemplified the model Nephite disciple of Christ. ...

"Implicit in Mormon's description of Moroni is the prophetic model of a man who understood the nature and value of covenant-making and keeping" (Valletta, "Captain and the Covenant," 223–24). ⊕

During the wars described in Alma, what was the difference in motivation between the Lamanites and the Nephites? (48:14) "A common objective of Lamanite warfare was to bring the Nephites into captivity. Nephites living under Lamanite control were normally required to pay tribute ..., and when captured in battle, they were usually taken back to become slaves or to be sacrificed. ... Nephite objectives ... were usually much different, at least as long as the people were living righteously. ... '[They] were inspired by a better cause, for they were not fighting for monarchy nor power but they were fighting for their homes and their liberties, their wives and their children, and their all, yea, for their rites of worship and their church' (Alma 43:45)" (Merrill, "Nephite Captains and Armies," 275–76). ⊕

children, and their peace, and that they might live unto the Lord their God, and that they might maintain that which was called by their enemies the cause of Christians.

11 And Moroni was a strong and a mighty man; he was a man of a perfect understanding; yea, a man that did not delight in bloodshed; a man whose soul did joy in the liberty and the freedom of his country, and his brethren from bondage and slavery;

12 Yea, a man whose heart did swell with thanksgiving to his God, for the many privileges and blessings which he bestowed upon his people; a man who did labor exceedingly for the welfare and safety of his people.

13 Yea, and he was a man who was firm in the faith of Christ, and he had sworn with an oath to defend his people, his rights, and his country, and his religion, even to the loss of his blood.

14 Now the Nephites were taught to defend themselves against their enemies, even to the shedding of blood if it were necessary; yea, and they were also taught never to give an offense, yea, and never to raise the sword except it were against an enemy, except it were to preserve their lives.

15 And this was their faith, that by so doing God would prosper them in the land, or in other words, if they were faithful in keeping the commandments of God that he would prosper them in the land; yea, warn them to flee, or to prepare for war, according to their danger;

16 And also, that God would make it known unto them whither they should go to defend themselves against their enemies, and by so doing, the Lord would deliver them; and this was the faith of Moroni, and his heart did glory in it; not in the shedding of blood but in doing good, in preserving his people, yea,

in keeping the commandments of God, yea, and resisting iniquity.

17 Yea, verily, verily I say unto you, if all men had been, and were, and ever would be, like unto Moroni, behold, the very powers of hell would have been shaken forever; yea, the devil would never have power over the hearts of the children of men.

18 Behold, he was a man like unto Ammon, the son of Mosiah, yea, and even the other sons of Mosiah, yea, and also Alma and his sons, for they were all men of God.

19 Now behold, Helaman and his brethren were no less serviceable unto the people than was Moroni; for they did preach the word of God, and they did baptize unto repentance all men whosoever would hearken unto their words.

20 And thus they went forth, and the people did humble themselves because of their words, insomuch that they were highly favored of the Lord, and thus they were free from wars and contentions among themselves, yea, even for the space of four years.

21 But, as I have said, in the latter end of the nineteenth year, yea, notwithstanding their peace amongst themselves, they were compelled reluctantly to contend with their brethren, the Lamanites.

22 Yea, and in fine, their wars never did cease for the space of many years with the Lamanites, notwithstanding their much reluctance.

23 Now, they were sorry to take up arms against the Lamanites, because they did not delight in the shedding of blood; yea, and this was not all—they were sorry to be the means of sending so many of their brethren out of this world into an eternal world, unprepared to meet their God.

Why was Moroni able to shake the powers of hell? (48:17) "Part of the reason we may not have sufficient priesthood bearers to save the Constitution, let alone to shake the powers of hell, is because unlike Moroni, I fear, our souls do not joy in keeping our country free, and we are not firm in the faith of Christ, nor have we sworn with an oath to defend our rights and the liberty of our country" (Benson, in Conference Report, Oct. 1966, 122).

How can we feel that we are "no less serviceable" when serving in less prominent positions? (48:19) "Even though Helaman was not as noticeable or conspicuous as Moroni, he was as serviceable; that is, he was as helpful or useful as Moroni. . . .

"Not all of us are going to be like Moroni, catching the acclaim of our colleagues all day every day. Most of us will be quiet, relatively unknown folks who come and go and do our work without fanfare. To those of you who may find that lonely or frightening or just unspectacular, I say, you are 'no less serviceable' than the most spectacular of your associates. You, too, are part of God's army" (Hunter, "No Less Serviceable," 64). ☉

Alma 48:21–25. The Nephites' Reaction to War Is Revealed

How frequently do the scriptures correlate prospering "in the land" with keeping God's commandments? (48:25) "The divine teaching—stated in the scriptures not once, but thirty-four times—[is] that people will prosper in the land only if they obey the commandments of God (see Lev. 26:3–15; Josh. 1:7–8; 1 Kgs. 2:3; 2 Kgs. 18:7; 2 Chr. 24:20; 26:5; 31:21; Ezra 6:14; Job 36:11; 1 Ne. 2:20; 4:14; 2 Ne. 1:9, 20, 31; 4:4; 5:10–11; Jarom 1:9; Omni 1:6; Mosiah 1:7; 2:22, 31; Alma 9:13; 36:1, 30; 37:13; 38:1; 45:6–8; 48:15, 25; 50:20; Hel. 3:20; 3 Ne. 5:22; D&C 9:13)" (Nelson, "Reverence for Life," 13).

Alma 49:1–11. The Lamanites Are Afraid to Attack the City of Ammonihah

Have archaeologists found anything similar to the kinds of fortifications Book of Mormon people used? (49:2–5) Proponents of various theories concerning the location of Book of Mormon lands suggest, some strongly, that Mesoamerica might be a logical fit. The Book of Mormon describes fortifications such as walled cites, ditches, and pickets. "A prime example of a topic on which expert views have changed dramatically to be more in agreement with the Book of Mormon is armed conflict. Until recently, the prevailing picture of Mesoamerica was that only peaceful societies existed . . . The big shift came with the 1970[s] . . . in the Yucatan Peninsula . . . The center of the site is surrounded by a ditch almost two kilometers in circumference and averaging sixteen meters across. The makers had piled the earth to form a ridge on the inner side of the ditch . . . 'To throw "uphill" from the outside is almost impossible. Defenders, possibly screened by a palisade, could

24 Nevertheless, they could not suffer to lay down their lives, that their wives and their children should be massacred by the barbarous cruelty of those who were once their brethren, yea, and had dissented from their church, and had left them and had gone to destroy them by joining the Lamanites.

25 Yea, they could not bear that their brethren should rejoice over the blood of the Nephites, so long as there were any who should keep the commandments of God, for the promise of the Lord was, if they should keep his commandments they should prosper in the land.

CHAPTER 49

The invading Lamanites are unable to take the fortified cities of Ammonihah and Noah—Amalickiah curses God and swears to drink the blood of Moroni—Helaman and his brethren continue to strengthen the Church. About 72 B.C.

1 And now it came to pass in the eleventh month of the nineteenth year, on the tenth day of the month, the armies of the Lamanites were seen approaching towards the land of Ammonihah.

2 And behold, the city had been rebuilt, and Moroni had stationed an army by the borders of the city, and they had cast up dirt round about to shield them from the arrows and the stones of the Lamanites; for behold, they fought with stones and with arrows.

3 Behold, I said that the city of Ammonihah had been rebuilt. I say unto you, yea, that it was in part rebuilt; and because the Lamanites had destroyed it once because of the iniquity of the people, they supposed that it would again become an easy prey for them.

4 But behold, how great was their disappointment; for behold, the Nephites had dug up a ridge of earth round about them, which

was so high that the Lamanites could not cast their stones and their arrows at them that they might take effect, neither could they come upon them save it was by their place of entrance.

5 Now at this time the chief captains of the Lamanites were astonished exceedingly, because of the wisdom of the Nephites in preparing their places of security.

6 Now the leaders of the Lamanites had supposed, because of the greatness of their numbers, yea, they supposed that they should be privileged to come upon them as they had hitherto done; yea, and they had also prepared themselves with shields, and with breastplates; and they had also prepared themselves with garments of skins, yea, very thick garments to cover their nakedness.

7 And being thus prepared they supposed that they should easily overpower and subject their brethren to the yoke of bondage, or slay and massacre them according to their pleasure.

8 But behold, to their uttermost astonishment, they were prepared for them, in a manner which never had been known among the children of Lehi. Now they were prepared for the Lamanites, to battle after the manner of the instructions of Moroni.

9 And it came to pass that the Lamanites, or the Amalickiahites, were exceedingly astonished at their manner of preparation for war.

10 Now, if king Amalickiah had come down out of the land of Nephi, at the head of his army, perhaps he would have caused the Lamanites to have attacked the Nephites at the city of Ammonihah; for behold, he did care not for the blood of his people.

11 But behold, Amalickiah did not come down himself to battle. And behold, his chief captains durst not attack the Nephites

have rained long-distance missiles on approaching enemies using spearthrowers and slings' [Webster, *Defensive Earthworks*, 96]. . . . This sounds almost like a paraphrase of Alma 49:18–20" (Sorenson, "Digging into the Book of Mormon," 33).

What does it mean to *cast* arrows? (49:4) "Surely the Indians of the northeastern United States that Joseph Smith knew about shot their arrows rather than 'cast them.' A primary war weapon among Mesoamerican peoples was the spear-thrower, or *atlatl*. . . . This implement consisted of a carved stick about eighteen inches long that was grasped at one end in the user's . . . hand as he extended his throwing arm behind him. The end of a relatively long, heavy arrow was placed with its blunt end against a notch at the far end of the atlatl, while two fingers of the user's hand held the projectile parallel to the throwing stick" (Sorenson, "How Could Joseph Smith Write So Accurately about Ancient American Civilization?" 295). ⊕

What does the fortifying of the Nephite cities teach us about following the guidance of spiritual leaders to prepare us for spiritual battle? (49:7–9) What counsel from your bishop, your stake president, or the prophet has helped you resist Satan's attacks? Can you recall a talk or counsel from a priesthood leader that gave you strength to resist a difficult temptation? Why do you think the Lord uses Church leaders to help us in our spiritual trials?

Alma 49:12–20. The Lamanites Take an Oath to Attack the City of Noah

In what ways can fortifying the city of Noah be compared to Ether 12:27? (49:13–14) In Ether 12:27 the Lord promises that if we humble ourselves before Him, He will turn our weaknesses to strengths. What weakness in your life has the Lord helped you fortify to make strong? What can you do to help others strengthen their weakness?

at the city of Ammonihah, for Moroni had altered the management of affairs among the Nephites, insomuch that the Lamanites were disappointed in their places of retreat and they could not come upon them.

12 Therefore they retreated into the wilderness, and took their camp and marched towards the land of Noah, supposing that to be the next best place for them to come against the Nephites.

13 For they knew not that Moroni had fortified, or had built forts of security, for every city in all the land round about; therefore, they marched forward to the land of Noah with a firm determination; yea, their chief captains came forward and took an oath that they would destroy the people of that city.

14 But behold, to their astonishment, the city of Noah, which had hitherto been a weak place, had now, by the means of Moroni, become strong, yea, even to exceed the strength of the city Ammonihah.

15 And now, behold, this was wisdom in Moroni; for he had supposed that they would be frightened at the city Ammonihah; and as the city of Noah had hitherto been the weakest part of the land, therefore they

What Have Latter-day Prophets Taught concerning War?

The First Presidency (Heber J. Grant, J. Reuben Clark Jr., and David O. McKay): "The Church is and must be against war. The Church itself cannot wage war, unless and until the Lord shall issue new commands. It cannot regard war as a righteous means of settling international disputes; these should and could be settled—the nations agreeing—by peaceful negotiation and adjustment.

"But the Church membership are citizens or subjects of sovereignties over which the Church has no control" ("Position of the Church on current issues such as war, military service . . . April 4, 1942," in Clark, *Messages of the First Presidency*, 6:158).

President David O. McKay: "There are . . . two conditions which may justify a truly Christian man to enter—mind you, I say *enter, not begin*—a war: (1) an attempt to dominate and to deprive another of his free agency, and (2) loyalty to his country. Possibly there is a third, viz., Defense of a weak nation that is being unjustly crushed by a strong, ruthless one. . . .

"*Paramount among these reasons, of course, is the defense of man's freedom.* An attempt to rob man of his free agency caused dissension even in heaven" (*Gospel Ideals*, 287, emphasis in original).

President Gordon B. Hinckley: "It is clear . . . that there are times and circumstances when nations are justified, in fact have an obligation, to fight for family, for liberty, and against tyranny, threat, and oppression" ("War and Peace," 80).

would march thither to battle; and thus it was according to his desires.

16 And behold, Moroni had appointed Lehi to be chief captain over the men of that city; and it was that same Lehi who fought with the Lamanites in the valley on the east of the river Sidon.

17 And now behold it came to pass, that when the Lamanites had found that Lehi commanded the city they were again disappointed, for they feared Lehi exceedingly; nevertheless their chief captains had sworn with an oath to attack the city; therefore, they brought up their armies.

18 Now behold, the Lamanites could not get into their forts of security by any other way save by the entrance, because of the highness of the bank which had been thrown up, and the depth of the ditch which had been dug round about, save it were by the entrance.

19 And thus were the Nephites prepared to destroy all such as should attempt to climb up to enter the fort by any other way, by casting over stones and arrows at them.

20 Thus they were prepared, yea, a body of their strongest men, with their swords and their slings, to smite down all who should attempt to come into their place of security by the place of entrance; and thus were they prepared to defend themselves against the Lamanites.

21 And it came to pass that the captains of the Lamanites brought up their armies before the place of entrance, and began to contend with the Nephites, to get into their place of security; but behold, they were driven back from time to time, insomuch that they were slain with an immense slaughter.

22 Now when they found that they could not obtain power over the Nephites by the pass, they began to dig down their banks of

Who was this Lehi? (49:16–17) Lehi was a "Nephite military commander [c. 74 B.C.]" who was highly trusted by Captain Moroni and played a major role in the Nephite-Lamanite wars (see "Index to the Triple Combination," ChurchofJesusChrist.org, s.v. "Lehi³"). Lehi encircled the Lamanites with his army (Alma 43:35) and was appointed chief captain over city of Noah (Alma 49:16–17). Lehi assisted Moroni in defeating the Lamanites (Alma 52:27–36; 62:32–34).

Alma 49:21–24. The Lamanites Are Defeated at the City of Noah

earth that they might obtain a pass to their armies, that they might have an equal chance to fight; but behold, in these attempts they were swept off by the stones and arrows which were thrown at them; and instead of filling up their ditches by pulling down the banks of earth, they were filled up in a measure with their dead and wounded bodies.

23 Thus the Nephites had all power over their enemies; and thus the Lamanites did attempt to destroy the Nephites until their chief captains were all slain; yea, and more than a thousand of the Lamanites were slain; while, on the other hand, there was not a single soul of the Nephites which was slain.

24 There were about fifty who were wounded, who had been exposed to the arrows of the Lamanites through the pass, but they were shielded by their shields, and their breastplates, and their head-plates, insomuch that their wounds were upon their legs, many of which were very severe.

How significant was the use of breastplates in Book of Mormon battles? (49:24) "Breastplates are the most common type of armor mentioned in the Book of Mormon. Most passages simply mention the use of breastplates and therefore offer no details as to their structure or material. Breastplates were said to protect the wearers from enemy weapons—'shielded from the strokes of the Lamanites by their breastplates' (Alma 43:38; 49:24)—but they could nonetheless be penetrated—'they did pierce many of their breastplates' (Alma 43:44). Breastplates were known to the Jaredites, at least in the last phases of their civilization (see Ether 15:15)" (Hamblin, "Armor in the Book of Mormon," 407).

Alma 49:25–30. The Nephites Thank the Lord for His Blessings

What led to Amalickiah's anger? (49:25–27) "So the great and carefully planned offensive with all its high hopes for a quick victory fizzled out, and a beaten army went back to report to the infuriated 'Führer.'... In a towering rage, 'exceedingly wroth ... he did curse God, and also Moroni, swearing with an oath that he would drink his blood' (Alma 49:27). At every step in his career he had found that man Moroni barring the way; at every step in the campaign his own army had played into the hands of that Moroni. No wonder Moroni began to be an obsession with him" (Nibley, *Since Cumorah*, 309).

25 And it came to pass, that when the Lamanites saw that their chief captains were all slain they fled into the wilderness. And it came to pass that they returned to the land of Nephi, to inform their king, Amalickiah, who was a Nephite by birth, concerning their great loss.

26 And it came to pass that he was exceedingly angry with his people, because he had not obtained his desire over the Nephites; he had not subjected them to the yoke of bondage.

27 Yea, he was exceedingly wroth, and he did curse God, and also Moroni, swearing with an oath that he would drink his blood; and this because Moroni had kept the commandments of God in preparing for the safety of his people.

28 And it came to pass, that on the other hand, the people of Nephi did thank the Lord their God, because of his matchless power in delivering them from the hands of their enemies.

29 And thus ended the nineteenth year of the reign of the judges over the people of Nephi.

30 Yea, and there was continual peace among them, and exceedingly great prosperity in the church because of their heed and diligence which they gave unto the word of God, which was declared unto them by Helaman, and Shiblon, and Corianton, and Ammon and his brethren, yea, and by all those who had been ordained by the holy order of God, being baptized unto repentance, and sent forth to preach among the people.

CHAPTER 50

Moroni fortifies the lands of the Nephites— They build many new cities—Wars and destructions befell the Nephites in the days of their wickedness and abominations—Morianton and his dissenters are defeated by Teancum— Nephihah dies, and his son Pahoran fills the judgment seat. About 72–67 B.C.

1 And now it came to pass that Moroni did not stop making preparations for war, or to defend his people against the Lamanites; for he caused that his armies should commence in the commencement of the twentieth year of the reign of the judges, that they should commence in digging up heaps of earth round about all the cities, throughout all the land which was possessed by the Nephites.

2 And upon the top of these ridges of earth he caused that there should be timbers, yea,

What is "being baptized unto repentance"? (49:30)
Adam was taught that repentance is a lifetime process, that "thou shalt repent and call upon God in the name of the Son forevermore" (Moses 5:8). "The Book of Mormon speaks repeatedly of being 'baptized unto repentance.' . . . The phrase appears in the Doctrine and Covenants as well (see D&C 35:5; 107:20). 'Baptism of or unto repentance' simply references the fact that baptism with its covenant of obedience is the capstone of repentance. With full repentance, including baptism, one is qualified for the laying on of hands for the gift of the Holy Ghost, and it is by the Holy Ghost that one receives the baptism of the Spirit (see John 3:5) and forgiveness of sins" (Christofferson, "Divine Gift of Repentance," 41n2).

Alma 50:1–6. Moroni's Armies Prepare for Attacks from the Lamanites

In what ways can Captain Moroni's example of continual preparation to protect his people teach us how to protect ourselves against sin? (50:1)
"There is another even more important preparation we must make for tests that are certain to come to each of us. . . .

"What we will need in our day of testing is a spiritual preparation. It is to have developed faith in Jesus Christ so powerful that we can pass the test of life upon which everything for us in eternity depends" (Eyring, "Spiritual Preparedness," 37). ☉

How do these ancient descriptions of fortifications match modern archaeological discoveries? (50:1–5) There are certain fascinating archaeological discoveries made after Joseph Smith's day that seem to parallel Book of Mormon descriptions. For example, in 1970, David L. Webster, who worked at one site in southeastern Mexico, described fortifications dating to about A.D. 250–300 that are similar to those mentioned in Alma 50: "The vertical distance from the top of the embankment to the bottom of the ditch . . . averaged something over [35 ft.]. . . . An enemy force caught in the bottom of the ditch would have been at the mercy of the defenders. . . . The attackers' approach would have been spotted by watchmen on tall towers, for which there is evidence" (Sorenson, "How Could Joseph Smith Write So Accurately about Ancient American Civilization?" 294–95).

Alma 50:7–12. Moroni's Armies Drive Out the Lamanites

Did Moroni build a physical structure between the Nephites and Lamanites? (50:7–12) Some have supposed "this line of defense to have been one continuous rampart, or wall—after the style of the Great Wall of China . . . [and] have argued that the completion of such an immense work in a few years was an impossibility. . . . The Book of Mormon conveys no such idea, it simply states that Moroni erected fortifications along this line. . . . Moroni took advantage of the natural features of the country, its wide rivers, far-reaching swamps, and high mountains, and built fortifications at every point where the Lamanites would find ingress. . . . There he stationed bodies of troops sufficiently strong to hold their posts, and, if necessary, defend the surrounding country" (Reynolds and Sjodahl, Commentary on the Book of Mormon, 5:65).

works of timbers built up to the height of a man, round about the cities.

3 And he caused that upon those works of timbers there should be a frame of pickets built upon the timbers round about; and they were strong and high.

4 And he caused towers to be erected that overlooked those works of pickets, and he caused places of security to be built upon those towers, that the stones and the arrows of the Lamanites could not hurt them.

5 And they were prepared that they could cast stones from the top thereof, according to their pleasure and their strength, and slay him who should attempt to approach near the walls of the city.

6 Thus Moroni did prepare strongholds against the coming of their enemies, round about every city in all the land.

7 And it came to pass that Moroni caused that his armies should go forth into the east wilderness; yea, and they went forth and drove all the Lamanites who were in the east wilderness into their own lands, which were south of the land of Zarahemla.

8 And the land of Nephi did run in a straight course from the east sea to the west.

9 And it came to pass that when Moroni had driven all the Lamanites out of the east wilderness, which was north of the lands of their own possessions, he caused that the inhabitants who were in the land of Zarahemla and in the land round about should go forth into the east wilderness, even to the borders by the seashore, and possess the land.

10 And he also placed armies on the south, in the borders of their possessions, and caused them to erect fortifications that they might secure their armies and their people from the hands of their enemies.

11 And thus he cut off all the strongholds of the Lamanites in the east wilderness, yea, and also on the west, fortifying the line between the Nephites and the Lamanites, between the land of Zarahemla and the land of Nephi, from the west sea, running by the head of the river Sidon—the Nephites possessing all the land northward, yea, even all the land which was northward of the land Bountiful, according to their pleasure.

12 Thus Moroni, with his armies, which did increase daily because of the assurance of protection which his works did bring forth unto them, did seek to cut off the strength and the power of the Lamanites from off the lands of their possessions, that they should have no power upon the lands of their possession.

13 And it came to pass that the Nephites began the foundation of a city, and they called the name of the city Moroni; and it was by the east sea; and it was on the south by the line of the possessions of the Lamanites.

14 And they also began a foundation for a city between the city of Moroni and the city of Aaron, joining the borders of Aaron and Moroni; and they called the name of the city, or the land, Nephihah.

15 And they also began in that same year to build many cities on the north, one in a particular manner which they called Lehi, which was in the north by the borders of the seashore.

16 And thus ended the twentieth year.

17 And in these prosperous circumstances were the people of Nephi in the commencement of the twenty and first year of the reign of the judges over the people of Nephi.

18 And they did prosper exceedingly, and they became exceedingly rich; yea, and they did multiply and wax strong in the land.

Alma 50:13–24. The Nephites Build Up Their Cities and Prosper

How is this unusual phrasing, "they called the name of the city . . . ," similar to Hebrew phrasing? (50:13–14) "When a child is born, we say in English that his [parents] 'called him X.' . . . The same is true in naming places, for example, 'He called his ranch Pleasant Valley.' But Hebrew expresses it quite differently: 'He called the name of his son X.' In Hebrew, it is the *name* that is 'called,' not the child or the place. Perhaps the best-known example from the Bible is the one found in Isaiah 7:14: 'Behold, a virgin shall conceive, and bear a son, and shall call his name Immanuel.' This idiom is found in a number of places in the Book of Mormon [1 Nephi 16:13; Mosiah 1:2; Alma 23:17 are quoted]" (Tvedtnes, "Hebrew Background," 89).

What blessings do faith and obedience bring in times of war? (50:20) "We forget that if we are righteous the Lord will either not suffer our enemies to come upon us—and this is the special promise to the inhabitants of the land of the Americas (see 2 Ne. 1:7)—or he will fight our battles for us" (Kimball, "False Gods We Worship," 6).

What is the relationship between peace and keeping the commandments? (50:21–23) "As we seek to understand the causes of wars, persecutions, and civil strife, we can see that they are almost always rooted in wickedness. . . .

"The blessings of the gospel are universal, and so is the formula for peace: keep the commandments of God. War and conflict are the result of wickedness; peace is the product of righteousness. . . .

"We have wars and conflicts, and everywhere they are rooted in violations of the commandments of God. . . .

"We cannot have peace among nations without achieving general righteousness among the people who comprise them. . . .

"If citizens do not have a basic goodness to govern their actions toward one another, we can never achieve peace in the world" (Oaks, "World Peace," 71–72).

Why do you think the people of Nephi were so happy during times of war? (50:22–23) How is it possible that happiness can be found in an atmosphere of war? How can people "be of good cheer" when dealing with calamity? Elder Neal A. Maxwell noted: "Jesus used the same encouraging words when, having healed a paralytic, He did not emphasize the health restored; rather, He said, 'Be of good cheer; thy sins is forgiven thee.' Like freedom from death, emancipation from error is always a special reason for being of good cheer" (Even As I Am, 100).

What brings true happiness? (50:23) Sister Linda K. Burton, general Relief Society president, taught that "keeping covenants is essential for true happiness." She explained: "President Thomas S. Monson taught, 'Sacred covenants are to be revered by us, and

19 And thus we see how merciful and just are all the dealings of the Lord, to the fulfilling of all his words unto the children of men; yea, we can behold that his words are verified, even at this time, which he spake unto Lehi, saying:

20 Blessed art thou and thy children; and they shall be blessed, inasmuch as they shall keep my commandments they shall prosper in the land. But remember, inasmuch as they will not keep my commandments they shall be cut off from the presence of the Lord.

21 And we see that these promises have been verified to the people of Nephi; for it has been their quarrelings and their contentions, yea, their murderings, and their plunderings, their idolatry, their whoredoms, and their abominations, which were among themselves, which brought upon them their wars and their destructions.

22 And those who were faithful in keeping the commandments of the Lord were delivered at all times, whilst thousands of their wicked brethren have been consigned to bondage, or to perish by the sword, or to dwindle in unbelief, and mingle with the Lamanites.

23 But behold there never was a happier time among the people of Nephi, since the days of Nephi, than in the days of Moroni, yea, even at this time, in the twenty and first year of the reign of the judges.

24 And it came to pass that the twenty and second year of the reign of the judges also ended in peace; yea, and also the twenty and third year.

faithfulness to them is a requirement for happiness.' In 2 Nephi we read, 'And it came to pass that we lived after the manner of happiness.' Earlier in this same chapter we learn that Nephi and his people had just built a temple. Surely they were joyful covenant keepers! [In Alma 50:22 we learn that these happy people] 'were faithful in keeping the commandments of the Lord.' Covenant keepers are commandment keepers!" ("Power, Joy, and Love of Covenant Keeping," 113).

Alma 50:25–36. The People of Morianton Rebel against the Nephites

Why was Moroni concerned about Morianton's contention and potential dissension? (50:25–28)
"Dissidents, in his view, were covenant-breakers. Their lack of trust in God or concern for the community of the saints put the whole people in jeopardy." Moroni "saw dissension as a root cause of Nephite problems. . . .

"'For it was his first care to put an end to such contentions and dissensions among the people for behold, this had been hitherto a cause of all their destruction' [Alma 51:16]. . . . One cannot blame Moroni for his sensitivity to dissension. Without exception, every enemy specifically identified by Mormon in Alma 43–63 is a body of Nephite dissenters or a group led by a Nephite dissenter (eg 43:5–8; 46:3–7; 50:25–28; 51:16; 52:3; 61:8)" (Valletta, "Captain and the Covenant," 244).

25 And it came to pass that in the commencement of the twenty and fourth year of the reign of the judges, there would also have been peace among the people of Nephi had it not been for a contention which took place among them concerning the land of Lehi, and the land of Morianton, which joined upon the borders of Lehi; both of which were on the borders by the seashore.

26 For behold, the people who possessed the land of Morianton did claim a part of the land of Lehi; therefore there began to be a warm contention between them, insomuch that the people of Morianton took up arms against their brethren, and they were determined by the sword to slay them.

27 But behold, the people who possessed the land of Lehi fled to the camp of Moroni, and appealed unto him for assistance; for behold they were not in the wrong.

28 And it came to pass that when the people of Morianton, who were led by a man whose name was Morianton, found that the people of Lehi had fled to the camp of Moroni, they were exceedingly fearful lest the army of Moroni should come upon them and destroy them.

29 Therefore, Morianton put it into their hearts that they should flee to the land which was northward, which was covered with large bodies of water, and take possession of the land which was northward.

30 And behold, they would have carried this plan into effect, (which would have been a cause to have been lamented) but behold, Morianton being a man of much passion, therefore he was angry with one of his maid servants, and he fell upon her and beat her much.

31 And it came to pass that she fled, and came over to the camp of Moroni, and told Moroni all things concerning the matter, and also concerning their intentions to flee into the land northward.

32 Now behold, the people who were in the land Bountiful, or rather Moroni, feared that they would hearken to the words of Morianton and unite with his people, and thus he would obtain possession of those parts of the land, which would lay a foundation for serious consequences among the people of Nephi, yea, which consequences would lead to the overthrow of their liberty.

33 Therefore Moroni sent an army, with their camp, to head the people of Morianton, to stop their flight into the land northward.

34 And it came to pass that they did not head them until they had come to the borders of the land Desolation; and there they did head them, by the narrow pass which led by the sea into the land northward, yea, by the sea, on the west and on the east.

35 And it came to pass that the army which was sent by Moroni, which was led by a man whose name was Teancum, did meet the people of Morianton; and so stubborn were the people of Morianton, (being inspired by his wickedness and his flattering words) that a battle commenced between them, in the which Teancum did slay Morianton and defeat his army, and took them prisoners, and returned to the camp of Moroni. And thus ended the twenty and fourth year of the reign of the judges over the people of Nephi.

Who was Teancum? (50:35) Teancum was a highly skilled Nephite military leader who led an elite squad of Nephite "warriors . . . in their strength and in their skill of war" (Alma 51:31). Teancum's warriors successfully prevented a small army of rebellious Nephites in their treacherous allegiance with the Lamanites (see Alma 50:35). In an effort to end the long Nephite-Lamanite wars, Teancum slew Amalickiah (see Alma 51:33–34) and eventually slew Amalickiah's brother Ammoron; however, Teancum was in turn slain (see Alma 62:35–36). A Nephite city was named after him (see Mormon 4:3-7, 14).

36 And thus were the people of Morianton brought back. And upon their covenanting to keep the peace they were restored to the land of Morianton, and a union took place between them and the people of Lehi; and they were also restored to their lands.

37 And it came to pass that in the same year that the people of Nephi had peace restored unto them, that Nephihah, the second chief judge, died, having filled the judgment-seat with perfect uprightness before God.

38 Nevertheless, he had refused Alma to take possession of those records and those things which were esteemed by Alma and his fathers to be most sacred; therefore Alma had conferred them upon his son, Helaman.

39 Behold, it came to pass that the son of Nephihah was appointed to fill the judgment-seat, in the stead of his father; yea, he was appointed chief judge and governor over the people, with an oath and sacred ordinance to judge righteously, and to keep the peace and the freedom of the people, and to grant unto them their sacred privileges to worship the Lord their God, yea, to support and maintain the cause of God all his days, and to bring the wicked to justice according to their crime.

40 Now behold, his name was Pahoran. And Pahoran did fill the seat of his father, and did commence his reign in the end of the twenty and fourth year, over the people of Nephi.

Alma 50:37–40. Pahoran Is Appointed Chief Judge

What is significant about the number twenty-four? (50:39–40) "Consider the significance of the number twenty-four in ancient Israel and in the Book of Mormon. Certain numbers were clearly meaningful in antiquity: seven was the number of spiritual perfection (as in the seven seals in the book of Revelation); twelve was a governmental number (as with the twelve tribes, twelve apostles). The number twenty-four, being a multiple of twelve, was associated with heavenly government, especially priestly judgment and temple service. . . .

"The text of the governmental oath of the Nephite chief judge to 'judge righteously' happens to be reported only in the account of the twenty-fourth year of the reign of Judges (Alma 50:39–40)" (Welch, "Number 24," 272–74).

Alma 51:1–8. A Group of Nephites Known as King-Men Desire a King to Rule over Them

How frequent were internal contentions among the Nephites? (51:1–8) "No fewer than four different internal rebellions occurred among the Nephites during the time when all their forces should have been marshaled to fight against the Lamanites (Alma 50:25–36; 51:1–8; 53:8–9; 61:3–4)" (Hansen, "Book of Alma as a Prototype," 278).

Who were the "king-men"? (51:5) "[This] group seemed to be citizens who simply desired some changes in the law. [Mormon] reveals them as the same kind of people who have cropped up throughout the history of the Nephites in Zarahemla.

"They want a king—which involves much more than a change in the style of government. A monarchy entails an entire lifestyle associated with kings. . . . The people who wanted a king were always the richest. . . . They want a king . . . because a king represented the way of life that supported the value of the wealth they had acquired. . . . [With] that wealth comes a set of values and concepts that include costly apparel, elitism, and a system of social classes" (Gardner, *Second Witness*, 4:558–59).

CHAPTER 51

The king-men seek to change the law and set up a king—Pahoran and the freemen are supported by the voice of the people—Moroni compels the king-men to defend their country or be put to death—Amalickiah and the Lamanites capture many fortified cities—Teancum repels the Lamanite invasion and slays Amalickiah in his tent. About 67–66 B.C.

1 And now it came to pass in the commencement of the twenty and fifth year of the reign of the judges over the people of Nephi, they having established peace between the people of Lehi and the people of Morianton concerning their lands, and having commenced the twenty and fifth year in peace;

2 Nevertheless, they did not long maintain an entire peace in the land, for there began to be a contention among the people concerning the chief judge Pahoran; for behold, there were a part of the people who desired that a few particular points of the law should be altered.

3 But behold, Pahoran would not alter nor suffer the law to be altered; therefore, he did not hearken to those who had sent in their voices with their petitions concerning the altering of the law.

4 Therefore, those who were desirous that the law should be altered were angry with him, and desired that he should no longer be chief judge over the land; therefore there arose a warm dispute concerning the matter, but not unto bloodshed.

5 And it came to pass that those who were desirous that Pahoran should be dethroned from the judgment-seat were called kingmen, for they were desirous that the law should be altered in a manner to overthrow the free government and to establish a king over the land.

6 And those who were desirous that Pahoran should remain chief judge over the land took upon them the name of freemen; and thus was the division among them, for the freemen had sworn or covenanted to maintain their rights and the privileges of their religion by a free government.

7 And it came to pass that this matter of their contention was settled by the voice of the people. And it came to pass that the voice of the people came in favor of the freemen, and Pahoran retained the judgment-seat, which caused much rejoicing among the brethren of Pahoran and also many of the people of liberty, who also put the king-men to silence, that they durst not oppose but were obliged to maintain the cause of freedom.

8 Now those who were in favor of kings were those of high birth, and they sought to be kings; and they were supported by those who sought power and authority over the people.

9 But behold, this was a critical time for such contentions to be among the people of Nephi; for behold, Amalickiah had again stirred up the hearts of the people of the Lamanites against the people of the Nephites, and he was gathering together soldiers from all parts of his land, and arming them, and preparing for war with all diligence; for he had sworn to drink the blood of Moroni.

10 But behold, we shall see that his promise which he made was rash; nevertheless, he did prepare himself and his armies to come to battle against the Nephites.

11 Now his armies were not so great as they had hitherto been, because of the many thousands who had been slain by the hand of the Nephites; but notwithstanding their great loss, Amalickiah had gathered together a wonderfully great army, insomuch that

In what ways does maintaining freedom of religion benefit society? (51:5–6) "Religious teachings and religious organizations are vital to our free society and therefore deserving of its special legal protection.

"Our country's robust private sector of charitable works originated with and is still sponsored most significantly by religious organizations and religious impulses. This includes education, hospitals, care for the poor, and countless other charities of great value to our country" (Oaks, "Strengthening the Free Exercise of Religion," 1). ⊕

Who were the "freemen"? (51:6) "[To] this point in Nephite history, the people have either been religiously united or separated into two factions: church-men and non-church-men. [Now] there are freemen and king-men. . . . The factions are sufficiently large and cohesive that they cannot only be named but be named in opposition to each other—opposition so severe that civil war is the next step. This is an absolute opposition of political, social, and religious worldviews. The dispute is so fundamental that mediation will not work. One side must win, and the other lose" (Gardner, *Second Witness*, 4:659).

Alma 51:9–12. Amalickiah Organizes a Lamanite Army to Fight the Nephites

Why did Amalickiah choose this particular time to gather his armies against the Nephites? (51:9–11) "Amalickiah . . . had not forgotten his ambitious dreams of subjecting the entire people of Nephi to his ungodly notions, and thereby make slaves of them. He had not relinquished any of his evil designs. . . .

"Neither had Amalickiah forgotten his boast that he would 'drink the blood of Moroni,' nor did he leave a thing undone that would bring about that end. The Sacred Record states that 'this was a critical time' for the Nephites to be torn by political strife, and that the contentions among them regarding the Chief Judge deprived them of a united effort in combating the serious menace always posed by the Lamanites" (Reynolds and Sjodahl, *Commentary on the Book of Mormon*, 5:91).

Alma 51:13–21. Captain Moroni Settles a Civil War Involving the King-Men

What are Church members' responsibilities to their countries during a time of war? (51:13–15) President Russell M. Nelson taught: "Members of this Church will be called into military service of many nations. . . .

"During the Second World War, when members of the Church were forced to fight on opposing sides, the First Presidency affirmed that 'the state is responsible for the civil control of its citizens or subjects, for their political welfare, and for the carrying forward of political policies, domestic and foreign. . . . But the Church itself, as such, has no responsibility for these policies, [other] than urging its members fully to render . . . loyalty to their country' (in Clark, *Messages of the First Presidency*, 6:155–56)" ("Blessed Are the Peacemakers," 40).

Why did Moroni enforce the law upon dissenters? (51:15–17) "Though some of Moroni's actions might be offensive to the more pacifistic of this modern age, he acted in harmony with what he felt was his and others' duty to God, even to the point of compelling dissenters to take up arms in support of the government during war (see Alma 51:15–16). At those times when he sensed that moral support for government or the cause of liberty was fading, Moroni single-handedly sought to foster enthusiasm and engender support for the government by reminding the people of their promises to God" (McConkie and Millet, *Doctrinal Commentary*, 3:323).

he feared not to come down to the land of Zarahemla.

12 Yea, even Amalickiah did himself come down, at the head of the Lamanites. And it was in the twenty and fifth year of the reign of the judges; and it was at the same time that they had begun to settle the affairs of their contentions concerning the chief judge, Pahoran.

13 And it came to pass that when the men who were called king-men had heard that the Lamanites were coming down to battle against them, they were glad in their hearts; and they refused to take up arms, for they were so wroth with the chief judge, and also with the people of liberty, that they would not take up arms to defend their country.

14 And it came to pass that when Moroni saw this, and also saw that the Lamanites were coming into the borders of the land, he was exceedingly wroth because of the stubbornness of those people whom he had labored with so much diligence to preserve; yea, he was exceedingly wroth; his soul was filled with anger against them.

15 And it came to pass that he sent a petition, with the voice of the people, unto the governor of the land, desiring that he should read it, and give him (Moroni) power to compel those dissenters to defend their country or to put them to death.

16 For it was his first care to put an end to such contentions and dissensions among the people; for behold, this had been hitherto a cause of all their destruction. And it came to pass that it was granted according to the voice of the people.

17 And it came to pass that Moroni commanded that his army should go against those king-men, to pull down their pride and their nobility and level them with the earth,

or they should take up arms and support the cause of liberty.

18 And it came to pass that the armies did march forth against them; and they did pull down their pride and their nobility, insomuch that as they did lift their weapons of war to fight against the men of Moroni they were hewn down and leveled to the earth.

19 And it came to pass that there were four thousand of those dissenters who were hewn down by the sword; and those of their leaders who were not slain in battle were taken and cast into prison, for there was no time for their trials at this period.

20 And the remainder of those dissenters, rather than be smitten down to the earth by the sword, yielded to the standard of liberty, and were compelled to hoist the title of liberty upon their towers, and in their cities, and to take up arms in defence of their country.

21 And thus Moroni put an end to those king-men, that there were not any known by the appellation of king-men; and thus he put an end to the stubbornness and the pride of those people who professed the blood of nobility; but they were brought down to humble themselves like unto their brethren, and to fight valiantly for their freedom from bondage.

22 Behold, it came to pass that while Moroni was thus breaking down the wars and contentions among his own people, and subjecting them to peace and civilization, and making regulations to prepare for war against the Lamanites, behold, the Lamanites had come into the land of Moroni, which was in the borders by the seashore.

23 And it came to pass that the Nephites were not sufficiently strong in the city of Moroni; therefore Amalickiah did drive them, slaying many. And it came to pass that

How did Moroni put an end to the king-men? (51:18–21) "Moroni's petition was not to kill whoever chose not to fight. Notice that there was not time for a trial (Alma 51:19). Five years later, the men of Pachus, also king-men, 'received their trial, according to the law' and those who would 'fight against [their country] were put to death.' This action was taken 'for the safety of their country' (Alma 62:9–10). In a similar situation today, the same action may be justified. Notice also that the dissenters were given the choice to defend their country or be put to death (Alma 51:15). Moroni's actions put an end to the king-men and to the stubbornness and pride of those 'who professed the blood of nobility' (v. 21)" (Nyman, *Record of Helaman*, 115).

Alma 51:22–37. Amalickiah's Lamanites Capture Many Nephite Cities, and Teancum Kills Amalickiah in His Tent

What erodes the peace of a nation and what does that erosion lead to? (51:22) "Mormon showed, by his account, that wickedness brought dissent, and dissent brought the threat of destruction from outside forces. The only way that the Nephites could stay free was to stay righteous" (Garrett, "Inspired by a Better Cause," 76).

Division and contention destroy peace. Consider those times when you have seen division and contention destroy peace in a family, circle of friends, or neighborhood. What helped solve the division or contention? What can you do to help put an end to the division and contention among those with whom you live, work, or attend school?

Amalickiah took possession of the city, yea, possession of all their fortifications.

24 And those who fled out of the city of Moroni came to the city of Nephihah; and also the people of the city of Lehi gathered themselves together, and made preparations and were ready to receive the Lamanites to battle.

25 But it came to pass that Amalickiah would not suffer the Lamanites to go against the city of Nephihah to battle, but kept them down by the seashore, leaving men in every city to maintain and defend it.

26 And thus he went on, taking possession of many cities, the city of Nephihah, and the city of Lehi, and the city of Morianton, and the city of Omner, and the city of Gid, and the city of Mulek, all of which were on the east borders by the seashore.

27 And thus had the Lamanites obtained, by the cunning of Amalickiah, so many cities, by their numberless hosts, all of which were strongly fortified after the manner of the fortifications of Moroni; all of which afforded strongholds for the Lamanites.

28 And it came to pass that they marched to the borders of the land Bountiful, driving the Nephites before them and slaying many.

29 But it came to pass that they were met by Teancum, who had slain Morianton and had headed his people in his flight.

30 And it came to pass that he headed Amalickiah also, as he was marching forth with his numerous army that he might take possession of the land Bountiful, and also the land northward.

31 But behold he met with a disappointment by being repulsed by Teancum and his men, for they were great warriors; for every man of Teancum did exceed the Lamanites in their strength and in their skill of war,

When did the Lamanites eventually capture Nephihah? (51:25–26) "Although the historian of this part of the record mentions in Alma 51:25 that the Lamanites decided not 'to go against the city of Nephihah to battle,' in the next verse the historian records that the Lamanites went on 'taking possession of many cities, the city of Nephihah, and the city of Lehi . . . ,' etc. Although it is not clear whether or not the historian intended to include the city of Nephihah in this list, it is evident that the city is captured later by the Lamanites (see Alma 59:7–9)" (Ludlow, *Companion to Your Study of the Book of Mormon*, 236).

insomuch that they did gain advantage over the Lamanites.

32 And it came to pass that they did harass them, insomuch that they did slay them even until it was dark. And it came to pass that Teancum and his men did pitch their tents in the borders of the land Bountiful; and Amalickiah did pitch his tents in the borders on the beach by the seashore, and after this manner were they driven.

33 And it came to pass that when the night had come, Teancum and his servant stole forth and went out by night, and went into the camp of Amalickiah; and behold, sleep had overpowered them because of their much fatigue, which was caused by the labors and heat of the day.

34 And it came to pass that Teancum stole privily into the tent of the king, and put a javelin to his heart; and he did cause the death of the king immediately that he did not awake his servants.

35 And he returned again privily to his own camp, and behold, his men were asleep, and he awoke them and told them all the things that he had done.

36 And he caused that his armies should stand in readiness, lest the Lamanites had awakened and should come upon them.

37 And thus endeth the twenty and fifth year of the reign of the judges over the people of Nephi; and thus endeth the days of Amalickiah.

What was the significance of Teancum's night raid? (51:33–34) "One interesting feature of this attack is that it was consistent with ancient custom. Hugh Nibley has noted that in ancient warfare, since set combat was usually forbidden after sundown, 'the wee small hours were reserved for the standard attack on the rival's tent, a vital maneuver, since once the tent had fallen, the enemy's morale, and often his resistance, was broken. . . . The ultimate in heroic gestures for the Arab was a night-raid on the tent of a chief'(Nibley, "Tenting, Toll, and Taxing," 618)" (Merrill, "Nephite Captains and Armies," 274). ◐

What do we know about the Nephite calendar system? (51:37) "The exact nature of the Nephite year . . . is not described. The Nephite year began with the 'first day' of the 'first month' (Alma 51:37–52:1; 56:1), and it probably had twelve months because the eleventh month was at 'the latter end' of the year (Alma 48:2, 21; 49:1), but the lengths of the months and of the year itself are not mentioned" (Ludlow, *Encyclopedia of Mormonism*, 1:169–70).

CHAPTER 52

Ammoron succeeds Amalickiah as king of the Lamanites—Moroni, Teancum, and Lehi lead the Nephites in a victorious war against the Lamanites—The city of Mulek is retaken, and Jacob the Zoramite is slain. About 66–64 B.C.

1 And now, it came to pass in the twenty and sixth year of the reign of the judges over the people of Nephi, behold, when the Lamanites awoke on the first morning of the first month, behold, they found Amalickiah was dead in his own tent; and they also saw that Teancum was ready to give them battle on that day.

2 And now, when the Lamanites saw this they were affrighted; and they abandoned their design in marching into the land northward, and retreated with all their army into the city of Mulek, and sought protection in their fortifications.

3 And it came to pass that the brother of Amalickiah was appointed king over the people; and his name was Ammoron; thus king Ammoron, the brother of king Amalickiah, was appointed to reign in his stead.

4 And it came to pass that he did command that his people should maintain those cities, which they had taken by the shedding of blood; for they had not taken any cities save they had lost much blood.

5 And now, Teancum saw that the Lamanites were determined to maintain those cities which they had taken, and those parts of the land which they had obtained possession of; and also seeing the enormity of their number, Teancum thought it was not expedient that he should attempt to attack them in their forts.

6 But he kept his men round about, as if making preparations for war; yea, and truly he was preparing to defend himself against

Alma 52:1–11. The Lamanites Appoint a New King While the Nephites Prepare for War

Why was the date of Amalickiah's death significant? (52:1–2) "In the ancient Old World, the New Year celebration was viewed as the birthday of the world. It was a day of coronation of divine and earthly kings, a day of victory over chaos, a day of renewal of covenant and the reenactment of the king's enthronement, and a day of temple dedication and record keeping. . . .

"Imagine the confusion caused when the Lamanites awoke on New Year's Day to find that King Amalickiah had been murdered on New Year's Eve" (Smith and Ricks, "New Year's Celebrations," 209).

Who was Ammoron? (52:3) Ammoron was a descendant of Zoram and a Nephite traitor who became king of the Lamanites (about 66–64 B.C.). After Teancum killed Amalickiah, Ammoron was appointed king (see Alma 52:3). Ammoron continued the campaign started by his brother to destroy all Nephites who would not be subjected to a life of servitude. During the war, Ammoron exchanged heated and threatening letters with Captain Moroni over the exchange of prisoners (see Alma 54; 55). In these letters, Ammoron's impure and revengeful motives are exposed. He threatens to subject "the Nephites to our authority or to their eternal extinction" (Alma 54:20). During the war, Ammoron is also slain by Teancum (Alma 62:36). Later we learn that Ammoron's son, Tubaloth becomes king of the Lamanites (see Helaman 1:16).

them, by casting up walls round about and preparing places of resort.

7 And it came to pass that he kept thus preparing for war until Moroni had sent a large number of men to strengthen his army.

8 And Moroni also sent orders unto him that he should retain all the prisoners who fell into his hands; for as the Lamanites had taken many prisoners, that he should retain all the prisoners of the Lamanites as a ransom for those whom the Lamanites had taken.

9 And he also sent orders unto him that he should fortify the land Bountiful, and secure the narrow pass which led into the land northward, lest the Lamanites should obtain that point and should have power to harass them on every side.

10 And Moroni also sent unto him, desiring him that he would be faithful in maintaining that quarter of the land, and that he would seek every opportunity to scourge the Lamanites in that quarter, as much as was in his power, that perhaps he might take again by stratagem or some other way those cities which had been taken out of their hands; and that he also would fortify and strengthen the cities round about, which had not fallen into the hands of the Lamanites.

11 And he also said unto him, I would come unto you, but behold, the Lamanites are upon us in the borders of the land by the west sea; and behold, I go against them, therefore I cannot come unto you.

12 Now, the king (Ammoron) had departed out of the land of Zarahemla, and had made known unto the queen concerning the death of his brother, and had gathered together a large number of men, and had marched forth against the Nephites on the borders by the west sea.

What was significant about the land of Bountiful? (52:9) "It marked and guarded the northern boundary of Nephite territory and held an important military position preventing the Lamanites from completely encircling the Nephites and thereby blocking their escape into the land northward. Because this outpost was of vital interest to Nephite security . . . and Lamanite prisoners were held there . . . , it is reasonable to assume that once Moroni fortified this site . . . , no one was stationed or allowed to live there who was not fiercely and unquestionably loyal to the Nephite cause. The fact that these settlers built, operated, and maintained a temple in this remote and obscure site confirms their devotion to the most orthodox Nephite values and traditional practices" (Welch, "The Temple," 367–68).

Alma 52:12–18. The Lamanites Gather Large Armies to Attack the Nephites

13 And thus he was endeavoring to harass the Nephites, and to draw away a part of their forces to that part of the land, while he had commanded those whom he had left to possess the cities which he had taken, that they should also harass the Nephites on the borders by the east sea, and should take possession of their lands as much as it was in their power, according to the power of their armies.

14 And thus were the Nephites in those dangerous circumstances in the ending of the twenty and sixth year of the reign of the judges over the people of Nephi.

15 But behold, it came to pass in the twenty and seventh year of the reign of the judges, that Teancum, by the command of Moroni—who had established armies to protect the south and the west borders of the land, and had begun his march towards the land Bountiful, that he might assist Teancum with his men in retaking the cities which they had lost—

16 And it came to pass that Teancum had received orders to make an attack upon the city of Mulek, and retake it if it were possible.

17 And it came to pass that Teancum made preparations to make an attack upon the city of Mulek, and march forth with his army against the Lamanites; but he saw that it was impossible that he could overpower them while they were in their fortifications; therefore he abandoned his designs and returned again to the city Bountiful, to wait for the coming of Moroni, that he might receive strength to his army.

18 And it came to pass that Moroni did arrive with his army at the land of Bountiful, in the latter end of the twenty and seventh year of the reign of the judges over the people of Nephi.

What important gospel truth can we derive from Teancum's abandoning his attack on the city of Mulek? (52:17) "Like these great Nephite military leaders, we must be wise and cautious as we battle against evil.... Some of our young people who are sincere in their desire to help their wayward friends may unwittingly end up going into the enemy's territory to try to bring them back to the gospel side of the line. They may think, 'If I go to such and such a party, I can be a positive influence by not drinking and thus encourage my struggling friends who will see my good example.' Unfortunately, they don't realize that by doing this they are entering into the adversary's stronghold, and ... they must realize that the odds are against them" (McClendon, "Captain Moroni's Wartime Strategies," 112).

19 And in the commencement of the twenty and eighth year, Moroni and Teancum and many of the chief captains held a council of war—what they should do to cause the Lamanites to come out against them to battle; or that they might by some means flatter them out of their strongholds, that they might gain advantage over them and take again the city of Mulek.

20 And it came to pass they sent embassies to the army of the Lamanites, which protected the city of Mulek, to their leader, whose name was Jacob, desiring him that he would come out with his armies to meet them upon the plains between the two cities. But behold, Jacob, who was a Zoramite, would not come out with his army to meet them upon the plains.

21 And it came to pass that Moroni, having no hopes of meeting them upon fair grounds, therefore, he resolved upon a plan that he might decoy the Lamanites out of their strongholds.

22 Therefore he caused that Teancum should take a small number of men and march down near the seashore; and Moroni and his army, by night, marched in the wilderness, on the west of the city Mulek; and thus, on the morrow, when the guards of the Lamanites had discovered Teancum, they ran and told it unto Jacob, their leader.

23 And it came to pass that the armies of the Lamanites did march forth against Teancum, supposing by their numbers to overpower Teancum because of the smallness of his numbers. And as Teancum saw the armies of the Lamanites coming out against him he began to retreat down by the seashore, northward.

24 And it came to pass that when the Lamanites saw that he began to flee, they took courage and pursued them with vigor. And while Teancum was thus leading away the

Alma 52:19–26. The Nephite Armies Recapture Mulek

What can we learn about Nephite decoy strategies from these passages? (52:19–26) "Keep in mind that you are not reading about the battles in chronological order. Many of the battles on the eastern front that you read about first actually occurred after some of the major battles on the western front. For example, the 'decoy method' of capturing cities was employed by Helaman and Antipus in their attempt to recapture the city of Antiparah on the western front (Alma 56:20, 27–57) before it was used successfully by Moroni and Teancum in recapturing the city of Mulek on the eastern front (Alma 52:19–26)" (Ludlow, *Companion to Your Study of the Book of Mormon*, 230).

How did Teancum formulate the strategy against the city of Mulek? (52:19) "Not all military conflict in antiquity was characterized by formal, set battles. What we in modern times call guerrilla war typified much ancient warfare. . . .

"Battles began with the dispatching of scouts to reconnoiter for food, trails, and the location of enemy troops. Most ancient armies used spies and other means to gain intelligence, and the Book of Mormon frequently mentions the importance of spies and other Nephite intelligence operations. Military leaders generally made battle plans shortly before the army encountered the enemy. Such plans were frequently formulated by a council of officers and professional soldiers who discussed the situation and offered suggestions" (Hamblin, "Importance of Warfare in Book of Mormon Studies," 491).

Who was Jacob? (52:20) Jacob, a Zoramite, was a military leader in the Lamanite army and was known for his "unconquerable spirit" (Alma 53:33). Jacob and his army were fooled by a military decoy launched by Moroni. Moroni effectively drew out the Lamanites by ordering Teancum and a small army to march in front of the Lamanite armies (see Alma 52:21–35). Jacob lost his life in a major battle with Moroni's troops (Alma 52:35).

Lamanites who were pursuing them in vain, behold, Moroni commanded that a part of his army who were with him should march forth into the city, and take possession of it.

25 And thus they did, and slew all those who had been left to protect the city, yea, all those who would not yield up their weapons of war.

26 And thus Moroni had obtained possession of the city Mulek with a part of his army, while he marched with the remainder to meet the Lamanites when they should return from the pursuit of Teancum.

27 And it came to pass that the Lamanites did pursue Teancum until they came near the city Bountiful, and then they were met by Lehi and a small army, which had been left to protect the city Bountiful.

28 And now behold, when the chief captains of the Lamanites had beheld Lehi with his army coming against them, they fled in much confusion, lest perhaps they should not obtain the city Mulek before Lehi should overtake them; for they were wearied because of their march, and the men of Lehi were fresh.

29 Now the Lamanites did not know that Moroni had been in their rear with his army; and all they feared was Lehi and his men.

30 Now Lehi was not desirous to overtake them till they should meet Moroni and his army.

31 And it came to pass that before the Lamanites had retreated far they were surrounded by the Nephites, by the men of Moroni on one hand, and the men of Lehi on the other, all of whom were fresh and full of strength; but the Lamanites were wearied because of their long march.

32 And Moroni commanded his men that they should fall upon them until they had given up their weapons of war.

Alma 52:27–40. The Lamanites Who Have Been Surrounded Surrender to Moroni

What is known about battles that would explain the Lamanites' confusion and fear of being overtaken by Lehi? (52:28) "If panic began to spread in the ranks, a complete and sudden collapse could result. . . . Most casualties occurred during the flight and pursuit, after the main units had broken up. Battles in the Book of Mormon often end with just such rout, flight, and destruction of an army (see Alma 52:28; 62:31)" (Hamblin, "Warfare in the Book of Mormon," 246).

What was one difference between Captain Moroni and the Zoramite military leaders? (52:32–39) "It was up to [the Lamanite leaders] to decide when to quit. . . . As soon as they gave [their weapons] up, that was it. There was not extermination here. Then

33 And it came to pass that Jacob, being their leader, being also a Zoramite, and having an unconquerable spirit, he led the Lamanites forth to battle with exceeding fury against Moroni.

34 Moroni being in their course of march, therefore Jacob was determined to slay them and cut his way through to the city of Mulek. But behold, Moroni and his men were more powerful; therefore they did not give way before the Lamanites.

35 And it came to pass that they fought on both hands with exceeding fury; and there were many slain on both sides; yea, and Moroni was wounded and Jacob was killed.

36 And Lehi pressed upon their rear with such fury with his strong men, that the Lamanites in the rear delivered up their weapons of war; and the remainder of them, being much confused, knew not whither to go or to strike.

37 Now Moroni seeing their confusion, he said unto them: If ye will bring forth your weapons of war and deliver them up, behold we will forbear shedding your blood.

38 And it came to pass that when the Lamanites had heard these words, their chief captains, all those who were not slain, came forth and threw down their weapons of war at the feet of Moroni, and also commanded their men that they should do the same.

39 But behold, there were many that would not; and those who would not deliver up their swords were taken and bound, and their weapons of war were taken from them, and they were compelled to march with their brethren forth into the land Bountiful.

40 And now the number of prisoners who were taken exceeded more than the number of those who had been slain, yea, more than those who had been slain on both sides.

notice the good old Zoramites. They were all Nephites to begin with; therefore, they were apostates and were very bitter. Jacob wants to go on fighting. The Lamanites don't, but he does. . . .

"Moroni said, 'If ye will bring forth your weapons of war . . . we will forbear shedding your blood.' He always does that" (Nibley, *Teachings of the Book of Mormon*, 3:158–59).

Alma 53:1–9. The Nephites Make the Lamanite Prisoners Work to Build Up Cities

What was the Nephite strategy with prisoners? (53:1–6) "When the Nephites took prisoners, they made good (but not excessive) use of them. Moroni had Lamanite prisoners both bury those slain in battle and fortify the city of Bountiful so that it became a suitable 'stronghold to retain . . . prisoners.' By doing so, he not only freed up Nephite troops for battle, but he also made guarding the prisoners easier (Alma 53:1–6). If prisoners did attempt to escape or revolt, they were slain (see Alma 57:30–34).

"Prisoners were not sought after, however, as a cheap form of slave labor. Instead, Nephites generally avoided taking prisoners by allowing captured troops to go free if they yielded up their weapons and covenanted not to fight again" (Welch, "Law and War in the Book of Mormon," 76–77). ◉

What lesson can we draw from the fortification of the Nephite cities for war? (53:4–5) "To avoid . . . temptations, be like Captain Moroni of old; set up 'fortifications' to strengthen your places of weakness. Instead of building walls of 'timbers and dirt' to protect a vulnerable city, build 'fortifications' in the form of personal ground rules to protect your priceless virtue. . . .

"One key fortification you can build is to decide now, before you face a challenge, where to draw the line. Our prophet teaches that if we decide now not to watch inappropriate media but instead to walk away, 'the challenge is behind us'" (Hinckley, "Prophet's Counsel and Prayer for Youth," 4)" (Sorensen, "You Can't Pet a Rattlesnake," 41–42). ◉

CHAPTER 53

The Lamanite prisoners are used to fortify the city Bountiful—Dissensions among the Nephites give rise to Lamanite victories—Helaman takes command of the two thousand stripling sons of the people of Ammon. About 64–63 B.C.

1 And it came to pass that they did set guards over the prisoners of the Lamanites, and did compel them to go forth and bury their dead, yea, and also the dead of the Nephites who were slain; and Moroni placed men over them to guard them while they should perform their labors.

2 And Moroni went to the city of Mulek with Lehi, and took command of the city and gave it unto Lehi. Now behold, this Lehi was a man who had been with Moroni in the more part of all his battles; and he was a man like unto Moroni, and they rejoiced in each other's safety; yea, they were beloved by each other, and also beloved by all the people of Nephi.

3 And it came to pass that after the Lamanites had finished burying their dead and also the dead of the Nephites, they were marched back into the land Bountiful; and Teancum, by the orders of Moroni, caused that they should commence laboring in digging a ditch round about the land, or the city, Bountiful.

4 And he caused that they should build a breastwork of timbers upon the inner bank of the ditch; and they cast up dirt out of the ditch against the breastwork of timbers; and thus they did cause the Lamanites to labor until they had encircled the city of Bountiful round about with a strong wall of timbers and earth, to an exceeding height.

5 And this city became an exceeding stronghold ever after; and in this city they did guard the prisoners of the Lamanites; yea, even within a wall which they had caused them to build with their own hands. Now Moroni was compelled to cause the Lamanites to labor, because it was easy to guard them while at their labor; and he desired all his forces when he should make an attack upon the Lamanites.

6 And it came to pass that Moroni had thus gained a victory over one of the greatest of the armies of the Lamanites, and had obtained possession of the city of Mulek, which was one of the strongest holds of the Lamanites in the land of Nephi; and thus he had also built a stronghold to retain his prisoners.

7 And it came to pass that he did no more attempt a battle with the Lamanites in that year, but he did employ his men in preparing for war, yea, and in making fortifications to guard against the Lamanites, yea, and also delivering their women and their children from famine and affliction, and providing food for their armies.

8 And now it came to pass that the armies of the Lamanites, on the west sea, south, while in the absence of Moroni on account of some intrigue amongst the Nephites, which caused dissensions amongst them, had gained some ground over the Nephites, yea, insomuch that they had obtained possession of a number of their cities in that part of the land.

9 And thus because of iniquity amongst themselves, yea, because of dissensions and intrigue among themselves they were placed in the most dangerous circumstances.

10 And now behold, I have somewhat to say concerning the people of Ammon, who, in the beginning, were Lamanites; but by Ammon and his brethren, or rather by the power and

Why did Mormon highlight dissension among the Nephites as a dangerous circumstance? (53:8–9) "Mormon views the conflict between the Nephites and Lamanites from a spiritual context. There is no mention here of the superior military strength of the Lamanites as a reason for their advantage in battle, but it comes from the dissensions among the Nephites. This message is consistent throughout the Book of Mormon—the Lord defended the Nephites (or His covenant people) when they were righteous. ... Hugh Nibley has observed: '[The Lamanites] were not the Nephite problem. They were merely kept there to remind the Nephites of their real problem which was to walk uprightly before the Lord' (Nibley, *Since Cumorah*, 376)" (Bassett, "Nephi's Freedom Thesis and the Sons of Helaman," 293).

Alma 53:10–23. The Two Thousand Stripling Soldiers Join the Army of the Nephites

Why did the people of Ammon consider breaking their oath by returning to their weapons of war? (53:10–13) "The Nephites protected them for many years, but eventually the Nephite army began to wear down, and reinforcements were gravely needed (see Alma 53:8–9; 56:10–17).

"The people of Ammon were at a critical moment of their spiritual lives. They had been true to their covenant never to take up arms. But they understood that fathers are responsible to provide protection to their families (see *Ensign*, Nov. 2010, 129). That need seemed great enough to merit consideration of breaking their covenant (see Alma 53:10–13)" (Scott, "Personal Strength through the Atonement," 82).

Why was it vital that the people of Ammon keep their promises to God? (53:14–16) "Their wise priesthood leader, Helaman, knew that breaking a covenant with the Lord is never justified" (Scott, "Personal Strength through the Atonement," 82).

"A covenant is an agreement between God and man. . . . In these divine agreements, God binds Himself to sustain, sanctify, and exalt us in return for our commitment to serve Him and keep His commandments. . . ."

Keeping covenants "[produces] the faith necessary to persevere and to do all things that are expedient in the Lord. Our willingness to take upon us the name of Christ and keep His commandments requires a degree of faith, but as we honor our covenants, that faith expands" (Christofferson, "Power of Covenants," 20–21).

word of God, they had been converted unto the Lord; and they had been brought down into the land of Zarahemla, and had ever since been protected by the Nephites.

11 And because of their oath they had been kept from taking up arms against their brethren; for they had taken an oath that they never would shed blood more; and according to their oath they would have perished; yea, they would have suffered themselves to have fallen into the hands of their brethren, had it not been for the pity and the exceeding love which Ammon and his brethren had had for them.

12 And for this cause they were brought down into the land of Zarahemla; and they ever had been protected by the Nephites.

13 But it came to pass that when they saw the danger, and the many afflictions and tribulations which the Nephites bore for them, they were moved with compassion and were desirous to take up arms in the defence of their country.

14 But behold, as they were about to take their weapons of war, they were overpowered by the persuasions of Helaman and his brethren, for they were about to break the oath which they had made.

15 And Helaman feared lest by so doing they should lose their souls; therefore all those who had entered into this covenant were compelled to behold their brethren wade through their afflictions, in their dangerous circumstances at this time.

16 But behold, it came to pass they had many sons, who had not entered into a covenant that they would not take their weapons of war to defend themselves against their enemies; therefore they did assemble themselves together at this time, as many as were able to take up arms, and they called themselves Nephites.

17 And they entered into a covenant to fight for the liberty of the Nephites, yea, to protect the land unto the laying down of their lives; yea, even they covenanted that they never would give up their liberty, but they would fight in all cases to protect the Nephites and themselves from bondage.

18 Now behold, there were two thousand of those young men, who entered into this covenant and took their weapons of war to defend their country.

19 And now behold, as they never had hitherto been a disadvantage to the Nephites, they became now at this period of time also a great support; for they took their weapons of war, and they would that Helaman should be their leader.

20 And they were all young men, and they were exceedingly valiant for courage, and also for strength and activity; but behold, this was not all—they were men who were true at all times in whatsoever thing they were entrusted.

21 Yea, they were men of truth and soberness, for they had been taught to keep the commandments of God and to walk uprightly before him.

22 And now it came to pass that Helaman did march at the head of his two thousand stripling soldiers, to the support of the people in the borders of the land on the south by the west sea.

23 And thus ended the twenty and eighth year of the reign of the judges over the people of Nephi.

Why was it important for the sons of the people of Ammon to keep their covenants like their fathers? (53:17–18) The fathers covenanted not to take up arms to kill. The sons covenanted never to give up their liberty and to protect their land, agreeing to fight in defense. Why were they both important covenants to keep?

What helps us to be "true at all times"? (53:20) President Dallin H. Oaks quoted Alma 53:20–21 and then suggested an application for those who have entered into sacred covenants: "Men and women who have made covenants to serve the Lord . . . are you being true to the faith? Do you have the faith and continuing commitment to demonstrate the principles of the gospel in your own lives, consistently? You have served well, but do you, like the pioneers, have the courage and the consistency to be true to the faith and to endure to the end?" ("Following the Pioneers," 73).

When might we have to be "valiant for courage" like Helaman's stripling warriors? (53:20–21) "There will be times when you . . . will have to demonstrate your righteous courage in plain view of your peers, the consequence of which may be ridicule and embarrassment. Additionally, . . . skirmishes with the adversary will also be fought on a silent, solitary battlefield in front of a screen. Technology with its substantial benefits also brings challenges not faced by generations before you" (Stevenson, "Be Valiant in Courage, Strength, and Activity," 52).

"Often you will experience much criticism and ridicule even by those who believe as you do, even though they may respect you for doing right. But remember that the Savior himself was tormented, ridiculed, spat upon, and finally crucified because he would not waver in his conviction" (Tanner, "'For They Loved the Praise of Men,'" 74). ◉

What made Helaman's soldiers so exceptional? (53:20–22) The spiritual environment in the homes of Helaman's soldiers was surely an important influence in the lives of these young men. Former Relief Society general president Julie B. Beck described the powerful influence of parents who teach the gospel in their homes: "A well-taught friend told me that he did not learn anything at church that he had not already learned at home. His parents used family scripture study, prayer, family home evening, mealtimes, and other gatherings to teach. Think of the power of our future missionary force if mothers considered their homes as a pre–missionary training center. Then the doctrines of the gospel taught in the MTC would be a review and not a revelation" ("Mothers Who Know," 77).

Alma 54:1–14. Moroni and Ammoron Correspond and Discuss Trading Prisoners

What are the real causes of war? (54:5) "The roots of the causes of war lie deeply bedded in vanity, selfishness, unjust commercialism, unrighteousness, and other things contrary to the spirit of the Gospel of Jesus Christ. O, if they could only apply the Gospel in their nationalism! But they consider it only as a thing apart from daily life—as something to be treated as a mere social function. They haven't felt that it is a vital force, the vital force in humanity" (McKay, *Pathways to Happiness*, 356).

CHAPTER 54

Ammoron and Moroni negotiate for the exchange of prisoners—Moroni demands that the Lamanites withdraw and cease their murderous attacks—Ammoron demands that the Nephites lay down their arms and become subject to the Lamanites. About 63 B.C.

1 And now it came to pass in the commencement of the twenty and ninth year of the judges, that Ammoron sent unto Moroni desiring that he would exchange prisoners.

2 And it came to pass that Moroni felt to rejoice exceedingly at this request, for he desired the provisions which were imparted for the support of the Lamanite prisoners for the support of his own people; and he also desired his own people for the strengthening of his army.

3 Now the Lamanites had taken many women and children, and there was not a woman nor a child among all the prisoners of Moroni, or the prisoners whom Moroni had taken; therefore Moroni resolved upon a stratagem to obtain as many prisoners of the Nephites from the Lamanites as it were possible.

4 Therefore he wrote an epistle, and sent it by the servant of Ammoron, the same who had brought an epistle to Moroni. Now these are the words which he wrote unto Ammoron, saying:

5 Behold, Ammoron, I have written unto you somewhat concerning this war which ye have waged against my people, or rather which thy brother hath waged against them, and which ye are still determined to carry on after his death.

6 Behold, I would tell you somewhat concerning the justice of God, and the sword of his almighty wrath, which doth hang over you except ye repent and withdraw your armies into your own lands, or the land of your possessions, which is the land of Nephi.

7 Yea, I would tell you these things if ye were capable of hearkening unto them; yea, I would tell you concerning that awful hell that awaits to receive such murderers as thou and thy brother have been, except ye repent and withdraw your murderous purposes, and return with your armies to your own lands.

8 But as ye have once rejected these things, and have fought against the people of the Lord, even so I may expect you will do it again.

9 And now behold, we are prepared to receive you; yea, and except you withdraw your purposes, behold, ye will pull down the wrath of that God whom you have rejected upon you, even to your utter destruction.

10 But, as the Lord liveth, our armies shall come upon you except ye withdraw, and ye shall soon be visited with death, for we will retain our cities and our lands; yea, and we will maintain our religion and the cause of our God.

11 But behold, it supposeth me that I talk to you concerning these things in vain; or it supposeth me that thou art a child of hell; therefore I will close my epistle by telling you that I will not exchange prisoners, save it be on conditions that ye will deliver up a man and his wife and his children, for one prisoner; if this be the case that ye will do it, I will exchange.

12 And behold, if ye do not this, I will come against you with my armies; yea, even I will arm my women and my children, and I will come against you, and I will follow you even

What is the underlying problem seen in the letters between Moroni and Ammoron? (54:6–11) "These letters between Moroni and Ammoron have to do less with exchange of prisoners than with the irreconcilable conflict between the powers of God and Satan, with Moroni appearing as the Christian champion....

"The issues Moroni outlines are these: The purposes of Ammoron and of Amalickiah before him are blatantly murderous. In spiritual terms, the Lamanites have fought against the people of the Lord, and unless they abandon their plans, they will incur the wrath of God to their destruction (in Book of Mormon terms, the ultimate curse—one that eventually comes to the Nephites). For their part, the Nephites vow to stand firm in their religion and with their God" (Rust, *Feasting on the Word*, 150–51). ☉

Who was required to fight in times of war? (54:12) "The only Book of Mormon group given an exemption from military service was the famous people of Ammon.... Normally one duty of ancient peoples was to take up arms in defense of their tribe or nation...."

Moroni had power to punish any person in the land of Zarahemla who would not 'defend [his] country' (Alma 51:15; Alma 46:35). . . . [Moroni] symbolically portrayed the brutal fate of those who would not fight (see Alma 46:21–22). Under extreme and desperate circumstances, this duty fell even upon old men, women, and children (see Mosiah 10:9; Alma 54:12)" (Welch, "Exemption from Military Duty," 189–90).

Why was Moroni's anger justified? (54:13–14) In righteously fulfilling his duty to protect the people, Moroni expressed justified anger toward Ammoron for his murderous attacks. President Gordon B. Hinckley observed: "Anger may be justified in some circumstances. The scriptures tell us that Jesus drove the moneychangers from the temple, saying, 'My house shall be called the house of prayer; but ye have made it a den of thieves' (Matthew 21:13).

"But even this was spoken more as a rebuke than as an outburst of uncontrolled anger" ("Slow to Anger," 66). ⊕

Alma 54:15–24. Ammoron Demands the Nephites' Surrender

What accounted for the Lamanite hatred toward the Nephites? (54:16–20) "Besides feeling personally obligated to avenge the blood of his brother, Ammoron went back to the origins of tribal conflict in the earliest days of the Nephite–Lamanite split. . . . While political aspirations were undoubtedly tied up in Ammoron's declaration, it is important to note that he appealed to a deeply rooted tribal or clan rivalry as the motivation for his political goals. In perpetuating this tribal antagonism, Ammoron promoted an ideology fundamentally at odds with the egalitarian and anti-tribal ideals of Nephite prophets (cf. 2 Nephi 26:33; Mosiah 4:19; 4 Nephi 1:2, 17)" (Book of Mormon Central, "Why Was Ammoron Determined to Avenge the Blood of His Brother?").

into your own land, which is the land of our first inheritance; yea, and it shall be blood for blood, yea, life for life; and I will give you battle even until you are destroyed from off the face of the earth.

13 Behold, I am in my anger, and also my people; ye have sought to murder us, and we have only sought to defend ourselves. But behold, if ye seek to destroy us more we will seek to destroy you; yea, and we will seek our land, the land of our first inheritance.

14 Now I close my epistle. I am Moroni; I am a leader of the people of the Nephites.

15 Now it came to pass that Ammoron, when he had received this epistle, was angry; and he wrote another epistle unto Moroni, and these are the words which he wrote, saying:

16 I am Ammoron, the king of the Lamanites; I am the brother of Amalickiah whom ye have murdered. Behold, I will avenge his blood upon you, yea, and I will come upon you with my armies for I fear not your threatenings.

17 For behold, your fathers did wrong their brethren, insomuch that they did rob them of their right to the government when it rightly belonged unto them.

18 And now behold, if ye will lay down your arms, and subject yourselves to be governed by those to whom the government doth rightly belong, then will I cause that my people shall lay down their weapons and shall be at war no more.

19 Behold, ye have breathed out many threatenings against me and my people; but behold, we fear not your threatenings.

20 Nevertheless, I will grant to exchange prisoners according to your request, gladly, that I may preserve my food for my men of war; and we will wage a war which shall be eternal, either to the subjecting the Nephites to our authority or to their eternal extinction.

21 And as concerning that God whom ye say we have rejected, behold, we know not such a being; neither do ye; but if it so be that there is such a being, we know not but that he hath made us as well as you.

22 And if it so be that there is a devil and a hell, behold will he not send you there to dwell with my brother whom ye have murdered, whom ye have hinted that he hath gone to such a place? But behold these things matter not.

23 I am Ammoron, and a descendant of Zoram, whom your fathers pressed and brought out of Jerusalem.

24 And behold now, I am a bold Lamanite; behold, this war hath been waged to avenge their wrongs, and to maintain and to obtain their rights to the government; and I close my epistle to Moroni.

CHAPTER 55

Moroni refuses to exchange prisoners—The Lamanite guards are enticed to become drunk, and the Nephite prisoners are freed—The city of Gid is taken without bloodshed. About 63–62 B.C.

1 Now it came to pass that when Moroni had received this epistle he was more angry, because he knew that Ammoron had a perfect knowledge of his fraud; yea, he knew that Ammoron knew that it was not a just cause that had caused him to wage a war against the people of Nephi.

2 And he said: Behold, I will not exchange prisoners with Ammoron save he will

Was Ammoron a Lamanite? (54:24) "Ammoron closes with an identification of his authority, just as Moroni did; however, he claims the authority of an identity created by separation from his Nephite roots. Even though he and his brother had been part of the Nephite political world before their defection to the Lamanites, he declares that he was never really Nephite, but rather a Zoramite who remembers the wrong done to Zoram by Nephi. Ammoron is now a 'bold Lamanite.' This war is justified by grudges from wrongs almost six centuries old" (Gardner, *Second Witness*, 4:694).

Alma 55:1–21. Moroni Refuses to Trade Prisoners and Instead Uses a Stratagem to Free the Nephite Prisoners

withdraw his purpose, as I have stated in my epistle; for I will not grant unto him that he shall have any more power than what he hath got.

3 Behold, I know the place where the Lamanites do guard my people whom they have taken prisoners; and as Ammoron would not grant unto me mine epistle, behold, I will give unto him according to my words; yea, I will seek death among them until they shall sue for peace.

4 And now it came to pass that when Moroni had said these words, he caused that a search should be made among his men, that perhaps he might find a man who was a descendant of Laman among them.

5 And it came to pass that they found one, whose name was Laman; and he was one of the servants of the king who was murdered by Amalickiah.

6 Now Moroni caused that Laman and a small number of his men should go forth unto the guards who were over the Nephites.

7 Now the Nephites were guarded in the city of Gid; therefore Moroni appointed Laman and caused that a small number of men should go with him.

8 And when it was evening Laman went to the guards who were over the Nephites, and behold, they saw him coming and they hailed him; but he saith unto them: Fear not; behold, I am a Lamanite. Behold, we have escaped from the Nephites, and they sleep; and behold we have taken of their wine and brought with us.

9 Now when the Lamanites heard these words they received him with joy; and they said unto him: Give us of your wine, that we may drink; we are glad that ye have thus taken wine with you for we are weary.

Why did Moroni need a Lamanite for his strategy to work? (55:4–8) "What could a Lamanite do that a non-Lamanite could not? For most readers, conditioned by years of assumptions, the assumption is that he is darker skinned while Nephites were 'white.' However, this reason is unlikely, given the actual working-out of the plan (v. 8). . . .

"According to the record, Laman does all of the talking, and the guards immediately accept his announcement that he is a Lamanite. Thus, there is a language difference between the two groups. . . . Lamanites identified Laman's voice as soon as they heard it as truly 'Lamanite'" (Gardner, *Second Witness*, 4:696–97).

10 But Laman said unto them: Let us keep of our wine till we go against the Nephites to battle. But this saying only made them more desirous to drink of the wine;

11 For, said they: We are weary, therefore let us take of the wine, and by and by we shall receive wine for our rations, which will strengthen us to go against the Nephites.

12 And Laman said unto them: You may do according to your desires.

13 And it came to pass that they did take of the wine freely; and it was pleasant to their taste, therefore they took of it more freely; and it was strong, having been prepared in its strength.

14 And it came to pass they did drink and were merry, and by and by they were all drunken.

15 And now when Laman and his men saw that they were all drunken, and were in a deep sleep, they returned to Moroni and told him all the things that had happened.

16 And now this was according to the design of Moroni. And Moroni had prepared his men with weapons of war; and he went to the city Gid, while the Lamanites were in a deep sleep and drunken, and cast in weapons of war unto the prisoners, insomuch that they were all armed;

17 Yea, even to their women, and all those of their children, as many as were able to use a weapon of war, when Moroni had armed all those prisoners; and all those things were done in a profound silence.

18 But had they awakened the Lamanites, behold they were drunken and the Nephites could have slain them.

19 But behold, this was not the desire of Moroni; he did not delight in murder or bloodshed, but he delighted in the saving of his people from destruction; and for this

Why did Moroni's plan to free the Nephite prisoners work so well? (55:10–18) "The trick exploited the well-known psychology of troops on permanent guard duty. Such troops must always be on the alert for what they never expect to happen and what, if they do their duty, never will happen. Their way of life becomes a stultifying bore, with the same dull routines from day to day and from week to week. Nothing offers a more welcome release to such misery than a little nip now and then, or, better still, a party. . . . It was a typical 'G.I.' binge with everybody getting happily drunk at the guardhouse since the stuff was doctored" (Nibley, *Since Cumorah*, 316).

What do these verses remind us about Moroni's character? (55:18–19) "Grounded in the faith of Jesus Christ, Captain Moroni defended his people, their rights, and their religion. He sustained the Nephite tradition to never give offense and to raise the sword only against aggressive enemies . . . after having approached the Lord for his help and guidance in fervent prayer" (Jenkins, "'Peaceable Followers of Christ' in Days of War and Contention," 91–93). ⊕

cause he might not bring upon him injustice, he would not fall upon the Lamanites and destroy them in their drunkenness.

20 But he had obtained his desires; for he had armed those prisoners of the Nephites who were within the wall of the city, and had given them power to gain possession of those parts which were within the walls.

21 And then he caused the men who were with him to withdraw a pace from them, and surround the armies of the Lamanites.

22 Now behold this was done in the nighttime, so that when the Lamanites awoke in the morning they beheld that they were surrounded by the Nephites without, and that their prisoners were armed within.

23 And thus they saw that the Nephites had power over them; and in these circumstances they found that it was not expedient that they should fight with the Nephites; therefore their chief captains demanded their weapons of war, and they brought them forth and cast them at the feet of the Nephites, pleading for mercy.

24 Now behold, this was the desire of Moroni. He took them prisoners of war, and took possession of the city, and caused that all the prisoners should be liberated, who were Nephites; and they did join the army of Moroni, and were a great strength to his army.

25 And it came to pass that he did cause the Lamanites, whom he had taken prisoners, that they should commence a labor in strengthening the fortifications round about the city Gid.

26 And it came to pass that when he had fortified the city Gid, according to his desires, he caused that his prisoners should be taken to the city Bountiful; and he also guarded that city with an exceedingly strong force.

Alma 55:22–26. Moroni's Army Captures the City of Gid

What does this account teach us about Moroni's character? (55:23–24) "Moroni 'did not delight in murder or bloodshed.' According to the Prophet Joseph Smith, 'When you find a spirit that wants bloodshed—murder, the same is not of God, but is of the devil' (*Teachings of the Prophet Joseph Smith*, 358)" (*The Book of Mormon for Latter-day Saint Families*, 426).

27 And it came to pass that they did, notwithstanding all the intrigues of the Lamanites, keep and protect all the prisoners whom they had taken, and also maintain all the ground and the advantage which they had retaken.

28 And it came to pass that the Nephites began again to be victorious, and to reclaim their rights and their privileges.

29 Many times did the Lamanites attempt to encircle them about by night, but in these attempts they did lose many prisoners.

30 And many times did they attempt to administer of their wine to the Nephites, that they might destroy them with poison or with drunkenness.

31 But behold, the Nephites were not slow to remember the Lord their God in this their time of affliction. They could not be taken in their snares; yea, they would not partake of their wine, save they had first given to some of the Lamanite prisoners.

32 And they were thus cautious that no poison should be administered among them; for if their wine would poison a Lamanite it would also poison a Nephite; and thus they did try all their liquors.

33 And now it came to pass that it was expedient for Moroni to make preparations to attack the city Morianton; for behold, the Lamanites had, by their labors, fortified the city Morianton until it had become an exceeding stronghold.

34 And they were continually bringing new forces into that city, and also new supplies of provisions.

35 And thus ended the twenty and ninth year of the reign of the judges over the people of Nephi.

Alma 55:27–35. The Nephites Are Protected As They Reclaim Their Lands

What opposition did the Nephites deal with after capturing the city of Gid? (55:27–30) "The Lamanites whom Moroni had captured were continually on the alert to regain their lost advantage, and were quick to attempt their escape from Nephite duress. The Nephites, on the other hand, were equally awake to the possibility that any pretext might be used by the Lamanite prisoners to effect their release. Therefore all the moves made by the Nephites were guarded, and a watchful care was taken that no Lamanite surprises would disrupt the orderly plan which Moroni had resolved. The Nephites by a constant vigilance were able to thwart any and all schemes of the Lamanites to regain the advantage they had lost to Moroni's men" (Reynolds and Sjodahl, *Commentary on the Book of Mormon*, 5:120–21).

How can we ensure that we are "not slow to remember the Lord"? (55:31) Why is it hard to remember God during times of ease? How does remembering Heavenly Father's love for us help us overcome adversity?

Alma 56:1–8. Helaman Tells of the Converted Lamanites' Covenant

How does the Nephite calendar correlate with our own? (56:1) If, as some hypothesize, the Nephite wars took place in Mesoamerica, then it may be relevant that "during the reign of the judges warfare was mostly limited to four consecutive Nephite months. These months can be approximately correlated with our calendar because even today warfare in Mesoamerica . . . is conducted mostly during the dry season after the fall harvest. This correlation implies that the Nephite year at that time began in December" (Ludlow, *Encyclopedia of Mormonism*, 1:170–71).

What should we remember when going to war to defend our country? (56:5) "As citizens of nations and members of the true church of Jesus Christ, we need to know and follow the Lord's counsel concerning our involvement in war. . . . 'Therefore, renounce war and proclaim peace, and seek diligently to turn the hearts of the children to their fathers, and the hearts of the fathers to the children' (D&C 98:16). The Lord's people are peacemakers and their message is one of peace. However, our ability to live in peace depends upon our retention of our freedom under the law. Sometimes our freedoms are threatened and we are required to defend our country, homes, families and God-given rights of free agency" (Otten and Caldwell, *Sacred Truths of the Doctrine and Covenants*, 2:168).

CHAPTER 56

Helaman sends an epistle to Moroni, recounting the state of the war with the Lamanites—Antipus and Helaman gain a great victory over the Lamanites—Helaman's two thousand stripling sons fight with miraculous power, and none of them are slain. Verse 1, about 62 B.C.; verses 2–19, about 66 B.C.; and verses 20–57, about 65–64 B.C.

1 And now it came to pass in the commencement of the thirtieth year of the reign of the judges, on the second day in the first month, Moroni received an epistle from Helaman, stating the affairs of the people in that quarter of the land.

2 And these are the words which he wrote, saying: My dearly beloved brother, Moroni, as well in the Lord as in the tribulations of our warfare; behold, my beloved brother, I have somewhat to tell you concerning our warfare in this part of the land.

3 Behold, two thousand of the sons of those men whom Ammon brought down out of the land of Nephi—now ye have known that these were descendants of Laman, who was the eldest son of our father Lehi;

4 Now I need not rehearse unto you concerning their traditions or their unbelief, for thou knowest concerning all these things—

5 Therefore it sufficeth me that I tell you that two thousand of these young men have taken their weapons of war, and would that I should be their leader; and we have come forth to defend our country.

6 And now ye also know concerning the covenant which their fathers made, that they would not take up their weapons of war against their brethren to shed blood.

7 But in the twenty and sixth year, when they saw our afflictions and our tribulations for them, they were about to break the covenant which they had made and take up their weapons of war in our defence.

8 But I would not suffer them that they should break this covenant which they had made, supposing that God would strengthen us, insomuch that we should not suffer more because of the fulfilling the oath which they had taken.

9 But behold, here is one thing in which we may have great joy. For behold, in the twenty and sixth year, I, Helaman, did march at the head of these two thousand young men to the city of Judea, to assist Antipus, whom ye had appointed a leader over the people of that part of the land.

10 And I did join my two thousand sons, (for they are worthy to be called sons) to the army of Antipus, in which strength Antipus did rejoice exceedingly; for behold, his army had been reduced by the Lamanites because their forces had slain a vast number of our men, for which cause we have to mourn.

11 Nevertheless, we may console ourselves in this point, that they have died in the cause of their country and of their God, yea, and they are happy.

12 And the Lamanites had also retained many prisoners, all of whom are chief captains, for none other have they spared alive. And we suppose that they are now at this time in the land of Nephi; it is so if they are not slain.

13 And now these are the cities of which the Lamanites have obtained possession by the shedding of the blood of so many of our valiant men:

14 The land of Manti, or the city of Manti, and the city of Zeezrom, and the city of Cumeni, and the city of Antiparah.

Why was Helaman adamant that the people of Ammon not break their covenant? (56:7–8) "Divine covenants make strong Christians. I urge each one to qualify for and receive all the priesthood ordinances you can and then faithfully keep the promises you have made by covenant. In times of distress, let your covenants be paramount and let your obedience be exact. Then you can ask in faith, nothing wavering, according to your need, and God will answer. He will sustain you as you work and watch. In His own time and way He will stretch forth his hand to you, saying, 'Here am I'" (Christofferson, "Power of Covenants," 22). ○

Alma 56:9–20. Helaman's Army Joins the Army of Antipus

Why did the Nephites find comfort in their worthy dead? (56:10–11) "There is no equivocation, no doubt, no uncertainty in our minds. Those who have been true and faithful in this life will not fall by the wayside in the life to come. If they keep their covenants here and now and depart this life firm and true in the testimony of our blessed Lord, they shall come forth with an inheritance of eternal life. We do not mean to say that those who die in the Lord, and who are true and faithful in this life, must be perfect in all things when they go into the next sphere of existence. There was only one perfect man—the Lord Jesus whose Father was God" (McConkie, "The Dead Who Die in the Lord," 107).

If Antipus and his men were depressed in spirit and body, why were they determined to conquer in this place or die? (56:16–18) Hugh Nibley noted that verse 16 illustrates a point made by the classic Prussian war theorist, Karl von Clausewitz: "Notice that Clausewitz says spirit is not the same as morale. Their [spirits were] low, but they were determined to go on fighting. This little force gave them great hopes. Their morale was high. Their spirits were low. They were exhausted, but they weren't going to give up. That's the difference between morale and spirit here" (*Teachings of the Book of Mormon*, 3:175).

What does this preservation of the Nephites teach us about our personal struggles? (56:17–19) How does our determination to do what is right compare to the army of Helaman? From what source did they receive "greater strength"? Where do we turn for strength against the evils we face? What blessing did the army of Antipus receive when they received that added strength? What have you experienced in your life that tells you that the Lord will be there to help you if you turn to Him in faith?

Alma 56:21–29. The Nephite Armies Increase in Number

Why would the Nephites prefer to be on the defensive rather than the offensive? (56:21) "Ammoron digs in at the cities his army has captured. Antipus and Helaman want to avoid the higher risks of open battle, or worse, of an attack on a fortified position. It would be greatly to their advantage should the Lamanites initiate an attack on Judea" (Gardner, *Second Witness*, 4:707). Hugh Nibley noted that this action supports the writings of Clausewitz, the Prussian war theorist, who postulated that "the defense position is always the strongest" (Nibley, *Teachings of the Book of Mormon*, 3:175).

15 And these are the cities which they possessed when I arrived at the city of Judea; and I found Antipus and his men toiling with their might to fortify the city.

16 Yea, and they were depressed in body as well as in spirit, for they had fought valiantly by day and toiled by night to maintain their cities; and thus they had suffered great afflictions of every kind.

17 And now they were determined to conquer in this place or die; therefore you may well suppose that this little force which I brought with me, yea, those sons of mine, gave them great hopes and much joy.

18 And now it came to pass that when the Lamanites saw that Antipus had received a greater strength to his army, they were compelled by the orders of Ammoron to not come against the city of Judea, or against us, to battle.

19 And thus were we favored of the Lord; for had they come upon us in this our weakness they might have perhaps destroyed our little army; but thus were we preserved.

20 They were commanded by Ammoron to maintain those cities which they had taken. And thus ended the twenty and sixth year. And in the commencement of the twenty and seventh year we had prepared our city and ourselves for defence.

21 Now we were desirous that the Lamanites should come upon us; for we were not desirous to make an attack upon them in their strongholds.

22 And it came to pass that we kept spies out round about, to watch the movements of the Lamanites, that they might not pass us by night nor by day to make an attack upon our other cities which were on the northward.

23 For we knew in those cities they were not sufficiently strong to meet them; therefore we

were desirous, if they should pass by us, to fall upon them in their rear, and thus bring them up in the rear at the same time they were met in the front. We supposed that we could overpower them; but behold, we were disappointed in this our desire.

24 They durst not pass by us with their whole army, neither durst they with a part, lest they should not be sufficiently strong and they should fall.

25 Neither durst they march down against the city of Zarahemla; neither durst they cross the head of Sidon, over to the city of Nephihah.

26 And thus, with their forces, they were determined to maintain those cities which they had taken.

27 And now it came to pass in the second month of this year, there was brought unto us many provisions from the fathers of those my two thousand sons.

28 And also there were sent two thousand men unto us from the land of Zarahemla. And thus we were prepared with ten thousand men, and provisions for them, and also for their wives and their children.

29 And the Lamanites, thus seeing our forces increase daily, and provisions arrive for our support, they began to be fearful, and began to sally forth, if it were possible to put an end to our receiving provisions and strength.

30 Now when we saw that the Lamanites began to grow uneasy on this wise, we were desirous to bring a stratagem into effect upon them; therefore Antipus ordered that I should march forth with my little sons to a

What does this act by the fathers of Helaman's stripling warriors suggest about their feelings about the war and their sons' participation in it? (56:27) "Under the direction of their prophet-leader, these young men took their fathers' place in defense of their families and homes. The events surrounding this critical decision demonstrate how the Atonement of Jesus Christ brings personal strength to the lives of the children of God. Consider the tender feelings of those fathers. How must they have felt to know that the rebellious actions of their past prevented them from protecting their wives and children at that moment of need? Knowing personally of the atrocities their sons would now face, they must have privately wept. Fathers, not children, are supposed to protect their families! Their sorrows must have been intense" (Scott, "Personal Strength through the Atonement," 83).

What does it mean to "sally forth"? (56:29) The 1828 *American Dictionary of the English Language* defines *sally* as "to issue or rush out, as a body of troops from a fortified place to attack besiegers." In the case of Alma 56:29, the Lamanites would send forth bodies of troops in attempts to prohibit the reinforcement of provisions and supplies by the Nephites.

Alma 56:30–43. The Nephite Armies Decoy the Lamanites

neighboring city, as if we were carrying provisions to a neighboring city.

31 And we were to march near the city of Antiparah, as if we were going to the city beyond, in the borders by the seashore.

32 And it came to pass that we did march forth, as if with our provisions, to go to that city.

33 And it came to pass that Antipus did march forth with a part of his army, leaving the remainder to maintain the city. But he did not march forth until I had gone forth with my little army, and came near the city Antiparah.

34 And now, in the city Antiparah were stationed the strongest army of the Lamanites; yea, the most numerous.

35 And it came to pass that when they had been informed by their spies, they came forth with their army and marched against us.

36 And it came to pass that we did flee before them, northward. And thus we did lead away the most powerful army of the Lamanites;

37 Yea, even to a considerable distance, insomuch that when they saw the army of Antipus pursuing them, with their might, they did not turn to the right nor to the left, but pursued their march in a straight course after us; and, as we suppose, it was their intent to slay us before Antipus should overtake them, and this that they might not be surrounded by our people.

38 And now Antipus, beholding our danger, did speed the march of his army. But behold, it was night; therefore they did not overtake us, neither did Antipus overtake them; therefore we did camp for the night.

39 And it came to pass that before the dawn of the morning, behold, the Lamanites were pursuing us. Now we were not sufficiently strong to contend with them; yea, I would not suffer that my little sons should fall into their hands; therefore we did continue our march, and we took our march into the wilderness.

40 Now they durst not turn to the right nor to the left lest they should be surrounded; neither would I turn to the right nor to the left lest they should overtake me, and we could not stand against them, but be slain, and they would make their escape; and thus we did flee all that day into the wilderness, even until it was dark.

41 And it came to pass that again, when the light of the morning came we saw the Lamanites upon us, and we did flee before them.

42 But it came to pass that they did not pursue us far before they halted; and it was in the morning of the third day of the seventh month.

43 And now, whether they were overtaken by Antipus we knew not, but I said unto my men: Behold, we know not but they have halted for the purpose that we should come against them, that they might catch us in their snare;

44 Therefore what say ye, my sons, will ye go against them to battle?

45 And now I say unto you, my beloved brother Moroni, that never had I seen so great courage, nay, not amongst all the Nephites.

46 For as I had ever called them my sons (for they were all of them very young) even so they said unto me: Father, behold our God is with us, and he will not suffer that we should fall; then let us go forth; we would not slay our brethren if they would let us alone; therefore let us go, lest they should overpower the army of Antipus.

What can we learn from this verse about avoiding temptation and sin? (56:40) Likewise, in the spiritual war that rages throughout the earth, Satan "maketh war with the saints of God, and encompasseth them round about" (D&C 76:29). How might obedience—turning neither to the left nor to the right—lead us away from temptation and from becoming surrounded by the enemy?

Alma 56:44–57. Helaman's Sons Fight in Righteousness

What moments in our lives might require "great courage" like that of Helaman's sons? (56:45) "Life's journey is not traveled on a freeway devoid of obstacles, pitfalls, and snares. Rather, it is a pathway marked by forks and turnings. Decisions are constantly before us. To make them wisely, courage is needed: the courage to say no, the courage to say yes. Decisions do determine destiny. The call for courage comes constantly to each of us. It has ever been so, and so shall it ever be" (Monson, "Courage Counts," 40).

Why did Helaman's sons not fear death or doubt even in their dire war situation? (56:47) Perhaps Helaman's young men had faith like that of Shadrach, Meshach, and Abed-nego who, while living in Babylonian captivity, faced a fiery furnace because they would not worship false idols: "They knew that they could trust God—even if things didn't turn out the way they hoped. They knew that faith is more than mental assent, more than an acknowledgment that God lives. Faith is total trust in Him. . . .

"Faith is believing that although we do not understand all things, He does. Faith is knowing that although our power is limited, His is not. Faith in Jesus Christ consists of complete reliance on Him" (Simmons, "But If Not . . . ," 73).

How does the example of the stripling warriors' mothers illustrate the importance of mothers today? (56:47–48) "The responsibility mothers have today has never required more vigilance. . . . When mothers know who they are and who God is and have made covenants with Him, they will have great power and influence for good on their children. . . . Mothers who know are always teachers. Since they are not babysitters, they are never off duty. . . . Think of the power of our future missionary force if mothers considered their homes as a pre-missionary training center. Then the doctrines of the gospel taught in the MTC would be a review and not a revelation. That is influence; that is power" (Beck, "Mothers Who Know," 76–77). ✚

Why is there a change in person in the middle of Helaman's letter? (56:52) "Alma 53 is narrated in third person by Mormon who is making an abridgement of the Large Plates of Nephi. But in Alma 56–58, Mormon chooses to give us the account on the sons of Helaman from the original source, which happens to be a letter from Helaman to the Captain of the Nephite army, Moroni. . . . With the exception of one verse of personal commentary (Alma 56:52), Mormon lets us see their battles through the pen of the man who saw the courage of these stripling warriors first hand" (Bassett, "Nephi's Freedom Thesis and the Sons of Helaman," 296).

47 Now they never had fought, yet they did not fear death; and they did think more upon the liberty of their fathers than they did upon their lives; yea, they had been taught by their mothers, that if they did not doubt, God would deliver them.

48 And they rehearsed unto me the words of their mothers, saying: We do not doubt our mothers knew it.

49 And it came to pass that I did return with my two thousand against these Lamanites who had pursued us. And now behold, the armies of Antipus had overtaken them, and a terrible battle had commenced.

50 The army of Antipus being weary, because of their long march in so short a space of time, were about to fall into the hands of the Lamanites; and had I not returned with my two thousand they would have obtained their purpose.

51 For Antipus had fallen by the sword, and many of his leaders, because of their weariness, which was occasioned by the speed of their march—therefore the men of Antipus, being confused because of the fall of their leaders, began to give way before the Lamanites.

52 And it came to pass that the Lamanites took courage, and began to pursue them; and thus were the Lamanites pursuing them with great vigor when Helaman came upon their rear with his two thousand, and began to slay them exceedingly, insomuch that the whole army of the Lamanites halted and turned upon Helaman.

53 Now when the people of Antipus saw that the Lamanites had turned them about, they gathered together their men and came again upon the rear of the Lamanites.

54 And now it came to pass that we, the people of Nephi, the people of Antipus, and I with my two thousand, did surround the

Lamanites, and did slay them; yea, insomuch that they were compelled to deliver up their weapons of war and also themselves as prisoners of war.

55 And now it came to pass that when they had surrendered themselves up unto us, behold, I numbered those young men who had fought with me, fearing lest there were many of them slain.

56 But behold, to my great joy, there had not one soul of them fallen to the earth; yea, and they had fought as if with the strength of God; yea, never were men known to have fought with such miraculous strength; and with such mighty power did they fall upon the Lamanites, that they did frighten them; and for this cause did the Lamanites deliver themselves up as prisoners of war.

57 And as we had no place for our prisoners, that we could guard them to keep them from the armies of the Lamanites, therefore we sent them to the land of Zarahemla, and a part of those men who were not slain of Antipus, with them; and the remainder I took and joined them to my stripling Ammonites, and took our march back to the city of Judea.

CHAPTER 57

Helaman recounts the taking of Antiparah and the surrender and later the defense of Cumeni—His Ammonite striplings fight valiantly; all are wounded, but none are slain—Gid reports the slaying and the escape of the Lamanite prisoners. About 63 B.C.

1 And now it came to pass that I received an epistle from Ammoron, the king, stating that if I would deliver up those prisoners of war whom we had taken that he would deliver up the city of Antiparah unto us.

What kind of strength did the Lord give the stripling warriors? (56:56) Ammon taught Limhi that "a man may have great power given him from God" (Mosiah 8:16). In this battle the stripling warriors were granted power beyond their own.

"Wendell Philips once said, 'One on God's side *is a majority*' (Ken Burns, Ric Burns, and Geoffery C. Ward, *The Civil War* [1990], 399). Mormon is making the same point by including the story of the sons of Helaman.... When the Lord is on your side, the size and strength of the opposition makes no difference" (Bassett, "Nephi's Freedom Thesis and the Sons of Helaman," 298).

Alma 57:1–12. Antiparah Is Taken without Bloodshed, and the Lamanites in Cumeni Surrender for Lack of Food

2 But I sent an epistle unto the king, that we were sure our forces were sufficient to take the city of Antiparah by our force; and by delivering up the prisoners for that city we should suppose ourselves unwise, and that we would only deliver up our prisoners on exchange.

3 And Ammoron refused mine epistle, for he would not exchange prisoners; therefore we began to make preparations to go against the city of Antiparah.

4 But the people of Antiparah did leave the city, and fled to their other cities, which they had possession of, to fortify them; and thus the city of Antiparah fell into our hands.

5 And thus ended the twenty and eighth year of the reign of the judges.

6 And it came to pass that in the commencement of the twenty and ninth year, we received a supply of provisions, and also an addition to our army, from the land of Zarahemla, and from the land round about, to the number of six thousand men, besides sixty of the sons of the Ammonites who had come to join their brethren, my little band of two thousand. And now behold, we were strong, yea, and we had also plenty of provisions brought unto us.

7 And it came to pass that it was our desire to wage a battle with the army which was placed to protect the city Cumeni.

8 And now behold, I will show unto you that we soon accomplished our desire; yea, with our strong force, or with a part of our strong force, we did surround, by night, the city Cumeni, a little before they were to receive a supply of provisions.

9 And it came to pass that we did camp round about the city for many nights; but we did sleep upon our swords, and keep guards, that the Lamanites could not come upon us by night and slay us, which they attempted

What implied principle do we learn from this imagery of the Nephites sleeping upon their swords and keeping guards before their enemies? (57:9) How can we be more cautious and watchful for such modern enemies as philosophies, practices, and behaviors that lead to sin?

many times; but as many times as they attempted this their blood was spilt.

10 At length their provisions did arrive, and they were about to enter the city by night. And we, instead of being Lamanites, were Nephites; therefore, we did take them and their provisions.

11 And notwithstanding the Lamanites being cut off from their support after this manner, they were still determined to maintain the city; therefore it became expedient that we should take those provisions and send them to Judea, and our prisoners to the land of Zarahemla.

12 And it came to pass that not many days had passed away before the Lamanites began to lose all hopes of succor; therefore they yielded up the city unto our hands; and thus we had accomplished our designs in obtaining the city Cumeni.

13 But it came to pass that our prisoners were so numerous that, notwithstanding the enormity of our numbers, we were obliged to employ all our force to keep them, or to put them to death.

14 For behold, they would break out in great numbers, and would fight with stones, and with clubs, or whatsoever thing they could get into their hands, insomuch that we did slay upwards of two thousand of them after they had surrendered themselves prisoners of war.

15 Therefore it became expedient for us, that we should put an end to their lives, or guard them, sword in hand, down to the land of Zarahemla; and also our provisions were not any more than sufficient for our own people, notwithstanding that which we had taken from the Lamanites.

What can we learn as we contrast how the Lamanites in Cumeni responded to their difficult situation with how the Nephites responded as they were pitched against the city of Manti? (57:12)
To see the Nephite response, read Alma 58:6–12 and study the difference in the responses. Why did the Nephites not lose their hope of succor (succor means help, relief, aid) when the Lamanites did? What is the difference between the two experiences?

Alma 57:13–23. The Lamanites Attack, but the Stripling Warriors Stand Firm

16 And now, in those critical circumstances, it became a very serious matter to determine concerning these prisoners of war; nevertheless, we did resolve to send them down to the land of Zarahemla; therefore we selected a part of our men, and gave them charge over our prisoners to go down to the land of Zarahemla.

17 But it came to pass that on the morrow they did return. And now behold, we did not inquire of them concerning the prisoners; for behold, the Lamanites were upon us, and they returned in season to save us from falling into their hands. For behold, Ammoron had sent to their support a new supply of provisions and also a numerous army of men.

18 And it came to pass that those men whom we sent with the prisoners did arrive in season to check them, as they were about to overpower us.

19 But behold, my little band of two thousand and sixty fought most desperately; yea, they were firm before the Lamanites, and did administer death unto all those who opposed them.

20 And as the remainder of our army were about to give way before the Lamanites, behold, those two thousand and sixty were firm and undaunted.

21 Yea, and they did obey and observe to perform every word of command with exactness; yea, and even according to their faith it was done unto them; and I did remember the words which they said unto me that their mothers had taught them.

22 And now behold, it was these my sons, and those men who had been selected to convey the prisoners, to whom we owe this great victory; for it was they who did beat the Lamanites; therefore they were driven back to the city of Manti.

What is meant by *undaunted*? (57:20) *Undaunted* means "not subdued or depressed by fear" (Webster, *American Dictionary*).

What can we learn about obedience from these sons of Helaman? (57:21) "Helaman was careful to let Moroni know that as the opposition grew darker, the light of obedience glowed as brightly as ever within his sons. . . . Could this be seen as blind obedience? Blind obedience is sheep following sheep, while following in exactness is sheep following the Shepherd; and Christ is the Good Shepherd (see Alma 5:37–39). . . . The stripling warriors must have been aware that their obedience to their leaders was an extension of their obedience to their God. . . . This is the ultimate test of obedience; to show one's allegiance to a perfect and infallible God by how we obey those less than perfect who are called to lead us" (Bassett, "Nephi's Freedom Thesis and the Sons of Helaman," 299).

23 And we retained our city Cumeni, and were not all destroyed by the sword; nevertheless, we had suffered great loss.

How can we develop the kind of faith expressed by the sons of Helaman? (57:21) "For some, faith is not understood and consequently not used to full advantage. Some feel that any discussion of religion and the guidance one can receive through robust faith have no rational basis. However, faith is not illusion nor magic but a power rooted in eternal principles. . . . One day a janitor entered while we were experimenting [with high energy particles]. In a spirit of disgust he said, 'You are all liars, pretending that you are doing something important, but you can't fool me. I know that if you can't see, hear, taste, smell, or touch it, it doesn't exist.' That attitude ruled out the possibility of his learning that there is much of worth that can't be identified by the five senses" (Scott, "Sustaining Power of Faith," 76).

24 And it came to pass that after the Lamanites had fled, I immediately gave orders that my men who had been wounded should be taken from among the dead, and caused that their wounds should be dressed.

Alma 57:24–27. The Stripling Warriors Are Saved by the Power of God

25 And it came to pass that there were two hundred, out of my two thousand and sixty, who had fainted because of the loss of blood; nevertheless, according to the goodness of God, and to our great astonishment, and also the joy of our whole army, there was not one

Why shouldn't we be surprised that not one of the stripling warriors perished? (57:25) "Having a testimony and having great faith in Christ does not guarantee that we won't suffer. Abraham, Job, Abinadi, Nephi, Joseph Smith, and countless other righteous people . . . all suffered. Jesus Christ suffered beyond them all, and he never did anything wrong. . . . We're

Discovering Implied Principles in the Story of Helaman's Stripling Warriors and Other Accounts in the Book of Mormon

"Many principles are not stated directly by the scriptural writer but are instead implied. Implied principles may come from an entire book of scripture, a chapter, or a single verse and may be couched in the scriptural story line, events, or parables. Identifying implied principles includes recognizing the truths being illustrated in a scriptural account and stating them clearly and succinctly. This often requires time and careful thought. Elder Richard G. Scott taught, 'It is worth great effort to organize the truth we gather to simple statements of principle' ('Acquiring Spiritual Knowledge,' 86).

"Implied principles can often be discovered by looking for cause-and-effect relationships within the scripture block. By analyzing the actions, attitudes, and behaviors of individuals or groups in the scriptural account, and identifying the blessings or consequences that came as a result, gospel principles become more apparent.

"Implied principles can also be identified by asking questions like:

"• What is the moral or point of the story?

"• Why do you think the writer included these events or passages?

"• What did the author intend for us to learn?

"• What are some of the fundamental truths taught in this passage?

"Some examples of implied principles include:

"From the events in the lives of Alma the Younger or Paul: A person who accepts the truth and repents of his sins can lead others to the blessings of the gospel (see Alma 36:10–21; Acts 9:4–20)" (*Gospel Teaching and Learning*, 27–28).

all going to go through some tough times; that's just the nature of life on earth. But our tough times cannot destroy our hope unless we let them. That is our option. We're all going to suffer, but we don't have to be miserable. Since all of the stripling warriors were wounded, we might expect that we'll also get some bumps and bruises as we go through life's battles" (Bytheway, *Righteous Warriors*, 120).

How were the two thousand sixty stripling warriors miraculously preserved? (57:26) "The faith of the stripling warriors kept them from dying. Sometimes, however, people of great faith die. Sometimes people are given priesthood blessings and they still die.... Abinadi had great faith, but he died. Joseph Smith had great faith, but he died.... When we exercise faith in [God], and in his timing, we can be assured that all things will work together for our good, however painful they may be for us at the moment. If someone you love dies, it does not necessarily mean that your faith was lacking.... The stripling warriors survived ... because of their faith in God and because, in this case, it was God's will that they survive" (Bytheway, *Righteous Warriors*, 118–19).

What can we learn from the preservation of the stripling warriors? (57:26) "Not everyone receives this same promise of preservation. Abinadi, for example, did not. But having received this assurance, the sons of Helaman acted upon it. They stand as a great central symbol of God's deliverance to those who trust in his word. Their preservation occurs even amidst a nation racked with turmoil. Their deliverance through believing and obeying the word of God offers hope" (Hansen, "Book of Alma as a Prototype," 279).

What does it mean to have a firm mind? (57:27) According to Jacob 3:2 and Moroni 7:29–30, what are some of the blessings granted to those who have a firm mind? What can we do to develop a firmer mind? "There is a great wealth of intelligence and guidance and safety available to you through regular, thoughtful prayer and scripture study. This keeps your minds firm and steadfast in holy places as you walk the halls at school or shop for clothing or surf the Internet" (Larsen, "Standing in Holy Places," 91). ☺

Alma 57:28–36. Gid Explains What Happened to the Lamanite Prisoners

26 And now, their preservation was astonishing to our whole army, yea, that they should be spared while there was a thousand of our brethren who were slain. And we do justly ascribe it to the miraculous power of God, because of their exceeding faith in that which they had been taught to believe—that there was a just God, and whosoever did not doubt, that they should be preserved by his marvelous power.

soul of them who did perish; yea, and neither was there one soul among them who had not received many wounds.

27 Now this was the faith of these of whom I have spoken; they are young, and their minds are firm, and they do put their trust in God continually.

28 And now it came to pass that after we had thus taken care of our wounded men, and had buried our dead and also the dead of the Lamanites, who were many, behold, we did inquire of Gid concerning the prisoners whom they had started to go down to the land of Zarahemla with.

29 Now Gid was the chief captain over the band who was appointed to guard them down to the land.

30 And now, these are the words which Gid said unto me: Behold, we did start to go down to the land of Zarahemla with our prisoners. And it came to pass that we did meet the spies of our armies, who had been sent out to watch the camp of the Lamanites.

31 And they cried unto us, saying—Behold, the armies of the Lamanites are marching towards the city of Cumeni; and behold, they will fall upon them, yea, and will destroy our people.

32 And it came to pass that our prisoners did hear their cries, which caused them to take courage; and they did rise up in rebellion against us.

33 And it came to pass because of their rebellion we did cause that our swords should come upon them. And it came to pass that they did in a body run upon our swords, in the which, the greater number of them were slain; and the remainder of them broke through and fled from us.

34 And behold, when they had fled and we could not overtake them, we took our march with speed towards the city Cumeni; and behold, we did arrive in time that we might assist our brethren in preserving the city.

35 And behold, we are again delivered out of the hands of our enemies. And blessed is the name of our God; for behold, it is he that has delivered us; yea, that has done this great thing for us.

36 Now it came to pass that when I, Helaman, had heard these words of Gid, I was filled with exceeding joy because of the goodness of God

When have you been filled with "exceeding joy" because God delivered or preserved you in some way? (57:36) President Henry B. Eyring taught the importance of remembering the goodness of God: "Before I would write, I would ponder this question: 'Have I seen the hand of God reaching out to touch us or our children or our family today?' . . . As I would cast my mind over the day, I would see evidence of what God had done for one of us that I had not recognized in the busy moments of the day. As that happened, and it happened often, I realized that trying to remember had allowed God to show me what He had done" ("O Remember, Remember," 67).

Alma 58:1–8. Helaman's Army Is Outnumbered and Starving

How did the Lamanites begin to thwart the tactics of the Nephite armies? (58:1) "Things settled down to a stalemate, with Helaman faced with the problem of containing greatly superior forces, who were now discouragingly familiar with the Nephite decoy tricks (Alma 58:1). He could only appeal to the capital for aid, which was forthcoming, but was largely canceled out by the Lamanite counter-buildup—for they too were receiving reinforcements, and had in the bargain begun copying the Nephites' own tactics of harassment (Alma 58:4–6). As in all long wars, the two opponents in their methods, armaments, tricks, and appearance had come to be more and more alike—for an enemy may not be allowed safely to monopolize any technical advantage for long" (Nibley, *Since Cumorah*, 321).

What is an embassy? (58:4) According to Noah Webster's 1828 *American Dictionary*, an "embassy" is "the message or public function of an embassador . . . ; the charge or employment of a public minister, whether ambassador or envoy." Apparently, Helaman sent a detailed message "concerning the affairs of [his] people" with an official envoy and waited for assistance.

in preserving us, that we might not all perish; yea, and I trust that the souls of them who have been slain have entered into the rest of their God.

CHAPTER 58

Helaman, Gid, and Teomner take the city of Manti by a stratagem—The Lamanites withdraw—The sons of the people of Ammon are preserved as they stand fast in defense of their liberty and faith. About 63–62 B.C.

1 And behold, now it came to pass that our next object was to obtain the city of Manti; but behold, there was no way that we could lead them out of the city by our small bands. For behold, they remembered that which we had hitherto done; therefore we could not decoy them away from their strongholds.

2 And they were so much more numerous than was our army that we durst not go forth and attack them in their strongholds.

3 Yea, and it became expedient that we should employ our men to the maintaining those parts of the land which we had regained of our possessions; therefore it became expedient that we should wait, that we might receive more strength from the land of Zarahemla and also a new supply of provisions.

4 And it came to pass that I thus did send an embassy to the governor of our land, to acquaint him concerning the affairs of our people. And it came to pass that we did wait to receive provisions and strength from the land of Zarahemla.

5 But behold, this did profit us but little; for the Lamanites were also receiving great strength from day to day, and also many provisions; and thus were our circumstances at this period of time.

6 And the Lamanites were sallying forth against us from time to time, resolving by

stratagem to destroy us; nevertheless we could not come to battle with them, because of their retreats and their strongholds.

7 And it came to pass that we did wait in these difficult circumstances for the space of many months, even until we were about to perish for the want of food.

8 But it came to pass that we did receive food, which was guarded to us by an army of two thousand men to our assistance; and this is all the assistance which we did receive, to defend ourselves and our country from falling into the hands of our enemies, yea, to contend with an enemy which was innumerable.

9 And now the cause of these our embarrassments, or the cause why they did not send more strength unto us, we knew not; therefore we were grieved and also filled with fear, lest by any means the judgments of God should come upon our land, to our overthrow and utter destruction.

10 Therefore we did pour out our souls in prayer to God, that he would strengthen us and deliver us out of the hands of our enemies, yea, and also give us strength that we might retain our cities, and our lands, and our possessions, for the support of our people.

11 Yea, and it came to pass that the Lord our God did visit us with assurances that he would deliver us; yea, insomuch that he did speak peace to our souls, and did grant unto us great faith, and did cause us that we should hope for our deliverance in him.

12 And we did take courage with our small force which we had received, and were fixed with a determination to conquer our enemies, and to maintain our lands, and our possessions, and our wives, and our children, and the cause of our liberty.

Alma 58:9–12. Helaman and His Men Place Their Trust in God

What might we learn from the prayers of Helaman and the Nephite army? (58:10) "The absolute Supreme Being, the most all-knowing, all-seeing, all-powerful personage, encourages you and me . . . to converse with Him as our Father. . . . He knows how desperately we need His guidance. . . . It matters not our circumstance, be we humble or arrogant, poor or rich, free or enslaved, learned or ignorant, loved or forsaken, we can address Him. We need no appointment. Our supplication can be brief or can occupy all the time needed. It can be an extended expression of love and gratitude or an urgent plea for help. He has created numberless cosmos and populated them with worlds, yet you and I can talk with Him personally, and He will ever answer" (Scott, "Using the Supernal Gift of Prayer," 8).

How did Heavenly Father answer the prayers of Helaman's army with subtle but significant blessings? (58:10–12) "Interestingly, the answers to these prayers did not produce additional weapons or an increased number of troops. Instead, God granted these faithful warriors assurance that He would deliver them, peace to their souls, and great faith and hope for their deliverance in Him (see Alma 58:11). . . . Assurance, peace, faith, and hope initially might not seem like the blessings warriors in battle might want, but they were precisely the blessings these valiant young men needed to press forward and prevail physically and spiritually" (Bednar, "Windows of Heaven," 18).

Why could the Nephite army take courage in these dire circumstances? (58:12) "It may be that the Nephites hoped for a miracle.... But what did they receive?.... The Lord put inside these men the will and the power to do what they desired—to begin with a strong resolve and then to see it through.... When the Lord instills hope and faith and peace and assurance in people, they can bring great things to pass. This, then, is often what we should look for when we ask for help—not a miracle to solve our problem for us, but a miracle inside, to help us come to the solution ourselves, with the Lord's help and the Lord's power" (Cook, *Receiving Answers to Our Prayers*, 156–57).

Alma 58:13–29. The Nephites Take Manti without Shedding Blood

What can we learn from the Nephite victory over the city of Manti? (58:13–29) "The events which transpired in regaining the city of Manti bore witness to the promise of deliverance made by the Lord. By once again drawing the Lamanites out of the city and then sending an army behind them into the defenseless city of Manti, 'they did take possession of the city of Manti without the shedding of blood' (Alma 58:28)" (Bassett, "Nephi's Freedom Thesis and the Sons of Helaman," 301).

13 And thus we did go forth with all our might against the Lamanites, who were in the city of Manti; and we did pitch our tents by the wilderness side, which was near to the city.

14 And it came to pass that on the morrow, that when the Lamanites saw that we were in the borders by the wilderness which was near the city, that they sent out their spies round about us that they might discover the number and the strength of our army.

15 And it came to pass that when they saw that we were not strong, according to our numbers, and fearing that we should cut them off from their support except they should come out to battle against us and kill us, and also supposing that they could easily destroy us with their numerous hosts, therefore they began to make preparations to come out against us to battle.

16 And when we saw that they were making preparations to come out against us, behold, I caused that Gid, with a small number of men, should secrete himself in the wilderness, and also that Teomner and a small number of men should secrete themselves also in the wilderness.

17 Now Gid and his men were on the right and the others on the left; and when they had thus secreted themselves, behold, I remained, with the remainder of my army, in that same place where we had first pitched our tents against the time that the Lamanites should come out to battle.

18 And it came to pass that the Lamanites did come out with their numerous army against us. And when they had come and were about to fall upon us with the sword, I caused that my men, those who were with me, should retreat into the wilderness.

19 And it came to pass that the Lamanites did follow after us with great speed, for they were exceedingly desirous to overtake us that they might slay us; therefore they did follow us into the wilderness; and we did pass by in the midst of Gid and Teomner, insomuch that they were not discovered by the Lamanites.

20 And it came to pass that when the Lamanites had passed by, or when the army had passed by, Gid and Teomner did rise up from their secret places, and did cut off the spies of the Lamanites that they should not return to the city.

21 And it came to pass that when they had cut them off, they ran to the city and fell upon the guards who were left to guard the city, insomuch that they did destroy them and did take possession of the city.

22 Now this was done because the Lamanites did suffer their whole army, save a few guards only, to be led away into the wilderness.

23 And it came to pass that Gid and Teomner by this means had obtained possession of their strongholds. And it came to pass that we took our course, after having traveled

What do we learn from the poor military decision the Lamanites made at this time? (58:22) A large army of Lamanites was led away by a small army of Nephites into the wilderness and out of the security of their strongholds. What seemingly small things may be leading us away out of our spiritual strongholds into the wilderness of temptation and sin? Elder Ian S. Arden thoughtfully observed, "For many of us, a barrier to revelation is being unwilling to truly repent of 'small things' the Spirit cannot tolerate. The so-called 'small things' include watching inappropriate movies, being immodest in dress and action, harboring unworthy thoughts, disregarding the teachings of the prophets, and doing what the Spirit warns us to avoid" ("Shunning Temptation," 56).

Alma 58:30–41. The Stripling Warriors Are Protected Because of Their Faith and Obedience

Why did Nephite record keepers refer to their lands by quarter? (58:30) "Book of Mormon writers commonly spoke of their land as being divided into four quarters (i.e., Mosiah 27:6; Alma 43:26; 52:10; 56:1; 58:30). They similarly thought of the earth as being divided into four quadrants (i.e., 1 Nephi 19:16; 22:25; 2 Nephi 10:8; 21:12; 3 Nephi 5:24; 5:26; 16:5; Ether 13:11). Accordingly, they described each area of their lands by reference to the cardinal directions, such as 'the land northward' and 'the land southward.' ...

much in the wilderness towards the land of Zarahemla.

24 And when the Lamanites saw that they were marching towards the land of Zarahemla, they were exceedingly afraid, lest there was a plan laid to lead them on to destruction; therefore they began to retreat into the wilderness again, yea, even back by the same way which they had come.

25 And behold, it was night and they did pitch their tents, for the chief captains of the Lamanites had supposed that the Nephites were weary because of their march; and supposing that they had driven their whole army therefore they took no thought concerning the city of Manti.

26 Now it came to pass that when it was night, I caused that my men should not sleep, but that they should march forward by another way towards the land of Manti.

27 And because of this our march in the night-time, behold, on the morrow we were beyond the Lamanites, insomuch that we did arrive before them at the city of Manti.

28 And thus it came to pass, that by this stratagem we did take possession of the city of Manti without the shedding of blood.

29 And it came to pass that when the armies of the Lamanites did arrive near the city, and saw that we were prepared to meet them, they were astonished exceedingly and struck with great fear, insomuch that they did flee into the wilderness.

30 Yea, and it came to pass that the armies of the Lamanites did flee out of all this quarter of the land. But behold, they have carried with them many women and children out of the land.

31 And those cities which had been taken by the Lamanites, all of them are at this period of time in our possession; and our fathers and our women and our children are returning to their homes, all save it be those who have been taken prisoners and carried off by the Lamanites.

32 But behold, our armies are small to maintain so great a number of cities and so great possessions.

33 But behold, we trust in our God who has given us victory over those lands, insomuch that we have obtained those cities and those lands, which were our own.

34 Now we do not know the cause that the government does not grant us more strength; neither do those men who came up unto us know why we have not received greater strength.

35 Behold, we do not know but what ye are unsuccessful, and ye have drawn away the forces into that quarter of the land; if so, we do not desire to murmur.

36 And if it is not so, behold, we fear that there is some faction in the government, that they do not send more men to our assistance; for we know that they are more numerous than that which they have sent.

37 But, behold, it mattereth not—we trust God will deliver us, notwithstanding the weakness of our armies, yea, and deliver us out of the hands of our enemies.

38 Behold, this is the twenty and ninth year, in the latter end, and we are in the possession of our lands; and the Lamanites have fled to the land of Nephi.

39 And those sons of the people of Ammon, of whom I have so highly spoken, are with me in the city of Manti; and the Lord has supported them, yea, and kept them from falling by the sword, insomuch that even one soul has not been slain.

"Good evidence exists that ancient Americans divided their territorial lands into four quadrants for administrative purposes" (Welch et al., "Four Quarters," 145).

How can we come to "trust in God" like Helaman and his army? (58:33–37) "This life is an experience in profound trust—trust in Jesus Christ, trust in His teachings, trust in our capacity as led by the Holy Spirit to obey those teachings for happiness now and for a purposeful, supremely happy eternal existence. To trust means to obey willingly without knowing the end from the beginning (see Prov. 3:5–7). . . . To exercise faith is to trust that the Lord knows what He is doing with you and that He can accomplish it for your eternal good even though you cannot understand how He can possibly do it" (Scott, "Trust in the Lord," 17).

What principle do we learn from Helaman's comment that "we do not desire to murmur"? (58:35) Helaman wondered "why the government had not sent the requested assistance. He feared lest the Nephite armies were too small to hold on to the cities they had recaptured. Then, almost as an apology for being negative he writes, 'we do not desire to murmur' (Alma 58:35). . . . Notice how Helaman has shared an unpleasant truth in a fashion that will still allow the lines of communication to remain open. His sensitivity to his leaders, as well as his subordinates, is commendable. . . . He is once again illustrating his total allegiance to his leaders; recognizing full well that he cannot expect God to stand by him if he doesn't stand by his leaders" (Bassett, "Nephi's Freedom Thesis and the Sons of Helaman," 301).

What encouragement do you receive knowing that God delivered the Nephites, "notwithstanding the weakness" of their armies? (58:37) When have you seen the Lord's hand as you faced tribulation in your weakness? How does Ether 12:27 help you understand this principle?

What was Mormon trying to teach through the account of Helaman's stripling warriors? (58:39) "Is it not obvious that Mormon has not only attempted to show us the problems we may face, but also the solutions to those problems? . . . The sons of Helaman represent a timeless solution to a modern challenge: even though the battlefield may be mortal, the most powerful weapon in our defense is obtained by serving 'the God of the land, who is Jesus Christ' (Ether 2:12)" (Bassett, "Nephi's Freedom Thesis and the Sons of Helaman," 302).

How can we, like the sons of the people of Ammon, remember God from day to day? (58:39–40) "How can you and I remember, always, the goodness of God . . . ? The Holy Ghost brings back memories of what God has taught us. . . . You could have an experience with the gift of the Holy Ghost today. You could begin a private prayer with thanks. . . . You could try the same thing as you write an entry in your book of remembrance. . . . As you start to write, you could ask yourself, 'How did God bless me today?' If you do that long enough and with faith, you will find yourself remembering blessings" (Eyring, *To Draw Closer to God*, 77–79).

Alma 59:1–13. The City of Nephihah Falls to the Lamanites

How does this first letter by Moroni help us better understand the account in Alma 60? (59:3) "Near the end of Helaman's letter, he expressed some frustration that the government 'does not grant us more strength' suggesting that 'some faction in the government' was not sending 'more men to our assistance' even though he had sent a message to Pahoran requesting aid (Alma 58:34, 36, 4). [Captain] Moroni had been wondering about the breakdown of communications

40 But behold, they have received many wounds; nevertheless they stand fast in that liberty wherewith God has made them free; and they are strict to remember the Lord their God from day to day; yea, they do observe to keep his statutes, and his judgments, and his commandments continually; and their faith is strong in the prophecies concerning that which is to come.

41 And now, my beloved brother, Moroni, may the Lord our God, who has redeemed us and made us free, keep you continually in his presence; yea, and may he favor this people, even that ye may have success in obtaining the possession of all that which the Lamanites have taken from us, which was for our support. And now, behold, I close mine epistle. I am Helaman, the son of Alma.

CHAPTER 59

Moroni asks Pahoran to strengthen the forces of Helaman—The Lamanites take the city of Nephihah—Moroni is angry with the government. About 62 B.C.

1 Now it came to pass in the thirtieth year of the reign of the judges over the people of Nephi, after Moroni had received and had read Helaman's epistle, he was exceedingly rejoiced because of the welfare, yea, the exceeding success which Helaman had had, in obtaining those lands which were lost.

2 Yea, and he did make it known unto all his people, in all the land round about in that part where he was, that they might rejoice also.

3 And it came to pass that he immediately sent an epistle to Pahoran, desiring that he should cause men to be gathered together to strengthen Helaman, or the armies of Helaman, insomuch that he might with ease maintain that part of the land which he had been so miraculously prospered in regaining.

4 And it came to pass when Moroni had sent this epistle to the land of Zarahemla, he began again to lay a plan that he might obtain the remainder of those possessions and cities which the Lamanites had taken from them.

5 And it came to pass that while Moroni was thus making preparations to go against the Lamanites to battle, behold, the people of Nephihah, who were gathered together from the city of Moroni and the city of Lehi and the city of Morianton, were attacked by the Lamanites.

6 Yea, even those who had been compelled to flee from the land of Manti, and from the land round about, had come over and joined the Lamanites in this part of the land.

7 And thus being exceedingly numerous, yea, and receiving strength from day to day, by the command of Ammoron they came forth against the people of Nephihah, and they did begin to slay them with an exceedingly great slaughter.

8 And their armies were so numerous that the remainder of the people of Nephihah were obliged to flee before them; and they came even and joined the army of Moroni.

9 And now as Moroni had supposed that there should be men sent to the city of Nephihah, to the assistance of the people to maintain that city, and knowing that it was easier to keep the city from falling into the hands of the Lamanites than to retake it from them, he supposed that they would easily maintain that city.

10 Therefore he retained all his force to maintain those places which he had recovered.

11 And now, when Moroni saw that the city of Nephihah was lost he was exceedingly sorrowful, and began to doubt, because of the wickedness of the people, whether they should not fall into the hands of their brethren.

also. At once he sat down and sent an urgent dispatch to Zarahemla, addressed directly to the chief of state, urging that help be sent to Helaman without further delay" (Nibley, *Since Cumorah*, 322–23).

How does Moroni's comment that it is "easier to keep the city . . . than to retake it" apply today? (59:9) President Ezra Taft Benson taught: "It is better to prepare and prevent than it is to repair and repent" ("Law of Chastity," 7).

How might this counsel apply to struggles faced by people we care about? How might we apply these truths to our own lives? One commentary draws the relation thus: "It is easier and better to remain faithful than it is to return to the faith after going astray" (*Book of Mormon Seminary Teacher Manual*, 362).

12 Now this was the case with all his chief captains. They doubted and marveled also because of the wickedness of the people, and this because of the success of the Lamanites over them.

13 And it came to pass that Moroni was angry with the government, because of their indifference concerning the freedom of their country.

CHAPTER 60

Moroni complains to Pahoran of the government's neglect of the armies—The Lord suffers the righteous to be slain—The Nephites must use all of their power and means to deliver themselves from their enemies—Moroni threatens to fight against the government unless help is supplied to his armies. About 62 B.C.

1 And it came to pass that he wrote again to the governor of the land, who was Pahoran, and these are the words which he wrote, saying: Behold, I direct mine epistle to Pahoran, in the city of Zarahemla, who is the chief judge and the governor over the land, and also to all those who have been chosen by this people to govern and manage the affairs of this war.

2 For behold, I have somewhat to say unto them by the way of condemnation; for behold, ye yourselves know that ye have been appointed to gather together men, and arm them with swords, and with cimeters, and all manner of weapons of war of every kind, and send forth against the Lamanites, in whatsoever parts they should come into our land.

3 And now behold, I say unto you that myself, and also my men, and also Helaman and his men, have suffered exceedingly great sufferings; yea, even hunger, thirst, and fatigue, and all manner of afflictions of every kind.

4 But behold, were this all we had suffered we would not murmur nor complain.

Alma 60:1–6. Moroni Describes His Army's Sufferings

What is Moroni's tone in his second letter to Pahoran? (60:1–6) "The letter seethes with the resentment of the man at the front for the easy-living ways of the VIP's back at the capital—the old misunderstandings between the 'office' and the 'field.' He starts out by reminding the governor of his duty to supply the armies in the field, and reminds him that both he and Helaman have suffered from short supplies from the beginning.... He admits his ignorance of the situation and asks for information, and yet he cannot resist passing judgment with a peevish and quite unjustified charge of negligence" (Nibley, *Since Cumorah*, 323).

5 But behold, great has been the slaughter among our people; yea, thousands have fallen by the sword, while it might have otherwise been if ye had rendered unto our armies sufficient strength and succor for them. Yea, great has been your neglect towards us.

6 And now behold, we desire to know the cause of this exceedingly great neglect; yea, we desire to know the cause of your thoughtless state.

7 Can you think to sit upon your thrones in a state of thoughtless stupor, while your enemies are spreading the work of death around you? Yea, while they are murdering thousands of your brethren—

8 Yea, even they who have looked up to you for protection, yea, have placed you in a situation that ye might have succored them, yea, ye might have sent armies unto them, to have strengthened them, and have saved thousands of them from falling by the sword.

9 But behold, this is not all—ye have withheld your provisions from them, insomuch that many have fought and bled out their lives because of their great desires which they had for the welfare of this people; yea, and this they have done when they were about to perish with hunger, because of your exceedingly great neglect towards them.

10 And now, my beloved brethren—for ye ought to be beloved; yea, and ye ought to have stirred yourselves more diligently for the welfare and the freedom of this people; but behold, ye have neglected them insomuch that the blood of thousands shall come upon your heads for vengeance; yea, for known unto God were all their cries, and all their sufferings—

11 Behold, could ye suppose that ye could

What is meant by *neglect***? (60:5)** Because Moroni uses this word several times in his letter to Pahoran, it is good to know that it means to be "heedless; careless; inattentive; accustomed or apt to omit what may or ought to be done" (Webster, *American Dictionary*). Even though Moroni wasn't entirely aware of Pahoran's situation, the caution against being neglectful can still apply today. What are some necessities, either spiritual or temporal, that sometimes are neglected? What can help us avoid being careless or inattentive toward these things?

Alma 60:7–13. Moroni Asks the Chief Judge Why No Help Has Been Sent to Him

How would most people respond to accusations like those posed here by Moroni? (60:7–13) Consider a time when you were unjustly accused and condemned by someone? What were your initial feelings? How did you respond? As you read Alma 61, ponder the lessons you can learn from Pahoran as he responds to Moroni's accusations.

What does *succored* **mean? (60:8)** The dictionary defines *succored* as being "assisted; relieved" (Webster, *American Dictionary*).

sit upon your thrones, and because of the exceeding goodness of God ye could do nothing and he would deliver you? Behold, if ye have supposed this ye have supposed in vain.

12 Do ye suppose that, because so many of your brethren have been killed it is because of their wickedness? I say unto you, if ye have supposed this ye have supposed in vain; for I say unto you, there are many who have fallen by the sword; and behold it is to your condemnation;

13 For the Lord suffereth the righteous to be slain that his justice and judgment may come upon the wicked; therefore ye need not suppose that the righteous are lost because they are slain; but behold, they do enter into the rest of the Lord their God.

Why are the righteous allowed to be slain by the wicked? (60:13) "Evil conduct is an element of agency. . . . [Captain Moroni] made it clear that the righteous are not lost. . . . The wicked will be held accountable for the atrocities they perpetrate. The Savior was clear that 'offences will come: but woe unto him, through whom they come!'" (Luke 17:1) (Cook, "Songs They Could Not Sing," 106). ●

Alma 60:14–23. Moroni Explains How a Lack of Unity Weakens the Nation

What are other scriptural terms that are similar to *slothfulness*? (60:14) Idleness, laziness, neglect, and procrastination are similar behaviors the Lord condemns in the scriptures. How would watching for these terms in the scriptures lead us to examine our personal spiritual, mental, and physical progress?

14 And now behold, I say unto you, I fear exceedingly that the judgments of God will come upon this people, because of their exceeding slothfulness, yea, even the slothfulness of our government, and their exceedingly great neglect towards their brethren, yea, towards those who have been slain.

15 For were it not for the wickedness which first commenced at our head, we could have withstood our enemies that they could have gained no power over us.

Why does Moroni lament the perceived lack of unity? (60:16) "Unity is strength. 'How pleasing it is for brethren to dwell together in unity!' Let the Saints of the Most High ever cultivate this principle, and the most glorious blessings must result, not only to them individually, but to the whole Church—the order of the kingdom will be maintained, its officers respected, and its requirements readily and cheerfully obeyed" (*Joseph Smith* [manual], 276).

16 Yea, had it not been for the war which broke out among ourselves; yea, were it not for these king-men, who caused so much bloodshed among ourselves; yea, at the time we were contending among ourselves, if we had united our strength as we hitherto have done; yea, had it not been for the desire of power and authority which those king-men had over us; had they been true to the cause of our freedom, and united with us, and gone forth against our enemies, instead of taking up their swords against us, which was the cause of so much bloodshed among ourselves; yea, if we had gone forth against them in the strength of the Lord, we should have dispersed our enemies, for it would have been done, according to the fulfilling of his word.

17 But behold, now the Lamanites are coming upon us, taking possession of our lands, and they are murdering our people with the sword, yea, our women and our children, and also carrying them away captive, causing them that they should suffer all manner of afflictions, and this because of the great wickedness of those who are seeking for power and authority, yea, even those king-men.

18 But why should I say much concerning this matter? For we know not but what ye yourselves are seeking for authority. We know not but what ye are also traitors to your country.

19 Or is it that ye have neglected us because ye are in the heart of our country and ye are surrounded by security, that ye do not cause food to be sent unto us, and also men to strengthen our armies?

20 Have ye forgotten the commandments of the Lord your God? Yea, have ye forgotten the captivity of our fathers? Have ye forgotten the many times we have been delivered out of the hands of our enemies?

21 Or do ye suppose that the Lord will still deliver us, while we sit upon our thrones and do not make use of the means which the Lord has provided for us?

22 Yea, will ye sit in idleness while ye are surrounded with thousands of those, yea, and tens of thousands, who do also sit in idleness, while there are thousands round about in the borders of the land who are falling by the sword, yea, wounded and bleeding?

What can we learn from Moroni's accusations against his political leaders? (60:18–23) "It was, to say the least, not the most tactful letter in the world, but Moroni's patience was worn out. Also, it turned out, he was right—on every point but one. And that point was an important one: he had accused the wrong man. Aside from that, he had the situation correctly sized up—his long experience with the king-men had not been for nothing" (Nibley, *Since Cumorah*, 326).

What does the "vessel" represent and what is the significance of the imagery? (Alma 60:23) "A vessel is a container like a cup or bowl. . . . The inside represents the government of the land. Moroni threatens to clean out the inner vessel, or overthrow the government, to keep the freedom of his country" (*Book of Mormon for Latter-day Saint Families*, 443).

On a more immediate level, President Ezra Taft Benson taught: "All is not well in Zion. As Moroni counseled, we must cleanse the inner vessel (see Alma 60:23), beginning first with ourselves, then with our families, and finally with the Church. . . . As we cleanse the inner vessel, there will have to be changes made in our own personal lives, in our families, and in the Church" ("Cleansing the Inner Vessel," 4–7).

Alma 60:24–36. Moroni Threatens to Overthrow the Government Leaders Unless They Help His Army

23 Do ye suppose that God will look upon you as guiltless while ye sit still and behold these things? Behold I say unto you, Nay. Now I would that ye should remember that God has said that the inward vessel shall be cleansed first, and then shall the outer vessel be cleansed also.

24 And now, except ye do repent of that which ye have done, and begin to be up and doing, and send forth food and men unto us, and also unto Helaman, that he may support those parts of our country which he has regained, and that we may also recover the

---

How was Captain Moroni's reference to cleansing the inner vessel of the Nephite nation in harmony with the Savior's teachings to the people of Israel in the Old World?

Portrait of Christ,
by Heinrich Hoffman

Captain Moroni's reference to cleansing the inner vessel of the Nephite nation is in harmony with the Savior's teachings:

"Woe unto you, scribes and Pharisees, hypocrites! for ye make clean the outside of the cup and of the platter, but within they are full of extortion and excess. Thou blind Pharisee, cleanse first that which is within the cup and platter, that the outside of them may be clean also" (Matthew 23:25–26).

"Ye are like unto whited sepulchres, which indeed appear beautiful outward, but are within full of dead men's bones, and of all uncleanness. Even so ye also outwardly appear righteous unto men, but within ye are full of hypocrisy and iniquity" (Matthew 23:27–28).

"Laying aside the commandment of God, ye hold the tradition of men, as the washing of pots and cups: and many other such like things ye do. . . . Full well ye reject the commandment of God, that ye may keep your own tradition" (Mark 7:8–9).

"Woe unto you, scribes and Pharisees, hypocrites! for ye are as graves which appear not, and the men that walk over them are not aware of them" (Luke 11:44).

"Extortion and excess" are related to a Greek word meaning rapacity (by force or greediness), self-indulgence, or lack of self-control (see notes *a* and *b* to Matthew 23:25). The washing (or worrying about the outside of the pot, cups, or vessels) is evidence that man is given to appearance, trends, and traditions rather than personal spiritual cleansing.

"Behold, vengeance cometh speedily upon the inhabitants of the earth, a day of wrath, a day of burning, a day of desolation, of weeping, of mourning, and of lamentation; and as a whirlwind it shall come upon all the face of the earth, saith the Lord. And upon my house shall it begin, and from my house shall it go forth, saith the Lord; First among those among you, saith the Lord, who have professed to know my name and have not known me, and have blasphemed against me in the midst of my house, saith the Lord" (D&C 112:24–26).

Public domain.

remainder of our possessions in these parts, behold it will be expedient that we contend no more with the Lamanites until we have first cleansed our inward vessel, yea, even the great head of our government.

25 And except ye grant mine epistle, and come out and show unto me a true spirit of freedom, and strive to strengthen and fortify our armies, and grant unto them food for their support, behold I will leave a part of my freemen to maintain this part of our land, and I will leave the strength and the blessings of God upon them, that none other power can operate against them—

26 And this because of their exceeding faith, and their patience in their tribulations—

27 And I will come unto you, and if there be any among you that has a desire for freedom, yea, if there be even a spark of freedom remaining, behold I will stir up insurrections among you, even until those who have desires to usurp power and authority shall become extinct.

28 Yea, behold I do not fear your power nor your authority, but it is my God whom I fear; and it is according to his commandments that I do take my sword to defend the cause of my country, and it is because of your iniquity that we have suffered so much loss.

29 Behold it is time, yea, the time is now at hand, that except ye do bestir yourselves in the defence of your country and your little ones, the sword of justice doth hang over you; yea, and it shall fall upon you and visit you even to your utter destruction.

30 Behold, I wait for assistance from you; and, except ye do administer unto our relief, behold, I come unto you, even in the land

Why is the "true spirit of freedom" so essential? (60:25) Lamanite aggressors and Nephite apostates wanted to suppress Nephite freedoms, particularly their freedom to worship God. "The Lord knows that without the spirit of freedom in the souls of men, there could be no willing response to the gospel plan. For it is in the culture of freedom and the use of agency in that freedom that men come to know the difference between good and evil. This progress leads to yearnings in the hearts of good men, and eventually to gospel dispensations. This is the pattern to be noted down through the era of the historical writings" (Dyer, "Last Dispensation," 53).

What did Moroni judge was the cause of such great loss among the Nephites? (60:28) Moroni testified, as did Limhi, about the cause of so much needless loss of life: "For behold how many of our brethren have been slain, and their blood has been spilt in vain, and all because of iniquity. For if this people had not fallen into transgression the Lord would not have suffered this great evil should come upon them, but behold, they would not hearken unto his words; but there arose contentions among them, even so much that they did shed blood among themselves" (Mosiah 7:24–25).

Was Moroni's use of "the sword" metaphorical or real? (60:29) "There are other, more symbolic reasons for Moroni's close identification with the sword. Book of Mormon writers often use the term 'sword' for a symbol of divine power, particularly as judgment" (Valletta, "Captain and the Covenant," 242).

of Zarahemla, and smite you with the sword, insomuch that ye can have no more power to impede the progress of this people in the cause of our freedom.

31 For behold, the Lord will not suffer that ye shall live and wax strong in your iniquities to destroy his righteous people.

32 Behold, can you suppose that the Lord will spare you and come out in judgment against the Lamanites, when it is the tradition of their fathers that has caused their hatred, yea, and it has been redoubled by those who have dissented from us, while your iniquity is for the cause of your love of glory and the vain things of the world?

33 Ye know that ye do transgress the laws of God, and ye do know that ye do trample them under your feet. Behold, the Lord saith unto me: If those whom ye have appointed your governors do not repent of their sins and iniquities, ye shall go up to battle against them.

34 And now behold, I, Moroni, am constrained, according to the covenant which I have made to keep the commandments of my God; therefore I would that ye should adhere to the word of God, and send speedily unto me of your provisions and of your men, and also to Helaman.

35 And behold, if ye will not do this I come unto you speedily; for behold, God will not suffer that we should perish with hunger; therefore he will give unto us of your food, even if it must be by the sword. Now see that ye fulfil the word of God.

36 Behold, I am Moroni, your chief captain. I seek not for power, but to pull it down. I seek not for honor of the world, but for the glory of my God, and the freedom and welfare of my country. And thus I close mine epistle.

What is notable about Moroni's threat to Pahoran? (60:36) "In this letter alone he has threatened Pahoran at least four times. He will march against Zarahemla and depose its rulers if they do not fulfill their rightful obligations. . . . While others might try to bring down the leader to usurp his power themselves (as Amalickiah did), Moroni's only goal is to 'pull it down'—'it' meaning, in this case, unrighteously exercised power" (Gardner, *Second Witness*, 4:748).

CHAPTER 61

Pahoran tells Moroni of the insurrection and rebellion against the government—The king-men take Zarahemla and are in league with the Lamanites—Pahoran asks for military aid against the rebels. About 62 B.C.

1 Behold, now it came to pass that soon after Moroni had sent his epistle unto the chief governor, he received an epistle from Pahoran, the chief governor. And these are the words which he received:

2 I, Pahoran, who am the chief governor of this land, do send these words unto Moroni, the chief captain over the army. Behold, I say unto you, Moroni, that I do not joy in your great afflictions, yea, it grieves my soul.

3 But behold, there are those who do joy in your afflictions, yea, insomuch that they have risen up in rebellion against me, and also those of my people who are freemen, yea, and those who have risen up are exceedingly numerous.

4 And it is those who have sought to take away the judgment-seat from me that have been the cause of this great iniquity; for they have used great flattery, and they have led away the hearts of many people, which will be the cause of sore affliction among us; they have withheld our provisions, and have daunted our freemen that they have not come unto you.

5 And behold, they have driven me out before them, and I have fled to the land of Gideon, with as many men as it were possible that I could get.

6 And behold, I have sent a proclamation throughout this part of the land; and behold, they are flocking to us daily, to their arms, in

Alma 61:1–8. Pahoran Writes That He Has Been Driven Out of Zarahemla

How did Pahoran respond to the unjustified scolding from Moroni? (61:1–2) "We must always realize that in a perfect church filled with imperfect people, there are bound to be some miscommunications at times. A noteworthy example occurred in ancient American Israel. Moroni wrote two times to Pahoran complaining of neglect because much-needed reinforcements did not arrive. Moroni used harsh language, accusing the governor of the land, Pahoran, of sitting on his throne in a state of 'thoughtless stupor' (Alma 60:7). Pahoran soon made a very patriotic reply, explaining why he could not do what Moroni wanted" (Maxwell, *All These Things Shall Give Thee Experience*, 119). ⊕

What conditions indicate the serious nature of Pahoran's situation? (61:3–7) "Why hadn't [Moroni] heard from them long before? [Pahoran] immediately explains why. There's a state of complete crisis—not only complete insecurity, but everything was totally disrupted, the communications and everything else. . . . They have taken over the government. 'And it is those who have sought to take away the judgment-seat from me that have been the cause of this great iniquity. . . . They have withheld our provisions, and have daunted our freemen that they have not come unto you.' They have blocked the way so that they couldn't come to you. It's not only intimidation, but they have taken over everything" (Nibley, *Teachings of the Book of Mormon*, 3:188).

Why is flattery so effective in leading people away from the Lord? (61:4) "Satan is the world's master in the use of flattery, and he knows the great power of speech (see Jacob 7:4)" (Faust, "Great Imitator," 34). President Harold B. Lee observed that flattery "ofttimes means to merely satisfy the individual's vanity and sometimes to ingratiate the flatterer into the good graces of the flattered" (*Teachings of Harold B. Lee*, 199).

the defence of their country and their freedom, and to avenge our wrongs.

7 And they have come unto us, insomuch that those who have risen up in rebellion against us are set at defiance, yea, insomuch that they do fear us and durst not come out against us to battle.

8 They have got possession of the land, or the city, of Zarahemla; they have appointed a king over them, and he hath written unto the king of the Lamanites, in the which he hath joined an alliance with him; in the which alliance he hath agreed to maintain the city of Zarahemla, which maintenance he supposeth will enable the Lamanites to conquer the remainder of the land, and he shall be placed king over this people when they shall be conquered under the Lamanites.

9 And now, in your epistle you have censured me, but it mattereth not; I am not angry, but do rejoice in the greatness of your heart. I, Pahoran, do not seek for power, save only to retain my judgment-seat that I may preserve the rights and the liberty of my people. My soul standeth fast in that liberty in the which God hath made us free.

10 And now, behold, we will resist wickedness even unto bloodshed. We would not shed the blood of the Lamanites if they would stay in their own land.

11 We would not shed the blood of our brethren if they would not rise up in rebellion and take the sword against us.

12 We would subject ourselves to the yoke of bondage if it were requisite with the justice of God, or if he should command us so to do.

13 But behold he doth not command us that we shall subject ourselves to our enemies, but that we should put our trust in him, and he will deliver us.

Alma 61:9–13. Pahoran Wants the Nephites to Continue to Be Free

What can we learn from Pahoran's choice to not be offended by Moroni's letter? (61:9) "One of the greatest indicators of our own spiritual maturity is revealed in how we respond to the weaknesses, the inexperience, and the potentially offensive actions of others. A thing, an event, or an expression may be offensive, but you and I can choose not to be offended—and to say with Pahoran, 'it mattereth not'" (Bednar, "And Nothing Shall Offend Them," 91). ⊕

How should we respond when a misinformed person unjustly corrects us? (61:9–13) Are you quick to point out the misinformation or do you respond like Pahoran? "Moroni was not the first underinformed leader to conclude that another leader was not doing enough (see Alma 60). Nor was Pahoran's sweet, generous response to his 'beloved brother' Moroni the last such that will be needed (Alma 61)" (Maxwell, "Notwithstanding My Weakness," 13–14).

How can Pahoran's example help us respond more wisely when misinformation is spoken about us or someone we love?

Alma 61:14–21. Pahoran Requests Help to Regain Control of the Government

14 Therefore, my beloved brother, Moroni, let us resist evil, and whatsoever evil we cannot resist with our words, yea, such as rebellions and dissensions, let us resist them with our swords, that we may retain our freedom, that we may rejoice in the great privilege of our church, and in the cause of our Redeemer and our God.

15 Therefore, come unto me speedily with a few of your men, and leave the remainder in the charge of Lehi and Teancum; give unto them power to conduct the war in that part of the land, according to the Spirit of God, which is also the spirit of freedom which is in them.

16 Behold I have sent a few provisions unto them, that they may not perish until ye can come unto me.

17 Gather together whatsoever force ye can upon your march hither, and we will go speedily against those dissenters, in the strength of our God according to the faith which is in us.

18 And we will take possession of the city of Zarahemla, that we may obtain more food to send forth unto Lehi and Teancum; yea, we will go forth against them in the strength of the Lord, and we will put an end to this great iniquity.

19 And now, Moroni, I do joy in receiving your epistle, for I was somewhat worried concerning what we should do, whether it should be just in us to go against our brethren.

20 But ye have said, except they repent the Lord hath commanded you that ye should go against them.

Why do we need to "resist evil" with our words and actions? (61:14) "We need to remember Edmund Burke's statement: 'The only thing necessary for the triumph of evil is for good men to do nothing' (attributed to John Bartlett, comp., *Familiar Quotations*, 15th ed. [1980], ix). We need to raise our voices with other concerned citizens throughout the world in opposition to current trends. We need to tell the sponsors of offensive media that we have had enough. We need to support programs and products that are positive and uplifting. Joining together with neighbors and friends who share our concerns, we can send a clear message to those responsible" (Ballard, "Let Our Voices Be Heard," 18).

Who was the supreme commander of the Nephite armies: Moroni or Pahoran? (61:15–17) "Alma 2:16 shows that . . . Alma, as 'the chief judge and the governor of the people of Nephi,' led '*his* armies, against the Amlicites to battle,' . . . Moroni had been 'appointed to be the chief captain' . . . and 'the chief captain took the command of all the armies of the Nephites' (Alma 43:16). Moroni would have been appointed to his post under the authority of the chief judge, who in turn received his authority by election from the people. With his right as commander-in-chief of the armies, Pahoran issued orders to Moroni (see Alma 61:15–18, 21)" (*Book of Mormon Student Manual* [1989], 103–4).

What words indicate that Pahoran was prayerful about his decision to end the rebellion in Zarahemla? (61:18–21) "We may conceive that Pahoran sent his request to Moroni for aid not without a prayer to Him whose servant he was. . . .

"Pahoran did not ask for help without giving his plans considerable thought. He had them already mapped out, probably inspired and in righteousness formulated. . . . Together [with Moroni] they could regain possession of Zarahemla. From its well-stocked supplies they then would send Lehi and Teancum adequate food; *Yea*, Pahoran confidently noted to Moroni in speaking of the rebels, *We will go forth against them in the strength of the Lord, and we will put an end to this great iniquity*" (Reynolds and Sjodahl, *Commentary on the Book of Mormon*, 5:169–70).

21 See that ye strengthen Lehi and Teancum in the Lord; tell them to fear not, for God will deliver them, yea, and also all those who stand fast in that liberty wherewith God hath made them free. And now I close mine epistle to my beloved brother, Moroni.

CHAPTER 62

Moroni marches to the aid of Pahoran in the land of Gideon—The king-men who refuse to defend their country are put to death—Pahoran and Moroni retake Nephihah—Many Lamanites join the people of Ammon—Teancum slays Ammoron and is in turn slain—The Lamanites are driven from the land, and peace is established—Helaman returns to the ministry and builds up the Church. About 62–57 B.C.

1 And now it came to pass that when Moroni had received this epistle his heart did take courage, and was filled with exceedingly great joy because of the faithfulness of Pahoran, that he was not also a traitor to the freedom and cause of his country.

2 But he did also mourn exceedingly because of the iniquity of those who had driven Pahoran from the judgment-seat, yea, in fine because of those who had rebelled against their country and also their God.

3 And it came to pass that Moroni took a small number of men, according to the desire of Pahoran, and gave Lehi and Teancum command over the remainder of his army, and took his march towards the land of Gideon.

4 And he did raise the standard of liberty in whatsoever place he did enter, and gained whatsoever force he could in all his march towards the land of Gideon.

Alma 62:1–6. Moroni Gathers an Army and Goes to the Aid of Pahoran

How can we be like Moroni in raising our voices to promote righteous standards today? (62:4) What standards can we raise to defend our God, religion, and families? "Send a clear message to those responsible. The Internet Web sites and their local affiliates will have their addresses. Letters and e-mails have more effect than most people realize, especially those like one sent by a Relief Society sister that stated, 'I represent a group of over a hundred women that meets every week and often talks about the harm your program is doing to our children'" (Ballard, "Let Our Voices Be Heard," 18).

In what ways can we join with others to raise standards of decency? ✦

5 And it came to pass that thousands did flock unto his standard, and did take up their swords in the defence of their freedom, that they might not come into bondage.

6 And thus, when Moroni had gathered together whatsoever men he could in all his march, he came to the land of Gideon; and uniting his forces with those of Pahoran they became exceedingly strong, even stronger than the men of Pachus, who was the king of those dissenters who had driven the freemen out of the land of Zarahemla and had taken possession of the land.

7 And it came to pass that Moroni and Pahoran went down with their armies into the land of Zarahemla, and went forth against the city, and did meet the men of Pachus, insomuch that they did come to battle.

8 And behold, Pachus was slain and his men were taken prisoners, and Pahoran was restored to his judgment-seat.

9 And the men of Pachus received their trial, according to the law, and also those king-men who had been taken and cast into prison; and they were executed according to the law; yea, those men of Pachus and those king-men, whosoever would not take up arms in the defence of their country, but would fight against it, were put to death.

10 And thus it became expedient that this law should be strictly observed for the safety of their country; yea, and whosoever was found denying their freedom was speedily executed according to the law.

11 And thus ended the thirtieth year of the reign of the judges over the people of Nephi; Moroni and Pahoran having restored peace to the land of Zarahemla, among their own people, having inflicted death upon all those who were not true to the cause of freedom.

How does this passage show strength in unity? (62:5–6) "After Moroni received Pahoran's gracious reply, 'his heart did take courage.' He began to march toward the land of Gideon, and 'thousands did flock unto his standard, and did take up their swords in the defence of their freedom' (Alma 62:1–5). As Moroni and Pahoran united their forces, 'they became exceedingly strong' and successfully rooted out the king-men, the internal dissenters who would have toppled the government from within. After being placed on trial in accordance with the laws of the land, 'those king-men, whosoever would not take up arms in the defence of their country, but would fight against it, were put to death' (Alma 62:6–9)" (Condie, "Righteous Oaths, Reproof, and Reconciliation," 89).

Alma 62:7–11. Moroni and Pahoran Defeat Pachus

What does the name Pachus mean? (62:7) "Pachus is a very interesting name. It's perfectly good Egyptian and means 'he who is praised.' It means a person who is 'praised, blessed or favored of God.' Mohammed means the same thing" (Nibley, *Teachings of the Book of Mormon*, 3:190).

Why were the king-men "executed according to the law"? (Alma 62:9–10) "Treason is a serious offense. Pachus and his king-men were committed to the overthrow of Nephite freedom. They insisted on trying to destroy the very thing Moroni's soldiers were fighting for and dying to preserve. This neither Moroni nor Pahoran could condone in the slightest. It was difficult enough to have to fight aggression from outside their country, but to have to battle foes within, as well, was unthinkable. Following their capture, the evil men of Pachus were executed if they would not take up arms to defend their country" (*Book of Mormon Student Manual* [1989], 104).

Alma 62:12–19. Moroni's Army Marches to Retake Nephihah

Why were Pahoran and Moroni able to capture "a large body of the men of the Lamanites"? (62:14–17) "Providence lent a helping hand in their undertaking. As they followed a course that would lead them to the stricken city, they came across a large company of Lamanitish warriors. . . . The army of Moroni's immediately attacked them, slew many, and took their provisions and weapons of war. To the number of 4000, the Nephites also took prisoners; indoctrinated them according to Nephite beliefs, and at their own request, sent them to join their brethren, the People of Ammon. . . . This incident in Moroni's campaign was not an accident. It proves that the Lord is willing to, and does help His people in their difficulties if they keep His commandments" (Reynolds and Sjodahl, Commentary on the Book of Mormon, 5:174).

12 And it came to pass in the commencement of the thirty and first year of the reign of the judges over the people of Nephi, Moroni immediately caused that provisions should be sent, and also an army of six thousand men should be sent unto Helaman, to assist him in preserving that part of the land.

13 And he also caused that an army of six thousand men, with a sufficient quantity of food, should be sent to the armies of Lehi and Teancum. And it came to pass that this was done to fortify the land against the Lamanites.

14 And it came to pass that Moroni and Pahoran, leaving a large body of men in the land of Zarahemla, took their march with a large body of men towards the land of Nephihah, being determined to overthrow the Lamanites in that city.

15 And it came to pass that as they were marching towards the land, they took a large body of men of the Lamanites, and slew many of them, and took their provisions and their weapons of war.

16 And it came to pass after they had taken them, they caused them to enter into a covenant that they would no more take up their weapons of war against the Nephites.

17 And when they had entered into this covenant they sent them to dwell with the people of Ammon, and they were in number about four thousand who had not been slain.

18 And it came to pass that when they had sent them away they pursued their march towards the land of Nephihah. And it came to pass that when they had come to the city of Nephihah, they did pitch their tents in the plains of Nephihah, which is near the city of Nephihah.

19 Now Moroni was desirous that the Lamanites should come out to battle against them, upon the plains; but the Lamanites, knowing

of their exceedingly great courage, and beholding the greatness of their numbers, therefore they durst not come out against them; therefore they did not come to battle in that day.

20 And when the night came, Moroni went forth in the darkness of the night, and came upon the top of the wall to spy out in what part of the city the Lamanites did camp with their army.

21 And it came to pass that they were on the east, by the entrance; and they were all asleep. And now Moroni returned to his army, and caused that they should prepare in haste strong cords and ladders, to be let down from the top of the wall into the inner part of the wall.

22 And it came to pass that Moroni caused that his men should march forth and come upon the top of the wall, and let themselves down into that part of the city, yea, even on the west, where the Lamanites did not camp with their armies.

23 And it came to pass that they were all let down into the city by night, by the means of their strong cords and their ladders; thus when the morning came they were all within the walls of the city.

24 And now, when the Lamanites awoke and saw that the armies of Moroni were within the walls, they were affrighted exceedingly, insomuch that they did flee out by the pass.

25 And now when Moroni saw that they were fleeing before him, he did cause that his men should march forth against them, and slew many, and surrounded many others, and took them prisoners; and the remainder of them fled into the land of Moroni, which was in the borders by the seashore.

26 Thus had Moroni and Pahoran obtained the possession of the city of Nephihah without the loss of one soul; and there were many of the Lamanites who were slain.

Alma 62:20–30. Moroni's Army Captures Nephihah

Why do you think these Lamanite prisoners wanted to be a free people? (62:27–28) Why did they forsake their homelands in order to live among the Nephites, who valued and protected freedom? What blessings and responsibilities come to those who live in countries that protect extensive freedoms of their people? How would it be if every government allowed "each individual the free exercise of conscience, the right and control of property, and the protection of life"? (D&C 134:2).

What can we learn from the Lamanites joining the Nephites in their daily labors? (62:29) Notice the harmony, peace and blessing that came to the prisoners and the people of Ammon by laboring together. Elder Maxwell taught: "'Behold, this is my *work* and my glory—to bring to pass the immortality and eternal life of man' (Moses 1:39; emphasis added). Consider the significance of the Lord's use of the word *work*. What He is doing so lovingly and redemptively is, nevertheless, work—even for Him! We, likewise, speak of 'working out our salvation,'... and of the 'sweat of the brow.'... These are not idle phrases. Instead, they underscore the importance of work. In fact, brethren, work is always a spiritual necessity even if, for some, work is not an economic necessity" (Maxwell, "Put Your Shoulder to the Wheel," 37).

Alma 62:31–38. In an Effort to End the War, Teancum Slays Ammoron and Is Overtaken and Slain

27 Now it came to pass that many of the Lamanites that were prisoners were desirous to join the people of Ammon and become a free people.

28 And it came to pass that as many as were desirous, unto them it was granted according to their desires.

29 Therefore, all the prisoners of the Lamanites did join the people of Ammon, and did begin to labor exceedingly, tilling the ground, raising all manner of grain, and flocks and herds of every kind; and thus were the Nephites relieved from a great burden; yea, insomuch that they were relieved from all the prisoners of the Lamanites.

30 Now it came to pass that Moroni, after he had obtained possession of the city of Nephihah, having taken many prisoners, which did reduce the armies of the Lamanites exceedingly, and having regained many of the Nephites who had been taken prisoners, which did strengthen the army of Moroni exceedingly; therefore Moroni went forth from the land of Nephihah to the land of Lehi.

31 And it came to pass that when the Lamanites saw that Moroni was coming against them, they were again frightened and fled before the army of Moroni.

32 And it came to pass that Moroni and his army did pursue them from city to city, until they were met by Lehi and Teancum; and the Lamanites fled from Lehi and Teancum, even down upon the borders by the seashore, until they came to the land of Moroni.

33 And the armies of the Lamanites were all gathered together, insomuch that they were all in one body in the land of Moroni. Now Ammoron, the king of the Lamanites, was also with them.

34 And it came to pass that Moroni and Lehi and Teancum did encamp with their armies

round about in the borders of the land of Moroni, insomuch that the Lamanites were encircled about in the borders by the wilderness on the south, and in the borders by the wilderness on the east.

35 And thus they did encamp for the night. For behold, the Nephites and the Lamanites also were weary because of the greatness of the march; therefore they did not resolve upon any stratagem in the night-time, save it were Teancum; for he was exceedingly angry with Ammoron, insomuch that he considered that Ammoron, and Amalickiah his brother, had been the cause of this great and lasting war between them and the Lamanites, which had been the cause of so much war and bloodshed, yea, and so much famine.

36 And it came to pass that Teancum in his anger did go forth into the camp of the Lamanites, and did let himself down over the walls of the city. And he went forth with a cord, from place to place, insomuch that he did find the king; and he did cast a javelin at him, which did pierce him near the heart. But behold, the king did awaken his servants before he died, insomuch that they did pursue Teancum, and slew him.

37 Now it came to pass that when Lehi and Moroni knew that Teancum was dead they were exceedingly sorrowful; for behold, he had been a man who had fought valiantly for his country, yea, a true friend to liberty; and he had suffered very many exceedingly sore afflictions. But behold, he was dead, and had gone the way of all the earth.

38 Now it came to pass that Moroni marched forth on the morrow, and came upon the Lamanites, insomuch that they did slay them with a great slaughter; and they did drive them out of the land; and they did flee, even that they did not return at that time against the Nephites.

Why was Teancum loved so dearly? (62:35–38)
"'When Lehi and Moroni knew that Teancum was dead they were exceeding sorrowful.'... In that glorious galaxy of patriot-priests, or warrior-prophets ... Teancum shines among the brightest. View him from whatever point we please, there is no mistaking the man. His ardent disposition, his fiery impetuosity, his zealous patriotism, his undaunted courage, his love of liberty, his entire disinterestedness [i.e., unselfishness], shine forth in every action. Indeed, we might almost call him rash, so little did he consider his personal safety when he thought the good of his country required the sacrifice" (Reynolds and Sjodahl, *Commentary on the Book of Mormon*, 5:178). ●

Alma 62:39–52. After Years of War, Peace Is Again Established throughout the Land

Why were some Nephites "hardened" by adversity, while others were "softened"? (62:39–41) "The same testing in troubled times can have quite opposite effects on individuals. Three verses from the Book of Mormon . . . teach us that . . . 'because of the exceedingly great length of the war between the Nephites and the Lamanites many had become *hardened*, because of the exceedingly great length of the war; and many were *softened* because of their afflictions . . .' (Alma 62:39–41; italics added).

"Surely you know some whose lives have been filled with adversity who have been mellowed and strengthened and refined by it, while others have come away from the same test bitter and blistered and unhappy" (Packer, "Mystery of Life," 18).

What does the Lord promise "because of the prayers of the righteous"? (62:40) "The Lord is far from the wicked: but he heareth the prayer of the righteous" (Proverbs 15:29). "It is by the prayers of the righteous that ye are spared" (Alma 10:23). "The Lord will remember the prayers of the righteous, which have been put up unto him for them" (Mormon 5:21). When have you felt the Lord's assistance in response to your humble prayers and faithful living?

How can afflictions bring us closer to God? (62:41) "Even as adversities inflict mortal hardships, they can also be the means of leading men and women to eternal blessings. Such large-scale adversities as natural disasters and wars seem to be inherent in the mortal experience. We cannot entirely prevent them, but we can determine how we will react to them. For example, the adversities of war and military service, which have been the spiritual destruction of some, have been the spiritual awakening of others" (Oaks, "Adversity," 7–8).

When was Moronihah, son of Moroni, appointed to be the next military leader? (62:43) "Moroni . . . became chief captain at the age of twenty-five (see Alma 43:17). Moroni had given up the command of the armies to his son Moronihah (see Alma 62:43), which implies that the position was inherited. Moroni himself became chief captain in the eighteenth year of the reign of the judges (see Alma 43:3) and his son Moronihah in about the thirty-first year (see Alma 62:39). If Moronihah was born when his father was twenty years of age, he would have been only eighteen when he succeeded him" (Tvedtnes, "Book of Mormon Tribal Affiliation and Military Castes," 318). ✪

39 And thus ended the thirty and first year of the reign of the judges over the people of Nephi; and thus they had had wars, and bloodsheds, and famine, and affliction, for the space of many years.

40 And there had been murders, and contentions, and dissensions, and all manner of iniquity among the people of Nephi; nevertheless for the righteous' sake, yea, because of the prayers of the righteous, they were spared.

41 But behold, because of the exceedingly great length of the war between the Nephites and the Lamanites many had become hardened, because of the exceedingly great length of the war; and many were softened because of their afflictions, insomuch that they did humble themselves before God, even in the depth of humility.

42 And it came to pass that after Moroni had fortified those parts of the land which were most exposed to the Lamanites, until they were sufficiently strong, he returned to the city of Zarahemla; and also Helaman returned to the place of his inheritance; and there was once more peace established among the people of Nephi.

43 And Moroni yielded up the command of his armies into the hands of his son, whose name was Moronihah; and he retired to his own house that he might spend the remainder of his days in peace.

44 And Pahoran did return to his judgment-seat; and Helaman did take upon him again to preach unto the people the word of God; for because of so many wars and contentions it had become expedient that a regulation should be made again in the church.

45 Therefore, Helaman and his brethren went forth, and did declare the word of God with much power unto the convincing of many people of their wickedness, which did

cause them to repent of their sins and to be baptized unto the Lord their God.

46 And it came to pass that they did establish again the church of God, throughout all the land.

47 Yea, and regulations were made concerning the law. And their judges, and their chief judges were chosen.

48 And the people of Nephi began to prosper again in the land, and began to multiply and to wax exceedingly strong again in the land. And they began to grow exceedingly rich.

49 But notwithstanding their riches, or their strength, or their prosperity, they were not lifted up in the pride of their eyes; neither were they slow to remember the Lord their God; but they did humble themselves exceedingly before him.

50 Yea, they did remember how great things the Lord had done for them, that he had delivered them from death, and from bonds, and from prisons, and from all manner of afflictions, and he had delivered them out of the hands of their enemies.

51 And they did pray unto the Lord their God continually, insomuch that the Lord did bless them, according to his word, so that they did wax strong and prosper in the land.

52 And it came to pass that all these things were done. And Helaman died, in the thirty and fifth year of the reign of the judges over the people of Nephi.

CHAPTER 63

Shiblon and later Helaman take possession of the sacred records—Many Nephites travel to the land northward—Hagoth builds ships, which sail forth in the west sea—Moronihah defeats the Lamanites in battle. About 56–52 B.C.

1 And it came to pass in the commencement of the thirty and sixth year of the reign of the

Alma 63:1–9. Hagoth Builds Ships That Carry People Northward

What does the name Shiblon mean? (63:1). Shiblon "is a good Arabic name. It means young lion. . . . He took possession of the sacred things, and he was a just man" (Nibley, *Teachings of the Book of Mormon*, 3:195).

We learn much about Shiblon's goodness from his father's words recorded in Alma 38, in which the young man was praised for his faithfulness, diligence, patience, and long-suffering.

What became of Hagoth? (63:5–9) In reference to "Hagoth and his party, President Spencer W. Kimball said: 'President Joseph F. Smith, the president of the Church reported, "You brethren and sisters from New Zealand, I want you to know that you are from the people of Hagoth." For New Zealand Saints, that was that. A prophet of the Lord had spoken' (in New Zealand Area Conference Report, 20–22 Feb. 1976, 3)" (*Book of Mormon Student Manual* [1989], 103–4).

judges over the people of Nephi, that Shiblon took possession of those sacred things which had been delivered unto Helaman by Alma.

2 And he was a just man, and he did walk uprightly before God; and he did observe to do good continually, to keep the commandments of the Lord his God; and also did his brother.

3 And it came to pass that Moroni died also. And thus ended the thirty and sixth year of the reign of the judges.

4 And it came to pass that in the thirty and seventh year of the reign of the judges, there was a large company of men, even to the amount of five thousand and four hundred men, with their wives and their children, departed out of the land of Zarahemla into the land which was northward.

5 And it came to pass that Hagoth, he being an exceedingly curious man, therefore he went forth and built him an exceedingly large ship, on the borders of the land Bountiful, by the land Desolation, and launched it forth into the west sea, by the narrow neck which led into the land northward.

6 And behold, there were many of the Nephites who did enter therein and did sail forth with much provisions, and also many women and children; and they took their course northward. And thus ended the thirty and seventh year.

7 And in the thirty and eighth year, this man built other ships. And the first ship did also return, and many more people did enter into it; and they also took much provisions, and set out again to the land northward.

8 And it came to pass that they were never heard of more. And we suppose that they were drowned in the depths of the sea. And it came to pass that one other ship also did sail forth; and whither she did go we know not.

9 And it came to pass that in this year there were many people who went forth into the land northward. And thus ended the thirty and eighth year.

10 And it came to pass in the thirty and ninth year of the reign of the judges, Shiblon died also, and Corianton had gone forth to the land northward in a ship, to carry forth provisions unto the people who had gone forth into that land.

11 Therefore it became expedient for Shiblon to confer those sacred things, before his death, upon the son of Helaman, who was called Helaman, being called after the name of his father.

12 Now behold, all those engravings which were in the possession of Helaman were written and sent forth among the children of men throughout all the land, save it were those parts which had been commanded by Alma should not go forth.

13 Nevertheless, these things were to be kept sacred, and handed down from one generation to another; therefore, in this year, they had been conferred upon Helaman, before the death of Shiblon.

14 And it came to pass also in this year that there were some dissenters who had gone forth unto the Lamanites; and they were stirred up again to anger against the Nephites.

15 And also in this same year they came down with a numerous army to war against the people of Moronihah, or against the army of Moronihah, in the which they were beaten and driven back again to their own lands, suffering great loss.

16 And thus ended the thirty and ninth year of the reign of the judges over the people of Nephi.

17 And thus ended the account of Alma, and Helaman his son, and also Shiblon, who was his son.

Alma 63:10–17. Shiblon Passes the Sacred Scriptural Record to Helaman's Son

How do we demonstrate reverence for the scriptures? (63:12–13) One way to show reverence is by treating the physical scriptures with the utmost of respect. More important, how do we hold the sacred words in our hearts? Do we carefully read the verses again and again and ponder what they mean? Do we pray for understanding, seeking for spiritual impressions?

Why do so many names in the Book of Mormon end with -iah and -ihah? (63:15) "A large proportion of Book of Mormon names end in -iah and -ihah. The same ending is peculiar to Palestinian names of Lehi's time but not so prevalent other times" (Nibley, *Teachings of the Book of Mormon*, 3:283).

THE BOOK OF HELAMAN

Introduction

The book of Helaman shows the Nephites and Lamanites frequently fluctuating between righteousness and wickedness. It shows the dangers of secret combinations and exposes the activities of the Gadianton robbers, whose works of darkness would lead to wars and eventually bring about the destruction of the Nephites (Helaman 2:13–14). Yet during this time of general wickedness, many of the Lamanites accept the gospel and are converted and become more righteous than the Nephites (Helaman 6:1).

The role of prophets is vividly portrayed in the book of Helaman. For example, Nephi reveals the murder of a chief judge and identifies the murderer by prophecy (Helaman 8–9). With priesthood power, the prophet Nephi brings about a famine and later ends it (Helaman 10–11). Mormon highlights the pride cycle, which so often afflicts the Nephites (Helaman 12). Samuel, a Lamanite prophet, foretells signs that will accompany the birth and death of Jesus Christ (Helaman 13–15). The believers are rewarded by witnessing the fulfillment of some of these signs, while unbelievers conclude that it is "not reasonable to believe" in Jesus Christ or the accompanying signs (Helaman 16). The book of Helaman covers the years from about 52 B.C. to 1 B.C.

The superscription to the book of Helaman, which appears just under the title, was part of the ancient record translated by the Prophet Joseph Smith (see also, for example, 2 Nephi, Mosiah 9, and 4 Nephi).

Distinct from the superscription is the chapter summary, which is presented in italics between the chapter number and the beginning of the scriptural text. Chapter summaries, originally added in the 1920 edition of the Book of Mormon, give the reader an overview of what each chapter contains.

An account of the Nephites. Their wars and contentions, and their dissensions. And also the prophecies of many holy prophets, before the coming of Christ, according to the records of Helaman, who was the son of Helaman, and also according to the records of his sons, even down to the coming of Christ. And also many of the Lamanites are converted. An account of their conversion. An account of the righteousness of the Lamanites, and the wickedness and abominations of the Nephites, according to the record of Helaman and his sons, even down to the coming of Christ, which is called the book of Helaman, and so forth.

CHAPTER 1

Pahoran the second becomes chief judge and is murdered by Kishkumen—Pacumeni fills the judgment seat—Coriantumr leads the Lamanite armies, takes Zarahemla, and slays

Pacumeni—Moronihah defeats the Lamanites and retakes Zarahemla, and Coriantumr is slain. About 52–50 B.C.

1 And now behold, it came to pass in the commencement of the fortieth year of the reign of the judges over the people of Nephi, there began to be a serious difficulty among the people of the Nephites.

2 For behold, Pahoran had died, and gone the way of all the earth; therefore there began to be a serious contention concerning who should have the judgment-seat among the brethren, who were the sons of Pahoran.

3 Now these are their names who did contend for the judgment-seat, who did also cause the people to contend: Pahoran, Paanchi, and Pacumeni.

4 Now these are not all the sons of Pahoran (for he had many), but these are they who did contend for the judgment-seat; therefore, they did cause three divisions among the people.

5 Nevertheless, it came to pass that Pahoran was appointed by the voice of the people to be chief judge and a governor over the people of Nephi.

6 And it came to pass that Pacumeni, when he saw that he could not obtain the judgment-seat, he did unite with the voice of the people.

7 But behold, Paanchi, and that part of the people that were desirous that he should be their governor, was exceedingly wroth; therefore, he was about to flatter away those people to rise up in rebellion against their brethren.

8 And it came to pass as he was about to do this, behold, he was taken, and was tried according to the voice of the people, and condemned unto death; for he had raised up in rebellion and sought to destroy the liberty of the people.

Helaman 1:1–8. The New Chief Judge, Pahoran, Is Murdered and His Brother Paanchi Is Tried for Rebellion

What were some of the consequences of contention among the Nephites? (1:1–8) "The contention of the sons of Pahoran for the judgment seat is a good example of what can happen in a democracy when men refuse to accept the will of the people. The contention for the judgment seat opened the way for much evil and eventually resulted in the downfall of the Nephite nation.

"Note the following points found in Helaman 1: . . .

"Those who sought to circumvent the law for personal power were willing to resort to murder to get their way (see v. 9).

"The contention over the judgment seat gave the attacking Lamanites an advantage against the Nephites (see vv. 18–20)" (*Book of Mormon Student Manual* [1989], 105).

What is the significance of the names Pahoran, Paanchi, and Pacumeni? (1:3) "There were three sons of Pahoran named Pahoran, Paanchi, and Pacumeni. Paanchi is the one indisputable Egyptian name in the Book of Mormon. Nobody can ever dispute that, either that Joseph Smith could have invented it or that it could not be pure, 100% Egyptian, because Paanchi [Piankhi] was a very important person in Egyptian history, just before Lehi's day. It means 'Amon is my life.' And Pacumeni and Pahoran mean the person is a Syrian. That's what an Egyptian would call a person from northern Palestine. These are familiar Egyptian names" (Nibley, *Teachings of the Book of Mormon*, 3:197–98). ●

Why was Paanchi tried for his crime "according to the voice of the people"? (1:7–8) "Had not Pahoran, the newly installed governor and chief judge, the right and the duty to judge all such cases? (Mosiah 29:25). . . . It may well have been that the law of conspiracy was not clearly settled under Nephite law. . . . Seeing the possible conflict between legal action on conspiracy and the rights afforded people to believe and to think what they wanted . . . Pahoran may have determined that this case needed to be submitted to the people for their determination" (Welch, *Legal Cases in the Book of Mormon*, 317–18). ●

Helaman 1:9–13. The Wicked Use Secret Combinations to Murder and Get Gain

What was the covenant of secrecy entered into by the followers of Paanchi? (1:9–11) "Beginning in the days of Cain and continuing through all generations, whenever there have been unrighteous and apostate peoples on earth, Satan has revealed unto them his oaths, vows, and secret combinations. . . . Murder, plunder, robbery, power, the destruction of freedom, and the persecution of the saints have been the objectives of these societies ever since (Moses 5:16–59; 6:15; Hela. 6:17–41).

"These secret societies flourished before the flood; they gained great strength among the Jaredites on this continent; the Gadianton robbers and the Lamanites reveled in them in Nephite days; and they are had in all parts of the earth today" (McConkie, *Mormon Doctrine*, 698). ⊕

Why do wicked men swear an oath to God? (1:11) "The conspirators then swore an oath of silence. Intriguingly, the Nephite record tells us that it was a religious oath, 'swearing by their everlasting Maker' (Hel. 1:11). This seems odd to those of us unaccustomed to thinking of murder as a religious act. But the very word *assassin* was given to us by a religious sect of the medieval Near East who bore it as a name. The 'Assassins' carried out daring murders for many years from mixed religious and political motives. And it would seem, from the story of Cain and Abel as recorded in the book of Moses, that such 'religious' oaths go back to the very beginning of human history" (Peterson, "Their Own Worst Enemies," 94). ⊕

Helaman 1:14–34. The Lamanites Attack and Defeat the Nephites in Zarahemla, and the Nephite Armies Regain Their Land

9 Now when those people who were desirous that he should be their governor saw that he was condemned unto death, therefore they were angry, and behold, they sent forth one Kishkumen, even to the judgment-seat of Pahoran, and murdered Pahoran as he sat upon the judgment-seat.

10 And he was pursued by the servants of Pahoran; but behold, so speedy was the flight of Kishkumen that no man could overtake him.

11 And he went unto those that sent him, and they all entered into a covenant, yea, swearing by their everlasting Maker, that they would tell no man that Kishkumen had murdered Pahoran.

12 Therefore, Kishkumen was not known among the people of Nephi, for he was in disguise at the time that he murdered Pahoran. And Kishkumen and his band, who had covenanted with him, did mingle themselves among the people, in a manner that they all could not be found; but as many as were found were condemned unto death.

13 And now behold, Pacumeni was appointed, according to the voice of the people, to be a chief judge and a governor over the people, to reign in the stead of his brother Pahoran; and it was according to his right. And all this was done in the fortieth year of the reign of the judges; and it had an end.

14 And it came to pass in the forty and first year of the reign of the judges, that the Lamanites had gathered together an innumerable army of men, and armed them with swords, and with cimeters and with bows, and with arrows, and with head-plates, and with breastplates, and with all manner of shields of every kind.

15 And they came down again that they might pitch battle against the Nephites. And they were led by a man whose name was Coriantumr; and he was a descendant of Zarahemla; and he was a dissenter from among the Nephites; and he was a large and a mighty man.

Who was Coriantumr? (1:15) "Coriantumr was a descendant of Zarahemla, and consequently was most likely of Judah. Originally he was a Nephite, but like many others during the days of the Judges, he dissented and went over to the Lamanites. He was a man of commanding presence, of more than ordinary stature and brilliant parts, with a reputation for wisdom which his later course scarcely appears to warrant. Tubaloth, . . . king of the Lamanites, gave him high office, and when (51 B.C.) the invasion of Zarahemla was determined upon, Coriantumr was placed in command of a vast host which was well armed and was raised particularly for that purpose.

"At this time through internal dissensions the Nephites were weak and distracted" (Reynolds and Sjodahl, *Commentary on the Book of Mormon*, 5:194).

16 Therefore, the king of the Lamanites, whose name was Tubaloth, who was the son of Ammoron, supposing that Coriantumr, being a mighty man, could stand against the Nephites, with his strength and also with his great wisdom, insomuch that by sending him forth he should gain power over the Nephites—

Who was Tubaloth and why did he appoint Coriantumr? (1:16) "It may be remembered that this king, named Tubaloth, was not really a Lamanite. Rather, he was the son of Ammoron, the brother and successor of the notoriously unscrupulous Nephite adventurer, Amalickiah. Tubaloth had chosen yet another dissenter from the Nephites, by the name of Coriantumr, to lead his warriors. It was certainly a common practice of those who would lead the Lamanites into battle against the Nephites to choose apostates as their assistants. . . . These apostates could be counted upon to feel a powerful hatred for the Nephites, which made them very useful to the great manipulators who appear with such appalling frequency in the pages of the Book of Mormon" (Peterson, "Their Own Worst Enemies," 94–95).

17 Therefore he did stir them up to anger, and he did gather together his armies, and he did appoint Coriantumr to be their leader, and did cause that they should march down to the land of Zarahemla to battle against the Nephites.

18 And it came to pass that because of so much contention and so much difficulty in the government, that they had not kept sufficient guards in the land of Zarahemla; for they had supposed that the Lamanites durst not come into the heart of their lands to attack that great city Zarahemla.

Why was Coriantumr's attempt to conquer and occupy Zarahemla unsuccessful? (1:17–34) "Coriantumr launched a kind of *blitzkrieg*, piercing the Nephite border defenses, and seized the capital city of Zarahemla. The conquest was quick and, for the moment, total. . . .

"As Hugh Nibley points out, his drive 'had been successful because it was completely unexpected; and it had been unexpected because it was utterly foolish.' It was utterly foolish because, having penetrated the Nephite defense on the circumference and seized the center of the land, Coriantumr was now, by the very nature of his own success, surrounded. . . . Following a bloody battle in which Coriantumr was killed, [it] left them no alternative but surrender. It was a humiliating defeat" (Peterson, "Their Own Worst Enemies," 95–96).

Why were the Nephites unable to defend them-selves against Coriantumr's initial attack on Zarahemla? (1:18–21) "Those who sought power in high places resorted to murder to gain that power. In so doing, they weakened the internal structure of the Nephite government, giving the Lamanites a decided advantage over the Nephites (see Hel. 1:18–20). The violent acts of murder by those in secret combinations were hard to prevent because the Nephites them-selves were in a degraded state....

"The Gadianton band never succeeded in their plans to overthrow the government when the Nephites were experiencing periods of spiritual growth in their society" (Black, *400 Questions and Answers*, 168).

19 But it came to pass that Coriantumr did march forth at the head of his numerous host, and came upon the inhabitants of the city, and their march was with such exceed-ingly great speed that there was no time for the Nephites to gather together their armies.

20 Therefore Coriantumr did cut down the watch by the entrance of the city, and did march forth with his whole army into the city, and they did slay every one who did op-pose them, insomuch that they did take pos-session of the whole city.

21 And it came to pass that Pacumeni, who was the chief judge, did flee before Coriantumr, even to the walls of the city. And it came to pass that Coriantumr did smite him against the wall, insomuch that he died. And thus ended the days of Pacumeni.

22 And now when Coriantumr saw that he was in possession of the city of Zarahemla, and saw that the Nephites had fled before them, and were slain, and were taken, and were cast into prison, and that he had ob-tained the possession of the strongest hold in all the land, his heart took courage insomuch that he was about to go forth against all the land.

23 And now he did not tarry in the land of Zarahemla, but he did march forth with a large army, even towards the city of Bountiful; for it was his determination to go forth and cut his way through with the sword, that he might obtain the north parts of the land.

24 And, supposing that their greatest strength was in the center of the land, therefore he did march forth, giving them no time to assemble themselves together save it were in small bod-ies; and in this manner they did fall upon them and cut them down to the earth.

25 But behold, this march of Coriantumr through the center of the land gave Moronihah great advantage over them, notwithstanding the greatness of the number of the Nephites who were slain.

26 For behold, Moronihah had supposed that the Lamanites durst not come into the center of the land, but that they would attack the cities round about in the borders as they had hitherto done; therefore Moronihah had caused that their strong armies should maintain those parts round about by the borders.

27 But behold, the Lamanites were not frightened according to his desire, but they had come into the center of the land, and had taken the capital city which was the city of Zarahemla, and were marching through the most capital parts of the land, slaying the people with a great slaughter, both men, women, and children, taking possession of many cities and of many strongholds.

28 But when Moronihah had discovered this, he immediately sent forth Lehi with an army round about to head them before they should come to the land Bountiful.

29 And thus he did; and he did head them before they came to the land Bountiful, and gave unto them battle, insomuch that they began to retreat back towards the land of Zarahemla.

30 And it came to pass that Moronihah did head them in their retreat, and did give unto them battle, insomuch that it became an exceedingly bloody battle; yea, many were slain, and among the number who were slain Coriantumr was also found.

31 And now, behold, the Lamanites could not retreat either way, neither on the north, nor on the south, nor on the east, nor on the west, for they were surrounded on every hand by the Nephites.

What is the significance of the word *nor*? (1:31)
Latter-day Saint scholar Donald W. Parry showed that this verse is an example of scriptural poetry: "*Working out* (Greek, *exergasia*) is a figure where two or more lines deliberate or explain what was first said in line one....

"Another example of working out exists in Helaman 1:31:

"'And now, behold, the Lamanites could not retreat either way,

"'neither on the north,

"'nor on the south,

"'nor on the east,

"'nor on the west,

"'for they were surrounded on every hand by the Nephites' (Helaman 1:31).

"The fact that the Lamanites were not able to 'retreat either way' is explained in the verses that follow" (*Book of Mormon Text Reformatted*, xxxiii–xxxiv).

Why were prisoners allowed to "depart out of the land in peace"? (1:33) How does the Lord expect us to treat others, even in times of war? "In contrast to the treatment of prisoners and innocent victims of war by the Lamanites (see Helaman 1:22), Moronihah allows the Lamanite prisoners of war to depart in peace. Those righteous military leaders who are disciples of Christ and are filled with the Spirit of the Lord treat even their enemies with kindness and compassion (see Alma 44:5–7). Even in most difficult circumstances, such as war, the Lord expects his disciples to 'love your enemies, . . . do good to them that hate you' (Matthew 5:44; 3 Nephi 12:44)" (McConkie and Millet, *Doctrinal Commentary*, 3:336).

Helaman 2:1–9. Kishkumen Is Killed When He Attempts to Murder Helaman

Who was this Helaman? (2:2) This Helaman was prophet, record-keeper (see Alma 63:11), and chief judge (see Hel. 2:2); he was the son of the prophet Helaman who led the stripling warriors, and the grandson of Alma the Younger. Helaman was preserved by his servant from the robber Kishkumen, and served righteously until his death (see Hel. 3:20, 37). He left a powerful testimony and blessing on his sons Nephi and Lehi that is often quoted (see Hel. 5:5–13).

What did Gadianton have in common with previous anti-Christs? (2:4) "Mormon describes Gadianton, the leader of the band formed by Kishkumen, as 'exceedingly expert in many words, and also in his craft.' It is significant that these traits are similar to those found in such anti-Christs as Sherem (see Jacob 7:4), Nehor (see Alma 1:3–6), and Korihor (see Alma 30:12–18).

32 And thus had Coriantumr plunged the Lamanites into the midst of the Nephites, insomuch that they were in the power of the Nephites, and he himself was slain, and the Lamanites did yield themselves into the hands of the Nephites.

33 And it came to pass that Moronihah took possession of the city of Zarahemla again, and caused that the Lamanites who had been taken prisoners should depart out of the land in peace.

34 And thus ended the forty and first year of the reign of the judges.

CHAPTER 2

Helaman, the son of Helaman, becomes chief judge—Gadianton leads the band of Kishkumen—Helaman's servant slays Kishkumen, and the Gadianton band flees into the wilderness. About 50–49 B.C.

1 And it came to pass in the forty and second year of the reign of the judges, after Moronihah had established again peace between the Nephites and the Lamanites, behold there was no one to fill the judgment-seat; therefore there began to be a contention again among the people concerning who should fill the judgment-seat.

2 And it came to pass that Helaman, who was the son of Helaman, was appointed to fill the judgment-seat, by the voice of the people.

3 But behold, Kishkumen, who had murdered Pahoran, did lay wait to destroy Helaman also; and he was upheld by his band, who had entered into a covenant that no one should know his wickedness.

4 For there was one Gadianton, who was exceedingly expert in many words, and also in his craft, to carry on the secret work of murder and of robbery; therefore he became the leader of the band of Kishkumen.

5 Therefore he did flatter them, and also Kishkumen, that if they would place him in the judgment-seat he would grant unto those who belonged to his band that they should be placed in power and authority among the people; therefore Kishkumen sought to destroy Helaman.

6 And it came to pass as he went forth towards the judgment-seat to destroy Helaman, behold one of the servants of Helaman, having been out by night, and having obtained, through disguise, a knowledge of those plans which had been laid by this band to destroy Helaman—

7 And it came to pass that he met Kishkumen, and he gave unto him a sign; therefore Kishkumen made known unto him the object of his desire, desiring that he would conduct him to the judgment-seat that he might murder Helaman.

8 And when the servant of Helaman had known all the heart of Kishkumen, and how that it was his object to murder, and also that it was the object of all those who belonged to his band to murder, and to rob, and to gain power, (and this was their secret plan, and their combination) the servant of Helaman said unto Kishkumen: Let us go forth unto the judgment-seat.

9 Now this did please Kishkumen exceedingly, for he did suppose that he should accomplish his design; but behold, the servant of Helaman, as they were going forth unto the judgment-seat, did stab Kishkumen even to the heart, that he fell dead without a groan. And he ran and told Helaman all the things which he had seen, and heard, and done.

10 And it came to pass that Helaman did send forth to take this band of robbers and secret murderers, that they might be executed according to the law.

Gadianton's use of many words and flattery to bring about his evil designs, as in the cases of the anti-Christs, was acquired through the tutelage of Satan. Gadianton was 'expert in his craft' because he had been taught and influenced 'according to the power of the devil' (Jacob 7:4)" (McConkie and Millet, *Doctrinal Commentary*, 3:337–38).

Why did Kishkumen's secret plans to kill the prophet fail? (2:6–9) Consider how the servant was able to frustrate the Gadianton robbers and protect the prophet. How can we also seek to sustain and pray for the prophet in our day?

Helaman 2:10–14. Gadianton and His Secret Band Flee into the Wilderness

How are the secret combinations of today like these Gadianton robbers of old? (2:13) "The Book of Mormon teaches that secret combinations engaged in crime present a serious challenge, not just to individuals and families but to entire civilizations. Among today's secret combinations are gangs, drug cartels, and organized crime families. The secret combinations of our day function much like the Gadianton robbers of the Book of Mormon times. They have secret signs and code words. They participate in secret rites and initiation ceremonies. Among their purposes are to 'murder, and plunder, and steal, and commit whoredoms and all manner of wickedness, contrary to the laws of their country and also the laws of their God' (Hel. 6:23)" (Ballard, "Standing for Truth and Right," 38). ◉

Helaman 3:1–12. Many Nephites and Ammonites Move to the Land Northward

What was Mormon's purpose for the first chapters in Helaman? (3:1–3) "Mormon's narrative structure communicates his overarching purpose in these two original chapters. . . . [His] purpose is to explain that Nephite contentions lead to the Gadiantons and that the Gadiantons destroy at least some aspect of Nephite government. This pattern parallels events in Mormon's day. Escalating contentions lead to the Gadiantons' rise to power, which leads in turn to the Nephites' total destruction. Mormon is telling us to look for the parallels between the events of his day and the events just preceding the Messiah's arrival in the New World. Both have something to do with the land northward" (Gardner, *Second Witness*, 5:59).

11 But behold, when Gadianton had found that Kishkumen did not return he feared lest that he should be destroyed; therefore he caused that his band should follow him. And they took their flight out of the land, by a secret way, into the wilderness; and thus when Helaman sent forth to take them they could nowhere be found.

12 And more of this Gadianton shall be spoken hereafter. And thus ended the forty and second year of the reign of the judges over the people of Nephi.

13 And behold, in the end of this book ye shall see that this Gadianton did prove the overthrow, yea, almost the entire destruction of the people of Nephi.

14 Behold I do not mean the end of the book of Helaman, but I mean the end of the book of Nephi, from which I have taken all the account which I have written.

CHAPTER 3

Many Nephites migrate to the land northward—They build houses of cement and keep many records—Tens of thousands are converted and baptized—The word of God leads men to salvation—Nephi the son of Helaman fills the judgment seat. About 49–39 B.C.

1 And now it came to pass in the forty and third year of the reign of the judges, there was no contention among the people of Nephi save it were a little pride which was in the church, which did cause some little dissensions among the people, which affairs were settled in the ending of the forty and third year.

2 And there was no contention among the people in the forty and fourth year; neither was there much contention in the forty and fifth year.

3 And it came to pass in the forty and sixth, yea, there was much contention and many dissensions; in the which there were an exceedingly great many who departed out of the land of Zarahemla, and went forth unto the land northward to inherit the land.

4 And they did travel to an exceedingly great distance, insomuch that they came to large bodies of water and many rivers.

5 Yea, and even they did spread forth into all parts of the land, into whatever parts it had not been rendered desolate and without timber, because of the many inhabitants who had before inherited the land.

6 And now no part of the land was desolate, save it were for timber; but because of the greatness of the destruction of the people who had before inhabited the land it was called desolate.

7 And there being but little timber upon the face of the land, nevertheless the people who went forth became exceedingly expert in the working of cement; therefore they did build houses of cement, in the which they did dwell.

8 And it came to pass that they did multiply and spread, and did go forth from the land southward to the land northward, and did spread insomuch that they began to cover the face of the whole earth, from the sea south to the sea north, from the sea west to the sea east.

9 And the people who were in the land northward did dwell in tents, and in houses of cement, and they did suffer whatsoever tree should spring up upon the face of the land that it should grow up, that in time they might have timber to build their houses, yea, their cities, and their temples, and their synagogues, and their sanctuaries, and all manner of their buildings.

Were the Nephites familiar with cement? (3:7)
"Once thought to be anachronistic, references to 'cement' in the Book of Mormon (Helaman 3:7,9,11) can be seen today as further evidence of the authenticity of the text. This is because today the presence of expert cement technology in pre-Hispanic America is a well-established archaeological fact. 'American technology in the manufacture of cement, its mixing and placement two thousand years ago, paralleled that of the Greeks and the Romans during the same period,' notes structural engineer David Hyman in a recent study devoted to the use of cement in Pre-Columbian Mexico" ("Right on Target: Boomerang Hits and the Book of Mormon," Fair Mormon Conference). ◉

Did the settlers in the north maintain contact with the people of Zarahemla? (3:10) "A thoughtful comment is made by Mormon in what is verse ten. He notes that many shiploads of timber were sent to the colonizers in the northern land by those who still dwelt in the land southward, or by those who were sent there for that purpose. Thus the Nephites still residing in the old homeland enabled the settlers of the land northward to continue their work of rehabilitation in a land that had been deforested by the pre-inhabitants thereof" (Reynolds and Sjodahl, *Commentary on the Book of Mormon*, 5:214).

Helaman 3:13–16. Many Books and Records Are Written and Kept by the Nephites

How did Mormon use the vast Nephite records? (3:13–16) "Mormon interjects the comment that many records have been kept concerning specifically these people who migrated northward and the Nephite nation generally. The doctrinal significance of these verses consists not so much in their informing the reader of the many historical records that deal with virtually every aspect of Nephite culture as in their reminding us that the primary purpose of the Book of Mormon is not one of history. Mormon's statement is that his record or abridgment does not contain a 'hundredth part' of all the history. He is not apologizing, but is again stating that his objective and his charge as an abridger and record-keeper is of a spiritual and not a secular nature" (McConkie and Millet, *Commentary on the Book of Mormon*, 3:340). ✛

10 And it came to pass as timber was exceedingly scarce in the land northward, they did send forth much by the way of shipping.

11 And thus they did enable the people in the land northward that they might build many cities, both of wood and of cement.

12 And it came to pass that there were many of the people of Ammon, who were Lamanites by birth, did also go forth into this land.

13 And now there are many records kept of the proceedings of this people, by many of this people, which are particular and very large, concerning them.

14 But behold, a hundredth part of the proceedings of this people, yea, the account of the Lamanites and of the Nephites, and their wars, and contentions, and dissensions, and their preaching, and their prophecies, and their shipping and their building of ships, and their building of temples, and of synagogues and their sanctuaries, and their righteousness, and their wickedness, and their murders, and their robbings, and their plundering, and all manner of abominations and whoredoms, cannot be contained in this work.

15 But behold, there are many books and many records of every kind, and they have been kept chiefly by the Nephites.

16 And they have been handed down from one generation to another by the Nephites, even until they have fallen into transgression and have been murdered, plundered, and hunted, and driven forth, and slain, and scattered upon the face of the earth, and mixed with the Lamanites until they are no more called the Nephites, becoming wicked, and wild, and ferocious, yea, even becoming Lamanites.

17 And now I return again to mine account; therefore, what I have spoken had passed after there had been great contentions, and disturbances, and wars, and dissensions, among the people of Nephi.

18 The forty and sixth year of the reign of the judges ended;

19 And it came to pass that there was still great contention in the land, yea, even in the forty and seventh year, and also in the forty and eighth year.

20 Nevertheless Helaman did fill the judgment-seat with justice and equity; yea, he did observe to keep the statutes, and the judgments, and the commandments of God; and he did do that which was right in the sight of God continually; and he did walk after the ways of his father, insomuch that he did prosper in the land.

21 And it came to pass that he had two sons. He gave unto the eldest the name of Nephi, and unto the youngest, the name of Lehi. And they began to grow up unto the Lord.

22 And it came to pass that the wars and contentions began to cease, in a small degree, among the people of the Nephites, in the latter end of the forty and eighth year of the reign of the judges over the people of Nephi.

23 And it came to pass in the forty and ninth year of the reign of the judges, there was continual peace established in the land, all save it were the secret combinations which Gadianton the robber had established in the

Helaman 3:17–30. Under Helaman's Leadership, Many People Join the Church

What actions are "right in the sight of God" for our day? (3:20) "We should be personal peacemakers. We should live peacefully—as couples, families, and neighbors. We should live by the Golden Rule. . . . We should . . . expand our circle of love to embrace the whole human family. We should bring divine love and revealed doctrines of restored religion to our neighbors and friends. We should serve them according to our abilities and opportunities. We should keep our principles on a high level and stand for the right. We should continue to gather scattered Israel from the four corners of the earth and offer the ordinances and covenants that seal families together forever. These blessings we are to bring to people of all nations" (Nelson, "Blessed Are the Peacemakers," 41).

Who were Nephi and Lehi? (3:21) "In Nephi we have one of the greatest prophets that ever trod the earth or to whom the God of our Salvation revealed His glorious will. He lived during the greater portion of the first century before Christ and disappeared from the knowledge of mankind but a short time before the advent of the Messiah in Bethlehem. He is first referred to in the Book of Mormon (44 B.C.) as the older of Helaman's two sons, Lehi being the younger. These two brothers appear to have been inseparable during their life; they are almost always mentioned as associated in the great and ofttimes perilous labors of the ministry undertaken for the Salvation of either Nephites or Lamanites" (Reynolds and Sjodahl, *Commentary on the Book of Mormon*, 5:215). ⊕

Why are secret combinations identified so often in the Book of Mormon? (3:23) "The Gadianton robbers are a specific instance of the larger set of events and concepts revolving around what the Book of Mormon calls *secret combinations*. These secret combinations show up in connection with the Jaredites, then they disappear. They reappear scant years prior to the arrival of the Savior in the New World, and then disappear for over two hundred years. Finally, they reappear to play a role in the final denouement of the Nephites. While the majority of the conflicts in the Book of Mormon occur with the Lamanites, the most destructive conflicts are those that come at the hands of the secret combinations, and specifically the Gadianton robbers" ("The Gadianton Robbers in Mormon's Theological History," Fair Mormon Conference). ⊕

What does it mean that the church prospered at this time? (3:24–28) "Frequently the first reaction to the word *prosperity* in the Book of Mormon is the concept of temporal blessings, or the 'good things of the earth.' Undoubtedly, such prosperity can be linked to some degree with righteousness (see Dean L. Larsen, *Ensign*, May 1991, 10–12). The context of this prosperity, however, makes it clearly spiritual in nature and linked to the blessings of the Church membership resulting from faithfulness. It is important that we not think of prosperity only in terms of material gain" (McConkie and Millet, *Doctrinal Commentary*, 3:342).

What is the "gate of heaven"? (3:28) "Jacob . . . had a dream in which he saw himself on the earth at the foot of a ladder that reached to heaven. . . . He beheld angels ascending and descending thereon, and Jacob realized that the covenants he made with the Lord there were the rungs on the ladder that he himself would have to climb in order to obtain the promised blessings—blessings that would entitle him to enter heaven and associate with the Lord. . . . Temples are to us all what Bethel was to Jacob. Even more, they are also the gates to heaven for all of our unendowed kindred dead. We should all do our duty in bringing our loved ones through them" (Romney, "Temples—the Gates of Heaven," 12).

Why is scripture study such an effective guide? (3:29) "Success in righteousness, the power to avoid deception and resist temptation, guidance in our daily lives, healing of the soul—these are but a few of the

more settled parts of the land, which at that time were not known unto those who were at the head of government; therefore they were not destroyed out of the land.

24 And it came to pass that in this same year there was exceedingly great prosperity in the church, insomuch that there were thousands who did join themselves unto the church and were baptized unto repentance.

25 And so great was the prosperity of the church, and so many the blessings which were poured out upon the people, that even the high priests and the teachers were themselves astonished beyond measure.

26 And it came to pass that the work of the Lord did prosper unto the baptizing and uniting to the church of God, many souls, yea, even tens of thousands.

27 Thus we may see that the Lord is merciful unto all who will, in the sincerity of their hearts, call upon his holy name.

28 Yea, thus we see that the gate of heaven is open unto all, even to those who will believe on the name of Jesus Christ, who is the Son of God.

29 Yea, we see that whosoever will may lay hold upon the word of God, which is quick and powerful, which shall divide asunder all the cunning and the snares and the wiles of the devil, and lead the man of Christ in a strait and narrow course across that everlasting gulf of misery which is prepared to engulf the wicked—

30 And land their souls, yea, their immortal souls, at the right hand of God in the kingdom of heaven, to sit down with Abraham, and Isaac, and with Jacob, and with all our holy fathers, to go no more out.

31 And in this year there was continual rejoicing in the land of Zarahemla, and in all the regions round about, even in all the land which was possessed by the Nephites.

32 And it came to pass that there was peace and exceedingly great joy in the remainder of the forty and ninth year; yea, and also there was continual peace and great joy in the fiftieth year of the reign of the judges.

33 And in the fifty and first year of the reign of the judges there was peace also, save it were the pride which began to enter into the church—not into the church of God, but into the hearts of the people who professed to belong to the church of God—

34 And they were lifted up in pride, even to the persecution of many of their brethren. Now this was a great evil, which did cause the more humble part of the people to suffer great persecutions, and to wade through much affliction.

promises the Lord has given to those who will come to His word. Does the Lord promise and not fulfill? Surely if He tells us that these things will come to us if we lay hold upon His word, then the blessings can be ours. And if we do not, then the blessings may be lost. However diligent we may be in other areas, certain blessings are to be found only in the scriptures" (Benson, "Power of the Word," 82). ✇

How do we become heirs with "all our holy fathers"? (3:30) "The covenant that the Lord first made to Abraham and reaffirmed to Isaac and Jacob is of transcendent significance. . . . We are also children of the covenant. We have received, as did they of old, the holy priesthood and the everlasting gospel. Abraham, Isaac, and Jacob are our ancestors. We are of Israel. We have the right to receive the gospel, blessings of the priesthood, and eternal life. Nations of the earth will be blessed by our efforts and by the labors of our posterity. The literal seed of Abraham and those who are gathered into his family by adoption receive these promised blessings—predicated upon . . . obedience to his commandments" (Nelson, "Children of the Covenant," 33).

Helaman 3:31–37. Some Proud and Wicked Nephites Persecute the Members of the Church

How does the pride of individual people detrimentally affect the whole Church? (3:33–35) President Ezra Taft Benson said: "Think of what pride has cost us in the past and what it is now costing us in our own lives . . . and the Church.

"Think of the repentance that could take place with lives changed, marriages preserved, and homes strengthened. . . .

"Think of the many who are less active members of the Church because they were offended and their pride will not allow them to forgive or fully sup at the Lord's table.

"Think of the tens of thousands of additional young men and couples who could be on missions. . . .

"Think how temple work would increase if the time spent in this godly service were more important than the many prideful pursuits that compete for our time" ("Beware of Pride," 6).

How did Helaman's people overcome their afflictions? (3:35) "The persecution and affliction came
from within the church (Helaman 3:34), but the formula to turn these negative conditions into a growth
pattern is given to us by Mormon. The first step of the
three-step formula is to 'fast and pray oft' (v. 35). . . .
The second step of the formula is to become stronger
in humility (v. 35). . . . The third step of the formula is to
become 'firmer in the faith of Christ' (v. 35). . . . Through
the above formula, the people's hearts were purified
and sanctified. . . . Thus the persecutions and the afflictions, although difficult to endure, brought them to
rely on the Lord . . . and helped them become firmer in
their conviction" (Nyman, *Record of Helaman*, 269–70).

**What was the legacy of this noble prophet
Helaman? (3:37)** See the commentary in this volume
on Helaman 5:6–7.

Helaman 4:1–10. Nephite Dissenters Join the Lamanites and Drive the Nephites Out of Zarahemla

**What was the source of the failure of the Nephite
society? (4:1–4)** "The presaged contentions begin
to occur in two places: (1) among church members
('dissensions in the church') and (2) in the body politic
('also a contention among the people'). It is highly
likely that the dividing line for the contentions was
similar for both the religious and political dissidents.
Mormon spells out the causal connection between
increasing prosperity and the desire for social differ-
entiation, even among church members. The pattern
is, at this point, completely familiar—a continuous
reminder of the larger culture's influence on the
Nephites" (Gardner, *Second Witness*, 5:77).

35 Nevertheless they did fast and pray oft,
and did wax stronger and stronger in their
humility, and firmer and firmer in the faith
of Christ, unto the filling their souls with joy
and consolation, yea, even to the purifying
and the sanctification of their hearts, which
sanctification cometh because of their yielding their hearts unto God.

36 And it came to pass that the fifty and
second year ended in peace also, save it were
the exceedingly great pride which had gotten into the hearts of the people; and it was
because of their exceedingly great riches and
their prosperity in the land; and it did grow
upon them from day to day.

37 And it came to pass in the fifty and third
year of the reign of the judges, Helaman
died, and his eldest son Nephi began to reign
in his stead. And it came to pass that he did
fill the judgment-seat with justice and equity;
yea, he did keep the commandments of God,
and did walk in the ways of his father.

CHAPTER 4

*Nephite dissenters and the Lamanites join forces
and take the land of Zarahemla—The Nephites'
defeats come because of their wickedness—The
Church dwindles, and the people become weak
like the Lamanites. About 38–30 B.C.*

1 And it came to pass in the fifty and fourth
year there were many dissensions in the
church, and there was also a contention
among the people, insomuch that there was
much bloodshed.

2 And the rebellious part were slain and
driven out of the land, and they did go unto
the king of the Lamanites.

3 And it came to pass that they did endeavor
to stir up the Lamanites to war against the
Nephites; but behold, the Lamanites were exceedingly afraid, insomuch that they would
not hearken to the words of those dissenters.

4 But it came to pass in the fifty and sixth year of the reign of the judges, there were dissenters who went up from the Nephites unto the Lamanites; and they succeeded with those others in stirring them up to anger against the Nephites; and they were all that year preparing for war.

5 And in the fifty and seventh year they did come down against the Nephites to battle, and they did commence the work of death; yea, insomuch that in the fifty and eighth year of the reign of the judges they succeeded in obtaining possession of the land of Zarahemla; yea, and also all the lands, even unto the land which was near the land Bountiful.

6 And the Nephites and the armies of Moronihah were driven even into the land of Bountiful;

7 And there they did fortify against the Lamanites, from the west sea, even unto the east; it being a day's journey for a Nephite, on the line which they had fortified and stationed their armies to defend their north country.

8 And thus those dissenters of the Nephites, with the help of a numerous army of the Lamanites, had obtained all the possession of the Nephites which was in the land southward. And all this was done in the fifty and eighth and ninth years of the reign of the judges.

9 And it came to pass in the sixtieth year of the reign of the judges, Moronihah did succeed with his armies in obtaining many parts of the land; yea, they regained many cities which had fallen into the hands of the Lamanites.

How did the Lamanites come into possession of Zarahemla? (4:5) "These years were some of the darkest in Nephite history. Owing to their great pride and iniquity the Lord left the people to themselves, and they became weak like unto the Lamanites, man for man. When war was commenced, the latter being much the more numerous, carried everything before them.... Zarahemla, with its hallowed associations, its glorious temples, where the daily sacrifice was unceasingly offered, its proud palaces, its luxurious homes, its Courts of Justice, where the Chief Judge sat in the magnificence of almost kingly authority to administer the law—Zarahemla, their Queen City, the seat of their government, the center of their civilization, the home of the High Priesthood, was in the hands of their ... foes" (Reynolds and Sjodahl, *Commentary on the Book of Mormon*, 5:223–24).

Who was Moronihah? (4:6–10) The Book of Mormon contains specific details regarding war between the Nephites and Lamanites, including their generals. Moronihah succeeded his father Moroni as the general of the Nephite armies (see Alma 62:43). The record also indicates that he not only led them in battle, but preached the gospel of repentance, along with Lehi and Nephi, in order to establish peace (see Helaman 4:14). "It appears that Book of Mormon military organization was aristocratic and dominated by a highly trained hereditary elite. Thus, for example, military leaders such as Moroni , his son Moronihah, and Mormon each became the chief captain at a young age (Alma 43:17; 62:39; Morm. 2:1)" (Ludlow, *Encyclopedia of Mormonism*, 1:163–64).

Helaman 4:11–20. The Nephites Repent, but Their Armies Regain Only Half Their Lands

What are the consequences of disobedience? (4:11–12) "Since the days of Adam, the Lord has spoken to His prophets, and while His message differs according to the specific needs of the time, there is one consistent, never-changing theme: Depart from iniquity and journey to higher ground.

"As people heed the words of the prophets, the Lord blesses them. When they disregard His word, however, distress and suffering often follow. Over and over, the Book of Mormon teaches this great lesson. . . .

"There is something about prosperity that brings out the worst in some people. In the book of Helaman, we learn of one group of Nephites who experienced great loss and slaughter. Of them we read, 'And it was because of the pride of their hearts, because of their exceeding riches'" (Wirthlin, "Journey to Higher Ground," 16).

How can we avoid becoming proud because of our possessions? (4:12–13) "It is a duty which every Saint ought to render to his brethren freely—to always love them, and ever succor them. To be justified before God we must love one another: we must overcome evil; we must visit the fatherless and the widow in their affliction, and we must keep ourselves unspotted from the world: for such virtues flow from the great fountain of pure religion" (*Joseph Smith* [manual], 426).

"Strengthening our faith by adding every good quality that adorns the children of the blessed Jesus, we can pray in the season of prayer; we can love our neighbor as ourselves, and be faithful in tribulation, knowing that the reward of such is greater in the kingdom of heaven" (*Joseph Smith* [manual], 353).

How did the Nephites make "a mock of that which was sacred"? (4:12–13) "At the beginning of the Book of Mormon, Nephi explained that the phrase 'to trample under their feet the God of Israel' means that 'they set him at naught, and hearken not to the voice of his counsels' (1 Nephi 19:7). This is what the Nephites had done. Despite their covenants, they had rejected the word of the Lord as delivered by past and present prophets. The apostle Paul also understood the consequences of rejecting the Lord in this manner when he said to the Hebrews, 'Of how much sorer punishment, suppose ye, shall he be thought worthy, who hath trodden underfoot the Son of God, and hath

10 And it came to pass in the sixty and first year of the reign of the judges they succeeded in regaining even the half of all their possessions.

11 Now this great loss of the Nephites, and the great slaughter which was among them, would not have happened had it not been for their wickedness and their abomination which was among them; yea, and it was among those also who professed to belong to the church of God.

12 And it was because of the pride of their hearts, because of their exceeding riches, yea, it was because of their oppression to the poor, withholding their food from the hungry, withholding their clothing from the naked, and smiting their humble brethren upon the cheek, making a mock of that which was sacred, denying the spirit of prophecy and of revelation, murdering, plundering, lying, stealing, committing adultery, rising up in great contentions, and deserting away into the land of Nephi, among the Lamanites—

13 And because of this their great wickedness, and their boastings in their own strength, they were left in their own strength; therefore they did not prosper, but were afflicted and smitten, and driven before the Lamanites, until they had lost possession of almost all their lands.

14 But behold, Moronihah did preach many things unto the people because of their iniquity, and also Nephi and Lehi, who were the sons of Helaman, did preach many things unto the people, yea, and did prophesy many things unto them concerning their iniquities, and what should come unto them if they did not repent of their sins.

15 And it came to pass that they did repent, and inasmuch as they did repent they did begin to prosper.

16 For when Moronihah saw that they did repent he did venture to lead them forth from place to place, and from city to city, even until they had regained the one-half of their property and the one-half of all their lands.

17 And thus ended the sixty and first year of the reign of the judges.

18 And it came to pass in the sixty and second year of the reign of the judges, that Moronihah could obtain no more possessions over the Lamanites.

19 Therefore they did abandon their design to obtain the remainder of their lands, for so numerous were the Lamanites that it became impossible for the Nephites to obtain more power over them; therefore Moronihah did employ all his armies in maintaining those parts which he had taken.

20 And it came to pass, because of the greatness of the number of the Lamanites the Nephites were in great fear, lest they should be overpowered, and trodden down, and slain, and destroyed.

21 Yea, they began to remember the prophecies of Alma, and also the words of Mosiah; and they saw that they had been a stiffnecked people, and that they had set at naught the commandments of God;

22 And that they had altered and trampled under their feet the laws of Mosiah, or that which the Lord commanded him to give unto the people; and they saw that their laws had become corrupted, and that they had become a wicked people, insomuch that they were wicked even like unto the Lamanites.

23 And because of their iniquity the church had begun to dwindle; and they began to disbelieve in the spirit of prophecy and in the spirit of revelation; and the judgments of God did stare them in the face.

counted the blood of the covenant, wherewith he was sanctified, an unholy thing, and hath done despite unto the Spirit of grace?' (Heb. 10:29)" (Fowles, "The Decline of the Nephites," 84).

What are the dangers of trusting in our own strength? (4:13) Do we ever make this same mistake and try to deal with all of life's challenges with our own strength and our own wisdom? Why is it so hard for some to acknowledge their total dependence on God? What kind of power are we passing up when we insist on doing things our way instead His way?

What can we learn from the Nephite failure to obtain their former lands? (4:19–20) "A lesson may be learned from the Nephites in their abandoning their quest for the remainder of the land (v. 19). Sometimes the making of restitution for sins committed is a long process. Had the Nephite nation been so wicked that the Lord required them not to be delivered until they had 'paid the uttermost senine' for their sins? Such may have been the case. Their living in great fear (v. 20) may have also been a part of that required payment" (Nyman, *Record of Helaman*, 290).

Helaman 4:21–26. The Nephites Realize That Because They Have Sinned, They Are as Weak as the Lamanites

What were the "prophecies of Alma" and the "laws of Mosiah"? (4:21–22) "The fulfillment of the prophecies of Alma are not specified. Mormon may have been referring to what is now Alma chapter 5. Such things as pride, persecution of their brethren, and neglecting the poor are referred to in Alma's great sermon to the people of Zarahemla (see Alma 5:53–56). The laws of Mosiah has reference to the new form of government revealed as a part of the reign of the judges (see Mosiah 29). Regardless of the generality used by Mormon in referring to both Alma and Mosiah, Alma's laws were the spiritual guidelines for the church and its members, and the laws of Mosiah were the political or governing laws revealed for a nation" (Nyman, *Record of Helaman*, 291).

What characterizes those who reject prophetic guidance? (4:23) "There are those within the Church who are disturbed when changes are made with which they disagree or when changes they propose are not made. They point to these as evidence that the leaders are not inspired. . . .

"Two things characterize them: they are always irritated by the word *obedience*, and always they question revelation. It has always been so. Helaman described those who 'began to disbelieve in the spirit of prophecy and in the spirit of revelation; and the judgments of God did stare them in the face' (Helaman 4:23). 'They were left in their own strength' (4:13), and 'the Spirit of the Lord did no more preserve them; yea, it had withdrawn from them' (4:24)" (Packer, "Revelation in a Changing World," 15).

What leads a people to become weak? (4:24–26)
"Alas, gross, individual selfishness is finally acculturated. Then societies can eventually become without order, without mercy, without love, perverted, and past feeling (see Moro. 9). Society thereby reflects a grim, cumulative tally which signals a major cultural decline. This happened anciently when a people actually became 'weak, because of their transgression' (Hel. 4:26). Speaking behaviorally, when what was once the lesser voice of the people becomes more dominant, then the judgments of God and the consequences of foolish selfishness follow (see Mosiah 29:26–27).

"Cultural decline is accelerated when single-interest segments of society become indifferent.... This drift is facilitated by the indifferent or the indulgent as society is led carefully down to hell (see 2 Ne. 28:21)" (Maxwell, "Repent of [Our] Selfishness," 23–24).

Helaman 5:1–4. Nephi Gives Up the Judgment-Seat to Preach

Who was Cezoram? (5:1) Cezoram was the eighth in the line of Nephite chief judges. In the sixty-second year of the reign of the judges, or about 30 B.C., Cezoram acceded to office when Nephi, son of

24 And they saw that they had become weak, like unto their brethren, the Lamanites, and that the Spirit of the Lord did no more preserve them; yea, it had withdrawn from them because the Spirit of the Lord doth not dwell in unholy temples—

25 Therefore the Lord did cease to preserve them by his miraculous and matchless power, for they had fallen into a state of unbelief and awful wickedness; and they saw that the Lamanites were exceedingly more numerous than they, and except they should cleave unto the Lord their God they must unavoidably perish.

26 For behold, they saw that the strength of the Lamanites was as great as their strength, even man for man. And thus had they fallen into this great transgression; yea, thus had they become weak, because of their transgression, in the space of not many years.

CHAPTER 5

Nephi and Lehi devote themselves to preaching—Their names invite them to pattern their lives after their forebears—Christ redeems those who repent—Nephi and Lehi make many converts and are imprisoned, and fire encircles them—A cloud of darkness overshadows three hundred people—The earth shakes, and a voice commands men to repent—Nephi and Lehi converse with angels, and the multitude is encircled by fire. About 30 B.C.

1 And it came to pass that in this same year, behold, Nephi delivered up the judgment-seat to a man whose name was Cezoram.

Helaman, relinquished the judgment-seat and devoted himself full time to "preach the word" (Helaman 5:4). Four years later, in 26 B.C., the Gadianton robbers murdered Cezoram. His son replaced him but in the same year was murdered also (Helaman 6:15). After that, the government fell into the hands of the Gadiantons (Helaman 6:38–39) until Nephi returned to call the Nephite people to repentance (Helaman 7–9). ⊕

What is our duty to our laws, community, and country? (5:2) "The Saints must be concerned with the maintenance of personal freedom, which the Lord has indicated is essential to individual salvation and exaltation.

"We must not assume that since the Constitution embodies a 'divinely inspired' political system the machinery of checks and balances, separation of powers, and other constitutional limitations will automatically preserve political and moral freedom for the individual. The prophets have made clear that no constitution or set of laws, written or unwritten, can by themselves protect a nation from corrupt leaders. Brigham Young remarked, 'No matter how good a government is, unless it is administered by righteous men, an evil government will be made of it'" (May, "Beyond Voting," 48). ⊕

What happens to law and justice when a wicked people choose evil? (5:2–3) "The Nephites, . . . by the exercise of their agency, brought themselves to such a state of affairs that their only course led to political bondage. This they did while living under a government providing for the freest exercise of agency. 'Their laws and their governments,' says the record, 'were established by the voice of the people, and they who chose evil were more numerous than they who chose good' (Hel. 5:2–3). . . . Under these circumstances, they chose as rulers wicked men, who would certainly destroy their political liberties, to replace righteous men who had in the past protected and preserved those liberties and would have continued to do so in the future" (Romney, "Perfect Law of Liberty," 43–44).

Helaman 5:5–14. Helaman Teaches His Sons to Remember Their Righteous Ancestors and to Remember Jesus Christ

What is the significance of repeating the word *remember* over and over again in this passage? (5:5–14) "Repetitive resumption refers to an editor's return to an original narrative following a deliberate

---

2 For as their laws and their governments were established by the voice of the people, and they who chose evil were more numerous than they who chose good, therefore they were ripening for destruction, for the laws had become corrupted.

3 Yea, and this was not all; they were a stiff-necked people, insomuch that they could not be governed by the law nor justice, save it were to their destruction.

4 And it came to pass that Nephi had become weary because of their iniquity; and he yielded up the judgment-seat, and took it upon him to preach the word of God all the remainder of his days, and his brother Lehi also, all the remainder of his days;

5 For they remembered the words which their father Helaman spake unto them. And these are the words which he spake:

interlude. Old Testament writers accomplished this by repeating a key word or phrase that immediately preceded the textual interruption.... A careful survey of editorial activity in the Book of Mormon shows that Nephite editors used repetitive resumption in a similar manner.... [An] example of repetitive resumption in the Book of Mormon occurs in Helaman 5:5–14. In this section the compiler inserts a direct report of Helaman's powerful discourse to his sons Nephi and Lehi (see vv. 6–12). This insertion is intentionally prefaced by the editorial introduction, 'For they remembered the words which their father Helaman spake unto them' (v. 5)" (Bokovoy, "Repetitive Resumption in the Book of Mormon"). ⊕

Why were Nephi and Lehi given their names?
(5:6–7) "We are not assured of the highest heaven in the celestial world because of our parentage, surname, or given name. Ancestry and heritage can guarantee nothing more than a great legacy, a memory, and a motivation to goodness. To be sure, all of us, whether reared in the Church or converts, are under covenant to be true to our shared heritage, to those who went before, who gave their lives that we might enjoy the privileges of Church membership today. We have a moral obligation to be loyal to the royal within us, to be true to our good names, to bear them with dignity and fidelity" (Millet, "Only Sure Foundation," 17). ⊕

What blessings come as we continually ponder and seek to understand the Atonement of Jesus Christ?
(5:9–13) "By understanding the Atonement, you will see that God is not a jealous being who delights in persecuting those who misstep. He is an absolutely perfect, compassionate, understanding, patient, and

6 Behold, my sons, I desire that ye should remember to keep the commandments of God; and I would that ye should declare unto the people these words. Behold, I have given unto you the names of our first parents who came out of the land of Jerusalem; and this I have done that when you remember your names ye may remember them; and when ye remember them ye may remember their works; and when ye remember their works ye may know how that it is said, and also written, that they were good.

7 Therefore, my sons, I would that ye should do that which is good, that it may be said of you, and also written, even as it has been said and written of them.

8 And now my sons, behold I have somewhat more to desire of you, which desire is, that ye may not do these things that ye may boast, but that ye may do these things to lay up for yourselves a treasure in heaven, yea, which is eternal, and which fadeth not away; yea, that ye may have that precious gift of eternal life, which we have reason to suppose hath been given to our fathers.

9 O remember, remember, my sons, the words which king Benjamin spake unto his people; yea, remember that there is no other way nor means whereby man can be saved, only through the atoning blood of Jesus

Christ, who shall come; yea, remember that he cometh to redeem the world.

10 And remember also the words which Amulek spake unto Zeezrom, in the city of Ammonihah; for he said unto him that the Lord surely should come to redeem his people, but that he should not come to redeem them in their sins, but to redeem them from their sins.

11 And he hath power given unto him from the Father to redeem them from their sins because of repentance; therefore he hath sent his angels to declare the tidings of the conditions of repentance, which bringeth unto the power of the Redeemer, unto the salvation of their souls.

12 And now, my sons, remember, remember that it is upon the rock of our Redeemer, who is Christ, the Son of God, that ye must build your foundation; that when the devil shall send forth his mighty winds, yea, his shafts in the whirlwind, yea, when all his hail and his mighty storm shall beat upon you, it shall have no power over you to drag you down to the gulf of misery and endless wo, because of the rock upon which ye are built, which is a sure foundation, a foundation whereon if men build they cannot fall.

13 And it came to pass that these were the words which Helaman taught to his sons; yea, he did teach them many things which are not written, and also many things which are written.

14 And they did remember his words; and therefore they went forth, keeping the commandments of God, to teach the word of God among all the people of Nephi, beginning at the city Bountiful;

15 And from thenceforth to the city of Gid; and from the city of Gid to the city of Mulek;

forgiving Father. He is willing to entreat, counsel, strengthen, lift, and fortify. He so loves each of us that He was willing to have His perfect, sinless, absolutely obedient, totally righteous Son experience indescribable agony and pain and give Himself in sacrifice for all [see Helaman 5:9]. Through that atonement we can live in a world where absolute justice reigns in its sphere so the world will have order. But that justice is tempered through mercy attainable by obedience to the teachings of Jesus Christ" (Scott, "Finding Forgiveness," 75). ◉

Are we saved *in* our sins or *from* our sins? (5:10) "Some Christians accuse Latter-day Saints . . . of denying the grace of God through claiming they can earn their own salvation. . . .

"We are not saved *in* our sins, as by being unconditionally saved through confessing Christ and then, inevitably, committing sins in our remaining lives (see Alma 11:36–37). We are saved *from* our sins (see Helaman 5:10) by a weekly renewal of our repentance and cleansing through the grace of God and His blessed plan of salvation (see 3 Nephi 9:20–22)" (Oaks, "Have You Been Saved?" 56). ◉

How is Jesus Christ the "rock" upon which we should build? (5:12) "Not upon any man, nor his words or claims, must we build the foundation of our Salvation. Christ, and Him alone, is the Rock upon which we build. It is not upon Revelation as some have supposed; it is not upon the Plan of Salvation, or the Everlasting Gospel, but on Him Who is revealed therein. On Christ, the Son of God, our hopes of Life Everlasting are centered, and upon Him power 'unto the Salvation of our souls' is given that through repentance we shall have peace and rest in God's Celestial Home.

"Upon Christ, and we repeat, Him alone, our foundation is sure" (Reynolds and Sjodahl, *Commentary on the Book of Mormon*, 5:237). ◉

Helaman 5:14–19. Nephi and Lehi Preach the Gospel

What was the source of Nephi and Lehi's preaching? (5:18–19) "As agents of the Lord they sought to be in tune so that they could speak the words of their Principal. They were led and guided by the power of the Holy Ghost, and as such had the very words divinely provided for them. Always and forever the counsel of the Master to his servants is, 'Treasure up in your minds continually the words of life, and it shall be given you in the very hour that portion that shall be meted unto every man' (D&C 84:85). . . . Christ commanded in a modern revelation: 'speak the thoughts that I shall put into your hearts, and you shall not be confounded before men' (D&C 100:5–6)" (McConkie and Millet, *Doctrinal Commentary*, 3:355).

Helaman 5:20–52. Nephi and Lehi Are Put in Prison and Are Miraculously Saved

What was the encircling fire? (5:23–24) "The encirclement 'as if by fire' (Helaman 5:23) was undoubtedly the glory of God that may not always be discernable

16 And even from one city to another, until they had gone forth among all the people of Nephi who were in the land southward; and from thence into the land of Zarahemla, among the Lamanites.

17 And it came to pass that they did preach with great power, insomuch that they did confound many of those dissenters who had gone over from the Nephites, insomuch that they came forth and did confess their sins and were baptized unto repentance, and immediately returned to the Nephites to endeavor to repair unto them the wrongs which they had done.

18 And it came to pass that Nephi and Lehi did preach unto the Lamanites with such great power and authority, for they had power and authority given unto them that they might speak, and they also had what they should speak given unto them—

19 Therefore they did speak unto the great astonishment of the Lamanites, to the convincing them, insomuch that there were eight thousand of the Lamanites who were in the land of Zarahemla and round about baptized unto repentance, and were convinced of the wickedness of the traditions of their fathers.

20 And it came to pass that Nephi and Lehi did proceed from thence to go to the land of Nephi.

21 And it came to pass that they were taken by an army of the Lamanites and cast into prison; yea, even in that same prison in which Ammon and his brethren were cast by the servants of Limhi.

22 And after they had been cast into prison many days without food, behold, they went forth into the prison to take them that they might slay them.

23 And it came to pass that Nephi and Lehi were encircled about as if by fire, even

insomuch that they durst not lay their hands upon them for fear lest they should be burned. Nevertheless, Nephi and Lehi were not burned; and they were as standing in the midst of fire and were not burned.

24 And when they saw that they were encircled about with a pillar of fire, and that it burned them not, their hearts did take courage.

25 For they saw that the Lamanites durst not lay their hands upon them; neither durst they come near unto them, but stood as if they were struck dumb with amazement.

26 And it came to pass that Nephi and Lehi did stand forth and began to speak unto them, saying: Fear not, for behold, it is God that has shown unto you this marvelous thing, in the which is shown unto you that ye cannot lay your hands on us to slay us.

27 And behold, when they had said these words, the earth shook exceedingly, and the walls of the prison did shake as if they were about to tumble to the earth; but behold, they did not fall. And behold, they that were in the prison were Lamanites and Nephites who were dissenters.

28 And it came to pass that they were overshadowed with a cloud of darkness, and an awful solemn fear came upon them.

29 And it came to pass that there came a voice as if it were above the cloud of darkness, saying: Repent ye, repent ye, and seek no more to destroy my servants whom I have sent unto you to declare good tidings.

30 And it came to pass when they heard this voice, and beheld that it was not a voice of thunder, neither was it a voice of a great tumultuous noise, but behold, it was a still voice of perfect mildness, as if it had been a whisper, and it did pierce even to the very soul—

to the physical eye. The Prophet Joseph Smith taught: 'Spirits can only be revealed in flaming fire and glory. Angels have advanced further, their light and glory being tabernacled; and hence they appear in bodily shape' ([*Teachings of the Prophet Joseph Smith*], 325). Apparently angels were attending to Nephi and Lehi. Nephi and Lehi recognized the presence of God in their midst (v. 26)" (Nyman, *Record of Helaman*, 299).

Why is the Lord's voice called a "still voice"? (5:30)
"The voice of the Spirit is described in the scripture as being neither 'loud' nor 'harsh.' . . . The Spirit does not get our attention by shouting or shaking us with a heavy hand. Rather it whispers. It caresses so gently that if we are preoccupied we may not feel it at all. (No wonder that the Word of Wisdom was revealed to us, for how could the drunkard or the addict feel such a voice?)

"Occasionally it will press just firmly enough for us to pay heed. But most of the time, if we do not heed the gentle feeling, the Spirit will withdraw and wait until we come seeking and listening" (Packer, "Candle of the Lord," 53). ⊕

What did Aminadab remember that was instrumental in the conversion of the Lamanites? (5:35–41) "Aminadab, who was a former Nephite and dissenter from the Church, remembered and knew they should pray till they had faith in Christ (see Helaman 5:35–41). Many more Lamanites were converted through the testimony of the 300 as they ministered unto the people, declaring what they had seen and heard (see Helaman 5: 49–50)" (Ringwood, "An Easiness and Willingness to Believe," 100). ⊕

What are we taught in these verses about how faith is obtained? (5:37–43) In Helaman 5:34 we are told the Lamanites could not move for fear. Now here in verse 37 power is given unto them to turn. When in our own lives we seem similarly unable to make the changes we know we ought to make, where can we find the strength to turn? Notice in verse 41 what the Lamanites had to do to be delivered from their "cloud of darkness." What are we taught there about how faith is obtained? How might you apply this experience to your own challenges? Is there someone you care about who could also benefit from these truths?

31 And notwithstanding the mildness of the voice, behold the earth shook exceedingly, and the walls of the prison trembled again, as if it were about to tumble to the earth; and behold the cloud of darkness, which had overshadowed them, did not disperse—

32 And behold the voice came again, saying: Repent ye, repent ye, for the kingdom of heaven is at hand; and seek no more to destroy my servants. And it came to pass that the earth shook again, and the walls trembled.

33 And also again the third time the voice came, and did speak unto them marvelous words which cannot be uttered by man; and the walls did tremble again, and the earth shook as if it were about to divide asunder.

34 And it came to pass that the Lamanites could not flee because of the cloud of darkness which did overshadow them; yea, and also they were immovable because of the fear which did come upon them.

35 Now there was one among them who was a Nephite by birth, who had once belonged to the church of God but had dissented from them.

36 And it came to pass that he turned him about, and behold, he saw through the cloud of darkness the faces of Nephi and Lehi; and behold, they did shine exceedingly, even as the faces of angels. And he beheld that they did lift their eyes to heaven; and they were in the attitude as if talking or lifting their voices to some being whom they beheld.

37 And it came to pass that this man did cry unto the multitude, that they might turn and look. And behold, there was power given unto them that they did turn and look; and they did behold the faces of Nephi and Lehi.

38 And they said unto the man: Behold, what do all these things mean, and who is it with whom these men do converse?

39 Now the man's name was Aminadab. And Aminadab said unto them: They do converse with the angels of God.

40 And it came to pass that the Lamanites said unto him: What shall we do, that this cloud of darkness may be removed from overshadowing us?

41 And Aminadab said unto them: You must repent, and cry unto the voice, even until ye shall have faith in Christ, who was taught unto you by Alma, and Amulek, and Zeezrom; and when ye shall do this, the cloud of darkness shall be removed from overshadowing you.

42 And it came to pass that they all did begin to cry unto the voice of him who had shaken the earth; yea, they did cry even until the cloud of darkness was dispersed.

43 And it came to pass that when they cast their eyes about, and saw that the cloud of darkness was dispersed from overshadowing them, behold, they saw that they were encircled about, yea every soul, by a pillar of fire.

44 And Nephi and Lehi were in the midst of them; yea, they were encircled about; yea, they were as if in the midst of a flaming fire, yet it did harm them not, neither did it take hold upon the walls of the prison; and they were filled with that joy which is unspeakable and full of glory.

Transforming Experiences in Lamanite History (Helaman 5:50–6:8)

"Notice the dramatic and transforming first-time experiences in the long history of the Lamanites:

"1. The majority of the Lamanites were converted to the gospel.

"2. The Lamanites laid down their weapons and their hatred and false traditions.

"3. They freely yielded up the land that belonged to the Nephites.

"4. The majority of the Lamanites became more righteous than the Nephites.

"5. The Lamanites began to preach the gospel to the Nephites.

"6. There was peace in all the land.

"7. The Lamanites and Nephites had open travel and free trade with one another" (Ogden and Skinner, *Book of Mormon*, 2:89).

Who are ministering angels? (5:48) "When messengers are sent to minister to the inhabitants of this earth, they are not strangers, but from the ranks of our kindred, friends, and fellow-beings and fellow-servants. The ancient prophets who died were those who came to visit their fellow creatures upon the earth. . . . In like manner our fathers and mothers, brothers, sisters and friends who have passed away from this earth, having been faithful, and worthy to enjoy these rights and privileges, may have a mission given them to visit their relatives and friends upon the earth again, bringing from the divine Presence messages of love, of warning, of reproof and instruction, to those whom they had learned to love in the flesh" (Smith, *Gospel Doctrine*, 435–37).

Why is it important to chose to believe? (5:50) "When problems come and questions arise, do not start your quest for faith by saying how much you do not have, leading as it were with your 'unbelief.' . . . I am not asking you to pretend to faith you do not have. I am asking you to be true to the faith you do have. Sometimes we act as if an honest declaration of doubt is a higher manifestation of moral courage than is an honest declaration of faith. It is not! . . . If you and your family want to be healed, don't let those questions stand in the way of faith working its miracle" (Holland, "Lord, I Believe," 94).

45 And behold, the Holy Spirit of God did come down from heaven, and did enter into their hearts, and they were filled as if with fire, and they could speak forth marvelous words.

46 And it came to pass that there came a voice unto them, yea, a pleasant voice, as if it were a whisper, saying:

47 Peace, peace be unto you, because of your faith in my Well Beloved, who was from the foundation of the world.

48 And now, when they heard this they cast up their eyes as if to behold from whence the voice came; and behold, they saw the heavens open; and angels came down out of heaven and ministered unto them.

49 And there were about three hundred souls who saw and heard these things; and they were bidden to go forth and marvel not, neither should they doubt.

50 And it came to pass that they did go forth, and did minister unto the people, declaring throughout all the regions round about all the things which they had heard and seen, insomuch that the more part of the Lamanites were convinced of them, because of the greatness of the evidences which they had received.

51 And as many as were convinced did lay down their weapons of war, and also their hatred and the tradition of their fathers.

52 And it came to pass that they did yield up unto the Nephites the lands of their possession.

CHAPTER 6

The righteous Lamanites preach to the wicked Nephites—Both peoples prosper during an era of peace and plenty—Lucifer, the author of sin, stirs up the hearts of the wicked and the Gadianton robbers in murder and wickedness—The robbers take over the Nephite government. About 29–23 B.C.

1 And it came to pass that when the sixty and second year of the reign of the judges had ended, all these things had happened and the Lamanites had become, the more part of them, a righteous people, insomuch that their righteousness did exceed that of the Nephites, because of their firmness and their steadiness in the faith.

2 For behold, there were many of the Nephites who had become hardened and impenitent and grossly wicked, insomuch that they did reject the word of God and all the preaching and prophesying which did come among them.

3 Nevertheless, the people of the church did have great joy because of the conversion of the Lamanites, yea, because of the church of God, which had been established among them. And they did fellowship one with another, and did rejoice one with another, and did have great joy.

4 And it came to pass that many of the Lamanites did come down into the land of Zarahemla, and did declare unto the people of the Nephites the manner of their conversion, and did exhort them to faith and repentance.

5 Yea, and many did preach with exceedingly great power and authority, unto the bringing down many of them into the depths of humility, to be the humble followers of God and the Lamb.

6 And it came to pass that many of the Lamanites did go into the land northward;

Helaman 6:1–6. Many Converted Lamanites Teach the Gospel to the Nephites

What caused this great conversion of Lamanites? (6:1–4) "As I pondered what caused this mighty change in the hearts of these Lamanites, I came to realize this easiness and willingness to believe in the word of God comes from a softness of heart. It comes from having a heart that is sensitive to the Holy Ghost. It comes from having a heart that can love. It comes from having a heart that will make and keep sacred covenants. It comes from a soft heart that can feel the power of the Atonement of Christ.

"This easiness to believe comes from the example of others who have soft hearts and who model this easiness to believe, such as Nephi and Lehi. Their father, Helaman, named them Nephi and Lehi to remind them of the faith of their fathers (see Helaman 5:6)" (Ringwood, "Easiness and Willingness to Believe," 100). ⊕

Helaman 6:7–14. The Nephites and Lamanites Enjoy a Time of Peace and Prosperity

How was peace finally attained by the Nephites and Lamanites? (6:7) "Peace is to be found in every land where righteousness prevails. Peace and righteousness . . . go hand-in-hand. It is therefore only natural that there is peace where the people keep the commandments of the Lord. Peace is God's most precious gift. . . .

"[The] Book of Mormon [bears] witness that where peace is founded upon truth, upheld and sustained by righteousness, the people prosper and the land is free from strife and contention" (Reynolds and Sjodahl, *Commentary on the Book of Mormon*, 5:248).

During times of peace, how did the Lamanites and Nephites interact with one another? (6:8–9) "Book of Mormon peoples apparently engaged in commerce on a substantial scale. By 130 B.C., after dissident Nephites who lived in the land of Nephi taught literacy to the Lamanites in the area, the latter 'began to increase in riches, and began to trade one with another and wax great, and began to be a cunning and a wise people' (Mosiah 24:7). A century later considerable intermixture of the two basic populations, Nephites and Lamanites, temporarily occurred, and 'they did have free intercourse one with another to buy and to sell, and to get gain.' As a result, 'they became exceeding rich, both the Lamanites and the Nephites' (Helaman 6:7–9)" (Sorenson, *Mormon's Codex*, 273–74).

and also Nephi and Lehi went into the land northward, to preach unto the people. And thus ended the sixty and third year.

7 And behold, there was peace in all the land, insomuch that the Nephites did go into whatsoever part of the land they would, whether among the Nephites or the Lamanites.

8 And it came to pass that the Lamanites did also go whithersoever they would, whether it were among the Lamanites or among the Nephites; and thus they did have free intercourse one with another, to buy and to sell, and to get gain, according to their desire.

9 And it came to pass that they became exceedingly rich, both the Lamanites and the Nephites; and they did have an exceeding plenty of gold, and of silver, and of all manner of precious metals, both in the land south and in the land north.

10 Now the land south was called Lehi, and the land north was called Mulek, which was after the son of Zedekiah; for the Lord did bring Mulek into the land north, and Lehi into the land south.

11 And behold, there was all manner of gold in both these lands, and of silver, and of precious ore of every kind; and there were also curious workmen, who did work all kinds of ore and did refine it; and thus they did become rich.

12 They did raise grain in abundance, both in the north and in the south; and they did flourish exceedingly, both in the north and in the south. And they did multiply and wax exceedingly strong in the land. And they

"In 1967, John W. Welch first encountered the study of chiasmus in the New Testament. This led within a few weeks to his landmark discovery of chiasmus in the Book of Mormon, followed by the publication of several well-known articles and a book on this subject. Today, the study of inverted parallel structures in the Book of Mormon still continues. Most recently, another fine example of chiasmus was discerned in Helaman 6:7–13, the annual report for the sixty-fourth year of the Reign of the Judges, whose main features can be displayed as follows:

"**A**, 'And behold, there was *peace* in all the land' (6:7)

  "**B**, [Freedom of travel and trade in *both lands* is discussed (6:7–8).]

    "**C**, 'And it came to pass that they became exceedingly *rich*, both the Lamanites and the Nephites;

      "**D**, and they did have an exceeding *plenty* of gold, and of *silver*, and of *all manner* of precious metals, *both* in the *land* south and in the *land* north' (6:9)

        "**E**, 'Now the land *south* was called *Lehi*, and the land north was called *Mulek* which was after the son of Zedekiah; for the *Lord* did bring *Mulek* into the land *north*, and *Lehi* into the land *south*' (6:11)

      "**D**, 'And behold, there was all manner of *gold* in both these lands, and of *silver*, and of *precious ore* of every kind;

    "**C**, and there were also curious workmen, who did work all kinds of ore and did refine it; and thus they did become *rich*' (6:11).

  "**B**, [Economic prosperity in *both lands* is discussed (6:12–13).]

"**A**, 'And thus the sixty and fourth year did pass away in *peace*' (6:13).

"This composition is remarkable in several ways. First, the report itself is beautifully executed. Words, phrases, and ideas that appear in the first half are repeated with precision and balance in the second half. This entry exhibits both fine quality and admirable length.

"Second, since the chiasm encompasses the entire report for the year, this unifying structure strongly suggests that the account was written as a single literary unit that Mormon copied verbatim from the Large Plates of Nephi into his abridgment. Apparently the contemporary historian used chiasmus to record an extraordinary year in the annals of his people. The report documents a great change that occurred during the sixty-fourth year involving prosperity, free travel, and peace between both the Nephites and Lamanites. Significant trade and peace treaties must have been entered into in order for this kind of peace and prosperity to occur, since before this time, restriction on travel was the norm in Nephite society, as is evidenced by Mosiah 7:1; 8:7; 28:1; Alma 23:2; 50:25; and Helaman 4:12. Official decrees of this type may be related to the misharum edicts of the Near East that typically proclaimed freedom for slaves and granted 'equity' for the land. In addition to marking an unprecedented turning point in Nephite history, using chiasmus would insure against additions to or deletions from the text, since any alteration would be strikingly apparent.

"Third, and most remarkable, the center of this chiasm involves two individual words. At the very apex, the words 'Zedekiah' and 'Lord' stand parallel to each other, which is intriguing since the Hebrew word for 'Lord' constitutes the theophoric suffix -*yah* at the end of the name 'Zedekiah.'

"Finally, it may be that other reports from antiquity were written in chiastic form. The Mesoamerican Chilam Balam of Chumayel, like Helaman 6, not only focuses chiastically on the migration of the people into the land they now occupy, but also similarly features, at the center, a word-play on the land's name, as J. E. S. Thompson has noted.

"This text deserves to take its place among the finest examples of chiasmus in the Book of Mormon and beyond. Through understanding this masterful composition, we can better appreciate the precision and richness of Old World stylistic influences in the Nephite historical records" (Welch, "Chiasmus in Helaman 6:7–13," 230–32; paragraphing altered).

did raise many flocks and herds, yea, many fatlings.

13 Behold their women did toil and spin, and did make all manner of cloth, of fine-twined linen and cloth of every kind, to clothe their nakedness. And thus the sixty and fourth year did pass away in peace.

14 And in the sixty and fifth year they did also have great joy and peace, yea, much preaching and many prophecies concerning that which was to come. And thus passed away the sixty and fifth year.

15 And it came to pass that in the sixty and sixth year of the reign of the judges, behold, Cezoram was murdered by an unknown hand as he sat upon the judgment-seat. And it came to pass that in the same year, that his son, who had been appointed by the people in his stead, was also murdered. And thus ended the sixty and sixth year.

16 And in the commencement of the sixty and seventh year the people began to grow exceedingly wicked again.

17 For behold, the Lord had blessed them so long with the riches of the world that they had not been stirred up to anger, to wars, nor to bloodshed; therefore they began to set their hearts upon their riches; yea, they began to seek to get gain that they might be lifted up one above another; therefore they began to commit secret murders, and to rob and to plunder, that they might get gain.

18 And now behold, those murderers and plunderers were a band who had been formed by Kishkumen and Gadianton. And now it had come to pass that there were many, even among the Nephites, of Gadianton's band. But behold, they were more numerous among the more wicked part of the Lamanites. And they were called Gadianton's robbers and murderers.

Helaman 6:15–30. The Gadianton Robbers Gain Power through Secret Combinations

Who caused the loss of peace and prosperity at this time? (6:15–17) "Mormon's moral is that this prosperity, which temporarily brings peace, will nevertheless lead directly and inevitably to conflict. This theme has been a persistent one for Mormon. In this case, the instrument of contention will be the Gadianton robbers, not the Lamanites. The Gadianton robbers are an internal Nephite problem, on whom Mormon blames the Nephite collapse just before the Messiah's arrival. . . . It suits Mormon's editorial purposes to ground the Gadianton dissension in the same destructive power of class distinctions and wealth as past conflicts. The players are changing, but the game is the same" (Gardner, *Second Witness*, 5:103–4). ⊕

19 And it was they who did murder the chief judge Cezoram, and his son, while in the judgment-seat; and behold, they were not found.

20 And now it came to pass that when the Lamanites found that there were robbers among them they were exceedingly sorrowful; and they did use every means in their power to destroy them off the face of the earth.

21 But behold, Satan did stir up the hearts of the more part of the Nephites, insomuch that they did unite with those bands of robbers, and did enter into their covenants and their oaths, that they would protect and preserve one another in whatsoever difficult circumstances they should be placed, that they should not suffer for their murders, and their plunderings, and their stealings.

22 And it came to pass that they did have their signs, yea, their secret signs, and their secret words; and this that they might distinguish a brother who had entered into the covenant, that whatsoever wickedness his brother should do he should not be injured by his brother, nor by those who did belong to his band, who had taken this covenant.

23 And thus they might murder, and plunder, and steal, and commit whoredoms and all manner of wickedness, contrary to the laws of their country and also the laws of their God.

24 And whosoever of those who belonged to their band should reveal unto the world of their wickedness and their abominations, should be tried, not according to the laws of their country, but according to the laws of their wickedness, which had been given by Gadianton and Kishkumen.

25 Now behold, it is these secret oaths and covenants which Alma commanded his son should not go forth unto the world, lest they

How is the word *covenant* used in the Book of Mormon? (6:21–22) "Of the 154 references to 'covenant' in the Book of Mormon, 113 of them explain some promises made between God and his children on the earth. Most of the remaining references describe honorable promises made between leaders and individuals, usually to end periods of conflict. But a third and smallest category of passages contains 17 references to evil, secret covenants made between men and the devil. Fifteen of these secret covenant references are found in the book of Helaman and the first chapters of 3 Nephi, where all three types of covenants are mentioned (see Alma 37:27, 29 for the other two secret covenant references)" (Ludlow, "Secret Covenant Teachings of Men and the Devil," 265–66). ◐

Why should we fear the rise of secret combinations? (6:23) "The Book of Mormon teaches that secret combinations engaged in crime present a serious challenge, not just to individuals and families but to entire civilizations. Among today's secret combinations are gangs, drug cartels, and organized crime families. . . . They have secret signs and code words. They participate in secret rites and initiation ceremonies. . . .

"If we are not careful, today's secret combinations can obtain power and influence just as quickly and just as completely as they did in Book of Mormon times. Do you remember the pattern? The secret combinations began among the 'more wicked part' of society, but eventually 'seduced the more part of the righteous' until the whole society was polluted (Hel. 6:38)" (Ballard, "Standing for Truth and Right," 38).

should be a means of bringing down the people unto destruction.

26 Now behold, those secret oaths and covenants did not come forth unto Gadianton from the records which were delivered unto Helaman; but behold, they were put into the heart of Gadianton by that same being who did entice our first parents to partake of the forbidden fruit—

27 Yea, that same being who did plot with Cain, that if he would murder his brother Abel it should not be known unto the world. And he did plot with Cain and his followers from that time forth.

28 And also it is that same being who put it into the hearts of the people to build a tower sufficiently high that they might get to heaven. And it was that same being who led on the people who came from that tower into this land; who spread the works of darkness and abominations over all the face of the land, until he dragged the people down to an entire destruction, and to an everlasting hell.

29 Yea, it is that same being who put it into the heart of Gadianton to still carry on the work of darkness, and of secret murder; and he has brought it forth from the beginning of man even down to this time.

30 And behold, it is he who is the author of all sin. And behold, he doth carry on his works of darkness and secret murder, and doth hand down their plots, and their oaths, and their covenants, and their plans of awful wickedness, from generation to generation according as he can get hold upon the hearts of the children of men.

31 And now behold, he had got great hold upon the hearts of the Nephites; yea, insomuch that they had become exceedingly wicked; yea, the more part of them had turned out of the way of righteousness, and

What was the consequence of Satan's plot with Cain? (6:27) "Cain, being the firstborn of his father's family ... might have been the head of this Priesthood, under his father, holding the right by birth; but instead of exercising his birthright on the principles of righteousness, and in accord with the powers of heaven, he was befogged and understood not his true position.... When Cain found that his offering was not accepted, and his brother, Abel's was accepted, Satan tempted him, and entered into him and led him into the way of all apostates—he became possessed with the spirit of murder. I mention it as the first apostasy of which we have record after the fall of man, through it Cain lost his privilege as firstborn" (Erastus Snow, in *Journal of Discourses*, 21:370).

Helaman 6:31–41. The Nephites Become Far More Wicked Than the Lamanites

What is Mormon trying to teach us about these events? (6:31–41) "Mormon gave the reader four 'thus we see' precepts as he recorded the events of the 68th year. The first lesson of life is the equation of unbelief and wickedness among the Nephites. He then equates the knowledge of God with walking in truth and

did trample under their feet the commandments of God, and did turn unto their own ways, and did build up unto themselves idols of their gold and their silver.

32 And it came to pass that all these iniquities did come unto them in the space of not many years, insomuch that a more part of it had come unto them in the sixty and seventh year of the reign of the judges over the people of Nephi.

33 And they did grow in their iniquities in the sixty and eighth year also, to the great sorrow and lamentation of the righteous.

34 And thus we see that the Nephites did begin to dwindle in unbelief, and grow in wickedness and abominations, while the Lamanites began to grow exceedingly in the knowledge of their God; yea, they did begin to keep his statutes and commandments, and to walk in truth and uprightness before him.

35 And thus we see that the Spirit of the Lord began to withdraw from the Nephites, because of the wickedness and the hardness of their hearts.

36 And thus we see that the Lord began to pour out his Spirit upon the Lamanites, because of their easiness and willingness to believe in his words.

37 And it came to pass that the Lamanites did hunt the band of robbers of Gadianton; and they did preach the word of God among the more wicked part of them, insomuch that this band of robbers was utterly destroyed from among the Lamanites.

38 And it came to pass on the other hand, that the Nephites did build them up and support them, beginning at the more wicked part of them, until they had overspread all the land of the Nephites, and had seduced the more part of the righteous until they had come down to believe in their works and

uprightness (v. 34). . . . The second lesson of life is the reason why the Spirit withdraws from us—wickedness (v. 35). . . . The third lesson of life [is that the] Spirit began to come 'upon the Lamanites because of their easiness and willingness to believe in his words' (Helaman 6:36). . . . The fourth lesson of life is more of a warning against the awful state and ripening for destruction that came upon the Nephites (Helaman 6:40)" (Nyman, *Record of Helaman*, 312–15).

Why is it important to "willingly believe" in God's words? (6:36) President Dieter F. Uchtdorf pleaded with the Saints: "Please, first doubt your doubts before you doubt your faith. We must never allow doubt to hold us prisoner and keep us from the divine love, peace, and gifts that come through faith in the Lord Jesus Christ" ("Come, Join with Us," 23). How can you become more willing to follow the Church and its teachings?

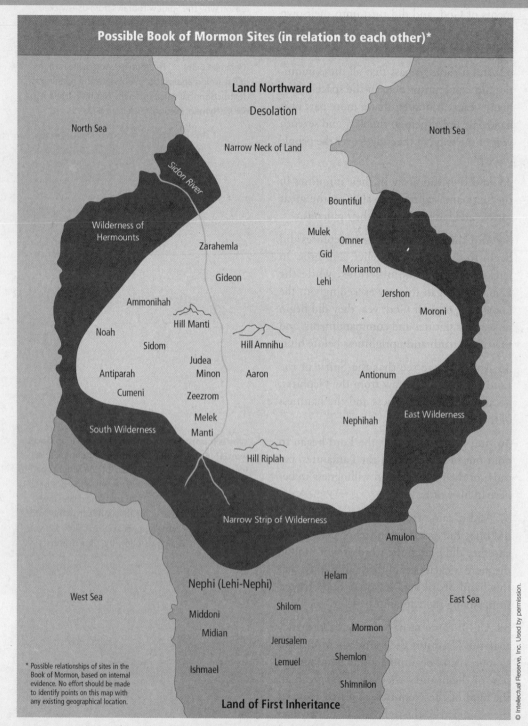

Possible Book of Mormon Sites (in relation to each other)*

Land Northward

Desolation

North Sea

Narrow Neck of Land

North Sea

Sidon River

Bountiful

Wilderness of Hermounts

Mulek

Omner

Zarahemla

Gid

Gideon

Morianton

Lehi

Jershon

Ammonihah

Moroni

Hill Manti

Noah

Hill Amnihu

Sidom

Judea

Antiparah

Minon

Aaron

Antionum

Cumeni

Zeezrom

Melek

Nephihah

East Wilderness

South Wilderness

Manti

Hill Riplah

Narrow Strip of Wilderness

Amulon

Helam

Nephi (Lehi-Nephi)

West Sea

Shilom

East Sea

Middoni

Midian

Mormon

Jerusalem

Shemlon

Lemuel

Ishmael

Shimnilon

Land of First Inheritance

* Possible relationships of sites in the Book of Mormon, based on internal evidence. No effort should be made to identify points on this map with any existing geographical location.

After Nephi, son of Helaman, was rejected by the people living in the land northward, he "returned again unto the land of his nativity" (Helaman 7:3).

partake of their spoils, and to join with them in their secret murders and combinations.

39 And thus they did obtain the sole management of the government, insomuch that they did trample under their feet and smite and rend and turn their backs upon the poor and the meek, and the humble followers of God.

40 And thus we see that they were in an awful state, and ripening for an everlasting destruction.

41 And it came to pass that thus ended the sixty and eighth year of the reign of the judges over the people of Nephi.

THE PROPHECY OF NEPHI, THE SON OF HELAMAN—God threatens the people of Nephi that he will visit them in his anger, to their utter destruction except they repent of their wickedness. God smiteth the people of Nephi with pestilence; they repent and turn unto him. Samuel, a Lamanite, prophesies unto the Nephites.

Comprising chapters 7 through 16.

CHAPTER 7

Nephi is rejected in the north and returns to Zarahemla—He prays upon his garden tower and then calls upon the people to repent or perish. About 23–21 B.C.

1 Behold, now it came to pass in the sixty and ninth year of the reign of the judges over the people of the Nephites, that Nephi, the son of Helaman, returned to the land of Zarahemla from the land northward.

2 For he had been forth among the people who were in the land northward, and did preach the word of God unto them, and did prophesy many things unto them;

3 And they did reject all his words, insomuch that he could not stay among them, but returned again unto the land of his nativity.

Superscription to Helaman 7

The superscription to Helaman 7 was part of the ancient record translated by the Prophet Joseph Smith and dictated by him to his scribe (see also, for example, 2 Nephi, Mosiah 9, and 4 Nephi). The phrase "Comprising chapters 7 through 16" was added to later editions of the Book of Mormon.

What does the superscription suggest about the book of Helaman? The "[superscription] before chapter seven tells us that Nephi wrote the chapters of the book of Helaman after that point. . . . This material was an extract from a separate record in Mormon's possession. Clearly a number of men had a significant hand in producing the book of Helaman" (Tvedtnes, "Colophons," 35–36).

Helaman 7:1–9. Nephi Mourns over the People's Wickedness

For what reasons did a large shift of governmental power occur? (7:4–5) "Greed and lust for power lead people to tamper with the laws designed to protect and prevent exploitation of all citizens.... If the majority permit changes in the laws, either by apathy or through ever growing numbers of people who are tempted and confused about right and wrong, the stage is set for the judgments of the Almighty, for he will not allow such wickedness to continue" (Brinley, "Promised Land and Its Covenant Peoples," 51). ●

How can the righteous endure such wicked and unfair circumstances? (7:5) "Even in our day, 'the guilty and the wicked go unpunished because of their money.' Some things just don't seem fair.

"With strong underpinnings, however, we are better able to reach upward for help, even when faced with questions without easy answers....

"Though we don't know all things, we know that God lives and that He loves us. Standing on that firm foundation, we can reach up and find strength to endure the heavy burdens of life" (Nelson, "How Firm Our Foundation," 76). ●

How can wickedness and apostasy occur so quickly in a society? (7:6) "Because the people lose the Spirit and fail to teach their children the doctrine of righteousness and to worship Jesus Christ. The rising generation will not know the history and the doctrine unless they are taught. And if not taught the doctrine, children are unprepared to cope with life's greatest problems. People need a reason not to commit sin; the gospel gives us that reason" (Matthews, "Patterns of Apostasy," 79).

Have you ever wished you lived in a more righteous time? (7:7–9) What do you learn about Nephi from his expression "I am consigned that these are my days"? How does it help you to remember that others, like Nephi, have lived faithfully through difficult and wicked times? As you read about Nephi's experiences, notice how he lived and ministered among the people even though his soul was often filled with sorrow because of the people's wickedness.

4 And seeing the people in a state of such awful wickedness, and those Gadianton robbers filling the judgment-seats—having usurped the power and authority of the land; laying aside the commandments of God, and not in the least aright before him; doing no justice unto the children of men;

5 Condemning the righteous because of their righteousness; letting the guilty and the wicked go unpunished because of their money; and moreover to be held in office at the head of government, to rule and do according to their wills, that they might get gain and glory of the world, and, moreover, that they might the more easily commit adultery, and steal, and kill, and do according to their own wills—

6 Now this great iniquity had come upon the Nephites, in the space of not many years; and when Nephi saw it, his heart was swollen with sorrow within his breast; and he did exclaim in the agony of his soul:

7 Oh, that I could have had my days in the days when my father Nephi first came out of the land of Jerusalem, that I could have joyed with him in the promised land; then were his people easy to be entreated, firm to keep the commandments of God, and slow to be led to do iniquity; and they were quick to hearken unto the words of the Lord—

8 Yea, if my days could have been in those days, then would my soul have had joy in the righteousness of my brethren.

9 But behold, I am consigned that these are my days, and that my soul shall be filled with

sorrow because of this the wickedness of my brethren.

10 And behold, now it came to pass that it was upon a tower, which was in the garden of Nephi, which was by the highway which led to the chief market, which was in the city of Zarahemla; therefore, Nephi had bowed himself upon the tower which was in his garden, which tower was also near unto the garden gate by which led the highway.

11 And it came to pass that there were certain men passing by and saw Nephi as he was pouring out his soul unto God upon the tower; and they ran and told the people what they had seen, and the people came together in multitudes that they might know the cause of so great mourning for the wickedness of the people.

12 And now, when Nephi arose he beheld the multitudes of people who had gathered together.

13 And it came to pass that he opened his mouth and said unto them: Behold, why have ye gathered yourselves together? That I may tell you of your iniquities?

14 Yea, because I have got upon my tower that I might pour out my soul unto my God, because of the exceeding sorrow of my heart, which is because of your iniquities!

15 And because of my mourning and lamentation ye have gathered yourselves together, and do marvel; yea, and ye have great need to marvel; yea, ye ought to marvel because ye are given away that the devil has got so great hold upon your hearts.

16 Yea, how could you have given way to the enticing of him who is seeking to hurl away your souls down to everlasting misery and endless wo?

Helaman 7:10–19. Nephi Commands the People to Repent

What is the significance of Nephi's garden tower? (7:10–11) "Nephi had a 'garden' ... near the highway that led to the 'chief market' in the city of Zarahemla. Such ideas have seemed incompatible with what was known about ancient American life. Recent discoveries about Mesoamerican urban settlements, however, have now made these features seem highly reasonable.

"The 'tower' might easily refer to pyramidal mounds, some built and used by families and lineage leaders for religious ceremonies, and which were referred to by the Spanish conquerors as 'towers'" (Sorenson, "Nephi's Garden and Chief Market," 236).

Why is it important that the text make note of the "chief market"? (7:10) "Significantly, this is the only place in the Book of Mormon where the word 'market' appears.

" ... Why add this description? If Joseph Smith were authoring the book, there would be no need to include such a description. ...

"We can, however, draw several conclusions from Mormon's inclusion of the phrase 'chief market.' First, the description was important to include, since he was limited for space and therefore would have included only words, phrases, and events that he felt were significant. Also, this description signifies that cities in this time period not only had more than one market, but that one of the markets was either larger or more significant than the others" (Hunt, "Marketplace," 138).

Why did the Nephites "marvel" at Nephi's accusations? (7:14–15) "The intolerant and unjust who have religion have often convinced themselves that God loves them because they do religious things. They are spiritually oblivious, or as God says to the wealthy, lukewarm members of the church in Laodicea, '[thou] knowest not that thou art wretched, and miserable, and poor, and blind, and naked' (Rev 3:17). The Nephites in the book of Helaman are a great example of this phenomenon. When Nephi severely chastised them, they marveled. In spite of their gross wickedness, they were shocked that he thought they were wicked (Hel 7:14–15)" (Hansen, "Terrifying Book of Helaman," 170). ⊕

What does the verb *hurl* in this verse tell you about Satan's attitude towards you? (7:16) According to Noah Webster, to "hurl" is "to throw with violence; to drive with great force" (*American Dictionary*). The devil rejoices when you are miserable (see 2 Nephi 2:27; Moroni 7:17). Once a person realizes the true nature of the devil, there is no desire to follow him or be like him.

Why does Nephi use the image of gathering and scattering? (7:19) "To illustrate the doctrines of gathering and scattering, Nephi used as a type the assembling of those who came to hear him. The faithful of all dispensations have gathered to be taught the gospel and also to facilitate the observance of their covenants. When they have rebelled against those teachings and broken their vows, their lands of promise have been taken from them and they have been driven, scattered, and often destroyed. Nephi applies that principle to his immediate audience—as they have gathered to hear him, so they must repent; and if they fail to do so they will be scattered" (McConkie and Millet, *Doctrinal Commentary*, 3:369).

Helaman 7:20–29. The Nephites Are Threatened with Destruction, but the Lamanites Are Promised Mercy

What is often the relationship between riches and forgetting God? (7:20–21) "President Heber J. Grant said that 'if we are faithful in keeping the commandments of God His promises will be fulfilled to the very letter. . . . The trouble is, the adversary of men's souls blinds their minds. He throws dust, so to speak, in their eyes, and they are blinded with the things of this world' (*Gospel Standards*, comp. G. Homer Durham [Salt Lake City: *Improvement Era*, 1941], 44–45). He tempts us with the transitory pleasures of the world so that we will not focus our minds and efforts on the things that bring eternal joy. The devil is a dirty fighter, and we must be aware of his tactics" (Ballard, "Purity Precedes Power," 36). ●

17 O repent ye, repent ye! Why will ye die? Turn ye, turn ye unto the Lord your God. Why has he forsaken you?

18 It is because you have hardened your hearts; yea, ye will not hearken unto the voice of the good shepherd; yea, ye have provoked him to anger against you.

19 And behold, instead of gathering you, except ye will repent, behold, he shall scatter you forth that ye shall become meat for dogs and wild beasts.

20 O, how could you have forgotten your God in the very day that he has delivered you?

21 But behold, it is to get gain, to be praised of men, yea, and that ye might get gold and silver. And ye have set your hearts upon the riches and the vain things of this world, for the which ye do murder, and plunder, and steal, and bear false witness against your neighbor, and do all manner of iniquity.

22 And for this cause wo shall come unto you except ye shall repent. For if ye will not repent, behold, this great city, and also all those great cities which are round about, which are in the land of our possession, shall be taken away that ye shall have no place in them; for behold, the Lord will not grant unto you strength, as he has hitherto done, to withstand against your enemies.

23 For behold, thus saith the Lord: I will not show unto the wicked of my strength, to one more than the other, save it be unto those who repent of their sins, and hearken unto

my words. Now therefore, I would that ye should behold, my brethren, that it shall be better for the Lamanites than for you except ye shall repent.

24 For behold, they are more righteous than you, for they have not sinned against that great knowledge which ye have received; therefore the Lord will be merciful unto them; yea, he will lengthen out their days and increase their seed, even when thou shalt be utterly destroyed except thou shalt repent.

25 Yea, wo be unto you because of that great abomination which has come among you; and ye have united yourselves unto it, yea, to that secret band which was established by Gadianton!

26 Yea, wo shall come unto you because of that pride which ye have suffered to enter your hearts, which has lifted you up beyond that which is good because of your exceedingly great riches!

27 Yea, wo be unto you because of your wickedness and abominations!

28 And except ye repent ye shall perish; yea, even your lands shall be taken from you, and ye shall be destroyed from off the face of the earth.

29 Behold now, I do not say that these things shall be, of myself, because it is not of myself that I know these things; but behold, I know that these things are true because the Lord God has made them known unto me, therefore I testify that they shall be.

What might be the significance of the three woes declared by Nephi? (7:25–28) Nephi's preaching of "woes" reminds us of some of the dire "woes" announced in the Book of Revelation regarding the last days (see Revelation 8: 13). "Woes" were usually pronounced when any of three sinful conditions were present: (1) joining the secret Gadianton bands; (2) exhibiting exceeding pride; or (3) committing wickedness and abominations. Any one of these would have been enough to topple the Nephite nation. But the combination of all three warranted the dire warning that "ye shall be destroyed from off the face of the land" (Helaman 7:28).

How can pride keep us from repenting? (7:26–28) "The first step in the repentance process has always been simply to recognize that we have done wrong. If we are so hedged about by pride, rationalization, machismo, or a misdirected sense of self-esteem as to prevent us from ever admitting that we are part of the problem, we are in trouble. We then may not even know of our need to repent. We will have no idea whether the Lord is pleased with us or not and may become 'past feeling' (1 Ne. 17:45). But all men, everywhere, must repent (see 3 Ne. 11:32). To fail to do so is to perish" (Howard, "Repentance," 13).

Helaman 8:1–10. Wicked Judges Try to Turn the People against Nephi, but Some People Believe He Is a Prophet

What did Nephi identify as the main source of corruption among the Nephites? (8:1–4) "Nephi fiercely denounced the evil that existed among them, and warned of impending disaster if they persisted in following iniquity's enticements and its empty promise of reward. His plainness and frankness enraged the corrupt judges who had been placed in office by equally corrupt men....

"Nephi...testified of the corruption [by] which their laws had ceremonially been made unclean, and that how through popular voice, the power to alter them from the Code of King Mosiah had been delegated to hearts, diseased and depraved, who had changed them to suit their own infatuation and greed" (Reynolds and Sjodahl, *Commentary on the Book of Mormon*, 5:264–65).

Why do some of the wicked react so strongly against the truth? (8:5–6) "Those whose wickedness was exposed by Nephi responded with the ferociousness of a trapped animal. They could not lay hands on him for fear of the people, so they sought to turn the people against him. Of Nephi's warning of impending destruction they said, 'this is impossible,' 'we are powerful,' 'our cities great,' 'our enemies can have no power over us.' Yet they trembled at the testimony of a lone man. Truth is more powerful than great cities" (McConkie and Millet, *Doctrinal Commentary*, 3:373).

Why is it important to support the prophet? (8:7) We can raise our voices in support of the prophet, even when it is not the popular thing to do. Have there

CHAPTER 8

Corrupt judges seek to incite the people against Nephi—Abraham, Moses, Zenos, Zenock, Ezias, Isaiah, Jeremiah, Lehi, and Nephi all testified of Christ—By inspiration Nephi announces the murder of the chief judge. About 23–21 B.C.

1 And now it came to pass that when Nephi had said these words, behold, there were men who were judges, who also belonged to the secret band of Gadianton, and they were angry, and they cried out against him, saying unto the people: Why do ye not seize upon this man and bring him forth, that he may be condemned according to the crime which he has done?

2 Why seest thou this man, and hearest him revile against this people and against our law?

3 For behold, Nephi had spoken unto them concerning the corruptness of their law; yea, many things did Nephi speak which cannot be written; and nothing did he speak which was contrary to the commandments of God.

4 And those judges were angry with him because he spake plainly unto them concerning their secret works of darkness; nevertheless, they durst not lay their own hands upon him, for they feared the people lest they should cry out against them.

5 Therefore they did cry unto the people, saying: Why do you suffer this man to revile against us? For behold he doth condemn all this people, even unto destruction; yea, and also that these our great cities shall be taken from us, that we shall have no place in them.

6 And now we know that this is impossible, for behold, we are powerful, and our cities great, therefore our enemies can have no power over us.

7 And it came to pass that thus they did stir up the people to anger against Nephi, and

raised contentions among them; for there were some who did cry out: Let this man alone, for he is a good man, and those things which he saith will surely come to pass except we repent;

8 Yea, behold, all the judgments will come upon us which he has testified unto us; for we know that he has testified aright unto us concerning our iniquities. And behold they are many, and he knoweth as well all things which shall befall us as he knoweth of our iniquities;

9 Yea, and behold, if he had not been a prophet he could not have testified concerning those things.

10 And it came to pass that those people who sought to destroy Nephi were compelled because of their fear, that they did not lay their hands on him; therefore he began again to speak unto them, seeing that he had gained favor in the eyes of some, insomuch that the remainder of them did fear.

11 Therefore he was constrained to speak more unto them saying: Behold, my brethren, have ye not read that God gave power unto one man, even Moses, to smite upon the waters of the Red Sea, and they parted hither and thither, insomuch that the Israelites, who were our fathers, came through upon dry ground, and the waters closed upon the armies of the Egyptians and swallowed them up?

12 And now behold, if God gave unto this man such power, then why should ye dispute among yourselves, and say that he hath given unto me no power whereby I may know concerning the judgments that shall come upon you except ye repent?

13 But, behold, ye not only deny my words, but ye also deny all the words which have been spoken by our fathers, and also the words which were spoken by this man,

been times in your life when you have raised your voice to support the living prophet, even though his teachings have been unpopular? How did this make a difference in your life? How did it influence others?

What influence did the people of Zarahemla have on Nephi's life when he voiced opposition to their judges? (8:7–10) "The great Nephi when he dared criticize the lawyers was in danger of his life at their hands and was only saved because there were a few common people who still preserved a lingering sense of justice and fair play (Helaman 8–9)" (Nibley, *Since Cumorah*, 359).

Helaman 8:11–23. Nephi Tells of Many Prophets Who Testified of Christ

Were the Nephites a highly literate culture? (8:11) "The Book of Mormon is a literate product of a literate culture. It references written texts. Nevertheless, behind the obvious literacy, there are clues to a primary orality in Nephite culture. The instances of text creation and most instances of reading texts suggest that documents were written by and for an elite class who were able to read and write.... Even as Mormon and Moroni wrote, they wrote as though speaking, using techniques appropriate to oral performance adapted to the written text" (Gardner, "Literacy and Orality," 84).

Why did Nephi appeal to many Old Testament prophets as witnesses of Christ? (8:13–23) Nephi listed these additional prophetic witnesses in order to show that he was not alone in testifying of Jesus Christ. If men deny Nephi's witness of Jesus Christ, they would also be denying the testimonies of these other great prophets. Moses bore record that Christ would come and be lifted up as the brazen serpent was in the wilderness (Helaman 8:15; see also Alma 33:19). Abraham rejoiced knowing that Christ would come (Helaman 8:17). Zenos boldly testified of Christ for which he was slain (Helaman 8:19, see also Alma 33:3–13). Zenock taught that mercy would come through the Son of God (Helaman 8:19; see also Alma 33:18). Ezias, Isaiah, and Jeremiah, thousands of years before Christ came, testified of His coming (Helaman 8:20).

What did the brazen serpent represent? (8:14–15)
"The incident is one of the best known of the Old Testament types. Christ interpreted it, saying: 'As Moses lifted up the serpent in the wilderness, even so must the Son of man be lifted up: That whosoever believeth in him should not perish, but have eternal life' (John 3:14–15)" (McConkie, *Gospel Symbolism*, 75). ⊙

What do we know about this "order of God"? (8:18)
See commentary in this volume on Alma 4:20.

Who were Zenos, Zenock, and Ezias? (8:19–20)
"Zenos, Zenock, and Ezias were prophets whose writings were found on the Plates of Brass but have been lost from the Old Testament. Their words are a part of the 'plain and precious' things spoken of by Nephi that have been lost from the record 'of the twelve apostles of the Lamb' (1 Nephi 13:24–29, 40). These prophets were descendants of Joseph, they testified of the Son of God, and sealed their testimonies with their blood. We look forward to the time when other manuscripts come forward and verify these restored losses from the Bible" (Nyman, "Restoration of Plain and Precious Parts," 153). ⊙

Who was Mulek and who were his descendants? (8:21) "Mulek was the son of Zedekiah, the king of Judah, who was spared at the time of the Babylonian

Moses, who had such great power given unto him, yea, the words which he hath spoken concerning the coming of the Messiah.

14 Yea, did he not bear record that the Son of God should come? And as he lifted up the brazen serpent in the wilderness, even so shall he be lifted up who should come.

15 And as many as should look upon that serpent should live, even so as many as should look upon the Son of God with faith, having a contrite spirit, might live, even unto that life which is eternal.

16 And now behold, Moses did not only testify of these things, but also all the holy prophets, from his days even to the days of Abraham.

17 Yea, and behold, Abraham saw of his coming, and was filled with gladness and did rejoice.

18 Yea, and behold I say unto you, that Abraham not only knew of these things, but there were many before the days of Abraham who were called by the order of God; yea, even after the order of his Son; and this that it should be shown unto the people, a great many thousand years before his coming, that even redemption should come unto them.

19 And now I would that ye should know, that even since the days of Abraham there have been many prophets that have testified these things; yea, behold, the prophet Zenos did testify boldly; for the which he was slain.

20 And behold, also Zenock, and also Ezias, and also Isaiah, and Jeremiah, (Jeremiah being that same prophet who testified of the destruction of Jerusalem) and now we know that Jerusalem was destroyed according to the words of Jeremiah. O then why not the Son of God come, according to his prophecy?

21 And now will you dispute that Jerusalem was destroyed? Will ye say that the sons of

Zedekiah were not slain, all except it were Mulek? Yea, and do ye not behold that the seed of Zedekiah are with us, and they were driven out of the land of Jerusalem? But behold, this is not all—

22 Our father Lehi was driven out of Jerusalem because he testified of these things. Nephi also testified of these things, and also almost all of our fathers, even down to this time; yea, they have testified of the coming of Christ, and have looked forward, and have rejoiced in his day which is to come.

23 And behold, he is God, and he is with them, and he did manifest himself unto them, that they were redeemed by him; and they gave unto him glory, because of that which is to come.

24 And now, seeing ye know these things and cannot deny them except ye shall lie, therefore in this ye have sinned, for ye have rejected all these things, notwithstanding so many evidences which ye have received; yea, even ye have received all things, both things in heaven, and all things which are in the earth, as a witness that they are true.

25 But behold, ye have rejected the truth, and rebelled against your holy God; and even at this time, instead of laying up for yourselves treasures in heaven, where nothing doth corrupt, and where nothing can come which is unclean, ye are heaping up for yourselves wrath against the day of judgment.

captivity and who later came to the Americas. The descendants of Mulek were included among the people of Zarahemla, and later they were numbered among the Nephites. Thus, among the combined Nephite-Lamanite-Mulekite peoples are represented at least three of the twelve tribes of ancient Israel: (1) the tribe of Manasseh, represented by the descendants of Lehi; (2) the tribe of Ephraim, represented by the descendants of Ishmael; (3) the tribe of Judah, represented by the descendants of Mulek" (Ludlow, *Companion to Your Study of the Book of Mormon*, 245).

In what sense is Jesus Christ God? (8:23) "Christ-Messiah is God! Such is the plain and pure pronouncement of all the prophets of all the ages. In our desire to avoid the false and absurd conclusions contained in the creeds of Christendom, we are wont to shy away from this pure and unadorned verity. . . . If we are to envision our Lord's true status and glory, we must come back to the pronouncement of pronouncements, the doctrine of doctrines, the message of messages, which is that Christ is God. And if it were not so, he could not save us" (McConkie, *Promised Messiah*, 98).

Helaman 8:24–28. Nephi Speaks against the Sins of the Judges and Announces That the Chief Judge Has Been Murdered

How did Nephi challenge the wickedness of his day? (8:24–26) "As the advent of Christ approached, social disorder increased, with burgeoning warfare, murder, and political disarray. To counter this trend and give hope, Nephi invoked the ancient teachings his people knew so well, testifying of these problems and the coming of the Messiah who would resolve them" (Holland, *Christ and the New Covenant*, 129).

26 Yea, even at this time ye are ripening, because of your murders and your fornication and wickedness, for everlasting destruction; yea, and except ye repent it will come unto you soon.

27 Yea, behold it is now even at your doors; yea, go ye in unto the judgment-seat, and search; and behold, your judge is murdered, and he lieth in his blood; and he hath been murdered by his brother, who seeketh to sit in the judgment-seat.

28 And behold, they both belong to your secret band, whose author is Gadianton and the evil one who seeketh to destroy the souls of men.

CHAPTER 9

Messengers find the chief judge dead at the judgment seat—They are imprisoned and later released—By inspiration Nephi identifies Seantum as the murderer—Nephi is accepted by some as a prophet. About 23–21 B.C.

1 Behold, now it came to pass that when Nephi had spoken these words, certain men who were among them ran to the judgment-seat; yea, even there were five who went, and they said among themselves, as they went:

2 Behold, now we will know of a surety whether this man be a prophet and God hath commanded him to prophesy such marvelous things unto us. Behold, we do not believe that he hath; yea, we do not believe that he is a prophet; nevertheless, if this thing which he has said concerning the chief judge be true, that he be dead, then will we believe that the other words which he has spoken are true.

3 And it came to pass that they ran in their might, and came in unto the judgment-seat; and behold, the chief judge had fallen to the earth, and did lie in his blood.

Helaman 9:1–15. Five Messengers Are Accused of Murder

4 And now behold, when they saw this they were astonished exceedingly, insomuch that they fell to the earth; for they had not believed the words which Nephi had spoken concerning the chief judge.

5 But now, when they saw they believed, and fear came upon them lest all the judgments which Nephi had spoken should come upon the people; therefore they did quake, and had fallen to the earth.

6 Now, immediately when the judge had been murdered—he being stabbed by his brother by a garb of secrecy, and he fled, and the servants ran and told the people, raising the cry of murder among them;

7 And behold the people did gather themselves together unto the place of the judgment-seat—and behold, to their astonishment they saw those five men who had fallen to the earth.

8 And now behold, the people knew nothing concerning the multitude who had gathered together at the garden of Nephi; therefore they said among themselves: These men are they who have murdered the judge, and God has smitten them that they could not flee from us.

9 And it came to pass that they laid hold on them, and bound them and cast them into prison. And there was a proclamation sent abroad that the judge was slain, and that the murderers had been taken and were cast into prison.

10 And it came to pass that on the morrow the people did assemble themselves together to mourn and to fast, at the burial of the great chief judge who had been slain.

11 And thus also those judges who were at the garden of Nephi, and heard his words, were also gathered together at the burial.

Why did these men fall to the earth? (9:4) "Every time you're afraid, do you fall flat on your face? Does fear have that effect on you? . . . How come these people all fall down when they're afraid? Well, this is routine. . . . Remember, [they lived] in a religious world, a sacral state. . . . So if something unexpected absolutely bowls you over, what happens? You're in the presence of some great or divine influence. You don't know whether it's good or bad, but you know it's powerful. It's more powerful than you are, so what do you do? You play safe. You take the position of complete submission. You fall on your face, and it becomes quite automatic" (Nibley, *Teachings of the Book of Mormon*, 3:260).

What challenges did this murder "by a garb of secrecy" present? (9:6) "Cases of unwitnessed murders presented special problems under the law of Moses. While the two-witness rule would seem to stand insurmountably in the way of ever obtaining a conviction in such cases, such slayings could not simply be ignored. If a person was found slain in the land and the murderer could not be found, solemn rituals, oaths of innocence, and special purification of all the men in the village had to be performed (see Deuteronomy 21:1–9). Things turned out differently in Seantum's case, however, for he was soon exposed in a way that opened the door to an exceptional rule of evidence that justified his conviction" (Welch, "Case of an Unobserved Murder," 242–43).

How is this account of a murdered chief judge evidence of the truthfulness of the Book of Mormon? (9:9–10) Immediately after the discovery of the murdered chief judge, "a public proclamation was then sent out by heralds announcing the murder and calling a day of fasting, mourning, and burial (see Helaman 9:10). The day after the death of a political leader was traditionally a day of fasting, mourning, and burial (see 1 Samuel 31:13; 2 Samuel 1:12)" (Welch, "Case of an Unobserved Murder," 242).

How did these witnesses bring comfort to those who followed Nephi as a prophet? (9:15) How is your faith increased when the words of prophets are verified? In what ways have you seen the words of ancient or modern prophets verified today?

Helaman 9:16–24. Nephi Is Accused of Assisting in the Murder of the Chief Judge

Why would the judges not believe that Nephi was a prophet? (9:16–20) Rational or even circumstantial evidence, although helpful at times, doesn't ultimately produce true faith, especially to these corrupt judges. The Lord has declared that true faith does not come by signs or wonders: "Behold, faith cometh not by signs, but signs follow those that believe" (D&C 63:7–9). Similarly in our day, even if the Lord showed the world the golden plates or other artifacts of the Book of Mormon, they would not believe it. "Behold, if they will not believe my words, they would not believe you, my servant Joseph, if it were possible that you should show them all these things which I have committed unto you" (D&C 5:6).

12 And it came to pass that they inquired among the people, saying: Where are the five who were sent to inquire concerning the chief judge whether he was dead? And they answered and said: Concerning this five whom ye say ye have sent, we know not; but there are five who are the murderers, whom we have cast into prison.

13 And it came to pass that the judges desired that they should be brought; and they were brought, and behold they were the five who were sent; and behold the judges inquired of them to know concerning the matter, and they told them all that they had done, saying:

14 We ran and came to the place of the judgment-seat, and when we saw all things even as Nephi had testified, we were astonished insomuch that we fell to the earth; and when we were recovered from our astonishment, behold they cast us into prison.

15 Now, as for the murder of this man, we know not who has done it; and only this much we know, we ran and came according as ye desired, and behold he was dead, according to the words of Nephi.

16 And now it came to pass that the judges did expound the matter unto the people, and did cry out against Nephi, saying: Behold, we know that this Nephi must have agreed with some one to slay the judge, and then he might declare it unto us, that he might convert us unto his faith, that he might raise himself to be a great man, chosen of God, and a prophet.

17 And now behold, we will detect this man, and he shall confess his fault and make known unto us the true murderer of this judge.

18 And it came to pass that the five were liberated on the day of the burial. Nevertheless, they did rebuke the judges in the words

which they had spoken against Nephi, and did contend with them one by one, insomuch that they did confound them.

19 Nevertheless, they caused that Nephi should be taken and bound and brought before the multitude, and they began to question him in divers ways that they might cross him, that they might accuse him to death—

20 Saying unto him: Thou art confederate; who is this man that hath done this murder? Now tell us, and acknowledge thy fault; saying, Behold here is money; and also we will grant unto thee thy life if thou wilt tell us, and acknowledge the agreement which thou hast made with him.

21 But Nephi said unto them: O ye fools, ye uncircumcised of heart, ye blind, and ye stiffnecked people, do ye know how long the Lord your God will suffer you that ye shall go on in this your way of sin?

22 O ye ought to begin to howl and mourn, because of the great destruction which at this time doth await you, except ye shall repent.

23 Behold ye say that I have agreed with a man that he should murder Seezoram, our chief judge. But behold, I say unto you, that this is because I have testified unto you that

What accusation were the judges making against Nephi in their declaration that he was "confederate"? (9:20) According to Webster's 1828 dictionary, to be *confederate* is to be "united in a league; allied by treaty" (*American Dictionary*). Here, Nephi's accusers suggest he is one of them, given to secret oaths and works of darkness. Their own darkness is evident when they offer him money and promise not to prosecute him if he will just tell them who killed the chief judge.

What does it mean to be "uncircumcised of heart"? (9:21) The apostle Paul taught circumcision, an outward ordinance, didn't profit a person unless he kept the law (see Romans 2:25). To be circumcised of the heart means to be a covenant keeper inwardly, "that of the heart, in the spirit, and not in the letter; whose praise is not of men, but of God" (Romans 9:29). "In modern times, Joseph Smith affirmed the perpetuity of the Abrahamic Covenant and defended the integrity of Judaism. Today, however, if Latter-day Saint males are circumcised, it is for cleanliness and health, not religious, reasons. From the beginning of the modern Church, the emphasis has been on circumcision of heart (cf. Deut. 10:16; 30:6; Jer. 4:4; Ezek. 44:9). Such a heart is taken as a sign or token of one's covenants with Christ. This may be the understanding of 'broken heart and contrite spirit' among Book of Mormon prophets (2 Ne. 2:7; 3 Ne. 12:19; Moro. 6:2) and in modern revelation (e.g., D&C 59:8)" (Ludlow, *Encyclopedia of Mormonism,* 1:283).

What do we glean from the imagery of the word *howl* **in this instance? (9:22)** This word, often used by Isaiah (see Isaiah 16:7; 23:1, 6, 14; 65:14), "implies that the wicked . . . are like dogs and wolves who howl while under distress" (Parry et al., *Understanding Isaiah,* 133).

What is the meaning and significance of the name Seezoram? (9:23) "The judge's name was Seezoram, and we had a Zeezrom before. That is the Egyptian word *zsr,* a very popular name, founded the third dynasty of Egypt. The name means holy, sacred. Our word Deseret comes from that. The land of Egypt, 'the holy land, the red land,' is called Deseret. And, of course, the symbol of the lowland is the bee. This is the Deseret name, the Zeezrom name. It pops up throughout the Book of Mormon" (Nibley, *Teachings of the Book of Mormon*, 3:262).

Helaman 9:25–41. Nephi Gives a Sign to Reveal the Murderer

ye might know concerning this thing; yea, even for a witness unto you, that I did know of the wickedness and abominations which are among you.

24 And because I have done this, ye say that I have agreed with a man that he should do this thing; yea, because I showed unto you this sign ye are angry with me, and seek to destroy my life.

25 And now behold, I will show unto you another sign, and see if ye will in this thing seek to destroy me.

26 Behold I say unto you: Go to the house of Seantum, who is the brother of Seezoram, and say unto him—

27 Has Nephi, the pretended prophet, who doth prophesy so much evil concerning this people, agreed with thee, in the which ye have murdered Seezoram, who is your brother?

28 And behold, he shall say unto you, Nay.

29 And ye shall say unto him: Have ye murdered your brother?

30 And he shall stand with fear, and wist not what to say. And behold, he shall deny unto you; and he shall make as if he were astonished; nevertheless, he shall declare unto you that he is innocent.

31 But behold, ye shall examine him, and ye shall find blood upon the skirts of his cloak.

32 And when ye have seen this, ye shall say: From whence cometh this blood? Do we not know that it is the blood of your brother?

33 And then shall he tremble, and shall look pale, even as if death had come upon him.

34 And then shall ye say: Because of this fear and this paleness which has come upon your face, behold, we know that thou art guilty.

35 And then shall greater fear come upon him; and then shall he confess unto you, and deny no more that he has done this murder.

36 And then shall he say unto you, that I, Nephi, know nothing concerning the matter save it were given unto me by the power of God. And then shall ye know that I am an honest man, and that I am sent unto you from God.

37 And it came to pass that they went and did, even according as Nephi had said unto them. And behold, the words which he had said were true; for according to the words he did deny; and also according to the words he did confess.

38 And he was brought to prove that he himself was the very murderer, insomuch that the five were set at liberty, and also was Nephi.

39 And there were some of the Nephites who believed on the words of Nephi; and there were some also, who believed because of the testimony of the five, for they had been converted while they were in prison.

40 And now there were some among the people, who said that Nephi was a prophet.

41 And there were others who said: Behold, he is a god, for except he was a god he could not know of all things. For behold, he has told us the thoughts of our hearts, and also has told us things; and even he has brought unto our knowledge the true murderer of our chief judge.

CHAPTER 10

The Lord gives Nephi the sealing power—He is empowered to bind and loose on earth and in heaven—He commands the people to repent or perish—The Spirit carries him from multitude to multitude. About 21–20 B.C.

1 And it came to pass that there arose a division among the people, insomuch that they divided hither and thither and went their ways, leaving Nephi alone, as he was standing in the midst of them.

Can your peers similarly attest to your honesty? (9:36) The Prophet Joseph Smith declared that "we believe in being honest, true, chaste, benevolent, virtuous, and in doing good to all men" (Articles of Faith 1:13). President Gordon B. Hinckley urged us to resist dishonesty: "How difficult for so many to resist the temptation to lie a little, cheat a little, steal a little, bear false witness in speaking gossipy words about others. Rise above it. . . . Be strong in the simple virtue of honesty" ("Building Your Tabernacle," 52). How have you exemplified being an honest person this past week?

What can we learn about self-incrimination and Mosaic law? (9:37–38) "Under the Talmud, no man could be put to death on his own testimony: 'No man may call himself a wrongdoer,' especially in a capital case. . . .

" . . . In the biblical period the normal two-witness rule could be overridden in the special case of a self-incriminating confession, if the confession occurred outside of court, or if God's will was evidenced in the matter by ordeal, lots, or otherwise in the detection of the offender, and if corroborating physical evidence of the crime could be produced.

"Seantum's self-incriminating confession satisfies all three of these requirements" (Welch, "Case of an Unobserved Murder," 243–44). ⊕

Helaman 10:1–11. The Lord Gives Nephi Power to Do Many Miracles to Help the People Repent

What are the blessings that come from pondering?
(10:2–3) "To ponder is to 'meditate and think deeply, often upon the scriptures or other things of God. When combined with prayer, pondering . . . may bring revelation and understanding' (*Guide to the Scriptures*, 'Ponder'). Nephi and other prophets received revelation while pondering. . . . [President] Russell M. Nelson . . . shared with us the benefits of pondering: 'As you ponder and pray about doctrinal principles, the Holy Ghost will speak to your mind and your heart [see D&C 8:2]. From events portrayed in the scriptures, new insights will come and principles relevant to your situation will distill upon your heart' (in Conference Report, Oct. 2000, 19; or *Ensign*, Nov. 2000, 18)" (*Book of Mormon Student Manual* [2009], 274).

What was the ultimate reward for Nephi's "unweariingness"? (10:4–5) Nephi was worthy of receiving the sealing power from the Lord. His faithfulness was rewarded as it is for those who have their calling and election made sure. Joseph Smith taught after a person is baptized and has received the first Comforter, "then let him continue to humble himself before God, hungering and thirsting after Righteousness. . . . When the Lord has thoro'ly proved him, and finds that the man is determined to serve him at all hazard, then the man will find his calling and Election made sure, then it will be his privilege to receive the other Comforter which the Lord hath promised the Saints, as is recorded in the testimony of St. John" ("History, 1838–1856, volume C-1 [2 November 1838–31 July 1842] [addenda]," p. 9 [addenda]).

How are these verses examples of poetry in the Book of Mormon? (10:6–11) Richard Dilworth Rust saw in these verses ancient poetry about God's power. First, the verses detail "increasing levels of physical power (famine, to pestilence, to destruction). Then it is given spiritual significance (sealed/loosed in heaven). Destructive power builds in intensity from rending the temple, to leveling a mountain, to the climax of divine power that will smite the people. With the confidence that comes from having seen the vision of God's power, Nephi was ready to declare the simple but meaningful message: 'Except ye repent ye shall be smitten, even unto destruction'" ("Poetry in the Book of Mormon," 107). ☉

What can we learn from Nephi's use of the sealing power? (10:7) President Joseph Fielding Smith taught: "We discover in the reading of the scriptures that the Lord conferred authority on some of his chosen servants and gave them exceptional powers

2 And it came to pass that Nephi went his way towards his own house, pondering upon the things which the Lord had shown unto him.

3 And it came to pass as he was thus pondering—being much cast down because of the wickedness of the people of the Nephites, their secret works of darkness, and their murderings, and their plunderings, and all manner of iniquities—and it came to pass as he was thus pondering in his heart, behold, a voice came unto him saying:

4 Blessed art thou, Nephi, for those things which thou hast done; for I have beheld how thou hast with unwearyingness declared the word, which I have given unto thee, unto this people. And thou hast not feared them, and hast not sought thine own life, but hast sought my will, and to keep my commandments.

5 And now, because thou hast done this with such unwearyingness, behold, I will bless thee forever; and I will make thee mighty in word and in deed, in faith and in works; yea, even that all things shall be done unto thee according to thy word, for thou shalt not ask that which is contrary to my will.

6 Behold, thou art Nephi, and I am God. Behold, I declare it unto thee in the presence of mine angels, that ye shall have power over this people, and shall smite the earth with famine, and with pestilence, and destruction, according to the wickedness of this people.

7 Behold, I give unto you power, that whatsoever ye shall seal on earth shall be sealed in heaven; and whatsoever ye shall loose on earth shall be loosed in heaven; and thus shall ye have power among this people.

8 And thus, if ye shall say unto this temple it shall be rent in twain, it shall be done.

9 And if ye shall say unto this mountain, Be thou cast down and become smooth, it shall be done.

10 And behold, if ye shall say that God shall smite this people, it shall come to pass.

11 And now behold, I command you, that ye shall go and declare unto this people, that thus saith the Lord God, who is the Almighty: Except ye repent ye shall be smitten, even unto destruction.

12 And behold, now it came to pass that when the Lord had spoken these words unto Nephi, he did stop and did not go unto his own house, but did return unto the multitudes who were scattered about upon the face of the land, and began to declare unto them the word of the Lord which had been spoken unto him, concerning their destruction if they did not repent.

13 Now behold, notwithstanding that great miracle which Nephi had done in telling them concerning the death of the chief judge, they did harden their hearts and did not hearken unto the words of the Lord.

14 Therefore Nephi did declare unto them the word of the Lord, saying: Except ye repent, thus saith the Lord, ye shall be smitten even unto destruction.

15 And it came to pass that when Nephi had declared unto them the word, behold, they did still harden their hearts and would not hearken unto his words; therefore they did revile against him, and did seek to lay their hands upon him that they might cast him into prison.

without the laying on of hands, but merely by his spoken edict. . . . The Lord gave similar authority to Nephi, son of Helaman, who likewise had authority to close the heavens and perform other mighty works, simply by his faith and the commandment from the Lord (Helaman 10:7). This wonderful power has been bestowed on but a few of the servants of the Lord" (*Answers to Gospel Questions*, 4:95). "Nephi received power to bind on earth as in heaven [see Hel. 10:7]. . . . Nephi used the sealing power to create 'a famine in the land, to stir up [the Nephites] in remembrance of the Lord their God' (Hel. 11:4).

"This same sealing power was later given to the ancient Apostles Peter, James, and John (see Matt. 16:19) and the Prophet Joseph Smith and Oliver Cowdery in the latter days (see D&C 128:8–10; D&C 132:46)" (Black, *400 Questions and Answers*, 171).

Helaman 10:12–19. Nephi Tells the People to Repent or They Will Be Destroyed

Why do you think Nephi decided not to return to his house? (10:12) "Characteristic of his complete submission to the will of God, Nephi did not go to his house to relax and experiment with his new power; rather, he immediately stopped his journey home and returned to preach repentance to the multitudes" (Pew, "Yield Your Heart to God," 216–17). How is Nephi's character revealed by how he responded to the will of the Father? When have you been blessed by setting aside personal conveniences, when necessary, for the benefit of others?

Were Nephi's physical body and spirit separated in this instance? (10:16–17) "The term 'in the Spirit,' which is used to indicate how Nephi taught the people, evidently means that Nephi went forth 'by the power of the Spirit.' It does not mean Nephi's body was separated from his spirit; rather it probably means he was protected in his missionary work by the power of the Spirit," much as the Savior was during His mortal labors (Ludlow, *Companion to Your Study of the Book of Mormon*, 245; see Luke 4:28–31).

Helaman 11:1–8. The Lord Stops the War and Sends a Famine

Why did Nephi ask the Lord to send a famine in the land? (11:4) As President Spencer W. Kimball taught: "The Lord uses the weather sometimes to discipline his people for the violation of his laws" ("The Lord Expects His Saints to Follow the Commandments," 4). How would a famine motivate the people to turn to God? Modern revelation confirms that God will use many ways to humble the rebellious through "the voice of thunderings, and by the voice of lightnings, and by the voice of tempests, and by the voice of

16 But behold, the power of God was with him, and they could not take him to cast him into prison, for he was taken by the Spirit and conveyed away out of the midst of them.

17 And it came to pass that thus he did go forth in the Spirit, from multitude to multitude, declaring the word of God, even until he had declared it unto them all, or sent it forth among all the people.

18 And it came to pass that they would not hearken unto his words; and there began to be contentions, insomuch that they were divided against themselves and began to slay one another with the sword.

19 And thus ended the seventy and first year of the reign of the judges over the people of Nephi.

CHAPTER 11

Nephi persuades the Lord to replace their war with a famine—Many people perish—They repent, and Nephi importunes the Lord for rain—Nephi and Lehi receive many revelations—The Gadianton robbers entrench themselves in the land. About 20–6 B.C.

1 And now it came to pass in the seventy and second year of the reign of the judges that the contentions did increase, insomuch that there were wars throughout all the land among all the people of Nephi.

2 And it was this secret band of robbers who did carry on this work of destruction and wickedness. And this war did last all that year; and in the seventy and third year it did also last.

3 And it came to pass that in this year Nephi did cry unto the Lord, saying:

4 O Lord, do not suffer that this people shall be destroyed by the sword; but O Lord, rather let there be a famine in the land, to stir them up in remembrance of the Lord their

God, and perhaps they will repent and turn unto thee.

5 And so it was done, according to the words of Nephi. And there was a great famine upon the land, among all the people of Nephi. And thus in the seventy and fourth year the famine did continue, and the work of destruction did cease by the sword but became sore by famine.

6 And this work of destruction did also continue in the seventy and fifth year. For the earth was smitten that it was dry, and did not yield forth grain in the season of grain; and the whole earth was smitten, even among the Lamanites as well as among the Nephites, so that they were smitten that they did perish by thousands in the more wicked parts of the land.

7 And it came to pass that the people saw that they were about to perish by famine, and they began to remember the Lord their God; and they began to remember the words of Nephi.

8 And the people began to plead with their chief judges and their leaders, that they would say unto Nephi: Behold, we know that thou art a man of God, and therefore cry unto the Lord our God that he turn away from us this famine, lest all the words which thou hast spoken concerning our destruction be fulfilled.

9 And it came to pass that the judges did say unto Nephi, according to the words which had been desired. And it came to pass that when Nephi saw that the people had repented and did humble themselves in sackcloth, he cried again unto the Lord, saying:

10 O Lord, behold this people repenteth; and they have swept away the band of Gadianton from amongst them insomuch that they have become extinct, and they have concealed their secret plans in the earth.

earthquakes, and great hailstorms, and by the voice of famines and pestilences of every kind" (D&C 43:25).

From this verse, what do we learn about Nephi's power? (11:5) Nephi's power came from his complete obedience to and faith on the Lord. The Lord knew Nephi would not ask anything that was not according to His will (see Hel. 10:5). The famine caused the people to repent. In a modern revelation the Lord said that "He that asketh in the Spirit asketh according to the will of God; wherefore it is done even as he asketh" (D&C 46:50).

Why does it often take extremes, such as a famine, to convince people to repent? (11:7–8) Incredibly, it took the Nephites more than two years to finally see the connection between their wickedness and the famine. Even then they had to plead with their leaders to ask Nephi for relief. In your opinion, would it take this length of time for our modern society to be humbled?

Helaman 11:9–16. Nephi Prays for the Famine to End

What can we learn from Nephi's repetition of "O Lord" in his prayer? (11:10–16) "According to Robert Alter, repetition of a word or phrase is one of the most common literary devices used in the narrative of the Bible. . . . Martin Buber noted this stylistic element and called it *Leitworter*, a German word meaning 'leading words,' 'guide words,' or 'theme words.'... Repetition of the phrase *O Lord* [in Helaman 11:4, 10–16] reminds the reader that Nephi is praying to the Lord, *even pleading* with him for his people" (Anderson, "*Leitworter* in Helaman and 3 Nephi," 241–44; emphasis added).

How did the Gadianton robbers conceal their secret plans? (11:10) During a Book of Mormon lecture on this issue, Dr. Hugh Nibley had this exchange with a student:

"Question: Nephi said that [the Gadianton robbers] had become extinct and they had concealed their secret plans in the earth. You said that meant they went underground?

"Answer: I mean they literally went underground if they buried their secrets in the earth. They will dig them up later on—don't worry. These things are hid and dug up. You find them. They put them in caves and their sacred places" (*Teachings of the Book of Mormon*, 3:267).

What is a "pestilence of the sword"? (11:14) Pestilence is "a fatal epidemic disease, esp. bubonic plague," but it can also be "something evil or destructive" (*Illustrated Oxford Dictionary*, 610). Years of war certainly must have seemed a fatal epidemic to Nephi.

Helaman 11:17–23. The Faithful Are Blessed with Peace and Prosperity

11 Now, O Lord, because of this their humility wilt thou turn away thine anger, and let thine anger be appeased in the destruction of those wicked men whom thou hast already destroyed.

12 O Lord, wilt thou turn away thine anger, yea, thy fierce anger, and cause that this famine may cease in this land.

13 O Lord, wilt thou hearken unto me, and cause that it may be done according to my words, and send forth rain upon the face of the earth, that she may bring forth her fruit, and her grain in the season of grain.

14 O Lord, thou didst hearken unto my words when I said, Let there be a famine, that the pestilence of the sword might cease; and I know that thou wilt, even at this time, hearken unto my words, for thou saidst that: If this people repent I will spare them.

15 Yea, O Lord, and thou seest that they have repented, because of the famine and the pestilence and destruction which has come unto them.

16 And now, O Lord, wilt thou turn away thine anger, and try again if they will serve thee? And if so, O Lord, thou canst bless them according to thy words which thou hast said.

17 And it came to pass that in the seventy and sixth year the Lord did turn away his anger from the people, and caused that rain should fall upon the earth, insomuch that it did bring forth her fruit in the season of her fruit. And it came to pass that it did bring forth her grain in the season of her grain.

18 And behold, the people did rejoice and glorify God, and the whole face of the land was filled with rejoicing; and they did no more seek to destroy Nephi, but they did

esteem him as a great prophet, and a man of God, having great power and authority given unto him from God.

19 And behold, Lehi, his brother, was not a whit behind him as to things pertaining to righteousness.

20 And thus it did come to pass that the people of Nephi began to prosper again in the land, and began to build up their waste places, and began to multiply and spread, even until they did cover the whole face of the land, both on the northward and on the southward, from the sea west to the sea east.

21 And it came to pass that the seventy and sixth year did end in peace. And the seventy and seventh year began in peace; and the church did spread throughout the face of all the land; and the more part of the people, both the Nephites and the Lamanites, did belong to the church; and they did have exceedingly great peace in the land; and thus ended the seventy and seventh year.

22 And also they had peace in the seventy and eighth year, save it were a few contentions concerning the points of doctrine which had been laid down by the prophets.

23 And in the seventy and ninth year there began to be much strife. But it came to pass that Nephi and Lehi, and many of their brethren who knew concerning the true points of doctrine, having many revelations daily, therefore they did preach unto the people, insomuch that they did put an end to their strife in that same year.

24 And it came to pass that in the eightieth year of the reign of the judges over the people of Nephi, there were a certain number of the dissenters from the people of Nephi, who had some years before gone over unto the Lamanites, and taken upon themselves the name of Lamanites, and also a certain number who

What important lesson is learned from this brief entry in the record concerning Lehi's righteousness? (11:19) President Howard W. Hunter taught: "Not all of us are going to be like Moroni, catching the acclaim of our colleagues all day every day. Most of us will be quiet, relatively unknown folks who come and go and do our work without fanfare.... You, too, are part of God's army....

"The great prophet Nephi, mentioned in the book of Helaman, had a brother named Lehi, who is seemingly mentioned only in passing but is noted as being 'not a whit behind him [Nephi] as to things pertaining to righteousness' (see Hel. 11:18–19)" ("No Less Serviceable," 64–65).

What are "points of doctrine"? (11:22–23) "One dictionary defines a *point* as a 'penetrating detail, a precise concept; a prominent or important item; the "telling part" of an argument or discussion; the salient feature; the precise thing; the "turning point."'... The Book of Mormon cannot be the 'most correct of any book on earth' and be wrong on the most important doctrines of the gospel.

"It is my observation that the points of doctrine given to us in the Book of Mormon and other latter-day scripture will answer all the major doctrinal questions that have been raised during, and as the result of, the Apostasy" (Matthews, *A Bible! A Bible!* 247).

Helaman 11:24–38. The Gadianton Robbers Return to Power

What motivated and enabled this "band of robbers" to defy the armies of two nations? (11:24–32) "As described in the Book of Mormon, the formation of trade networks for the accumulation of wealth was also accompanied by the rise of violent groups such as the Gadianton Robbers who sought control for personal gain. The Gadianton Society was a far more powerful and complex group than their description as robbers implies. They often commanded huge armies capable of defying the armed forces of both the Nephite and Lamanite nations. . . . The motivation of the Gadiantons was primarily economic and tied to the newfound wealth flowing into Nephite society through international trade. They therefore operated both among the Nephites and the Lamanite kingdoms" (Christenson, "Nephite Trade Networks and the Dangers of a Class Society," 236). ✪

The Nephite Pride Cycle

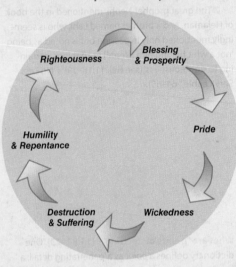

Righteousness

Blessing & Prosperity

Pride

Humility & Repentance

Destruction & Suffering

Wickedness

were real descendants of the Lamanites, being stirred up to anger by them, or by those dissenters, therefore they commenced a war with their brethren.

25 And they did commit murder and plunder; and then they would retreat back into the mountains, and into the wilderness and secret places, hiding themselves that they could not be discovered, receiving daily an addition to their numbers, inasmuch as there were dissenters that went forth unto them.

26 And thus in time, yea, even in the space of not many years, they became an exceedingly great band of robbers; and they did search out all the secret plans of Gadianton; and thus they became robbers of Gadianton.

27 Now behold, these robbers did make great havoc, yea, even great destruction among the people of Nephi, and also among the people of the Lamanites.

28 And it came to pass that it was expedient that there should be a stop put to this work of destruction; therefore they sent an army of strong men into the wilderness and upon the mountains to search out this band of robbers, and to destroy them.

29 But behold, it came to pass that in that same year they were driven back even into their own lands. And thus ended the eightieth year of the reign of the judges over the people of Nephi.

30 And it came to pass in the commencement of the eighty and first year they did go forth again against this band of robbers, and did destroy many; and they were also visited with much destruction.

31 And they were again obliged to return out of the wilderness and out of the mountains unto their own lands, because of the exceeding greatness of the numbers of those robbers who infested the mountains and the wilderness.

32 And it came to pass that thus ended this year. And the robbers did still increase and wax strong, insomuch that they did defy the whole armies of the Nephites, and also of the Lamanites; and they did cause great fear to come unto the people upon all the face of the land.

33 Yea, for they did visit many parts of the land, and did do great destruction unto them; yea, did kill many, and did carry away others captive into the wilderness, yea, and more especially their women and their children.

34 Now this great evil, which came unto the people because of their iniquity, did stir them up again in remembrance of the Lord their God.

35 And thus ended the eighty and first year of the reign of the judges.

36 And in the eighty and second year they began again to forget the Lord their God. And in the eighty and third year they began to wax strong in iniquity. And in the eighty and fourth year they did not mend their ways.

37 And it came to pass in the eighty and fifth year they did wax stronger and stronger in their pride, and in their wickedness; and thus they were ripening again for destruction.

38 And thus ended the eighty and fifth year.

CHAPTER 12

Men are unstable and foolish and quick to do evil—The Lord chastens His people—The nothingness of men is compared with the power of God—In the day of judgment, men will gain everlasting life or everlasting damnation. About 6 B.C.

1 And thus we can behold how false, and also the unsteadiness of the hearts of the children of men; yea, we can see that the Lord in his great infinite goodness doth bless and prosper those who put their trust in him.

What lessons can we learn from the Nephites' quick turn from remembering the Lord to forgetting Him? (11:33–38) Elder Neal A. Maxwell observed: "Significant moral decay can happen within a single generation—whether in a nation or in a family" ("For I Will Lead You Along," 7). How are you able to remember the Lord every day? In what ways can daily prayer and scripture study help you remember?

Helaman 12:1–6. God's Children Often Forget Him When Life Goes Well

What can we learn from comparing the "unsteadiness" of the Nephites in Helaman 12:1–5 and the "unwearyingness" of Nephi in Helaman 10:1–5? (12:1–5) Why do you think Nephi was able to stand faithful, even when he stood alone? Why were the Nephites so quick to forget God's great blessings and sink into sin? What examples of unwavering faithfulness have you seen in your life? What examples have you seen of people forgetting God when times are good? What could you and your family do to be more constantly faithful? ⊕

How do Mormon's writings reflect his view on life? (12:2–3) "Mormon has a providential philosophy of history that greatly influences his selection and interpretation of individuals, events, and society. In composing his monumental summary of Nephite history, Mormon has left, as it were, 'DNA fingerprints' that portray his own attitude toward life, toward the consequences of men's faith or disobedience, toward God's blessings or punishment, toward prophecy and its fulfillment, and toward the recurrence of debilitating and destructive social forces. As a prophet, he places his focus more on matters of righteousness than on material manifestations of achievement" (Mackay, "Mormon's Philosophy of History," 129). ⊕

How can we improve our ability to remember God's goodness? (12:5) "How can we remember even a part of all God has done for us? . . .

"The Holy Ghost brings back memories of what God has taught us. And one of the ways God teaches us is with His blessings; and so, if we choose to exercise faith, the Holy Ghost will bring God's kindnesses to our remembrance.

"You could test that in prayer today. You could follow the command 'Thou shalt thank the Lord thy God in all things' (D&C 59:7)" (Eyring, "Recognize, Remember, and Give Thanks," 4). ⊕

Helaman 12:7–19. The Earth Is Obedient to the Commands of God

Why must we recognize that we are nothing without God? (12:7) "We may defy our nothingness and attempt to become something without God. We may

2 Yea, and we may see at the very time when he doth prosper his people, yea, in the increase of their fields, their flocks and their herds, and in gold, and in silver, and in all manner of precious things of every kind and art; sparing their lives, and delivering them out of the hands of their enemies; softening the hearts of their enemies that they should not declare wars against them; yea, and in fine, doing all things for the welfare and happiness of his people; yea, then is the time that they do harden their hearts, and do forget the Lord their God, and do trample under their feet the Holy One—yea, and this because of their ease, and their exceedingly great prosperity.

3 And thus we see that except the Lord doth chasten his people with many afflictions, yea, except he doth visit them with death and with terror, and with famine and with all manner of pestilence, they will not remember him.

4 O how foolish, and how vain, and how evil, and devilish, and how quick to do iniquity, and how slow to do good, are the children of men; yea, how quick to hearken unto the words of the evil one, and to set their hearts upon the vain things of the world!

5 Yea, how quick to be lifted up in pride; yea, how quick to boast, and do all manner of that which is iniquity; and how slow are they to remember the Lord their God, and to give ear unto his counsels, yea, how slow to walk in wisdom's paths!

6 Behold, they do not desire that the Lord their God, who hath created them, should rule and reign over them; notwithstanding his great goodness and his mercy towards them, they do set at naught his counsels, and they will not that he should be their guide.

7 O how great is the nothingness of the children of men; yea, even they are less than the dust of the earth.

8 For behold, the dust of the earth moveth hither and thither, to the dividing asunder, at the command of our great and everlasting God.

9 Yea, behold at his voice do the hills and the mountains tremble and quake.

10 And by the power of his voice they are broken up, and become smooth, yea, even like unto a valley.

11 Yea, by the power of his voice doth the whole earth shake;

12 Yea, by the power of his voice, do the foundations rock, even to the very center.

13 Yea, and if he say unto the earth—Move—it is moved.

14 Yea, if he say unto the earth—Thou shalt go back, that it lengthen out the day for many hours—it is done;

15 And thus, according to his word the earth goeth back, and it appeareth unto man that the sun standeth still; yea, and behold, this is so; for surely it is the earth that moveth and not the sun.

16 And behold, also, if he say unto the waters of the great deep—Be thou dried up—it is done.

17 Behold, if he say unto this mountain—Be thou raised up, and come over and fall upon that city, that it be buried up—behold it is done.

18 And behold, if a man hide up a treasure in the earth, and the Lord shall say—Let it be accursed, because of the iniquity of him who hath hid it up—behold, it shall be accursed.

19 And if the Lord shall say—Be thou accursed, that no man shall find thee from this time henceforth and forever—behold, no man getteth it henceforth and forever.

try in many vain ways to prove our worth by seeking wealth, power, or praise of men.

"Yet, when we can finally admit that we are nothing without God, the Savior invites us to lay on the altar the great burden of trying to do everything on our own or of assuming more responsibility than we have. Our meekness and dependence on the Lord, our hunger to know what is right, draw the Lord and his solutions to us" (Thomas, "Blessed Are Ye . . . ," 6). ☉

In what way is man "less than the dust"? (12:7–8) "This statement should not be interpreted that Mormon believes men are worth even less than the dust of the earth. Rather Mormon is saying that men sometimes appear to be less wise than the dust of the earth. When the Lord tells the dust of the earth to move, it obeys, whereas when the Lord tells men to do something, they frequently do not obey" (Ludlow, *Companion to Your Study of the Book of Mormon*, 246).

Did Mormon understand our solar system? (12:14–15) "The knowledge of astronomy was well developed among the ancients upon the American continent. . . .

"We know, then, that the prevalent notion in the world today that the ancients from the dawn of history to the days of Galileo believed that the earth is flat and the center of the universe, around which the sun and stars revolve, is a most stupendous error. The ignorance made manifest in the days of Galileo and Columbus, and for centuries preceding their time, was the result of apostasy from and rebellion against the truth which in the beginning was plainly revealed from the heavens" (Smith, *Progress of Man*, 184–85).

Helaman 12:20–26. Repentance Is the Only Way to Happiness

Why do you think this warning and promise are repeated so many times? (12:21–23) What are some other commandments or promises that are repeated over and over again in scripture? What do these repetitions teach us about our Heavenly Father and His desires for us?

In what way is grace dependent upon works? (12:24) "Theologically, the grace of God is his goodwill toward us, his predisposition to act in our best interest even before we can earn or deserve such consideration....

"Nevertheless, the term *grace* is sometimes used in a different sense to describe a quality that *is* responsive or reactive to human behavior. When spoken of in this sense, God's favor or grace is not a preexisting given but is something that can be sought after, increased, decreased, or even lost completely....John explains that believers receive grace for grace, or in other words they receive increased favor from God as they react positively (graciously) to grace already received (see John 1:16; see also D&C 93:12, 19–20)" (Robinson, *Believing Christ*, 63–64). ⊕

What are everlasting life and everlasting damnation? (12:26) "Eternal life is God's life. It is that gift by which the righteous not only dwell in his presence, but by which they become like him....

"As all things have their opposites, there is a punishment which is the opposite to eternal life....This is the second or spiritual death, which is banishment from the presence of God and from his light and truth forever. In speaking of the second death as eternal death, we do not mean that those who partake of it are doomed eternally to the dissolution of the body and also of the spirit. The spirit of man is eternal and cannot die in the sense of ceasing to exist" (Smith, *Doctrines of Salvation*, 2:217–18).

20 And behold, if the Lord shall say unto a man—Because of thine iniquities, thou shalt be accursed forever—it shall be done.

21 And if the Lord shall say—Because of thine iniquities thou shalt be cut off from my presence—he will cause that it shall be so.

22 And wo unto him to whom he shall say this, for it shall be unto him that will do iniquity, and he cannot be saved; therefore, for this cause, that men might be saved, hath repentance been declared.

23 Therefore, blessed are they who will repent and hearken unto the voice of the Lord their God; for these are they that shall be saved.

24 And may God grant, in his great fulness, that men might be brought unto repentance and good works, that they might be restored unto grace for grace, according to their works.

25 And I would that all men might be saved. But we read that in the great and last day there are some who shall be cast out, yea, who shall be cast off from the presence of the Lord;

26 Yea, who shall be consigned to a state of endless misery, fulfilling the words which say: They that have done good shall have everlasting life; and they that have done evil shall have everlasting damnation. And thus it is. Amen.

The prophecy of Samuel, the Lamanite, to the Nephites.

Comprising chapters 13 through 15.

CHAPTER 13

Samuel the Lamanite prophesies the destruction of the Nephites unless they repent—They and their riches are cursed—They reject and stone the prophets, are encircled about by demons, and seek for happiness in doing iniquity. About 6 B.C.

1 And now it came to pass in the eighty and sixth year, the Nephites did still remain in wickedness, yea, in great wickedness, while the Lamanites did observe strictly to keep the commandments of God, according to the law of Moses.

2 And it came to pass that in this year there was one Samuel, a Lamanite, came into the land of Zarahemla, and began to preach unto the people. And it came to pass that he did preach, many days, repentance unto the people, and they did cast him out, and he was about to return to his own land.

3 But behold, the voice of the Lord came unto him, that he should return again, and prophesy unto the people whatsoever things should come into his heart.

4 And it came to pass that they would not suffer that he should enter into the city; therefore he went and got upon the wall thereof, and stretched forth his hand and cried with a loud voice, and prophesied unto the people whatsoever things the Lord put into his heart.

Superscription to Helaman 13

The superscription to Helaman 13 was part of the ancient record translated by the Prophet Joseph Smith and dictated by him to his scribe, except the phrase "Comprising chapters 13 through 15." "The 1830 edition presents the entire prophecy of Samuel as a single chapter, so the note is required to explain this next unit" (Gardner, *Second Witness*, 5:172).

Helaman 13:1–4. Samuel the Lamanite Declares the Word of God to the Nephites

What was Samuel the Lamanite's warning to the Nephites? (13:2) "He warned the Nephites that within 400 years the sword of justice would hang over them because of their rejection of the word of God or covenant of the Lord (Hel. 13:5). Specifically, because of the hardness of the hearts of the people, the Lord would take away his word and Spirit from among them (v. 8). The Nephites not only rejected the word of the Lord, but they also rejected Samuel, a living prophet, who had come to testify of their sins and iniquities. Instead of repenting, they were angry with him because he forced them to acknowledge their wickedness (vv. 26–27)" (Fowles, "The Decline of the Nephites," 86).

What do we learn from Samuel's experience about the Lord's love and patience? (13:3) Why does the Lord try so hard to save His children? If the Lord tried to reach the rebellious Nephites by sending Samuel a second time, what will He do for those who stumble and fall today? President James E. Faust observed that "many of us backslide, many stumble, and I believe firmly in the gospel of the second chance. But the gospel of the second chance means that having once been found weak . . . thereafter we become steadfast . . . 'and immovable, willing with all diligence to keep the commandments of the Lord' [3 Nephi 6:14]" ("Stand Up and Be Counted," 71).

Helaman 13:5–10. Samuel Prophesies the Destruction of the Nephites in Four Hundred Years If They Do Not Repent

What was the source of Samuel's divine message? (13:5–7) President Boyd K. Packer described how the voice of the Lord often comes: "Revelation comes as words we feel more than hear. Nephi told his wayward brothers, who were visited by an angel, 'Ye were past *feeling*, that ye could not *feel* his words' [1 Nephi 17:45; italics added].

"The scriptures are full of such expressions as 'The veil was taken from our minds, and the eyes of our understanding were opened' [D&C 110:1], or 'I will tell you in your mind and in your heart' [D&C 8:2], or 'I did enlighten thy mind' [D&C 6:15], or 'Speak the thoughts that I shall put into your hearts' [D&C 100:5]. There are hundreds of verses which teach of revelation" ("Personal Revelation," 60).

Do we see repentance as a burden or a blessing? (13:6–7) "There is an essential aspect of the plan of happiness of our Father in Heaven that is often ignored even though it invariably yields peace and joy. . . . This subject is widely misunderstood and often feared. Some feel that it is to be employed only by those in serious transgression, while the Lord intended that it be consistently used by every one of His children. . . . I refer to the blessing of true, sincere, continuing repentance, the path to peace and joy. It is a conduit to the reforming power of the Lord and, when understood and used, a dear and precious friend" (Scott, "Path to Peace and Joy," 25). 🔊

What is the result when the Spirit withdraws? (13:8) "Book of Mormon prophets stressed again and again that hardened hearts are simply unable to perceive and then receive the quiet whisperings of the Spirit (see 2 Nephi 33:2; Alma 13:4; 40:13). In time, what love they do have will be lost, and their crudeness will be transformed and translated into perversion and murder. They shall become like the Nephites who, within four centuries after the coming of Christ, were described by Mormon as being 'without civilization' . . . (Moroni 9:11, 18, 20). 'For the Spirit of the Lord will not always strive with man. And when the Spirit ceaseth to strive with man then cometh speedy destruction' (2 Nephi 26:11; compare Helaman 13:8; Ether 2:15)" (Millet, *Power of the Word*, 241).

5 And he said unto them: Behold, I, Samuel, a Lamanite, do speak the words of the Lord which he doth put into my heart; and behold he hath put it into my heart to say unto this people that the sword of justice hangeth over this people; and four hundred years pass not away save the sword of justice falleth upon this people.

6 Yea, heavy destruction awaiteth this people, and it surely cometh unto this people, and nothing can save this people save it be repentance and faith on the Lord Jesus Christ, who surely shall come into the world, and shall suffer many things and shall be slain for his people.

7 And behold, an angel of the Lord hath declared it unto me, and he did bring glad tidings to my soul. And behold, I was sent unto you to declare it unto you also, that ye might have glad tidings; but behold ye would not receive me.

8 Therefore, thus saith the Lord: Because of the hardness of the hearts of the people of the Nephites, except they repent I will take away my word from them, and I will withdraw my Spirit from them, and I will suffer them no longer, and I will turn the hearts of their brethren against them.

9 And four hundred years shall not pass away before I will cause that they shall be smitten; yea, I will visit them with the sword and with famine and with pestilence.

10 Yea, I will visit them in my fierce anger, and there shall be those of the fourth generation who shall live, of your enemies, to behold your utter destruction; and this shall surely come except ye repent, saith the Lord; and those of the fourth generation shall visit your destruction.

11 But if ye will repent and return unto the Lord your God I will turn away mine anger, saith the Lord; yea, thus saith the Lord, blessed are they who will repent and turn unto me, but wo unto him that repenteth not.

12 Yea, wo unto this great city of Zarahemla; for behold, it is because of those who are righteous that it is saved; yea, wo unto this great city, for I perceive, saith the Lord, that there are many, yea, even the more part of this great city, that will harden their hearts against me, saith the Lord.

13 But blessed are they who will repent, for them will I spare. But behold, if it were not for the righteous who are in this great city, behold, I would cause that fire should come down out of heaven and destroy it.

14 But behold, it is for the righteous' sake that it is spared. But behold, the time cometh, saith the Lord, that when ye shall cast out the righteous from among you, then shall ye be ripe for destruction; yea, wo be unto this great city, because of the wickedness and abominations which are in her.

15 Yea, and wo be unto the city of Gideon, for the wickedness and abominations which are in her.

16 Yea, and wo be unto all the cities which are in the land round about, which are possessed by the Nephites, because of the wickedness and abominations which are in them.

17 And behold, a curse shall come upon the land, saith the Lord of Hosts, because of the people's sake who are upon the land, yea, because of their wickedness and their abominations.

Helaman 13:11–14. It Is Only Because of the Righteous among Them That Zarahemla Has Not Already Been Destroyed

What does it mean to turn unto God? (13:11) "When we sin, we turn away from God. When we repent, we turn back toward God.

"The invitation to repent is rarely a voice of chastisement but rather a loving appeal to turn around and to 're-turn' toward God. It is the beckoning of a loving Father and His Only Begotten Son to be more than we are, to reach up to a higher way of life, to change, and to feel the happiness of keeping the commandments. Being disciples of Christ, we rejoice in the blessing of repenting and the joy of being forgiven. They become part of us, shaping the way we think and feel" (Andersen, "Repent . . . That I May Heal You," 40). ◉

Why does destruction await those who cast out the righteous? (13:13–14) "All sin has the effect of weakening the fabric of society. Because of this, it is inevitable that the righteous will suffer because of the transgressions of others. Nevertheless the Lord goes to great lengths to protect and spare the righteous. . . . As sin, be it public or private, weakens the fabric of society, so all that is wholesome and good reaches out to bless and even preserve it (see Genesis 18:23–32; see also Alma 10:22; 3 Nephi 9:11)" (McConkie and Millet, *Doctrinal Commentary*, 3:401–2).

Helaman 13:15–23. The Lord Will Curse the Riches of the Wicked

What does it mean to hide up treasures unto the Lord? (13:18–19) "Here we have a concrete and indisputable example of an ancient Israelite practice. . . . If we hide [our treasures] unto the Lord, that's a good thing; he wants us to hide treasures to him, in regular old Jewish fashion. Again, Baruch, the secretary of Jeremiah, writes that when Jerusalem was destroyed (referring to the destruction of Jerusalem at the time of Lehi), the Lord wanted the treasures to be buried up unto him. It's a rule, and now we know from the *Copper Scroll* that it was actually done. . . . When we flee before our enemies, we hide our treasure up unto the Lord; it's a commandment" (Nibley, *Temple and Cosmos*, 217). ✛

Is prosperity bad? (13:21–23) "Many have asked why God would consistently reward the virtues of the Nephites with a prosperity which almost infallibly destroyed that virtue. The answer is in the 'almost'—there is no paradox here; wealth need not be destructive. A person in exuberant health is certainly more likely to be tempted of the flesh than one suffering from a dire disease. And yet exuberant good health is a reward of right living. The temptations of health and the temptations of wealth are real, to be sure, but they are *not* irresistible, and they *are* necessary to test mankind in this life of probation" (Nibley, *Since Cumorah*, 355). ✛

18 And it shall come to pass, saith the Lord of Hosts, yea, our great and true God, that whoso shall hide up treasures in the earth shall find them again no more, because of the great curse of the land, save he be a righteous man and shall hide it up unto the Lord.

19 For I will, saith the Lord, that they shall hide up their treasures unto me; and cursed be they who hide not up their treasures unto me; for none hideth up their treasures unto me save it be the righteous; and he that hideth not up his treasures unto me, cursed is he, and also the treasure, and none shall redeem it because of the curse of the land.

20 And the day shall come that they shall hide up their treasures, because they have set their hearts upon riches; and because they have set their hearts upon their riches, and will hide up their treasures when they shall flee before their enemies; because they will not hide them up unto me, cursed be they and also their treasures; and in that day shall they be smitten, saith the Lord.

21 Behold ye, the people of this great city, and hearken unto my words; yea, hearken unto the words which the Lord saith; for behold, he saith that ye are cursed because of your riches, and also are your riches cursed because ye have set your hearts upon them, and have not hearkened unto the words of him who gave them unto you.

22 Ye do not remember the Lord your God in the things with which he hath blessed you, but ye do always remember your riches, not to thank the Lord your God for them; yea, your hearts are not drawn out unto the Lord, but they do swell with great pride, unto boasting, and unto great swelling, envyings, strifes, malice, persecutions, and murders, and all manner of iniquities.

23 For this cause hath the Lord God caused that a curse should come upon the land, and also upon your riches, and this because of your iniquities.

24 Yea, wo unto this people, because of this time which has arrived, that ye do cast out the prophets, and do mock them, and cast stones at them, and do slay them, and do all manner of iniquity unto them, even as they did of old time.

25 And now when ye talk, ye say: If our days had been in the days of our fathers of old, we would not have slain the prophets; we would not have stoned them, and cast them out.

26 Behold ye are worse than they; for as the Lord liveth, if a prophet come among you and declareth unto you the word of the Lord, which testifieth of your sins and iniquities, ye are angry with him, and cast him out and seek all manner of ways to destroy him; yea, you will say that he is a false prophet, and that he is a sinner, and of the devil, because he testifieth that your deeds are evil.

27 But behold, if a man shall come among you and shall say: Do this, and there is no iniquity; do that and ye shall not suffer; yea, he will say: Walk after the pride of your own hearts; yea, walk after the pride of your eyes, and do whatsoever your heart desireth—and if a man shall come among you and say this, ye will receive him, and say that he is a prophet.

28 Yea, ye will lift him up, and ye will give unto him of your substance; ye will give unto him of your gold, and of your silver, and ye will clothe him with costly apparel; and

Helaman 13:24–30. The Nephites Cast Out True Prophets and Support False Prophets Instead

Why are living prophets often rejected? (13:24)
"We wonder how often hearers first rejected the prophets because they despised them, and finally despised the prophets even more because they had rejected them....

"Sometimes people let their hearts get so set upon things and the honors of this world.... Simple truths are often rejected in favor of the much less demanding philosophies of men....

"The holy prophets have not only refused to follow erroneous human trends, but have pointed out these errors. No wonder the response to the prophets has not always been one of indifference. So often the prophets have been rejected because they first rejected the wrong ways of their own society" (Kimball, "Listen to the Prophets," 77). ◉

Do the wicked really honor past prophets? (13:25–26) "What pure, unadulterated hypocrisy it is for those who reject the living prophets to say: 'If we had lived in former days, we would have accepted the prophets whom others rejected.' Prophets are prophets, truth is truth, and rebellion is rebellion. The spirit which leads men to fight God in one age is the same that operates in every age. Those who reject the Lord's anointed today would have done so anciently. Compare Luke 16:27–31" (McConkie, *Doctrinal New Testament Commentary*, 1:622). ◉

Why are false prophets often honored? (13:27–28) "In the very nature of things, persecution of true prophets includes the acceptance of false prophets. It is a philosophical impossibility to reject truth without accepting error, to depart from true teachers without cleaving to false ones, to reject the Lord's ministers without giving allegiance to those who follow the other master [see Helaman 13:27–28]" (McConkie, *Promised Messiah*, 37).

"The world loves and honors its own, and living prophets have never been received by it. Christ promised the meridian Apostles that they would be hated of all nations for his name's sake and that they would be delivered up and killed (Joseph Smith–Matthew 1:7).

Only when death has silenced the voice of a prophet does the world erect shrines in his honor. Similarly, it has been observed that many who eulogize George Washington or Abraham Lincoln would have been bitter opponents of these men had they lived in their day. Most who profess to reverence or worship Christ today do so very selectively, ignoring that which would have brought them into conflict with him had they been contemporaries" (McConkie and Millet, *Doctrinal Commentary*, 3:404). ⊕

What examples have you seen today of those who hold fast to "foolish and blind guides"? (13:29) What habits or behaviors are vigorously defended today despite evidence of their destructive consequences? What examples do you see today of "blind guides" that many follow as if they were prophets? How are "freedom" and "personal choice" used to defend behaviors that are destructive to society as a whole?

Helaman 13:31–39. It Is Impossible to Find Happiness in Wickedness

because he speaketh flattering words unto you, and he saith that all is well, then ye will not find fault with him.

29 O ye wicked and ye perverse generation; ye hardened and ye stiffnecked people, how long will ye suppose that the Lord will suffer you? Yea, how long will ye suffer yourselves to be led by foolish and blind guides? Yea, how long will ye choose darkness rather than light?

30 Yea, behold, the anger of the Lord is already kindled against you; behold, he hath cursed the land because of your iniquity.

31 And behold, the time cometh that he curseth your riches, that they become slippery, that ye cannot hold them; and in the days of your poverty ye cannot retain them.

Prophecies of the Birth and Death of Jesus Christ

Prophecy of the Savior's Birth		Fulfillment
Helaman 14:2	Birth in five years	3 Nephi 1:13
Helaman 14:3–4	No darkness the night before the birth	3 Nephi 1:15
Helaman 14:5	New star	3 Nephi 1:21
Helaman 14:6	Many signs and wonders in heaven	Helaman 16:13; 3 Nephi 2:1
Helaman 14:7	All people amazed and fall to the earth	3 Nephi 1:16–17

Prophecy of the Savior's Death		Fulfillment
Helaman 14:20, 27	Sun darkened for three days	3 Nephi 8:19–23
Helaman 14:21	Thunder, lightning, earthquakes	3 Nephi 8:6–7
Helaman 14:22	Earth broken up	3 Nephi 8:12, 17–18
Helaman 14:23	Great tempests; mountains laid low and valleys become mountains	3 Nephi 8:5–6
Helaman 14:24	Highways and cities destroyed	3 Nephi 8:8–11, 13–14
Helaman 14:25	Graves open and resurrected Saints minister to people	3 Nephi 23:9–13

(*Book of Mormon Student Manual*, [2009], 283.)

32 And in the days of your poverty ye shall cry unto the Lord; and in vain shall ye cry, for your desolation is already come upon you, and your destruction is made sure; and then shall ye weep and howl in that day, saith the Lord of Hosts. And then shall ye lament, and say:

33 O that I had repented, and had not killed the prophets, and stoned them, and cast them out. Yea, in that day ye shall say: O that we had remembered the Lord our God in the day that he gave us our riches, and then they would not have become slippery that we should lose them; for behold, our riches are gone from us.

34 Behold, we lay a tool here and on the morrow it is gone; and behold, our swords are taken from us in the day we have sought them for battle.

35 Yea, we have hid up our treasures and they have slipped away from us, because of the curse of the land.

36 O that we had repented in the day that the word of the Lord came unto us; for behold the land is cursed, and all things are become slippery, and we cannot hold them.

37 Behold, we are surrounded by demons, yea, we are encircled about by the angels of him who hath sought to destroy our souls. Behold, our iniquities are great. O Lord, canst thou not turn away thine anger from us? And this shall be your language in those days.

38 But behold, your days of probation are past; ye have procrastinated the day of your salvation until it is everlastingly too late, and your destruction is made sure; yea, for ye have sought all the days of your lives for that which ye could not obtain; and ye have sought for happiness in doing iniquity, which thing is contrary to the nature of that righteousness which is in our great and Eternal Head.

Can it ever be too late to repent? (13:38) "Every wrong decision one makes restricts the area in which he can thereafter exercise his agency. The further one goes in the making of wrong decisions in the exercise of free agency, the more difficult it is for him to recover the lost ground. One can, by persisting long enough, reach the point of no return. He then becomes an abject slave. By the exercise of his free agency, he has decreased the area in which he can act, almost to the vanishing point" (Romney, "Perfect Law of Liberty," 45). ☉

Why can we not be happy in sin? (13:38) "Our yearnings for happiness were implanted in our hearts by Deity. They represent a kind of homesickness, for we have a residual memory of our premortal existence. They are also a foretaste of the fulness of joy that is promised to the faithful. . . .

"Words such as *reap, restored,* and *desire* imply that happiness is a consequence, not a reward. We are restored to a state of happiness when we have chosen to live according to the plan of happiness [see Alma 42:16]. Our joy in God's kingdom will be a natural extension of the happiness we cultivate in this life" (Goaslind, "Happiness," 52–53). ◉

Helaman 14:1–8. Samuel Prophesies of Jesus Christ's Birth

Why were these signs given? (14:2) "The pivotal occasions when Christ has come to the earth, meaning both his first and his second comings, have been preceded by signs, so that the faithful may know and be blessed. Signs help the Lord's people to be prepared and, because they know what to watch for, to avoid deception [see also Helaman 14:28–29]" (Parry and Parry, *Understanding the Signs of the Times*, 1).

Why were "great lights" an appropriate sign of the birth of the Messiah into the world? (14:3–5) "All things testify of Christ. At his birth the heavens resounded forth in magnificent splendor with all manner of signs and wonders. Here Samuel foretells a day without night following it, and a new star, along with the other signs and wonders, all of which would attest to the birth of the Prince of Light. How appropriate and typical—with the coming of the Light of Life into the world there would be no darkness!" (McConkie and Millet, *Doctrinal Commentary*, 3:408). ◉

39 O ye people of the land, that ye would hear my words! And I pray that the anger of the Lord be turned away from you, and that ye would repent and be saved.

CHAPTER 14

Samuel predicts light during the night and a new star at Christ's birth—Christ redeems men from temporal and spiritual death—The signs of His death include three days of darkness, the rending of the rocks, and great upheavals of nature. About 6 B.C.

1 And now it came to pass that Samuel, the Lamanite, did prophesy a great many more things which cannot be written.

2 And behold, he said unto them: Behold, I give unto you a sign; for five years more cometh, and behold, then cometh the Son of God to redeem all those who shall believe on his name.

3 And behold, this will I give unto you for a sign at the time of his coming; for behold, there shall be great lights in heaven, insomuch that in the night before he cometh there shall be no darkness, insomuch that it shall appear unto man as if it was day.

4 Therefore, there shall be one day and a night and a day, as if it were one day and there were no night; and this shall be unto you for a sign; for ye shall know of the rising of the sun and also of its setting; therefore they shall know of a surety that there shall be two days and a night; nevertheless the night shall not be darkened; and it shall be the night before he is born.

5 And behold, there shall a new star arise, such an one as ye never have beheld; and this also shall be a sign unto you.

6 And behold this is not all, there shall be many signs and wonders in heaven.

7 And it shall come to pass that ye shall all be amazed, and wonder, insomuch that ye shall fall to the earth.

8 And it shall come to pass that whosoever shall believe on the Son of God, the same shall have everlasting life.

9 And behold, thus hath the Lord commanded me, by his angel, that I should come and tell this thing unto you; yea, he hath commanded that I should prophesy these things unto you; yea, he hath said unto me: Cry unto this people, repent and prepare the way of the Lord.

10 And now, because I am a Lamanite, and have spoken unto you the words which the Lord hath commanded me, and because it was hard against you, ye are angry with me and do seek to destroy me, and have cast me out from among you.

11 And ye shall hear my words, for, for this intent have I come up upon the walls of this city, that ye might hear and know of the judgments of God which do await you because of your iniquities, and also that ye might know the conditions of repentance;

12 And also that ye might know of the coming of Jesus Christ, the Son of God, the Father of heaven and of earth, the Creator of all things from the beginning; and that ye might know of the signs of his coming, to the intent that ye might believe on his name.

Helaman 14:9–19. Samuel Cries Repentance to the Nephites

Why did Samuel rely so heavily on the exact words of past prophets? (14:12) There are "extensive, intricate consistencies found in the Book of Mormon.

"Passages tie together precisely and accurately though separated from each other by hundreds of pages of text and dictated weeks apart.

"[In Helaman 14:12] Samuel the Lamanite spoke of the coming of Christ, so that the people in the city of Zarahemla 'might know of the coming of *Jesus Christ, the Son of God, the Father of heaven and of earth, the Creator of all things from the beginning.*' The twenty-one words in italic appear to be standard Nephite religious terminology derived from the words given to Benjamin by an angel from God [see Mosiah 3:8]" (Welch, "Textual Consistency," 21–22). ◉

How is repentance tied to faith? (14:13) "The most basic expression of what faith produces is found in the teachings of Samuel the Lamanite [see Helaman 14:13]. Samuel explains that if we have faith, then we will repent—the two are inseparable. This 'if-then' relationship also makes clear that if we do not repent it is because we do not have faith in Christ, we do not 'believe on his name.' Our choice to believe on the atonement of Christ gives us the desire to change 'that thereby ye may have a remission of them [your sins] through his merits' (Helaman 14:13). Faith in Christ produces repentance" (Lane, "Faith unto Repentance," 183–84).

Will all people, including the wicked, be brought back into God's presence? (14:15–17) "The sacrifice and 'righteousness of the redeemer' (2 Nephi 2:3) brings everyone back into the presence of God; whether we are allowed to remain (or dwell) in the presence of the Father depends upon the degree to which we have accepted the sacrifice of the Son and have been willing to keep His commandments" (Judd, "Righteousness of the Redeemer," 155). ◉

What is the "second death"? (14:18–19) "After the separation of body and spirit, which is the natural death, the wicked and ungodly die a second death, a spiritual death, meaning they are cast out of the presence of the Lord and are dead as pertaining to the things of righteousness (D&C 63:17–18). . . .

"But when those here designated have suffered for their own sins . . . they shall come forth in the second resurrection and receive their inheritance in the telestial kingdom (D&C 76:103–106). That is, the allotted period of their spiritual death shall cease: and all men, except the sons of perdition, shall receive their part in the kingdoms which are prepared" (McConkie, *Doctrinal New Testament Commentary*, 3:584–85). ◉

13 And if ye believe on his name ye will repent of all your sins, that thereby ye may have a remission of them through his merits.

14 And behold, again, another sign I give unto you, yea, a sign of his death.

15 For behold, he surely must die that salvation may come; yea, it behooveth him and becometh expedient that he dieth, to bring to pass the resurrection of the dead, that thereby men may be brought into the presence of the Lord.

16 Yea, behold, this death bringeth to pass the resurrection, and redeemeth all mankind from the first death—that spiritual death; for all mankind, by the fall of Adam being cut off from the presence of the Lord, are considered as dead, both as to things temporal and to things spiritual.

17 But behold, the resurrection of Christ redeemeth mankind, yea, even all mankind, and bringeth them back into the presence of the Lord.

18 Yea, and it bringeth to pass the condition of repentance, that whosoever repenteth the same is not hewn down and cast into the fire; but whosoever repenteth not is hewn down and cast into the fire; and there cometh upon them again a spiritual death, yea, a second death, for they are cut off again as to things pertaining to righteousness.

19 Therefore repent ye, repent ye, lest by knowing these things and not doing them ye shall suffer yourselves to come under condemnation, and ye are brought down unto this second death.

20 But behold, as I said unto you concerning another sign, a sign of his death, behold, in that day that he shall suffer death the sun shall be darkened and refuse to give his light unto you; and also the moon and the stars; and there shall be no light upon the face of this land, even from the time that he shall suffer death, for the space of three days, to the time that he shall rise again from the dead.

21 Yea, at the time that he shall yield up the ghost there shall be thunderings and lightnings for the space of many hours, and the earth shall shake and tremble; and the rocks which are upon the face of this earth, which are both above the earth and beneath, which ye know at this time are solid, or the more part of it is one solid mass, shall be broken up;

22 Yea, they shall be rent in twain, and shall ever after be found in seams and in cracks, and in broken fragments upon the face of the whole earth, yea, both above the earth and beneath.

23 And behold, there shall be great tempests, and there shall be many mountains laid low, like unto a valley, and there shall be many places which are now called valleys which shall become mountains, whose height is great.

24 And many highways shall be broken up, and many cities shall become desolate.

25 And many graves shall be opened, and shall yield up many of their dead; and many saints shall appear unto many.

26 And behold, thus hath the angel spoken unto me; for he said unto me that there should be thunderings and lightnings for the space of many hours.

27 And he said unto me that while the thunder and the lightning lasted, and the tempest, that these things should be, and that darkness should cover the face of the whole earth for the space of three days.

Helaman 14:20–31. Samuel Gives the Signs of the Death of Jesus Christ

How is the breaking of the rocks a symbol of the world rejecting Christ? (14:21–22) "It is prophesied that at the death of Christ the Rock, 'the rocks . . . the more part of it is one solid mass, shall be broken up' (Hel. 14:21). In the fulfillment of this prophecy, at the time of the Crucifixion 'the rocks were rent in twain; they were broken up upon the face of the whole earth' (3 Ne. 8:18). On the other hand, in its wholeness a rock is associated with Christ, the rock of salvation (1 Ne. 15:15). . . . It is upon the rock of the Redeemer and his doctrine we may confidently build (Hel. 5:12; 3 Ne. 11:39–40)" (Rust, *Feasting on the Word*, 188).

What is the relationship between evidence and faith? (14:28–29) "Elder John A. Widtsoe taught that evidence can remove honest doubt and give assurances that build faith. 'After proper inquiries, using all the powers at our command,' he said, 'the weight of evidence is on one side or the other. Doubt is removed.' 'Doubt of the right kind—that is, honest questioning—leads to faith' and 'opens the door to truth,' for where there is doubt, faith cannot thrive [*Evidences and Reconciliations*, 28–29]. Elder Joseph Fielding Smith likewise affirmed that evidence, as convincing as in any court in the land, proves 'beyond the possibility of doubt that Joseph Smith and Oliver Cowdery spoke the truth' [*Doctrines of Salvation*, 2:124]" (Welch, Power of Evidence in the Nurturing of Faith," 155). ✚

What is agency and what conditions are required for it to exist? (14:30–31) "Agency is the ability and freedom to choose good or evil. It is an eternal principle. . . .

"Four great principles must be in force if there is to be agency: 1. Laws must exist, laws ordained by an Omnipotent power, laws which can be obeyed or disobeyed; 2. Opposites must exist—good and evil, virtue and vice, right and wrong—that is, there must be an opposition, one force pulling one way and another pulling the other; 3. A knowledge of good and evil must be had by those who are to enjoy the agency, that is, they must know the difference between the opposites; and 4. An unfettered power of choice must prevail" (McConkie, *Mormon Doctrine*, 26). ✚

Helaman 15:1–4. The Lord Rebukes the Nephites

28 And the angel said unto me that many shall see greater things than these, to the intent that they might believe that these signs and these wonders should come to pass upon all the face of this land, to the intent that there should be no cause for unbelief among the children of men—

29 And this to the intent that whosoever will believe might be saved, and that whosoever will not believe, a righteous judgment might come upon them; and also if they are condemned they bring upon themselves their own condemnation.

30 And now remember, remember, my brethren, that whosoever perisheth, perisheth unto himself; and whosoever doeth iniquity, doeth it unto himself; for behold, ye are free; ye are permitted to act for yourselves; for behold, God hath given unto you a knowledge and he hath made you free.

31 He hath given unto you that ye might know good from evil, and he hath given unto you that ye might choose life or death; and ye can do good and be restored unto that which is good, or have that which is good restored unto you; or ye can do evil, and have that which is evil restored unto you.

CHAPTER 15

The Lord chastened the Nephites because He loved them—Converted Lamanites are firm and steadfast in the faith—The Lord will be merciful unto the Lamanites in the latter days. About 6 B.C.

1 And now, my beloved brethren, behold, I declare unto you that except ye shall repent your houses shall be left unto you desolate.

2 Yea, except ye repent, your women shall have great cause to mourn in the day that they shall give suck; for ye shall attempt to flee and there shall be no place for refuge;

yea, and wo unto them which are with child, for they shall be heavy and cannot flee; therefore, they shall be trodden down and shall be left to perish.

3 Yea, wo unto this people who are called the people of Nephi except they shall repent, when they shall see all these signs and wonders which shall be showed unto them; for behold, they have been a chosen people of the Lord; yea, the people of Nephi hath he loved, and also hath he chastened them; yea, in the days of their iniquities hath he chastened them because he loveth them.

4 But behold my brethren, the Lamanites hath he hated because their deeds have been evil continually, and this because of the iniquity of the tradition of their fathers. But behold, salvation hath come unto them through the preaching of the Nephites; and for this intent hath the Lord prolonged their days.

5 And I would that ye should behold that the more part of them are in the path of their duty, and they do walk circumspectly before God, and they do observe to keep his commandments and his statutes and his judgments according to the law of Moses.

6 Yea, I say unto you, that the more part of them are doing this, and they are striving with unwearied diligence that they may bring the remainder of their brethren to the knowledge of the truth; therefore there are many who do add to their numbers daily.

7 And behold, ye do know of yourselves, for ye have witnessed it, that as many of them as are brought to the knowledge of the truth, and to know of the wicked and abominable traditions of their fathers, and are led to believe the holy scriptures, yea, the prophecies of the holy prophets, which are written, which leadeth them to faith on the Lord, and unto repentance, which faith and repentance bringeth a change of heart unto them—

Doesn't God love all His children unconditionally? (15:3–4) "While divine love can be called perfect, infinite, enduring, and universal, it cannot correctly be characterized as unconditional. . . . On the other hand, many verses affirm that the higher levels of love the Father and the Son feel for each of us—and certain divine blessings stemming from that love—are conditional. . . .

"Thanks to the Atonement, the gift of immortality is unconditional. The greater gift of eternal life, however, is conditional. In order to qualify, one must deny oneself of ungodliness and honor the ordinances and covenants of the temple. The resplendent bouquet of God's love—including eternal life—includes blessings for which we must qualify" (Nelson, "Divine Love," 24). ◉

Helaman 15:5–10. The Converted Lamanites Are Faithful

How extensive was this conversion of Lamanites? (15:5–8) "While some casual readers of the Book of Mormon may assume that Samuel was an exception, it is clear from what Samuel says in his prophecy to the Nephites that he was just one of many examples of reversed roles among the Nephites and Lamanites [see Helaman 15:5–8]" (Cowan, "Lamanites," 258).

How can the scriptures lead us to increase our faith, repent, and have a change of heart? (15:7–8) "The scriptures hold the keys to spiritual protection. They contain the doctrine and laws and ordinances that will bring each child of God to a testimony of Jesus Christ as the Savior and Redeemer. . . .

"We seek to make them available to all who wish to learn. They teach us where to go and what to do. They offer hope and knowledge" (Packer, "Key to Spiritual Protection," 26–27). ◉

8 Therefore, as many as have come to this, ye know of yourselves are firm and steadfast in the faith, and in the thing wherewith they have been made free.

9 And ye know also that they have buried their weapons of war, and they fear to take them up lest by any means they should sin; yea, ye can see that they fear to sin—for behold they will suffer themselves that they be trodden down and slain by their enemies, and will not lift their swords against them, and this because of their faith in Christ.

10 And now, because of their steadfastness when they do believe in that thing which they do believe, for because of their firmness when they are once enlightened, behold, the Lord shall bless them and prolong their days, notwithstanding their iniquity—

11 Yea, even if they should dwindle in unbelief the Lord shall prolong their days, until the time shall come which hath been spoken of by our fathers, and also by the prophet Zenos, and many other prophets, concerning the restoration of our brethren, the Lamanites, again to the knowledge of the truth—

12 Yea, I say unto you, that in the latter times the promises of the Lord have been extended to our brethren, the Lamanites; and notwithstanding the many afflictions which they shall have, and notwithstanding they shall be driven to and fro upon the face of the earth, and be hunted, and shall be smitten and scattered abroad, having no place for refuge, the Lord shall be merciful unto them.

13 And this is according to the prophecy, that they shall again be brought to the true knowledge, which is the knowledge of their Redeemer, and their great and true shepherd, and be numbered among his sheep.

14 Therefore I say unto you, it shall be better for them than for you except ye repent.

Helaman 15:11–17. The Lord Will Bless the Lamanites in the Last Days

In what ways is this prophecy of the children of Lehi returning to the Lord being fulfilled today? (15:11–16) Some years ago, Elder Gene R. Cook said: "My family and I are presently living in South America among the Lamanites—the children of Lehi, the people of the Book of Mormon, a people of great promise. For a number of years we have been witnesses to spiritual miracles among that people:

"1. We have seen thousands converted to the Lord who had his law put into their minds and written in their hearts (see Heb. 8:10).

"2. We have seen them organized into numerous stakes of Zion.

"3. We have truly seen them 'blossom as the rose' as prophecy has been fulfilled through them (see D&C 49:24).

"4. We have literally seen the Lord perform miracles among them by their faith" ("Miracles among the Lamanites," 67). ⊕

15 For behold, had the mighty works been shown unto them which have been shown unto you, yea, unto them who have dwindled in unbelief because of the traditions of their fathers, ye can see of yourselves that they never would again have dwindled in unbelief.

16 Therefore, saith the Lord: I will not utterly destroy them, but I will cause that in the day of my wisdom they shall return again unto me, saith the Lord.

17 And now behold, saith the Lord, concerning the people of the Nephites: If they will not repent, and observe to do my will, I will utterly destroy them, saith the Lord, because of their unbelief notwithstanding the many mighty works which I have done among them; and as surely as the Lord liveth shall these things be, saith the Lord.

CHAPTER 16

The Nephites who believe Samuel are baptized by Nephi—Samuel cannot be slain with the arrows and stones of the unrepentant Nephites—Some harden their hearts, and others see angels—The unbelievers say it is not reasonable to believe in Christ and His coming in Jerusalem. About 6–1 B.C.

1 And now, it came to pass that there were many who heard the words of Samuel, the Lamanite, which he spake upon the walls of the city. And as many as believed on his word went forth and sought for Nephi; and when they had come forth and found him they confessed unto him their sins and denied not, desiring that they might be baptized unto the Lord.

2 But as many as there were who did not believe in the words of Samuel were angry with him; and they cast stones at him upon the wall, and also many shot arrows at him as he stood upon the wall; but the Spirit of the Lord was with him, insomuch that they

Helaman 16:1–12. Many Believe the Teachings of Samuel and Nephi and Are Baptized

What caused the people to be angry and seek Samuel's destruction? (16:1–2) Nephi said, "I knew that I had spoken hard things against the wicked, according to the truth; and the righteous have I justified, and testified that they should be lifted up at the last day; wherefore, the guilty taketh the truth to be hard, for it cutteth them to the very center" (1 Nephi 16:2).

Jacob warned, "Do not say that I have spoken hard things against you; for if ye do, ye will revile against the truth; for I have spoken the words of your Maker. I know that the words of truth are hard against all uncleanness; but the righteous fear them not, for they love the truth and are not shaken" (2 Nephi 9:40). ●

What is the role of prophets today? (16:4–5) "In the words of President James E. Faust . . . : 'We have been promised that the President of the Church will receive guidance for all of us as the revelator for the Church. Our safety lies in paying heed to that which he says and following his counsel'" (Williams, "Following the Prophet," 22). ⊕

How does Samuel's life typify the life of Jesus Christ? (16:6) Compare Helaman 16:6 and John 7:20. In what way was Samuel like the Savior? "Not only did the prophets of Old Testament times believe in Christ and worship the Father in his name but they also lived in such a way that each could say of the promised Messiah, as did Moses, he shall be 'like unto me' (Deuteronomy 18:15). From Adam to Malachi, their lives constituted marvelous prophetic types of the life of Christ" (McConkie, *Gospel Symbolism*, 146).

Can you think of other ways Samuel's life was like the Savior's?

could not hit him with their stones neither with their arrows.

3 Now when they saw that they could not hit him, there were many more who did believe on his words, insomuch that they went away unto Nephi to be baptized.

4 For behold, Nephi was baptizing, and prophesying, and preaching, crying repentance unto the people, showing signs and wonders, working miracles among the people, that they might know that the Christ must shortly come—

5 Telling them of things which must shortly come, that they might know and remember at the time of their coming that they had been made known unto them beforehand, to the intent that they might believe; therefore as many as believed on the words of Samuel went forth unto him to be baptized, for they came repenting and confessing their sins.

6 But the more part of them did not believe in the words of Samuel; therefore when they saw that they could not hit him with their stones and their arrows, they cried unto their captains, saying: Take this fellow and bind him, for behold he hath a devil; and because of the power of the devil which is in him we cannot hit him with our stones and our arrows; therefore take him and bind him, and away with him.

7 And as they went forth to lay their hands on him, behold, he did cast himself down from the wall, and did flee out of their lands, yea, even unto his own country, and began to preach and to prophesy among his own people.

8 And behold, he was never heard of more among the Nephites; and thus were the affairs of the people.

9 And thus ended the eighty and sixth year of the reign of the judges over the people of Nephi.

10 And thus ended also the eighty and seventh year of the reign of the judges, the more part of the people remaining in their pride and wickedness, and the lesser part walking more circumspectly before God.

11 And these were the conditions also, in the eighty and eighth year of the reign of the judges.

12 And there was but little alteration in the affairs of the people, save it were the people began to be more hardened in iniquity, and do more and more of that which was contrary to the commandments of God, in the eighty and ninth year of the reign of the judges.

13 But it came to pass in the ninetieth year of the reign of the judges, there were great signs given unto the people, and wonders; and the words of the prophets began to be fulfilled.

14 And angels did appear unto men, wise men, and did declare unto them glad tidings of great joy; thus in this year the scriptures began to be fulfilled.

15 Nevertheless, the people began to harden their hearts, all save it were the most believing part of them, both of the Nephites and also of the Lamanites, and began to depend upon their own strength and upon their own wisdom, saying:

16 Some things they may have guessed right, among so many; but behold, we know that all these great and marvelous works cannot come to pass, of which has been spoken.

17 And they began to reason and to contend among themselves, saying:

18 That it is not reasonable that such a being as a Christ shall come; if so, and he be the Son of God, the Father of heaven and of earth, as it has been spoken, why will he not show himself unto us as well as unto them who shall be at Jerusalem?

Helaman 16:13–25. Despite Great Signs and Wonders, Many Still Do Not Believe

How can the Book of Mormon help us prepare for the Second Coming? (16:13) "In the Book of Mormon we find a pattern for preparing for the Second Coming. A major portion of the book centers on the few decades just prior to Christ's coming to America. By careful study of that time period we can determine why some were destroyed in the terrible judgments that preceded His coming and what brought others to stand at the temple in the land of Bountiful and thrust their hands into the wounds of His hands and feet. . . .

"Can anyone doubt that this book was meant for us and that in it we find great power, great comfort, and great protection?" (Benson, "Book of Mormon—Keystone of Our Religion," 6–7).

What is the relationship between reason and faith? (16:15–18) "The knowledge of God and His plan of salvation is the kind of knowledge that saves, and this kind of knowledge can be obtained only in the Lord's way.

"God reveals Himself and His eternal truths—the spiritual food that the scriptures call the bread of life and the living water—to those who seek, who serve, who keep His commandments, and who wait and listen in humility for His teaching. Study and reason are appropriate to begin this process, but 'the things of God cannot be learned solely by study and reason'" (Oaks, "Nourishing the Spirit," 9). ⊕

19 Yea, why will he not show himself in this land as well as in the land of Jerusalem?

20 But behold, we know that this is a wicked tradition, which has been handed down unto us by our fathers, to cause us that we should believe in some great and marvelous thing which should come to pass, but not among us, but in a land which is far distant, a land which we know not; therefore they can keep us in ignorance, for we cannot witness with our own eyes that they are true.

21 And they will, by the cunning and the mysterious arts of the evil one, work some great mystery which we cannot understand, which will keep us down to be servants to their words, and also servants unto them, for we depend upon them to teach us the word; and thus will they keep us in ignorance if we will yield ourselves unto them, all the days of our lives.

22 And many more things did the people imagine up in their hearts, which were foolish and vain; and they were much disturbed, for Satan did stir them up to do iniquity continually; yea, he did go about spreading rumors and contentions upon all the face of the land, that he might harden the hearts of the people against that which was good and against that which should come.

23 And notwithstanding the signs and the wonders which were wrought among the people of the Lord, and the many miracles which they did, Satan did get great hold upon the hearts of the people upon all the face of the land.

24 And thus ended the ninetieth year of the reign of the judges over the people of Nephi.

25 And thus ended the book of Helaman, according to the record of Helaman and his sons.

How does Satan use contention to harden hearts today? (16:22–23) "Scriptures repeatedly warn that the father of contention opposes the plan of our Heavenly Father. Satan's method relies on the infectious canker of contention. Satan's motive: to gain personal acclaim even over God Himself.

"The work of the adversary may be likened to loading guns in opposition to the work of God. Salvos containing germs of contention are aimed and fired at strategic targets essential to that holy work. These vital targets include—in addition to the individual—the family, leaders of the Church, and divine doctrine" (Nelson, "Canker of Contention," 69). ●

THIRD NEPHI
THE BOOK OF NEPHI

THE SON OF NEPHI, WHO WAS THE SON OF HELAMAN

Nephi, son of Nephi and great-grandson of Helaman, wrote 3 Nephi. Dr. Sidney B. Sperry observed: "The book known to us as Third Nephi was originally called 'The Book of Nephi' as the caption immediately below the title in our modern editions indicates. The title '3 Nephi' was first added by Elder Orson Pratt in the 1879 edition to distinguish this book from the first two books in the Nephite record, known respectively as 'The First Book of Nephi' and 'The Second Book of Nephi.' In other words, 'Third Nephi' is not a part of the original text of the Book of Mormon" (*Book of Mormon Compendium*, 389).

Beginning with the miraculous fulfillment of the prophecies of Samuel the Lamanite concerning the birth of Christ (see 3 Nephi 1), the record concludes with Mormon's discourse on the nature of translated beings and his plea to those who read these sacred words (see 3 Nephi 28–30). The opening chapters contrast those who are righteous, converted to the Church, and led by the prophet Nephi with the wicked, who infiltrate and corrupt the government. Eventually the wicked succeed in creating anarchy, which divides the people into family tribes and bands of robbers. This collapse is followed by a physical destruction and cleansing of the land before the coming of Jesus Christ. His appearance is the dramatic and spiritual zenith of the Book of Mormon.

Third Nephi also highlights both the Savior's mortal life and miraculous post-Resurrection appearance: His miraculous birth in Bethlehem (see 3 Nephi 1) and His postmortal ministry as the resurrected Lord visiting and teaching the Nephites (see 3 Nephi 11–27). Third Nephi contains the Lord's inspiring account of the points of His doctrine (see 3 Nephi 11) and His two-day sermon at the temple in Bountiful. Jesus heals the sick, and angels minister to Nephite children (3 Nephi 17). Christ institutes the sacrament (3 Nephi 18) and calls twelve special disciples (3 Nephi 19), three of whom are translated (28:16–23).

And Helaman was the son of Helaman, who was the son of Alma, who was the son of Alma, being a descendant of Nephi who was the son of Lehi, who came out of Jerusalem in the first year of the reign of Zedekiah, the king of Judah.

CHAPTER 1

Nephi, the son of Helaman, departs out of the land, and his son Nephi keeps the records—Though signs and wonders abound, the wicked plan to slay the righteous—The night of Christ's birth arrives—The sign is given, and a new star arises—Lyings and deceivings increase, and the Gadianton robbers slaughter many. About A.D. 1–4.

The superscription to 3 Nephi, which appears just under the title, was part of the ancient record translated by the Prophet Joseph Smith and dictated by him to his scribe (see also, for example, 1 Nephi, Alma 5, and 4 Nephi).

Distinct from the superscription is the chapter summary, which is presented in italics between the chapter number and the beginning of the scriptural text. Chapter summaries, originally added in the 1920 edition of the Book of Mormon, give the reader an overview of what each chapter contains.

3 Nephi 1:1–3. Handing Down the Records

Who was the new keeper of the records? (1:2) The chart below illustrates the lineage of the new record keeper, Nephi.

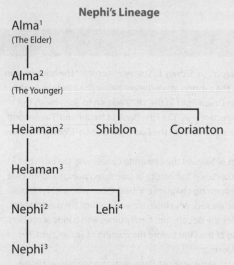

Nephi's Lineage

Alma¹
(The Elder)

Alma²
(The Younger)

Helaman²   Shiblon   Corianton

Helaman³

Nephi²   Lehi⁴

Nephi³

What were some of the things that had been kept sacred? (1:2) David Whitmer recalled: "The fact is, it was just as though Joseph, Oliver and I were sitting just here on a log, when we were overshadowed by a light. It was not the light of the sun, nor like that of a fire, but more glorious and beautiful. It extended away around us . . . in the midst of this light . . . there appeared as it were a table with many records or plates upon it, besides the plates of the Book of Mormon; also the sword of Laban, the Directors (i.e., the ball which Lehi had) and the Interpreters" (Smith, *Life of Joseph F. Smith*, 242). ●

What happened to Nephi, son of Helaman? (1:3) "What happened to Nephi? Was he slain under mysterious circumstances and his body never recovered, or was he translated? We are not specifically told, but one gets the distinct impression that some great spiritual incident lies behind the disappearance of Nephi" (Sperry, *Book of Mormon Compendium*, 393; see also commentary in this volume on 3 Nephi 2:9).

1 Now it came to pass that the ninety and first year had passed away and it was six hundred years from the time that Lehi left Jerusalem; and it was in the year that Lachoneus was the chief judge and the governor over the land.

2 And Nephi, the son of Helaman, had departed out of the land of Zarahemla, giving charge unto his son Nephi, who was his eldest son, concerning the plates of brass, and all the records which had been kept, and all those things which had been kept sacred from the departure of Lehi out of Jerusalem.

3 Then he departed out of the land, and whither he went, no man knoweth; and his son Nephi did keep the records in his stead, yea, the record of this people.

4 And it came to pass that in the commencement of the ninety and second year, behold, the prophecies of the prophets began to be fulfilled more fully; for there began to be greater signs and greater miracles wrought among the people.

5 But there were some who began to say that the time was past for the words to be fulfilled, which were spoken by Samuel, the Lamanite.

6 And they began to rejoice over their brethren, saying: Behold the time is past, and the words of Samuel are not fulfilled; therefore, your joy and your faith concerning this thing hath been vain.

7 And it came to pass that they did make a great uproar throughout the land; and the people who believed began to be very sorrowful, lest by any means those things which had been spoken might not come to pass.

8 But behold, they did watch steadfastly for that day and that night and that day which should be as one day as if there were no night, that they might know that their faith had not been vain.

9 Now it came to pass that there was a day set apart by the unbelievers, that all those who believed in those traditions should be put to death except the sign should come to pass, which had been given by Samuel the prophet.

10 Now it came to pass that when Nephi, the son of Nephi, saw this wickedness of his people, his heart was exceedingly sorrowful.

11 And it came to pass that he went out and bowed himself down upon the earth, and cried mightily to his God in behalf of his people, yea, those who were about to be destroyed because of their faith in the tradition of their fathers.

3 Nephi 1:4–14. The Faithful, under a Death Sentence, Anxiously Await the Signs of Christ's Coming

Why is it important that we study this record? (1:4)
"A record of anarchy and the collapse of government is found in 3 Nephi 1 to 10, preceding the coming of the Lord. This pattern, which can also be seen in many prophecies of the last days, seems to foreshadow a similar pattern of events in our time (see Rev. 17–19; D&C 45:22–44; D&C 88:87–95; JS–M 1:23–37)" (Garrett, "Peace Within," 21).

Why would the unbelievers want to put to death the believers? (1:9) "Here we witness a phenomenon which is repeated ad nauseam in the Book of Mormon: the wicked who refuse to believe dare not allow others to believe. There is no room in their tightly controlled epistemological system for faith or spirit or revelation or hope. They do not know so they conclude that no one else knows. They cannot feel, so they dare not allow others to feel. In this case they shun the light of evidence that comes from God and refuse others the right to wait patiently on the Lord for the signs to be given" (McConkie et al., *Doctrinal Commentary*, 4:5). ❂

How did Christ fulfill both the will of the Father and the Son? (1:14) "This is a most difficult passage. It sounds as though the Lord is stating that he will come into the world to fulfill two wills—the will of Jehovah, the premortal God of the ancients (perhaps referred to here as 'me'), and the will of the mortal Messiah (the person of 'flesh'). Of course we know that they, Jehovah and Jesus, are one and the same being. At the same time, this statement dramatizes the separate and severable roles that would be played by the Master, that of the Holy One of Israel (premortal) and that of Jesus of Nazareth (mortal)" (McConkie et al., *Doctrinal Commentary*, 4:7). ⊕

3 Nephi 1:15–21. The Signs Are Given

What do we learn from the remarkable display of light in the New World that accompanied Christ's birth in the Holy Land? (1:15) "How fitting that the Savior's birth in Bethlehem was accompanied by miraculous displays of light in the Western Hemisphere. At the time of His birth, 'at the going down of the sun there was no darkness; and the people began to be astonished because . . . there was no darkness in all that night' (3 Nephi 1:15, 19). This celebration of light stood in stark contrast to that which occurred at His Crucifixion, when 'there was thick darkness upon all the face of the land, insomuch that the inhabitants thereof . . . could feel the vapor of darkness' (3 Nephi 8:20; see also verses 21–23)" (Jensen, "Lead, Kindly Light," 62).

What important truth was illustrated on this miraculous night? (1:16) "We are told that Nephi 'cried mightily unto the Lord' (3 Ne. 1:12), whereupon the Lord came unto him and answered him that the time was at hand for all that had been spoken by his holy prophets to be fulfilled. All the signs came to pass, the new star appeared in the sky, and the unbelievers 'fell to the earth and became as if they were dead' (3 Ne. 1:16). Here is one of the first lessons we learn. The words of God's prophets are always fulfilled" (Tanner, "Christ in America," 34–35).

12 And it came to pass that he cried mightily unto the Lord all that day; and behold, the voice of the Lord came unto him, saying:

13 Lift up your head and be of good cheer; for behold, the time is at hand, and on this night shall the sign be given, and on the morrow come I into the world, to show unto the world that I will fulfil all that which I have caused to be spoken by the mouth of my holy prophets.

14 Behold, I come unto my own, to fulfil all things which I have made known unto the children of men from the foundation of the world, and to do the will, both of the Father and of the Son—of the Father because of me, and of the Son because of my flesh. And behold, the time is at hand, and this night shall the sign be given.

15 And it came to pass that the words which came unto Nephi were fulfilled, according as they had been spoken; for behold, at the going down of the sun there was no darkness; and the people began to be astonished because there was no darkness when the night came.

16 And there were many, who had not believed the words of the prophets, who fell to the earth and became as if they were dead, for they knew that the great plan of destruction which they had laid for those who believed in the words of the prophets had been frustrated; for the sign which had been given was already at hand.

17 And they began to know that the Son of God must shortly appear; yea, in fine, all the people upon the face of the whole earth from the west to the east, both in the land north and in the land south, were so exceedingly astonished that they fell to the earth.

18 For they knew that the prophets had testified of these things for many years, and that the sign which had been given was already at hand; and they began to fear because of their iniquity and their unbelief.

19 And it came to pass that there was no darkness in all that night, but it was as light as though it was mid-day. And it came to pass that the sun did rise in the morning again, according to its proper order; and they knew that it was the day that the Lord should be born, because of the sign which had been given.

20 And it had come to pass, yea, all things, every whit, according to the words of the prophets.

21 And it came to pass also that a new star did appear, according to the word.

22 And it came to pass that from this time forth there began to be lyings sent forth among the people, by Satan, to harden their hearts, to the intent that they might not believe in those signs and wonders which they had seen; but notwithstanding these lyings and deceivings the more part of the people did believe, and were converted unto the Lord.

23 And it came to pass that Nephi went forth among the people, and also many others, baptizing unto repentance, in the which there was a great remission of sins. And thus the people began again to have peace in the land.

24 And there were no contentions, save it were a few that began to preach, endeavoring to prove by the scriptures that it was no more expedient to observe the law of Moses. Now

3 Nephi 1:22–30. Satan Causes False Doctrine to Flourish and Gadianton Robbers to Increase

How does Satan respond to great spiritual experiences? (1:22) "Don't assume that a great revelation, some marvelous illuminating moment, or the opening of an inspired path is the end of it. . . .

"I wish to encourage every one of you today regarding opposition that so often comes after enlightened decisions have been made, after moments of revelation and conviction have given us a peace and an assurance we thought we would never lose. . . .

"Opposition turns up almost anyplace something good has happened" (Holland, "Cast Not Away Therefore Your Confidence").

Why is it dangerous to privately interpret the scriptures? (1:24) Some assumed the law of Moses was fulfilled in the birth of Christ and began to preach this untruth without the authority of leaders. "President Wilford Woodruff urged the Church flock to follow the

Brethren because, he said, 'the very moment that men in this kingdom attempt to run ahead or cross the path of their leaders, ... they are in danger of being injured by the wolves. ... I have never in my life known it to fail' (in *Journal of Discourses*, 5:83)" (Maxwell, "Behold, the Enemy Is Combined," 78). ⊕

Why did Mormon include this warning against secret combinations? (1:27) "If we are not careful, today's secret combinations can obtain power and influence just as quickly and just as completely as they did in Book of Mormon times. Do you remember the pattern? The secret combinations began among the 'more wicked part' of society, but eventually 'seduced the more part of the righteous' until the whole society was polluted" (Ballard, "Standing for Truth and Right," 38).

How do we guard against becoming "for ourselves"? (1:29) "Let the Saints remember that great things depend on their individual exertion, and that they are called to be co-workers with us and the Holy Spirit in accomplishing the great work of the last days; and ... let every selfish feeling be not only buried, but annihilated; and let love to God and man predominate, and reign triumphant in every mind, that their hearts may become like unto Enoch's of old" (Jensen, "Keep an Eternal Perspective," 27).

in this thing they did err, having not understood the scriptures.

25 But it came to pass that they soon became converted, and were convinced of the error which they were in, for it was made known unto them that the law was not yet fulfilled, and that it must be fulfilled in every whit; yea, the word came unto them that it must be fulfilled; yea, that one jot or tittle should not pass away till it should all be fulfilled; therefore in this same year were they brought to a knowledge of their error and did confess their faults.

26 And thus the ninety and second year did pass away, bringing glad tidings unto the people because of the signs which did come to pass, according to the words of the prophecy of all the holy prophets.

27 And it came to pass that the ninety and third year did also pass away in peace, save it were for the Gadianton robbers, who dwelt upon the mountains, who did infest the land; for so strong were their holds and their secret places that the people could not overpower them; therefore they did commit many murders, and did do much slaughter among the people.

28 And it came to pass that in the ninety and fourth year they began to increase in a great degree, because there were many dissenters of the Nephites who did flee unto them, which did cause much sorrow unto those Nephites who did remain in the land.

29 And there was also a cause of much sorrow among the Lamanites; for behold, they had many children who did grow up and began to wax strong in years, that they became for themselves, and were led away by some who were Zoramites, by their lyings and their flattering words, to join those Gadianton robbers.

30 And thus were the Lamanites afflicted also, and began to decrease as to their faith and righteousness, because of the wickedness of the rising generation.

CHAPTER 2

Wickedness and abominations increase among the people—The Nephites and Lamanites unite to defend themselves against the Gadianton robbers—Converted Lamanites become white and are called Nephites. About A.D. 5–16.

1 And it came to pass that thus passed away the ninety and fifth year also, and the people began to forget those signs and wonders which they had heard, and began to be less and less astonished at a sign or a wonder from heaven, insomuch that they began to be hard in their hearts, and blind in their minds, and began to disbelieve all which they had heard and seen—

2 Imagining up some vain thing in their hearts, that it was wrought by men and by the power of the devil, to lead away and deceive the hearts of the people; and thus did Satan get possession of the hearts of the people again, insomuch that he did blind their eyes and lead them away to believe that the doctrine of Christ was a foolish and a vain thing.

3 And it came to pass that the people began to wax strong in wickedness and abominations; and they did not believe that there should be any more signs or wonders given; and Satan did go about, leading away the hearts of the people, tempting them and

Why was this mention about the rising generation included? (1:30) "While we do not think of it this way very often, the rising generation has some genuine responsibilities to the older generation still living. We are not immune to influence from you. We not only regard you as the seedbearers of a celestial culture to come, but our own journey can be hastened by your pressing forward. . . . Lowering standards in the rising generations can create an undertow that affects all ages.

"We have seen, in just the past decade, various youth movements wash over shaky adults who gave way under pressure. Some adults, strangely enough, replaced their old values, of all things, with youth worship! The last thing youth needs is to be envied or worshiped" (Maxwell, *Wherefore, Ye Must Press Forward*, 84).

3 Nephi 2:1–10. The People Forget the Signs of Christ's Birth and Return to Wickedness

Why do signs fail to provide a lasting conversion? (2:1) President Dallin H. Oaks taught: "The obtaining of faith by signs was not God's way, because 'faith cometh not by signs, but signs follow those that believe.' . . . The viewing of signs or miracles is not a secure foundation for conversion. Scriptural history attests that people converted by signs and wonders soon forget them and again become susceptible to the lies and distortions of Satan and his servants (Hel. 16:23; 3 Ne. 1:22; 2:1; 8:4)" (*The Lord's Way*, 82–87). ◉

What is the pattern so often repeated among the Nephites? (2:2–3) "Some things never seem to change. For the next thirty years, Nephite civilization proceeded according to their long-established pattern—moments of righteousness and consequent prosperity followed by transgression and alienation. But the transcendent moments were transcendent indeed" (Holland, *Christ and the New Covenant*, 253).

How does the fluctuating faith of the Nephites compare to faith manifested in our day? (2:2–3) What happens to the level of religious feeling and activity among people today after a natural or man-made disaster? How long do such renewed religious feelings usually last? Why do you think this might be so? What can you do in your family to remember and be faithful regardless of world conditions?

causing them that they should do great wickedness in the land.

4 And thus did pass away the ninety and sixth year; and also the ninety and seventh year; and also the ninety and eighth year; and also the ninety and ninth year;

5 And also an hundred years had passed away since the days of Mosiah, who was king over the people of the Nephites.

6 And six hundred and nine years had passed away since Lehi left Jerusalem.

7 And nine years had passed away from the time when the sign was given, which was spoken of by the prophets, that Christ should come into the world.

8 Now the Nephites began to reckon their time from this period when the sign was given, or from the coming of Christ; therefore, nine years had passed away.

What methods did the Nephites use to determine their time? (2:8) "The Nephites used three systems of reckoning time:

"(1) The first method was to determine the number of years since father Lehi left Jerusalem; this system was used from 600 B.C. to 92 B.C. (Mosiah 29:44–47; Alma 1:1).

"(2) The second method was to calculate the number of years from the beginning of the reign of the judges; this system was used for about 100 years, from 91 B.C. to A.D. 9 (3 Nephi 2:5–7).

"(3) The last method was to 'reckon their time from this period when the sign was given, or from the coming of Christ' (3 Nephi 2:7–8); this system was used for the remainder of their record" (Ludlow, *Companion to Your Study of the Book of Mormon*, 254).

What happened to Nephi, the son of Helaman and father of Nephi? (2:9) "Third Nephi begins with an interesting statement about Nephi the son of Helaman. . . . [He] 'departed out of the land, and whither he went, no man knoweth' (3 Ne. 1:3) and . . . he 'did not return to the land of Zarahemla, and could nowhere be found in all the land' (3 Ne. 2:9). This is reminiscent of a similar passage about Nephi's great-grandfather Alma the younger. . . . In Alma's day the church members speculated that he might have been 'taken up' by the Lord as was Moses. Although there is no similar declaration in the Book of Mormon about Nephi the son of Helaman, he was certainly a candidate for translation considering the type of life he led" (Szink, "Just and True Record," 125).

9 And Nephi, who was the father of Nephi, who had the charge of the records, did not return to the land of Zarahemla, and could nowhere be found in all the land.

10 And it came to pass that the people did still remain in wickedness, notwithstanding the much preaching and prophesying which was sent among them; and thus passed away the tenth year also; and the eleventh year also passed away in iniquity.

11 And it came to pass in the thirteenth year there began to be wars and contentions throughout all the land; for the Gadianton robbers had become so numerous, and did slay so many of the people, and did lay waste so many cities, and did spread so much death and carnage throughout the land, that it became expedient that all the people, both the Nephites and the Lamanites, should take up arms against them.

12 Therefore, all the Lamanites who had become converted unto the Lord did unite with their brethren, the Nephites, and were compelled, for the safety of their lives and their women and their children, to take up arms against those Gadianton robbers, yea, and also to maintain their rights, and the privileges of their church and of their worship, and their freedom and their liberty.

13 And it came to pass that before this thirteenth year had passed away the Nephites were threatened with utter destruction because of this war, which had become exceedingly sore.

14 And it came to pass that those Lamanites who had united with the Nephites were numbered among the Nephites;

15 And their curse was taken from them, and their skin became white like unto the Nephites;

16 And their young men and their daughters became exceedingly fair, and they were numbered among the Nephites, and were called Nephites. And thus ended the thirteenth year.

17 And it came to pass in the commencement of the fourteenth year, the war between the robbers and the people of Nephi did continue and did become exceedingly sore; nevertheless, the people of Nephi did gain some advantage of the robbers, insomuch that they did drive them back out of their lands into the mountains and into their secret places.

3 Nephi 2:11–19. Righteous Nephites and Lamanites Join in Fighting the Gadianton Robbers

What was the promised blessing these Lamanites received? (2:15) "The mark of God's curse, the dark skin (see 1 Nephi 2:23; 2 Nephi 5:21–23) was taken away. This was consistent with the prophetic word which declared that when the Lamanites are restored to the knowledge of Jesus Christ and his gospel, 'their scales of darkness shall begin to fall from their eyes; and many generations shall not pass away among them'" (McConkie et al., *Doctrinal Commentary*, 4:12).

"The Nephite society was on the brink of annihilation, or as Mormon put it, 'the sword of destruction
did hang over them' (3 Ne. 2:19)" (Szink, "Just and True
Record," 128).

3 Nephi 3:1–10. Giddianhi Writes a Threatening Letter to Lachoneus

**What do we learn about ancient military prac-
tice from Giddianhi's letter? (3:1)** "Among Book
of Mormon peoples, military commanders typically
corresponded with each other before launching any
attacks. Even where hatred ran deep, and even when
there was no chance that the proposed terms would
be accepted, the parties asked for capitulation or
extended terms of surrender before going to battle"
(Welch, "Law and War," 59). ☉

**Why did Giddianhi fail to see divine intervention
among the Nephites? (3:2–4)** President Boyd K. Packer
helped us understand why skeptics don't understand
divine intervention: "One thing is for sure: the skeptic
will never know, for he will not meet the requirement
of faith, humility, and obedience to qualify him for the
visitation of the Spirit" (*That All May Be Edified*, 340).

What motivated Giddianhi to invite the Nephites
to unite with them? (3:6–7) "The ambitious did not
seek power for its sake alone. It was a means to earth-
ier satisfactions: Giddianhi was at least as concerned
with 'possessions' and 'all our substance' as he was with
'rights' and rulership (3 Nephi 3:2–12); the secret group
under Gadianton and successors were 'robbers' and
'plunderers' (Helaman 2:10; 6:18) who 'set their hearts
upon their riches' (Helaman 6:17)" (Sorenson, *Ancient
American Setting*, 164). ☉

18 And thus ended the fourteenth year. And
in the fifteenth year they did come forth
against the people of Nephi; and because of
the wickedness of the people of Nephi, and
their many contentions and dissensions, the
Gadianton robbers did gain many advantages
over them.

19 And thus ended the fifteenth year, and
thus were the people in a state of many afflictions; and the sword of destruction did hang
over them, insomuch that they were about to
be smitten down by it, and this because of
their iniquity.

CHAPTER 3

*Giddianhi, the Gadianton leader, demands that
Lachoneus and the Nephites surrender them-
selves and their lands—Lachoneus appoints
Gidgiddoni as chief captain of the armies—The
Nephites assemble in Zarahemla and Bountiful
to defend themselves. About A.D. 16–18.*

1 And now it came to pass that in the sixteenth year from the coming of Christ,
Lachoneus, the governor of the land, received
an epistle from the leader and the governor
of this band of robbers; and these were the
words which were written, saying:

2 Lachoneus, most noble and chief governor
of the land, behold, I write this epistle unto
you, and do give unto you exceedingly great
praise because of your firmness, and also the
firmness of your people, in maintaining that
which ye suppose to be your right and liberty; yea, ye do stand well, as if ye were supported by the hand of a god, in the defence
of your liberty, and your property, and your
country, or that which ye do call so.

3 And it seemeth a pity unto me, most noble
Lachoneus, that ye should be so foolish and
vain as to suppose that ye can stand against
so many brave men who are at my command, who do now at this time stand in their

arms, and do await with great anxiety for the word—Go down upon the Nephites and destroy them.

4 And I, knowing of their unconquerable spirit, having proved them in the field of battle, and knowing of their everlasting hatred towards you because of the many wrongs which ye have done unto them, therefore if they should come down against you they would visit you with utter destruction.

5 Therefore I have written this epistle, sealing it with mine own hand, feeling for your welfare, because of your firmness in that which ye believe to be right, and your noble spirit in the field of battle.

6 Therefore I write unto you, desiring that ye would yield up unto this my people, your cities, your lands, and your possessions, rather than that they should visit you with the sword and that destruction should come upon you.

7 Or in other words, yield yourselves up unto us, and unite with us and become acquainted with our secret works, and become our brethren that ye may be like unto us—not our slaves, but our brethren and partners of all our substance.

8 And behold, I swear unto you, if ye will do this, with an oath, ye shall not be destroyed; but if ye will not do this, I swear unto you with an oath, that on the morrow month I will command that my armies shall come down against you, and they shall not stay their hand and shall spare not, but shall slay you, and shall let fall the sword upon you even until ye shall become extinct.

9 And behold, I am Giddianhi; and I am the governor of this the secret society of Gadianton; which society and the works thereof I know to be good; and they are of ancient date and they have been handed down unto us.

Why did Giddianhi swear an oath? (3:8) "These legal notices declaring war—in effect initiating a lawsuit between the gods of the respective sides, to be decided through the ordeal of battle—were to be lodged according to Jewish law at least two or three days before opening hostilities. Thus, it was consonant with such principles that Giddianhi gave Lachoneus until the 'morrow month' to consider his proposal before his armies would come down against the Nephites and make them 'extinct' (3 Nephi 3:8)" (Welch, "Law and War," 61). ✦

3 Nephi 3:11–26. Lachoneus Refuses to Surrender and Asks His People to Repent and Pray for Help

Why was it important to designate Giddianhi as a robber? (3:12) "Although there is only little difference between a thief and a robber in most modern minds, there were considerable differences between the two under ancient Near Eastern law. A thief (*ganab*) was usually a local person who stole from his neighbor. He was dealt with judicially. He was tried and punished civilly, most often by a court composed of his fellow townspeople. A robber, on the other hand, was treated as an outsider, as a brigand or highwayman. He was dealt with militarily, and he could be executed summarily" (Welch and Ward, "Thieves and Robbers," 248).

10 And I write this epistle unto you, Lachoneus, and I hope that ye will deliver up your lands and your possessions, without the shedding of blood, that this my people may recover their rights and government, who have dissented away from you because of your wickedness in retaining from them their rights of government, and except ye do this, I will avenge their wrongs. I am Giddianhi.

11 And now it came to pass when Lachoneus received this epistle he was exceedingly astonished, because of the boldness of Giddianhi demanding the possession of the land of the Nephites, and also of threatening the people and avenging the wrongs of those that had received no wrong, save it were they had wronged themselves by dissenting away unto those wicked and abominable robbers.

12 Now behold, this Lachoneus, the governor, was a just man, and could not be frightened by the demands and the threatenings of a robber; therefore he did not hearken to the epistle of Giddianhi, the governor of the robbers, but he did cause that his people should cry unto the Lord for strength against the time that the robbers should come down against them.

13 Yea, he sent a proclamation among all the people, that they should gather together their women, and their children, their flocks and their herds, and all their substance, save it were their land, unto one place.

14 And he caused that fortifications should be built round about them, and the strength thereof should be exceedingly great. And he caused that armies, both of the Nephites and of the Lamanites, or of all them who were numbered among the Nephites, should be placed as guards round about to watch them, and to guard them from the robbers day and night.

15 Yea, he said unto them: As the Lord liveth, except ye repent of all your iniquities, and cry unto the Lord, ye will in nowise be delivered out of the hands of those Gadianton robbers.

16 And so great and marvelous were the words and prophecies of Lachoneus that they did cause fear to come upon all the people; and they did exert themselves in their might to do according to the words of Lachoneus.

17 And it came to pass that Lachoneus did appoint chief captains over all the armies of the Nephites, to command them at the time that the robbers should come down out of the wilderness against them.

18 Now the chiefest among all the chief captains and the great commander of all the armies of the Nephites was appointed, and his name was Gidgiddoni.

19 Now it was the custom among all the Nephites to appoint for their chief captains, (save it were in their times of wickedness) some one that had the spirit of revelation and also prophecy; therefore, this Gidgiddoni was a great prophet among them, as also was the chief judge.

20 Now the people said unto Gidgiddoni: Pray unto the Lord, and let us go up upon the mountains and into the wilderness, that we may fall upon the robbers and destroy them in their own lands.

21 But Gidgiddoni saith unto them: The Lord forbid; for if we should go up against them the Lord would deliver us into their hands; therefore we will prepare ourselves in the center of our lands, and we will gather all our armies together, and we will not go against them, but we will wait till they shall come against us; therefore as the Lord liveth, if we do this he will deliver them into our hands.

How did Lachoneus respond to Giddianhi's threats? (3:15) "Though there is no direct response by Lachoneus to Giddianhi that would reveal a contrast in personalities, we are given part of Lachoneus's proclamation to his people. He calls on them to gather into one central location with their families and enough substance for seven years, and he says they must repent or they will 'in nowise be delivered out of the hands of those Gadianton robbers' (3 Ne. 3:15). His plan is successful. Giddianhi is slain, and the robbers are eventually defeated" (Rust, *Feasting on the Word*, 162).

Why were the Nephites careful to appoint a captain who had the spirit of revelation and prophecy? (3:19) "Religion and warfare were closely connected in the Book of Mormon. Certain elements of the Israelite patterns of 'holy war' were continued in the Book of Mormon, such as the important ancient idea that success in war was due fundamentally to the will of God and the righteousness of the people (Alma 2:28; 44:4–5; 50:21; 56:47; 57:36; 58:33; Morm. 2:26). Nephite armies consulted prophets before going to battle (Alma 16:5; 43:23–24; 3 Ne. 3:19) and entered into covenants with God before battle" (Ludlow, *Encyclopedia of Mormonism*, 1:163).

Why did Gidgiddoni refuse to attack the robbers "in their own lands"? (3:20–21) "Although the people had faith in Gidgiddoni as a prophet, they misunderstood his role in leading them. They assumed he could lead them in a successful offensive battle against the Gadianton robbers; however, he explained that the Lord would not help them launch a first-strike attack against their enemies but would only help them defend themselves" (Szink, "Just and True Record," 131). ☉

What do we know about the place where Lachoneus gathered his people? (3:23) "Northward, beyond the borders of the land of Zarahemla, lay an unnamed 'land which was between the land Zarahemla and the land Bountiful.' The place is mentioned only in 3 Nephi 3:23. (The line containing these words was omitted from the printed text for many years, apparently because of a typesetter's error, but has been replaced in the 1981 edition of the Book of Mormon.) The land of Bountiful as a whole seems to have been quite narrow, since Alma 22:31–33 describes it mostly as a zone that ran across the narrow neck of land. Little more is said about it" (Sorenson, *Ancient American Setting*, 12).

Why did Lachoneus assemble the Nephites together in one place? (3:25) In this intriguing account, the Nephites "gather together . . . unto one place" (v. 13), "in the center of [their] lands" (v. 21), "to the place which had been appointed" (v. 22), "in one body" (v. 25), and did "repent of all their sins" and "put up their prayers" to God (v. 25). This passage reminds us of Enoch's city, whose gathered people "were of one heart and one mind, and dwelt in righteousness" (Moses 7:18). In what way might these events forecast the last days when the Saints establish "a land of peace, a city of refuge, a place of safety for the saints of the Most High God"? (D&C 45:65).

22 And it came to pass in the seventeenth year, in the latter end of the year, the proclamation of Lachoneus had gone forth throughout all the face of the land, and they had taken their horses, and their chariots, and their cattle, and all their flocks, and their herds, and their grain, and all their substance, and did march forth by thousands and by tens of thousands, until they had all gone forth to the place which had been appointed that they should gather themselves together, to defend themselves against their enemies.

23 And the land which was appointed was the land of Zarahemla, and the land which was between the land Zarahemla and the land Bountiful, yea, to the line which was between the land Bountiful and the land Desolation.

24 And there were a great many thousand people who were called Nephites, who did gather themselves together in this land. Now Lachoneus did cause that they should gather themselves together in the land southward, because of the great curse which was upon the land northward.

25 And they did fortify themselves against their enemies; and they did dwell in one land, and in one body, and they did fear the words which had been spoken by Lachoneus, insomuch that they did repent of all their sins; and they did put up their prayers unto the Lord their God, that he would deliver them in the time that their enemies should come down against them to battle.

26 And they were exceedingly sorrowful because of their enemies. And Gidgiddoni did cause that they should make weapons of war of every kind, and they should be strong with armor, and with shields, and with bucklers, after the manner of his instruction.

CHAPTER 4

The Nephite armies defeat the Gadianton rob-bers—Giddianhi is slain, and his successor, Zemnarihah, is hanged—The Nephites praise the Lord for their victories. About A.D. 19–22.

1 And it came to pass that in the latter end of the eighteenth year those armies of robbers had prepared for battle, and began to come down and to sally forth from the hills, and out of the mountains, and the wilderness, and their strongholds, and their secret places, and began to take possession of the lands, both which were in the land south and which were in the land north, and began to take possession of all the lands which had been deserted by the Nephites, and the cities which had been left desolate.

2 But behold, there were no wild beasts nor game in those lands which had been deserted by the Nephites, and there was no game for the robbers save it were in the wilderness.

3 And the robbers could not exist save it were in the wilderness, for the want of food; for the Nephites had left their lands desolate, and had gathered their flocks and their herds and all their substance, and they were in one body.

4 Therefore, there was no chance for the robbers to plunder and to obtain food, save it were to come up in open battle against the Nephites; and the Nephites being in one body, and having so great a number, and having reserved for themselves provisions, and horses and cattle, and flocks of every kind, that they might subsist for the space of seven years, in the which time they did hope to destroy the robbers from off the face of the land; and thus the eighteenth year did pass away.

5 And it came to pass that in the nineteenth year Giddianhi found that it was expedient that he should go up to battle against the Nephites, for there was no way that they

3 Nephi 4:1–6. The Robbers Are Forced to Attack the Nephite Strongholds or Starve

How do we, like the Nephites, prepare for the coming struggles? (4:4) "For years we have been counseled to have on hand a year's supply of food. Yet there are some today who will not start storing until the Church comes out with a detailed monthly home storage program. Now, suppose that never happens. We still cannot say we have not been warned. . . . The revelation to produce and store food may be as essential to our temporal welfare today as boarding the ark was to the people in the days of Noah" (*Teachings of Ezra Taft Benson*, 265–66).

3 Nephi 4:7–29. A Great Battle Ensues, and Giddianhi Is Slain

Why were the Nephites prepared to meet their enemies? (4:7) Joseph Smith promised, "If we will but cleanse ourselves and covenant before God, to serve him, it is our privilege to have an assurance that God will protect us at all times" (*Far West Record*, 20). ⊕

Why do you think fearing God was a stronger motivator for the Nephites than fearing their brutal mortal enemy? (4:10) What kinds of things do people today tend to "fear" more than God? What choices have you seen people make who are more concerned about the people around them than they are about God? What are some of the tragic consequences of those choices?

Why was there so much slaughter in the war with the Gadianton robbers? (4:11) "The robbers in the land of Zarahemla were militant. They came as invading armies, in siege warfare (see 3 Nephi 4:16),

could subsist save it were to plunder and rob and murder.

6 And they durst not spread themselves upon the face of the land insomuch that they could raise grain, lest the Nephites should come upon them and slay them; therefore Giddianhi gave commandment unto his armies that in this year they should go up to battle against the Nephites.

7 And it came to pass that they did come up to battle; and it was in the sixth month; and behold, great and terrible was the day that they did come up to battle; and they were girded about after the manner of robbers; and they had a lamb-skin about their loins, and they were dyed in blood, and their heads were shorn, and they had head-plates upon them; and great and terrible was the appearance of the armies of Giddianhi, because of their armor, and because of their being dyed in blood.

8 And it came to pass that the armies of the Nephites, when they saw the appearance of the army of Giddianhi, had all fallen to the earth, and did lift their cries to the Lord their God, that he would spare them and deliver them out of the hands of their enemies.

9 And it came to pass that when the armies of Giddianhi saw this they began to shout with a loud voice, because of their joy, for they had supposed that the Nephites had fallen with fear because of the terror of their armies.

10 But in this thing they were disappointed, for the Nephites did not fear them; but they did fear their God and did supplicate him for protection; therefore, when the armies of Giddianhi did rush upon them they were prepared to meet them; yea, in the strength of the Lord they did receive them.

11 And the battle commenced in this the sixth month; and great and terrible was the battle thereof, yea, great and terrible was the slaughter thereof, insomuch that there never was known so great a slaughter among all the people of Lehi since he left Jerusalem.

12 And notwithstanding the threatenings and the oaths which Giddianhi had made, behold, the Nephites did beat them, insomuch that they did fall back from before them.

13 And it came to pass that Gidgiddoni commanded that his armies should pursue them as far as the borders of the wilderness, and that they should not spare any that should fall into their hands by the way; and thus they did pursue them and did slay them, to the borders of the wilderness, even until they had fulfilled the commandment of Gidgiddoni.

14 And it came to pass that Giddianhi, who had stood and fought with boldness, was pursued as he fled; and being weary because of his much fighting he was overtaken and slain. And thus was the end of Giddianhi the robber.

15 And it came to pass that the armies of the Nephites did return again to their place of security. And it came to pass that this nineteenth year did pass away, and the robbers did not come again to battle; neither did they come again in the twentieth year.

16 And in the twenty and first year they did not come up to battle, but they came up on all sides to lay siege round about the people of Nephi; for they did suppose that if they should cut off the people of Nephi from their lands, and should hem them in on every side, and if they should cut them off from all their outward privileges, that they could cause them to yield themselves up according to their wishes.

17 Now they had appointed unto themselves another leader, whose name was Zemnarihah; therefore it was Zemnarihah that did cause that this siege should take place.

with military power capable of defying 'whole armies' (Helaman 11:32; cf. 3 Nephi 2:11, 17; 4:1, 11). They suffered from shortages of supplies, for they, like the Near Eastern robbers, lived off the land (see 3 Nephi 4:3, 19–20). Their military strength was terrifying—they were the most feared of all Nephite enemies. Mormon identifies them as the primary cause of the overthrow and almost the entire destruction of the Nephites (see Helaman 2:13)" (Welch, "Law and War," 89).

What lessons can we learn from the Nephites about the importance of preparation? (4:16–20) The Lord has revealed that like the Nephites we "shall be gathered in unto one place upon the face of this land, to prepare our hearts and be prepared in all things against the day when tribulation and desolation are sent forth upon the wicked" (D&C 29:8). No wonder He later promised: "If ye are prepared ye shall not fear" (D&C 38:30).

18 But behold, this was an advantage to the Nephites; for it was impossible for the robbers to lay siege sufficiently long to have any effect upon the Nephites, because of their much provision which they had laid up in store,

19 And because of the scantiness of provisions among the robbers; for behold, they had nothing save it were meat for their subsistence, which meat they did obtain in the wilderness;

20 And it came to pass that the wild game became scarce in the wilderness insomuch that the robbers were about to perish with hunger.

21 And the Nephites were continually marching out by day and by night, and falling upon their armies, and cutting them off by thousands and by tens of thousands.

22 And thus it became the desire of the people of Zemnarihah to withdraw from their design, because of the great destruction which came upon them by night and by day.

23 And it came to pass that Zemnarihah did give command unto his people that they should withdraw themselves from the siege, and march into the furthermost parts of the land northward.

24 And now, Gidgiddoni being aware of their design, and knowing of their weakness because of the want of food, and the great slaughter which had been made among them, therefore he did send out his armies in the night-time, and did cut off the way of their retreat, and did place his armies in the way of their retreat.

25 And this did they do in the night-time, and got on their march beyond the robbers, so that on the morrow, when the robbers began their march, they were met by the armies of the Nephites both in their front and in their rear.

26 And the robbers who were on the south were also cut off in their places of retreat. And all these things were done by command of Gidgiddoni.

27 And there were many thousands who did yield themselves up prisoners unto the Nephites, and the remainder of them were slain.

28 And their leader, Zemnarihah, was taken and hanged upon a tree, yea, even upon the top thereof until he was dead. And when they had hanged him until he was dead they did fell the tree to the earth, and did cry with a loud voice, saying:

29 May the Lord preserve his people in righteousness and in holiness of heart, that they may cause to be felled to the earth all who shall seek to slay them because of power and secret combinations, even as this man hath been felled to the earth.

30 And they did rejoice and cry again with one voice, saying: May the God of Abraham, and the God of Isaac, and the God of Jacob, protect this people in righteousness, so long as they shall call on the name of their God for protection.

31 And it came to pass that they did break forth, all as one, in singing, and praising their God for the great thing which he had done for them, in preserving them from falling into the hands of their enemies.

32 Yea, they did cry: Hosanna to the Most High God. And they did cry: Blessed be the name of the Lord God Almighty, the Most High God.

33 And their hearts were swollen with joy, unto the gushing out of many tears, because of the great goodness of God in delivering them out of the hands of their enemies; and they knew it was because of their repentance and their humility that they had been delivered from an everlasting destruction.

Why did they chop down the tree after hanging Zemnarihah? (4:28–29) John W. Welch pointed out that the hanging of this war criminal "upon a tree . . . even upon the top thereof" and then the chopping down of the tree with the dead criminal still in it, were elements of a "public execution [that] followed ancient ceremony and law" ("Execution of Zemnarihah," 250). ◉

3 Nephi 4:30–33. Victorious Nephites Praise God for Their Success

Why are their hearts "swollen with joy"? (4:33) Through this experience, the Nephites discovered that God is true to His word. If they "repent" and "cry unto the Lord" they would be delivered from their enemy (see 3 Nephi 3:15). "After the victory, the Nephites [here] recognized the source of their strength. . . . That recognition on the part of the Nephites is important because it is plain that they knew what they were doing and what God had done" (Riddle, "Days of Wickedness and Vengeance," 193).

CHAPTER 5

The Nephites repent and forsake their sins—Mormon writes the history of his people and declares the everlasting word to them—Israel will be gathered in from her long dispersion. About A.D. *22–26.*

3 Nephi 5:1–3. The Nephites Repent, Believe Signs, and Return to God

How quickly can changing circumstances affect people's faith? (5:1–3) "Changing circumstances can . . . affect nearly a whole people's faith. . . . 'There was not a living soul among . . . the Nephites who did doubt in the least the words of all the holy prophets' (3 Nephi 5:1). . . .

"Now . . . 'There began to be great doubtings and disputations among the people, notwithstanding so many signs had been given' (3 Nephi 8:4).

"As I check the years of these two verses, I note that this decline happened in the space of a mere ten years or less! Circumstances changed from one in which 'not a living soul' doubted the prophecies to a time in which there were 'great doubtings.' It isn't very confidence inspiring, is it?" (Maxwell, *We Talk of Christ*, 64). ✚

3 Nephi 5:4–7. Secret Combinations Are Crushed

How effective was the Nephite treatment of the Gadianton criminals? (5:4–6) "The Nephite approach to the captured Gadianton members was remarkable in light of many trends in our present society. Modern societies expend millions of dollars trying to psychoanalyze and rehabilitate criminals. Notice the twofold approach of the Nephites, who understood the Gadianton conspiracy posed a real threat to both the government and the Church. The Nephites preached the gospel to the robbers to see if they would be converted. If converted, the Gadiantons were freed—a remarkable bit of jurisprudence in and of itself! If the Gadiantons refused to repent, they 'were condemned and punished according to the law'" (*Book of Mormon Student Manual* [1996], 113).

1 And now behold, there was not a living soul among all the people of the Nephites who did doubt in the least the words of all the holy prophets who had spoken; for they knew that it must needs be that they must be fulfilled.

2 And they knew that it must be expedient that Christ had come, because of the many signs which had been given, according to the words of the prophets; and because of the things which had come to pass already they knew that it must needs be that all things should come to pass according to that which had been spoken.

3 Therefore they did forsake all their sins, and their abominations, and their whoredoms, and did serve God with all diligence day and night.

4 And now it came to pass that when they had taken all the robbers prisoners, insomuch that none did escape who were not slain, they did cast their prisoners into prison, and did cause the word of God to be preached unto them; and as many as would repent of their sins and enter into a covenant that they would murder no more were set at liberty.

5 But as many as there were who did not enter into a covenant, and who did still continue to have those secret murders in their hearts, yea, as many as were found breathing out threatenings against their brethren were condemned and punished according to the law.

6 And thus they did put an end to all those wicked, and secret, and abominable combinations, in the which there was so much wickedness, and so many murders committed.

7 And thus had the twenty and second year passed away, and the twenty and third year also, and the twenty and fourth, and the twenty and fifth; and thus had twenty and five years passed away.

8 And there had many things transpired which, in the eyes of some, would be great and marvelous; nevertheless, they cannot all be written in this book; yea, this book cannot contain even a hundredth part of what was done among so many people in the space of twenty and five years;

9 But behold there are records which do contain all the proceedings of this people; and a shorter but true account was given by Nephi.

10 Therefore I have made my record of these things according to the record of Nephi, which was engraven on the plates which were called the plates of Nephi.

11 And behold, I do make the record on plates which I have made with mine own hands.

12 And behold, I am called Mormon, being called after the land of Mormon, the land in which Alma did establish the church among the people, yea, the first church which was established among them after their transgression.

13 Behold, I am a disciple of Jesus Christ, the Son of God. I have been called of him to declare his word among his people, that they might have everlasting life.

14 And it hath become expedient that I, according to the will of God, that the prayers of those who have gone hence, who were the holy ones, should be fulfilled according to their faith, should make a record of these things which have been done—

15 Yea, a small record of that which hath taken place from the time that Lehi left Jerusalem, even down until the present time.

3 Nephi 5:8–20. Mormon Relates Record-Keeping Practices and Testimony

What does Mormon explain about his record? (5:8–10) "When Mormon abridged these records, he noted that he could not write a 'hundredth part' of their proceedings (Words of Mormon 1:5). Thus, historical aspects of the book assume secondary significance. . . .

"This explanation was repeated five more times (see Jacob 3:13; Helaman 3:14; 3 Nephi 5:8; 26:6; Ether 15:33). Jacob, who received the plates from his brother Nephi, provided additional insight, noting that he 'should not touch, save it were lightly, concerning the history of this people,' but that he was to touch upon sacred or great things 'as much as it were possible, for Christ's sake, and for the sake of our people' (Jacob 1:2, 4)" (Nelson, "Testimony of the Book of Mormon," 69, note 7).

How does being a disciple influence our service? (5:13) "We are engaged in the work of the Lord Jesus Christ. We, like those of olden times, have answered His call. We are on His errand. We shall succeed in the solemn charge given by Mormon to declare the Lord's word among His people. He wrote: [see 3 Ne 5:13]. May we ever remember the truth, 'Who honors God, God honors'" (Monson, "Who Honors God, God Honors," 50).

Why did Mormon introduce himself as the editor? (5:16–18) "A careful analysis of Mormon's statements suggests that both his discussion of records and his self-introduction in 3 Nephi 5 can be seen as part of the same narrative goal—to legitimize both the record and the record keepers of the Book of Mormon . . . Mormon likewise certified his own record as being 'just and true' (3 Nephi 5:18) . . . and that his record of his own day was "of the things which I have seen with mine own eyes" (v. 17). This language was clearly intended to establish Mormon as a credible abridger and as a primary witness, perhaps analogous to the Eight Witnesses to the Book of Mormon who saw and hefted the plates for themselves" (Book of Mormon Central, "Why Did Mormon Introduce Himself in 3 Nephi 5?").

Mormon Abridges the Plates

What did Mormon's appreciation for a righteous ancestor do for him? (5:20) Do you have a righteous ancestor whose life has inspired you? Which ancestor led your family to the Church? Which one has influenced your relationship with the Lord?

16 Therefore I do make my record from the accounts which have been given by those who were before me, until the commencement of my day;

17 And then I do make a record of the things which I have seen with mine own eyes.

18 And I know the record which I make to be a just and a true record; nevertheless there are many things which, according to our language, we are not able to write.

19 And now I make an end of my saying, which is of myself, and proceed to give my account of the things which have been before me.

20 I am Mormon, and a pure descendant of Lehi. I have reason to bless my God and my Savior Jesus Christ, that he brought our fathers out of the land of Jerusalem, (and no one knew it save it were himself and those whom he brought out of that land) and that he hath given me and my people so much knowledge unto the salvation of our souls.

21 Surely he hath blessed the house of Jacob, and hath been merciful unto the seed of Joseph.

22 And insomuch as the children of Lehi have kept his commandments he hath blessed them and prospered them according to his word.

23 Yea, and surely shall he again bring a remnant of the seed of Joseph to the knowledge of the Lord their God.

24 And as surely as the Lord liveth, will he gather in from the four quarters of the earth all the remnant of the seed of Jacob, who are scattered abroad upon all the face of the earth.

25 And as he hath covenanted with all the house of Jacob, even so shall the covenant wherewith he hath covenanted with the house of Jacob be fulfilled in his own due time, unto the restoring all the house of Jacob unto the knowledge of the covenant that he hath covenanted with them.

26 And then shall they know their Redeemer, who is Jesus Christ, the Son of God; and then shall they be gathered in from the four quarters of the earth unto their own lands, from whence they have been dispersed; yea, as the Lord liveth so shall it be. Amen.

CHAPTER 6

The Nephites prosper—Pride, wealth, and class distinctions arise—The Church is rent with dissensions—Satan leads the people in open rebellion—Many prophets cry repentance and are slain—Their murderers conspire to take over the government. About A.D. 26–30.

1 And now it came to pass that the people of the Nephites did all return to their own lands in the twenty and sixth year, every man, with his family, his flocks and his herds, his horses and his cattle, and all things whatsoever did belong unto them.

3 Nephi 5:21–26. Mormon Prophesies That the House of Israel and Lehi's Family Will Be Gathered

Why does the Book of Mormon often refer to the "four quarters of the earth"? (5:24) "Book of Mormon writers commonly spoke of their land as being divided into four quarters. . . . Accordingly they described each area of their lands by reference to the cardinal directions, such as 'the land northward' and 'the land southward.' Recent research . . . shows that similar ideas existed in pre-Columbian America and the Old World" (Wirth, "Four Quarters," 145). ⊕

What role does Mormon's record play in gathering Israel? (5:26) President Russell M. Nelson taught: "The Book of Mormon is central to this work. It declares the doctrine of the gathering. It causes people to learn about Jesus Christ, to believe His gospel, and to join His Church. In fact, if there were no Book of Mormon, the promised gathering of Israel would not occur" ("Gathering of Scattered Israel," 80). ⊕

3 Nephi 6:1–9. The Nephites Prosper in Peace

2 And it came to pass that they had not eaten up all their provisions; therefore they did take with them all that they had not devoured, of all their grain of every kind, and their gold, and their silver, and all their precious things, and they did return to their own lands and their possessions, both on the north and on the south, both on the land northward and on the land southward.

3 And they granted unto those robbers who had entered into a covenant to keep the peace of the land, who were desirous to remain Lamanites, lands, according to their numbers, that they might have, with their labors, wherewith to subsist upon; and thus they did establish peace in all the land.

4 And they began again to prosper and to wax great; and the twenty and sixth and seventh years passed away, and there was great order in the land; and they had formed their laws according to equity and justice.

5 And now there was nothing in all the land to hinder the people from prospering continually, except they should fall into transgression.

6 And now it was Gidgiddoni, and the judge, Lachoneus, and those who had been appointed leaders, who had established this great peace in the land.

7 And it came to pass that there were many cities built anew, and there were many old cities repaired.

8 And there were many highways cast up, and many roads made, which led from city to city, and from land to land, and from place to place.

9 And thus passed away the twenty and eighth year, and the people had continual peace.

10 But it came to pass in the twenty and ninth year there began to be some disputings among the people; and some were lifted up unto pride and boastings because of their

In what ways do you think transgression stops people from "prospering continually"? (6:5) What do you think it means to prosper continually? How can a person be wealthy and still righteous? What difference might there be between being wealthy and prospering continually?

3 Nephi 6:10–19. The Nephites Become Lifted Up in Pride

Why is pride such a serious problem? (6:10–12) "Pride adversely affects all our relationships—our relationship with God and His servants, between husband and wife, parent and child, employer and employee, teacher and student, and all mankind. Our degree

exceedingly great riches, yea, even unto great persecutions;

11 For there were many merchants in the land, and also many lawyers, and many officers.

12 And the people began to be distinguished by ranks, according to their riches and their chances for learning; yea, some were ignorant because of their poverty, and others did receive great learning because of their riches.

13 Some were lifted up in pride, and others were exceedingly humble; some did return railing for railing, while others would receive railing and persecution and all manner of afflictions, and would not turn and revile again, but were humble and penitent before God.

14 And thus there became a great inequality in all the land, insomuch that the church began to be broken up; yea, insomuch that in the thirtieth year the church was broken up in all the land save it were among a few of the Lamanites who were converted unto the true faith; and they would not depart from it, for they were firm, and steadfast, and immovable, willing with all diligence to keep the commandments of the Lord.

15 Now the cause of this iniquity of the people was this—Satan had great power, unto the stirring up of the people to do all manner of iniquity, and to the puffing them up with pride, tempting them to seek for power, and authority, and riches, and the vain things of the world.

of pride determines how we treat our God and our brothers and sisters. Christ wants to lift us to where He is. Do we desire to do the same for others?

"Pride fades our feelings of sonship to God and brotherhood to man. It separates and divides us by 'ranks,' according to our 'riches' and our 'chances for learning' (3 Ne. 6:12). Unity is impossible for a proud people, and unless we are one we are not the Lord's" (Benson, "Beware of Pride," 6). ●

How do we avoid pride and become united? (6:12) "Where people have that Spirit with them, we may expect harmony. The Spirit puts the testimony of truth in our hearts, which unifies those who share that testimony. The Spirit of God never generates contention (see 3 Ne. 11:29). It never generates the feelings of distinctions between people which lead to strife (see Joseph F. Smith, *Gospel Doctrine*, 13th ed. [1963], 131). It leads to personal peace and a feeling of union with others. It unifies souls. A unified family, a unified Church, and a world at peace depend on unified souls" (Eyring, "That We May Be One," 67). ●

How can someone humbly endure persecution? (6:13) "Most of us will experience injustice. But the Savior's Atonement can redeem us not only from our own sins but also from the pain caused by the sins of other people. 'And he cometh into the world that he may save all men if they will hearken unto his voice; for behold, he suffereth the pains of all men, yea, the pains of every living creature, both men, women, and children, who belong to the family of Adam' (2 Ne. 9:21). If we meekly and humbly strive to be peaceful and forgiving, the Holy Ghost will enter our hearts, melt the pain of insults and injuries, and quench our resentment and desire for revenge" (Dunlop, "Book of Mormon Principles: Turning the Other Cheek," 34).

Why are vain desires among Satan's most common tools? (6:15–16) "As so often happens, the people rejected the Lord. Pride became commonplace. Dishonesty and immorality were widespread. Secret combinations flourished because, as Helaman tells us, the Gadianton robbers 'had seduced the more part of the righteous until they had come down to believe in their works and partake of their spoils' (Hel. 6:38). 'The people began to be distinguished by ranks, according to their riches and their chances for learning' (3 Ne. 6:12). And 'Satan had great power, unto the stirring up of the people to do all manner of iniquity, . . .' even as today (3 Ne. 6:15)" (Benson, "Savior's Visit to America," 4).

Why is Satan allowed to tempt us in mortality? (6:17) "Surely it should give us more pause . . . to think of how casually we sometimes give to him who could not control his own ego in the pre-mortal world such awful control over our egos here. We often let the adversary do *indirectly* now what we refused to let him do *directly* then.

"Thus we can expect no immunity from either trial or temptation, because these are the common lot of mankind. Mortality without the dimension of tempta-tion or trial would not be full proving; it would be a school with soft credits and no hard courses. These features of mortality were among the very conditions we agreed to before we undertook this mortal experi-ence" (Maxwell, *We Will Prove Them Herewith*, 45).

Why is it ironic when a person willfully submits to the devil's will? (6:18) "Whereas the Spirit of Christ is typified by his submission to the will of the Father, the spirit of Lucifer was captured in his rebellion against God. Again, it is ironic that many who refuse to submit to the will of our Father in Heaven bow so submis-sively to the will of the father of darkness" (McConkie, et al., *Doctrinal Commentary*, 4:27–28).

3 Nephi 6:20–30. The Wicked Kill the Prophets and Set Up Secret Combinations to Destroy the People of God

Typically, how do those with worldly power respond to the prophetic invitation to repent? (6:20–23) Like their counterparts in the New Testament, these Nephite leaders reject the Lord's anointed. "The implications of the Savior's chastisement of the lawyers, priests, and Pharisees runs deep in the lives of every generation, as the Book of Mormon testifies. Rejecting the 'key of knowledge' and 'hindering' others who are seeking the plan of salvation is a serious transgression. . . . Nor is it a wise strategy to reject the reality of a Supreme Being in order to become a law unto ourselves so that we will have no one to answer to except ourselves (D&C 1:15–17). We may be unable to escape choosing between the twin trinities of governance—power, pleasure, and possessions versus sacrifice, suffering, and service" (Flinders, "The Key of Knowledge," 31).

16 And thus Satan did lead away the hearts of the people to do all manner of iniquity; therefore they had enjoyed peace but a few years.

17 And thus, in the commencement of the thirtieth year—the people having been deliv-ered up for the space of a long time to be carried about by the temptations of the devil whithersoever he desired to carry them, and to do whatsoever iniquity he desired they should—and thus in the commencement of this, the thirtieth year, they were in a state of awful wickedness.

18 Now they did not sin ignorantly, for they knew the will of God concerning them, for it had been taught unto them; therefore they did wilfully rebel against God.

19 And now it was in the days of Lachoneus, the son of Lachoneus, for Lachoneus did fill the seat of his father and did govern the people that year.

20 And there began to be men inspired from heaven and sent forth, standing among the people in all the land, preaching and testify-ing boldly of the sins and iniquities of the people, and testifying unto them concerning the redemption which the Lord would make for his people, or in other words, the resur-rection of Christ; and they did testify boldly of his death and sufferings.

21 Now there were many of the people who were exceedingly angry because of those who testified of these things; and those who were angry were chiefly the chief judges, and they who had been high priests and lawyers; yea, all those who were lawyers were angry with those who testified of these things.

22 Now there was no lawyer nor judge nor high priest that could have power to condemn any one to death save their condemnation was signed by the governor of the land.

23 Now there were many of those who testified of the things pertaining to Christ who testified boldly, who were taken and put to death secretly by the judges, that the knowledge of their death came not unto the governor of the land until after their death.

24 Now behold, this was contrary to the laws of the land, that any man should be put to death except they had power from the governor of the land—

25 Therefore a complaint came up unto the land of Zarahemla, to the governor of the land, against these judges who had condemned the prophets of the Lord unto death, not according to the law.

26 Now it came to pass that they were taken and brought up before the judge, to be judged of the crime which they had done, according to the law which had been given by the people.

27 Now it came to pass that those judges had many friends and kindreds; and the remainder, yea, even almost all the lawyers and the high priests, did gather themselves together, and unite with the kindreds of those judges who were to be tried according to the law.

28 And they did enter into a covenant one with another, yea, even into that covenant which was given by them of old, which covenant was given and administered by the devil, to combine against all righteousness.

29 Therefore they did combine against the people of the Lord, and enter into a covenant to destroy them, and to deliver those who were guilty of murder from the grasp of justice, which was about to be administered according to the law.

How is the Church affected when people unite in wickedness? (6:27–30) "Shortly before the appearance of the resurrected Savior in the New World, apostate high priests attempted to set up a king in alliance with officials who were in a position to administer the government's economic policies (3 Nephi 6:27, 30). As a result, the church as a moderating social influence was effectively destroyed" (Christenson, "Nephite Trade Networks and the Dangers of a Class Society," 235). ⊕

30 And they did set at defiance the law and the rights of their country; and they did covenant one with another to destroy the governor, and to establish a king over the land, that the land should no more be at liberty but should be subject unto kings.

CHAPTER 7

The chief judge is murdered, the government is destroyed, and the people divide into tribes—Jacob, an anti-Christ, becomes king of a secret combination—Nephi preaches repentance and faith in Christ—Angels minister to him daily, and he raises his brother from the dead—Many repent and are baptized. About A.D. 30–33.

1 Now behold, I will show unto you that they did not establish a king over the land; but in this same year, yea, the thirtieth year, they did destroy upon the judgment-seat, yea, did murder the chief judge of the land.

2 And the people were divided one against another; and they did separate one from another into tribes, every man according to his family and his kindred and friends; and thus they did destroy the government of the land.

3 And every tribe did appoint a chief or a leader over them; and thus they became tribes and leaders of tribes.

4 Now behold, there was no man among them save he had much family and many kindreds and friends; therefore their tribes became exceedingly great.

5 Now all this was done, and there were no wars as yet among them; and all this iniquity had come upon the people because they did yield themselves unto the power of Satan.

6 And the regulations of the government were destroyed, because of the secret combination of the friends and kindreds of those who murdered the prophets.

3 Nephi 7:1–8. The Government of Judges Is Destroyed, and the People Divide into Tribes

What does this division of the people into tribes teach us about their culture? (7:2–4) "The descendants of Lehi's party consistently divided themselves into seven tribes [see Jacob 1:13; 4 Nephi 1:38; Mormon 1:8]. . . . Significantly, these references come from the earliest as well as the latest periods of Nephite history, indicating the importance and persistence of kinship as a basic element in this society. . . .

"Though different forms of government might come and go in Nephite history, the underlying family fabric of this society remained permanent. Even in the darkest days of political collapse, all the people still had 'much family,' and the tribal structure was present to supplant the collapsed government (see 3 Nephi 7:2–4)" (Sorenson et al., "Seven Tribes," 93–94).

7 And they did cause a great contention in the land, insomuch that the more righteous part of the people had nearly all become wicked; yea, there were but few righteous men among them.

8 And thus six years had not passed away since the more part of the people had turned from their righteousness, like the dog to his vomit, or like the sow to her wallowing in the mire.

9 Now this secret combination, which had brought so great iniquity upon the people, did gather themselves together, and did place at their head a man whom they did call Jacob;

10 And they did call him their king; therefore he became a king over this wicked band; and he was one of the chiefest who had given his voice against the prophets who testified of Jesus.

11 And it came to pass that they were not so strong in number as the tribes of the people, who were united together save it were their leaders did establish their laws, every one according to his tribe; nevertheless they were enemies; notwithstanding they were not a righteous people, yet they were united in the hatred of those who had entered into a covenant to destroy the government.

12 Therefore, Jacob seeing that their enemies were more numerous than they, he being the king of the band, therefore he commanded his people that they should take their flight into the northernmost part of the land, and there build up unto themselves a kingdom, until they were joined by dissenters, (for he flattered them that there would be many dissenters) and they become sufficiently strong to contend with the tribes of the people; and they did so.

13 And so speedy was their march that it could not be impeded until they had gone

3 Nephi 7:9–14. The Secret Combinations Flee to the North As the Other Tribes Unite to Defend Themselves

How were these tribes governed? (7:11) "The tribal and kinship structure had always been in place (see Jacob 1:13). . . . What we see in 3 Nephi 7 is a default government, not centralized like that formerly headed by kings or chief judges, yet sufficiently capable to enact and administer 'their laws, every one according to his tribe' (3 Nephi 7:11). A version of that dispersed political structure surely continued following the appearance of Jesus Christ, because nothing is said of any central government from then until possibly the time of Mormon (see Mormon 2:2)" (Sorenson, "How Could Joseph Smith Write So Accurately about Ancient American Civilization?" 284–85).

forth out of the reach of the people. And thus ended the thirtieth year; and thus were the affairs of the people of Nephi.

14 And it came to pass in the thirty and first year that they were divided into tribes, every man according to his family, kindred and friends; nevertheless they had come to an agreement that they would not go to war one with another; but they were not united as to their laws, and their manner of government, for they were established according to the minds of those who were their chiefs and their leaders. But they did establish very strict laws that one tribe should not trespass against another, insomuch that in some degree they had peace in the land; nevertheless, their hearts were turned from the Lord their God, and they did stone the prophets and did cast them out from among them.

15 And it came to pass that Nephi—having been visited by angels and also the voice of the Lord, therefore having seen angels, and being eye-witness, and having had power given unto him that he might know concerning the ministry of Christ, and also being eye-witness to their quick return from righteousness unto their wickedness and abominations;

16 Therefore, being grieved for the hardness of their hearts and the blindness of their minds—went forth among them in that same year, and began to testify, boldly, repentance and remission of sins through faith on the Lord Jesus Christ.

17 And he did minister many things unto them; and all of them cannot be written, and a part of them would not suffice, therefore they are not written in this book. And Nephi did minister with power and with great authority.

18 And it came to pass that they were angry with him, even because he had greater power than they, for it were not possible that they

3 Nephi 7:15–20. Nephi Preaches with Great Power, and Many People Become Angry at Him

What are some ways angels minister to us? (7:15)
"The word 'angel' is used in the scriptures for any heavenly being bearing God's message. . . . The scriptures recite numerous instances where an angel appeared personally. Angelic appearances to Zacharias and Mary (see Luke 1) and to King Benjamin and Nephi, the grandson of Helaman (see Mosiah 3:2; 3 Ne. 7:17–18) are only a few examples. . . .

"But the ministering of angels can also be unseen. Angelic messages can be delivered by a voice or merely by thoughts or feelings communicated to the mind. President John Taylor described 'the action of the angels, or messengers of God, upon our minds, so that the heart can conceive . . . revelations from the eternal world'" (Oaks, "Aaronic Priesthood and the Sacrament," 38–39). ✛

could disbelieve his words, for so great was his faith on the Lord Jesus Christ that angels did minister unto him daily.

19 And in the name of Jesus did he cast out devils and unclean spirits; and even his brother did he raise from the dead, after he had been stoned and suffered death by the people.

20 And the people saw it, and did witness of it, and were angry with him because of his power; and he did also do many more miracles, in the sight of the people, in the name of Jesus.

21 And it came to pass that the thirty and first year did pass away, and there were but few who were converted unto the Lord; but as many as were converted did truly signify unto the people that they had been visited by the power and Spirit of God, which was in Jesus Christ, in whom they believed.

22 And as many as had devils cast out from them, and were healed of their sicknesses and their infirmities, did truly manifest unto the people that they had been wrought upon by the Spirit of God, and had been healed; and they did show forth signs also and did do some miracles among the people.

What does Nephi's priesthood power tell us about him and others who wish to gain the same power? (7:19) "I know of a great man who held his dead son in his arms, and said, 'In the name of Jesus Christ and by the power and authority of the Holy Melchizedek Priesthood, I command you to live.' And the dead boy opened his eyes.

"This great brother could not have possibly done that had he been looking at a pornographic piece of material a few nights before or if he had been involved in any other transgression of that kind. The priesthood has to have a pure conduit to operate" (Featherstone, "Self-Inflicting Purge," 66). See commentary on 3 Nephi 8:1.

What do we learn about signs and conversion from the people's response to Nephi's miracles? (7:20) "The prophet Nephi of approximately A.D. 32 was so righteous and had such great faith that 'angels did minister unto him daily' (3 Nephi 7:18). Although Nephi used this power to try to bless his people (he even raised his own brother from the dead), the wicked people 'were angry with him because of his power' (3 Nephi 7:20). Thus, despite the great signs and miracles that had been performed for the people, they still disbelieved. Once again this indicates that signs do not convert unless the conversion of faith follows" (Ludlow, *Companion to Your Study of the Book of Mormon*, 258).

3 Nephi 7:21–26. Many People Believe Nephi and Are Baptized

What is true conversion unto the Lord? (7:21) President Marion G. Romney explained that conversion means "to turn from one belief or course of action to another. Conversion is a spiritual and moral change. Converted implies not merely mental acceptance of Jesus and his teachings but also a motivating faith in him and his gospel. A faith which works a transformation, an actual change in one's understanding of life's meaning and in his allegiance to God in interest, in thought, and in conduct" (in *Book of Mormon Student Manual* [2009], 294).

Why did the Lord once again send His prophet to preach to the Nephites? (7:23) "In this final state of wickedness the Lord sought yet a third time to recover his people, the Nephites. He sent his faithful servant Nephi, and others, to bear a final witness before the day of wrath and vengeance. . . .

"The few who were righteous hearkened to the words of the prophets and Nephi; the many who were wicked stonily rejected both them and God, ultimately rejecting their own redemption. Now it was the time for the Lord to do his great work of vengeance" (Riddle, "Days of Wickedness and Vengeance," 199).

3 Nephi 8:1–4. The People Begin to Doubt and Argue about the Signs of Christ's Crucifixion

What do we learn from Nephi about personal righteousness? (8:1) "It is an eternal principle that the powers of heaven are inseparably connected with righteousness (D&C 121:36). The working of miracles in the name of Jesus is an evidence that one is 'cleansed every whit from his iniquity' and thus worthy of the companionship of the Holy Ghost and the powers of God. The wonders of God—the signs and miracles which always attend a dispensation of the gospel—require righteousness in the human instrument (see D&C 50:27–30)" (McConkie et al., *Doctrinal Commentary*, 4:35). ☉

How does the detailed account of darkness in the New World testify as a witness of the death of Christ? (8:3) "No single historical event in the whole Book of Mormon account is recorded in so great detail or such extended length as the fulfillment of the signs signifying that Jesus had been lifted up upon the cross

23 Thus passed away the thirty and second year also. And Nephi did cry unto the people in the commencement of the thirty and third year; and he did preach unto them repentance and remission of sins.

24 Now I would have you to remember also, that there were none who were brought unto repentance who were not baptized with water.

25 Therefore, there were ordained of Nephi, men unto this ministry, that all such as should come unto them should be baptized with water, and this as a witness and a testimony before God, and unto the people, that they had repented and received a remission of their sins.

26 And there were many in the commencement of this year that were baptized unto repentance; and thus the more part of the year did pass away.

CHAPTER 8

Tempests, earthquakes, fires, whirlwinds, and physical upheavals attest the crucifixion of Christ—Many people are destroyed—Darkness covers the land for three days—Those who remain bemoan their fate. About A.D. 33–34.

1 And now it came to pass that according to our record, and we know our record to be true, for behold, it was a just man who did keep the record—for he truly did many miracles in the name of Jesus; and there was not any man who could do a miracle in the name of Jesus save he were cleansed every whit from his iniquity—

2 And now it came to pass, if there was no mistake made by this man in the reckoning of our time, the thirty and third year had passed away;

3 And the people began to look with great earnestness for the sign which had been given by the prophet Samuel, the Lamanite, yea, for

the time that there should be darkness for the space of three days over the face of the land.

4 And there began to be great doubtings and disputations among the people, notwithstanding so many signs had been given.

5 And it came to pass in the thirty and fourth year, in the first month, on the fourth day of the month, there arose a great storm, such an one as never had been known in all the land.

6 And there was also a great and terrible tempest; and there was terrible thunder, insomuch that it did shake the whole earth as if it was about to divide asunder.

7 And there were exceedingly sharp lightnings, such as never had been known in all the land.

8 And the city of Zarahemla did take fire.

9 And the city of Moroni did sink into the depths of the sea, and the inhabitants thereof were drowned.

10 And the earth was carried up upon the city of Moronihah, that in the place of the city there became a great mountain.

11 And there was a great and terrible destruction in the land southward.

12 But behold, there was a more great and terrible destruction in the land northward; for behold, the whole face of the land was changed, because of the tempest and the whirlwinds, and the thunderings and the lightnings, and the exceedingly great quaking of the whole earth;

13 And the highways were broken up, and the level roads were spoiled, and many smooth places became rough.

14 And many great and notable cities were sunk, and many were burned, and many were shaken till the buildings thereof had fallen to the earth, and the inhabitants thereof were slain, and the places were left desolate.

and had voluntarily laid down his life for the world" (McConkie, *Promised Messiah*, 542). ●

3 Nephi 8:5–18. A Great Storm Arises, and There Is a Great Earthquake in Which Many Cities Are Destroyed

How does the Book of Mormon inform us about which month the Crucifixion occurred? (8:5) "According to the Nephite calendar system, the Savior was crucified 'in the thirty and fourth year, in the first month, on the fourth day of the month' (3 Nephi 8:5). Although we are not certain when the first month of the Nephite calendar would occur, if the Nephites were using the same calendar system as the Hebrews, the first month would be in the spring of the year sometime between about the middle of March and the middle of April" (Ludlow, *Companion to Your Study of the Book of Mormon*, 259).

What is the historical evidence for the events described in 3 Nephi 8? (8:11–18) "The account of the great destruction given in 3 Nephi 8 finds remarkable parallels with what modern seismology and vulcanology show about cataclysmic geological events and with historical reports of such catastrophes. Yet Joseph Smith never saw a volcano and never experienced a significant earthquake, nor is it likely he had read any substantial literature on the subject.

"But the region of Mesoamerica . . . is a place of continuing volcanic and seismic activity" (Peterson, "Mounting Evidence for the Book of Mormon," 22). ●

15 And there were some cities which remained; but the damage thereof was exceedingly great, and there were many in them who were slain.

16 And there were some who were carried away in the whirlwind; and whither they went no man knoweth, save they know that they were carried away.

17 And thus the face of the whole earth became deformed, because of the tempests, and the thunderings, and the lightnings, and the quaking of the earth.

18 And behold, the rocks were rent in twain; they were broken up upon the face of the whole earth, insomuch that they were found in broken fragments, and in seams and in cracks, upon all the face of the land.

19 And it came to pass that when the thunderings, and the lightnings, and the storm, and the tempest, and the quakings of the earth did cease—for behold, they did last for about the space of three hours; and it was said by some that the time was greater; nevertheless,

3 Nephi 8:19–25. A Thick Darkness Covers the Land for Three Days

What might have caused this darkness? (8:19–22)
"The ash from a volcano can rise to great heights (many thousands of feet) and then spread out in the stratosphere to cover a large region with an impenetrable cloud of dust. . . . Volcanic ash, smoke, and gases, along with dust and debris rising into the air from a large earthquake, could have produced the 'vapor

The Coming of Christ to the Nephites Is a Pattern of His Second Coming

"In the Book of Mormon we find a pattern for preparing for the Second Coming. A major portion of the book centers on the few decades just prior to Christ's coming to America. By careful study of that time period, we can determine why some were destroyed in the terrible judgments that preceded His coming and what brought others to stand at the temple in the land of Bountiful and thrust their hands into the wounds of His hands and feet" (Benson, "Book of Mormon—Keystone of Our Religion," 6–7).

Christ's Visit to the Nephites	Events	Christ's Future Coming
3 Nephi 6:17–18; 7:7	Wickedness increases among the people.	Joseph Smith–Matthew 1:30
3 Nephi 7:14	People reject the prophets.	D&C 1:14
3 Nephi 8:4	Skepticism increases concerning Christ's coming.	D&C 45:26
3 Nephi 8:6, 10–19	Earthquakes and other disturbances accompany His coming.	D&C 45:48
3 Nephi 8:20–23	Darkness covers the earth.	D&C 45:42
3 Nephi 8:24, 25	Christ comes as a thief in the night.	2 Peter 3:10
3 Nephi 9:1–13; 10:12	The wicked are destroyed at His coming; the righteous are preserved.	D&C 29:11

(Adapted from *Book of Mormon Student Manual* [2009], 395.)

all these great and terrible things were done in about the space of three hours—and then behold, there was darkness upon the face of the land.

20 And it came to pass that there was thick darkness upon all the face of the land, insomuch that the inhabitants thereof who had not fallen could feel the vapor of darkness;

21 And there could be no light, because of the darkness, neither candles, neither torches; neither could there be fire kindled with their fine and exceedingly dry wood, so that there could not be any light at all;

22 And there was not any light seen, neither fire, nor glimmer, neither the sun, nor the moon, nor the stars, for so great were the mists of darkness which were upon the face of the land.

23 And it came to pass that it did last for the space of three days that there was no light seen; and there was great mourning and howling and weeping among all the people continually; yea, great were the groanings of the people, because of the darkness and the great destruction which had come upon them.

24 And in one place they were heard to cry, saying: O that we had repented before this great and terrible day, and then would our brethren have been spared, and they would not have been burned in that great city Zarahemla.

25 And in another place they were heard to cry and mourn, saying: O that we had repented before this great and terrible day, and had not killed and stoned the prophets, and cast them out; then would our mothers and our fair daughters, and our children have been spared, and not have been buried up in that great city Moronihah. And thus were the howlings of the people great and terrible.

of darkness' spoken of in 3 Nephi 8:20 and 10:13. . . . Furthermore, volcanic ash and lava can be carried *up* to bury cities . . . and Nephi records that the earth was carried *up* on the city Moronihah (3 Nephi 8:10) and not down, as one would expect in a landslide" (Benson, "Geological Upheaval and Darkness," 64). ⊕

3 Nephi 9:1–12. The Lord Destroys Nephite Cities and Their Inhabitants Because of Their Wickedness

What is unique about this voice being heard?
(9:1–2) "Twice during that terrible night of darkness that attested to the death of Christ in the Old World, the voice of the Redeemer spoke to those in the New World. I do not think I overstate the matter in suggesting that the world has never known a more dramatic teaching moment. The audible voice of the Lord had been heard speaking from the heavens before, but never to such an extensive and numerous audience" (McConkie, "Doctrine of a Covenant People," 162).

What does this event teach us about the justice of Jesus Christ? (9:6–12) We often think of Jesus as the Savior, the Good Shepherd, the God of Mercy, and the God of Love. Those name-titles are all true and accurate, but what do we learn in these verses about Jesus Christ as a God of Justice? What are the reasons He gives for destroying these cities? Are there people today who are guilty of the same sins and yet believe that God is too kind to call them to judgment?

CHAPTER 9

In the darkness, the voice of Christ proclaims the destruction of many people and cities for their wickedness—He also proclaims His divinity, announces that the law of Moses is fulfilled, and invites men to come unto Him and be saved. About A.D. 34.

1 And it came to pass that there was a voice heard among all the inhabitants of the earth, upon all the face of this land, crying:

2 Wo, wo, wo unto this people; wo unto the inhabitants of the whole earth except they shall repent; for the devil laugheth, and his angels rejoice, because of the slain of the fair sons and daughters of my people; and it is because of their iniquity and abominations that they are fallen!

3 Behold, that great city Zarahemla have I burned with fire, and the inhabitants thereof.

4 And behold, that great city Moroni have I caused to be sunk in the depths of the sea, and the inhabitants thereof to be drowned.

5 And behold, that great city Moronihah have I covered with earth, and the inhabitants thereof, to hide their iniquities and their abominations from before my face, that the blood of the prophets and the saints shall not come any more unto me against them.

6 And behold, the city of Gilgal have I caused to be sunk, and the inhabitants thereof to be buried up in the depths of the earth;

7 Yea, and the city of Onihah and the inhabitants thereof, and the city of Mocum and the inhabitants thereof, and the city of Jerusalem and the inhabitants thereof; and waters have I caused to come up in the stead thereof, to hide their wickedness and abominations from before my face, that the blood of the prophets and the saints shall not come up any more unto me against them.

8 And behold, the city of Gadiandi, and the city of Gadiomnah, and the city of Jacob, and the city of Gimgimno, all these have I caused to be sunk, and made hills and valleys in the places thereof; and the inhabitants thereof have I buried up in the depths of the earth, to hide their wickedness and abominations from before my face, that the blood of the prophets and the saints should not come up any more unto me against them.

9 And behold, that great city Jacobugath, which was inhabited by the people of king Jacob, have I caused to be burned with fire because of their sins and their wickedness, which was above all the wickedness of the whole earth, because of their secret murders and combinations; for it was they that did destroy the peace of my people and the government of the land; therefore I did cause them to be burned, to destroy them from before my face, that the blood of the prophets and the saints should not come up unto me any more against them.

10 And behold, the city of Laman, and the city of Josh, and the city of Gad, and the city of Kishkumen, have I caused to be burned with fire, and the inhabitants thereof, because of their wickedness in casting out the prophets, and stoning those whom I did send to declare unto them concerning their wickedness and their abominations.

11 And because they did cast them all out, that there were none righteous among them, I did send down fire and destroy them, that their wickedness and abominations might be hid from before my face, that the blood of the prophets and the saints whom I sent among them might not cry unto me from the ground against them.

12 And many great destructions have I caused to come upon this land, and upon this people, because of their wickedness and their abominations.

3 Nephi 9:13–22. The Lord Pleads with Those Who Are Left to Repent and Be Healed

In what ways can we "come unto [the Savior]"? (9:14) "Whoever we are and whatever we reply, [Christ's] response is *always* the same: 'Come,' He says lovingly. 'Come, follow me.' Wherever you are going, first come and see what I do, see where and how I spend my time. Learn of me, walk with me, talk with me, believe. Listen to me pray. In turn you will find answers to your own prayers. God will bring rest to your souls. Come, follow me" (Holland, "He Hath Filled the Hungry with Good Things," 65).

What does it mean that Christ is the light of the world? (9:18) "'Then spake Jesus again unto them, saying, I am the light of the world: he that followeth me shall not walk in darkness, but shall have the light of life' (John 8:12). This is 'the light which is in all things, which giveth life to all things, which is the law by which all things are governed' (D&C 88:13). Light and darkness cannot occupy the same space at the same time. Where the light of Christ is found, the darkness of Lucifer, even Satan, must depart, defeated" (Hales, "In Remembrance of Jesus," 25–26).

What is meant by "a broken heart and a contrite spirit"? (9:19–20) "The Savior said He would no longer accept burnt offerings of animals. The gift or sacrifice He will accept now is 'a broken heart and a contrite spirit' [3 Nephi 9:20]. . . . You can offer the Lord the gift of your broken, or repentant, heart and your contrite, or obedient, spirit. In reality, it is the gift of yourself—what you are and what you are becoming.

"Is there something in you or in your life that is impure or unworthy? When you get rid of it, that is a gift to the Savior" (Christofferson, "When Thou Art Converted," 12).

13 O all ye that are spared because ye were more righteous than they, will ye not now return unto me, and repent of your sins, and be converted, that I may heal you?

14 Yea, verily I say unto you, if ye will come unto me ye shall have eternal life. Behold, mine arm of mercy is extended towards you, and whosoever will come, him will I receive; and blessed are those who come unto me.

15 Behold, I am Jesus Christ the Son of God. I created the heavens and the earth, and all things that in them are. I was with the Father from the beginning. I am in the Father, and the Father in me; and in me hath the Father glorified his name.

16 I came unto my own, and my own received me not. And the scriptures concerning my coming are fulfilled.

17 And as many as have received me, to them have I given to become the sons of God; and even so will I to as many as shall believe on my name, for behold, by me redemption cometh, and in me is the law of Moses fulfilled.

18 I am the light and the life of the world. I am Alpha and Omega, the beginning and the end.

19 And ye shall offer up unto me no more the shedding of blood; yea, your sacrifices and your burnt offerings shall be done away, for I will accept none of your sacrifices and your burnt offerings.

20 And ye shall offer for a sacrifice unto me a broken heart and a contrite spirit. And whoso cometh unto me with a broken heart and a contrite spirit, him will I baptize with fire and with the Holy Ghost, even as the Lamanites,

because of their faith in me at the time of their conversion, were baptized with fire and with the Holy Ghost, and they knew it not.

21 Behold, I have come unto the world to bring redemption unto the world, to save the world from sin.

22 Therefore, whoso repenteth and cometh unto me as a little child, him will I receive, for of such is the kingdom of God. Behold, for such I have laid down my life, and have taken it up again; therefore repent, and come unto me ye ends of the earth, and be saved.

CHAPTER 10

There is silence in the land for many hours—The voice of Christ promises to gather His people as a hen gathers her chickens—The more righteous part of the people have been preserved. About A.D. *34–35.*

1 And now behold, it came to pass that all the people of the land did hear these sayings, and did witness of it. And after these sayings there was silence in the land for the space of many hours;

2 For so great was the astonishment of the people that they did cease lamenting and howling for the loss of their kindred which had been slain; therefore there was silence in all the land for the space of many hours.

3 And it came to pass that there came a voice again unto the people, and all the people did hear, and did witness of it, saying:

4 O ye people of these great cities which have fallen, who are descendants of Jacob, yea,

How is it possible for a person to be baptized with the Holy Ghost and yet not know it? (9:20) "Too many of us are like those whom the Lord said '[came] with a broken heart and a contrite spirit . . . [and] at the time of their conversion, were baptized with fire and with the Holy Ghost, and *they knew it not.*'

"Imagine that: 'And they knew it not.' It is not unusual for one to have received the gift and not really know it. . . .

"The voice of the Spirit is a still, small voice—a voice that is felt rather than heard. It is a spiritual voice that comes into the mind as a thought put into your heart" (Packer, "Cloven Tongues of Fire," 8). ⊕

How are we saved "from" our sins? (9:21–22) "We are not saved *in* our sins, as by being unconditionally saved through confessing Christ and then, inevitably, committing sins in our remaining lives (see Alma 11:36–37). We are saved *from* our sins (see Hel. 5:10) by a weekly renewal of our repentance and cleansing through the grace of God and His blessed plan of salvation (see 3 Ne. 9:20–22)" (Oaks, "Have You Been Saved?" 56).

3 Nephi 10:1–8. The Voice of Christ Breaks the Silence, and He Promises to Gather His People

What parallel is found in these verses between the Savior's coming to the Nephites and His Second Coming to the world? (10:1–2) Many hours of silence preceded Christ's visit to the Nephites. In modern revelation, the Lord said before His Second Coming, "There shall be silence in heaven for the space of half an hour . . . and the face of the Lord shall be unveiled" (D&C 88:95). The book of Revelation states that after the seventh seal is opened, there will be silence in heaven for the space of about half an hour (see Revelation 8:1).

who are of the house of Israel, how oft have I gathered you as a hen gathereth her chickens under her wings, and have nourished you.

5 And again, how oft would I have gathered you as a hen gathereth her chickens under her wings, yea, O ye people of the house of Israel, who have fallen; yea, O ye people of the house of Israel, ye that dwell at Jerusalem, as ye that have fallen; yea, how oft would I have gathered you as a hen gathereth her chickens, and ye would not.

6 O ye house of Israel whom I have spared, how oft will I gather you as a hen gathereth her chickens under her wings, if ye will repent and return unto me with full purpose of heart.

7 But if not, O house of Israel, the places of your dwellings shall become desolate until the time of the fulfilling of the covenant to your fathers.

8 And now it came to pass that after the people had heard these words, behold, they began to weep and howl again because of the loss of their kindred and friends.

9 And it came to pass that thus did the three days pass away. And it was in the morning, and the darkness dispersed from off the face of the land, and the earth did cease to tremble, and the rocks did cease to rend, and the dreadful groanings did cease, and all the tumultuous noises did pass away.

10 And the earth did cleave together again, that it stood; and the mourning, and the weeping, and the wailing of the people who were spared alive did cease; and their mourning was turned into joy, and their lamentations into the praise and thanksgiving unto the Lord Jesus Christ, their Redeemer.

11 And thus far were the scriptures fulfilled which had been spoken by the prophets.

How does this repeated teaching of the Savior's invitation "to gather" apply to us? (10:6–7) "More than once [Christ] said that He would gather us to Him as a hen would gather her chickens under her wings. He says that we must choose to come to Him in meekness and with enough faith in Him to repent 'with full purpose of heart' [3 Nephi 10:6].

"One way to do that is to gather with the Saints in His Church. Go to your meetings, even when it seems hard. If you are determined, He will help you find the strength to do it" (Eyring, "In the Strength of the Lord," 18). ◐

3 Nephi 10:9–13. The More Righteous People Are Saved from Destruction

What important blessings can come from enduring darkness and tribulation well? (10:9–10) "Out of the darkness of destruction came the voice the Nephite nation had waited more than six hundred years to hear. 'Behold, I am Jesus Christ the Son of God,' he said. . . . As should be expected, such an introductory pronouncement from the great Jehovah/Jesus himself is laden with doctrinal significance [see 3 Nephi 9:15–22]. . . . Concurrent with these and other such magnificent declarations, the darkness lifted and the earth ceased to tremble. The light of the world had come. The more righteous part of the people had been saved, through their obedience, and were now prepared to receive the visitation of the Son of God himself" (Holland, *Christ and the New Covenant*, 256–58). ◐

12 And it was the more righteous part of the people who were saved, and it was they who received the prophets and stoned them not; and it was they who had not shed the blood of the saints, who were spared—

13 And they were spared and were not sunk and buried up in the earth; and they were not drowned in the depths of the sea; and they were not burned by fire, neither were they fallen upon and crushed to death; and they were not carried away in the whirlwind; neither were they overpowered by the vapor of smoke and of darkness.

14 And now, whoso readeth, let him understand; he that hath the scriptures, let him search them, and see and behold if all these deaths and destructions by fire, and by smoke, and by tempests, and by whirlwinds, and by the opening of the earth to receive them, and all these things are not unto the fulfilling of the prophecies of many of the holy prophets.

15 Behold, I say unto you, Yea, many have testified of these things at the coming of Christ, and were slain because they testified of these things.

16 Yea, the prophet Zenos did testify of these things, and also Zenock spake concerning these things, because they testified particularly concerning us, who are the remnant of their seed.

17 Behold, our father Jacob also testified concerning a remnant of the seed of Joseph. And behold, are not we a remnant of the seed of Joseph? And these things which testify of us, are they not written upon the plates of brass which our father Lehi brought out of Jerusalem?

Why is it vital to follow living prophets? (10:12)
"The Lord promised: 'If my people will hearken unto my voice, and unto the voice of my servants whom I have appointed to lead my people, behold, verily, I say unto you, they shall not be moved out of their place.

"'But if they will not hearken to my voice, nor unto the voice of these men whom I have appointed, they shall not be blest' (D&C 124:45–46).

"I bear witness, . . . that the leaders of the Church were called of God by proper authority, and it is known to the Church that they have that authority and have been properly ordained by the regularly ordained heads of the Church. If we follow them we will be saved. If we stray from them we will surely be lost" (Packer, "'From Such Turn Away,'" 35).

3 Nephi 10:14–19. Mormon Explains That These Destructions Were Prophesied

What have we been commanded to do to know for ourselves? (10:14) The Savior commanded us to search the scriptures. The Prophet Joseph Smith counseled: "Search the scriptures—search the revelations . . . and ask your Heavenly Father, in the name of His Son Jesus Christ, to manifest the truth unto you, and if you do it with an eye single to His glory, nothing doubting, He will answer you by the power of His Holy Spirit. You will then know for yourselves and not for another. You will not then be dependent on man for the knowledge of God; nor will there be any room for speculation" (*History of the Church*, 1:282). ●

Why did Mormon, the historian, quote from the lost prophets called Zenos and Zenock? (10:16–17) "The prophets Zenos and Zenock are quoted several times by the prophets of the Book of Mormon. A possible reason for this propensity in quoting them becomes evident in [3 Nephi 10:16–17]: the Nephites are descendants of the prophets Zenos and Zenock! The historian records: ' . . . the prophet Zenos did testify of these things, and also Zenock spake concerning these things, because *they testified particularly concerning us, who are the remnant of their seed*' (3 Nephi 10:16; italics added)" (Ludlow, *Companion to Your Study of the Book of Mormon*, 260).

When did Jesus Christ appear to the Nephites? (10:18) "The Nephites adjusted their calendar so as to begin a new dating era with the birth of Jesus; and according to their chronology, the storms and the darkness and the crucifixion came to pass on the fourth day of the first month of the thirty-fourth year (3 Ne. 8). Then 'in the ending' of that year (3 Ne. 10:18–19), several months after the Ascension on Olivet, Jesus ministered personally among the Nephites for many hours on many days" (McConkie, *Mortal Messiah*, 4:306–7).

Superscription to 3 Nephi 11

The superscription to 3 Nephi 11 was part of the ancient record translated by the Prophet Joseph Smith and dictated by him to his scribe, except for the phrase "comprising chapters 11 through 26" (see also, for example, 2 Nephi, Mosiah 9, and 4 Nephi).

3 Nephi 11:1–17. The Resurrected Christ Appears to the People at the Temple in Bountiful

How were those at Bountiful prepared to receive the Lord? (11:1) "Those who survived the tumult and witnessed these events were the more righteous ones. The wicked were slain in the destruction (3 Nephi 9:12–13; 10:12–13). . . . After all these things had happened to them, they could not ever be casual or indifferent about the gospel of Jesus Christ and the true purpose of life. They were ready to see, hear, and participate in the personal ministry of Jesus, their Lord and Redeemer" (Matthews, "Jesus the Savior," 27).

18 And it came to pass that in the ending of the thirty and fourth year, behold, I will show unto you that the people of Nephi who were spared, and also those who had been called Lamanites, who had been spared, did have great favors shown unto them, and great blessings poured out upon their heads, insomuch that soon after the ascension of Christ into heaven he did truly manifest himself unto them—

19 Showing his body unto them, and ministering unto them; and an account of his ministry shall be given hereafter. Therefore for this time I make an end of my sayings.

Jesus Christ did show himself unto the people of Nephi, as the multitude were gathered together in the land Bountiful, and did minister unto them; and on this wise did he show himself unto them.

Comprising chapters 11 through 26.

CHAPTER 11

The Father testifies of His Beloved Son—Christ appears and proclaims His Atonement—The people feel the wound marks in His hands and feet and side—They cry Hosanna—He sets forth the mode and manner of baptism—The spirit of contention is of the devil—Christ's doctrine is that men should believe and be baptized and receive the Holy Ghost. About A.D. 34.

1 And now it came to pass that there were a great multitude gathered together, of the people of Nephi, round about the temple which was in the land Bountiful; and they were marveling and wondering one with another, and were showing one to another the great and marvelous change which had taken place.

2 And they were also conversing about this Jesus Christ, of whom the sign had been given concerning his death.

3 And it came to pass that while they were thus conversing one with another, they heard a voice as if it came out of heaven; and they cast their eyes round about, for they understood not the voice which they heard; and it was not a harsh voice, neither was it a loud voice; nevertheless, and notwithstanding it being a small voice it did pierce them that did hear to the center, insomuch that there was no part of their frame that it did not cause to quake; yea, it did pierce them to the very soul, and did cause their hearts to burn.

4 And it came to pass that again they heard the voice, and they understood it not.

5 And again the third time they did hear the voice, and did open their ears to hear it; and their eyes were towards the sound thereof; and they did look steadfastly towards heaven, from whence the sound came.

6 And behold, the third time they did understand the voice which they heard; and it said unto them:

7 Behold my Beloved Son, in whom I am well pleased, in whom I have glorified my name—hear ye him.

8 And it came to pass, as they understood they cast their eyes up again towards heaven; and behold, they saw a Man descending out of heaven; and he was clothed in a white robe; and he came down and stood in the midst of them; and the eyes of the whole multitude were turned upon him, and they durst not open their mouths, even one to another, and wist not what it meant, for they thought it was an angel that had appeared unto them.

9 And it came to pass that he stretched forth his hand and spake unto the people, saying:

10 Behold, I am Jesus Christ, whom the prophets testified shall come into the world.

11 And behold, I am the light and the life of the world; and I have drunk out of that bitter

---

Why is hearing or understanding the voice of the Spirit sometimes hard to do? (11:3–4) President Boyd K. Packer taught: "We do not have the words (even the scriptures do not have words) which perfectly describe the Spirit. The scriptures generally use the word voice, which does not exactly fit. These delicate, refined spiritual communications are not seen with our eyes, nor heard with our ears. And even though it is described as a voice, it is a voice that one feels, more than one hears" ("Candle of the Lord," 52). ●

How do we prepare to understand and obey the voice of the Lord? (11:5–6) President James E. Faust said: "The more righteous part of the Nephites had to learn to focus attention in order to hear the voice....

"If we are to hearken to the voice of the Spirit, we too must open our ears, turn the eye of faith to the source of the voice, and look steadfastly towards heaven" ("Voice of the Spirit," 4–5).

What is Heavenly Father's message on the rare occasions His voice is heard by men on this earth? (11:7) "All revelation since the fall has come through Jesus Christ, who is the Jehovah of the Old Testament. In all of the scriptures, where God is mentioned and where he has appeared, it was Jehovah.... The Father has never dealt with man directly and personally since the fall, and he has never appeared except to introduce and bear record of the Son" (Smith, *Doctrines of Salvation* 1:27).

How does the declaration "I am Jesus Christ" shape the Nephites? (11:10–12) "He speaks and says simply, with a voice that penetrates the very marrow of your bones, 'I am Jesus Christ.'...

"There it is—or, more correctly speaking, there he is. The focal point and principal figure behind every fireside and devotional and family home evening held by those Nephites for the last six hundred years. . . .

"Everyone has talked of him and sung of him and dreamed of him and prayed—but here he actually is. This is the day and yours is the generation. What a moment! But you find you are less inclined to check the film in your camera than you are to check the faith in your heart" (Holland and Holland, *On Earth As It Is in Heaven*, 125).

What does the "bitter cup" represent? (11:11) "It is doctrinally significant to note what the Savior did as he appeared to the people and for what purposes he did it. He taught and testified of himself. . . . He is the Christ, the Messiah who every prophet had testified would come into the world. . . . The 'bitter cup'—which is the symbolic representation of the painful demands of justice that had to be met in order for the infinite and eternal sacrifice to be fulfilled—had been drunk" (McConkie, et al., *Doctrinal Commentary*, 4:52).

Why did Jesus retain the physical signs of the Atonement in His resurrected body? (11:14–15) "These wounds are the principal way we are to recognize Him when He comes. He may invite us forward, as He has invited others, to see and to feel those marks. If not before, then surely at that time, we will remember with Isaiah that it was for us that a God was 'despised and rejected . . . ; a man of sorrows, and acquainted with grief,' that 'he was wounded for our transgressions, he was bruised for our iniquities: the chastisement of our peace was upon him; and with his stripes we are healed' (Isaiah 53:3, 5)" (Holland, "Teaching, Preaching, Healing," 42). ⊕

What does the word *Hosanna* mean? (11:16–17) "Whether in the heavens—and on earth in this dispensation—the [hosanna] shout expressed unspeakable, sublime, and deeply sacred joy, in Jewish usage it became more nearly a cry of supplication" (Woodbury, "The Origin of the Sacred Hosanna Shout," 18). See commentary in this volume on 1 Nephi 11:6.

cup which the Father hath given me, and have glorified the Father in taking upon me the sins of the world, in the which I have suffered the will of the Father in all things from the beginning.

12 And it came to pass that when Jesus had spoken these words the whole multitude fell to the earth; for they remembered that it had been prophesied among them that Christ should show himself unto them after his ascension into heaven.

13 And it came to pass that the Lord spake unto them saying:

14 Arise and come forth unto me, that ye may thrust your hands into my side, and also that ye may feel the prints of the nails in my hands and in my feet, that ye may know that I am the God of Israel, and the God of the whole earth, and have been slain for the sins of the world.

15 And it came to pass that the multitude went forth, and thrust their hands into his side, and did feel the prints of the nails in his hands and in his feet; and this they did do, going forth one by one until they had all gone forth, and did see with their eyes and did feel with their hands, and did know of a surety and did bear record, that it was he, of whom it was written by the prophets, that should come.

16 And when they had all gone forth and had witnessed for themselves, they did cry out with one accord, saying:

17 Hosanna! Blessed be the name of the Most High God! And they did fall down at the feet of Jesus, and did worship him.

18 And it came to pass that he spake unto Nephi (for Nephi was among the multitude) and he commanded him that he should come forth.

19 And Nephi arose and went forth, and bowed himself before the Lord and did kiss his feet.

20 And the Lord commanded him that he should arise. And he arose and stood before him.

21 And the Lord said unto him: I give unto you power that ye shall baptize this people when I am again ascended into heaven.

22 And again the Lord called others, and said unto them likewise; and he gave unto them power to baptize. And he said unto them: On this wise shall ye baptize; and there shall be no disputations among you.

23 Verily I say unto you, that whoso repenteth of his sins through your words, and desireth to be baptized in my name, on this wise shall ye baptize them—Behold, ye shall go down and stand in the water, and in my name shall ye baptize them.

24 And now behold, these are the words which ye shall say, calling them by name, saying:

25 Having authority given me of Jesus Christ, I baptize you in the name of the Father, and of the Son, and of the Holy Ghost. Amen.

26 And then shall ye immerse them in the water, and come forth again out of the water.

27 And after this manner shall ye baptize in my name; for behold, verily I say unto you, that the Father, and the Son, and the Holy Ghost are one; and I am in the Father, and the Father in me, and the Father and I are one.

28 And according as I have commanded you thus shall ye baptize. And there shall be no disputations among you, as there have

3 Nephi 11:18–30. Jesus Teaches the Nephite Disciples about Baptism

Why was the power to baptize one of the first things the Savior gave to the Nephites? (11:21–23) Joseph Smith solemnly declared: "Baptism is a sign to God, to angels, and to heaven that we do the will of God, and there is no other way beneath the heavens whereby God hath ordained for man to come to Him to be saved, and enter into the kingdom of God, except faith in Jesus Christ, repentance, and baptism for the remission of sins. . . . Then you have the promise of the gift of the Holy Ghost" (*Joseph Smith* [manual], 91).

Why do some prayers have prescribed wording? (11:24–25) "By revelation the Lord has given the Church three set prayers for use in our sacred ordinances. Except for these prayers, the Lord seems to expect us to express ourselves in our own words as we approach him in supplication.

"All three of these revealed prayers relate to the atonement of the Lord Jesus Christ, his crucifixion, and his burial and resurrection. All of the ordinances in which we use these prayers place us under solemn covenants of obedience to God. They are the sacrament of the Lord's Supper and the ordinance of baptism" (Petersen, "Sacred, Set Prayers," 56).

In teaching the gospel, why is it crucial to avoid contention? (11:28–30) The Prophet Joseph Smith warned: "Let the elders be exceedingly careful about unnecessarily disturbing and harrowing up the feelings of the people.

" . . . Avoid contentions and vain disputes with men of corrupt minds who do not desire to know the truth. Remember that 'it is a day of warning, and not a day of many words.' If they receive not your testimony in one place, flee to another, remembering to cast no reflections, nor throw out any bitter sayings. If you do your duty, it will be just as well with you, as though all men embraced the Gospel" (*History of the Church*, 1:468; see also "The Elders in Kirtland, to Their Brethren Abroad," in *The Evening and the Morning Star*, Dec. 1833, 120).

3 Nephi 11:31–41. Jesus Christ Declares His Doctrine

What do we learn in these verses about the doctrine of Christ? (11:32–35) "It is clear at the outset that the sermon in the Book of Mormon is built upon one overwhelmingly important premise that is not so obvious in the New Testament—that the doctrines taught and the blessings promised are predicated upon first principles, on saving ordinances and covenants of the gospel, including the baptismal covenant, which brings people through 'the gate' to the strait and narrow path leading to eternal life. As Christ taught here, so Nephi taught earlier—that these first principles and ordinances constitute the 'doctrine of Christ'" (Holland, *Christ and the New Covenant*, 261–62). ✪

hitherto been; neither shall there be disputations among you concerning the points of my doctrine, as there have hitherto been.

29 For verily, verily I say unto you, he that hath the spirit of contention is not of me, but is of the devil, who is the father of contention, and he stirreth up the hearts of men to contend with anger, one with another.

30 Behold, this is not my doctrine, to stir up the hearts of men with anger, one against another; but this is my doctrine, that such things should be done away.

31 Behold, verily, verily, I say unto you, I will declare unto you my doctrine.

32 And this is my doctrine, and it is the doctrine which the Father hath given unto me; and I bear record of the Father, and the Father beareth record of me, and the Holy Ghost beareth record of the Father and me; and I bear record that the Father commandeth all men, everywhere, to repent and believe in me.

33 And whoso believeth in me, and is baptized, the same shall be saved; and they are they who shall inherit the kingdom of God.

34 And whoso believeth not in me, and is not baptized, shall be damned.

35 Verily, verily, I say unto you, that this is my doctrine, and I bear record of it from the Father; and whoso believeth in me believeth

The Doctrine of Christ

Nephi Taught	Christ Taught
2 Nephi 31:2; 4–21	3 Nephi 11:31–41
Doctrine of Christ (2)	This is my doctrine (31)
Repent and be baptized (4–6, 11)	Repent and be baptized (32–33)
Holy Ghost (12)	Be visited with fire and the Holy Ghost (35)
Take upon you the name of Christ (13, 21)	In my name (37)
Endure to the end in faith (14–16, 21)	Inherit the kingdom of God (33)

in the Father also; and unto him will the Father bear record of me, for he will visit him with fire and with the Holy Ghost.

36 And thus will the Father bear record of me, and the Holy Ghost will bear record unto him of the Father and me; for the Father, and I, and the Holy Ghost are one.

37 And again I say unto you, ye must repent, and become as a little child, and be baptized in my name, or ye can in nowise receive these things.

38 And again I say unto you, ye must repent, and be baptized in my name, and become as a little child, or ye can in nowise inherit the kingdom of God.

39 Verily, verily, I say unto you, that this is my doctrine, and whoso buildeth upon this buildeth upon my rock, and the gates of hell shall not prevail against them.

40 And whoso shall declare more or less than this, and establish it for my doctrine, the same cometh of evil, and is not built upon my rock; but he buildeth upon a sandy foundation, and the gates of hell stand open to receive such when the floods come and the winds beat upon them.

41 Therefore, go forth unto this people, and declare the words which I have spoken, unto the ends of the earth.

What do we promise when we are baptized in Christ's name? (11:37–38) "At baptism we make a covenant with our Heavenly Father that we are willing to come into His kingdom and keep His commandments from that time forward, even though we still live in the world. We are reminded from the Book of Mormon that our baptism is a covenant to 'stand as witnesses of God [and His kingdom] *at all times and in all things, and in all places* that ye may be in, even until death, that ye may be redeemed of God, and be numbered with those of the first resurrection, that ye may have eternal life' (Mosiah 18:9; emphasis added)" (Hales, "Covenant of Baptism," 7). ⊕

What do the "gates of hell" symbolize? (11:40) "The gates of hell, then, does not refer to the devil at all; though his snares and wiles might lead men sooner or later to their death, delivering them 'to the destruction of the *flesh*,' his power ends there. The gates of hell are—the 'holding back' of those who are in the spirit world from attaining the object of their desire" (Nibley, *Mormonism and Early Christianity*, 108).

"Baptism for the dead, then, was the key to the gates of hell which no church claimed to possess until the nineteenth century, the gates remaining inexorably closed against those very dead of whose salvation the early Christians had been so morally certain" (Nibley, *Mormonism and Early Christianity*, 106).

3 Nephi 12:1–12. Jesus Teaches the Beatitudes

Why were these people chosen to receive this magnificent discourse? (12:1) "It may well be that the most perfect and elaborate sermon was delivered to the Nephites, for their congregation was composed only of spiritually attuned souls" (McConkie, *Mortal Messiah*, 2:117). ⊕

How can being "poor in spirit" or having reason to "mourn" be a blessing? (12:3–4) Notice that in verse 3 the Lord included a phrase that is not found in the New Testament version of this sermon. The poor in spirit (meaning the humble) will receive the kingdom of heaven if they "come unto" the Savior. Humility alone is not sufficient. Would that also apply to those who mourn? Does feeling sorrowful for a loved one's fall into sin or death bring comfort? In what ways does turning to the Savior in your sorrow make a difference?

CHAPTER 12

Jesus calls and commissions the twelve disciples—He delivers to the Nephites a discourse similar to the Sermon on the Mount—He speaks the Beatitudes—His teachings transcend and take precedence over the law of Moses—Men are commanded to be perfect even as He and His Father are perfect—Compare Matthew 5. About A.D. 34.

1 And it came to pass that when Jesus had spoken these words unto Nephi, and to those who had been called, (now the number of them who had been called, and received power and authority to baptize, was twelve) and behold, he stretched forth his hand unto the multitude, and cried unto them, saying: Blessed are ye if ye shall give heed unto the words of these twelve whom I have chosen from among you to minister unto you, and to be your servants; and unto them I have given power that they may baptize you with water; and after that ye are baptized with water, behold, I will baptize you with fire and with the Holy Ghost; therefore blessed are ye if ye shall believe in me and be baptized, after that ye have seen me and know that I am.

2 And again, more blessed are they who shall believe in your words because that ye shall testify that ye have seen me, and that ye know that I am. Yea, blessed are they who shall believe in your words, and come down into the depths of humility and be baptized, for they shall be visited with fire and with the Holy Ghost, and shall receive a remission of their sins.

3 Yea, blessed are the poor in spirit who come unto me, for theirs is the kingdom of heaven.

4 And again, blessed are all they that mourn, for they shall be comforted.

5 And blessed are the meek, for they shall inherit the earth.

6 And blessed are all they who do hunger and thirst after righteousness, for they shall be filled with the Holy Ghost.

7 And blessed are the merciful, for they shall obtain mercy.

8 And blessed are all the pure in heart, for they shall see God.

9 And blessed are all the peacemakers, for they shall be called the children of God.

10 And blessed are all they who are persecuted for my name's sake, for theirs is the kingdom of heaven.

11 And blessed are ye when men shall revile you and persecute, and shall say all manner of evil against you falsely, for my sake;

12 For ye shall have great joy and be exceedingly glad, for great shall be your reward in heaven; for so persecuted they the prophets who were before you.

13 Verily, verily, I say unto you, I give unto you to be the salt of the earth; but if the salt shall lose its savor wherewith shall the earth be salted? The salt shall be thenceforth good for nothing, but to be cast out and to be trodden under foot of men.

What does it mean to be meek? (12:5) Meekness is "gentleness; submission to divine will. A quality that the Lord attributes to himself (Matt. 11:29); a childlike quality (Mosiah 3:19; Matt. 11:29), often coupled with [lowliness of heart] (e.g., Alma 37:33; Moro. 7:43). Meekness characterizes those who have faith in Christ (Moro. 7:39), and is one of the fruits of the Spirit (Alma 13:28; D&C 19:23; Gal. 5:22–23)" (Largey, *Book of Mormon Reference Companion*, 534).

How can we become more merciful? (12:7) "Let us be more merciful. Let us get the arrogance out of our lives, the conceit, and the egotism. Let us be more compassionate, gentler, filled with forbearance and patience and a greater measure of respect one for another. In so doing our very example will cause others to be more merciful, and we shall have greater claim upon the mercy of God who in His love will be generous toward us" (*Teachings of Gordon B. Hinckley*, 338).

How do we qualify for the blessing that comes to those who have a pure heart? (12:8) "The promises of the gospel are uplifting and ennobling, even exalting. We receive those promises by covenants which are conditioned on our living lives of purity and morality. When we live right and seek to purify our hearts, we draw closer to God and the Spirit. The condition of our heart determines how much evidence of divinity we see in the world now and qualifies us for the eventual realization of the promise that the pure 'shall see God.' Ours is a quest for purity" (Clayton, "Blessed Are All the Pure in Heart," 52–53).

How does having a pure heart and being a peacemaker bring you closer to God? (12:8–12) Can you think of others who are pure in heart and who obtained "great joy" despite persecution? What do you learn from the life of Christ? How about "the prophets who were before you"? What can you do to more fully purify your heart?

3 Nephi 12:13–48. Jesus Compares the Law of Moses with the Gospel

What does it mean to be the salt of the earth? (12:13) "The 'salt of the earth' consists of those members of the Church who are the true seasoning and preservatives of mankind. Their actions bring out the best in themselves and others and help guard against decay and corrosion in society" (Brewster, *Doctrine and Covenants Encyclopedia*, 489).

What are ways in which we can be a light to the world? (12:14–16) The Savior later answered that question: "Therefore, hold up your light that it may shine unto the world. Behold I am the light which ye shall hold up—that which ye have seen me do" (3 Nephi 18:24). What have you seen or experienced in your life that demonstrates to you that Christlike behavior really does bring light into a dark world? ●

What was Jesus's relationship with the law of Moses? (12:17–18) "Jesus came to restore that gospel fulness which men had enjoyed before the day of Moses, before the time of the lesser order. Obviously he did not come to destroy what he himself had revealed to Moses anymore than a college professor destroys arithmetic by revealing the principles of integral calculus to his students. Jesus came to build on the foundation Moses laid. By restoring the fulness of the gospel he fulfilled the need for adherence to the terms and conditions of the preparatory gospel. No one any longer needed to walk by the light of the moon, for the sun had risen in all its splendor" (McConkie, *Doctrinal New Testament Commentary*, 1:219–20).

What is a broken heart? (12:19–20) "A broken heart is a submissive heart, an obedient heart, a heart open to the Savior. Why would any of us ever hesitate to go where the Lord would lead us, knowing what price he has paid for us because of his love for us?" (Wilcox, "Beatitudes, Pathway to the Savior," 23).

Why is it important that the conditional phrase "without a cause" does not appear in this passage, even though it appears in the Bible? (12:22) "The Lord expects us to make the choice *not* to become angry.

---

14 Verily, verily, I say unto you, I give unto you to be the light of this people. A city that is set on a hill cannot be hid.

15 Behold, do men light a candle and put it under a bushel? Nay, but on a candlestick, and it giveth light to all that are in the house;

16 Therefore let your light so shine before this people, that they may see your good works and glorify your Father who is in heaven.

17 Think not that I am come to destroy the law or the prophets. I am not come to destroy but to fulfil;

18 For verily I say unto you, one jot nor one tittle hath not passed away from the law, but in me it hath all been fulfilled.

19 And behold, I have given you the law and the commandments of my Father, that ye shall believe in me, and that ye shall repent of your sins, and come unto me with a broken heart and a contrite spirit. Behold, ye have the commandments before you, and the law is fulfilled.

20 Therefore come unto me and be ye saved; for verily I say unto you, that except ye shall keep my commandments, which I have commanded you at this time, ye shall in no case enter into the kingdom of heaven.

21 Ye have heard that it hath been said by them of old time, and it is also written before you, that thou shalt not kill, and whosoever shall kill shall be in danger of the judgment of God;

22 But I say unto you, that whosoever is angry with his brother shall be in danger of his judgment. And whosoever shall say to his brother, Raca, shall be in danger of the council; and whosoever shall say, Thou fool, shall be in danger of hell fire.

23 Therefore, if ye shall come unto me, or shall desire to come unto me, and rememberest that thy brother hath aught against thee—

24 Go thy way unto thy brother, and first be reconciled to thy brother, and then come unto me with full purpose of heart, and I will receive you.

25 Agree with thine adversary quickly while thou art in the way with him, lest at any time he shall get thee, and thou shalt be cast into prison.

26 Verily, verily, I say unto thee, thou shalt by no means come out thence until thou hast paid the uttermost senine. And while ye are in prison can ye pay even one senine? Verily, verily, I say unto you, Nay.

27 Behold, it is written by them of old time, that thou shalt not commit adultery;

28 But I say unto you, that whosoever looketh on a woman, to lust after her, hath committed adultery already in his heart.

29 Behold, I give unto you a commandment, that ye suffer none of these things to enter into your heart;

30 For it is better that ye should deny yourselves of these things, wherein ye will take up your cross, than that ye should be cast into hell.

31 It hath been written, that whosoever shall put away his wife, let him give her a writing of divorcement.

32 Verily, verily, I say unto you, that whosoever shall put away his wife, saving for the cause of fornication, causeth her to commit adultery; and whoso shall marry her who is divorced committeth adultery.

"Nor can becoming angry be justified. In Matthew 5, verse 22, the Lord says: 'But I say unto you, That whosoever is angry with his brother *without a cause* shall be in danger of the judgment' (emphasis added). How interesting that the phrase 'without a cause' is not found in the inspired Joseph Smith Translation . . . nor in the 3 Nephi 12:22 version. When the Lord eliminates the phrase 'without a cause,' He leaves us without an excuse" (Robbins, "Agency and Anger," 80). ❂

Why should we agree with our adversaries? (12:25–26) "Often this phrase is interpreted to mean that we should be conciliatory with adversaries in order to avoid contention, lawsuits, or persecution. Certainly, we should be peacemakers—'easy to be intreated' (James 3:17) and cooperative with all people of goodwill. We should even absorb worldly hurt and unfairness when doing so would help advance the cause of righteousness (see 1 Pet. 2:12–23; 1 Pet. 3:13–17; 1 Pet. 4:14–19). But surely we are not to compromise truth and righteous purpose to achieve peaceful coexistence with our fellow beings" (Dahl, "The Higher Law," 7). ❂

Why is controlling our thoughts so important? (12:27–30) "Next to murder in seriousness was adultery, expressly forbidden by God. Jesus also noted the seriousness of lust. . . . The thoughts precede the actions: 'For as he thinketh in his heart, so is he' (Prov. 23:7). Jesus was teaching accountability for thoughts as well as actions; either of these could cost one's salvation. Controlling the mind and impulses could obliterate the outward commission of serious sin" (Farley, "Appearance of Christ to the People of Nephi," 155–56).

What did this command condemning divorce mean in Jesus's day? (12:31–32) "This strict law governing divorce was . . . to the disciples only. . . . Further, Jesus expressly limited its application. All men could not live such a high standard; it applied only to those 'to whom it is given'" (McConkie, *Doctrinal New Testament Commentary*, 1:548–49). ❂

What is included in swearing? (12:33–37) "We do not take the name of the Lord in vain (see Ex. 20:7), nor do we condone the misuse of any terms referring to Deity. We follow the admonition of the Savior to 'swear not at all' in our dealings with each other (see Matt. 5:34–37). Therefore, in the conduct of our daily affairs we do not make vain oaths in the name of sacred things. Rather, our communications with one another are simple and honest and straightforward. We also feel that those who follow Christ will avoid the use of vulgar, foul, uncouth language—as well as avoid the use of any expression reserved for Deity in any improper way" (Wells, "We Are Christians Because . . . ," 17).

Why must we "turn the other cheek"? (12:38–44) "When we do not retaliate—when we turn the other cheek and resist feelings of anger—we too stand with the Savior. We show forth His love, which is the only power that can subdue the adversary and answer our accusers without accusing them in return. That is not weakness. *That* is Christian courage" (Hales, "Christian Courage: The Price of Discipleship," 72). ◉

33 And again it is written, thou shalt not forswear thyself, but shalt perform unto the Lord thine oaths;

34 But verily, verily, I say unto you, swear not at all; neither by heaven, for it is God's throne;

35 Nor by the earth, for it is his footstool;

36 Neither shalt thou swear by thy head, because thou canst not make one hair black or white;

37 But let your communication be Yea, yea; Nay, nay; for whatsoever cometh of more than these is evil.

38 And behold, it is written, an eye for an eye, and a tooth for a tooth;

39 But I say unto you, that ye shall not resist evil, but whosoever shall smite thee on thy right cheek, turn to him the other also;

40 And if any man will sue thee at the law and take away thy coat, let him have thy cloak also;

41 And whosoever shall compel thee to go a mile, go with him twain.

42 Give to him that asketh thee, and from him that would borrow of thee turn thou not away.

43 And behold it is written also, that thou shalt love thy neighbor and hate thine enemy;

44 But behold I say unto you, love your enemies, bless them that curse you, do good to them that hate you, and pray for them who despitefully use you and persecute you;

45 That ye may be the children of your Father who is in heaven; for he maketh his sun to rise on the evil and on the good.

46 Therefore those things which were of old time, which were under the law, in me are all fulfilled.

47 Old things are done away, and all things have become new.

48 Therefore I would that ye should be perfect even as I, or your Father who is in heaven is perfect.

CHAPTER 13

Jesus teaches the Nephites the Lord's Prayer—They are to lay up treasures in heaven—The twelve disciples in their ministry are commanded to take no thought for temporal things—Compare Matthew 6. About A.D. *34.*

1 Verily, verily, I say that I would that ye should do alms unto the poor; but take heed that ye do not your alms before men to be seen of them; otherwise ye have no reward of your Father who is in heaven.

2 Therefore, when ye shall do your alms do not sound a trumpet before you, as will hypocrites do in the synagogues and in the streets, that they may have glory of men. Verily I say unto you, they have their reward.

3 But when thou doest alms let not thy left hand know what thy right hand doeth;

4 That thine alms may be in secret; and thy Father who seeth in secret, himself shall reward thee openly.

5 And when thou prayest thou shalt not do as the hypocrites, for they love to pray, standing in the synagogues and in the corners of the streets, that they may be seen of men. Verily I say unto you, they have their reward.

6 But thou, when thou prayest, enter into thy closet, and when thou hast shut thy door, pray to thy Father who is in secret; and thy Father, who seeth in secret, shall reward thee openly.

What type of perfection does Jesus require of us? (12:48) "We need not be dismayed if our earnest efforts toward perfection now seem so arduous and endless. Perfection is pending. It can come in full only after the Resurrection and only through the Lord. It awaits all who love him and keep his commandments. It includes thrones, kingdoms, principalities, powers, and dominions. It is the end for which we are to endure. It is the eternal perfection that God has in store for each of us" (Nelson, "Perfection Pending," 86). ●

3 Nephi 13:1–4. Jesus Teaches about Giving

What attitude should we avoid when giving our gifts to others? (13:1–2) "The tossing of alms to a beggar . . . to be seen of men, and similar displays of affected liberality, were fashionable among certain classes in the time of Christ; and the same Spirit is manifest today. Some there be now who cause a trumpet to be sounded, . . . to call attention to their giving, that they may have glory of men—to win political favor, to increase their trade or influence, to get what in their estimation is worth more than that from which they part. With logical incisiveness the Master demonstrated that such givers have their reward" (Talmage, *Jesus the Christ*, 237).

3 Nephi 13:5–18. Jesus Teaches about Prayer and Fasting

What is the difference between "vain repetitions" and sincere pleadings with the Lord in prayer? (13:7) "The problem is in the vainness, not in repetition. In how many different ways can we bless our food? How many original prayers—original in the sense of novel or unusual language—can we offer? God is not offended by repetition, so long as the words are spoken from the heart and are sincere. The heavens withdraw themselves, however, in the face of vanity. Something is vain when it is empty, meaningless, or hollow. Whenever our prayers are meaningless and thus become trite or ritualistic religious jargon, having no feeling or emanating from a duplicitous heart, they accomplish little" (McConkie et al., *Doctrinal Commentary*, 4:81).

Why is forgiveness such an integral part of the Lord's Prayer? (13:11, 14–15) "Forgiveness is too precious a pearl to be cast at the feet of the unforgiving; and, without the sincerity that springs from a contrite heart, no man may justly claim mercy. If others owe us, either in actual money or goods as suggested by debts and debtors, or through some infringement upon our rights included under the broader designation as a trespass, our mode of dealing with them will be taken into righteous account in the judgment of our own offenses" (Talmage, *Jesus the Christ*, 240). ☉

3 Nephi 13:19–24. Disciples of Christ Seek First the Kingdom of God

7 But when ye pray, use not vain repetitions, as the heathen, for they think that they shall be heard for their much speaking.

8 Be not ye therefore like unto them, for your Father knoweth what things ye have need of before ye ask him.

9 After this manner therefore pray ye: Our Father who art in heaven, hallowed be thy name.

10 Thy will be done on earth as it is in heaven.

11 And forgive us our debts, as we forgive our debtors.

12 And lead us not into temptation, but deliver us from evil.

13 For thine is the kingdom, and the power, and the glory, forever. Amen.

14 For, if ye forgive men their trespasses your heavenly Father will also forgive you;

15 But if ye forgive not men their trespasses neither will your Father forgive your trespasses.

16 Moreover, when ye fast be not as the hypocrites, of a sad countenance, for they disfigure their faces that they may appear unto men to fast. Verily I say unto you, they have their reward.

17 But thou, when thou fastest, anoint thy head, and wash thy face;

18 That thou appear not unto men to fast, but unto thy Father, who is in secret; and thy Father, who seeth in secret, shall reward thee openly.

19 Lay not up for yourselves treasures upon earth, where moth and rust doth corrupt, and thieves break through and steal;

20 But lay up for yourselves treasures in heaven, where neither moth nor rust doth

corrupt, and where thieves do not break through nor steal.

21 For where your treasure is, there will your heart be also.

22 The light of the body is the eye; if, therefore, thine eye be single, thy whole body shall be full of light.

23 But if thine eye be evil, thy whole body shall be full of darkness. If, therefore, the light that is in thee be darkness, how great is that darkness!

24 No man can serve two masters; for either he will hate the one and love the other, or else he will hold to the one and despise the other. Ye cannot serve God and Mammon.

25 And now it came to pass that when Jesus had spoken these words he looked upon the twelve whom he had chosen, and said unto them: Remember the words which I have spoken. For behold, ye are they whom I have chosen to minister unto this people. Therefore I say unto you, take no thought for your life, what ye shall eat, or what ye shall drink; nor yet for your body, what ye shall put on. Is not the life more than meat, and the body than raiment?

26 Behold the fowls of the air, for they sow not, neither do they reap nor gather into barns; yet your heavenly Father feedeth them. Are ye not much better than they?

27 Which of you by taking thought can add one cubit unto his stature?

What characterizes serving God over Satan? (13:24) "The worship of God is an act of love towards God. Jesus emphasized that in praying, giving of alms, and fasting, true disciples do not make a big scene about their worship. They know that God sees all and is aware of the intent of their hearts. Worship acts that are dressed up to impress others are offered out of self-love and not as loving acts to God. This is emphasized by Jesus' statement that a man cannot serve two masters (3 Nephi 13:24). Either we serve God out of love or we are serving the devil, the author of vanity and pride" (Whiting, "Commandment to Be Perfect," 114).

3 Nephi 13:25–34. Jesus Gives Special Instructions to His Twelve Disciples

To whom did Jesus direct his teaching to "take no thought for your life"? (13:25–32) Elder Jeffrey R. Holland wrote: "In a general sense these verses can apply to all believers, but at their most literal level they apply to those the Lord has called as his full-time witnesses. Most people must give some thought to what they will eat and what they will wear; the necessities of life require it. But the twelve disciples were not to do so, for they were chosen 'to minister unto [the] people.' Their call was to give complete devotion to their spiritual ministry and to trust in God's—and the people's—providence for their temporal needs" (*Christ and the New Covenant*, 264–65).

What does God promise if we put Him first in our lives? (13:33) President Henry B. Eyring taught: "The Lord loves you and watches over you. He is all-powerful, and He promised you this: 'But seek ye first the kingdom of God, and his righteousness; and all these things shall be added unto you.' (*Matthew 6:33*).

"That is a true promise. When we put God's purposes first, He will give us miracles. If we pray to know what He would have us do next, He will multiply the effects of what we do in such a way that time seems to be expanded. He may do it in different ways for each individual, but I know from long experience that He is faithful to His word" (Eaton and Eyring, *I Will Lead You Along*, 84–85).

Why should we not be concerned with tomorrow? (13:34) "Don't worry about tomorrow, because you may have no tomorrows. . . . And if you can always witness honestly that whatever you did, you did to the best of your ability, and next day try improvement on that, when your life's end comes, of you it can be said in truth, his was a successful life because he lived to the best that was in him. That's all the Lord expects of any one of His children. We are all born with different capacities, some to do one thing, some to do the other, and all He asks is that we do our best; and that's the measure by which we'll be judged when that time comes" (*Teachings of Harold B. Lee*, 64–65).

3 Nephi 14:1–6. Judge Others the Way You Would Like God to Judge You

What type of judging is forbidden? (14:1–2) "I have been puzzled that some scriptures command us not to judge and others instruct us that we should judge and even tell us how to do it. But as I have studied these passages I have become convinced that these seemingly contradictory directions are consistent when we view them with the perspective of eternity. The key is to understand that there are two kinds of judging: final judgments, which we are forbidden to make, and intermediate judgments, which we are directed to make, but upon righteous principles" (Oaks, "'Judge Not' and Judging," 7). 🟢

What is the difference between a "mote" and a "beam"? (14:3–5) "A mote is a tiny sliver like a small portion from a toothpick, while the beam is usually

28 And why take ye thought for raiment? Consider the lilies of the field how they grow; they toil not, neither do they spin;

29 And yet I say unto you, that even Solomon, in all his glory, was not arrayed like one of these.

30 Wherefore, if God so clothe the grass of the field, which today is, and tomorrow is cast into the oven, even so will he clothe you, if ye are not of little faith.

31 Therefore take no thought, saying, What shall we eat? or, What shall we drink? or, Wherewithal shall we be clothed?

32 For your heavenly Father knoweth that ye have need of all these things.

33 But seek ye first the kingdom of God and his righteousness, and all these things shall be added unto you.

34 Take therefore no thought for the morrow, for the morrow shall take thought for the things of itself. Sufficient is the day unto the evil thereof.

CHAPTER 14

Jesus commands: Judge not; ask of God; beware of false prophets—He promises salvation to those who do the will of the Father—Compare Matthew 7. About A.D. 34.

1 And now it came to pass that when Jesus had spoken these words he turned again to the multitude, and did open his mouth unto them again, saying: Verily, verily, I say unto you, Judge not, that ye be not judged.

2 For with what judgment ye judge, ye shall be judged; and with what measure ye mete, it shall be measured to you again.

3 And why beholdest thou the mote that is in thy brother's eye, but considerest not the beam that is in thine own eye?

4 Or how wilt thou say to thy brother: Let me pull the mote out of thine eye—and behold, a beam is in thine own eye?

5 Thou hypocrite, first cast the beam out of thine own eye; and then shalt thou see clearly to cast the mote out of thy brother's eye.

6 Give not that which is holy unto the dogs, neither cast ye your pearls before swine, lest they trample them under their feet, and turn again and rend you.

7 Ask, and it shall be given unto you; seek, and ye shall find; knock, and it shall be opened unto you.

8 For every one that asketh, receiveth; and he that seeketh, findeth; and to him that knocketh, it shall be opened.

9 Or what man is there of you, who, if his son ask bread, will give him a stone?

10 Or if he ask a fish, will he give him a serpent?

11 If ye then, being evil, know how to give good gifts unto your children, how much more shall your Father who is in heaven give good things to them that ask him?

12 Therefore, all things whatsoever ye would that men should do to you, do ye even so to them, for this is the law and the prophets.

13 Enter ye in at the strait gate; for wide is the gate, and broad is the way, which leadeth to destruction, and many there be who go in thereat;

14 Because strait is the gate, and narrow is the way, which leadeth unto life, and few there be that find it.

a great, strong timber or metal which runs from wall to wall to support the heavy roof of the building" (Kimball, *Miracle of Forgiveness*, 269).

How do "dogs" and "swine" figure in ancient scripture? (14:6) "The dog being an unclean animal the name was used as a term of reproach" (Brewster, *Doctrine and Covenants Encyclopedia*, 142). Additionally, "'swine' and 'sow' are mentioned in the Nephite portion of the Book of Mormon with a tone of disgust (3 Nephi 7:8; 14:6). That's what we would expect among people who even nominally followed the constraints of the law of Moses on eating pork" (Sorenson, *Ancient American Setting*, 297). ⊕

3 Nephi 14:7–14. Jesus Teaches about Prayer and the Golden Rule

What are we to do for others? (14:12) "This rule embodies the entire moral code of the Gospel of Christ and the Kingdom of God, equally binding upon nations and associations, as in individuals.

"... [This] precept, as delivered by the Savior, enjoins us not only to avoid harming our brother, but to do that which benefits him" (Reynolds and Sjodahl, *Commentary on the Book of Mormon*, 7:158). ⊕

3 Nephi 14:15–20. True Prophets Are Known by Their Good Works

How can we identify false prophets? (14:15–20) "Let us beware of false prophets and false teachers, both men and women, who are self-appointed declarers of the doctrines of the Church and who seek to spread their false gospel and attract followers by sponsoring symposia, books, and journals whose contents challenge fundamental doctrines of the Church. Beware of those who speak and publish in opposition to God's true prophets and who actively proselyte others with reckless disregard for the eternal well-being of those whom they seduce" (Ballard, "Beware of False Prophets and False Teachers," 63). ✚

3 Nephi 14:21–27. The Savior Teaches That Disciples Must Hear and Obey

Why will some who claim faithfulness to the Lord not enter into His presence? (14:21–22) "Some people are weak in their faith and testimonies but are not even aware of how precarious their situation is. Many of them likely would be offended at the suggestion. They raise their right hand to sustain Church leaders and then murmur and complain when a decision does not square with their way of thinking. They claim to be obedient to God's commandments but do not feel at all uncomfortable about purchasing food at the store on Sunday and then asking the Lord to bless it. Some say they would give their lives for the Lord, yet they refuse to serve in the nursery" (Wirthlin, "Spiritual Bonfires of Testimony," 35).

What did these people do so the Savior would say that He never knew them? (14:23) "Jesus is saying: 'I never knew you as true disciples, for you never received the fulness of my gospel and came into my Church, and hence, Ye never knew me'; or, 'Ye never knew me so fully as to be sealed up unto eternal life with your callings and elections made sure, and since you did not magnify your callings in the priesthood, you shall be cast out and be made as though I never knew you'" (McConkie, *Doctrinal New Testament Commentary* 1:255).

15 Beware of false prophets, who come to you in sheep's clothing, but inwardly they are ravening wolves.

16 Ye shall know them by their fruits. Do men gather grapes of thorns, or figs of thistles?

17 Even so every good tree bringeth forth good fruit; but a corrupt tree bringeth forth evil fruit.

18 A good tree cannot bring forth evil fruit, neither a corrupt tree bring forth good fruit.

19 Every tree that bringeth not forth good fruit is hewn down, and cast into the fire.

20 Wherefore, by their fruits ye shall know them.

21 Not every one that saith unto me, Lord, Lord, shall enter into the kingdom of heaven; but he that doeth the will of my Father who is in heaven.

22 Many will say to me in that day: Lord, Lord, have we not prophesied in thy name, and in thy name have we cast out devils, and in thy name done many wonderful works?

23 And then will I profess unto them: I never knew you; depart from me, ye that work iniquity.

24 Therefore, whoso heareth these sayings of mine and doeth them, I will liken him unto a wise man, who built his house upon a rock—

25 And the rain descended, and the floods came, and the winds blew, and beat upon that house; and it fell not, for it was founded upon a rock.

26 And every one that heareth these sayings of mine and doeth them not shall be likened unto a foolish man, who built his house upon the sand—

27 And the rain descended, and the floods came, and the winds blew, and beat upon that house; and it fell, and great was the fall of it.

CHAPTER 15

Jesus announces that the law of Moses is fulfilled in Him—The Nephites are the other sheep of whom He spoke in Jerusalem—Because of iniquity, the Lord's people in Jerusalem do not know of the scattered sheep of Israel. About A.D. 34.

1 And now it came to pass that when Jesus had ended these sayings he cast his eyes round about on the multitude, and said unto them: Behold, ye have heard the things which I taught before I ascended to my Father; therefore, whoso remembereth these sayings of mine and doeth them, him will I raise up at the last day.

2 And it came to pass that when Jesus had said these words he perceived that there were some among them who marveled, and wondered what he would concerning the law of Moses; for they understood not the saying that old things had passed away, and that all things had become new.

3 And he said unto them: Marvel not that I said unto you that old things had passed away, and that all things had become new.

4 Behold, I say unto you that the law is fulfilled that was given unto Moses.

5 Behold, I am he that gave the law, and I am he who covenanted with my people Israel; therefore, the law in me is fulfilled, for I have come to fulfil the law; therefore it hath an end.

6 Behold, I do not destroy the prophets, for as many as have not been fulfilled in me, verily I say unto you, shall all be fulfilled.

3 Nephi 15:1–10. Jesus Explains How the Law of Moses Is Fulfilled in Him

What does the phrase "ye have heard the things which I taught before I ascended to my Father" suggest? (15:1) To understand the context and intent of these verses, notice when Jesus Christ is speaking to the twelve disciples and when His words are given to the multitude. For example, in verse 11, the Savior directs His words to the Twelve. How does it help you to better understand the intent of these verses when studying this account in this way?

What can we learn from the statement by the Savior that "these sayings" were His? (15:1) "This indicates that the Sermon in Bountiful was an intentional repetition and that both the teachings and their frame were the Savior's own and not the literary work of the evangelist Matthew" (Cloward, "Savior's Missionary Training Sermon," 121). ●

What was the relationship between the law of Moses and the new law? (15:2–5) Elder Jeffrey R. Holland explained: "It is crucial to understand that the law of Moses was overlaid upon, and thereby included, many basic parts of the gospel of Jesus Christ, which had existed before it. It was never intended to be something apart or separated from, and certainly not something antagonistic to, the gospel of Jesus Christ. It was more elementary than the full gospel—thus its schoolmaster's role in bringing people to the gospel—but its purpose was never to have been different from the higher law. Both were to bring people to Christ" (*Christ and the New Covenant*, 147). ●

What is the distinction between the covenant and the law? (15:8) "Jesus clarifies some important distinctions between the law and the covenant. He explains that the law, which was given to Moses about 1300 years earlier, had been fulfilled by him, the Savior. Yahweh, the premortal Lord, had given the law to Moses at Mount Sinai. And Jesus, the Anointed One, had fulfilled the law at Gethsemane, Golgotha, and the Garden Tomb. But, Christ goes on to explain, the covenant he had made with his people was not yet all fulfilled. The covenant, which was given to Abraham around 1900 B.C., had been partially fulfilled in the intervening two millennia, but there were many wonderful covenant promises waiting to be fulfilled, especially in these latter days" (Ludlow, "Covenant Teachings of the Scriptures").

In what ways is the Savior both the "law" and the "light" to you? (15:9) How does the Savior's law influence you for good? How do you access His light? How does keeping His law affect your ability to obtain light? According to this verse, what ultimate blessing can you receive?

3 Nephi 15:11–24. The Nephites Are Some of the Other Sheep Jesus Promised to Visit

In what way were the Nephite Twelve to be a light to the people? (15:12) "Both the Jerusalem apostles and the Nephite disciples were to be the channel of light through which Israel would receive Christ's true doctrinal word and the ordinances of his gospel....

"For today's technological world, the light of the Twelve might be thought of as something like a laser. The Light of Christ through the Twelve emits a coherent beam of one color directed on a salvational path. This light is emitted so precisely that it marks a glowing course of safety for Israel. In the hierarchy of available lights of this life, that light from the Twelve stands supreme next to Christ's" (Anderson, "The Twelve," 150–51).

7 And because I said unto you that old things have passed away, I do not destroy that which hath been spoken concerning things which are to come.

8 For behold, the covenant which I have made with my people is not all fulfilled; but the law which was given unto Moses hath an end in me.

9 Behold, I am the law, and the light. Look unto me, and endure to the end, and ye shall live; for unto him that endureth to the end will I give eternal life.

10 Behold, I have given unto you the commandments; therefore keep my commandments. And this is the law and the prophets, for they truly testified of me.

11 And now it came to pass that when Jesus had spoken these words, he said unto those twelve whom he had chosen:

12 Ye are my disciples; and ye are a light unto this people, who are a remnant of the house of Joseph.

13 And behold, this is the land of your inheritance; and the Father hath given it unto you.

14 And not at any time hath the Father given me commandment that I should tell it unto your brethren at Jerusalem.

15 Neither at any time hath the Father given me commandment that I should tell unto them concerning the other tribes of the house of Israel, whom the Father hath led away out of the land.

16 This much did the Father command me, that I should tell unto them:

17 That other sheep I have which are not of this fold; them also I must bring, and they shall hear my voice; and there shall be one fold, and one shepherd.

18 And now, because of stiffneckedness and unbelief they understood not my word; therefore I was commanded to say no more of the Father concerning this thing unto them.

19 But, verily, I say unto you that the Father hath commanded me, and I tell it unto you, that ye were separated from among them because of their iniquity; therefore it is because of their iniquity that they know not of you.

20 And verily, I say unto you again that the other tribes hath the Father separated from them; and it is because of their iniquity that they know not of them.

21 And verily I say unto you, that ye are they of whom I said: Other sheep I have which are not of this fold; them also I must bring, and they shall hear my voice; and there shall be one fold, and one shepherd.

22 And they understood me not, for they supposed it had been the Gentiles; for they understood not that the Gentiles should be converted through their preaching.

23 And they understood me not that I said they shall hear my voice; and they understood me not that the Gentiles should not at any time hear my voice—that I should not manifest myself unto them save it were by the Holy Ghost.

24 But behold, ye have both heard my voice, and seen me; and ye are my sheep, and ye are numbered among those whom the Father hath given me.

Why is the Savior often called a shepherd? (15:17) "Jesus Christ is often called the Good Shepherd (see D&C 50:44; John 10:7–18; Alma 5:38–60; Helaman 7:18). The metaphor of the shepherd and his relationship to his sheep connotes personal care and concern" (*Book of Mormon Student Manual* [2009], 313).

In what way was the Savior showing His personal concern for His sheep in the Americas? How has He shown His personal concern in your life? ⊕

Where are these "other tribes" that are separated from the house of Israel? (15:20) "There is something mysterious and fascinating about believing the Ten Tribes are behind an iceberg somewhere in the land of the north, or that they are on some distant planet that will one day join itself with the earth, or that the tribe of Dan is in Denmark, the tribe of Reuben in Russia, and so forth. . . . True it is that they are lost from the knowledge of the world; they are not seen and recognized as the kingdom they once were; but in general terms, their whereabouts is known. They are scattered in all the nations of the earth, primarily in the nations north of the lands of their first inheritance" (McConkie, *New Witness*, 520).

Why did the Jews mistake the "other sheep" as Gentiles? (15:22–23) "Those of the Old World supposed that Christ was referring to the Gentiles in his reference to 'other sheep.' This indicates that they did not fully understand the implications of the Abrahamic covenant. In the divine economy of things, those of Israel were to be accorded the privilege of his personal appearance while others [Gentiles] were to obtain their assurance of saving truths by and through the Holy Ghost" (McConkie, "Doctrine of a Covenant People," 170). ⊕

3 Nephi 16:1–3. Jesus Christ Speaks of Other People He Will Visit

Why does the Savior personally visit His scattered sheep? (16:1–3) "Earlier in the Book of Mormon (2 Nephi 29:11–14), the Lord promises that in the mouths of three great scriptural witnesses the divinity of Christ would be established. It is of interest to note that evidently the resurrected Jesus Christ appeared to all of the peoples who were to write these great scriptural witnesses. He appeared as a resurrected being to the Jews, from whom we get the Bible; he appeared as a resurrected being to the Nephites, from whom we get the Book of Mormon; and he promises here that he is going to appear as a resurrected being to the lost tribes of Israel, from whom shall come the third great scriptural witness" (Ludlow, *Companion to Your Study of the Book of Mormon*, 271).

3 Nephi 16:4–20. In the Latter Days, the Gospel Shall Go First to the Gentiles and Then to the House of Israel

Who are the Gentiles? (16:4) "After the Kingdom of Israel was destroyed and the Ten Tribes were led away into Assyrian captivity, those of the Kingdom of Judah called themselves Jews and designated all others as Gentiles. It is this concept that would have been taught to Lehi, Mulek and the other Jews who came to the Western Hemisphere to found the great Nephite and Lamanite civilizations" (McConkie, *Mormon Doctrine*, 311).

What is the "fulness of the Gentiles"? (16:4) "The 'fulness of the Gentiles' is a term for a doctrine taught in the New Testament, the Book of Mormon, and the Doctrine and Covenants. It refers to a process whereby, after Jesus' ministry among his Jewish countrymen, the gospel was preached to Gentiles in the meridian of time" (Nyman, "Gentiles, Fulness of," in Ludlow, *Encyclopedia of Mormonism*, 4:541).

CHAPTER 16

Jesus will visit others of the lost sheep of Israel— In the latter days the gospel will go to the Gentiles and then to the house of Israel—The Lord's people will see eye to eye when He brings again Zion. About A.D. 34.

1 And verily, verily, I say unto you that I have other sheep, which are not of this land, neither of the land of Jerusalem, neither in any parts of that land round about whither I have been to minister.

2 For they of whom I speak are they who have not as yet heard my voice; neither have I at any time manifested myself unto them.

3 But I have received a commandment of the Father that I shall go unto them, and that they shall hear my voice, and shall be numbered among my sheep, that there may be one fold and one shepherd; therefore I go to show myself unto them.

4 And I command you that ye shall write these sayings after I am gone, that if it so be that my people at Jerusalem, they who have seen me and been with me in my ministry, do not ask the Father in my name, that they may receive a knowledge of you by the Holy Ghost, and also of the other tribes whom they know not of, that these sayings which ye shall write shall be kept and shall be manifested unto the Gentiles, that through the fulness of the Gentiles, the remnant of their seed, who shall be scattered forth upon the face of the earth because of their unbelief, may be brought in, or may be brought to a knowledge of me, their Redeemer.

5 And then will I gather them in from the four quarters of the earth; and then will I fulfil the covenant which the Father hath made unto all the people of the house of Israel.

6 And blessed are the Gentiles, because of their belief in me, in and of the Holy Ghost, which witnesses unto them of me and of the Father.

7 Behold, because of their belief in me, saith the Father, and because of the unbelief of you, O house of Israel, in the latter day shall the truth come unto the Gentiles, that the fulness of these things shall be made known unto them.

8 But wo, saith the Father, unto the unbelieving of the Gentiles—for notwithstanding they have come forth upon the face of this land, and have scattered my people who are of the house of Israel; and my people who are of the house of Israel have been cast out from among them, and have been trodden under feet by them;

9 And because of the mercies of the Father unto the Gentiles, and also the judgments of the Father upon my people who are of the house of Israel, verily, verily, I say unto you, that after all this, and I have caused my people who are of the house of Israel to be smitten, and to be afflicted, and to be slain, and to be cast out from among them, and to become hated by them, and to become a hiss and a byword among them—

10 And thus commandeth the Father that I should say unto you: At that day when the Gentiles shall sin against my gospel, and shall reject the fulness of my gospel, and shall be lifted up in the pride of their hearts above all nations, and above all the people of the whole earth, and shall be filled with all manner of lyings, and of deceits, and of mischiefs, and all manner of hypocrisy, and murders, and priestcrafts, and whoredoms, and of secret abominations; and if they shall do all those things, and shall reject the fulness of my gospel, behold, saith the Father, I will bring the fulness of my gospel from among them.

What blessing and warning will come to the Gentiles in the last days? (16:6–10) "One of the purposes of scattering the house of Israel among all the nations of the earth was to fulfill the covenant made to Abraham to bless all the kindreds of the earth (1 Nephi 22:9; Gen. 12:3). In fulfilling the covenant to gather Israel from among the nations, Gentile and other, those nations are given the opportunity to gather with Israel and receive the blessings of the gospel (see 3 Nephi 16:6–7, 13). Those Gentiles who reject the gospel will have the covenant people of the Lord gathered from among them and the gospel will be taken out of their midst (vv. 8–12)" (Nyman, "Designations Jesus Gives Himself in 3 Nephi," 55–56). ●

What happens to the Gentiles if they refuse to repent? (16:11–15) "Except for a few who are the humble followers of Christ, the Gentiles will not repent. They will revel in their abominations and sin against the restored gospel, and they will be burned by the brightness of our Lord's coming while the righteous—here called the remnant of Jacob—shall abide the day. And then, in the prophetic imagery, it will be as though the remnant of Israel overthrew their enemies as a young lion among the flocks of sheep" (McConkie, *Millennial Messiah*, 248). ✪

To whom was Isaiah referring as "watchmen"? (16:18) "Elder George Q. Cannon described the 'officers of the Church of Jesus Christ of Latter-day Saints' as 'watchmen' (GT 1:269). Speaking as one of the Lord's chosen servants, President Spencer W. Kimball said, 'We continue to warn the people and plead with them, for we are watchmen upon the towers, and in our hands we have a trumpet which we must blow loudly and sound the alarm' (CR, Oct. 1975, 8)" (Brewster, *Doctrine and Covenants Encyclopedia*, 626). As to seeing "eye to eye," it means that "the prophets shall see with their own eyes the return of the Lord's people to the Land of Zion. It may also mean that there will be no difference of opinion among the *watchmen*" (Reynolds and Sjodahl, *Commentary on the Book of Mormon*, 7:168).

What is Jerusalem? (16:18–19) "Both the New Testament and the modern scriptures speak of a New Jerusalem to be built in the latter days. Some have assumed that this refers to only one new city, but a careful reading indicates that there are several 'new' Jerusalems, including (1) the city in Enoch's day, which will come with Jesus Christ at the time of his second coming; (2) the old city of Jerusalem in Israel, which will be rebuilt and thus will become new; and (3) a city called New Jerusalem, which will be built in Zion—the Americas" (Ludlow, *A Companion to Your Study of the Doctrine and Covenants*, 190).

11 And then will I remember my covenant which I have made unto my people, O house of Israel, and I will bring my gospel unto them.

12 And I will show unto thee, O house of Israel, that the Gentiles shall not have power over you; but I will remember my covenant unto you, O house of Israel, and ye shall come unto the knowledge of the fulness of my gospel.

13 But if the Gentiles will repent and return unto me, saith the Father, behold they shall be numbered among my people, O house of Israel.

14 And I will not suffer my people, who are of the house of Israel, to go through among them, and tread them down, saith the Father.

15 But if they will not turn unto me, and hearken unto my voice, I will suffer them, yea, I will suffer my people, O house of Israel, that they shall go through among them, and shall tread them down, and they shall be as salt that hath lost its savor, which is thenceforth good for nothing but to be cast out, and to be trodden under foot of my people, O house of Israel.

16 Verily, verily, I say unto you, thus hath the Father commanded me—that I should give unto this people this land for their inheritance.

17 And then the words of the prophet Isaiah shall be fulfilled, which say:

18 Thy watchmen shall lift up the voice; with the voice together shall they sing, for they shall see eye to eye when the Lord shall bring again Zion.

19 Break forth into joy, sing together, ye waste places of Jerusalem; for the Lord hath comforted his people, he hath redeemed Jerusalem.

20 The Lord hath made bare his holy arm in the eyes of all the nations; and all the ends of the earth shall see the salvation of God.

CHAPTER 17

Jesus directs the people to ponder His words and pray for understanding—He heals their sick—He prays for the people, using language that cannot be written—Angels minister to and fire encircles their little ones. About A.D. 34.

1 Behold, now it came to pass that when Jesus had spoken these words he looked round about again on the multitude, and he said unto them: Behold, my time is at hand.

2 I perceive that ye are weak, that ye cannot understand all my words which I am commanded of the Father to speak unto you at this time.

3 Therefore, go ye unto your homes, and ponder upon the things which I have said, and ask of the Father, in my name, that ye may understand, and prepare your minds for the morrow, and I come unto you again.

4 But now I go unto the Father, and also to show myself unto the lost tribes of Israel, for they are not lost unto the Father, for he knoweth whither he hath taken them.

5 And it came to pass that when Jesus had thus spoken, he cast his eyes round about again on the multitude, and beheld they were in tears, and did look steadfastly upon him as if they would ask him to tarry a little longer with them.

6 And he said unto them: Behold, my bowels are filled with compassion towards you.

7 Have ye any that are sick among you? Bring them hither. Have ye any that are lame, or blind, or halt, or maimed, or leprous, or that

3 Nephi 17:1–4. Jesus Commands the People to Go to Their Homes and Prepare for the Morrow

Why are we taught spiritual concepts gradually, line upon line? (17:2) The Savior had just finished teaching about the scattering and gathering of Israel. "In spite of their [spiritual] preparation they were not taught all of the doctrine of the gathering until the second day. . . . The gathering of Israel is a profound doctrine filled with implications about God, his plan, and our place in it. It reminds members of the kingdom of God that they are a covenant people and implies that they will be saved only by keeping those covenants" (Hansen, "Gathering to the Temple," 212). Therefore, the Savior did not give the Nephites all of this information at one time.

What is the purpose of pondering? (17:3) "Man must take time to meditate, to sweep the cobwebs from his mind, so that he might get a more firm grip on the truth and spend less time chasing phantoms and dallying in projects of lesser worth. . . .

"Take time to meditate. Ponder the meaning of the work in which you are engaged. The Lord has counseled, 'Let the solemnities of eternity rest upon your minds' (D&C 43:34). You cannot do that when your minds are preoccupied with the worries and cares of the world" (*Teachings of Ezra Taft Benson*, 390).

3 Nephi 17:5–10. Jesus Heals the Sick and Afflicted

What is the context of the term *bowels*? (17:6–7) "In the Bible the Hebrew and Greek words translated as 'bowels' imply compassion, sympathy, love, or pity. Thus the bowels are most often associated with one's feelings or emotions" (Gaskill, *Lost Language of Symbolism*, 32).

What led to this outpouring of spiritual power? (17:7–10) "Sensing with divine insight that these people desired to behold the miracles he had performed for their brothers and sisters in Jerusalem, and recognizing instantly that their faith was sufficient for them to be healed, Christ responded to each need within the multitude, 'and he did heal them every one as they were brought forth unto him.' In response to such an outpouring of compassion and mercy, all of the congregation, the healed as well as the whole, did 'bow down at his feet, and did worship him'" (Holland, *Christ and the New Covenant*, 268–69). ⊕

What can we learn from the Savior's very personal ministry among the Nephites? (17:9) The Savior has the power to heal people in groups or at a distance without touching them (see Luke 7:1–19; Mark 7:24–30). "The Lord chose among the Nephites, however, to have the sick brought close to him, and as the record implies, he touched each one personally" (Holzapfel, "One by One," 187). In what ways have you experienced the Savior's healing power?

are withered, or that are deaf, or that are afflicted in any manner? Bring them hither and I will heal them, for I have compassion upon you; my bowels are filled with mercy.

8 For I perceive that ye desire that I should show unto you what I have done unto your brethren at Jerusalem, for I see that your faith is sufficient that I should heal you.

9 And it came to pass that when he had thus spoken, all the multitude, with one accord, did go forth with their sick and their afflicted, and their lame, and with their blind, and with their dumb, and with all them that were afflicted in any manner; and he did heal them every one as they were brought forth unto him.

10 And they did all, both they who had been healed and they who were whole, bow down at his feet, and did worship him; and as many as could come for the multitude did kiss his feet, insomuch that they did bathe his feet with their tears.

Interpreting God's Promises to His Covenant Children

"Third Nephi contains some key passages relative to the promises of the Lord to the house of Israel. I have particular reference to chapters 16, 20, and 21. These passages have been misunderstood and misused. . . . To that end, perhaps these observations ought be made:

"1. The Book of Mormon came forth to gather Israel—all Israel, not a particular or exclusive part of Israel. On the title page Moroni states that the purpose of the book is 'to show unto the remnant of the House of Israel what great things the Lord hath done for their fathers; and that they may know the covenants of the Lord, that they are not cast off forever.' Note that the emphasis is on *the* remnant of Israel, not *a* remnant. Long before Christ visited the Nephites, Israel had been scattered throughout the earth (see 1 Nephi 22:4), thus, Christ's announcement to the Nephites that there were still others that he had been commanded of the Father to visit. All these scattered remnants of Jacob have claim on the promises made to their fathers. Each is 'a remnant of Jacob,' and collectively, they are 'the remnant.' . . .

"2. These chapters cannot be properly understood in isolation from the rest of the covenant sermon. They assume an understanding of the call and ordination of the Twelve (see 3 Nephi 18:36; Moroni 2:2). The whole idea of there being 'twelve' instead of some other number is their symbolic representation of the twelve tribes of Israel. The unity with which they stand at the head of the Church was and is to be a constant reminder of the Lord's promise to unite all of Israel in his millennial kingdom. The gathering of Israel and building of Zion must take place under their direction. Any doctrine that holds that some remnant of Israel can do some portion of the gathering or the building

11 And it came to pass that he commanded that their little children should be brought.

12 So they brought their little children and set them down upon the ground round about him, and Jesus stood in the midst; and the multitude gave way till they had all been brought unto him.

13 And it came to pass that when they had all been brought, and Jesus stood in the midst, he commanded the multitude that they should kneel down upon the ground.

14 And it came to pass that when they had knelt upon the ground, Jesus groaned within himself, and said: Father, I am troubled because of the wickedness of the people of the house of Israel.

15 And when he had said these words, he himself also knelt upon the earth; and behold he prayed unto the Father, and the things which he prayed cannot be written, and the multitude did bear record who heard him.

16 And after this manner do they bear record: The eye hath never seen, neither hath the ear heard, before, so great and marvelous things as we saw and heard Jesus speak unto the Father;

3 Nephi 17:11–25. Jesus Prays and Blesses the Little Children

Why is the Lord so concerned about little children? (17:11–14) "We cannot know exactly what the Savior was feeling in such a poignant moment, but we do know that He was 'troubled' and that He 'groaned within himself' over the destructive influences always swirling around the innocent. We know He felt a great need to pray for and bless the children.

"In such times as we are in, . . . I too pray for the children. Some days it seems that a sea of temptation and transgression inundates them, simply washes over them before they can successfully withstand it, before they should have to face it. . . .

"Well, some of [these things] may be beyond our control, but I testify with faith in the living God that they are not beyond His" (Holland, "Prayer for the Children," 85).

Why were the Savior's emotions so strong on this occasion? (17:15–22) "Jesus concluded his supplication on behalf of the children and arose from his prayer. However, because of their overwhelming joy, the multitude did not—or could not—rise. Jesus bade them arise, saying that because of *their* faith *his joy* was full. What a remarkable gift to the Savior of the world to be so faithful and devoted, so humble and respectful, that he, the Man of Sorrows, who weeps so often for the sins of the world, could weep because his joy was full" (Holland, *Christ and the New Covenant,* 270). ⊕

of Zion independent of the direction of the Twelve, . . . is out of harmony with the covenant of baptism and the covenant to sustain the Twelve . . . , with which the Savior began his instruction to the Nephites (3 Nephi 12:1).

"It ought also to be observed that the same pattern and principle exists in our dispensation. The keys of the gathering of Israel and the building of Zion rest with the First Presidency, the Twelve, and none others. . . .

"3. Spiritual stability and sound understanding are not found in strained phrases. We ought to be inherently suspicious of interpretations that aggrandize a particular group or some marvelous or mighty leader that is going to come onto the scene to straighten out the Church. The Twelve are in place. . . .

"4. Wisdom suggests moderation and caution in scriptural interpretation. In discussing chapters 16, 20, and 21, . . . Elder McConkie observed: 'It is not always possible for us in our present state of spiritual enlightenment to put every event into an exact category or time frame.' He also noted that some of these texts 'apply to both pre- and post-millennial events; some have an initial and partial fulfillment in our day and shall have a second and grander completion in the days ahead' (*Millennial Messiah,* 251).

"5. In a past General Conference we were warned about false views relative to the gathering. The warning was specifically against 'cults' and 'colonies' ([Packer, 'To Be Learned Is Good If . . . ,'] 73). The caution was to beware of those who think themselves a part of some inner circle, who think their understanding is ahead of those called to hold the keys of the gathering of Israel, and thus, who think they are to preside over all that takes place relative to it" (McConkie, "Doctrine of a Covenant People," 177–79).

17 And no tongue can speak, neither can there be written by any man, neither can the hearts of men conceive so great and marvelous things as we both saw and heard Jesus speak; and no one can conceive of the joy which filled our souls at the time we heard him pray for us unto the Father.

18 And it came to pass that when Jesus had made an end of praying unto the Father, he arose; but so great was the joy of the multitude that they were overcome.

19 And it came to pass that Jesus spake unto them, and bade them arise.

20 And they arose from the earth, and he said unto them: Blessed are ye because of your faith. And now behold, my joy is full.

21 And when he had said these words, he wept, and the multitude bare record of it, and he took their little children, one by one, and blessed them, and prayed unto the Father for them.

22 And when he had done this he wept again;

23 And he spake unto the multitude, and said unto them: Behold your little ones.

24 And as they looked to behold they cast their eyes towards heaven, and they saw the heavens open, and they saw angels descending out of heaven as it were in the midst of fire; and they came down and encircled those little ones about, and they were encircled about with fire; and the angels did minister unto them.

25 And the multitude did see and hear and bear record; and they know that their record is true for they all of them did see and hear, every man for himself; and they were in number about two thousand and five hundred souls; and they did consist of men, women, and children.

What did the encircling fire represent? (17:24)
"This chapter [3 Nephi 17] certifies that religion is more than doctrine, more than theology, more even than selfless service. Religion is a thing of the heart. Religion is lived. And religion is felt. Being encircled about with fire is a tangible symbol of the outpouring of the Holy Spirit (compare Nephi and Lehi's experience in Helaman 5:23–49)" (McConkie et al., *Doctrinal Commentary*, 4:118).

Why did Mormon record the exact number of people present? (17:25) "[This] concluding testimony suggests something of the urgency Mormon must have felt in trying to convey that this really did happen. After this vivid description from his own words, he invoked witnesses—two thousand five hundred of them, 'men, women, and children,'—stressing twice that the entire multitude 'did see and hear and bear record' of this unprecedented experience" (Holland, *Christ and the New Covenant*, 270–71).

CHAPTER 18

Jesus institutes the sacrament among the Nephites —They are commanded to pray always in His name—Those who eat His flesh and drink His blood unworthily are damned—The disciples are given power to confer the Holy Ghost. About A.D. 34.

1 And it came to pass that Jesus commanded his disciples that they should bring forth some bread and wine unto him.

2 And while they were gone for bread and wine, he commanded the multitude that they should sit themselves down upon the earth.

3 And when the disciples had come with bread and wine, he took of the bread and brake and blessed it; and he gave unto the disciples and commanded that they should eat.

4 And when they had eaten and were filled, he commanded that they should give unto the multitude.

5 And when the multitude had eaten and were filled, he said unto the disciples: Behold there shall one be ordained among you, and to him will I give power that he shall break bread and bless it and give it unto the people of my church, unto all those who shall believe and be baptized in my name.

6 And this shall ye always observe to do, even as I have done, even as I have broken bread and blessed it and given it unto you.

7 And this shall ye do in remembrance of my body, which I have shown unto you. And it shall be a testimony unto the Father that ye do always remember me. And if ye do always remember me ye shall have my Spirit to be with you.

8 And it came to pass that when he said these words, he commanded his disciples that they should take of the wine of the cup and drink of it, and that they should also give unto the multitude that they might drink of it.

3 Nephi 18:1–14. Jesus Institutes the Sacrament among the Nephites

What are the blessings of partaking of the sacrament? (18:6) "Those who would deny themselves the blessing of the sacrament by not attending sacrament meeting or by not thinking of the Savior during the services surely must not understand the great opportunity to be forgiven, to have his Spirit to guide and comfort them! What more could anyone ask?

"As we worthily partake of the sacrament, we will sense those things we need to improve in and receive the help and determination to do so. No matter what our problems, the sacrament always gives hope" (Groberg, "Beauty and Importance of the Sacrament," 38). ⊕

Why did the sacrament replace animal sacrifices? (18:6–7) "As sacrifice was thus to cease [see 3 Nephi 15:2–5] with the occurrence of the great event toward which it pointed, there must needs be a new ordinance to replace it, an ordinance which also would center the attention of the saints on the infinite and eternal atonement. . . . Sacrifice stopped and sacrament started. It was the end of the old era, the beginning of the new. Sacrifice looked forward to the shed blood and bruised flesh of the Lamb of God. The sacrament was to be in remembrance of his spilt blood and broken flesh, the emblems, bread and wine, typifying such as completely as had the shedding of the blood of animals in their days" (McConkie, *Doctrinal New Testament Commentary*, 1:719–20).

What can we do to "always remember" Him? (18:11) "I wish to elaborate on three aspects of what it means to 'always remember him': first, seeking to know and follow His will; second, recognizing and accepting our obligation to answer to Christ for every thought, word, and action; and third, living with faith and without fear so that we can always look to the Savior for the help we need" (Christofferson, "To Always Remember Him," 49). ☉

How can the Spirit bless my life? (18:11) "By participating weekly and appropriately in the ordinance of the sacrament we qualify for the promise that we will 'always have his Spirit to be with [us]' (D&C 20:77). That Spirit is the foundation of our testimony. It testifies of the Father and the Son, brings all things to our remembrance, and leads us into truth. It is the compass

9 And it came to pass that they did so, and did drink of it and were filled; and they gave unto the multitude, and they did drink, and they were filled.

10 And when the disciples had done this, Jesus said unto them: Blessed are ye for this thing which ye have done, for this is fulfilling my commandments, and this doth witness unto the Father that ye are willing to do that which I have commanded you.

11 And this shall ye always do to those who repent and are baptized in my name; and ye shall do it in remembrance of my blood, which I have shed for you, that ye may witness unto the Father that ye do always remember me. And if ye do always remember me ye shall have my Spirit to be with you.

"And This Shall Ye Do in Remembrance of [Me]" (3 Nephi 18:7)

The Mosaic sacrifices pointed forward to the atoning sacrifice of the Lamb of God that was to come.

The ordinance of the sacrament reminds the faithful of that great and last sacrifice of Jesus Christ, our Redeemer.

Courtesy Church History Museum.

All ordinances before and after the sacrifice of the Lamb of God point to Jesus Christ.

12 And I give unto you a commandment that ye shall do these things. And if ye shall always do these things blessed are ye, for ye are built upon my rock.

13 But whoso among you shall do more or less than these are not built upon my rock, but are built upon a sandy foundation; and when the rain descends, and the floods come, and the winds blow, and beat upon them, they shall fall, and the gates of hell are ready open to receive them.

14 Therefore blessed are ye if ye shall keep my commandments, which the Father hath commanded me that I should give unto you.

15 Verily, verily, I say unto you, ye must watch and pray always, lest ye be tempted by the devil, and ye be led away captive by him.

16 And as I have prayed among you even so shall ye pray in my church, among my people who do repent and are baptized in my name. Behold I am the light; I have set an example for you.

17 And it came to pass that when Jesus had spoken these words unto his disciples, he turned again unto the multitude and said unto them:

to guide us on our path. This gift of the Holy Ghost, President Wilford Woodruff taught, 'is the greatest gift that can be bestowed upon man'" (Oaks, "Sacrament Meeting and the Sacrament," 17).

How can you experience all you should through the ordinance of the sacrament? (18:12) Think of times when the sacrament has been especially meaningful to you. What was happening in your life that made it so? What attitudes or actions make a spiritual sacrament experience more difficult? What could you do to make partaking of the sacrament more meaningful?

We often see people do less than is commanded, but is it possible to go too far in our religious observance? (18:13) "Another sign of spiritual immaturity and sometimes apostasy is when one focuses on certain gospel principles or pursues 'gospel hobbies' with excess zeal. Almost any virtue taken to excess can become a vice. . . .

"An example might be when one advocates additions to the Word of Wisdom that are not authorized by the Brethren and proselytes others to adopt these interpretations. If we turn a health law or any other principle into a form of religious fanaticism, we are looking beyond the mark.

"Some who are not authorized want to speak for the Brethren and imply that their message contains the 'meat' the Brethren would teach if they were not constrained to teach only the 'milk'" (Cook, "Looking beyond the Mark," 42).

3 Nephi 18:15–25. Jesus Teaches the Multitude to Pray

How is it possible to "pray always"? (18:15) "Praying always entails constantly being conscious of God and his plan of salvation. It consists of having a continual attitude which directs us during every waking moment of mortality, of maintaining a spiritual posture of thankfulness and reliance on the Lord, of desiring the companionship of the Holy Ghost. Brigham Young noted that to pray always is to live as we pray: 'I do not know any other way for the Latter-day Saints than for every breath to be virtually a prayer for God to guide and direct his people. . . . Every breath should virtually be a prayer that God will preserve us from sin and from the effects of sin'" (Parry, "'Pray Always,'" 144).

How do I pray more effectively and how does prayer shield me from temptation? (18:18–19)
"Prayer is the act by which the will of the Father and the will of the child are brought into correspondence with each other. The object of prayer is not to change the will of God but to secure for ourselves and for others blessings that God is already willing to grant but that are made conditional on our asking for them" (Bible Dictionary, "Prayer," 707).

"If you will earnestly seek guidance from your Heavenly Father, morning and evening, you will be given the strength to shun any temptation" (Benson, "Message to the Rising Generation," 32). ⊕

What are the blessings of family prayer? (18:21)
"Parents should teach their children to pray. The child learns both from what the parents do and what they say. The child who sees a mother or a father pass through the trials of life with fervent prayer to God and then hears a sincere testimony that God answered in kindness will remember what he or she saw and heard. When trials come, that individual will be prepared" (Eyring, "That He May Write upon Our Hearts," 5). ⊕

How can I help my ward or branch be more welcoming? (18:22–23) "The Savior's commandment to the Nephites to 'not forbid any man from coming unto you when ye shall meet together' has special application to us in the Church today. While we may not verbally 'forbid' others—members and nonmembers alike—from our fellowship in the Church, they may feel 'forbidden' by reason of our attitudes and our actions. [President] M. Russell Ballard observed: 'I believe we members do not have the option to extend the hand of fellowship only to relatives, close friends, certain Church members and those selected nonmembers who express an interest in the Church. Limiting or withholding our fellowship seems to me to be contrary to the gospel of Jesus Christ'" (McConkie et al., *Doctrinal Commentary*, 4:127). ⊕

How can I possibly do what Jesus did? (18:24)
"What had the Nephites seen Him do, and could I possibly do those things in my home? When the people desired for Him to tarry with them a little longer, He had compassion upon them and lingered with them. Then He healed them, prayed with them, taught them, wept with them, blessed their little children one by one, fed them, and administered and shared the sacrament that they might covenant to always remember Him. His ministry among them was about teaching and caring for each individual, and about completing

18 Behold, verily, verily, I say unto you, ye must watch and pray always lest ye enter into temptation; for Satan desireth to have you, that he may sift you as wheat.

19 Therefore ye must always pray unto the Father in my name;

20 And whatsoever ye shall ask the Father in my name, which is right, believing that ye shall receive, behold it shall be given unto you.

21 Pray in your families unto the Father, always in my name, that your wives and your children may be blessed.

22 And behold, ye shall meet together oft; and ye shall not forbid any man from coming unto you when ye shall meet together, but suffer them that they may come unto you and forbid them not;

23 But ye shall pray for them, and shall not cast them out; and if it so be that they come unto you oft ye shall pray for them unto the Father, in my name.

24 Therefore, hold up your light that it may shine unto the world. Behold I am the light which ye shall hold up—that which ye have seen me do. Behold ye see that I have prayed unto the Father, and ye all have witnessed.

25 And ye see that I have commanded that none of you should go away, but rather have commanded that ye should come unto me, that ye might feel and see; even so shall ye do

unto the world; and whosoever breaketh this commandment suffereth himself to be led into temptation.

26 And now it came to pass that when Jesus had spoken these words, he turned his eyes again upon the disciples whom he had chosen, and said unto them:

27 Behold verily, verily, I say unto you, I give unto you another commandment, and then I must go unto my Father that I may fulfil other commandments which he hath given me.

28 And now behold, this is the commandment which I give unto you, that ye shall not suffer any one knowingly to partake of my flesh and blood unworthily, when ye shall minister it;

29 For whoso eateth and drinketh my flesh and blood unworthily eateth and drinketh damnation to his soul; therefore if ye know that a man is unworthy to eat and drink of my flesh and blood ye shall forbid him.

30 Nevertheless, ye shall not cast him out from among you, but ye shall minister unto him and shall pray for him unto the Father, in my name; and if it so be that he repenteth and is baptized in my name, then shall ye receive him, and shall minister unto him of my flesh and blood.

31 But if he repent not he shall not be numbered among my people, that he may not destroy my people, for behold I know my sheep, and they are numbered.

32 Nevertheless, ye shall not cast him out of your synagogues, or your places of worship, for unto such shall ye continue to minister; for ye know not but what they will return and repent, and come unto me with full purpose of heart, and I shall heal them; and ye shall be the means of bringing salvation unto them.

33 Therefore, keep these sayings which I have commanded you that ye come not under

the work His Father had commanded Him to do. There was no thought for Himself" (Tanner, "'I Am the Light Which Ye Shall Hold Up,'" 103).

3 Nephi 18:26–39. Jesus Gives His Disciples Power to Confer the Holy Ghost

What does it mean to partake of the sacrament worthily? (18:28–29) Or how do we know if we are unworthy? "If we desire to improve (which is to repent) and are not under priesthood restriction, then, in my opinion, we are worthy. If, however, we have no desire to improve, if we have no intention of following the guidance of the Spirit, we must ask: Are we worthy to partake, or are we making a mockery of the very purpose of the sacrament, which is to act as a catalyst for personal repentance and improvement?" (Groberg, "Beauty and Importance of the Sacrament," 38–39). ☉

How should we "minister" to those who have left the fold? (18:30–32) "As the Lord says, to 'not cast out' is, by itself, an inadequate response; we must, additionally, make room for them and give them a place among us. Always we must 'continue to minister,' because, for some, we 'shall be the means of bringing salvation to them.' No wonder this effort does not involve a new program. Rather, it involves a principle—the fundamental and regular keeping of the second, great commandment" (Maxwell, "Continue to Minister," 10). ☉

For whom should you "continue to minister"? (18:32) Think of the people you care about or for whom you have a responsibility. Is there someone who might be reached or could be blessed by a renewed effort to reach out in love and concern? What is the Spirit urging you to do for him or her? What more might you do to make him or her feel valued and needed? How does love help us minister to those who may have left the fold of Christ? "After all is said and done, true ministering is accomplished one by one with love as the motivation. . . . With love as the motivation, miracles will happen, and we will find ways to bring our 'missing' sisters and brothers into the all-inclusive embrace of the gospel of Jesus Christ" (Bingham, "Ministering as the Savior Does," 106).

What is the significance of the Savior's "touching" of each of His disciples? (18:36–37) "It appears from verse 37 that the touching here referred to is a laying on of hands—a setting apart or ordination [see Moroni 2:1–3].

"As a result of the fulfillment of the law and as part of the establishment of a new dispensation and new Church, the Savior ordains and sets apart his disciples and gives them authority to confer the gift of the Holy Ghost and set in order the new organization. The words spoken by Christ to the Twelve—which were not heard by the multitude—were preserved (see Moroni 2)" (McConkie et al., *Doctrinal Commentary*, 4:131). ☉

What can we learn from the first day of the Savior's visit? (18:39) "Thus ended the first day. The incomparable Sermon at the Temple was over. It was a manifestation of divine will and presence never to be forgotten. From this experience come many things: teachings of practical ethical value; an understanding of that which was fulfilled and that which remained yet to be fulfilled; a comprehension of the continuity and transition from the old law to the new; knowledge and testimony of the resurrection and exaltation of Jesus Christ; commandments and covenants; and also a basis for religious ritual" (Welch, *Sermon at the Temple*, 82). ☉

3 Nephi 19:1–10. The Twelve Disciples Organize, Teach, and Pray with the People

condemnation; for wo unto him whom the Father condemneth.

34 And I give you these commandments because of the disputations which have been among you. And blessed are ye if ye have no disputations among you.

35 And now I go unto the Father, because it is expedient that I should go unto the Father for your sakes.

36 And it came to pass that when Jesus had made an end of these sayings, he touched with his hand the disciples whom he had chosen, one by one, even until he had touched them all, and spake unto them as he touched them.

37 And the multitude heard not the words which he spake, therefore they did not bear record; but the disciples bare record that he gave them power to give the Holy Ghost. And I will show unto you hereafter that this record is true.

38 And it came to pass that when Jesus had touched them all, there came a cloud and overshadowed the multitude that they could not see Jesus.

39 And while they were overshadowed he departed from them, and ascended into heaven. And the disciples saw and did bear record that he ascended again into heaven.

CHAPTER 19

The twelve disciples minister unto the people and pray for the Holy Ghost—The disciples are baptized and receive the Holy Ghost and the ministering of angels—Jesus prays using words that cannot be written—He attests to the exceedingly great faith of these Nephites. About A.D. 34.

1 And now it came to pass that when Jesus had ascended into heaven, the multitude did disperse, and every man did take his wife and his children and did return to his own home.

2 And it was noised abroad among the people immediately, before it was yet dark, that the multitude had seen Jesus, and that he had ministered unto them, and that he would also show himself on the morrow unto the multitude.

3 Yea, and even all the night it was noised abroad concerning Jesus; and insomuch did they send forth unto the people that there were many, yea, an exceedingly great number, did labor exceedingly all that night, that they might be on the morrow in the place where Jesus should show himself unto the multitude.

4 And it came to pass that on the morrow, when the multitude was gathered together, behold, Nephi and his brother whom he had raised from the dead, whose name was Timothy, and also his son, whose name was Jonas, and also Mathoni, and Mathonihah, his brother, and Kumen, and Kumenonhi, and Jeremiah, and Shemnon, and Jonas, and Zedekiah, and Isaiah—now these were the names of the disciples whom Jesus had chosen—and it came to pass that they went forth and stood in the midst of the multitude.

5 And behold, the multitude was so great that they did cause that they should be separated into twelve bodies.

6 And the twelve did teach the multitude; and behold, they did cause that the multitude should kneel down upon the face of the earth, and should pray unto the Father in the name of Jesus.

7 And the disciples did pray unto the Father also in the name of Jesus. And it came to pass that they arose and ministered unto the people.

8 And when they had ministered those same words which Jesus had spoken—nothing varying from the words which Jesus had spoken—behold, they knelt again and prayed to the Father in the name of Jesus.

How long had the Savior been with the Nephites during this visit? (19:2) It is instructive to note that all the events recorded between 3 Nephi 11:1 and 3 Nephi 19:2 occurred on the first day of the Savior's visit to the land Bountiful.

What does it mean to "minister those same words"? (19:8) "The disciples prayed and arose and ministered to the people. What would they do? They gave the speech here. Notice, the next verse proves what we mean by ministering: 'And when they had ministered those same words which Jesus had spoken.' They ministered the words, see. They came and told them what the teaching was. They told [the people] what the Lord had told them before, so they ministered the words. That's what you do when you minister. In other words, you come and teach" (Nibley, *Teachings of the Book of Mormon*, 3:356).

What makes the Holy Ghost a "most desired" gift? (19:9) "It is most significant that it was this for which the Nephite twelve prayed above all else. As Christ had not yet appeared to them for this second day (and because the Father and Son could not permanently be with them—or us—in a telestial world), the next best companionship came from that member of the Godhead who *can* be with mortals permanently—the Holy Ghost . . . who is the spiritual extension and telestial representative of the Father and the Son" (Holland, *Christ and the New Covenant*, 278). ●

3 Nephi 19:11–18. The Savior Appears and Commands His Disciples to Pray

Why were the people baptized again? (19:11–13) "When Christ appeared to the Nephites on this continent, he commanded them to be baptized, although they had been baptized previously for the remission of their sins. We read how Nephi beheld angels who came and ministered to him daily; how he baptized all who came to be baptized for the remission of sins; how he organized the Church; and how he even raised his brother from the dead, since he held the priesthood. Then we read that the Savior commanded Nephi and the people to be baptized again, because he had organized anew the Church under the gospel. Before that it had been organized under the law" (Smith, *Doctrines of Salvation*, 2:336).

Why does fire represent the Holy Ghost? (19:13–14) "The symbolism of receiving the gift of the Holy Ghost is that of lighting a perpetual flame within the soul, one which provides light and warmth while constantly purging that which is unclean from it" (McConkie, *Gospel Symbolism*, 197).

Why was the Nephites' experience with the Savior so unique in earth's history? (19:15) "In our view, these marvelous happenings—when the Holy Ghost fell mightily upon the people; when the sanctifying power of the Holy Spirit of God cleansed their souls;

9 And they did pray for that which they most desired; and they desired that the Holy Ghost should be given unto them.

10 And when they had thus prayed they went down unto the water's edge, and the multitude followed them.

11 And it came to pass that Nephi went down into the water and was baptized.

12 And he came up out of the water and began to baptize. And he baptized all those whom Jesus had chosen.

13 And it came to pass when they were all baptized and had come up out of the water, the Holy Ghost did fall upon them, and they were filled with the Holy Ghost and with fire.

14 And behold, they were encircled about as if it were by fire; and it came down from heaven, and the multitude did witness it, and did bear record; and angels did come down out of heaven and did minister unto them.

15 And it came to pass that while the angels were ministering unto the disciples, behold, Jesus came and stood in the midst and ministered unto them.

when mortal men were quickened by the Spirit until their countenances shone (as did that of Moses after he was with the Lord for forty days in the holy mount); when Jesus spoke words that could not be written and could only be understood by the power of the Spirit—these marvelous events were the high point of Jesus' ministry among his 'other sheep.' Seldom, if ever, has there been such a scene on planet earth" (McConkie, *Mortal Messiah*, 4:329). ●

How might the Nephites' experience with the Savior apply to us? (19:15) Notice the process on this second day. The multitude gathers together (v. 4). They are taught by the Lord's chosen servants and unite in prayer for their greatest desire, which is to receive the Holy Ghost (vv. 6–9). They are baptized with water and then are "filled with the Holy Ghost and with fire" (v. 13). Angels minister unto them and then Jesus appears and also ministers unto them (vv. 10–15). Though we may not expect a personal visit from the Savior, are there parts in this pattern that might allow you to have the Holy Ghost and the Savior as a more significant influence in your life?

Why did the Nephites pray to Jesus instead of the Father? (19:18) "On that Pentecostal occasion when the Nephites received the gift of the Holy Ghost, they offered approved prayers directly to Jesus and not to the Father. But there was a special reason why this was done in this instance. . . . Jesus was present before them as the symbol of the Father [see 3 Nephi 19:22]. Seeing him, it was as though they saw the Father; praying to him, it was as though they prayed to the Father. It was a special and unique situation that as far as we know has taken place only once on earth during all the long ages of the Lord's hand-dealings with his children" (McConkie, *Promised Messiah*, 560–61).

3 Nephi 19:19–36. The Savior Prays for His Disciples

16 And it came to pass that he spake unto the multitude, and commanded them that they should kneel down again upon the earth, and also that his disciples should kneel down upon the earth.

17 And it came to pass that when they had all knelt down upon the earth, he commanded his disciples that they should pray.

18 And behold, they began to pray; and they did pray unto Jesus, calling him their Lord and their God.

19 And it came to pass that Jesus departed out of the midst of them, and went a little way off from them and bowed himself to the earth, and he said:

20 Father, I thank thee that thou hast given the Holy Ghost unto these whom I have chosen; and it is because of their belief in me that I have chosen them out of the world.

21 Father, I pray thee that thou wilt give the Holy Ghost unto all them that shall believe in their words.

What does the companionship of the Holy Ghost mean to you? (19:20) What have you experienced in your life that confirms to you the truth that the gift of the Holy Ghost is "most desired"? What inspiration have you received, what warnings have you felt, or what insight have you gained from listening to the promptings of the Spirit? What do you feel you could do to be more receptive to those promptings?

How can we make sure we are praying for that which is right? (19:24) "We must have the Spirit with us, so that the Holy Ghost can prompt us to pray for that which is right. Nephi advised us that the Spirit 'teacheth a man to pray' (2 Nephi 32:8). There is, therefore, a definite connection between our righteousness and our capacity to draw upon the Spirit so that we will ask for what we should ask for. The Lord told Joseph Smith in 1831, 'And if ye are purified and cleansed from all sin, ye shall ask whatsoever you will in the name of Jesus, and it shall be done. But know this, it shall be *given* you what you shall ask' (D&C 50:29–30; italics added)" (Maxwell, "What Should We Pray For?" 44–45). ●

What caused the disciples to become as white as the countenance and garments of Jesus? (19:25–30) "The Holy Ghost performs two of his functions in these passages: he fills those praying with catalytic desire, and he burns out impurities and cleanses them. In this process the disciples were transfigured, being empowered to endure the presence of heavenly elements and beings without being wholly consumed (D&C 76:118)" (Thomas, "Theophany," 180). ●

22 Father, thou hast given them the Holy Ghost because they believe in me; and thou seest that they believe in me because thou hearest them, and they pray unto me; and they pray unto me because I am with them.

23 And now Father, I pray unto thee for them, and also for all those who shall believe on their words, that they may believe in me, that I may be in them as thou, Father, art in me, that we may be one.

24 And it came to pass that when Jesus had thus prayed unto the Father, he came unto his disciples, and behold, they did still continue, without ceasing, to pray unto him; and they did not multiply many words, for it was given unto them what they should pray, and they were filled with desire.

25 And it came to pass that Jesus blessed them as they did pray unto him; and his countenance did smile upon them, and the light of his countenance did shine upon them, and behold they were as white as the countenance and also the garments of Jesus; and behold the whiteness thereof did exceed all the whiteness, yea, even there could be nothing upon earth so white as the whiteness thereof.

26 And Jesus said unto them: Pray on; nevertheless they did not cease to pray.

27 And he turned from them again, and went a little way off and bowed himself to the earth; and he prayed again unto the Father, saying:

28 Father, I thank thee that thou hast purified those whom I have chosen, because of their faith, and I pray for them, and also for them who shall believe on their words, that they may be purified in me, through faith on their words, even as they are purified in me.

29 Father, I pray not for the world, but for those whom thou hast given me out of the world, because of their faith, that they may be purified in me, that I may be in them as thou, Father, art in me, that we may be one, that I may be glorified in them.

30 And when Jesus had spoken these words he came again unto his disciples; and behold they did pray steadfastly, without ceasing, unto him; and he did smile upon them again; and behold they were white, even as Jesus.

31 And it came to pass that he went again a little way off and prayed unto the Father;

32 And tongue cannot speak the words which he prayed, neither can be written by man the words which he prayed.

33 And the multitude did hear and do bear record; and their hearts were open and they did understand in their hearts the words which he prayed.

34 Nevertheless, so great and marvelous were the words which he prayed that they cannot be written, neither can they be uttered by man.

35 And it came to pass that when Jesus had made an end of praying he came again to the disciples, and said unto them: So great faith have I never seen among all the Jews; wherefore I could not show unto them so great miracles, because of their unbelief.

36 Verily I say unto you, there are none of them that have seen so great things as ye have seen; neither have they heard so great things as ye have heard.

What is remarkable about the Savior's prayers? (19:31–36) "Even more impressive in Chapter 19 is its description of an ineffable outpouring of prayer when Jesus again stood in the midst of the people (19:15–34). In all scripture there can be found no description of a prayer service as powerful and marvelous as this. Only [those] with a high degree of spirituality can begin to comprehend and appreciate it. . . .

"On account of its drama, loveliness, and high spirituality, I rank this chapter (19) as one of the greatest in the Book of Mormon" (Sperry, *Book of Mormon Compendium*, 411–12).

CHAPTER 20

Jesus provides bread and wine miraculously and again administers the sacrament unto the people—The remnant of Jacob will come to the knowledge of the Lord their God and will inherit the Americas—Jesus is the prophet like unto Moses, and the Nephites are children of the prophets—Others of the Lord's people will be gathered to Jerusalem. About A.D. 34.

1 And it came to pass that he commanded the multitude that they should cease to pray, and also his disciples. And he commanded them that they should not cease to pray in their hearts.

2 And he commanded them that they should arise and stand up upon their feet. And they arose up and stood upon their feet.

3 And it came to pass that he brake bread again and blessed it, and gave to the disciples to eat.

4 And when they had eaten he commanded them that they should break bread, and give unto the multitude.

5 And when they had given unto the multitude he also gave them wine to drink, and commanded them that they should give unto the multitude.

6 Now, there had been no bread, neither wine, brought by the disciples, neither by the multitude;

7 But he truly gave unto them bread to eat, and also wine to drink.

3 Nephi 20:1–9. Jesus Miraculously Provides Bread and Wine for the People

Why is it important to pray always in our hearts? (20:1) "We were not placed on this earth to walk alone. What an amazing source of power, of strength, and of comfort is available to each of us. He who knows us better than we know ourselves, He who sees the larger picture and who knows the end from the beginning, has assured us that He will be there for us to provide help if we but ask. . . . Of course, prayer is not just for times of trouble. We are told repeatedly in the scriptures to 'pray always' and to keep a prayer in our hearts" (Monson, "We Never Walk Alone," 121–22).

How were the sacrament's emblems provided? (20:6–7) "Certainly the Savior's providing bread and wine for the sacrament could be termed a miracle. The Savior did not circumvent natural law; rather, he used the law in a way we do not fully understand. Many people can make bread by taking wheat and adding other ingredients such as yeast and sugar; this process also requires the presence of the ingredients plus heat and time. However, Jesus Christ, the Creator of the heavens and the earth, was able to apply these natural laws almost instantaneously. That is, although there was no bread present, he was able to reach out his hands, gather the elements, and break bread that could be used in the sacrament" (Ludlow, *Companion to Your Study of the Book of Mormon*, 277).

8 And he said unto them: He that eateth this bread eateth of my body to his soul; and he that drinketh of this wine drinketh of my blood to his soul; and his soul shall never hunger nor thirst, but shall be filled.

9 Now, when the multitude had all eaten and drunk, behold, they were filled with the Spirit; and they did cry out with one voice, and gave glory to Jesus, whom they both saw and heard.

10 And it came to pass that when they had all given glory unto Jesus, he said unto them: Behold now I finish the commandment which the Father hath commanded me concerning this people, who are a remnant of the house of Israel.

11 Ye remember that I spake unto you, and said that when the words of Isaiah should be fulfilled—behold they are written, ye have them before you, therefore search them—

12 And verily, verily, I say unto you, that when they shall be fulfilled then is the fulfilling of the covenant which the Father hath made unto his people, O house of Israel.

13 And then shall the remnants, which shall be scattered abroad upon the face of the earth, be gathered in from the east and from the west, and from the south and from the north; and they shall be brought to the knowledge of the Lord their God, who hath redeemed them.

14 And the Father hath commanded me that I should give unto you this land, for your inheritance.

15 And I say unto you, that if the Gentiles do not repent after the blessing which they shall receive, after they have scattered my people—

16 Then shall ye, who are a remnant of the house of Jacob, go forth among them; and ye shall be in the midst of them who shall

How can we be "filled" by partaking of the sacrament? (20:8–9) "Such intense focusing on the life of the Savior, and in particular his Atonement, is designed to produce a supreme spiritual feast. Brigham Young declared, 'The Lord has planted within us a divinity; and that divine immortal spirit requires to be fed. . . . That divinity within us needs food from the Fountain from which it emanated.' That food may be found at the sacrament table. But Elder Melvin J. Ballard cautions, 'We must come . . . to the sacrament table hungry'" (Callister, *Infinite Atonement*, 287–88). ⊕

3 Nephi 20:10–24. Jesus Teaches How the Covenant with Israel Will Be Fulfilled

Is the gathering of Israel literal or allegorical? (20:10–13) "These comments of the Savior certainly affirm that neither he nor his Father has forgotten the covenants made to our ancient progenitors. The promises God made to the posterity of Abraham, Isaac, and Jacob are real! The Abrahamic covenant is not an allegory; it is not a Bible story that is to be spiritualized away. The gathering of Israel will be literal, and it is literal Israel that is to be gathered. The promises given to the seed of Abraham are as real as the dirt and dust upon which he set his feet of flesh and blood" (McConkie, "Final Gathering to Christ," 193–94).

To what land was Jesus referring? (20:14) "America [north and south] is the land of Joseph. The Nephites are of the house of Joseph; and they, along with us, who also have that tribal ancestry, are destined to inherit these lands which are choice above all other lands" (McConkie, *Mortal Messiah*, 4:334). ⊕

Who will tread down the unrepentant Gentiles? (20:15–17) "These words of our Lord to the Nephites are quoted from Micah 5:8–9 and have reference to the desolations and ultimate burning that shall destroy the wicked at the Second Coming. Except for a few who are the humble followers of Christ, the Gentiles will not repent. They will revel in their abominations and sin against the restored gospel, and they will be burned by the brightness of our Lord's coming while the righteous—here called the remnant of Jacob—shall abide the day. And then, in the prophetic imagery, it will be as though the remnant of Israel overthrew their enemies as a young lion among the flocks of sheep" (McConkie, *Millennial Messiah*, 248). ●

When will this gathering take place and how will it happen? (20:18–19) "This is the great gathering destined to occur after our Lord's return. By way of further explanation of the triumphant events involved, Jesus now says: 'For I will make my people with whom the Father hath covenanted, yea, I will make thy horn iron, and I will make thy hoofs brass. And thou shalt beat in pieces many people; and I will consecrate their gain unto the Lord, and their substance unto the Lord of the whole earth. And behold, I am he who doeth it.' Again the prophetic imagery comes from the Old Testament. It is taken from Micah 4:13" (McConkie, *Millennial Messiah*, 248). ●

What is the "New Jerusalem"? (20:22) "The terms City of Zion and Zion are frequently used synonymously with the New Jerusalem. According to President Joseph Fielding Smith, the terms City of Zion and New Jerusalem 'have reference to the same sanctified place' (DS 3:67). This will be a millennial city 'from whence the law and the word of the Lord shall go forth to all people' (DS 3:68–69). It will be one of two world capitals, the other being the old Jerusalem (Isa. 2:2–5; Micah 4:1–7; 2 Ne. 12:2–5). The inhabitants of these holy cities will be 'they whose garments are white through the blood of the Lamb' (Ether 13:10–11)" (Brewster, *Doctrine and Covenants Encyclopedia*, 383).

be many; and ye shall be among them as a lion among the beasts of the forest, and as a young lion among the flocks of sheep, who, if he goeth through both treadeth down and teareth in pieces, and none can deliver.

17 Thy hand shall be lifted up upon thine adversaries, and all thine enemies shall be cut off.

18 And I will gather my people together as a man gathereth his sheaves into the floor.

19 For I will make my people with whom the Father hath covenanted, yea, I will make thy horn iron, and I will make thy hoofs brass. And thou shalt beat in pieces many people; and I will consecrate their gain unto the Lord, and their substance unto the Lord of the whole earth. And behold, I am he who doeth it.

20 And it shall come to pass, saith the Father, that the sword of my justice shall hang over them at that day; and except they repent it shall fall upon them, saith the Father, yea, even upon all the nations of the Gentiles.

21 And it shall come to pass that I will establish my people, O house of Israel.

22 And behold, this people will I establish in this land, unto the fulfilling of the covenant which I made with your father Jacob; and it shall be a New Jerusalem. And the powers of heaven shall be in the midst of this people; yea, even I will be in the midst of you.

23 Behold, I am he of whom Moses spake, saying: A prophet shall the Lord your God raise up unto you of your brethren, like unto me; him shall ye hear in all things whatsoever he shall say unto you. And it shall come to pass that every soul who will not hear that prophet shall be cut off from among the people.

24 Verily I say unto you, yea, and all the prophets from Samuel and those that follow after, as many as have spoken, have testified of me.

25 And behold, ye are the children of the prophets; and ye are of the house of Israel; and ye are of the covenant which the Father made with your fathers, saying unto Abraham: And in thy seed shall all the kindreds of the earth be blessed.

26 The Father having raised me up unto you first, and sent me to bless you in turning away every one of you from his iniquities; and this because ye are the children of the covenant—

27 And after that ye were blessed then fulfilleth the Father the covenant which he made with Abraham, saying: In thy seed shall all the kindreds of the earth be blessed—unto the pouring out of the Holy Ghost through me upon the Gentiles, which blessing upon the Gentiles shall make them mighty above all, unto the scattering of my people, O house of Israel.

28 And they shall be a scourge unto the people of this land. Nevertheless, when they shall have received the fulness of my gospel, then if they shall harden their hearts against me I will return their iniquities upon their own heads, saith the Father.

3 Nephi 20:25–46. Israel Will Be Gathered Again When They Accept Jesus Christ

What is one of the greatest blessings of keeping the Abrahamic covenant? (20:25) "Every covenant contains promises and blessings. The Lord promised Abraham that his seed would be granted the blessings of the priesthood (Abr. 1:18). The Savior told the Nephites, who were a part of covenant Israel, that he would 'bless' them by 'turning away every one of you from his iniquities.' That is a wonderful promise. What turns people from their iniquities, whether it be Old Testament Israel, Book of Mormon Nephites, or Latter-day Saints? Only the principles of truth and righteousness contained in the gospel can keep a society or an individual righteous. And righteousness is the only means to happiness, peace, and rest" (Wilcox, "Abrahamic Covenant," 272). ●

Can our covenants save our wayward children? (20:26) "The influence of parents who honor covenants and obey commandments indeed can have a decisive spiritual impact upon children who stray by activating the tentacles of divine Providence—in ways that have not been revealed fully and are not understood completely. However, righteous parental influence (1) does not replace in the life of an individual the need for the redeeming and strengthening power of the Atonement of Jesus Christ, (2) does not overrule the consequences of the unrighteous exercise of moral agency, and (3) does not negate the responsibility of an individual as an agent 'to act . . . and not to be acted upon' (2 Nephi 2:26)" (Bednar, "Faithful Parents and Wayward Children: Sustaining Hope While Overcoming Misunderstanding," 32). ●

How does one become of the house of Israel to receive the blessings of the gospel? (20:27) "Every person who embraces the gospel becomes of the house of Israel. In other words, they become members of the chosen lineage, or Abraham's children through Isaac and Jacob unto whom the promises were made. The great majority of those who become members of the Church are literal descendants of Abraham through Ephraim, son of Joseph. Those who are not literal descendants of Abraham and Israel must become such, and when they are baptized and confirmed they are grafted into the tree and are entitled to all the rights and privileges as heirs" (Smith, *Doctrines of Salvation*, 3:245–46).

How will the Jews be gathered to Jerusalem?
(20:29–33) "This gathering will consist of accepting
Christ, joining the Church, and receiving anew the
Abrahamic covenant as it is administered in holy
places [see Bible Dictionary, 'Abraham, covenant of,'
585]. The present assembling of people of Jewish
ancestry into the Palestinian nation of Israel is not the
scriptural gathering of Israel or of Judah. It may be
prelude thereto, and some of the people so assembled
may in due course be gathered into the true church
and kingdom of God on earth, and they may then
assist in building the temple that is destined to grace
Jerusalem's soil. But a political gathering is not a spiritual gathering, and the Lord's kingdom is not of this
world" (McConkie, *New Witness*, 519–20). ⊕

**What is the meaning of the symbolism behind the
words and phrases in these verses? (20:36–37)** "*Put
on thy strength.* Joseph Smith explained . . . [that] to
put on her strength is to put on the authority of the
priesthood, which she, Zion, has a right to by lineage
. . . (D&C 113:8). . . .
"*Uncircumcised/unclean.* These words refer to the
disobedient, sinners, or disbelieving Gentiles. Such will
not be found in Zion . . .
"*Arise/sit down.* The Lord's people are instructed
to get up from the dust, where slaves must sit, and sit
instead in a place of honor, as on a throne. In contrast,
Babylon has been cast from a throne into the dust . . .
"*Bands.* . . . The bands of her neck are the curses
of God upon her, or the remnants of Israel in their
scattered condition among the Gentiles'" (D&C
113:10). These are images of Israel coming forth
from both physical and spiritual slavery" (Parry, et al.
Understanding Isaiah, 460–61). ⊕

29 And I will remember the covenant which
I have made with my people; and I have covenanted with them that I would gather them
together in mine own due time, that I would
give unto them again the land of their fathers
for their inheritance, which is the land of
Jerusalem, which is the promised land unto
them forever, saith the Father.

30 And it shall come to pass that the time
cometh, when the fulness of my gospel shall
be preached unto them;

31 And they shall believe in me, that I am
Jesus Christ, the Son of God, and shall pray
unto the Father in my name.

32 Then shall their watchmen lift up their
voice, and with the voice together shall they
sing; for they shall see eye to eye.

33 Then will the Father gather them together
again, and give unto them Jerusalem for the
land of their inheritance.

34 Then shall they break forth into joy—
Sing together, ye waste places of Jerusalem;
for the Father hath comforted his people, he
hath redeemed Jerusalem.

35 The Father hath made bare his holy arm
in the eyes of all the nations; and all the ends
of the earth shall see the salvation of the
Father; and the Father and I are one.

36 And then shall be brought to pass that
which is written: Awake, awake again, and
put on thy strength, O Zion; put on thy
beautiful garments, O Jerusalem, the holy
city, for henceforth there shall no more come
into thee the uncircumcised and the unclean.

37 Shake thyself from the dust; arise, sit down,
O Jerusalem; loose thyself from the bands of
thy neck, O captive daughter of Zion.

38 For thus saith the Lord: Ye have sold yourselves for naught, and ye shall be redeemed
without money.

39 Verily, verily, I say unto you, that my people shall know my name; yea, in that day they shall know that I am he that doth speak.

40 And then shall they say: How beautiful upon the mountains are the feet of him that bringeth good tidings unto them, that publisheth peace; that bringeth good tidings unto them of good, that publisheth salvation; that saith unto Zion: Thy God reigneth!

41 And then shall a cry go forth: Depart ye, depart ye, go ye out from thence, touch not that which is unclean; go ye out of the midst of her; be ye clean that bear the vessels of the Lord.

42 For ye shall not go out with haste nor go by flight; for the Lord will go before you, and the God of Israel shall be your rearward.

43 Behold, my servant shall deal prudently; he shall be exalted and extolled and be very high.

44 As many were astonished at thee—his visage was so marred, more than any man, and his form more than the sons of men—

45 So shall he sprinkle many nations; the kings shall shut their mouths at him, for that which had not been told them shall they see; and that which they had not heard shall they consider.

46 Verily, verily, I say unto you, all these things shall surely come, even as the Father hath commanded me. Then shall this covenant which the Father hath covenanted with his people be fulfilled; and then shall Jerusalem be inhabited again with my people, and it shall be the land of their inheritance.

What is the ultimate blessing that the gospel of Jesus Christ brings to a troubled world? (20:39–40) "Peace and good tidings; good tidings and peace. These are among the ultimate blessings that the gospel of Jesus Christ brings a troubled world and the troubled people who live in it, solutions to personal struggles and human sinfulness, a source of strength for days of weariness and hours of genuine despair....

"Ultimately it is Christ who is beautiful upon the mountain. And it is His merciful promise of 'peace in this world,' His good tidings of 'eternal life in the world to come' that make us fall at His feet and call His name blessed and give thanks for the restoration of His true and living Church" (Holland, "Peaceable Things of the Kingdom," 82). ✛

What is the relationship between personal purity and priesthood power? (20:41) "Receiving the authority of the priesthood by the laying on of hands is an important beginning, but it is not enough. Ordination confers authority, but righteousness is required to act with power as we strive to lift souls, to teach and testify, to bless and counsel, and to advance the work of salvation [see also D&C 38:42; 121:34–40]" (Bednar, "Powers of Heaven," 50). ✛

What difference could it make to you to be surrounded by divine protection? (20:42) As the world becomes increasingly unsafe and hostile to righteousness, how comforting is the Lord's promise to go before you and guard behind you? (see also D&C 84:88). From what you have learned in the Savior's teachings to the Nephites, what must we do to ensure that promise will apply to us?

Why will people be astonished at Christ's coming? (20:43–45) "In these words we see a triumphant millennial Christ—one whose visage was marred and whose form was mangled when he dwelt among men—we see him in glory and dominion, in whose presence kings remain silent and before whom their mouths are shut. We see his cleansing blood sprinkle all nations, with devout men everywhere turning to the saving truths that they have not before heard and to the words of truth that they have not theretofore considered" (McConkie, *Mortal Messiah*, 4:344). ✛

3 Nephi 21:1–8. The Gathering of Israel Is a Sign of the Lord's Second Coming

What event signals the start of the gathering of Israel? (21:1–7) "The coming forth of the Book of Mormon is a sign to the entire world that the Lord has commenced to gather Israel and fulfill covenants He made to Abraham, Isaac, and Jacob. . . . The Book of Mormon is central to this work. It declares the doctrine of the gathering. It causes people to learn about Jesus Christ, to believe His gospel, and to join His Church. In fact, if there were no Book of Mormon, the promised gathering of Israel would not occur" (Nelson, "Gathering of Scattered Israel," 80). ✛

Why establish the Gentiles in this land? (21:4) Elder Mark E. Petersen testified about why America is the land of the restoration: "And why was freedom so necessary in connection with the restoration of the gospel and its promulgation among the children of men? In order that those to whom the gospel would be restored might have the freedom of speech to preach the gospel; the freedom of the press to publish the gospel; freedom of assembly so they could gather together in congregations and worship the Lord; and religious freedom so that they could worship God according to the dictates of their own conscience" (in Conference Report, Apr. 1946, 169). ✛

CHAPTER 21

Israel will be gathered when the Book of Mormon comes forth—The Gentiles will be established as a free people in America—They will be saved if they believe and obey; otherwise, they will be cut off and destroyed—Israel will build the New Jerusalem, and the lost tribes will return. About A.D. 34.

1 And verily I say unto you, I give unto you a sign, that ye may know the time when these things shall be about to take place—that I shall gather in, from their long dispersion, my people, O house of Israel, and shall establish again among them my Zion;

2 And behold, this is the thing which I will give unto you for a sign—for verily I say unto you that when these things which I declare unto you, and which I shall declare unto you hereafter of myself, and by the power of the Holy Ghost which shall be given unto you of the Father, shall be made known unto the Gentiles that they may know concerning this people who are a remnant of the house of Jacob, and concerning this my people who shall be scattered by them;

3 Verily, verily, I say unto you, when these things shall be made known unto them of the Father, and shall come forth of the Father, from them unto you;

4 For it is wisdom in the Father that they should be established in this land, and be set up as a free people by the power of the Father, that these things might come forth from them unto a remnant of your seed, that the covenant of the Father may be fulfilled which he hath covenanted with his people, O house of Israel;

5 Therefore, when these works and the works which shall be wrought among you hereafter shall come forth from the Gentiles, unto your seed which shall dwindle in unbelief because of iniquity;

6 For thus it behooveth the Father that it should come forth from the Gentiles, that he may show forth his power unto the Gentiles, for this cause that the Gentiles, if they will not harden their hearts, that they may repent and come unto me and be baptized in my name and know of the true points of my doctrine, that they may be numbered among my people, O house of Israel;

7 And when these things come to pass that thy seed shall begin to know these things—it shall be a sign unto them, that they may know that the work of the Father hath already commenced unto the fulfilling of the covenant which he hath made unto the people who are of the house of Israel.

8 And when that day shall come, it shall come to pass that kings shall shut their mouths; for that which had not been told them shall they see; and that which they had not heard shall they consider.

How will prominent individuals respond to the Lord's work? (21:8) "The great and mighty shall be so amazed at the Lord's latter-day work that they shall not know what to say and shall feel impelled to consider the wondrous work which rolls before their eyes. So far there has been a small amount of this; what the future holds is limitless" (McConkie, *Mortal Messiah*, 4:353). ☉

3 Nephi 21:9–19. Those Who Reject the Restored Gospel Will Be Cut Off

9 For in that day, for my sake shall the Father work a work, which shall be a great and a marvelous work among them; and there shall be among them those who will not believe it, although a man shall declare it unto them.

Why did Heavenly Father restore the gospel in the last days? (21:9) "In that day, Christ said, it would be for his sake—for the success of his mission and the full efficacy of his life—that the Father would restore the gospel and reestablish his church" (Holland, *Christ and the New Covenant*, 287). ☉

10 But behold, the life of my servant shall be in my hand; therefore they shall not hurt him, although he shall be marred because of them. Yet I will heal him, for I will show unto them that my wisdom is greater than the cunning of the devil.

11 Therefore it shall come to pass that whosoever will not believe in my words, who am Jesus Christ, which the Father shall cause him to bring forth unto the Gentiles, and shall give unto him power that he shall bring them forth unto the Gentiles, (it shall be

Who is the "marred" servant spoken of in this verse? (21:10) Victor L. Ludlow suggests at least four possibilities: (1) It may "refer to Israel as a whole." (2) Perhaps it could be "the same servant described throughout Isaiah 53. If so, these verses describe Christ, his great works, and the persecutions and suffering he endured." (3) It could refer to Joseph Smith, the prophet of the restoration: "As the Savior comments upon these verses later in 3 Nephi 21:7–11, it appears obvious that he is not talking about himself, but about his servant." (4) Maybe it refers to "another modern prophet" (*Isaiah*, 438–41). ☉

done even as Moses said) they shall be cut off from among my people who are of the covenant.

12 And my people who are a remnant of Jacob shall be among the Gentiles, yea, in the midst of them as a lion among the beasts of the forest, as a young lion among the flocks of sheep, who, if he go through both treadeth down and teareth in pieces, and none can deliver.

13 Their hand shall be lifted up upon their adversaries, and all their enemies shall be cut off.

14 Yea, wo be unto the Gentiles except they repent; for it shall come to pass in that day, saith the Father, that I will cut off thy horses out of the midst of thee, and I will destroy thy chariots;

15 And I will cut off the cities of thy land, and throw down all thy strongholds;

16 And I will cut off witchcrafts out of thy land, and thou shalt have no more soothsayers;

17 Thy graven images I will also cut off, and thy standing images out of the midst of thee, and thou shalt no more worship the works of thy hands;

18 And I will pluck up thy groves out of the midst of thee; so will I destroy thy cities.

19 And it shall come to pass that all lyings, and deceivings, and envyings, and strifes, and priestcrafts, and whoredoms, shall be done away.

20 For it shall come to pass, saith the Father, that at that day whosoever will not repent and come unto my Beloved Son, them will I cut off from among my people, O house of Israel;

21 And I will execute vengeance and fury upon them, even as upon the heathen, such as they have not heard.

22 But if they will repent and hearken unto my words, and harden not their hearts, I

3 Nephi 21:20–29. The Gentiles Will Help Build the New Jerusalem and Gather Scattered Israel

Who is the "remnant of Jacob" that will help the Gentiles build the New Jerusalem? (21:20–23) "This [3 Nephi 21:20–23] has been interpreted to mean that the remnant of Jacob are those of the descendants of Lehi, but there is nothing in the passage as I read it which should convey this thought. Remember that all through the Lord has been speaking of the remnant of Jacob or Israel, and of the great promises made to the gentiles who are on this land and in all other lands, if they will only come into the Church and be numbered with the house of Israel. Their privileges would be to

will establish my church among them, and they shall come in unto the covenant and be numbered among this the remnant of Jacob, unto whom I have given this land for their inheritance;

23 And they shall assist my people, the remnant of Jacob, and also as many of the house of Israel as shall come, that they may build a city, which shall be called the New Jerusalem.

24 And then shall they assist my people that they may be gathered in, who are scattered upon all the face of the land, in unto the New Jerusalem.

25 And then shall the power of heaven come down among them; and I also will be in the midst.

26 And then shall the work of the Father commence at that day, even when this gospel shall be preached among the remnant of this people. Verily I say unto you, at that day shall the work of the Father commence among all the dispersed of my people, yea, even the tribes which have been lost, which the Father hath led away out of Jerusalem.

27 Yea, the work shall commence among all the dispersed of my people, with the Father to prepare the way whereby they may come unto me, that they may call on the Father in my name.

28 Yea, and then shall the work commence, with the Father among all nations in preparing the way whereby his people may be gathered home to the land of their inheritance.

29 And they shall go out from all nations; and they shall not go out in haste, nor go by flight, for I will go before them, saith the Father, and I will be their rearward.

assist in building the New Jerusalem" (Smith, *Doctrines of Salvation*, 2:250). ⊕

When will the Saints be gathered "in unto the New Jerusalem"? (21:24) Elder Bruce R. McConkie wrote: "The building up of Old Jerusalem in Palestine and the establishment of the New Jerusalem in America are both destined to occur before our Lord returns. Both events are yet future. As to the American Zion that is to be, one of our scriptures proclaims: 'The Son of Man cometh.... But before the great day of the Lord shall come, Jacob shall flourish in the wilderness.... Zion shall flourish upon the hills and rejoice upon the mountains and shall be assembled together unto the place which I have appointed' (D&C 49:22, 24–25). We, as the seed of Jacob, now flourish in the wilderness of western America, and at the appointed time the saints shall gather to their promised Zion in Missouri" (*New Witness*, 362).

What does "the power of heaven come down among them" mean? (21:25) Elder Bruce R. McConkie noted that this phrase means "that the Lord will reign personally upon the earth during the Millennium" (*Millennial Messiah*, 303).

In what day shall this work of the Father commence? (21:26–28) "This is a millennial setting. It is a setting in which wickedness and crime and vengeance are no longer on earth. It is an era when goodness and decency and integrity are the order of the day. In this setting, in this day, the work of the Father—the work of the gathering of Israel—shall commence. Commence? Has not the work of gathering ... been in full operation since the days of Joseph Smith? Yes, the work of the Father shall commence in the great millennial day, in the sense that its magnitude shall be infinitely greater than anything we can even identify with today" (McConkie et al., *Doctrinal Commentary*, 4:152). ⊕

What is a "rearward"? (21:29) "The promise of the Lord to be Israel's rearward is found in the Doctrine and Covenants (D&C 49:27), Book of Mormon (3 Ne. 20:42; 21:29), and Old Testament (Isa. 52:12).... Not only will the Lord be the 'rearward' of his people but he will also go before them. Thus, he will be the vanguard of protection on the front, as well as the rearguard (rearward). In addition, he will be in their midst, thus protecting both flanks from attack" (Brewster, *Doctrine and Covenants Encyclopedia*, 453).

3 Nephi 22:1–5. The Lord's Church Shall Grow, and Nothing Will Stop It

Who is the barren woman? (22:1) "The barren woman seems to be Israel, who had not previously borne the promised fruit of her covenant with God. She has never travailed with child but will rejoice to have children (meaning the blessings of the covenant) as a result of another's travail, that of Christ" (Parry et al., *Understanding Isaiah*, 480). Elder Jeffrey R. Holland taught: "Even though there has been barrenness and sometimes unfaithfulness, yet will the husband (Christ) reclaim and redeem his bride (Israel). The imagery of Jehovah as bridegroom and Israel as bride is among the most commonly used metaphors in scripture, being used by the Lord and his prophets to describe the relationship between Deity and the children of the covenant" (*Christ and the New Covenant*, 290).

Why should the tent be enlarged? (22:2) "The clarion call to 'enlarge' and 'strengthen' the stakes of Zion was given anciently to Isaiah (Isa. 54:2), repeated to the Nephites (3 Ne. 22:2), and reiterated in our day (D&C 109:59; 133:9). . . . [Stakes] are places where the Saints of God may be instructed more perfectly in the doctrines of salvation. As the number of stakes increases, the influence of the protective tent expands to reach more of the earth's inhabitants. The ultimate goal is to stretch it over the entire earth, to gather all people under its protection" (Brewster, *Isaiah Plain and Simple*, 263). ✦

What was the shame of Israel's youth? (22:4) "This refers to her unfaithfulness in her earlier years, when she

CHAPTER 22

In the last days, Zion and her stakes will be established, and Israel will be gathered in mercy and tenderness—They will triumph—Compare Isaiah 54. About A.D. 34.

1 And then shall that which is written come to pass: Sing, O barren, thou that didst not bear; break forth into singing, and cry aloud, thou that didst not travail with child; for more are the children of the desolate than the children of the married wife, saith the Lord.

2 Enlarge the place of thy tent, and let them stretch forth the curtains of thy habitations; spare not, lengthen thy cords and strengthen thy stakes;

3 For thou shalt break forth on the right hand and on the left, and thy seed shall inherit the Gentiles and make the desolate cities to be inhabited.

4 Fear not, for thou shalt not be ashamed; neither be thou confounded, for thou shalt

God's Promises and Israel's Millennial Hope

"By chapter's end [3 Nephi 22], the relationship between the Lord and his children of covenant is seen fully and poetically. Consider this summary of God's promises and Israel's millennial hope":

Verses	Husband Provides Wife	Jehovah Provides Israel
1–3	Children	Gathering and great growth
4–8	Love	Mercy and redemption
9–10	Commitment	Unbreakable covenant
11–12	Material comfort	Splendor in a New Jerusalem
13–17	Protection for the family	Peace, freedom from fear and oppression for Zion

(Holland, *Christ and the New Covenant*, 291.)

not be put to shame; for thou shalt forget the shame of thy youth, and shalt not remember the reproach of thy youth, and shalt not remember the reproach of thy widowhood any more.

5 For thy maker, thy husband, the Lord of Hosts is his name; and thy Redeemer, the Holy One of Israel—the God of the whole earth shall he be called.

6 For the Lord hath called thee as a woman forsaken and grieved in spirit, and a wife of youth, when thou wast refused, saith thy God.

7 For a small moment have I forsaken thee, but with great mercies will I gather thee.

8 In a little wrath I hid my face from thee for a moment, but with everlasting kindness will I have mercy on thee, saith the Lord thy Redeemer.

9 For this, the waters of Noah unto me, for as I have sworn that the waters of Noah should no more go over the earth, so have I sworn that I would not be wroth with thee.

10 For the mountains shall depart and the hills be removed, but my kindness shall not depart from thee, neither shall the covenant of my peace be removed, saith the Lord that hath mercy on thee.

11 O thou afflicted, tossed with tempest, and not comforted! Behold, I will lay thy stones with fair colors, and lay thy foundations with sapphires.

12 And I will make thy windows of agates, and thy gates of carbuncles, and all thy borders of pleasant stones.

sought after false gods rather than remaining true to her covenant Husband the Lord God Jehovah. This was a time not only of shameful conduct, but also of spiritual sterility, when she was not blessed with increase. Some commentators have suggested this shame could mean her periods of captivity, such as the Egyptian bondage" (Brewster, *Isaiah Plain and Simple*, 265). ⊕

3 Nephi 22:6–17. The Lord Will Again Gather and Protect His Children in the Last Days

What is meant by the forsaken woman? (22:6)
"Because of her unfaithfulness, Israel, a bride chosen in her early or youthful years, had become a forsaken wife. Be it remembered, however, that it was she who left the house of her Husband" (Brewster, *Isaiah Plain and Simple*, 266).

What is the Lord's promise to Israel? (22:7–8)
"Compassion and mercy always return and prevail in a most reassuring way. The mountains and the hills may disappear. The water of the great seas may dry up. The least likely things in the world may happen, but the Lord's kindness and peace will never be taken from his covenant people. He has sworn with a heavenly oath that he will not be wroth with them forever" (Holland, *Christ and the New Covenant*, 290). ⊕

What is "the covenant of my peace"? (22:10)
"Although there are many temporary strategies for finding peace amidst adversity, the only way to experience the 'peace of God, which passeth all understanding' (Philippians 4:7) is through the 'merits, and mercy, and grace of the Holy Messiah' (2 Nephi 2:8). The counsel of the Savior and of prophets ancient and modern points us to what the Lord described as 'the covenant of my peace' (3 Nephi 22:10), which nurtures a spirit of optimism, inspires hope, increases faith, strengthens families, and helps maintain or reclaim sanity in the lives of those who face hard questions and seek to implement the answers the Lord has provided" (Judd, *Hard Questions, Prophetic Answers*, 215–16). ⊕

What do the windows, agates, carbuncles, and precious stones symbolize in Isaiah? (22:12)
"'Windows [pinnacles or turrets] of agates [rubies], gates of carbuncles [sparkling jewels], borders [walls] of pleasant [precious] stones.' These could symbolize

the beauty of the holy city, or dwelling place of the Saints of God, and the material blessings that will be poured out upon the righteous" (Brewster, *Isaiah Plain and Simple*, 269). ⊕

Who was a latter-day "smith" that served as an instrument for the Lord? (22:16) "Joseph [Smith, Jr.] was surely the smith who forged the instrument by which the Lord's people continue to prepare individually and collectively for the Savior's return—and that instrument is The Church of Jesus Christ of Latter-day Saints" (Lund, "Prophet for the Fulness of Times," 54).

What is the ultimate destiny of this great latter-day work? (22:17) "No unhallowed hand can stop the work from progressing; persecutions may rage, mobs may combine, armies may assemble, calumny may defame, but the truth of God will go forth boldly, nobly, and independent, till it has penetrated every clime, swept every country, and sounded in every ear, till the purposes of God shall be accomplished, and the Great Jehovah shall say the work is done" (*Joseph Smith* [manual], 444). ⊕

3 Nephi 23:1–5. Everything Isaiah Taught about the House of Israel Will Be Fulfilled

Why are the words of Isaiah important for us? (23:1) Elder Bruce R. McConkie wrote: "If our eternal salvation depends upon our ability to understand the writings of Isaiah as fully and truly as Nephi understood them—and who shall say that such is not the case!—how shall we fare in that great day when with Nephi we shall stand before the pleasing bar of Him who said: 'Great are the words of Isaiah'? . . . It just may be that my salvation (and yours also!) does in fact depend upon our ability to understand the writings of Isaiah as fully and truly as Nephi understood them" ("Keys to Understanding Isaiah," 78). ⊕

13 And all thy children shall be taught of the Lord; and great shall be the peace of thy children.

14 In righteousness shalt thou be established; thou shalt be far from oppression for thou shalt not fear, and from terror for it shall not come near thee.

15 Behold, they shall surely gather together against thee, not by me; whosoever shall gather together against thee shall fall for thy sake.

16 Behold, I have created the smith that bloweth the coals in the fire, and that bringeth forth an instrument for his work; and I have created the waster to destroy.

17 No weapon that is formed against thee shall prosper; and every tongue that shall revile against thee in judgment thou shalt condemn. This is the heritage of the servants of the Lord, and their righteousness is of me, saith the Lord.

CHAPTER 23

Jesus approves the words of Isaiah—He commands the people to search the prophets—The words of Samuel the Lamanite concerning the Resurrection are added to their records. About A.D. 34.

1 And now, behold, I say unto you, that ye ought to search these things. Yea, a commandment I give unto you that ye search these things diligently; for great are the words of Isaiah.

2 For surely he spake as touching all things concerning my people which are of the house of Israel; therefore it must needs be that he must speak also to the Gentiles.

3 And all things that he spake have been and shall be, even according to the words which he spake.

4 Therefore give heed to my words; write the things which I have told you; and according to the time and the will of the Father they shall go forth unto the Gentiles.

5 And whosoever will hearken unto my words and repenteth and is baptized, the same shall be saved. Search the prophets, for many there be that testify of these things.

6 And now it came to pass that when Jesus had said these words he said unto them again, after he had expounded all the scriptures unto them which they had received, he said unto them: Behold, other scriptures I would that ye should write, that ye have not.

7 And it came to pass that he said unto Nephi: Bring forth the record which ye have kept.

8 And when Nephi had brought forth the records, and laid them before him, he cast his eyes upon them and said:

9 Verily I say unto you, I commanded my servant Samuel, the Lamanite, that he should testify unto this people, that at the day that the Father should glorify his name in me that there were many saints who should arise from the dead, and should appear unto many, and should minister unto them. And he said unto them: Was it not so?

10 And his disciples answered him and said: Yea, Lord, Samuel did prophesy according to thy words, and they were all fulfilled.

How can it be said that all things that Isaiah spoke "have been" and also "shall be"? (23:3) Isaiah is written in such a way as to have multiple fulfillments. One event can be historical as well as foretelling or shadowing the future. Elder Bruce R. McConkie explained: "Similarly, many chapters [of Isaiah] dealing with latter-day apostasy and the second coming of Christ are written relative to ancient nations whose destruction was but a symbol, a type, and a shadow, of that which would fall upon all nations when the great and dreadful day of the Lord finally came" ("Ten Keys To Understanding Isaiah," 83). Consider D&C 1:37–38.

Why is it crucial that we study the scriptures? (23:4–5) "The Lord is not trifling with us when he gives us these things, for 'unto whomsoever much is given, of him shall be much required' (Luke 12:48). Access to these things means responsibility for them. We must study the scriptures according to the Lord's commandment (see 3 Ne. 23:1–5); and we must let them govern our lives" (*Teachings of Spencer W. Kimball*, 127).

3 Nephi 23:6–14. Jesus Commands That the Missing Words of Samuel the Lamanite Be Added to the Nephite Scriptures

What corroborating evidence to the Resurrection took place in America? (23:9–10) "After he came forth from his borrowed tomb, the risen Lord appeared to various of his saints, among them both men and women, so that they might become witnesses, first, that he was in fact raised from death to life, and second, as to the nature and kind of being he had then become. And as to the resurrection of others than our Lord, ' . . . many bodies of the saints which slept arose, . . . and appeared unto many' (Matt. 27:52–53). Each person to whom such a resurrected saint ministered became a witness both of the resurrection and of such revealed knowledge relative to resurrected beings as he then received (Hel. 14:25; 3 Ne. 23:7–13)" (McConkie, *Promised Messiah*, 278). ○

What do you learn from the Savior's pointed question about the Resurrection? (23:11) "When [the Lord] came to the Nephites he made a big thing about keeping records. He went through the records himself and made sure that all the prophecies were mentioned. Samuel the Lamanite had prophesied something that was fulfilled. You didn't put it down here, he says to Nephi. Nephi's face turned red and he said, Well, we'll see that it gets put down! (cf. 3 Nephi 23:6–13). It was very embarrassing, believe me, when the Lord himself was there! But he wants those records complete" (Nibley, *Temple and Cosmos*, 321–22). ⊕

What evidence is there in the Book of Mormon that Nephi inserted Samuel's prophecy, according to the Lord's request? (23:13) D. Lynn Johnson argues that the "broken symmetry, as it occurs in Helaman 14:20–27 as the text reads today, is unusual in scripture. In particular, careful analysis reveals that the balance of the record of Samuel's discourse is highly patterned, primarily in the inverse order of chiasmus, with no other similar instances of out-of-place elements. . . . An even more compelling argument that the prophecy was inserted later lies in the literary structure of verses 20–27" (Johnson, "The Missing Scripture," 86–88). This broken symmetry may indicate this passage is Nephi's later insertion. ⊕

What does it mean to "expound all scriptures in one"? (23:14) "To 'expound all scriptures in one' perhaps means to bring all the revealed word of God to one focal point, laying stress on that toward which all scripture points—the mission of Jesus Christ. Having done this, Jesus commanded his disciples that they teach to others what he had taught them, thus building a chain of pure doctrinal understanding that would continue into subsequent generations" (Jackson, "Teaching from the Words of the Prophets," 197).

3 Nephi 24:1–5. The Lord Will Send His Messenger to Prepare Us for the Second Coming

Why were the Nephites commanded to include Malachi's writings? (24:1) "The prophecies of Malachi were given approximately 430 B.C., almost two centuries after Lehi left Jerusalem. These prophecies were considered so significant that the Father commanded that they be included in the Nephite scriptures. . . . Just

11 And Jesus said unto them: How be it that ye have not written this thing, that many saints did arise and appear unto many and did minister unto them?

12 And it came to pass that Nephi remembered that this thing had not been written.

13 And it came to pass that Jesus commanded that it should be written; therefore it was written according as he commanded.

14 And now it came to pass that when Jesus had expounded all the scriptures in one, which they had written, he commanded them that they should teach the things which he had expounded unto them.

CHAPTER 24

The Lord's messenger will prepare the way for the Second Coming—Christ will sit in judgment—Israel is commanded to pay tithes and offerings—A book of remembrance is kept—Compare Malachi 3. About A.D. 34.

1 And it came to pass that he commanded them that they should write the words which the Father had given unto Malachi, which he should tell unto them. And it came to pass that after they were written he expounded them. And these are the words which he did tell unto them, saying: Thus said the Father unto Malachi—Behold, I will send my messenger, and he shall prepare the way before me, and the Lord whom ye seek shall suddenly come to his temple, even the messenger of the covenant, whom ye delight in; behold, he shall come, saith the Lord of Hosts.

2 But who may abide the day of his coming, and who shall stand when he appeareth? For he is like a refiner's fire, and like fuller's soap.

3 And he shall sit as a refiner and purifier of silver; and he shall purify the sons of Levi, and purge them as gold and silver, that they may offer unto the Lord an offering in righteousness.

4 Then shall the offering of Judah and Jerusalem be pleasant unto the Lord, as in the days of old, and as in former years.

as the Savior . . . quoted from Isaiah and Malachi, so did Moroni quote from them as he counseled Joseph Smith concerning the work of the Restoration (see Joseph Smith–History 1:36–40). This demonstrates the significance of these prophecies about the work of the last days in preparation for the Savior's second coming" (McConkie et al., *Doctrinal Commentary*, 4:163).

Who is the "messenger of the covenant"? (24:1)
"Christ, who is the great 'messenger of the covenant,' did come to the first temple in this dispensation, in Kirtland, Ohio, on April 3, 1836. He has, of course, come to other temples and will yet do so—particularly in Jerusalem and Jackson County, Missouri—as part of the culmination of his majestic second coming" (Holland, *Christ and the New Covenant*, 294). ◕

What is fuller's soap? (24:2) "Anciently, a fuller was one who cleansed and whitened garments. 'The process of fulling or cleansing clothes consisted in treading or stamping on the garments with the feet or with bats in tubs of water, in which some alkaline substance answering the purpose of soap had been dissolved' (Peloubet, 203–4).

"Christ's blood is the only 'fuller's soap' strong enough to remove all stains of sin from those who repent and fully accept his atoning sacrifice (1 Ne. 12:11; Mosiah 3:11–18; Alma 5:27; 13:11). . . . However, the blood of Christ will have no cleansing effect upon the wicked, for the stain of sin shall remain on their garments (D&C 29:17)" (Brewster, *Doctrine and Covenants Encyclopedia*, 195–96).

What might be the sacrifice that the "sons of Levi" will offer? (24:3) "We are living in the dispensation of the fulness of times into which all things are to be gathered, and all things are to be restored since the beginning. Even this earth is to be restored to the condition which prevailed before Adam's transgression. Now in the nature of things, the law of sacrifice will have to be restored. . . . It will be necessary, therefore, for the sons of Levi, who offered the blood sacrifices anciently in Israel, to offer such a sacrifice again to round out and complete this ordinance in this dispensation. Sacrifice by the shedding of blood was instituted in the days of Adam and of necessity will have to be restored.

"Blood sacrifices will be performed long enough to complete the fullness of the restoration of this dispensation. Afterwards sacrifice will be of some other character"(*Doctrines of Salvation*, 3:94). ◕

How does the Lord feel about the treatment of the widows? (24:5) "The word *widow* appears to have had a most significant meaning to our Lord. He cautioned his disciples to beware the example of the scribes, who feigned righteousness by their long apparel and their lengthy prayers, but who devoured the houses of widows (see Luke 20:46–47).

"To the Nephites came the direct warning, 'I will come near to you to judgment; and I will be a swift witness against . . . those that oppress . . . the widow' (3 Ne. 24:5).

"And to the Prophet Joseph Smith he directed, 'The storehouse shall be kept by the consecrations of the church; and widows and orphans shall be provided for, as also the poor' (D&C 83:6)" (Monson, "The Fatherless and the Widows," 70).

3 Nephi 24:6–12. Israel Will Be Blessed for Paying Tithes and Offerings

How does man rob God? (24:8) "We do not rob God by withholding our gift in the sense that we deprive Him of the substance of earth. He always has that substance, never relinquishing it. But we rob Him of the satisfaction and the joy that He must feel when His children respond to His mandates and open their hearts in giving and in worship" (Richards, *Church in War and Peace*, 117). ✪

How is bringing "tithes into the storehouse" different from a charitable contribution? (24:10) "We pay tithing, as the Savior taught, by bringing the tithes 'into the storehouse' (3 Nephi 24:10; Malachi 3:10). We do this by paying our tithing to our bishop or branch president. We do not pay tithing by contributing to our favorite charities. The contributions we should make to charities come from our own funds, not from the tithes we are commanded to pay to the storehouse of the Lord" (Oaks, "Tithing," 35).

To what might the "windows of heaven" refer? (24:10) "The imagery of the 'windows' of heaven used by Malachi is most instructive. Windows allow natural light to enter into a building. In like manner, spiritual illumination and perspective are poured out through the windows of heaven and into our lives as we honor the law of tithing" (Bednar, "Windows of Heaven," 18). ✪

5 And I will come near to you to judgment; and I will be a swift witness against the sorcerers, and against the adulterers, and against false swearers, and against those that oppress the hireling in his wages, the widow and the fatherless, and that turn aside the stranger, and fear not me, saith the Lord of Hosts.

6 For I am the Lord, I change not; therefore ye sons of Jacob are not consumed.

7 Even from the days of your fathers ye are gone away from mine ordinances, and have not kept them. Return unto me and I will return unto you, saith the Lord of Hosts. But ye say: Wherein shall we return?

8 Will a man rob God? Yet ye have robbed me. But ye say: Wherein have we robbed thee? In tithes and offerings.

9 Ye are cursed with a curse, for ye have robbed me, even this whole nation.

10 Bring ye all the tithes into the storehouse, that there may be meat in my house; and prove me now herewith, saith the Lord of Hosts, if I will not open you the windows of heaven, and pour you out a blessing that there shall not be room enough to receive it.

11 And I will rebuke the devourer for your sakes, and he shall not destroy the fruits of your ground; neither shall your vine cast her fruit before the time in the fields, saith the Lord of Hosts.

12 And all nations shall call you blessed, for ye shall be a delightsome land, saith the Lord of Hosts.

13 Your words have been stout against me, saith the Lord. Yet ye say: What have we spoken against thee?

14 Ye have said: It is vain to serve God, and what doth it profit that we have kept his ordinances and that we have walked mournfully before the Lord of Hosts?

15 And now we call the proud happy; yea, they that work wickedness are set up; yea, they that tempt God are even delivered.

16 Then they that feared the Lord spake often one to another, and the Lord hearkened and heard; and a book of remembrance was written before him for them that feared the Lord, and that thought upon his name.

17 And they shall be mine, saith the Lord of Hosts, in that day when I make up my jewels; and I will spare them as a man spareth his own son that serveth him.

18 Then shall ye return and discern between the righteous and the wicked, between him that serveth God and him that serveth him not.

How does the Lord "rebuke the devourer"? (24:11) "The Lord has promised that he will rebuke the devourer for our sakes. . . . May not that rebuke of the devourer apply to various of our personal efforts and concerns?

"There is the great blessing of wisdom, of knowledge, even hidden treasures of knowledge. We are promised that ours shall be a delightsome land if we will walk in obedience to this law. I can interpret the word *land* as people, that those who walk in obedience shall be a delightsome people. What a marvelous condition to be a delightsome people whom others would describe as blessed!" (Hinckley, "Tithing," 40).

3 Nephi 24:13–18. A Book of Remembrance Is Written for the Righteous

How does the Lord answer the wicked who think it is foolish to serve Him? (24:14) "The fact that the wicked often seem to profit and do very well in this life may fill us with questions: 'Ye have said, It is vain to serve God: and what profit is it that we have kept his ordinance, and that we have walked mournfully before the Lord of hosts?' (Malachi 3:14).

"Yet is it not true that 'the triumphing of the wicked is short, and the joy of the hypocrite but for a moment'? (Job 20:5). The Lord Himself confirmed that those who follow the ways of man have 'joy in their works [but] for a season' (3 Nephi 27:11)" (Maxwell, *Men and Women of Christ*, 116–17).

3 Nephi 25:1–6. The Wicked Will Be Burned at the Second Coming, and the Righteous Will Be Saved

What do the root and branch represent in Malachi's prophecy? (25:1) "In order to understand this passage of scripture, for root read 'progenitors' or 'ancestors' and for branch read 'posterity' or 'children.' Unless, then, through obedience to the laws of God you can qualify yourself to go to the temple and have your family sealed to you, you will live forever separately and singly in an unmarried state. It seems to me that would be a very lonesome type of existence—to live without the warming influence of family life among those you love, who in turn love you" (Burton, "Salvation and Exaltation," 79).

How shall God come to the rescue of this generation? (25:5) "He will send Elijah the prophet.... Elijah shall reveal the covenants to seal the hearts of the fathers to the children, and the children to the fathers....

"In the days of Noah, God destroyed the world by a flood, and He has promised to destroy it by fire in the last days: but before it should take place, Elijah should first come and turn the hearts of the fathers to the children" (*Joseph Smith* [manual], 311, 313). ✛

What does it mean to "turn the heart of the fathers to the children"? (25:6) "Now, the word *turn* here should be translated *bind*, or seal. But what is the object of this important mission? or how is it to be fulfilled? The keys are to be delivered, the spirit of Elijah is to come, the Gospel to be established, the Saints of God gathered, Zion built up, and the Saints to come up as saviors on Mount Zion" (*Joseph Smith* [manual], 472–73). ✛

CHAPTER 25

At the Second Coming, the proud and wicked will be burned as stubble—Elijah will return before that great and dreadful day—Compare Malachi 4. About A.D. 34.

1 For behold, the day cometh that shall burn as an oven; and all the proud, yea, and all that do wickedly, shall be stubble; and the day that cometh shall burn them up, saith the Lord of Hosts, that it shall leave them neither root nor branch.

2 But unto you that fear my name, shall the Son of Righteousness arise with healing in his wings; and ye shall go forth and grow up as calves in the stall.

3 And ye shall tread down the wicked; for they shall be ashes under the soles of your feet in the day that I shall do this, saith the Lord of Hosts.

4 Remember ye the law of Moses, my servant, which I commanded unto him in Horeb for all Israel, with the statutes and judgments.

5 Behold, I will send you Elijah the prophet before the coming of the great and dreadful day of the Lord;

6 And he shall turn the heart of the fathers to the children, and the heart of the children to their fathers, lest I come and smite the earth with a curse.

CHAPTER 26

Jesus expounds all things from the beginning to the end—Babes and children utter marvelous things that cannot be written—Those in the Church of Christ have all things in common among them. About A.D. 34.

1 And now it came to pass that when Jesus had told these things he expounded them unto the multitude; and he did expound all things unto them, both great and small.

2 And he saith: These scriptures, which ye had not with you, the Father commanded that I should give unto you; for it was wisdom in him that they should be given unto future generations.

3 And he did expound all things, even from the beginning until the time that he should come in his glory—yea, even all things which should come upon the face of the earth, even until the elements should melt with fervent heat, and the earth should be wrapt together as a scroll, and the heavens and the earth should pass away;

4 And even unto the great and last day, when all people, and all kindreds, and all nations and tongues shall stand before God, to be judged of their works, whether they be good or whether they be evil—

5 If they be good, to the resurrection of everlasting life; and if they be evil, to the resurrection of damnation; being on a parallel, the one on the one hand and the other on the other hand, according to the mercy, and the justice, and the holiness which is in Christ, who was before the world began.

3 Nephi 26:1–5. Jesus Christ Reveals All Things from the Beginning of the World to the Final Judgment

To what scriptures was Jesus Christ referring? (26:2) Jesus Christ referred to the words of Malachi, a prophet who lived in Jerusalem after Lehi and Nephi traveled to the promised land. Malachi's prophecies were therefore not on the brass plates. The Savior made it clear that the Father wanted Malachi's words preserved for future generations. All the words of Malachi 3–4 are recorded in 3 Nephi 24–25; in addition, this prophecy of Malachi 4 is in all four standard works (see D&C 2 and Joseph Smith–History 1:37–39).

What is meant by the phrase "the heavens and the earth should pass away"? (26:3) Modern revelation explains: "And every corruptible thing, both of man, or of the beasts of the field, or of the fowls of the heavens, or of the fish of the sea, that dwells upon all the face of the earth, shall be consumed. . . . And also that of element shall melt with fervent heat; and all things shall become new, that my knowledge and glory may dwell upon all the earth" (D&C 101:24–34).

3 Nephi 26:6–12. Mormon Writes Only a Small Part of Jesus's Teachings

Why should we believe and trust in what the Lord has already revealed? (26:9) "In the Lord's mercy, he has revealed to us what in his wisdom he knows that we need (Alma 29:8). If we feast on—and believe in—what has been revealed already, more will be revealed to us, either through the inspiration of the Holy Spirit or through the revelation of more scripture at a later time. If we do not learn—and thus do not gain faith in—what the Lord has made known to the world already, we are closing the door on wonderful opportunities. It is no wonder, then, that modern prophets have counseled us repeatedly to make scripture study an important part of our lives" (Jackson, "Teaching from the Words of the Prophets," 204).

What do we learn from what Mormon says about what he did not write? (26:11–12) "From this statement and all the other reasons given by Book of Mormon authors for not including certain things, two points can be easily drawn about the book and what the Lord intended that we get from it. One is the fact that the Book of Mormon is the Lord's book and that a correct understanding of it comes from him alone. The other is that there is much more knowledge and truth available which we will receive only as we live in accordance with that which we already have" (Brown, "'I Speak Somewhat,'" 63).

3 Nephi 26:13–16. Jesus Blesses the Children, and They Speak Marvelous Things

What were the "marvelous things" the children uttered? (26:14–16) "One can scarcely imagine such deeply spiritual and profound things being uttered by little children. We are left to conjecture about their

6 And now there cannot be written in this book even a hundredth part of the things which Jesus did truly teach unto the people;

7 But behold the plates of Nephi do contain the more part of the things which he taught the people.

8 And these things have I written, which are a lesser part of the things which he taught the people; and I have written them to the intent that they may be brought again unto this people, from the Gentiles, according to the words which Jesus hath spoken.

9 And when they shall have received this, which is expedient that they should have first, to try their faith, and if it shall so be that they shall believe these things then shall the greater things be made manifest unto them.

10 And if it so be that they will not believe these things, then shall the greater things be withheld from them, unto their condemnation.

11 Behold, I was about to write them, all which were engraven upon the plates of Nephi, but the Lord forbade it, saying: I will try the faith of my people.

12 Therefore I, Mormon, do write the things which have been commanded me of the Lord. And now I, Mormon, make an end of my sayings, and proceed to write the things which have been commanded me.

13 Therefore, I would that ye should behold that the Lord truly did teach the people, for the space of three days; and after that he did show himself unto them oft, and did break bread oft, and bless it, and give it unto them.

14 And it came to pass that he did teach and minister unto the children of the multitude

of whom hath been spoken, and he did loose their tongues, and they did speak unto their fathers great and marvelous things, even greater than he had revealed unto the people; and he loosed their tongues that they could utter.

15 And it came to pass that after he had ascended into heaven—the second time that he showed himself unto them, and had gone unto the Father, after having healed all their sick, and their lame, and opened the eyes of their blind and unstopped the ears of the deaf, and even had done all manner of cures among them, and raised a man from the dead, and had shown forth his power unto them, and had ascended unto the Father—

16 Behold, it came to pass on the morrow that the multitude gathered themselves together, and they both saw and heard these children; yea, even babes did open their mouths and utter marvelous things; and the things which they did utter were forbidden that there should not any man write them.

17 And it came to pass that the disciples whom Jesus had chosen began from that time forth to baptize and to teach as many as did come unto them; and as many as were baptized in the name of Jesus were filled with the Holy Ghost.

18 And many of them saw and heard unspeakable things, which are not lawful to be written.

19 And they taught, and did minister one to another; and they had all things common among them, every man dealing justly, one with another.

20 And it came to pass that they did do all things even as Jesus had commanded them.

21 And they who were baptized in the name of Jesus were called the church of Christ.

messages. Was the veil parted to allow them to speak of life in the first estate? Did they discourse upon life among the Gods in a celestial environment? Did they reveal doctrinal mysteries which today's world could not receive? . . . This was such a sacred manifestation, the content of these inspired utterances were of such a nature, that mortal language could not adequately capture the true meaning and intent. In this sense, things of the Spirit are unspeakable (compare 3 Nephi 17:15–18)" (McConkie et al., *Doctrinal Commentary*, 4:172).

3 Nephi 26:17–21. The Twelve Disciples Teach and Baptize

Why do you think the Lord desires some sacred experiences not be spoken of or written about? (26:18) "Remember that that which cometh from above is sacred, and must be spoken with care, and by constraint of the Spirit; and in this there is no condemnation, and ye receive the Spirit through prayer; wherefore, without this there remaineth condemnation" (D&C 64:64).

CHAPTER 27

Jesus commands them to call the Church in His name—His mission and atoning sacrifice constitute His gospel—Men are commanded to repent and be baptized that they may be sanctified by the Holy Ghost—They are to be even as Jesus is. About A.D. 34–35.

3 Nephi 27:1–8. Jesus Christ Names His Church

What are the blessings that come individually and collectively to those who pray and fast? (27:1)
"Fasting, coupled with mighty prayer, is powerful. It can fill our minds with the revelations of the Spirit. It can strengthen us against times of temptation. Fasting and prayer can help develop within us courage and confidence. It can strengthen our character and build self restraint and discipline. Often when we fast, our righteous prayers and petitions have greater power. . . . Fasting in the proper spirit and in the Lord's way will energize us spiritually, strengthen our self-discipline, fill our homes with peace, lighten our hearts with joy, fortify us against temptation, prepare us for times of adversity, and open the windows of heaven" (Wirthlin, "Law of the Fast," 73–74).

Why is the name of the Church so important? (27:3–8) President M. Russell Ballard commented on the name of the Church: "I have thought a lot about why the Savior gave the nine-word name to His restored Church. It may seem long, but if we think of it as a descriptive overview of what the Church is, it suddenly becomes wonderfully brief, candid, and straightforward. How could any description be more direct and clear and yet expressed in such few words? . . .

1 And it came to pass that as the disciples of Jesus were journeying and were preaching the things which they had both heard and seen, and were baptizing in the name of Jesus, it came to pass that the disciples were gathered together and were united in mighty prayer and fasting.

2 And Jesus again showed himself unto them, for they were praying unto the Father in his name; and Jesus came and stood in the midst of them, and said unto them: What will ye that I shall give unto you?

3 And they said unto him: Lord, we will that thou wouldst tell us the name whereby we shall call this church; for there are disputations among the people concerning this matter.

4 And the Lord said unto them: Verily, verily, I say unto you, why is it that the people should murmur and dispute because of this thing?

The Name of the Church

In 1838 the Lord revealed through the Prophet Joseph Smith: "For thus shall my church be called in the last days, even The Church of Jesus Christ of Latter-day Saints" (D&C 115:4).

President Russell M. Nelson taught the great importance of using the correct name of the Church:

"Joseph Smith did not name the Church restored through him; neither did Mormon. It was the Savior Himself. . . .

"'Even earlier, in AD 34, our resurrected Lord gave similar instruction to members of His Church when He visited them in the Americas. At that time He said:

"'Ye shall call the church in my name. . . .

"'And how be it my church save it be called in my name? For if a church be called in Moses' name then it be Moses' church; or if it be called in the name of a man then it be the church of a man; but if it be called in my name then it is my church [3 Nephi 27:7–8].'

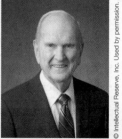

President Russell M. Nelson

"The name the Savior has given to His Church tells us exactly who we are and what we believe. We believe that Jesus Christ is the Savior and the Redeemer of the world. He atoned for all who would repent of their sins, and He broke the bands of death and provided the resurrection from the dead. We follow Jesus Christ" (Ballard, "Importance of a Name," 80). ⊕

5 Have they not read the scriptures, which say ye must take upon you the name of Christ, which is my name? For by this name shall ye be called at the last day;

6 And whoso taketh upon him my name, and endureth to the end, the same shall be saved at the last day.

7 Therefore, whatsoever ye shall do, ye shall do it in my name; therefore ye shall call the church in my name; and ye shall call upon the Father in my name that he will bless the church for my sake.

8 And how be it my church save it be called in my name? For if a church be called in Moses' name then it be Moses' church; or if it be called in the name of a man then it be the church of a man; but if it be called in my name then it is my church, if it so be that they are built upon my gospel.

What is the danger of failing to read and study the scriptures? (27:5) "If only each of us would be wise enough to say that we aren't able to answer any question unless we can find a doctrinal answer in the scriptures! And if we hear someone teaching something that is contrary to what is in the scriptures, each of us may know whether the things spoken are false—it is as simple as that. But the unfortunate thing is that so many of us are not reading the scriptures. We do not know what is in them, and therefore we speculate about the things that we ought to have found in the scriptures themselves. I think that therein is one of our biggest dangers of today" (Lee, "Find the Answers in the Scriptures," 3).

"Thus, the name of the Church is not negotiable. When the Savior clearly states what the name of His Church should be and even precedes His declaration with, 'Thus shall my church be called,' He is serious. And if we allow nicknames to be used or adopt or even sponsor those nicknames ourselves, He is offended.

"What's in a name or, in this case, a nickname? When it comes to nicknames of the Church, such as the 'LDS Church,' the 'Mormon Church,' or the 'Church of the Latter-day Saints,' the most important thing *in* those names is the *absence* of the Savior's name. To remove the Lord's name from the Lord's Church is a major victory for Satan. When we *discard* the Savior's name, we are subtly *disregarding* all that Jesus Christ did for us—even His Atonement. . . .

"When we omit His name from His Church, we are inadvertently removing *Him* as the central focus of our lives. . . .

"So, what's in a name? When it comes to the name of the Lord's Church, the answer is 'Everything!' Jesus Christ directed us to call the Church by His name because it is His Church, filled with His power" ("The Correct Name of the Church," *Ensign,* Nov. 2018, 87–89).

3 Nephi 27:9–22. Jesus Christ Explains His Gospel

What is meant by the word *gospel*? (27:9) "Gospel, means Good Tidings, especially the good news concerning Christ, the Kingdom of God, and Salvation; hence the teachings of Christ" (Reynolds and Sjodahl, *Commentary on the Book of Mormon*, 7:215).

The Doctrine and Covenants says: "And this is the gospel, the glad tidings, which the voice out of the heavens bore record unto us—That he came into the world, even Jesus, to be crucified for the world, and to bear the sins of the world, and to sanctify the world, and to cleanse it from all unrighteousness; That through him all might be saved whom the Father had put into his power and made by him" (D&C 76:40–42).

What does the often-mentioned phrase "hewn down and cast into the fire" mean? (27:11–12, 17) "In Doctrine and Covenants 97:7, the Lord says metaphorically that his people, Zion, are like the trees of the vineyard (see also Matthew 3:10). Men are like trees in that they are known by their fruits or their works (see Matthew 7:16–20). Good fruit is brought forth by good trees, and evil fruit is brought forth by evil trees. Such evil trees are eliminated from the vineyard so that 'they cumber not the ground' (Jacob 5:66). The Lord speaks of hewing down 'every tree that bringeth not forth good fruit' (D&C 97:7)" (*Doctrine and Covenants Student Manual*, (1981), 228).

What points of doctrine in verses 13–21 define the Savior's gospel? (27:13–21) Take a moment to list or mark those points of doctrine the Savior emphasizes as defining His gospel.

What did the Savior's mortal life teach us about His relationship with His Father? (27:13–14) Elder Bruce R. McConkie explained: "The Son came to do the will of the Father in all things. Jesus said: 'I came down from heaven, not to do mine own will, but the will of him that sent me' (John 6:38). Also [quotes 3 Nephi 27:13–14]. And Paul said of him: He 'made himself of no reputation, and took upon him the form of a servant, and was made in the likeness of men: And being found in fashion as a man. He humbled himself, and became obedient unto death, even the death of the cross' (Philip. 2:7–8). How better could his relationship with his Father be stated?" (*Doctrines of the Restoration*, 62).

9 Verily I say unto you, that ye are built upon my gospel; therefore ye shall call whatsoever things ye do call, in my name; therefore if ye call upon the Father, for the church, if it be in my name the Father will hear you;

10 And if it so be that the church is built upon my gospel then will the Father show forth his own works in it.

11 But if it be not built upon my gospel, and is built upon the works of men, or upon the works of the devil, verily I say unto you they have joy in their works for a season, and by and by the end cometh, and they are hewn down and cast into the fire, from whence there is no return.

12 For their works do follow them, for it is because of their works that they are hewn down; therefore remember the things that I have told you.

13 Behold I have given unto you my gospel, and this is the gospel which I have given unto you—that I came into the world to do the will of my Father, because my Father sent me.

14 And my Father sent me that I might be lifted up upon the cross; and after that I had been lifted up upon the cross, that I might draw all men unto me, that as I have been lifted up by men even so should men be lifted up by the Father, to stand before me, to be judged of their works, whether they be good or whether they be evil—

15 And for this cause have I been lifted up; therefore, according to the power of the Father I will draw all men unto me, that they may be judged according to their works.

16 And it shall come to pass, that whoso repenteth and is baptized in my name shall be filled; and if he endureth to the end, behold, him will I hold guiltless before my Father at that day when I shall stand to judge the world.

17 And he that endureth not unto the end, the same is he that is also hewn down and cast into the fire, from whence they can no more return, because of the justice of the Father.

18 And this is the word which he hath given unto the children of men. And for this cause he fulfilleth the words which he hath given, and he lieth not, but fulfilleth all his words.

19 And no unclean thing can enter into his kingdom; therefore nothing entereth into his rest save it be those who have washed their garments in my blood, because of their faith, and the repentance of all their sins, and their faithfulness unto the end.

20 Now this is the commandment: Repent, all ye ends of the earth, and come unto me and be baptized in my name, that ye may be sanctified by the reception of the Holy Ghost, that ye may stand spotless before me at the last day.

21 Verily, verily, I say unto you, this is my gospel; and ye know the things that ye must do in my church; for the works which ye have seen me do that shall ye also do; for that which ye have seen me do even that shall ye do;

How do we become clean in order to enter into God's kingdom? (27:19) "The exaltation to the celestial kingdom is so great that the Father is fully justified in making it dependent upon strict obedience to all of his commandments. The celestial kingdom is a kingdom of perfection. All who enter there must be thoroughly tried and proved and become perfect to inherit it. The Lord has said that through their obedience those who enter must be sanctified from all unrighteousness. Every law governing it must be obeyed. There can be no opposition to divine law, nor could anyone receiving this reward have any desire to change or disagree with anything prevailing there, for these laws are perfect" (Smith, *Man, His Origin and Destiny*, 532). ●

What makes sanctification possible? (27:20) "Sanctification is the process of becoming pure and spotless before God through the power of the Sanctifier, who is the Holy Ghost. It is made possible through the grace of Christ (D&C 20:31; 3 Ne. 27:19–20; Moro. 10:32–33). It occurs when men yield 'their hearts unto God' (Hel. 3:35). Sanctification is brought to those whose complete repentance and love of that which is good have whitened their garments through the blood of Christ's atonement. . . . One who is sanctified through the Spirit has 'no more disposition to do evil, but to do good continually' (Mosiah 5:2)" (Brewster, *Doctrine and Covenants Encyclopedia*, 490). ●

Which of the Savior's works can we do? (27:21) "The Savior's mortal mission we know as the Atonement. The Savior's mortal ministry includes everything else that He did—His teachings, expressions of love, attention to ordinances, patterns of prayer, perseverance, and more. He lived to be our

Exemplar. . . . 'This is my gospel,' He said, ' . . . for the works which ye have seen me do that shall ye also do.' Thus, faith; repentance; baptism by water, fire, and of the Holy Ghost; the gathering of the elect; and enduring to the end are all part of the gospel. [See D&C 33:6–12; 39:6.] All of us can emulate the Lord's example, regardless of age, status, or location" (Nelson, "Senior Missionaries and the Gospel," 81).

3 Nephi 27:23–27. Jesus Christ Teaches the Importance of Keeping Records

By which book or books will we be judged? (27:24–26) "The tithing records will name the full tithe payers; the books on Sabbath observance will tell those who went to the house of prayer on the Lord's day to pay their devotions to the Most High. . . . Even beyond this, every man will be judged out of the book of his own life, out of the record of obedience or disobedience that is written in the flesh and sinews and soul of his own body. And however imperfect the records kept on earth may be, all things are written by the Father, into the very body and spirit of each person, so that none will be judged amiss or from an imperfect ledger" (McConkie, *Mortal Messiah*, 4:384). ◉

Who will be the judges of the house of Israel? **(27:27)** "Jesus is the Judge of all. The Father judgeth no man but hath committed all judgment unto the Son. But the Twelve in Jerusalem shall sit on twelve thrones judging the whole house of Israel; the Nephite Twelve, having been so judged, will in turn judge the Nephite nation; and we may well conclude that the hierarchy of judgment expands out to other legal administrators in the various dispensations. Just as the noble and great participated with the Great Creator in the creation, so those who are chosen and worthy shall participate with the Great Judge in the day of judgment. That the lesser judges must be as the Great Judge is self-evident" (McConkie, *Mortal Messiah*, 4:385). ◉

3 Nephi 27:28–33. The Savior Goes to the Father

What is the significance of praying in Jesus's name? **(3 Nephi 27:28)** "When we use these sacred words, 'in the name of Jesus Christ,' . . . [w]e are on holy ground. . . . We are using a name most sublime, most holy, and most wonderful—the very name of the Son of God. We are now able to come unto the Father through His Beloved Son. What power and reassurance and peace come when we really pray in His name. This conclusion

22 Therefore, if ye do these things blessed are ye, for ye shall be lifted up at the last day.

23 Write the things which ye have seen and heard, save it be those which are forbidden.

24 Write the works of this people, which shall be, even as hath been written, of that which hath been.

25 For behold, out of the books which have been written, and which shall be written, shall this people be judged, for by them shall their works be known unto men.

26 And behold, all things are written by the Father; therefore out of the books which shall be written shall the world be judged.

27 And know ye that ye shall be judges of this people, according to the judgment which I shall give unto you, which shall be just. Therefore, what manner of men ought ye to be? Verily I say unto you, even as I am.

28 And now I go unto the Father. And verily I say unto you, whatsoever things ye shall ask the Father in my name shall be given unto you.

29 Therefore, ask, and ye shall receive; knock, and it shall be opened unto you; for he that asketh, receiveth; and unto him that knocketh, it shall be opened.

30 And now, behold, my joy is great, even unto fulness, because of you, and also this generation; yea, and even the Father rejoiceth, and also all the holy angels, because of you and this generation; for none of them are lost.

31 Behold, I would that ye should understand; for I mean them who are now alive of this generation; and none of them are lost; and in them I have fulness of joy.

32 But behold, it sorroweth me because of the fourth generation from this generation, for they are led away captive by him even as was the son of perdition; for they will sell me for silver and for gold, and for that which moth doth corrupt and which thieves can break through and steal. And in that day will I visit them, even in turning their works upon their own heads.

33 And it came to pass that when Jesus had ended these sayings he said unto his disciples: Enter ye in at the strait gate; for strait is the gate, and narrow is the way that leads to life, and few there be that find it; but wide is the gate, and broad the way which leads to death, and many there be that travel therein, until the night cometh, wherein no man can work.

to the prayer may, in many ways, be the most important part of the prayer. We can appeal to the Father through His victorious Son with confidence that our prayers will be heard. We can ask and receive, we can seek and find and subsequently find the open door" (Brown, "Pray unto the Father in My Name," 79).

How do we confidently pray to have the heavens opened? (27:29) "For each of you to receive revelation unique to your own needs and responsibilities, certain guidelines prevail. The Lord asks you to develop 'faith, hope, charity and love, with an eye single to the glory of God.' Then with your firm 'faith, virtue, knowledge, temperance, patience, brotherly kindness, godliness, charity, humility, [and] diligence,' you may ask, and you will receive; you may knock, and it will be opened unto you. Revelation from God is always compatible with His eternal law. It never contradicts His doctrine. It is facilitated by proper reverence for Deity. . . . Every Latter-day Saint may merit personal revelation" (Nelson, "Ask, Seek, Knock," 83).

What was Jesus Christ alluding to when He said the "fourth generation from this generation" of Nephites would sell Him for silver and gold? (27:32) According to one commentary, the Savior was saying, in essence: "This generation has seen and believed in the Atoning Messiah. Their faith will continue to be strong. But after four generations, their descendants will go astray. That apostasy again alludes to the Sermon at the Temple (3 Ne. 13:19). The Savior sorrowfully spells out the reason for their defection. It will be the same problem that has always plagued the Nephites—their desire for worldly status" (Gardner, *Second Witness*, 5:581–82).

CHAPTER 28

Nine of the twelve disciples desire and are promised an inheritance in Christ's kingdom when they die—The Three Nephites desire and are given power over death so as to remain on the earth until Jesus comes again—They are translated and see things not lawful to utter, and they are now ministering among men. About A.D. 34–35.

1 And it came to pass when Jesus had said these words, he spake unto his disciples, one by one, saying unto them: What is it that ye desire of me, after that I am gone to the Father?

3 Nephi 28:1–3. Jesus Christ Blesses Nine of His Twelve Disciples to Find Rest in His Heavenly Kingdom

What can we learn from the righteous desires of these disciples? (28:1) "The trust level was so high that our Resurrected Lord let his disciples ask, and it was given not simply because Jesus knew their thoughts, but because true disciples do not use their fervent faith to ask for anything which is not right. . . . If we can achieve a significant milestone in discipleship, we will find that 'he that asketh in the Spirit asketh according to the will of God; wherefore it is done even as he asketh' (D&C 46:30). . . . God only shares his power with those who will not abuse it, nor use it to cover their sins, gratify their pride, ambition, or control other men" (Maxwell, *Time to Choose*, 29).

What is the significance of the designation "the age of man"? (28:2–3) "The nine Nephite Apostles desired the same thing as Peter had desired: to come speedily into the Lord's kingdom. Perhaps what they are requesting is the blessing of being resurrected soon after mortal death and taken into celestial glory with their Lord." The Savior said this was a good desire (see D&C 7:5). "The significance, if any, of the specified age at which the nine would die—seventy-two years—is unknown" (McConkie et al., *Doctrinal Commentary*, 4:189).

2 And they all spake, save it were three, saying: We desire that after we have lived unto the age of man, that our ministry, wherein thou hast called us, may have an end, that we may speedily come unto thee in thy kingdom.

3 And he said unto them: Blessed are ye because ye desired this thing of me; therefore, after that ye are seventy and two years old ye shall come unto me in my kingdom; and with me ye shall find rest.

3 Nephi 28:4–12. Jesus Christ Promises Three Disciples That They Will Not Taste Death

4 And when he had spoken unto them, he turned himself unto the three, and said unto them: What will ye that I should do unto you, when I am gone unto the Father?

5 And they sorrowed in their hearts, for they durst not speak unto him the thing which they desired.

6 And he said unto them: Behold, I know your thoughts, and ye have desired the thing which John, my beloved, who was with me in my ministry, before that I was lifted up by the Jews, desired of me.

7 Therefore, more blessed are ye, for ye shall never taste of death; but ye shall live to behold all the doings of the Father unto the children of men, even until all things shall be fulfilled according to the will of the Father, when I shall come in my glory with the powers of heaven.

8 And ye shall never endure the pains of death; but when I shall come in my glory ye shall be changed in the twinkling of an eye from mortality to immortality; and then shall ye be blessed in the kingdom of my Father.

9 And again, ye shall not have pain while ye shall dwell in the flesh, neither sorrow save it be for the sins of the world; and all this will I do because of the thing which ye have desired of me, for ye have desired that ye might bring the souls of men unto me, while the world shall stand.

10 And for this cause ye shall have fulness of joy; and ye shall sit down in the kingdom of my Father; yea, your joy shall be full, even as the Father hath given me fulness of joy; and ye shall be even as I am, and I am even as the Father; and the Father and I are one;

11 And the Holy Ghost beareth record of the Father and me; and the Father giveth the Holy Ghost unto the children of men, because of me.

12 And it came to pass that when Jesus had spoken these words, he touched every one of them with his finger save it were the three who were to tarry, and then he departed.

13 And behold, the heavens were opened, and they were caught up into heaven, and saw and heard unspeakable things.

14 And it was forbidden them that they should utter; neither was it given unto them power that they could utter the things which they saw and heard;

How are translated beings similar to resurrected beings? (28:7) "Translated beings serve as types and shadows of celestial resurrected beings.... Like translated beings, those who are resurrected do not experience physical pain, and Satan has no power over them. Resurrected personages have the power to hide or 'veil' their true identity from others, as do those who have been translated. And resurrected beings possess power over the earth's elements; there is no power on earth that can hold them. The same is also true of translated beings" (Parry and Parry, *Understanding Death and the Resurrection*, 178). ⊕

Did these three disciples experience death? (28:8) "This change from mortality to immortality, though almost instantaneous, is both a death and a resurrection. Thus, translated beings do not suffer death as we normally define it, meaning the separation of body and spirit; nor do they receive a resurrection as we ordinarily describe it, meaning that the body rises from the dust and the spirit enters again into its fleshly home. But they do pass through death and are changed from mortality to immortality, in the eternal sense, and they thus both die and are resurrected in the eternal sense" (McConkie, *Mortal Messiah*, 4:389).

3 Nephi 28:13–16. The Three Disciples Are Translated

What is the difference between transfiguration and translation? (28:15) "Transfiguration for mortals consists of a temporary physical and spiritual change, allowing them not only to behold the glory of God but to enter his presence. . . . Transfiguration should not be confused with translation of the body, though both possibly affect the body in similar ways. Transfiguration describes a momentary change, whereas translated beings experience a long-term change that ends only when they pass from mortality to immortality (3 Ne. 28:8)" (Ludlow, *Encyclopedia of Mormonism*, 4:1485).

3 Nephi 28:17–40. Mormon Writes of the Ministry of the Three Disciples

What is the primary responsibility of the three translated Nephite disciples? (28:18) "This verse teaches an important principle, one that was made known early in this final dispensation: 'The thing which will be of the most worth unto you will be to declare repentance unto this people, that you may bring souls unto me, that you may rest with them in the kingdom of my Father' (D&C 15:6; D&C 16:6). The primary responsibility of the Three Nephites is missionary work, the gathering of Israel into the true church and fold of God" (McConkie et al., *Doctrinal Commentary*, 4:192).

15 And whether they were in the body or out of the body, they could not tell; for it did seem unto them like a transfiguration of them, that they were changed from this body of flesh into an immortal state, that they could behold the things of God.

16 But it came to pass that they did again minister upon the face of the earth; nevertheless they did not minister of the things which they had heard and seen, because of the commandment which was given them in heaven.

17 And now, whether they were mortal or immortal, from the day of their transfiguration, I know not;

18 But this much I know, according to the record which hath been given—they did go forth upon the face of the land, and did minister unto all the people, uniting as many to the church as would believe in their preaching; baptizing them, and as many as were baptized did receive the Holy Ghost.

19 And they were cast into prison by them who did not belong to the church. And the prisons could not hold them, for they were rent in twain.

20 And they were cast down into the earth; but they did smite the earth with the word of God, insomuch that by his power they were delivered out of the depths of the earth; and therefore they could not dig pits sufficient to hold them.

Transfiguration, Translation, and Resurrection

Transfiguration	Translation	Resurrection
The condition of persons who are temporarily changed in appearance and nature—that is, lifted to a higher spiritual level—so that they can endure the presence and glory of heavenly beings (see *Guide to the Scriptures*).	Persons who are changed so that they do not experience pain or death until their resurrection to immortality. Elijah was taken to heaven without tasting death (D&C 110:13; see *Guide to the Scriptures*).	The reuniting of the spirit body with the physical body of flesh and bones after death. After resurrection, the spirit and body will never again be separated, and the person will become immortal (see *Guide to the Scriptures*).

21 And thrice they were cast into a furnace and received no harm.

22 And twice were they cast into a den of wild beasts; and behold they did play with the beasts as a child with a suckling lamb, and received no harm.

23 And it came to pass that thus they did go forth among all the people of Nephi, and did preach the gospel of Christ unto all people upon the face of the land; and they were converted unto the Lord, and were united unto the church of Christ, and thus the people of that generation were blessed, according to the word of Jesus.

24 And now I, Mormon, make an end of speaking concerning these things for a time.

25 Behold, I was about to write the names of those who were never to taste of death, but the Lord forbade; therefore I write them not, for they are hid from the world.

26 But behold, I have seen them, and they have ministered unto me.

27 And behold they will be among the Gentiles, and the Gentiles shall know them not.

28 They will also be among the Jews, and the Jews shall know them not.

29 And it shall come to pass, when the Lord seeth fit in his wisdom that they shall minister unto all the scattered tribes of Israel, and unto all nations, kindreds, tongues and people, and shall bring out of them unto Jesus many souls, that their desire may be fulfilled, and also because of the convincing power of God which is in them.

30 And they are as the angels of God, and if they shall pray unto the Father in the name of Jesus they can show themselves unto whatsoever man it seemeth them good.

What do these verses confirm about the identity of translated beings? (28:26–28) "The fact that the Three Nephites appeared to the prophet Mormon as well as to his son Moroni illustrates that translated beings 'can show themselves unto whatsoever man it seemeth them good,' especially to the prophets (see 3 Nephi 28:24–26; Mormon 8:10–11). But the implication of 3 Nephi 28:27–28 remains that translated individuals will not normally be recognized by the general populace" (Judd and Szink, "John the Beloved in Latter-day Scripture," 102–3).

In what way are the three Nephites like the angels of God? (28:30) Like angels, the three Nephites (1) cannot be harmed physically by mortals, (2) minister as directed by Jesus Christ and are subject to Him, and (3) are free from the sins of this world. "All are under sin, except those which I have reserved unto myself, holy men that ye know not of" (D&C 49:8).

What is the central message of Mormon's insertion about receiving the Savior's words? (28:34–35) "It is an offense to God when we refuse to receive the words of the Twelve he has called to lead us. . . . A central message from Christ in 3 Nephi is clear: our Heavenly Father gave his glorious gospel plan to his Son. Jesus gave that same gospel plan, with its true doctrine and ordinances to the twelve disciples; and the twelve disciples, in turn, made the same eternal fulness available to all the Nephite Saints. Through the Twelve all of Israel (Church members) may become one with the God of heaven. This unity and oneness of the Saints is an evidence of the truth of the Lord's work" (Anderson, "The Twelve," 157–58).

What did Joseph Smith say about translated beings, which is the condition of the three Nephite disciples? (28:36) "Now the doctrine of translation is a power which belongs to this [the Melchizedek] Priesthood. Many have supposed that the doctrine of translation was a doctrine whereby men were taken immediately into the presence of God, and into an eternal fulness, but this is a mistaken idea. Their place of habitation is that of the terrestrial order, and a place prepared for such characters He held in reserve to be ministering angels unto many planets" (History of the Church, 4:210).

What can Mormon's experience teach us about receiving personal revelation? (28:36–37) In 3 Nephi 28:17, Mormon had a question he did not know the answer to. What did Mormon do about his question in the interval between verse 17 and verses 36–37? Why do you suppose that even prophets are not given the answers to all their questions right when the question comes up? How would you apply this

31 Therefore, great and marvelous works shall be wrought by them, before the great and coming day when all people must surely stand before the judgment-seat of Christ;

32 Yea even among the Gentiles shall there be a great and marvelous work wrought by them, before that judgment day.

33 And if ye had all the scriptures which give an account of all the marvelous works of Christ, ye would, according to the words of Christ, know that these things must surely come.

34 And wo be unto him that will not hearken unto the words of Jesus, and also to them whom he hath chosen and sent among them; for whoso receiveth not the words of Jesus and the words of those whom he hath sent receiveth not him; and therefore he will not receive them at the last day;

35 And it would be better for them if they had not been born. For do ye suppose that ye can get rid of the justice of an offended God, who hath been trampled under feet of men, that thereby salvation might come?

36 And now behold, as I spake concerning those whom the Lord hath chosen, yea, even three who were caught up into the heavens, that I knew not whether they were cleansed from mortality to immortality—

37 But behold, since I wrote, I have inquired of the Lord, and he hath made it manifest unto me that there must needs be a change wrought upon their bodies, or else it needs be that they must taste of death;

38 Therefore, that they might not taste of death there was a change wrought upon their bodies, that they might not suffer pain nor sorrow save it were for the sins of the world.

39 Now this change was not equal to that which shall take place at the last day; but there was a change wrought upon them, insomuch that Satan could have no power over them, that he could not tempt them; and they were sanctified in the flesh, that they were holy, and that the powers of the earth could not hold them.

40 And in this state they were to remain until the judgment day of Christ; and at that day they were to receive a greater change, and to be received into the kingdom of the Father to go no more out, but to dwell with God eternally in the heavens.

CHAPTER 29

The coming forth of the Book of Mormon is a sign that the Lord has commenced to gather Israel and fulfill His covenants—Those who reject His latter-day revelations and gifts will be cursed. About A.D. 34–35.

1 And now behold, I say unto you that when the Lord shall see fit, in his wisdom, that these sayings shall come unto the Gentiles according to his word, then ye may know that the covenant which the Father hath made with the children of Israel, concerning their restoration to the lands of their inheritance, is already beginning to be fulfilled.

2 And ye may know that the words of the Lord, which have been spoken by the holy prophets, shall all be fulfilled; and ye need not say that the Lord delays his coming unto the children of Israel.

3 And ye need not imagine in your hearts that the words which have been spoken are vain, for behold, the Lord will remember his covenant which he hath made unto his people of the house of Israel.

experience to those who think that because God did not answer their question right away, they will never get an answer?

What will be the "greater change" for the three translated disciples? (28:38–40) "God changed the mortal bodies of the three Nephites so their bodies were similar to those of immortal souls. . . . Their bodies became translated bodies, not resurrected souls. . . . The 'greater change' refers to the resurrection. At the judgment day, the three Nephites will receive the greater change to their bodies; they will become glorious, resurrected souls" (Parry and Parry, *Understanding Death and the Resurrection*, 182).

3 Nephi 29:1–3. The Coming Forth of the Book of Mormon Is a Sign That God Will Keep His Promise to Gather Israel

What are "these sayings" that will come to the Gentiles in the latter days? (29:1–3) "These sayings" are the whole of the Book of Mormon which has come to us in our day. "Indeed, the Lord has not forgotten! He has blessed us and others throughout the world with the Book of Mormon. . . . It helps us to make covenants with God. It invites us to remember Him and to know His Beloved Son. It is another testament of Jesus Christ" (Nelson, "Covenants," 88).

Why is it important to believe the words spoken by the holy prophets? (29:2) Why do you think some people doubt that God speaks through inspired servants? In what ways have you seen the words of holy prophets fulfilled? Consider these words: "What I the Lord have spoken, I have spoken, and I excuse not myself; . . . my word shall not pass away, but shall all be fulfilled, whether by mine own voice or by the voice of my servants, it is the same" (D&C 1:38).

Why does the Book of Mormon emphasize that God will remember His covenants with Israel? (29:3) "This book, written for our day, states as one of its purposes that 'ye may know that the covenant which the Father hath made with the children of Israel . . . is already beginning to be fulfilled. . . . For behold, the Lord will remember his covenant which he hath made unto his people of the house of Israel" (Nelson, "Covenants," 88). "When you read the Book of Mormon, concentrate on the principal figure in the book—from its first chapter to the last—the Lord Jesus Christ, Son of the Living God. And look for a second undergirding theme: God will keep His covenants with the remnants of the house of Israel" (Nelson, "Testimony of the Book of Mormon," 69).

3 Nephi 29:4–9. Those Who Reject God's Work in the Last Days Will Be Cursed

How does someone profit by denying the miracles and gospel of Jesus Christ? (29:7) "[Mormon] saw that at that time wicked and crafty men would turn preaching the messages of Life and Salvation from a duty of love towards Christ to a money-making proposition. To do so is to turn religion into an industrial craft, and that is 'priestcraft.'

"Priestcraft means, not only crafty and wicked ruses to lead the unwary astray, but also the making of religion a profession in which the aim is to obtain worldly honor, gold, and silver, and the plaudits of men" (Reynolds and Sjodahl, *Commentary on the Book of Mormon*, 7:236).

Rather than "make game of the Jews," why should Christians be thankful for their sacrifice? (29:8) "'Do they remember the travails, and the labors, and the pains of the Jews, and their diligence unto me, in bringing forth salvation unto the Gentiles?' (2 Nephi 29:2–4). If the hearts of the Christians of the world were truly centered on the Bible, as they profess, would they not have an entirely different feeling toward the Jews? Did not Jesus say that 'salvation is of the Jews'? (John 4:22). Was not Jesus a Jew, and did not the Bible come to us through Jewish hands? Can anyone truly believe and reverence the Bible without honoring and thanking the Jews?" (McConkie, *New Witness*, 462–63).

4 And when ye shall see these sayings coming forth among you, then ye need not any longer spurn at the doings of the Lord, for the sword of his justice is in his right hand; and behold, at that day, if ye shall spurn at his doings he will cause that it shall soon overtake you.

5 Wo unto him that spurneth at the doings of the Lord; yea, wo unto him that shall deny the Christ and his works!

6 Yea, wo unto him that shall deny the revelations of the Lord, and that shall say the Lord no longer worketh by revelation, or by prophecy, or by gifts, or by tongues, or by healings, or by the power of the Holy Ghost!

7 Yea, and wo unto him that shall say at that day, to get gain, that there can be no miracle wrought by Jesus Christ; for he that doeth this shall become like unto the son of perdition, for whom there was no mercy, according to the word of Christ!

8 Yea, and ye need not any longer hiss, nor spurn, nor make game of the Jews, nor any of the remnant of the house of Israel; for behold, the Lord remembereth his covenant unto them, and he will do unto them according to that which he hath sworn.

9 Therefore ye need not suppose that ye can turn the right hand of the Lord unto the left, that he may not execute judgment unto the fulfilling of the covenant which he hath made unto the house of Israel.

CHAPTER 30

The latter-day Gentiles are commanded to repent, come unto Christ, and be numbered with the house of Israel. About A.D. 34–35.

1 Hearken, O ye Gentiles, and hear the words of Jesus Christ, the Son of the living God, which he hath commanded me that I should speak concerning you, for, behold he commandeth me that I should write, saying:

2 Turn, all ye Gentiles, from your wicked ways; and repent of your evil doings, of your lyings and deceivings, and of your whoredoms, and of your secret abominations, and your idolatries, and of your murders, and your priestcrafts, and your envyings, and your strifes, and from all your wickedness and abominations, and come unto me, and be baptized in my name, that ye may receive a remission of your sins, and be filled with the Holy Ghost, that ye may be numbered with my people who are of the house of Israel.

3 Nephi 30:1–2. The Gentiles in the Latter Days Are Invited to Turn Away from Wickedness, Repent, and Be Numbered with the House of Israel

What does *hearken* mean? (30:1) To *hearken* is "to attend; to regard; to give heed to what is uttered; to observe or obey" (Webster, *American Dictionary*).

"Above all, God's children should learn to listen, then listen to learn from the Lord. . . . Scriptures recorded in all dispensations teach that we show our *love* of God as we *hearken* to His commandments and *obey* them. These actions are closely connected. In fact, the Hebrew language of the Old Testament in most instances uses the same term for both *hearkening* (to the Lord) and *obedience* (to His word)" (Nelson, "Listen to Learn," 24). What does it show the Lord when we hearken to Him?

Why does 3 Nephi end with a strong warning, pronouncing curses upon the wicked? (30:2) The Book of Mormon, as an ancient text, naturally reflects the form, function, and style of ancient writing. Hugh Nibley noted: "In many ancient Near Eastern covenant or treaty documents, it's appropriate to end with a number of wo's—wo to people who don't live up worthily to these things, wo to those who spurn the works of God, wo to them who deny the revelations of God" (*Teachings of the Book of Mormon*, 4:157).

What blessings come to Gentiles who are gathered and numbered with the people of the house of Israel? (30:2) "The prophets proclaim . . . that all men and women, if they are to achieve true happiness, must 'come unto Christ, and be perfected in him' (Moroni 10:32). Indeed, that is the very purpose of The Church of Jesus Christ of Latter-day Saints to invite, encourage, and assist all of God's children, both living and dead, to come to Christ . . . that 'ye may receive a remission of your sins, and be filled with the Holy Ghost, that ye may be numbered with my people who are of the house of Israel' (3 Nephi 30:2). That is why we do missionary work" (Morrison, "Dawning of a New Day in Africa," 25). ☉

FOURTH NEPHI
THE BOOK OF NEPHI

WHO IS THE SON OF NEPHI—
ONE OF THE DISCIPLES OF JESUS CHRIST

An account of the people of Nephi, according to his record.

Introduction

In only forty-nine verses, the book of 4 Nephi covers a lengthy period of nearly three hundred years, which is approximately one-third of the entire Nephite history. The book contrasts the righteousness of the people immediately following Jesus Christ's ministry with the wickedness of the people a few generations later.

Fourth Nephi begins with the good news that "the people were all converted unto the Lord" and have "all things common" (4 Nephi 1:2–3). The people experience peace, prosperity, miracles, and live in unity and happiness for many years (see 4 Nephi 1:4–18). After Nephi dies, his son Amos keeps the records and then passes the records to his son Amos (see 4 Nephi 1:19–21). Mormon mentions that the people then "become exceedingly rich" and wear "costly apparel" (4 Nephi 1:23–24). Sadly, at that point, the people no longer have all things in common and begin to be "divided into classes." Satan begins to "get hold upon their hearts" (4 Nephi 1:26–28). The wicked persecute the members of the true Church and the apostles of Jesus Christ, smiting the former and attempting to torture and imprison the latter (4 Nephi 1:29–34). Eventually, the people return to the previous divisions as Nephites and Lamanites. The Lamanites "willfully rebel against the gospel," teach their children to "hate the children of Nephi," and begin "again to build up the secret oaths and combinations of Gadianton" (4 Nephi 1:35–42). The book of 4 Nephi ends tragically, as both the Nephites and the Lamanites join the Gadianton robbers, who spread over the face of all the land until "there were none that were righteous save it were the disciples of Jesus" (4 Nephi 1:43–46). Amos dies, and his brother Ammaron keeps the records for a time before being directed by the Holy Ghost to hide them to come forth at a later time (4 Nephi 1:47–49).

Fourth Nephi allows us to follow the narrative immediately after the remarkable visit of Jesus Christ down to the life of young Mormon. In this book, we sense a longing by Mormon for the golden years of Nephite civilization and his regret that pride, division, and corruption began the ruin of his people.

The superscription to the book of 4 Nephi is a single line that appears just under the title. It was part of the ancient record translated by the Prophet Joseph Smith and dictated by him to his scribe (see also, for example, 1 Nephi, Alma 5, and Moroni 9).

Distinct from the superscription is the chapter summary, which is presented in italics between the chapter number and the beginning of the scriptural text. Chapter summaries, originally added in the 1920 edition of the Book of Mormon, give the reader an overview of what each chapter contains.

4 Nephi 1:1–13. Everyone Was Converted to the Church of Jesus Christ

CHAPTER 1

The Nephites and the Lamanites are all converted unto the Lord—They have all things in common, work miracles, and prosper in the land—After two centuries, divisions, evils, false churches, and persecutions arise—After three hundred years, both the Nephites and the Lamanites are wicked—Ammaron hides up the sacred records. About A.D. 35–321.

1 And it came to pass that the thirty and fourth year passed away, and also the thirty and fifth, and behold the disciples of Jesus had formed a church of Christ in all the lands round about. And as many as did come unto them, and did truly repent of their sins, were baptized in the name of Jesus; and they did also receive the Holy Ghost.

2 And it came to pass in the thirty and sixth year, the people were all converted unto the Lord, upon all the face of the land, both Nephites and Lamanites, and there were no contentions and disputations among them, and every man did deal justly one with another.

3 And they had all things common among them; therefore there were not rich and poor, bond and free, but they were all made free, and partakers of the heavenly gift.

4 And it came to pass that the thirty and seventh year passed away also, and there still continued to be peace in the land.

5 And there were great and marvelous works wrought by the disciples of Jesus, insomuch that they did heal the sick, and raise the dead, and cause the lame to walk, and the blind to receive their sight, and the deaf to hear; and all manner of miracles did they work among the children of men; and in nothing did they work miracles save it were in the name of Jesus.

6 And thus did the thirty and eighth year pass away, and also the thirty and ninth, and forty and first, and the forty and second, yea, even until forty and nine years had passed away, and also the fifty and first, and the fifty and second; yea, and even until fifty and nine years had passed away.

7 And the Lord did prosper them exceedingly in the land; yea, insomuch that they did build cities again where there had been cities burned.

8 Yea, even that great city Zarahemla did they cause to be built again.

What responsibility do we have to deal justly and honestly in all our associations? (1:2) "We are our brother's keeper, even in the marketplace. . . . We cannot allow ourselves to do less for our partners, our customers, our employees, and others with whom we deal in the marketplace. What a beautiful and happy world this would be if all of us would strive to live these principles to the fullest. Our efforts and influence would affect millions. Examples improve society more than sermons. . . . In those brilliant generations that followed the appearance of the resurrected Christ in the New World, 'there were no contentions and disputations among [the people], and every man did deal justly one with another' (4 Ne. 1:2)" (Oaks, "Brother's Keeper," 22–23).

Is it possible today to have "all things common," with no rich and no poor? (1:3) "We may not yet be the Zion of which our prophets foretold . . . , but we long for it and we keep working toward it. I do not know whether a full implementation of such a society can be realized until Christ comes, but I know that when He did come to the Nephites, His majestic teachings . . . led to the happiest of all times, a time in which ' . . . they had all things common among them; therefore there were not rich and poor. . . .' That blessed circumstance was, I suppose, achieved on only one other occasion of which we know—the city of Enoch [see Moses 7:21]" (Holland, "Handful of Meal and a Little Oil," 30).

Book of Mormon Pages and Time Periods

This chart shows how many pages in the Book of Mormon correspond with each author and time period.

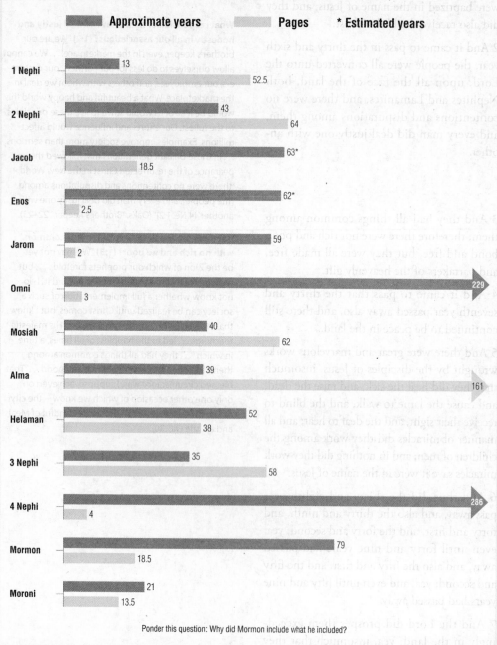

Legend:
- Approximate years
- Pages
- * Estimated years

Author	Approximate years	Pages
1 Nephi	13	52.5
2 Nephi	43	64
Jacob	63*	18.5
Enos	62*	2.5
Jarom	59	2
Omni	229	3
Mosiah	40	62
Alma	39	161
Helaman	52	38
3 Nephi	35	58
4 Nephi	286	4
Mormon	79	18.5
Moroni	21	13.5

Ponder this question: Why did Mormon include what he included?

9 But there were many cities which had been sunk, and waters came up in the stead thereof; therefore these cities could not be renewed.

10 And now, behold, it came to pass that the people of Nephi did wax strong, and did multiply exceedingly fast, and became an exceedingly fair and delightsome people.

11 And they were married, and given in marriage, and were blessed according to the multitude of the promises which the Lord had made unto them.

12 And they did not walk any more after the performances and ordinances of the law of Moses; but they did walk after the commandments which they had received from their Lord and their God, continuing in fasting and prayer, and in meeting together oft both to pray and to hear the word of the Lord.

13 And it came to pass that there was no contention among all the people, in all the land; but there were mighty miracles wrought among the disciples of Jesus.

14 And it came to pass that the seventy and first year passed away, and also the seventy and second year, yea, and in fine, till the seventy and ninth year had passed away; yea, even an hundred years had passed away, and the disciples of Jesus, whom he had chosen, had all gone to the paradise of God, save it were the three who should tarry; and there were other disciples ordained in their stead; and also many of that generation had passed away.

15 And it came to pass that there was no contention in the land, because of the love of God which did dwell in the hearts of the people.

16 And there were no envyings, nor strifes, nor tumults, nor whoredoms, nor lyings, nor murders, nor any manner of lasciviousness;

Why is marriage such a blessing? (1:11) "One of the sweetest verses in the Book of Mormon states simply, 'And they were married, and given in marriage, and were blessed according to the multitude of the promises which the Lord had made unto them.' The promises of the Lord are extended to all those who follow the pattern of life that builds happy, holy marriage relationships. Such blessings come as the delightful, predictable consequences of faithfully living the gospel of Jesus Christ. . . . Marriage is a gift from God to us; the quality of our marriages is a gift from us to Him" (Clayton, "Marriage," 85).

How were the Nephites and Lamanites able to have a society without contention? (1:13) According to verse 2, there was "no contention" because everyone was "converted unto the Lord." In verse 13, "no contention" is connected with "mighty miracles," perhaps as an outcome. Thus, in addition to peace, another blessing appears to come with conversion to the gospel and having the love of God in one's heart: mighty miracles. ☉

4 Nephi 1:14–22. The New Generation Remains Faithful

How can labels and nicknames be misused? (1:15–17) "When we know who we are and what God expects of us . . . we are spiritually protected. We become better people. When the Nephites were truly righteous, they avoided divisive nicknames and 'there was no contention in the land, because of the love of God which did dwell in the hearts of the people' (4 Nephi 1:15).

"'There were no . . . Lamanites, nor any manner of -ites; but they were in one, the children of Christ, and heirs to the kingdom of God' (4 Nephi 1:17). That lesson from history suggests that we also delete from our personal vocabularies names that segregate and hyphens that separate" (Nelson, "Children of the Covenant," 34). ⊕

and surely there could not be a happier people among all the people who had been created by the hand of God.

17 There were no robbers, nor murderers, neither were there Lamanites, nor any manner of -ites; but they were in one, the children of Christ, and heirs to the kingdom of God.

18 And how blessed were they! For the Lord did bless them in all their doings; yea, even they were blessed and prospered until an hundred and ten years had passed away; and the first generation from Christ had passed away, and there was no contention in all the land.

19 And it came to pass that Nephi, he that kept this last record, (and he kept it upon the plates of Nephi) died, and his son Amos kept it in his stead; and he kept it upon the plates of Nephi also.

20 And he kept it eighty and four years, and there was still peace in the land, save it were a small part of the people who had revolted from the church and taken upon them the name of Lamanites; therefore there began to be Lamanites again in the land.

21 And it came to pass that Amos died also, (and it was an hundred and ninety and four years from the coming of Christ) and his son

Steps to Apostasy

"The small book of Fourth Nephi provides a classic example of the steps that lead to apostasy. [Just like the collapse of Nephite society recorded in 4 Nephi, any nation can decay and fall into destruction.] In the first part of this book the historian [describes] an almost perfect society. . . . [then] step by step the things that led the people from the state of nearly perfect happiness to a state of exceeding wickedness:

"(1) A small part of the people revolted from the church—verse 20.

"(2) The people became 'exceeding rich'—verse 23.

"(3) Some of the people began to be 'lifted up in pride, such as the wearing of costly apparel'—verse 24.

"(4) After the people were built up in pride, 'from that time forth they did have their goods and their substance no more common among them'—verse 25.

"(5) The people began to be divided into classes—verse 26.

"(6) The people began to 'build up churches unto themselves to get gain, and began to deny the true church of Christ'—verse 26.

"(7) Many churches were established 'which professed to know the Christ, and yet they did deny the more parts of his gospel'—verse 27.

Amos kept the record in his stead; and he also kept it upon the plates of Nephi; and it was also written in the book of Nephi, which is this book.

22 And it came to pass that two hundred years had passed away; and the second generation had all passed away save it were a few.

23 And now I, Mormon, would that ye should know that the people had multiplied, insomuch that they were spread upon all the face of the land, and that they had become exceedingly rich, because of their prosperity in Christ.

24 And now, in this two hundred and first year there began to be among them those who were lifted up in pride, such as the wearing of costly apparel, and all manner of fine pearls, and of the fine things of the world.

25 And from that time forth they did have their goods and their substance no more common among them.

26 And they began to be divided into classes; and they began to build up churches unto themselves to get gain, and began to deny the true church of Christ.

27 And it came to pass that when two hundred and ten years had passed away there were

4 Nephi 1:23–35. The People Are Lifted Up in Pride and Become Wicked

What is the greatest stumbling block to establishing Zion? (1:24) "It was essentially the sin of pride that kept us from establishing Zion in the days of the Prophet Joseph Smith. It was the same sin of pride that brought consecration to an end among the Nephites (see 4 Ne. 1:24–25).

"Pride is the great stumbling block to Zion. I repeat: Pride is the great stumbling block to Zion.

"We must cleanse the inner vessel by conquering pride (see Alma 6:2–4; Matt. 23:25–26).

"We must yield 'to the enticings of the Holy Spirit,' put off the prideful 'natural man,' become 'a saint through the atonement of Christ the Lord,' and become 'as a child, submissive, meek, humble' [Mosiah 3:19]" (Benson, "Beware of Pride," 7).

How was pride manifest among the Nephites? How is it manifested today? (1:24–35) As you study

"(8) These churches which professed to know Christ did administer 'that which was sacred [the sacrament] unto him whom it had been forbidden because of unworthiness. And this church did multiply exceedingly because of iniquity, and because of the power of Satan who did get hold upon their hearts'—verses 27–28.

"(9) Another church was established 'which denied the Christ; and they did persecute the true church of Christ, . . . and they did despise them because of the many miracles which were wrought among them'—verse 29.

"(10) '. . . the people did harden their hearts and seek to kill' the few remaining righteous people, including the three Nephite disciples—verse 31.

"(11) The 'wicked part of the people began again to build up the secret oaths and combinations of Gadianton'—verse 42.

"(12) And finally, the people became 'proud in their hearts' and 'vain like unto their brethren,' thus 'both the people of Nephi and the Lamanites had become exceeding wicked one like unto another . . . ; and there were none that were righteous save it were the disciples of Jesus'—verses 43–46" (Ludlow, *Companion to Your Study of the Book of Mormon*, 296–97).

4 Nephi 1:24–35, ponder the effects of pride among the people. Consider the negative effects of wearing costly apparel, dividing into social classes, building up churches to get gain, denying the true church, persecuting the faithful, and establishing secret combinations. How does each manifestation of pride become progressively worse? Have you seen this pattern? How are people today, perhaps even in the Church, exhibiting similar manifestations of pride?

many churches in the land; yea, there were many churches which professed to know the Christ, and yet they did deny the more parts of his gospel, insomuch that they did receive all manner of wickedness, and did administer that which was sacred unto him to whom it had been forbidden because of unworthiness.

28 And this church did multiply exceedingly because of iniquity, and because of the power of Satan who did get hold upon their hearts.

29 And again, there was another church which denied the Christ; and they did persecute the true church of Christ, because of their humility and their belief in Christ; and they did despise them because of the many miracles which were wrought among them.

30 Therefore they did exercise power and authority over the disciples of Jesus who did tarry with them, and they did cast them into prison; but by the power of the word of God, which was in them, the prisons were rent in twain, and they went forth doing mighty miracles among them.

31 Nevertheless, and notwithstanding all these miracles, the people did harden their hearts, and did seek to kill them, even as the Jews at Jerusalem sought to kill Jesus, according to his word.

32 And they did cast them into furnaces of fire, and they came forth receiving no harm.

33 And they also cast them into dens of wild beasts, and they did play with the wild beasts even as a child with a lamb; and they did come forth from among them, receiving no harm.

34 Nevertheless, the people did harden their hearts, for they were led by many priests and false prophets to build up many churches, and to do all manner of iniquity. And they did smite upon the people of Jesus; but the people of Jesus did not smite again. And thus they did dwindle in unbelief and wickedness, from year to year, even until two hundred and thirty years had passed away.

35 And now it came to pass in this year, yea, in the two hundred and thirty and first year, there was a great division among the people.

36 And it came to pass that in this year there arose a people who were called the Nephites, and they were true believers in Christ; and among them there were those who were called by the Lamanites—Jacobites, and Josephites, and Zoramites;

37 Therefore the true believers in Christ, and the true worshipers of Christ, (among whom were the three disciples of Jesus who should tarry) were called Nephites, and Jacobites, and Josephites, and Zoramites.

38 And it came to pass that they who rejected the gospel were called Lamanites, and Lemuelites, and Ishmaelites; and they did not dwindle in unbelief, but they did wilfully rebel against the gospel of Christ; and they did teach their children that they should not believe, even as their fathers, from the beginning, did dwindle.

39 And it was because of the wickedness and abomination of their fathers, even as it was in the beginning. And they were taught to hate the children of God, even as the Lamanites were taught to hate the children of Nephi from the beginning.

40 And it came to pass that two hundred and forty and four years had passed away, and thus were the affairs of the people. And the more wicked part of the people did wax strong, and became exceedingly more numerous than were the people of God.

41 And they did still continue to build up churches unto themselves, and adorn them with all manner of precious things. And thus did two hundred and fifty years pass away, and also two hundred and sixty years.

4 Nephi 1:36–49. The People Divide into Tribes and Seek Out Secret Combinations

What does it mean to be "true believers in Christ"? (1:36) "In our time, the words 'true believer' have sometimes come to denote 'fanatic.' But many years ago, a similar phrase was used by Alma and by the Apostle Nephi, who wrote of 'true believers in Christ' as a definition of those who belong 'to the church of God' and are 'true worshipers' (Alma 46:14, 4 Ne. 1:36)" (Maxwell, "True Believers," 20). ❂

Why do these seven tribes keep appearing in Nephite history? (1:37–38) "Three times in the Book of Mormon these seven [tribes] are mentioned, each time in . . . rigid order. . . . Significantly, these references come from the earliest as well as the latest periods of Nephite history, indicating the importance and persistence of kinship as a basic element in society" (Sorenson et al., "Seven Tribes," 93).

What is the effect of teaching children to hate others? (1:39) "The Lamanites in 4 Nephi were reviving old prejudices and teaching their children again to hate, 'even as the Lamanites were taught to hate the children of Nephi from the beginning' [4 Nephi 1:39]. And so the polarizing process began all over again.

"I hope that we may learn this important lesson and delete segregating names from our personal vocabularies. . . . [Remember,] 'all are alike unto God' [2 Ne. 26:33]" (Nelson, "More Excellent Hope," 63).

42 And it came to pass that the wicked part of the people began again to build up the secret oaths and combinations of Gadianton.

43 And also the people who were called the people of Nephi began to be proud in their hearts, because of their exceeding riches, and become vain like unto their brethren, the Lamanites.

44 And from this time the disciples began to sorrow for the sins of the world.

45 And it came to pass that when three hundred years had passed away, both the people of Nephi and the Lamanites had become exceedingly wicked one like unto another.

46 And it came to pass that the robbers of Gadianton did spread over all the face of the land; and there were none that were righteous save it were the disciples of Jesus. And gold and silver did they lay up in store in abundance, and did traffic in all manner of traffic.

47 And it came to pass that after three hundred and five years had passed away, (and the people did still remain in wickedness) Amos died; and his brother, Ammaron, did keep the record in his stead.

48 And it came to pass that when three hundred and twenty years had passed away, Ammaron, being constrained by the Holy Ghost, did hide up the records which were sacred—yea, even all the sacred records which had been handed down from generation to generation, which were sacred—even until the three hundred and twentieth year from the coming of Christ.

49 And he did hide them up unto the Lord, that they might come again unto the remnant of the house of Jacob, according to the prophecies and the promises of the Lord. And thus is the end of the record of Ammaron.

What is one of the main reasons why the Book of Mormon was preserved? (1:49) The Lord revealed to the Prophet Joseph Smith that he "should translate . . . the engravings of Nephi, and send forth . . . this work [which contains] all those parts of my gospel which my holy prophets . . . desired in their prayers should come forth unto this people. And I said unto them, that it should be granted unto them according to their faith in their prayers" (D&C 10:45–47; see also D&C 3:16–20).

How has the Book of Mormon fulfilled the faith and prayers of its writers? How does knowing that the Lord will fulfill His promises increase your faith in what you pray for?

THE BOOK OF MORMON

Introduction

Mormon's record includes seven chapters of his own writing (Mormon 1–7) and two chapters from his son Moroni (Mormon 8–9). The events Mormon describes occurred between A.D. 321 and 385. The record speaks of Mormon's life and the demise of the Nephite nation due to its wickedness, which he witnessed firsthand. He personally observed the degradation of Nephite society and Nephite conflicts with the Lamanites for about sixty-five years. His record is only a small part of what he knew and saw (see Mormon 5:9).

This book contains a shorter version of Mormon's record written on the large plates of Nephi (see Mormon 2:18; 5:9). Mormon mercifully wrote to the descendants of the people who killed him, his family, and his nation. He invites latter-day descendants of Lehi to believe in Christ, accept His gospel, and be saved. He promises that those who truly believe the Bible will also believe the Book of Mormon. Moroni added to his father's record, likely in about A.D. 401 (see Mormon 8:6), urging latter-day readers to receive the Book of Mormon and believe in Christ.

CHAPTER 1

Ammaron instructs Mormon concerning the sacred records—War commences between the Nephites and the Lamanites—The Three Nephites are taken away—Wickedness, unbelief, sorceries, and witchcraft prevail. About A.D. 321–326.

1 And now I, Mormon, make a record of the things which I have both seen and heard, and call it the Book of Mormon.

2 And about the time that Ammaron hid up the records unto the Lord, he came unto me, (I being about ten years of age, and I began to be learned somewhat after the manner of the learning of my people) and Ammaron said unto me: I perceive that thou art a sober child, and art quick to observe;

3 Therefore, when ye are about twenty and four years old I would that ye should remember the things that ye have observed

Mormon 1:1–5. Mormon, While Yet a Child, Is Given Responsibility for Sacred Records

What are we to understand from this description of Mormon as "quick to observe"? (1:2) Elder David A. Bednar taught: "When we are quick to observe, we promptly look or notice and obey. Both of these fundamental elements—looking and obeying—are essential to being quick to observe. And the prophet Mormon is an impressive example of this gift in action" ("Quick to Observe," 32). ○

What insight does the name *Shim* add to this account? (1:3) "The hill of Shim is very interesting. What's the Arabic word for *shim*? It means *north*, north country. *Shim* is *north* in any Semitic language. . . . So here's another one of those places where the Book of Mormon just casually tosses off just a bit of evidence at no extra charge. But people don't notice these things.

"Therefore, go to the hill Shim 'and there have I deposited unto the Lord all the sacred engravings concerning this people.' He knew that the movement would be northward. It wouldn't be safe for them to remain south when they start into this long tragic retreat here" (Nibley, *Teachings of the Book of Mormon*, 4:192).

Mormon 1:6–12. War Begins between the Nephites and the Lamanites

What did Mormon mean by his description of the population of Zarahemla? (1:6–7) "He was eleven years old, and he was taken by his father to a land southward to Zarahemla—the big city, the big capital. . . . The land was covered with buildings, and he [had] never seen anything like that. . . . As an eleven-year-old, he's impressed. You'd be impressed with these things. So we have to be very careful and not be simplistic when we read the Book of Mormon. When this kid tells us that people in Zarahemla were as numerous as the sands of the sea, how many hundred trillion people are there? It doesn't mean that at all. It's a metaphor here, as it were the sands of the sea" (Nibley, *Teachings of the Book of Mormon*, 4:192–93).

concerning this people; and when ye are of that age go to the land Antum, unto a hill which shall be called Shim; and there have I deposited unto the Lord all the sacred engravings concerning this people.

4 And behold, ye shall take the plates of Nephi unto yourself, and the remainder shall ye leave in the place where they are; and ye shall engrave on the plates of Nephi all the things that ye have observed concerning this people.

5 And I, Mormon, being a descendant of Nephi, (and my father's name was Mormon) I remembered the things which Ammaron commanded me.

6 And it came to pass that I, being eleven years old, was carried by my father into the land southward, even to the land of Zarahemla.

7 The whole face of the land had become covered with buildings, and the people were as numerous almost, as it were the sand of the sea.

8 And it came to pass in this year there began to be a war between the Nephites, who consisted of the Nephites and the Jacobites and the Josephites and the Zoramites; and this war was between the Nephites, and the Lamanites and the Lemuelites and the Ishmaelites.

The Boyhood of the Prophet Mormon

"1. He was born probably in A.D. 310 or 311. (He was about ten years of age in A.D. 321—see 4 Nephi [1:]48 and Mormon 1:2.)

"2. He was a descendant of Nephi (Mormon 1:5).

"3. His father's name was Mormon, and he was named after the land of Mormon (Mormon 1:5 and 3 Nephi 5:12).

"4. He was evidently born in the land northward (Mormon 1:2, 6).

"5. At the age of fifteen he was 'visited of the Lord' (Mormon 1:15).

"6. Despite his testimony of the divinity of Christ, he was 'forbidden' [for a time] to preach repentance unto the wicked people (Mormon 1:16).

"7. In his 'sixteenth year' he was appointed leader of the Nephite armies, and he and his armies defended the Nephites from the Lamanites (Mormon 2:2)" (Ludlow, *Companion to Your Study of the Book of Mormon*, 298).

9 Now the Lamanites and the Lemuelites and the Ishmaelites were called Lamanites, and the two parties were Nephites and Lamanites.

10 And it came to pass that the war began to be among them in the borders of Zarahemla, by the waters of Sidon.

11 And it came to pass that the Nephites had gathered together a great number of men, even to exceed the number of thirty thousand. And it came to pass that they did have in this same year a number of battles, in which the Nephites did beat the Lamanites and did slay many of them.

12 And it came to pass that the Lamanites withdrew their design, and there was peace settled in the land; and peace did remain for the space of about four years, that there was no bloodshed.

13 But wickedness did prevail upon the face of the whole land, insomuch that the Lord did take away his beloved disciples, and the work of miracles and of healing did cease because of the iniquity of the people.

14 And there were no gifts from the Lord, and the Holy Ghost did not come upon any, because of their wickedness and unbelief.

15 And I, being fifteen years of age and being somewhat of a sober mind, therefore I was visited of the Lord, and tasted and knew of the goodness of Jesus.

16 And I did endeavor to preach unto this people, but my mouth was shut, and I was forbidden that I should preach unto them; for behold they had wilfully rebelled against

Mormon 1:13–19. Because of the Wickedness of the People, the Three "Beloved Disciples" Are Taken Away and Mormon Is Forbidden to Preach

Why did the Lord call Mormon at such a young age? (1:15) What was going on in Nephite society that such a young prophet was necessary? Elder Jeffrey R. Holland observed: "The maturing Mormon, by then fifteen years of age, stood beyond the sinfulness around him and rose above the despair of his time. Consequently, he 'was visited of the Lord, and tasted and knew of the goodness of Jesus,' trying valiantly to preach to his people" (*Christ and the New Covenant*, 318). Why does the Lord often choose "the weak things of the world" (D&C 1:19) to accomplish his purpose? Might this help explain why He calls such young people to serve full-time missions in our day? ⊕

What are the consequences of willfully rebelling against God and His teachings? (1:16) "Those who have willfully rebelled against the light and truth of the gospel will suffer spiritual death." Spiritual death is "separation from God and his influences." It is "to die as to things pertaining to righteousness." All is not lost, however, if individuals become humble and repentant. "Through the atonement of Jesus Christ and by obedience to the principles and ordinances of the gospel, men and women can become clean from sin and overcome spiritual death" (*Guide to the Scriptures*, s.v., "Death, Spiritual").

Why was Mormon forbidden to preach to his people? (1:16–17) "During his mortal ministry, Jesus taught his disciples, 'Give not that which is holy unto the dogs, neither cast ye your pearls before swine, lest they trample them under their feet, and turn again and rend you' (Matthew 7:6). What the disciples, both ancient and modern, are allowed by the Spirit to teach is determined by the spiritual readiness of the listeners. The Lord has cautioned against presenting more than the listeners are prepared to hear and heed. Mormon was forbidden to preach the gospel not only because of the people's spiritual unpreparedness but also perhaps because the hardness of their hearts would have prompted them to 'turn again and rend' Mormon" (McConkie et al., *Doctrinal Commentary*, 4:211–12). ⊕

Why is there danger in becoming involved with sorceries, witchcraft, and other powers of the evil one? (1:19) Mormon was born in a time of spiritual corruption. We are likewise living in a similar environment. President James E. Faust cautioned against taking interest in Satan's devices: "It is not good practice to become intrigued by Satan and his mysteries. No good can come from getting close to evil. Like playing with fire, it is too easy to get burned. . . . The only safe course is to keep well distanced from him and any of his wicked activities or nefarious practices. The mischief of devil worship, sorcery, casting spells, witchcraft, voodooism, black magic, and all other forms of demonism should be avoided like the plague" ("The Great Imitator," 33).

Mormon 2:1–9. At Age Sixteen, Mormon Leads the Nephite Armies

How can young men and women follow Mormon's example? (2:1–2) Like Mormon, "you will reach out to your friends who are not of our faith and help prepare them to join the Church. . . . You will watch over and

their God; and the beloved disciples were taken away out of the land, because of their iniquity.

17 But I did remain among them, but I was forbidden to preach unto them, because of the hardness of their hearts; and because of the hardness of their hearts the land was cursed for their sake.

18 And these Gadianton robbers, who were among the Lamanites, did infest the land, insomuch that the inhabitants thereof began to hide up their treasures in the earth; and they became slippery, because the Lord had cursed the land, that they could not hold them, nor retain them again.

19 And it came to pass that there were sorceries, and witchcrafts, and magics; and the power of the evil one was wrought upon all the face of the land, even unto the fulfilling of all the words of Abinadi, and also Samuel the Lamanite.

CHAPTER 2

Mormon leads the Nephite armies—Blood and carnage sweep the land—The Nephites lament and mourn with the sorrowing of the damned—Their day of grace is passed—Mormon obtains the plates of Nephi—Wars continue. About A.D. 327–350.

1 And it came to pass in that same year there began to be a war again between the Nephites and the Lamanites. And notwithstanding I being young, was large in stature; therefore the people of Nephi appointed me that I should be their leader, or the leader of their armies.

2 Therefore it came to pass that in my sixteenth year I did go forth at the head of an army of the Nephites, against the Lamanites; therefore three hundred and twenty and six years had passed away.

3 And it came to pass that in the three hundred and twenty and seventh year the Lamanites did come upon us with exceedingly great power, insomuch that they did frighten my armies; therefore they would not fight, and they began to retreat towards the north countries.

4 And it came to pass that we did come to the city of Angola, and we did take possession of the city, and make preparations to defend ourselves against the Lamanites. And it came to pass that we did fortify the city with our might; but notwithstanding all our fortifications the Lamanites did come upon us and did drive us out of the city.

5 And they did also drive us forth out of the land of David.

6 And we marched forth and came to the land of Joshua, which was in the borders west by the seashore.

7 And it came to pass that we did gather in our people as fast as it were possible, that we might get them together in one body.

8 But behold, the land was filled with robbers and with Lamanites; and notwithstanding the great destruction which hung over my people, they did not repent of their evil doings; therefore there was blood and carnage spread throughout all the face of the land, both on the part of the Nephites and also on the part of the Lamanites; and it was one complete revolution throughout all the face of the land.

strengthen them. You will lead out in the rescue of other[s] . . . who have lost their way. . . .

"You will be a force for good at all times and in every circumstance. Your righteous example . . . will be a powerful way to invite all who know you to come unto Christ.

"In their most critical time, the Nephites looked to a young man, Mormon, for leadership and inspiration. . . . Today, we look to you to be a great strength to the Church and a force for good on the earth" (Beck, "Magnificent Aaronic Priesthood," 55). ✚

Why might lands in the New World have been given names similar to those of the Holy Land? (2:5–6) "All the names we give to our lands and cities are those we had in the old country. As far as naming them after heroes of the Old Testament, this is exactly what people would do. In upstate New York, Joseph Smith's country, you have a Rome, an Athens, and a Syracuse. You have all the old classical names of towns up there. We carry our old names over, and we keep our traditions. We don't invent names cold, unless they describe either the founder of the city or some peculiar thing about it" (Nibley, *Teachings of the Book of Mormon*, 4:195).

Mormon 2:10–15. Mormon Is Saddened by the Wickedness of His People

What is the difference between the sorrow of Mormon's people and the sorrow that leads to a true change of heart and life? (2:12–13) "The prophet Mormon at first thought his people were sorrowing unto repentance (see Morm. 2:12–13). Yet he soon discerned that theirs was not actually the sorrowing unto repentance but the 'sorrowing of the damned,' stranding them in a 'no-man's-land.' Compare that episode to the prodigal son's solitary working through of his own repentance; since his sorrow was real, he truly 'came to himself' (Luke 15:17). Sometimes we learn 'by sad experience,' but sometimes not! (D&C 121:39)" (Maxwell, "Content with the Things Allotted unto Us," 73). ●

What attitude is characteristic of a broken heart and a contrite spirit? (2:12–14) "Godly sorrow—the broken heart and contrite spirit—is much more than remorse or regret over having sinned. Mormon observed anguish in his own people and described it as 'the sorrowing of the damned' (see Morm. 2:12–14). It was a sorrow born of sins and circumstances but which did not produce 'faith unto repentance.' Many may be remorseful for past actions and regret the consequences that have befallen them but do nothing to change, to come unto Christ and partake of his mercy and to comply with the requirements of the gospel. A 'broken heart and contrite spirit' is an attitude that always leads to a commitment to change" (Top, "Faith unto Repentance," 199).

9 And now, the Lamanites had a king, and his name was Aaron; and he came against us with an army of forty and four thousand. And behold, I withstood him with forty and two thousand. And it came to pass that I beat him with my army that he fled before me. And behold, all this was done, and three hundred and thirty years had passed away.

10 And it came to pass that the Nephites began to repent of their iniquity, and began to cry even as had been prophesied by Samuel the prophet; for behold no man could keep that which was his own, for the thieves, and the robbers, and the murderers, and the magic art, and the witchcraft which was in the land.

11 Thus there began to be a mourning and a lamentation in all the land because of these things, and more especially among the people of Nephi.

12 And it came to pass that when I, Mormon, saw their lamentation and their mourning and their sorrow before the Lord, my heart did begin to rejoice within me, knowing the mercies and the long-suffering of the Lord, therefore supposing that he would be merciful unto them that they would again become a righteous people.

13 But behold this my joy was vain, for their sorrowing was not unto repentance, because of the goodness of God; but it was rather the sorrowing of the damned, because the Lord would not always suffer them to take happiness in sin.

14 And they did not come unto Jesus with broken hearts and contrite spirits, but they did curse God, and wish to die. Nevertheless they would struggle with the sword for their lives.

15 And it came to pass that my sorrow did return unto me again, and I saw that the day of grace was passed with them, both temporally and spiritually; for I saw thousands of them hewn down in open rebellion against their God, and heaped up as dung upon the face of the land. And thus three hundred and forty and four years had passed away.

16 And it came to pass that in the three hundred and forty and fifth year the Nephites did begin to flee before the Lamanites; and they were pursued until they came even to the land of Jashon, before it was possible to stop them in their retreat.

17 And now, the city of Jashon was near the land where Ammaron had deposited the records unto the Lord, that they might not be destroyed. And behold I had gone according to the word of Ammaron, and taken the plates of Nephi, and did make a record according to the words of Ammaron.

18 And upon the plates of Nephi I did make a full account of all the wickedness and abominations; but upon these plates I did forbear to make a full account of their wickedness and abominations, for behold, a continual scene of wickedness and abominations has been before mine eyes ever since I have been sufficient to behold the ways of man.

19 And wo is me because of their wickedness; for my heart has been filled with sorrow because of their wickedness, all my days; nevertheless, I know that I shall be lifted up at the last day.

20 And it came to pass that in this year the people of Nephi again were hunted and driven. And it came to pass that we were

How does one allow the "day of grace" to pass, or procrastinate repentance until it is too late? (2:15) "'One of the greatest principles of the gospel of Jesus Christ is the principle of repentance,' said President Harold B. Lee. 'However, if one has sinned so seriously and becomes habitually a sinner, the spirit of repentance leaves, and he may or may not be able to repent' (*Church News*, March 3, 1973, 4). Amulek had previously warned against procrastinating the day of repentance. His great sermon teaches of a 'night of darkness' wherein additional labor (that is, faith, repentance, ordinances, etc.) is not forthcoming because the Spirit of the Lord is withdrawn and Satan 'doth seal you his' and 'hath all power over you' (Alma 34:33–35)" (McConkie et al., *Doctrinal Commentary*, 4:217). ⊙

Mormon 2:16–29. Mormon Continues to Lead the Nephites in Battle

Why was Mormon filled with such immense sorrow? (2:18–19) "In one of the loneliest scenes in scriptural history, a silent, war-weary soldier looked out across time and the unspeakable tragedy his family and followers faced. Mormon, the man destined before the world was formed to abridge and summarize the Nephite story—and in so doing to have his name forever immortalized with this additional testament of Jesus Christ—surveyed the casualties of a nation that had turned from the Lord. As sobering as the account is, it does not give a full account of all the sin and sadness Mormon had seen. Indeed, such an account probably would have been impossible to record" (Holland, *Christ and the New Covenant*, 317).

From whom might Mormon have found inspiration for his leadership? (2:22–23) "Frustrated with the cowardice and wickedness of his people, . . . Mormon looked for inspiration to another young general, who lived over 400 years earlier and was able to inspire his people to victory through righteousness. Captain Moroni, chief captain of the Nephite armies, is a man Mormon greatly admired. He devotes a large part of his abridgment to the wars fought by Captain Moroni and may even have named his son after this courageous captain. The description of Captain Moroni in the book of Alma gives some insight into Mormon's personality. He admires Moroni for his skill as a general but even more for his faith in God" (Hatch, "Mormon and Moroni," 107). ⊕

What are the dangers of living without the Lord's help and being "left to ourselves"? (2:26) "As the Nephite general, Mormon tried to maintain what military defense he could. . . . Although there was an occasional temporary gain, Mormon faced the most hopeless of all military tasks—fighting when 'the strength of the Lord was not with us'" (Holzapfel, "Mormon," 121). What trends and practices in our day are leaving people without the Lord's help? What consequences are often the result of this way of life? "The Lord has noted three natural consequences of having one's heart set on the things of the world: First, we seek to hide our sins instead of repenting of them. Next, we seek to gratify our pride and vain ambitions rather than seeking the things of God. Finally, we begin to exercise unrighteous dominion over others. . . .

"In the Liberty Jail revelation, the Lord described the effect of a worldly heart: 'Behold, the heavens withdraw themselves; the Spirit of the Lord is grieved; and . . . behold, ere he is aware, he is left unto himself.' Brothers and sisters, in these very 'perilous times,' we cannot afford to grieve the Spirit and be left to ourselves" (Lund, "Opening Our Hearts," 34).

driven forth until we had come northward to the land which was called Shem.

21 And it came to pass that we did fortify the city of Shem, and we did gather in our people as much as it were possible, that perhaps we might save them from destruction.

22 And it came to pass in the three hundred and forty and sixth year they began to come upon us again.

23 And it came to pass that I did speak unto my people, and did urge them with great energy, that they would stand boldly before the Lamanites and fight for their wives, and their children, and their houses, and their homes.

24 And my words did arouse them somewhat to vigor, insomuch that they did not flee from before the Lamanites, but did stand with boldness against them.

25 And it came to pass that we did contend with an army of thirty thousand against an army of fifty thousand. And it came to pass that we did stand before them with such firmness that they did flee from before us.

26 And it came to pass that when they had fled we did pursue them with our armies, and did meet them again, and did beat them; nevertheless the strength of the Lord was not with us; yea, we were left to ourselves, that the Spirit of the Lord did not abide in us; therefore we had become weak like unto our brethren.

27 And my heart did sorrow because of this the great calamity of my people, because of their wickedness and their abominations. But behold, we did go forth against the Lamanites and the robbers of Gadianton, until we had again taken possession of the lands of our inheritance.

28 And the three hundred and forty and ninth year had passed away. And in the three hundred and fiftieth year we made a treaty with the Lamanites and the robbers of Gadianton, in which we did get the lands of our inheritance divided.

29 And the Lamanites did give unto us the land northward, yea, even to the narrow passage which led into the land southward. And we did give unto the Lamanites all the land southward.

CHAPTER 3

Mormon cries repentance unto the Nephites—They gain a great victory and glory in their own strength—Mormon refuses to lead them, and his prayers for them are without faith—The Book of Mormon invites the twelve tribes of Israel to believe the gospel. About A.D. *360–362.*

1 And it came to pass that the Lamanites did not come to battle again until ten years more had passed away. And behold, I had employed my people, the Nephites, in preparing their lands and their arms against the time of battle.

2 And it came to pass that the Lord did say unto me: Cry unto this people—Repent ye, and come unto me, and be ye baptized, and build up again my church, and ye shall be spared.

3 And I did cry unto this people, but it was in vain; and they did not realize that it was the Lord that had spared them, and granted unto them a chance for repentance. And behold they did harden their hearts against the Lord their God.

4 And it came to pass that after this tenth year had passed away, making, in the whole, three hundred and sixty years from the coming of Christ, the king of the Lamanites sent an epistle unto me, which gave unto me to know that they were preparing to come again to battle against us.

Mormon 3:1–10. Mormon Asks His People to Repent as They Prepare for Battle

What made Mormon's people insensitive to the source of their protection? (3:3) "Mormon's people were so steeped in sin, and had become so hardened to sensibility that they were no longer able to choose between good and evil, let alone see the right when opposed by that which was wrong. They had the idea that whatsoever pleased the fancy or gratified the demands of their carnal selves would bring happiness. . . . Notwithstanding the offer the Lord made to spare them, if they would repent, . . . 'They did harden their hearts against the Lord their God'" (Reynolds and Sjodahl, *Commentary on the Book of Mormon*, 7:263).

How did Mormon, who had compiled the Book of Mormon, feel about being the aggressor in war? (3:9–10) At one point, Mormon's armies began to swear that "they would avenge themselves" of fellow Nephites killed in battle. "When the Nephite soldiers decided to attack the Lamanites first, Mormon refused to lead them in offensive war. This position was not only justified by earlier teachings of the prophets and the counsel of the Lord (see 3 Nephi 3:20–21; Alma 43:46; Alma 48:14), but was also vindicated by subsequent events: the Nephite armies began to be defeated from that time forth" (Ludlow, *Companion to Your Study of the Book of Mormon*, 300). ⊕

Mormon 3:11–16. Mormon Refuses to Lead His People Because of Their Wickedness

What caused Mormon to eventually refuse to be the Nephites' military leader? (3:11–12) "At one point Mormon 'utterly refuse[d]' to be the commander and leader of a people so wicked, so ignorant, so bent on self-destruction. It was a wrenching time for him because these *were* his people, and he loved them. Indeed, he loved them 'with all [his] heart.' Furthermore, he had poured out his soul in prayer 'all

5 And it came to pass that I did cause my people that they should gather themselves together at the land Desolation, to a city which was in the borders, by the narrow pass which led into the land southward.

6 And there we did place our armies, that we might stop the armies of the Lamanites, that they might not get possession of any of our lands; therefore we did fortify against them with all our force.

7 And it came to pass that in the three hundred and sixty and first year the Lamanites did come down to the city of Desolation to battle against us; and it came to pass that in that year we did beat them, insomuch that they did return to their own lands again.

8 And in the three hundred and sixty and second year they did come down again to battle. And we did beat them again, and did slay a great number of them, and their dead were cast into the sea.

9 And now, because of this great thing which my people, the Nephites, had done, they began to boast in their own strength, and began to swear before the heavens that they would avenge themselves of the blood of their brethren who had been slain by their enemies.

10 And they did swear by the heavens, and also by the throne of God, that they would go up to battle against their enemies, and would cut them off from the face of the land.

11 And it came to pass that I, Mormon, did utterly refuse from this time forth to be a commander and a leader of this people, because of their wickedness and abomination.

12 Behold, I had led them, notwithstanding their wickedness I had led them many times to battle, and had loved them, according to the love of God which was in me, with all my heart; and my soul had been poured out in prayer unto my God all the day long for

them; nevertheless, it was without faith, because of the hardness of their hearts.

13 And thrice have I delivered them out of the hands of their enemies, and they have repented not of their sins.

14 And when they had sworn by all that had been forbidden them by our Lord and Savior Jesus Christ, that they would go up unto their enemies to battle, and avenge themselves of the blood of their brethren, behold the voice of the Lord came unto me, saying:

15 Vengeance is mine, and I will repay; and because this people repented not after I had delivered them, behold, they shall be cut off from the face of the earth.

16 And it came to pass that I utterly refused to go up against mine enemies; and I did even as the Lord had commanded me; and I did stand as an idle witness to manifest unto the world the things which I saw and heard, according to the manifestations of the Spirit which had testified of things to come.

17 Therefore I write unto you, Gentiles, and also unto you, house of Israel, when the work shall commence, that ye shall be about to prepare to return to the land of your inheritance;

18 Yea, behold, I write unto all the ends of the earth; yea, unto you, twelve tribes of Israel, who shall be judged according to your works by the twelve whom Jesus chose to be his disciples in the land of Jerusalem.

19 And I write also unto the remnant of this people, who shall also be judged by the twelve whom Jesus chose in this land; and they shall be judged by the other twelve whom Jesus chose in the land of Jerusalem.

20 And these things doth the Spirit manifest unto me; therefore I write unto you all. And for this cause I write unto you, that ye may know that ye must all stand before the

the day long for them.' But alas, such earnest prayer—and we can scarcely imagine a more loving and faithful effort on behalf of a people—was by Mormon's own admission uttered 'without faith' because of the hardness of the hearts of the people" (Holland, *Christ and the New Covenant*, 320).

Who may properly impose vengeance? (3:14–15) President Joseph F. Smith taught: "Men are not called upon to curse mankind; that is not our mission; it is our mission to preach righteousness to them. It is our business to love and to bless them, and to redeem them from the fall and from the wickedness of the world. This is our mission and our special calling. God will curse and will exercise his judgment in those matters. 'Vengeance is mine,' saith the Lord, 'and I will repay.' We are perfectly willing to leave vengeance in the hands of God and let him judge between us and our enemies, and let him reward them according to his own wisdom and mercy" (*Gospel Doctrine*, 140).

Mormon 3:17–22. Mormon Invites the Gentiles and Latter-day Israel to Come unto Christ

How does the Book of Mormon have a part in the return, or gathering, spoken of by Mormon? (3:17–21) "The process of gathering is now and always will be one in which the scattered remnants of Jacob—those of all tribes—believe the Book of Mormon, accept the restored gospel, and come to the latter-day Zion....

"As far as the gathering of Israel is concerned, the Book of Mormon is the most important book that ever has been or ever will be written. It is the book that gathers Israel.... It is the Book of Mormon that causes people to believe the gospel and join the Church, and, as we have heretofore seen, it is the power that brings to pass the gathering of Israel" (McConkie, *New Witness*, 457, 554). ☉

What part will the original Twelve Apostles and the twelve Nephite disciples play in the Judgment? (3:19) "The reality is that there will be a whole hierarchy of judges who, under Christ, shall judge the righteous. He alone shall issue the decrees of damnation for the wicked" (McConkie, *Millennial Messiah*, 520). "The Apostle John taught that 'the Father judgeth no man, but hath committed all judgment unto the Son'

(John 5:22). The Son, in turn, will call upon others to assist in the Judgment. The Twelve who were with Him in His ministry will judge the twelve tribes of Israel (see Matthew 19:28; Luke 22:30). The twelve Nephite disciples will judge the Nephite and Lamanite people (see 1 Nephi 12:9–10; Mormon 3:18–19)" (*Gospel Principles*, 271).

How are you preparing for the Final Judgment? (3:20) "The tenor of our times is permissiveness. All around us we see the idols of the movie screen, the heroes of the athletic field—those whom many young people long to emulate—as disregarding the laws of God and rationalizing away sinful practices, seemingly with no ill effect. Don't you believe it! There is a time of reckoning—even a balancing of the ledger. Every Cinderella has her midnight—it's called Judgment Day, even the Big Exam of Life. Are you prepared? Are you pleased with your own performance?" (Monson, "Be Thou an Example," 113–14).

Mormon 4:1–17. The Nephites Become More Wicked, and the Lamanites Begin to Conquer Them

What was the significance of the name of the city of Teancum? (4:3) In the waning years of Nephite civilization (about A.D. 363–375), the city Teancum, a coastal community near the city Desolation, was the setting for tragedy as Nephites unsuccessfully gathered there for safety from an invading Lamanite army. After the city

judgment-seat of Christ, yea, every soul who belongs to the whole human family of Adam; and ye must stand to be judged of your works, whether they be good or evil;

21 And also that ye may believe the gospel of Jesus Christ, which ye shall have among you; and also that the Jews, the covenant people of the Lord, shall have other witness besides him whom they saw and heard, that Jesus, whom they slew, was the very Christ and the very God.

22 And I would that I could persuade all ye ends of the earth to repent and prepare to stand before the judgment-seat of Christ.

CHAPTER 4

War and carnage continue—The wicked punish the wicked—Greater wickedness prevails than ever before in all Israel—Women and children are sacrificed to idols—The Lamanites begin to sweep the Nephites before them. About A.D. 363–375.

1 And now it came to pass that in the three hundred and sixty and third year the Nephites did go up with their armies to battle against the Lamanites, out of the land Desolation.

2 And it came to pass that the armies of the Nephites were driven back again to the land of Desolation. And while they were yet weary, a fresh army of the Lamanites did come upon them; and they had a sore battle, insomuch that the Lamanites did take possession of the city Desolation, and did slay many of the Nephites, and did take many prisoners.

3 And the remainder did flee and join the inhabitants of the city Teancum. Now the city Teancum lay in the borders by the seashore; and it was also near the city Desolation.

fell, Lamanite soldiers offered Nephite women and children "as sacrifices unto their idol gods" (Morm. 4:6–14).

The city was named after Teancum, a famous Nephite general who faithfully served with Captain Moroni during the Lamanite/Nephite wars (see Alma 50–53). Teancum was fearless in battle and on two occasions, subtly stole into Lamanite camps to slay their leaders, which eventually took his life (see Alma 62:36). Teancum "fought valiantly for his country" and was "a true friend of liberty" (Alma 62:37).

What are the effects of an offensive war? (4:4–5)

"Once the Nephite soldiers started to wage offensive war they soon became so bloodthirsty they were concerned only with the taking of human life. . . . The leaders of this dispensation have also warned against the dangers of starting an offensive war. President Charles W. Penrose has said:

"'We Latter-day Saints must watch ourselves and not give way to passion and desire to shed blood and to destroy, for that is the power of the evil one. We do not want to imitate any nation that is bent on a policy of destruction, . . . to break down and trample under foot where they cannot dominate. If we have that desire, it is the spirit of the wicked one' (Conference Report, April 1917, 21–22)" (Ludlow, *Companion to Your Study of the Book of Mormon*, 301). ☉

4 And it was because the armies of the Nephites went up unto the Lamanites that they began to be smitten; for were it not for that, the Lamanites could have had no power over them.

5 But, behold, the judgments of God will overtake the wicked; and it is by the wicked that the wicked are punished; for it is the wicked that stir up the hearts of the children of men unto bloodshed.

6 And it came to pass that the Lamanites did make preparations to come against the city Teancum.

7 And it came to pass in the three hundred and sixty and fourth year the Lamanites did come against the city Teancum, that they might take possession of the city Teancum also.

8 And it came to pass that they were repulsed and driven back by the Nephites. And when the Nephites saw that they had driven the Lamanites they did again boast of their own strength; and they went forth in their own might, and took possession again of the city Desolation.

9 And now all these things had been done, and there had been thousands slain on both sides, both the Nephites and the Lamanites.

10 And it came to pass that the three hundred and sixty and sixth year had passed away, and the Lamanites came again upon the Nephites to battle; and yet the Nephites

How does the boasting of these Nephite soldiers contrast with Ammon's boasting? (4:8) Elder

Bruce R. McConkie explained: "There is a difference between boasting after the manner of the world and glorying in the Lord. One is a form of self-righteous pride, the other a song of praise and thanksgiving to that Holy Being whose mercy endureth forever" (McConkie, *Doctrinal New Testament Commentary*, 2:438). Contrast the boasting of the Nephite soldiers in Mormon 4 with that of Ammon, who said, "Yea, I know that I am nothing; as to my strength I am weak; therefore I will not boast of myself, but I will boast of my God, for in his strength I can do all things" (Alma 26:12).

repented not of the evil they had done, but persisted in their wickedness continually.

11 And it is impossible for the tongue to describe, or for man to write a perfect description of the horrible scene of the blood and carnage which was among the people, both of the Nephites and of the Lamanites; and every heart was hardened, so that they delighted in the shedding of blood continually.

12 And there never had been so great wickedness among all the children of Lehi, nor even among all the house of Israel, according to the words of the Lord, as was among this people.

13 And it came to pass that the Lamanites did take possession of the city Desolation, and this because their number did exceed the number of the Nephites.

14 And they did also march forward against the city Teancum, and did drive the inhabitants forth out of her, and did take many prisoners both women and children, and did offer them up as sacrifices unto their idol gods.

15 And it came to pass that in the three hundred and sixty and seventh year, the Nephites being angry because the Lamanites had sacrificed their women and their children, that they did go against the Lamanites with exceedingly great anger, insomuch that they did beat again the Lamanites, and drive them out of their lands.

16 And the Lamanites did not come again against the Nephites until the three hundred and seventy and fifth year.

17 And in this year they did come down against the Nephites with all their powers; and they were not numbered because of the greatness of their number.

18 And from this time forth did the Nephites gain no power over the Lamanites, but began to be swept off by them even as a dew before the sun.

What distortion of doctrine has led to the practice of human sacrifice? (4:14–15) "The most horrifying and revolting perversion of the divine sacrificial system has been human sacrifice, the shedding of mortal blood by mortal man on one religious pretext or another. As Amulek said, 'There is not any man that can sacrifice his own blood which will atone for the sins of another' (Alma 34:11). Nor is God appeased, nor are the forces of nature controlled, by the most sincere slaying of the purest virgins or others. Such acts are the basest form of false worship....

"Satan has such great hold on the hearts of men that he has prevailed upon them to sacrifice each other by the thousands in the name of religion" (McConkie, *Promised Messiah*, 256–57).

Mormon 4:18–23. The Nephites Begin to Flee before the Lamanite Armies

What is the meaning of the metaphor "a dew before the sun"? (4:18) "A very powerful expression. There's nothing left. Everything is swept away as the dew before the sun, combing the land. It wasn't just a spot engagement here and there that would lead to a conference

19 And it came to pass that the Lamanites did come down against the city Desolation; and there was an exceedingly sore battle fought in the land Desolation, in the which they did beat the Nephites.

20 And they fled again from before them, and they came to the city Boaz; and there they did stand against the Lamanites with exceeding boldness, insomuch that the Lamanites did not beat them until they had come again the second time.

21 And when they had come the second time, the Nephites were driven and slaughtered with an exceedingly great slaughter; their women and their children were again sacrificed unto idols.

22 And it came to pass that the Nephites did again flee from before them, taking all the inhabitants with them, both in towns and villages.

23 And now I, Mormon, seeing that the Lamanites were about to overthrow the land, therefore I did go to the hill Shim, and did take up all the records which Ammaron had hid up unto the Lord.

CHAPTER 5

Mormon again leads the Nephite armies in battles of blood and carnage—The Book of Mormon will come forth to convince all Israel that Jesus is the Christ—Because of their unbelief, the Lamanites will be scattered, and the Spirit will cease to strive with them—They will receive the gospel from the Gentiles in the latter days. About A.D. 375–384.

1 And it came to pass that I did go forth among the Nephites, and did repent of the oath which I had made that I would no more assist them; and they gave me command again of their armies, for they looked upon me as though I could deliver them from their afflictions.

between the rulers, or something like that. No, it was a total thing. The most violent element of war, like a violent natural force, like a plague sweeping a nation, appears when, 'freed from all conventional restrictions, it [breaks] loose with all its natural force. It is a natural phenomenon. There are no more artificial or other restraints. War is much nearer to real nature in absolutes'" (Nibley, *Teachings of the Book of Mormon*, 3:136).

Why did Mormon remove the sacred records from the hill Shim? (4:23) "Seeing that the Lamanites were about to overthrow the land, he went to the hill Shim and removed from it all of the sacred records which Ammaron had hid up unto the Lord. Sometime later under commandment from God, Mormon began to make an abridgment from those records which work was near completion and yet unfinished by the time of his death" (Berrett, *Teachings of the Book of Mormon,* 3).

Mormon 5:1–7. Mormon Leads the Nephites into Battle Again

How did Mormon "repent"? (5:1–2) "Mormon refused to be [the Nephites'] military leader in A.D. 362 (see Mormon 3:8–11). Therefore, if our assumption concerning the time is correct, he had not been leading the armies for thirteen or more years. He had undoubtedly been writing and abridging during this time. . . . That he 'did repent of the oath' (Mormon 5:1) means he reversed his decision, not that his previous decision was wrong or sinful. The people were just as wicked, and probably more wicked, but he came back knowing it was a lost cause (v. 2). However, his return apparently inspired the men to fight more fiercely for their cities, and they were successful (vv. 3–4)" (Nyman, *I, Mormon, Make a Record*, 82).

What is happening to the Nephite society? (5:5–7)
"Here you have a clear picture of Nephite society. Separate 'lands' living their own lives, now in this last crisis terribly reluctant to move and join the swelling host in the retreat to the north. Those who refused to

2 But behold, I was without hope, for I knew the judgments of the Lord which should come upon them; for they repented not of their iniquities, but did struggle for their lives without calling upon that Being who created them.

3 And it came to pass that the Lamanites did come against us as we had fled to the city of Jordan; but behold, they were driven back that they did not take the city at that time.

4 And it came to pass that they came against us again, and we did maintain the city. And there were also other cities which were maintained by the Nephites, which strongholds did cut them off that they could not get into the country which lay before us, to destroy the inhabitants of our land.

5 But it came to pass that whatsoever lands we had passed by, and the inhabitants thereof were not gathered in, were destroyed by the Lamanites, and their towns, and villages, and

"The Gentiles Who Shall Possess the Land" (Mormon 5:19)

English colonists land in 1620 at what became Plymouth, Massachusetts. By Charles Lucy

The ancient prophets Nephi and Isaiah had seen and foretold that which Mormon prophesied concerning the destiny of both the Lamanites and the land of America—that the Lord would reserve the blessings the wicked Lamanites might have received "in the land" for the future Gentiles who would "possess the land" (Mormon 5:16–20; see also 1 Nephi 13:13–15; 2 Nephi 12:2).

cities were burned with fire; and thus three hundred and seventy and nine years passed away.

6 And it came to pass that in the three hundred and eightieth year the Lamanites did come again against us to battle, and we did stand against them boldly; but it was all in vain, for so great were their numbers that they did tread the people of the Nephites under their feet.

7 And it came to pass that we did again take to flight, and those whose flight was swifter than the Lamanites' did escape, and those whose flight did not exceed the Lamanites' were swept down and destroyed.

8 And now behold, I, Mormon, do not desire to harrow up the souls of men in casting before them such an awful scene of blood and carnage as was laid before mine eyes; but I, knowing that these things must surely be

pull up stakes were one by one completely wiped out by the Lamanites. This was no planned migration but a forced evacuation, like dozens of such we read about in the grim and terrible times of the 'Invasion of the Barbarians' that destroyed the classic civilizations of the Old World. . . . The fitful but continual falling back of the Nephites towards the north . . . became something like a rout, with speed the only hope of survival" (Nibley, *Approach to the Book of Mormon*, 267).

Mormon 5:8–24. The Book of Mormon Will Come Forth to Bring People to Christ

What does it mean to "harrow up"? (5:8) A harrow is "an instrument of agriculture, formed of pieces of timber sometimes crossing each other, and set with iron teeth." It is the process of drawing the instrument "over plowed land to level it and break the clods, and to cover seed when sown" (Webster, *American*

The history of the early discovery and colonization of America illustrates the fulfillment of Mormon's prophecy. Recent revisions in estimates of native populations north of Mexico suggest as few as two million and as many as ten million, most scholars generally accepting the indigenous population to have been approximately five million in 1492 (see Taylor, *American Colonies*, 40). Through three periods of contact and interaction—the early age of discovery, of settlement and colonization, and of pre-Revolutionary emigration from Europe (see Morison, *European Discovery of America*; Morgan, *Wilderness at Dawn*; and Bailyn, *Peopling of British North America*)—a disastrous depopulation of Native America ensued, mostly due to disease. Within the first decade, studies suggest, half of the native population had been decimated. After fifty years, only one-tenth remained (see Taylor, *American Colonies*, 39–40).

By contrast, the various immigrations created a "Gentile" population of one quarter of a million by 1700. By 1775 the early settlers had increased ten-fold to approximately two million and continued to double every twenty-five years thereafter (see Current et al., *American History*, 33). One scholar noted: "Although disastrous for the American natives, the post-1492 New and Old World exchange of microbes and plants provided a double boon to Europeans. First, they obtained an expanded food supply that permitted their reproduction at an unprecedented rate. Second, they acquired access to fertile and extensive new lands largely emptied of native peoples by the exported diseases. In effect, the post-Columbian exchange depleted people on the American side of the Atlantic while swelling those on the European . . . shores. Eventually, the surplus population flowed westward to refill the demographic vacuum created on the American side of the Atlantic World" (Taylor, *American Colonies*, 46).

The repopulation of America by the "Gentiles" with the accompanying conquest of the "land" are a direct fulfillment of Mormon's prophecy upon the Lamanite people who were "led about by Satan, even as chaff is driven before the wind" (Mormon 5:18). Nephi described this circumstance in no uncertain terms: "I beheld many multitudes of the Gentiles upon the land of promise; and I beheld the wrath of God, that it was upon the seed of my brethren; and they were scattered before the Gentiles and *smitten*. . . . I beheld the Spirit of the Lord, that it was upon the Gentiles, and they did prosper and obtain the land for their inheritance" (1 Nephi 13:14–15, emphasis added).

Dictionary). Mormon seems to be using the word as both the instrument and the process. He did not wish "to tear; to lacerate; to torment" the tender souls of his readers with the horrors of his day.

How will all things be revealed which have been hidden? (5:8) "Mormon tells us he purposely did not record all the detail of the 'blood and carnage' of those terrible years, this in order to prevent the latter-day reader from having an unnecessary and soul-troubling view of it all. His statement that all things 'must be revealed' has a dual meaning. Several scriptural passages testify that at the Judgment all deeds, words, thoughts, and intents of the heart—both righteous and wicked—will be revealed, will be shouted from the housetops, as it were, for all to know (see Matthew 10:26–27; D&C 1:3; D&C 88:108–10)" (McConkie et al., *Doctrinal Commentary*, 4:230). ✸

What is the "abridgment" spoken of here? (5:9) "When Mormon is acting as an abridger, he interacts extensively with the underlying documents he is abridging. It is usually possible (although not always) to distinguish Mormon's own words and comments from the words that he draws from the materials he is condensing. As one reads along in many sections of the Book of Mormon abridged by Mormon, one often senses that a subtle shift has taken place as a smooth, almost imperceptible transition has occurred from the underlying historical narrative to Mormon's commentary on that narrative" (Keller, "Mormon and Moroni as Authors and Abridgers," 269). In this verse, however, Mormon seems to be "abridging" himself as witness to the horrific events of his last days.

How are we "clasped in the arms of Jesus"? (5:11) "The Lord's protective and redemptive embrace is described in the Book of Mormon as being 'encircled' or 'clasped' in the Lord's arms:

"'But behold, the Lord hath redeemed my soul from hell; I have beheld his glory, and I am encircled about eternally in the arms of his love (2 Nephi 1:15).'

"'And thus mercy can satisfy the demands of justice, and encircles them in the arms of safety, while he that exercises no faith unto repentance is exposed to the whole law of the demands of justice (Alma 34:16). . . .'

"The embracing arms in these passages and the extended arm(s) of mercy both depend on the human addressee's repentance" (Calabro, "'Stretch Forth Thy Hand and Prophesy,'" 55).

made known, and that all things which are hid must be revealed upon the house-tops—

9 And also that a knowledge of these things must come unto the remnant of these people, and also unto the Gentiles, who the Lord hath said should scatter this people, and this people should be counted as naught among them—therefore I write a small abridgment, daring not to give a full account of the things which I have seen, because of the commandment which I have received, and also that ye might not have too great sorrow because of the wickedness of this people.

10 And now behold, this I speak unto their seed, and also to the Gentiles who have care for the house of Israel, that realize and know from whence their blessings come.

11 For I know that such will sorrow for the calamity of the house of Israel; yea, they will sorrow for the destruction of this people; they will sorrow that this people had not repented that they might have been clasped in the arms of Jesus.

12 Now these things are written unto the remnant of the house of Jacob; and they are written after this manner, because it is known of God that wickedness will not bring them forth unto them; and they are to be hid up unto the Lord that they may come forth in his own due time.

13 And this is the commandment which I have received; and behold, they shall come forth according to the commandment of the Lord, when he shall see fit, in his wisdom.

14 And behold, they shall go unto the unbelieving of the Jews; and for this intent shall they go—that they may be persuaded that Jesus is the Christ, the Son of the living God; that the Father may bring about, through his most Beloved, his great and eternal purpose, in restoring the Jews, or all the house of Israel, to the land of their inheritance, which the Lord their God hath given them, unto the fulfilling of his covenant;

15 And also that the seed of this people may more fully believe his gospel, which shall go forth unto them from the Gentiles; for this people shall be scattered, and shall become a dark, a filthy, and a loathsome people, beyond the description of that which ever hath been amongst us, yea, even that which hath been among the Lamanites, and this because of their unbelief and idolatry.

16 For behold, the Spirit of the Lord hath already ceased to strive with their fathers; and they are without Christ and God in the world; and they are driven about as chaff before the wind.

17 They were once a delightsome people, and they had Christ for their shepherd; yea, they were led even by God the Father.

What did the Lord promise about Mormon's record? (5:12–15) "In the title-page-preface the promise is made that this record would be preserved to come forth by the power of God to the convincing of the Lamanite, and also the Jew, and also the Gentile, that Jesus Christ is the Son of God. Throughout the Book of Mormon the prediction is made that this record would be preserved for that purpose and, moreover, to bear witness of the inspiration and sacredness of the Hebrew scriptures [Mormon 5:12–15; 7:8–9]. . . .

"Nephi wrote that the day would come 'that the words of the book which were sealed shall be read upon the house tops; and they shall be read by the power of Christ' [2 Nephi 27:11]" (Smith, *Doctrines of Salvation*, 3:211). ⊕

What is meant by the phrase that the Spirit "hath already ceased to strive" with the Nephites? (5:16) President Harold B. Lee taught: "Mormon described some people, his people, from whom the spirit of the Lord had departed, and when I read . . . it seems clear to me that what he was talking about was not merely the inability to have the companionship of or the gift of the Holy Ghost, but he was talking of that light of truth to which every one born into the world is entitled and will never cease to strive with the individual unless he loses it through his own sinning" (in Conference Report, Apr. 1956, 108). This was also the ultimate cause of the destruction of the Jaredite civilization (see Ether 15:18–19). ⊕

What do we need as an anchor to our souls? (5:18)
Hope through Jesus Christ is the anchor with which we can secure our lives. President James E. Faust observed: "Hope is the anchor of our souls. I know of no one who is not in need of hope—young or old, strong or weak, rich or poor. As the prophet Ether exhorted, 'Wherefore, whoso believeth in God might with surety hope for a better world, yea, even a place at the right hand of God, which hope cometh of faith, maketh an anchor to the souls of men, which would make them sure and steadfast, always abounding in good works, being led to glorify God'" ("Hope, an Anchor of the Soul," 59).

How will the earth "be rolled together as a scroll"?
(5:23) "At least three possible interpretations might explain the phrase 'the heavens shall be rolled together as a scroll':

"1. The weather phenomena of the last days (D&C 43:25; 133:69) or the manifestations in the skies (Rev. 6:14; D&C 29:14).

"2. The sealing of the heavens after the completion of one phase or glory of the earth; or the opening of the veil of heaven, indicating a new age (D&C 77:8; 133:69).

"3. The completion of the work of the telestial world in anticipation of the Millennium and the Second Coming (D&C 88:95; 101:23)" (Ludlow, *Companion to Your Study of the Old Testament*, 298).

18 But now, behold, they are led about by Satan, even as chaff is driven before the wind, or as a vessel is tossed about upon the waves, without sail or anchor, or without anything wherewith to steer her; and even as she is, so are they.

19 And behold, the Lord hath reserved their blessings, which they might have received in the land, for the Gentiles who shall possess the land.

20 But behold, it shall come to pass that they shall be driven and scattered by the Gentiles; and after they have been driven and scattered by the Gentiles, behold, then will the Lord remember the covenant which he made unto Abraham and unto all the house of Israel.

21 And also the Lord will remember the prayers of the righteous, which have been put up unto him for them.

22 And then, O ye Gentiles, how can ye stand before the power of God, except ye shall repent and turn from your evil ways?

23 Know ye not that ye are in the hands of God? Know ye not that he hath all power, and at his great command the earth shall be rolled together as a scroll?

24 Therefore, repent ye, and humble yourselves before him, lest he shall come out in justice against you—lest a remnant of the seed of Jacob shall go forth among you as a lion, and tear you in pieces, and there is none to deliver.

CHAPTER 6

The Nephites gather to the land of Cumorah for the final battles—Mormon hides the sacred records in the hill Cumorah—The Lamanites are victorious, and the Nephite nation is destroyed—Hundreds of thousands are slain with the sword. About A.D. 385.

1 And now I finish my record concerning the destruction of my people, the Nephites. And it came to pass that we did march forth before the Lamanites.

2 And I, Mormon, wrote an epistle unto the king of the Lamanites, and desired of him that he would grant unto us that we might gather together our people unto the land of Cumorah, by a hill which was called Cumorah, and there we could give them battle.

3 And it came to pass that the king of the Lamanites did grant unto me the thing which I desired.

4 And it came to pass that we did march forth to the land of Cumorah, and we did pitch our tents around about the hill Cumorah; and it was in a land of many waters, rivers, and fountains; and here we had hope to gain advantage over the Lamanites.

5 And when three hundred and eighty and four years had passed away, we had gathered in all the remainder of our people unto the land of Cumorah.

6 And it came to pass that when we had gathered in all our people in one to the land of Cumorah, behold I, Mormon, began to be old; and knowing it to be the last struggle of my people, and having been commanded of the Lord that I should not suffer the records which had been handed down by our fathers, which were sacred, to fall into the hands of the Lamanites, (for the Lamanites would destroy them) therefore I made this record out

Mormon 6:1–15. The Nephites Gather to Cumorah for Their Last Battle

Where was the "land of Cumorah"? (6:2–4) "There are many theories about precisely where the land of Cumorah was located, and those who advocate each view are very sure about their views. The North America theorists believe this is a clear reference to the Great Lakes and . . . the northeast part of the United States. The South America theorists posit that this is a reference to the plains of Imbabura in Ecuador's lake country. . . . The Mesoamerica theorists identify an area of southern Mexico on the eastern shore of the continent just north of the Yucatan Peninsula. . . . But when it comes to Book of Mormon geography, the only *official* statements that have been made by Church authorities say that we do not know" (Chase, *Making Precious Things Plain*, 3:212–13). ⊕

How old was Mormon? (6:6) At this time, Mormon was about seventy-four years old (ca. A.D. 311–385). He had been "about ten years of age" when Ammaron hid up the plates in the hill Shim and gave the young Mormon charge over them, ca. A.D. 321 (see 4 Nephi 1:48; Mormon 1:2–4). It was about A.D. 385 when Mormon concealed the plates in the hill Cumorah and gave charge of them to his son Moroni.

Why do the wicked fear death? (6:7)
The Prophet Joseph Smith once remarked: "There is no pain so awful as that of suspense. This is the punishment of the wicked; their doubt, anxiety and suspense cause weeping, wailing and gnashing of teeth" (Joseph Smith [manual], 224). ⊕

How great was the slaughter of Mormon's people? (6:11–15) "Mormon himself fell wounded, but his life, for a time, was spared as the Lamanite armies swept on. Only he, Moroni, and twenty-two other Nephites remained; 230,000 of their nation had fallen.

"The scope and significance of that horrible slaughter may be seen more readily when we realize that the great American Civil War of the 1860s, the costliest war, in terms of human life, that the United States has ever known, took the lives of 140,000 [Union soldiers] in a five-year period. Here, 230,000 fell in a single day" (Holland, "Mormon," 18).

of the plates of Nephi, and hid up in the hill Cumorah all the records which had been entrusted to me by the hand of the Lord, save it were these few plates which I gave unto my son Moroni.

7 And it came to pass that my people, with their wives and their children, did now behold the armies of the Lamanites marching towards them; and with that awful fear of death which fills the breasts of all the wicked, did they await to receive them.

8 And it came to pass that they came to battle against us, and every soul was filled with terror because of the greatness of their numbers.

9 And it came to pass that they did fall upon my people with the sword, and with the bow, and with the arrow, and with the ax, and with all manner of weapons of war.

10 And it came to pass that my men were hewn down, yea, even my ten thousand who were with me, and I fell wounded in the midst; and they passed by me that they did not put an end to my life.

11 And when they had gone through and hewn down all my people save it were twenty and four of us, (among whom was my son Moroni) and we having survived the dead of our people, did behold on the morrow, when the Lamanites had returned unto their camps, from the top of the hill Cumorah, the ten thousand of my people who were hewn down, being led in the front by me.

12 And we also beheld the ten thousand of my people who were led by my son Moroni.

13 And behold, the ten thousand of Gidgiddonah had fallen, and he also in the midst.

14 And Lamah had fallen with his ten thousand; and Gilgal had fallen with his ten thousand; and Limhah had fallen with his ten thousand; and Jeneum had fallen with his ten

thousand; and Cumenihah, and Moronihah, and Antionum, and Shiblom, and Shem, and Josh, had fallen with their ten thousand each.

15 And it came to pass that there were ten more who did fall by the sword, with their ten thousand each; yea, even all my people, save it were those twenty and four who were with me, and also a few who had escaped into the south countries, and a few who had deserted over unto the Lamanites, had fallen; and their flesh, and bones, and blood lay upon the face of the earth, being left by the hands of those who slew them to molder upon the land, and to crumble and to return to their mother earth.

16 And my soul was rent with anguish, because of the slain of my people, and I cried:

17 O ye fair ones, how could ye have departed from the ways of the Lord! O ye fair ones, how could ye have rejected that Jesus, who stood with open arms to receive you!

18 Behold, if ye had not done this, ye would not have fallen. But behold, ye are fallen, and I mourn your loss.

19 O ye fair sons and daughters, ye fathers and mothers, ye husbands and wives, ye fair ones, how is it that ye could have fallen!

20 But behold, ye are gone, and my sorrows cannot bring your return.

21 And the day soon cometh that your mortal must put on immortality, and these bodies which are now moldering in corruption must soon become incorruptible bodies; and then ye must stand before the judgment-seat of Christ, to be judged according to your works; and if it so be that ye are righteous, then are ye blessed with your fathers who have gone before you.

22 O that ye had repented before this great destruction had come upon you. But behold, ye are gone, and the Father, yea, the Eternal

Mormon 6:16–22. Mormon Mourns the Destruction of His People

How can we be received by Jesus? (6:17) "We long for the ultimate blessing of the Atonement—to become one with Him, to be in His divine presence, to be called individually by name as He warmly welcomes us home with a radiant smile, beckoning us with open arms to be enfolded in His boundless love. How gloriously sublime this experience will be if we can feel worthy enough to be in His presence! The free gift of His great atoning sacrifice for each of us is the only way we can be exalted enough to stand before Him and see Him face-to-face. The overwhelming message of the Atonement is the perfect love the Savior has for each and all of us" (Faust, "The Atonement," 20). ☉

What tendencies do you see in your culture, your community, and yourself that are similar to those of the fallen Nephites? (6:17–22) Mormon seems to change audience in these verses. No longer is he speaking to the "fair ones" fallen in the great destruction but to those who would later receive his words. After reading Mormon's plea to be always aware that you inevitably "must stand before the judgment-seat of Christ," how should you read the account in these verses of the fair ones who have fallen! What changes must be made to assure that you do not suffer the same fate as the Nephite people?

What is Mormon's message to latter-day readers? (6:21) "In a soliloquy of death, Mormon reached across time and space to all, especially to that 'remnant of the house of Israel' who would one day read his majestic record. Those of another time and place must learn what those lying before him had forgotten—that all must 'believe in Jesus Christ, that he is the Son of God,' that following his crucifixion in Jerusalem he had, 'by the power of the Father . . . risen again, whereby he hath gained the victory over the grave; and also in him is the sting of death swallowed up'" (Holland, *Christ and the New Covenant*, 321–22).

What is the lesson for today of the destruction of the Nephites? (6:22) "Read the Book of Mormon and learn what it says in regard to the ancient Nephites. The whole nation of the Nephites were slain, because they departed from the Lord their God and did wickedly. In the last great and tremendous battle between the Nephites and the Lamanites, over two millions of the Nephites were slain and the residue were hunted and slain until not a single person, except Moroni was left of a high and mighty nation. . . . Blood answered to blood until the land was cleansed, and few men were left. And so will it be with this nation who have slain the Prophets and have sought continually to destroy the people of God" (Young, in *Journal of Discourses*, 10:287).

Mormon 7:1–10. Mormon Explains What the Lamanites Must Do to Be Saved

Who is the "remnant" to whom Mormon wrote? (7:1–10) As the prophet Mormon's life draws to a close, he writes to the "remnant of this people who are spared" who are a "remnant of the house of Israel" (Mormon 7:1) and invites them to believe in Christ and accept His gospel. This invitation is remarkable in that these people to whom he is speaking are the descendants of the very Lamanites who had destroyed Mormon's people (see Mormon 6). Mormon's son "Moroni, on the title page of the Book of Mormon [also] calls the Lamanites 'a remnant of the house of Israel.' And the Lord himself identifies the Lamanites— the seed of father Lehi—as the 'remnant' of whom he spoke in Nephi's writings (1 Ne. 13:34)" (Brewster, *Doctrine and Covenants Encyclopedia*, 459).

How can we "come unto repentance" and be saved? (7:3) "The gospel teaches us that relief from torment and guilt can be earned through repentance. Save for

Father of heaven, knoweth your state; and he doeth with you according to his justice and mercy.

CHAPTER 7

Mormon invites the Lamanites of the latter days to believe in Christ, accept His gospel, and be saved—All who believe the Bible will also believe the Book of Mormon. About A.D. 385.

1 And now, behold, I would speak somewhat unto the remnant of this people who are spared, if it so be that God may give unto them my words, that they may know of the things of their fathers; yea, I speak unto you, ye remnant of the house of Israel; and these are the words which I speak:

2 Know ye that ye are of the house of Israel.

3 Know ye that ye must come unto repentance, or ye cannot be saved.

those few who defect to perdition after having known a fulness, there is no habit, no addiction, no rebellion, no transgression, no offense exempted from the promise of complete forgiveness.

"'Come now, and let us reason together, saith the Lord: though your sins be as scarlet, they shall be as white as snow; though they be red like crimson, they shall be as wool.' That is, Isaiah continued, 'if ye be willing and obedient.' Even that grace of God promised in the scriptures comes only 'after all we can do'" (Packer, "Brilliant Morning of Forgiveness," 19).

4 Know ye that ye must lay down your weapons of war, and delight no more in the shedding of blood, and take them not again, save it be that God shall command you.

5 Know ye that ye must come to the knowledge of your fathers, and repent of all your sins and iniquities, and believe in Jesus Christ, that he is the Son of God, and that he was slain by the Jews, and by the power of the Father he hath risen again, whereby he hath gained the victory over the grave; and also in him is the sting of death swallowed up.

Why should we follow the counsel to lay down our weapons of war? (7:4) President Spencer W. Kimball declared: "We are a warlike people, easily distracted from our assignment of preparing for the coming of the Lord. When enemies rise up, we commit vast resources to the fabrication of gods of stone and steel—ships, planes, missiles, fortifications—and depend on them for protection and deliverance. When threatened, we become anti-enemy instead of pro-kingdom of God; we train a man in the art of war and call him a patriot, thus, in the manner of Satan's counterfeit of true patriotism, perverting the Savior's teaching: ... 'That ye may be the children of your Father which is in heaven' (Matt. 5:44–45)" ("False Gods We Worship," 6). ☉

How will the latter-day Lamanites who are a remnant of the House of Israel be saved? (7:2, 3, 5, 8) Mormon pleads to the remnant of the Lamanites in the latter days to repent and believe in Jesus Christ and "be baptized in the name of Jesus, and lay hold upon the gospel of Christ" (v. 8). The Lord in modern-day revelation explained the doctrine just as Mormon had: "That the Lamanites might come to the knowledge of their fathers, and that they might know the promises of the Lord, and that they may believe the gospel and rely upon the merits of Jesus Christ, and be glorified through faith in his name, and that through their repentance they might be saved" (D&C 3:20).

Mormon's Final Counsel to Latter-day Israel (Mormon 7)

1. Remember always that "ye are of the house of Israel" (Mormon 7:2).
2. "Come unto repentance," for it is the only path to salvation (v. 3).
3. Do not be a people of war unless God commands (v. 4).
4. Obtain "knowledge of your fathers" and their failings (v. 5).
5. Believe in Jesus Christ and the power of the Atonement (v. 5).
6. Be baptized in the name of Jesus Christ (v. 8).
7. "Lay hold" upon the gospel of Jesus Christ as it shall come forth in the Bible and the Book of Mormon (v. 8).
8. Know what it means to be a "covenant" people and that as the seed of Jacob, you are inheritors of the "first covenant" (v. 10).

What is one of the purposes of resurrection? (7:6) Mormon reminds us that one of the purposes of resurrection is to enable us to stand before God to be judged of what we did with our bodies in mortality. President Dallin H. Oaks taught: "The principle of restoration also means that persons who are not righteous in mortal life will not rise up righteous in the resurrection. . . . Moreover, unless our mortal sins have been cleansed and blotted out by repentance and forgiveness . . . we will be resurrected with a 'bright recollection . . .' and a 'perfect knowledge of all of our guilt, and our uncleanness. . . .' The seriousness of that reality is emphasized by the many scriptures suggesting that the resurrection is followed immediately by the Final Judgment" ("Resurrection," 16).

What is the relationship between the nature of God and a state of happiness? (7:7) God lives in a never-ending state of happiness. Conversely, those who are separated from God in any degree are to that degree in a state of unhappiness. Alma taught that "wickedness never was happiness" (Alma 41:10). "The Book of Mormon speaks of men that are in a 'carnal state . . . and in the bonds of iniquity; they are without God in the world, and they have gone contrary to the nature of God; therefore, they are in a state contrary to the nature of happiness' (Alma 41:11). . . .

"If we are not pure, we would be miserable in the presence of God and Christ, who are by their very nature happy and joyful and cannot look upon sin with any allowance" (Goaslind, "Happiness," 53).

What is the promise of the record preserved by Mormon? (7:8–9) See commentary in this volume on Mormon 5:12–15.

6 And he bringeth to pass the resurrection of the dead, whereby man must be raised to stand before his judgment-seat.

7 And he hath brought to pass the redemption of the world, whereby he that is found guiltless before him at the judgment day hath it given unto him to dwell in the presence of God in his kingdom, to sing ceaseless praises with the choirs above, unto the Father, and unto the Son, and unto the Holy Ghost, which are one God, in a state of happiness which hath no end.

8 Therefore repent, and be baptized in the name of Jesus, and lay hold upon the gospel of Christ, which shall be set before you, not only in this record but also in the record which shall come unto the Gentiles from the Jews, which record shall come from the Gentiles unto you.

9 For behold, this is written for the intent that ye may believe that; and if ye believe that ye will believe this also; and if ye believe this ye will know concerning your fathers, and also the marvelous works which were wrought by the power of God among them.

10 And ye will also know that ye are a remnant of the seed of Jacob; therefore ye are numbered among the people of the first covenant; and if it so be that ye believe in Christ, and are baptized, first with water, then with fire and with the Holy Ghost, following the example of our Savior, according to that which he hath commanded us, it shall be well with you in the day of judgment. Amen.

CHAPTER 8

The Lamanites seek out and destroy the Nephites—The Book of Mormon will come forth by the power of God—Woes pronounced upon those who breathe out wrath and strife against the work of the Lord—The Nephite record will come forth in a day of wickedness, degeneracy, and apostasy. About A.D. 400–421.

1 Behold I, Moroni, do finish the record of my father, Mormon. Behold, I have but few things to write, which things I have been commanded by my father.

2 And now it came to pass that after the great and tremendous battle at Cumorah, behold, the Nephites who had escaped into the country southward were hunted by the Lamanites, until they were all destroyed.

3 And my father also was killed by them, and I even remain alone to write the sad tale of the destruction of my people. But behold, they are gone, and I fulfil the commandment of my father. And whether they will slay me, I know not.

4 Therefore I will write and hide up the records in the earth; and whither I go it mattereth not.

5 Behold, my father hath made this record, and he hath written the intent thereof. And behold, I would write it also if I had room upon the plates, but I have not; and ore I have none, for I am alone. My father hath been slain in battle, and all my kinsfolk, and I have not friends nor whither to go; and how long the Lord will suffer that I may live I know not.

6 Behold, four hundred years have passed away since the coming of our Lord and Savior.

7 And behold, the Lamanites have hunted my people, the Nephites, down from city to city and from place to place, even until they are no more; and great has been their fall;

Mormon 8:1–11. Mormon Is Killed, and Moroni Is Left Alone

Who was Moroni? (8:1) "Moroni was probably born close to the middle of the fourth century A.D. The only other member of his family mentioned is his father Mormon, the Nephite military commander-in-chief and the Lord's chosen prophet. We do not know his mother's name or whether he had siblings or was married. Mormon, who was well aware of the prophecies about his people, knew that his newly born son would experience a lifetime of bloodshed, turmoil, and strife. . . .

"Knowing the difficulties his son would encounter, Mormon, no doubt, named his infant son after the legendary prophet and military leader Captain Moroni, whose history he had abridged (see Alma 43:16–62:43)" (Peterson, "Moroni, the Last of the Nephite Prophets," 235–36).

For whom was Moroni writing? (8:1) "Following this dismaying decline of Nephite civilization documented by his father, Moroni picked up the recorder's task, but he did not write to any living audience. Rather, he directed his final testimony—in fact, three final testimonies—to those who would receive the record in the last days. . . . Moroni's experience was painful, for he observed in life, in history, and in vision the pollution and destruction of three glorious civilizations—his own Nephite world, the Jaredite nation, and our latter-day dispensation" (Holland, *Christ and the New Covenant*, 323). ◉

What did it mean for Moroni to be the last survivor of his people? (8:3, 7) "Who can sense the depth of his pain, the poignant loneliness that constantly overshadowed him as he moved about, a fugitive relentlessly hunted by his enemies? For how long he actually was alone we do not know, but the record would indicate that it was for a considerable period. His conversation was prayer to the Lord. His companion was the Holy Spirit. There were occasions when the Three Nephites ministered to him. But with all of this, there is an element of terrible tragedy in the life of this man who became a lonely wanderer" (Hinckley, "Moroni," 197). ◉

What was the state of the inhabitants of the land following the Nephite defeat? (8:7–9) "The Lamanites . . . would not let what was left of the people of Nephi rest in the ignominy of defeat, but hunted them down wherever they might be, until all had been found and slain. . . . The Lamanites, not content with the defeat of the Nephites, began a war among themselves. Their bloodthirstiness, and the love they had for killing, were not gratified in the slaying of their enemies, but that measure of their want was in a way gratified only with them taking the lives of their neighbors" (Reynolds and Sjodahl, *Commentary on the Book of Mormon*, 7:289–90).

What do we learn in these verses about the mission of the three disciples who tarried? (8:10–11) "The disciples of Jesus who knew the true God were the three who were blessed to remain on the earth until Christ came again. Their mission was to bring souls unto Christ (see 3 Nephi 28:4–10). Thus their purpose in ministering to Mormon and Moroni was undoubtedly in this capacity. They had either ministered to them earlier, and Moroni is recollecting their visit, or they had ministered to them in regards to their keeping the records. The three disciples may have been among the lost tribes since they had departed from the Nephites because of the wickedness of the people (Mormon 8:9; see Mormon 1:13)" (Nyman, *I, Mormon, Make a Record*, 119).

Mormon 8:12–16. The Book of Mormon Will Come to Light

What does "this record" refer to? (8:12) "This record" refers to the Book of Mormon, which Mormon compiled, his son Moroni completed, and the Prophet Joseph Smith translated. What will the Book of Mormon do for you if you do not condemn it despite its imperfections? (see Mormon 9:31). What do you consider to be the greater things Moroni promises?

Why does Moroni identify himself again? (8:13–14) "There is something remarkable that has happened between these verses. . . . The Moroni of verse 13 is not the Moroni of verse 14, by which I mean, he is the same person, the same individual, but something remarkable has happened to him. All of a sudden, Moroni has a sense of mission that is not apparent in the first thirteen verses. He has received a call from God telling him what he must do with this record and

yea, great and marvelous is the destruction of my people, the Nephites.

8 And behold, it is the hand of the Lord which hath done it. And behold also, the Lamanites are at war one with another; and the whole face of this land is one continual round of murder and bloodshed; and no one knoweth the end of the war.

9 And now, behold, I say no more concerning them, for there are none save it be the Lamanites and robbers that do exist upon the face of the land.

10 And there are none that do know the true God save it be the disciples of Jesus, who did tarry in the land until the wickedness of the people was so great that the Lord would not suffer them to remain with the people; and whether they be upon the face of the land no man knoweth.

11 But behold, my father and I have seen them, and they have ministered unto us.

12 And whoso receiveth this record, and shall not condemn it because of the imperfections which are in it, the same shall know of greater things than these. Behold, I am Moroni; and were it possible, I would make all things known unto you.

13 Behold, I make an end of speaking concerning this people. I am the son of Mormon, and my father was a descendant of Nephi.

14 And I am the same who hideth up this record unto the Lord; the plates thereof are of no worth, because of the commandment of the Lord. For he truly saith that no one shall have them to get gain; but the record

thereof is of great worth; and whoso shall bring it to light, him will the Lord bless.

15 For none can have power to bring it to light save it be given him of God; for God wills that it shall be done with an eye single to his glory, or the welfare of the ancient and long dispersed covenant people of the Lord.

16 And blessed be he that shall bring this thing to light; for it shall be brought out of darkness unto light, according to the word of God; yea, it shall be brought out of the earth, and it shall shine forth out of darkness, and come unto the knowledge of the people; and it shall be done by the power of God.

17 And if there be faults they be the faults of a man. But behold, we know no fault; nevertheless God knoweth all things; therefore, he that condemneth, let him be aware lest he shall be in danger of hell fire.

18 And he that saith: Show unto me, or ye shall be smitten—let him beware lest he commandeth that which is forbidden of the Lord.

19 For behold, the same that judgeth rashly shall be judged rashly again; for according to his works shall his wages be; therefore, he that smiteth shall be smitten again, of the Lord.

20 Behold what the scripture says—man shall not smite, neither shall he judge; for judgment is mine, saith the Lord, and vengeance is mine also, and I will repay.

21 And he that shall breathe out wrath and strifes against the work of the Lord, and against the covenant people of the Lord who are the house of Israel, and shall say: We will destroy the work of the Lord, and the Lord will not remember his covenant which he hath made unto the house of Israel—the

what his responsibilities are. He now begins to speak with power, as if he were a prophet. We never hear the words of loneliness from him again in his writing" (Merrill, "Moroni," 8).

Who is the "blessed" person who brings the Book of Mormon to light? (8:16) "Mormon 8:16 refers to the Prophet Joseph Smith, who was chosen to bring the Book of Mormon to the world (see D&C 3:5–10). Many of the ancient prophets were aware of Joseph Smith and prayed for his success to translate and publish the gold plates, thus fulfilling the purposes of God (see Mormon 8:22, 24–25; D&C 10:46)" (*Book of Mormon Student Manual* [2009], 356).

Mormon 8:17–25. Moroni Counsels Future Readers to Search the Book of Mormon

What faults might the Book of Mormon have? (8:17) "The Book of Mormon is a translation of the originals. . . .

"Skeptics and students of sacred literature may point to the errors they allege to have found in the Book of Mormon, to the wrongful use of words, to improper forms of speech, but in doing this they fail to point out, 'If there are faults they are the mistakes of men,' (Inspired Preface) and not the inspirations of God. They do not say, 'This is the finger of man, and not the Finger of God.'

"'Wherefore, condemn not the things of God, that ye may be found spotless at the Judgment-Seat of Christ'" (Reynolds and Sjodahl, *Commentary on the Book of Mormon*, 7:8, 10). ⊕

What should be our attitude toward the modern-day descendants of the Lamanites? (8:21–22) President Spencer W. Kimball declared: "I remember that the Lord was long-suffering with ancient Israel. . . . Here [the Lord] has the Indian or Lamanite, with a background of twenty-five centuries of superstition, degradation, idolatry, and indolence. He has loathed their wickedness, chastised them, brought the Gentiles to them for nursing fathers and mothers, and (it would seem) has finally forgiven them. Their sufferings have been sore, their humiliation complete, their punishment severe and long, their heartaches many, and their opportunities reduced. Has he not now forgiven them and accepted them? Can we not now forgive and accept them?" (in Conference Report, Apr. 1954, 106). ●

Which prophecies of Isaiah does Moroni admonish us to search? (8:23) See commentary in this volume on 3 Nephi 23:1. ●

Who are those who shall cry from the dust? (8:23–25) "The saints who will 'cry unto the Lord' from the dust are those whose actual words were written upon the plates as well as others who were referred to in the accounts of the Nephite records. Isaiah had foretold their crying from the dust or speaking out of the ground (see Isaiah 29:4)" (Nyman, *I, Mormon, Make a Record*, 124–25). ●

same is in danger to be hewn down and cast into the fire;

22 For the eternal purposes of the Lord shall roll on, until all his promises shall be fulfilled.

23 Search the prophecies of Isaiah. Behold, I cannot write them. Yea, behold I say unto you, that those saints who have gone before me, who have possessed this land, shall cry, yea, even from the dust will they cry unto the Lord; and as the Lord liveth he will remember the covenant which he hath made with them.

24 And he knoweth their prayers, that they were in behalf of their brethren. And he knoweth their faith, for in his name could they remove mountains; and in his name could they cause the earth to shake; and by the power of his word did they cause prisons to tumble to the earth; yea, even the fiery furnace could not harm them, neither wild beasts nor poisonous serpents, because of the power of his word.

Moroni Sees Our Day

Moroni acknowledged that the day in which the Book of Mormon would come forth would be a time of great difficulty and unbelief. In Mormon 8:26–41, he describes the circumstances that might inhibit acceptance of the ancient record:

1. It will be a time when miracles are denied (v. 26).

2. It will be in a day when the rise of secret combinations and works of darkness shall cause the blood of the saints to be shed and cry from the earth (v. 27).

3. It will come in a day when the power of God shall be denied (v. 28).

4. It will be a time when churches and their leaders shall be defiled and lifted up with pride, envy, and corruption (vv. 28, 32).

5. The earth will tremble because of fires and tempests and "vapors of smoke in foreign lands" (v. 29).

6. There will be widespread war and "rumors of wars" among the nations (v. 30).

7. There will be earthquakes "in divers places" (v. 30).

8. There will be "great pollutions" upon all the earth (v. 31).

9. In that day there will be rampant wickedness—murders, robbings, lying, deceiving, whoredoms, "and all manner of abominations" (v. 31).

10. It will be a time when people reject accountability for their behavior (v. 31).

Nonetheless, Moroni noted that notwithstanding the wickedness of the last days, the ancient record—the Book of Mormon—would indeed come forth by the hand of the Lord, "and none can stay it" (Mormon 8:26). Moroni admonished those living in these difficult days to pay heed to the revelations of God, for "all these things must be fulfilled" (Mormon 8:33).

25 And behold, their prayers were also in behalf of him that the Lord should suffer to bring these things forth.

26 And no one need say they shall not come, for they surely shall, for the Lord hath spoken it; for out of the earth shall they come, by the hand of the Lord, and none can stay it; and it shall come in a day when it shall be said that miracles are done away; and it shall come even as if one should speak from the dead.

27 And it shall come in a day when the blood of saints shall cry unto the Lord, because of secret combinations and the works of darkness.

28 Yea, it shall come in a day when the power of God shall be denied, and churches become defiled and be lifted up in the pride of their hearts; yea, even in a day when leaders of churches and teachers shall rise in the pride of their hearts, even to the envying of them who belong to their churches.

29 Yea, it shall come in a day when there shall be heard of fires, and tempests, and vapors of smoke in foreign lands;

30 And there shall also be heard of wars, rumors of wars, and earthquakes in divers places.

31 Yea, it shall come in a day when there shall be great pollutions upon the face of the earth; there shall be murders, and robbing, and lying, and deceivings, and whoredoms, and all manner of abominations; when there shall be many who will say, Do this, or do that, and it mattereth not, for the Lord will uphold such at the last day. But wo unto such, for they are in the gall of bitterness and in the bonds of iniquity.

32 Yea, it shall come in a day when there shall be churches built up that shall say: Come unto me, and for your money you shall be forgiven of your sins.

33 O ye wicked and perverse and stiffnecked people, why have ye built up churches unto

Mormon 8:26–41. Moroni Sees Our Day

What prophesied events are beginning to unfold in our day? (8:26–33) How might you live in this time of increasing wickedness and not be tainted or overwhelmed by attitudes and behaviors of those who have lost faith and denied God? How specifically can the scriptures enable you to maintain your faith in Heavenly Father and remain clean and pure?

What pollutions or deteriorating spiritual conditions did Mormon see in our day? (8:31) Elder Joe J. Christensen commented on the moral and spiritual pollution addressed by Moroni: "We all hear and read a great deal these days about our polluted physical environment—acid rain, smog, toxic wastes. But . . . there is another kind of pollution that is much more dangerous—the moral and spiritual.

"In a recent conference, Elder Boyd K. Packer said, 'As we test the moral environment, we find the pollution index is spiraling upward' (*Ensign*, May 1992, 66). The Apostle Paul foresaw 'that in the last days perilous times shall come' (2 Tim 3:1). And speaking of the last days, the prophet Moroni declared, 'Yea, it shall come in a day when there shall be great pollutions upon the face of the earth' (Morm. 8:31" ("Rearing Children in a Polluted Environment," 11). ●

How should knowing that Moroni and other Book of Mormon prophets saw our day in vision influence our study of this sacred record? (8:34–35) "We must make the Book of Mormon a center focus of study because it was written for our day. The Nephites never had the book, neither did the Lamanites of ancient times. It was meant for us. . . . [Mormon and] Moroni, the last of the inspired writers, actually saw our day and time. . . . If they saw our day, and chose those things which would be of greatest worth to us, is not that how we should study the Book of Mormon? We should constantly ask ourselves . . . [w]hat lesson can I learn from that to help me live in this day and age?" (*Teachings of Ezra Taft Benson*, 58–59). ⊕

Why does Moroni call some practices of our day "pollutions"? (8:38) President Spencer W. Kimball remarked: "I have traveled much in various assignments over the years, and when I pass through the lovely countryside or fly over the vast and beautiful expanses of our globe, I compare these beauties with many of the dark and miserable practices of men, and I have the feeling that the good earth can hardly bear our presence upon it. I recall the occasion when Enoch heard the earth mourn, saying, 'Wo, wo is me, the mother of men; I am pained, I am weary, because of the wickedness of my children. When shall I rest, and be cleansed from the filthiness which is gone forth out of me?' (Moses 7:48)" ("False Gods We Worship," 4). ⊕

Why do these warnings from Moroni apply to members of The Church of Jesus Christ of Latter-day Saints? (8:38–41) "This prophecy is a solemn warning . . . to the Latter-day Saints. . . . The Saints of

yourselves to get gain? Why have ye transfigured the holy word of God, that ye might bring damnation upon your souls? Behold, look ye unto the revelations of God; for behold, the time cometh at that day when all these things must be fulfilled.

34 Behold, the Lord hath shown unto me great and marvelous things concerning that which must shortly come, at that day when these things shall come forth among you.

35 Behold, I speak unto you as if ye were present, and yet ye are not. But behold, Jesus Christ hath shown you unto me, and I know your doing.

36 And I know that ye do walk in the pride of your hearts; and there are none save a few only who do not lift themselves up in the pride of their hearts, unto the wearing of very fine apparel, unto envying, and strifes, and malice, and persecutions, and all manner of iniquities; and your churches, yea, even every one, have become polluted because of the pride of your hearts.

37 For behold, ye do love money, and your substance, and your fine apparel, and the adorning of your churches, more than ye love the poor and the needy, the sick and the afflicted.

38 O ye pollutions, ye hypocrites, ye teachers, who sell yourselves for that which will canker, why have ye polluted the holy church of God? Why are ye ashamed to take upon you the name of Christ? Why do ye not think that greater is the value of an endless happiness than that misery which never dies—because of the praise of the world?

39 Why do ye adorn yourselves with that which hath no life, and yet suffer the hungry, and the needy, and the naked, and the sick and the afflicted to pass by you, and notice them not?

40 Yea, why do ye build up your secret abominations to get gain, and cause that widows should mourn before the Lord, and also orphans to mourn before the Lord, and also the blood of their fathers and their husbands to cry unto the Lord from the ground, for vengeance upon your heads?

41 Behold, the sword of vengeance hangeth over you; and the time soon cometh that he avengeth the blood of the saints upon you, for he will not suffer their cries any longer.

CHAPTER 9

Moroni calls upon those who do not believe in Christ to repent—He proclaims a God of miracles, who gives revelations and pours out gifts and signs upon the faithful—Miracles cease because of unbelief—Signs follow those who believe—Men are exhorted to be wise and keep the commandments. About A.D. 401–421.

1 And now, I speak also concerning those who do not believe in Christ.

2 Behold, will ye believe in the day of your visitation—behold, when the Lord shall come, yea, even that great day when the earth shall be rolled together as a scroll, and the elements shall melt with fervent heat, yea, in that great day when ye shall be brought to stand before the Lamb of God—then will ye say that there is no God?

3 Then will ye longer deny the Christ, or can ye behold the Lamb of God? Do ye suppose that ye shall dwell with him under a consciousness of your guilt? Do ye suppose that ye could be happy to dwell with that holy Being, when your souls are racked with a consciousness of guilt that ye have ever abused his laws?

4 Behold, I say unto you that ye would be more miserable to dwell with a holy and just God, under a consciousness of your filthiness

God need to labor day and night to retain purity of heart and thus propriety in their dealings with God and with one another. Zion can only be established among a people who are pure in heart, a people who search out the poor and needy, who see to those needs, and who focus their attention, their loyalties, and their time on people and on things which have eternal relevance and worth [see D&C 105:5]" (McConkie et al., *Doctrinal Commentary*, 4:250).

What do you need to do to enable yourself to more firmly establish the principles of Zion and the celestial kingdom in your home and in your own life? In what ways can you help the hungry and needy? ❂

Mormon 9:1–6. Moroni Invites Unbelievers in the Last Days to Repent

What does Moroni desire unbelievers to understand? (9:1) "Moroni at first evidently intended this chapter to be the last one in the entire Book of Mormon. Thus he addresses himself to 'those who do not believe in Christ' (Mormon 9:1). Then in a powerful, logical, and forceful manner he outlines the major teachings of the gospel of Jesus Christ and indicates why all men must understand and apply these principles if they are to find the peace and happiness they desire. He says the gospel is not restricted to a chosen few, but is available 'unto all, even unto the ends of the earth' (Mormon 9:21)" (Ludlow, *Companion to Your Study of the Book of Mormon*, 307).

What is Moroni's message to those who do not believe in Christ? (9:1–6) "Moroni wrote with an apocalyptic view to the future. Though his audience was centuries removed, he addressed them directly. His message, echoing his father's warnings, emphasized the reality of the final judgment" (Mackay, "Mormon and the Destruction of Nephite Civilization," 242). Elder L. Tom Perry described Moroni's voice of warning as coming from one who "witnessed the wickedness and destruction which comes from unbelief, when men's and women's souls are not anchored to the teachings of the gospel" (Perry, "'Behold, the Lord Hath Shown unto Me Great and Marvelous Things,'" 16).

How does true repentance begin? (9:5–6) President Spencer W. Kimball taught: "As repentance gets under way, there must be a deep consciousness of guilt, and in that consciousness of guilt may come suffering to the mind, the spirit, and sometimes even to the body. In order to live with themselves, people who transgress must follow one or the other of two alternatives. The one is to sear their conscience or dull their sensitivity with mental tranquilizers so that their transgression may be continued. Those who choose this alternative eventually become calloused and lose their desire to repent. The other alternative is to permit remorse to lead one to total sorrow, then to repentance, and finally on to eventual forgiveness" (Kimball, "Gospel of Repentance," 4). ●

Mormon 9:7–10. Moroni Testifies That God Has Always Performed Miracles and Given Revelations

Why do some deny the revelations and gifts of God? (9:7–8) "Whoever rejects the revelations and gifts of God—the miracles and signs and wonders—does so in either absolute ignorance of the holy scriptures or in absolute rebellion and defiance against the order of things in the Lord's kingdom. If there is a God, and if he is a possessor of all knowledge and all power, and if we

before him, than ye would to dwell with the damned souls in hell.

5 For behold, when ye shall be brought to see your nakedness before God, and also the glory of God, and the holiness of Jesus Christ, it will kindle a flame of unquenchable fire upon you.

6 O then ye unbelieving, turn ye unto the Lord; cry mightily unto the Father in the name of Jesus, that perhaps ye may be found spotless, pure, fair, and white, having been cleansed by the blood of the Lamb, at that great and last day.

7 And again I speak unto you who deny the revelations of God, and say that they are done away, that there are no revelations, nor prophecies, nor gifts, nor healing, nor speaking with tongues, and the interpretation of tongues;

The Doctrine of an Unchangeable God (Mormon 9:9)

The Bible hints that one of the characteristics of God is that he does not vary or lack consistency (see James 1:7; Malachi 3:6). However, the presentation of this important concept is so scattered and fragmented that it has been largely ignored by the Christian world—otherwise they would not have ceased to believe in miracles or in modern prophets and revelation. On the other hand, the knowledge that God is the same unchangeable God generation after generation, dispensation to dispensation, "yesterday, today, and forever," is a powerful doctrine mostly unique to modern revelation, particularly the Book of Mormon. Note the clarity and sustained presentation of this doctrine in modern-day revelation:

1. 1 Nephi 10:18: "For he is the same yesterday, today, and forever."
2. 2 Nephi 2:4: "For the Spirit is the same, yesterday, today, and forever."
3. 2 Nephi 27:23: "I am a God of miracles; and I will show unto the world that I am the same yesterday, today, and forever."
4. 2 Nephi 29:9: "I do this that I may prove unto many that I am the same yesterday, today, and forever."
5. Alma 31:17 "Thou art the same yesterday, today, and forever."
6. Mormon 9:9–10 "For do we not read that God is the same yesterday, today, and forever, and in him there is no variableness neither shadow of changing?"
7. Moroni 10:7–8 "I would exhort you that ye deny not the power of God; for he worketh by power, according to the faith of the children of men, the same today, and tomorrow, and forever."
8. Moroni 10:19 "I would exhort you . . . that ye remember that he is the same yesterday, today, and forever."

In April 1830, as the time for the formal organization of the Church approached, the Lord highlighted for Joseph Smith and the early Saints the key doctrines and principles in the Book of Mormon (D&C 20:8–35). One of those governing principles is "God does inspire men and call them to his holy work in this age and generation, as well as in generations of old; thereby showing that he is the same God yesterday, today, and forever, amen" (D&C 20:11–12).

8 Behold I say unto you, he that denieth these things knoweth not the gospel of Christ; yea, he has not read the scriptures; if so, he does not understand them.

9 For do we not read that God is the same yesterday, today, and forever, and in him there is no variableness neither shadow of changing?

10 And now, if ye have imagined up unto yourselves a god who doth vary, and in whom there is shadow of changing, then have ye imagined up unto yourselves a god who is not a God of miracles.

11 But behold, I will show unto you a God of miracles, even the God of Abraham, and the God of Isaac, and the God of Jacob; and it is that same God who created the heavens and the earth, and all things that in them are.

12 Behold, he created Adam, and by Adam came the fall of man. And because of the fall of man came Jesus Christ, even the Father and the Son; and because of Jesus Christ came the redemption of man.

13 And because of the redemption of man, which came by Jesus Christ, they are brought back into the presence of the Lord; yea, this is wherein all men are redeemed, because the death of Christ bringeth to pass the resurrection, which bringeth to pass a redemption from an endless sleep, from which sleep all men shall be awakened by the power of God when the trump shall sound; and they shall come forth, both small and great, and all shall stand before his bar, being redeemed and loosed from this eternal band of death, which death is a temporal death.

are his children, then it is inconceivable that he would not want to reveal himself and manifest his power among his offspring. If such things are no more, if they have in some way been done away, then it is because of the lack of faith on the part of those on earth" (McConkie et al., *Doctrinal Commentary*, 4:254). ✛

Why is it important to know that God does not change? (9:9–10) "[God] changes not, neither is there variableness with him; but that he is the same from everlasting to everlasting, being the same yesterday, to-day, and for ever; and that his course is one eternal round, without variation.... It is ... necessary that men should have the idea that he is a God who changes not, in order to have faith in him ... for without the idea of unchangeableness in the character of the Deity, doubt would take the place of faith. But with the idea that he changes not, faith lays hold upon the excellences in his character with unshaken confidence" (*Lectures on Faith*, [41–42]).

Mormon 9:11–21. Miracles and Signs Come to Those Who Believe in Christ

What are miracles? (9:11) "A miracle has been defined as 'a beneficial event brought about through divine power that mortals do not understand and of themselves cannot duplicate.' The idea that events are brought about through divine power is rejected by most irreligious people and even by some who are religious....

"Miracles worked by the power of the priesthood are always present in the true Church of Jesus Christ" (Oaks, "Miracles," 6, 8).

14 And then cometh the judgment of the Holy One upon them; and then cometh the time that he that is filthy shall be filthy still; and he that is righteous shall be righteous still; he that is happy shall be happy still; and he that is unhappy shall be unhappy still.

15 And now, O all ye that have imagined up unto yourselves a god who can do no miracles, I would ask of you, have all these things passed, of which I have spoken? Has the end come yet? Behold I say unto you, Nay; and God has not ceased to be a God of miracles.

16 Behold, are not the things that God hath wrought marvelous in our eyes? Yea, and who can comprehend the marvelous works of God?

17 Who shall say that it was not a miracle that by his word the heaven and the earth should be; and by the power of his word man was created of the dust of the earth; and by the power of his word have miracles been wrought?

18 And who shall say that Jesus Christ did not do many mighty miracles? And there were many mighty miracles wrought by the hands of the apostles.

19 And if there were miracles wrought then, why has God ceased to be a God of miracles and yet be an unchangeable Being? And behold, I say unto you he changeth not; if so he would cease to be God; and he ceaseth not to be God, and is a God of miracles.

20 And the reason why he ceaseth to do miracles among the children of men is because that they dwindle in unbelief, and depart from the right way, and know not the God in whom they should trust.

21 Behold, I say unto you that whoso believeth in Christ, doubting nothing, whatsoever he shall ask the Father in the name of Christ it shall be granted him; and this promise is unto all, even unto the ends of the earth.

Why do miracles cease in certain ages? (9:19–21)
"Why are [miracles] not found at all times and among all peoples? Were those of old entitled to greater blessings than those of us who now dwell on the same earth that once was theirs . . . ? They worship false gods whom they define in their creeds, and they no longer walk in the same paths pursued by the saints of former days.

"It is men who have changed, not God; he is the same everlastingly. All men who have the same faith and live the same law will reap the same blessings" (McConkie, *New Witness*, 367). ⊕

Mormon 9:22–29. Moroni Teaches That It Is Wise to Keep the Commandments

22 For behold, thus said Jesus Christ, the Son of God, unto his disciples who should tarry, yea, and also to all his disciples, in the hearing of the multitude: Go ye into all the world, and preach the gospel to every creature;

23 And he that believeth and is baptized shall be saved, but he that believeth not shall be damned;

24 And these signs shall follow them that believe—in my name shall they cast out devils; they shall speak with new tongues; they shall take up serpents; and if they drink any deadly thing it shall not hurt them; they shall lay hands on the sick and they shall recover;

25 And whosoever shall believe in my name, doubting nothing, unto him will I confirm all my words, even unto the ends of the earth.

26 And now, behold, who can stand against the works of the Lord? Who can deny his sayings? Who will rise up against the almighty power of the Lord? Who will despise the works of the Lord? Who will despise the children of Christ? Behold, all ye who are

Why were these words of the Savior not recorded in 3 Nephi? (9:22–24) "Moroni is presumably quoting here from words spoken by our Lord to the Nephites during his American ministry. They are not to be found in our present text, Mormon's abridgment of the plates of Nephi, though we do have a record of the Master speaking such words on the Eastern Hemisphere (see Mark 16:15–18). Mormon himself explained: 'And now there cannot be written in this book even a hundredth part of the things which Jesus did truly teach unto the people; but behold the [unabridged, large] plates of Nephi do contain the more part of the things which he taught the people' (3 Nephi 26:6–7)" (McConkie et al., *Doctrinal Commentary*, 4:256).

What is the purpose of signs? (9:24) "Signs flow from faith. They may incidentally have the effect of strengthening the faith of those who are already spiritually inclined, but their chief purpose is not to convert people to the truth, but to reward and bless those already converted. . . . Signs are sacred grants of divine favor reserved for the faithful and concerning which the recipients are commanded not to boast. 'A commandment I give unto them,' the Lord says, 'that they shall not boast themselves of these things, neither speak them before the world; for these things are given unto you for your profit and for salvation' (D&C 84:73)" (McConkie, *Mormon Doctrine*, 714).

Moroni's Summary of the Plan of Salvation

1. God created the heavens and the earth and all things that are in them (Mormon 9:11).
2. He created Adam, and by Adam came the fall of man (v. 12).
3. Because of the Fall, God sent His Son Jesus Christ to redeem mankind (v. 12).
4. Because of the redemption, we can return to the presence of God (v. 13).
5. Because of the death and resurrection of Christ, all will be resurrected (v. 13).
6. Jesus Christ will judge both the righteous and the wicked (v. 14).
7. The worthy Saints will receive a reward according to their righteousness (v. 14).

Though not directly quoting from these passages, elements in Moroni's summary of the plan of salvation were concisely identified by Elder Bruce R. McConkie as the "three pillars of eternity." Elder McConkie stated: "God himself, the Father of us all, ordained and established a plan of salvation whereby his spirit children might advance and progress and become like him. It is the gospel of God, the plan of Eternal Elohim, the system that saves and exalts, and it consists of three things. These three are the very pillars of eternity itself. They are the most important events that ever have or will occur in all eternity. They are the Creation, the Fall, and the Atonement. . . . We must know how and in what manner these three eternal verities—the Creation, the Fall, and the Atonement—are inseparably woven together to form one plan of salvation. No one of them stands alone; each of them ties into the other two; and without a knowledge of all of them, it is not possible to know the truth about any one of them" ("Christ and the Creation," 9).

despisers of the works of the Lord, for ye shall wonder and perish.

27 O then despise not, and wonder not, but hearken unto the words of the Lord, and ask the Father in the name of Jesus for what things soever ye shall stand in need. Doubt not, but be believing, and begin as in times of old, and come unto the Lord with all your heart, and work out your own salvation with fear and trembling before him.

28 Be wise in the days of your probation; strip yourselves of all uncleanness; ask not, that ye may consume it on your lusts, but ask with a firmness unshaken, that ye will yield to no temptation, but that ye will serve the true and living God.

29 See that ye are not baptized unworthily; see that ye partake not of the sacrament of Christ unworthily; but see that ye do all things in worthiness, and do it in the name of Jesus Christ, the Son of the living God; and if ye do this, and endure to the end, ye will in nowise be cast out.

30 Behold, I speak unto you as though I spake from the dead; for I know that ye shall have my words.

31 Condemn me not because of mine imperfection, neither my father, because of his imperfection, neither them who have written before him; but rather give thanks unto God that he hath made manifest unto you our imperfections, that ye may learn to be more wise than we have been.

32 And now, behold, we have written this record according to our knowledge, in the characters which are called among us the reformed Egyptian, being handed down and altered by us, according to our manner of speech.

33 And if our plates had been sufficiently large we should have written in Hebrew; but the Hebrew hath been altered by us also; and

Mormon 9:30–37. Moroni Speaks concerning the Language of the Book of Mormon

How familiar were Book of Mormon authors with the Egyptian language? (9:32–34) "The Book of Mormon indicates that it was written using Egyptian characters, called by Moroni 'reformed Egyptian,' though the Nephites also knew Hebrew (see Mormon 9:32–34). Nephi made 'a record in the language of [his] father, which consists of the learning of the Jews and the language of the Egyptians' (1 Nephi 1:2). Evidently, the brass plates of Laban also contained Egyptian characters, for King Benjamin informed his sons that, if we could have written in Hebrew, behold, ye would have had no imperfection in our record.

34 But the Lord knoweth the things which we have written, and also that none other people knoweth our language; and because that none other people knoweth our language, therefore he hath prepared means for the interpretation thereof.

35 And these things are written that we may rid our garments of the blood of our brethren, who have dwindled in unbelief.

36 And behold, these things which we have desired concerning our brethren, yea, even their restoration to the knowledge of Christ, are according to the prayers of all the saints who have dwelt in the land.

37 And may the Lord Jesus Christ grant that their prayers may be answered according to their faith; and may God the Father remember the covenant which he hath made with the house of Israel; and may he bless them forever, through faith on the name of Jesus Christ. Amen.

without a knowledge of Egyptian, Lehi would not have been able to read them (see Mosiah 1:3–4)" (Ricks, "Pressing Forward with the Book of Mormon," 2). ◉

What means were prepared and used for the interpretation of the Nephite record? (9:34) Mormon states that "none other people knoweth our language," therefore the Lord prepared means to translate the record. Elder James E. Talmage testified: "The translation of the Book of Mormon was effected through the power of God manifested in the bestowal of the gift of revelation. . . . Joseph Smith received from the angel other sacred treasures, including a breastplate, to which were attached the Urim and Thummim . . . and by the use of these he was enabled to translate the ancient records into our modern tongue" (*Articles of Faith*, 273). Elder Talmage also wrote: "There will be, there can be, no absolutely reliable translation of . . . scriptures unless it be effected through the gift of translation, as one of the endowments of the Holy Ghost. The translator must have the spirit of the prophet if he would render in another tongue the prophet's words; and human wisdom alone leads not to that possession" (*Articles of Faith*, 241).

THE BOOK OF ETHER

Introduction

Mormon promises that an account from the record of the Jaredites translated by Mosiah (see Mosiah 28:17) from twenty-four gold plates found by the people of Limhi (see Mosiah 8:7–8) would be written in a future day. He records that "it is expedient that all people should know the things which are written in this account" (Mosiah 28:19). Mormon's son Moroni eventually fulfills this promise in his abridgment of the book of Ether—the record of a group of people called the Jaredites (see Title Page of the Book of Mormon). More than two thousand years before the mortal ministry of Jesus Christ, the Lord led a man named Jared and his family and friends away from the Tower of Babel to a choice land (the Americas). The account records the rise and fall of a great nation. The book is named after the last great Jaredite prophet, who witnessed the destruction of his people and wrote the record (see Ether 1:6; 5:33–34). The book of Ether "serves as a microcosm of the whole Book of Mormon" (Rust, *Feasting on the Word*, 226) and is therefore a second witness of the importance of following and serving the God of Heaven.

What is the origin of the superscription in italics that precedes the opening text of the book of Ether? Unlike the superscriptions to other books and sections of books within the Book of Mormon, this one is not part of the ancient record translated by Joseph Smith. This superscription "is wanting in all but the current editions of the Book of Mormon and is not to be regarded as part of the original text. The note seems to have been inserted by the committee appointed to edit the text now in common use" (Sperry, *Book of Mormon Compendium*, 460–61).

The chapter summary is presented in italics between the chapter number and the beginning of the scriptural text. The chapter summaries, first added in the 1920 edition of the Book of Mormon, give the reader an overview of what each chapter contains.

Ether 1:1–5. Moroni Begins His Abridgment of the Jaredite Record

How might Moroni's life experience have influenced what he chose to abridge from the Jaredite record? (1:1–2) "Moroni is one of the most tantalizing characters in scripture. His life bridges two eras: one that spanned the last decades of his civilization, ending

The record of the Jaredites, taken from the twenty-four plates found by the people of Limhi in the days of King Mosiah.

CHAPTER 1

Moroni abridges the writings of Ether—Ether's genealogy is set forth—The language of the Jaredites is not confounded at the Tower of Babel—The Lord promises to lead them to a choice land and make them a great nation.

1 And now I, Moroni, proceed to give an account of those ancient inhabitants who were destroyed by the hand of the Lord upon the face of this north country.

2 And I take mine account from the twenty and four plates which were found by the people of Limhi, which is called the Book of Ether.

3 And as I suppose that the first part of this record, which speaks concerning the creation of the world, and also of Adam, and an account from that time even to the great tower, and whatsoever things transpired among the children of men until that time, is had among the Jews—

4 Therefore I do not write those things which transpired from the days of Adam until that time; but they are had upon the plates; and whoso findeth them, the same will have power that he may get the full account.

5 But behold, I give not the full account, but a part of the account I give, from the tower down until they were destroyed.

with its utter annihilation, and one in which the only civilizing influences were those of his enemies. . . .

"Although Moroni was raised in one of the most notable families of his era, it made little difference. It was the worst of times" (Brown, *Voices from the Dust*, 180).

Richard Dilworth Rust helps us understand how Moroni's difficult life shaped the abridgment of the book of Ether: "We get closer to the essence of the book of Ether by looking at its structure in the 1830 edition of the Book of Mormon. Originally it was made up of six chapters: 1 (chapters 1–4 in our current Book of Mormon), 2 (our chapter 5), 3 (chapters 6–8), 4 (chapters 9–11), 5 (chapter 12), and 6 (chapters 13–15). All but one of these chapters begin with 'And now I, Moroni,' and the fourth sentence of the remaining chapter (5) begins with 'And now I, Moroni'—emphasizing the central position of Moroni in the presentation and structure of the book of Ether" (Rust, *Feasting on the Word*, 238–239). ✦

Did Moroni translate his account from Ether's plates or did he rely on Mosiah's translation? (1:2)
"It is not absolutely clear in the Book of Mormon whether Moroni made his abridgment of the record of Ether from Mosiah's earlier translation (see Mosiah 28:1–20) or whether Moroni took his account directly from the plates of Ether—in which case he would have needed to translate the record as well as abridge it" (Ludlow, *Companion to Your Study of the Book of Mormon*, 308).

Where did the the first part of the Jaredite record regarding the creation come from? (1:3)
"Also among the ancient Jaredites was a record which had been 'brought across the great deep' from Mesopotamia by Jared and his people (8:9). It contained a creation account down to the time of 'the great tower' (1:3) and also set forth the 'secret plans' of evil men aimed at obtaining kingdoms and glory (8:9). None of this early scriptural information, however, is found in our book of Ether, for it was supposed by Moroni that it would be had among the Jews (1:3)" (Welch, "Preliminary Comments on the Sources behind the Book of Ether," 5).

Ether 1:6–32. Moroni Lists Ether's Genealogy

What can we learn from Ether's genealogy? (1:6–32)
"*Lineage* as used here means a group of people recognizing descent from a common progenitor and using that shared descent as the basis for their social identity....

"The record of the Jaredites is similar. Nothing makes that clearer than the genealogy we find in Ether 1:6–32. Some of the leaders listed were kings and some others claimants to the throne, but all of them were of the lineage of Jared. Jared's descendants carried the right to rule (Ether 6:22–25), as with Nephi's descendants—the ruling line—who kept the official account during the much later era" (Sorenson, *Ancient American Setting*, 50, 52). ✚

6 And on this wise do I give the account. He that wrote this record was Ether, and he was a descendant of Coriantor.

7 Coriantor was the son of Moron.

8 And Moron was the son of Ethem.

9 And Ethem was the son of Ahah.

10 And Ahah was the son of Seth.

11 And Seth was the son of Shiblon.

12 And Shiblon was the son of Com.

13 And Com was the son of Coriantum.

14 And Coriantum was the son of Amnigaddah.

15 And Amnigaddah was the son of Aaron.

16 And Aaron was a descendant of Heth, who was the son of Hearthom.

17 And Hearthom was the son of Lib.

18 And Lib was the son of Kish.

19 And Kish was the son of Corom.

The Book of Ether—A Second Witness

The book of Ether covers 1,500 years of history. One purpose of the book of Ether is to serve as a second witness, along with the Nephite record, that those who live in a land "choice above all other lands" (see 1 Nephi 2:20; Ether 1:38, 42) must either serve God or be destroyed (see Ether 2:8–11). (See Joseph Fielding McConkie and Robert L. Millet, *Doctrinal Commentary*, 4:259.) Consider the following comparison between the Jaredites and the people of Lehi:

Jaredites	Similarity	Lehites
Ether 1:38, 42	Both peoples were brought by the Lord to a promised land which was "choice above all other lands"	1 Nephi 2:20
Ether 3:13	Both groups were led by mighty prophets who saw the Lord	1 Nephi 1:8
Ether 6:27–28; 7:1	Both peoples experienced prosperity during times of righteousness	4 Nephi 1:2–23
Ether 3:9–19	Both testified of the reality of Jesus Christ	3 Nephi 11–28
Ether 7:20	Both experienced a major division of the people into two groups	2 Nephi 5:5–7
Ether 13:20–21	Both experienced great destruction because of wickedness	Mormon 6:17–18
Ether 13:22	Both destructions are survived by a lone prophet–record keeper who was rejected and hunted by his people	Mormon 8:3

(Garner, *Search These Things Diligently*, 307. Used by permission.)

20 And Corom was the son of Levi.

21 And Levi was the son of Kim.

22 And Kim was the son of Morianton.

23 And Morianton was a descendant of Riplakish.

24 And Riplakish was the son of Shez.

25 And Shez was the son of Heth.

26 And Heth was the son of Com.

27 And Com was the son of Coriantum.

28 And Coriantum was the son of Emer.

29 And Emer was the son of Omer.

30 And Omer was the son of Shule.

31 And Shule was the son of Kib.

32 And Kib was the son of Orihah, who was the son of Jared;

33 Which Jared came forth with his brother and their families, with some others and their families, from the great tower, at the time the Lord confounded the language of the people, and swore in his wrath that they should be scattered upon all the face of the earth; and according to the word of the Lord the people were scattered.

34 And the brother of Jared being a large and mighty man, and a man highly favored of the Lord, Jared, his brother, said unto him: Cry unto the Lord, that he will not confound us that we may not understand our words.

35 And it came to pass that the brother of Jared did cry unto the Lord, and the Lord had compassion upon Jared; therefore he

Ether 1:33–37. The Brother of Jared Asks the Lord Not to Change Their Language

What has this "great tower" in Babel come to symbolize? (1:33) "Under the direction of the Lord, the brother of Jared and his followers were separated from the confounding curse that fell upon the builders of Babel. From that day to ours, Babel, or Babylon, the ancient capital of Babylonia, has been a symbol of all that is corrupt and confused; specifically, it connotes the false religion of all schemes or denominations that promise an entrance into heaven which they cannot deliver" (Middleton, "Gatherings in the Last Days," 187).

What do we know about the brother of Jared? (1:34) The "life and legacy [of the brother of Jared] have become synonymous with bold, consummate, perfect faith" (Holland, *Christ and the New Covenant*, 14). "The book of Ether employs the phrase 'the brother of Jared' as a type for Jesus Christ. The exclusion of the name draws attention to the fact that Jared was not left alone, but had a very special brother who intervened in his and his family's behalf. . . .

"It should not be surprising that the brother of Jared could be a type of Jesus Christ, as all of God's prophets typify Jesus Christ ([see] McConkie, *Gospel Symbolism*, 146–72)" (Valletta, "Jared and His Brother," 307). ✪

What was the blessing of not having their language confounded? (1:35–37) "Jared and his brother made the request of the Lord that their language be not changed at the time of the confusion of tongues at the Tower of Babel. Their request was granted, and they carried with them the speech of their fathers, the Adamic language, which was powerful even in its written form, so that the things [the brother of Jared] wrote 'were mighty even unto the overpowering of man to read them.' That was the kind of language Adam had and this was the language with which Enoch was able to accomplish his mighty work" (Smith, *Way to Perfection*, 69).

Ether 1:38–43. The Brother of Jared Prays to Be Led to a Choice Land

What might be the intent behind the word "drive"? (1:38) "Jared's phrase, 'drive us out of the land,' is like the language used to describe Adam and Eve's being driven from the Garden of Eden (Ether 1:38; Gen. 3:24; Moses 4:31), as well as the expression Cain used when he was driven from 'the face of the Lord' (Moses 5:39; Gen. 4:14). . . . The Hebrew word used in these verses is *garash*, which means to 'drive out,' 'cast out,' 'separate,' 'divorce' or 'expel,' sometimes suggesting 'forcible or violent expulsion' (Harris 1:173)" (Valletta, "Jared and His Brother," 309).

did not confound the language of Jared; and Jared and his brother were not confounded.

36 Then Jared said unto his brother: Cry again unto the Lord, and it may be that he will turn away his anger from them who are our friends, that he confound not their language.

37 And it came to pass that the brother of Jared did cry unto the Lord, and the Lord had compassion upon their friends and their families also, that they were not confounded.

38 And it came to pass that Jared spake again unto his brother, saying: Go and inquire of the Lord whether he will drive us out of the land, and if he will drive us out of the land, cry unto him whither we shall go. And who knoweth but the Lord will carry us forth into a land which is choice above all the earth? And if it so be, let us be faithful unto the Lord, that we may receive it for our inheritance.

39 And it came to pass that the brother of Jared did cry unto the Lord according to that which had been spoken by the mouth of Jared.

40 And it came to pass that the Lord did hear the brother of Jared, and had compassion upon him, and said unto him:

41 Go to and gather together thy flocks, both male and female, of every kind; and also of the seed of the earth of every kind; and thy families; and also Jared thy brother and his family; and also thy friends and their families, and the friends of Jared and their families.

42 And when thou hast done this thou shalt go at the head of them down into the valley which is northward. And there will I meet thee, and I will go before thee into a land which is choice above all the lands of the earth.

43 And there will I bless thee and thy seed, and raise up unto me of thy seed, and of the seed of thy brother, and they who shall go with thee, a great nation. And there shall be none greater than the nation which I will raise up unto me of thy seed, upon all the face of the earth. And thus I will do unto thee because this long time ye have cried unto me.

CHAPTER 2

The Jaredites prepare for their journey to a promised land—It is a choice land whereon men must serve Christ or be swept off—The Lord talks to the brother of Jared for three hours—The Jaredites build barges—The Lord asks the brother of Jared to propose how the barges will be lighted.

1 And it came to pass that Jared and his brother, and their families, and also the friends of Jared and his brother and their families, went down into the valley which was northward, (and the name of the valley was Nimrod, being called after the mighty hunter) with their flocks which they had gathered together, male and female, of every kind.

2 And they did also lay snares and catch fowls of the air; and they did also prepare a vessel, in which they did carry with them the fish of the waters.

3 And they did also carry with them deseret, which, by interpretation, is a honey bee; and thus they did carry with them swarms of bees, and all manner of that which was upon the face of the land, seeds of every kind.

Ether 2:1–3. The Jaredites Prepare for Their Journey

What do we know about the name Nimrod? (2:1) "The name 'Nimrod' evoked strong feelings among the ancients and was usually associated with 'rebellion.' It may have carried more meaning than simply a name-title for a valley. Nimrod, who 'founded the kingdom of Babel,' had 'established false priesthood and false kingship in the earth in imitation of God's rule and 'made all men to sin' (Nibley, *Lehi in the Desert*, 165). He typified Satan" (Valletta, "Jared and His Brother," 310). ☉

What is the significance of the word *deseret* in the Book of Mormon? (2:3) "By all odds the most interesting and attractive passenger in Jared's company is *deseret*, the honeybee. . . . The word *deseret*, we are told (Ether 2:3), 'by interpretation is a honeybee,' the word plainly coming from the Jaredite language, since Ether (or Moroni) must interpret it. Now it is a remarkable coincidence that the word *deseret*, or something very close to it, enjoyed a position of ritual prominence among the founders of the classical Egyptian civilization, who associated it very closely with the symbol of the bee" ("Echoes and Evidences from Hugh Nibley," in *Echoes and Evidences in the Book of Mormon*, 462–63).

Ether 2:4–7. The Lord Directs the Jaredites to the Promised Land

What is the symbolism of "the wilderness"? (2:5)
"The idea of the people of God escaping into the wilderness is a common pattern. Adam and Eve are driven into a world of thorns and thistles (Moses 4:24). The Israelites wandered forty years in the wilderness. Even the Savior preceded his mission by going out into the wilderness to commune with God. . . . [One] scholar of antiquity has suggested that . . . 'The desert is the world one passes through. It is nothing in itself, it is barren and inhospitable. It is not meant for people to remain in. One travels through the wilderness as one travels through time. Just like time, so does the desert lead to a new world, to the promised land' (Weinreb, [*Roots of the Bible*,] 125)" (Valletta, "Jared and His Brother," 311). ⊕

Why did the Lord direct Jared's company to a "choice" and "preserved" land? (2:6–7) "God does not rejoice in the suffering of his children, and in his kindness has set aside places where those qualified to be happy could enjoy happiness even in this life: 'He leadeth away the righteous into precious lands' (1 Nephi 17:38), where 'the hand of providence' pours blessings upon them in almost embarrassing abundance (Jacob 2:13). Those who come to the land of promise come by invitation: 'There shall none come into this land save they shall be brought by the hand of the Lord' (2 Nephi 1:6). Hence they are expected to behave themselves" (Nibley, *Since Cumorah*, 391).

Ether 2:8–15. Jesus Will Protect Those Living in the Promised Land Who Serve Him

What can we learn from the warning given to the Jaredites in these verses? (2:8–12) "The Lord has reserved this land as the place for the restoration of his church. For this land to achieve its full potential, its citizens must remain rooted firmly in the principles that made it great. The enemies of God are attacking the core foundations of this land. The Lord's law for this land is declared in the Book of Mormon, where we read that this land is a 'land of promise' that ' . . . whatsoever nation shall possess it shall serve God, or they shall be swept off.' The only power strong enough

4 And it came to pass that when they had come down into the valley of Nimrod the Lord came down and talked with the brother of Jared; and he was in a cloud, and the brother of Jared saw him not.

5 And it came to pass that the Lord commanded them that they should go forth into the wilderness, yea, into that quarter where there never had man been. And it came to pass that the Lord did go before them, and did talk with them as he stood in a cloud, and gave directions whither they should travel.

6 And it came to pass that they did travel in the wilderness, and did build barges, in which they did cross many waters, being directed continually by the hand of the Lord.

7 And the Lord would not suffer that they should stop beyond the sea in the wilderness, but he would that they should come forth even unto the land of promise, which was choice above all other lands, which the Lord God had preserved for a righteous people.

8 And he had sworn in his wrath unto the brother of Jared, that whoso should possess this land of promise, from that time henceforth and forever, should serve him, the true and only God, or they should be swept off when the fulness of his wrath should come upon them.

9 And now, we can behold the decrees of God concerning this land, that it is a land of

promise; and whatsoever nation shall possess it shall serve God, or they shall be swept off when the fulness of his wrath shall come upon them. And the fulness of his wrath cometh upon them when they are ripened in iniquity.

10 For behold, this is a land which is choice above all other lands; wherefore he that doth possess it shall serve God or shall be swept off; for it is the everlasting decree of God. And it is not until the fulness of iniquity among the children of the land, that they are swept off.

11 And this cometh unto you, O ye Gentiles, that ye may know the decrees of God—that ye may repent, and not continue in your iniquities until the fulness come, that ye may not bring down the fulness of the wrath of God upon you as the inhabitants of the land have hitherto done.

12 Behold, this is a choice land, and whatsoever nation shall possess it shall be free from bondage, and from captivity, and from all other nations under heaven, if they will but serve the God of the land, who is Jesus Christ, who hath been manifested by the things which we have written.

13 And now I proceed with my record; for behold, it came to pass that the Lord did bring Jared and his brethren forth even to that great sea which divideth the lands. And as they came to the sea they pitched their tents; and they called the name of the place Moriancumer; and they dwelt in tents, and dwelt in tents upon the seashore for the space of four years.

14 And it came to pass at the end of four years that the Lord came again unto the brother of Jared, and stood in a cloud and talked with him. And for the space of three hours did the Lord talk with the brother of Jared, and chastened him because he remembered not to call upon the name of the Lord.

to withstand a fulness of iniquity is the fulness of the gospel of Jesus Christ" (Wirthlin, "Deep Roots," 77).

What is the significance of the name Moriancumer? (2:13) "The Lord finally brought Jared and his brethren safely to the shores of the 'great sea which divideth the lands' (2:13). Here they pitched their tents and named the place 'Moriancumer.' Inasmuch as it was quite customary in ancient times—even now at times for that matter—to name a place after the name of the most prominent individual who helped settle it, we may rightly guess that the name of the brother of Jared was Moriancumer" (Sperry, Book of Mormon Compendium, 456).

What can we learn from the brother of Jared's experience with prayer? (2:14–15) "In the dispersion from the Tower of Babel, the people of Jared arrived at 'that great sea which divideth the lands,' where they pitched their tents, awaiting further revelation about crossing the mighty ocean. For four years they awaited divine direction, but apparently they waited too casually, without supplication and exertion. Then came this remarkable encounter. . . .

"It is difficult to imagine what a three-hour rebuke from the Lord might be like, but the brother of Jared endured it. With immediate repentance and prayer, this prophet again sought guidance for the journey they had been assigned and those who were to pursue it. God accepted his repentance and lovingly gave further direction for their crucial mission" (Holland, *Christ and the New Covenant*, 14–15). ●

Ether 2:16–25. The Jaredites Build according to the Instructions of the Lord

What is meant by the phrase "tight like unto a dish"? (2:16–17) For their long sea voyage the Lord instructed the brother of Jared to build watertight "seaworthy crafts . . . small, light, dish-shaped vessels identical in design above and beneath so they were capable of staying afloat even if overturned by the waves. These 'exceedingly tight' crafts were obviously of unprecedented design and capability, made under the direction of him who rules the seas and the winds" (Holland, *Christ and the New Covenant*, 15).

How can you liken this situation experienced by the brother of Jared to yourself? (2:18–23) "Like the brother of Jared, each of us faces challenges in life. At times we may plead with the Lord: 'Will ye have me go through this life without light to understand why things are the way they are?' His answer to us might be the same question He asked the brother of Jared: 'What would ye that I should do to put light into your spiritual vessels?'" (Garrett, "Light in Our Vessels," 81).

Why do you think the Lord often insists that we figure things out on our own? ●

15 And the brother of Jared repented of the evil which he had done, and did call upon the name of the Lord for his brethren who were with him. And the Lord said unto him: I will forgive thee and thy brethren of their sins; but thou shalt not sin any more, for ye shall remember that my Spirit will not always strive with man; wherefore, if ye will sin until ye are fully ripe ye shall be cut off from the presence of the Lord. And these are my thoughts upon the land which I shall give you for your inheritance; for it shall be a land choice above all other lands.

16 And the Lord said: Go to work and build, after the manner of barges which ye have hitherto built. And it came to pass that the brother of Jared did go to work, and also his brethren, and built barges after the manner which they had built, according to the instructions of the Lord. And they were small, and they were light upon the water, even like unto the lightness of a fowl upon the water.

17 And they were built after a manner that they were exceedingly tight, even that they would hold water like unto a dish; and the bottom thereof was tight like unto a dish; and the sides thereof were tight like unto a dish; and the ends thereof were peaked; and the top thereof was tight like unto a dish; and the length thereof was the length of a tree; and the door thereof, when it was shut, was tight like unto a dish.

18 And it came to pass that the brother of Jared cried unto the Lord, saying: O Lord, I have performed the work which thou hast commanded me, and I have made the barges according as thou hast directed me.

19 And behold, O Lord, in them there is no light; whither shall we steer? And also we shall perish, for in them we cannot breathe, save it is the air which is in them; therefore we shall perish.

20 And the Lord said unto the brother of Jared: Behold, thou shalt make a hole in the top, and also in the bottom; and when thou shalt suffer for air thou shalt unstop the hole and receive air. And if it be so that the water come in upon thee, behold, ye shall stop the hole, that ye may not perish in the flood.

21 And it came to pass that the brother of Jared did so, according as the Lord had commanded.

22 And he cried again unto the Lord saying: O Lord, behold I have done even as thou hast commanded me; and I have prepared the vessels for my people, and behold there is no light in them. Behold, O Lord, wilt thou suffer that we shall cross this great water in darkness?

23 And the Lord said unto the brother of Jared: What will ye that I should do that ye may have light in your vessels? For behold, ye cannot have windows, for they will be dashed in pieces; neither shall ye take fire with you, for ye shall not go by the light of fire.

24 For behold, ye shall be as a whale in the midst of the sea; for the mountain waves shall dash upon you. Nevertheless, I will bring you up again out of the depths of the sea; for the winds have gone forth out of my mouth, and also the rains and the floods have I sent forth.

25 And behold, I prepare you against these things; for ye cannot cross this great deep save I prepare you against the waves of the sea, and the winds which have gone forth, and the floods which shall come. Therefore what will ye that I should prepare for you that ye may have light when ye are swallowed up in the depths of the sea?

What do we learn from the question asked by the Lord in this verse? (2:25) Maybe what the Lord was asking was, "What will ye do, Mahonri?" Speaking of this event, President Harold B. Lee taught: "This is the principle in action. If you want the blessing, don't just kneel down and pray about it. Prepare yourself in every conceivable way you can in order to make yourselves worthy to receive the blessing you seek" (*Teachings of Harold B. Lee*, 129). ☉

CHAPTER 3

The brother of Jared sees the finger of the Lord as He touches sixteen stones—Christ shows His spirit body to the brother of Jared—Those who have a perfect knowledge cannot be kept from within the veil—Interpreters are provided to bring the Jaredite record to light.

Ether 3:1–5. The Brother of Jared Asks the Lord to Touch Sixteen Stones

What were the stones that shone and gave light? (3:1) "The Jaredites begin their journey by placing stones that have been blessed by the Lord's touch in their ships so that they might have light.... Of course, the Lord could have provided light for the travelers by many other methods, but He used the stones the brother of Jared brought to Him. These stones may serve to remind those in the barges, and us as well, that all light comes from the Savior, that He is the rock of our salvation (see Psalm 89:26; 2 Nephi 4:30)" (Swift, "The Literary Power of the Book of Mormon," in *Living the Book of Mormon*, 80). ✪

What is meant by "our natures [are] evil continually"? (3:2) "We all have inherited Adam and Eve's fallen nature, which includes the ability and the propensity to sin....

"Conception, which clothes us in the flesh, is the mechanism of transmission, the means by which Adam and Eve's fallen nature (both physical and spiritual death) is transferred from generation to generation. The propensity for and susceptibility to sin are implanted in our nature at conception, just as death is" (Millet, *Power of the Word*, 73). ✪

Is there any precedence for inviting the Lord to touch stones with His finger? (3:4) "There are fascinating rabbinic legends to the effect that Noah enjoyed light in the ark because he carried with him divinely given shining stones. If such stones are true,

1 And it came to pass that the brother of Jared, (now the number of the vessels which had been prepared was eight) went forth unto the mount, which they called the mount Shelem, because of its exceeding height, and did molten out of a rock sixteen small stones; and they were white and clear, even as transparent glass; and he did carry them in his hands upon the top of the mount, and cried again unto the Lord, saying:

2 O Lord, thou hast said that we must be encompassed about by the floods. Now behold, O Lord, and do not be angry with thy servant because of his weakness before thee; for we know that thou art holy and dwellest in the heavens, and that we are unworthy before thee; because of the fall our natures have become evil continually; nevertheless, O Lord, thou hast given us a commandment that we must call upon thee, that from thee we may receive according to our desires.

3 Behold, O Lord, thou hast smitten us because of our iniquity, and hast driven us forth, and for these many years we have been in the wilderness; nevertheless, thou hast been merciful unto us. O Lord, look upon me in pity, and turn away thine anger from this thy people, and suffer not that they shall go forth across this raging deep in darkness; but behold these things which I have molten out of the rock.

4 And I know, O Lord, that thou hast all power, and can do whatsoever thou wilt for the benefit of man; therefore touch these stones, O Lord, with thy finger, and prepare

them that they may shine forth in darkness; and they shall shine forth unto us in the vessels which we have prepared, that we may have light while we shall cross the sea.

5 Behold, O Lord, thou canst do this. We know that thou art able to show forth great power, which looks small unto the understanding of men.

6 And it came to pass that when the brother of Jared had said these words, behold, the Lord stretched forth his hand and touched the stones one by one with his finger. And the veil was taken from off the eyes of the brother of Jared, and he saw the finger of the Lord; and it was as the finger of a man, like unto flesh and blood; and the brother of Jared fell down before the Lord, for he was struck with fear.

7 And the Lord saw that the brother of Jared had fallen to the earth; and the Lord said unto him: Arise, why hast thou fallen?

8 And he saith unto the Lord: I saw the finger of the Lord, and I feared lest he should smite me; for I knew not that the Lord had flesh and blood.

9 And the Lord said unto him: Because of thy faith thou hast seen that I shall take upon me flesh and blood; and never has man come before me with such exceeding faith as thou hast; for were it not so ye could not have seen my finger. Sawest thou more than this?

10 And he answered: Nay; Lord, show thyself unto me.

11 And the Lord said unto him: Believest thou the words which I shall speak?

then the brother of Jared was acting in harmony with the deeds of a prophet who was less than a century and a half removed from him" (McConkie et al., *Doctrinal Commentary*, 4:273).

Footnote a. to Genesis 6:16 in the Latter-day Saint edition of the Bible states: "HEB *tsohar;* some rabbis believed it was a precious stone that shone in the ark. Ether 2:23 (23–24)." ◉

Ether 3:6–16. The Brother of Jared Sees the Spirit Body of Jesus Christ

What significant doctrine is contained in the brother of Jared's experience of seeing the Lord's finger? (3:6–8) "Among the fundamental doctrinal truths contained in [this] passage, we find that a spirit has the appearance of flesh and blood even though it is spirit material. We know from Doctrine and Covenants 129 that if the brother of Jared had tried to touch the finger of the Lord he could not have felt it, since mortals cannot physically feel a spirit body" (Matthews, "Mission of Jesus Christ," 23; see also D&C 88:68).

How was the brother of Jared's faith unique? (3:9–13) "As a rule, prophets are *invited* into the presence of the Lord, are bidden to enter his presence by him and only with his sanction. The brother of Jared, on the other hand, seems to have thrust himself through the veil, not as an unwelcome guest but perhaps technically as an uninvited one. . . . Obviously the Lord himself was linking unprecedented faith with this unprecedented vision. If the vision itself was not unique, then it had to be the faith and how the vision was obtained that was so unparalleled. The only way that faith could be so remarkable was its ability to take the prophet, uninvited, where others had been able to go only with God's bidding" (Holland, *Christ and the New Covenant*, 23). ◉

What does the Lord's question to the brother of Jared suggest about the doctrine of faith? (3:11) "Preparatory faith is formed by experiences in the past—by the known, which provides a basis for belief. But redemptive faith must often be exercised toward experiences in the future—the unknown, which provides an opportunity for the miraculous. Exacting faith, mountain-moving faith, faith like that of the brother of Jared, *precedes* the miracle and the knowledge. . . . Faith is to agree unconditionally—and in advance—to whatever conditions God may require in both the near and distant future" (Holland, *Christ and the New Covenant*, 18–19).

How does the brother of Jared's redemption show the power of the Atonement? (3:13) "[Ether 3:13] underscores the eternal nature of the Atonement, its impact reaching out to all who lived before the Savior's birth as well as all who lived after it. All those in Old Testament times who were baptized in Christ's name had the same claim upon eternal life that the brother of Jared had, even though Christ had not yet even been born" (Holland, *Christ and the New Covenant*, 27).

In the 1981 edition of the Book of Mormon the word *light* in verse 14 was changed to *life*. Why? (3:14) "During the preparation of the 1981 edition, it was brought to the attention of the Brethren that even though all printed editions of the Book of Mormon to this time had read *light*, the printer's manuscript, from which the type was set for the first edition of the Book of Mormon, clearly said *life*. The Scriptures Publications Committee . . . unanimously agreed that . . . since the manuscript read *life*, the correction should be made. An examination of the context also justifies this correction, for they who believe will become the sons and daughters of Christ. They are thus spiritually begotten by him and are given eternal life" (Matthews, "Mission of Jesus Christ," 25).

What does the Savior showing His body to the brother of Jared teach us about the spirit and the body? (3:15–16) The 1909 First Presidency statement titled "The Origin of Man" states the following: "'God created man in His own image.' This is just as true of the spirit as it is of the body, which is only the clothing of the spirit, its complement; the two together constituting the soul. The spirit of man is in the form of man, and the spirits of all creatures are in the likeness of their bodies" ("Origin of Man," 29).

12 And he answered: Yea, Lord, I know that thou speakest the truth, for thou art a God of truth, and canst not lie.

13 And when he had said these words, behold, the Lord showed himself unto him, and said: Because thou knowest these things ye are redeemed from the fall; therefore ye are brought back into my presence; therefore I show myself unto you.

14 Behold, I am he who was prepared from the foundation of the world to redeem my people. Behold, I am Jesus Christ. I am the Father and the Son. In me shall all mankind have life, and that eternally, even they who shall believe on my name; and they shall become my sons and my daughters.

15 And never have I showed myself unto man whom I have created, for never has man believed in me as thou hast. Seest thou that ye are created after mine own image? Yea, even all men were created in the beginning after mine own image.

16 Behold, this body, which ye now behold, is the body of my spirit; and man have I created after the body of my spirit; and even as I appear unto thee to be in the spirit will I appear unto my people in the flesh.

17 And now, as I, Moroni, said I could not make a full account of these things which are written, therefore it sufficeth me to say that Jesus showed himself unto this man in the spirit, even after the manner and in the likeness of the same body even as he showed himself unto the Nephites.

18 And he ministered unto him even as he ministered unto the Nephites; and all this, that this man might know that he was God, because of the many great works which the Lord had showed unto him.

19 And because of the knowledge of this man he could not be kept from beholding within the veil; and he saw the finger of Jesus, which, when he saw, he fell with fear; for he knew that it was the finger of the Lord; and he had faith no longer, for he knew, nothing doubting.

20 Wherefore, having this perfect knowledge of God, he could not be kept from within the veil; therefore he saw Jesus; and he did minister unto him.

21 And it came to pass that the Lord said unto the brother of Jared: Behold, thou shalt not suffer these things which ye have seen and heard to go forth unto the world, until the time cometh that I shall glorify my name in the flesh; wherefore, ye shall treasure up the things which ye have seen and heard, and show it to no man.

Ether 3:17–20. Moroni Explains Why the Brother of Jared Could See Jesus Christ

Why did Moroni frequently insert his name into the text? (3:17) "Moroni is usually careful about marking the beginning and ending of the comments that he has inserted into the abridged record. For example, his comments in Ether 3:17–20; 4:1–6:1; 8:18–26; and 12:6–13:1 are readily distinguishable from the abridged portions in the book of Ether. His frequent use of the phrase 'I, Moroni' in Ether 1:1; 3:17; 5:1; 6:1; 8:20; 8:26; 9:1; 12:6; 12:29; 12:38; and 13:1 makes it easy to tell what Moroni has written and what he has abridged" (Keller, "Mormon and Moroni as Authors and Abridgers," 270).

In what way can faith be replaced by knowledge? (3:19) Elder Bruce R. McConkie observed: "In the eternal sense, because faith is the power of God himself, it embraces within its fold a knowledge of all things. This measure of faith, the faith by which the worlds are and were created and which sustains and upholds all things, is found only among resurrected persons. It is the faith of saved beings. But mortals are in process, through faith, of gaining eternal salvation. Their faith is based on a knowledge of the truth, within the meaning of Alma's statement that 'faith is not to have a perfect knowledge of things,' but that men have faith when they 'hope for things which are not seen, which are true.' In this sense faith is both preceded and supplanted by knowledge, and when any person gains a perfect knowledge on any given matter, then, as pertaining to that thing, he has faith no longer; or, rather, his faith is dormant; it has been supplanted by pure knowledge (see Alma 32:21–34). . . . The brother of Jared stands out as a good illustration of how the knowledge of God is gained by faith, and also of how that perfect knowledge, from a mortal perspective, replaces faith" (New Witness, 209–11; see also McConkie et al., Doctrinal Commentary, 4:278–79).

Ether 3:21–28. The Lord Shows the Brother of Jared All Things

What were these "two stones"? (3:23) The two stones mentioned here have been identified as "Urim and Thummim" (D&C 17:1). "The Hebrew plural nouns *urim* and *thummim* mean 'lights' and 'perfections.' . . . The Urim and Thummim is an instrument used to receive revelation" (Millet, et al., *LDS Beliefs*, 647).

How was the brother of Jared able to see "all the inhabitants of the earth"? (3:25) "When Moriancumer had received the Urim and Thummim, the Lord opened his vision, . . . and he was shown the human race, past and future, passing as if in a panorama.

"Enoch had a similar view of *many generations* upon Mt. Simeon [Moses 7:2–6, 22–69]. Abraham, who received a second Urim and Thummim while he was in Ur of the Chaldees, had marvelous visions and revelations concerning the Creation of the Universe, and the intelligences that were organized *before the world was* [Abraham 3:1–28]. . . . Moses, too, who may have been the possessor of the same Urim and Thummim that had first been given to Abraham, had similar visions [Moses 1:1–7]" (Reynolds and Sjodahl, *Commentary on the Book of Mormon*, 6:87–88).

Why could nothing be withheld from the brother of Jared? (3:26) "After the prophet stepped through the veil to behold the Savior of the world, he was not limited in seeing the rest of what the eternal world revealed. . . . The staying power and source of privilege for such an extraordinary experience was once again the faith of the brother of Jared, for '*the Lord could not withhold anything from him,* for he knew that the Lord could show him all things'" (Holland, *Christ and the New Covenant*, 27).

What does the brother of Jared's sacred experience mean for you? (3:27–28) "What is the value to us in knowing of these things that happened so long ago? I cannot speak for others, but when I read of the experiences of the brother of Jared there wells up within me a desire to have faith like he had and my testimony and love for the Lord increase. My soul 'hungers' and wants to feast upon the same kind of spiritual food that the brother of Jared ate. Reading the brief account . . . is an appetizer which arouses a desire to someday have such an experience myself" (Matthews, "Mission of Jesus Christ," 28).

22 And behold, when ye shall come unto me, ye shall write them and shall seal them up, that no one can interpret them; for ye shall write them in a language that they cannot be read.

23 And behold, these two stones will I give unto thee, and ye shall seal them up also with the things which ye shall write.

24 For behold, the language which ye shall write I have confounded; wherefore I will cause in my own due time that these stones shall magnify to the eyes of men these things which ye shall write.

25 And when the Lord had said these words, he showed unto the brother of Jared all the inhabitants of the earth which had been, and also all that would be; and he withheld them not from his sight, even unto the ends of the earth.

26 For he had said unto him in times before, that if he would believe in him that he could show unto him all things—it should be shown unto him; therefore the Lord could not withhold anything from him, for he knew that the Lord could show him all things.

27 And the Lord said unto him: Write these things and seal them up; and I will show them in mine own due time unto the children of men.

28 And it came to pass that the Lord commanded him that he should seal up the two stones which he had received, and show them not, until the Lord should show them unto the children of men.

CHAPTER 4

Moroni is commanded to seal up the writings of the brother of Jared—They will not be revealed until men have faith even as the brother of Jared—Christ commands men to believe His words and those of His disciples—Men are commanded to repent, believe the gospel, and be saved.

1 And the Lord commanded the brother of Jared to go down out of the mount from the presence of the Lord, and write the things which he had seen; and they were forbidden to come unto the children of men until after that he should be lifted up upon the cross; and for this cause did king Mosiah keep them, that they should not come unto the world until after Christ should show himself unto his people.

2 And after Christ truly had showed himself unto his people he commanded that they should be made manifest.

3 And now, after that, they have all dwindled in unbelief; and there is none save it be the Lamanites, and they have rejected the gospel of Christ; therefore I am commanded that I should hide them up again in the earth.

4 Behold, I have written upon these plates the very things which the brother of Jared saw; and there never were greater things made manifest than those which were made manifest unto the brother of Jared.

5 Wherefore the Lord hath commanded me to write them; and I have written them. And he commanded me that I should seal them up; and he also hath commanded that I should seal up the interpretation thereof; wherefore I have sealed up the interpreters, according to the commandment of the Lord.

6 For the Lord said unto me: They shall not go forth unto the Gentiles until the day that they shall repent of their iniquity, and become clean before the Lord.

Ether 4:1–7. Moroni Is Commanded to Seal Up the Record of the Brother of Jared

When did the Lord say the sealed plates will be revealed? (4:4–6) Moroni wrote that "there never were greater things made manifest" than what was shown Jared's brother (see also 2 Nephi 27:10). What were they? "When, during the Millennium, the sealed portion of the Book of Mormon is translated, it will give an account of life in the premortal existence; of the creation of all things; of the fall and the Atonement and the Second Coming; of temple ordinances, in their fulness; of the ministry and mission of translated beings; of life in the spirit world, in both paradise and hell; of the kingdoms of glory to be inhabited by resurrected beings; and many such like things" (McConkie, *Doctrines of the Restoration*, 277).

How can we qualify ourselves to receive the sealed portion of the Book of Mormon? (4:6–7) "Our faith is on trial. The indications point to the fact that our faith is weak, and therefore we are not prepared to receive these greater revelations [the sealed portion] which will come forth when men are sufficiently humbled, prayerful, obedient, and filled with faith, such as the brother of Jared had. Then they will be revealed in that day when the people are willing to accept *all* the words of the Lord without doubts and mental reservations" (Smith, *Way to Perfection*," 339). ⊕

Who will see what the brother of Jared saw? (4:7)
Elder Bruce R. McConkie testified: "Revelations are not reserved for a limited few or for those called to positions of importance in the Church. . . . Rather it is personal righteousness; it is keeping the commandments; it is seeking the Lord while he may be found.

"God is no respecter of persons. He will give revelation to me and to you on the same terms and conditions. . . . I can entertain angels and see God, I can receive an outpouring of the gifts of the Spirit—and so can you" (quoted in Ludlow, *Companion to Your Study of the Doctrine and Covenants*, 1:4).

Ether 4:8–19. Jesus Christ Commands All People to Repent, Come unto Him, and Be Saved

7 And in that day that they shall exercise faith in me, saith the Lord, even as the brother of Jared did, that they may become sanctified in me, then will I manifest unto them the things which the brother of Jared saw, even to the unfolding unto them all my revelations, saith Jesus Christ, the Son of God, the Father of the heavens and of the earth, and all things that in them are.

8 And he that will contend against the word of the Lord, let him be accursed; and he that shall deny these things, let him be accursed; for unto them will I show no greater things, saith Jesus Christ; for I am he who speaketh.

9 And at my command the heavens are opened and are shut; and at my word the earth shall shake; and at my command the inhabitants thereof shall pass away, even so as by fire.

10 And he that believeth not my words believeth not my disciples; and if it so be that I do not speak, judge ye; for ye shall know that it is I that speaketh, at the last day.

11 But he that believeth these things which I have spoken, him will I visit with the manifestations of my Spirit, and he shall know and bear record. For because of my Spirit he shall know that these things are true; for it persuadeth men to do good.

12 And whatsoever thing persuadeth men to do good is of me; for good cometh of none save it be of me. I am the same that leadeth men to all good; he that will not believe my words will not believe me—that I am; and he that will not believe me will not believe

the Father who sent me. For behold, I am the Father, I am the light, and the life, and the truth of the world.

13 Come unto me, O ye Gentiles, and I will show unto you the greater things, the knowledge which is hid up because of unbelief.

14 Come unto me, O ye house of Israel, and it shall be made manifest unto you how great things the Father hath laid up for you, from the foundation of the world; and it hath not come unto you, because of unbelief.

15 Behold, when ye shall rend that veil of unbelief which doth cause you to remain in your awful state of wickedness, and hardness of heart, and blindness of mind, then shall the great and marvelous things which have been hid up from the foundation of the world from you—yea, when ye shall call upon the Father in my name, with a broken heart and a contrite spirit, then shall ye know that the Father hath remembered the covenant which he made unto your fathers, O house of Israel.

16 And then shall my revelations which I have caused to be written by my servant John be unfolded in the eyes of all the people. Remember, when ye see these things, ye shall know that the time is at hand that they shall be made manifest in very deed.

17 Therefore, when ye shall receive this record ye may know that the work of the Father has commenced upon all the face of the land.

18 Therefore, repent all ye ends of the earth, and come unto me, and believe in my gospel, and be baptized in my name; for he that believeth and is baptized shall be saved; but he that believeth not shall be damned; and signs shall follow them that believe in my name.

19 And blessed is he that is found faithful unto my name at the last day, for he shall be lifted up to dwell in the kingdom prepared for him from the foundation of the world. And behold it is I that hath spoken it. Amen.

What does it mean to "rend [the] veil of unbelief"? (4:13–15) The Book of Mormon is predicated on the willingness of men and women to 'rend that veil of unbelief' in order to behold the revelations—and the Revelation—of God. The brother of Jared may not have had great belief in himself, but his belief in God was unprecedented. In that there is hope for us all. His faith was without doubt or limit. . . .

"Once and for all it was declared that ordinary people with ordinary challenges could rend the veil of unbelief and enter the realms of eternity" (Holland, *Christ and the New Covenant*, 29).

What shall be revealed as "the work of the Father commences?" (4:16–17) "For the Lord is nigh at hand and not afar off. He has commenced the great work of restitution, and will roll it on to its consummation. He will restore every power and every gift and grace, every key, revelation and inspiration that has ever been enjoyed by the ancient Saints. Is that all? No, my brethren and sisters, it is not all; for after God has restored everything that has been lost, He will, in this dispensation, reveal things kept hidden from the foundations of the world. He will reveal them 'to babes and sucklings,' to the children born in Zion who are heirs to the holy priesthood, trained up in the way they should go, not trained up as some of our children are, but in the way God has appointed" (Penrose, "The Work of Restoration of All Things," 20:297). ◉

What is the "work of the Father" and how will it be fulfilled? (4:17) "The process of gathering is one in which the scattered remnants of Jacob—those of all tribes—believe the Book of Mormon, accept the restored gospel, and come to the latter-day Zion. . . . This gathering will be one person here, and two there, and a few somewhere else—all by the power of a book, the stick of Joseph joined with the stick of Judah" (McConkie, *New Witness*, 457).

Ether 5:1–6. Three Witnesses Will Testify of the Book of Mormon Plates

What is in the sealed portion? (5:1) Elder Jeffrey R. Holland has written: "After [the brother of Jared] stepped through the veil to behold the Savior of the world, he was not limited in seeing the rest of what the eternal world revealed....

"This vision . . . was similar to that given Moses and others of the prophets (see Moses 1:27–29). In this case, however, it was written down in great detail and then sealed up.... Of this vision given to the brother of Jared, Moroni wrote, 'There never was greater things made manifest than those which were made manifest unto the brother of Jared' (Ether 4:4).

"Those sealed plates constitute the sealed protion of the Book of Mormon which Joseph Smith did not translate" (*A Book of Mormon Treasury*, 62–63). ◉

Why is the testimony of the Three Witnesses such a crucial part of the Restoration? (5:2–3) The "testimony of the Three Witnesses . . . stands forth in great strength. Each of the three had ample reason and opportunity to renounce his testimony if it had been false, or to equivocate on details if any had been inaccurate.... Each one of these three witnesses was excommunicated from The Church of Jesus Christ of Latter-day Saints by about eight years after the publication of their testimony. All three went their separate ways, with no common interest to support a collusive effort. Yet to the end of their lives—periods ranging from 12 to 50 years after their excommunications—not one of these witnesses deviated from his published testimony" (Oaks, "The Witness: Martin Harris," 36).

CHAPTER 5

Three witnesses and the work itself will stand as a testimony of the truthfulness of the Book of Mormon.

1 And now I, Moroni, have written the words which were commanded me, according to my memory; and I have told you the things which I have sealed up; therefore touch them not in order that ye may translate; for that thing is forbidden you, except by and by it shall be wisdom in God.

2 And behold, ye may be privileged that ye may show the plates unto those who shall assist to bring forth this work;

3 And unto three shall they be shown by the power of God; wherefore they shall know of a surety that these things are true.

"Unto Three Shall They Be Shown" (Ether 5:3)

"[One] morning, after attending to the usual services, namely, reading, singing and praying, Joseph arose from his knees, and approaching Martin Harris with a solemnity that thrills through my veins to this day, when it occurs to my recollection, said, 'Martin Harris, you have got to humble yourself before God this day, that you may obtain a forgiveness of your sins. If you do, it is the will of God that you should look upon the plates, in company with Oliver Cowdery and David Whitmer.'

"In a few minutes after this, Joseph, Martin, Oliver and David, repaired to a grove, a short distance from the house, where they commenced calling upon the Lord, and continued in earnest supplication, until he permitted an angel to come down from his presence, and declare to them, that all which Joseph had testified of concerning the plates was true.

"When they returned to the house it was between three and four o'clock P.M. Mrs. Whitmer, Mr. Smith and myself, were sitting in a bedroom at the time. On coming in, Joseph threw himself down beside me, and exclaimed, 'Father,

4 And in the mouth of three witnesses shall these things be established; and the testimony of three, and this work, in the which shall be shown forth the power of God and also his word, of which the Father, and the Son, and the Holy Ghost bear record—and all this shall stand as a testimony against the world at the last day.

5 And if it so be that they repent and come unto the Father in the name of Jesus, they shall be received into the kingdom of God.

6 And now, if I have no authority for these things, judge ye; for ye shall know that I have authority when ye shall see me, and we shall stand before God at the last day. Amen.

CHAPTER 6

The Jaredite barges are driven by the winds to the promised land—The people praise the Lord for His goodness—Orihah is appointed king over them—Jared and his brother die.

1 And now I, Moroni, proceed to give the record of Jared and his brother.

2 For it came to pass after the Lord had prepared the stones which the brother of Jared had carried up into the mount, the brother of Jared came down out of the mount, and he did put forth the stones into the vessels which were prepared, one in each end thereof; and behold, they did give light unto the vessels.

Who are other witnesses to the Book of Mormon?
(5:4) "Traditionally, we think of the three witnesses to the Book of Mormon as Oliver Cowdery, Martin Harris, and David Whitmer. . . . However, there are additional sets of three witnesses to this sacred record. Moroni declared that the 'Father, and the Son, and the Holy Ghost bear record' (Ether 5:4). Also, three branches of the House of Israel, the Jews, the Nephites, and the lost tribes, each kept a record, and each branch will eventually receive the others' records (2 Nephi 29:12–14). These three branches of the House of Israel will also become a set of three witnesses in the latter-days" (Donaldson, "Plates of Ether and the Covenant of the Book of Mormon," 74).

Ether 6:1–12. The Jaredites Cross the Sea and Arrive in the Promised Land

What might the Jaredites' journey in barges typify?
(6:2–6) "Essentially every event or person in the Book of Mormon may well remind us of another event or person; the book is like a beautifully composed symphony with repeated themes and motifs. . . . Directed or lighted by objects requiring faith for their operation, Nephi's ship and the Jaredite barges are connected with Noah's ark in being types of rebirth and

mother, you do not know how happy I am: the Lord has now caused the plates to be shown to three more besides myself. They have seen an angel, who has testified to them, and they will have to bear witness to the truth of what I have said, for now they know for themselves, that I do not go about to deceive the people, and I feel as if I was relieved of a burden which was almost too heavy for me to bear, and it rejoices my soul, that I am not any longer to be entirely alone in the world.' Upon this, Martin Harris came in: he seemed almost overcome with joy, and testified boldly to what he had both seen and heard. And so did David and Oliver, adding that no tongue could express the joy of their hearts, and the greatness of the things which they had both seen and heard" (Smith, *History of Joseph Smith by His Mother*, 151–53).

How do you bear witness of the truthfulness of the Book of Mormon? In what ways can you testify of the Book of Mormon?

baptism (1 Peter 3:20–21); further, the Jaredite vessels 'were tight like unto the ark of Noah' (Ether 6:7). They all bring the occupants through the water into a new life, representing in the process the death, burial, and resurrection of Christ (Colossians 2:12)" (Rust, *Feasting on the Word*, 196–206). ◐

How can we be protected from the storms of life like the Jaredites? (6:7) "In our time there are vessels that protect against these terrible spiritual tempests, and they are our temples, homes, quorums, wards, and stakes" (Faust, "We Believe in You!" 6).

How was the "furious wind" mentioned in verse 5 a blessing to the Jaredites? (6:8) Sister Ardeth Kapp observed: "Note that it [the furious wind] never did cease to blow *towards the promised land* (Ether 6:8; emphasis added). They were driven forth before the wind toward their goal. Once they understood the purpose for the wind and knowing that their vessels were tight, we read further, 'And they did sing praises unto the Lord'" (*Rejoice! His Promises Are Sure*, 69). ◐

3 And thus the Lord caused stones to shine in darkness, to give light unto men, women, and children, that they might not cross the great waters in darkness.

4 And it came to pass that when they had prepared all manner of food, that thereby they might subsist upon the water, and also food for their flocks and herds, and whatsoever beast or animal or fowl that they should carry with them—and it came to pass that when they had done all these things they got aboard of their vessels or barges, and set forth into the sea, commending themselves unto the Lord their God.

5 And it came to pass that the Lord God caused that there should be a furious wind blow upon the face of the waters, towards the promised land; and thus they were tossed upon the waves of the sea before the wind.

6 And it came to pass that they were many times buried in the depths of the sea, because of the mountain waves which broke upon them, and also the great and terrible tempests which were caused by the fierceness of the wind.

7 And it came to pass that when they were buried in the deep there was no water that could hurt them, their vessels being tight like unto a dish, and also they were tight like unto the ark of Noah; therefore when they were encompassed about by many waters they did cry unto the Lord, and he did bring them forth again upon the top of the waters.

8 And it came to pass that the wind did never cease to blow towards the promised land while they were upon the waters; and thus they were driven forth before the wind.

9 And they did sing praises unto the Lord; yea, the brother of Jared did sing praises unto the Lord, and he did thank and praise the Lord all the day long; and when the night came, they did not cease to praise the Lord.

10 And thus they were driven forth; and no monster of the sea could break them, neither whale that could mar them; and they did have light continually, whether it was above the water or under the water.

11 And thus they were driven forth, three hundred and forty and four days upon the water.

12 And they did land upon the shore of the promised land. And when they had set their feet upon the shores of the promised land they bowed themselves down upon the face of the land, and did humble themselves before the Lord, and did shed tears of joy before the Lord, because of the multitude of his tender mercies over them.

13 And it came to pass that they went forth upon the face of the land, and began to till the earth.

14 And Jared had four sons; and they were called Jacom, and Gilgah, and Mahah, and Orihah.

15 And the brother of Jared also begat sons and daughters.

16 And the friends of Jared and his brother were in number about twenty and two souls; and they also begat sons and daughters before they came to the promised land; and therefore they began to be many.

17 And they were taught to walk humbly before the Lord; and they were also taught from on high.

18 And it came to pass that they began to spread upon the face of the land, and to multiply and to till the earth; and they did wax strong in the land.

What can we learn from the multitude of the Lord's tender mercies experienced by the Jaredites? (6:12) "The various scriptures tell us vital things about God's 'tender mercies' (1 Ne. 1:20; Ether 6:12; see also Luke 1:78) and His dealings with our predecessors. What is past is truly prologue; hence an unvarying, all-seeing God, desiring to save mercurial and myopic man, is not interested in our retroactive adulation, but in preventing our prospective ruination" (Maxwell, "God Will Yet Reveal," 53). ✹

Ether 6:13–30. The Jaredites Choose to Establish a King to Rule over Them

Why mention tilling the earth? (6:13) "Tilling the ground seems like such an ordinary thing to do. Why, then, would one waste time and space writing about such things? Such an apparently superfluous piece of information becomes more meaningful when we realize that tilling the earth had symbolic significance among various ancient societies. Mircea Eliade has noticed in his studies of ancient cultures and religions that ' . . . rites are performed that symbolically repeat the act of Creation.' . . . Thus, tilling the ground may symbolize the act of creation to the author/editor of the Jaredite record and therefore warrants inclusion" (Thompson, "The Jaredite Exodus," 106–7). ✹

How may we be taught from on high? (6:17) President Harold B. Lee explained that "one may readily understand that learning by faith requires the bending of the whole soul through worthy living to become attuned to the Holy Spirit of the Lord, the calling up from the depths of one's own mental searching, and the linking of our own efforts to receive the true witness of the Spirit" (*Teachings of Harold B. Lee*, 92–93).

Why did the Jaredite leaders gather their people together? (6:19) "Jaredite history in the New World was formally inaugurated by a general assembly and census of the entire nation (Ether 6:19), a thoroughly Asiatic practice which goes back to the days of prehistoric hunters and which lies at the root of all ancient political organization. . . . Strictly in accordance with the ancient pattern, this assembly was the occasion for the choosing of a king, and the establishment of a dynasty, which as the brother of Jared clearly foresaw, could only lead straight to the slough of Old World intrigue and turmoil from which the Jaredites had already been once delivered (Ether 6:23)" (Nibley, *Lehi in the Desert*, 224).

19 And the brother of Jared began to be old, and saw that he must soon go down to the grave; wherefore he said unto Jared: Let us gather together our people that we may number them, that we may know of them what they will desire of us before we go down to our graves.

20 And accordingly the people were gathered together. Now the number of the sons and the daughters of the brother of Jared were twenty and two souls; and the number of sons and daughters of Jared were twelve, he having four sons.

21 And it came to pass that they did number their people; and after that they had numbered them, they did desire of them the things which they would that they should do before they went down to their graves.

22 And it came to pass that the people desired of them that they should anoint one of their sons to be a king over them.

23 And now behold, this was grievous unto them. And the brother of Jared said unto them: Surely this thing leadeth into captivity.

24 But Jared said unto his brother: Suffer them that they may have a king. And therefore he said unto them: Choose ye out from among our sons a king, even whom ye will.

25 And it came to pass that they chose even the firstborn of the brother of Jared; and his name was Pagag. And it came to pass that he refused and would not be their king. And the people would that his father should constrain him, but his father would not; and he commanded them that they should constrain no man to be their king.

26 And it came to pass that they chose all the brothers of Pagag, and they would not.

27 And it came to pass that neither would the sons of Jared, even all save it were one; and Orihah was anointed to be king over the people.

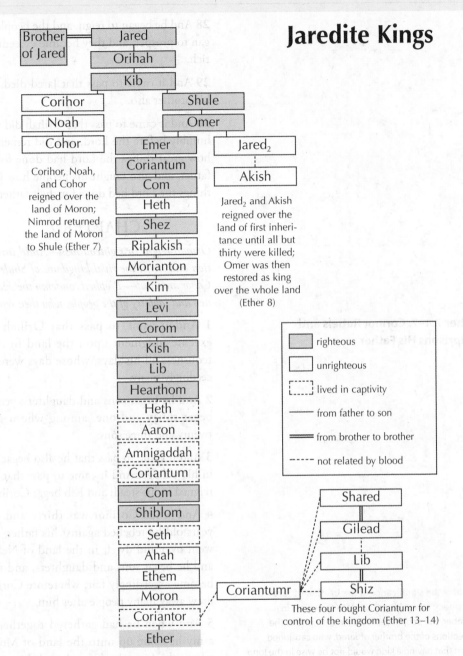

Jaredite Kings

Brother of Jared = Jared
Orihah
Kib

Corihor
Noah
Cohor

Corihor, Noah, and Cohor reigned over the land of Moron; Nimrod returned the land of Moron to Shule (Ether 7)

Shule
Omer

Emer
Coriantum
Com
Heth
Shez
Riplakish
Morianton
Kim
Levi
Corom
Kish
Lib
Hearthom
Heth
Aaron
Amnigaddah
Coriantum
Com
Shiblom
Seth
Ahah
Ethem
Moron
Coriantor
Ether

Jared₂
Akish

Jared₂ and Akish reigned over the land of first inheritance until all but thirty were killed; Omer was then restored as king over the whole land (Ether 8)

Legend:
- █ righteous
- ☐ unrighteous
- ┄ lived in captivity
- ── from father to son
- ═ from brother to brother
- --- not related by blood

Shared
Gilead
Lib
Shiz

Coriantumr

These four fought Coriantumr for control of the kingdom (Ether 13–14)

(Welch and Welch [expanded from the work of Lee Prince], *Charting the Book of Mormon*, chart 31; used by permission.)

28 And he began to reign, and the people began to prosper; and they became exceedingly rich.

29 And it came to pass that Jared died, and his brother also.

30 And it came to pass that Orihah did walk humbly before the Lord, and did remember how great things the Lord had done for his father, and also taught his people how great things the Lord had done for their fathers.

CHAPTER 7

Orihah reigns in righteousness—Amid usurpation and strife, the rival kingdoms of Shule and Cohor are set up—Prophets condemn the wickedness and idolatry of the people, who then repent.

1 And it came to pass that Orihah did execute judgment upon the land in righteousness all his days, whose days were exceedingly many.

2 And he begat sons and daughters; yea, he begat thirty and one, among whom were twenty and three sons.

3 And it came to pass that he also begat Kib in his old age. And it came to pass that Kib reigned in his stead; and Kib begat Corihor.

4 And when Corihor was thirty and two years old he rebelled against his father, and went over and dwelt in the land of Nehor; and he begat sons and daughters, and they became exceedingly fair; wherefore Corihor drew away many people after him.

5 And when he had gathered together an army he came up unto the land of Moron where the king dwelt, and took him captive, which brought to pass the saying of the brother of Jared that they would be brought into captivity.

6 Now the land of Moron, where the king dwelt, was near the land which is called Desolation by the Nephites.

Ether 7:1–7. Corihor Rebels and Imprisons His Father

What is the significance of the brother of Jared's prophecy about kings? (7:5) "As they grew in number, the people desired a king, in spite of the objections of the brother of Jared, who cautioned them that having a king would not be wise in the long run (see Ether 6:23; 7:5). At a much later date, Mosiah, the Nephite seer . . . also warned the Nephites of the dangers of a kingship. . . .

"Under Mosiah's wise counsel, and after he had translated the account of the Jaredites, the Nephites changed their form of government to judges rather than kings" (Brinley, "The Jaredites—A Case Study in Following the Brethren," 47–48).

7 And it came to pass that Kib dwelt in captivity, and his people under Corihor his son, until he became exceedingly old; nevertheless Kib begat Shule in his old age, while he was yet in captivity.

8 And it came to pass that Shule was angry with his brother; and Shule waxed strong, and became mighty as to the strength of a man; and he was also mighty in judgment.

9 Wherefore, he came to the hill Ephraim, and he did molten out of the hill, and made swords out of steel for those whom he had drawn away with him; and after he had armed them with swords he returned to the city Nehor, and gave battle unto his brother Corihor, by which means he obtained the kingdom and restored it unto his father Kib.

10 And now because of the thing which Shule had done, his father bestowed upon him the kingdom; therefore he began to reign in the stead of his father.

11 And it came to pass that he did execute judgment in righteousness; and he did spread his kingdom upon all the face of the land, for the people had become exceedingly numerous.

12 And it came to pass that Shule also begat many sons and daughters.

13 And Corihor repented of the many evils which he had done; wherefore Shule gave him power in his kingdom.

14 And it came to pass that Corihor had many sons and daughters. And among the sons of Corihor there was one whose name was Noah.

15 And it came to pass that Noah rebelled against Shule, the king, and also his father

Is there evidence of captured kings being allowed to live in captivity? (7:7) "Such is the practice, mentioned many times in the book, of keeping a king prisoner throughout his entire lifetime, allowing him to beget and raise a family in captivity, even though the sons thus brought up would be almost sure to seek vengeance for their parent and power for themselves upon coming of age. . . . It seems to us a perfectly ridiculous system, yet it is in accordance with the immemorial Asiatic usage" (Nibley, *Lehi in the Desert*, 207–8).

Ether 7:8–13. Shule Frees His Father, Who Then Grants Shule the Kingdom

Do we have evidence of swords of steel at this time? (7:9) "'It seems evident,' notes one recent authority, 'that by the beginning of the tenth century B.C. blacksmiths were intentionally steeling iron.' In 1987, the *Ensign* reported that archaeologists had unearthed a long steel sword near Jericho dating back to the late seventh century B.C., probably to the reign of King Josiah who died shortly before Lehi began to prophesy. This sword is now on display at Jerusalem's Israel Museum. The museum's explanatory sign reads in part, 'The sword is made of iron hardened into steel, attesting to substantial metallurgical know-how'" (Christofferson, "Prophet Joseph Smith"). ⊕

Ether 7:14–20. Rebellion and War Result in Two Rival Kingdoms

What do we learn of the Jaredite civilization from the rebellion and intrigues of Noah and King Shule? (7:14–20) "You read your book of Ether and you'll find the whole history is a tale of fierce and unrelenting struggle for power. It's dark with intrigue and violence particularly of the Asiatic brand. When the rival for a kingdom is bested, he goes off by himself in the wilderness, bides his time, and gathers an army of outcasts. . . .

"A grand cycle running from unity of the nations to division, and conflict, and hence to paralysis or extinction is repeated at least a dozen times" (Nibley, *Teachings of the Book of Mormon*, 4:256).

Ether 7:21–27. King Shule Rules in Righteousness, and the People Follow Prophets and Repent

What does the sending of prophets during the reign of Shule teach us? (7:23) "Because the Lord is kind, He calls servants to warn people of danger. That call to warn is made harder and more important by the fact that the warnings of most worth are about

Corihor, and drew away Cohor his brother, and also all his brethren and many of the people.

16 And he gave battle unto Shule, the king, in which he did obtain the land of their first inheritance; and he became a king over that part of the land.

17 And it came to pass that he gave battle again unto Shule, the king; and he took Shule, the king, and carried him away captive into Moron.

18 And it came to pass as he was about to put him to death, the sons of Shule crept into the house of Noah by night and slew him, and broke down the door of the prison and brought out their father, and placed him upon his throne in his own kingdom.

19 Wherefore, the son of Noah did build up his kingdom in his stead; nevertheless they did not gain power any more over Shule the king, and the people who were under the reign of Shule the king did prosper exceedingly and wax great.

20 And the country was divided; and there were two kingdoms, the kingdom of Shule, and the kingdom of Cohor, the son of Noah.

21 And Cohor, the son of Noah, caused that his people should give battle unto Shule, in which Shule did beat them and did slay Cohor.

22 And now Cohor had a son who was called Nimrod; and Nimrod gave up the kingdom of Cohor unto Shule, and he did gain favor in the eyes of Shule; wherefore Shule did bestow great favors upon him, and he did do in the kingdom of Shule according to his desires.

23 And also in the reign of Shule there came prophets among the people, who were sent from the Lord, prophesying that the wickedness and idolatry of the people was bringing a curse upon the land, and they should be destroyed if they did not repent.

24 And it came to pass that the people did revile against the prophets, and did mock them. And it came to pass that king Shule did execute judgment against all those who did revile against the prophets.

25 And he did execute a law throughout all the land, which gave power unto the prophets that they should go whithersoever they would; and by this cause the people were brought unto repentance.

26 And because the people did repent of their iniquities and idolatries the Lord did spare them, and they began to prosper again in the land. And it came to pass that Shule begat sons and daughters in his old age.

27 And there were no more wars in the days of Shule; and he remembered the great things that the Lord had done for his fathers in bringing them across the great deep into the promised land; wherefore he did execute judgment in righteousness all his days.

CHAPTER 8

There is strife and contention over the kingdom—Akish forms an oath-bound secret combination to slay the king—Secret combinations are of the devil and result in the destruction of nations—Modern Gentiles are warned against the secret combination that will seek to overthrow the freedom of all lands, nations, and countries.

1 And it came to pass that he begat Omer, and Omer reigned in his stead. And Omer begat Jared; and Jared begat sons and daughters.

2 And Jared rebelled against his father, and came and dwelt in the land of Heth. And it came to pass that he did flatter many people, because of his cunning words, until he had gained the half of the kingdom.

dangers that people don't yet think are real" (Eyring, "Voice of Warning," 32). ⊕

What happens when the prophets are protected by civil law? (7:25–27) "Among the Jaredites, 'the people were brought unto repentance' when the king protected the prophets (Ether 7:25). In contrast, when a later king did not protect the prophets, 'the people hardened their hearts' and 'did reject all the words of the prophets' (Ether 11:13, 22), with the result that 'the Spirit of the Lord had ceased striving with them, and Satan had full power over the hearts of the people' (Ether 15:19). They then reached 'the fulness of iniquity,' which brought down upon them 'the fulness of the wrath of God' (Ether 2:10–11)" (Merrill, "They Wrote to Us As If We Were Present," 15).

Ether 8:1–7. Jared's Desire for Power Leads to Great Suffering in His Family

How can we be protected against flattery? (8:2) Flattery may be defined as "False praise; commendation bestowed for the purpose of gaining favor and influence, or to accomplish some purpose" (Webster, *American Dictionary*). President Joseph F. Smith identified flattery as one of the three great temptations facing the Latter-day Saints (see *Gospel Doctrine*, 312). How can you protect yourself from those who practice flattery?

3 And when he had gained the half of the kingdom he gave battle unto his father, and he did carry away his father into captivity, and did make him serve in captivity;

4 And now, in the days of the reign of Omer he was in captivity the half of his days. And it came to pass that he begat sons and daughters, among whom were Esrom and Coriantumr;

5 And they were exceedingly angry because of the doings of Jared their brother, insomuch that they did raise an army and gave battle unto Jared. And it came to pass that they did give battle unto him by night.

6 And it came to pass that when they had slain the army of Jared they were about to slay him also; and he pled with them that they would not slay him, and he would give up the kingdom unto his father. And it came to pass that they did grant unto him his life.

7 And now Jared became exceedingly sorrowful because of the loss of the kingdom, for he had set his heart upon the kingdom and upon the glory of the world.

8 Now the daughter of Jared being exceedingly expert, and seeing the sorrows of her father, thought to devise a plan whereby she could redeem the kingdom unto her father.

9 Now the daughter of Jared was exceedingly fair. And it came to pass that she did talk with her father, and said unto him: Whereby hath my father so much sorrow? Hath he not read the record which our fathers brought across the great deep? Behold, is there not an account concerning them of old, that they by their secret plans did obtain kingdoms and great glory?

10 And now, therefore, let my father send for Akish, the son of Kimnor; and behold, I am fair, and I will dance before him, and I will please him, that he will desire me to

Ether 8:8–17. Jared and His Daughter Initiate a Secret Combination

Why does Jared's daughter's dance before a ruler seem so familiar? (8:8–10) "There is one tale of intrigue in the book of Ether that presents very ancient and widespread (though but recently discovered) parallels. That is the story of Jared's daughter. . . .

"Historically, the whole point of this story is that it is highly unoriginal. It is supposed to be. . . .

"The thing to note especially is that there actually seems to have been a succession rite of great antiquity that followed this pattern. . . . The episode of the dancing princess is at all times essentially a ritual, and the name of Salome (in reference to Herodias' daughter) is perhaps no accident, for her story is anything but unique" (Nibley, *Lehi in the Desert*, 212). ⊕

wife; wherefore if he shall desire of thee that ye shall give unto him me to wife, then shall ye say: I will give her if ye will bring unto me the head of my father, the king.

11 And now Omer was a friend to Akish; wherefore, when Jared had sent for Akish, the daughter of Jared danced before him that she pleased him, insomuch that he desired her to wife. And it came to pass that he said unto Jared: Give her unto me to wife.

12 And Jared said unto him: I will give her unto you, if ye will bring unto me the head of my father, the king.

13 And it came to pass that Akish gathered in unto the house of Jared all his kinsfolk, and said unto them: Will ye swear unto me that ye will be faithful unto me in the thing which I shall desire of you?

14 And it came to pass that they all sware unto him, by the God of heaven, and also by the heavens, and also by the earth, and by their heads, that whoso should vary from the assistance which Akish desired should lose his head; and whoso should divulge whatsoever thing Akish made known unto them, the same should lose his life.

15 And it came to pass that thus they did agree with Akish. And Akish did administer unto them the oaths which were given by them of old who also sought power, which

The Dangers of Secret Combinations (Ether 8)

1. Founded on ancient and secret plans (Ether 8:9).
2. Joined with a secret oath (v. 14).
3. Maintain loyalty and secrecy by threats of violence (v. 14).
4. Kept up by the devil (v. 16).
5. Established to "obtain kingdoms and great glory" (v. 9), "to gain power, and to murder, and to plunder, and to lie, and to commit all manner of wickedness and whoredoms" (v. 16).
6. Forbidden by the Lord as wicked (vv. 18–19).
7. Had "among all people" (v. 20).
8. "Caused the destruction" of both the Jaredite and Nephite nations (v. 21).
9. Promised destruction for whatever nation upholds secret combinations (v. 22).

had been handed down even from Cain, who was a murderer from the beginning.

16 And they were kept up by the power of the devil to administer these oaths unto the people, to keep them in darkness, to help such as sought power to gain power, and to murder, and to plunder, and to lie, and to commit all manner of wickedness and whoredoms.

17 And it was the daughter of Jared who put it into his heart to search up these things of old; and Jared put it into the heart of Akish; wherefore, Akish administered it unto his kindred and friends, leading them away by fair promises to do whatsoever thing he desired.

Ether 8:18–26. The Laws of God Regarding Secret Combinations

18 And it came to pass that they formed a secret combination, even as they of old; which combination is most abominable and wicked above all, in the sight of God;

19 For the Lord worketh not in secret combinations, neither doth he will that man should shed blood, but in all things hath forbidden it, from the beginning of man.

20 And now I, Moroni, do not write the manner of their oaths and combinations, for it hath been made known unto me that they are had among all people, and they are had among the Lamanites.

What caused the destruction of both the Nephites and Jaredites? (8:20–22) "Moroni could have pointed out many factors that led to the destruction of the people, but notice how he singled out the secret combinations, just as the Church today could point out many threats to peace, prosperity, and the spread of God's work, but it has singled out the greatest threat as the godless conspiracy.... This scripture should alert us to what is ahead unless we repent" (Benson, *God, Family, and Country*, 321–22).

21 And they have caused the destruction of this people of whom I am now speaking, and also the destruction of the people of Nephi.

22 And whatsoever nation shall uphold such secret combinations, to get power and gain, until they shall spread over the nation, behold, they shall be destroyed; for the Lord will not suffer that the blood of his saints, which shall be shed by them, shall always cry unto him from the ground for vengeance upon them and yet he avenge them not.

23 Wherefore, O ye Gentiles, it is wisdom in God that these things should be shown unto you, that thereby ye may repent of your sins, and suffer not that these murderous combinations shall get above you, which are built up to get power and gain—and the work, yea, even the work of destruction come upon you, yea, even the sword of the justice of the Eternal God shall fall upon you, to your overthrow and destruction if ye shall suffer these things to be.

24 Wherefore, the Lord commandeth you, when ye shall see these things come among you that ye shall awake to a sense of your awful situation, because of this secret combination which shall be among you; or wo be unto it, because of the blood of them who have been slain; for they cry from the dust for vengeance upon it, and also upon those who built it up.

25 For it cometh to pass that whoso buildeth it up seeketh to overthrow the freedom of all lands, nations, and countries; and it bringeth to pass the destruction of all people, for it is built up by the devil, who is the father of all lies; even that same liar who beguiled our first parents, yea, even that same liar who hath caused man to commit murder from the beginning; who hath hardened the hearts of men that they have murdered the prophets, and stoned them, and cast them out from the beginning.

26 Wherefore, I, Moroni, am commanded to write these things that evil may be done away, and that the time may come that Satan may have no power upon the hearts of the children of men, but that they may be persuaded to do good continually, that they may come unto the fountain of all righteousness and be saved.

How should we view our "awful situation"? (8:24) "We live in dangerously troubled times. The values that steadied mankind in earlier times are being tossed away. We must not ignore Moroni's words when he saw our day and said, 'Ye [must] awake to a sense of your awful situation' (Ether 8:24). We cannot take lightly this warning from the Book of Mormon" (Packer, "Do Not Fear," 77–78).

Why did Satan use secret combinations to destroy both the Jaredite and the Nephite civilizations? (8:25) "As the enemies of honest men and women governed by the rule of law, such secret combinations seek to subvert public virtue and legally constituted authority. They defile, defraud, murder, deceive, and destroy elements of good government, religious or secular. Their goal is to seize power and to rule over all people (3 Ne. 6:27–30), which results in the destruction of human freedom and agency and the paralysis of peaceful and just communities.

"Secret combinations and their practices have a scriptural and historic tradition that extends from the days of Cain's secret covenant with Satan to modern times" (Ludlow, et al., *Encyclopedia of Mormonism*, 1291).

Why did Moroni encourage his readers to "come unto the fountain of all righteousness and be saved"? (8:26) "Jesus Christ is the *Fountain of all Righteousness.* . . . *Fountain* is properly the source or springhead of waters. . . . Metaphorically, God is called the Fountain of Living Waters (Jeremiah 2:18). Springs or fountains are called *living,* when they never cease, but are always sending forth their waters" (Reynolds and Sjodahl, *Commentary on the Book of Mormon,* 6:169). Isaiah similarly invited God's children to "draw water out of the wells of salvation" (2 Nephi 22:3; Isaiah 12:3) which is an invitation to partake of eternal life.

CHAPTER 9

The kingdom passes from one to another by descent, intrigue, and murder—Emer saw the Son of Righteousness—Many prophets cry repentance—A famine and poisonous serpents plague the people.

Ether 9:1–13. The Jaredites Suffer Because of Sin and Wicked Leaders

How are dreams an avenue of revelation? (9:3)
"Dreams confirm premonitions or show something that is about to happen. An inspired dream might entail a warning—a rebuke for course correction—it might convey a direct command to do something, or it might serve as spiritual assurance or bestow a promise. In every dispensation dreams have been a prevalent spiritual gift, and the gift is validated in scripture. The Prophet Joseph Smith conveyed: 'We believe that we have a right to revelations, visions, and *dreams from God*, our Heavenly Father; and light and intelligence, through the gift of the Holy Ghost . . . on all subjects pertaining to our spiritual welfare; if it so be that we keep his commandments, so as to render ourselves worthy in his sight'" (Jenkins, "Quiet Slumber," 74).

1 And now I, Moroni, proceed with my record. Therefore, behold, it came to pass that because of the secret combinations of Akish and his friends, behold, they did overthrow the kingdom of Omer.

2 Nevertheless, the Lord was merciful unto Omer, and also to his sons and to his daughters who did not seek his destruction.

3 And the Lord warned Omer in a dream that he should depart out of the land; wherefore Omer departed out of the land with his family, and traveled many days, and came over and passed by the hill of Shim, and came over by the place where the Nephites were destroyed, and from thence eastward, and came to a place which was called Ablom, by the seashore, and there he pitched his tent, and also his sons and his daughters, and all his household, save it were Jared and his family.

4 And it came to pass that Jared was anointed king over the people, by the hand of wickedness; and he gave unto Akish his daughter to wife.

5 And it came to pass that Akish sought the life of his father-in-law; and he applied unto those whom he had sworn by the oath of the ancients, and they obtained the head of his father-in-law, as he sat upon his throne, giving audience to his people.

6 For so great had been the spreading of this wicked and secret society that it had corrupted the hearts of all the people; therefore Jared was murdered upon his throne, and Akish reigned in his stead.

7 And it came to pass that Akish began to be jealous of his son, therefore he shut him up in prison, and kept him upon little or no food until he had suffered death.

8 And now the brother of him that suffered death, (and his name was Nimrah) was angry with his father because of that which his father had done unto his brother.

9 And it came to pass that Nimrah gathered together a small number of men, and fled out of the land, and came over and dwelt with Omer.

10 And it came to pass that Akish begat other sons, and they won the hearts of the people, notwithstanding they had sworn unto him to do all manner of iniquity according to that which he desired.

11 Now the people of Akish were desirous for gain, even as Akish was desirous for power; wherefore, the sons of Akish did offer them money, by which means they drew away the more part of the people after them.

12 And there began to be a war between the sons of Akish and Akish, which lasted for the space of many years, yea, unto the destruction of nearly all the people of the kingdom, yea, even all, save it were thirty souls, and they who fled with the house of Omer.

13 Wherefore, Omer was restored again to the land of his inheritance.

14 And it came to pass that Omer began to be old; nevertheless, in his old age he begat Emer; and he anointed Emer to be king to reign in his stead.

15 And after that he had anointed Emer to be king he saw peace in the land for the space of two years, and he died, having seen exceedingly many days, which were full of sorrow. And it came to pass that Emer did reign in his stead, and did fill the steps of his father.

What were the consequences of the war between Akish and his sons? (9:12) "A war of the most horrible character broke out, which lasted for several years, and ended when nearly every soul was slain. Of the Kingdom of Akish, for which he had sinned so much, there remained but thirty souls. All the rest—men, women, and children, had been swept by bloody hands into untimely graves. The people of Akish having been thus destroyed, Omer, with his friends, returned from his exile and reigned over the feeble remnant of a wasted people" (Reynolds and Sjodahl, *Commentary on the Book of Mormon*, 6:136).

Ether 9:14–22. Emer, a Righteous King, Sees the Lord

16 And the Lord began again to take the curse from off the land, and the house of Emer did prosper exceedingly under the reign of Emer; and in the space of sixty and two years they had become exceedingly strong, insomuch that they became exceedingly rich—

17 Having all manner of fruit, and of grain, and of silks, and of fine linen, and of gold, and of silver, and of precious things;

18 And also all manner of cattle, of oxen, and cows, and of sheep, and of swine, and of goats, and also many other kinds of animals which were useful for the food of man.

19 And they also had horses, and asses, and there were elephants and cureloms and cumoms; all of which were useful unto man, and more especially the elephants and cureloms and cumoms.

20 And thus the Lord did pour out his blessings upon this land, which was choice above all other lands; and he commanded that whoso should possess the land should possess it unto the Lord, or they should be destroyed when they were ripened in iniquity; for upon such, saith the Lord: I will pour out the fulness of my wrath.

Were there horses in the New World at the time of the Jaredites? (9:19) "Horses are mentioned only once in the land northward during the Jaredite period—that is, during the prosperous reign of King Emer around 2500 B.C. and before the great drought sometime in the third millennium B.C. (see Ether 9:19, 30–35). Since horses are not mentioned again in the Jaredite record, it is possible that they became extinct in the region north of the narrow neck of land following that time" (Bennett, "Horses in the Book of Mormon"). ⊕

What are *cureloms* and *cumoms*? (9:19) "These animals were unknown to the Nephites, and so Moroni leaves the words untranslated, or else though known to the Nephites, they are out of our experience so that our language has no name to call them by. They were simply breeds of those 'many other kinds of animals which were useful for the food of man' (Ether 9:18)" (Nibley, *Lehi in the Desert*, 220).

Were there elephants in early America? (9:19) "Mastodons and mammoths once lived throughout North America and part of South America. They are unquestionably elephants in the eyes of zoologists. The question is how late they lived. Most experts assume they failed to survive down to the time of the Jaredites. The only place they are mentioned in the Book of Mormon is in the Book of Ether, near the beginning of that record (by my calculations of Jaredite chronology, the date must have been before 2500 B.C.). Experts agree that the mammoth and mastodon could have survived in favored spots much later than the time normally assigned for their extinction" (Sorensen, *Ancient American Setting*, 297).

21 And Emer did execute judgment in righteousness all his days, and he begat many sons and daughters; and he begat Coriantum, and he anointed Coriantum to reign in his stead.

22 And after he had anointed Coriantum to reign in his stead he lived four years, and he saw peace in the land; yea, and he even saw the Son of Righteousness, and did rejoice and glory in his day; and he died in peace.

23 And it came to pass that Coriantum did walk in the steps of his father, and did build many mighty cities, and did administer that which was good unto his people in all his days. And it came to pass that he had no children even until he was exceedingly old.

24 And it came to pass that his wife died, being an hundred and two years old. And it came to pass that Coriantum took to wife, in his old age, a young maid, and begat sons and daughters; wherefore he lived until he was an hundred and forty and two years old.

25 And it came to pass that he begat Com, and Com reigned in his stead; and he reigned forty and nine years, and he begat Heth; and he also begat other sons and daughters.

26 And the people had spread again over all the face of the land, and there began again to be an exceedingly great wickedness upon the face of the land, and Heth began to embrace the secret plans again of old, to destroy his father.

What does Moroni's insertion about Emer's righteousness during wicked times convey? (9:21–22) "The experiences of Emer are some of the most promising moments in these chapters of rampant wickedness among the Jaredites. As a very righteous leader of his people, Emer was privileged to have the veil parted and see the Lord Himself. . . . Moroni may have desired to show us through Emer that not only righteousness but perfect faith is possible in a world sandwiched in on all sides by wickedness" (Judd, "Jaredite Zion Societies," 150).

Ether 9:23–29. The Lord Sends Prophets to Warn the People

How do secret combinations thrive? (9:26) "Secret combinations are formed to implement the ambitions of individuals, seeking power through gain and gain through power. Hence they produce and thrive in an atmosphere of conflict, within the groups and between them, assassination being, as the Book of Mormon makes very clear, the cornerstone of their dire economy" (Nibley, *Since Cumorah*, 395).

The Jaredite Pride Cycle: Prosperity to Wickedness (Ether 9)

1. During the righteous reigns of Emer and Coriantum the people prospered exceedingly (Ether 9:15–25).
2. Under the reign of Heth, the people began to join together in secret combinations, and they turned to wickedness (vv. 26–27).
3. The Lord sent prophets to warn the people of their terrible circumstances (v. 28).
4. The people of Heth rejected the prophets (v. 29).
5. The judgments of God fell upon the people (vv. 30–33).
6. The people humbled themselves and repented and the Lord blessed them again with prosperity (vv. 34–35).

Why are there people in nearly every generation who do not believe prophets? (9:29) "In keeping with the Savior's own experience, there has been a long history of rejection and a painfully high price paid by prophets and apostles, missionaries and members in every generation. . . . So here we have the burden of those called to bear the messianic message. In addition to teaching, encouraging, and cheering people on (that is the pleasant part of discipleship), from time to time these same messengers are called upon to worry, to warn, and sometimes just to weep (that is the painful part of discipleship). . . . Unfortunately, messengers of divinely mandated commandments are often no more popular today than they were anciently" (Holland, "Cost—and Blessings—of Discipleship," 6–7).

Ether 9:30–35. The Jaredites Suffer a Famine and a Plague of Poisonous Snakes

What brought about the plague of poisonous snakes? (9:31) "The description of how people were driven out of a land by a plague of serpents that then 'hedge up the way that the people could not pass' (Ether 9:31–35) may put a strain on your scientific credulity. . . . In the thirteenth century A.D. Shah Sadrudin set his heart on the building of a capital which should surpass all other cities in splendor; yet the project had to be abandoned after enormous expense when during a period of drought the place so swarmed with serpents that no one could live in it. It is interesting in this connection that the plague of serpents in Ether is described as following upon a period of extreme drought (Ether 9:30)" (Nibley, *Lehi in the Desert*, 221). ⊕

27 And it came to pass that he did dethrone his father, for he slew him with his own sword; and he did reign in his stead.

28 And there came prophets in the land again, crying repentance unto them—that they must prepare the way of the Lord or there should come a curse upon the face of the land; yea, even there should be a great famine, in which they should be destroyed if they did not repent.

29 But the people believed not the words of the prophets, but they cast them out; and some of them they cast into pits and left them to perish. And it came to pass that they did all these things according to the commandment of the king, Heth.

30 And it came to pass that there began to be a great dearth upon the land, and the inhabitants began to be destroyed exceedingly fast because of the dearth, for there was no rain upon the face of the earth.

31 And there came forth poisonous serpents also upon the face of the land, and did poison many people. And it came to pass that their flocks began to flee before the poisonous serpents, towards the land southward, which was called by the Nephites Zarahemla.

32 And it came to pass that there were many of them which did perish by the way; nevertheless, there were some which fled into the land southward.

33 And it came to pass that the Lord did cause the serpents that they should pursue them no more, but that they should hedge

up the way that the people could not pass, that whoso should attempt to pass might fall by the poisonous serpents.

34 And it came to pass that the people did follow the course of the beasts, and did devour the carcasses of them which fell by the way, until they had devoured them all. Now when the people saw that they must perish they began to repent of their iniquities and cry unto the Lord.

35 And it came to pass that when they had humbled themselves sufficiently before the Lord he did send rain upon the face of the earth; and the people began to revive again, and there began to be fruit in the north countries, and in all the countries round about. And the Lord did show forth his power unto them in preserving them from famine.

CHAPTER 10

One king succeeds another—Some of the kings are righteous; others are wicked—When righteousness prevails, the people are blessed and prospered by the Lord.

1 And it came to pass that Shez, who was a descendant of Heth—for Heth had perished by the famine, and all his household save it were Shez—wherefore, Shez began to build up again a broken people.

2 And it came to pass that Shez did remember the destruction of his fathers, and he did build up a righteous kingdom; for he remembered what the Lord had done in bringing Jared and his brother across the deep; and he did walk in the ways of the Lord; and he begat sons and daughters.

3 And his eldest son, whose name was Shez, did rebel against him; nevertheless, Shez was smitten by the hand of a robber, because of his exceeding riches, which brought peace again unto his father.

Ether 10:1–4. Shez Remembers the Lord and Rebuilds the Kingdom in Righteousness

How was the famine that humbled the people actually a blessing? (10:1–2) What led Shez to rebuild "a broken people"? What blessings has the Lord given to help you and others build upon a foundation of righteousness?

Ether 10:5–8. Riplakish Makes His People Pay Heavy Taxes

What do we learn from these verses about the pattern of unrighteous kings? (10:5–8) How is Riplakish similar to King Noah (see Mosiah 11:1–15)? Why did King Mosiah suggest the Nephites do away with kings? Why are multiple judges more likely to rule fairly than a single king? (See Mosiah 29:11–14, 16–19; see also Deuteronomy 17:13–20 for Moses's account of unrighteous kings.)

Ether 10:9–19. The People Are Most Prosperous When Their Rulers Are Righteous

4 And it came to pass that his father did build up many cities upon the face of the land, and the people began again to spread over all the face of the land. And Shez did live to an exceedingly old age; and he begat Riplakish. And he died, and Riplakish reigned in his stead.

5 And it came to pass that Riplakish did not do that which was right in the sight of the Lord, for he did have many wives and concubines, and did lay that upon men's shoulders which was grievous to be borne; yea, he did tax them with heavy taxes; and with the taxes he did build many spacious buildings.

6 And he did erect him an exceedingly beautiful throne; and he did build many prisons, and whoso would not be subject unto taxes he did cast into prison; and whoso was not able to pay taxes he did cast into prison; and he did cause that they should labor continually for their support; and whoso refused to labor he did cause to be put to death.

7 Wherefore he did obtain all his fine work, yea, even his fine gold he did cause to be refined in prison; and all manner of fine workmanship he did cause to be wrought in prison. And it came to pass that he did afflict the people with his whoredoms and abominations.

8 And when he had reigned for the space of forty and two years the people did rise up in rebellion against him; and there began to be war again in the land, insomuch that Riplakish was killed, and his descendants were driven out of the land.

9 And it came to pass after the space of many years, Morianton, (he being a descendant of Riplakish) gathered together an army of outcasts, and went forth and gave battle unto the people; and he gained power over many cities; and the war became exceedingly sore, and did last for the space of many years; and he did gain power over all the land, and did establish himself king over all the land.

10 And after that he had established himself king he did ease the burden of the people, by which he did gain favor in the eyes of the people, and they did anoint him to be their king.

11 And he did do justice unto the people, but not unto himself because of his many whoredoms; wherefore he was cut off from the presence of the Lord.

12 And it came to pass that Morianton built up many cities, and the people became exceedingly rich under his reign, both in buildings, and in gold and silver, and in raising grain, and in flocks, and herds, and such things which had been restored unto them.

13 And Morianton did live to an exceedingly great age, and then he begat Kim; and Kim did reign in the stead of his father; and he did reign eight years, and his father died. And it came to pass that Kim did not reign in righteousness, wherefore he was not favored of the Lord.

14 And his brother did rise up in rebellion against him, by which he did bring him into captivity; and he did remain in captivity all his days; and he begat sons and daughters in captivity, and in his old age he begat Levi; and he died.

15 And it came to pass that Levi did serve in captivity after the death of his father, for the space of forty and two years. And he did make war against the king of the land, by which he did obtain unto himself the kingdom.

16 And after he had obtained unto himself the kingdom he did that which was right in the sight of the Lord; and the people did prosper in the land; and he did live to a good old age, and begat sons and daughters; and he also begat Corom, whom he anointed king in his stead.

What lesson can we learn from Morianton? (10:10–12) "Foregoing trends are further accelerated by the fashionable nonjudgmentalism which excuses whatever wrong individuals do—as long as they do anything else commendable. . . . Violators of the seventh commandment may still make useful contributions, but they pay a hidden, personal cost. . . . Apparently a fair, no-respecter-of-persons leader, Morianton did not respect himself! His self-inflicted wounds were masked by the outward ornamentation of riches and buildings. . . .

"The revelations tell us that commensurate with their own sins, unrepentant sinners must suffer even as [Jesus] did for ours, as they one day personally experience the full justice of God" (Maxwell, "Seventh Commandment," 80).

What do we know about the land southward?
(10:19) Although the exact location of the Book of
Mormon lands is unknown, Moroni noted that the
land southward was the place the Nephites called
Zarahemla (see Ether 9:31).

Ether 10:20–28. The People Are Blessed and Prospered Because They Are Righteous

**What is one reason why Moroni described the
prosperity of these people?** (10:22–28) "There is a
big difference between the way this people prospered
compared with the deceptive and bloodthirsty means
by which previous wicked men murdered to get gain.
. . . The language which Moroni used to describe the
state of the people of Lib is remarkably similar to the
language his father Mormon used to describe the Zion
society of the Nephites in 4 Nephi (4 Nephi 1:16). . . . It
seems possible that Moroni was trying to bring to our
memory the precious experiences of those Nephites
as he describes the righteousness among the people
of Lib" (Judd, "Jaredite Zion Societies," 152). ✚

17 And it came to pass that Corom did that
which was good in the sight of the Lord all
his days; and he begat many sons and daughters; and after he had seen many days he did
pass away, even like unto the rest of the earth;
and Kish reigned in his stead.

18 And it came to pass that Kish passed away
also, and Lib reigned in his stead.

19 And it came to pass that Lib also did that
which was good in the sight of the Lord. And
in the days of Lib the poisonous serpents
were destroyed. Wherefore they did go into
the land southward, to hunt food for the
people of the land, for the land was covered
with animals of the forest. And Lib also himself became a great hunter.

20 And they built a great city by the narrow
neck of land, by the place where the sea divides the land.

21 And they did preserve the land southward
for a wilderness, to get game. And the whole
face of the land northward was covered with
inhabitants.

22 And they were exceedingly industrious,
and they did buy and sell and traffic one with
another, that they might get gain.

23 And they did work in all manner of ore,
and they did make gold, and silver, and iron,
and brass, and all manner of metals; and they
did dig it out of the earth; wherefore, they did
cast up mighty heaps of earth to get ore, of
gold, and of silver, and of iron, and of copper.
And they did work all manner of fine work.

24 And they did have silks, and fine-twined
linen; and they did work all manner of cloth,
that they might clothe themselves from their
nakedness.

25 And they did make all manner of tools
to till the earth, both to plow and to sow, to
reap and to hoe, and also to thrash.

26 And they did make all manner of tools with which they did work their beasts.

27 And they did make all manner of weapons of war. And they did work all manner of work of exceedingly curious workmanship.

28 And never could be a people more blessed than were they, and more prospered by the hand of the Lord. And they were in a land that was choice above all lands, for the Lord had spoken it.

29 And it came to pass that Lib did live many years, and begat sons and daughters; and he also begat Hearthom.

30 And it came to pass that Hearthom reigned in the stead of his father. And when Hearthom had reigned twenty and four years, behold, the kingdom was taken away from him. And he served many years in captivity, yea, even all the remainder of his days.

31 And he begat Heth, and Heth lived in captivity all his days. And Heth begat Aaron, and Aaron dwelt in captivity all his days; and he begat Amnigaddah, and Amnigaddah also dwelt in captivity all his days; and he begat Coriantum, and Coriantum dwelt in captivity all his days; and he begat Com.

32 And it came to pass that Com drew away the half of the kingdom. And he reigned over the half of the kingdom forty and two years; and he went to battle against the king, Amgid, and they fought for the space of many years, during which time Com gained power over Amgid, and obtained power over the remainder of the kingdom.

33 And in the days of Com there began to be robbers in the land; and they adopted the old plans, and administered oaths after the

What are we to understand by the image of the "hand of the Lord" in the Book of Mormon? (10:28) "The image of the hand of God . . . stands for the Lord's power to intervene in the affairs of men and the events of history. . . . The hand of God is also cited often as the agent of judgment as well as the means of deliverance. . . . The hand of the Lord was what once made the Jaredites prosperous (see Ether 10:28) but later destroyed them (see Ether 1:1)" (Seely, "Image of the Hand of God," 140–41). ⊕

Ether 10:29–34. War Begins Again, and Secret Bands of Robbers Infest the Land

Why did the Jaredites return so often to secret oaths? (10:33) Why do you suppose Mosiah, Alma, and Helaman purposely kept "these secret plans of their oaths and their covenants from this people"? (Alma

37:29). Why is it important not to seek after wickedness, even out of curiosity? Can you think of examples of materials that are better off not read or studied?

Ether 11:1–7. Wicked Jaredites Kill the Prophets and Are Cursed with a Great Destruction

What can we learn from the Lord's sending prophets to a wicked people? (11:1) Nephi said, "And as one generation hath been destroyed among the Jews because of iniquity, even so have they been destroyed from generation to generation according to their iniquities; and never hath any of them been destroyed save it were foretold them by the prophets of the Lord" (2 Nephi 25:9).

What must the Lord's servants often face as they call people to repentance? How does your reaction to prophets reflect how much you love the Lord or reject Him?

manner of the ancients, and sought again to destroy the kingdom.

34 Now Com did fight against them much; nevertheless, he did not prevail against them.

CHAPTER 11

Wars, dissensions, and wickedness dominate Jaredite life—Prophets predict the utter destruction of the Jaredites unless they repent—The people reject the words of the prophets.

1 And there came also in the days of Com many prophets, and prophesied of the destruction of that great people except they should repent, and turn unto the Lord, and forsake their murders and wickedness.

2 And it came to pass that the prophets were rejected by the people, and they fled unto Com for protection, for the people sought to destroy them.

3 And they prophesied unto Com many things; and he was blessed in all the remainder of his days.

4 And he lived to a good old age, and begat Shiblom; and Shiblom reigned in his stead. And the brother of Shiblom rebelled against him, and there began to be an exceedingly great war in all the land.

5 And it came to pass that the brother of Shiblom caused that all the prophets who prophesied of the destruction of the people should be put to death;

6 And there was great calamity in all the land, for they had testified that a great curse should come upon the land, and also upon the people, and that there should be a great destruction among them, such an one as never had been upon the face of the earth, and their bones should become as heaps of earth upon the face of the land except they should repent of their wickedness.

7 And they hearkened not unto the voice of the Lord, because of their wicked combinations; wherefore, there began to be wars and contentions in all the land, and also many famines and pestilences, insomuch that there was a great destruction, such an one as never had been known upon the face of the earth; and all this came to pass in the days of Shiblom.

8 And the people began to repent of their iniquity; and inasmuch as they did the Lord did have mercy on them.

9 And it came to pass that Shiblom was slain, and Seth was brought into captivity, and did dwell in captivity all his days.

10 And it came to pass that Ahah, his son, did obtain the kingdom; and he did reign over the people all his days. And he did do all manner of iniquity in his days, by which he did cause the shedding of much blood; and few were his days.

11 And Ethem, being a descendant of Ahah, did obtain the kingdom; and he also did do that which was wicked in his days.

12 And it came to pass that in the days of Ethem there came many prophets, and prophesied again unto the people; yea, they did prophesy that the Lord would utterly destroy them from off the face of the earth except they repented of their iniquities.

13 And it came to pass that the people hardened their hearts, and would not hearken unto their words; and the prophets mourned and withdrew from among the people.

14 And it came to pass that Ethem did execute judgment in wickedness all his days; and he begat Moron. And it came to pass that Moron did reign in his stead; and Moron did that which was wicked before the Lord.

15 And it came to pass that there arose a rebellion among the people, because of that

Ether 11:8–23. The Jaredites Repent for a Short Time and Then Become Wicked Again, Despite Prophets' Warnings

Why did the Jaredite people reject the prophets? (11:12–13) The Jaredites followed a pattern of prophetic rejection evident in all ages. "[The Jaredites] would say with the corrupt Ahab, 'I hate [the prophet Micaiah]; for he never prophesied good unto me, but always [prophesied] evil.' That kind of hate for a prophet's honesty cost Abinadi his life. As he said to King Noah: 'Because I have told you the truth ye are angry with me. . . . Because I have spoken the word of God ye have judged me that I am mad' or, we might add, provincial, patriarchal, bigoted, unkind, narrow, outmoded, and elderly" (Holland, "Cost—and Blessings—of Discipleship," 7).

secret combination which was built up to get power and gain; and there arose a mighty man among them in iniquity, and gave battle unto Moron, in which he did overthrow the half of the kingdom; and he did maintain the half of the kingdom for many years.

16 And it came to pass that Moron did overthrow him, and did obtain the kingdom again.

17 And it came to pass that there arose another mighty man; and he was a descendant of the brother of Jared.

18 And it came to pass that he did overthrow Moron and obtain the kingdom; wherefore, Moron dwelt in captivity all the remainder of his days; and he begat Coriantor.

19 And it came to pass that Coriantor dwelt in captivity all his days.

20 And in the days of Coriantor there also came many prophets, and prophesied of great and marvelous things, and cried repentance unto the people, and except they should repent the Lord God would execute judgment against them to their utter destruction;

21 And that the Lord God would send or bring forth another people to possess the land, by his power, after the manner by which he brought their fathers.

22 And they did reject all the words of the prophets, because of their secret society and wicked abominations.

23 And it came to pass that Coriantor begat Ether, and he died, having dwelt in captivity all his days.

What other people besides the Jaredites does the Book of Mormon certify were brought here to possess the land? (11:21) "The Book of Mormon itself ... does not claim that the peoples it describes were either the predominant or the exclusive inhabitants of the lands they occupied. In fact, cultural and demographic clues in its text hint at the presence of other groups [like the Nephites and Mulekites]....

"The 2006 update of the Introduction to the Book of Mormon reflects this understanding by stating that Book of Mormon peoples were 'among the ancestors of the American Indians'" ("Book of Mormon and DNA Studies").

CHAPTER 12

The prophet Ether exhorts the people to believe in God—Moroni recounts the wonders and marvels done by faith—Faith enabled the brother of Jared to see Christ—The Lord gives men weakness that they may be humble—The brother of Jared moved Mount Zerin by faith—Faith, hope, and charity are essential to salvation—Moroni saw Jesus face to face.

1 And it came to pass that the days of Ether were in the days of Coriantumr; and Coriantumr was king over all the land.

2 And Ether was a prophet of the Lord; wherefore Ether came forth in the days of Coriantumr, and began to prophesy unto the people, for he could not be restrained because of the Spirit of the Lord which was in him.

3 For he did cry from the morning, even until the going down of the sun, exhorting the people to believe in God unto repentance lest they should be destroyed, saying unto them that by faith all things are fulfilled—

4 Wherefore, whoso believeth in God might with surety hope for a better world, yea, even a place at the right hand of God, which hope cometh of faith, maketh an anchor to the souls of men, which would make them sure and steadfast, always abounding in good works, being led to glorify God.

5 And it came to pass that Ether did prophesy great and marvelous things unto the people, which they did not believe, because they saw them not.

6 And now, I, Moroni, would speak somewhat concerning these things; I would show unto the world that faith is things which are hoped for and not seen; wherefore, dispute not because ye see not, for ye receive no witness until after the trial of your faith.

Ether 12:1–5. Ether Urges His People to Repent and Have Faith

What is important to remember about Ether's background? (12:2–3) "Ether was a direct descendant of Jared.... His grandfather, Moron, was overthrown as king of the Jaredites ... and his father, Coriantor, spent all his days as a political prisoner (Ether 11:23). We do not know whether Ether's father was righteous, but the record does state that Ether's grandfather, Moron, and the three previous kings were wicked.... Ether, the heir apparent to the Jaredite throne, was rejected by the people in power, and they even tried to kill him" (LeBaron, "Ether and Mormon," 154).

What is meant by the phrase "hope for a better world"? (12:4) "Hoping for a better world should not be viewed as passively putting up with the problems and pains of this life, being fixated only on the next life. It implies living in such a way that our hope for a better world can be to some degree realized in this life. Hope, like faith, implies action. Hoping for a better world will, of necessity, motivate us to love our fellowmen and seek to eliminate, where possible, the suffering of our brothers and sisters around us. Hope will lead us to greater compassion and more merciful dealings with those around us. In this practical way we can hope for a better world here and now" (McConkie et al., *Doctrinal Commentary*, 4:295).

Ether 12:6–22. Moroni Tells How Faith Blesses the Lives of Saints

How can we try our faith? (12:6) "Every time you try your faith, that is, act in worthiness on an impression, you will receive the confirming evidence of the Spirit. Those feelings will fortify your faith. As you repeat that pattern, your faith will become stronger.... When you ask with honesty and real intent, He will prompt you to do that which will increase your ability to act in faith. As you walk to the boundary of your understanding into the twilight of uncertainty, exercising faith, you will be led to find solutions you would not obtain otherwise. . . . I have experienced the grueling, anguishing struggle that precedes a confirming answer. Yet those trying experiences have been edifying" (Scott, "Sustaining Power of Faith," 76). ⊕

What may be one meaning of Moroni's use of the word "witness" in verse 6? (12:6–7) Note that in the very next line, in verse 7, Moroni makes reference to Jesus Christ showing Himself to others as they exercise great faith. Study the following passages of scripture: Doctrine and Covenants 67:10; 76:116–18; 88:67–69; 93:1; 110:7–8. How can we each become a "witness" in this way?

Who are the "partakers of the heavenly gift"? (12:8–10) "The heavenly gift of which Moroni speaks is the forgiveness of sins, the companionship of the Holy Ghost (see Hebrews 6:4), and the accompanying gifts of the Spirit that are bestowed upon the just and faithful Saints of God. The Apostle Peter spoke of this gift as 'the divine nature' (see 2 Peter 1:4) that, through the atoning grace of Christ, swallows up the natural man. Through faith and acceptance of Christ's atoning plan of mercy people can be cleansed of iniquity, transformed into 'new creatures.' During the golden era of the Nephite Zion society the people partook of the heavenly gift, which produced a society free from contention and disputation, injustices and inequities, lasciviousness and crime. . . . From the words and examples of faith of these holy men of God as found in the scriptures, Moroni desires that others may also come to have that kind of faith and hope and thereby partake of this heavenly gift (see verses 8–9)" (McConkie et al., *Doctrinal Commentary*, 4:298).

What was the whole purpose of the law of Moses? (12:11) The whole purpose of the law of Moses was to bring the people to Christ, the more excellent way: "The Doctrine and Covenants says that the law of Moses consists of the preparatory gospel and the law of carnal commandments. The preparatory gospel includes the elements of faith in Jesus Christ, repentance, and baptism. We are counseled to 'come unto Christ,' which ultimately means to become Christlike. The Lord has established a path to help us achieve that end. There are many significant steps along the way, all centered in the gospel of Jesus Christ" (Brandt, "Law of Moses and the Law of Christ," 135). ⊕

7 For it was by faith that Christ showed himself unto our fathers, after he had risen from the dead; and he showed not himself unto them until after they had faith in him; wherefore, it must needs be that some had faith in him, for he showed himself not unto the world.

8 But because of the faith of men he has shown himself unto the world, and glorified the name of the Father, and prepared a way that thereby others might be partakers of the heavenly gift, that they might hope for those things which they have not seen.

9 Wherefore, ye may also have hope, and be partakers of the gift, if ye will but have faith.

10 Behold it was by faith that they of old were called after the holy order of God.

11 Wherefore, by faith was the law of Moses given. But in the gift of his Son hath God prepared a more excellent way; and it is by faith that it hath been fulfilled.

12 For if there be no faith among the children of men God can do no miracle among them; wherefore, he showed not himself until after their faith.

13 Behold, it was the faith of Alma and Amulek that caused the prison to tumble to the earth.

14 Behold, it was the faith of Nephi and Lehi that wrought the change upon the Lamanites, that they were baptized with fire and with the Holy Ghost.

15 Behold, it was the faith of Ammon and his brethren which wrought so great a miracle among the Lamanites.

16 Yea, and even all they who wrought miracles wrought them by faith, even those who were before Christ and also those who were after.

17 And it was by faith that the three disciples obtained a promise that they should not taste of death; and they obtained not the promise until after their faith.

18 And neither at any time hath any wrought miracles until after their faith; wherefore they first believed in the Son of God.

19 And there were many whose faith was so exceedingly strong, even before Christ came, who could not be kept from within the veil, but truly saw with their eyes the things which they had beheld with an eye of faith, and they were glad.

20 And behold, we have seen in this record that one of these was the brother of Jared; for so great was his faith in God, that when God put forth his finger he could not hide it from the sight of the brother of Jared, because of his word which he had spoken unto him, which word he had obtained by faith.

21 And after the brother of Jared had beheld the finger of the Lord, because of the promise

What kind of faith leads to miracles? (12:12–18) "I believe there are basically two kinds of faith. The kind of which I have spoken—faith that God lives and rules in the heavens—sustains us in life's challenges. It enables us to endure without yielding, and bear the trials common to us all. . . .

"There is another kind of faith: more powerful, less known, infrequently observed. This faith in God compounds our ability to accomplish our righteous desires. It is the creative, and generative kind of faith. This is the faith save for the exercise of which things would not happen. This is the great causative force in human lives. . . .

"The Lord's ability to help us succeed is limited only by our faith in him" (Tuttle, "A Prophet's Faith," 23).

Why is there a veil and how can faith penetrate it? (12:19–21) "One is inclined to say that surely God could block such an experience if he wished to. But the text suggests otherwise: 'this man . . . could not be kept from within the veil.' This may be an unprecedented case of a mortal man's desire, will, and purity so closely approaching the heavenly standard that God could not but honor his devotion. Given such faith, we should not be surprised that the Lord would show . . . him visions that would be relevant to the mission of all the Book of Mormon prophets and to the events of the latter-day dispensation" (Holland, *Christ and the New Covenant*, 23–24). ⊙

Ether 12:23–27. Moroni Is Concerned about His Ability to Write the Book of Mormon

What must believers remember when people mock the Book of Mormon? (12:23–25) "Science will not be able to prove or disprove holy writ. However, enough plausible evidence will come forth to prevent scoffers from having a field day, but not enough to remove the requirement of faith. . . . Writers and editors of the Book of Mormon repeatedly indicated the selectivity used in choosing, under the inspiration of heaven, what to include in that precious volume. It is understandable that some scholars would like even more contextual material about the life, times, and culture of the peoples in the Book of Mormon. Yet such attending history . . . is not the purpose for which the book has been brought forward" (Maxwell, *Plain and Precious Things*, 4). ☺

Why does humility qualify us for God's grace? (12:27) "Humility is that quality that permits us to be taught from on high through the Spirit or to be taught from sources whose origin was inspiration from the Lord, such as the scriptures and the comments of the prophets. Humility is the precious fertile soil of righteous character. In it the seeds of personal growth

which the brother of Jared had obtained by faith, the Lord could not withhold anything from his sight; wherefore he showed him all things, for he could no longer be kept without the veil.

22 And it is by faith that my fathers have obtained the promise that these things should come unto their brethren through the Gentiles; therefore the Lord hath commanded me, yea, even Jesus Christ.

23 And I said unto him: Lord, the Gentiles will mock at these things, because of our weakness in writing; for Lord thou hast made us mighty in word by faith, but thou hast not made us mighty in writing; for thou hast made all this people that they could speak much, because of the Holy Ghost which thou hast given them;

24 And thou hast made us that we could write but little, because of the awkwardness of our hands. Behold, thou hast not made us mighty in writing like unto the brother of Jared, for thou madest him that the things which he wrote were mighty even as thou art, unto the overpowering of man to read them.

25 Thou hast also made our words powerful and great, even that we cannot write them; wherefore, when we write we behold our weakness, and stumble because of the placing of our words; and I fear lest the Gentiles shall mock at our words.

26 And when I had said this, the Lord spake unto me, saying: Fools mock, but they shall mourn; and my grace is sufficient for the meek, that they shall take no advantage of your weakness;

27 And if men come unto me I will show unto them their weakness. I give unto men weakness that they may be humble; and my grace is sufficient for all men that humble themselves before me; for if they humble themselves before me, and have faith in me, then will I make weak things become strong unto them.

28 Behold, I will show unto the Gentiles their weakness, and I will show unto them that faith, hope and charity bringeth unto me—the fountain of all righteousness.

29 And I, Moroni, having heard these words, was comforted, and said: O Lord, thy righteous will be done, for I know that thou workest unto the children of men according to their faith;

30 For the brother of Jared said unto the mountain Zerin, Remove—and it was removed. And if he had not had faith it would not have moved; wherefore thou workest after men have faith.

31 For thus didst thou manifest thyself unto thy disciples; for after they had faith, and did speak in thy name, thou didst show thyself unto them in great power.

32 And I also remember that thou hast said that thou hast prepared a house for man, yea, even among the mansions of thy Father,

germinate. When cultivated through the exercise of faith, pruned by repentance, and fortified by obedience and good works, such seeds produce the cherished fruit of spiritual direction. Divine inspiration and power then result—inspiration to know the will of the Lord, power to provide the ability to accomplish that inspired will" (Scott, "Transforming Power of Faith and Character," 46). ✚

Why would the Lord want to show us our weakness? (12:27) "When we read in the scriptures of man's 'weakness,' this term includes the . . . weakness inherent in the general human condition in which the flesh has such an incessant [or constant] impact upon the spirit (see Ether 12:28–29). Weakness likewise includes, however, our specific, individual weaknesses, which we are expected to overcome (see D&C 66:3; Jacob 4:7). Life has a way of exposing these weaknesses" (Maxwell, *Lord, Increase Our Faith* [1994], 84). "Whereas Satan would have us avoid facing our faults so that we may appear better than we really are, the Lord requires us to acknowledge our faults so that we may actually become better" (Bednar and Peterson, *Doing the Right Things for the Right Reasons*, 124).

Ether 12:28–41. We Must Have Faith, Hope, and Charity to Be Saved

What does the moving of the mountain Zerin teach us about the brother of Jared? (12:30) The Savior compared such faith to a person with faith the size of a mustard seed (see Matthew 17:20). Was the Savior using the brother of Jared to illustrate what great things we can do with our faith? "Faith is power; by faith the worlds were made; nothing is impossible to those who have faith. If the earth itself came rolling into existence by faith, surely a mere mountain can be removed by that same power" (McConkie, *Mortal Messiah*, 3:73).

in which man might have a more excellent hope; wherefore man must hope, or he cannot receive an inheritance in the place which thou hast prepared.

33 And again, I remember that thou hast said that thou hast loved the world, even unto the laying down of thy life for the world, that thou mightest take it again to prepare a place for the children of men.

34 And now I know that this love which thou hast had for the children of men is charity; wherefore, except men shall have charity they cannot inherit that place which thou hast prepared in the mansions of thy Father.

35 Wherefore, I know by this thing which thou hast said, that if the Gentiles have not charity, because of our weakness, that thou wilt prove them, and take away their talent, yea, even that which they have received, and give unto them who shall have more abundantly.

36 And it came to pass that I prayed unto the Lord that he would give unto the Gentiles grace, that they might have charity.

37 And it came to pass that the Lord said unto me: If they have not charity it mattereth not unto thee, thou hast been faithful; wherefore, thy garments shall be made clean. And because thou hast seen thy weakness thou shalt be made strong, even unto the sitting down in the place which I have prepared in the mansions of my Father.

38 And now I, Moroni, bid farewell unto the Gentiles, yea, and also unto my brethren whom I love, until we shall meet before the judgment-seat of Christ, where all men shall know that my garments are not spotted with your blood.

39 And then shall ye know that I have seen Jesus, and that he hath talked with me face to face, and that he told me in plain humility,

What is important to remember as we see and confront our weakness? (12:37) "We should not be discouraged or depressed by our shortcomings. No one is without weakness. As part of the divine plan, we are tested to see whether we master weakness or let weakness master us. Proper diagnosis is essential to proper treatment. . . . But wishing for strength won't make us strong. It takes faith and work to shore up a weakened cord of integrity. We know the process of self-repair called repentance" (Nelson, *Perfection Pending and Other Favorite Discourses*, 25–26).

How many people, like Moroni, have seen Jesus Christ face to face? (12:39) "We have no way of knowing how many mortal persons have seen the Lord. Individual saints and prophets have seen him in

"When Joseph Smith and his brother Hyrum started for Carthage to face what they knew would be an imminent martyrdom, Hyrum read these words to comfort the heart of his brother [see Ether 12:36–38], . . . a few short verses from the 12th chapter of Ether in the Book of Mormon. Before closing the book, Hyrum turned down the corner of the page from which he had read, marking it as part of the everlasting testimony for which these two brothers were about to die. . . . Later, when actually incarcerated in the jail, Joseph the Prophet turned to the guards who held him captive and bore a powerful testimony of the divine authenticity of the Book of Mormon. Shortly thereafter pistol and ball would take the lives of these two testators.

"As one of a thousand elements of my own testimony of the divinity of the Book of Mormon, I submit this as yet one more evidence of its truthfulness. In this their greatest—and last—hour of need, I ask you: would these men blaspheme before God by continuing to fix their lives, their honor, and their own search for eternal salvation on a book (and by implication a church and a ministry) they had fictitiously created out of whole cloth?

"Never mind that their wives are about to be widows and their children fatherless. Never mind that their little band of followers will yet be 'houseless, friendless and homeless' and that their children will leave footprints of blood across frozen rivers and an untamed prairie floor. Never mind that legions will die and other legions live declaring in the four quarters of this earth that they know the Book of Mormon and the Church which espouses it to be true. Disregard all of that, and tell me whether in this hour of death these two men would enter the presence of their Eternal Judge quoting from and finding solace in a book which, if not the very word of God, would brand them as imposters and charlatans until the end of time? They would not do that! They were willing to die rather than deny the divine origin and the eternal truthfulness of the Book of Mormon" (Holland, "Safety for the Soul," 88–89).

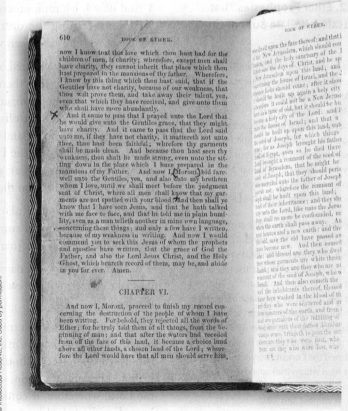

The Book of Mormon that once belonged to Hyrum Smith. He folded down page 610 in Ether the day he left for Carthage with his brother Joseph.

all dispensations, and sometimes he has appeared to large congregations. We know that 'many, exceeding great many' (Alma 13:12), as Alma expressed it, have enjoyed this privilege. We are left to assume that there are far more occasions—thousands or tens of thousands of times over—that we do not know of than those of which we do have knowledge" (McConkie, *Promised Messiah*, 605).

Ether 13:1–12. Ether Prophesies That the New Jerusalem Will Be Built in the Americas

What is required of those who dwell in this choice land? (13:2) President Gordon B. Hinckley taught: "Great are the promises concerning this land of America. We are told unequivocally that it 'is a choice land, and whatsoever nation shall possess it shall be free from bondage, and from captivity, and from all other nations under heaven, if they will but serve the God of the land, who is Jesus Christ' (Ether 2:12). This is the crux of the entire matter—obedience to the commandments of God" ("Times in Which We Live," 73). ☉

Where is the choice land and for what purpose did God choose it? (13:2–3) "The eventful destiny of America has also been revealed to God's prophets. To Joseph Smith the Lord revealed that 'the whole of America is Zion itself from north to south.'... Further, the Lord decreed this land to be 'the place of the New Jerusalem, which should come down out of heaven, ... the holy sanctuary of the Lord' (Ether 13:3). To serve God's eternal purposes and to prepare this land of Zion, God 'established the Constitution of this land, by the hands of wise men whom [He] raised up ... and redeemed the land by the shedding of blood' (D&C 101:80)" (Benson, "A Witness and a Warning," 31).

even as a man telleth another in mine own language, concerning these things;

40 And only a few have I written, because of my weakness in writing.

41 And now, I would commend you to seek this Jesus of whom the prophets and apostles have written, that the grace of God the Father, and also the Lord Jesus Christ, and the Holy Ghost, which beareth record of them, may be and abide in you forever. Amen.

CHAPTER 13

Ether speaks of a New Jerusalem to be built in America by the seed of Joseph—He prophesies, is cast out, writes the Jaredite history, and foretells the destruction of the Jaredites—War rages over all the land.

1 And now I, Moroni, proceed to finish my record concerning the destruction of the people of whom I have been writing.

2 For behold, they rejected all the words of Ether; for he truly told them of all things, from the beginning of man; and that after the waters had receded from off the face of this land it became a choice land above all other lands, a chosen land of the Lord; wherefore the Lord would have that all men should serve him who dwell upon the face thereof;

3 And that it was the place of the New Jerusalem, which should come down out of heaven, and the holy sanctuary of the Lord.

4 Behold, Ether saw the days of Christ, and he spake concerning a New Jerusalem upon this land.

5 And he spake also concerning the house of Israel, and the Jerusalem from whence Lehi should come—after it should be destroyed it should be built up again, a holy city unto the Lord; wherefore, it could not be a new Jerusalem for it had been in a time of old; but it should be built up again, and become a holy city of the Lord; and it should be built unto the house of Israel—

6 And that a New Jerusalem should be built up upon this land, unto the remnant of the seed of Joseph, for which things there has been a type.

7 For as Joseph brought his father down into the land of Egypt, even so he died there; wherefore, the Lord brought a remnant of the seed of Joseph out of the land of Jerusalem, that he might be merciful unto the seed of Joseph that they should perish not, even as he was merciful unto the father of Joseph that he should perish not.

8 Wherefore, the remnant of the house of Joseph shall be built upon this land; and it shall be a land of their inheritance; and they shall build up a holy city unto the Lord, like unto the Jerusalem of old; and they shall no more be confounded, until the end come when the earth shall pass away.

9 And there shall be a new heaven and a new earth; and they shall be like unto the old save the old have passed away, and all things have become new.

10 And then cometh the New Jerusalem; and blessed are they who dwell therein, for it is they whose garments are white through the blood of the Lamb; and they are they who are numbered among the remnant of the seed of Joseph, who were of the house of Israel.

11 And then also cometh the Jerusalem of old; and the inhabitants thereof, blessed are they, for they have been washed in the blood of the Lamb; and they are they who were scattered

How many Jerusalems did Ether prophesy about? (13:3–6) "Ether, whose teachings are summarized for us by Moroni, speaks of the New Jerusalem (Enoch's city) that shall come down out of heaven, of the New Jerusalem to be built upon the American continent, and of the building up anew of the Old Jerusalem in Palestine. His words show the relationship of these three Jerusalems to the Second Coming" (McConkie, *New Witness*, 589). ⊕

When will the earth become new and "receive its paradisiacal glory" (Articles of Faith 1:10)? (13:9) "Eventually, 'the earth will be renewed and receive its paradisiacal glory.' At the Second Coming of the Lord, the earth will be changed once again. It will be returned to its paradisiacal state and be made new. There will be a new heaven and a new earth" (Nelson, "The Creation," 85).

What is the symbolism of having our clothing washed in the blood of the Lamb? (13:10) "It is interesting to note the symbols used here by the Savior to teach the sanctifying, cleansing power of the infinite and eternal sacrifice of the Lamb of God. How do sin-stained garments become pure white when immersed in the blood of Christ? Mortal blood is a staining agent itself, but somehow, spiritually speaking, the blood spilled by a God in our behalf becomes the only true cleansing agent" (McConkie et al., *Doctrinal Commentary*, 4:180).

How is the gathering of Israel an event different from the restoration of the ten tribes? (13:11) "'We believe in the literal gathering of Israel and in the restoration of the Ten Tribes.' ... This inspired language leaves the clear impression that the gathering of Israel is one thing and the restoration of the Ten Tribes another. . . .

"We are gathering Israel now in all nations and counseling them to stay where they are, . . . there to build up stakes of Zion in their own lands and among their own people. But with the Ten Tribes, . . . it will be another thing. They are destined to return . . . to the same soil where the feet of their forebears walked during the days of their mortal pilgrimage. They are to return to Palestine" (McConkie, *Millennial Messiah*, 319–21).

What does the phrase "they who were first, who shall be last; and they who were last, who shall be first" mean regarding taking the gospel to the nations of the earth? (13:12) "Those offered the gospel first, the Jews, have been reserved for redemption last because they were so tardy in accepting their Savior; the Gentiles, last to be taught the gospel in ancient times, will have been saved first" (Thomas, "More Excellent Way," 279). See also the parable of the certain householder which planted a vineyard in Matthew 21:33–46, as well as JST, Matthew 21:47–56.

Ether 13:13–19. Ether Is Rejected and Cast Out, and His People Continue Their War

What does Moroni tell us about Ether? (13:13) "Other things Ether saw were simply too 'great and marvelous' for Moroni to record (Ether 13:13). How marvelous these must have been—in view of the great things Moroni was able to record!

"Ether had a special perspective in his life. A fellow prophet, Moroni, paid Ether this compliment: 'And now I, Moroni, proceed to finish my record concerning the destruction of the people of whom I have been writing.

"'For behold, they rejected all the words of Ether; for he truly told them of all things, from the beginning of man.' . . .

and gathered in from the four quarters of the earth, and from the north countries, and are partakers of the fulfilling of the covenant which God made with their father, Abraham.

12 And when these things come, bringeth to pass the scripture which saith, there are they who were first, who shall be last; and there are they who were last, who shall be first.

13 And I was about to write more, but I am forbidden; but great and marvelous were the prophecies of Ether; but they esteemed him as naught, and cast him out; and he hid himself in the cavity of a rock by day, and by night he went forth viewing the things which should come upon the people.

The New Jerusalem

"Ether was shown many marvelous things by the Lord, including the establishment of a New Jerusalem prior to the Second Coming. Note what Ether said about the New Jerusalem:

"1. It will be 'the holy sanctuary of the Lord' (Ether 13:2).

"2. It will be built on the American continent for the remnant of the seed of Joseph (see verses 4–6).

"3. It will be a holy city like the Jerusalem built unto the Lord (see verses 8–9).

"4. It will stand until the earth is celestialized (see verse 8).

"5. It will be a city for the pure and righteous (see verse 10)" (*Book of Mormon Student Manual* [2009], 380).

"Ether's degree of disclosure to those he taught no doubt made for sweeping sermons" (Maxwell, "Three Jaredites," 7).

What is the irony and significane of Ether dwelling in a cave? (13:14) "Ether, the heir apparent to the Jaredite throne, was rejected by the people in power. . . . The fact that Ether was the grandson of a deposed king and that he was making accusations against king Coriantumr must have created a strong bias against him. Because both his person and his message were unwelcome in Coriantumr's court, Ether had to flee for his life (Ether 13:20–22). He lived without influence among the people rather than as a king in a castle. In fact, he was considered to be an enemy, and lived as a recluse in a cave. He warned the people, observed the war by night, and recorded the tragic events (Ether 13:13–14)" (LeBaron, "Ether and Mormon," 154). ☉

14 And as he dwelt in the cavity of a rock he made the remainder of this record, viewing the destructions which came upon the people, by night.

15 And it came to pass that in that same year in which he was cast out from among the people there began to be a great war among the people, for there were many who rose up, who were mighty men, and sought to destroy Coriantumr by their secret plans of wickedness, of which hath been spoken.

16 And now Coriantumr, having studied, himself, in all the arts of war and all the cunning of the world, wherefore he gave battle unto them who sought to destroy him.

17 But he repented not, neither his fair sons nor daughters; neither the fair sons and daughters of Cohor; neither the fair sons and daughters of Corihor; and in fine, there were none of the fair sons and daughters upon the face of the whole earth who repented of their sins.

18 Wherefore, it came to pass that in the first year that Ether dwelt in the cavity of a rock, there were many people who were slain by the sword of those secret combinations, fighting against Coriantumr that they might obtain the kingdom.

19 And it came to pass that the sons of Coriantumr fought much and bled much.

20 And in the second year the word of the Lord came to Ether, that he should go and prophesy unto Coriantumr that, if he would repent, and all his household, the Lord would give unto him his kingdom and spare the people—

21 Otherwise they should be destroyed, and all his household save it were himself. And

Ether 13:20–31. Ether Prophesies of the Destruction of His People

he should only live to see the fulfilling of the prophecies which had been spoken concerning another people receiving the land for their inheritance; and Coriantumr should receive a burial by them; and every soul should be destroyed save it were Coriantumr.

22 And it came to pass that Coriantumr repented not, neither his household, neither the people; and the wars ceased not; and they sought to kill Ether, but he fled from before them and hid again in the cavity of the rock.

23 And it came to pass that there arose up Shared, and he also gave battle unto Coriantumr; and he did beat him, insomuch that in the third year he did bring him into captivity.

24 And the sons of Coriantumr, in the fourth year, did beat Shared, and did obtain the kingdom again unto their father.

25 Now there began to be a war upon all the face of the land, every man with his band fighting for that which he desired.

26 And there were robbers, and in fine, all manner of wickedness upon all the face of the land.

27 And it came to pass that Coriantumr was exceedingly angry with Shared, and he went against him with his armies to battle; and they did meet in great anger, and they did meet in the valley of Gilgal; and the battle became exceedingly sore.

28 And it came to pass that Shared fought against him for the space of three days. And it came to pass that Coriantumr beat him, and did pursue him until he came to the plains of Heshlon.

29 And it came to pass that Shared gave him battle again upon the plains; and behold, he did beat Coriantumr, and drove him back again to the valley of Gilgal.

How is the destruction of the Jaredite nation a warning to us today? (13:25) "Finally, in Ether's time too, the anarchy became absolute: 'Now there began to be a war upon all the face of the land, every man with his band fighting for that which he desired' (Ether 13:25). Destruction produced its own intoxication: 'And when the night came they were drunken with anger, even as a man who is drunken with wine; and they slept again upon their swords' (Ether 15:22).

"Preceding the second coming, will there be such similar and widespread violence, disorder, and anarchy again? Yet even in the midst of such destruction, the Lord's purposes unfold, not only generally but individually, as He keeps His individualized promises to His servants" (Maxwell, *Plain and Precious Things*, 90).

30 And Coriantumr gave Shared battle again in the valley of Gilgal, in which he beat Shared and slew him.

31 And Shared wounded Coriantumr in his thigh, that he did not go to battle again for the space of two years, in which time all the people upon the face of the land were shedding blood, and there was none to restrain them.

CHAPTER 14

The iniquity of the people brings a curse upon the land—Coriantumr engages in warfare against Gilead, then Lib, and then Shiz—Blood and carnage cover the land.

1 And now there began to be a great curse upon all the land because of the iniquity of the people, in which, if a man should lay his tool or his sword upon his shelf, or upon the place whither he would keep it, behold, upon the morrow, he could not find it, so great was the curse upon the land.

2 Wherefore every man did cleave unto that which was his own, with his hands, and would not borrow neither would he lend; and every man kept the hilt of his sword in his right hand, in the defence of his property and his own life and of his wives and children.

3 And now, after the space of two years, and after the death of Shared, behold, there arose the brother of Shared and he gave battle unto Coriantumr, in which Coriantumr did beat him and did pursue him to the wilderness of Akish.

4 And it came to pass that the brother of Shared did give battle unto him in the wilderness of Akish; and the battle became exceedingly sore, and many thousands fell by the sword.

How does this verse describe the terrible state the Jaredites had fallen to? (13:31) "When people think of the book of Ether in the Book of Mormon, they often remember scenes of deception, darkness, and bloodshed. This is not all that surprising, for indeed the book of Ether contains much of these kinds of things. The text speaks of a time of terrible wickedness when 'all the people upon the face of the land were shedding blood, and there was none to restrain them' (Ether 13:31). All the men kept their swords in their hands and no one would lend anything to another because no one was trustworthy in all the land (14:1–2)" (Judd, "Jaredite Zion Societies," 147).

Ether 14:1–8. Coriantumr Fights against Secret Combinations

How does the battle between the brother of Shared and Coriantumr exemplify the evil and horrors of the war? (14:3–8) "[This] chapter recounts the ferocious battles that raged between Coriantumr and the rebels who sought to overthrow him and who were supported in their rebellion by secret combinations. Terrible bloodshed enveloped the land, and the sights and scents of death permeated the entire area. Perhaps millions of Jaredite men, women, and children were slaughtered in these battles, and their bodies covered the landscape. It was impossible for any inhabitants to escape the horrors of these wars" (McConkie et al., *Doctrinal Commentary*, 4:313).

Ether 14:9–16. Lib Murders Gilead and Takes His Throne

How is the assassination of Gilead typical of the ancient world? (14:9) "The success of any conspiracy against such watchful royalty depends . . . on secrecy and surprise . . . , and so we have as the unfailing adjunct and nemesis of Asiatic kingship the secret society, investing all life with a paralyzing sense of insecurity, . . . overthrowing dynasties and empires in a single night. . . . The case of the brother of Shared . . . (Ether 14:9), is, then, thoroughly typical, and that by no mere coincidence. For we are . . . told that the system was inherited 'from them of old' and perpetuated by the same methods of secret societies, family compacts, bribes, oaths, assassinations, etc., as in the Old World" (Nibley, *Lehi in the Desert*, 203).

5 And it came to pass that Coriantumr did lay siege to the wilderness; and the brother of Shared did march forth out of the wilderness by night, and slew a part of the army of Coriantumr, as they were drunken.

6 And he came forth to the land of Moron, and placed himself upon the throne of Coriantumr.

7 And it came to pass that Coriantumr dwelt with his army in the wilderness for the space of two years, in which he did receive great strength to his army.

8 Now the brother of Shared, whose name was Gilead, also received great strength to his army, because of secret combinations.

9 And it came to pass that his high priest murdered him as he sat upon his throne.

10 And it came to pass that one of the secret combinations murdered him in a secret pass, and obtained unto himself the kingdom; and his name was Lib; and Lib was a man of great stature, more than any other man among all the people.

11 And it came to pass that in the first year of Lib, Coriantumr came up unto the land of Moron, and gave battle unto Lib.

12 And it came to pass that he fought with Lib, in which Lib did smite upon his arm that he was wounded; nevertheless, the army of Coriantumr did press forward upon Lib, that he fled to the borders upon the seashore.

13 And it came to pass that Coriantumr pursued him; and Lib gave battle unto him upon the seashore.

14 And it came to pass that Lib did smite the army of Coriantumr, that they fled again to the wilderness of Akish.

15 And it came to pass that Lib did pursue him until he came to the plains of Agosh. And Coriantumr had taken all the people

with him as he fled before Lib in that quarter of the land whither he fled.

16 And when he had come to the plains of Agosh he gave battle unto Lib, and he smote upon him until he died; nevertheless, the brother of Lib did come against Coriantumr in the stead thereof, and the battle became exceedingly sore, in the which Coriantumr fled again before the army of the brother of Lib.

17 Now the name of the brother of Lib was called Shiz. And it came to pass that Shiz pursued after Coriantumr, and he did overthrow many cities, and he did slay both women and children, and he did burn the cities.

18 And there went a fear of Shiz throughout all the land; yea, a cry went forth throughout the land—Who can stand before the army of Shiz? Behold, he sweepeth the earth before him!

19 And it came to pass that the people began to flock together in armies, throughout all the face of the land.

20 And they were divided; and a part of them fled to the army of Shiz, and a part of them fled to the army of Coriantumr.

21 And so great and lasting had been the war, and so long had been the scene of bloodshed and carnage, that the whole face of the land was covered with the bodies of the dead.

22 And so swift and speedy was the war that there was none left to bury the dead, but they did march forth from the shedding of blood to the shedding of blood, leaving the bodies of both men, women, and children strewed upon the face of the land, to become a prey to the worms of the flesh.

23 And the scent thereof went forth upon the face of the land, even upon all the face of the land; wherefore the people became troubled by day and by night, because of the scent thereof.

Ether 14:17–31. Coriantumr Battles Shiz as Death and Destruction Cover the Land

What are the effects of seeking revenge? (14:17–18) "Our first encounter with Shiz in the scriptures introduces his insensitivity, for he 'did slay both women and children, and he did burn the cities' (Ether 14:17).

"We see in the rivalry of Shiz and Coriantumr, as in other Book of Mormon episodes, an awful cycle of family vengeance. Those who are caught up in revenge lose all perspective concerning the sanctity of life.

"Shiz swore to 'avenge himself upon Coriantumr of the blood of his brother' (Ether 14:24). That Shiz was an intimidating individual is made perfectly clear by the quailing question, 'Who can stand before the army of Shiz?' (Ether 14:18)" (Maxwell, "Three Jaredites," 9).

Why do divisions among people escalate in war? (14:20) "Coriantumr and Shared became obsessed with the necessity of ridding the world of each other. When Shared defeated one of Coriantumr's armies, he raced to the capital and put himself on the man's throne. But the process of polarization then began in earnest. Coriantumr gathered 'great strength to his army' . . . while Gilead, the brother and successor of Shared, was doing the same, assisted by secret combinations. The[y] were dangerous associates, however, for they soon murdered Gilead and then . . . his murderer, while a giant by the name of Lib . . . became king. He was killed fighting Coriantumr, but his brother continued the feud—he was the famous Shiz. . . . Always this steady, progressive process of polarization goes on" (Nibley, *Teachings of the Book of Mormon*, 4:257–58).

What was the real cause of the strife and blood-shed among the Jaredites? (14:24) "Jaredite society, like every other heroic society, is a feudal organization bound together by an elaborate system of oaths.... Since in heroic ages one becomes a leader by proving his prowess in open competition, personal rivalry and ambition are the ordinary and accepted motives for war and need no excuse. Throughout our Jaredite history the perennial source of strife and bloodshed is the purely personal rivalry between great leaders" (Nibley, *Lehi in the Desert*, 410).

What does the phrase "and thus we see" help us understand about the distinctiveness of Mormon's and Moroni's writings? (14:25) "Recent research ... has taken a closer look at the works of Mormon and Moroni to analyze these writers as authors and abridgers comparing their techniques and identifying unique and distinctive characteristics in the editorial styles of each....

"Another significant difference is found in the use of the well-known but characteristic expression 'and thus we see that....' Mormon used it over twenty times to insert moral conclusions in the sections he wrote or abridged.... Moroni used the phrase only once (see Ether 14:25)" (Keller, "Mormon and Moroni as Authors and Abridgers," 269–71).

What brings on the "fulness" of the Lord's wrath? (14:25) "These painful consequences of war were the direct result of their own wickedness, which in turn produced a literal fulfillment of earlier prophecies wherein the Lord had promised peace and protection to the inhabitants of this land if they would obey him and destruction if they did not.... Much if not all of the pain and suffering that could be viewed as 'the wrath of God' came by means of the meanness, the cruelty, and the thirst for blood that filled the hearts of the spiritually sick and dead" (McConkie et al., *Doctrinal Commentary*, 4:313).

24 Nevertheless, Shiz did not cease to pursue Coriantumr; for he had sworn to avenge himself upon Coriantumr of the blood of his brother, who had been slain, and the word of the Lord which came to Ether that Coriantumr should not fall by the sword.

25 And thus we see that the Lord did visit them in the fulness of his wrath, and their wickedness and abominations had prepared a way for their everlasting destruction.

26 And it came to pass that Shiz did pursue Coriantumr eastward, even to the borders by the seashore, and there he gave battle unto Shiz for the space of three days.

27 And so terrible was the destruction among the armies of Shiz that the people began to be frightened, and began to flee before the armies of Coriantumr; and they fled to the land of Corihor, and swept off the inhabitants before them, all them that would not join them.

28 And they pitched their tents in the valley of Corihor; and Coriantumr pitched his tents in the valley of Shurr. Now the valley of Shurr was near the hill Comnor; wherefore, Coriantumr did gather his armies together upon the hill Comnor, and did sound a trumpet unto the armies of Shiz to invite them forth to battle.

29 And it came to pass that they came forth, but were driven again; and they came the second time, and they were driven again the second time. And it came to pass that they came again the third time, and the battle became exceedingly sore.

30 And it came to pass that Shiz smote upon Coriantumr that he gave him many deep wounds; and Coriantumr, having lost his blood, fainted, and was carried away as though he were dead.

31 Now the loss of men, women and children on both sides was so great that Shiz commanded his people that they should not pursue the armies of Coriantumr; wherefore, they returned to their camp.

CHAPTER 15

Millions of the Jaredites are slain in battle— Shiz and Coriantumr assemble all the people to mortal combat—The Spirit of the Lord ceases to strive with them—The Jaredite nation is utterly destroyed—Only Coriantumr remains.

1 And it came to pass when Coriantumr had recovered of his wounds, he began to remember the words which Ether had spoken unto him.

2 He saw that there had been slain by the sword already nearly two millions of his people, and he began to sorrow in his heart; yea, there had been slain two millions of mighty men, and also their wives and their children.

3 He began to repent of the evil which he had done; he began to remember the words which had been spoken by the mouth of all the prophets, and he saw them that they were fulfilled thus far, every whit; and his soul mourned and refused to be comforted.

4 And it came to pass that he wrote an epistle unto Shiz, desiring him that he would spare the people, and he would give up the kingdom for the sake of the lives of the people.

5 And it came to pass that when Shiz had received his epistle he wrote an epistle unto Coriantumr, that if he would give himself up, that he might slay him with his own sword, that he would spare the lives of the people.

6 And it came to pass that the people repented not of their iniquity; and the people

Ether 15:1–4. Coriantumr Sorrows over the Deaths of So Many People

Why does Coriantumr finally remember the words of Ether? (15:1–3) Faced with the entire destruction of his people, Coriantumr remembers the words of Ether. Why are people more willing to listen to the words of prophets in times of difficulty? (see D&C 101:8). How can you guard against making a similar mistake in your own life?

Ether 15:5–10. The People Are Filled with Anger, and War Continues

How could the destruction of the Jaredite people have been averted? (15:5) "There for us to ponder also is a clear case in which personal pride and rage kept two principals from acting for the welfare of their people. Shiz insisted on 'getting his man,' even if it meant the destruction of his own people; and Coriantumr offered his kingdom but not his life for his people. Each said, in effect, that the ultimate object of his selfishness was nonnegotiable! Neither was willing to play the role of the intervener and say of the circumstances, 'This has gone too far—enough is enough.' How often on a lesser scale in human affairs do tinier tragedies occur for want of this selfless intervention?" (Maxwell, "Three Jaredites," 11).

What were the rules of war for the Jaredites? (15:8) "'A dignified and fastidious tone' prevails in the dealings of these men with each other, and strict rules of chivalry are observed, especially in war and duels. So we are told in Ether how Shiz and Coriantumr pitch formal camps and 'invite' each other's armies forth to combat by regulated trumpet blasts . . . , exchange letters in an attempt to avoid needless bloodshed . . . , and rest at night without attempting to attack each other, fighting only at the proper and agreed times. . . . As in all epics, including Ether, 'the waging of war is not incidental but essential to the heroic way of life'" (Nibley, *Lehi in the Desert*, 409).

Ether 15:11–14. For Four Years Ether Watches the People Gather into Two Armies

What is the relationship between the hill Ramah and the hill Cumorah? (15:11) The Hill Ramah and the Hill Cumorah are the same hill where both the Jaredites and Nephites fought their final battles. Ramah is the Jaredite name given to the "same hill where my father Mormon did hide up the records" (Ether 15:11). During the final battles of the Jaredites between Coriantumr and Shiz, the armies of Coriantumr "did pitch their tents by the hill Ramah" and here gathered the people for four years (Ether 15:11, 14). However, hundreds of years later after the destruction of the Jaredites, it became known to the Nephites as the Hill Cumorah where they too were destroyed as a people (see Mormon 6:2–11; 8:2).

of Coriantumr were stirred up to anger against the people of Shiz; and the people of Shiz were stirred up to anger against the people of Coriantumr; wherefore, the people of Shiz did give battle unto the people of Coriantumr.

7 And when Coriantumr saw that he was about to fall he fled again before the people of Shiz.

8 And it came to pass that he came to the waters of Ripliancum, which, by interpretation, is large, or to exceed all; wherefore, when they came to these waters they pitched their tents; and Shiz also pitched his tents near unto them; and therefore on the morrow they did come to battle.

9 And it came to pass that they fought an exceedingly sore battle, in which Coriantumr was wounded again, and he fainted with the loss of blood.

10 And it came to pass that the armies of Coriantumr did press upon the armies of Shiz that they beat them, that they caused them to flee before them; and they did flee southward, and did pitch their tents in a place which was called Ogath.

11 And it came to pass that the army of Coriantumr did pitch their tents by the hill Ramah; and it was that same hill where my father Mormon did hide up the records unto the Lord, which were sacred.

12 And it came to pass that they did gather together all the people upon all the face of the land, who had not been slain, save it was Ether.

13 And it came to pass that Ether did behold all the doings of the people; and he beheld that the people who were for Coriantumr were gathered together to the army of Coriantumr; and the people who were for Shiz were gathered together to the army of Shiz.

14 Wherefore, they were for the space of four years gathering together the people, that they might get all who were upon the face of the land, and that they might receive all the strength which it was possible that they could receive.

15 And it came to pass that when they were all gathered together, every one to the army which he would, with their wives and their children—both men, women and children being armed with weapons of war, having shields, and breastplates, and head-plates, and being clothed after the manner of war—they did march forth one against another to battle; and they fought all that day, and conquered not.

16 And it came to pass that when it was night they were weary, and retired to their camps; and after they had retired to their camps they took up a howling and a lamentation for the loss of the slain of their people; and so great were their cries, their howlings and lamentations, that they did rend the air exceedingly.

17 And it came to pass that on the morrow they did go again to battle, and great and terrible was that day; nevertheless, they conquered not, and when the night came again they did rend the air with their cries, and their howlings, and their mournings, for the loss of the slain of their people.

18 And it came to pass that Coriantumr wrote again an epistle unto Shiz, desiring that he would not come again to battle, but that he would take the kingdom, and spare the lives of the people.

19 But behold, the Spirit of the Lord had ceased striving with them, and Satan had full power over the hearts of the people; for they were given up unto the hardness of their hearts, and the blindness of their minds that they might be destroyed; wherefore they went again to battle.

Ether 15:15–34. Ether Witnesses the War Continue Until All the Jaredites Are Destroyed except Coriantumr

How do the last Jaredite battles compare to the last Nephite battles? (15:15–17) "The chapters recounting the Jaredite demise (Ether 13–15) feature a rejection of God's prophets, escalating warfare, a polarized society in which everyone is swept up by one side or the other, a gathering for the final battle, and then a cataclysmic conclusion. It . . . sounds somewhat like Mormon's account of the end of the Nephites. However, Moroni never points out the rather significant differences: Jaredite troubles arose from rival factions among the leadership rather than from competing ethnic groups, the last prophet had no role in the struggles, the two forces were fairly evenly matched, and one side did not successfully conquer the other" (Hardy, *Understanding the Book of Mormon*, 229).

What happens when Satan has full power over the hearts of the people? (15:19) "Civil order had collapsed. In reflection of the slipperiness and the utter perishability of their lives and works, they held on to nothing but their swords; no security offered itself. The relentless law of the harvest rolled upon them, and they lived out their remaining days like specters in a terrifying nightmare of anger—sickness, howling, stench, and blood. The lives they had chosen had filled them, not with desire for peace and abundant thriving life, but with hatred and self-destruction. The ultimate end of evil is death" (Thomas, "More Excellent Way," 279–80).

Was it unusual for the kings to be the last survivors? (15:25–28) "The whole population was cut down to fifty-nine souls, . . . and these slew each other . . . leaving the two kings as the last survivors. This is not a fantastic coincidence at all. We have seen that the common and established rule of heroic warfare demanded that the king be the last survivor in any conflict. Since the entire host had taken a solemn oath to die in defense of his person, in theory the king had to be the last to go, and in practice he sometimes actually was" (Nibley, *Lehi in the Desert*, 413).

As you reflect on the end of this mighty nation, what important lessons have you learned? (15:29) "The only power strong enough to withstand a fulness of iniquity is the fulness of the gospel of Jesus Christ" (Wirthlin, "Deep Roots," 77).

20 And it came to pass that they fought all that day, and when the night came they slept upon their swords.

21 And on the morrow they fought even until the night came.

22 And when the night came they were drunken with anger, even as a man who is drunken with wine; and they slept again upon their swords.

23 And on the morrow they fought again; and when the night came they had all fallen by the sword save it were fifty and two of the people of Coriantumr, and sixty and nine of the people of Shiz.

24 And it came to pass that they slept upon their swords that night, and on the morrow they fought again, and they contended in their might with their swords and with their shields, all that day.

25 And when the night came there were thirty and two of the people of Shiz, and twenty and seven of the people of Coriantumr.

26 And it came to pass that they ate and slept, and prepared for death on the morrow. And they were large and mighty men as to the strength of men.

27 And it came to pass that they fought for the space of three hours, and they fainted with the loss of blood.

28 And it came to pass that when the men of Coriantumr had received sufficient strength that they could walk, they were about to flee for their lives; but behold, Shiz arose, and also his men, and he swore in his wrath that he would slay Coriantumr or he would perish by the sword.

29 Wherefore, he did pursue them, and on the morrow he did overtake them; and they fought again with the sword. And it came to pass that when they had all fallen by the

sword, save it were Coriantumr and Shiz, behold Shiz had fainted with the loss of blood.

30 And it came to pass that when Coriantumr had leaned upon his sword, that he rested a little, he smote off the head of Shiz.

31 And it came to pass that after he had smitten off the head of Shiz, that Shiz raised up on his hands and fell; and after that he had struggled for breath, he died.

32 And it came to pass that Coriantumr fell to the earth, and became as if he had no life.

33 And the Lord spake unto Ether, and said unto him: Go forth. And he went forth, and beheld that the words of the Lord had all been fulfilled; and he finished his record; (and the hundredth part I have not written) and he hid them in a manner that the people of Limhi did find them.

34 Now the last words which are written by Ether are these: Whether the Lord will that I be translated, or that I suffer the will of the Lord in the flesh, it mattereth not, if it so be that I am saved in the kingdom of God. Amen.

What do some find unbelievable about the death of Shiz? (15:31) "Unfriendly critics of the Book of Mormon have objected to this account of the death of Shiz as incredible. A decapitated human body cannot, in their opinion, have acted as here represented. The obvious reply is that the case may be exceptional, even unique, but that is not a reason why we should doubt the veracity, or accuracy, of the chronicler. Exceptions to well-known rules are of daily occurrence" (Reynolds and Sjodahl, *Commentary on the Book of Mormon*, 6:201). ◉

What truth is emphasized by the deaths of Coriantumr and Shiz? (15:32) "Coriantumr and Shiz shared the last scene together. Ether, looking on secretly from his hiding place, saw Coriantumr behead Shiz in a memorably gory scene, after which Coriantumr fell to the earth 'as if he had no life' (Ether 15:32). But he was not dead, as the Lord foresaw. Coriantumr appeared again among the Mulekites as one who pathetically straddled that tradition from a fallen group to a new chosen people (Omni 1:21). One of the great lessons of the Book of Mormon is that whatever the Lord prophesies is fulfilled, every whit, in every specific detail, nothing omitted" (Thomas, "More Excellent Way," 280).

Why do you think Ether was so faithful to his message that he continued to teach it to his fellowmen, even amidst their wars? (15:33) "A great prophet, Ether, prophesied great things 'unto the people' but 'they did not believe because they saw them not.' Such is the recurring and fatal flaw of the faithless. Such, also, is the love of prophets, like Ether, who nevertheless continue to strive lovingly with their fellowmen 'from the morning, even until the going down of the sun' [Ether 12:3]" (Maxwell, "Three Jaredites," 11).

Was Ether translated? (15:34) "We see in the book of Ether intimations that this very special prophet might have been translated, but we never do learn what actually happened to him. The silence concerning his circumstance is not unlike the disappearance of Alma the Younger, of which it was written, 'And when Alma had done this he departed out of the land of Zarahemla, ... And it came to pass that he was never heard of more; as to his death or burial we know not of'" (Maxwell, "Three Jaredites," 9).

THE BOOK OF MORONI

Moroni, after abridging the record of the Jaredites, which is known as the book of Ether, wrote his own book. This last Book of Mormon prophet described some of the Savior's teachings and commandments during His visit to the Nephites, which include the doctrine of receiving the Holy Ghost, priesthood ordinations, sacrament prayers, and baptism. In many ways, the book of Moroni acted as a blueprint for Joseph Smith on how to establish the true Church of Jesus Christ. Many of the doctrines and principles set forth in Moroni's own book were the source for Doctrine and Covenants 20. Moroni's last remarks exemplify charity toward his enemies, the Lamanites. Even as they seek his life, he still mercifully writes to their descendants in love and compassion. The book of Moroni also contains a promise to anyone who sincerely reads the Book of Mormon that God will reveal the truth of the work through the power of the Holy Ghost. Moroni concludes with a powerful witness of Jesus Christ.

Moroni 1:1–4. Moroni's Final Words Are to the Lamanites

What do we know about Moroni? (1:1) See commentary in this volume on Mormon 8:1 and Ether 1:1–2.

In what way might the Nephite wars be similar to ancient "holy" wars? (1:2) Most of the Nephite wars were over spiritual issues, not temporal concerns. William Hamblin observed: "Religion and warfare were closely connected in the Book of Mormon. Certain elements of the Israelite patterns of 'holy war' were continued in the Book of Mormon, such as the important ancient idea that success in war was due fundamentally to the will of God and the righteousness of the people (Alma 2:28; 44:4–5; 50:21; 56:47; 57:36; 58:33; Mormon 2:26)" (Ludlow, *Encyclopedia of Mormonism*, 1:163).

CHAPTER 1

Moroni writes for the benefit of the Lamanites—The Nephites who will not deny Christ are put to death. About A.D. 401–421.

1 Now I, Moroni, after having made an end of abridging the account of the people of Jared, I had supposed not to have written more, but I have not as yet perished; and I make not myself known to the Lamanites lest they should destroy me.

2 For behold, their wars are exceedingly fierce among themselves; and because of their hatred they put to death every Nephite that will not deny the Christ.

3 And I, Moroni, will not deny the Christ; wherefore, I wander whithersoever I can for the safety of mine own life.

4 Wherefore, I write a few more things, contrary to that which I had supposed; for I had supposed not to have written any more; but I write a few more things, that perhaps they may be of worth unto my brethren, the Lamanites, in some future day, according to the will of the Lord.

CHAPTER 2

Jesus gave the twelve Nephite disciples power to confer the gift of the Holy Ghost. About A.D. 401–421.

1 The words of Christ, which he spake unto his disciples, the twelve whom he had chosen, as he laid his hands upon them—

2 And he called them by name, saying: Ye shall call on the Father in my name, in mighty prayer; and after ye have done this ye shall have power that to him upon whom ye shall lay your hands, ye shall give the Holy Ghost; and in my name shall ye give it, for thus do mine apostles.

3 Now Christ spake these words unto them at the time of his first appearing; and the multitude heard it not, but the disciples heard it; and on as many as they laid their hands, fell the Holy Ghost.

CHAPTER 3

Elders ordain priests and teachers by the laying on of hands. About A.D. 401–421.

1 The manner which the disciples, who were called the elders of the church, ordained priests and teachers—

What were included in the "few more things" Moroni wanted to write? (1:4) "What Moroni first recorded in the book carrying his own name were vignettes—a brief catalog, if you will—of things he felt needed to be recorded before he died and the Book of Mormon saga ended. These included the words of Christ to his twelve disciples when they were commissioned to bestow the Holy Ghost by the laying on of hands, the prayer by which priests and teachers were ordained, the sacrament prayers, and instructions as to how those who were baptized were to be received into the 'church of Christ' and numbered among the 'people of Christ'" (Holland, *Christ and the New Covenant*, 332). ⊕

Moroni 2:1–3. Jesus Gives His Twelve Nephite Disciples the Power to Confer the Gift of the Holy Ghost

In what ways were the twelve Nephite disciples Apostles? (2:2) "While in every instance the Nephite twelve are spoken of as disciples, the fact remains that they had been endowed with divine authority to be special witnesses for Christ among their own people. Therefore, they were virtually apostles to the Nephite race, although their jurisdiction was, as revealed to Nephi, eventually to be subject to the authority and jurisdiction of Peter and the twelve chosen in Palestine (see Mormon 3:18–19). According to the definition prevailing in the world an apostle is a witness for Christ, or one who evangelizes a certain nation or people.... Therefore the Nephite twelve became apostles, as special witnesses, just as did Joseph Smith and Oliver Cowdery in the Dispensation of the Fulness of Times" (Smith, *Answers to Gospel Questions*, 1:122).

Moroni 3:1–4. Moroni Explains How the Nephites Ordained Men to the Priesthood

What priesthood did the Nephites hold? (3:1) "Even during the Mosaic dispensation there were no Aaronic Priesthood holders among the Nephites, for there were no Levites among them. The priests and teachers among the Nephites held the Melchizedek Priesthood" (McConkie, *New Witness*, 348). ⊕

How were priests ordained in Moroni's day? (3:2–4)
"The Christian world lays on unauthorized hands, confers divinity degrees to bestow authority, or assumes power by simple desire. . . .

"There can be no question as to how one is ordained with the power to minister for Christ and how that power is used to bestow the Holy Ghost. Another plain and precious teaching has been restored in the Book of Mormon, and we can now read biblical statements on receiving the priesthood and bestowing the Holy Ghost without misunderstanding" (Parsons, "Practices of the Church," 283–84). ⊕

Moroni 4:1–3. Jesus Christ Gives Instructions on How to Bless the Bread for the Sacrament

What similarities are there between Moroni's teachings on the sacrament and those of the resurrected Lord? (4:1) "The close relationship between the words of Jesus in 3 Nephi 18 and the basic terms of the sacrament prayers found in Moroni 4–5 is readily apparent. Virtually every component in the two sacrament prayers has a precise counterpart in the express words of Jesus himself" (Welch, "From Presence to Practice," 124).

Why is it important to "always remember" the Savior? (4:3) "The Book of Mormon provide[s] us with direction from prophets who warn us to preserve and enlarge our own memory of God's mighty deeds and with the terms of the covenant that make us the people of God. These records teach us that we must neither forget what God has done nor what we have covenanted to do. The result of forgetting is to begin following some unholy tradition into darkness and sin. Instead, we must 'always remember him, and keep his commandments' (Moroni 4:3) and be willing to take upon us the name of Jesus Christ, for to forget the sacrifice offered by our Lord for our sins by not keeping the commandments is to offend God" (Midgley, "Ways of Remembrance," 176). ⊕

2 After they had prayed unto the Father in the name of Christ, they laid their hands upon them, and said:

3 In the name of Jesus Christ I ordain you to be a priest (or if he be a teacher, I ordain you to be a teacher) to preach repentance and remission of sins through Jesus Christ, by the endurance of faith on his name to the end. Amen.

4 And after this manner did they ordain priests and teachers, according to the gifts and callings of God unto men; and they ordained them by the power of the Holy Ghost, which was in them.

CHAPTER 4

How elders and priests administer the sacramental bread is explained. About A.D. 401–421.

1 The manner of their elders and priests administering the flesh and blood of Christ unto the church; and they administered it according to the commandments of Christ; wherefore we know the manner to be true; and the elder or priest did minister it—

2 And they did kneel down with the church, and pray to the Father in the name of Christ, saying:

3 O God, the Eternal Father, we ask thee in the name of thy Son, Jesus Christ, to bless and sanctify this bread to the souls of all those who partake of it; that they may eat in remembrance of the body of thy Son, and witness unto thee, O God, the Eternal Father, that they are willing to take upon them the name of thy Son, and always remember him, and keep his commandments which he hath given them, that they may always have his Spirit to be with them. Amen.

CHAPTER 5

The mode of administering the sacramental wine is set forth. About A.D. 401–421.

1 The manner of administering the wine—Behold, they took the cup, and said:

2 O God, the Eternal Father, we ask thee, in the name of thy Son, Jesus Christ, to bless and sanctify this wine to the souls of all those who drink of it, that they may do it in remembrance of the blood of thy Son, which was shed for them; that they may witness unto thee, O God, the Eternal Father, that they do always remember him, that they may have his Spirit to be with them. Amen.

CHAPTER 6

Repentant persons are baptized and fellowshipped—Church members who repent are forgiven—Meetings are conducted by the power of the Holy Ghost. About A.D. 401–421.

1 And now I speak concerning baptism. Behold, elders, priests, and teachers were baptized; and they were not baptized save they brought forth fruit meet that they were worthy of it.

2 Neither did they receive any unto baptism save they came forth with a broken heart and a contrite spirit, and witnessed unto the church that they truly repented of all their sins.

Moroni 5:1–2. Jesus Christ Teaches the Nephites How to Bless the Wine for the Sacrament

When did water replace wine in the sacrament emblems of the Church? (5:1) "The Lord revealed to Joseph Smith that 'it mattereth not what ye shall eat or what ye shall drink when ye partake of the sacrament, if it so be that ye do it with an eye single to my glory—remembering unto the Father my body which was laid down for you, and my blood which was shed for the remission of your sins' [D&C 27:2]. . . .

"It took a number of years before the congregations of the Saints totally abolished the use of wine in the sacrament, but by the end of President Brigham Young's administration, the use of water for the sacrament was generally the practice" (Haight, "Remembering the Savior's Atonement," 11).

What are the covenants and promises in the sacramental prayer? (5:2) "At the conclusion of Benjamin's speech, his people entered into a covenant, saying 'we are willing . . . to be obedient to [God's] commandments in all things that he shall command us,' after which they agreed to 'take upon [themselves] the name of Christ' and obligated themselves to 'remember to retain the name written always in [their] hearts' (Mosiah 5:5–12). These three specific promises not only reappear in Moroni 4, but are still the essential elements of the sacramental prayers as they are used today" (Welch, "Our Nephite Sacrament Prayers," 286).

Moroni 6:1–4. Moroni Teaches about Baptism

Why did Moroni stress worthiness as a requirement for baptism? (6:1) "No price is too great to pay for the privilege of receiving this holy ordinance. We must prepare ourselves for baptism; we must be worthy to make a covenant with the Holy One; we must have a fixed and unalterable determination to conform to his will. Otherwise baptism profiteth nothing. No ordinance is binding on earth and in heaven unless it is ratified and sealed by the Holy Spirit of Promise, and this Spirit is given only to those who are just and true. Just as those who partake unworthily of the sacrament eat and drink damnation to their souls, so those who are baptized unworthily receive cursings instead of blessings" (McConkie, *New Witness*, 248).

What does it mean to take upon us the name of Jesus Christ? (6:3) "When we witness our willingness to take upon us the name of Jesus Christ, we are signifying our commitment to do all that we can to achieve eternal life in the kingdom of our Father. We are expressing our candidacy—our determination to strive for—exaltation in the celestial kingdom" (Oaks, "Taking upon Us the Name of Jesus Christ," 82).

How should new converts be remembered and nourished? (6:4) "With the ever-increasing number of converts, we must make an increasingly substantial effort to assist them as they find their way. Every one of them needs three things: a friend, a responsibility, and nurturing with 'the good word of God' (Moro. 6:4). It is our duty and opportunity to provide these things" (Hinckley, "Converts and Young Men," 47). ◉

Moroni 6:5–9. Moroni Writes about Church Practices

What is the purpose of the church meeting together often? (6:5) "Ours is the commandment and the blessing to 'meet together oft, to fast and to pray, and to speak one with another concerning the welfare of [our] souls.' In general conferences and in other Church meetings around the world, we come together seeking companionship—the good company of brothers and sisters in the gospel and the comfort of sweet communion with the Spirit of God. In our worship services, the presence of that Spirit fills our hearts with love for God and for our fellow Saints" (Wirthlin, "Valued Companions," 32).

What should all people experience as they attend church meetings? (6:9) "We have begun a great effort to 'invite all to come unto Christ' (D&C 20:59). As the members meet—the active and the less active, the poor in spirit, the singles and the married, the handicapped, and those who have been disciplined—they ought to feel the Spirit, love, and forgiveness. For all of us, this ought to be a time of prayerful meditation and thanksgiving" (Haight, "Remembering the Savior's Atonement," 13). ◉

3 And none were received unto baptism save they took upon them the name of Christ, having a determination to serve him to the end.

4 And after they had been received unto baptism, and were wrought upon and cleansed by the power of the Holy Ghost, they were numbered among the people of the church of Christ; and their names were taken, that they might be remembered and nourished by the good word of God, to keep them in the right way, to keep them continually watchful unto prayer, relying alone upon the merits of Christ, who was the author and the finisher of their faith.

5 And the church did meet together oft, to fast and to pray, and to speak one with another concerning the welfare of their souls.

6 And they did meet together oft to partake of bread and wine, in remembrance of the Lord Jesus.

7 And they were strict to observe that there should be no iniquity among them; and whoso was found to commit iniquity, and three witnesses of the church did condemn them before the elders, and if they repented not, and confessed not, their names were blotted out, and they were not numbered among the people of Christ.

8 But as oft as they repented and sought forgiveness, with real intent, they were forgiven.

9 And their meetings were conducted by the church after the manner of the workings of the Spirit, and by the power of the Holy Ghost; for as the power of the Holy Ghost led them whether to preach, or to exhort, or to pray, or to supplicate, or to sing, even so it was done.

CHAPTER 7

An invitation is given to enter into the rest of the Lord—Pray with real intent—The Spirit of Christ enables men to know good from evil—Satan persuades men to deny Christ and do evil—The prophets manifest the coming of Christ—By faith, miracles are wrought and angels minister—Men should hope for eternal life and cleave unto charity. About A.D. 401–421.

1 And now I, Moroni, write a few of the words of my father Mormon, which he spake concerning faith, hope, and charity; for after this manner did he speak unto the people, as he taught them in the synagogue which they had built for the place of worship.

2 And now I, Mormon, speak unto you, my beloved brethren; and it is by the grace of God the Father, and our Lord Jesus Christ, and his holy will, because of the gift of his calling unto me, that I am permitted to speak unto you at this time.

3 Wherefore, I would speak unto you that are of the church, that are the peaceable followers of Christ, and that have obtained a sufficient hope by which ye can enter into the rest of the Lord, from this time henceforth until ye shall rest with him in heaven.

4 And now my brethren, I judge these things of you because of your peaceable walk with the children of men.

Moroni 7:1–4. Mormon Speaks to the Peaceable Followers of Christ

Why did Moroni write the words of his father's sermon? (7:1) "One of the most tightly woven and forceful sermons in the Book of Mormon is that recorded by Moroni as given by his father, Mormon, on faith, hope, and charity. The topic is particularly poignant in its context: Mormon has been killed by the Lamanites, and Moroni is the solitary survivor, recording these words out of his own generosity of spirit. We can also imagine that Moroni is rereading this sermon to strengthen his own faith, hope, and charity—a topic Moroni addresses in his concluding words in the Book of Mormon" (Rust, *Feasting on the Word*, 140–41).

Why do you think Mormon viewed his calling as a gift from Heavenly Father? (7:2) How do you feel about the callings the Lord gives to you? Why should you feel gratitude for the opportunity to serve God and your brothers and sisters? ●

What is the "rest of the Lord" and how do we enter it? (7:3) "The rest here referred to is not physical rest, for there is no such thing as physical rest in the Church of Jesus Christ. Reference is made to the spiritual rest and peace which are born from a settled conviction of the truth in the minds of men. We may thus enter into the rest of the Lord today, by coming to an understanding of the truths of the gospel" (Smith, *Gospel Doctrine*, 126).

Why does Mormon connect "peace" with those who follow Christ? (7:3–4) "This is the spiritual endowment of hope—of perspective, of patience, of an inner serenity, a sure inner sight, that is 'not weary in well-doing' (D&C 64:33). Such hope is bestowed by the power of the Holy Ghost, 'which Comforter filleth with hope' (Moroni 8:26). . . . It is the hope that Mormon recognized as a sustaining, God-given source of strength in the maturing stages of spiritual development: [Moroni 7:3–4]. Not perfect, not frantic; not pessimistic and not artificially cheerful. The walk of those who walk with the endowment of hope is 'peaceable'" (Hafen, *Broken Heart*, 183–84).

Moroni 7:5–11. We Must Serve with Real Intent

How does God judge gifts that are given grudgingly? (7:5–11) President Dallin H. Oaks cited President David O. McKay, who taught: "Mere compliance with the word of the Lord, without a corresponding inward desire, will avail but little. Indeed, such outward actions and pretending phrases may disclose hypocrisy, a sin that Jesus most vehemently condemned" (in Conference Report, Oct. 1951, 6, cited in Oaks, *Pure in Heart*, 33).

President Oaks concluded, "There are no blessings in supposedly good acts that are performed for the wrong reasons" (*Pure in Heart*, 33). ◉

What difference do our intentions make when we give a gift or provide service? (7:11) How is someone who serves grudgingly like a bitter fountain? Why do you think obedience with a sincere heart is a vital part of the gospel?

Moroni 7:12–20. Mormon Teaches How We Can Know Good from Evil

How can we know if something is good or evil? (7:12–13) President Thomas S. Monson offered: "May I provide a simple formula by which you can measure the choices which confront you. It's easy to remember: 'You can't be right by doing wrong; you can't be wrong by doing right.' Your personal conscience always warns you as a friend before it punishes you as a judge" ("Pathways to Perfection," 100).

5 For I remember the word of God which saith by their works ye shall know them; for if their works be good, then they are good also.

6 For behold, God hath said a man being evil cannot do that which is good; for if he offereth a gift, or prayeth unto God, except he shall do it with real intent it profiteth him nothing.

7 For behold, it is not counted unto him for righteousness.

8 For behold, if a man being evil giveth a gift, he doeth it grudgingly; wherefore it is counted unto him the same as if he had retained the gift; wherefore he is counted evil before God.

9 And likewise also is it counted evil unto a man, if he shall pray and not with real intent of heart; yea, and it profiteth him nothing, for God receiveth none such.

10 Wherefore, a man being evil cannot do that which is good; neither will he give a good gift.

11 For behold, a bitter fountain cannot bring forth good water; neither can a good fountain bring forth bitter water; wherefore, a man being a servant of the devil cannot follow Christ; and if he follow Christ he cannot be a servant of the devil.

12 Wherefore, all things which are good cometh of God; and that which is evil cometh of the devil; for the devil is an enemy unto God, and fighteth against him continually, and inviteth and enticeth to sin, and to do that which is evil continually.

13 But behold, that which is of God inviteth and enticeth to do good continually; wherefore, every thing which inviteth and enticeth to do good, and to love God, and to serve him, is inspired of God.

14 Wherefore, take heed, my beloved brethren, that ye do not judge that which is evil to be of God, or that which is good and of God to be of the devil.

15 For behold, my brethren, it is given unto you to judge, that ye may know good from evil; and the way to judge is as plain, that ye may know with a perfect knowledge, as the daylight is from the dark night.

16 For behold, the Spirit of Christ is given to every man, that he may know good from evil; wherefore, I show unto you the way to judge; for every thing which inviteth to do good, and to persuade to believe in Christ, is sent forth by the power and gift of Christ; wherefore ye may know with a perfect knowledge it is of God.

17 But whatsoever thing persuadeth men to do evil, and believe not in Christ, and deny him, and serve not God, then ye may know with a perfect knowledge it is of the devil; for after this manner doth the devil work, for he persuadeth no man to do good, no, not one; neither do his angels; neither do they who subject themselves unto him.

18 And now, my brethren, seeing that ye know the light by which ye may judge, which light is the light of Christ, see that ye do not judge wrongfully; for with that same judgment which ye judge ye shall also be judged.

19 Wherefore, I beseech of you, brethren, that ye should search diligently in the light of Christ that ye may know good from evil; and if ye will lay hold upon every good thing, and condemn it not, ye certainly will be a child of Christ.

20 And now, my brethren, how is it possible that ye can lay hold upon every good thing?

Of what are we to "take heed" when judging good and evil? (7:14–19) President Harold B. Lee declared: "It seemed necessary in every dispensation to set up the measure by which the world could know falsehood from truth (see Moroni 7; D&C 50)" (*Teachings of Harold B. Lee,* 464).

As you study the "measure" provided in these verses by Mormon, consider how it might help you discern the difference between falsehood and truth.

Why is it important to act on the knowledge taught through the Light of Christ? (7:15–16) "All are born with the Light of Christ, a guiding influence which permits each person to recognize right from wrong. What we do with that light and how we respond to those promptings to live righteously is part of the test of mortality" (Packer, "These Things I Know," 8). ✪

What does it mean that we should not wrongfully judge others? (7:18) "Sometimes people feel that it is wrong to judge others in any way. While it is true that you should not condemn others or judge them unrighteously, you will need to make judgments of ideas, situations, and people throughout your life. The Lord has given many commandments that you cannot keep without making judgments. . . .

"Judgment is an important use of your agency and requires great care, especially when you make judgments about other people. All your judgments must be guided by righteous standards. Remember that only God, who knows each individual's heart, can make final judgments of individuals. . . .

"The Lord gave a warning to guide us in our judgment of others [see 3 Nephi 14:2–5]" (*True to the Faith,* 90).

Moroni 7:21–39. Mormon Speaks about Faith in Jesus Christ

Why does God still send angels? (7:22) "From the beginning down through the dispensations, God has used angels as His emissaries in conveying love and concern for His children. . . .

"Usually such beings are *not* seen. Sometimes they are. But seen or unseen they are *always* near. Sometimes their assignments are very grand and have significance for the whole world. Sometimes the messages are more private. Occasionally the angelic purpose is to warn. But most often it is to comfort, to provide some form of merciful attention, guidance in difficult times. . . .

"I testify that angels are *still* sent to help *us*, even as they were sent to help Adam and Eve, to help the prophets, and indeed to help the Savior of the world Himself" (Holland, "Ministry of Angels," 29).

How is the faith of those who lived before Christ's birth similar to those who live after He was born? (7:25–26) "In every age of the world, and all parts of the Earth, holy angels sent from God and commissioned by Him, have declared Salvation to all men through Jesus Christ, our Lord. Those who lived before His coming looked forward to that great event; we look back. Both visions are effectual to the working of grace in the hearts of men" (Reynolds and Sjodahl, *Commentary on the Book of Mormon*, 7:341).

21 And now I come to that faith, of which I said I would speak; and I will tell you the way whereby ye may lay hold on every good thing.

22 For behold, God knowing all things, being from everlasting to everlasting, behold, he sent angels to minister unto the children of men, to make manifest concerning the coming of Christ; and in Christ there should come every good thing.

23 And God also declared unto prophets, by his own mouth, that Christ should come.

24 And behold, there were divers ways that he did manifest things unto the children of men, which were good; and all things which are good cometh of Christ; otherwise men were fallen, and there could no good thing come unto them.

25 Wherefore, by the ministering of angels, and by every word which proceeded forth out of the mouth of God, men began to exercise faith in Christ; and thus by faith, they did lay hold upon every good thing; and thus it was until the coming of Christ.

26 And after that he came men also were saved by faith in his name; and by faith, they become the sons of God. And as surely as Christ liveth he spake these words unto our fathers, saying: Whatsoever thing ye shall ask the Father in my name, which is good, in faith believing that ye shall receive, behold, it shall be done unto you.

27 Wherefore, my beloved brethren, have miracles ceased because Christ hath ascended into heaven, and hath sat down on the right hand of God, to claim of the Father his rights of mercy which he hath upon the children of men?

28 For he hath answered the ends of the law, and he claimeth all those who have faith in him; and they who have faith in him will

cleave unto every good thing; wherefore he advocateth the cause of the children of men; and he dwelleth eternally in the heavens.

29 And because he hath done this, my beloved brethren, have miracles ceased? Behold I say unto you, Nay; neither have angels ceased to minister unto the children of men.

30 For behold, they are subject unto him, to minister according to the word of his command, showing themselves unto them of strong faith and a firm mind in every form of godliness.

31 And the office of their ministry is to call men unto repentance, and to fulfil and to do the work of the covenants of the Father, which he hath made unto the children of men, to prepare the way among the children of men, by declaring the word of Christ unto the chosen vessels of the Lord, that they may bear testimony of him.

32 And by so doing, the Lord God prepareth the way that the residue of men may have faith in Christ, that the Holy Ghost may have place in their hearts, according to the power thereof; and after this manner bringeth to pass the Father, the covenants which he hath made unto the children of men.

33 And Christ hath said: If ye will have faith in me ye shall have power to do whatsoever thing is expedient in me.

34 And he hath said: Repent all ye ends of the earth, and come unto me, and be baptized in my name, and have faith in me, that ye may be saved.

35 And now, my beloved brethren, if this be the case that these things are true which I have spoken unto you, and God will show unto you, with power and great glory at the last day, that they are true, and if they are true has the day of miracles ceased?

What important principle should accompany our faith in Jesus Christ? (7:33–34) "The combination of faith in Christ plus *faith unto repentance* is vitally important. . . . Apparently faith great enough to move mountains is not required; faith enough to speak in tongues or to heal the sick is not needed; all that we need is just enough faith to recognize that we have sinned and to repent of our sins, to feel remorse for them, and to desire to sin no more but to please Christ the Lord. Then the greatest miracle of all, the Atonement, whereby Christ rescues us from our deserved punishment, is in effect in our behalf" (Wells, "The Liahona Triad," 6–7). ✪

Moroni 7:40–42. Mormon Speaks about Hope

What is the relationship between faith and hope? (7:40–42) "It is certainly much more than wishful thinking. It is to have 'hope through the atonement of Christ and the power of his resurrection, to be raised unto life eternal, and this because of your faith in him according to the promise' [Moroni 7:41]. *That* is the theological meaning of hope in the faith-hope-charity sequence. With an eye to that meaning, Moroni 7:42 then clearly reads, 'If a man have faith [in Christ and his atonement] he must needs [as a consequence] have hope [in the promise of the Resurrection, because the two are inextricably linked]; for without faith [in Christ's atonement] there cannot be any hope [in the Resurrection]'" (Holland, *Christ and the New Covenant*, 334–35). ☉

Moroni 7:43–48. Charity Is the Pure Love of Christ

What does it mean to be meek? (7:43–44) Elder Ulisses Soares described meekness as "the quality of those who are 'Godfearing, righteous, humble, teachable, and patient under suffering' [*Guide to the*

36 Or have angels ceased to appear unto the children of men? Or has he withheld the power of the Holy Ghost from them? Or will he, so long as time shall last, or the earth shall stand, or there shall be one man upon the face thereof to be saved?

37 Behold I say unto you, Nay; for it is by faith that miracles are wrought; and it is by faith that angels appear and minister unto men; wherefore, if these things have ceased wo be unto the children of men, for it is because of unbelief, and all is vain.

38 For no man can be saved, according to the words of Christ, save they shall have faith in his name; wherefore, if these things have ceased, then has faith ceased also; and awful is the state of man, for they are as though there had been no redemption made.

39 But behold, my beloved brethren, I judge better things of you, for I judge that ye have faith in Christ because of your meekness; for if ye have not faith in him then ye are not fit to be numbered among the people of his church.

40 And again, my beloved brethren, I would speak unto you concerning hope. How is it that ye can attain unto faith, save ye shall have hope?

41 And what is it that ye shall hope for? Behold I say unto you that ye shall have hope through the atonement of Christ and the power of his resurrection, to be raised unto life eternal, and this because of your faith in him according to the promise.

42 Wherefore, if a man have faith he must needs have hope; for without faith there cannot be any hope.

43 And again, behold I say unto you that he cannot have faith and hope, save he shall be meek, and lowly of heart.

44 If so, his faith and hope is vain, for none is acceptable before God, save the meek and lowly in heart; and if a man be meek and lowly in heart, and confesses by the power of the Holy Ghost that Jesus is the Christ, he must needs have charity; for if he have not charity he is nothing; wherefore he must needs have charity.

45 And charity suffereth long, and is kind, and envieth not, and is not puffed up, seeketh not her own, is not easily provoked, thinketh no evil, and rejoiceth not in iniquity but rejoiceth in the truth, beareth all things, believeth all things, hopeth all things, endureth all things.

46 Wherefore, my beloved brethren, if ye have not charity, ye are nothing, for charity never faileth. Wherefore, cleave unto charity, which is the greatest of all, for all things must fail—

47 But charity is the pure love of Christ, and it endureth forever; and whoso is found possessed of it at the last day, it shall be well with him.

48 Wherefore, my beloved brethren, pray unto the Father with all the energy of heart, that ye may be filled with this love, which he hath bestowed upon all who are true followers of his Son, Jesus Christ; that ye may become the sons of God; that when he shall appear we shall be like him, for we shall see him as he is; that we may have this hope; that we may be purified even as he is pure. Amen.

Scriptures, "Meek, Meekness"; scriptures.lds.org]. Those who possess this attribute are willing to follow Jesus Christ, and their temperament is calm, docile, tolerant, and submissive....

"Being meek does not mean weakness, but it does mean behaving with goodness and kindness, showing strength, serenity, healthy self-worth, and self-control" (Soares, "Be Meek and Lowly of Heart," 9). ✦

What is charity? (7:45–47) Charity is "the highest, noblest, strongest kind of love, not merely affection; the pure love of Christ. It is never used [in the scriptures] to denote alms or deeds of benevolence, although it may be a prompting motive" (Bible Dictionary, "Charity," 614).

"This love is more than just a willingness to share time or possessions with another human being; rather, it is a deep and lasting devotion for and to God and his Son (Moroni 7:47). Thus, more than an act, charity is an attitude, a state of heart and mind that accompanies our works and is proffered unceasingly (1 Cor. 13:4–7; D&C 121:45)" (Garrett, "Light in Our Vessels," 86). ✦

What is the ultimate purpose of charity? (7:48) "The purpose of charity is not merely to cause a proper motivation for charitable acts toward other people.... The ultimate purpose is to make Christ's followers *like him....*

"The ultimate purpose of the gospel of Jesus Christ is to cause the sons and daughters of God to become as Christ is.... We can give without loving, but we cannot love without giving. If our vertical relationship with God is complete, then, by the fruit of that relationship, the horizontal relationship with our fellow beings will also be complete. We then act charitably toward others, not merely because we think we should, but because that is the way we are" (Hafen, *Broken Heart,* 196–97).

Moroni 8:1–3. Moroni Records a Letter from His Father

Why did Moroni include letters from his father? (8:1) "It is appropriate that these letters [Moroni 8, 9] follow Mormon's sermon on faith, hope, and charity [Moroni 7] because they put the essence of that sermon to the test. . . .

"Mormon's first letter is like a Pauline epistle in giving counsel to help regulate the Church. . . .

"In harmony with his argument and his previously quoted sermon, Mormon's dominant characteristic revealed in this letter is love. . . .

"The second letter reveals the full strength of Mormon's position. His people, he says, 'have lost their love, one towards another; and they thirst after blood and revenge continually' (Moro. 9:5). Yet Mormon preserves his 'perfect love' (Moro. 8:16) and remains uncontaminated by the evil around him" (Rust, *Feasting on the Word*, 163–64). ◉

What does the word *ministry* mean? (8:1–2) "Brethren holding the priesthood are called to the *ministry*. As the Lord's agents, his ambassadors, they serve him by serving their fellow men. The various offices in the priesthood are so designed that ministers will be available to perform all the diverse and specialized labors which aid the rolling forth of the Lord's purposes" (McConkie, *Mormon Doctrine*, 505).

What do we know about the bond between Mormon and his son Moroni? (8:2–3) "Moroni seems to exhibit a deep sense of love and admiration for his father. The inclusion of two letters and a sermon by his father in his own record shows this respect and admiration. He is also fiercely loyal to the charge his father gave him concerning the record. . . .

"All in all, the letters provide more evidence of a powerful parental bond between father and son as Mormon honors his son by addressing him, 'my beloved son' (see Moroni 8:1, 9). In this letter, Mormon addresses Moroni six times as 'my son' (see vv. 6, 24, 27–30)" (Holzapfel, "Mormon," 127). ◉

CHAPTER 8

The baptism of little children is an evil abomination—Little children are alive in Christ because of the Atonement—Faith, repentance, meekness and lowliness of heart, receiving the Holy Ghost, and enduring to the end lead to salvation. About A.D. 401–421.

1 An epistle of my father Mormon, written to me, Moroni; and it was written unto me soon after my calling to the ministry. And on this wise did he write unto me, saying:

2 My beloved son, Moroni, I rejoice exceedingly that your Lord Jesus Christ hath been mindful of you, and hath called you to his ministry, and to his holy work.

3 I am mindful of you always in my prayers, continually praying unto God the Father in the name of his Holy Child, Jesus, that he, through his infinite goodness and grace, will keep you through the endurance of faith on his name to the end.

4 And now, my son, I speak unto you concerning that which grieveth me exceedingly; for it grieveth me that there should disputations rise among you.

5 For, if I have learned the truth, there have been disputations among you concerning the baptism of your little children.

6 And now, my son, I desire that ye should labor diligently, that this gross error should be removed from among you; for, for this intent I have written this epistle.

7 For immediately after I had learned these things of you I inquired of the Lord concerning the matter. And the word of the Lord came to me by the power of the Holy Ghost, saying:

8 Listen to the words of Christ, your Redeemer, your Lord and your God. Behold, I came into the world not to call the righteous but sinners to repentance; the whole need no physician, but they that are sick; wherefore, little children are whole, for they are not capable of committing sin; wherefore the curse of Adam is taken from them in me, that it hath no power over them; and the law of circumcision is done away in me.

9 And after this manner did the Holy Ghost manifest the word of God unto me; wherefore, my beloved son, I know that it is solemn mockery before God, that ye should baptize little children.

10 Behold I say unto you that this thing shall ye teach—repentance and baptism unto those who are accountable and capable of committing sin; yea, teach parents that they must repent and be baptized, and humble themselves as their little children, and they shall all be saved with their little children.

11 And their little children need no repentance, neither baptism. Behold, baptism is unto repentance to the fulfilling the commandments unto the remission of sins.

Moroni 8:4–24. Little Children Are Saved by Jesus Christ and Do Not Need Baptism

Why is baptism of little children a "gross error"? (8:5–8) "We're born good; we learn to sin as we grow older. And if you need evidence of the truth of that doctrine, please see your nearest infant. Look deeply into the child's eyes. Have you ever seen such sweetness and purity? It's like you can look through a baby's eyes right into heaven.

"Of course, that changes a little later in their lives when wide-eyed innocence turns into wild-eyed mischievousness. That's when children become accountable and capable of sin—when they know and understand the difference between right and wrong. Through the Prophet Joseph Smith the Lord revealed that the age of accountability is eight years old" (Ballard, *Our Search for Happiness*, 87). ✛

In what ways can parents be "as their little children"? (8:9–10) "In the pattern set by the Savior's own teachings, it is telling that both [Mormon and King Benjamin (see Mosiah 3:16, 18, 21)] invite adults—Mormon said specifically 'parents'—to become more like little children, not the other way around. An infant's purity and innocence, a baby's sense of wonder, a little one's willingness to believe, a toddler's inherent trust in a Father and Mother, a child's ability to almost instantly forgive and forget, to laugh again and see the very best in the world—these are just a few of the ways adults need to be more like children" (Holland, *Christ and the New Covenant*, 217). ✛

Why is repentance and baptism not necessary for little children? (8:11–12) "The Lord extends special protection to children and shares jurisdiction with earthly parents, even as we enjoy their presence. They cannot sin until they reach the age of accountability, which the Lord has declared to be eight years (see D&C 18:42; D&C 29:47). In fact, the power to even tempt them to commit sin has been taken from Satan. The prophet Mormon taught that 'little children are whole, for they are not capable of committing sin.'...

"Because they cannot sin, they have no need of repentance, neither baptism. Adam's original transgression has no claim as a result of the atonement of Jesus Christ" (Lybbert, "The Status of Little Children," 31). ☉

Why is the idea of baptizing an infant such a damning doctrine to believe? (8:14–16, 20–21)
"It is Lucifer who is behind this doctrine and who seeks to pervert the ways of God and distort the true nature of Deity. Satan, the father of this lie and all lies is the one who is without faith, hope, and charity.... In this epistle Mormon is exercising all his power and authority to preach against Lucifer's false and damning doctrine concerning the salvation of little children and exhorting all to repent and come to a true understanding and acceptance of the mercies of the Messiah" (McConkie et al., *Doctrinal Commentary*, 4:352–53).

12 But little children are alive in Christ, even from the foundation of the world; if not so, God is a partial God, and also a changeable God, and a respecter to persons; for how many little children have died without baptism!

13 Wherefore, if little children could not be saved without baptism, these must have gone to an endless hell.

14 Behold I say unto you, that he that supposeth that little children need baptism is in the gall of bitterness and in the bonds of iniquity; for he hath neither faith, hope, nor charity; wherefore, should he be cut off while in the thought, he must go down to hell.

15 For awful is the wickedness to suppose that God saveth one child because of baptism, and the other must perish because he hath no baptism.

16 Wo be unto them that shall pervert the ways of the Lord after this manner, for they shall perish except they repent. Behold, I speak with boldness, having authority from God; and I fear not what man can do; for perfect love casteth out all fear.

17 And I am filled with charity, which is everlasting love; wherefore, all children are alike unto me; wherefore, I love little children with a perfect love; and they are all alike and partakers of salvation.

18 For I know that God is not a partial God, neither a changeable being; but he is unchangeable from all eternity to all eternity.

19 Little children cannot repent; wherefore, it is awful wickedness to deny the pure mercies of God unto them, for they are all alive in him because of his mercy.

20 And he that saith that little children need baptism denieth the mercies of Christ, and setteth at naught the atonement of him and the power of his redemption.

21 Wo unto such, for they are in danger of death, hell, and an endless torment. I speak it boldly; God hath commanded me. Listen unto them and give heed, or they stand against you at the judgment-seat of Christ.

22 For behold that all little children are alive in Christ, and also all they that are without the law. For the power of redemption cometh on all them that have no law; wherefore, he that is not condemned, or he that is under no condemnation, cannot repent; and unto such baptism availeth nothing—

23 But it is mockery before God, denying the mercies of Christ, and the power of his Holy Spirit, and putting trust in dead works.

24 Behold, my son, this thing ought not to be; for repentance is unto them that are under condemnation and under the curse of a broken law.

25 And the first fruits of repentance is baptism; and baptism cometh by faith unto the fulfilling the commandments; and the fulfilling the commandments bringeth remission of sins;

26 And the remission of sins bringeth meekness, and lowliness of heart; and because of meekness and lowliness of heart cometh the visitation of the Holy Ghost, which Comforter filleth with hope and perfect love, which love endureth by diligence unto prayer, until the end shall come, when all the saints shall dwell with God.

Who are those who are "without the law" and how are they similar to little children? (8:22) "All little children are alive in Christ, as are those 'that are without the law. For the power of redemption cometh on all them that have no law' (Moroni 8:22). Two groups of people in scripture are referred to as dying 'without law.' The first group consists of the heathen nations, those who will not receive the fulness of gospel light and understanding and who thereby qualify for a terrestrial inheritance (see D&C 45:54; 76:72). The other group consists of those who never have an opportunity to receive the gospel in this life but who would have done so had the opportunity presented itself (D&C 137:7–8)" (Millet, "Alive in Christ," 9). ☉

What are "dead works"? (8:23) "[Dead] works are symbolic of that which has no life now nor power to grant life hereafter. . . . Participation in dead works has no saving power, no matter how sincere the recipient may have been" (Brewster, *Doctrine & Covenants Encyclopedia*, 128–129). The prophet Mormon instructed his son Moroni regarding the "dead works" of infant baptism. This ordinance is not authorized by God and is unnecessary. Heavenly Father declared that "little children are redeemed from the foundation of the world through mine Only Begotten" (D&C 29:46). Such baptism, taught Mormon, "is mockery before God, denying the mercies of Christ, and the power of his Holy Spirit" (Moroni 8:23).

Moroni 8:25–30. Moroni Explains the Fruits of Repentance

27 Behold, my son, I will write unto you again if I go not out soon against the Lamanites. Behold, the pride of this nation, or the people of the Nephites, hath proven their destruction except they should repent.

28 Pray for them, my son, that repentance may come unto them. But behold, I fear lest the Spirit hath ceased striving with them; and in this part of the land they are also seeking to put down all power and authority which cometh from God; and they are denying the Holy Ghost.

29 And after rejecting so great a knowledge, my son, they must perish soon, unto the fulfilling of the prophecies which were spoken by the prophets, as well as the words of our Savior himself.

30 Farewell, my son, until I shall write unto you, or shall meet you again. Amen.

The second epistle of Mormon to his son Moroni.
Comprising chapter 9.

CHAPTER 9

Both the Nephites and the Lamanites are depraved and degenerate—They torture and murder each other—Mormon prays that grace and goodness may rest upon Moroni forever. About A.D. 401.

1 My beloved son, I write unto you again that ye may know that I am yet alive; but I write somewhat of that which is grievous.

2 For behold, I have had a sore battle with the Lamanites, in which we did not conquer; and Archeantus has fallen by the sword, and also Luram and Emron; yea, and we have lost a great number of our choice men.

3 And now behold, my son, I fear lest the Lamanites shall destroy this people; for they

---

Why did Mormon instruct Moroni to pray for the Nephites, that the spirit of repentance might come to them? (8:28) "When we begin to follow a path that will lead us to ultimate destruction and a wider spiritual separation from the Father, if we yield to the power and influence of the Holy Ghost, it will work on our hearts and souls to motivate and direct us to return to the path of the Father, to repent and cleanse our lives before the Lord. The essence of the purifying attributes of the Holy Ghost reside within us and entice us to cleanse our natural selves through repentance. . . . Yielding to the Holy Ghost and its influence will provide us the strength we need to bring true repentance into our lives" (Pew, "'Yield Your Heart to God,'" 212).

Superscription to Moroni 9

Who wrote the superscription to Moroni 9 and why is it important? The superscription to Moroni 9 was part of the ancient record translated by the Prophet Joseph Smith and dictated by him to his scribe. The superscription "reads, 'The second epistle of Mormon to his son, Moroni.' If the ninth chapter of the book of Moroni is considered 'the second epistle,' then this [superscription to chapter 9] seems to imply that chapter 8 of the book of Moroni is the first epistle" (Miner, *Step by Step through the Book of Mormon*).

Moroni 9:1–10. Mormon Describes the Evil Acts of the Nephites and Lamanites

What is the origin of the name Luram? (9:2) Another evidence of the correctness of the translation of the Book of Mormon comes from the now discovered Hebrew names contained in it. "Luram is the name of a Nephite military leader who served with Mormon (see Moroni 9:2). The name is reflected in the second element of the name *'dn-Lrm*, 'Lord of LRM,' known from a seal of ca. 720 B.C. found during excavations at Hama (Hamath) in Syria. The name is also known from graffiti on three bricks from the same level at Hama"

do not repent, and Satan stirreth them up continually to anger one with another.

4 Behold, I am laboring with them continually; and when I speak the word of God with sharpness they tremble and anger against me; and when I use no sharpness they harden their hearts against it; wherefore, I fear lest the Spirit of the Lord hath ceased striving with them.

5 For so exceedingly do they anger that it seemeth me that they have no fear of death; and they have lost their love, one towards another; and they thirst after blood and revenge continually.

6 And now, my beloved son, notwithstanding their hardness, let us labor diligently; for if we should cease to labor, we should be brought under condemnation; for we have a labor to perform whilst in this tabernacle of clay, that we may conquer the enemy of all righteousness, and rest our souls in the kingdom of God.

7 And now I write somewhat concerning the sufferings of this people. For according to the knowledge which I have received from Amoron, behold, the Lamanites have many prisoners, which they took from the tower of Sherrizah; and there were men, women, and children.

8 And the husbands and fathers of those women and children they have slain; and they feed the women upon the flesh of their husbands, and the children upon the flesh of their fathers; and no water, save a little, do they give unto them.

9 And notwithstanding this great abomination of the Lamanites, it doth not exceed that of our people in Moriantum. For behold, many of the daughters of the Lamanites have they taken prisoners; and after depriving them of that which was most dear and

(Tvedtnes, Gee, and Roper, "Book of Mormon Names Attested in Ancient Hebrew Inscriptions," 49).

What have you noticed is the typical reaction of Book of Mormon people and those in our day when they are called to repentance? (9:4) "Just as the word of God can be comforting to those who accept it, it can be discomforting—'hard,' 'sharp,' or 'strict'—to those who reject it. This dichotomy is a prevalent theme in the Book of Mormon" (Taylor, "Word of God," 58).

Consider discomfort with the word of God in the following passages: 1 Nephi 16:2; 2 Nephi 1:26; Jacob 2:35; Mosiah 13:7; Alma 35:15. ⊕

What did Mormon understand about continuing to do our duty despite the hardness of others? (9:6) "After we have done all we could do for the cause of truth and withstood the evil that men have brought upon us, and we have been overwhelmed by their wrongs, it is still our duty to stand. We cannot give up; we must not lie down. . . . To stand firm in the face of overwhelming opposition, when you have done all you can, is the courage of faith" (Smith, *Gospel Doctrine*, 119).

Why are chastity and virtue "most dear and precious above all things"? (9:9) President Marion G. Romney taught: "Jesus spoke of specific rewards for different virtues but reserved the greatest, so it seems to me, for the pure in heart, 'for they,' said he, 'shall see God' (Matt. 5:8). And not only shall they see the Lord, but they shall feel at home in his presence. . . . 'Let virtue garnish thy thoughts unceasingly; then shall thy confidence wax strong in the presence of God' (D&C 121:45)" ("Trust in the Lord," 42). Elder David A. Bednar said: "Disciplining the natural man in each of us makes possible a richer, a deeper, and a more enduring love of God and of His children. Love increases through righteous restraint" ("We Believe in Being Chaste," 43).

Moroni 9:11–21. Mormon Feels Sorrow for a Once Great People

What conditions caused Mormon to believe his people would soon be destroyed? (9:11–19) What do you think caused these people to become so brutal to each other? How could Mormon still love these people despite their wickedness? What helps you love those who may not treat you well?

precious above all things, which is chastity and virtue—

10 And after they had done this thing, they did murder them in a most cruel manner, torturing their bodies even unto death; and after they have done this, they devour their flesh like unto wild beasts, because of the hardness of their hearts; and they do it for a token of bravery.

11 O my beloved son, how can a people like this, that are without civilization—

12 (And only a few years have passed away, and they were a civil and a delightsome people)

13 But O my son, how can a people like this, whose delight is in so much abomination—

14 How can we expect that God will stay his hand in judgment against us?

15 Behold, my heart cries: Wo unto this people. Come out in judgment, O God, and hide their sins, and wickedness, and abominations from before thy face!

16 And again, my son, there are many widows and their daughters who remain in Sherrizah; and that part of the provisions which the Lamanites did not carry away, behold, the army of Zenephi has carried away, and left them to wander whithersoever they can for food; and many old women do faint by the way and die.

17 And the army which is with me is weak; and the armies of the Lamanites are betwixt Sherrizah and me; and as many as have fled to the army of Aaron have fallen victims to their awful brutality.

18 O the depravity of my people! They are without order and without mercy. Behold, I am but a man, and I have but the strength of a man, and I cannot any longer enforce my commands.

19 And they have become strong in their perversion; and they are alike brutal, sparing none, neither old nor young; and they delight in everything save that which is good; and the suffering of our women and our children upon all the face of this land doth exceed everything; yea, tongue cannot tell, neither can it be written.

20 And now, my son, I dwell no longer upon this horrible scene. Behold, thou knowest the wickedness of this people; thou knowest that they are without principle, and past feeling; and their wickedness doth exceed that of the Lamanites.

21 Behold, my son, I cannot recommend them unto God lest he should smite me.

22 But behold, my son, I recommend thee unto God, and I trust in Christ that thou wilt be saved; and I pray unto God that he will spare thy life, to witness the return of his people unto him, or their utter destruction; for I know that they must perish except they repent and return unto him.

23 And if they perish it will be like unto the Jaredites, because of the wilfulness of their hearts, seeking for blood and revenge.

24 And if it so be that they perish, we know that many of our brethren have deserted over unto the Lamanites, and many more will also desert over unto them; wherefore, write somewhat a few things, if thou art spared and I shall perish and not see thee; but I trust that I may see thee soon; for I have sacred records that I would deliver up unto thee.

To what depths did Nephite civilization plunge? (9:20–21) "In Proverbs, we read, 'For the commandment is a lamp' (Prov. 6:23). Once darkened, a society loses its capacity to distinguish between right and wrong and the will to declare that some things are wrong per se. . . . [In] all their eagerness to experience certain things, hedonists become desensitized. People who wrongly celebrate their capacity to feel finally reach a point where they lose much of their capacity to feel! In the words of three different prophets, such individuals become 'past feeling' (see 1 Ne. 17:45; Eph. 4:19; Moro. 9:20).

"When people proceed 'without principle,' erelong they will be 'without civilization,' 'without mercy,' and 'past feeling' (see Moro. 9:11–20)" (Maxwell, "Deny Yourselves of All Ungodliness," 67–68). Such individuals do not experience real joy.

Moroni 9:22–26. Mormon Expresses Hope for His Righteous Son Moroni

How can we encourage and reassure others in times of trial? (9:22) Mormon expressed support and confidence in his son Moroni. President Gordon B. Hinckley emphasized the importance of such words: "In your associations one with another, build and strengthen one another. 'No man is an island; no man stands alone.' We so need help and encouragement and strength, one from another" (*Teachings of Gordon B. Hinckley*, 45).

How should we respond to challenges and despair?
(9:25) "Both Mormon and Moroni were facing days
of difficulty. . . . Mormon knew his son might be overcome with gloom and foreboding, so he told him the
perfect antidote. He told him that he could choose,
by what he put in his mind, to become an example
of hope. Here is what he wrote: 'My son, be faithful in
Christ; and may not the things which I have written
grieve thee, to weigh thee down unto death; but may
Christ lift thee up, and may his sufferings and death,
and the showing his body unto our fathers, and his
mercy and long-suffering, and the hope of his glory
and of eternal life, rest in your mind forever'" (Eyring,
To Draw Closer to God, 133).

Moroni 10:1–5. Prayerful Readers Can Know If the Book of Mormon Is True

Why is it important to read the Book of Mormon
before trying to gain a testimony of its divinity?
(10:3) President Boyd K. Packer testified: "After you
have read the Book of Mormon, you become qualified
to inquire of the Lord, in the way that He prescribes.
. . . You will be eligible, on the conditions He has established, to receive that personal revelation" ("Things of
My Soul," 61). ◉

25 My son, be faithful in Christ; and may
not the things which I have written grieve
thee, to weigh thee down unto death; but
may Christ lift thee up, and may his sufferings and death, and the showing his body
unto our fathers, and his mercy and long-
suffering, and the hope of his glory and of
eternal life, rest in your mind forever.

26 And may the grace of God the Father,
whose throne is high in the heavens, and our
Lord Jesus Christ, who sitteth on the right
hand of his power, until all things shall become subject unto him, be, and abide with
you forever. Amen.

CHAPTER 10

*A testimony of the Book of Mormon comes by
the power of the Holy Ghost—The gifts of the
Spirit are dispensed to the faithful—Spiritual
gifts always accompany faith—Moroni's words
speak from the dust—Come unto Christ, be
perfected in Him, and sanctify your souls.
About A.D. 421.*

1 Now I, Moroni, write somewhat as seemeth me good; and I write unto my brethren,
the Lamanites; and I would that they should
know that more than four hundred and
twenty years have passed away since the sign
was given of the coming of Christ.

2 And I seal up these records, after I have
spoken a few words by way of exhortation
unto you.

3 Behold, I would exhort you that when ye
shall read these things, if it be wisdom in
God that ye should read them, that ye would
remember how merciful the Lord hath been
unto the children of men, from the creation
of Adam even down until the time that ye
shall receive these things, and ponder it in
your hearts.

4 And when ye shall receive these things, I would exhort you that ye would ask God, the Eternal Father, in the name of Christ, if these things are not true; and if ye shall ask with a sincere heart, with real intent, having faith in Christ, he will manifest the truth of it unto you, by the power of the Holy Ghost.

5 And by the power of the Holy Ghost ye may know the truth of all things.

6 And whatsoever thing is good is just and true; wherefore, nothing that is good denieth the Christ, but acknowledgeth that he is.

7 And ye may know that he is, by the power of the Holy Ghost; wherefore I would exhort you that ye deny not the power of God; for he worketh by power, according to the faith of the children of men, the same today and tomorrow, and forever.

What does it mean to ask with "real intent"? (10:4)
"To access information from heaven, one must first have a firm faith and a deep desire. One needs to 'ask with a sincere heart [and] real intent, having faith in [Jesus] Christ' (Moroni 10:4). 'Real intent' means that one *really intends* to follow the divine direction given" (Nelson, "Ask, Seek, Knock," 81).

How may we receive the promise that the Holy Ghost will teach us the "truth of all things"? (10:5)
"The Book of Mormon teaches that God will manifest the truth of spiritual things unto us by the power of the Holy Ghost (see Moroni 10:4–5). In modern revelation God promises us that we will receive 'knowledge' by His telling us in our mind and in our heart 'by the Holy Ghost' (D&C 8:1–2).

"One of the greatest things about our Heavenly Father's plan for His children is that each of us can know the truth of that plan for ourselves. That revealed knowledge does not come from books, from scientific proof, or from intellectual pondering. As with the Apostle Peter, we can receive that knowledge directly from our Heavenly Father through the witness of the Holy Ghost" (Oaks, "Testimony," 26). ◉

Moroni 10:6–19. The Gifts of the Spirit Are Given to People Who Believe

The Importance of a Testimony

Public domain.

President Heber C. Kimball

Moroni 10:3–5 contains an invitation and a promise from Moroni about coming to know the truth of the Book of Mormon. A similar process can be used to build one's personal testimony of the gospel. Why is it important to have such a testimony?

"President Heber C. Kimball, a [counselor to Brigham Young in] the First Presidency, prophesied: 'Let me say to you, that many of you will see the time when you will have all the trouble, trial and persecution that you can stand, and plenty of opportunities to show that you are true to God and his work. This Church has before it many close places through which it will have to pass before the work of God is crowned with victory. . . .

"'The time will come when no man nor woman will be able to endure on borrowed light. Each will have to be guided by the light within himself. If you do not have it, how can you stand?'" (Whitney, *Life of Heber C. Kimball*, 449–50).

Why is it important to "deny not the gifts of God"? (10:8) Elder Robert D. Hales observed: "To find the gifts we have been given, we must pray and fast. Often patriarchal blessings tell us the gifts we have received and declare the promise of gifts we can receive if we seek after them. I urge you each to discover your gifts and to seek after those that will bring direction to your life's work and that will further the work of heaven.

"During our time here on earth, we have been charged to develop the natural gifts and capabilities Heavenly Father has blessed us with. Then it will be our opportunity to use these gifts to become teachers and leaders of God's children wherever they may be found on earth. To exercise these gifts, we must develop a purity of heart" ("Gifts of the Spirit," 16).

How are we to obtain spiritual gifts and to whom are they given? (10:17) President Boyd K. Packer explained: "I take the word *he* to refer to us, meaning that the gifts will be received as we will." President Packer further explained the reception of gifts of the Spirit: "I must emphasize that the word *gift* is of great significance, for a gift may not be demanded or it ceases to be a gift. It may only be accepted when proffered.... Spiritual gifts ... are a product of our faith, and if we do not have them, something is less than it should be [see Moroni 7:35–38; 10:24]" (*Shield of Faith*, 94–104). ●

8 And again, I exhort you, my brethren, that ye deny not the gifts of God, for they are many; and they come from the same God. And there are different ways that these gifts are administered; but it is the same God who worketh all in all; and they are given by the manifestations of the Spirit of God unto men, to profit them.

9 For behold, to one is given by the Spirit of God, that he may teach the word of wisdom;

10 And to another, that he may teach the word of knowledge by the same Spirit;

11 And to another, exceedingly great faith; and to another, the gifts of healing by the same Spirit;

12 And again, to another, that he may work mighty miracles;

13 And again, to another, that he may prophesy concerning all things;

14 And again, to another, the beholding of angels and ministering spirits;

15 And again, to another, all kinds of tongues;

16 And again, to another, the interpretation of languages and of divers kinds of tongues.

17 And all these gifts come by the Spirit of Christ; and they come unto every man severally, according as he will.

18 And I would exhort you, my beloved brethren, that ye remember that every good gift cometh of Christ.

19 And I would exhort you, my beloved brethren, that ye remember that he is the same yesterday, today, and forever, and that all these gifts of which I have spoken, which are spiritual, never will be done away, even as long as the world shall stand, only according to the unbelief of the children of men.

20 Wherefore, there must be faith; and if there must be faith there must also be hope; and if there must be hope there must also be charity.

21 And except ye have charity ye can in nowise be saved in the kingdom of God; neither can ye be saved in the kingdom of God if ye have not faith; neither can ye if ye have no hope.

22 And if ye have no hope ye must needs be in despair; and despair cometh because of iniquity.

23 And Christ truly said unto our fathers: If ye have faith ye can do all things which are expedient unto me.

24 And now I speak unto all the ends of the earth—that if the day cometh that the power and gifts of God shall be done away among you, it shall be because of unbelief.

Moroni 10:20–23. We Must Have Faith, Hope, and Charity

In what ways are faith, hope, and charity related? (10:20–21) "Hope is often linked with faith. Hope and faith are commonly connected to charity. Why? Because hope is essential to faith; faith is essential to hope; faith and hope are essential to charity. They support one another like legs on a three-legged stool. All three relate to our Redeemer.

"*Faith* is rooted in Jesus Christ. *Hope* centers in his Atonement. *Charity* is manifest in the 'pure love of Christ' [Moroni 7:47]. These three attributes are intertwined like strands in a cable and may not always be precisely distinguished. Together they become our tether to the celestial kingdom" (Nelson, "More Excellent Hope," 61).

How does hope triumph over despair? (10:22) "Admittedly, we have ample reason to be deeply concerned because we see no immediate answers to the seemingly unsolvable problems confronting the human family. But regardless of this dark picture, which will ultimately get worse, we must never allow ourselves to give up hope! Moroni, having seen our day, counseled, 'Wherefore, there must be faith; and if there must be faith there must also be hope (Moro. 10:20)" (Ballard, "Joy of Hope Fulfilled," 31).

What can we do to develop the faith necessary to "do all things which are expedient" to the Lord? (10:23) "If you will let your heart be drawn to the Savior and always remember Him, and if you will draw near to our Heavenly Father in prayer, you will have put on spiritual armor. You will be protected against pride because you will know that any success comes not from your human powers. And you will be protected against the thoughts which come rushing in upon us that we are too weak, too inexperienced, too unworthy to do what we are called of God to do to serve and help save His children. We can have come into our hearts [this promise recorded by] Moroni" (Eyring, *Because He First Loved Us*, 74).

Moroni 10:24–29. All People Will See Moroni at the Judgment and Know His Words Are True

What is the significance of Moroni's warning to heed the precepts and teachings of the Book of Mormon? (10:24–29) "Any group which has access to [the Book of Mormon] is enormously accountable. . . . The Book of Mormon testifies that God will judge the nations that possess [it] . . . (2 Nephi 25:22). In fact, Nephi, Jacob, Mormon, and Moroni, the four most prominent writers of the book, all testify in sobering farewell statements that we will stand with them at the judgment bar of God to answer for what we have done with the teachings of the Book of Mormon (see 2 Nephi 33:10–15; Jacob 6:5–13; Mormon 7:5–10; Moroni 10:24–34). These prophets want us to know that part of our judgment will be based on how well we have used their teachings in our lives" (Hansen, "Preparing for the Judgment," 98). ⊕

Moroni 10:30–34. Moroni Invites All People to Come unto Christ and Be Perfected in Him

What do "beautiful garments" represent? (10:31)
"The Lord states: 'For Zion must increase in beauty, and in holiness; her borders must be enlarged; her

25 And wo be unto the children of men if this be the case; for there shall be none that doeth good among you, no not one. For if there be one among you that doeth good, he shall work by the power and gifts of God.

26 And wo unto them who shall do these things away and die, for they die in their sins, and they cannot be saved in the kingdom of God; and I speak it according to the words of Christ; and I lie not.

27 And I exhort you to remember these things; for the time speedily cometh that ye shall know that I lie not, for ye shall see me at the bar of God; and the Lord God will say unto you: Did I not declare my words unto you, which were written by this man, like as one crying from the dead, yea, even as one speaking out of the dust?

28 I declare these things unto the fulfilling of the prophecies. And behold, they shall proceed forth out of the mouth of the everlasting God; and his word shall hiss forth from generation to generation.

29 And God shall show unto you, that that which I have written is true.

30 And again I would exhort you that ye would come unto Christ, and lay hold upon every good gift, and touch not the evil gift, nor the unclean thing.

31 And awake, and arise from the dust, O Jerusalem; yea, and put on thy beautiful

The Importance of the Book of Mormon

After spending a day in council with the Twelve Apostles at the home of President Brigham Young, the Prophet said, "I told the brethren that the Book of Mormon was the most correct of any book on earth, and the keystone of our religion, and a man would get nearer to God by abiding by its precepts, than by any other book" (*Joseph Smith* [manual], 64).

"Take away the Book of Mormon and the revelations, and where is our religion? We have none" (*Joseph Smith* [manual], 196).

The Prophet Joseph Smith, by Alvin Gittens

garments, O daughter of Zion; and strengthen thy stakes and enlarge thy borders forever, that thou mayest no more be confounded, that the covenants of the Eternal Father which he hath made unto thee, O house of Israel, may be fulfilled.

32 Yea, come unto Christ, and be perfected in him, and deny yourselves of all ungodliness; and if ye shall deny yourselves of all ungodliness, and love God with all your might, mind and strength, then is his grace sufficient for you, that by his grace ye may be perfect in Christ; and if by the grace of God ye are perfect in Christ, ye can in nowise deny the power of God.

33 And again, if ye by the grace of God are perfect in Christ, and deny not his power, then are ye sanctified in Christ by the grace of God, through the shedding of the blood of Christ, which is in the covenant of the Father unto the remission of your sins, that ye become holy, without spot.

34 And now I bid unto all, farewell. I soon go to rest in the paradise of God, until my spirit and body shall again reunite, and I am brought forth triumphant through the air, to meet you before the pleasing bar of the great Jehovah, the Eternal Judge of both quick and dead. Amen.

stakes must be strengthened; yea, verily I say unto you, Zion must arise and put on her beautiful garments' (D&C 82:14).

"Here the Lord declares another great purpose of a stake: to be a beautiful emblem for all the world to see. The phrase 'put on her beautiful garments' refers, of course, to the inner sanctity that must be attained by every member who calls himself or herself a Saint. Zion is 'the pure in heart' (D&C 97:21).

"Stakes in Zion are strengthened and Zion's borders enlarged as members reflect the standard of holiness that the Lord expects of His chosen people" (Benson, "'Strengthen Thy Stakes,'" 2). ◉

How do we become perfected in Christ? (10:32–33) "We will not attain a state of perfection in this life, but we can and should press forward with faith in Christ along the strait and narrow path and make steady progress toward our eternal destiny. The Lord's pattern for spiritual development is 'line upon line, precept upon precept, here a little and there a little' (2 Nephi 28:30). Small, steady, incremental spiritual improvements are the steps the Lord would have us take. Preparing to walk guiltless before God is one of the primary purposes of mortality and the pursuit of a lifetime; it does not result from sporadic spurts of intense spiritual activity" (Bednar, "Clean Hands and a Pure Heart," 82). ◉

Why did Moroni refer to the judgment of the Lord as "pleasing"? (10:34) If you love the Lord and others and seek to keep His commandments, "He will see and reward it. If you do this often enough and long enough, you will feel a change in your very nature through the Atonement of Jesus Christ. Not only will you feel closer to Him, but you will also feel more and more that you are becoming like Him. Then, when you do see Him, as we all will, it will be for you as it was for Moroni. . . .

"If we serve with faith, humility, and a desire to do God's will, I testify that the judgment bar of the great Jehovah will be pleasing. We will see our loving Father and His Son as They see us now—with perfect clarity and with perfect love" (Eyring, "Where Is the Pavilion?" 75).

PRONUNCIATION GUIDE

Following are suggestions for pronouncing Book of Mormon names and terms. This guide is provided to assist the reader and is not intended as an authoritative source on how these names were pronounced originally.

KEY

a   *a*bout
ă   *a*sk, p*a*t, m*a*p
ā   *a*ble, b*a*ke, w*a*y
ä   *a*lms, f*a*ther, c*a*ll
ĕ   *e*bb, m*e*t, s*e*cond
ē   *ea*t, m*e*te, m*e*
er   p*er*mit

ĭ   *i*t, h*i*m, m*i*rror
ī   *i*dle, f*i*ne, den*y*
ō   *o*ver, b*o*ne, kn*o*w
ou   ab*ou*t
u   j*u*mp
ū   r*u*le, b*oo*t, tw*o*

Aaron ĕr´an
Abel ā´bul
Abinadi a-bĭn´a-dī
Abinadom a-bĭn´a-dum
Abish ā´bĭsh
Ablom ăb´lum
Abraham ā´bra-hăm
Adam ăd´um
Agosh ā´gäsh
Aha ā´hä
Ahah ā´hä
Ahaz ā´hăz
Aiath ī´uth
Akish ā´kĭsh
Alma ăl´ma
Alpha ăl´fa
Amaleki a-măl´a-kī
Amalekite a-măl´a-kīt
Amalickiah a-măl´a-kī´a
Amalickiahite a-măl´a-kī´a-īt
Amaron a-mä´rän
Amgid ăm´gĭd
Aminadab a-mĭn´a-dăb
Aminadi a-mĭn´a-dī
Amlici ăm´lĭ-sī

Amlicite ăm´lĭ-sīt
Ammah ăm´mä
Ammaron ăm´a-rän
Ammon ăm´un
Ammonihah ăm-a-nī´hä
Ammonihahite ăm-a-nī´hä-īt
Ammonite ăm´a-nīt
Ammoron ăm´ōr-än
Amnigaddah ăm-nĭ-găd´ä
Amnihu ăm-nī´hū
Amnor ăm´nōr
Amoron a-mōr´än
Amos ā´mus
Amoz ā´muz
Amulek ăm´yū-lĕk
Amulon ăm´yū-län
Amulonites ăm´ya-län´īts
Anathoth ăn´a-tōth
Angola ăn-gō´la
Ani-Anti ăn´ī–ăn´tī
Anti-Nephi-Lehi ăn´tī–nē´fi-lē´hī
Anti-Nephi-Lehies ăn´tī–nē´fi-lē´hīz
Antiomno ăn-tē-äm´nō
Antion ăn´tē-än
Antionah ăn-tē-än´a

Antionum ăn-tē-ō´num	Carchemish kär-kĕm´ĭsh
Antiparah ăn-tĭ-pär´a	Cezoram sē-zōr´um
Antipas ăn´tĭ-päs	Chaldeans kăl-dē´unz
Antipus ăn´tĭ-pus	Chaldees kăl-dēz´
Antum ăn´tum	Chemish kĕm´ĭsh
Archeantus är-kē-ăn´tus	Cherubim chĕr´a-bĭm
Arpad är´păd	Cohor kō´hōr
Assyria a-sĭr´ē-a	Com kōm
	Comnor kōm´nōr
Babylon băb´ĭ-län	Corianton kōr-ē-ăn´tun
Bashan bā´shän	Coriantor kōr-ē-ăn´tōr
Benjamin bĕn´ja-mĭn	Coriantum kōr-ē-ăn´tum
Bethabara bĕth-ăb´a-ra	Coriantumr kōr-ē-ăn´ta-mer
Boaz bō´ăz	Corihor kōr´ĭ-hōr
Bountiful boun´tĭ-ful	Corom kōr´um
	Cumeni kū´ma-nī
Cain kān	Cumenihah kū-ma-nī´hä
Calno kăl´nō	Cumom kū´mum

CHRONOLOGY OF THE PRONUNCIATION GUIDE

Various attempts have been made to standardize the pronunciation of proper names found in the text of the Book of Mormon. Efforts to standardize the pronunciation of proper names have reflected language conventions at each of those various times. The Pronunciation Guide available in the 2013 edition of the scriptures relied on current trends among English-speaking members of the Church with an emphasis on American pronunciation.

1827–1829: During the translation process, Joseph may have spelled some of the names rather than pronouncing them. This most likely occurred when he didn't know the pronunciation. Based on interviews given by David Whitmer and Emma Smith, some have suggested that Joseph spelled out the proper names in the text (see Whitmer, *David Whitmer Interviews*, 126, 128; Nibley, *Lehi in the Desert*, 29, 31). Recent research suggests that Joseph likely spoke some names and later corrected the spelling in the manuscript (Skousen, "How Joseph Smith Translated the Book of Mormon," 27).

1829–1869: Though it may be presumed that early Latter-day Saints heard the Prophet Joseph Smith pronounce Book of Mormon names and places, no evidence of these pronunciations is extant.

1869: Publication of the Book of Mormon in the Deseret Alphabet suggests how mid–nineteenth century Latter-day Saints pronounced certain names. For instance, Dē-sē-rĕt, as opposed to our current Dĕz´-a-rĕt, and Ĭs-a-bĕl, to our current Iz´-a-bĕl (Huchel, "Deseret Alphabet as an Aid in Pronouncing Book of Mormon Names," 58).

1891: George Reynolds publishes his *Dictionary of the Book of Mormon*, including proper names. Elder Reynolds's work does not offer suggestions for pronunciation.

1903: On May 23, a convention for students of the Book of Mormon begins at Brigham Young University under the direction of Church President Joseph F. Smith. A significant part of the convention deals with developing a standardized pronunciation guide for proper names in the Book of Mormon. A committee is appointed, consisting of Elder George Reynolds, Charles W. Penrose, J. E. Hickman, Benjamin Cluff Jr., and M. H. Hardy. The following day, May 24, the committee offers several rules to govern pronunciation. The following guidelines are representative:

- Accepted pronunciation of Bible names to be followed.
- "Ch" always to be pronounced "K."
- "I" as the final letter always to be pronounced long.
- "G" at the beginning of a word is always pronounced hard ("Book of Mormon Students Meet," *Deseret News*, 3).

Cumorah   ka-mōr´a

Curelom   kū-rē´lum

Deseret   dĕz-a-rĕt´

Desolation   dĕs-ō-lā´shun

Edom   ē´dum

Egypt   ē´jĭpt

Egyptian   ē-jĭp´shun

Elam   ē´lum

Elijah   ē-lī´ja

Emer   ē´mer

Emron   ĕm´rän

Enos   ē´nus

Ephah   ē´fä

Ephraim   ē´frĕm *or* ē´frum

Esrom   ĕz´rum

Ethem   ē´thum

Ether   ē´ther

Eve   ēv

Ezias   ē-zī´us

Ezrom   ĕz´rum

Gad   găd

Gadiandi   găd-ē-ăn´dī

Gadianton   găd-ē-ăn´tun

Gadiomnah   găd-ē-äm´na

Gallim   găl´ĭm

Gazelem   ga-zā´lĭm

Geba   gē´ba

Gebim   gē´bĭm

Gibeah   gĭb´ē-a

Gid   gĭd

Giddianhi   gĭd-ē-ăn´hī

Giddonah   gĭd-dō´nä

Gideon   gĭd´ē-un

Gidgiddonah   gĭd-gĭd-dō´nä

1903–1910: The Deseret Sunday School Board appoints a committee to produce a pronouncing vocabulary based on the rules established in 1903. The Committee members are Elder Anthon H. Lund, James E. Talmage, and John M. Mills. The Committee states that their purpose is to arrive at the correct pronunciation based "solely in the interest of uniformity" (Woodger, "English Pronunciation of Book of Mormon Names," 57; Parry, "I Have a Question," 60).

1910: The results of the recommendations of the Sunday School Committee are published in the 1910 edition of George Reynolds's *Dictionary of the Book of Mormon*.

1920: The Church announces that it will publish a new edition of the Book of Mormon. The First Presidency assigns a committee of members of the Quorum of the Twelve Apostles to examine all previous editions, including references and footnotes, for any corrections needing to be made. A pronunciation guide similar to the 1910 recommendations of the Sunday School Committee first appears in the Book of Mormon in 1920.

1920–1981: No changes in the pronunciation guide are made.

1970–1981: Church President Spencer W. Kimball appoints a committee to improve doctrinal scholarship in the Church (Anderson, "Church Publishes First LDS Edition of the Bible," 9). Dr. George Horton, director of curriculum for the Church Educational System (later Seminaries and Institutes), approaches Elder Bruce R. McConkie of the Scripture Committee to suggest a new pronunciation guide for the Bible and the Book of Mormon. After review, the existing pronunciation guide is removed from the Bible, and a committee is appointed to revise the pronunciation guide for the upcoming new edition of the Book of Mormon. Brigham Young University English professor Soren Cox is appointed to review all previous material and suggests several revisions, additions, and guidelines (Woodger, "English Pronunciation of Book of Mormon Names," 56). A general American dialect is chosen as a basis for the revision. The resulting Pronunciation Guide is approved by the First Presidency and the Quorum of the Twelve Apostles.

1981: The 1981 edition of the Book of Mormon includes the new, approved Pronunciation Guide. The phonetic spelling for each of 344 names appears in the guide, as do examples of the pronunciation of each phonetic symbol. The names *Ishmael*, *Israel*, and *Mosiah* have two suggested pronunciations, reflecting the ways those names are pronounced among English-speaking Church members.

1981–Present: The Pronunciation Guide published in the 1981 edition of the Book of Mormon continues to be included in the scriptures.

Gidgiddoni gĭd-gĭd-dō´nī
Gilead gĭl´ē-ud
Gilgah gĭl´gä
Gilgal gĭl´gäl
Gimgimno gĭm-gĭm´nō
Gomorrah ga-mōr´a

Hagoth hā´gäth
Hamath hā´muth
Hearthom hē-är´thum
Helam hē´lum
Helaman hē´la-mun
Helem hē´lĕm
Helorum hē-lōr´um
Hem hĕm
Hermounts her´mounts
Heshlon hĕsh´län
Heth hĕth
Himni hĭm´nī
Horeb hōr´ĕb

Immanuel ĭm-măn´yū-ĕl
Irreantum ĭ-rē-ăn´tum
Isaac ī´zĭk
Isabel ĭz´a-bĕl
Isaiah ī-zā´a
Ishmael ĭsh´mul or ĭsh´mĕl
Ishmaelite ĭsh´mul-īt or ĭsh´mĕl-īt
Israel ĭz´rĕl or ĭz´rul
Israelite ĭz´rĕl-īt or ĭz´rul-īt

Jacob jā´kub
Jacobite jā´kub-īt
Jacobugath jā´ka-bū´găth
Jacom jā´kum
Jared jĕr´ud
Jaredite jĕr´a-dīt
Jarom jĕr´um
Jashon jā´shän
Jeberechiah jĕb-a-ra-kī´a
Jehovah jē-hō´va
Jeneum jĕn´ē-um
Jeremiah jĕr-a-mī´a
Jershon jĕr´shän

Jerusalem ja-rū´sa-lĕm
Jesse jĕs´ē
Jew jū
John jän
Jonas jō´nus
Jordan jōr´dun
Joseph jō´zĕf
Josephite jō´zĕf-īt
Josh jäsh
Joshua jäsh´ū-wa
Jotham jō´thum
Judah jū´da
Judea jū-dē´a

Kib kĭb
Kim kĭm
Kimnor kĭm´nōr
Kish kĭsh
Kishkumen kĭsh-kū´mun
Korihor kō´rĭ-hōr
Kumen kū´mun
Kumenonhi kū´ma-nän´hī

Laban lā´bun
Lachoneus la-kō´nē-us
Laish lā´ĭsh
Lamah lā´mä
Laman lā´mun
Lamanite lā´mun-īt
Lamoni la-mō´nī
Lebanon lĕb´a-nän
Lehi lē´hī
Lehi-Nephi lē´hī–nē´fī
Lehonti lē-hän´tī
Lemuel lĕm´yūl
Lemuelite lĕm´yūl-īt
Levi lē´vī
Liahona lē´a-hō´na
Lib lĭb
Limhah lĭm´hä
Limher lĭm´her
Limhi lĭm´hī
Limnah lĭm´nä
Luram lūr´um

Madmenah măd-měn´a

Mahah mā´hä

Maher-shalal-hash-baz mā´her–shăl-ăl–hăsh´bäz

Malachi măl´a-kī

Manasseh ma-năs´a

Manti măn´tī

Mary mĕ´rē

Mathoni ma-thō´nī

Mathonihah măth-ō-nī´hä

Medes mēdz

Melchizedek měl-kĭz´a-dĭk

Melek mē´lĕk

Michmash mĭk´măsh

Middoni mĭd-dō´nī

Midian mĭd´ē-un

Migron mī´grän

Minon mī´nän

Moab mō´ăb

Mocum mō´kum

Moriancumer mōr-ē-ăn´ka-mer

Morianton mōr-ē-ăn´tun

Moriantum mōr-ē-ăn´tum

Mormon mōr´mun

Moron mōr´un

Moroni mō-rō´nī

Moronihah mō-rō-nī´hä

Moses mō´zus

Mosiah mō-sī´a or mō-zī´a

Mulek myū´lĕk

Muloki myū´la-kī

Nahom nā´hum

Naphtali năf´ta-lī

Nazareth năz´a-rĕth

Neas nē´äs

Nehor nē´hōr

Nephi nē´fī

Nephihah nē-fī´hä

Nephite nē´fīt

Neum nē´um

Nimrah nĭm´rä

Nimrod nĭm´räd

Noah nō´a

Ogath ō´găth

Omega ō-mā´ga

Omer ō´mer

Omner äm´ner

Omni äm´nī

Onidah ō-nī´da

Onihah ō-nī´hä

Onti än´tī

Ophir ō´fer

Oreb ōr´ĕb

Orihah ō-rī´hä

Paanchi pā-ăn´kī

Pachus pā´kus

Pacumeni pā-kyū´měn-ī

Pagag pā´gäg

Pahoran pa-hōr´un

Palestina păl-a-stī´na

Pathros pā´thrōs

Pekah pē´kä

Pharaoh fā´rō or fĕ´rō

Philistine fĭl´a-stēn

Rabbanah ra-băn´a

Rahab rā´hăb

Ramah rä´mä

Ramath rä´muth

Rameumptom răm-ē-ump´tum

Remaliah rĕm-a-lī´a

Rezin rē´zĭn

Riplah rĭp´lä

Riplakish rĭp-lā´kĭsh

Ripliancum rĭp-lē-ăn´kum

Salem sā´lĕm

Sam săm

Samaria sa-mĕr´ē-a

Samuel săm´yū-ĕl

Sarah sĕr´a

Sariah sa-rī´a

Saul säl

Seantum sē-ăn´tum

Sebus sē´bus

Seezoram sē-zōr´um

Senine sē′nīn	Siron sī′run
Senum sē′num	Syria sĭr′ē-a
Seraphim sĕr′a-fĭm	
Seth sĕth	Tarshish tär′shĭsh
Shared shā′rud	Teancum tē-ăn′kum
Shazer shā′zer	Teomner tē-äm′ner
Shearjashub shĭr-jā′shub	Thummim thum′ĭm
Shelem shē′lĕm	Timothy tĭm′a-thē
Shem shĕm	Tubaloth tū′ba-läth
Shemlon shĕm′län	
Shemnon shĕm′nän	Uriah yū-rī′a
Sherem shĕr′um	Urim yūr′ĭm
Sherrizah shĕr-ī′za	Uzziah yū-zī′a
Sheum shē′um	
Shez shĕz	Zarahemla zĕr-a-hĕm′la
Shiblom shĭb′lum	Zebulun zĕb′yū-lun
Shiblon shĭb′lun	Zechariah zĕk′a-rī′a
Shiblum shĭb′lum	Zedekiah zĕd′a-kī′a
Shiloah shī-lō′a	Zeezrom zē-ĕz′rum
Shilom shī′lum	Zemnarihah zĕm-na-rī′hä
Shim shĭm	Zenephi zēn′a-fī
Shimnilom shĭm-nī′läm	Zeniff zē′nĭf
Shinar shī′när	Zenock zē′nuk
Shiz shĭz	Zenos zē′nus
Shule shūl	Zerahemnah zĕr-a-hĕm′nä
Shum shum	Zeram zē′rum
Shurr sher	Zerin zē′rĭn
Sidom sī′dum	Ziff zĭf
Sidon sī′dun	Zion zī′un
Sinai sī′nī	Zoram zō′rum
Sinim sī′nĭm	Zoramite zōr′um-īt

CHARTS

MAJOR LEADERS DURING NEPHITE HISTORY

Year-Reign of Judges	Christian Year	King, Chief Judge, or Governor	Historical or Church Leader	Military Leader
	600 B.C.	Nephi (2 Nephi 5:18–19)	Nephi (1 Nephi 1:1–3; 19:1–4)	Nephi (2 Nephi 5:14; Jacob 1:10)
	544 B.C.	Others designated (Jacob 1:9)	Jacob (2 Nephi 5:26; Jacob 1:1–4, 17–18)	
	544–420 B.C.		Enos and many prophets (Enos 1:22, 26)	
	399 B.C.	"Mighty men in the faith of the Lord" (Jarom 1:7)	Jarom and the prophets of the Lord (Jarom 1:1, 10–11)	"Mighty men in the faith of the Lord" (Jarom 1:7)
	361 B.C.		Omni (Omni 1:1–3)	
	317 B.C.		Amaron (Omni 1:4–8) Chemish (Omni 1:9)	
	279–130 B.C.	Mosiah[1] (Omni 1:12–23) Benjamin (Omni 1:23–25; Words of Mormon)	Abinadom (Omni 1:10–11) Amaleki (Omni 1:12) Benjamin with the holy prophets (Words of Mormon 1:16–18; Mosiah 1–6)	Mosiah[1] (Omni 1:12–23) Benjamin (Omni 1:23–25)
	124 B.C.	Mosiah[2] (Mosiah 1:15)	Mosiah[2] (Mosiah 6:3)	
	122 B.C.		Alma[1] (Mosiah 25:19; 26:28)	
1	91 B.C.	Alma[2] (Mosiah 29:44)	Alma[2] (Mosiah 29:42)	Alma[2] (Alma 2:16)
9	83 B.C.	Nephihah (Alma 4:17, 20)		
18	74 B.C.			Moroni (Alma 43:17)
19	73 B.C.		Helaman[1] (Alma 37:1; 45:20–23)	
24	68–67 B.C.	Pahoran (Alma 50:39–40)		
32	60 B.C.			Moronihah (Alma 62:43)
36	56 B.C.		Shiblon (Alma 63:1)	
39	53 B.C.		Helaman[2] (Alma 63:11)	
40	52 B.C.	Pahoran[2] (Helaman 1:1, 5) and Pacumeni (Helaman 1:13)		
42	50 B.C.	Helaman[2] (Helaman 2:1–2)		
53	39 B.C.	Nephi[1] (Helaman 3:37)	Nephi[1] (Helaman 3:37)	
62	30 B.C.	Cezoram (Helaman 4:18; 5:1)		Last reference to Moronihah (Helaman 4:18)
66	26 B.C.	Cezoram's son (Helaman 6:15)		
?	?	Seezoram (Helaman 6:39; 9:23)		

Year-Reign of Judges	Christian Year	King, Chief Judge, or Governor	Historical or Church Leader	Military Leader
92	A.D. 1	Lachoneus[1] (3 Nephi 1:1)	Nephi[2] (3 Nephi 1:1–2)	
	A.D. 16			Gidgiddoni (3 Nephi 3:18)
	A.D. 30	Lachoneus[2] (3 Nephi 6:19)		
	?		Nephi[3] (?) (Superscription to 4 Nephi)	
	A.D. 110		Amos[1] (4 Nephi 1:19–20)	
	A.D. 194		Amos[2] (4 Nephi 1:21)	
	A.D. 305		Ammaron (4 Nephi 1:47)	
	circa A.D. 321–335		Mormon (Mormon 1:1–3)	
	A.D. 326			Mormon (Mormon 2:2)
	A.D. 385		Moroni (Mormon 6:6)	

BOOK OF MORMON RECORD KEEPERS

Nephi
Prophet, leader, teacher, and initiator of Nephite record (1–2 Nephi)

	Small plates of Nephi	Large plates of Nephi
	Personal journals of prophecy and spiritual experiences	Social, political, military, and religious history
ABOUT 600 B.C.	▼ Nephi, son of Lehi Prophet and author of 1–2 Nephi	▼ Kept by the kings
544 B.C.	▶ Jacob, brother of Nephi Prophet and author of book of Jacob	▼
544–421 B.C.	▼ Enos, son of Jacob Prophet and author of book of Enos	▼
420 B.C.	▼ Jarom, son of Enos Prophet and author of book of Jarom	▼
361 B.C.	▼ Omni, son of Jarom Nephite warrior who wrote first 3 verses of book of Omni	▼
279 B.C.	▼ Amaron, son of Omni Wrote 5 verses noting the Lord's destruction of the wicked of his generation	▼
279 B.C.	▶ Chemish, brother of Amaron Wrote only 1 verse	▼
	▼ Abinadom, son of Chemish Wrote only 2 verses	▼ Mosiah¹ King who united the Nephites with the Mulekites
130 B.C.	▼ Amaleki, son of Abinadom Wrote 19 verses, bore fervent testimony of the Savior, and turned small plates of Nephi over to King Benjamin ————	○ Benjamin, son of Mosiah¹

130 B.C. 191–124 B.C.	▼ Mosiah², son of Benjamin Last of the Nephite kings	
91–72 B.C.	○ Alma², son of Alma¹ Prophet and first chief judge	
72–56 B.C.	▼ Helaman¹, son of Alma² Prophet and military leader	
	▶ Shiblon, son of Alma²	
56–53 B.C.	▶ Helaman², son of Helaman¹	
53–59 B.C.	▼ Nephi², son of Helaman² Contemporary with Samuel the Lamanite	
39–1 B.C.	▼ Nephi³, son of Nephi² Chief Nephite disciple and Apostle of the resurrected Lord	
?–A.D. 111	▼ Nephi⁴, son of Nephi³	
A.D. 111–194	▼ Amos¹, son of Nephi⁴	
A.D. 194–306	▼ Amos², son of Amos¹	
A.D. 306–321	▶ Ammaron, brother of Amos² Hid plates in the hill Shim in A.D. 321 Commissioned 10-year-old Mormon to continue record upon turning 24 years of age	
A.D. 345–385	○ Mormon Made an abridgment of Nephite plates	
A.D. 385–421	▼ Moroni, son of Mormon² Completed the record of his father Added his own writings Abridged the Jaredite record (book of Ether) Sealed the abridged records in the Hill Cumorah	

The following indicate relationships:
▼ Father to son
▶ Brother to brother
○ Plates passed outside family relationships

SOURCES

BOOKS AND ARTICLES

Adams, William J., Jr. "Nephi's Jerusalem and Laban's Sword." In Welch and Thorne, *Pressing Forward with the Book of Mormon.*

———. "Synagogues in the Book of Mormon." *Journal of Book of Mormon Studies 9*, no. 1 (2000): 4–13, 76.

Albrea, Angel. "Your Own Personal Testimony." *Ensign*, May 2000, 41–42.

Allen, Joseph L. *Exploring the Lands of the Book of Mormon.* 1989.

Allred, Philip A. "Moses' Charge to Remember." In *Covenants, Prophecies, and Hymns of the Old Testament.*

Allred, Sylvia. "Holy Temples, Sacred Covenants." *Ensign*, Nov. 2008, 112–14.

Allred, William. "Recollections of the Prophet Joseph Smith." *Juvenile Instructor* 27, no. 15 (1 Aug. 1892): 471, in *Presidents of the Church Teacher Manual.* 2005.

Andersen, Neil L. "A Classroom of Faith, Hope, and Charity." Address to Church Educational System religious educators, Feb. 28, 2014.

———. "Overcoming the World." *Ensign*, May 2017, 58–62.

———. "'Repent . . . That I May Heal You.'" *Ensign*, Nov. 2009, 40–43.

———. "Reverence for God Is the Beginning of Wisdom." *Ensign*, Jan. 2013, 32–39.

———. "Trial of Your Faith." *Ensign*, Nov. 2012, 39–42.

Anderson, Kenneth W. "The Twelve: A Light unto This People." In Nyman and Tate, *3 Nephi 9–30.*

Anderson, Lavina Fielding. "The Church Publishes First LDS Edition of the Bible." *Ensign*, Oct. 1979, 8–11.

Anderson, Ronald D. "*Leitworter* in Helaman and 3 Nephi." In Nyman and Tate, *Helaman through 3 Nephi 8.*

Anderson, Richard Lloyd. "Attempts to Redefine the Experience of the Eight Witnesses." *Journal of Book of Mormon Studies* 14, no. 1 (2005): 18–31, 125–27.

———. *Investigating the Book of Mormon Witnesses.* 1981.

Anderson, Scott, and Angelle Anderson. "One by One." In *Eternal Families.* Edited by Daniel K Judd and Douglas E. Brinley. 1996.

Archibald, Dallas N. "Born of Goodly Parents." *Ensign*, Nov. 1992, 25–26.

Arden, Ian S. "Shunning Temptation: A Key to Receiving Revelation." *Ensign*, Nov. 2014, 56–59.

Asay, Carlos E. *Family Pecan Trees: Planting a Legacy of Faith at Home.* 1992.

———. "Golden Threads of the Book of Mormon." In *Heroes from the Book of Mormon.*

———. "Opposition to the Work." *Ensign*, Nov.1981, 67–69.

———. "Parent-Child Interviews." *Ensign*, Nov. 1983, 14–15.

———. *Seven M's of Missionary Service: Proclaiming the Gospel as a Member or Full-time Missionary.* 1996.

Ashton, Marvin J. "Neither Boast of Faith Nor Mighty Works." *Ensign*, May 1990, 65–67.

———. "No Time for Contention." *Ensign*, May 1978, 7–9.

———. "Power of Plainness." *Ensign*, May 1977, 66–68.

——. *Teaching, Mentoring, and Things of the Spirit.* Brigham Young University Annual University Conference, Aug. 24, 1992.

Aston, Warren P. "A History of NaHoM." *Brigham Young University Studies* 51, no. 2 (2012): 78–98.

Aston, Warren P., and Michaela J. Aston. "Lehi's Trail and Nahom Revisited." In Welch, *Reexploring the Book of Mormon.*

——. *In the Footsteps of Lehi: New Evidence for Lehi's Journey Across Arabia to Bountiful.* 1994.

Bailyn, Bernard. *The Peopling of British North America: An Introduction.* 1988.

Ball, Terry. "Isaiah's Imagery of Plants and Planting." In *Thy People Shall Be My People.*

——. "Old Testament Prophets in the Book of Mormon (Lehi, Zenock, Neum, Zenos, Ezias)." In Jackson, *1 Kings to Malachi.*

Ball, Terry B., and Wilford M. Hess. "Agriculture in Lehi's World: Some Textual, Historical, Archaeological, and Botanical Insights." In Welch et al., *Glimpses of Lehi's Jerusalem.*

Ball, Terry, and Nathan Winn. *Making Sense of Isaiah.* 2009.

Ballard, Melvin J. "Classic Discourses from the General Authorities: The Sacramental Covenant." *New Era*, Jan. 1976, 66–67.

——. *Sermons and Missionary Services of Melvin J. Ballard.* Edited by Bryant S. Hinckley. 1949.

Ballard, M. Russell. "Beware of False Prophets and False Teachers." *Ensign*, Nov. 1999, 62–64.

——. "A Chance to Start Over: Church Disciplinary Councils and the Restoration of Blessings." *Ensign*, Sep. 1990, 12–19.

——. "Creating a Gospel-Sharing Home." *Ensign*, May 2006, 84–87.

——. "Feasting at the Lord's Table." *Ensign*, May 1996, 80–82.

——. "Finding Joy through Loving Service." *Ensign*, May 2011, 46–49.

——. "The Greatest Generation of Missionaries." *Ensign*, Nov. 2002, 46–49.

——. "The Hand of Fellowship." *Ensign*, Nov. 1988, 28–30.

——. "The Importance of a Name." *Ensign*, Nov. 2011, 79–82.

——. "The Joy of Hope Fulfilled." *Ensign*, Nov. 1992, 31–33.

——. "Let Our Voices Be Heard." *Ensign*, Nov. 2003, 16–18.

——. "O Be Wise." *Ensign*, Nov. 2006, 17–20.

——. *Our Search for Happiness.* 1993.

——. "Pure Testimony." *Ensign*, Nov. 2004, 40–43.

——. "Purity Precedes Power." *Ensign*, Nov. 1990, 35–38.

——. "Small and Simple Things." *Ensign*, May 1990, 6–8.

——. "Standing for Truth and Right." *Ensign*, Nov. 1997, 37–40.

Barney, Kevin L. "Understanding Old Testament Poetry." *Ensign*, June 1990, 51–54.

Bassett, Douglas. "Faces of Worldly Pride in the Book of Mormon." *Ensign*, Oct. 2000, 48–54.

Bassett, K. Douglas. "Four Faces of Pride in the Book of Mormon." In *Doctrines of the Book of Mormon.*

——. "Nephi's Freedom Thesis and the Sons of Helaman." In Nyman and Tate, *Alma.*

Bateman, Merrill J. "Coming unto Christ by Searching the Scriptures." *Ensign*, Nov. 1992, 27–28.

Beck, David L. "The Magnificent Aaronic Priesthood." *Ensign*, May 2010, 54–56.

Beck, Julie B. "Mothers Who Know." *Ensign*, Nov. 2007, 76–78.

Bednar, David A. "And Nothing Shall Offend Them." *Ensign*, Nov. 2006, 89–92.

——. "Arise and Shine Forth." Brigham Young University–Idaho devotional, June 28, 2003.

——. "The Atonement and the Journey of Mortality." *Ensign*, Apr. 2012, 40–47.

——. "Clean Hands and a Pure Heart." *Ensign*, Nov. 2007, 80–83.

———. "Converted unto the Lord." *Ensign,* Nov. 2012, 106–9.

———. "Faithful Parents and Wayward Children: Sustaining Hope While Overcoming Misunderstanding." *Ensign*, Mar. 2014, 28–33.

———. "Honorably Hold a Name and Standing." *Ensign*, Apr. 2009, 97–100.

———. "In the Strength of the Lord." *Ensign*, Nov. 2004, 76–78.

———. "Lehi's Dream: Holding Fast to the Rod." *Ensign*, Oct. 2011, 32–37.

———. "The Powers of Heaven." *Ensign*, May 2012, 48–51.

———. "Quick to Observe." *Ensign*, Dec. 2006, 31–36.

———. "A Reservoir of Living Water." Church Educational System fireside, Feb. 4, 2007.

———. "Seek Learning by Faith." *Ensign*, Sep. 2007, 60–68.

———. "The Spirit of Revelation." *Ensign*, May 2011, 87–90.

———. "The Tender Mercies of the Lord." *Ensign*, May 2005, 99–102.

———. "That We May Always Have His Spirit to Be with Us." *Ensign*, May 2006, 28–31.

———. "Therefore They Hushed Their Fears." *Ensign*, May 2015, 46–49.

———. "To Sweep the Earth as with a Flood." Address at Brigham Young University, Aug. 19, 2014.

———. "Watching with All Perseverance." *Ensign*, May 2010, 40–43.

———. "We Believe in Being Chaste." *Ensign,* May 2013, 41–44.

———. "The Windows of Heaven." *Ensign*, Nov. 2013, 17–20.

———. "Ye Must Be Born Again." *Ensign,* May 2007, 19–22.

Bednar, Richard L., and Scott R. Peterson. *Doing the Right Things for the Right Reasons*. 1995.

Belnap, Daniel L. "'A Wise Man Built His House upon a Rock.'" In Strathearn et al., *Sermon on the Mount in Latter-day Scripture*.

Bennett, Richard E. "Martin Harris and Three Wise Men." Brigham Young University devotional, June 29, 2010.

Bennett, Robert R. "Horses in the Book of Mormon." Neal A. Maxwell Institute for Religious Scholarship, August 2000.

Bennett, Wallace F. "The Constitution and the Bill of Rights." Brigham Young University forum, Feb. 15, 1961.

Benson, Alvin K. "Geological Upheaval and Darkness in 3 Nephi 8–10." In Nyman and Tate, *3 Nephi 9–30*.

Benson, Ezra Taft. "Beware of Pride." *Ensign*, May 1989, 4–7.

———. "The Book of Mormon and the Doctrine and Covenants." *Ensign*, May 1987, 83–85.

———. "The Book of Mormon Is the Word of God." *Ensign*, Jan. 1988, 3–5.

———. "The Book of Mormon—Keystone of Our Religion." *Ensign*, Nov. 1986, 4–7.

———. "Born of God." *Ensign*, Nov. 1985, 5–7.

———. "Civic Standards for the Faithful Saints." *Ensign*, July 1972, 59–61.

———. "Cleansing the Inner Vessel." *Ensign*, May 1986, 4–7.

———. *Come unto Christ*. 1983.

———. "Do Not Despair." *Ensign*, Nov. 1974, 65–68.

———. *God, Family, and Country: Our Three Great Loyalties*. 1974.

———. "The Great Commandment—Love the Lord." *Ensign*, May 1988, 4–6.

———. "I Testify." *Ensign*, Nov. 1988, 85–87.

———. In Conference Report, Apr. 1968, 49–54.

———. In Conference Report, Oct. 1962, 14–19.

———. In Conference Report, Oct. 1966, 120–25.

———. "Jesus Christ—Gifts and Expectations." *Ensign*, Dec. 1988, 2–6.

———. "The Law of Chastity." *New Era*, Jan. 1998, 4–7.

———. "Listen to a Prophet's Voice." *Ensign*, Jan. 1973, 57–59.

———. "A Marvelous Work and a Wonder." *Ensign*, May 1980, 32–34.

———. "A Message to Judah from Joseph." *Ensign*, Dec. 1976, 67–72.

———. "A Message to the Rising Generation." *Ensign*, Nov. 1977, 30–32.

———. "A Mighty Change of Heart." *Ensign*, Oct. 1989, 2–5.

———. "A New Witness for Christ." *Ensign*, Nov. 1984, 6–8.

———. "Our Divine Constitution." *Ensign*, Nov. 1987, 4–7.

———. "The Power of the Word." *Ensign*, May 1986, 79–82.

———. "Pray Always." *Ensign*, Feb. 1990, 2–6.

———. "The Savior's Visit to America." *Ensign*, May 1987, 4–7.

———. "'Strengthen Thy Stakes.'" *Ensign*, Jan.1991, 2–5.

———. *The Teachings of Ezra Taft Benson*. Edited by Reed Benson. 1988.

———. "This Is a Day of Sacrifice." *Ensign*, May 1979, 32–33.

———. *Title of Liberty*. 1964.

———. *This Nation Shall Endure*. 1977.

———. "To the Rising Generation." *New Era*, June 1986, 5.

———. "To the 'Youth of the Noble Birthright.'" *Ensign*, May 1986, 45–48.

———. "What I Hope You Will Teach Your Children about the Temple." *Ensign*, Aug. 1985, 6–10.

———. "A Witness and a Warning." *Ensign*, Nov. 1979, 31–33.

———. *A Witness and a Warning: A Modern-Day Prophet Testifies of the Book of Mormon*. 1988.

———. "Worthy Fathers, Worthy Sons." *Ensign*, Nov. 1985, 35–37.

Berrett, William E. *Teachings of the Book of Mormon*. 1962.

Best, Brian. "Nephi, Lehi, and Samuel the Lamanite." *Ensign*, Dec. 1977, 44–51.

Bible Dictionary. Holy Bible: The Church of Jesus Christ of Latter-day Saints. 2013.

Bingham, Jean B. "Ministering as the Savior Does." *Ensign*, May 2018, 104–7.

Black, Susan Easton. *400 Questions and Answers about the Book of Mormon*. 2011.

———. "King Benjamin: In the Service of God." In Nyman and Tate, *Mosiah*.

Blanch, Mae. "Samuel the Lamanite." In Jackson, *Alma 30 to Moroni*.

Bokovoy, David E. "Repetitive Resumption in the Book of Mormon." *Insights* 27, no. 1 (2007).

"Book of Mormon Anachronisms: Jeremiah Being Put into Prison." Fairmormon.org.

"Book of Mormon and DNA Studies." Gospel Topics.

Book of Mormon Central. "Ammonihah."

———. "Did Lehi Use the Poetry of the Ancient Bedouin?" KnoWhy 5.

———. "How Is the Day of Atonement Understood in the Book of Mormon?" KnoWhy 479.

———. "Pillar of Fire."

———. "What Parts of the Old Testament Were on the Plates of Brass?" KnoWhy 410.

———. "Who Were the 'Elders of the Jews' Mentioned by Zoram?" KnoWhy 464.

———. "Why Are There So Many War Chapters in the Book of Mormon?" KnoWhy 157.

———. "Why Did Lehi Divide His People into Seven Tribes?" KnoWhy 319.

———. "Why Did Mormon See Captain Moroni as a Hero?" KnoWhy 155.

———. "Why Did Mormon Introduce Himself in 3 Nephi 5?" KnoWhy 194.

———. "Why Was Ammoron Determined to Avenge the Blood of His Brother?" KnoWhy 162.

———. "Why Would Zerahemnah Not Swear an Oath to Moroni?" KnoWhy 152.

The Book of Mormon for Latter-day Saint Families. Edited by Thomas R. Valletta et al. 1999.

"Book of Mormon Geography." Gospel Topics.

"Book of Mormon Reaches Another Milestone: 150 Million and Counting." April 18, 2011.

Book of Mormon Seminary Teacher Manual. 2012.

Book of Mormon Seminary Student Study Guide. 2000.

Book of Mormon Student Manual, Religion 121–122. 1989.

Book of Mormon Student Manual, Religion 121–122. 1996.

Book of Mormon Student Manual, Religion 121–122. 2009.

"Book of Mormon Students Meet." *Deseret Evening News,* May 25, 1903, 3–4.

The Book of Mormon: The Foundation of Our Faith. Sperry Symposium series. 1999.

A Book of Mormon Treasury: Gospel Insights from General Authorities and Religious Educators. 2003.

Bowen, Matthew L. "Internal Textual Evidence for the Egyptian Origin of Nephi's Name." *Insights* 22, no. 11 (2002).

———. "'They Came Forth and Fell Down and Partook of the Fruit of the Tree': Proskynesis in 3 Nephi 11:12–19 and 17:9–10 and Its Significance." In Skinner and Strathearn, *Third Nephi.*

Bradley, Carol Pratt. "Women, the Book of Mormon, and the Law of Moses." *Studia Antiqua.* Summer 2004.

Brandt, Edward J. "The Law of Moses and the Law of Christ." In *Sperry Symposium Classics: The Old Testament.* Edited by Paul Y. Hoskisson. 2005.

Brewster, Hoyt W., Jr. *Behold, I Come Quickly.* 1994.

———. *Doctrine and Covenants Encyclopedia.* 1989.

———. *Isaiah Plain and Simple: The Message of Isaiah in the Book of Mormon.* 1995.

Brigham, Kay, trans. *Christopher Columbus's Book of Prophecies: Reproduction of the Original Manuscript with English Translation.* Quincentenary edition. 1991.

Brinley, Douglas E. "The Jaredites—A Case Study in Following the Brethren." In Nyman and Tate, *Fourth Nephi through Moroni.*

———. "The Promised Land and Its Covenant Peoples." In Nyman and Tate, *Helaman through 3 Nephi 8.*

Bromiley, Geoffrey W. *Theological Dictionary of the New Testament.* 1 vol. 1985.

Brown, Cheryl. "'I Speak Somewhat Concerning That Which I Have Written.'" In Nyman and Tate, *Jacob through Words of Mormon.*

Brown, Hugh B. "The Currant Bush." *New Era,* Jan. 1973, 14–15.

———. In Conference Report, Oct. 1962, 83–85.

Brown, L. Edward. "Pray unto the Father in My Name." *Ensign,* May 1997, 78–79.

Brown, Matthew B. "Girded About with a Lambskin." *Journal of Book of Mormon Studies* 6, no. 2 (1997).

Brown, Raymond E. *The Birth of the Messiah: A Commentary on the Infancy Narratives in the Gospels of Matthew and Luke.* 1999.

Brown, S. Kent. "Alma's Conversion: Reminiscences in His Sermons." In Nyman and Tate, *Alma.*

———. "A Case for Lehi's Bondage in Arabia." *Journal of Book of Mormon Studies* 6, no. 2 (2000): 205–17.

———. "The Exodus Pattern in the Book of Mormon." *Brigham Young University Studies* 30, no. 3 (1990): 111–26.

———. "The Exodus: Seeing It as a Test, a Testimony, and a Type." *Ensign,* Feb. 1990, 54–57.

———. "Lehi's Personal Record: Quest for a Missing Source." *Brigham Young University Studies* 24, no. 1 (1984): 19–42.

———. "Marriage and Treaty in the Book of Mormon: The Case of the Abducted Lamanite Daughters." In *The Disciple as Scholar: Essays on Scripture and the Ancient World in Honor of Richard Lloyd Anderson.* Edited by Stephen D. Ricks, Donald W. Parry, and Andrew H. Hedges. 2000.

———. "Moses and Jesus: The Old Adorns the New." In Nyman and Tate, *3 Nephi 9–30.*

———. "Nephi's Use of Lehi's Record." In Sorenson and Thorne, *Rediscovering the Book of Mormon.*

———. "New Light from Arabia on Lehi's Trail." In Parry et al., *Echoes and Evidences.*

———. "Refining the Spotlight on Lehi and Sariah." *Journal of Book of Mormon Studies* 15/2 (2006): 44–57, 116–20.

———. *Voices from the Dust: Book of Mormon Insights.* 2004.

———. "What Were Those Sacrifices Offered by Lehi?" In *From Jerusalem to Zarahemla: Literary and Historical Studies of the Book of Mormon.* 1998.

Buehner, Carl W. In Conference Report, Apr. 1953, 114–17.

Burton, H. David. "Go, and Do Thou Likewise." *Ensign,* May 1997, 75–77.

Burton, Linda K. "The Power, Joy, and Love of Covenant Keeping." *Ensign,* Nov. 2013, 111–14.

Burton, Rulon T. *We Believe.* 1994.

Burton, Theodore M. "Salvation and Exaltation." *Ensign,* July 1972, 78–79.

Bushman, Richard L. "The Book of Mormon and the American Revolution." *Brigham Young University Studies* 17, no. 1 (Autumn 1976): 3–20.

Butler, John M. "The 'Author' and the 'Finisher' of the Book of Mormon." In Nyman and Tate, *Fourth Nephi through Moroni.*

Bytheway, John. *Righteous Warriors: Lessons from the War Chapters in the Book of Mormon.* 2004.

Calabro, David. "'Stretch Forth Thy Hand and Prophesy': Hand Gestures in the Book of Mormon." *Journal of the Book of Mormon and Other Restoration Scripture* 21, no. 1 (2012): 46–59.

Caldwell, C. Max. "The Path That Leads to Christ." *Ensign,* Apr. 1996, 27–30.

Call, Gail. "Antenantiosis in the Book of Mormon." In Welch, *Reexploring the Book of Mormon.*

Callister, Tad R. *The Inevitable Apostasy and the Promised Restoration.* 2006.

———. *The Infinite Atonement.* 2000.

———. "Our Identity and Our Destiny." Brigham Young University devotional, Aug. 14, 2012.

Cannon, George Q. In Conference Report, Oct. 1897, 64–71.

———. *Gospel Truth: Discourses and Writings of President George Q. Cannon.* Edited by Jerreld L. Newquist. 1987.

Card, Orson Scott. "Three Kings and a Captain: Nephite Leaders in the Land of Nephi." *Ensign,* Jan. 1977, 76–82.

Cazier, Donald A. "I Have a Question." *Ensign,* Aug. 1992, 60–61.

Chadwick, Jeffrey R. "The Names Lehi and Sariah—Language and Meaning." *Journal of Book of Mormon Studies* 9, no. 1 (2000): 32–34.

Chase, Randal S. *Making Precious Things Plain: Book of Mormon Study Guide.* 3 vols. 2010.

Cheesman, Paul R., ed. *The Book of Mormon: The Keystone Scripture.* Book of Mormon Symposium series. 1988.

———. "Lehi's Journeys." In Nyman and Tate, *First Nephi.* 1988.

Childs, Larry G. "Epanalepsis in the Book of Mormon." In Welch, *Reexploring the Book of Mormon.*

Child, Sheldon F. "A Sure Foundation." *Ensign,* Nov. 2003, 8–10.

Christensen, Joe J. "Greed, Selfishness, and Overindulgence." *Ensign*, May 1999, 10–12.

———. "Rearing Children in a Polluted Environment." *Ensign*, Nov. 1993, 11–13.

———. "The Savior Is Counting on You." *Ensign*, Nov. 1996, 39–41.

Christenson, Allen J. "Nephite Trade Networks and the Dangers of a Class Society." In Nyman and Tate, *Helaman through 3 Nephi 8*.

Christiansen, Elray L. "The Laws of God Are Blessings." *Ensign*, May 1975, 23–24.

Christofferson, D. Todd. "As Many as I Love, I Rebuke and Chasten." *Ensign*, May 2011, 97–100.

———. "The Blessing of Scripture." *Ensign*, May 2010, 32–35.

———. "Come to Zion." *Ensign,* Nov. 2008, 37–40.

———. "The Divine Gift of Repentance." *Ensign*, Nov. 2011, 38–41.

———. "Firm and Steadfast in the Faith of Christ." *Ensign*, Nov. 2018, 30–33.

———. "Let Us Be Men." *Ensign*, Oct. 2006, 46–48.

———. "The Power of Covenants." *Ensign*, May 2009, 19–23.

———. "The Prophet Joseph Smith." Brigham Young University–Idaho devotional, Sep. 24, 2013.

———. "Redemption." *Ensign*, May 2013, 109–12.

———. "To Always Remember Him." *Ensign*, Apr. 2011, 49–55.

———. "When Thou Art Converted." *Ensign*, May, 2004, 11–13.

Cinelli, Catherine. "Living by the Scriptures." In *Church News*, Jan. 20, 1996.

Clark, James R., comp. *Messages of the First Presidency of The Church of Jesus Christ of Latter-day Saints*. 6 vols. 1965–75.

Clark, John E. "A Key for Evaluating Nephite Geographies." *FARMS Review* 1, no. 1, 1989.

Clark, J. Reuben, Jr. In Conference Report, Oct. 1955, 83–84.

Clark, Kim B. "Three Invitations." Brigham Young University–Hawaii Devotional, 15 Dec. 2017.

Clark, Robert E. "The Type at the Border: An Inquiry into Book of Mormon Typology." *Journal of Book of Mormon Studies* 2, no. 2 (1993), 63–77.

Clarke, Don R. "Becoming Instruments in the Hands of God." *Ensign*, Nov. 2006, 97–99.

Clayton, L. Whitney. "Blessed Are All the Pure in Heart." *Ensign,* Nov. 2007, 51–53.

———. "Marriage: Watch and Learn." *Ensign,* May 2013, 83–85.

———. "That Your Burdens May Be Light." *Ensign*, Nov. 2009, 12–14.

Cloward, Robert A. "The Savior's Missionary Training Sermon in 3 Nephi." In Nyman and Tate, *3 Nephi 9–30*.

Clyde, Aileen H. "Covenant of Love." *Ensign*, May 1995, 26–28.

Collected Discourses. Edited by Brian H. Stuy. 5 vols. 1987.

Condie, Spencer J. "Righteous Oaths, Reproof, and Reconciliation (Alma 50–63)." In Jackson, *Alma 30 to Moroni*.

———. *Your Agency: Handle with Care*. 1996.

Conkling, Chris. "The Gentle Power of Jacob." *Ensign*, Feb. 1992, 7–10.

Cook, Carl B. "It's Better to Look Up." *Ensign*, Nov. 2011, 33–35.

Cook, Gene R. *Living by the Power of Faith*. 1985.

———. "Miracles among the Lamanites." *Ensign*, Nov. 1980, 67–69.

———. "Moroni's Promise." *Ensign*, Apr. 1994, 12–16.

———. *Receiving Answers to Our Prayers*. 1996.

———. *Searching the Scriptures: Bringing Power to Your Personal and Family Study*. 1997.

———. "Spiritual Guides for Teachers of Righteousness." *Ensign*, May 1982, 25–27.

Cook, Quentin L. "In Tune with the Music of Faith." *Ensign,* May 2012, 41–44.

———. "Looking beyond the Mark." *Ensign,* March 2003, 41–44.

———. "The Restoration of Morality and Religious Freedom." BYU–Idaho commencement address, Dec. 16, 2011.

———. "Restoring Morality and Religious Freedom." *Ensign,* Sep. 2012, 33–37.

———. "The Songs They Could Not Sing." *Ensign,* Nov. 2011, 104–7.

———. "Valiant in the Testimony of Jesus." *Ensign,* Nov. 2016, 40–43.

Coutts, Alison V. P. "From a Convert's Viewpoint." In Parry et al., *Echoes and Evidences.*

Covenants, Prophecies, and Hymns of the Old Testament. Edited by Frank F. Judd Jr. and Gaye Strathearn. Sperry Symposium series. 2001.

Cowan, Richard O. *The Church in the Twentieth Century.* 1985.

———. *The Doctrine and Covenants, Our Modern Scripture.* 1984.

———. "The Lamanites—a More Accurate Image." In Nyman and Tate, *Helaman through 3 Nephi 8.*

———. "A New Meaning of 'Restoration.'" In Nyman and Tate, *Alma.*

———. "Restoration, Redemption, and Resurrection: Three R's of the Book of Mormon." In *Living the Book of Mormon.*

———. "Sacred Temples Ancient and Modern." In *The Temple in Time and Eternity.* Edited by Donald W. Parry and Stephen D. Ricks. 1999.

Cowley, Matthias F. *Cowley's Talks on Doctrine.* 1902.

Cramer, Lew W. "Abinadi." In Ludlow, *Encyclopedia of Mormonism.*

Current, Richard N., Harry T. Williams, and Frank Freidel. *American History: A Survey.* 1966.

Dahl, Larry E. "The Higher Law." *Ensign,* Feb. 1991, 7–11.

———. "The Plan of Redemption—Taught and Rejected." In Jackson, *1 Nephi to Alma 29.*

Dahl, Larry E., and Donald Q. Cannon. *Encyclopedia of Joseph Smith's Teachings.* 1997.

Dew, Sheri. *If Life Were Easy, It Wouldn't Be Hard.* 2005.

———. *No Doubt about It.* 2002.

———. "Our Only Chance." *Ensign,* May 1999, 66–67.

"Did Lehi Use the Poetry of the Ancient Bedouin?" Book of Mormon Central. KnoWhy 5.

DK Illustrated Oxford Dictionary. 2003.

Doctrine and Covenants Student Manual. 2001.

Doctrines of the Book of Mormon. Edited by Bruce A. Van Orden and Brent L. Top. Sperry Symposium series. 1992.

Donaldson, Lee. "'After the Manner of Their Language': A Look at the Language of Joseph Smith." Address to Church Educational System religious educators, Aug. 10–12, 1993.

———. "Benjamin and Noah: The Principle of Dominion." In Nyman and Tate, *Mosiah.*

———. "The Plates of Ether and the Covenant of the Book of Mormon." In Nyman and Tate, *Fourth Nephi through Moroni.*

Dunlop, James. "Book of Mormon Principles: Turning the Other Cheek." *Ensign,* Sep. 2004, 32–34.

Durham, W. Cole, Jr. "Moroni." *Ensign,* June 1978, 56–61.

Dyer, Alvin R. "The Last Dispensation." *Ensign,* July 1972, 52–53.

Eastmond, Mark Elbert. "Images of Mercy in the Writings of Isaiah." In *Covenants, Prophecies, and Hymns of the Old Testament.*

Eaton, Robert I., and Henry J. Eyring. *I Will Lead You Along: The Life of Henry B. Eyring.* 2013.

Edersheim, Alfred. *The Life and Times of Jesus the Messiah.* 1993.

Edgley, Richard C. "The Empowerment of Humility." *Ensign*, Nov. 2003, 97–99.

———. "Satan's Bag of Snipes." *Ensign*, Nov. 2000, 42–43.

———. "Three Towels and a 25-Cent Newspaper." *Ensign*, Nov. 2006, 72–74.

Edwards, Kay P. "The Kingdom of God and the Kingdoms of Men." In Jackson, *1 Nephi to Alma 29*.

Edwards, Keith R. "That They Might Know Thee." *Ensign*, Nov. 2006, 66–67.

"The Elders in Kirtland, to Their Brethren Abroad." *The Evening and the Morning Star*, Dec. 1833.

Eliade, Mircea. *The Myth of the Eternal Return; or, Cosmos and History.* 1954.

England, Eugene. "Moroni and His Captains: Men of Peace in a Time of War." *Ensign*, Sep. 1977, 29–36.

Esplin, Scott C. "Millions Shall Know Brother Joseph Again: Joseph Smith's Place among the Prophets." In *Joseph Smith and the Doctrinal Restoration.* Sperry Symposium series. 2005.

Eternal Families. Edited by Daniel K Judd and Douglas E. Brinley. 1996.

Eubank, Sharon. "Turn On Your Light." *Ensign*, Nov. 2017, 6–9.

Evans, Richard L. "Should the Commandments Be Rewritten?" *Ensign*, Dec. 1971, 57.

Eyring, Henry B. "Adversity." *Ensign*, May 2009, 23–27.

———. "Always." *Ensign,* Oct. 1999, 7–12.

———. "Amulek: The Blessings of Obedience." In *Heroes from the Book of Mormon.*

———. *Because He First Loved Us.* 2002.

———. "The Book of Mormon Will Change Your Life." *Ensign*, Feb. 2004, 9–14.

———. "A Child and a Disciple." *Ensign,* May 2003, 29–32.

———. "Do Not Delay." *Ensign*, Nov. 1999, 33–35.

———. "Finding Safety in Counsel." *Ensign*, May 1997, 24–26.

———. "Gifts of the Spirit for Hard Times." *Ensign*, June 2007, 18–24.

———. "Helping Students Inquire of the Lord." Address to Church Educational System religious educators, Feb. 2, 2001.

———. "In the Strength of the Lord." *Ensign*, May 2004, 16–19.

———. "Opportunities to Do Good." *Ensign*, May 2011, 22–26.

———. "O Remember, Remember." *Ensign,* Nov. 2007, 66–69.

———. "Our Hearts Knit as One." *Ensign*, Oct. 2008, 68–71.

———. "Recognize, Remember, and Give Thanks." *Ensign*, Aug. 2013, 4–5.

———. "Safety in Counsel." *Ensign*, June 2008, 5–9.

———. "Spiritual Preparedness: Start Early and Be Steady." *Ensign*, Nov. 2005, 37–40.

———. "That He May Write upon Our Hearts." *Ensign*, Aug. 2009, 5–9.

———. "That We May Be One." *Ensign*, May 1998, 66–68.

———. *To Draw Closer to God: A Collection of Discourses.* 1997.

———. "A Voice of Warning." *Ensign*, Nov. 1998, 32–34.

———. "We Must Raise Our Sights." *Ensign*, Sep. 2004, 14–19.

———. "Where Is the Pavilion?" *Ensign*, Nov. 2012, 72–75.

Fair Mormon Conference. "The Gadianton Robbers in Mormon's Theological History: Their Structural Role and Plausible Identification."

———. "Right on Target: Boomerang Hits and the Book of Mormon."

"The Family: A Proclamation to the World." *Ensign*, Nov. 2010, 129.

Farley, S. Brent. "The Appearance of Christ to the People of Nephi." In Jackson, *Alma 30 to Moroni.*

Far West Record: Minutes of The Church of Jesus Christ of Latter-day Saints, 1830–1844. Edited by Lyndon W. Cook and Donald Q. Cannon. 1983.

Faulring, Scott H. "An Examination of the 1829 'Articles of the Church of Christ' in Relation to Section 20 of the Doctrine and Covenants." *Brigham Young University Studies* 43, no. 4 (2004): 57–74.

Faust, James E. "The Atonement: Our Greatest Hope." *Ensign*, Nov. 2001, 18–20.

———. "The Blessings We Receive as We Meet the Challenges of Economic Stress." *Ensign*, Nov. 1982, 87–90.

———. "The Enemy Within." *Ensign*, Nov. 2000, 44–46.

———. "Father, Come Home." *Ensign*, May 1993, 35–37.

———. "The Forces That Will Save Us." *Ensign*, Jan. 2007, 5–9.

———. "The Great Imitator." *Ensign*, Nov. 1987, 33–36.

———. "Heirs to the Kingdom of God." *Ensign*, May 1995, 61–63.

———. "Hope, an Anchor of the Soul." *Ensign*, Nov. 1999, 59–61.

———. "The Importance of Bearing Testimony." *Ensign*, Mar. 1997, 2–5.

———. "The Keystone of Our Religion." *Ensign*, Nov. 1983, 9–11.

———. "The Lifeline of Prayer." *Ensign*, May 2002, 59–62.

———. "A Royal Priesthood." *Ensign*, May 2006, 50–53.

———. "Stand Up and Be Counted." *Ensign*, Feb. 1982, 69–71.

———. "The Voice of the Spirit." Brigham Young University fireside, Sep. 5, 1993.

———. "We Believe in You!" Church Educational System fireside, Nov. 1, 1998.

———. "Woman, Why Weepest Thou?" *Ensign*, Nov. 1996, 50–53.

Featherstone, Vaughn J. "The King's Son." *New Era*, Nov. 1975, 34–38.

———. "A Self-Inflicting Purge." *Ensign*, May 1975, 66–68.

Federer, William J., comp. *America's God and Country: Encyclopedia of Quotations.* 1994.

First Presidency of The Church of Jesus Christ of Latter-day Saints [Joseph F. Smith, John R. Winder, and Anthon H. Lund]. "The Origin of Man." *Improvement Era,* Nov. 1909, 75–81. Reprint, *Ensign*, Feb. 2002, 26–30.

Fisher, David Hackett. *Paul Revere's Ride.* 1994.

Flammer, Philip M. "A Land of Promise, Choice above All Other Lands." In Nyman and Tate, *First Nephi.*

Flinders,Neil J. "The Key of Knowledge." In *The Book of Mormon and the Message of the Four Gospels.* 2001.

For the Strength of Youth [booklet]. 2011.

Fowles, John L. "The Decline of the Nephites: Rejection of the Covenant and Word of God." In Nyman and Tate, *The Book of Mormon: Helaman Through 3 Nephi 8, According To Thy Word.* 81–92.

———. "Zenos' Prophetic Allegory of Israel." In *Book of Mormon.* Church Educational System Religious Educators Symposium. 1986.

Franklin, Benjamin. "Motion for Prayers in the Convention." In *Benjamin Franklin Writings.* Edited by J. A. Leo Lemay. 1987.

Fronk, Camille. "Desert Epiphany: Sariah and the Women in 1 Nephi." *Journal of Book of Mormon Studies* 9, no. 2 (2000): 4–15.

———. "Show Forth Good Examples in Me." In Jackson, *1 Nephi to Alma 29.*

The Fulness of the Gospel: Foundational Teachings from the Book of Mormon. Sperry Symposium series. 2003.

Galbraith, David B., D. Kelly Ogden, and Andrew C. Skinner. *Jerusalem, the Eternal City.* 1996.

Gardner, Brant A. "Literacy and Orality in the Book of Mormon." *Interpreter: A Journal of Mormon Scripture* 9 (2014): 29–85.

———. "Musings on the Making of Mormon's Book: 1 Nephi 6." *Mormon Interpreter*, Sep. 2013.

———. *Second Witness: Analytical and Textual Commentary on the Book of Mormon.* 6 vols. 2007.

Garner, Brian D. *Search These Things Diligently: A Personal Study Guide to the Book of Mormon.* 2003.

Garrett, H. Dean. "Inspired by a Better Cause." In Jackson, *Alma 30 to Moroni.*

———. "Light in Our Vessels: Faith, Hope, and Charity." In Nyman and Tate, *Fourth Nephi through Moroni.*

———. "Nephi's Farewell." In Nyman and Tate, *Second Nephi.*

———. "Peace Within." *Ensign,* Sep. 1988, 20–25.

Gaskill, Alonzo L. *The Lost Language of Symbolism.* 2003.

Gee, John. "Book of Mormon Word Usage: 'Seal You His.'" *Insights* 22, no. 1 (2002).

Gee, John, and Daniel C. Peterson. "Graft and Corruption: On Olives and Olive Culture in the Pre-Modern Mediterranean." In Ricks and Welch, *Allegory of the Olive Tree.*

Gentry, Leland. "God Will Fulfill His Covenants with the House of Israel." In Nyman and Tate, *Second Nephi.*

Goaslind, Jack H. "Happiness." *Ensign,* May 1986, 52–54.

Goff, Alan. "Historical Narrative, Literary Narrative—Expelling Poetics from the Republic of History." *Journal of Book of Mormon Studies* 5, no. 1 (Spring 1996): 50–102.

———. "The Stealing of the Daughters of the Lamanites." In Sorenson and Thorne, *Rediscovering the Book of Mormon.*

Gospel Principles [manual]. 2011.

Gospel Teaching and Learning: A Handbook for Teachers and Leaders in Seminaries and Institutes of Religion. 2012.

Grant, Heber J. *Gospel Standards: Selections from the Sermons and Writings of Heber J. Grant.* Edited by G. Homer Durham. 1941.

———. In Conference Report, Apr. 1909, 108–116.

———. In Conference Report, Oct. 1936, 2–16.

Grant, Heber J., J. Reuben Clark Jr., and David O. McKay. In Conference Report, Apr. 1942, 88–97.

Great American Documents for Latter-day Saint Families. Edited by Thomas R. Valletta et al. 2011.

Griggs, C. Wilfred. "The Tree of Life in Ancient Cultures." *Ensign,* June 1988, 26–31.

Groberg, John H. "The Beauty and Importance of the Sacrament." *Ensign,* May 1989, 38–40.

———. "The Power of Family Prayer." *Ensign,* May 1982, 50–52.

———. "Right for the Climate." *New Era,* March 1992, 4–7.

Guide to the Scriptures.

Hadfield, Gary M., and John W. Welch. "The 'Decapitation' of Shiz." *FARMS Update,* Nov. 1994.

Hafen, Bruce C. "The Atonement: All for All." *Ensign,* May 2004, 97–99.

———. *The Believing Heart: Nourishing the Seed of Faith.* 1986.

———. *The Broken Heart: Applying the Atonement to Life's Experiences.* 1989.

Hafen, Bruce C., and Marie K. Hafen. *The Belonging Heart: The Atonement and Relationships with God and Family.* 1994.

———. "Bridle All Your Passions." *Ensign,* Feb. 1994, 14–18.

Haight, David B. "Remembering the Savior's Atonement." *Ensign,* Apr. 1988, 6–13.

———. "The Sacrament—and the Sacrifice." *Ensign,* Nov. 1989, 59–61.

———. "Spiritual Crevasses." *Ensign,* Nov. 1986, 36–38.

Hales, Robert D. "The Aaronic Priesthood: Return with Honor." *Ensign,* May 1990, 39–41.

———. "Becoming a Disciple of Our Lord Jesus Christ." *Ensign,* May 2017, 46–48.

———. "Being a More Christian Christian." *Ensign,* Nov. 2012, 90–92.

———. "Christian Courage: The Price of Discipleship." *Ensign*, Nov. 2008, 72–75.

———. "The Covenant of Baptism: To Be in the Kingdom and of the Kingdom." *Ensign*, Nov. 2000, 6–9.

———. "Faith through Tribulation Brings Peace." *Ensign*, May 2003, 15–18.

———. "Finding Faith in the Lord Jesus Christ." *Ensign*, Nov. 2004, 70–73.

———. "Gifts of the Spirit." *Ensign,* Feb. 2002, 12–25.

———. "A Gospel Vision of Welfare: Faith in Action." In *Basic Principles of Welfare and Self-Reliance.* 2009.

———. "Gratitude for the Goodness of God." *Ensign*, May 1992, 63–65.

———. "Healing Soul and Body." *Ensign*, Nov. 1998, 14–17.

———. "If Thou Wilt Enter into Life, Keep the Commandments." *Ensign*, May 1996, 35–37.

———. "In Remembrance of Jesus." *Ensign*, Nov. 1997, 24–26.

———. "Out of the Darkness into His Marvelous Light." *Ensign*, May 2002, 69–72.

———. "Some Have Compassion, Making a Difference." *Ensign*, May 1987, 75–77.

———. "Waiting upon the Lord: Thy Will Be Done." *Ensign*, Nov. 2011, 71–74.

———. "Welfare Principles to Guide Our Lives: An Eternal Plan for the Welfare of Men's Souls." *Ensign*, May 1996, 28–30.

———. "With All the Feeling of a Tender Parent: A Message of Hope to Families." *Ensign*, May 2004, 88–91.

Hamblin, William J. "Armor in the Book of Mormon." In Ricks and Hamblin, *Warfare in the Book of Mormon.*

———. "The Importance of Warfare in Book of Mormon Studies." In Ricks and Hamblin, *Warfare in the Book of Mormon.*

———. "Nephi's Bows and Arrows." In Welch, *Reexploring the Book of Mormon.*

———. "Warfare in the Book of Mormon." In Sorenson and Thorne, *Rediscovering the Book of Mormon.*

Hamblin, William J., and A. Brent Merrill. "Swords in the Book of Mormon." In Ricks and Hamblin, *Warfare in the Book of Mormon.*

Handbook 2: Administering the Church. 2010.

Hanks, Marion D. "Conquer the Darkness." *Improvement Era*, May 1961, 321.

———. "Hard to Be Understood." *Improvement Era*, Aug. 1961, 586–87.

———. In Conference Report, Apr. 1957, 125–29.

———. "A Loving, Communicating God." *Ensign*, Nov. 1992, 63–65.

———. "Steps to Learning." Brigham Young University devotional, May 4, 1960.

Hansen, Gerald, Jr. "The Book of Alma as a Prototype." In Nyman and Tate, *Alma.*

———. "Gathering to the Temple: Teachings of the Second Day." In Nyman and Tate, *3 Nephi 9–30.*

———. "Preparing for the Judgment." In Nyman and Tate, *Fourth Nephi through Moroni.*

———. "The Terrifying Book of Helaman." In Nyman and Tate, *Helaman through 3 Nephi 8.*

Hardy, Grant R. "Mormon's Agenda." In Welch, *Reexploring the Book of Mormon.*

———. *Understanding the Book of Mormon.* 2010.

Hardy, Grant R., and Robert E. Parsons. "Plates and Records in the Book of Mormon." In Ludlow, *Encyclopedia of Mormonism.*

Harris, De Verle P. "Religion and Science of Mineral and Environmental Resources." In *Of Heaven and Earth: Reconciling Scientific Thought with LDS Theology.* Edited by David Clark. 1998.

Harrison, E. L. T. "A Real Representative of the Most High." *Millennial Star* 20, no. 41 (9 Oct. 1858): 641–44.

Hart, Richard K. "The Marriage Metaphor." *Ensign*, Jan. 1995, 22–27.

Hatch, Gary Layne. "Mormon and Moroni: Father and Son." In Nyman and Tate, *Fourth Nephi through Moroni.*

Hauglid, Brian M. "Foreordination in the Book of Mormon." In *The Book of Mormon: The Foundation of Our Faith.*

Hawkins, Lisa Bolin, and Gordon Thomasson. "'I Only Am Escaped Alone to Tell Thee': Survivor Witnesses in the Book of Mormon." Preliminary Report, Foundation for Ancient Research and Mormon Studies (FARMS), 1984.

Henrichsen, Kirk. "What Did the Golden Plates Look Like?" *New Era*, July 2007, 29–33.

Heroes from the Book of Mormon. 1995.

Hess, Wilford M. "Recent Notes about Olives in Antiquity." *Brigham Young University Studies* 39, no. 4 (Fall 2000): 115–26.

Higbee, Kenneth L. "Five Ways to Bear Testimony." *Ensign*, Feb. 1977, 89.

Hill, Keith K. "Sorrow and Joy." *Ensign*, Jan. 1988, 30–33.

Hilton, Lynn M., and Hope A. Hilton "In Search of Lehi's Trail—Part 1: The Preparation." *Ensign*, Sep. 1976, 32–54.

Hilton, Matthew, M. F. Flinders, and Neil J. Flinders. "The Impact of Shifting Cultural Assumptions on the Military Policies Directing Armed Conflict Reported in the Book of Alma." In Ricks and Hamblin, *Warfare in the Book of Mormon.*

Hinckley, Clark B. *Christopher Columbus: "A Man among the Gentiles."* 2014.

Hinckley, Gordon B. "Be Not Faithless." *Ensign*, May 1978, 58–61.

———. "Bring in Solid Converts; Help Them Remain." *Church News*, 15 March 1997.

———. "Building Your Tabernacle." *Ensign*, Nov. 1992, 50–52.

———. "Converts and Young Men." *Ensign*, May 1997, 47–50.

———. *Discourses of Gordon B. Hinckley.* 2 vols. 2005.

———. "'Except the Lord Build the House . . .'" *Ensign*, June 1971, 71–72.

———. *Faith, the Essence of True Religion.* 1989.

———. "Find the Lambs, Feed the Sheep." *Ensign*, May 1999, 108–9.

———. "If Ye Are Prepared Ye Shall Not Fear." *Ensign*, Nov. 2005, 60–62.

———. In Conference Report, Apr. 1968, 21–24.

———. In Conference Report, Oct. 1959, 118–20.

———. "'In . . . Counsellors There Is Safety.'" *Ensign*, Nov. 1990, 50–52.

———. "Latter-day Counsel: Excerpts from Addresses of Gordon B. Hinckley." *Ensign*, October 2000, 73.

———. "Loyalty." *Ensign*, May 2003, 58–60.

———. "Moroni." In *Heroes from the Book of Mormon.*

———. "A Prophet's Counsel and Prayer for Youth." *Ensign*, Jan. 2001, 2–11.

———. "Rejoice in This Great Era of Temple Building." *Ensign*, Nov. 1985, 53–60.

———. "Reverence and Morality." *Ensign,* May 1987, 45–48.

———. "Save the Children." *Ensign*, Nov. 1994, 52–54.

———. "Slow to Anger." *Ensign*, Nov. 2007, 62–66.

———. "Stand True and Faithful." *Ensign*, May 1996, 92–96.

———. "The Symbol of Our Faith." *Ensign*, Apr. 2005, 3–6.

———. *Teachings of Gordon B. Hinckley.* 1997.

———. "The Times in Which We Live." *Ensign,* Nov. 2001, 72–74.

————. "Tithing: An Opportunity to Prove Our Faithfulness." *Ensign*, May 1982, 40–42.

————. "To Men of the Priesthood." *Ensign*, Nov. 2002, 56–59.

————. "War and Peace." *Ensign*, May 2003, 78–81.

————. "We Look to Christ." *Ensign*, May 2002, 90–91.

————. "The Wondrous and True Story of Christmas." *Ensign*, Dec. 2000, 2–5.

————. "Your Greatest Challenge, Mother." *Ensign*, Nov. 2000, 97–98.

"History, 1838–1856, volume C-1 [2 November 1838–31 July 1842] [addenda]," p. 9 [addenda]. The Joseph Smith Papers. Accessed December 5, 2018.

Hlavaty, Lauri. "The Religion of Moses and the Book of Mormon." In Nyman and Tate, *Jacob through Words of Mormon*.

Holbrook, Brett L. "The Sword of Laban as a Symbol of Divine Authority and Kingship." *Journal of Book of Mormon Studies* 2, no. 1 (1993): 39–72.

Holland, Jeffrey R. "The Atonement of Jesus Christ." *Ensign*, Mar. 2008, 32–38.

————. "The Bitter Cup and the Bloody Baptism." Brigham Young University devotional, 13 Jan. 1987.

————. "Broken Things to Mend." *Ensign*, May 2006, 70–73.

————. *Broken Things to Mend*. 2008.

————. "'Cast Not Away Therefore Your Confidence.'" Brigham Young University devotional, Mar. 2, 1999.

————. *Christ and the New Covenant: The Messianic Message of the Book of Mormon*. 1997.

————. "Come unto Me." *Ensign*, April 1998, 16–23.

————. "The Cost—and Blessings—of Discipleship." *Ensign*, May 2014, 6–9.

————. "Daddy, Donna, and Nephi." *Ensign*, Sep. 1976, 6–11.

————. "For a Wise Purpose." *Ensign*, Jan. 1996, 12–14.

————. *For Times of Trouble: Spiritual Solace from the Psalms*. 2012.

————. "The Grandeur of God." *Ensign*, Nov. 2003, 70–73.

————. "A Handful of Meal and a Little Oil." *Ensign*, May 1996, 29–31.

————. "He Hath Filled the Hungry with Good Things." *Ensign*, Nov. 1997, 64–66.

————. *However Long and Hard the Road*. 1985.

————. "Jacob the Unshakable." In *Heroes from the Book of Mormon*.

————. "The Laborers in the Vineyard." *Ensign*, May 2012, 31–33.

————. "Lord, I Believe." *Ensign*, May 2013, 93–95.

————. "The Ministry of Angels." *Ensign*, Nov. 2008, 29–31.

————. "Mormon: The Man and the Book, Part 1." *Ensign*, Mar. 1978, 15–18.

————. "My Words . . . Never Cease." *Ensign*, May 2008, 90–94.

————. "The Only True God and Jesus Christ Whom He Hath Sent." *Ensign*, Oct. 2007, 40–42.

————. "The Other Prodigal." *Ensign*, May 2002, 62–64.

————. "The Peaceable Things of the Kingdom." *Ensign*, Nov. 1996, 82–84.

————. "Personal Purity." *Ensign*, Nov. 1998, 76–78.

————. "A Prayer for the Children." *Ensign*, May 2003, 85–87.

————. "President Gordon B. Hinckley: Stalwart and Brave He Stands." *Ensign*, June 1995, 2–13.

————. "Safety for the Soul." *Ensign*, Nov. 2009, 88–90.

————. "Sanctify Yourselves." *Ensign*, Nov. 2000, 38–40.

————. "A Standard unto My People." Church Educational System Religious Educators Symposium, Aug. 9, 1994.

———. "Teaching, Preaching, Healing." *Ensign*, Jan. 2003, 33–42.

———. "That Our Children May Know." Brigham Young University devotional, Aug. 25, 1981.

———. "The Tongue of Angels." *Ensign*, May 2007, 16–18.

———. *Trusting Jesus.* 2003.

———. "Whom Say Ye That I Am?" *Ensign*, Sep. 1974, 66–69.

Holland, Jeffrey R., and Patricia T. Holland. *On Earth as It Is in Heaven.* 1989.

Holzapfel, Richard Neitzel. "Mormon: the Man and the Message." In Nyman and Tate, *Fourth Nephi through Moroni.*

———. "One by One: The Fifth Gospel's Model of Service." In Nyman and Tate, *3 Nephi 9–30.*

Horton, George. "Understanding Textual Changes in the Book of Mormon." *Ensign,* Dec. 1983, 26–28.

Hoskisson, Paul Y. "The Allegory of the Olive Tree in Jacob." In Ricks and Welch, *Allegory of the Olive Tree.*

———. "The 'Familiar Spirit' in 2 Nephi 26:16." *Insights* 28, no. 6 (2008).

Hoskisson, Paul Y., John W. Welch, Robert F. Smith, Bruce W. Warren, Roger R. Keller, David Fox, and Deloy Pack. "Words and Phrases." In Welch, *Reexploring the Book of Mormon.*

Howard, F. Burton. "Ammon: Reflections on Faith and Testimony." In *Heroes from the Book of Mormon.*

———. *Marion G. Romney: His Life and Faith.* 1988.

———. "Repentance." *Ensign,* May 1991, 12–14.

Huchel, Federick M. "The Deseret Alphabet as an Aid in Pronouncing Book of Mormon Names." *Journal of Book of Mormon Studies* 9, no. 1 (2000): 58–80.

Hunt, Wallace E., Jr. "Notes and Communications: the Marketplace." *Journal of Book of Mormon Studies* 4, no. 2 (Fall 1995): 138–41.

Hunter, Howard W. In Conference Report, Apr. 1964, 33–36.

———. "No Less Serviceable." *Ensign,* April 1992, 64–67.

———. *The Teachings of Howard W. Hunter.* Edited by Clyde J. Williams. 1997.

Hunter, Milton R. In Conference Report, Apr. 1952, 123–25.

Huntsman, Eric D. "The Six Antitheses: Attaining the Purpose of the Law through the Teachings of Jesus." In Strathearn et al., *The Sermon on the Mount in Latter-day Scripture.*

Hurd, Jerrie W. *Our Sisters in the Latter-day Scriptures.* 1987.

Interpreter's Bible. *12 vols. 1951–57.*

Isaacson, Thorpe B. In Conference Report. Oct. 1948, 19–22.

Ivins, Anthony W. In Conference Report, Apr. 1929, 8–16.

Jack, Elaine L. "Ponder the Path of Thy Feet." *Ensign,* Nov. 1993, 98–101.

Jackson, Kent P. "Comfort My People (Isaiah 34–50)." In Jackson, *1 Kings to Malachi.*

———. "Nourished by the Good Word of God." In Jackson, *1 Nephi to Alma 29.*

———. "Teaching from the Words of the Prophets (3 Nephi 23–26)." In Jackson, *Alma 30 to Moroni.*

Jackson, Kent P., and Darrell L. Matthews. "The Lamanite Converts Firm in the Faith of Christ." In Jackson, *1 Nephi to Alma 29.*

Jackson, Kent P., and Morgan W. Tanner. "Zeniff and Noah." In Jackson, *1 Nephi to Alma 29.*

Jackson, Kent P., ed. *Alma 30 to Moroni.* Vol. 8 of Studies in Scripture series. 1988.

———, ed. *1 Kings to Malachi.* Vol. 4 of Studies in Scripture series. 1993.

———, ed. *1 Nephi to Alma 29.* Vol. 7 of Studies in Scripture series. 1987.

Jenkins, Ryan. "'Peaceable Followers of Christ' in Days of War and Contention." *Religious Educator* 10, no. 3 (2009): 87–102.

———. "Quiet Slumber: Revelation through Dreams." *Religious Educator* 12, no. 1 (2011): 73–89.

Jensen, Jay E. "Bearing Testimony." *Ensign*, Oct. 2005, 22–25.

———. "Keep an Eternal Perspective." *Ensign*, May 2000, 27–28.

Jensen, Marlin K. "Remember and Perish Not." *Ensign*, May 2007, 36–38.

———. "To Walk Humbly with Thy God." *Ensign*, May 2001, 9–11.

Jensen, Virginia U. "Lead, Kindly Light." *Ensign*, Nov. 2000, 62–63.

Johnson, D. Lynn. "The Missing Scripture." *Journal of Book of Mormon Studies* (Fall 1994): 84–93.

Johnson, Edward. *Wonder-Working Providence of Sion's Saviour in New England, 1628–1651*. 1974.

Jones, Spencer V. "Overcoming the Stench of Sin." *Ensign*, May 2003, 88–89.

Journal of Discourses. 26 vols. 1854–86.

Judd, Daniel K. *Fortunate Fall: Understanding the Blessings and Burdens of Adversity*. 2011.

———. *Hard Questions, Prophetic Answers*. 2004.

———. "The Righteousness of the Redeemer." In *The Book of Mormon: The Foundation of Our Faith*.

———. "The Spirit of Christ: A Light amidst the Darkness." In Nyman and Tate, *Fourth Nephi through Moroni*.

Judd, Frank F., Jr. "Jaredite Zion Societies: Hope for a Better World." In Nyman and Tate, *Fourth Nephi through Moroni*.

———. "The Parables of Matthew 13: Revealing and Concealing the Kingdom of God." In *Life and Teachings of Jesus Christ*, vol. 2. Edited by Thomas A. Wayment and Richard Neitzel Holzapfel. 2006.

Judd, Frank F., Jr., and Terry L. Szink. "John the Beloved in Latter-day Scripture (D&C 7)." In *The Doctrine and Covenants: Revelations in Context*. Edited by Alonzo L. Gaskill, Spencer J. Fluhman, and Andrew H. Hedges. Sperry Symposium series. 2008.

Kapp, Ardeth, G. *Rejoice! His Promises Are Sure*. 1997.

Keil, C. F., and Franz Delitzsch. *Commentary on the Old Testament*. 10 vols. 1989.

Keller, Roger R. "Mormon and Moroni as Authors and Abridgers." In Welch, *Reexploring the Book of Mormon*.

Kerr, Todd R. "Ancient Aspects of Nephite Kingship in the Book of Mormon." *Journal of Book of Mormon Studies* 1, no. 2 (Fall 1992): 85–118.

Kimball, Spencer W. "Absolute Truth." *Ensign*, Sep. 1978, 3–8.

———. "Becoming the Pure in Heart." *Ensign*, May 1978, 79–81.

———. "Boys Need Heroes Close By." *Ensign*, May 1976, 45–47.

———. "Circles of Exaltation." Address to Church Educational System religious educators, June 28, 1968.

———. "The False Gods We Worship." *Ensign*, June 1976, 3–6.

———. "The Fruit of Our Welfare Services Labors." *Ensign*, Nov. 1978, 74–77.

———. "The Gospel of Repentance." *Ensign*, Oct. 1982, 2–5.

———. "Guidelines to Carry Forth the Work of God in Cleanliness." *Ensign*, May 1974, 4–8.

———. "How Rare a Possession—the Scriptures." *Ensign*, Sep. 1976, 2–5.

———. "Humility." Brigham Young University devotional, Jan. 16, 1963.

———. In Conference Report, April 1949, 103–13.

———. In Conference Report, April 1954, 103–8.

———. In Conference Report, Oct. 1949, 123–37.

———. In Conference Report, Oct. 1961, 29–34.

———. "The Lamanites Are Progressing." *Improvement Era*, June 1953, 433–35.

———. "Listen to the Prophets." *Ensign*, May 1978, 76–78.

———. "The Lord Expects His Saints to Follow the Commandments." *Ensign*, May 1977, 4–7.

———. *The Miracle of Forgiveness*. 1969.

———. "Ocean Currents and Family Influences." *Ensign*, Nov. 1974, 110–13.

———. "Our Paths Have Met Again." *Ensign*, Dec. 1975, 2–7.

———. "Prayer." Brigham Young University devotional, Oct. 11, 1961.

———. *Spencer W. Kimball* [manual]. Teachings of Presidents of the Church series. 2006.

———. *The Teachings of Spencer W. Kimball*. 1982.

———. "Voices of the Past, of the Present, and of the Future." *Ensign*, June 1971, 16–19.

———. "'When the World Will Be Converted.'" *Ensign*, Oct. 1974, 2–14.

Kramer, Neal W. "Prophetic Principles for Building Zion." In *Living the Book of Mormon*.

Lambert, Neal E. "The Symbolic Unity of Christ's Ministry in 3 Nephi." In Nyman and Tate, *Third Nephi 9–30*.

Lane, Jennifer C. "Faith unto Repentance: The Fulness of the Simple Way" In *The Fulness of the Gospel*.

———. "The Lord Will Redeem His People: Adoptive Covenant and Redemption in the Old Testament and Book of Mormon." *Journal of Book of Mormon Studies* 2, no. 2 (1993): 39–62.

Larsen, David J. "Pillar of Fire." Book of Mormon Central.

Larsen, Dean L. "Likening the Scriptures unto Us." In Nyman and Tate, *Alma*.

———. "A Royal Generation." *Ensign*, May 1983, 33–35.

———. "Zeezrom." In Heroes from the Book of Mormon.

Larsen, Sharon G. "Standing in Holy Places." *Ensign*, May 2002, 91–93.

Larsen, Val. "In His Footsteps: Ammon1 and Ammon2." *Interpreter: A Journal of Mormon Scripture* 3 (2013).

The Latter-day Saints Psalmody: A Collection of Original and Selected Tunes. 1912.

LeBaron, E. Dale. "Ether and Mormon: Parallel Prophets of Warning and Witness." In Nyman and Tate, *Fourth Nephi through Moroni*.

Lectures on Faith. 1985.

Lee, Harold B. "Find the Answers in the Scriptures." *Ensign*, Dec. 1972, 2–3.

———. "How to Receive a Blessing from God." *Improvement Era*, Oct. 1966, 862–63, 896–99.

———. In Conference Report, Apr. 1943, 124–30.

———. In Conference Report, Apr. 1956, 107–11.

———. In Conference Report, Oct. 1972, 123–31.

———. *Stand Ye in Holy Places*. 1974.

———. "Strengthen the Stakes of Zion." *Ensign*, July 1973, 2–6.

———. *The Teachings of Harold B. Lee*. Edited by Clyde J. Williams. 1996.

———. "The Way to Eternal Life." *Ensign*, Nov. 1971, 9–17.

Living the Book of Mormon: Abiding by Its Precepts. Edited by Gaye Strathearn and Charles Swift. Sperry Symposium series. 2007.

Lloyd, R. Scott. "Revelation Rewarded Those Who Waited." *Church News*, Dec. 18, 1999.

Ludlow, Daniel H. *A Companion to Your Study of the Book of Mormon*. 1976.

———. *A Companion to Your Study of the Doctrine and Covenants*. 1978.

———. *A Companion to Your Study of the Old Testament*. 1981.

———. "The Message to the Jews with Special Emphasis on 2 Nephi 25." In Nyman and Tate, *Second Nephi*.

———. *Selected Writings of Daniel H. Ludlow*. Gospel Scholars Series. 2000.

Ludlow, Daniel H., et al., eds. *Encyclopedia of Mormonism*. 4 vols. 1992.

Ludlow, Victor L. "Covenant Teachings of the Scriptures." *BYU Speeches*, Oct 13, 1988.

———. "The Father's Covenant People Sermon: 3 Nephi 20:10–23:5." In Skinner and Strathearn, *Third Nephi*.

———. *Isaiah: Prophet, Seer, and Poet*. 1982.

———. *Principles and Practices of the Restored Gospel*. 1992.

———. "Scribes and Scriptures: Enos, Jarom, Omni, and the Words of Mormon." In Jackson, *1 Nephi to Alma 29*.

———. "Secret Covenant Teachings of Men and the Devil." In Nyman and Tate, *Helaman through 3 Nephi 8*.

———. *Unlocking Isaiah in the Book of Mormon*. 2003.

———. *Unlocking the Old Testament*. 1981.

Lund, Gerald N. "An Anti-Christ in the Book of Mormon—the Face May Be Strange, but the Voice Is Familiar: Korihor and the Word of God." In Nyman and Tate, *Alma*.

———. "Countering Korihor's Philosophy." *Ensign*, July 1992, 16–21.

———. "The Fall of Man and His Redemption." In Nyman and Tate, *Second Nephi*.

———. *Jesus Christ, Key to the Plan of Salvation*. 2009.

———. "Opening Our Hearts." *Ensign*, May 2008, 32–34.

———. "The Opportunity to Serve." *Ensign*, May 2002, 85.

———. "A Prophet for the Fulness of Times." *Ensign*, Jan. 1997, 52–54.

———. *Selected Writings of Gerald N. Lund*. Gospel Scholars series. 1999.

———. "Understanding Scriptural Symbols." *Ensign*, Oct. 1986, 23–27.

———. "The Voice of the Lord." Brigham Young University devotional, Dec. 2, 1997.

Lundquist, John M., and John W. Welch. "Ammon and Cutting Off the Arms of Enemies." In Welch, *Reexploring the Book of Mormon*.

———. "Kingship and Temple in 2 Nephi 5–10." In Welch, *Reexploring the Book of Mormon*.

Lybbert, Merlin R. "The Status of Little Children." *Ensign*, May 1994, 31–33.

Mackay, Thomas W. "Mormon and the Destruction of Nephite Civilization (Mormon 3–9)." In Jackson, *Alma 30 to Moroni*.

———. "Mormon's Philosophy of History: Helaman 12 in the Perspective of Mormon's Editing Procedure." In Nyman and Tate, *Helaman through 3 Nephi 8*.

Madsen, Truman G. "The Olive Press." *Ensign*, Dec. 1982, 57–62.

———. "The Olive Press: A Symbol of Christ." In Ricks and Welch, *Allegory of the Olive Tree*.

———. *The Radiant Light*. 1994.

Marble, Brian. "From Mission to Military." *New Era*, June 2006, 34–36.

Marlowe, Eric. "The Golden Rule: A Moral Searchlight." In Strathearn et al., *The Sermon on the Mount in Latter-day Scripture*.

Marsh, David Brent. "Peace through Christ: Divine Perspective on War." In *The Fulness of the Gospel*.

Matsumori, Vicki F. "A Lesson from the Book of Mormon." *Ensign*, May 2007, 76–77.

Matthews, Robert J. "Abinadi: The Prophet and Martyr." *Ensign*, Apr. 1992, 25–31.

———. "Abinadi: The Prophet and Martyr." In Nyman and Tate, *Mosiah*.

———. "The Atonement of Jesus Christ: 2 Nephi 9." In Nyman and Tate, *Second Nephi*.

———. *Behold the Messiah*. 1984.

———. *A Bible! A Bible!: How Latter-day Revelation Helps Us Understand the Scriptures and the Savior*. 1990.

———. *A Burning Light: The Life and Ministry of John the Baptist*. 1972.

———. "Establishing the Truth of the Bible." In Nyman and Tate, *First Nephi*.

———. "Jacob: Prophet, Theologian, Historian." In Nyman and Tate, *Jacob through Words of Mormon*.

———. "Jesus the Savior in 3 Nephi." In Nyman and Tate, *3 Nephi 9–30*.

———. "The Mission of Jesus Christ—Ether 3 and 4:2." In Nyman and Tate, *Fourth Nephi through Moroni*.

———. "The New Publications of the Standard Works—1979, 1981." *Brigham Young University Studies* 22, no. 4 (Fall 1982): 387–423.

———. "Patterns of Apostasy in the Book of Helaman." In Nyman and Tate, *Helaman through 3 Nephi 8*.

———. "The Power and the Purpose of the Written Record." In *Nurturing Faith*.

———. "The Probationary Nature of Mortality." In Nyman and Tate, *Alma*.

———. *Selected Writings of Robert J. Matthews*. Gospel Scholars series. 1999.

———. "Two Ways in the World: The Warfare between God and Satan." In Jackson, *1 Nephi to Alma 29*.

Maxwell, Neal A. "According to the Desire of [Our] Hearts." *Ensign*, Nov. 1996, 21–23.

———. *All These Things Shall Give Thee Experience*. 1979.

———. "Answer Me." *Ensign*, Nov. 1988, 31–33.

———. "Behold, the Enemy Is Combined." *Ensign*, May 1993, 76–78.

———. "Be of Good Cheer." *Ensign*, May 1991, 64–66.

———. "The Book of Mormon: A Great Answer to 'The Great Question.'" In Nyman and Tate, *First Nephi*.

———. "Brightness of Hope." *Ensign*. Nov. 1994, 34–36.

———. "Brim with Joy." Brigham Young University devotional, Jan. 23, 1996.

———. "A Brother Offended." *Ensign*, May 1982, 37–39.

———. "But a Few Days." Address to Church Educational System religious educators, Sep. 10, 1982.

———. *But for a Small Moment*. 1986.

———. "By the Gift and Power of God." *Ensign,* Jan. 1997, 36–41.

———. "The Children of Christ." In Nyman and Tate, *Mosiah*.

———. "Content with the Things Allotted unto Us." *Ensign,* May 2000, 72–74.

———. "Continue to Minister." *Ensign,* June 1987, 10–11.

———. "Deny Yourselves of All Ungodliness." *Ensign*, May 1995, 66–69.

———. *Deposition of a Disciple*. 1976.

———. "Discipleship and Scholarship." *BYU Studies* 32, no. 3 (Summer 1992): 5–9.

———. "Endure It Well." *Ensign*, May 1990, 33–36.

———. "Enduring Well." *Ensign*, April 1997, 7–10.

———. *Even as I Am*. 1982.

———. "For I Will Lead You Along." *Ensign*, May 1988, 7–9.

———. *For the Power Is in Them . . .* : Mormon Musings. 1970.

———. "God Will Yet Reveal." *Ensign*, Nov. 1986, 52–59.

———. "The Great Plan of the Eternal God." *Ensign*, May 1984, 21–23.

———. "How Choice a Seer!" *Ensign*, Nov. 2003, 99–102.

———. *If Thou Endure It Well*. 1996.

———. *"King Benjamin." In* Heroes from the Book of Mormon.

———. "King Benjamin's Manual of Discipleship." *Ensign*, Jan. 1992, 8–13.

———. "Lessons from Laman and Lemuel." *Ensign*, Nov. 1999, 6–8.

———. "Lest Ye Be Wearied and Faint in Your Minds." *Ensign*, May 1991, 88–90.

———. *Lord, Increase Our Faith*. 1994.

———. "Make Calling Focus of Your Mission." *Church News*, Sep. 17, 1994, 4.

———. "The Man of Christ." *Ensign*, May 1975, 101–2.

———. *Meek and Lowly*. 1987.

———. *Men and Women of Christ*. 1991.

———. *The Neal A. Maxwell Quote Book*. Edited by Cory H. Maxwell. 1997.

———. "The Net Gathers of Every Kind." *Ensign*, Nov. 1980, 66–69.

———. "Notwithstanding My Weakness." *Ensign*, Nov. 1976, 12–14.

———. *Notwithstanding My Weakness*. 1981.

———. *One More Strain of Praise*. 1999.

———. *Plain and Precious Things*. 1983.

———. *The Promise of Discipleship*. 2001.

———. "Put Your Shoulder to the Wheel." *Ensign*, May 1998, 37–39.

———. "Repent of [Our] Selfishness." *Ensign*, May 1999, 23–25.

———. "The Richness of the Restoration." *Ensign,* March 1998, 8–13.

———. "The Seventh Commandment: A Shield." *Ensign*, Nov. 2001, 78–80.

———. *That My Family Should Partake*. 1974.

———. *Things as They Really Are*. 1978.

———. "Three Jaredites: Contrasting Contemporaries." *Ensign*, Aug. 1978, 6–11.

———. *A Time to Choose*. 1972.

———. "True Believers." *New Era*, April 1994, 20–24.

———. *We Talk of Christ, We Rejoice in Christ*. 1984.

———. *We Will Prove Them Herewith*. 1982.

———. "What Should We Pray For?" In *Prayer*.

———. *Wherefore, Ye Must Press Forward*. 1977.

———. "Willing to Submit." *Ensign*, May 1985, 70–72.

———. *A Wonderful Flood of Light*. 1990.

May, Cheryll Lynn. "Beyond Voting: Some Duties of the LDS Citizen." *Ensign*, June 1976, 46–48.

McClendon, Richard. "Captain Moroni's Wartime Strategies: An Application for the Spiritual Battles of Our Day." *Religious Educator* 3, no. 3 (2002): 99–114.

McConkie, Bruce R. "Behold the Condescension of God." *New Era*, Dec. 1984, 34–39.

———. "Be Valiant in the Fight of Faith." *Ensign*, Nov. 1974, 33–35.

———. "Christ and the Creation." *Ensign*, June 1982, 9–15.

———. "The Dead Who Die in the Lord." *Ensign*, Nov. 1976, 106–8.

———. *Doctrinal New Testament Commentary*. 3 vols. 1971–73.

———. "The Doctrinal Restoration." In *The Joseph Smith Translation: The Restoration of Plain and Precious Things*. Edited by Monte S. Nyman and Robert L. Millet. 1985.

———. "The Doctrine of the Priesthood." *Ensign*, May 1982, 32–34.

———. *Doctrines of the Restoration: Sermons and Writings of Bruce R. McConkie*. Edited and arranged by Mark L. McConkie. 1989.

———. "Eve and the Fall." In *Woman*. 1979.

———. *Millennial Messiah: The Second Coming of the Son of Man*. 1982.

———. *Mormon Doctrine*. 2d ed. 1978.

———. *Mortal Messiah: From Bethlehem to Calvary.* 4 vols. 1980.

———. *A New Witness for the Articles of Faith.* 1985.

———. *The Promised Messiah: The First Coming of Christ.* 1978.

———. "The Purifying Power of Gethsemane." *Ensign,* May 1985, 9–11.

———. "The Salvation of Little Children." *Ensign,* Apr. 1977, 3–7.

———. "Stand Independent above All Other Creatures." *Ensign,* May 1979, 92–94.

———. "Ten Keys to Understanding Isaiah." *Ensign,* Oct. 1973, 80–83.

———. "The Three Pillars of Eternity." Brigham Young University devotional, Feb. 17, 1981.

———. "Who Shall Declare His Generation?" *Brigham Young University Studies* 16, no. 4 (Fall 1976): 553–60.

McConkie, Joseph Fielding. *Answers: Straightforward Answers to Tough Gospel Questions.* 1998.

———. "Chosen Vessels and the Order of the Priesthood." In *The Lectures on Faith in Historical Perspective.* Edited by Larry E. Dahl and Charles D. Tate Jr. 1990.

———. "The Doctrine of a Covenant People." In Nyman and Tate, *3 Nephi 9–30.*

———. "The Final Gathering to Christ." In Jackson, *Alma 30 to Moroni.*

———. *Gospel Symbolism.* 1985.

———. *Here We Stand.* 1995.

———. "The Promise of Eternal Life." In Jackson, *1 Nephi to Alma 29.*

———. "The Testimony of Christ through the Ages." In Nyman and Tate, *Jacob through Words of Mormon.*

McConkie, Joseph Fielding, and Craig J. Ostler. *Revelations of the Restoration.* 2000.

McConkie, Joseph Fielding, and Donald W. Parry. *A Guide to Scriptural Symbols.* 1990.

McConkie, Joseph Fielding, and Robert L. Millet. *Sustaining and Defending the Faith.* 1985.

———. Vols. 1–3 of *Doctrinal Commentary on the Book of Mormon.* 1987–91.

McConkie, Joseph Fielding, Robert L. Millet, and Brent L. Top. Vol. 4 of *Doctrinal Commentary on the Book of Mormon.* 1992.

McConkie, Oscar W. *Angels.* 1975.

McKay, David O. *Cherished Experiences from the Writings of President David O. McKay.* Compiled by Clare Middlemiss. 1955.

———. "Consciousness of God: Supreme Goal of Life." *Improvement Era,* June 1967, 80–82.

———. *Gospel Ideals.* Compiled by the editors of the *Improvement Era.* 1953.

———. In Conference Report, Apr. 1956, 6–8.

———. *Pathway to Happiness.* Compiled by Llewelyn R. McKay. 1957.

McNeely, Brent E. "The Book of Mormon and the Heavenly Book Motif." In Welch, *Reexploring the Book of Mormon.*

Merrill, A. Brent. "Nephite Captains and Armies." In Ricks and Hamblin, *Warfare in the Book of Mormon.*

Merrill, Byron R. "Government by the Voice of the People." In Nyman and Tate, *Mosiah.*

———. "Moroni: The Man and the Message." FARMS Book of Mormon Lecture Series (Transcript). 1996.

———. "They Wrote to Us as If We Were Present." *Ensign,* Jan. 2000, 12–17.

Meservy, Keith H. "God Is with Us." In Jackson, *1 Kings to Malachi.*

———. "Jerusalem at the Time of Lehi and Jeremiah." *Ensign,* Jan. 1988, 23–25.

Mickelsen, Lynn A. "The Atonement, Repentance, and Dirty Linen." *Ensign,* Nov. 2003, 10–13.

Middleton, Michael W. "Gatherings in the Last Days." In Nyman and Tate, *Fourth Nephi through Moroni.*

Midgley, Louis C. "'O Man, Remember, and Perish Not' (Mosiah 4:30)." In Welch, *Reexploring the Book of Mormon*.

———. "Prophetic Messages or Dogmatic Theology? Commenting on the Book of Mormon: A Review Essay." *FARMS Review* 1, no. 1 (1989).

———. "The Ways of Remembrance." In Sorenson and Thorne, *Rediscovering the Book of Mormon*.

Millet, Robert L. "Abinadi's Messianic Sermon." In *Book of Mormon*. Church Educational System Religious Educators Symposium. 1986.

———. "Alive in Christ: The Miracle of Spiritual Rebirth. *1997*.

———. "Alive in Christ: The Salvation of Little Children." In Nyman and Tate, *Fourth Nephi through Moroni*.

———. "The Brass Plates: An Inspired and Expanded Version of the Old Testament." In *Old Testament and the Latter-day Saints*.

———. "The Gathering of Israel in the Book of Mormon: A Consistent Pattern." In Sorenson and Thorne, *Rediscovering the Book of Mormon*.

———. *Grace Works.* 2003.

———. "The Holy Order of God." In Nyman and Tate, *Alma*.

———. *Life in Christ.* 1990.

———. "The Ministry of the Father and the Son." In Cheesman, *Book of Mormon*.

———. "Nephi on the Destiny of Israel." In Jackson, *1 Nephi to Alma 29*.

———. "The Only Sure Foundation: Building on the Rock of Our Redeemer." In Nyman and Tate, *Helaman through 3 Nephi 8*.

———. *The Power of the Word: Saving Doctrines from the Book of Mormon.* 1994.

———. "Sherem the Anti-Christ." In Nyman and Tate, *Jacob through Words of Mormon*.

———. *Steadfast and Immovable: Striving for Spiritual Maturity.* 1992.

———. *Watch and Be Ready: Preparing for the Second Coming of the Lord.* 1994.

———. *When a Child Wanders.* 1996.

Millet, Robert L., and Joseph Fielding McConkie. *The Life Beyond.* 1986.

Millet, Robert L., Camille Fronk Olson, Andrew C. Skinner, and Brent L. Top. *LDS Beliefs: A Doctrinal Reference.* 2011.

Miner, Alan C. *Step by Step through the Book of Mormon: A Cultural Commentary through the Wilderness to the Promised Land.* 7 vols. 1996.

Monson, Thomas S. "Be Thou an Example." *Ensign,* May 2005, 112–15.

———. "Choose You This Day." *Ensign,* Nov. 2004, 67–70.

———. "Come All Ye Sons of God." *Ensign,* May 2013, 66–69.

———. "Courage Counts." *Ensign,* Nov. 1986, 40–42.

———. "Dare to Stand Alone." *Ensign,* Nov. 2011, 60–67.

———. "Examples of Righteousness." *Ensign,* May 2008, 65–68.

———. "The Fatherless and the Widows—Beloved of God." *Ensign,* Nov. 1994, 69–71.

———. "Hastening the Work." *Ensign,* June 2014, 4–5.

———. *Pathways to Perfection.* 1973.

———. "Pathways to Perfection." *Ensign,* May 2002, 99–101.

———. "True Shepherds." *Ensign,* Nov. 2013, 61–62.

———. "We Never Walk Alone." *Ensign,* Nov. 2013, 121–24.

———. "Who Honors God, God Honors." *Ensign,* Nov. 1995, 48–50.

———. "Willing and Worthy to Serve." *Ensign*, May 2012, 66–69.

———. "Your Eternal Voyage." *Ensign*, May 2000, 46–48.

———. "Your Patriarchal Blessing: A Liahona of Light." *Ensign*, Nov. 1986, 65–67.

Moore, Heather B. "Abish: A Common Servant, a True Testimony." *Ensign*, July 2012, 52–55.

Morgan, Ted. *Wilderness at Dawn: The Settling of the North American Continent.* 1993.

Morison, Samuel Eliot. *Admiral of the Ocean Sea: A Life of Christopher Columbus.* 1942.

———. *The European Discovery of America: The Northern Voyages.* 1971.

Morrise, Mark J. "Simile Curses in the Ancient Near East, Old Testament, and Book of Mormon." *Journal of Book of Mormon Studies* 2, no. 1 (1993): 124–38.

Morrison, Alexander B. "The Dawning of a New Day in Africa." *Ensign*, Nov. 1987, 25–26.

———. *Feed My Sheep: Leadership Ideas for Latter-day Shepherds.* 1992.

———. "'For This Cause Came I into the World.'" *Ensign,* Nov. 1999, 25–27.

Moyle, Henry D. In Conference Report, Apr. 1949, 60–65.

Nelson, Russell M. "Ask, Seek, Knock." *Ensign*, Nov. 2009, 81–84.

———. "The Atonement." *Ensign*, Nov. 1996, 34–37.

———. "Blessed Are the Peacemakers." *Ensign*, Nov. 2002, 39–42.

———. "Call to the Holy Apostleship." *Ensign*, May 1984, 52–53.

———. "The Canker of Contention." *Ensign*, May 1989, 68–71.

———. "Children of the Covenant." *Ensign*, May 1995, 32–35.

———. "Choices." *Ensign*, Nov. 1990, 73–75.

———. "The Correct Name of the Church." *Ensign,* Nov. 2018, 87–89.

———. "Covenants." *Ensign*, Nov. 2011, 86–89.

———. "The Creation." *Ensign*, May 2000, 84–86.

———. "Divine Love." *Ensign*, Feb. 2003, 20–25.

———. "The Gathering of Scattered Israel." *Ensign,* Nov. 2006, 79–82.

———. "Getting Where You Want to Go." *New Era*, May 2003, 4–7.

———. "How Firm Our Foundation." *Ensign,* May 2002, 75–78.

———. "Joy Cometh in the Morning." *Ensign*, Nov. 1986, 67–70.

———. "Listen to Learn." *Ensign*, May 1991, 22–25.

———. "A More Excellent Hope." *Ensign*, Feb. 1997, 60–64.

———. "Nephi, Son of Lehi." In *Heroes from the Book of Mormon.*

———. "Now Is the Time to Prepare." *Ensign*, May 2005, 16–18.

———. *Perfection Pending and Other Favorite Discourses.* 1998.

———. "Perfection Pending." *Ensign,* Nov. 1995, 86–88.

———. "Repentance and Conversion." *Ensign*, May 2007, 102–5.

———. "Reverence for Life." *Ensign,* May 1985, 11–14.

———. "Senior Missionaries and the Gospel." *Ensign*, Nov. 2004, 79–81.

———. "Sisters' Participation in the Gathering of Israel." Ensign, Nov. 2018, 68–70.

———. "Sweet Power of Prayer." *Ensign*, May 2003, 7–9.

———. "Teach Us Tolerance and Love." *Ensign*, May 1994, 69–71.

———. "A Testimony of the Book of Mormon." *Ensign*, Nov. 1999, 69–72.

———. "Thanks Be to God." *Ensign,* May 2012, 77–79.

———. "Thus Shall My Church Be Called." *Ensign*, May 1990, 16.

———. "The Transforming Power of Faith and Character." *Ensign*, Nov. 2010, 43–45.

———. "With God Nothing Shall Be Impossible." *Ensign*, May 1988, 35–37.

Nibley, Hugh. *Ancient Documents and the Pearl of Great Price*. 1986.

———. *Approaching Zion*. Edited by Don E. Norton. Vol. 9, The Collected Works of Hugh Nibley. 1989.

———. *An Approach to the Book of Mormon*. Edited by John W. Welch. Vol. 6, The Collected Works of Hugh W. Nibley. 1964.

———. *Brother Brigham Challenges the Saints*. Edited by Don E. Norton and Shirley S. Ricks. Vol. 13, The Collected Works of Hugh Nibley. 1994.

———. "Columbus and Revelation." *Instructor*, Oct. 1953, 319–20.

———. "Echoes and Evidences from Hugh Nibley." In Parry et al., *Echoes and Evidences*.

———. *Eloquent Witness: Nibley on Himself, Others, and the Temple*. Edited by Stephen D. Ricks. Vol. 17, The Collected Works of Hugh Nibley. 2008.

———. *Lehi in the Desert/The World of the Jaredites/There Were Jaredites*. Edited by John W. Welch, Darrell L. Matthews, and Stephen R. Callister. Vol. 5, The Collected Works of Hugh W. Nibley. 1988.

———. *Mormonism and Early Christianity*. Edited by Todd M. Compton and Stephen D. Ricks. Vol. 4, The Collected Works of Hugh Nibley. 1987.

———. *Nibley on the Timely and the Timeless*. 1978.

———. *The Prophetic Book of Mormon*. Edited by John W. Welch. Vol. 8, The Collected Works of Hugh Nibley. 1989.

———. "Scriptural Perspectives on How to Survive the Calamities of the Last Days." *Brigham Young University Studies* 25, no. 1 (Winter 1985).

———. *Since Cumorah*. Edited by John W. Welch. Vol. 7, The Collected Works of Hugh Nibley. 1988.

———. *Teachings of the Book of Mormon*. 4 vols. 1993.

———. *Temple and Cosmos: Beyond This Ignorant Present*. Edited by Don E. Norton. Vol. 12, The Collected Works of Hugh Nibley. 1992.

———. "Warfare and the Book of Mormon." In Ricks and Hamblin, *Warfare in the Book of Mormon*.

Nielsen, S. Gifford. "Hastening the Lord's Game Plan." *Ensign*, Nov. 2013, 33–35.

Nielson, Brent H. "A Call to the Rising Generation." *Ensign*, Nov. 2009, 95–97.

Nurturing Faith through the Book of Mormon. *Sperry Symposium series. 1995.*

Nyman, Monte S. "Bondage and Deliverance." In Jackson, *1 Nephi to Alma 29*.

———. "Come to Understanding and Learn Doctrine." In Nyman and Tate, *Second Nephi*.

———. "The Designations Jesus Gives Himself in 3 Nephi." In Nyman and Tate, *3 Nephi 9–30*.

———. *Great Are the Words of Isaiah*. 1980.

———. "I Have a Question." *Ensign*, Aug. 1994, 61–62.

———. *I, Mormon, Make a Record*. Vol. 6 of Book of Mormon Commentary series. 2004.

———. *I, Nephi, Wrote This Record*. Vol. 1 of Book of Mormon Commentary series. 2003.

———. *Isaiah and the Prophets: Inspired Voices from the Old Testament*. 1984.

———. "The Judgment Seat of Christ." In Nyman and Tate, *Fourth Nephi*.

———. "Lehi and Nephi: Faith unto Salvation." In Nyman and Tate, *First Nephi*, 1988.

———. "The Most Correct Book." *Ensign*, June 1984, 20–22.

———. *The Most Correct Book: Why the Book of Mormon Is the Keystone Scripture*. 1991.

———. *The Record of Alma*. Vol. 3 of Book of Mormon Commentary series. 2004.

———. *The Record of Helaman*. Vol. 4 of Book of Mormon Commentary series. 2004.

———. "The Restoration of Plain and Precious Parts." In Nyman and Tate, *Helaman through 3 Nephi 8*.

———. *These Records Are True*. Vol. 2 of Book of Mormon Commentary series. 2004.

———. "To Learn with Joy: Sacred Preaching, Great Revelation, Prophesying." In Nyman and Tate, *Jacob through Words of Mormon*.

Nyman, Monte S., and Charles D. Tate Jr., eds. *Alma: The Testimony of the Word*. Book of Mormon Symposium series, 1992.

———, eds. *First Nephi: The Doctrinal Foundation*. Book of Mormon Symposium series, 1986.

———, eds. *Fourth Nephi through Moroni: From Zion to Destruction*. Book of Mormon Symposium series, 1995.

———, eds. *Helaman through 3 Nephi 8: According to Thy Word*. Book of Mormon Symposium series, 1992.

———, eds. *Jacob through Words of Mormon: To Learn with Joy*. Book of Mormon Symposium series, 1990.

———, eds. *Mosiah: Salvation Only through Christ*. Book of Mormon Symposium series, 1991.

———, eds. *Second Nephi: The Doctrinal Structure*. Book of Mormon Symposium series, 1989.

———, eds. *3 Nephi 9–30: This Is My Gospel*. Book of Mormon Symposium series, 1993.

Oaks, Dallin H. "The Aaronic Priesthood and the Sacrament." *Ensign*. Nov. 1998, 37–40.

———. "Adversity." *Ensign*, July 1998, 7–8.

———. "All Men Everywhere." *Ensign*, May 2006, 77–80.

———. "Alternate Voices." *Ensign*, May 1989, 27–30.

———. "Another Testament of Jesus Christ." *Ensign*, Mar. 1994, 60–67.

———. "Be Not Deceived." *Ensign*, Nov. 2004, 43–46.

———. "Bible Stories and Personal Protection." *Ensign*, Nov. 1992, 37–40.

———. "Brother's Keeper." *Ensign*, Nov. 1986, 20–23.

———. "The Challenge to Become." *Ensign*, Nov. 2000, 32–34.

———. "Desires." *Ensign*, May 2011, 42–45.

———. "The Desires of Our Hearts." *Ensign*, June 1986, 64–67.

———. "Following the Pioneers." *Ensign*, Nov. 1997, 72–74.

———. "Free Agency and Freedom." In *2 Nephi, the Doctrinal Structure*, edited by Monte S. Nyman and Charles D. Tate. Vol. 3 of Book of Mormon Symposium series. 1989.

———. "Good, Better, Best." *Ensign*, Nov. 2007, 104–8.

———. "Gospel Teaching." *Ensign*, Nov. 1999, 78–80.

———. "The Great Plan of Happiness." *Ensign*, Nov. 1993, 72–75.

———. "Have You Been Saved?" *Ensign*, May 1998, 55–57.

———. "He Heals the Heavy Laden." *Ensign*, Nov. 2006, 6–9.

———. "'Judge Not' and Judging." *Ensign*, Aug. 1999, 7–11.

———. *Life's Lessons Learned*. 2011.

———. *The Lord's Way*. 1991.

———. "Miracles." *Ensign*, June 2001, 6–17.

———. "No Other Gods." *Ensign*, Nov. 2013, 72–75.

———. "Nourishing the Spirit." *Ensign*, Dec. 1998, 7–13.

———. "Opposition in All Things." *Ensign*, May 2016, 114–17.

———. "Preparation for the Second Coming." *Ensign*, May 2004, 7–10.

———. *Pure in Heart*. 1988.

———. "Resurrection." *Ensign*, May 2000, 14–16.

———. "Sacrament Meeting and the Sacrament." *Ensign*, Nov. 2008, 17–20.

———. "Scripture Reading and Revelation." *Ensign*, Jan. 1995, 6–9.

———. "Sin and Suffering." *Ensign*, July 1992, 70–74.

———. "Sins, Crimes, and Atonement." Address to Church Educational System religious educators, Feb. 7, 1992.

———. "Spiritual Gifts." *Ensign*, Sep. 1986, 70–73.

———. "Strengthening the Free Exercise of Religion." Address to Becket Fund for Religious Liberty, Canterbury Medal Dinner, New York City, May 16, 2013.

———. "Taking Upon Us the Name of Jesus Christ." *Ensign*, May 1985, 80–83.

———. "Testimony." *Ensign*, May 2008, 26–29.

———. "Things They're Saying." *New Era*, Feb. 1974, 18–20.

———. "Timing." *Ensign*, Oct. 2003, 10–17.

———. "Tithing." *Ensign*, May 1994, 33–35.

———. "Why Do We Serve?" *Ensign*, Nov. 1984, 12–15.

———. "The Witness: Martin Harris." *Ensign*, May 1999, 35–37.

———. "World Peace." *Ensign*, May 1990, 71–73.

The Old Testament and the Latter-day Saints. Sperry Symposium series. 1986.

Old Testament Student Manual: 1 King through Malachi, Religion 302. 2003.

Olmstead, Jacob W. "From Pentecost to Administration: A Reappraisal of the History of the Hosanna Shout." *Mormon Historical Studies* 2 (Fall 2001): 7–36.

Osguthorpe, Russell T. "The Power of Inspired Invitations." In *The Things Which My Father Saw: Approaches to Lehi's Dream and Nephi's Vision.* Edited by Daniel Belnap, Gaye Strathearn, and Stanley A. Johnson. Sperry Symposium series. 2011.

Ostler, Blake T. "The Throne-Theophany and Prophetic Commission in 1 Nephi: A Form-Critical Analysis." *Brigham Young University Studies* 26, no. 4 (Fall 1986): 67–95.

Ostler, Craig J. "Isaiah's Voice on the Promised Millennium." In *Voices of Old Testament Prophets.*

Otten, L. G., and C. M. Caldwell. *Sacred Truths of the Doctrine and Covenants.* 2 vols. 1982–83.

Pace, Glenn L. *Spiritual Plateaus.* 1991.

———. "They're Not Really Happy." *Ensign*, Nov. 1987, 39–41.

———. "A Thousand Times." *Ensign*, Nov. 1990, 8–10.

Packard, Dennis, and Sandra Packard. *Feasting on the Word.* 1981.

———. "Pondering the Word." *Journal of Book of Mormon Studies* 2, no. 1 (1999): 48–59, 86.

Packer, Boyd K. "And a Little Child Shall Lead Them." *Ensign*, May 2012, 6–9.

———. "The Balm of Gilead." *Ensign*, Nov. 1977, 59–61.

———. "The Book of Mormon: Another Testament of Jesus Christ—Plain and Precious Things." *Ensign*, May 2005, 6–9.

———. "The Brilliant Morning of Forgiveness." *Ensign.* Nov. 1995, 18–21.

———. "Called to Serve." *Ensign*, Nov. 1997, 6–8.

———. "The Candle of the Lord." *Ensign,* Jan. 1983, 51–56.

———. "The Cloven Tongues of Fire." *Ensign*, May 2000, 7–9.

———. "Counsel to Youth." *Ensign,* Nov. 2011, 16–19.

———. "Covenants." *Ensign*, May 1987, 22–25.

———. "A Defense and Refuge." *Ensign,* Nov. 2006, 85–88.

———. "Do Not Fear." *Ensign*, May 2004, 77–80.

———. "Finding Ourselves in Lehi's Dream." *Ensign*, Aug. 2010, 21–25.

———. "From Such Turn Away." *Ensign,* May 1985, 33–35.

———. "Funerals—a Time for Reverence." *Ensign*, Nov. 1988, 18–21.

———. "The Great Plan of Happiness." *Doctrine and Covenants and Church History*. 1993.

———. In Conference Report, Apr. 1968, 33–36.

———. "I Will Remember Your Sins No More." *Ensign*, May 2006, 25–28.

———. "The Key to Spiritual Protection." *Ensign*, Nov. 2013, 26–28.

———. *Let Not Your Heart Be Troubled*. 1978.

———. "The Library of the Lord." *Ensign*, May 1990, 36–38.

———. "Little Children." *Ensign*, Nov. 1986, 16–18.

———. "The Mediator." *Ensign*, May 1977, 54–56.

———. "The Mystery of Life." *Ensign*, Nov. 1983, 16–18.

———. "The One Pure Defense." Address to Church Educational System religious educators, Feb. 6, 2004.

———. "Our Moral Environment." *Ensign*, May 1992, 66–68.

———. "Personal Revelation: The Gift, the Test, and the Promise." *Ensign*, Nov. 1994, 59–60.

———. "The Plan of Happiness." *Ensign*, Nov. 2015, 26–28.

———. "Revelation in a Changing World." *Ensign*, Nov., 1989, 14–16.

———. *The Shield of Faith*. 1998.

———. "Teach Them Correct Principles." *Ensign*, May 1990, 89–91.

———. *That All May Be Edified*. 1982.

———. "These Things I Know." *Ensign*, May 2013, 6–8.

———. "The Things of My Soul." *Ensign*, May 1986, 59–61.

———. *The Things of the Soul*. 1996.

———. "'To Be Learned Is Good If . . .'" *Ensign*, Nov. 1992, 71–73.

———. "The Touch of the Master's Hand." *Ensign*, May 2001, 22–24.

———. "Washed Clean." *Ensign*, May 1997, 9–12.

———. "Who Is Jesus Christ?" *Ensign*, Mar. 2008, 12–19.

Packer, Cameron J. "Cumorah's Cave." *Journal of Book of Mormon Studies* 13, no. 1 (2004).

Paramore, James M. "They Taught and Did Minister One to Another." *Ensign*, May 1986, 69–70.

Parker, Todd B. "Abinadi: The Man and the Message." 1996, In *FARMS Preliminary Reports*.

Parkin, Bonnie D. "Gratitude: A Path to Happiness." *Ensign*, May 2007, 34–36.

Parrish, Alan K. "Lehi and the Covenant of the Promised Land: A Modern Appraisal." In Nyman and Tate, *Second Nephi*.

Parry, Donald W. *The Book of Mormon Text Reformatted according to Parallelistic Patterns*. 1992.

———. "Climactic Forms in the Book of Mormon." In Welch, *Reexploring the Book of Mormon*.

———. "Hebraisms and Other Ancient Peculiarities in the Book of Mormon." In Parry et al., *Echoes and Evidences*.

———. "Hebrew Literary Patterns in the Book of Mormon." *Ensign*, Oct. 1989, 58–61.

———. "I Have a Question." *Ensign*, July 1996, 60–61.

———. "'Pray Always': Learning to Pray as Jesus Prayed." In Nyman and Tate, *3 Nephi 9–30*.

———. "Symbolic Action as Prophetic Curse." In Welch, *Reexploring the Book of Mormon*.

———. "Teaching in Black and White: Antithetic Parallel Structure in the Book of Alma, Its Forms and Function." In Nyman and Tate, *Alma*.

Parry, Donald W., and Jay A. Parry. *Symbols and Shadows: Unlocking a Deeper Understanding of the Atonement*. 2009.

Parry, Donald W., Jay A. Parry, and Tina M. Peterson. *Understanding Isaiah*. 1998.

Parry, Donald W., Daniel C. Peterson, and John W. Welch, eds. *Echoes and Evidences of the Book of Mormon*. 2002.

Parry, Jay A., and Donald W. Parry. *Understanding Death and the Resurrection*. 2003.

———. *Understanding the Signs of the Times*. 1999.

Parsons, Robert E. "The Practices of the Church." In Jackson, *Alma 30 to Moroni*.

Pearson, Glenn L., and Reid E. Bankhead, *Building Faith with the Book of Mormon*. 1986.

Penrose, Charles W. In Conference Report, Oct. 1914, 34–44.

———. "The Work of Restoration of All Things." *Journal of Discourses*, 20:292–99.

Perkins, Anthony D. "Beware concerning Yourselves." *Ensign*, Nov. 2012, 54–56.

———. "The Great and Wonderful Love." *Ensign*, Nov. 2006, 76–78.

Perkins, Keith. "Why Are We Here in New England?" In *New England*. Edited by Donald Q. Cannon. Regional Studies in Church History series. 1988.

Perry, L. Tom. "Back to Gospel Basics." *Ensign*, May 1993, 90–92.

———. "Becoming Self-Reliant." *Ensign*, Nov. 1991, 64–66.

———. "'Behold, the Lord Hath Shown unto Me Great and Marvelous Things.'" *Ensign,* November 1992, 15–17.

———. "Blessings Resulting from Reading the Book of Mormon." *Ensign*, Nov. 2005, 7–8.

———. "Discipleship." *Ensign*, Nov. 2000, 60–62.

———. "Learning to Serve." *Ensign*, Aug. 1996, 10–16.

———. *Living with Enthusiasm*. 1996.

———. "The Peaceable Followers of Christ." *Ensign*, Nov. 1989, 70–72.

———. "The Power of Deliverance." *Ensign*, May 2012, 94–97.

———. "Proclaim My Gospel from Land to Land." *Ensign*, May 1989, 13–14.

Petersen, Mark E. In Conference Report, Apr. 1946, 167–72.

———. In Conference Report, Apr. 1951, 60–64.

———. "The Sabbath Day." *Ensign*, May 1975, 47–49.

———. "Sacred, Set Prayers." In *Prayer*.

Peterson, Daniel C. "Authority in the Book of Mosiah." In *FARMS Review* 18, Issue 1 (2006): 149–85.

———. "Mounting Evidence for the Book of Mormon." *Ensign*, Jan. 2000, 18–24.

———. "Priesthood in Mosiah." In Nyman and Tate, *Mosiah*.

———. "Their Own Worst Enemies." In Jackson, *Alma 30 to Moroni*.

Peterson, H. Donl. "Church Discipline in the Book of Mosiah." In Nyman and Tate, *Mosiah*.

———. "Moroni, the Last of the Nephite Prophets." In Nyman and Tate, *Fourth Nephi through Moroni*.

Peterson, Janet, and Eduardo Ayala. "Friend to Friend." *Friend*, Mar. 1996, 6–7.

Pew, W. Ralph. "'Yield Your Heart to God'—the Process of Sanctification." In Nyman and Tate, *Helaman through 3 Nephi 8*.

Phillips, R. Douglas. "I Have a Question." *Ensign*, Jan. 1978, 17–18.

Pike, Dana M. "Israelite Inscriptions from the Time of Jeremiah and Lehi." In Welch et al., *Glimpses of Lehi's Jerusalem*.

Porter, Bruce D. "A Broken Heart and a Contrite Spirit." *Ensign*, Nov. 2007, 31–32.

Porter, L. Aldin. "Our Destiny." *Ensign*, Nov. 1999, 65–66.

———. "The Spirit of Prophecy." *Ensign*, Nov. 1996, 9–11.

Pratt, Parley P. *Autobiography of Parley Parker Pratt*. Edited by Parley P. Pratt Jr. 1938.

———. *Key to the Science of Theology*. 1855.

Prayer. 1977.

Preach My Gospel. 2004.

Presidents of the Church Teacher Manual. 2005.

Rasband, Ronald A. "Our Rising Generation." *Ensign*, May 2006, 46–47.

Rappleye, Neal. "Learning Nephi's Language: Creating a Context." *Interpreter: A Journal of Mormon Scripture* 16 (2015), 151–59.

Rasmussen, Ellis T. *A Latter-day Saint Commentary on the Old Testament*. 1993.

Rector, Hartman, Jr. "The Gospel." *Ensign*, Nov. 1985, 74–77.

Reeve, Rex C., Jr. "The Book of Mormon Plates." In Nyman and Tate, *First Nephi*.

———. "Dealing with Opposition to the Church." In Nyman and Tate, *Alma*.

———. "God's Way or Man's: The Ultimate Choice." In Jackson, *Alma 30 to Moroni*.

———. "We Labor Diligently to Persuade Our Children to Believe in Christ: 2 Nephi 25:21 to 26:11." In Nyman and Tate, *Second Nephi*.

"Research and Perspectives: Recent Studies on the Book of Mormon." *Ensign*, July 1989, 65.

Reynolds, George. *A Dictionary of the Book of Mormon*. 1929.

Reynolds, George, and Janne M. Sjodahl. *Commentary on the Book of Mormon*. 7 vols. 1962.

Reynolds, Noel B. "The Authorship of the Book of Mormon." Brigham Young University forum, May 27, 1997.

———, ed. *Book of Mormon Authorship Revisited: The Evidence for Ancient Origins*. 1997.

———. "The Gospel as Taught by Nephite Prophets." In Welch, *Reexploring the Book of Mormon*.

———. "Nephi's Political Testament." In Sorenson and Thorne, *Rediscovering the Book of Mormon*.

Richards, Franklin D. "Origin of American Aborigines." *Contributor* 17 (May 1896): 425–28.

Richards, Franklin D., and James A. Little. *Compendium of the Doctrines of the Gospel*. 1857.

Richards, Kent F. "The Atonement Covers All Pain." *Ensign*, May 2011, 15–17.

Richards, LeGrand. In Conference Report, Apr. 1954, 52–56.

———. In Conference Report, Oct. 1956, 22–26.

———. *Israel! Do You Know?* 1954.

———. *Just to Illustrate*. 1961.

———. "Prophets and Prophecy." *Ensign*, Nov. 1975, 50–52.

Richards, Stephen L. *The Church in War and Peace*. 1943.

Richardson, E. LV. "What Is a Jew?" *Ensign*, May 1972, 12–17.

Ricks, Eldin. *Book of Mormon Commentary, Volume 1: Comprising the Complete Text of The First Book of Nephi with Explanatory Notes*. 1953.

———. "The Small Plates of Nephi and the Words of Mormon." In Nyman and Tate, *Jacob through Words of Mormon*.

Ricks, Stephen D. "The Coronation of Kings." In Welch, *Reexploring the Book of Mormon*.

———. "I Have a Question." *Ensign*, Aug. 1988, 27–28.

———. "Pressing Forward with the Book of Mormon: Semitic Texts Written in Egyptian Characters." *Insights* 12 (Mar. 1992): 2.

Ricks, Stephen D., and William J. Hamblin. *Warfare in the Book of Mormon*. 1990.

Ricks, Stephen D., and John A. Tvedtnes. "Notes and Communications: The Hebrew Origin of Some Book of Mormon Place Names." *Journal of Book of Mormon Studies* 6, no. 2 (1997): 255–59.

Ricks, Stephen D., and John W. Welch. *The Allegory of the Olive Tree*. 1994.

Riddle, Chauncey. "Days of Wickedness and Vengeance." In Nyman and Tate, *Helaman through 3 Nephi 8*.

Ringger, Hans B. "Choose You This Day." *Ensign,* May 1990, 25–26.

Ringwood, Michael T. "An Easiness and Willingness to Believe." *Ensign,* Nov. 2009, 100–102.

Robbins, Lynn G. "Agency and Anger." *Ensign,* May 1998, 80–81.

Roberts, B. H. *A Comprehensive History of The Church of Jesus Christ of Latter-day Saints, Century One.* 6 vols. 1965.

———. *The Seventy's Course in Theology: Outline History of the Dispensations of the Gospel, Second Year.* 1976.

Robinson, Stephen E. *Believing Christ.* 1992.

———. "Early Christianity and 1 Nephi 13–14." In Nyman and Tate, *First Nephi*.

———. "Eternities That Come and Go." *Religious Educator* 8, no. 3 (May 1994): 1–4.

Romney, Marion G. "According to the Covenants." *Ensign,* Nov. 1975, 71–73.

———. In Conference Report, Apr. 1949, 35–41.

———. In Conference Report, Oct. 1948, 110–13.

———. In Conference Report, Oct. 1970, 27–30.

———. *Learning for the Eternities.* 1977.

———. "The Light of Christ." *Ensign,* May 1977, 66–68.

———. "The Perfect Law of Liberty." *Ensign,* Nov. 1981, 43–45.

———. "Temples—the Gates of Heaven." *Ensign,* March 1971, 12–16.

———. "Trust in the Lord." *Ensign,* May 1979, 40–43.

Roper, Matthew. "On Cynics and Swords." *FARMS Review* 9, no. 1 (1997).

———. "Was Aminadab a Zoramite?" *Insights* 24, no. 1 (2004).

Rust, Richard Dilworth. "Book of Mormon Imagery." In Sorenson and Thorne, *Rediscovering the Book of Mormon*.

———. *Feasting on the Word: The Literary Testimony of the Book of Mormon.* 1997.

———. "Poetry in the Book of Mormon." In Sorenson and Thorne, *Rediscovering the Book of Mormon*.

Samuelson, Cecil O. "Appropriate Zeal." Brigham Young University devotional, Sep. 7, 2010.

Satterfield, Bruce. "The Publication History of the Book of Mormon." In *Church News.* Jan. 1, 2000.

Scott, Richard G. "The Atonement Can Secure Your Peace and Happiness." *Ensign,* Nov. 2006, 40–42.

———. "Acquiring Spiritual Knowledge." *Ensign,* Nov. 1993, 86–88.

———. "Finding Forgiveness." *Ensign,* May 1995, 75–77.

———. "How to Live Well Amid Increasing Evil." *Ensign,* May 2004, 100–102.

———. "How to Obtain Revelation and Inspiration for Your Personal Life." *Ensign,* May 2012, 45–47.

———. "Jesus Christ, Our Redeemer." *Ensign,* May 1997, 53–59.

———. "Making the Right Choices." *Ensign,* Nov. 1994, 37–39.

———. "Obtaining Help from the Lord." *Ensign,* Nov. 1991, 84–86.

———. "The Path to Peace and Joy." *Ensign,* Nov. 2000, 25–27.

———. "Peace of Conscience and Peace of Mind." *Ensign,* Nov. 2004, 15–18.

———. "Personal Strength through the Atonement of Jesus Christ." *Ensign,* Nov. 2013, 82–85.

———. "The Power of Righteousness." *Ensign,* Nov. 1998, 69–70.

———. "The Power of Scripture." *Ensign,* Nov. 2011, 6–8.

———. "Removing Barriers to Happiness." *Ensign,* May 1998, 85–87.

———. "The Sustaining Power of Faith in Times of Uncertainty and Testing." *Ensign,* May 2003, 75–78.

———. "To Acquire Spiritual Guidance." *Ensign,* Nov. 2009, 6–8.

———. "To Be Free of Heavy Burdens." *Ensign*, Nov. 2002, 86–88.

———. "To Be Healed." *Ensign,* May 1994, 7–9.

———. "The Transforming Power of Faith and Character." *Ensign*, Nov. 2010, 43–46.

———. "Trust in the Lord." *Ensign*, Nov. 1995, 16–18.

———. "Truth: The Foundations of Correct Decisions." *Ensign*, Nov. 2007, 90–92.

———. "Using the Supernal Gift of Prayer." *Ensign*, May 2007, 8–11.

Seely, David Rolph. "The Image of the Hand of God in the Book of Mormon and the Old Testament." In Sorenson and Thorne, *Rediscovering the Book of Mormon.*

———. "The Lord Will Bring Salvation." In Jackson, *1 Kings to Malachi.*

Seely, David Rolph, and Fred E. Woods. "How Could Jerusalem, 'That Great City,' Be Destroyed?" In Welch et al., *Glimpses of Lehi's Jerusalem.*

The Sermon on the Mount in Latter-day Scripture. Edited by Gaye Strathearn, Thomas A. Wayment, and Daniel L. Belnap. 2010.

Simmons, Dennis E. "But If Not . . ." *Ensign*, May 2004, 73–75.

———. "His Peace." *Ensign*, May 1997, 31–32.

Sitati, Joseph W. "Blessings of the Gospel Available to All." *Ensign*, Nov. 2009, 103–5.

Skinner, Andrew C., and Gaye Strathearn, eds. *Third Nephi: An Incomparable Scripture.* 2012.

Skousen, Royal. *Analysis of Textual Variants of the Book of Mormon.* 6 vols. 2004.

———. "How Joseph Smith Translated the Book of Mormon: Evidence from the Original Manuscript." *Journal of Book of Mormon Studies* 1 (Summer 1998): 23–31.

———. "Translating the Book of Mormon: Evidence from the Original Manuscript." In Reynolds, *Book of Mormon Authorship Revisited.*

Smith, George Albert. *Sharing the Gospel with Others.* 1948.

Smith, Hyrum M., and Janne M. Sjodahl. *Doctrine and Covenants Commentary.* 1972.

Smith, Joseph. *History of The Church of Jesus Christ of Latter-day Saints.* Edited by B. H. Roberts. 2d ed. rev. 7 vols. 1932–51.

———. "A History of the Life of Joseph Smith, Jr." In *An American Prophet's Record: The Diaries and Journals of Joseph Smith.* Edited by Scott H. Faulring. 1989.

———. *Joseph Smith* [manual]. Teachings of Presidents of the Church series. 2007.

———. *Papers of Joseph Smith.* Edited by Dean C. Jessee. 2 vols. 1989–92.

———. *Personal Writings of Joseph Smith.* Edited by Dean C. Jessee. 1984.

———. *Teachings of the Prophet Joseph Smith.* Selected by Joseph Fielding Smith. 1976.

———. *The Words of Joseph Smith.* Edited by Andrew F. Ehat and Lyndon W. Cook. 1980.

Smith, Joseph F. *Gospel Doctrine.* 1986.

———. In Conference Report, Apr. 1900, 46–50.

———. In Conference Report, Apr. 1901, 68–74.

———. *Joseph F. Smith* [manual]. Teachings of Presidents of the Church series. 1998.

Smith, Joseph Fielding. *Answers to Gospel Questions.* 5 vols. 1957–66.

———. *Doctrines of Salvation.* Edited by Bruce R. McConkie. 3 vols. 1955.

———. In Conference Report, Apr. 1943, 11–16.

———. In Conference Report, Apr. 1969, 121–23.

———. In Conference Report, Oct. 1961, 18–20.

———. *The Life of Joseph F. Smith.* 1938.

———. *Man, His Origin and Destiny.* 1954.

————. *The Progress of Man.* 1936.

————. *Seek Ye Earnestly.* 1970.

————. *The Way to Perfection.* 1975.

Smith, Lucy Mack. *Biographical Sketches of Joseph Smith the Prophet and His Progenitors for Many Generations.*

————. *History of Joseph Smith by His Mother.* Edited by Preston Nibley. 1958.

Smith, Robert F. "New Information about Mulek, Son of the King." In Welch, *Reexploring the Book of Mormon.*

————. "Textual Criticism of the Book of Mormon." In Welch, *Reexploring the Book of Mormon.*

Smith, Robert F., and Stephen D. Ricks. "New Year's Celebrations." In Welch, *Reexploring the Book of Mormon.*

Smith, Robert F., Gordon C. Thomasson, and John W. Welch. "What Did Charles Anthon Really Say?" In Welch, *Reexploring the Book of Mormon.*

Smith, William. *William Smith on Mormonism: A Sketch of the History, Experience, and Ministry of Elder William Smith.* 1883.

Snow, Eliza R. Biography and Family Record of Lorenzo Snow. 1884.

Soares, Ulisses. "Be Meek and Lowly of Heart." *Ensign,* Nov. 2013, 9–11.

Sorensen, David E. "You Can't Pet a Rattlesnake." *Ensign,* May 2001, 41–42.

Sorenson, John L. *An Ancient American Setting for the Book of Mormon.* 1985.

————. "Barley in Ancient America." In Welch, *Reexploring the Book of Mormon.*

————. "The Book of Mormon as a Mesoamerican Record." In Reynolds, *Book of Mormon Authorship Revisited.*

————. "Digging into the Book of Mormon." *Ensign,* Sep. 1984, 26–37.

————. "How Could Joseph Smith Write So Accurately about Ancient American Civilization?" In Parry et al., *Echoes and Evidences.*

————. "Latest Discoveries." In Welch, *Reexploring the Book of Mormon.*

————. *Mormon's Codex.* 2013.

————. "Nephi's Garden and Chief Market." In Welch, *Reexploring the Book of Mormon.*

————. "Seasons of War, Seasons of Peace in the Book of Mormon." In Sorenson and Thorne, *Rediscovering the Book of Mormon.*

————. "When Lehi's Party Arrived in the Land, Did They Find Others There?" In *Journal of Book of Mormon Studies* 1, no. 1 (Fall 1992).

Sorenson, John L., John A. Tvedtnes, and John W. Welch. "Seven Tribes: An Aspect of Lehi's Legacy." In Welch, *Reexploring the Book of Mormon.*

Sorenson, John L., and Melvin J. Thorne, eds. *Rediscovering the Book of Mormon.* 1991.

Sperry, Sidney B. *Book of Mormon Compendium.* 1968.

————. "Moroni the Lonely: The Story of the Writing of the Title Page of the Book of Mormon." *Improvement Era,* Feb. 1944, 83, 116–18.

————. "The Problem of the 'Rod' and the 'Root of Jesse' in Isaiah 11." *Improvement Era,* Oct. 1966, 869, 914–17.

————. *The Problems of the Book of Mormon.* 1964.

Staheli, Donald L. "Securing Our Testimonies." *Ensign,* Nov. 2004, 38–39.

Staley, Jenna L. "The Winds That Blow." *Ensign,* April 2005, 61.

Stapley, Delbert L. "The Savior's Ministry." *Ensign,* May 1974, 101–3.

Stevenson, Gary E. "Be Valiant in Courage, Strength, and Activity." *Ensign,* Nov. 2012, 51–53.

Strong, James. *Strong's Exhaustive Concordance to the Bible.* 2009.

Swift, Charles. "The Literary Power of the Book of Mormon." In *Living the Book of Mormon: Abiding by its Precepts.* Edited by Gaye Strathearn and Charles Swift. Sperry Symposium series. 2007.

Swiss, Ralf E. "The Tame and Wild Olive Trees—An Allegory of Our Savior's Love." *Ensign,* August 1988, 50–52.

Szink, Terrence L. "A Just and True Record." In Jackson, *Alma 30 to Moroni.*

———. "Nephi and the Exodus." In Sorenson and Thorne, *Rediscovering the Book of Mormon.*

Talmage, James E. *Articles of Faith.* 1971.

———. *The Great Apostasy.* 1909.

———. *Jesus the Christ.* 1915.

———. *Vitality of Mormonism.* 1919.

Tanner, John S. "Jacob and His Descendants as Authors." In Sorenson and Thorne, *Rediscovering the Book of Mormon.*

———. "Literary Reflections on Jacob and His Descendants." In Nyman and Tate, *Jacob through Words of Mormon.*

Tanner, N. Eldon. "Christ in America." *Ensign,* May 1975, 34–36.

———. In Conference Report, Oct. 1970, 49–53.

———. "'For They Loved the Praise of Men More Than the Praise of God.'" *Ensign,* Nov. 1975, 74–77.

———. "If They Will But Serve the God of the Land." *Ensign,* May 1976, 48–51.

———. "Our Responsibility to the Transgressor." *Ensign,* Nov. 1974, 76–79.

Tanner, Susan W. "'I Am the Light Which Ye Shall Hold Up.'" *Ensign,* May 2006, 103–5.

Tate, Lucile C. *LeGrand Richards, Beloved Apostle.* 1982.

Taylor, Alan. *American Colonies: The Settling of North America.* 2001.

Taylor, John. *The Mediation and Atonement of Our Lord and Savior Jesus Christ.* 1882.

Taylor, Leslie A. "The Word of God." *Journal of Book of Mormon Studies* 12, no. 1 (2003): 52–63, 116.

Thomas, Brett P. "They Did Remember His Words." In Nyman and Tate, *Helaman through 3 Nephi 8.*

———. "The Weak Things of the World." In *The Heavens Are Opened.* Sperry Symposium series. 1992.

Thomas, M. Catherine. "Benjamin and the Mysteries of Godliness." In Welch and Ricks, *King Benjamin's Speech.*

———. "Blessed Are Ye . . ." *Ensign,* June 1987, 6–9.

———. "Jacob's Allegory: The Mystery of Christ." In Ricks and Welch, *Allegory of the Olive Tree.*

———. "A More Excellent Way." In Jackson, *Alma 30 to Moroni.*

———. "Theophany." In Jackson, *Alma 30 to Moroni.*

———. "Types and Shadows of Deliverance in the Book of Mormon." In *Doctrines of the Book of Mormon.*

Thompson, John S. "The Jaredite Exodus: A Literary Perspective of a Historical Narrative." *Journal of Book of Mormon Studies,* Spring 1994.

Thy People Shall Be My People and Thy God My God. Edited by Paul Y. Hoskisson. Sperry Symposium series. 1994.

Tingey, Earl C. "The Great Plan of Happiness." *Ensign,* May, 2006, 72–74.

Top, Brent L. "Faith unto Repentance." In *Doctrines of the Book of Mormon.*

———. *A Peculiar Treasure.* 1997.

True to the Faith: A Gospel Reference. 2004.

Turner, Rodney. "A Faith unto Salvation." In Jackson, *Alma 30 to Moroni.*

———. "The Great Conversion." In Jackson, *1 Nephi to Alma 29.*

———. "The Imperative and Unchanging Nature of God." In *The Lectures on Faith in Historical Perspective.* Edited by Larry E. Dahl and Charles D. Tate Jr. 1990.

———. "The Lamanite Mark." In Nyman and Tate, *Second Nephi.*

———. "The Prophet Nephi." In Nyman and Tate, *First Nephi.* 1988.

Tuttle, A. Theodore. "Developing Faith." *Ensign,* Nov. 1986, 66–67.

———. "A Prophet's Faith." *Ensign,* Nov. 1975, 23–24.

Tvedtnes, John A. "Ancient Texts in Support of the Book of Mormon." In Parry et al., *Echoes and Evidences.*

———. "As a Garment in a Hot Furnace." *Journal of Book of Mormon Studies* 6, no. 1 (1997): 76–79.

———. *The Book of Mormon and Other Hidden Books.* 2000.

———. "Book of Mormon Tribal Affiliation and Military Castes." In Ricks and Hamblin, *Warfare in the Book of Mormon.*

———. "Colophons in the Book of Mormon." In Sorenson and Thorne, *Rediscovering the Book of Mormon.*

———. "Drought and Serpents." *Journal of Book of Mormon Studies* 6, no. 1 (Fall 1997).

———. "The Hebrew Background of the Book of Mormon." In Sorenson and Thorne, *Rediscovering the Book of Mormon.*

———. "I Have a Question." *Ensign,* Oct. 1986, 64–67.

———. "Isaiah Variants in the Book of Mormon." In *Isaiah and the Prophets: Inspired Voices from the Old Testament.* Edited by Monte S. Nyman. 1984.

———. "Mormon's Editorial Promises." In Sorenson and Thorne, *Rediscovering the Book of Mormon.*

———. *The Most Correct Book.* 2003.

———. "Notes and Communications: Cities and Lands in the Book of Mormon." *Journal of Book of Mormon Studies* 4, no. 2 (1995): 147–50.

———. "A Review of 'New Approaches to the Book of Mormon: Explorations in Critical Methodology.'" *FARMS Review* 6, no. 1 (1994): 8–50.

———. "*Rod* and *Sword* as the Word of God." *Journal of Book of Mormon Studies* 5, no. 2 (1996): 148–55.

———. "That Which Is to Come." *Journal of Book of Mormon Studies* 6, no. 2 (1997): 245–50.

———. "Why Were Israel and Judah Carried Away Captive?" *Ensign,* Aug. 1982, 25–26.

Tvedtnes, John A., John Gee, and Matthew Roper. "Book of Mormon Names Attested in Ancient Hebrew Inscriptions." *Journal of Book of Mormon Studies* 9, no. 1 (2000): 40–51, 78–79.

Uchtdorf, Dieter F. "Come, Join with Us." *Ensign,* Nov. 2013, 21–24.

———. "The Fruits of the First Vision." *Ensign,* May 2005, 36–38.

———. "Have We Not Reason to Rejoice?" *Ensign,* Nov. 2007, 18–21.

———. "Heeding the Voice of the Prophets." *Ensign,* July 2008, 5–7.

———. "The Infinite Power of Hope." *Ensign,* Nov. 2008, 21–24.

———. "The Merciful Obtain Mercy." *Ensign,* May 2012, 70–77.

———. "Point of Safe Return." *Ensign,* May 2007, 99–101.

———. "The Power of a Personal Testimony." *Ensign,* Nov. 2006, 37–39.

———. "Pride and the Priesthood." *Ensign,* Nov. 2010, 55–58.

———. "The Way of the Disciple." *Ensign,* May 2009, 75–78.

———. "The Why of Priesthood Service." *Ensign,* May 2012, 58–61.

Valletta, Thomas R. "Conflicting Orders: Alma and Amulek in Ammonihah." In *The Temple in Time and Eternity.* Edited by Donald W. Parry and Stephen D. Ricks. Vol. 2 of Temples through the Ages series. 1999.

———. "The Captain and the Covenant." In Nyman and Tate, *Alma*.

———. "The Exodus: Prophetic Type and the Plan of Redemption." In *Thy People Shall Be My People*.

———. "I Have a Question." *Ensign*, Feb. 1994, 61–62.

———. "Jared and His Brother." In Nyman and Tate, *Fourth Nephi through Moroni*.

Vandenberg, John H. In Conference Report, Oct. 1968, 31–34.

Van Orden, Bruce A. "The Law of Witnesses in 2 Nephi." In Nyman and Tate, *Second Nephi*.

Voices of Old Testament Prophets. Sperry Symposium series. 1997.

von Clausewitz, Karl. *War, Politics, and Power: Selections from "On War," and "I Believe and Profess."* Tr. and ed. Edward M. Collins. N.d.

Walker, Gary Lee. "The Downfall of the Nephite Nation: Lessons for Our Time." In Jackson, *Alma 30 to Moroni*.

Wardle, Lynn D. "Dissent: Perspectives from the Book of Mormon." *Journal of Book of Mormon Studies* 3, no. 1 (1994): 53–73.

Washington, George. *George Washington Writings*. Edited by John Rhodehamel. 1997.

Watson, Wilfred G. E. *Classical Hebrew Poetry*. 1984.

Watts, Pauline. "Prophecy and Discovery: On the Spiritual Origins of Christopher Columbus's 'Enterprise of the Indies.'" *American Historical Review* 90, no. 1 (Feb. 1985): 73–102.

Webster, David L. *Defensive Earthworks at Becan, Campeche, Mexico: Implications for Maya Warfare*. Tulane, LA: Tulane University, Middle American Research Institute, Publication 41, 1976.

Webster, Noah. *An American Dictionary of the English Language*. 1828. Reprint, 1980.

Webster's Ninth New Collegiate Dictionary. *1983*.

Weinreb, Friedrich. *Roots of the Bible: An Ancient View for a New Outlook*. 1986.

Welch, John W. "Benjamin's Covenant as a Precursor of the Sacrament Prayers." In Welch and Ricks, *King Benjamin's Speech*.

———. "Benjamin, the Man: His Place in Nephite History." In Welch, John W. and Ricks, Stephen D., eds. *King Benjamin's Speech*. 1998.

———. "The Calling of a Prophet." In Nyman and Tate, *First Nephi*.

———. "The Case of an Unobserved Murder." In Welch, *Reexploring the Book of Mormon*.

———. "Chiasmus in Helaman 6:7–13." In Welch, *Reexploring the Book of Mormon*.

———. "Colophons in the Book of Mormon." Reexploring the Book of Mormon. 13–15. Salt Lake City: Deseret Book Company, 1992.

———. "Decorative Iron in Early Israel." In Welch, *Reexploring the Book of Mormon*.

———. "Democratizing Forces in King Benjamin's Speech." In Welch and Thorne, *Pressing Forward with the Book of Mormon*.

———. "The Destruction of Ammonihah and the Law of Apostate Cities." In Welch, *Reexploring the Book of Mormon*.

———. "Doubled, Sealed, and Witnessed Documents." *Insights* 21, no. 6 (2001).

———. "The Execution of Zemnarihah." In Welch, *Reexploring the Book of Mormon*.

———. "Exemption from Military Duty." In Welch, *Reexploring the Book of Mormon*.

———. "From Presence to Practice: Jesus, the Sacrament Prayers, the Priesthood, and Church Discipline in 3 Nephi 18 and Moroni 2–6." *Journal of Book of Mormon Studies* 5, no. 1 (Spring 1996): 123–24.

———. "Isaiah 53, Mosiah 14, and the Book of Mormon." In *Isaiah in the Book of Mormon*. Edited by Donald W. Parry. 1998.

———. "Jacob's Ten Commandments." In Welch, *Reexploring the Book of Mormon*.

———. "King Benjamin's Speech: A Masterful Oration." In Welch and Ricks, *King Benjamin's Speech*.

———. "'The Lamb of God' in Pre-Christian Texts." In Welch and Thorne, *Pressing Forward with the Book of Mormon*.

———. "Law and War in the Book of Mormon." In Ricks and Hamblin, *Warfare in the Book of Mormon*.

———. "The Law of Mosiah." In Welch, *Reexploring the Book of Mormon*.

———. *The Legal Cases in the Book of Mormon*. 2008.

———. "Legal Perspectives on the Slaying of Laban." *Journal of Book of Mormon Studies* 1, no. 1 (1992): 119–41.

———. "Lehi's Council Vision and the Mysteries of God." In Welch, *Reexploring the Book of Mormon*.

———. "Lehi's Last Will and Testament: A Legal Approach." In Nyman and Tate, *Second Nephi*.

———. "A Masterpiece: Alma 36." In Sorenson and Thorne, *Rediscovering the Book of Mormon*.

———. "Number 24." In Welch, *Reexploring the Book of Mormon*.

———. "Our Nephite Sacrament Prayers." In Welch, *Reexploring the Book of Mormon*.

———. "The Power of Evidence in the Nurturing of Faith." In *Nurturing Faith*.

———. "Preliminary Comments on the Sources behind the Book of Ether." *FARMS Manuscript Collection*. 1986.

———, ed. *Reexploring the Book of Mormon*. 1992.

———. "Seeing Third Nephi as the Holy of Holies of the Book of Mormon." *Journal of the Book of Mormon and Other Restoration* 19, no. 1 (2010).

———. *The Sermon at the Temple and the Sermon on the Mount: A Latter-day Saint Approach*. 1990.

———. "The Sermon at the Temple." In Welch, *Reexploring the Book of Mormon*.

———. "Sherem's Accusations against Jacob." *Pressing Forward with the Book of Mormon: The FARMS Updates of the 1990's*. 1999.

———. "A Steady Stream of Significant Recognitions." In Parry et al., *Echoes and Evidences*.

———. "Synagogues in the Book of Mormon" In Welch, *Reexploring the Book of Mormon*.

———. "The Temple in the Book of Mormon: The Temples at the Cities of Nephi, Zarahemla, and Bountiful." In *Temples of the Ancient World*. Edited by Donald W. Parry. 1994.

———. "Ten Testimonies of Jesus Christ from the Book of Mormon." In *Book of Mormon Treasury*.

———. "Ten Testimonies of Jesus Christ." *In Doctrines of the Book of Mormon*. 1992.

———. "Textual Consistency." In Welch, *Reexploring the Book of Mormon*.

———. "Unintentional Sin in Benjamin's Discourse." *Insights* 16, no. 2 (1996): 2.

———. "Was Helaman 7–8 an Allegorical Funeral Sermon?" In Welch, *Reexploring the Book of Mormon*.

———. "Weighing and Measuring in the Worlds of the Book of Mormon." *Journal of Book of Mormon Studies* 8, no. 2 (1999): 36–45, 86.

———. "What Does Chiasmus in the Book of Mormon Prove?" In Reynolds, *Book of Mormon Authorship Revisited*.

———. "What Was a 'Mosiah'?" In Welch, *Reexploring the Book of Mormon*.

———. "When Did Nephi Write the Small Plates?" In Welch and Thorne, *Pressing Forward with the Book of Mormon*.

Welch, John W., and Daryl R. Hague. "Benjamin's Sermon as a Traditional Ancient Farewell Address." In Welch and Ricks, *King Benjamin's Speech*.

Welch, John W., and Daniel McKinlay. "Getting Things Strai[gh]t." In Welch, *Reexploring the Book of Mormon*.

Welch, John W., and Heidi Harkness Parker. "Better That One Man Perish." In Welch and Thorne, *Pressing Forward with the Book of Mormon*.

Welch, John W., and Tim Rathbone. "How Long Did It Take to Translate the Book of Mormon?" In Welch, *Reexploring the Book of Mormon*.

Welch, John W., and Stephen D. Ricks. "Complete Text of Benjamin's Speech with Notes and Comments." In Welch and Ricks, *King Benjamin's Speech*.

———. *King Benjamin's Speech: "That Ye May Learn Wisdom."* 1998.

Welch, John W., and Kelly Ward. "Thieves and Robbers." In Welch, *Reexploring the Book of Mormon*.

Welch, John W., and J. Gregory Welch. *Charting the Book of Mormon: Visual Aids for Personal Study and Teaching*. 1999.

Welch, John W., Neal Rappleye, Stephen O. Smoot, David J. Larsen, and Taylor Halverson, eds. *Knowing Why: 137 Evidences That the Book of Mormon Is True*. 2017.

Welch, John W., David Rolph Seely, and Jo Ann H. Seely, eds. *Glimpses of Lehi's Jerusalem*. 2004.

Welch, John W., Robert F. Smith, and Gordon C. Thomasson. "Dancing Maidens and the Fifteenth of Av." In Welch, *Reexploring The Book of Mormon*.

Welch, John W., Gordon C. Thomasson, and Robert F. Smith. "Abinadi and Pentecost." In Welch, *Reexploring the Book of Mormon*.

Welch, John W., and Melvin J. Thorne, eds. *Pressing Forward with the Book of Mormon*. 1999.

Wells, Matthew G., and John W. Welch. "Concrete Evidence for the Book of Mormon." In Welch, *Reexploring the Book of Mormon*.

Wells, Robert E. *"The Liahona Triad." In Book of Mormon Treasury*.

———. *The Mount and the Master*. 1981.

———. "Our Message to the World." *Ensign*, Nov. 1995, 65–66.

———. "We Are Christians Because . . ." *Ensign*, Jan. 1984, 17–19.

"What Parts of the Old Testament Were on the Plates of Brass?" Book of Mormon Central, KnoWhy 410.

Whetten, Robert J. "Strengthen Thy Brethren." *Ensign*, May 2005, 91–93.

Whiting, Gary R. "The Commandment to Be Perfect." In Nyman and Tate, *3 Nephi 9–30*.

Whitmer, David. *David Whitmer Interviews: A Restoration Witness*. Edited by Lyndon W. Cook. 1991.

Whitney, Orson F. In Conference Report, Apr. 1928, 56–61.

———. *Life of Heber C. Kimball*. 1945.

Widtsoe, John A. "Alma Speaks to the Twentieth Century." *Improvement Era*, Nov. 1927, 20–31.

———. *Evidences and Reconciliations*. Arranged by G. Homer Durham. 3 Vols. in one. 1960.

Wilcox, S. Michael. "The Abrahamic Covenant." In *Witness of Jesus Christ*.

———. "The Beatitudes, Pathway to the Savior." *Ensign*, Jan. 1991, 18–23.

———. "I Have a Question." *Ensign*, June 1991, 51–52.

———. "Nephi's Message to the 'Gentiles.'" In Nyman and Tate, *Second Nephi*.

———. *Who Shall Be Able to Stand?* 2003.

Wilford Woodruff's Journal, 1833–1898 [typescript]. Edited by Scott G. Kenny. 9 vols. 1987.

Williams, Clyde J. "The Book of Mormon and Overcoming Satan." In *Doctrines of the Book of Mormon*.

———. "Deliverance from Bondage." In Nyman and Tate, *Mosiah*.

———. "Following the Prophet: A Book of Mormon Perspective." *Ensign*, July 2000, 19–23.

———. "Insights from Moroni's Visits in 1823." In *Joseph: Exploring the Life and Ministry of the Prophet*. Edited by Andrew C. Skinner and Susan Easton Black. 2005.

———. "Instruments in the Hands of God: The Message of Alma 17–27." In Nyman and Tate, *Alma*.

————. "A Shield against Evil." *Ensign*, Jan. 1996, 28–33.

————. *Teachings of Harold B. Lee*. 1996.

————. "Using the Book of Mormon to Meet Today's Challenges." In *Living the Book of Mormon*.

Wirth, Diane E. "Four Quarters." In Welch, *Reexploring the Book of Mormon*.

Wirthlin, Joseph B. "Alma the Elder: A Role Model for Today." In *Heroes from the Book of Mormon*.

————. "Christians in Belief and Action." *Ensign*, Nov. 1996, 70–71.

————. "Come What May, and Love It." *Ensign*, Nov. 2008, 26–28.

————. "Deep Roots." *Ensign*, Nov. 1994, 75–77.

————. "Improving Our Prayers." Brigham Young University devotional, Jan. 21, 2003.

————. "Journey to Higher Ground." *Ensign*, Nov. 2005, 16–19.

————. "The Law of the Fast." *Ensign*, May 2001, 73–75.

————. "Live in Thanksgiving Daily." *Ensign*, Sep. 2001, 6–13.

————. "Living Water to Quench Spiritual Thirst." *Ensign*, May 1995, 18–20.

————. "Spiritual Bonfires of Testimony." *Ensign*, Nov. 1992, 34–36.

————. "Sunday Will Come." *Ensign*, Nov. 2006, 28–30.

————. "Valued Companions." *Ensign*, Nov. 1997, 32–34.

Witness of Jesus Christ. Edited by Richard D. Draper. Sperry Symposium series. 1990.

Wood, Fred E. "The Record of Alma: A Prophetic Pattern of the Principles Governing Testimony." In Nyman and Tate, *Alma*.

Wood, Robert S. "Instruments of the Lord's Peace." *Ensign*, May 2006, 93–95.

————. "On the Responsible Self." *Ensign*, Mar. 2002, 27–31.

————. "The Tongue of Angels." *Ensign*, Nov. 1999, 83–84.

Woodbury, Lael A. "The Origin and Uses of the Sacred Hosanna Shout." In *Sperry Lecture Series*. 1975.

Woodger, Mary Jane. "How the Guide to English Pronunciation of Book of Mormon Names Came About." *Journal of Book of Mormon Studies* 9, no. 1 (2000): 52–57, 79.

Woodruff, Wilford. *The Discourses of Wilford Woodruff*. Edited by G. Homer Durham. 1946.

————. In Conference Report, Apr. 1898, 88–90.

Workman, H. Ross. "Beware of Murmuring." *Ensign*, Nov. 2001, 85–86.

Young, Brigham. *Brigham Young* [manual]. Teachings of Presidents of the Church series. 1997.

————. *Discourses of Brigham Young*. Edited by John A. Widtsoe. 1954.

WEBSITES CONSULTED

bookofmormoncentral.org

books.google.com

byui.edu

byustudies.byu.edu

ChurchofJesusChrist.org

fairmormon.org

gospelink.com

maxwellinstitute.byu.edu

olivercowdery.com

publications.maxwellinstitute.byu.edu

rsc.byu.edu

speeches.byu.edu

INDEX

of, 71–72; Nephi's vision of, 71–73; Bible brought to, 72–73; New Jerusalem to be built upon, 118; as choice land, 127, 1050; prospering of gospel in, 173–75; European invasion of, 222, 974–75; in allegory of olive tree, 276; as land of Joseph, 915; names in, 963; Gentiles to possess, 974–75; people of, 1042; requirements for inhabitants of, 1050. *See also* Jesus Christ: visit to Nephites; Promised land(s); United States of America

Aminadab, 780

Aminadi, 481

Amiss, asking, 149

Amlici, 440–42

Amlicites, 441–44, 446–47

Ammon: leads search party to land of Lehi-Nephi, 336–37; significance of name of, 337; imprisonment of, 337–40; lineage of, 339; teaches words of King Benjamin, 343; Limhi tells his story to, 396–98; becomes servant to Lamoni, 520–21; as type of Jesus Christ, 521; saves Lamoni's flocks, 521–23; arm of, 523; Lord's protection of, 523; mistaken for great spirit, 524–25; faithfulness of, 525; answers Lamoni's questions, 526–27; gains influence, 527; teaches Lamoni plan of salvation, 528–29; Lamoni believes, 529–30; overcome by Spirit, 531–32; life of, saved by Lord, 533–34; sent to deliver brethren from prison, 536–37; meets Lamoni's father, 537–38; and sons of Mosiah's release from prison, 539–40; returns to land of Ishmael, 544; blessed as missionary, 563; boasting of, 564, 971; missionary success of, 564; praises God, 565–66; reminds brothers of missionary experiences, 566–67; asks how to save Anti-Nephi-Lehies, 569–70; meets Alma, 570–71; Anti-Nephi-Lehies become known as people of, 572–73. *See also* Sons of Mosiah

Ammonihah, 472–73, 476–79, 482–83, 504–9, 513–16, 678–80

Ammonites, 764–66

Ammoron: as Lamanite leader, 650; background of, 696; Moroni's correspondence with, 706–8;

appeals to Lamanite hatred of Nephites, 708; demands Nephites' surrender, 708–9; nationality of, 709; slain by Teancum, 750–51

Amon, 299

Amulek: Alma meets, 474; background of, 474, 481–82; called to preach gospel, 475, 481–82; lawyers try to deceive, 482–83; tells of people's wickedness, 483–85; calls Zeezrom wicked, 488; learning from example of, 488; teachings on salvation, 489–90; teachings on resurrection, 490–91; exposes Zeezrom's evil plan, 491–93; brought before chief judge, 504–5; forced to watch burning of righteous, 505–6; set free by power of God, 508–9; finds Zeezrom sick, 510; sacrifice of, 512; Alma provides for, 512–13; preaches to all who will listen, 515–16; testifies of Christ, 603–4; teachings of mercy and service, 605–6; encourages people to obey Lord, 608; Jershon as refuge for, 609; on putting off repentance, 965

Amulon, 405–7, 540

Amulonites, 541

Anachronisms: *church* as, 39; horses as, 107, 1032; cement as, 765

Anarchy, 181, 1054

Anchor, hope as, 978

Andersen, Neil L., 294, 406, 438, 644, 819

Anderson, Richard Lloyd, 7

"And of" phrases, 151

"And thus we see," 1058

Angel(s): protects Nephi and Sam, 34–35; forgetting visitation of, 46–47; tongue of, 245, 247; calls Alma the Younger to repentance, 419–20; as God's emissaries, 473, 496, 1072; appear to Book of Mormon people, 503; appear to just and holy men, 541–42; similarities between missionaries and, 569; purpose of, 596, 612–13; ministering, 782, 864; Three Nephites compared to, 945

Anger: of Nephi, 148; against Israel, 198–99; rage and stirring up, 234–35; at words of prophets, 250; of Amalickiah, 682; justified, 708; of

Jared, 1025–28. *See also* Brother of Jared

Jaredites: as people of Coriantumr, 300; Limhi finds record of, 343–44; Mosiah translates plates of, 425–26; lands of, 550; Alma tells Helaman about, 621–22; Moroni begins abridgment of records of, 998–99; similarities between Lehites and, 1000; prepare for journey, 1003; warning given to, 1004–5; build ship, 1006–7; cross sea and arrive in promised land, 1017–19; tender mercies experienced by, 1019; kings of, 1019–22; general assembly of, 1020; Corihor rebels and imprisons father, 1022–23; Shule frees father and gains kingdom, 1023; civilization of, 1023–24; rival kingdoms of, 1023–24; Shule rules in righteousness, 1024–25; consequences of Jared's desire for power, 1025–26; destruction of, 1028, 1029, 1040–41, 1053–55, 1057–62; wickedness of, 1030–31, 1033, 1040–42, 1054–55; Emer sees Lord, 1031–33; prophets sent to warn, 1033–34; suffer famine and plague of snakes, 1034–35; Shez rebuilds kingdom in righteousness, 1035; taxed heavily under Riplakish, 1036; prosper under righteous rulers, 1036–38; blessed for righteousness, 1038–39; war and secret combinations infest, 1039–40; repent then become wicked again, 1041–42; Coriantumr fights against secret combinations, 1055–56; Coriantumr battles Shiz as destruction covers land, 1057–59; cause of strife and bloodshed among, 1058; Coriantumr sorrows over deaths of, 1059; anger and war among, 1059–60; gather into armies, 1060; rules of war for, 1060; Nephite battles compared to those of, 1061; Satan has full power over, 1061–62. *See also* Brother of Jared; Ether (book); Ether, plates of

Jarom, 295

Jehovah, 370, 577. *See also* Jesus Christ; Messiah

Jenkins, Ryan C., 445, 711, 1030

Jensen, Jay E., 840

Jensen, Marlin K., 128–29

Jeremiah, 47

Jershon, 571, 581–82, 609

Jerusalem: at time of Lehi's departure, 21; destruction of, 24, 28, 155, 216, 820; Lehi leaves, 25–26; return to, for brass plates, 30–31; "land of" versus "city of," 31; failure to obtain brass plates in, 31–34; return from, 40–42; return to, for Ishmael's family, 45–46, 88–89; warning against returning to, 46–47; prophecy concerning destruction of, 56–57, 181–82; duties of Twelve Apostles in, 67–68; suffering of, 160; guidance for, 160–61; promise to, 161; synagogues in, 541, 589; gathering of Jews to, 918; building up of, 923. *See also* New Jerusalem

Jesse: stem of, 203; root of, 204

Jesus Christ. *See also* Atonement; Jehovah; Light of Christ; Messiah; Second Coming

Book of Mormon brings people to, viii, 241–42, 975–78; tender mercies of, 24–25; visits Nephi, 28; coming unto, 51, 169–71, 459, 872, 969–70, 1014–15, 1088–89; cast off from presence of, 54; Nephi₁ desires to know more about, 59–60; as Son of God, 63, 497; condescension of, 64–65; as Lamb of God, 65; garments made white through blood of, 68, 1051; as light, 95, 116, 872, 884; remembering, 110–11, 347, 775–77, 813, 904, 1066; bearing name of, 113; and missionary work in spirit prison, 117; will not forget His children, 117–18; standard of, 118–19; to lead righteous, 124–25; mortal ministry of, 132, 157–58, 371; salvation through, 133, 217–18, 324, 327–28, 362, 604, 626; as great Mediator, 137–38; walking in light of, 158; submission to, 163, 325; significance of resurrection of, 164; as keeper of gate, 169; Book of Mormon as testament of, 171–72, 218, 306; as Judge, 182, 940; Isaiah stands before, 189; similarities between callings of Isaiah and, 190–91; name-titles of, 197, 323; to bring light into darkened world, 197–98; outstretched hand of,

57–59; prophesies about scattering and gathering of Israel, 59; family rebels against, 92–93; journeys to promised land, 103–4; arrives in promised land, 106–7; prophesies about promised land, 126–29; testimony of, 129–30; counsels sons to be righteous, 130–31; first blessing of, 131; speaks to Zoram, 131; speaks to Jacob, 132; blesses Joseph, 138–39; as "righteous branch," 139; counsels Joseph, 142–43; blesses children and dies, 144–46; children of, to return to Lord, 830; similarities between Jaredites and people of, 1000

Lehi (Nephite military commander), 681

Lehi (son of Helaman): background of, 767; name of, 776, 783; preaches gospel, 777–78; imprisoned and miraculously saved, 778–82; righteousness of, 811

Lehi-Nephi, land of. *See* Nephi, land of

"Lehi's paradox," 574

Lehonti, 671–72

Lemuel (son of Lehi). *See* Laman and Lemuel

Lemuel (valley), 88

Levites, 512, 929

Liahona, 89–90, 91–92, 623–24

Lib, 1056

Liberty: importance of, 174; achieving and maintaining blessings of, 402; and spread of Nehor's teachings, 437; preserving, 552, 775; title of, 663–64; standard of, 668; Moroni rejoices in, 676–77. *See also* Agency; Freedom; Religious freedom

Light of Christ, 469–70, 524–25, 1071

"Light of the glory of God," 531

Light(s): Jesus Christ as, 95, 116, 872, 884; to the Gentiles, 116; walking in, 158, 179; Jesus Christ to bring, 197–98; of Lord as fire, 201; as sign of Christ's birth, 824, 838–39; to the world, 884; Nephite Twelve as, 894; from stones, 1008

Limhi: background of, 339; speaks to people, 340–42; reason for story of, in Book of Mormon, 341; people of, prepare to escape, 343; finds Jaredite record, 343–44; captured

by Lamanites, 387–88; oath of, 389; succession to throne, 389; Lamanites attack people of, 390–91; king of Lamanites pleads for people of, 391–93; reason for bondage of people of, 392; attempts to escape from Lamanites, 393–94; humility of people of, 394–95; tells story to Ammon, 396–98; Gideon's plan for people of, 398–99; delivered from Lamanites, 399–400; comparison of bondage of Alma and, 409

List, 320

Literacy, 797

Locke, John, 552

"Loins, girdle of his," 242

Lord's Prayer, 888

Lots, casting, 32

Love: of God, 62–64, 99, 262, 274, 277, 565, 817, 829; for God, 170; of wealth, 259; song of redeeming, 457; between Ammon and Lamoni, 539, 544; power of, 539; and bridling passions, 627

Ludlow, Daniel H., 5, 14, 15, 21, 26, 28, 30, 32, 98, 104, 139, 188, 209, 226–27, 235–36, 241, 269, 310–11, 346, 348, 361, 400, 402, 420, 425, 427, 440, 481, 486, 490, 491, 492, 526, 527, 532, 541, 558, 569, 590, 613, 614, 623, 694, 695, 699, 714, 771, 798–99, 803, 808, 815, 842, 847, 865, 867, 875, 896, 898, 914, 944, 954–55, 960, 968, 971, 978, 991, 999, 1014, 1029, 1064

Ludlow, Victor L., 180, 181–82, 183, 184, 186, 189, 190, 192, 193, 198, 201, 209, 211, 787, 894, 921

Lund, Gerald, 112, 167, 327, 436, 580, 584, 926, 966

Lundquist, John M., 151, 523

Luram, 1080–81

"Lust of your eyes," 629–30

Mackay, Thomas W., 814, 991

Maher-shalal-hash-baz, 191, 194

Malachi, 928–29, 932, 933

Mammoths, 1032

"Management of the creature," 580

Nicknames, 953–54

Night raids, 695

Nimrod, 1003

Noah (city), 680–82

Noah (prophet), 1008–9

Noah, King: reigns in wickedness, 353–55; palace and buildings of, 355; armies of, delight in bloodshed, 356; spiritual condition of people of, 356; Abinadi prophesies destruction of, 358–59; and trial of Abinadi, 360; Abinadi defends himself before, 361–62; warned to repent, 378; Alma's people flee, 386–87; Gideon confronts, 386–87; moral character of leadership of, 387; execution of, 388–89; compared to King Benjamin, 428–29

Nor, 761

Nursing fathers and mothers, Gentiles as, 119

Nyman, Monte S., 4, 26, 55, 61, 65, 65, 76, 81, 85, 102, 109, 112, 119, 131, 144, 160, 185, 190, 196, 206, 213, 220, 236, 241, 250, 281, 282, 292, 299–300, 305, 311, 314–15, 323, 326, 340, 354, 358, 361–62, 365, 369, 380, 389, 391, 398–99, 406, 421, 450, 460, 469–70, 473, 500, 520, 600, 621, 636–37, 640, 648, 652, 654, 693, 770, 773, 778–79, 788–89, 798, 896, 897, 973–74, 986, 988

Oaks, Dallin H.: 6, 114, 120, 136, 137, 187, 224, 225, 236, 264, 286–87, 317, 329, 363, 366–67, 377, 401, 407, 547, 641, 671–72, 686, 691, 752, 777, 833, 864, 873, 890, 904–5, 930, 951, 993, 1016, 1068, 1085; on gospel, vii; on desires, priorities, choices, and actions, 60; on opposition in all things, 134; on being subject to Savior, 163; on Fall, 163; on Isaiah's prophecies, 204; on false doctrine, 233; on church discipline, 416–17; on making choices, 427; on types, 601; on keeping covenants, 705; on faith by signs, 841; on resurrection, 984; on gifts grudgingly given, 1070

Oaks of Bashan, 180

Oak trees, 191–92

Oath(s): sworn by Nephi, 32; binding power of, 39; of King Limhi, 389, 391; of

Anti-Nephi-Lehies, 556–58, 703–5, 714–15, 717; Zerahemnah refuses to swear, 655; breaking, 704; of wicked to God, 758; sworn by Giddianhi, 845

Obedience: and acting in faith, 31, 35–36, 56; taught by Nephi, 125; of Nephites, 129; blessings of, 318, 686; becoming child of Christ through, 334; prompt, 473; peace through, 578–79, 686; prosperity through, 612, 678; of Helaman, 658–59; and avoiding temptation, 719; of stripling warriors, 724, 732–34; of earth, 814–15. See also Commandments; Disobedience

Offense, 744

Offensive war, 968, 971

Offerings: sacrifice versus burnt, 41–42; tithes and, 930–31. See also Sacrifice(s)

Old Testament: insights from brass plates into, 42; understanding, 214; witnesses of Christ in, 797–98

Olive tree: Israel compared to, 59, 83–84, 272; allegory of, 85, 185, 269–82

Olson, Camille Fronk, 623–24, 1012. See also Fronk, Camille

Omer, 1031

Omni, 299

One eternal round, 60

Only Begotten Son, 497

Opposition: brought on by faithful actions, 25; need for, 134–35; at time of great spiritual experiences, 839; continuing in spite of, 1081. See also Afflictions; Compound in one; Suffering; Trials

Order: in serving Lord, 331–32; in resurrection, 375

Order of the Nehors, 542

Ore, 95

Other sheep, 894–96

Overzealousness, 340, 341, 347

Paanchi, 757, 758

Pace, Glenn L., 53

Pachus, 747

Packard, Dennis, 49

207–8; destruction of, 208–9, 220; warning before destruction of, 214–17; and binding of Satan, 230; false and foolish doctrines of, 232–33; punishment of, 234; and second death, 264; found among Nephites, 295–96; unquenchable fire for, 321; redemption of, 374, 490; gnashing of teeth of, 376; reactions of, against divine messengers, 541; angels will not appear to, 541–42; in spirit world, 633; agency of, 738; oath of, to God, 758; use secret combinations and murder to get gain, 758; impact on law and justice, 775; reaction of, against truth, 796; cursing of riches of, 819–20; and honor for past prophets, 821; returned to God's presence, 826; and religious freedom, 837; kill prophets and set up secret combinations, 860–62; prosperity of, 931; to be burned at Second Coming, 932; fear death, 980

Wickedness: leading to destruction of Jerusalem, 24; of Laman and Lemuel, 100; in promised land, 128–29; daughters of Zion punished for, 183; of Israel, 199–200; in last days, 225–26; of Nephites, 256–57, 258, 263–64, 788–91, 955–57; King Noah reigns in, 353–55; and happiness, 376, 638, 822–24; Amulek tells of Ammonihah's, 483–85; Zeezrom falls ill due to, 510; Nephi₂ mourns over, 791–92; rapidity of decline into, 792; righteous during times of, 792; challenged by Nephi₂, 799–800; unity in, 861; Gentiles invited to turn away from, 949; consequences of, 961–62; Mormon saddened by, 964–65; Mormon refuses to lead people due to, 968–69; of Jaredites, 1030–31, 1033, 1040–42, 1054–55

Widows, 930

Widtsoe, John A., 345, 828

Wilcox, S. Michael, 221, 884, 917

Wilderness: Lehites' journey through, 94; Lehites' children born in, 104; and deliverance of God's people, 147; Nephi and faithful flee into, 149–50; Alma's people flee into, 386–87, 400–401, 408; as prayer location, 606; Gadianton robbers flee into, 763–64; symbolism of, 1004

Williams, Clyde J., 8, 9, 223, 288, 341, 371, 392, 394–95, 409, 446, 502, 526, 533, 539, 547, 564, 832

Will of God: pride and, 66; fulfilled by Jesus Christ, 838

Wind, furious, 1018

Windows, 925–26

"Windows of heaven," 930

Wine, 1067

"Wine and milk without money and without price," 171

Wirthlin, Joseph B., 138, 205, 233, 379, 401, 472, 608, 772, 892, 936, 1004–5, 1062, 1068

Wisdom: in your own eyes, 187; being wise, 284; in serving Lord, 331–32; seeking after, 406; learning, 623; boasting in, 628

Witchcraft, 962

Witnesses: law of, 194, 476; of truth, 460–61; becoming, 1044; face-to-face, of Jesus Christ, 1048–50. See also Eight Witnesses; Three Witnesses

Wives, murder of, 208

"Wo," 186

Woes, three, 234, 795

Women: seven, to take hold of one man, 184; as victims of unchastity, 261–62; carried away by wicked priests, 390; dancing, 390, 1026; barren woman, 924; forsaken woman, 925

"Wonderful contention," 440

Wood, Robert S., 234–35, 431

Woodger, Mary Jane, 1093

Woodruff, Wilford, 183, 214–15, 542, 839–40, 905

Woods, Fred E., 28

Word of God: clinging to versus holding fast to, 52; holding fast to, 52, 53; hardening heart against, 493–94; maintenance of, 653–54; rejected by Nephites, 772–73; willing belief in, 789

Word of Wisdom, 905

Words: kind, 245; judgment according to, 493–94; resisting evil with, 745

Work, importance of, 750. See also Action(s)

Working out, 761